Financial Accounting and Reporting

Visit the *Financial Accounting and Reporting, tenth edition*
Companion Website at
www.booksites.net/elliott_elliott
to find valuable **student** learning material including:

- Case studies with solutions
- Extracts from financial press

Financial Accounting and Reporting

TENTH EDITION

Barry Elliott and Jamie Elliott

FT Prentice Hall
FINANCIAL TIMES

An imprint of **Pearson Education**
Harlow, England • London • New York • Boston • San Francisco • Toronto • Sydney • Singapore • Hong Kong
Tokyo • Seoul • Taipei • New Delhi • Cape Town • Madrid • Mexico City • Amsterdam • Munich • Paris • Milan

Pearson Education Limited

Edinburgh Gate
Harlow
Essex CM20 2JE
England

and Associated Companies throughout the world

Visit us on the World Wide Web at:
www.pearsoned.co.uk

First published 1993
Second edition 1996
Third edition 1999
Fourth edition 2000
Fifth edition 2001
Sixth edition 2002
Seventh edition 2003
Eighth edition 2004
Ninth edition published 2005
Tenth edition published 2006

ISBN-13: 978-0-273-70364-8
ISBN-10: 0-273-70364-1

British Library Cataloguing-in-Publication Data
A catalogue record for this book is available from the British Library.

10 9 8 7 6 5 4 3 2
10 09 08 07 06

Typeset in 9/12pt Ehrhardt by 25.
Printed by Ashford Colour Press Ltd, Gosport

Brief Contents

Full Contents

Preface and acknowledgements

Our objective is to provide a balanced and comprehensive framework to enable students to acquire the requisite knowledge and skills to appraise current practice critically and to evaluate proposed changes from a theoretical base. To this end, the text contains:

- current standards,
- illustrations from published accounts,
- a range of review questions,
- exercises of varying difficulty,
- outline solutions to selected exercises in an Appendix at the end of the book,
- extensive references.

We have assumed that readers will have an understanding of financial accounting to a foundation or first-year level, although the text and exercises have been designed on the basis that a brief revision is still helpful.

Lecturers are using the text selectively to support a range of teaching programmes for second-year and final-year undergraduate and postgraduate programmes. We have therefore attempted to provide subject coverage of sufficient breadth and depth to assist selective use.

The text has been adopted for financial accounting, reporting and analysis modules on:

- second-year undergraduate courses for Accounting, Business Studies and Combined Studies;
- final-year undergraduate courses for Accounting, Business Studies and Combined Studies;
- MBA courses;
- specialist MSc courses; and
- professional courses preparing students for professional accountancy examinations.

Changes to the tenth edition

Accounting standards

UK listed companies, together with those non-listed companies that so choose, will apply international standards from January 2005.

For non-listed companies that choose to continue to apply UK GAAP, the ASB has stated its commitment to progressively bringing UK GAAP into line with international standards and the seven FRSs 20–26 that have been issued since April 2004 are part of this process.

For companies currently applying FRSSE, this will continue but the IASB are looking in the medium term at the possibility of issuing an international equivalent.

Accounting standards – tenth edition updates

Chapters 5 and 6 cover the evolution of the regulatory framework in the UK and the evolution of international standards.

Topics and International Standards are covered as follows:

Chapter 8	Published accounts of companies	IAS 1, IAS 14, IAS 37, IFRS 1 and IFRS 5
Chapter 9	Preparation of published accounts	IAS 1, IAS 8, IAS 24 and IAS 35
Chapter 12	Off balance sheet finance	IAS 37
Chapter 13	Financial instruments	IAS 32 and IAS 39
Chapter 14	Employee benefits	IAS 19 and IAS 26
Chapter 15	Taxation in company accounts	IAS 12
Chapter 16	Property, plant and equipment (PPE)	IAS 16, IAS 20, IAS 23, IAS 36, IAS 40 and IFRS 5
Chapter 17	Leasing	IAS 17
Chapter 18	R&D; goodwill and intangible assets; brands	IAS 38 and IFRS 3
Chapter 19	Inventories	IAS 2
Chapter 20	Construction contracts	IAS 11
Chapters 21 to 25	Consolidation	IAS 21, IAS 27, IAS 28, IAS 31 and IFRS 3
Chapter 26	Earnings per share	IAS 33
Chapter 27	Cash flow statements	IAS 7
Chapter 31	Corporate governance	IFRS 2

Income and asset value measurement systems

Chapters 1 to 4 continue to cover accounting and reporting on a cash flow and accrual basis, the economic income approach and accounting for changing price levels.

The UK regulatory framework and analysis

UK listed companies will continue to be subject to national company law, and mandatory and best practice requirements such as the *Operating and Financial Review* and the *Combined Code*.

UK regulatory framework and analysis – tenth edition changes

The following chapters have been retained and updated as appropriate:
Chapter 10 Share capital, capital maintenance and distributable profits
Chapter 11 Reduction of share capital
Chapter 12 Off balance sheet finance
Chapter 28 Review of financial ratio analysis
Chapter 29 Trend analysis and multivariate analysis

A new chapter has been written, Chapter 30 Financial Reporting on the Internet
Chapter 31 Corporate governance
Chapter 32 Environmental and social reporting
Chapter 33 Ethics for accountants

Our emphasis has been on keeping the text current and responsive to constructive comments from reviewers.

Recent developments

In addition to the steps being taken towards the development of IFRSs that will receive broad consensus support, regulators have been active in developing further requirements concerning corporate governance. These have been prompted by the accounting scandals in the USA and, more recently, in Europe and by shareholder activism fuelled by the apparent lack of any relationship between increases in directors' remuneration and company performance.

The content of financial reports continues to be subjected to discussion with a tension between preparers, stakeholders, auditors, academic accountants and standard setters; this is mirrored in the tension that exists between theory and practice.

- Preparers favour reporting transactions on a historical cost basis which is reliable but does not provide shareholders with relevant information to appraise past performance or to predict future earnings.
- Stakeholders favour forward-looking reports relevant in estimating future dividend and capital growth and in understanding environmental and social impacts.
- Auditors favour reports that are verifiable so that the figures can be substantiated to avoid them being proved wrong at a later date.
- Academic accountants favour reports that reflect economic reality and are relevant in appraising management performance and in assessing the capacity of the company to adapt.
- Standard setters lean towards the academic view and favour reporting according to the commercial substance of a transaction.

In order to understand the tensions that exist, students need:

- the skill to prepare financial statements in accordance with the historical cost and current cost conventions, both of which appear in annual financial reports;
- an understanding of the main thrust of mandatory and voluntary standards;
- an understanding of the degree of flexibility available to the preparers and the impact of this on reported earnings and the balance sheet figures;
- an understanding of the limitations of these financial reports in portraying economic reality; and
- an exposure to source material and other published material in so far as time permits.

Instructor's Manual

A separate Instructor's Manual has been written to accompany this text. It contains fully worked solutions to all the exercises and is of a quality that allows them to be used as overhead transparencies. The Manual is available at no cost to lecturers on application to the publishers.

Website

An electronic version of the Manual is also available for download at www.booksites.net/elliott_elliott.

Acknowledgements

Financial reporting is a dynamic area and we see it as extremely important that the text should reflect this and be kept current. Assistance has been generously given by colleagues and many others in the preparation and review of the text and assessment material. This tenth edition is very much a result of the authors, colleagues, reviewers and Pearson editorial and production staff working as a team and we are grateful to all concerned for their assistance in achieving this.

We owe particular thanks to Sally Aisbitt of the Open University, who has updated the chapter 'Financial reporting – evolution of international standards' (Chapter 6); Ron Altshul of Leeds Metropolitan University, who has updated 'Taxation in company accounts' (Chapter 15); Charles Batchelor of the Financial Training Company for 'Employee benefits' (Chapter 14) and Financial Instruments (Chapter 13); Steve Dungworth of De Montfort University, for 'Ethics for accountants' (Chapter 33), which first appeared in the third edition; Ozer Erman of Kingston University, for 'Share capital, capital maintenance and distributable profits' (Chapter 10); and 'Reduction of share capital' (Chapter 11), which first appeared in the second edition; Mike O'Meara of the Regents Business School for consolidation chapters; Paul Robins of University of Wales College Newport for 'Property, plant and equipment' (Chapter 16) and 'Construction contracts' (Chapter 20); Professor Garry Tibbits of the University of Western Sydney for Leasing (Chapter 17); Hendrika Tibbits of the University of Western Sydney for An Introduction to Financial Reporting on the Internet (Chapter 30); David Towers, formerly of Keele University, for R&D; Goodwill and intangible assets and 'Corporate governance' (Chapter 30); and Martin Howes for inputs to financial analysis.

The authors are grateful for the constructive comments received from the following reviewers which have assisted us in making improvements: Iain Fleming of the University of Paisley, John Morley of the University of Brighton, John Forker of Queen's University, Belfast, Breda Sweeney of Cork University, Patricia McCourt Larres of Queen's University, Belfast, and Dave Knight of Leeds Metropolitan University.

Thanks are owed to A.T. Benedict of the South Bank University, Keith Brown of De Montfort University, Kenneth N. Field of the University of Leeds, Sue McDermott of London Guildhall University, David Murphy of Manchester Metropolitan University, Bahadur Najak of the University of Durham, Graham Sara of Coventry University, Laura Spira of Oxford Brookes University, Ken Trunkfield, formerly of the University of Derby, and Martin Tuffy of the University of Brighton.

Thanks are also due to the following organisations: the Accounting Standards Board, the International Accounting Standards Board, the Association of Chartered Certified Accountants, the Chartered Institute of Management Accountants, the Institute of Chartered Accountants of Scotland, Chartered Institute of Public Finance and

Accountancy, Chartered Institute of Bankers and the Institute of Investment Management and Research.

We would also like to thank the authors of some of the end-of-chapter exercises. Some of these exercises have been inherited from a variety of institutions with which we have been associated, and we have unfortunately lost the identities of the originators of such material with the passage of time. We are sorry that we cannot acknowledge them by name and hope that they will excuse us for using their material.

We are indebted to Paula Harris and Verina Pettigrew of Pearson Education for active support in keeping us largely to schedule and the attractively produced and presented text.

Finally we thank our wives, Di and Jacklin, for their continued good humoured support during the period of writing and revisions, and Giles Elliott for his critical comment at the commencement of the project. We alone remain responsible for any errors and for the thoughts and views that are expressed.

Barry and Jamie Elliott
August 2006

Companion Website resources

Visit the Companion Website at www.booksites.net/elliott_elliott

For students
• Case studies with solutions
• Extracts from financial press

For lecturers
• Downloadable Instructor's Manual which includes worked solutions to all exercises
• PowerPoint slides that can be downloaded and used as OHTs

PART I

Income and asset value measurement systems

CHAPTER **1**

Accounting and reporting on a cash flow basis

1.1 Introduction

Accountants are communicators. Accountancy is the art of communicating financial information about a business entity to users such as shareholders and managers. The communication is generally in the form of financial statements that show in money terms the economic resources under the control of the management. The art lies in selecting the information that is relevant to the user and is reliable.

Shareholders require periodic information that the managers are accounting properly for the resources under their control. This information helps the shareholders to evaluate the performance of the managers. The performance measured by the accountant shows the extent to which the economic resources of the business have grown or diminished during the year.

The shareholders also require information to **predict future performance**. At present companies are not required to publish forecast financial statements on a regular basis and the shareholders use the report of past performance when making their predictions.

Managers require information in order **to control the business and make investment decisions**.

In this chapter we will consider both categories of user, and the extent to which cash flow accounting would satisfy their information needs, under the following headings:

- Shareholders
- What skills does an accountant require in respect of external reports?
- Managers
- What skills does an accountant require in respect of internal reports?
- Procedural steps when reporting to internal users
- Illustration of operating cash flows
- Illustration continued with statement of financial position
- Treatment of fixed assets in the cash flow model
- What are the characteristics of these data that make them reliable?
- Reports to external users.

1.2 Shareholders

Shareholders are external users. As such, they are unable to obtain access to the same amount of detailed historical information as the managers, e.g. total administration costs are disclosed in the published profit and loss account, but not an analysis to show how the figure is made up. Shareholders are also unable to obtain associated information, e.g. budgeted sales and costs. Even though the shareholders own a company, their entitlement to information is restricted.

The information to which shareholders are entitled is restricted to that specified by statute, e.g. the Companies Acts, or by professional regulation, e.g. Financial Reporting Standards, or by market regulations, e.g. Listing requirements. This means that there may be a tension between the **amount** of information that a shareholder would like to receive and the amount that the directors are prepared to provide. For example, shareholders might consider that forecasts of future cash flows would be helpful in predicting future dividends, but the directors might be concerned that such forecasts could help competitors or make directors open to criticism if forecasts are not met. As a result, this information is not disclosed.

There may also be a tension between the **quality** of information that shareholders would like to receive and that which directors are prepared to provide. For example, the shareholders might consider that judgements made by the directors in the valuation of long-term contracts should be fully explained, whereas the directors might prefer not to reveal this information given the high risk of error that often attaches to such estimates. In practice, companies tend to compromise: they do not reveal the judgements to the shareholders, but maintain confidence by relying on the auditor to give a clean audit report.

The financial reports presented to the shareholders are also used by other parties such as lenders and trade creditors, and they have come to be regarded as general-purpose reports. However, it may be difficult or impossible to satisfy the needs of all users. For example, users may have different time-scales – shareholders may be interested in the long-term trend of earnings over three years, whereas creditors may be interested in the likelihood of receiving cash within the next three months.

The information needs of the shareholders are regarded as the primary concern. The government perceives shareholders to be important because they provide companies with their economic resources. It is shareholders' needs that take priority in deciding on the nature and detailed content of the general-purpose reports.[1]

1.3 What skills does an accountant require in respect of external reports?

For external reporting purposes the accountant has a two-fold obligation:

- an obligation to ensure that the financial statements comply with statutory, professional and Listing requirements; this requires the accountant to possess **technical expertise**;
- an obligation to ensure that the financial statements present the substance of the commercial transactions the company has entered into; this requires the accountant to have **commercial awareness**.[2]

1.4 Managers

Managers are internal users. As such, they have access to detailed financial statements showing the current results, the extent to which these vary from the budgeted results and the future budgeted results. Examples of internal users are sole traders, partners and, in a company context, directors and managers.

There is no statutory restriction on the amount of information that an internal user may receive; the only restriction would be that imposed by the company's own policy. Frequently, companies operate a 'need to know' policy and only the directors see all the financial statements; employees, for example, would be most unlikely to receive information that would assist them in claiming a salary increase – unless, of course, it happened to be a time of recession, when information would be more freely provided by management as a means of containing claims for an increase.

1.5 What skills does an accountant require in respect of internal reports?

For the internal user, the accountant is able to tailor his or her reports. The accountant is required to produce financial statements that are specifically relevant to the user requesting them.

The accountant needs to be skilled in identifying the information that is needed and conveying its implication and meaning to the user. The user needs to be confident that the accountant understands the user's information needs and will satisfy them in a language that is understandable. The accountant must be a skilled communicator who is able to instil confidence in the user that the information is:

● relevant to the user's needs;

● measured objectively;

● presented within a time-scale that permits decisions to be made with appropriate information;

● verifiable, in that it can be confirmed that the report represents the transactions that have taken place;

● reliable, in that it is as free from bias as is possible;

● a complete picture of material items;

● a fair representation of the business transactions and events that have occurred or are being planned.

The accountant is a trained reporter of financial information. Just as for external reporting, the accountant needs commercial awareness. It is important, therefore, that he or she should not operate in isolation.

1.5.1 Accountant's reporting role

The accountant's role is to ensure that the information provided is useful for making decisions. For external users, the accountant achieves this by providing a general-purpose financial statement that complies with statute and is reliable. For internal users, this is done by interfacing with the user and establishing exactly what financial information is relevant to the decision that is to be made.

We now consider the steps required to provide relevant information for internal users.

1.6 Procedural steps when reporting to internal users

A number of user steps and accounting action steps can be identified within a financial decision model. These are shown in Figure 1.1.

Figure 1.1 General financial decision model to illustrate the user/accountant interface

USER	USER/ACCOUNTANT INTERFACE	ACCOUNTANT
User step 1 Identify decision and how it is to be made *User step 2* Establish with the accountant the information necessary for decision making *User step 3* Seek relevant data from the accountant	**USER/ACCOUNTANT INTERFACE**	Identify the material information needed by the user Measure the relevant information Prepare report for user to allow user to make decision Provide an understandable report to the user

Note that, although we refer to an accountant/user interface, this is not a single occurrence because the user and accountant interface at each of the user decision steps.

At **step 1**, the accountant attempts to ensure that the decision is based on the appropriate appraisal methodology. However, the accountant is providing a service to a user and, while the accountant may give guidance, the final decision about methodology rests with the user.

At **step 2**, the accountant needs to establish the information necessary to support the decision that is to be made.

At **step 3**, the accountant needs to ensure that the user **understands** the full impact and financial implications of the accountant's report taking into account the user's level of understanding and prior knowledge. This may be overlooked by the accountant, who feels that the task has been completed when the written report has been typed.

It is important to remember in following the model that the accountant is attempting to satisfy the information needs of the individual user rather than those of a 'user group'. It is tempting to divide users into groups with apparently common information needs, without recognising that a group contains individual users with different information needs. We return to this later in the chapter, but for the moment we continue by studying a situation where the directors of a company are considering a proposed capital investment project.

Let us assume that there are three companies in the retail industry: Retail A Ltd, Retail B Ltd and Retail C Ltd. The directors of each company are considering the purchase of a warehouse. We could assume initially that, because the companies are operating in the same industry and are faced with the same investment decision, they have identical information needs. However, enquiry might establish that the directors of each company have a completely different attitude to, or perception of, the primary business objective.

For example, it might be established that Retail A Ltd is a large company and under the Fisher/Hirshleifer separation theory the directors seek to maximise profits for the benefit of the equity investors; Retail B Ltd is a medium-sized company in which the directors seek to obtain a satisfactory return for the equity shareholders; and Retail C Ltd is a smaller company in which the directors seek to achieve a satisfactory return for a wider range of stakeholders, including, perhaps, the employees as well as the equity shareholders.

The accountant needs to be aware that these differences may have a significant effect on the information required. Let us consider this diagrammatically in the situation where a capital investment decision is to be made, referring particularly to user step 2: 'Establish with the accountant the information necessary for decision making'.

Figure 1.2 Impact of different user attitudes on the information needed in relation to a capital investment proposal

	USER A Directors of Retail A Ltd	USER B Directors of Retail B Ltd	USER C Directors of Retail C Ltd
User attitude	PROFIT MAXIMISER for SHAREHOLDERS	PROFIT SATISFICER for SHAREHOLDERS	PROFIT SATISFICER for SHAREHOLDERS/ STAFF
Relevant data to measure	CASH FLOWS	CASH FLOWS	CASH FLOWS
Appraisal method (decided on by user)	IRR	NPV	NPV
Appraisal criterion (decided on by user)	HIGHEST IRR	NPV but only if positive	NPV possibly even if negative

We can see from Figure 1.2 that the accountant has identified that:

● the relevant financial data are the same for each of the users, i.e. cash flows; but
● the appraisal methods selected, i.e. internal rate of return (IRR) and net present value (NPV), are different; and
● the appraisal criteria employed by each user, i.e. higher IRR and NPV, are different.

In practice, the user is likely to use more than one appraisal method, as each has advantages and disadvantages. However, we can see that, even when dealing with a single group of apparently homogeneous users, the accountant has first to identify the information needs of the particular user. Only then is the accountant able to identify the relevant financial data and the appropriate report. It is the **user's** needs that are predominant.

If the accountant's view of the appropriate appraisal method or criterion differs from the user's view, the accountant might decide to report from **both** views. This approach affords the opportunity to improve the user's understanding and encourages good practice.

The diagrams can be combined (Figure 1.3) to illustrate the complete process. The user is assumed to be Retail A Ltd, a company that has directors who are profit maximisers.

Figure 1.3 User/accountant interface where the user is a profit maximiser

General model USER	Specific application for Retail A Ltd A PROFIT MAXIMISER		General model ACCOUNTANT	Specific application for Retail A Ltd ACCOUNTANT
Step 1 Decision to be made	Appraise which project warrants capital investment		Identify information needed by the user	User decision criterion is IRR
Step 2 Information needed		**USER/** **ACCOUNTANT** **INTERFACE**	Measure	Measure the project cash flows
Step 3 Seek relevant data	Project with the highest IRR		Prepare report	Prepare report of highest IRR
	Report of IRR project		Provide report	Submit report of project with highest IRR per £ invested

The accountant is reactive when reporting to an internal user. We observe this characteristic in the Norman example set out in section 1.8. Because the cash flows are identified as relevant to the user, it is these flows that the accountant will record, measure and appraise.

The accountant can also be proactive, by giving the user advice and guidance in areas where the accountant has specific expertise, such as the appraisal method that is most appropriate to the circumstances.

1.7 Agency costs[3]

The information in Figure 1.2 assumes that the directors have made their investment decision based on the assumed preferences of the shareholders. However, in real life, the directors might also be influenced by how the decision impinges on their own position. If, for example, their remuneration is a fixed salary, they might select not the investment with the highest IRR, but the one that maintains their security of employment. The result might be suboptimal investment and financing decisions based on risk aversion and over-retention. To the extent that the potential cash flows have been reduced, there will be an agency cost to the shareholders. This agency cost is an opportunity cost – the amount that was forgone because the decision making was suboptimal – and, as such, it will not be recorded in the books of account and will not appear in the financial statements.

1.8 Illustration of periodic financial statements prepared under the cash flow concept to disclose realised operating cash flows

In the above example of Retail A, B and C, the investment decision for the acquisition of a warehouse was based on an appraisal of cash flows. This raises the question: 'Why not continue with the cash flow concept and report the financial changes that occur after the investment has been undertaken using that same concept?'

To do this, the company will record the consequent cash flows through a number of subsequent accounting periods; report the cash flows that occur in each financial period; and produce a balance sheet at the end of each of the financial periods. For illustration we follow this procedure in paras 1.8.1 and 1.8.2 for transactions entered into by Mr S. Norman.

1.8.1 Appraisal of the initial investment decision

Mr Norman is considering whether to start up a retail business by acquiring the lease of a shop for five years at a cost of £80,000.

Our first task has been set out in Figure 1.1 above. It is to establish the information that Mr Norman needs, so that we can decide what data it will be necessary to collect and measure. Let us assume that, as a result of a discussion with Mr Norman, it has been ascertained that he is a profit satisficer who is looking to achieve at least a 10% return, which represents the time value of money. This indicates that, as illustrated in Figure 1.2:

● the relevant data to be measured are **cash flows**, represented by the outflow of cash invested in the lease and the inflow of cash represented by the realised operating cash flows;
● the appropriate appraisal method is **NPV**; and
● the appraisal criterion is a **positive NPV** using the discount rate of 10%.

Let us further assume that the cash to be invested in the lease is £80,000 and that the realised operating cash flows over the life of the investment in the shop are as shown in Figure 1.4. This shows that there is a forecast of £30,000 annually for five years and a final receipt of £29,000 in 20X6 when he proposes to cease trading.

Figure 1.4 Forecast of realised operating cash flows

	Annually years 20X1–20X5 £	Cash in year 20X6 after shop closure £
Receipts from Customers	400,000	55,000
Payments to		
Suppliers	(342,150)	(20,000)
Expense creditors	(21,600)	(3,000)
Rent	(6,250)	(3,000)
Total payments	(370,000)	(26,000)
Realised operating cash flows	30,000	29,000

We already know that Mr Norman's investment criterion is a positive NPV using a discount factor of 10%. A calculation (Figure 1.5) shows that the investment easily satisfies that criterion.

Figure 1.5 NPV calculation using discount tables

	£	£
Cost of lease		(80,000)
£30,000 annually for 5 years (30,000 × 3.79)	113,700	
£29,000 received in year 6 (29,000 × 0.564)	16,356	
		130,056
Positive net present value		50,056

1.8.2 Preparation of periodic financial statements under the cash flow concept

Having **predicted** the realised operating cash flows for the purpose of making the investment decision, we can assume that the owner of the business will wish to obtain **feedback** to evaluate the correctness of the investment decision. He does this by reviewing the actual results on a regular **timely** basis and **comparing** these with the predicted forecast. Actual results should be reported quarterly, half-yearly or annually in the same format as used when making the decision in Figure 1.4. The actual results provide management with the feedback information required to audit the initial decision; it is a technique for achieving accountability. However, frequently, companies do not provide a report of actual cash flows to compare with the forecast cash flows, and fail to carry out an audit review.

In some cases, the transactions relating to the investment cannot be readily separated from other transactions, and the information necessary for the audit review of the investment cannot be made available. In other cases, the routine accounting procedures fail to collect such cash flow information because the reporting systems have not been designed to provide financial reports on a cash flow basis; rather, they have been designed to produce reports prepared on an accrual basis.

What would financial reports look like if they were prepared on a cash flow basis?

To illustrate cash flow period accounts, we will prepare half-yearly accounts for Mr Norman. To facilitate a comparison with the forecast that underpinned the investment decision, we will redraft the forecast annual statement on a half-yearly basis. The data for the first year given in Figure 1.4 have therefore been redrafted to provide a forecast for the half-year to 30 June, as shown in Figure 1.6.

We assume that, having applied the net present value appraisal technique to the cash flows and ascertained that the NPV was positive, Mr Norman proceeded to set up the business on 1 January 20X1. He introduced capital of £50,000, acquired a five-year lease for £80,000 and paid £6,250 in advance as rent to occupy the property to 31 December 20X1. He has decided to prepare financial statements at half-yearly intervals. The information given in Figure 1.7 concerns his trading for the half-year to 30 June 20X1.

Figure 1.6 Forecast of realised operating cash flows

	Half-year to 30 June 20X1 £
Receipts from	
Customers	165,000
Payments to	
Suppliers	(124,000)
Expense creditors	(18,000)
Rent	(6,250)
Total payments	(148,250)
Realised operating cash flows	16,750

Figure 1.7 Monthly sales, purchases and expenses for six months ended 30 June 20X1

Month	Sales invoiced £	Cash received £	Purchases invoiced £	Cash paid £	Expenses invoiced £	Cash paid £
January	15,000	7,500	16,000		3,400	3,100
February	20,000	17,500	19,000	16,000	3,500	3,400
March	35,000	27,500	29,000	19,000	3,800	3,500
April	40,000	37,500	32,000	29,000	3,900	3,800
May	40,000	40,000	33,000	32,000	3,900	3,900
June	45,000	42,500	37,000	33,000	4,000	3,900
TOTAL	195,000	172,500	166,000	129,000	22,500	21,600

Note: The following items were included under the Expenses invoiced heading:
Expense creditors   – amount
Wages   – £3,100 per month paid in the month
Commission   – 2% of sales invoiced payable one month in arrears

Figure 1.8 Monthly realised operating cash flows

	Jan £	Feb £	Mar £	Apr £	May £	Jun £	Total £
Receipts							
Customers	7,500	17,500	27,500	37,500	40,000	42,500	172,500
Less payments							
Suppliers		16,000	19,000	29,000	32,000	33,000	129,000
Expense creditors	3,100	3,400	3,500	3,800	3,900	3,900	21,600
Rent	6,250						6,250
Realised	(1,850)	(1,900)	5,000	4,700	4,100	5,600	15,650

Mr Norman was naturally eager to determine whether the business was achieving its forecast cash flows for the first six months of trading, so he produced the statement of realised operating cash flows (Figure 1.8) from the information provided in Figure 1.7. From this statement we can see that the business generated positive cash flows after the end of February. These are, of course, only the cash flows relating to the trading transactions.

The information in the 'Total' row of Figure 1.7 can be extracted to provide the financial statement for the six months ended 30 June 20X1, as shown in Figure 1.9.

Figure 1.9 Realised operating cash flows for the six months ended 30 June 20X1

		£
Receipts from		
Customers		172,500
Payments to		
Suppliers	(129,000)	
Expense creditors	(21,600)	
Rent	(6,250)	
		156,850
Realised operating cash flow		15,650

The figure of £15,650 needs to be compared with the forecast cash flows used in the investment appraisal. This is a form of auditing. It allows the assumptions made on the initial investment decision to be confirmed. The forecast/actual comparison (based on the information in Figures 1.6 and 1.9) is set out in Figure 1.10.

Figure 1.10 Forecast/actual comparison

		Actual £		Forecast £
Receipts from				
Customers		172,500		165,000
Payment to				
Suppliers	(129,000)			(124,000)
Expense creditors	(21,600)			(18,000)
Rent	(6,250)			(6,250)
Total payments		(156,850)		(148,250)
Realised operating cash flow		15,650		16,750

What are the characteristics of these data that make them relevant?

● The data are **objective**. There is no judgement involved in deciding the values to include in the financial statement, as each value or amount represents a verifiable cash transaction with a third party.

- The data are **consistent**. The statement incorporates the same cash flows within the periodic financial report of trading as the cash flows that were incorporated within the initial capital investment report. This permits a logical comparison and confirmation that the decision was realistic.
- The results have a **confirmatory** value by helping users confirm or correct their past assessments.
- The results have a **predictive** value, in that they provide a basis for revising the initial forecasts if necessary.[4]
- There is **no requirement for accounting standards** or disclosure of accounting policies that are necessary to regulate accrual accounting practices, e.g. depreciation methods.

1.9 Illustration of preparation of balance sheet under the cash flow concept

Although the information set out in Figure 1.10 permits us to compare and evaluate the initial decision, it does not provide a sufficiently sound basis for the following:

- assessing the stewardship over the total cash funds that have been employed within the business;
- signalling to management whether its working capital policies are appropriate.

1.9.1 Stewardship

To assess the stewardship over the total cash funds we need to:

(a) evaluate the effectiveness of the accounting system to make certain that all transactions are recorded;

(b) extend the cash flow statement to take account of the capital cash flows; and

(c) prepare a statement of financial position or balance sheet as at 30 June 20X1.

The additional information for (b) and (c) above is set out in Figures 1.11 and 1.12 respectively.

The cash flow statement and statement of financial position, taken together, are a means of assessing stewardship. They identify the movement of **all** cash and derive a **net** balance figure. These statements are a normal feature of a sound system of internal control, but they have not been made available to external users.

Figure 1.11 Cash flow statement to calculate the net cash balance

	Jan £	Feb £	Mar £	Apr £	May £	Jun £	Total £
Operating cash	(1,850)	(1,900)	5,000	4,700	4,100	5,600	15,650
New capital	50,000						50,000
Lease payment	(80,000)						(80,000)
Cash balance	(31,850)	(33,750)	(28,750)	(24,050)	(19,950)	(14,350)	(14,350)

Figure 1.12 Statement of financial position

	Opening 1 Jan 20X1 £	Closing 30 Jun 20X1 £
Capital introduced	50,000	50,000
Net operating cash flow		15,650
	50,000	65,650
Lease		80,000
Net cash balance	50,000	−14,350
	50,000	65,650

1.9.2 Working capital policies

By 'working capital' we mean the current assets and current liabilities of the business. In addition to providing a means of making management accountable, cash flows are the raw data required by financial managers when making decisions on the management of working capital. One of the decisions would be to set the appropriate terms for credit policy. For example, Figure 1.11 shows that the business will have a £14,350 overdraft at 30 June 20X1. If this is not acceptable, management will review its working capital by reconsidering the credit given to customers, the credit taken from suppliers, stock-holding levels and the timing of capital cash inflows and outflows.

If, in the example, it were possible to obtain 45 days' credit from suppliers, then the creditors at 30 June would rise from £37,000 to a new total of £53,500. This increase in trade credit of £16,500 means that half of the May purchases (£33,000/2) would not be paid for until July, which would convert the overdraft of £14,350 into a positive balance of £2,150. As a new business it might not be possible to obtain credit from all of the suppliers. In that case, other steps would be considered, such as phasing the payment for the lease of the warehouse or introducing more capital.

An interesting research report[5] identified that for small firms survival and stability were the main objectives rather than profit maximisation. This, in turn, meant that cash flow indicators and managing cash flow were seen as crucial to survival. In addition, cash flow information was perceived as important to external bodies such as banks in evaluating performance.

1.10 Treatment of non-current assets in the cash flow model

The statement of financial position in Figure 1.12 does not take into account any **unrealised** cash flows. Such flows are deemed to occur as a result of any rise or fall in the realisable value of the lease. This could rise if, for example, the annual rent payable under the lease were to be substantially lower than the rate payable under a new lease entered into on 30 June 20X1. It could also fall with the passing of time, with six months having expired by 30 June 20X1. We need to consider this further and examine the possible treatment of non-current assets in the cash flow model.

Using the cash flow approach, we require an independent verification of the realisable value of the lease at 30 June 20X1. If the lease has fallen in value, the difference between the original outlay and the net realisable figure could be treated as a negative unrealised operating cash flow.

For example, if the independent estimate was that the realisable value was £74,000, then the statement of financial position would be prepared as in Figure 1.13. The fall of £6,000 in realisable value is an unrealised cash flow and, while it does not affect the calculation of the net cash balance, it does affect the statement of financial position.

Figure 1.13 Statement of financial position as at 30 June 20X1 (assuming that there were unrealised operating cash flows)

	£
Capital introduced	50,000
Net operating flow: realised	15,650
: unrealised	(6,000)
	59,650
Lease: net realisable value	74,000
Net cash balance	−14,350
	59,650

The additional benefit of the statement of financial position, as revised, is that the owner is able clearly to identify the following:

- the operating cash inflows of £15,650 that have been realised from the business operations;
- the operating cash outflow of £6,000 that has not been realised, but has arisen as a result of investing in the lease;
- the net cash balance of −£14,350;
- the statement provides a **stewardship-orientated** report: that is, it is a means of making the management accountable for the cash within its control.

1.11 What are the characteristics of these data that make them reliable?

We have already discussed some characteristics of cash flow reporting which indicate that the data in the financial statements are **relevant**, e.g. their predictive and confirmatory roles. We now introduce five more characteristics of cash flow statements which indicate that the information is also **reliable**, i.e. free from bias.[6] These are prudence, neutrality, completeness, faithful representation and substance over form.

1.11.1 Prudence characteristic

Revenue and profits are included in the cash flow statement only when they are realised. Realisation is deemed to occur when cash is received. In our Norman example, the £172,500 cash received from debtors represents the revenue for the half-year ended 30 June 20X1. This policy is described as prudent because it **does not anticipate** cash flows: cash flows are recorded only when they actually occur and not when they are reasonably certain to occur. This is one of the factors that distinguishes cash flow from accrual accounting.

1.11.2 Neutrality characteristic

Financial statements are not neutral if, by their selection or presentation of information, they influence the making of a decision in order to achieve a predetermined result or outcome. With cash flow accounting, the information is not subject to management selection criteria.

Cash flow accounting avoids the tension that can arise between prudence and neutrality because, whilst neutrality involves freedom from deliberate or systematic bias, prudence is a potentially biased concept that seeks to ensure that, under conditions of uncertainty, gains and assets are not overstated and losses and liabilities are not understated.[7]

1.11.3 Completeness characteristic

The cash flows can be verified for completeness provided there are adequate internal control procedures in operation. In small and medium-sized enterprises there can be a weakness if one person, typically the owner, has control over the accounting system and is able to under-record cash receipts.

1.11.4 Faithful representation characteristic

Cash flows can be depended upon by users to represent faithfully what they purport to represent provided, of course, that the completeness characteristic has been satisfied.

1.11.5 Substance over form

Cash flow accounting does not necessarily possess this characteristic which requires that transactions should be accounted for and presented in accordance with their substance and economic reality and not merely their legal form.[8]

1.12 Reports to external users

1.12.1 Stewardship orientation

Cash flow accounting provides objective, consistent and prudent financial information about a business's transactions. It is stewardship-orientated and offers a means of achieving accountability over cash resources and investment decisions.

1.12.2 Prediction orientation

External users are also interested in the ability of a company to pay dividends. It might be thought that the past and current cash flows are the best indicators of future cash flows and dividends. However, the cash flow might be misleading, in that a declining company might sell fixed assets and have a better **net cash position** than a growing company that buys fixed assets for future use. There is also no matching of cash inflows and outflows, in the sense that a benefit is matched with the sacrifice made to achieve it.

Consequently, it has been accepted accounting practice to view the income statement prepared on the accrual accounting concept as a better predictor of future cash flows to an investor than the cash flow statements that we have illustrated in this chapter.

However, the operating cash flows arising from trading and the cash flows arising from the introduction of capital and the acquisition of fixed assets can become significant to investors, e.g. they may threaten the company's ability to survive or may indicate growth.

In the next chapter, we revise the preparation of the same three statements using the **accrual accounting** model.

Summary

To review our understanding of this chapter, we should ask ourselves the following questions.

How useful is cash flow accounting for internal decision making?

Forecast cash flows are relevant for the appraisal of proposals for capital investment.

Actual cash flows are relevant for the confirmation of the decision for capital investment.

Cash flows are relevant for the management of working capital. Financial managers might have a variety of mathematical models for the efficient use of working capital, but cash flows are the raw data upon which they work.

How useful is cash flow accounting for making management accountable?

The cash flow statement is useful for confirming decisions and, together with the statement of financial position, provides a stewardship report. Lee states that 'Cash flow accounting appears to satisfy the need to supply owners and others with stewardship-orientated information as well as with decision-orientated information.'[9]

Lee further states that:

By reducing judgements in this type of financial report, management can report factually on its stewardship function, whilst at the same time disclosing data of use in the decision-making process. In other words, cash flow reporting eliminates the somewhat artificial segregation of stewardship and decision-making information.

This is exactly what we saw in our Norman example – the same realised operating cash flow information was used for both the investment decision and financial reporting. However, for stewardship purposes it was necessary to extend the cash flow to include **all** cash movements and to extend the statement of financial position to include the **unrealised** cash flows.

How useful is cash flow accounting for reporting to external users?

Cash flow information is relevant:

● as a basis for making internal management decisions in relation to both fixed assets and working capital; and
● for stewardship and accountability.

Cash flow information is reliable, being:

● objective;
● consistent;

- prudent; and
- neutral.

However, professional accounting practice requires reports to external users to be on an accrual accounting basis. This is because the accrual accounting profit figure is a better predictor for investors of the future cash flows likely to arise from the dividends paid to them by the business, and of any capital gain on disposal of their investment. It could also be argued that cash flows may not be a fair representation of the commercial substance of transactions, e.g. if a business allowed a year's credit to all its customers there would be no income recorded.

REVIEW QUESTIONS

1 Explain why it is the user who should determine the information that the accountant collects, measures and reports, rather than the accountant who is the expert in financial information.

2 'Yuji Ijiri rejects decision usefulness as the main purpose of accounting and puts in its place accountability. Ijiri sees the accounting relationship as a tripartite one, involving the accountor, the accountee, and the accountant ... the decision useful approach is heavily biased in favour of the accountee ... with little concern for the accountor ... in the central position Ijiri would put fairness.'[10] Discuss Ijiri's view in the context of cash flow accounting.

3 Discuss the extent to which you consider that accounts for a small businessperson who is carrying on business as a sole trader should be prepared on a cash flow basis.

4 Explain why your decision in question 3 might be different if the business entity were a medium-sized limited company.

5 'Realised operating cash flows are only of use for internal management purposes and are irrelevant to investors.' Discuss.

6 'While accountants may be free from bias in the measurement of economic information, they cannot be unbiased in identifying the economic information that they consider to be relevant.' Discuss.

7 Explain the effect on the statement of financial position in Figure 1.13 if the fixed asset consisted of expenditure on industry-specific machine tools rather than a lease.

8 'It is essential that the information in financial statements has a prudent characteristic if the financial statements are to be objective.' Discuss.

EXERCISES

An extract from the solution is provided in the Appendix at the end of the text for exercises marked with an asterisk (*).

* Question 1

Jane Parker is going to set up a new business on 1 January 20X1. She estimates that her first six months in business will be as follows:

 (i) She will put £150,000 into a bank account for the firm on 1 January 20X1.

 (ii) On 1 January 20X1 she will buy machinery £30,000, motor vehicles £24,000 and premises £75,000, paying for them immediately.

 (iii) All purchases will be effected on credit. She will buy £30,000 goods on 1 January and will pay for these in February. Other purchases will be: rest of January £48,000; February, March, April, May and June £60,000 each month. Other than the £30,000 worth bought in January, all other purchases will be paid for two months after purchase.

 (iv) Sales (all on credit) will be £60,000 for January and £75,000 for each month after. Customers will pay for the goods in the fourth month after purchase, i.e. £60,000 is received in May.

 (v) She will make drawings of £1,200 per month.

 (vi) Wages and salaries will be £2,250 per month and will be paid on the last day of each month.

 (vii) General expenses will be £750 per month, payable in the month following that in which they are incurred.

 (viii) Rates will be paid as follows: for the three months to 31 March 20X1 by cheque on 28 February 20X1; for the 12 months ended 31 March 20X2 by cheque on 31 July 20X1. Rates are £4,800 per annum.

 (ix) She will introduce new capital of £82,500 on 1 April 20X1.

 (x) Insurance covering the 12 months of 20X1 of £2,100 will be paid for by cheque on 30 June 20X1.

 (xi) All receipts and payments will be by cheque.

 (xii) Inventory on 30 June 20X1 will be £30,000.

 (xiii) The net realisable value of the vehicles is £19,200, machinery £27,000 and premises £75,000.

Required: Cash flow accounting
 (i) Draft a cash budget (includes bank) month by month for the period January to June, showing clearly the amount of bank balance or overdraft at the end of each month.
 (ii) Draft an operating cash flow statement for the six-month period.
 (iii) Assuming that Jane Parker sought your advice as to whether she should actually set up in business, state what further information you would require.

* Question 2

Mr Norman set up a new business on 1 January 20X8. He invested £50,000 in the new business on that date. The following information is available.

1 Gross profit was 20% of sales. Monthly sales were as follows:

Month	Sales £	Month	Sales £
January	15,000	May	40,000
February	20,000	June	45,000
March	35,000	July	50,000
April	40,000		

2 50% of sales were for cash. Credit customers (50% of sales) pay in month following sale.

3 The supplier allowed one month's credit.

4 Monthly payments were made for rent and rates £2,200 and wages £600.

5 On 1 January 20X8 the following payments were made: £80,000 for a five-year lease of business premises and £3,500 for insurances on the premises for the year. The realisable value of the lease was estimated to be £76,000 on 30 June 20X8 and £70,000 on 31 December 20X8.

6 Staff sales commission of 2% of sales was paid in the month following the sale.

Required:
(a) A purchases budget for each of the first six months.
(b) A cash flow statement for the first six months.
(c) A statement of operating cash flows and financial position as at 30 June 20X8.
(d) Write a brief letter to the bank supporting a request for an overdraft.

Question 3

Fred and Sally own a profitable business that deals in windsurfing equipment. They are the only UK agents to import 'Dryline' sails from Germany, and in addition to this they sell a variety of boards and miscellaneous equipment that they buy from other dealers in the UK.

Two years ago they diversified into custom-made boards built to individual customer requirements, each of which was supplied with a 'Dryline' sail. In order to build the boards they have had to take over larger premises, which consist of a shop front with a workshop at the rear, and employ two members of staff to help.

Demand is seasonal and Fred and Sally find that there is insufficient work during the winter months to pay rent for the increased accommodation and also wages to the extra two members of staff. The four of them could spend October to March in Lanzarote as windsurf instructors and close the UK operation down in this period. If they did, however, they would lose the 'Dryline' agency, as Dryline insists on a retail outlet in the UK for twelve months of the year. Dryline sails constitute 40% of their turnover and carry a 50% mark-up.

Trading has been static and the pattern is expected to continue as follows for 1 April 20X5 to 31 March 20X6:

Sales of boards and equipment (non-custom-built) with Dryline agency: 1 April–30 September £120,000; of this 30% was paid by credit card, which involved one month's delay in receiving cash and 4% deduction at source.

Sixty custom-built boards 1 April–30 September £60,000; of this 15% of the sales price was for the sail (a 'Dryline' 6 m² sail costs Fred and Sally £100; the average price for a sail of the same size and quality is £150 (cost to them)).

Purchasers of custom-built boards take an average of two months to pay and none pays by credit card.

Sales 1 October–31 March of boards and equipment (non-custom-built) £12,000, 30% by credit card as above.

Six custom-built boards were sold for a total of £6,000 and customers took an unexplainable average of three months to pay in the winter.

Purchases were made monthly and paid for two months in arrears.

The average mark-up on goods for resale excluding 'Dryline' sails was 25%. If they lose the agency, they expect that they will continue to sell the same number of sails, but at their average mark-up of 25%. The variable material cost of each custom-made board (excluding the sail) was £500.

Other costs were:
    Wages to employees £6,000 p.a. each (gross including insurance).
    Rent for premises £6,000 p.a. (six-monthly renewable lease) payable on the first day of each
    month.
    Other miscellaneous costs:
        1 April–30 September   £3,000
        1 October–31 March   £900.

Bank balance on 1 April was £100.

Salary earnable over whole period in Lanzarote:
    Fred and Sally £1,500 each + living accommodation
    Two employees £1,500 each + living accommodation

All costs and income accruing evenly over time.

Required:
(i)   Prepare a cash budget for 1 April 20X5 to 31 March 20X6 assuming that:
      (a)   Fred and Sally close the business in the winter months.
      (b)   They stay open all year.
(ii)   What additional information would you require before you advised Fred and Sally of the best
      course of action to take?

References

1 *Framework for the Preparation and Presentation of Financial Statements*, IASC, 1989, para. 10.
2 *Ibid.*, para. 35.
3 G. Whittred and I. Zimmer, *Financial Accounting: Incentive Effects and Economic Consequences*,
    Holt, Rinehart & Winston, 1992, p. 27.
4 IASC, *op. cit.*, para. 27.
5 R. Jarvis, J. Kitching, J. Curran and G. Lightfoot, *The Financial Management of Small Firms:
    An Alternative Perspective*, ACCA Research Report No. 49.
6 IASC, *op. cit.*, para. 34.
7 *Ibid.*, para. 37.
8 *Ibid.*, para. 35.
9 T.A. Lee, *Income and Value Measurement: Theory and Practice* (3rd edition), Van Nostrand
    Reinhold (UK), 1985, p. 173.
10 D. Solomons, *Making Accounting Policy*, Oxford University Press, 1986, p. 79.

CHAPTER 2

Accounting and reporting on an accrual accounting basis

2.1 Introduction

In this chapter we consider the following:

- Historical cost convention
- Accrual accounting concept
- Mechanics of accrual accounting – adjusting cash receipts and payments
- Subjective judgements required in accrual accounting
  1 Adjusting cash receipts in accordance with IAS 18
  2 Adjusting cash payments in accordance with the matching principle
- Mechanics of accrual accounting – the balance sheet
- Reformatting the statement of financial position into a balance sheet
- Accounting for the sacrifice of fixed assets
- Reconciliation of cash flow and accrual accounting data.

2.1.1 Objective of financial statements

The International Accounting Standards Committee (IASC) has stated that the objective of financial statements is to provide information about the financial position, performance and capability of an enterprise that is useful to a wide range of users in making economic decisions.[1]

Common information needs for decision making

The IASC recognises that all the information needs of all users cannot be met by financial statements, but it takes the view that some needs are common to all users: in particular, they have some interest in the financial position, performance and adaptability of the enterprise as a whole. This leaves open the question of which user is the primary target; the IASC states that, as investors are providers of risk capital, financial statements that meet their needs would also meet the needs of other users.[2]

Stewardship role of financial statements

In addition to assisting in making economic decisions, financial statements also show the results of the stewardship of management: that is, the accountability of management for the resources entrusted to it. The IASC view[3] is that users who assess the stewardship do so in order to make economic decisions, e.g. whether to hold or sell shares in a particular company or change the management.

Decision makers need to assess ability to generate cash

The IASC considers that economic decisions also require an evaluation of an enterprise's ability to generate cash, and of the timing and certainty of its generation.[4] It believes that users are better able to make the evaluation if they are provided with information that focuses on the financial position, performance and cash flow of an enterprise.

2.1.2 Financial information to evaluate the ability to generate cash differs from financial information on actual cash flows

The IASC approach differs from the cash flow model used in Chapter 1, in that, in addition to the cash flows and statement of financial position, it includes within its definition of performance a reference to profit. It states that this information is required to assess changes in the economic resources that the enterprise is likely to control in the future. This is useful in predicting the capacity of the enterprise to generate cash flows from its existing resource base.[5]

2.1.3 Statements making up the financial statements published for external users

The IASC suggests that the financial statements published by a company for external users should consist of the following:

- an income statement,
- a statement of changes in equity,[6]
- a balance sheet,
- a statement of changes in financial position, e.g. a cash flow statement.[7]

In this chapter we consider two of the conventions under which the income statement and balance sheet are prepared: the historical cost convention and the accrual accounting concept.

2.2 Historical cost convention

The historical cost convention results in an appropriate measure of the economic resource that has been withdrawn or replaced.

Under it, transactions are reported at the £ amount recorded at the date the transaction occurred. Financial statements produced under this convention provide a basis for determining the outcome of agency agreements with reasonable certainty and predictability because the data are relatively objective.[8]

By this we mean that various parties who deal with the enterprise, such as lenders, will know that the figures produced in any financial statements are objective and not manipulated by subjective judgements made by the directors. A typical example occurs when a lender attaches a covenant to a loan that the enterprise shall not exceed a specified level of gearing.

At an operational level, revenue and expense in the income statement are stated at the £ amount that appears on the invoices. This amount is objective and verifiable. Because of this, the historical cost convention has strengths for stewardship purposes, but inflation-adjusted figures may well be more appropriate for decision usefulness.

2.3 Accrual basis of accounting

The accrual basis dictates when transactions with third parties should be recognised and, in particular, determines the accounting periods in which they should be incorporated into the financial statements. Under this concept the cash receipts from customers and payments to creditors are replaced by revenue and expenses respectively.

Revenue and expenses are derived by adjusting the realised operating cash flows to take account of business trading activity that has occurred during the accounting period, but has not been converted into cash receipts or payments by the end of the period.

2.3.1 Accrual accounting is a better indicator than cash flow accounting of ability to generate cash

The accounting profession generally supports the view expressed by the Financial Accounting Standards Board (FASB) in the USA that accrual accounting provides a better indication of an enterprise's present and continuing ability to generate favourable cash flows than information limited to the financial aspects of cash receipts and payments.[9]

The IASC supported the FASB view in 1989 when it stated that financial statements prepared on an accrual basis inform users not only of past transactions involving the payment and receipt of cash, but also of obligations to pay cash in the future and of resources that represent cash to be received in the future, and that they provide the type of information about past transactions and other events that is most useful in making economic decisions.[10]

Having briefly considered why accrual accounting is more useful than cash flow accounting, we will briefly revise the preparation of financial statements under the accrual accounting convention.

2.4 Mechanics of accrual accounting – adjusting cash receipts and payments

We use the cash flows set out in Figure 1.7 on page 11. The derivation of the revenue and expenses for this example is set out in Figures 2.1 and 2.2. We assume that the enterprise has incomplete records, so that the revenue is arrived at by keeping a record of unpaid invoices and adding these to the cash receipts. Clearly, if the invoices are not adequately controlled, there will be no assurance that the £22,500 figure is correct. This is a relatively straightforward process at a mechanistic level. The uncertainty is not how to adjust the cash flow figures, but when to adjust them. This decision requires managers to make subjective judgements. We now look briefly at the nature of such judgements.

Figure 2.1   Derivation of revenue

	£
Cash received	172,500
Invoices not paid (= Sales invoiced – Cash received)	22,500
Revenue = Total invoiced	195,000

Figure 2.2 Derivation of expense

	Materials £	Services £
Cash paid	129,000	21,600
Invoices not paid	37,000	900
Expense = Total invoiced	166,000	22,500

2.5 Subjective judgements required in accrual accounting – adjusting cash receipts in accordance with IAS 18

In Figure 2.1 we assumed that revenue was derived simply by adding unpaid invoices to the cash receipts. In practice, however, this is influenced by the commercial facts underlying the transactions. For example, if the company is a milk producer, the point at which it should report the milk production as revenue will be influenced by the existence of a supply contract. If there is a contract with a buyer, the revenue might be recognised immediately on production.

So that financial statements are comparable, the IASC[11] has set out revenue recognition criteria in IAS 18 *Revenue* in an attempt to identify when performance was sufficient to warrant inclusion in the revenue for the period. It stated that:

> In a transaction involving the sale of goods, performance should be regarded as being achieved when the following conditions have been fulfilled:
> (a) the seller of the goods has transferred to the buyer the significant risks and rewards of ownership, in that all significant acts have been completed and the seller retains no continuing managerial involvement in, or effective control of, the goods transferred to a degree usually associated with ownership; and
> (b) no significant uncertainty exists regarding:
>   (i) the consideration that will be derived from the sale of the goods;
>   (ii) the associated costs incurred or to be incurred in producing or purchasing the goods;
>   (iii) the extent to which the goods are returned.

The criteria are simple in their intention, but difficult in their application. For instance, at what exact point in the sales cycle is there no significant uncertainty? The enterprise has to decide on the critical event that can support an assumption that revenue may be recognised.

To assist with these decisions, the standard provided an appendix with a number of examples. Figure 2.3 gives examples of critical events.

The amount of detail in the accounting policy for turnover will depend on the range of activities within a business and events occurring during the financial year. For example, the relevant section of the 2004 Annual Report of the Chloride Group, which tests and assembles electronic products, simply reads:

> Turnover represents the amounts, excluding VAT and similar sales-related taxes, receivable by the Group for goods and services supplied to customers in the ordinary course of business. Turnover is recognised when persuasive evidence of an

Figure 2.3   Extracts from IAS 18 *Revenue* illustrating critical events

Transaction	Critical event
Services	
Servicing fees included in the price of the product[12]	When the selling price of a product includes an identifiable amount for subsequent servicing for, say, a warranty period, it will normally be appropriate to defer the relevant portion of the selling price and to recognise it as revenue over the appropriate period.
Sales of goods	
Shipment made giving the buyer right of return[13]	Recognition of revenue in such circumstances will depend on the substance of the agreement. In the case of normal retail sales (e.g. chain store offering money back if not satisfied) it may be appropriate to recognise the sale but to make a suitable provision for returns based on previous experience. In other cases the substance of the agreement may amount to a sale on consignment, in which case the revenue should not be recognised until the goods are sold to a third party.

arrangement with a customer exists, products have been delivered or services have been rendered and collectability is reasonably assured.

Cadbury Schweppes in its 2003 Annual Report is more specific with a reference to inter-company sales and sales returns as follows:

Turnover
This represents the invoiced value of sales and royalties excluding inter-company sales, value added tax and sales taxes that arise as a result of the Group's sale of branded chocolate, sugar and gum confectionery products and branded soft drinks. Turnover is stated net of trade discounts, sales incentives, up-front payments, slotting fees and other non-discretionary payments. Revenue is recognised when persuasive evidence of an arrangement with a customer exists, delivery has occurred, the price is fixed or determinable and collection of the amount due is reasonably assured. A provision for sales returns is estimated on the basis of historical returns and recorded so as to allocate these returns to the same period as the original turnover is recorded.

Turnover accounting policy for Balfour Beatty plc, which carries on business in building construction, civil and rail engineering, is stated in its 2003 Annual Report as:

Turnover represents amounts invoiced to outside customers, net of trade discounts, value added and similar sales-based taxes, except in respect of contracting activities where turnover represents the value of work carried out during the year including amounts not invoiced. Turnover is recognised on property developments when they are subject to substantially unconditional contracts for sale.

There can be some uncertainty over the treatment of items that are to be netted off to arrive at turnover. For example, the Novartis Group disclosed in its 2002 Annual

Report that it had changed its treatment of discounts allowed to customers:

> Sales are recognised when the significant risks and rewards of ownership of the assets have been transferred to a third party and are reported net of sales taxes and rebates. ... Sales have been restated for all periods presented to treat certain sales incentives and discounts to retailers as sales deductions instead of marketing and distribution expenses.

Note that this does not affect the bottom line but does have an impact on the sales and gross profit figures.

2.6 Subjective judgements required in accrual accounting – adjusting cash payments in accordance with the matching principle

We have seen that the enterprise needs to decide when to recognise the revenue. It then needs to decide when to include an item as an expense in the profit and loss account. This decision is based on an application of the matching principle.

The matching principle means that financial statements must include costs related to the achievement of the reported revenue. These include the internal transfers required to ensure that reductions in the assets held by a business are recorded at the same time as the revenues.

The expense might be more or less than the cash paid. For example, in the Norman example, £37,000 was invoiced but not paid on materials, and £900 on services; £3,125 was prepaid on rent for the six months after June. The cash flow information therefore needs to be adjusted as in Figure 2.4.

Figure 2.4 Income statement for the six months ended 30 June 20X1

	Operating cash flow £	ADJUST cash flow £	Business activity £
Revenue from business activity	172,500	22,500	195,000
Less: Matching expenses			
Transactions for materials	129,000	37,000	166,000
Transactions for services	21,600	900	22,500
Transaction with landlord	6,250	(3,125)	3,125
OPERATING CASH FLOW from business activity	15,650		
Transactions NOT converted to cash or relating to a subsequent period		(12,275)	
PROFIT from business activity			3,375

2.7 Mechanics of accrual accounting – the balance sheet

The balance sheet or statement of financial position, as set out in Figure 1.12, needs to be amended following the change from cash flow to accrual accounting. It needs to include the £ amounts that have arisen from trading but have not been converted to cash, and the £ amounts of cash that have been received or paid but relate to a subsequent period. The adjusted statement of financial position is set out in Figure 2.5.

Figure 2.5   Statement of financial position adjusted to an accrual basis

	£
Capital	50,000
Net operating cash flow: **realised**	15,650
Net operating cash flow: **to be realised next period**	(12,275)
	53,375
Lease	80,000
Net cash balance (refer to Figure 1.11)	(14,350)
Net amount of activities not converted to cash or relating to subsequent periods	(12,275)
	53,375

2.8 Reformatting the statement of financial position into a balance sheet

The item 'net amount of activities not converted to cash or relating to subsequent periods' is the net debtor/creditor balance. If we wished, the statement of financial position could be reframed into the customary balance sheet format, where items are classified as assets or liabilities. The IASC defines assets and liabilities in its *Framework*:[14]

Figure 2.6   Balance sheet as at 30 June

		Reframed
	£	£
CAPITAL	50,000	50,000
Net operating cash flow: **realised**	15,650	
Net operating cash flow: **to be realised**	(12,275)	
NET INCOME		3,375
	53,375	53,375
NON-CURRENT ASSETS	80,000	80,000
NET CURRENT ASSETS		
Net amount of activities not converted to cash	(12,275)	
CURRENT ASSETS		
Trade receivables		22,500
Other receivables: Prepaid rent		3,125
CURRENT LIABILITIES		
Trade payables		(37,000)
Other payables: service suppliers		(900)
Net cash balance	(14,350)	(14,350)
	53,375	53,375

● An asset is a resource:
- controlled by the enterprise
- as a result of past events
- from which future economic benefits are expected to flow
● A liability is a present obligation:
- arising from past events
- the settlement of which is expected to result in an outflow of resources.

The reframed balance sheet set out in Figure 2.6 is in accordance with these definitions. Note that the same amount of £3,375 results from calculating the difference in the opening and closing net assets in the balance sheets as from calculating the residual amount in the income statement. When the amount derived from both approaches is the same, the balance sheet and income statement are said to **articulate**. The income statement provides the detailed explanation for the difference in the net assets and the amount is the same because the same concepts have been applied to both statements.

2.9 Accounting for the sacrifice of non-current assets

The income statement and balance sheet have both been prepared using verifiable data that have arisen from transactions with third parties outside the business. However, in order to determine the full sacrifice of economic resources that a business has made to achieve its revenue, it is necessary also to take account of the use made of the non-current assets during the period in which the revenue arose.

In the Norman example, the non-current asset is the lease. The extent of the sacrifice is a matter of judgement by the management. This is influenced by the prudence principle, which regulates the matching principle. The prudence principle determines the extent to which transactions that have already been included in the accounting system should be recognised in the income statement.

2.9.1 Treatment of non-current assets in accrual accounting

Applying the matching principle, it is necessary to estimate how much of the initial outlay should be assumed to have been revenue expenditure, i.e. used in achieving the revenue of the accounting period. The provisions of IAS 16 on **depreciation** assist by defining depreciation and stating the duty of allocation, as follows:

> Depreciation is the systematic allocation of the depreciable amount of an asset over its useful life.[15]

> Depreciable amount is the cost of an asset, or other amount substituted for cost in the financial statements, less its residual value.[16]

> The depreciation method used should reflect the pattern in which the asset's economic benefits are consumed by the enterprise.[17]

This sounds a rather complex requirement. It is therefore surprising, when one looks at the financial statements of a multinational company such as BP plc, to find that depreciation on tangible assets other than mineral production is simply provided on a straight-line basis of an equal amount each year, calculated so as to write off the cost by equal instalments. In the UK, this treatment is recognised in FRS 15 which states that where the pattern of consumption of an asset's economic benefits is uncertain, a straight-line method of depreciation is usually adopted.[18] The reason is that, in accrual accounting, the depreciation charged to the income statement is a measure of the amount of the economic benefits that have been consumed, rather than a measure of the fall in realisable value. In estimating the amount of service potential expired, a business is following the **going concern assumption**.

2.9.2 Going concern assumption

The going concern assumption is that the business enterprise will continue in operational existence for the foreseeable future. This assumption introduces a constraint on the prudence concept by allowing the account balances to be reported on a depreciated cost basis rather than on a net realisable value basis.

It is more relevant to use the loss of service potential than the change in realisable value because there is no intention to cease trading and to sell the fixed assets at the end of the accounting period.

In our Norman example, the procedure would be to assume that, in the case of the lease, the economic resource that has been consumed can be measured by the amortisation that has occurred due to the effluxion of time. The time covered by the accounts is half a year: this means that one-tenth of the lease has expired during the half-year. As a result, £8,000 is treated as revenue expenditure in the half-year to 30 June.

This additional revenue expenditure reduces the income in the income account and the asset figure in the balance sheet. The effects are incorporated into the two statements in Figures 2.7 and 2.8. The asset amounts and the income figure in the balance sheet are also affected by the exhaustion of part of the fixed assets, as set out in Figure 2.8.

It is current accounting practice to apply the same concepts to determining the entries in both the income statement and the balance sheet. The amortisation charged in the income statement at £8,000 is the same as the amount deducted from the fixed assets in the balance sheet. As a result, the two statements articulate: the income statement explains the reason for the reduction of £4,625 in the net assets.

Figure 2.7   Income statement for the six months ending 30 June

	Operating cash flow CURRENT period £	Adjust cash flow £	Business activity CURRENT period £
Revenue from business activity	172,500	22,500	195,000
Less			
Expenditure to support this activity:			
Transactions with suppliers	129,000	37,000	166,000
Transactions with service providers	21,600	900	22,500
Transactions with landlord	6,250	(3,125)	3,125
OPERATING CASH FLOW from activity	15,650		
TRANSACTIONS NOT CONVERTED TO CASH		(12,275)	
INCOME from business activity			3,375
Allocation of fixed asset cost to this period			8,000
INCOME			(4,625)

Figure 2.8 Balance sheet as at 30 June

	Transaction cash flows £	Notional flows £	Reported £
CAPITAL	50,000		50,000
Net operating cash flow: **realised**	15,650		
Net operating cash flow: **to be realised**	(12,275)		
Net income before depreciation		3,375	
AMORTISATION		(8,000)	
Net income after amortisation			(4,625)
	53,375		45,375
NON-CURRENT ASSETS	80,000	80,000	
Less amortisation		(8,000)	
Net book value			72,000
NET CURRENT ASSETS			
Net amount not converted to cash	(12,275)		
CURRENT ASSETS			
Trade receivables			22,500
Other receivables – prepaid rent			3,125
CURRENT LIABILITIES			
Trade payables			(37,000)
Other payables: service suppliers			(900)
Net cash balance	(14,350)		(14,350)
	53,375		45,375

How decision-useful to the management is the income figure that has been derived after deducting a depreciation charge?

The loss of £4,625 indicates that the distribution of any amount would further deplete the financial capital of £50,000 which was invested in the company by Mr Norman on setting up the business. This is referred to as **capital maintenance**; the particular capital maintenance concept that has been applied is the **financial capital maintenance concept**.

2.9.3 Financial capital maintenance concept

The financial capital maintenance concept recognises a profit only after the original monetary investment has been maintained. This means that, as long as the cost of the assets representing the initial monetary investment is recovered against the profit, by way of a depreciation charge, the initial monetary investment is maintained.

The concept has been described in the IASC *Framework for the Presentation and Preparation of Financial Statements*:

> a profit is earned only if the financial or money amount of the net assets at the end of the period exceeds the financial or money amount of the net assets at the beginning of the period, after excluding any distributions to, and contributions from,

owners during the period. Financial capital maintenance can be measured in either nominal monetary units [as we are doing in this chapter] or in units of constant purchasing power [as we will be doing in Chapter 4].[19]

2.9.4 Summary of views on accrual accounting

Standard setters:

The profit (loss) is considered to be a guide when assessing the amount, timing and uncertainty of prospective cash flows as represented by future income amounts. The IASC, FASB in the USA and ASB in the UK clearly state that the accrual accounting concept is more useful in predicting future cash flows than cash flow accounting.

Academic researchers:

Academic research provides conflicting views. In 1986, research carried out in the USA indicated that the FASB view was inconsistent with its findings and that cash flow information was a better predictor of future operating cash flows;[20] research carried out in the UK, however, indicated that accrual accounting using the historical cost convention was 'a more relevant basis for decision making than cash flow measures'.[21]

2.10 Reconciliation of cash flow and accrual accounting data

The accounting profession attempted to provide users of financial statements with the benefits of both types of data, by requiring a cash flow statement to be prepared as well as the income statement and balance sheet prepared on an accrual basis.

From the income statement prepared on an accrual basis (as in Figure 2.7) an investor is able to obtain an indication of a business's present ability to generate favourable cash flows; from the balance sheet prepared on an accrual basis (as in Figure 2.8) an investor is able to obtain an indication of a business's continuing ability to generate favourable cash flows; from the cash flow statement (as in Figure 2.9) an investor is able to reconcile the income figure with the change in net cash balance.

Figure 2.9   Reconciliation of income figure with net cash balance

	£
Income per income statement	(4,625)
Add: unrealisable cash outflow	8,000
	3,375
Add: unrealised operating cash flows	12,275
Operating cash flow	15,650
Other sources:	
Capital	50,000
Total cash available	65,650
Applications	
Lease	(80,000)
Net cash balance	(14,350)

Figure 2.9 reconciles the information produced in Chapter 1 under the cash flow basis with the information produced under the accrual basis. It could be expanded to provide information more clearly, as in Figure 2.10. Here we are using the information from Figures 1.9 and 1.12, but within a third statement rather than the income statement and balance sheet.

Figure 2.10   Cash flow statement netting amounts that have not been converted to cash

	£	£
Sales	195,000	
Trade receivables	(22,500)	172,500
Purchases	166,000	
Trade payables	(37,000)	(129,000)
Expenses	22,500	
Other payables	(900)	(21,600)
Rent	3,125	
Other receivables: Prepaid rent	3,125	(6,250)
Net cash inflow from operating activities		15,650
Cash flows from investing activities		
Lease		(80,000)
Cash flows from financing activities		
Issue of capital		50,000
Decrease in cash		(14,350)

2.10.1 Published cash flow statement

IAS 7 *Cash Flow Statements*[22] specifies the standard headings under which cash flows should be classified. They are:

● cash flows from operating activities;
● cash flows from investing activities;
● cash flows from financing activities;
● net increase in cash and cash equivalents.

To comply with IAS 7, the cash flows from Figure 2.10 would be set out as in Figure 2.11. IAS 7 is mentioned at this stage only to illustrate that cash flows can be reconciled to the accrual accounting data. There is further discussion of IAS 7 in Chapter 27.

Figure 2.11   Cash flow statement in accordance with IAS 7 *Cash Flow Statements*

	£
Net cash inflow from operating activities	15,650
Investing activities	
Payment to acquire lease	(80,000)
Net cash outflow before financing	(64,350)
Financing	
Issue of capital	50,000
Decrease in cash	(14,350)
Reconciliation of operating loss to net cash inflow from operating activities	£
Operating profit/loss	(4,625)
Amortisation charges	8,000
Increase in trade receivables	(22,500)
Increase in prepayments	(3,125)
Increase in trade payables	37,000
Increase in accruals	900
	15,650

REVIEW QUESTIONS

1   *The Framework for the Preparation and Presentation of Financial Statements* identified seven user groups: investors, employees, lenders, suppliers and other trade creditors, customers, government and the public.

Discuss which of the financial statements illustrated in Chapters 1 and 2 would be most useful to each of these seven groups if they could only receive one statement.

2   'Accrual accounting is preferable to cash flow accounting because the information is more relevant to all users of financial statements.' Discuss.

3   'Cash flow accounting and accrual accounting information are both required by a potential shareholder.' Discuss.

4   'Information contained in a profit and loss account and a balance sheet prepared under accrual accounting concepts is factual and objective.' Discuss.

5   'The asset measurement basis applied in accrual accounting can lead to financial difficulties when assets are due for replacement.' Discuss.

6   'Accountants preparing financial statements in the UK do not require a standard such as IAS 18 *Revenue*.' Discuss.

7   Explain the revenue recognition principle and discuss the effect of alternative treatments on the reported results of a company.

8   The annual financial statements of companies are used by various parties for a wide variety of purposes. For each of the seven different 'user groups', explain their presumed interest with reference to the performance of the company and its financial position.

EXERCISES

An extract from the solution is provided in the Appendix at the end of the text for exercises marked with an asterisk (*).

* Question 1

Jane Parker is going to set up a new business in Bruges on 1 January 20X1. She estimates that her first six months in business will be as follows:

   (i)   She will put €150,000 into the firm on 1 January 20X1.

   (ii) On 1 January 20X1 she will buy machinery €30,000, motor vehicles €24,000 and premises €75,000, paying for them immediately.

   (iii) All purchases will be effected on credit. She will buy €30,000 goods on 1 January and she will pay for these in February. Other purchases will be: rest of January €48,000; February, March, April, May and June €60,000 each month. Other than the €30,000 worth bought in January, all other purchases will be paid for two months after purchase, i.e. €48,000 in March.

   (iv) Sales (all on credit) will be €60,000 for January and €75,000 for each month after that. Customers will pay for goods in the third month after purchase, i.e. €60,000 in April.

   (v)   Inventory on 30 June 20X1 will be €30,000.

   (vi) Wages and salaries will be €2,250 per month and will be paid on the last day of each month.

   (vii) General expenses will be €750 per month, payable in the month following that in which they are incurred.

   (viii) She will introduce new capital of €75,000 on 1 June 20X1. This will be paid into the business bank account immediately.

   (ix) Insurance covering the 12 months of 20X1 of €26,400 will be paid for by cheque on 30 June 20X1.

   (x)   Local taxes will be paid as follows: for the three months to 31 March 20X1 by cheque on 28 February 20X2, delay due to an oversight by Parker; for the 12 months ended 31 March 20X2 by cheque on 31 July 20X1. Local taxes are €8,000 per annum.

   (xi) She will make drawings of €1,500 per month by cheque.

   (xii) All receipts and payments are by cheque.

   (xiii) Depreciate motor vehicles by 20% per annum and machinery by 10% per annum, using the straight-line depreciation method.

   (xiv) She has been informed by her bank manager that he is prepared to offer an overdraft facility of €30,000 for the first year.

Required:

(a) Draft a cash budget (for the firm) month by month for the period January to June, showing clearly the amount of bank balance at the end of each month.

(b) Draft the projected income statement for the first six months' trading, and a balance sheet as at 30 June 20X1.

(c) Advise Jane on the alternative courses of action that could be taken to cover any cash deficiency that exceeds the agreed overdraft limit.

* Question 2

Mr Norman is going to set up a new business in Singapore on 1 January 20X8. He will invest $150,000 in the business on that date and has made the following estimates and policy decisions:

1   Forecast sales (in units) made at a selling price of $50 per unit are:

Month	Sales units	Month	Sales units
January	1,650	May	4,400
February	2,200	June	4,950
March	3,850	July	5,500
April	4,400		

2   50% of sales are for cash. Credit terms are payment in the month following sale.

3   The units cost $40 each and the supplier is allowed one month's credit.

4   It is intended to hold inventory at the end of each month sufficient to cover 25% of the following month's sales.

5   Administration $8,000 and wages $17,000 are paid monthly as they arise.

6   On 1 January 20X8, the following payments will be made: $80,000 for a five-year lease of the business premises and $350 for insurance for the year.

7   Staff sales commission of 2% of sales will be paid in the month following sale.

Required:
(a) A purchases budget for each of the first six months.
(b) A cash flow forecast for the first six months.
(c) A budgeted income statement for the first six months' trading and a budgeted balance sheet as at 30 June 20X8.
(d) Advise Mr Norman on the investment of any excess cash.

Question 3

The Piano Warehouse Company Limited was established in the UK on 1 January 20X7 for the purpose of making pianos. Jeremy Holmes, the managing director, had twenty years' experience in the manufacture of pianos and was an acknowledged technical expert in the field. He had invested his life's savings of £15,000 in the company, and his decision to launch the company reflected his desire for complete independence.

Nevertheless, his commitment to the company represented a considerable financial gamble. He paid close attention to the management of its financial affairs and ensured that a careful record of all transactions was kept.

The company's activities during the year ended 31 December 20X7 were as follows:

(i)   Four pianos had been built and sold for a total sum of £8,000. Holmes calculated their cost of manufacture as follows:

Materials	£2,000
Labour	£2,800
Overhead costs	£800

(ii) Two pianos were 50% completed at 31 December 20X7. Madrigal Music Limited had agreed to buy them for a total of £4,500 and had made a down-payment amounting to 20% of the agreed sale price. Holmes estimated their costs of manufacture to 31 December 20X7 as follows:

Materials	£900
Labour	£800
Overhead costs	£100

(iii) Two pianos had been rebuilt and sold for a total of £3,000. Holmes paid £1,800 for them at an auction and had spent a further £400 on rebuilding them. The sale of these two pianos was made under a hire purchase agreement under which The Piano Warehouse Company received £1,000 on delivery and two payments over the next two years plus interest of 15% on the outstanding balance.

At the end of the company's first financial year, Jeremy Holmes was anxious that the company's net profit to 31 December 20X7 should be represented in the most accurate manner. There appeared to be several alternative bases on which the transactions for the year could be interpreted. It was clear to him that, in simple terms, the net profit for the year should be calculated by deducting expenses from revenues. As far as cash sales were concerned he saw no difficulty. But how should the pianos that were 50% completed be treated? Should the value of the work done up to 31 December 20X7 be included in the profit of that year, or should it be carried forward to the next year, when the work would be completed and the pianos sold? As regards the pianos sold under the hire purchase agreement, should profit be taken in 20X7 or spread over the years in which a proportion of the revenue is received?

Required:
(a) Prepare an income statement for the year ended 31 December 20X7 on a basis that would reflect conventional accounting principles.
(b) Examine the problems implied in the timing of the recognition of revenues, illustrating your answer by the facts in the case of The Piano Warehouse.
(c) Discuss the significant accounting conventions that would be relevant to profit determination in this case, and discuss their limitations in this context.
(d) Advise the company on alternative accounting treatments that could increase the profit for the year.

Question 4

The following is an extract from the Financial Reporting Review Panel website (www.frrp.org.uk) relating to the Wiggins Group showing the restated financial results.

		Year					
		1995	1996	1997	1998	1999	2000
Turnover	As published	6.4	6.9	19.9	17.8	26.7	49.8
(£m)	Adjustments	(1.5)	(2.6)	(15.6)	(6.7)	(21.6)	(42.5)
	Restated	4.9	4.3	4.3	11.1	5.1	7.3
Profit/(loss)	As published	0.7	1.0	4.9	5.1	12.1	25.1
before tax	Adjustments	(1.3)	(1.9)	(10.2)	(8.5)	(17.2)	(35.0)
(£m)	Restated	(0.6)	(0.9)	(5.3)	(3.4)	(5.1)	(9.9)
Basic EPS	As published	0.14	0.20	0.66	0.64	1.21	2.87
(pence)	Adjustments	(0.26)	(0.38)	(1.67)	(1.14)	(1.91)	(4.06)
	Restated	(0.12)	(0.18)	(1.01)	(0.50)	(0.70)	(1.19)
Net assets	As published	10.2	11.4	17.5	37.5	52.2	45.8
(£m)	Adjustments	(1.3)	(3.2)	(12.0)	(19.8)	(33.8)	(35.4)
	Restated	8.9	8.2	5.5	17.7	18.4	10.4

Revenue recognition

The 1999 accounts contained an accounting policy for turnover in the following terms:

> Commercial property sales are recognised at the date of exchange of contract, providing the Group is reasonably assured of the receipt of the sale proceeds.

The FRRP accepted that this wording was similar to that used by many other companies and was not on the face of it objectionable. In reviewing the company's 1999 accounts the FRRP noted that the turnover and profits recognised under this policy were not reflected in similar inflows of cash; indeed, operating cash flow was negative and the amount receivable within debtors of £46m represented more than the previous two years' turnover of £44m. As a result, the FRRP enquired into the detailed application of the policy.

Required:
Refer to the website and discuss the significance of the revenue recognition criteria on the published results.

References

1 *Framework for the Preparation and Presentation of Financial Statements*, IASC, 1989, para. 12.
2 *Ibid.*, para. 10.
3 *Ibid.*, para. 14.
4 *Ibid.*, para. 15.
5 *Ibid.*, para. 17.
6 IAS 1 *Presentation of Financial Statements*, IASC, revised 1997, para. 86.
7 *Framework for the Preparation and Presentation of Financial Statements*, IASC, 1989, para. 7.
8 M. Page, *British Accounting Review*, vol. 24(1), 1992, p. 80.
9 *Statement of Financial Accounting Concepts No. 1, Objectives of Financial Reporting by Business Enterprises*, Financial Accounting Standards Board, 1978.
10 *Framework for the Preparation and Presentation of Financial Statements*, IASC, 1989, para. 20.
11 IAS 18 *Revenue*, IASC, 1993, para. 14.
12 *Ibid.*, para. 11 of the Appendix.

13 *Ibid.*, para. 2 of the Appendix.
14 *Framework for the Preparation and Presentation of Financial Statements*, IASC, 1989, para. 49.
15 IAS 16 *Property, Plant and Equipment*, IASC, revised 1998, para. 6.
16 *Ibid.*, para. 6.
17 *Ibid.*, para. 41.
18 FRS 15 *Tangible Fixed Assets*, ASB, 1999, para. 81.
19 *Framework for the Preparation and Presentation of Financial Statements*, IASC, 1989, para. 102.
20 R.M. Bowen, D. Burgstahller and L.A. Daley, 'Evidence on the relationship between earnings and various measures of cash flow', *Accounting Review*, October 1986, pp. 713–725.
21 J.I.G. Board and J.F.S. Day, 'The information content of cash flow figures', *Accounting and Business Research*, Winter 1989, pp. 3–11.
22 *Cash Flow Statements*, IASC, 1994.

CHAPTER 3

Income and asset value measurement: an economist's approach

3.1 Introduction

This chapter discusses the need for income measurement. It compares the methods of measurement adopted by the accountant with those of the economist, the reasons for the different approaches, the relationship of income to capital and the impact of the concept of value on these measures. The prime objective is to engender an understanding of the rule of income and capital within the commercial enterprise, and to prevent misunderstanding of what initially may appear to be a conflict of method between the two disciplines. Economic value was initially perceived as an academic subject but we now see it being applied by the IASC within financial reporting, e.g. in IAS 36 *Impairment of Assets* where it is referred to as value in use. In this chapter we consider the following:

- Role and objective of income measurement
- Accountant's view of income, capital and value
- Critical comment on the accountant's measure
- Economist's view of income, capital and value
- Critical comment on the economist's measure
- Income, capital and changing price levels.

3.2 Role and objective of income measurement

Although accountancy has played a part in business reporting for centuries, it is only since the Companies Act 1929 that financial reporting has become income orientated. Prior to that Act an income statement was of minor importance. It was the balance sheet that mattered, providing a list of capital, assets and liabilities that revealed the financial soundness and solvency of the business.

According to some commentators,[1] this scenario may be attributed to the sources of capital funding. Until the late 1920s, as in present-day Germany, external capital finance in the UK was mainly in the hands of bankers, other lenders and trade creditors. As the main users of published financial statements, they focused on the company's ability to pay trade creditors and the interest on loans, and to meet the scheduled dates of loan repayment: they were interested in the short-term liquidity and longer-term solvency of the entity.

Thus the balance sheet was the prime document of interest. Perhaps in recognition of this, the English balance sheet, until recent times, tended to show liabilities on the left-hand side, thus making them the first part of the balance sheet read.

The gradual evolution of a sophisticated investment market, embracing a range of financial institutions, together with the growth in the number of individual investors, caused a reorientation of priorities. Investor protection and investor decision-making needs started to dominate the financial reporting scene, and the revenue statement replaced the balance sheet as the sovereign reporting document.

Consequently, attention became fixed on the income statement and on concepts of accounting for profit. Moreover, investor protection assumed a new meaning. It changed from simply protecting the **capital** that had **been invested** to protecting the **income information** used by investors when making an investment decision.

However, the sight of major companies experiencing severe liquidity problems over the past decade has revived interest in the balance sheet; while its light is perhaps not of the same intensity as that of the profit and loss account, it cannot be said to be totally subordinate to its accompanying statement of income.

The main objectives of income measurement are to provide:

- a means of control in a micro- and macroeconomic sense;
- a means of prediction;
- a basis for taxation.

We consider each of these below.

3.2.1 Income as a means of control

Assessment of stewardship performance

Managers are the stewards appointed by shareholders. Income, in the sense of net income or net profit, is the crystallisation of their accountability. Maximisation of income is seen as a major aim of the entrepreneurial entity, but the capacity of the business to pursue this aim may be subject to political and social constraints in the case of large public monopolies, and private semi-monopolies such as British Telecommunications plc.

Maximisation of net income is reflected in the earnings per share (EPS) figure, which is shown on the face of the published profit and loss account. The importance of this figure to the shareholders is evidenced by contracts that tie directors' remuneration to growth in EPS. A rising EPS may result in an increased salary or bonus for directors and upward movement in the market price of the underlying security. The effect on the market price is indicated by another extremely important statistic, which is influenced by the income statement: namely, the price/earnings (PE) ratio. The PE ratio reveals the numerical relationship between the share's current market price and the last reported EPS.

Actual performance versus predicted performance

This comparison enables the management and the investing public to use the lessons of the past to improve future performance. The public, as shareholders, may initiate a change in the company directorate if circumstances necessitate it. This may be one reason why management is generally loath to give a clear, quantified estimate of projected results – such an estimate is a potential measure of efficiency. The comparison of actual with projected results identifies apparent underachievement.

The macroeconomic concept

Good government is, of necessity, involved in managing the macroeconomic scene and as such is a user of the income measure. State policies need to be formulated concerning the allocation of economic resources and the regulation of firms and industries, as illustrated by the measures taken by Oftel and Ofwat to regulate the size of earnings by British Telecom and the water companies.

3.2.2 Income as a means of prediction

Dividend and retention policy

The payment of a dividend, its scale and that of any residual income after such dividend has been paid are influenced by the profit generated for the financial year. Other influences are also active, including the availability of cash resources within the entity, the opportunities for further internal investment, the dividend policies of capital-competing entities with comparable shares, the contemporary cost of capital and the current tempo of the capital market.

However, some question the soundness of using the profit generated for the year when making a decision to invest in an enterprise. Their view is that such a practice misunderstands the nature of income data, and that the appropriate information is the prospective cash flows. They regard the use of income figures from past periods as defective because, even if the future accrual accounting income could be forecast accurately, 'it is no more than an imperfect surrogate for future cash flows'.[2]

The counter-argument is that there is considerable resistance by both managers and accountants to the publication of future operating flows and dividend payments.[3] This means that, in the absence of relevant information, an investor needs to rely on a surrogate. The question then arises: which is the best surrogate?

In the short term, the best surrogate is the information that is currently available, i.e. income measured according to the accrual concept. In the longer term, management will be pressed by the shareholders to provide the actual forecast data on operating cash flows and dividend distribution, or to improve the surrogate information.

Suggestions for improving the surrogate information have included the provision of cash earnings per share. More fundamentally, Revsine has suggested that ideal information for investors would indicate the economic value of the business (and its assets) based on expected future cash flows. However, the Revsine suggestion itself requires information on future cash flows that it is not possible to obtain at this time.[4] Instead, he considered the use of replacement cost as a surrogate for the economic value of the business, and we return to this later in the chapter.

Future performance

While history is not a faultless indicator of future events and their financial results, it does have a role to play in assessing the level of future income. In this context, historic income is of assistance to existing investors, prospective investors and management.

Identifying maintainable profit by the analysis of matched costs

Subject to the requirement of enforced disclosure via the Companies Acts 1985 and 1989, as supplemented by various accounting standards, the measurement of income discloses items of income and expenditure necessarily of interest in assessing stewardship success and future prospects. In this respect, exceptional items, extraordinary items and other itemised costs and turnover are essential information.

3.2.3 Basis for taxation

The contemporary taxation philosophy, in spite of criticism from some economists, uses income measurement to measure the taxable capacity of a business entity.

However, the determination of income by the Inland Revenue is necessarily influenced by socioeconomic fiscal factors, among others, and thus accounting profit is subject to adjustment in order to achieve taxable profit. As a tax base, it has been continually eroded as the difference between accounting income and taxable income has grown.[5]

The Inland Revenue in the UK has tended to disallow expenses that are particularly susceptible to management judgement. For example, a uniform capital allowance is substituted for the subjective depreciation charge that is made by management, and certain provisions that appear as a charge in the profit and loss account are not accepted as an expense for tax purposes until the loss crystallises, e.g. a charge to increase the doubtful debts provision may not be allowed until the debt is recognised as bad.

3.3 Accountant's view of income, capital and value

Variations between accountants and economists in measuring income, capital and value are caused by their different views of these measures. In this section, we introduce the accountant's view and, in the next, the economist's, in order to reconcile variations in methods of measurement.

3.3.1 The accountant's view

Income is an important part of accounting theory and practice, although until 1970, when a formal system of propagating standard accounting practice throughout the accountancy profession began, it received little attention in accountancy literature. The characteristics of measurement were basic and few, and tended to be of an intuitive, traditional nature, rather than being spelled out precisely and given mandatory status within the profession.

Accounting tradition of historical cost

The income statement is based on the actual costs of business transactions, i.e. the costs incurred in the currency and at the price levels pertaining at the time of the transactions.

Accounting income is said to be historical income, i.e. it is an *ex post* measure because it takes place after the event. The traditional profit and loss account is historical in two senses: because it concerns a past period, and because it utilises historical cost, being the cost of the transactions on which it is based. It follows that the balance sheet, being based on the residuals of transactions not yet dealt with in the profit and loss account, is also based on historical cost.

In practice, certain amendments may be made to historical cost in both profit and loss account and balance sheet, but historical cost still predominates in both statements. It is justified on a number of counts which, in principle, guard against the manipulation of data.

The main characteristics of historical cost accounting are as follows:

● **Objectivity**. It is a predominantly objective system, although it does exhibit aspects of subjectivity. Its nature is generally understood and it is invariably supported by independent documentary evidence, e.g. an invoice, statement, cheque, cheque counterfoil, receipt or voucher.

● **Factual**. As a basis of fact (with exceptions such as when amended in furtherance of revaluation), it is verifiable and to that extent is beyond dispute.

- **Profit or income concept**. Profit as a concept is generally well understood in a capital market economy, even if its precise measurement may be problematic. It constitutes the difference between revenue and expenditure or, in the economic sense, between opening and closing net assets.

Unfortunately, historical cost is not without its weaknesses. It is not always objective, owing to alternative definitions of revenue and costs and the need for estimates.

We saw in the preceding chapter that revenue could be determined according to a choice of criteria. There is also a choice of criteria for defining costs. For example, although inventories are valued at the lower of cost or net realisable value, the **cost** will differ depending upon the definition adopted, e.g. first-in-first-out, last-in-first-out or standard cost.

Estimation is needed in the case of inventory valuation, assessing possible bad debts, accruing expenses, providing for depreciation and determining the profit attributable to long-term contracts. So, although it is transaction based, there are aspects of historical cost reporting that do not result from an independently verifiable business transaction. This means that profit is not always a unique figure.

Assets are often subjected to revaluation. In an economy of changing price levels, the historical cost system has been compromised by a perceived need to restate the carrying value of those assets that comprise a large proportion of a company's capital employed; e.g. land and buildings. This practice is controversial, not least because it is said to imply that a balance sheet is a list of assets at market valuation, rather than a statement of unamortised costs not yet charged against revenue.

However, despite conventional accountancy income being partly the result of subjectivity, it is largely the product of the historical cost concept. A typical accounting policy specified in the published accounts of companies now reads as follows:

> The financial statements are prepared under the historical cost conventions as modified by the revaluation of certain fixed assets.

Nature of accounting income

Accounting income is defined in terms of the business entity. It is the excess of revenue from sales over direct and allocated indirect costs incurred in the achievement of such sales. Its measure results in a net figure. It is the numerical result of the matching and accruals concepts discussed in the preceding chapter.

We saw in the preceding chapter that accounting income is transaction based and therefore can be said to be factual, in as much as the revenue and costs have been realised and will be reflected in cash inflow and outflow, although not necessarily within the financial year.

We also saw that, under accrual accounting, the sales for a financial period are offset by the expenses incurred in generating such sales. Objectivity is a prime characteristic of accrual accounting, but the information cannot be entirely objective because of the need to break up the ongoing performance of the business entity into calendar periods or financial years for purposes of accountability reporting. The allocation of expenses between periods requires a prudent estimate of some costs, e.g. the provision for depreciation and bad debts attributable to each period.

Accounting income is presented in the form of the conventional profit and loss account or income statement. This income statement, in being based on actual transactions, is concerned with a past-defined period of time. Thus accounting profit is said to be historic income, i.e. an *ex post* measure because it is after the event.

Nature of accounting capital

The business enterprise requires the use of non-monetary assets, e.g. buildings, plant and machinery, office equipment, motor vehicles, stock of raw materials and work-in-progress.

Such assets are not consumed in any one accounting period, but give service over a number of periods; therefore, the unconsumed portions of each asset are carried forward from period to period and appear in the balance sheet. This document itemises the unused asset balances at the date of the financial year-end. In addition to listing unexpired costs of non-monetary assets, the balance sheet also displays monetary assets such as debtor and cash balances, together with monetary liabilities, i.e. moneys owing to trade creditors, other creditors and lenders. Funds supplied by shareholders and retained income following the distribution of dividend are also shown. Retained profits are usually added to shareholders' capital, resulting in what is known as shareholders' funds. These represent the company's equity capital.

The net assets of the firm, i.e. that fund of unconsumed assets which exceeds moneys attributable to creditors and lenders, constitutes the company's net capital, which is the same as its equity capital. Thus the profit and loss account of a financial period can be seen as a linking statement between that period's opening and closing balance sheets: in other words, income may be linked with opening and closing capital. This linking may be expressed by formula, as follows:

$$Y_{0-1} = NA_1 - NA_0 + D_{0-1}$$

where Y_{0-1} = income for the period of time t_0 to t_1; NA_0 = net assets of the entity at point of time t_0; NA_1 = net assets of the entity at point of time t_1; D_{0-1} = dividends or distribution during period t_{0-1}.

Less formally: Y = income of financial year; NA_0 = net assets as shown in the balance sheet at beginning of financial year; NA_1 = net assets as shown in the balance sheet at end of financial year; D_{0-1} = dividends paid and proposed for the financial year. We can illustrate this as follows:

Income Y_{0-1} for the financial year t_{0-1} as compiled by the accountant was £1,200
Dividend D_{0-1} for the financial year t_{0-1} was £450
Net assets NA_0 at the beginning of the financial year were £6,000
Net assets NA_1 at the end of the financial year were £6,750.

The income account can be linked with opening and closing balance sheets, namely:

$$Y_{0-1} = NA_1 - NA_0 + D_{0-1}$$
$$= £6,750 - £6,000 + £450$$
$$= £1,200 = Y_{0-1}$$

Thus Y has been computed by using the opening and closing capitals for the period where capital equals net assets.

In practice, however, the accountant would compute income Y by compiling a profit and loss account. So, of what use is this formula? For reasons to be discussed later, the economist finds use for the formula when it is amended to take account of what we call **present values**. Computed after the end of a financial year, it is the *ex post* measure of income.

Nature of traditional accounting value

As the values of assets still in service at the end of a financial period have been based on the unconsumed costs of such assets, they are the by-product of compiling the income financial statement. These values have been fixed not by direct measurement, but simply by an assessment of costs consumed in the process of generating period turnover. We can say, then, that the balance sheet figure of net assets is a residual valuation after measuring income.

However, it is not a value in the sense of worth or market value as a buying price or selling price; it is merely a **value of unconsumed costs of assets**. This is an important point that will be encountered again later.

3.4 Critical comment on the accountant's measure

3.4.1 Virtues of the accountant's measure

As with the economist's, the accountant's measure is not without its virtues. These are invariably aspects of the historical cost concept, such as objectivity, being transaction based and being generally understood.

3.4.2 Faults of the accountant's measure

Principles of historical cost and profit realisation

The historical cost and profit realisation concepts are firmly entrenched in the transaction basis of accountancy. However, in practice, the two concepts are not free of adjustments. Because of such adjustments, some commentators argue that the system produces a heterogeneous mix of values and realised income items.[6]

For example, in the case of asset values, certain assets such as land and buildings may have a carrying figure in the balance sheet based on a revaluation to market value, while other assets such as motor vehicles may still be based on a balance of unallocated cost. The balance sheet thus pretends on the one hand to be a list of resultant costs pending allocation over future periods, and on the other hand to be a statement of current values.

Prudence concept

This concept introduces caution into the recognition of assets and income for financial reporting purposes. The cardinal rule is that income should not be recorded or recognised within the system until it is realised, but unrealised losses should be recognised immediately.

However, not all unrealised profits are excluded. For example, practice is that attributable profit on long-term contracts still in progress at the financial year-end may be taken into account. As with fixed assets, rules are not applied uniformly.

Unrealised capital profits

Capital profits are ignored as income until they are realised, when, in the accounting period of sale, they are acknowledged by the reporting system. However, all the profit is recognised in one financial period when, in truth, the surplus was generated over successive periods by gradual growth, albeit unrealised until disposal of the asset. Thus a portion of what are now realised profits applies to prior periods. Not all of this profit should be attributed to the period of sale.

Going concern

The going concern concept is fundamental to accountancy and operates on the assumption that the business entity has an indefinite life. It is used to justify basing the periodic reports of asset values on carrying forward figures that represent unallocated costs, i.e. to justify the non-recognition of the realisable or disposal values of non-monetary assets and, in so doing, the associated unrealised profits/losses. Although the life of an entity is deemed indefinite, there is uncertainty, and accountants are reluctant to predict the future. When they are matching costs with revenue for the current accounting period, they follow the prudence concept of reasonable certainty.

In the long term, economic income and accountancy income are reconciled. The unrealised profits of the economic measure are eventually realised and, at that point, they will be recognised by the accountant's measure. In the short term, however, they give different results for each period.

What if we cannot assume that a business will continue as a going concern?

There may be circumstances, as in the case of Gretag Imaging Holdings AG which in its 2001 Annual Report referred to falling sales and losses, which require a judgement to be made as to the validity of the going concern assumption. The assumption can be supported by showing that active steps are being taken such as restructuring, cost reduction and raising additional share capital which will ensure the survival of the business. If survival is not possible, the business will prepare its accounts using net realisable values, which are discussed in the next chapter.

The key considerations for shareholders are whether there will be sufficient profits to support dividend distributions and whether they will be able to continue to dispose of their shares in the open market. The key consideration for the directors is whether there will be sufficient cash to allow the business to trade profitably. We can see all these considerations being addressed in the following extract from the 2003 Annual Report of Royal Numico N.V.

> **Going concern**
> The negative shareholders' equity ... results from the impairment of intangible fixed assets ... Management remains confident that it will be able to sufficiently strengthen shareholders' equity and return to positive shareholders' equity through retained profits ... and that the negative shareholders' equity will not have an impact on the group's operations, access to funding nor its stock exchange listing.
>
> Based on the cash flow generating capacity of the company and its current financing structure, management is convinced that the company will continue as a going concern. Therefore the valuation principles for assets and liabilities applied are consistent with the prior year and are based on going concern.

3.5 Economist's view of income, capital and value

Let us now consider the economist's tradition of present value and the nature of economic income.

3.5.1 Economist's tradition of present value

Present value is a technique used in valuing a future money flow, or in measuring the money value of an existing capital stock in terms of a predicted cash flow *ad infinitum*.

Present value (PV) constitutes the nature of economic capital and, indirectly, economic income. Given the choice of receiving £100 now or £100 in one year's time, the rational person will opt to receive £100 now. This behaviour exhibits an intuitive appreciation of the fact that £100 today is worth more than £100 one year hence. Thus the mind has **discounted** the value of the future sum: £100 today is worth £100; but compared with today, i.e. **compared with present value**, a similar sum receivable in twelve months' time is worth less than £100. How much less is a matter of subjective evaluation, but compensation for the time element may be found by reference to interest: a person forgoing the spending of £1 today and spending it one year later may earn interest of, say, 10% per annum in compensation for the sacrifice undergone by deferring consumption.

So £1 today invested at 10% p.a. will be worth £1.10 one year later, £1.21 two years later, £1.331 three years later, and so on. This is the concept of compound interest. It may be calculated by the formula $(1 + r)^n$, where 1 = the sum invested; r = the rate of interest; n = the number of periods of investment (in our case years). So for £1 invested at 10% p.a. for four years:

$$(1 + r)^n = (1 + 0.10)^4$$
$$= (1.1)^4$$
$$= £1.4641$$

and for five years:

$$= (1.1)^5$$
$$= £1.6105, \text{ and so on.}$$

Notice how the **future value** increases because of the compound interest element – it **varies** over time – whereas the investment of £1 remains constant. So, conversely, the sum of £1.10 received at the end of year one has a PV of £1, as does £1.21 received at the end of year two and £1.331 at the end of year three.

It has been found convenient to construct tables to ease the task of calculating present values. These show the cash flow, i.e. the future values, at a constant figure of £1 and allow the investment to vary. So:

$$PV = \frac{CF}{(1 + r)^n}$$

where CF = anticipated cash flow; r = the discount (i.e. interest) rate. So the PV of a cash flow of £1 receivable at the end of one year at 10% p.a. is:

$$\frac{£1}{(1 + r)^1} = £0.9091$$

and £1 at the end of two years:

$$\frac{£1}{(1 + r)^2} = £0.8264$$

and so on over successive years. The appropriate present values for years three, four and five would be £0.7513, £0.6830, £0.6209 respectively.

£0.9091 invested today at 10% p.a. will produce £1 at the end of one year. The PV of £1 receivable at the end of two years is £0.8264 and so on.

Tables presenting data in this way are called 'PV tables', while the earlier method compiles tables usually referred to as 'compound interest tables'. Both types of table are compound interest tables; only the presentation of the data has changed.

To illustrate the ease of computation using PV tables, we can compute the PV of £6,152 receivable at the end of year five, given a discount rate of 10%, as being £6,152 × £0.6209 = £3,820. Thus £3,820 will total £6,152 in five years given an interest rate of 10% p.a. So the PV of that cash flow of £6,152 is £3,820, because £3,820 would generate interest of £2,332 (i.e. 6,152 – 3,820) as compensation for losing use of the principal sum for five years. Future flows must be discounted to take cognisance of the time element separating cash flows. Only then are we able to compare like with like by reducing all future flows to the comparable loss of present value.

This concept of PV has a variety of applications in accountancy and will be encountered in many different areas requiring financial measurement, comparison and decision. It originated as an economist's device within the context of economic income and economic capital models, but in accountancy it assists in the making of valid comparisons and decisions. For example, two machines may each generate an income of £10,000 over three years. However, timing of the cash flows may vary between the machines. This is illustrated in Figure 3.1.

If we simply compare the profit-generating capacity of the machines over the three-year span, each produces a total profit of £10,000. But if we pay regard to the time element of the money flows, the machines are not so equal.

Figure 3.1 Dissimilar cash flows

Cash flows		
Machine A	Machine B	Receivable end of year
£	£	
1,000	5,000	1
2,000	4,000	2
7,000	1,000	3
10,000	10,000	

However, the technique has its faults. Future money flows are invariably the subject of **estimation** and thus the actual flow experienced may show variations from forecast. Also, the element of **interest**, which is crucial to the calculation of present values, is **subjective**. It may, for instance, be taken as the average prevailing rate operating within the economy or a rate peculiar to the firm and the element of risk involved in the particular decision. In this chapter we are concerned only with PV as a tool of the economist in evaluating economic income and economic capital.

3.5.2 Nature of economic income

Economics is concerned with the economy in general, raising questions such as: how does it function? how is wealth created? how is income generated? why is income generated? The economy as a whole is activated by income generation. The individual is motivated to generate income because of a need to satisfy personal wants by consuming goods and services. Thus the economist becomes concerned with the individual consumer's psychological state of personal **enjoyment and satisfaction**. This creates a need to treat the economy as a **behavioural entity**.

The behavioural aspect forms a substantial part of micro- and macroeconomic thought, emanating particularly from the microeconomic. We can say that the economist's version of income measurement is microeconomics orientated in contrast to the accountant's business entity orientation.

The origination of the economic measure of income commenced with Irving Fisher in 1930.[7] He saw income in terms of consumption, and consumption in terms of individual perception of personal enjoyment and satisfaction. His difficulty in formulating a standard measure of this personal psychological concept of income was overcome by equating this individual experience with the consumption of goods and services and assuming that the cost of such goods and services formed the measure.

Thus, he reasoned, consumption (C) equals income (Y); so $Y = C$. He excluded savings from income because savings were not consumed. There was no satisfaction derived from savings; enjoyment necessitated consumption, he argued. Money was worthless until spent; so growth of capital was ignored, but reductions in capital became part of income because such reductions had to be spent.

In Fisher's model, capital was a stock of wealth existing at a point in time, and as a stock it generated income. Eventually, he reconciled the value of capital with the value of income by employing the concept of present value. He assessed the PV of a future flow of income by **discounting** future flows using the discounted cash flow (DCF) technique. Fisher's model adopted the prevailing average market rate of interest as the discount factor.

Economists since Fisher have introduced savings as part of income. Sir John Hicks played a major role in this area.[8] He introduced the idea that income was the maximum consumption enjoyed by the individual without reducing the individual's capital stock, i.e. the amount a person could consume during a period of time that still left him or her with the same value of capital stock at the end of the period as at the beginning. Hicks also used the DCF technique in the valuation of capital.

If capital increases, the increase constitutes savings and grants the opportunity of consumption. The formula illustrating this was given in section 3.3, i.e. $Y_{0-1} = NA_1 - NA_0 + D_{0-1}$.

However, in the Hicksian model, $NA_1 - NA_0$, given as £6,750 and £6,000 respectively in the aforementioned example, would have been discounted to achieve present values.

The same formula may be expressed in different forms. The economist is likely to show it as $Y - C + (K_1 - K_0)$ where C = consumption, having been substituted for dividend, and K_1 and K_0 have been substituted for NA_1 and NA_0 respectively.

Hicks's income model is often spoken of as an *ex ante* model because it is usually used for the measurement of **expected** income in advance of the time period concerned. Of course, because it specifically introduces the present value concept, present values replace the balance sheet values of net assets adopted by the accountant. Measuring income **before the event** enables the individual to estimate the level of consumption that may be achieved without depleting capital stock. Before-the-event computations of income necessitate predictions of future cash flows.

Suppose that an individual proprietor of a business anticipated that his investment in the enterprise would generate earnings over the next four years as specified in Figure 3.2.

Figure 3.2 Business cash flows for four years

Years	Cash inflows
	£
1	26,000
2	29,000
3	35,000
4	41,000

Furthermore, such earnings would be retained by the business for the financing of new equipment with a view to increasing potential output.

We will assume that the expected rate of interest on capital employed in the business is 8% p.a.

The economic value of the business at K_0 (i.e. at the beginning of year one) will be based on the discounted cash flow of the future four years. Figure 3.3 shows that K_0 is £106,853, calculated as the present value of anticipated earnings of £131,000 spread over a four-year term.

The economic value of the business at K_1 (i.e. at the end of year one, which is the same as saying the beginning of year two) is calculated in Figure 3.4. This shows that K_1 is £115,403 calculated as the present value of anticipated earnings of £131,000 spread over a four-year term.

Figure 3.3 Economic value at K_0

Year	(a) Cash flow £	(b) $DCF = \dfrac{1}{(1+r)^n}$	(c) PV (a) × (b) £
K_1	26,000	$\dfrac{1}{(1.08)^1} = 0.9259$	24,073
K_2	29,000	$\dfrac{1}{(1.08)^2} = 0.8573$	24,862
K_3	35,000	$\dfrac{1}{(1.08)^3} = 0.7938$	27,783
K_4	41,000	$\dfrac{1}{(1.08)^4} = 0.7350$	30,135
	131,000		106,853

Figure 3.4 Economic value at K_1

Year	(a) Cash flow £	(b) $DCF = \dfrac{-1}{(1+r)^n}$	(c) PV (a) × (b) £
K_1	26,000	1.0000	26,000
K_2	29,000	$\dfrac{1}{(1+r)^1} = 0.9259$	26,851
K_3	35,000	$\dfrac{1}{(1+r)^2} = 0.8573$	30,006
K_4	41,000	$\dfrac{1}{(1+r)^3} = 0.7938$	32,546
	131,000		115,403

From this information we are able to calculate Y for the period Y_1, as in Figure 3.5. Note that C (consumption) is nil because, in this exercise, dividends representing consumption have not been payable for Y_1. In other words, income Y_1 is entirely in the form of projected capital growth, i.e. savings.

Figure 3.5 Calculation of Y for the period Y_1

$$Y = C + (K_1 - K_0)$$
$$Y = 0 + (115,403 - 106,853)$$
$$= 0 + 8,550$$
$$= £8,550$$

By year-end K_1, earnings of £26,000 will have been received; in projecting the capital at K_2 such earnings will have been reinvested and at the beginning of year K_2 will have a PV of £26,000. These earnings will no longer represent a **predicted** sum because they will have been **realised** and therefore will no longer be subjected to discounting.

The income of £8,550 represents an anticipated return of 8% p.a. on the economic capital at K_0 of £106,853 (8% of £106,853 is £8,548, the difference of £2 between this figure and the figure calculated above being caused by rounding).

As long as the expectations of future cash flows and the chosen interest rate do not change, then Y_1 will equal 8% of £106,853.

What will the anticipated income for the year Y_2 amount to?

Applying the principle explained above, the anticipated income for the year Y_2 will equal 8% of the capital at the end of K_1 amounting to £115,403 = £9,233. This is proved in Figure 3.6, which shows that K_2 is £124,636 calculated as the present value of anticipated earnings of £131,000 spread over a four-year term.

Figure 3.6 Economic value at K_2

Year	(a) Cash flow	(b) $DCF = \dfrac{1}{(1+r)^n}$	(c) $PV = (a) \times (b)$
	£	£	£
K_1	26,000	1.08	28,080
K_2	29,000	1.0000	29,000
K_3	35,000	0.9259	32,407
K_4	41,000	0.8573	35,149
	131,000		124,636

From this information we are able to calculate Y for the period Y_2 as in Figure 3.7. Note that capital value attributable to the end of the year K_2 is being assessed at the beginning of K_2. This means that the £26,000 due at the end of year K_1 will have been received and reinvested, earning interest of 8% p.a. Thus by the end of year K_2 it will be worth £28,080. The sum of £29,000 will be realised at the end of year K_2 so its present value at that time will be £29,000.

If the anticipated future cash flows change, the expected capital value at the successive points in time will also change. Accordingly, the actual value of capital may vary from that forecast by the *ex ante* model.

Figure 3.7 Calculation of Y for the period Y_2

$$Y = C + (K_2 - K_1)$$
$$Y = 0 + (124,636 - 115,403)$$
$$= 0 + 9,233$$
$$= £9,233$$

3.6 Critical comment on the economist's measure

While the income measure enables us to formulate theories regarding the behaviour of the economy, it has inherent shortcomings not only in the economic field, but particularly in the accountancy sphere.

● The calculation of economic capital, hence economic income, is subjective in terms of the present value factor, often referred to as the DCF element. The factor may be based on any one of a number of factors, such as opportunity cost, the current return on the firm's existing capital employed, the contemporary interest payable on a short-term loan such as a bank overdraft, the average going rate of interest payable in the economy at large, or a rate considered justified on the basis of the risk attached to a particular investment.

● Investors are not of one mind or one outlook. For example, they possess different risk and time preferences and will therefore employ different discount factors.

● The model constitutes a compound of unrealised and realised flows, i.e. profits. Because of the unrealised element, it has not been used as a base for computing tax or for declaring a dividend.

● The projected income is dependent upon the success of a planned financial strategy. Investment plans may change, or fail to attain target.

● Windfall gains cannot be foreseen, so they cannot be accommodated in the *ex ante* model. Our prognostic cash flows may therefore vary from the actual flows generated, e.g. an unexpected price movement.

● It is difficult to construct a satisfactory, meaningful balance sheet detailing the unused stock of net assets by determining the present values of individual assets. Income is invariably the consequence of deploying a group of assets working in unison.

3.7 Income, capital and changing price levels

A primary concern of income measurement to both economist and accountant is the maintenance of the capital stock, i.e. the maintenance of capital values. The assumption is that income can only arise **after** the capital stock has been maintained at the same amount as at the beginning of the accounting period.

However, this raises the question of how we should define the capital that we are attempting to maintain. There are a number of possible definitions:

● **Money capital.** Should we concern ourselves with maintaining the fund of capital resources initially injected by the entrepreneur into the new enterprise? This is indeed one of the aims of traditional, transaction-based accountancy.

● **Potential consumption capital.** Is it this that should be maintained, i.e. the economist's present value philosophy expressed via the discounted cash flow technique?

● **Operating capacity capital.** Should maintenance of productive capacity be the rule, i.e. capital measured in terms of tangible or physical assets? This measure would utilise the current cost accounting system.

Revsine attempted to construct an analytical bridge between replacement cost accounting that maintains the operating capacity, and the economic concepts of **income** and **value**, by demonstrating that the distributable operating flow component of economic income is equal to the current operating component of replacement cost income, and that the unexpected income component of economic income is equal to the unrealisable cost savings of replacement cost income.[9] This will become clearer when the replacement cost model is dealt with in the next chapter.

- **Financial capital**. Should capital be maintained in terms of a fund of general purchasing power (sometimes called 'real' capital)? In essence this is the consumer purchasing power (or general purchasing power) approach, but not in a strict sense as it can be measured in a variety of ways. The basic method uses a general price index. This concept is likely to satisfy the criteria of the proprietor/shareholders of the entity. The money capital and the financial capital concepts are variations of the same theme, the former being founded on the historic cost principle and the latter applying an adjustment mechanism to take account of changing price levels.

The money capital concept has remained the foundation stone of traditional accountancy reporting, but the operating and financial capital alternatives have played a controversial secondary role over the past twenty-five years.

Potential consumption capital is peculiar to economics in terms of measurement of the business entity's aggregate capital, although, as discussed on pages 49–52, it has a major role to play as a decision-making model in financial management.

3.7.1 Why are these varying methods of concern?

The problem tackled by these devices is that plague of the economy known as 'changing price levels', particularly the upward spiralling referred to as **inflation**. Throughout this chapter we have assumed that there is a stable monetary unit and that income, capital and value changes over time have been in response to operational activity and the interaction of supply and demand or changes in expectations.

Following the historic cost convention, capital maintenance has involved a comparison of opening and closing capital in each accounting period. It has been assumed that the purchasing power of money has remained constant over time.

If we take into account moving price levels, particularly the fall in the purchasing power of the monetary unit due to inflation, then our measure of **income** is affected if we insist upon **maintaining capital in real terms**.

3.7.2 Is it necessary to maintain capital in real terms?

Undoubtedly it is necessary if we wish to prevent an erosion of the operating capacity of the entity and thus its ability to maintain real levels of income. If we do not maintain the capacity of capital to generate the current level of profit, then the income measure, being the difference between opening and closing capitals, will be overstated or overvalued. This is because the capital measure is being understated or undervalued. In other words, there is a danger of dividends being paid out of real capital rather than out of real income. It follows that, if the need to retain profits is overlooked, the physical assets will be depleted.

In accountancy there is no theoretical difficulty in measuring the impact of changing price levels. There are, however, two practical difficulties:

- There are a number of methods, or mixes of methods, available and it has proved impossible to obtain consensus support for one method or compound of methods.

- There is a high element of subjectivity, which detracts from the objectivity of the information.

In the next chapter we deal with inflation and analyse the methods formulated, together with the difficulties that they in turn introduce into the financial reporting system.

Summary

In measuring income, capital and value, the accountant's approach varies from the sister discipline of the economist, yet both are trying to achieve similar objectives.

The accountant uses a traditional transaction-based model of computing income, capital being the residual of this model.

The economist's viewpoint is anchored in a behavioural philosophy that measures capital and deduces income to be the difference between the capital at commencement of a period and that at its end.

The objectives of income measurement are important because of the existence of a highly sophisticated capital market. These objectives involve the assessment of stewardship performance, dividend and retention policies, comparison of actual results with those predicted, assessment of future prospects, payment of taxation and disclosure of matched costs against revenue from sales.

The natures of income, capital and value must be appreciated if we are to understand and achieve measurement. The apparent conflict between the two measures can be seen as a consequence of the accountant's need for periodic reporting to shareholders. In the longer term, both methods tend to agree.

Present value as a concept is the foundation stone of the economist, while historical cost, adjusted for prudence, is that of the accountant. Present value demands a subjective discount rate and estimates that time may prove incorrect; historical cost ignores unrealised profits and in application is not always transaction based.

The economist's measure, of undoubted value in the world of micro- and macroeconomics, presents difficulty in the accountancy world of annual reports. The accountant's method, with its long track record of acceptance, ignores any generated profits, which caution and the concept of the going concern deem not to exist.

The economic trauma of changing price levels is a problem that both measures can embrace, but consensus support for a particular model of measurement has proved elusive.

REVIEW QUESTIONS

1 What is the purpose of measuring income?

2 Explain the nature of economic income.

3 The historical cost concept has withstood the test of time. Specify the reasons for this success, together with any aspects of historical cost that you consider are detrimental in the sphere of financial reporting.

4 What is meant by present value? Does it take account of inflation?

5 A company contemplates purchasing a machine that will generate an income of £25,000 per year over each of the next five years. A scrap value of £2,000 is anticipated on disposal. How much would you advise the company to pay for the asset?

6 Discuss the arguments for and against revaluing fixed assets and recognising the gain or loss.

7 To an accountant, net income is essentially a historical record of the past. To an economist, net income is essentially a speculation about the future. Examine the relative merits of these two approaches for financial reporting purposes.

8 Examine and contrast the concepts of profit that you consider to be relevant to:

(a)   an economist;   (b)   a speculator;

(c)   a business executive;   (d)   the managing director of a company;

(e)   a shareholder in a private company; (f)   a shareholder in a large public company.

EXERCISES

An extract from the solution is provided in the Appendix at the end of the text for exercises marked with an asterisk (*).

Question 1

(a)   'Measurement in financial statements', Chapter 6 of the ASB's *Statement of Principles,* was published in 1999. Amongst the theoretical valuation systems considered is value in use – more commonly known as economic value.

Required:
Describe the Hicksian economic model of income and value, and assess its usefulness for financial reporting.

(b)   Jim Bowater purchased a parcel of 30,000 ordinary shares in New Technologies plc for £36,000 on 1 January 20X5. Jim, an Australian on a four-year contract in the UK, has it in mind to sell the shares at the end of 20X7, just before he leaves for Australia. Based on the company's forecast growth and dividend policy, his broker has advised him that his shares are likely to fetch only £35,000 then.

In its annual report for the year ended 31 December 20X4 the company had forecast annual dividend pay-outs as follows:

Year ended: 31 December 20X5, 25p per share
              31 December 20X6, 20p per share
              31 December 20X7, 20p per share

Required:
Using the economic model of income:
(i)   Compute Jim's economic income for each of the three years ending on the dates indicated above.
(ii)   Show that Jim's economic capital will be preserved at 1 January 20X5 level. Jim's cost of capital is 20%.

* Question 2

(a)   Describe briefly the theory underlying Hicks's economic model of income and capital. What are its practical limitations?

(b) Spock purchased a space invader entertainment machine at the beginning of year one for £1,000. He expects to receive at annual intervals the following receipts: at the end of year one £400; end of year two £500; end of year three £600. At the end of year three he expects to sell the machine for £400.

Spock could receive a return of 10% in the next best investment.

The present value of £1 receivable at the end of a period discounted at 10% is as follows:

End of year one   £0.909
End of year two   £0.826
End of year three   £0.751

Required:
Calculate the ideal economic income, ignoring taxation and working to the nearest £.

Your answer should show that Spock's capital is maintained throughout the period and that his income is constant.

* Question 3

Jason commenced with £135,000 cash. He acquired an established shop on 1 January 20X1. He agreed to pay £130,000 for the fixed and current assets and the goodwill. The replacement cost of the shop premises was £100,000, stock £10,000 and debtors £4,000; the balance of the purchase price was for the goodwill. He paid legal costs of £5,000. No liabilities were taken over. Jason could have resold the business immediately for £135,000. Legal costs are to be expensed in 20X1.

Jason expected to draw £25,000 per year from the business for three years and to sell the shop at the end of 20X3 for £150,000.

At 31 December 20X1 the books showed the following tangible assets and liabilities:

Cost to the business before any drawings by Jason:		He estimated that the net realisable values were:	
	£		£
Shop premises	100,000		85,000
Stock	15,500		20,000
Debtors	5,200		5,200
Cash	40,000		40,000
Creditors	5,000		5,000

Based on his experience of the first year's trading, he revised his estimates and expected to draw £35,000 per year for three years and sell the shop for £175,000 on 31 December 20X3.

Jason's opportunity cost of capital was 20%.

Required:
(a) Calculate the following income figures for 20X1:
    (i)   accounting income;
    (ii)   income based on net realisable values;
    (iii)   economic income *ex ante*;
    (iv)   economic income *ex post*.
       State any assumptions made.
(b) Evaluate each of the four income figures as indicators of performance in 20X1 and as a guide to decisions about the future.

Question 4

The following information relates to Ozone Ltd at 1 January 20X0:

Expected net receipts for 20X0	£240,000
Expected net receipts for subsequent years	£400,000 p.a.
Cost of capital	10%

Further information becomes available at 31 December 20X0:

Expected future net receipts revised to	£440,000 p.a.
Actual net receipts for 20X0	£200,000

Additionally, a decision has been taken to begin a project on 31 December 20X0 at a cost of £40,000, with estimated net receipts at £20,000 p.a. for the next four years.

Information is also available concerning the company's net assets at the start and end of 20X0:

	1 Jan 20X0 £	31 Dec 20X0 £
Net historical cost	2,920,000	2,800,000
Net replacement cost	3,800,000	2,600,000
Net realisable value	3,280,000	4,040,000

Required:
(a) Using Hicks's concept of income:
    (i)   calculate the budgeted income for the year;
    (ii) calculate the actual income for the year (two versions);
    (iii) reconcile the budgeted and actual outcomes with brief narrative explanations.
(b) Briefly assess the economist's contribution to accounting measurement of income and capital.

References

1 T.A. Lee, *Income and Value Measurement: Theory and Practice* (3rd edition), Van Nostrand Reinhold (UK), 1985, p. 20.
2 D. Solomons, *Making Accounting Policy*, Oxford University Press, 1986, p. 132.
3 R.W. Scapens, *Accounting in an Inflationary Environment* (2nd edition), Macmillan, 1981, p. 125.
4 *Ibid.*, p. 127.
5 D. Solomons, *op. cit.*, p. 132.
6 T.A. Lee, *op. cit.*, pp. 52–54.
7 I. Fisher, *The Theory of Interest*, Macmillan, 1930, pp. 171–181.
8 J.R. Hicks, *Value and Capital* (2nd edition), Clarendon Press, 1946.
9 R.W. Scapens, *op. cit.*, p. 127.

Bibliography

American Institute of Certified Public Accountants, *Objectives of Financial Statements*, Report of the Study Group, 1973.

The Corporate Report, ASC, 1975, pp. 28–31.

N. Kaldor, 'The concept of income in economic theory', in R.H. Parker and G.C. Harcourt (eds), *Readings in the Concept and Measurement of Income*, Cambridge University Press, 1969.

T.A. Lee, 'The accounting entity concept, accounting standards and inflation accounting', *Accounting and Business Research*, Spring 1980, pp. 1–11.

J.R. Little, 'Income measurement: an introduction', *Student Newsletter*, June 1988.

D. Solomons, 'Economic and accounting concepts of income', in R.H. Parker and G.C. Harcourt (eds), *Readings in the Concept and Measurement of Income*, Cambridge University Press 1969.

R.R. Sterling, *Theory of the Measurement of Enterprise Income*, University of Kansas Press, 1970.

CHAPTER 4

Accounting for inflation

4.1 Introduction

In this chapter we discuss the impact of inflation on profit and capital measurement and the concepts that have been suggested to incorporate these movements into the financial reports. These concepts are still undergoing development and have not yet achieved general support among practitioners in the field. In this chapter we consider the following:

● A review of the problems of historical cost accounting (HCA)
● Inflation accounting
● The concepts in principle
● The concepts illustrated for one year's transactions – cash transations
● A critique of each model
● A comprehensive example of current cost accounts
● A critique of current cost accounting (CCA) financial statements
● The ASB approach
● The IASB approach
● Future developments.

4.2 Review of the problems of historical cost accounting (HCA)

The transaction-based historical cost concept was unchallenged in the UK until price levels started to hedge upwards at an ever-increasing pace during the 1950s and reached an annual rate of increase of 20% in the mid 1970s. The historical cost base for financial reporting witnessed growing criticism. The inherent faults of the system were discussed in Chapter 3, but inflation exacerbates the problem in the following ways:

● Profit is overstated when inflationary changes in the value of assets are ignored.
● Comparability of business entities, which is so necessary in the assessment of performance and growth, becomes distorted.
● The decision-making process, the formulation of plans and the setting of targets may be suboptimal if financial base data are out of date.
● Financial reports become confusing at best, misleading at worst, because revenue is mismatched with differing historical cost levels as the monetary unit becomes unstable.
● Unrealised profits arising in individual accounting periods are increased as a result of inflation.

In order to combat these serious defects, current value accounting became the subject of research and controversy as to the most appropriate method to use for financial reporting.

4.3 Inflation accounting

A number of versions of current value accounting (CVA) were eventually identified, but the current value postulate was said to suffer from the following disadvantages:

● It destroys the factual nature of HCA, which is transaction based: the factual characteristic is to all intents and purposes lost as transaction-based historic values are replaced by judgemental values.

● It is not as objective as HCA because it is less verifiable from auditable documentation.

● It entails recognition of unrealised profit, a practice that is anathema to the traditionalist.

● The claimed improvement in comparability between commercial entities is a myth because of the degree of subjectivity in measuring current value by each.

● The lack of a single accepted method of computing current values compounds the subjectivity aspect. One fault-laden system is being usurped by another that is also faulty.

In spite of these criticisms, the search for a system of financial reporting devoid of the defects of HCA and capable of coping with inflation has produced a number of CVA models.

4.4 The concepts in principle

Several current income and value models have been proposed to replace or operate in tandem with the historical cost convention. However, in terms of basic characteristics, they may be reduced to the following three models:

● current purchasing power (CPP) or general purchasing power (GPP);

● current entry cost or replacement cost (RC);

● current exit cost or net realisable value (NRV).

We discuss each of these models below.

4.4.1 Current purchasing power accounting (CPPA)

The CPP model measures income and value by adopting a price index system. Movements in price levels are gauged by reference to price changes in a group of goods and services in **general** use within the economy. The aggregate price value of this **basket** of commodities-cum-services is determined at a base point in time and indexed as 100. Subsequent changes in price are compared on a regular basis with this base period price and the change recorded. For example, the price level of our chosen range of goods and services may amount to £76 on 31 March 20X1, and show changes as follows:

£76   at 31 March 20X1
£79   at 30 April 20X1
£81   at 31 May 20X1
£84   at 30 June 20X1
and so on.

The change in price may be indexed with 31 March as the base:

20X1	Calculation	Index
31 March	i.e. £76	100
30 April	i.e. $\dfrac{79}{76} \times 100$	103.9
31 May	i.e. $\dfrac{81}{76} \times 100$	106.6
30 June	i.e. $\dfrac{84}{76} \times 100$	110.5

In the UK, an index system similar in construction to this is known as the Retail Price Index (RPI). It is a barometer of fluctuating price levels covering a miscellany of goods and services as used by the average household. Thus it is a **general** price index. It is amended from time to time to take account of new commodities entering the consumer's range of choice and needs. As a model, it is unique owing to the introduction of the concept of gains and losses in **purchasing power**.

4.4.2 Current entry or replacement cost accounting (RCA)

The replacement cost (RC) model assesses income and value by reference to entry costs or current replacement costs of materials and other assets utilised within the business entity. The valuation attempts to replace like with like and thus takes account of the quality and condition of the existing assets. A motor vehicle, for instance, may have been purchased brand new for £25,000 with an expected life of five years, an anticipated residual value of nil and a straight-line depreciation policy. Its HCA carrying value in the balance sheet at the end of its first year would be £25,000 less £5,000 = £20,000. However, if a similar new replacement vehicle cost £30,000 at the end of year one, then its gross RC would be £30,000; depreciation for one year based on this sum would be £6,000 and the net RC would be £24,000. The increase of £4,000 is a holding gain and the vehicle with a HCA carrying value of £20,000 would be revalued at £24,000.

4.4.3 Current exit cost or net realisable value accounting (NRVA)

The net realisable value (NRV) model is based on the economist's concept of opportunity cost. It is a model that has had strong academic support, most notably in Australia from Professor Ray Chambers who referred to this approach as Continuous Contemporary Accounting (CoCoA). If an asset cost £25,000 at the beginning of year one and at the end of that year it had a NRV of £21,000 after meeting selling expenses, it would be carried in the NRV balance sheet at £21,000. This amount represents the cash forgone by holding the asset, i.e. the opportunity of possessing cash of £21,000 has been sacrificed in favour of the asset. Depreciation for the year would be £25,000 less £21,000 = £4,000.

4.5 The four models illustrated for a company with cash purchases and sales

We will illustrate the effect on the profit and net assets of Entrepreneur Ltd.

Entrepreneur Ltd commenced business on 1 January 20X1 with a capital of £3,000 to buy and sell second-hand computers. The company purchased six computers on 1 January 20X1 for £500 each and sold three of the computers on 15 January for £900 each.

The following data are available for January 20X1:

	Retail Price Index	Replacement cost per computer £	Net realisable value £
1 January	100		
15 January	112	610	
31 January	130	700	900

The income statements and balance sheets are set out in Figure 4.1 with the detailed workings in Figure 4.2.

Figure 4.1 Trading account for the month ended 31 January 20X1

Income statements for the month ended 31 January 20X1

	HCA £		CPP CPP£		RCA £		NRVA £	
Sales	2,700	W1	3,134	W5	2,700	W1	2,700	W1
Opening inventory	—		—		—		—	
Purchases	3,000	W2	3,900	W6	3,000	W2	3,000	W2
Closing inventory	(1,500)	W3	(1,950)	W7	(1,500)	W3	(1,500)	W3
COSA	na		na		330	W10	na	
Cost of sales	1,500		1,950		1,830		1,500	
Holding gain	na		na		na		1,200	W15
Profit	**1,200**		**1,184**		**870**		**2,400**	

Balance sheets as at 31 January 20X1

	£		CPP£		£		£	
Current assets								
Inventory	1,500	W3	1,950	W7	2,100	W11	2,700	W14
Cash	2,700	W4	2,700		2,700		2,700	
Capital employed	**4,200**		**4,650**		**4,800**		**5,400**	
Capital	3,000		3,900	W8	3,000		3,000	
Holding gains								
On inventory consumed	na		na		330	W12		
On inventory in hand	na		na		600	W13		
Profit	1,200		1,184		870		2,400	
Loss on monetary items	na		(434)	W9	na		na	
	4,200		4,650		4,800		5,400	

na = not applicable

Figure 4.2 Workings (W)

HCA

W1 Sales:	3 × £900 = £2,700	
W2 Purchases:	6 × £500 = £3,000	
W3 Closing inventory:	3 × £500 = £1,500	
W4 Cash:	1 January 20X1 Capital	3,000
	1 January 20X1 Purchases	(3,000)
	1 January 20X1 Balance	nil
	15 January 20X1 Sales	
	3 × £900 =	£2,700
	31 January 20X1 Balance	£2,700

CPP

		CPP£
W5 Sales	£2,700 × 130/112 =	3,134
W6 Purchases	£3,000 × 130/100 =	3,900
W7 Closing inventory	£1,500 × 130/100 =	1,950
W8 Capital	£3,000 × 130/100 =	3,900

W9   Balance of cash was nil until 15 January when sales generated £2,700. This sum was held until 31 January during which period cash, a monetary item, lost purchasing power. The loss of purchasing power is measured by applying the general index to the cash held.
£2,700 × 130/112 − £2,700 = CPP £434.

RCA

W10   Additional replacement cost of inventory consumed as at the date of sale is measured as a cost of sales adjustment (COSA). COSA is calculated as follows:

	3 × £610 =	1,830
Less:	3 × £500 =	1,500
	COSA	£330

W11   Closing inventory: 3 × £700 = £2,100
W12   Holding gains on inventory consumed: as for W10   = £330

W13	Inventory at replacement cost	= 3 × £700 = 2,100
	Less: inventory at cost	= 3 × £500 = 1,500
	Holding gains on closing inventory	£600

NRVA

W14   Closing inventory at net realisable value = 900 × 3 = £2,700

W15	3 × £900 =	2,700
	3 × £500 =	1,500
	Holding gain	£1,200

4.5.1 Financial capital maintence concept

HCA and CPP are both transaction-based models that apply the financial capital maintenance concept. This means that profit is the difference between the opening and closing net assets (expressed in HC £) or the opening and closing net assets (expressed in HC £ indexed for RPI changes) adjusted for any capital introduced or withdrawn during the month.

CPP adjustments

- All historical cost values are adjusted to a common index level for the month. In theory this can be the index applicable to any day of the financial period concerned. However, in practice it has been deemed preferable to use the last day of the period; thus the financial statements show the latest price level appertaining to the period.

- The application of a general price index as an adjusting factor results in the creation of an **alien** currency of **purchasing power**, which is used in place of sterling. Note, particularly, the impact on the entity's sales and capital compared with the other models. **Actual** sales shown on **invoices** will still read £2,700.

- Note the application of the concept of gain or loss on holding monetary items. In this example there is a monetary loss of CPP £434 as shown in Working 9.

4.5.2 Operating capital maintenance concept

Under this concept capital is only maintained if sufficient income is retained to maintain the business entity's physical operating capacity, i.e. its ability to produce the existing level of goods or services. Profit is, therefore, the residual after increasing the cost of sales to the cost applicable at the date of sale.

- Basically, only two adjustments are involved: the additional replacement cost of inventory consumed and holding gains on closing inventories. However, in a comprehensive exercise an adjustment will be necessary regarding fixed assets and you will also encounter a gearing adjustment.

- Notice the concept of holding gains. This model introduces, in effect, unrealised profits in respect of closing inventories. The holding gain concerning inventory consumed at the time of sale has been realised and deducted from what would have been a profit of £1,200. The statement discloses profits of £870.

4.5.3 Capacity to adapt concept

The HCA, CPP and RCA models have assumed that the business will continue as a going concern and only distribute realised profits after retaining sufficient profits to maintain either the financial or operating capital.

The NRVA concept is that a business has the capacity to realise its net assets at the end of each financial period and reinvest the proceeds and that the NRV accounts provide management with this information.

- This produces the same initial profit as HCA, namely £1,200, but a peculiarity of this system is that this realised profit is supplemented by **unrealised** profit generated by holding stocks. Under RCA accounting, such gains are shown in a separate account and are not treated as part of real income.

● This simple exercise has ignored the possibility of investment in fixed assets, thus depreciation is not involved. A reduction in the NRV of fixed assets at the end of a period compared with the beginning would be treated in a similar fashion to depreciation by being charged to the revenue account, and consequently profits would be reduced. An increase in the NRV of such assets would be included as part of the profit.

4.5.4 The four models compared

Dividend distribution

We can see from Figure 4.1 that if the business were to distribute the profit reported under HCA, CPP or NRVA the physical operating capacity of the business would be reduced and it would be paying dividends out of capital:

	HCA	CPP	RCA	NRVA
Realised profit:	1,200	1,184	870	1,200
Unrealised profit	—	—	—	1,200
Profit for month	1,200	1,184	870	2,400

Shareholder orientation

The CPP model is shareholder orientated in that it shows whether shareholders' funds are keeping pace with inflation by maintaining their purchasing power. Only CPP changes the value of the share capital.

Management orientation

The RCA model is management orientated in that it identifies holding gains which represent the amounts required to be retained in order to simply maintain the operating capital.

RCA measures the impact of inflation on the individual firm, in terms of the change in price levels of its **raw materials and assets**, i.e. inflation peculiar to the company, whereas CPP measures general inflation in the economy as a whole. CPP may be meaningless in the case of an individual company. Consider a firm that carries a constant volume of stock valued at £100 in HCA terms. Now suppose that price levels double when measured by a general price index (GPI), so that its inventory is restated to £200 in a CPP system. If, however, the cost of that **particular** inventory has sustained a price change consisting of a five-fold increase, then under the RCA model the value of the stock should be £500.

In the mid 1970s, when the accountancy profession was debating the problem of changing price level measurement, the general price level had climbed by some 23% over a period during which petroleum-based products had risen by 500%.

4.6 Critique of each model

A critique of the various models may be formulated in terms of their characteristics and peculiarities as virtues and defects in application.

4.6.1 HCA

This model's virtues and defects have been discussed in Chapter 3 and earlier in this chapter.

4.6.2 CPP

Virtues

- It is an **objective measure** since it is still transaction based, as with HCA, and the possibility of subjectivity is constrained if a GPI is used that has been constructed by a central agency such as a government department. This applies in the UK, where the Retail Price Index is constructed by the Department of Employment.

- It is a **measure of shareholders' capital** and that capital's maintenance in terms of purchasing power units. Profit is the residual value after maintaining the money value of capital funds, taking account of changing price levels. Thus it is a measure readily understood by the shareholder/user of the accounts. It can prevent payment of a dividend out of real capital as measured by GPPA.

- It **introduces the concept of monetary items** as distinct from non-monetary items and the attendant concepts of gains and losses in holding net monetary liabilities compared with holding net monetary assets. Such gains and losses are experienced on a disturbing scale in times of inflation. They are **real** gains and losses. The **basic RCA and NRV models** do not recognise such 'surpluses' and 'deficits'.

Defects

- It is **HCA based but adjusted** to reflect general price movements. Thus it possesses the characteristics of HCA, good and bad, but with its values updated in the light of an arithmetic measure of general price changes. The major defect of becoming out of date is mitigated to a degree, but the impact of inflation on the entity's income and capital may be at variance with the rate of inflation affecting the economy in general.

- It may be **wrongly assumed that the CPP balance sheet is a current value statement**. It is not a current value document because of the defects discussed above; in particular, asset values may be subject to a different rate of inflation than that reflected by the GPI.

- It **creates an alien unit of measurement** still labelled by the £ sign. Thus we have the HCA £ and the CPP £. They are different pounds: one is the bona fide pound, the other is a synthetic unit. This may not be fully appreciated or understood by the user when faced with the financial accounts for the recent accounting period.

- Its **concept of profit is dangerous**. It pretends to cater for changing prices, but at the same time it fails to provide for the additional costs of replacing stocks sold or additional depreciation due to the escalating replacement cost of assets. The inflation encountered by the business entity will not be the same as that encountered by the whole economy. Thus the maintenance of the CPP of shareholders' capital via this concept of profit is not the maintenance of the entity's operating capital in physical terms, i.e. its capacity to produce the same volume of goods and services. The use of CPP profit as a basis for decision making without regard to RCA profit can have disastrous consequences.

4.6.3 RCA

Virtues

- Its **unit of measurement** is the monetary unit and consequently it is understood and accepted by the user of accountancy reports. In contrast, the CPP system employs an artificial unit based on arithmetic relationships, which is different and thus unfamiliar.

- It **identifies and isolates holding gains** from operating income. Thus it can prevent the inadvertent distribution of dividends in excess of operating profit. It satisfies the prudence criterion of the traditional accountant and **maintains the physical operating capacity** of the entity.

- It introduces **realistic current values** of assets in the balance sheet, thus making the balance sheet a 'value' statement and consequently more meaningful to the user. This contrasts sharply with the balance sheet as a list of unallocated carrying costs in the HCA system.

Defects

- It is a **subjective measure**, in that replacement costs are often necessarily based on estimates or assessments. It does not possess the factual characteristics of HCA. It is open to manipulation within constraints. Often it is based on index numbers which themselves may be based on a compound of prices of a mixture of similar commodities used as raw material or operating assets. This subjectivity is exacerbated in circumstances where rapid technological advance and innovation are involved in the potential new replacement asset, e.g. computers, printers.

- It **assumes replacement of assets** by being based on their replacement cost. Difficulties arise if such assets are not to be replaced by similar assets. Presumably, it will then be assumed that a replacement of equivalent value to the original will be deployed, however differently, as capital within the firm.

4.6.4 NRVA

Virtues

- It is a concept readily understood by the user. The value of any item invariably has two measures – a buying price and a selling price – and the twain do not usually meet. However, when considering the value of an **existing** possession, the owner instinctively considers its 'value' to be that in potential sale, i.e. NRV.

- It **avoids the need to estimate depreciation** and, in consequence, the attendant problems of assessing life-span and residual values. Depreciation is treated as the arithmetic difference between the NRV at the end of a financial period and the NRV at its beginning.

- It is **based on opportunity cost** and so can be said to be more meaningful. It is the **sacrificial** cost of possessing an asset, which, it can be argued, is more authentic in terms of being a true or real cost. If the asset were not possessed, its cash equivalent would exist instead and that cash would be deployed in other opportunities. Therefore, NRV = cash = opportunity = cost.

Defects

- It is a **subjective measure** and in this respect it possesses the same major fault as RCA. It can be said to be less prudent than RCA because NRV will tend to be higher in some cases than RCA. For example, when valuing finished inventories, a profit content will be involved.
- It is **not a realistic measure** as most assets, except finished goods, are possessed in order to be utilised, not sold. Therefore, NRV is irrelevant.
- It is **not always determinable**. The assets concerned may be highly specialist and there may be no ready market by which a value can be easily assessed. Consequently, any particular value may be fictitious or erroneous, containing too high a holding gain or, indeed, too low a holding loss.
- It **violates the concept of the going concern**, which demands that the accounts are drafted on the basis that there is no intention to liquidate the entity. Admittedly, this concept was formulated with HCA in view, but the acceptance of NRV implies the possibility of a cessation of trading.

4.7 Operating capital maintenance – a comprehensive example

In Figure 4.1 we considered the effect of inflation on a cash business without fixed assets, credit customers or credit suppliers. In the following example, Economica plc, we now consider the effect where there are fixed assets and credit transactions.

The HCA balance sheets as at 31 December 20X4 and 20X5 are set out in Figure 4.3 and index numbers required to restate the fixed assets, inventory and monetary items in Figure 4.4.

4.7.1 Restating the opening balance sheet to current cost

The non-current assets and inventory are restated to their current cost as at the date of the opening balance as shown in W1 and W2 below. The increase from HC to CC represents an unrealised holding gain which is debited to the asset account and credited to a reserve account called a current cost reserve, as in W3 below.

The calculations are as follows. First we shall convert the HCA balance sheet in Figure 4.3, as at 31 December 20X4, to the CCA basis, using the index data in Figure 4.4.

The **non-monetary items**, comprising the fixed assets and inventory, are converted and the converted amounts are taken to the CC balance sheet and the increases taken to the current cost reserve, as follows.

(W1) Property, Plant and Equipment

	HCA £000	Index	CCA £000	Increase £000
Cost	85,000	$\times \dfrac{165}{100} =$	140,250	55,250
Depreciation	25,500	$\times \dfrac{165}{100} =$	42,075	16,575
	59,500		98,175	38,675

The CCA valuation at 31 December 20X4 shows a net increase in terms of numbers of pounds sterling of £38,675,000. The £59,500,000 in the HCA balance sheet will be replaced in the CCA balance sheet by £98,175,000.

Figure 4.3 Economica plc HCA balance sheets

Balance sheets as at 31 December on the basis of HCA		20X5		20X4
	£000	£000	£000	£000
Non-current assets:				
Cost	85,000		85,000	
Depreciation	34,000		25,500	
		51,000		59,500
Current assets:				
Inventory	25,500		17,000	
Trade receivables	34,000		23,375	
Cash and bank	17,000		1,875	
	76,500		42,250	
Current liabilities:				
Trade payables	25,500		17,000	
Income tax	8,500		4,250	
Dividend proposed	5,000		4,000	
	39,000		25,250	
Net current assets	37,500		17,000	
Less: 8% debentures	11,000		11,000	
		26,500		6,000
		77,500		65,500
Share capital and reserves:				
Authorised and issued £1 ordinary shares		50,000		50,000
Share premium		1,500		1,500
Retained earnings		26,000		14,000
		77,500		65,500

Figure 4.4 Index data relating to Economica plc

1.   Index numbers as prepared by the Central Statistical Office for non-current assets:

1 January 20X2	100
1 January 20X5	165
1 January 20X6	185
Average for 20X4	147
Average for 20X5	167

2.   All non-current assets were acquired on 1 January 20X2. There were no further acquisitions or disposals during the four years ended 31 December 20X5.

3.   Indices as prepared by the Central Statistical Office for inventories and monetary working capital adjustments were:

1 October 20X4	115
31 December 20X4	125
15 November 20X4	120
1 October 20X5	140
31 December 20X5	150
15 November 20X5	145
Average for 20X5	137.5

4.   Three months' inventory is carried.

5.   Depreciation: historical cost based on 10% pa straight-line with residual value of nil:

	£HCA
20X4	8,500,000
20X5	8,500,000

(W2) Inventories

HCA		Index		CCA		Increase
£000				£000		£000
17,000	×	$\dfrac{125}{120}$	=	17,708	=	708

Note that Figure 4.4 specifies that three months' inventories are held. Thus on average they will have been purchased on 15 November 20X4, on the assumption that they have been acquired and consumed evenly throughout the calendar period. Hence the index at the time of purchase would have been 120. The £17,000,000 in the HCA balance sheet will be replaced in the CCA balance sheet by £17,708,000.

(W3) Current cost reserve

The total increase in CCA carrying values for non-monetary items is £39,383,000, which will be credited to CC reserves in the CC balance sheet. It comprises £38,675,000 on the fixed assets and £708,000 on the inventory.

Note that monetary items do not change by virtue of inflation. Purchasing power will be lost or gained, but the carrying values in the CCA balance sheet will be identical to those in its HCA counterpart. We can now compile the CCA balance sheet as at 31 December 20X4 – this will show net assets of £104,883,000.

4.7.2 Adjustments that affect the profit for the year

The income statement for the year ended 31 December 20X5 set out in Figure 4.5 discloses a profit before interest and tax of £26,350,000. We need to deduct realised holding gains from this profit to avoid the distribution of dividends that would reduce the operating capital. These deductions are a cost of sales adjustment (COSA), a depreciation adjustment (DA) and a monetary working capital adjustment (MWCA). The accounting treatment is to debit the income statement and credit the current cost reserve.

Figure 4.5 Economica plc HCA income statement

	Income statement for the year ended 31 December 20X5, on the basis of HCA		
		20X5	20X4
		£000	£000
Turnover		42,500	38,250
Less: Cost of sales		(12,070)	(23,025)
Gross profit		30,430	15,225
Less: Distribution costs	2,460		2,210
Less: Administrative expenses	1,620		1,540
		(4,080)	(3,750)
Profit before interest and tax		26,350	11,475
Interest		(880)	(880)
Profit before tax		25,470	10,595
Income tax expense		(8,470)	(4,250)
Profit after tax		17,000	6,345
Dividend		(5,000)	(4,000)
Retentions		12,000	2,345
Balance b/f		14,000	11,655
Balance c/f		26,000	14,000
EPS		34p	13p

The adjustments are calculated as follows.

(W4) Cost of sales adjustment (COSA) using the average method

We will compute the cost of sales adjustment by using the average method. The average purchase price index for 20X5 is 137.5. If price increases have moved at an even pace throughout the period, this implies that consumption occurred, on average, at 30 June, the mid-point of the financial year.

	HCA £000	Adjustment		CCA £000	Difference £000
Opening inventory	17,000	×	$\dfrac{137.5}{120}$ =	19,479	2,479
Purchases	—		—	—	—
	17,000			19,479	
Closing inventory	(25,500)	×	$\dfrac{137.5}{145}$ =	24,181	1,319
	(8,500)			(4,702)	3,798

The impact of price changes on the cost of sales would be an increase of £3,798,000, causing a profit decrease of like amount and a current cost reserve increase of like amount.

(W5) Depreciation adjustment: average method

As assets are consumed throughout the year, the CCA depreciation charge should be based on average current costs.

	HCA £000	Adjustment		CCA £000		Difference £000
Depreciation	8,500	×	$\dfrac{167}{100}$ =	14,195	=	5,695

(W6) Monetary working capital adjustment (MWCA)

The objective is to transfer from the income statement to CC reserve the amount by which the need for monetary working capital (MWC) has increased due to rising price levels. The change in MWC from one balance sheet to the next will be the consequence of a combination of changes in volume and escalating price movements. Volume change may be segregated from the price change by using an average index.

	20X5 £000	20X4 £000		Change £000
Trade receivables	34,000	23,375		
Trade payables	25,500	17,000		
MWC =	8,500	6,375	Overall change =	2,125

The MWC is now adjusted by the average index for the year.

This adjustment will reveal the change in volume.

$$\left(8,500 \times \frac{137.5}{150}\right) - \left(6,375 \times \frac{137.5}{125}\right)$$

=	7,792	− 7,012	= Volume change	780
	So price change =			1,345

The profit before interest and tax will be reduced as follows:

	£000	£000
Profit before interest and tax		26,350
Less:		
COSA	(3,798)	
DA	(5,695)	
MWCA	(1,345)	
Current cost operating adjustments		(10,838)
Current cost operating profit		15,512

The adjustments will be credited to the current cost reserve.

4.7.3 Unrealised holding gains on non-monetary assets as at 31 December 20X5

The holding gains as at 31 December 20X4 were calculated in 4.7.1 above for non-current assets and inventory. A similar calculation is required to restate these at 20X5 current costs for the closing balance sheet. The calculations are as in Working 7 below.

(W7) Non-monetary assets

		£000
(i)	Holding gain on non-current assets	
	Revaluation at year-end	
	Non-current assets at 1 January 20X5 (as W1) at CCA revaluation	140,250
	CCA value at 31 December 20X5 = $140,250 \times \dfrac{185}{165} =$	157,250
	Revaluation holding gain for 20X5 to CC reserve in W8	**17,000**

This holding gain of £17,000,000 is transferred to CC reserves.

		£000
(ii)	Backlog depreciation on non-current assets	
	CCA aggregate depreciation at 31 December 20X5 for CC balance sheet	
	= £HCA 34,000,000 $\times \dfrac{185}{100}$ in CC balance sheet	62,900
	Less: CCA aggregate depreciation at 1 January 20X5 (as per W1 and balance sheet at 1 January 20X5)	42,075
	Being CCA depreciation as revealed between opening and closing balance sheets	20,825
	But CCA depreciation charged in revenue accounts (i.e. £8,500,000 in £HCA plus additional depreciation of £5,695,000 per W5) =	14,195
	So total backlog depreciation to CC reserve in W8	**6,630**

	£000
The CCA value of non-current assets at 31 December 20X5:	
Gross CCA value (above)	157,250
Depreciation (above)	62,900
Net CCA carrying value in the CC balance sheet in W8	**94,350**

This £6,630,000 is backlog depreciation for 20X5. Total backlog depreciation is not expensed (i.e. charged to revenue account) as an adjustment of HCA profit, but is charged against CCA reserves. The net effect is that the CC reserve will increase by £10,370,000, i.e. £17,000,000 – £6,630,000.

(iii)   Inventory valuation at year-end

CCA valuation at 31 December 20X5

£HCA000	£CCA000	£CCA000
= 25,500 × 150/145 = 26,379 = increase of		879

CCA valuation at 1 January 20X5 (per W2)

= 17,000 × 125/120 = 17,708 = increase of		708
Inventory holding gain occurring during 20X5 to W8		171

4.7.4 Current cost balance sheet as at 31 December 20X5

The current cost balance sheet as at 31 December 20X5 now discloses non-current assets and inventory adjusted by index to their current cost and the retained profits reduced by the current cost operating adjustments. It appears as in Working 8 below.

(W8) Economica plc: CCA balance sheet as at 31 December 20X5

		20X5		20X4
Non-current assets	£000	£000	£000	£000
Cost	157,250 (W7(i))		140,250 (W1)	
Depreciation	62,900 (W7(ii))		42,075 (W1)	
		94,350 (W7(ii))		98,175
Current assets				
Inventory	26,379 (W7(iii))		17,708 (W2)	
Trade receivables	34,000		23,375	
Cash	17,000		1,875	
	77,379		42,958	
Current liabilities				
Trade payables	25,500		17,000	
Income tax	8,500		4,250	
Dividend proposed	5,000		4,000	
	39,000		25,250	
Net current assets	38,379		17,708	
Less: 8% debentures	11,000		11,000	
		27,379		6,708
		121,729		104,883
Financed by				
Share capital: authorised and issued £1 shares		50,000		50,000
Share premium		1,500		1,500
*CC reserve		55,067		39,383
** Retained profit		15,162		14,000
Shareholders' funds		121,729		104,883

*CC reserve	£000	£000
Opening balance		39,383 (W3)
Holding gains		
Non-current assets	17,000 (W7(i))	
Inventory	171 (W7(iii))	
		17,171
COSA	3,798 (W4)	
MWCA	1,345 (W6)	
Less: backlog depreciation	(6,630) (W7(ii))	(1,487)
		55,067

**Retained profit		
Opening balance		14,000 (Figure 4.5)
HCA profit for 20X5	12,000	
COSA	(3,798)(W4)	
Extra depreciation	(5,695)(W5)	
MWCA	(1,345)(W6)	
		1,162
CCA profit for 20X5		15,162

4.7.5 How to take the level of borrowings into account

We have assumed that the company will need to retain £10,838,000 from the current year's earnings in order to maintain the physical operating capacity of the company. However, if the business is part financed by borrowings then part of the amount required may be assumed to come from the lenders. One of the methods advocated is to make a gearing adjustment. The gearing adjustment that we illustrate here has the effect of reducing the impact of the adjustments on the profit after interest, i.e. it is based on the realised holding gains only.

The gearing adjustment will change the carrying figures of CC reserves and retained profit, but not the shareholders' funds, as the adjustment is compensating. The gearing adjustment cannot be computed before the determination of the shareholders' interest because that figure is necessary in order to complete the gearing calculation.

Gearing adjustment

The CC operating profit of the business is quantified after making such retentions from the historical profit as are required in order to maintain the physical operating capacity of the entity. However, from a shareholder standpoint, there is no need to maintain in real terms the portion of the entity financed by loans that are fixed in monetary values. Thus, in calculating profit attributable to shareholders, that part of the CC adjustments relating to the proportion of the business financed by loans can be deducted:

(W9) Gearing adjustment =

$$\frac{\text{Average net borrowings for year}}{\left(\begin{array}{c}\text{Average net borrowings}\\ \text{for year}\end{array}\right) + \left(\begin{array}{c}\text{Average shareholders'}\\ \text{funds for year}\end{array}\right)} \times \begin{array}{c}\text{Aggregate}\\ \text{adjustments}\end{array}$$

This formula is usually expressed as $\dfrac{L}{(L + S)} \times A$

where L = loans (i.e. net borrowings); S = shareholders' interest or funds; A = adjustments (i.e. extra depreciation + COSA + MWCA). Note that $L/(L + S)$ is often expressed as a percentage of A (see example below where it is 6.31%).

Net borrowings

This is the sum of all liabilities less current assets, excluding items included in MWC or utilised in computing COSA. In this instance it is as follows:

	Closing balance £000	Opening balance £000
Debentures	11,000	11,000
Income tax	8,500	4,250
Cash	(17,000)	(1,875)
Total net borrowings, the average of which equals L	2,500	13,375

Average net borrowings $= \dfrac{2,500,000 + 13,375,000}{2} = £7,937,500$

Note: in some circumstances (e.g. new issue of debentures occurring during the year) a weighted average will be used.

Net borrowings plus shareholders' funds

	Closing balance £000	Opening balance £000
Shareholders' funds in CC £ (inclusive of proposed dividends)	126,729	108,883
Add: net borrowings	2,500	13,375
	129,229	122,258

Or, alternatively:

	£000	£000
Non-current assets	94,350	98,175
Inventory	26,379	17,708
MWC	8,500	6,375
	129,229	122,258

Average $L + S = \dfrac{129,229,000 + 122,258,000}{2}$

$= 125,743,500$

So gearing $= \dfrac{L}{L+S} \times A$

$= \dfrac{£7,937,500}{125,743,500} \times \dfrac{\text{(COSA} + \text{MWCA} + \text{Extra depreciation)}}{(3,798,000 + 1,345,000 + 5,695,000)}$

$= 6.31\%$ of £10,838,000 = £683,877, say **£684,000**

Thus the CC adjustment of £10,838,000 charged against historical profit may be reduced by £684,000 due to a gain being derived from net borrowings during a period of inflation as shown in Figure 4.6. The £684,000 is shown as a deduction from interest payable.

Figure 4.6 Economica plc CCA income statement

Economica plc CCA income statement for year ended 31 December 20X5 (i.e. under the operating capital maintenance concept)		£000
Turnover		42,500
Cost of sales		(12,070)
Gross profit		30,430
Distribution costs		(2,460)
Administrative expenses		(1,620)
Historical cost operating profit		26,350
Current cost operating adjustments		**(10,838)**
Current cost operating profit		15,512
Interest payable	(880)	
Gearing adjustment	**684**	(196)
Current profit on ordinary activities before taxation		15,316
Tax on profit on ordinary activities		(8,470)
Current cost profit for the financial year		6,846
Proposed dividends		(5,000)
Current cost profit retained		1,846
EPS		13.7p

4.7.6 The closing current cost balance sheet

The closing balance sheet with the non-current assets and inventory restated at current cost and the retained profit adjusted for current cost operating adjustments as reduced by the gearing adjustment is set out in Figure 4.7.

4.7.7 Real Terms System

The Real Terms System combines both CPP and current cost concepts. This requires a calculation of total unrealised holding gains and an inflation adjustment as calculated in Workings 10 and 11 below.

(W10) Total unrealised holding gains to be used in Figure 4.8

[Closing balance sheet at CC – Closing balance sheet at HC] – [Opening balance sheet at CC – Opening balance sheet at HC]
= (£121,729,000 – £77,500,000) – (£104,883,000 – £65,500,000) = £4,846,000
    (W8)   (Figure 4.3)   (Working 8)   (Figure 4.3)

Figure 4.7 Economica plc CCA balance sheet

Economica plc CCA balance sheet as at 31 December 20X5

20X4			20X5	
£000	£000	*Non-current assets*	£000	£000
140,250		Property, Plant and Equipment	157,250	
42,075		Depreciation	62,900	
	98,175			94,350
		Current assets		
17,708		Inventory	26,379	
23,375		Trade receivables	34,000	
1,875		Cash	17,000	
42,958			77,379	
		Current liabilities		
17,000		Trade payables	25,500	
		Other payables		
4,250		— income tax	8,500	
4,000		— proposed dividend	5,000	
25,250			39,000	
	17,708	*Net current assets*		38,379
		Non-current liabilities		
	(11,000)			(11,000)
	6,708			27,379
	104,883			121,729
	£000	*Capital and reserves*		£000
	50,000	Called-up share capital		50,000
	1,500	Share premium account		1,500
	53,383	Total of other reserves		70,229
	104,883			121,729

Analysis of 'Total of other reserves'

£000		£000
14,000	Income statement	15,846
39,383	Current cost reserve	54,383
53,383		70,229

continued

Figure 4.7 (*cont.*)

Movements on reserves

(a) Income statement: £000

    Balance at 1 January 20X5   14,000 (from Figure 4.5)

    Current cost retained profit   1,846 (from Figure 4.6)

    Balance at 31 December 20X5   15,846

(b) Current cost reserve:

	Total £000	Non-current assets £000	Inventory £000	MWCA £000	Gearing £000
Balance as at 1 January 20X5	39,383	38,675	708		
Movements during the year:					
Unrealised holding gains in the year	10,541	10,370	171		
Gearing adjustment	(684)				(684)
MWCA	1,345			1,345	
COSA	3,798		3,798		
Balance as at 31 December 20X5	54,383	49,045	4,677	1,345	(684)

(W11) General price index numbers to be used to calculate the inflation adjustment in Figure 4.8

General price index at 1 January 20X5   = 317.2

General price index at 31 December 20X5 = 333.2

Opening shareholders' funds at CC × Percentage change in GPI during the year =

$$104{,}883{,}000 \times \frac{333.2 - 317.2}{317.2} = £5{,}290{,}435, \text{ say } £5{,}290{,}000$$

The GPP (or CPP) real terms financial capital

The real terms financial capital maintenance concept may be incorporated within the CCA system as in Figure 4.8 by calculating an inflation adjustment.

4.8 Critique of CCA statements

Considerable effort and expense are involved in compiling and publishing CCA statements. Does their usefulness justify the cost? CCA statements have the following uses:

1 The operating capital maintenance statement reveals CCA profit. Such profit has removed inflationary price increases in raw materials and other inventories, and thus is more realistic than the alternative HCA profit.

2 Significant increases in a company's buying and selling prices will give the HCA profit a holding gains content. That is, the reported HCA profit will include gains consequent upon holding inventories during a period when the cost of buying such

Figure 4.8 Economica plc real terms income statement

*Economica plc CCA income statement under the real terms system
for the year ended 31 December 20X5*

	£000	£000
Historical cost profit after tax for the financial year		17,000
Add: Total unrealised holding gains arising during the year (see W10)	4,846	
Less: Realised holding gains previously recognised as unrealised	none	
	4,846	
Less: Inflation adjustment to CCA shareholders' funds (W11)	(5,290)	
Real holding gains		(444)
Total real gains		16,556
Deduct: proposed dividends		5,000
Amount retained		11,556

Real terms system: analysis of reserves

20X4 £000		20X5 £000
53,383	Income statement	64,939
—	Financial capital maintenance reserve	5,290
53,383		70,229

Movements on reserves

	Income statement £000	Financial capital maintenance reserve £000
Balances at 1 January 20X5	53,383	—
Amount retained	11,556	—
Inflation adjustment for year		5,290
Balances as at 31 December 20X5	64,939	5,290

inventories increases. Conversely, if specific inventory prices fall, HCA profit will be reduced as it takes account of losses sustained by holding inventory while its price drops. Holding gains and losses are quite different from operating gains and losses. HCA profit does not distinguish between the two, whereas CCA profit does.

3 HCA profit might be adjusted to reflect the moving price level syndrome:
   (a) by use of the operating capital maintenance approach, which regards only the CCA **operating** profit as the authentic result for the period and which treats any holding gain or loss as a movement on reserves;
   (b) by adoption of the real terms **financial** capital maintenance approach, which applies a general inflation measure via the RPI, combined with CCA information regarding holding gains.

Thus the statement can reveal information to satisfy the demands of the management of the entity itself – as distinct from the shareholder/proprietor, whose awareness of inflation may centre on the RPI. In this way the concern of operating management can be accommodated with the different interest of the shareholder. The HCA profit would fail on both these counts.

4 CC profit is important because:

(a) it quantifies cost of sales and depreciation after allowing for changing price levels; hence trading results, free of inflationary elements, grant a clear picture of entity activities and management performance;

(b) resources are maintained, having eliminated the possibility of paying dividend out of real capital;

(c) yardsticks for management performance are more comparable as a time series within the one entity and between entities, the distortion caused by moving prices having been alleviated.

4.9 The ASB approach

The ASB has been wary of this topic. It is only too aware that standard setters in the past have been unsuccessful in obtaining a consensus on the price level adjusting model to be used in financial statements. The chronology in Figure 4.9 illustrates the previous attempts to deal with the topic. Consequently, the ASB has clearly decided to follow a gradualist approach and to require uniformity in the treatment of specific assets and liabilities where it is current practice to move away from historical costs.

The ASB view was set out in a Discussion Paper, *The Role of Valuation in Financial Reporting*, issued in 1993.[1] The ASB had three options when considering the existing system of modified historic costs:

● to remove the right to modify cost in the balance sheet;

● to introduce a coherent current value system immediately;

● to make *ad hoc* improvements to the present modified historic cost system.

4.9.1 Remove the right to modify cost in the balance sheet

This would mean pruning the system back to one rigorously based on the principles of historical costs, with current values shown by way of note.

This option has strong support from the profession not only in the UK, e.g. 'in our view ... the most significant advantage of historical cost over current value accounting ... is that it is based on the actual transactions which the company has undertaken and the cash flows that it has generated ... this is an advantage not just in terms of reliability, but also in terms of relevance',[2] but also in the USA, e.g. 'a study showed that users were opposed to replacing the current historic cost based accounting model ... because it provides them with a stable and consistent benchmark that they can rely on to establish historical trends'.[3]

Although this would have brought UK practice into line with that of the USA and some of the EU countries, it has been rejected by the ASB. This is no doubt on the basis that the ASB wishes to see current values established in the UK in the longer term.

Figure 4.9 Standard setters' unsuccessful attempts to replace HCA

1940s ICAEW Recommendation on Accounting Principles No. 12 *Rising Price Levels in Relation to Accounts.*

1950s ICAEW Recommendation on Accounting Principles No. 15 *Accounting for Changes in the Purchasing Power of Money.*

1974 Statement of Accounting Practice SSAP 7 *Accounting for Changes in the Purchasing Power of Money* advocating the CPP model.

1975 *Inflation Accounting,* Report of the Inflation Accounting Committee (The Sandilands Report) advocating current cost accounting (CCA) rather than the CPP, RCA or NRVA model. The CCA system recommended by Sandilands was based on the deprival value of an asset, i.e. the value based on the loss, direct or indirect, sustainable by an entity if it were to be deprived of the asset concerned. In effect, the CCA model became a compound of the concepts of RC, NRV and PV, with a heavy bias towards RC. The committee believed that, where RC could be estimated, it would represent the value of an asset to the business. The government, the standard setters and the accountancy profession in general accepted the report and a new committee was set up, the Morpeth Committee.

1976 The Morpeth Committee produced precise proposals for the adoption of a CCA system together with the abandonment of the HCA model of financial reporting.

1977 ED 18 was published but it failed to obtain ratification by the ICAEW in open forum because of its complexity, particularly with regard to the valuation of capital assets and stocks, its non-recognition of monetary items, and its mandatory abandonment of HCA.

1978 The standard setters produced *Interim Recommendation of the ASC* (referred to as The Hyde Guidelines). This was a holding operation until detailed proposals could be produced.

1979 ED 24 *Current Cost Accounting* was issued by the ASC to be followed by a standard, SSAP 16 *Current Cost Accounting.*

1984 SSAP 16 *Current Cost Accounting* was issued by the ASC requiring listed companies to produce CCA accounts as their primary financial report. There was widespread non-compliance and a new exposure draft ED 35 was issued effectively retaining HCA accounts as the primary financial report with supplementary current cost information.

1985 SSAP 16 was withdrawn and the ASC issued *Accounting for the Effects of Changing Prices: A Handbook.* The Handbook was interesting in that it set out four valuation bases if the financial capital maintenance concept was applied and four valuation bases if the operating capital maintenance concept was applied. Its preferred options were CCA under the financial capital maintenance concept which it referred to as real terms accounting (RTA) and CCA under the operating capital maintenance concept.

4.9.2 Introduce a coherent current value system immediately

This would mean developing the system into one more clearly founded on principles embracing current values. One such system, advocated by the ASB in Chapter 6 of its *Statement of Accounting Principles*, is based on **value to the business**. The value to the business measurement model is eclectic in that it draws on various current value systems. The approach to establishing the value to the business of a specific asset is quite logical:

● If an asset is worth replacing, then use replacement cost (RC).

● If it is **not** worth replacing, then use:
  value in use (economic value) if it is worth keeping, **or**
  net realisable value (NRV) if it is **not** worth keeping.

However, the ASB did not see it as feasible to implement this system at that time because 'there is much work to be done to determine whether or not it is possible to devise a system that would be of economic relevance and acceptable to users and preparers of financial statements in terms of sufficient reliability without prohibitive cost'.[4]

Make *ad hoc* improvements to the present modified historical cost system

The Board favoured this option for removing anomalies, on the basis that practice should be evolutionary and should follow various ASB pronouncements (e.g. on the revaluation of properties and quoted investments) on an *ad hoc* basis. The *Statement of Accounting Principles* continues to envisage that a mixed measurement system will be used and it focuses on the mix of historical cost and current value to be adopted.[5]

It is influenced in choosing this option by the recognition that there are anxieties about the costs and benefits of moving to a full current value system, and by the belief that a considerable period of experimentation and learning would be needed before such a major change could be successfully introduced.[6]

Given the inability of the standard setters to implement a uniform current value system in the past, it seems a sensible, pragmatic approach for the ASB to recognise that it would fail if it made a similar attempt now.

This approach has been applied in FRS 3 with the requirement for a new primary financial statement, the statement of total recognised gains and losses (see Chapter 8 for further discussion) to report unrealised gains and losses arising from revaluation.

The historical cost based system and the current value based system have far more to commend them than the *ad hoc* option chosen by the ASB. However, as a short-term measure, it leaves the way open for the implementation in the longer term of its preferred value to the business model.

4.10 The IASC/IASB approach

The IASB has struggled in the same way as the ASB in the UK in deciding how to respond to inflation rates that have varied so widely over time. Theoretically there is a case for inflation-adjusting financial statements whatever the rate of inflation but standard setters need to carry the preparers and users of accounts with them – this means that there has to be a consensus that the traditional HCA financial statements are failing to give a true and fair view. Such a consensus is influenced by the current rate of inflation.

When the rates around the world were in double figures there was pressure for a **mandatory** standard so that financial statements were comparable. This led to the issue in 1983 of IAS 15 *Information Reflecting the Effects of Changing Prices* which required companies to restate the HCA accounts using either a general price index or replacement costs with adjustments for depreciation, cost of sales and monetary items.

As the inflation rates fell below double figures there was less willingness by companies to prepare inflation-adjusted accounts and so, in 1989, the mandatory requirement was relaxed and the application of IAS 15 became **optional**.

In recent years the inflation rates in developed countries have ranged between 1% and 4% and so in 2003, twenty years after it was first issued, IAS 15 was **withdrawn** as part of the ASB Improvement Project.

These low rates have not been universal outside the developed world and there has remained a need to prepare inflation-adjusted financial statements where the rates are so high that HCA would be misleading.

4.10.1 The IASB position where there is hyperinflation

What do we mean by hyperinflation?

IAS 29 *Financial Reporting in Hyperinflationary Economies* states that hyperinflation occurs when money loses purchasing power at such a rate that comparison of amounts from transactions that have occurred at different times, even within the same accounting period, is misleading.

What rate indicates that hyperinflation exists?

IAS 29 does not specify an absolute rate – this is a matter of qualitative judgement – but it sets out certain pointers, such as people preferring to keep their wealth in non-monetary assets, people preferring prices to be stated in terms of an alternative stable currency rather than the domestic currency, wages and prices being linked to a price index, or the cumulative inflation rate over three years approaching 100%.

Countries where hyperinflation has occurred recently include Angola, Burma and Turkey.

How are financial statements adjusted?

The current year financial statements, whether HCA or CCA, must to be restated using the domestic measuring unit current at the balance sheet date; if the current year should be the first year that restatement takes place then the opening balance sheet also has to be restated.

Illustration of disclosures in IAS 29 adjusted accounts

The following is an extract from the 2002 accounts of Turkiye Petrol Rafinerileri.

IAS 29 requires that financial statements prepared in the currency of a hyperinflationary economy be stated in terms of the measuring unit current at the balance sheet date and the corresponding figures for previous periods be restated in the same terms. One characteristic that leads to the classification of an economy as hyperinflationary is a cumulative three-year inflation rate approaching 100%. Such cumulative rate in Turkey was 227% for the three years ended 31 December 2002 based on the wholesale price index announced by the Turkish State Institute of Statistics. The restatement has been calculated by means of conversion factors based on the Turkish countrywide wholesale price index (WPI).

The index and corresponding conversion factors for year-ends are as follows (1994 average = 100)

	Index	Conversion factor
Year ended 31 December 1999	1,979.5	3.2729
Year ended 31 December 2000	2,626.0	2.4672
Year ended 31 December 2001	4,951.7	1.3083
Year ended 31 December 2002	6,478.8	1.0000

- Monetary assets and liabilities are not restated.
- Non-monetary assets and liabilities are restated by applying to the initial acquisition cost and any accumulated depreciation for fixed assets the relevant conversion factors reflecting the increase in WPI from date of acquisition.
- All items in the statements of income are restated.

4.11 Future developments

A mixed picture emerges when we try to foresee the future of changing price levels and financial reporting. The accounting profession has been reluctant to abandon the HC concept in favour of a 'valuation accounting' approach. In the UK and Australia many companies have stopped revaluing their non-current assets, with a large proportion opting instead to revert to the historical cost basis with the two main factors influencing management's decision being cost effectiveness and future reporting flexibility.[7]

The pragmatic approach is prevailing with each class of asset and liability being considered on an individual basis, e.g. fixed assets reported at depreciated replacement cost unless this is higher than the economic value we discussed in Chapter 3; financial assets being reported at market value (exit value in the NRV model); current assets reported at lower of HC and NRV. In each case the resulting changes, both realised and unrealised, in value will find their way into the financial performance statement(s).

This means that in the future historical cost and realisation will be regarded as less relevant[8] and investors, analysts and management will need to come to terms with increased volatility in reported annual performance.

Summary

The traditional HCA system reveals disturbing inadequacies in times of changing price levels, calling into question the value of financial reports using this system. Considerable resources and energy have been expended in searching for a substitute model able to counter the distortion and confusion caused by an unstable monetary unit.

Three basic models have been developed: RCA, NRVA and CPP. Each has its merits and defects; each produces a different income value and a different capital value. However, it is important that inflation-adjusted values be computed in order to avoid a possible loss of entity resources and the collapse of the going concern.

The contemporary financial reporting scene is beset by problems such as the emergence of brand accounting, the debate on accounting for goodwill, the need for more informative revenue accounts and a sudden spate of financial scandals involving major industrial conglomerations. These have combined to raise questions regarding the adequacy of the annual accounts and the intrinsic validity of the auditors' report.

In assessing future prospects it would seem that more useful financial information is needed. This need will be met by changes in the reporting system, which are beginning to include some form of 'value accounting' as distinct from HC accounting. Such value accounting will probably embrace inflationary adjustments to enable comparability to be maintained, as far as possible, in an economic environment of changing prices.

REVIEW QUESTIONS

1 (a) Explain the limitations of HCA when prices are rising.

   (b) Why has the HCA model survived in spite of its shortcomings in times of inflation?

2 Explain the features of the CPP model in contrast with those of the CCA model.

3 What factors should be taken into account when designing a system of accounting for inflation?

4 To what extent are CCA statements useful to an investor?

5 Compare the operating and financial capital maintenance concepts.

6 'Historical cost accounting is the worst possible accounting convention, until one considers the alternatives.' Discuss this statement in relation to CPP, CCA and NRVA.

7 'To be relevant to investors, the profit for the year should include both realised and unrealised gains/losses.' Discuss.

8 Discuss the effect on setting performance bonuses for staff if financial performance for a period contains both realised and unrealised gains/losses.

9 'The relevant financial performance figure for an investor is the amount available for distribution at the balance sheet date.' Discuss.

10 'Financial statements should reflect realistically the performance and position of an organisation, but most of the accountant's rules conflict directly with the concept of realism.' Discuss.

11 Explain why financial reports prepared under the historical cost convention are subject to the following major limitations:

   ● inventory is undervalued

   ● the depreciation charge to the income statement is understated

   ● gains and losses on net monetary assets are undisclosed

   ● balance sheet values are understated

   ● periodic comparisons are invalidated.

12 Explain how each of the limitations in question 11 could be overcome.

13 In April 2000 the G4 + 1 Group acknowledged that market exit value is generally regarded as the basis for fair value measurement of financial instruments and was discussing the use of the deprival value model for the measurement of non-financial assets or liabilities, especially in cases in which the item is highly specialised and not easily transferable in the market in its current condition. The deprival value model would require that an asset or liability be measured at its replacement cost, net realisable value, or value in use, depending on the particular circumstances.

   (a) Discuss reasons why financial and non-financial assets should be measured using different bases.

   (b) Explain what is meant by 'depending on the particular circumstances'.

14 Explain the criteria for determining whether hyperinflation exists.

EXERCISES

An extract from the solution is provided in the Appendix at the end of the text for exercises marked with an asterisk (*).

* Question I

Shower Ltd was incorporated towards the end of 20X2, but it did not start trading until 20X3. Its historical cost balance sheet at 1 January 20X3 was as follows:

	£
Share capital, £1 shares	2,000
Loan (interest free)	8,000
	£10,000
Fixed assets, at cost	6,000
Inventory, at cost (4,000 units)	4,000
	£10,000

A summary of Shower Limited's bank account for 20X3 is given below:

		£	£
1 Jan 20X3	Opening balance		nil
30 Jun 20X3	Sales (8,000 units)		20,000
Less			
29 Jun 20X3	Purchase (6,000 units)	9,000	
	Sundry expenses	5,000	14,000
31 Dec 20X3	Closing balance		£6,000

All the company's transactions are on a cash basis.

The fixed assets are expected to last for five years and the company intends to depreciate its fixed assets on a straight-line basis. The fixed assets had a resale value of £2,000 at 31 December 20X3.

Notes

1   The closing inventory is 2,000 units and the inventory is sold on a first-in-first-out basis.

2   All prices remained constant from the date of incorporation to 1 January 20X3, but thereafter, various relevant price indices moved as follows:

		Specific indices	
	General price level	*Inventory*	*Fixed assets*
1 January 20X3	100	100	100
30 June 20X3	120	150	140
31 December 20X3	240	255	200

Required:

Produce balance sheets as at December 20X3 and income statements for the year ended on that date on the basis of:

(i)   historical cost;
(ii) current purchasing power (general price level);
(iii) replacement cost;
(iv) continuous contemporary accounting (NRVA).

Question 2

The finance director of Toy plc has been asked by a shareholder to explain items that appear in the current cost income statement for the year ended 31.8.20X9 and the balance sheet as at that date:

		£	£
Historical cost profit			143,000
Cost of sales adjustment	(1)	10,000	
Additional depreciation	(2)	6,000	
Monetary working capital adjustment	(3)	2,500	18,500
Current cost operating profit before tax			124,500
Gearing adjustment	(4)		2,600
CCA operating profit			127,100
Non-current assets at gross replacement cost		428,250	
Accumulated current cost depreciation	(5)	(95,650)	332,600
Net current assets			121,400
12% debentures			(58,000)
			396,000
Issued share capital			250,000
Current cost reserve	(6)		75,000
Retained earnings			71,000
			396,000

Required:

(a) Explain what each of the items numbered 1–6 represents and the purpose of each.
(b) What do you consider to be the benefits to users of providing current cost information?

* Question 3

The balance sheets of Parkway plc for 20X7 and 20X8 are given below, together with the profit and loss account for the year ended 30 June 20X8.

	Balance Sheet					
	20X8			20X7		
	£000	£000	£000	£000	£000	£000
Non-current assets	Cost	Depn	NBV	Cost	Depn	NBV
Freehold land	60,000	—	60,000	60,000	—	60,000
Buildings	40,000	8,000	32,000	40,000	7,200	32,800
Plant and machinery	30,000	16,000	14,000	30,000	10,000	20,000
Vehicles	40,000	20,000	20,000	40,000	12,000	28,000
	170,000	44,000	126,000	170,000	29,200	140,800

	£000	£000
Current assets		
Inventory	80,000	70,000
Trade receivables	60,000	40,000
Short-term investments	50,000	—
Cash at bank and in hand	5,000	5,000
	195,000	115,000
Current liabilities		
Trade payables	90,000	60,000
Bank overdraft	50,000	45,000
Taxation	28,000	15,000
Dividends	15,000	10,000
	183,000	130,000
Net current assets	12,000	(15,000)
	138,000	125,800
Financed by		
Ordinary share capital	80,000	80,000
Share premium	10,000	10,000
Retained profits	28,000	15,800
	118,000	105,800
Long-term loans	20,000	20,000
	138,000	125,800

Income statement of Parkway plc for
the year ended 30 June 20X8

	£000
Sales	738,000
Cost of sales	620,000
Gross profit	118,000

Notes

1. The freehold land and buildings were purchased on 1 July 20X0. The company policy is to depreciate buildings over fifty years and to provide no depreciation on land.
2. Depreciation on plant and machinery and motor vehicles is provided at the rate of 20% per annum on a straight-line basis.
3. Depreciation on buildings and plant and equipment has been included in administration expenses, while that on motor vehicles is included in distribution expenses.
4. The directors of Parkway plc have provided you with the following information relating to price rises:

	RPI	Inventory	Land	Buildings	Plant	Vehicles
1 July 20X0	100	60	70	50	90	120
1 July 20X7	170	140	290	145	135	180
30 June 20X8	190	180	310	175	165	175
Average for year ending 30 June 20X8	180	160	300	163	145	177

Required:

(a) Making and stating any assumptions that are necessary, and giving reasons for those assumptions, calculate the monetary working capital adjustment for Parkway plc.

(b) Critically evaluate the usefulness of the monetary working capital adjustment.

* Question 4

Raiders plc prepares accounts annually to 31 March. The following figures, prepared on a conventional historical cost basis, are included in the company's accounts to 31 March 20X5.

1. In the profit and loss account:

	£000	£000
(i) Cost of goods sold:		
Inventory at 1 April 20X4	9,600	
Purchases	39,200	
	48,800	
Inventory at 31 March 20X5	11,300	37,500
(ii) Depreciation of equipment		8,640

2. In the balance sheet:

	£000	£000
(iii) Equipment at cost	57,600	
Less: Accumulated depreciation	16,440	41,160
(iv) Inventory		11,300

The inventory held on 31 March 20X4 and 31 March 20X5 was in each case purchased evenly during the last six months of the company's accounting year.

Equipment is depreciated at a rate of 15% per annum, using the straight-line method. Equipment owned on 31 March 20X5 was purchased as follows: on 1 April 20X2 at a cost of £16 million; on 1 April 20X3 at a cost of £20 million; and on 1 April 20X4 at a cost of £21.6 million.

The following indices are available:

	Current cost of inventory	Current cost of equipment	Retail Price Index
1 April 20X2	109	145	313
1 April 20X3	120	162	328
30 September 20X3	128	170	339
31 December 20X3	133	175	343
31 March/1 April 20X4	138	180	345
30 September 20X4	150	191	355
31 December 20X4	156	196	360
31 March 20X5	162	200	364

Required:
(a) Calculate the following current cost accounting figures:
   (i)   The cost of goods sold of Raiders plc for the year ended 31 March 20X5.
   (ii) The balance sheet value of inventory at 31 March 20X5.
   (iii) The equipment depreciation charge for the year ended 31 March 20X5.
   (iv) The net balance sheet value of equipment at 31 March 20X5.
(b) Discuss the extent to which the figures you have calculated in (a) above (together with figures calculated on a similar basis for earlier years) provide information over and above that provided by the conventional historical cost income statement and balance sheet figures.
(c) Outline the main reasons why the standard setters have experienced so much difficulty in their attempts to develop an accounting standard on accounting for changing prices.

Question 5

The historical cost accounts of Smith plc are as follows:

Smith plc Income statement for the year ended 31 December 20X8

	£000	£000
Sales		2,000
Cost of sales:		
Opening inventory 1 January 20X8	320	
Purchases	1,680	
	2,000	
Closing inventory at 31 December 20X8	280	
		1,720
Gross profit		280
Depreciation	20	
Administration expenses	100	
		120
Net profit		160

Balance Sheet of Smith plc as at 31 December 20X8

	20X7	20X8
	£000	£000
Fixed assets		
Land and buildings at cost	1,360	1,360
Less aggregate depreciation	(160)	(180)
	1,200	1,180

		20X7		20X8	
Current assets					
Inventory	320		280		
Trade receivables	80		160		
Cash at bank	40		120		
	440		560		
Trade payables	200		140		
		240		420	
		1,440		1,600	
Ordinary share capital		800		800	
Retained profit		640		800	
		1,440		1,600	

Notes

1 Land and buildings were acquired in 20X0 with the buildings component costing £800,000 and depreciated over forty years.
2 Share capital was issued in 20X0.
3 Closing inventories were acquired in the last quarter of the year.
4 RPI numbers were:

Average for 20X0	120
20X7 last quarter	216
At 31 December 20X7	220
20X8 last quarter	232
Average for 20X8	228
At 31 December 20X8	236

Required:
(i) Explain the basic concept of the CPP accounting system.
(ii) Prepare CPP accounts for Smith plc for the year ended 20X8.
    The following steps will assist in preparing the CPP accounts:
    (a) Restate the income statement for the current year in terms of £CPP at the year-end.
    (b) Restate the closing balance sheet in £CPP at year-end, but excluding monetary items, i.e. trade receivables, trade payables, cash at bank.
    (c) Restate the opening balance sheet in £CPP at year-end, but including monetary items, i.e. trade receivables, trade payables and cash at bank, and showing equity as the balancing figure.
    (d) Compare the opening and closing equity figures derived in (b) and (c) above to arrive at the total profit/loss for the year in CPP terms. Compare this figure with the CPP profit calculated in (a) above to determine the monetary gain or monetary loss.
    (e) Reconcile monetary gains/loss in (d) with the increase/decrease in net monetary items during the year expressed in £CPP compared with the increase/decrease expressed in £HC.

* Question 6

Aspirations Ltd commenced trading as wholesale suppliers of office equipment on 1 January 20X1, issuing ordinary shares of £1 each at par in exchange for cash. The shares were fully paid on issue, the number issued being 1,500,000.

The following financial statements, based on the historical cost concept, were compiled for 20X1.

Aspirations Ltd

Income statement for the year ended 31 December 20X1

	£	£
Sales		868,425
Purchases	520,125	
Less: Inventory 31 December 20X1	24,250	
Cost of sales		495,875
Gross profit		372,550
Expenses	95,750	
Depreciation	25,250	
		121,000
Net profit		251,550

Balance Sheet as at 31 December 20X1

	Cost	Depreciation	
Non-current assets	£	£	£
Freehold property	650,000	6,500	643,500
Office equipment	375,000	18,750	356,250
	1,025,000	25,250	999,750
Current assets			
Inventories		24,250	
Trade receivables		253,500	
Cash		1,090,300	
		1,368,050	
Current liabilities		116,250	
		1,251,800	
Non-current liabilities		500,000	751,800
			1,751,550
Issued share capital			1,500,000
1,500,000 £1 ordinary shares			251,550
Retained earnings			1,751,550

The year 20X1 witnessed a surge of inflation and in consequence the directors became concerned about the validity of the revenue account and balance sheet as income and capital statements. Index numbers reflecting price changes were:

Specific index numbers reflecting replacement costs

	1 January 20X1	31 December 20X1	Average for 20X1
Inventory	115	150	130
Freehold property	110	165	127
Office equipment	125	155	145
General price index numbers	135	170	155

Regarding current exit costs

Inventory is anticipated to sell at a profit of 75% of cost.

The value of assets at 31 December 20X1 was

	£
Freehold property	640,000
Office equipment	350,000

Initial purchases of inventory were effected on 1 January 20X1 amounting to £34,375; the balance of purchases was evenly spread over the twelve-month period. The non-current assets were acquired on 1 January 20X1 and, together with the initial inventory, were paid for in cash on that day.

Required:
Prepare the accounts adjusted for current values using each of the three proposed models of current value accounting: namely, the accounting methods known as replacement cost, general (or current) purchasing power and net realisable value.

References

1 *The Role of Valuation in Financial Reporting*, ASB, 1993.
2 Ernst & Young, *UK GAAP* (4th edition), 1994, p. 91.
3 *The Information Needs of Investors and Creditors*, AICPA Special Committee on Financial Reporting.
4 *The Role of Valuation in Financial Reporting*, ASB, 1993, para. 31(ii).
5 *Statement of Accounting Principles*, ASB, December 1999, para. 6.4.
6 *The Role of Valuation in Financial Reporting*, ASB, 1993, para. 33.
7 Ernst & Young, 'Revaluation of non-current assets', Accounting Standard, Ernst & Young, January 2002, www.ey.com/Global/gcr.nsf/Australia.
8 A. Wilson, 'IAS: the challenge for measurement', *Accountancy*, December 2001, p. 90.

Bibliography

Accounting for Changes in the Purchasing Power of Money, SSAP 7, ASC, 1974.
Accounting for Stewardship in a Period of Inflation, The Research Foundation of the ICAEW, 1968.

R.J. Chambers, *Accounting Evaluation and Economic Behaviour*, Prentice Hall, 1966.

R.J. Chambers, 'Second thoughts on continuous contemporary accounting', *Abacus*, September 1970.

R.A. Hill, 'Economic income and value: the price level problem', *ACCA Students' Newsletter*, November 1987.

T.A. Lee, *Income and Value Measurement: Theory and Practice* (3rd edition), Van Nostrand Reinhold (UK), 1985, Chapter 5.

'A quickfall: the elementary arithmetic of measuring real profit', *Management Accounting*, April 1980.

F. Sandilands (Chairman), *Inflation Accounting – Report of the Inflation Accounting Committee*, HMSO Cmnd 6225, 1975, pp. 139–155 and Chapter 9.

D. Tweedie and G. Whittington, *Capital Maintenance Concepts*, ASC, 1985.

G. Whittington, 'Inflation accounting: all the answers from Deloitte, Haskins and Sells', distinguished lecture series, Cardiff, 5 March 1981, reproduced in *Contemporary Issues in Accounting*, Pitman/Farringdon, 1984.

PART 2

Regulatory framework – an attempt to achieve uniformity

CHAPTER 5

Financial reporting – evolution of the regulatory framework in the UK

5.1 Introduction

There has been much discussion of the move to International Standards in 2005 for many listed companies. However, we should not lose sight of the fact that there remain many UK-specific regulatory requirements. For example, there are UK SSAPs and FRSs for companies which choose not to apply International Standards, the FRSSE for small companies, Stock Exchange listing requirements including compliance with the Combined Code, mandatory statements such as the Operating and Financial Review, and ASB Statements of Best Practice such as that on interim reports.

In this chapter we will discuss:

● Mandatory regulations
● Arguments for and against standards
● The structure of the UK regulatory framework
● The Operating and Financial Review
● The Combined Code on Corporate Governance
● The FRSSE
● Interim reports.

5.2 Mandatory regulations

Mandatory regulations take the form of Statements of Standard Accounting Practice (SSAPs) and Financial Reporting Standards (FRSs) issued by the Accounting Standards Board. Such regulations are important because users of accounting numbers need to be able to have confidence that the numbers are a fair representation and have not been manipulated by management.

5.2.1 Role of accounting numbers in defining contractual entitlements

Contracting parties frequently define the rights between themselves in terms of accounting numbers.[1] For example, the remuneration of directors and managers might be expressed in terms of a salary plus a bonus based on an agreed performance measure, e.g. Interbrew's 2002 Annual Report states:

An annual bonus plan is approved each year. Payment levels are linked to audited consolidated earnings before interest and taxes, and to year over year changes, both positive and negative, in return on cash capital employed and/or market share.

However, if there is a risk that earnings for the year will not grow at a rate that is attractive to the directors and managers, there could be a temptation to improve the earnings for the period by taking measures that might not be in the interest of the shareholders.

Typical measures include: **deferring discretionary expenditure**, e.g. research, advertising, training expenditure; **deferring amortisation**, e.g. making optimistic sales projections in order to classify research as development expenditure which can be capitalised; and **reclassifying** deteriorating current assets as fixed assets to avoid the need to recognise a loss under the lower of cost and net realisable value rule applicable to current assets.

The introduction of a mandatory standard that changes management's ability to adopt such measures **affects wealth distribution** within the firm. For example, if managers are unable to delay the amortisation of development expenditure, then bonuses related to profit will be lower and there will effectively have been a transfer of wealth from managers to shareholders.

This effect of changes in mandatory standards on wealth distribution is a major reason why standards are required, and also why it is difficult to obtain a consensus. Each party considers the economic consequences, real or imagined, on their personal position.

5.2.2 Need for mandatory standards

Mandatory standards are needed to define the way in which accounting numbers are presented in financial statements, so that their measurement and presentation are less subjective. It had been thought that the accountancy profession could obtain uniformity of disclosure by persuasion but, in reality, the profession found it difficult to resist management pressures.

During the 1960s the financial sector of the UK economy lost confidence in the accountancy profession when internationally known UK-based companies were seen to have published financial data that were materially incorrect. Shareholders are normally unaware that this occurs and it tends only to become public knowledge in restricted circumstances, e.g. when a third party has a **vested interest** in revealing adverse facts following a takeover, or when a company falls into the hands of an administrator, inspector or liquidator, **whose duty it is to enquire and report** on shortcomings in the management of a company.

Two scandals which disturbed the public at the time, GEC/AEI and Pergamon Press,[2] were both made public in the restricted circumstances referred to above, when financial reports prepared from the same basic information disclosed a materially different picture.

GEC takeover of AEI in 1967

The first calamity for the profession involved GEC Ltd in its takeover bid for AEI Ltd when the pre-takeover accounts prepared by the old AEI directors differed materially from the post-takeover accounts prepared by the new AEI directors.

AEI profit forecast for 1967 as determined by the old AEI directors
AEI Ltd produced a **profit forecast of £10 million** in November 1967 and recommended its shareholders to reject the GEC bid. The forecast had the blessing of

the auditors, in as much as they said that it had been prepared on a fair and reasonable basis and in a manner consistent with the principles followed in preparing the annual accounts. The investing public would normally have been quite satisfied with the forecast figure and the process by which it was produced. Clearly, AEI would not subsequently have produced other information to show that the picture was materially different from that forecast.

However, GEC was successful with its bid and as a result it was GEC's directors who had control over the preparation of the AEI accounts for 1967.

AEI profit for 1967 as determined by the new AEI directors

Under the control of the directors of GEC the accounts of AEI were produced for 1967 showing **a loss of £4.5 million**. Unfortunately, this was from basic information that was largely the same as that used by AEI when producing its profit forecast.

There can be two reasons for the difference between the figures produced. Either the facts have changed or the judgements made by the directors have changed. In this case, it seems there was a change in the facts to the extent of a post-acquisition closure of an AEI factory; this explained £5 million of the £14.5 million difference between the forecast profit and the actual loss. The remaining £9.5 million arose because of differences in judgement. For example, the new directors took a different view of the value of stock and work-in-progress.

Pergamon Press

Audited accounts were produced by Pergamon Press Ltd for 1968 showing a profit of approximately £2 million.

An independent investigation by Price Waterhouse suggested that this profit should be reduced by 75% because of a number of unacceptable valuations, e.g. there had been a failure to reduce certain stock to the lower of cost and net realisable value, and there had been a change in policy on the capitalisation of printing costs of back issues of scientific journals – they were treated as a cost of closing stock in 1968, but not as a cost of opening stock in 1968.

Public view of the accounting profession following these cases

It had long been recognised that accountancy is not an exact science, but it had not been appreciated just how much latitude there was for companies to produce vastly different results based on the same transactions. Given that the auditors were perfectly happy to sign that accounts showing either a £10 million profit or a £4.5 million loss were true and fair, the public felt the need for action if investors were to have any trust in the figures that were being published.

The difficulty was that each firm of accountants tended to rely on precedents within its own firm in deciding what was true and fair. This is fine until the public becomes aware that profits depend on the particular firm or partner who happens to be responsible for the audit. The auditors were also under pressure to agree to practices that the directors wanted because there were no professional mandatory standards.

This was the scenario that galvanised the City press and the investing public. An embarrassed, disturbed profession announced in 1969, via the ICAEW, that there was a pressing need for the introduction of Statements of Standard Accounting Practice to supplement the legislation.

5.2.3 Creation of a standard-setting body

In this section we briefly consider the ASSC, the ASC, the Dearing Committee, the Dearing Report and the ASB.

The Accounting Standards Steering Committee (ASSC)

The Accounting Standards Steering Committee was formed by the ICAEW in 1970. The committee later increased its membership to include other professional accounting bodies. The objectives of the ASSC were as follows:

- **Damage limitation** by narrowing the areas of difference in accounting practice that had been bringing the profession into disrepute.
- The **development of a consensus** by encouraging wider exposure and discussion of proposals for standards. This was a vital step because failure to carry directors or the profession would lead to non-compliance or rejection, as happened when unsuccessful attempts were made to make either CPP or CCA inflation-adjusted financial statements compulsory.
- To **encourage disclosure** by requiring companies to disclose the accounting policies they have adopted, e.g. depreciation policy, and also to disclose if they change a policy.
- To **improve standards** by developing a continuing programme.

The Accounting Standards Committee (ASC)

By 1976 the procedure was for the ASSC (renamed the ASC) to prepare a draft standard; the draft was adopted if all six professional accountancy bodies were unanimous; each of the professional accounting bodies then issued the SSAP to its own members.

By 1982 it was felt that the professional accounting bodies had too great a control over the process. Consequently, the terms of reference of the ASC were widened, e.g. to consult representatives of finance, commerce, industry and government, and other persons concerned with financial reporting; the membership was reduced to twenty, including five users of financial reports who were not required to be accountants; and government officials, e.g. representatives from the Department of Trade and Industry, could be co-opted as non-voting members.

The process was also organised to give users full opportunity to make their inputs to the standard setting. The aims of the process were as follows:

- Topics that were to be the subject of a standard were made public.
- Consultation was encouraged by the issue of discussion documents.
- An exposure draft prepared by the ASC was published.
- A draft standard was prepared by the ASC, taking into account reactions to the discussion documents and exposure drafts.

The Dearing Committee[3]

Although the ASC had produced twenty-five standards by 1991, there was criticism that it was not adequately staffed, had no ground-plan and was reactive rather than proactive. However, it had operated as effectively as possible given its resources, and had indeed been ambitious in attempting to address areas where the profession was itself divided, e.g. inflation accounting.

The political climate changed in the 1980s with wider share ownership and the growing use of watchdog organisations to encourage self-regulation, e.g. Oftel in the telecommunications industry and Ofwat in the water industry. Changes in the way in which the accounting profession ensured conformity to universal standards were only to be expected and so the Dearing Committee was set up to review the standard-setting process in the light of future changes in the financial markets, i.e. recognising that financial statements are a prerequisite for a properly functioning capital market, and taking account of the current attitude of the state and public to the regulation of companies. The committee reported in 1988.

The Dearing Report

The report recommended the creation of a conceptual framework by developing work that had already taken place, e.g. FASB statements produced in the USA. It is a noticeable feature of the evolution of a conceptual framework that the ASB has been eclectic in making use of material from a wide range of sources, e.g. the FASB statements and the IASC document *Framework for the Presentation and Preparation of Financial Statements*.[4]

It also recommended a structure by proposing setting up the following:

- a Financial Reporting Council with professional accountants and users to be responsible for giving the ASB guidance on priorities and advising it on areas of public concern;
- an Accounting Standards Board (ASB) with a salaried staff comprising accountants responsible for issuing standards which were to be founded on stated **principles** wherever possible so as to avoid standards becoming a cookbook of detailed, legalistic rules;
- an Urgent Issues Task Force to amend or expand on standards if the need suddenly arose;
- a Review Panel reporting to the Council to examine departures from standards by large companies. This would allow the auditor to make reference for guidance where the directors proposed to depart from a standard and where the auditor disagreed with their proposed treatment or agreed and considered that the standard needed to be amended.

Accounting Standards Board (ASB)

The ASC consequently ceased to exist on 1 August 1990 when it was replaced by the new Accounting Standards Board (ASB).

5.3 Arguments in support of standards

The setting of standards has both supporters and opponents. In this section we discuss comparability, credibility, influence and discipline.

Comparability

Financial statements should allow a user to make predictions of future cash flows, make comparisons with other companies[5] and evaluate the management's performance.

In order to be able to make valid inter-company comparisons of performance and trends, investment decision makers must be supplied with relevant and reliable data that have been standardised. Such comparisons would be distorted and valueless if companies were permitted to select accounting policies at random or, even worse, with the intention of disguising changes in performance and trends.

Credibility

The accountancy profession would lose all credibility if it permitted companies experiencing similar events to produce financial reports that disclosed markedly different results simply because they could select different accounting policies. Uniformity is essential if financial reports are to disclose a true and fair view. However, the ASC had emphasised that the standards were not intended to be a comprehensive code of rigid rules – they did not want them to supersede the exercise of informed judgement in determining what constituted a true and fair view in each circumstance.

Influence

The process of formulating standards has encouraged a constructive appraisal of the policies being proposed for individual reporting problems and has stimulated the development of a conceptual framework. For example, the standard on leasing introduced the idea in UK standards of considering the commercial substance of a transaction rather than simply the legal position.

When the ASC was set up in the 1970s there was no clear statement of accounting principles other than that accounts should be prudent, be consistent, follow accrual accounting procedures and be based on the initial assumption that the business would remain a going concern.

The immediate task was to bring some order into accounting practice. The challenge of this task is illustrated by the ASC report *A Conceptual Framework for Financial Accounting and Reporting: The Possibilities for an Agreed Structure* by R. Macve, published in 1981, which considered that the possibility of an agreed body of accounting principles was remote at that time.

However, the process of setting standards has stimulated accounting thought and literature to the point where, by 1994, the ASB had produced its exposure drafts of *Statement of Accounting Principles*, which appeared in final form in December 1999.

Discipline

Companies left to their own devices without the need to observe standards will eventually be disciplined by the financial market: e.g. incorrect classification of research as development expenditure will eventually become apparent when sales growth is not as expected by the market. Mandatory standards will impose systematic ongoing regulation, which should prevent serious loss to the entity and those who rely on the annual accounts when making credit, loan and investment decisions.

There is a tension between the desire that standards should not be a comprehensive code of rigid rules and the desire to regulate accounting practices that are imaginatively devised by directors and their financial advisers to create a picture that they may consider true and fair – but which others may not. Directors are under pressure to maintain and improve the market valuation of their company's securities; they will attempt to influence any financial statistic that has an impact on the market valuation, such as the trend in the EPS figure, the net asset backing for the shares or the gearing ratios.

The Financial Reporting Council showed awareness of the need to impose discipline when it stated in its annual review, November 1991, para. 2.4, that the high level of company failures in the then recession, some of which were associated with obscure financial reporting, damaged confidence in the high standard of reporting by the majority of companies.

5.4 Arguments against standards

We have so far discussed the arguments in support of standard setting. However, there are also arguments against.

Adverse allocative effects

Adverse allocative effects could occur if standard setters did not take account of the economic consequences flowing from the standards they issued.[6] For example, additional costs could be imposed on preparers, and suboptimal managerial decisions might be taken to avoid any reduction in reported earnings or net assets. Furthermore, the adverse effects might be felt by people who did not actually use the accounts, e.g. a leasing standard that caused a fall in the lessee's reported profits might, as a consequence, depress the leasing industry, leading to the loss of employment by staff engaged in manufacturing assets supplied under lease, or in servicing the leasing industry.

Consensus-seeking

Consensus-seeking can lead to the issuing of standards that are over-influenced by those with easiest access to the standard setters – particularly as the subject matter becomes more complex, as with e.g. capital instruments. It could be argued that the ASB is attempting to minimise such influences by basing its standards on the *Statement of Principles*, but there is a counter-argument that the *Statement of Principles* is too general to fulfil this role effectively.

Overload

Standard overload is not a new charge. However, it takes a number of conflicting forms, e.g.:

- There are too many/too few standards.
- Standards are too detailed/not sufficiently detailed.
- Standards are general-purpose and fail to recognise the differences between large and small entities and interim and final accounts.
- There are too many standard setters with differing requirements, e.g. FASB, IASB, ASB, national Stock Exchange listing requirements.

5.5 Structure of regulatory framework

Financial statements prepared in the UK are subject to regulation by a number of different regulatory bodies, e.g. the Financial Reporting Council, the Financial Services Authority and Company Law.

5.5.1 The Financial Reporting Council (FRC)

The FRC was set up in 1990 as an independent regulator to set and enforce accounting standards. It operated through the Accounting Standards Board (ASB) and the Financial

Reporting Review Panel (FRRP) to encourage high-quality financial reporting. Due to its success in doing this, the government decided, following corporate disasters such as Enron in the USA, to give it a more proactive role from 2004 onwards in the areas of corporate governance, compliance with statutes and accounting and auditing standards.

The FRC's new structure is shown in Figure 5.1.

Figure 5.1 The Financial Reporting Council structure showing subsidiary boards

5.5.2 The Accounting Standards Board

The ASB issues mandatory standards (SSAPs and FRSs), confirms that SORPs are not in conflict with its mandatory standards and issues statements of best practice (such as those on OFR and Interim Reports).

5.5.3 SSAPs and FRSs

Extant standards are shown in Figure 5.2. Breaks in the numerical sequence are a consequence of standards being withdrawn and/or renumbered on reissue. Note that FRSs 20–26 are based on IFRSs.

5.5.4 Statements of Recommended Practice (SORPs)

SORPs are produced for specialised industries or sectors to supplement accounting standards and other regulatory requirements. SORPs are issued by SORP-making bodies that have satisfied criteria laid down by the ASB and developed their SORP in accordance with the ASB's code of practice. The ASB considers a proposed SORP

Figure 5.2 Extant standards

SSAP 4	Accounting for Government Grants
SSAP 5	Accounting for Value Added Tax
SSAP 9	Stocks and Long-Term Contracts
SSAP 13	Accounting for Research and Development
SSAP 17	Accounting for Post Balance Sheet Events
SSAP 19	Accounting for Investment Properties
SSAP 20	Foreign Currency Translation
SSAP 21	Accounting for Leases and Hire Purchase Contracts
SSAP 25	Segmental Reporting
FRS 1	Cash Flow Statements
FRS 2	Accounting for Subsidiary Undertakings
FRS 3	Reporting Financial Performance
FRS 4	Capital Instruments
FRS 5	Reporting the Substance of Transactions
FRS 6	Acquisitions and Mergers
FRS 7	Fair Values in Acquisition Accounting
FRS 8	Related Party Disclosures
FRS 9	Associates and Joint Ventures
FRS 10	Goodwill and Intangible Assets
FRS 11	Impairment of Fixed Assets and Goodwill
FRS 12	Provisions, Contingent Liabilities and Contingent Assets
FRS 13	Derivatives and Other Financial Instruments: Disclosures
FRS 14	Earnings per Share
FRS 15	Tangible Fixed Assets
FRS 16	Current Tax
FRS 17	Retirement Benefits
FRS 18	Accounting Policies
FRS 19	Deferred Tax
FRS 20 (IFRS 2)	Share-based Payment
FRS 21 (IAS 10)	Events After the Balance Sheet Date
FRS 22 (IAS 33)	Earnings per Share
FRS 23 (IAS 21)	The Effects of Changes in Foreign Exchange Rates
FRS 24 (IAS 29)	Financial Reporting in Hyperinflationary Economies
FRS 25 (IAS 32)	Financial Instruments: Disclosure and Presentation
FRS 26 (IAS 39)	Financial Instruments: Measurement
FRS 27	Life Assurance
FRSSE	Financial Reporting Standard for Smaller Entities

through one of its two advisory committees, the Financial Sector and Other Special Industries Committee and the Public Sector and Not-for-Profit Committee, to check that it is not in conflict with current accounting practice, current or future FRSs and does not override the legal provisions, FRSs or UITF Abstracts.

Each SORP-making body is required to satisfy the ASB that it has financial reporting problems that require ASB pronouncements to be supplemented, and that the body represents a major part of the industry and shares the ASB commitment to maintaining standards.

Figure 5.3 gives a list of extant SORPs which indicates why there are special industry reporting requirements.

Figure 5.3 Extant SORPs

SORP-making body	SORP	Issued
British Bankers Association	Advances	November 1997
	Contingent Liabilities	February 1996
	Derivatives	December 2001
	Segmental Reporting	January 1993
Charity Commission	Accounting and Reporting	Updated January 2003
Universities UK	Accounting for Further and Higher Education	October 2003
Association of British Insurers	Accounting for Insurance Business	Revised November 2003
Association of Investment Trust Companies	Financial Statements of Investment Trust Companies	Revised January 2003
Finance and Leasing Association	Accounting Issues in the Asset Finance and Leasing Industry	April 2000
CIPFA	Code of Practice on Local Authority Accounting in the United Kingdom	July 2004
Oil Industry Accounting Committee	Accounting for Oil and Gas Exploration, Development, Production and Decommissioning Activities	June 2001
Pensions Research Accountants Group	Financial Reports of Pension Schemes	Revised November 2002
National Housing Federation	Accounting by Registered Social Landlords	Updated November 2002
Consultative Committee of Accountancy Bodies	Limited Liability Partnerships	May 2002

5.6 The operating and financial review (OFR)

The *Operating and Financial Review*[7] statement was issued by the ASB in 1993 to encourage the development of best practice. It was intended to have persuasive rather than mandatory force. The format was not prescriptive and directors were encouraged to develop the presentation of their OFR in a way that best complements the format of their annual accounts. It was not an accounting standard and was mainly for listed companies for which its use had been recommended by the Financial Reporting Council, the Hundred Group of Finance Directors and the London Stock Exchange.

The OFR was intended to provide a discussion and interpretation of the main factors and uncertainties of the business and the structure of its financing. While it was not a forecast, it should bring out those aspects of the year under review that were relevant to an assessment of future prospects, to provide a more consistent foundation for investment decisions. Companies were not required to disclose information that would allow competitors to damage their business.

Because the intention was to assist investors, the OFR should not be merely a numerical analysis. The emphasis was on providing a readily understood discussion that dealt with both good and bad aspects of the business; that commented on trends, factors and uncertainties that had affected or would affect the results; and that explained the reasons for and the effect of changes in accounting policies.

The statement also offered detailed guidance to support these general principles. For example, a discussion of factors affecting future results could include capital expenditure and the likely benefits expected from it; a discussion of uncertainties affecting future results could include scarcity of raw materials, dependence on major suppliers, skill shortages and product liability. The user needs to know what steps a company has taken to counter such uncertainties. The following is an extract from the Bayer Annual Report 2003:

> To counter risks that could arise from the numerous tax, competition, patent, antitrust and environmental regulations and laws, we make our decisions and engineer our business processes on the basis of comprehensive legal advice provided by both our own experts and by acknowledged external specialists. We establish provisions in the balance sheet for risks resulting from new laws or legal judgments that apply retroactively.

The financial review part of the statement was intended to explain the capital structure of the business, its treasury policy and the dynamics of its financial position – its sources of liquidity and their application, including the implications of the financing requirements arising from its capital expenditure plans. The following is an extract from the BOC 2003 Annual Report:

> The Group has access to a diverse range of debt finance including commercial paper, public bonds and bank borrowings which, it believes, will be available to meet long-term financing needs. The Group has sufficient facilities to cover likely borrowing needs. Management anticipates that capital expenditure in 2004 will be at a slightly higher level than in 2003 and will be covered by cash inflow from operating activities.

5.6.1 How successful has the OFR been in encouraging companies to disclose risk?

The ASB recommended that companies identify **their principal risks** and comment on the **approach to managing these risks and, in qualitative terms, the nature of the potential impact on results**.

It is important, for example, to be aware of how a company manages financial risk. In the age of multinational accounting and economic cycles, important factors are the currencies in which borrowings are made, the use of financial instruments for hedging purposes and the current liquidity position. Risks relating to financial instruments have been the subject of FRS 13 because of the perceived high risks attached to financial instruments. The following is a brief extract from the BOC 2003 Annual Report:

Management of financial risk
The board of directors sets the treasury policies and objectives of the Group which includes controls over the procedures used to manage currency, interest rate and credit risk.

Interest rate risk

In order to manage interest rate risk the Group maintains both floating rate and fixed rate debt. At 30 September 2003 there is a 32:68 ratio (2002: 28:62) between floating rate and fixed rate net debt.

5.6.2 How successful has the OFR been in informing investors of risk?

Although the reporting of risks attaching to financial instruments is being addressed, the reporting of business risks and how management is dealing with them has been woefully lacking. The OFR has, in general, been treated as a PR document, being bland, with little significant effort to highlight in advance the real sources of uncertainties that had the major impacts on returns. The previous OFR of every company that reports **unexpected** worsening of turnover, profits or liquidity should be examined to determine how these risks were presented in the annual report. Invariably there is little comment until after the event.

5.6.3 How has the OFR been improved?

Mandatory status

In a 1994 research report *Operating and Financial Review: Views of Analysts and Institutional Investors*,[8] some analysts believed the OFR would contain useful information, but that market forces would not be sufficient to get companies to produce high-quality reports on a voluntary basis.

The view has been put forward by Zeff[9] that whilst 'one of the widely applauded leadership steps the ASB has taken is the recommendation that companies include an operating and financial review in their annual reports there is a need for the OFR to be made mandatory and thus subject to the true and fair view'.

The Final Report from The Company Law Review Steering Committee issued in July 2001 proposed in para. 3.34 that there should be a new mandatory OFR and in para. 8.32 that it should contain:

- a review by the directors of the company's operations and finances modelled on current ASB guidance and best practice
- a discussion and analysis of the performance of the business and main trends and factors
  - underlying the results and financial position, and
  - likely to affect future performance.

Audited status

Some believed that an entirely new set of audit skills was needed to audit an OFR properly.[10] This has been addressed and the Final Report[11] recommends that the OFR should be subject to review by the company's auditors.

Disclosure of business risks

The profession

The ICAEW's Financial Reporting Committee produced a discussion paper in 1997, *Financial Reporting of Risk – Proposals for a Statement of Business Risk.*

This paper proposed that there should be an additional report in which directors identified key risks and explained how they measured them and how they proposed to deal with them. Such a report would allow investors to understand the uncertainties that their board faced, e.g. cheap foreign imports, difficulty in obtaining supplies of components and raw materials, effect of adverse publicity about products, expiry of patents for major products. There would, of course, need to be the normal relief from reporting commercially sensitive information, e.g. early negotiations to establish trading alliances where a company's major product is losing the protection of patents.

The government

The objective is to enable users to assess the strategies adopted by the business and the potential for successfully achieving them.

The Final Report proposed that the OFR should include as mandatory items:

● A fair review of the company's business over the year, operating performance, its position at the year-end and material post-year-end events with details of market changes, new products, changes in market positioning, new and discontinued products and services, and acquisitions and disposals.

● The company's purpose, strategy and principal drivers to allow users to see the criteria by reference to which its success is evaluated, the source from which it derives its success, segmental performance against objectives and competitive positioning.

The Report also proposes further disclosures of material for the following:

● An account of the company's key relationships with employees, customers, suppliers and others on which its success depends, with details of employment policies and practices and policies on creditor payment.

● Corporate governance – values and structures, with details of the company's structures for securing an effective working relationship between members, directors and senior management.

● Dynamics of business such as trends and uncertainties which may affect future performance or investment programmes with details of risks and opportunities, competition and customer/supplier dependency, technological change, financial risks, environmental costs and liabilities and investment in training, research and development, brands, intellectual property.

● Environmental policies and performance, including compliance with regulations.

● Policies and performance on community, social, ethical and reputational issues.

● Receipts from, and returns to, shareholders covering distributions and distribution policy and share repurchases.

The above appears detailed but the Report is careful to emphasise that a substantial measure of discretion has been left for directors to determine how usefully to analyse and assess their business and deliberately avoids overprescription, with the risk that involves of rigidity and a 'cookbook' approach.

The proposals appear to follow existing ASB guidelines and best practice and will be welcomed by existing and potential investors.

5.6.4 The revised OFR

The ASB issued a revised statement *Operating and Financial Review* in January 2003 which reflected the main thrust of the Company Law Review with its added emphasis on providing information about the business objectives and strategy, the expected effect of known trends, the potential effect of risks facing the business and the key performance indicators used by management. The Statement also requires those accounting policies to be highlighted which entailed the particular exercise of judgement in their application and to which the results are most sensitive.

However, given the results of one research project[12] which analysed over 6,000 narrative disclosures in the food processing sector and revealed that only 1% were quantified and forward-looking, it was clear that companies would not provide decision-useful, forward-looking and quantified disclosures without a statutory requirement to do so.

5.6.5 OFR Reporting Standard RS 1

The government requires all listed companies to publish an OFR as from 1 April 2005 which complies with a standard to be issued by the ASB. The ASB published RS 1 in May 2005 which, in the main, follows the requirements of the Final Report discussed above. The intention is that directors should focus on the information needs specific to their company and its shareholders rather than follow a rigid list of items to be disclosed. RS 1 assists directors in this approach by setting down certain principles and providing illustrations of Key Performance Indicators.

The OFR's guiding principles

The seven principles are that the OFR should:

1 reflect the directors' view of the business;

2 focus on matters that are relevant to investors in assessing the strategies adopted and the potential for those strategies to succeed. Whilst maintaining the primacy of meeting investors' needs, directors should take a 'broad view' in deciding what should be included in their OFR, on the grounds that the decisions and agendas of other stakeholders can influence the performance and value of a company;

3 have a forward-looking orientation with an analysis of the main trends and factors which are likely to affect the entity's future development, performance and position;

4 complement as well as supplement the financial statements with additional explanations of amounts included in the financial statements;

5 be comprehensive and understandable but avoid the inclusion of too much information that is not directly relevant;

6 be balanced and neutral – in this way the OFR can produce reliable information;

7 be comparable over time – the ability to compare with other entities in the same industry or sector is encouraged.

Key Performance Indicators (KPIs)

There has been a concern that OFR would lack quantifiable information. This has been addressed in RED 1 with a list of potentially useful KPIs. These cover a wide range of interests including:

● Economic measures of ability to create value (with the terms defined)
  – Return on capital employed

   Capital employed defined as Intangible assets/property, plant and equipment + investments + accumulated goodwill amortisation + inventories + trade accounts receivable + other assets including prepaid expenses – non-interesting bearing provisions/liabilities

- Economic profit type measures

  Economic profit = Profit after tax and minority interests, excluding goodwill amortisation – cost of capital

● Market positioning

- Market position

- Market share

  Market share, being company revenue over estimated market revenue

● Development, performance and position

- A number of the measures used to monitor the development, performance and position of the company may be traditional financial measures

  - Cash conversion rate: rate at which profit is converted into cash

  - Asset turnover rates

- Directors often supplement these with other measures common to their industry to monitor their progress towards stated objectives, e.g.

  - Average revenue per user (customer)

  - Number of subscribers

  - Sales per square foot

  - Percentage of revenue from new products

  - Number of products sold per customer

  - Products in the development pipeline

  - Cost per unit produced

● Persons with whom the entity has relations and which could have a significant impact

- Customers: how do they view the service provided?

  - Measure customer retention

- Alien employees: how do they feel about the company?

  - Employee satisfaction surveys

  - Health and safety measures

- Suppliers: how do they view the company?

- Regulators: how do they view the company?

● Environmental matters

- Quantified measures of water and energy usage

● Social and community issues

- Public health issues, such as obesity, perceived safety issues related to high use of mobile phones

- Social risks existing in the supply chain such as the use of child labour and payment of fair wages

- Diversity in either the employee or customer base

- Impact on the local community, e.g. noise, pollution, transport congestion

- Indigenous and human rights issues relating to communities local to overseas operations

● Receipts from and payments to shareholders

● Other resources
   – Brand strength
   – Intellectual property
   – Intangible assets.

5.7 The Financial Reporting Review Panel

The Financial Reporting Review Panel (FRRP) is completely independent of the ASB. It has a solicitor as chairman and the other members include accountants, bankers and lawyers. Its role is to review material departures from accounting standards and, where financial statements are defective, to require the company to take appropriate remedial action. It operates under section 245B of the Companies Act 1985, which has given the courts power to order a company to rectify defective accounts. However, it has to date made no such court application and has instead relied on its opinion to be persuasive.

The FRRP prefers to deal with defects by agreement, although it has threatened applying to the courts. For example, in the accounts of Trafalgar House for the year ended 30 September 1991 certain fixed assets had been reclassified from current to fixed assets – these properties were then written down in value and the reduction charged to reserves, so avoiding the profit and loss account. The FRRP disagreed with this treatment and, following an apparent reluctance by the directors of Trafalgar House to accept their opinion, informed the directors that they were 'minded to make an application to the court ... requiring the directors of the company to prepare revised accounts'. The directors then agreed to make requisite changes to their 30 September 1992 accounts. As a result of the FRRP action the 1992 revised accounts saw a reported £122.5m profit turned into a £30m loss. This was clearly a significant intervention by the regulators and a warning to companies that the FRRP was not toothless.

The FRRP cannot create standards. If a company has used an inappropriate accounting policy that contravenes a standard, the FRRP can act. If there is no standard and a company chooses the most favourable from two or more accounting policies, the FRRP cannot act.

It has a policing role with responsibility for overseeing some 2,500 companies. Until 2003 it only became involved as a result of a complaint by an individual, a referral from the Stock Exchange, e.g. where accounts have been qualified by an auditor for non-compliance, or following media comment.

FRRP public statements

The FRRP has made a number of public statements setting out its findings. Some of these are listed in Figure 5.4.

A research study[13] into companies that have been the subject of a public statement suggests that when a firm's performance comes under severe strain, even apparently well-governed firms can succumb to the pressure for creative accounting, and that good governance alone is not a sufficient condition for ensuring high-quality financial reporting. The researchers compared these companies with a control group and a further interesting finding was that there were fewer Big Five auditors in the FRRP population – the researchers commented that this could be interpreted in different ways, e.g. it could be an indication that the Panel prefers to avoid confrontation with the large audit firms

Figure 5.4 FRRP – public statements

Date	Company	Matter under enquiry
14/02/2003	Kensington Group	Treatment of quasi-subsidiaries
31/01/2003	Finelot plc	Treatment of start-up costs
26/07/2002	Equator Group	The amortisation of intangible assets
26/02/2002	Liberty International	Use of true and fair override
06/11/2001	QA Services (No. 2) Ltd	Disclosure of fair values on acquisition
26/09/2001	Groupe Chez Gerard plc	Treatment of changes to depreciation policies

because of an increased risk of losing the case or a reflection of the fact that these audit firms are better at managing the politics of the investigation process and negotiating a resolution that does not lead to a public censure.

Criticism of the FRRP for being reactive

The FRRP has, since its establishment in 1988, been a reactive body responding to issues appearing in individual sets of accounts to which it is alerted by public or specific complaint. This led to the criticism that the FRRP was not addressing significant financial reporting issues and was simply dealing with disclosure matters that had readily been detected. The Panel consequently commissioned a pilot study in 2000 which reviewed selected companies for non-compliance. The pilot study revealed no major incidents of non-compliance and in November 2001 the FRRP decided that a proactive approach was unnecessary.

Investor pressure for a more proactive stance

However, regulatory bodies have to be responsive to a material change in investor attitudes and act if there is likely to be a loss of confidence in financial reports which could damage the capital markets. Such a loss of confidence arose following the US accounting scandals such as Enron. Regulators could no longer be simply reactive even though there had been no evidence in the UK of material non-compliance.

Proactive stance – European initiative

The Committee of European Securities Regulators (CESR), at the request of the Commission, has developed proposals which would require enforcement bodies to take a proactive approach. In its *Proposed Statement of Principles of Enforcement of Accounting Standards in Europe* issued in 2002, it proposed that there should be a selection of companies and documents to be examined using a risk-based approach or a mixed model where a risk-based approach is combined with a rotation and/or a sampling approach – a pure rotation approach or a pure reactive approach would not be acceptable.[14]

Proactive stance – UK initiative

The Coordinating Group on Accounting and Auditing Issues recommended in its Final Report in 2003 that the FRRP should press ahead urgently with developing a proactive element to its work.[15]

The FRRP response to the new requirement for a proactive approach

The Panel proposed that there should be:

- a stepped implementation with a minimum of 300 accounts being reviewed from 2004;
- the development of a risk-based approach to the selection of published accounts taking account of the risk that a particular set of accounts will not give a true and fair view of market stability and investor confidence.

Reviews should comprise an initial desk-check of selected risk areas or whole sets of accounts followed, where appropriate, with correspondence to chairpersons.

Whilst adopting a proactive approach, the FRRP has raised concerns that stakeholders might have a false expectation that the Panel is providing a guarantee that financial statements are true and fair, stressing that no system of enforcement can or should guarantee the integrity of a financial reporting regime.

The Financial Reporting Review Panel has announced that in selecting company accounts for review in 2005 it will focus on:

- the automobile, pharmaceutical, retail, transport and utilities sectors;
- targeted reviews to check compliance with specific accounting requirements – in 2005 it proposes to pay particular attention to interim reports with a view to identifying companies whose year-end accounts are expected to be subject to significant changes following the adoption of international accounting standards from 1 January 2005; and also
- taking company-specific risk factors into account.

5.8 The Financial Services Authority

The Stock Exchange was probably the earliest promulgator of rules and regulations governing financial statements. Many of its requirements have been incorporated into statute and standards, although there are still additional demands that are not yet in either.

The role of UK listing authority was transferred to the Financial Services Authority (FSA) on 1 May 2000.

Any public company wishing to have its shares bought and sold on the Stock Exchange must first secure what is called a **quotation** or **listing** on the Exchange. Securing such a listing is not a formality. The protection of prospective shareholders is the prime objective of the Exchange and in furtherance of this objective a company wishing to be listed is subjected to a prolonged and deep investigation. The investigation looks at its history, the calibre of its management, its financial condition, its future prospects and its constitution. A successful applicant must then conform with the rules of the Stock Exchange. These rules are incorporated in the *Stock Exchange (Listing) Regulations* and its *Admission of Securities to Listing*.

The rules cover a wide range of information, e.g.:

- from the short-term objective of maintaining fair trading conditions with the requirement that price-sensitive information must be released in a way that ensures all users have simultaneous access to the same information;
- to the longer-term objective of enforcing good corporate governance with the requirement for companies to state how they have applied the principles set out in the Combined Code.

The Combined Code is having an increasingly significant influence and we briefly discuss its development and structure below.

5.9 The Revised Combined Code (July 2003)

The Financial Reporting Council has revised the original Combined Code[16] which was issued in 1998. The original Code was largely based on the Cadbury Report (1992) supplemented by additional requirements such as those arising from the Greenbury Report (1995) which dealt with directors' remuneration and the Hampel Report (1998) which dealt with directors' contracts (see Chapter 31 for more detailed discussion of these reports). The current revision is, therefore, part of an evolving process.

5.9.1 The Cadbury Committee Report[17]

The process started in 1991 with the setting up by the Financial Reporting Council, the London Stock Exchange and the accounting profession of the Cadbury Committee to report on the financial aspects of corporate governance. A year later the committee produced the Cadbury Committee Report, which set out a voluntary Code of Best Practice based on openness, integrity and accountability.

Although the Code was voluntary, boards of directors were responsible for applying its provisions, stating whether the accounts comply with the Code, and explaining if they did not.

The Code made proposals in four areas relating to (1) the board of directors, (2) non-executive directors, (3) executive directors and (4) controls and reporting. The general thrust of the proposals was that there should be key safeguards. These were as follows:

● The board should retain control over important decisions such as major capital expenditure programmes, bank borrowings and material loans.

● Non-executive directors should be able to exert significant influence by virtue of number and experience.

● Audit committees consisting of non-executive directors should have clear terms of reference.

● The position of chairman should be separate from that of chief executive.

● Financial reporting and auditing systems should provide full disclosure at an appropriate time to affect decisions.

5.9.2 The structure of the original Combined Code

The original Code made an interesting development by separating its proposals into two parts:

● Part 1 containing Principles of Good Governance relating to
  A: Directors
  B: Directors' Remuneration
  C: Relations with Shareholders
  D: Accountability and Audit

- Part 2 containing Codes of Best Practice with procedures to make the Principles operational.

5.9.3 The Revised Combined Code

When revising the Code in 2003, the FRC continued to distinguish between broad principles (which companies are largely free to choose their own method of implementing) and detailed code provisions (which companies are required to say whether they have complied with and, where they have not complied, to explain why not). The intention was to combine flexibility over detailed implementation with clarity where there was non-compliance.

The Revised Code separates the Principles into Main Principles and Supporting Principles with detailed Code Provisions. The six Principles that relate to Directors cover:

A1   The Board

A2   Chairman and Chief Executive

A3   Board balance and independence

A4   Appointments to the Board

A5   Information and professional development

A6   Performance evaluation

As an illustration of the level of detail specified in the Revised Code, the Principles (A1) and Provisions (A1.1 to A1.5) relating to **The Board** are set out below.

A.1   The Board

Main Principle
Every company should be headed by an effective board, which is collectively responsible for the success of the company.

Supporting Principles
- The board's role is to provide entrepreneurial leadership of the company within a framework of prudent and effective controls which enables risk to be assessed and managed.
- The board should
  - set the company's strategic aims
  - ensure that the necessary financial and human resources are in place for the company to meet its objectives; and
  - review management performance.
- The board should
  - set the company's values and standards; and
  - ensure that its obligations to its shareholders and others are understood and met.
- All directors must take decisions objectively in the interests of the company.
- As part of their role as members of a unitary board, non-executive directors should
  - constructively challenge and help develop proposals on strategy.
  - scrutinise the performance of management in meeting agreed goals and objectives and monitor the reporting of performance

- satisfy themselves on the integrity of financial information and that financial controls and systems of risk management are robust and defensible.
- As non-executive directors they
  - are responsible for determining appropriate levels of remuneration of executive directors; and
  - have a prime role in appointing, and where necessary removing, executive directors, and in succession planning.

Code Provisions

A.1.1 The board should meet sufficiently regularly to discharge its duties effectively. There should be a formal schedule of matters specifically reserved for its decision. The annual report should include a statement of how the board operates, including a high level statement of which types of decisions are to be taken by the board and which are to be delegated to management.

A.1.2 The annual report should identify the chairman, the deputy chairman (where there is one), the chief executive, the senior independent director and the chairmen and members of the nomination, audit and remuneration committees. It should also set out the number of meetings of the board and those committees, and individual attendance by directors.

A.1.3 The chairman should hold meetings with the non-executive directors without the executives present. Led by the senior independent director, the non-executive directors should meet without the chairman present at least annually to appraise the chairman's performance (as described in A.6.1) and on such other occasions as are deemed appropriate.

A.1.4 Where directors have concerns which cannot be resolved about the running of the company or a proposed action, they should ensure that their concerns are recorded in the board minutes. On resignation, a non-executive director should provide a written statement to the chairman, for circulation to the board, if they have any such concerns.

A.1.5 The company should arrange appropriate insurance cover in respect of legal action against its directors.

5.10 Interim reports following Cadbury

The Cadbury Committee recommended in 1992 that the ASB, in conjunction with the London Stock Exchange, should clarify the accounting principles that companies should follow in preparing Interim Reports. At the request of the ASB, the Financial Reporting Committee of the ICAEW published a consultative paper in 1993 which formed the basis for the ASB's 1996 Exposure Draft. The Exposure Draft was developed in consultation with the London Stock Exchange, The Hundred Group of Finance Directors, the Institute of Investment Management and Research, the National Association of Pension Funds, the Big Six accounting firms and the Auditing Practices Board.

There has also been significant academic research, for example by Hussey and Woolfe.[18]

As Sir David Tweedie commented, 'Producing the ASB Statement has been very much a co-operative effort. It carries the commendation of the Financial Reporting Council, the Hundred Group and both the London and Irish Stock Exchanges. The authoritative backing of these bodies gives the Statement the best possible start in life and we greatly appreciate their support.'

In 1998 the ASB published its 'best practice' Statement on *Interim Reports*.[19] Like the Operating and Financial Review it is non-mandatory.

What is best practice?

● A shorter period for publishing.
The London Stock Exchange allowed four months to publish. The ASB propose that this should be reduced to two months.

● Use of the **discrete** method.
The ASB does not support the **integral** approach which is sometimes followed. Under this approach the interim report is merely a proportion of the estimate of the full year's results.

Instead, it favours the **discrete** method which uses the same measurement and recognition bases and accounting policies as used in the annual accounts. Consequently, the interim report should show what actually happened in the period; e.g. seasonal businesses will disclose results which differ markedly between the first half and second half of the year.

What does the ASB recommend to appear in interim reports?

The Statement recommends that interim reports should contain:

(i) **A management commentary** to highlight and explain significant events and trends as required already by the London Stock Exchange but, in addition, to follow the end-of-year practice by disclosing turnover and profit by segment and the turnover and profits of discontinued operations and acquisitions.

(ii) **A summarised profit and loss account and balance sheet** with classifications consistent with the year-end accounts and supported by a **Statement of Total Recognised Gains and Losses**.

(iii) **A summarised cash flow statement** using FRS 1 *Cash Flow Statements* headings and reconciling operating profit to operating cash flow and cash in period to movement in net debt.

The Statement was much needed. Current practice varied widely and did not always show what actually happened in the period and did not provide investors with information that was either timely or relevant. The Statement should go a long way towards securing a general improvement in consistency, comparability and quality of interim reporting. It reflects a welcome and fruitful collaborative exercise.[20]

As a result of the Statement, companies are encouraged to highlight and explain the most relevant and appropriate figures in their interim reports, to give a succinct but balanced picture with an emphasis on reporting trends and the impact of events and activities since the last full annual report.

The ASB has also addressed preliminary announcements and issued a 'best practice' Statement on *Preliminary Announcements* in 1997 aimed at improving the timeliness, quality, relevance and consistency of preliminary announcements whilst complying with the need for reliability.

Will there be further developments?

The US Securities and Exchange Commission requires listed companies to publish quarterly reports and UK companies with a US listing are already complying.[21] A similar requirement will no doubt be made for UK listed companies to keep London abreast of best international practice. Although preliminary and interim results are highly price-sensitive, there has been no requirement for them to be audited or reviewed. In the USA there is a suggestion that the quarterly reports should be reviewed and, if this is adopted, a review by the auditors of UK companies would seem to be a natural sequel.

European requirements

Under the Financial Services Action Plan a Directive on Transparency Obligations for Security Issuers was adopted in December 2004 [http://europa.eu.int] aimed at raising the quality of information available to investors on companies' performance and financial position in order to provide better investor protection, increase investor trust, enhance investor confidence and create better functioning European capital markets.

There was an initial proposal that there should be quarterly reports similar in content to half-yearly reports. However, there was a contrary view that such quarterly reporting had not prevented Enron occurring and that it encourages short-termism, e.g. Porsche AG has refused to provide quarterly reports, arguing that such a requirement was a significant cause of high volatility of share prices on the stock market.[22]

In taking account of such resistance the Directive has set minimum requirements, namely, that there should be quarterly financial information to include those key data currently required under existing Community law for half-yearly reporting, i.e. net turnover, profit and loss before or after deduction of tax, supplemented by trend information on the future company development – thus enabling investors to judge achieved results and also to take due account of any long-term strategy.

Whilst recognising the arguments that were made against quarterly reporting in formulating the Directives minimum approach, it should be noted there are already higher requirements set in some jurisdictions, e.g. the UK, and by some stock exchanges, e.g. Euronext.

Impact on UK practice

The Directive must be implemented by Member States by 2007 and both HM Treasury and the FSA are working out a timetable for consultation and implementation of the Directive in the UK.

Has the Cadbury Report resolved the problems of corporate governance?

Critics could argue with some justification that it is futile to rely on non-executive directors to monitor executive directors. Executive and non-executive directors are perceived to be playing musical chairs at each other's boards, with little time or facility for any detailed role. For example, a minister of the Crown who acted as non-executive director for a company in the defence industry has gone on record saying that he was unaware of major business decisions made by the company. This only adds force to the view that they are engaged only for their contacts and not for any major corporate governance role. Even executive directors question whether it is feasible for part-time directors to make any valid comment on the work of the full-time professional directors, and successful entrepreneurs have been known to see them simply as a waste of money. However, there is clearly important progress being made by the ASB in developing voluntary 'best practice' statements such as *Interim Reports*.

An indication that the ASB's best practice statement is taking effect is provided by a survey of interim reports comparing 1995 with 1999 which showed that 78% of companies now give cash flow information (1995: 61%) and there has been an increase in explanatory narrative sections, with 38% of companies exceeding 1,000 words (1995: 14%).[23]

5.11 Developments for small companies

Small firms play a major role in the UK economy and are seen to be the main job creators. Statistics published by the DTI (*Small and Medium Enterprise (SME) Statistics for the United Kingdom, 1997*, URN 98/92, July 1998) showed that in 1997 there were around 3.7 million businesses in the UK. Of these, 2.5 million were sole traders or partners without employees. There were 1.2 million companies on the Companies House register and, of these, around 12,000 (1%) were public companies (*Companies in 1997/98* (The Companies Annual Report 1997-1998), The Stationery Office) with only about 2,450 listed on the Stock Exchange. Of the companies on the register, around 7,000 had more than 250 employees, 26,000 had between 50 and 250 employees, and around 1.01 million had nine or fewer employees.

Certain companies are relieved of statutory and mandatory requirements on account of their size.

5.11.1 Statutory requirements

Every year the directors are required to submit accounts to the shareholders and file a copy with the Registrar of Companies. In recognition of the cost implications and need for different levels of privacy, there is provision for small and medium-sized companies to file abbreviated accounts.

A small company satisfies two or more of the following conditions:

● Turnover does not exceed £5.6m.
● Assets do not exceed £2.8m.
● Average number of employees does not exceed 50.

The company is excused from filing a profit and loss account, and the directors' report and balance sheet need only be an abbreviated version disclosing major asset and liability headings. Its privacy is protected by excusing disclosure of directors' emoluments.

A medium-sized company satisfies two or more of the following conditions:

● Turnover does not exceed £22.8m.
● Assets do not exceed £11.4m.
● Average number of employees does not exceed 250.

It is excused far less than a small company: the major concession is that it need not disclose sales turnover and cost of sales, and the profit and loss account starts with the gross profit figure. This is to protect its competitive position.

5.11.2 Mandatory requirements

The approach by the standard setters has generally been to require all companies to comply with SSAPs and FRSs. This can be justified on the grounds that compliance is necessary in order to present a true and fair view. Critics maintain that small companies might well never enter into transactions that fall within a standard, e.g. finance leasing, and that they should therefore be excused from compliance with the majority of standards. This is a weak position to take. After all, if a company actually does enter into a transaction for which a standard exists, it is difficult to see how it could be permitted to account for it in a non-standard way.

However, there is a legitimate interest in deregulation and a working party was set up by the CCAB at the request of the ASB to carry out a consultation exercise to assess whether companies should be excused from complying on the grounds of size or public interest.

From the consultations[24] there was clear support for some relief from accounting standards to be based on size or a combination of size and public interest. The ASB accepted the recommendations of the CCAB Working Party and issued the FRSSE[25] in November 1997. Recognising that there was concern as to the legality of setting different measurement and disclosure requirements, the ASB took legal advice which confirmed that smaller entities can properly be allowed exemptions or differing treatments in standards and UITFs provided such differences were justified **on rational grounds**.

How can rational grounds be established?

The test as to whether a decision is rational is based on obtaining answers to nine questions. If there are more negative responses than positive, there are rational grounds for a different treatment. The nine questions can be classified as follows:

Generic relevance

1. Is the standard essential practice for all entities?
2. Is the standard likely to be widely relevant to small entities?

Proprietary relevance

3. Would the treatment required by the standard be readily recognised by the proprietor or manager as corresponding to their understanding of the transaction?

Relevant measurement requirements

4. Is the treatment compatible with that used by the Inland Revenue in computing tax?
5. Are the measurement methods in a standard reasonably practical for small entities?
6. Is the accounting treatment the least cumbersome?

User relevance

7. Is the standard likely to meet information needs and legitimate expectations of the users?
8. Is the disclosure likely to be meaningful and comprehensible to users?

Expanding statutory provision

9. Do the requirements of the standard significantly augment the treatment required by statute?

How are individual standards dealt with in the FRSSE?

Standards have been dealt with in seven ways as explained in (a) to (g) below:

(a) Adopted without change

FRSSE adopted certain standards and UITFs without change, e.g. SSAP 17 *Accounting for Post Balance Sheet Events*, UITF 14 *Disclosure of Changes in Accounting Policy*, UITF 24 *Accounting for Start-Up Costs*.

(b) Not addressed

Certain standards were not addressed in the FRSSE, e.g. SSAP 5 *Accounting for Value Added Tax*, SSAP 25 *Segmental Reporting*, FRS 1 (Revised 1996) *Cash Flow Statements*, UITF 4 *Presentation of Long-Term Debtors in Current Assets* and UITF 5, UITF 9-11, UITF 13, UITF 15-19, UITF 22, UITF 25-27, 29-30; FRS 13 *Derivatives and Other Financial Instruments: Disclosures*; FRS 14 *Earnings per Share*.

(c) Statements relating to groups are cross-referenced

If group accounts are to be prepared the FRSSE contains the cross-references required to FRS 2 *Accounting for Subsidiary Undertakings*, FRS 6 *Acquisitions and Mergers* and FRS 7 *Fair Values in Acquisition Accounting*.

(d) Disclosure requirements removed

Certain standards apply but the disclosure requirement is removed, e.g. FRS 10 *Goodwill and Intangible Assets*.

(e) Disclosure requirements reduced

Certain standards apply but there is a reduced disclosure requirement, e.g.

- SSAP 9 *Stocks and Long-Term Contracts* applies but there is no requirement to sub-classify stock nor to disclose the accounting policy.
- FRS 3 *Reporting Financial Performance* applies but:
  - no requirement to analyse the turnover, costs and results into continuing operations, acquisitions and discontinued operations;
  - no reference to earnings per share;
  - no requirement for a note of historical cost profits and losses or a reconciliation of movements in shareholders' funds.
- FRS 16 and 19 where detailed disclosure is replaced by the requirement to disclose material components of the current tax charges.

(f) Increased requirements

Certain standards are included with certain of the requirements reduced and other requirements increased, e.g. under FRS 8 *Related Party Disclosures* a new paragraph has been added, clarifying that the standard requires the disclosure of directors' personal guarantees for their company's borrowings.

(g) Main requirements included

Certain standards have their main requirements included, e.g. FRS 16 *Current Tax*, FRS 18 *Accounting Policies*, FRS 19 *Deferred Tax*.

How unanimous was the response to the consultation exercise?

As one would expect, reactions were mixed with supporters both for excluding and for retaining a particular standard. For example, some commentators who represented the main users suggested that the cash flow statement should also be required from smaller entities. Their argument was that the management of cash is crucial in small, as well as large, businesses and that a cash flow statement provided a useful focus for discussions with management as well as a reference point for subsequent more detailed analysis.

The CCAB Working Party, however, accepted the arguments of those commentators who supported the exclusion of cash flow statements. Their arguments were:

- FRS 1 already exempts small entities from preparing a statement.
- For many small businesses in which transactions are straightforward, the cash flow statement adds little to what was already apparent from the balance sheet and profit and loss account.
- The gap between the period-end and the date of finalising the financial statements may be of such a length (up to ten months) as to limit the usefulness of any cash flow information.
- Managers in small businesses are well aware of the need to manage cash effectively. Their mechanisms for doing so may be informal but little would be added by a requirement for a cash flow statement in annual accounts prepared some months after period-end.

The ASB itself, whilst recognising that cash flow statements were not mandatory under FRS 1 for smaller entities, believed that a cash flow statement is an important aid to the understanding of an entity's financial position and performance and therefore included in the FRSSE a **Voluntary Disclosures** section which recommended that smaller entities present a simplified cash flow statement using the indirect method.

Does the FRSSE improve the information provided to users?

It is interesting to note that only one of the FRSs issued by the ASB, namely FRS 8 *Related Party Disclosures*, was deemed by the CCAB and ASB to have any relevance to smaller entities. It would seem reasonable to deduce from this that the ASB exists primarily to regulate the financial reporting of the 2,450 or so companies listed on the London Stock Exchange and has had little time to consider the million other companies that prepare and file accounts.

There are two clear adverse effects of this:

- The lack of adequate research by the ASB into the information needs of the users of accounts of smaller and medium-sized companies means, according to some researchers,[26] that the FRSSE has been produced without proper regard to those needs.
- The exercise started from the wrong end of the scale, according to the Small Practitioners Association,[27] in that it started with the standards designed for large public companies and then went through the nine questions approach to decide which of these to include in the FRSSE. A more logical approach would have been to have carried out the research suggested by Dugdale, Hussey and Jarvis[28] and developed positive standards that satisfied identified user needs.

However, given the pressure to establish appropriate FRSs for listed companies and to maintain a presence in the international standard-setting scene, there seems little prospect that ASB resources could be stretched to embrace the needs of the one million non-listed companies.

One could reasonably ask questions such as:

- Why should non-listed companies require ten months to prepare and file accounts?

- Why should this be accepted by the CCAB working party as actual justification for not requiring a cash flow statement?

- Is it feasible, or indeed even desirable, to expect the ASB to be concerned with non-listed company reporting given that almost 100% of the time since it was set up has been devoted to the reporting requirements of listed companies?

How will the FRSSE be kept up to date?

The ASB has set up an advisory committee, the Committee on Accounting for Smaller Entities, chaired by Professor Whittington, to assist in updating and revising the FRSSE periodically but any change in the FRSSE as a result of new standards, e.g. FRS 10, will be the subject of public consultation.

In December 2001 the ASB issued a revised FRSSE which came into effect in June 2002. Although the FRSSE is revised annually it does lag behind the issue of individual FRSs. It has been suggested that one way to overcome this would be to insert a note in each new FRS as to its applicability to small enterprises.[29]

The basic principles remain unchanged:

- Smaller entities may properly be allowed exemptions or different treatment provided such differences are justified on rational grounds, as discussed above.

- The objective of the FRSSE is to ensure that the reporting entity provides information about the financial position, performance and financial adaptability of the entity that is useful to users in assessing the stewardship of management and for making economic decisions, recognising that the balance between users' needs in respect of stewardship and economic decision making for smaller entities is different from that for other reporting entities.

- The financial statements should present a true and fair view which takes account of the substance of any arrangement or transaction, i.e. after identifying whether the transaction has changed existing, or given rise to new, assets or liabilities.

In February 2001 the ASB published for comment a discussion paper reviewing its FRSSE. The objective of the paper was to seek respondents' views on whether, in its present form, the FRSSE best met users' needs and whether any fundamental changes should be considered to the way in which it was prepared and presented. The response was that it was widely used and generally valued by practitioners. There is the view that accounts prepared in accordance with the FRSSE can provide information that is more meaningful and understandable to owner-managers than accounts complying with Big GAAP. However, there is a contrary view[30] that whilst external accountants may consider and adopt the FRSSE, it is questionable whether directors have been involved in such consideration as they are too busy running their businesses and surviving.

Company Law Review

The Company Law Review Steering Group[31] acknowledged that there appeared to be serious problems which required remedy arising from fact that the Companies Act:

- is structured around the needs of larger, publicly owned companies with a separation between the shareholders/investors and the directors with many provisions imposing duties on directors to provide protection for shareholders against abuses of directors' powers (Section 5.2.3);

● is opaque and inaccessible to small business users and requires a thorough knowledge of the whole Act to understand what exemptions and adaptations are available (Section 5.2.5);

● lays down regulatory requirements for the protection of the company's creditors that are overly burdensome and fail to serve the purposes for which they were designed (Section 5.2.7);

● with regard to the work of the ASB, *The Strategic Framework* recognises that a considerable amount of piecemeal work has been done on improving approaches within the existing framework, e.g. the FRSSE (Section 5.2.8). It also recognises the view expressed by some directors of small companies that statutory accounts are a tiresome irrelevance but, whilst being open to consultation, reminds us that the Fourth Directive requires all limited companies to publish accounts and that any replacement of this requirement would require a change in EU law (Section 5.2.14).

It has been interesting to see the responses[32] to the questions raised by *The Strategic Framework*. Selected questions with responses included:

Qn 9: Is it agreed that the difficulties met by small and closely-held companies in operating within the Act are serious and worthy of remedy?
Responses: The overwhelming majority supported the proposition, feeling that the present law was opaque, unwieldy, unnecessarily complex and therefore ripe for review.

Qn 10(a): Is it agreed that it is not desirable to restrict access to limited liability?
Responses: A significant majority took the view that it was not desirable to restrict access to limited liability, seeing limited liability status as a spur to entrepreneurship and innovation.

Qn 10(b): If not, then what restraints should be considered?
Responses: It was thought desirable by respondents to (b) to require a minimum capital threshold as a practical and useful measure to cause proprietors of small businesses to consider whether they needed to be incorporated.

Qn 11(a): Should the current accounting exemptions for small and medium-sized companies be removed or amended?
Responses: The vast majority took the view that some change was necessary but there was a wide divergence as to the nature of the change that was desirable. Responses ranged from complete exemption from preparing and filing accounts to replacing with alternative forms of financial information such as cash flow statements, ratios and graphical presentation, to requiring the same compliance as that required of large companies.

11(b): Do current exempt accounts provide proportionate, or any, protection to creditors, bearing in mind the cost of preparation?
Responses: The overwhelming view was that abbreviated accounts filed by small and medium-sized companies provided little or no protection to creditors.

5.11.3 ASB's one stop shop approach

A Discussion Paper, *A 'One Stop Shop' Financial Reporting Standard for Smaller Entities (FRSSE)*, was issued by the ASB in March 2004 which proposed that the accounting requirements of the Companies Act 1985 should be included within the FRSSE to provide a single source for both legislation and accounting standards. This was followed by an Exposure Draft *Amendment to the FRSSE* which adopted the one stop approach as well as including updating amendments relating to FRS 5 *Application Note G (revenue recognition)* and FRS 21 *Events After the Balance Sheet Date*. Responses to the Discussion Paper indicated strong support for the one stop approach.

5.11.4 How does the UK approach compare with that in the developing world?

The United Nations Conference on Trade and Development (UNCTAD) has a working group of experts on international standards of accounting and reporting (ISAR) which continued to discuss the accounting needs of small and medium-sized enterprises in 2001.[33] This is because such enterprises are regarded by governments in developing countries as important generators of employment and economic growth. Many countries have many businesses that keep no records and pay no taxes, but when they want to grow they come within regulations and are subject to additional costs and regulatory requirements.[34] As far as accounting requirements are concerned, it is suggested that a way forward would be to follow the system being developed in West Africa where the micro-business starts with simple cash accounting, and then progresses to accrual accounting and finally compliance with International Accounting Standards. In the developing world, it is felt that accounting hurdles are too high and a progressive system of accounting is required as seen in West Africa. Many small and medium-sized enterprises in the UK are halfway along the spectrum with accrual accounting and audited accounts but, as we have seen above, there are still calls in the UK for a reduction in the regulatory burden and many small enterprises are operating outside the formal system, keeping no records and paying no tax.

5.11.5 What is the IASB position?

The IASB issued a Discussion Paper 'Preliminary Views on Accounting Standards for Small and Medium-sized Entities' in June 2004. They propose to move away from the size tests towards a definition based on qualitative factors such as public accountability whereby an SME would be a business that does not have public accountability. Public accountability is implied if outside stakeholders have a high degree of either investment, commercial or social interest and if the majority of stakeholders have no alternative to the external financial report for financial information. Suggested criteria that indicate that public accountability exists include the provision of a public service, the holding of funds in a fiduciary capacity and the intention to raise funds publicly.

Given the move from a size test to a qualitative test it is proposed to describe companies that satisfy the criteria for adopting SME standards with a different term to SME.

The decision whether a business should be permitted to adopt IASB SME standards will be left to national jurisdictions subject to the right of any of the owners to require compliance with the full IFRSs.

It is interesting to note some of the responses to the Discussion Paper – these showed that:

● an overwhelming majority of respondents believed that full IFRS was not suitable for all entities;

● a majority agreed that the IASB should complete the SME project by starting with full IFRS and working back to SME standards; there was very little support for starting from scratch;

● a majority of respondents agreed that a 'characteristics' approach was a better method of defining SMEs, rather than issuing quantitative guidelines;

● a clear majority agreed that it was likely that disclosure and presentation modifications to full IFRS would be needed in respect of SMEs having taken into account user needs and cost/benefit analyses.

Taking account of user needs and cost/benefit can be a complex task[35] and requires judgements to be made. For example:

User needs

Non-publicly accountable companies have a narrower range of users of their financial statements than publicly accountable companies which frequently have a detailed knowledge of the company with the facility to obtain information beyond the financial statements. This means that they may have less need to rely on the published financial statements.

However, whereas with publicly accountable companies there is a clear understanding that the primary user is the equity investor, the question remains for SMEs as to (a) the primary user, e.g. is it the non-managing owner, the long-term lender, the trade creditor or the tax authorities, and (b) what are the primary user's needs, e.g. maximising long-term growth, medium term viability or short-term liquidity. Questions remain such as whether the financial statements need to be a stewardship report or decision-useful and, then, how are the characteristics such as relevance, reliability and comparability to be ranked and prioritised.

The approach to SME reporting has varied around the world. For example, in the USA there has not been an SME reporting regime in the sense of compliance with FRSs and IFRSs but SMEs have been permitted to prepare financial statements that are tax compliant; the IASB has only recently addressed the topic of SME reporting; in the UK the ASB has produced FRSSE, in drafting which it has taken a pragmatic approach when deciding which FRS provisions need not be applied by SMEs.

There is now a general awareness that the users of non-publicly-accountable companies are extremely diverse and steps are being taken to involve them in the standard-setting process, e.g. in Canada the Accounting Standards Board (AcSB) established a Differential Reporting Advisory Committee (DRAC) in 2000 as a standing committee to provide input to the standard-setting process by acting as a communication conduit for users, preparers and auditors of SMEs.

However, it appears that the research necessary to provide a rationale and conceptual approach to user needs is still some way off and the pragmatic approach taken by the ASB will inform financial reporting standards for SMEs for some time to come.

Cost/benefit analyses

The benefit versus cost test is particularly relevant for non-publicly-accountable companies and will be an important consideration when deciding on the appropriate reporting disclosure and measurement standards. However, just as it is difficult to identify user needs, so there is a problem identifying the relevant costs and benefits.

First, the costs have to be identified, e.g. those incurred in preparation, review and audit; then quantified and a judgement made as to whether these can be considered high, moderate or low; then the benefits have to be identified, quantified and a similar judgement made as to the level of benefits. This might give a simple rationale for non-compliance with standards if the costs are high and benefits are low but leaves a grey area if there other combinations such as costs low and benefits moderate.

It can be seen from this that there is a large element of estimation involved in identifying the users and their needs, quantifying their benefits, identifying costs and quantifying them and finally agreeing on respective levels and determining what impact this should have on the reporting standards applied by publicly accountable companies. However, this does provide a framework for input by users, preparers and auditors and transparency in the standard-setting process.

5.12 Evaluation of effectiveness of mandatory regulations

The events in the Sketchley plc takeover in 1990 suggest that mandatory regulations will not be effective.[36]

● In November 1989 Sketchley reported a fall in pre-tax profits for the half-year ended 30 December 1989 from £7.2m to £5.4m.
● In February 1990 Godfrey Davis Holdings made a bid to take over Sketchley.
● In March 1990 Sketchley issued a defence document forecasting pre-tax profits for the year ended 31 March 1990 of £6m. Godfrey Davis Holdings withdrew in the light of these poor results.
● In March 1990, one week later, the Compass Group made a bid. Sketchley appointed a new management team and this second bid was defeated.

The new management team decided that the company had not made a profit of £6m for the year ended 31 March 1990 after all – they had made a loss of £2m.

This has a familiar ring. It is very like the AEI situation of 1967, almost 25 years before. The adjustments made are shown in Figure 5.5.

Figure 5.5 Sketchley plc 1990 preliminary results

Sketchley plc 1990 preliminary results	
(a) Effect of more prudent accounting judgement (exercised by the new management team)	£000
Reassessment of bad and doubtful debts	3,358
Reassessment of stock provisions	2,770
Write-off of fixed assets	773
	6,901
(b) Provision for redundancy costs	554
(c) Other items, including the effect of accounting policy changes	557
	8,012
Profit before taxation, as forecast	6,000
Loss before taxation, as reported	2,012

Of course, it is not too difficult to visualise the motivation of the old and new management teams. The old team would take as favourable a view as possible of the asset values in order to resist a bid. The new team would take as unfavourable a view as possible, so that their performance would appear that much better in the future. It is clear, however, that the adjustments only arose on the change of management control, and without such a change we would have been basing investment decisions on a set of accounts that showed a £6m profit rather than a £2m loss.

There is often mention of the expectation gap, whereby shareholders appear to have lost faith in financial statements. The situation just discussed does little to persuade them that they are wrong. After all, what is the point of a regulatory system that ensures that the accounts are true and fair until the very moment when such a requirement is really necessary?

The area of provisioning and the exercise of judgement has finally been addressed by the regulators with the issue of national and international standards dealing with provisions.

5.12.1 Has the need for standards and effective enforcement fallen since 1990?

We only need to look at the unfortunate events with Enron and Ahold to arrive at an answer.

Enron

This is a company that was formed in the mid 1980s and became by the end of the 1990s the seventh-largest company in revenue terms in the USA. However, this concealed the fact that it had off balance sheet debts and that it had overstated its profits by more than $500,000,000 – falling into bankruptcy (the largest in US corporate history) in 2001.

Ahold

In 2003 Ahold, the world's third-largest grocer, reported that its earnings for the past two years were overstated by more than $500 million as a result of local managers recording promotional allowances provided by suppliers to promote their goods at a figure greater than the cash received. This may reflect on the pressure to inflate profits when there are option schemes for managers.

The need for standards and effective enforcement remains.

Summary

It is evident from cases such as AEI/GEC and the Wiggins Group (see Question 4 in Chapter 2) that management cannot be permitted to have total discretion in the way in which it presents financial information in its accounts and rules are needed to ensure uniformity in the reporting of similar commercial transactions. Decisions must then be made as to the nature of the rules and how they are to be enforced.

In the UK the standard-setting bodies have tended to lean towards rules being framed as general principles and accepting the culture of voluntary compliance.

Although there is a preference on the part of the standard setters to concentrate on general principles, there is a growing pressure from the preparers of the accounts for more detailed illustrations and explanations in how the standards are to be applied. This is apparent from FRS 4 with its Application Notes and the increasing number of Urgent Issue Task Force Abstracts.

With regard to voluntary compliance, The Combined Code supports the continuance of this approach but there is evidence that the government will require increasing mandatory compliance as seen with the proposal to make the OFR mandatory.

REVIEW QUESTIONS

1 Why is it necessary for financial reporting to be subject to (a) mandatory control and (b) statutory control?

2 How is it possible to make shareholders aware of the significance of the exercise of judgement by directors which can turn profits of £6m into losses of £2m?

3 Discuss the main arguments for dispensing with all SSAPs and FRSs.

4 'The effective working of the financial aspects of a market economy rests on the validity of the underlying premises of integrity in the conduct of business and reliability in the provision of information. Even though in the great majority of cases that presumption is wholly justified, there needs to be strong institutional underpinning.

'That institutional framework has been shown to be inadequate. The last two to three years have accordingly seen a series of measures by the financial and business community to strengthen it. Amongst these has been the creation of the Financial Reporting Council and the bodies which it in turn established.'[37]

Discuss the above statement with particular reference to one of the following institutions: Accounting Standards Board, Financial Reporting Review Panel, Urgent Issues Task Force. Illustrate with reference to publications or decisions from the institution you have chosen to discuss.

5 To what extent do you think FRSs should take economic consequences into account?

6 (a) Name four companies that have been the subject of FRRP pronouncements and explain the reason for FRRP involvement.

(b) 'Shorter accounting standards are not a realistic option until both companies and the accountancy profession can be trusted to "fully honour an approach limited to basic principles".' Discuss why companies and the profession cannot be so trusted.

7 Explain the main changes to interim reports following the ASB Statement of Best Practice.

8 'The most favoured way to reduce information overload was to have the company filter the available information set based on users' specifications of their needs.'[38] Discuss how this can be achieved.

9 Review a SORP and discuss the reasons why existing FRSs need to be supplemented.

10 'Quarterly reporting is essential in the interest of transparency and can, therefore, only be beneficial for investors.' Discuss.

11 'Every European company should be required to prepare their financial reports in accordance with an IFRSSE similar in content to the UK's FRSSE.' Discuss.

12 'Measurement criteria are more important than disclosure requirements for small entities.' Discuss.

EXERCISES

Question 1

Constructive review of the regulators.

Required:
(a) Obtain a copy of the Financial Reporting Council's Annual Review.
(b) Prepare a profile of the members of the Financial Reporting Council, the ASB and the Financial Reporting Review Panel.
(c) Comment on the strengths and weaknesses revealed by the profile.
(d) Advise (with reasons) on changes that you consider would strengthen one or more of these bodies.

References

1 G. Whittred and I. Zimmer, *Financial Accounting Incentive Effects and Economic Consequences*, Holt, Rinehart & Winston, 1992, p. 8.
2 E.R. Farmer, *Making Sense of Company Reports*, Van Nostrand Reinhold, 1986, p. 16.
3 Dearing Report, *The Making of Accounting Standards*, CCAB, 1988.
4 *Framework for the Presentation and Preparation of Financial Statements*, IASC, 1989.
5 *Ibid.*, para. 40.
6 M. Bromwich, *The Economics of Accounting Standard Setting*, Prentice Hall, 1985, p. 78.
7 *Operating and Financial Review*, ASB, 1993.
8 P. Weetman, Bill Collins and E. Davie, *Operating and Financial Review: Views of Analysts and Institutional Investors*, ICAS, 1994.
9 S. Zeff, 'Good so far but difficult decisions ahead', *Accountancy*, October 1995, p. 96.
10 P. Weetman *et al.*, *op. cit.*
11 *Modern Company Law for a Competitive Economy - The Final Report*, Company Law Review Steering Committee, July 2001, para. 8.63.
12 V. Beattie, B. McInnes and S. Fearnley, *Through the Eyes of Management: A Study of Narrative Disclosures*, Centre for Business Performance, ICAEW, June 2002.
13 K. Peasnell, P. Pope and S. Young, 'Breaking the rules', *Accountancy International*, February 2000, p. 76.
14 CESR, *Proposed Statement of Principles of Enforcement of Accounting Standards in Europe*, CESR02–188b Principle 13, October 2002.
15 Coordinating Group on Accounting and Auditing Issues, *Final Report*, January 2003, para 4.22.
16 *Committee on Corporate Governance: The Combined Code*, Gee, 1998.
17 *Report of the Committee on the Financial Aspects of Corporate Governance*, Gee, 1992.
18 R. Hussey and S. Woolfe, *Interim Statements and Preliminary Profit Announcements*, ICAEW Research Board, 1994.
19 *Interim Reports*, ASB, 1998.
20 Hannah King, 'What's the latest on interim reports?', *Accountancy*, October 1997, p. 88.

21 K. Bagshaw, *Preliminary Announcements: A Guide to Best Practice* and *Interim Financial Reporting: A Guide to Best Practice*, Accountancy Books, 1999.

22 *The Times*, 'Porsche files lawsuit against Deutsche Bourse', 8 April 2003, p. 21.

23 *Progress in the Interim: Surveying Corporate Half Yearly Reporting*, Arthur Andersen, 1999.

24 A consultative document *Exemptions from Standards on Grounds of Size or Public Interest*, CCAB, November 1994; and a paper *Designed to Fit – A Financial Reporting Standard for Smaller Entities*, CCAB, December 1995.

25 *Financial Reporting Standard for Smaller Entities*, ASB, 1997.

26 D. Dugdale, J. Hussey and R. Jarvis, 'Can less mean more?', *Certified Accountant*, November 1997, pp. 32–33.

27 'FRSSE: OK, not perfect', *Accountancy*, December 1997, p. 11.

28 D. Dugdale *et al.*, *loc. cit.*

29 N. Sleigh-Johnson, 'In defence of the FRSSE', *Accountancy*, December 2001, p. 92.

30 J. Morley, 'Who wants a FRSSE?', *Accountancy*, September 2001, p. 104.

31 *The Strategic Framework: A Consultation Document from the Company Law Steering Group*, DTI, February 1999.

32 *Responses to the Consultation Document Published by the Company Law Review Steering Group*, February, 1999, DTI, December 1999.

33 ISAR, *Accounting by SMEs*, United Nations Conference on Trade and Development (UNCTAD), 13 July 2001.

34 P. Walton, 'UN research into the accounting needs of SMEs', *Accounting and Business*, February 2000, p. 34.

35 G. Edwards, 'Performance measures', *CA Magazine*, October 2004.

36 *Student Financial Reporting*, ICAEW, 1991/2, p. 17.

37 *The State of Financial Reporting*, Financial Reporting Council Second Annual Review, November 1992.

38 V. Beattie, *Business Reporting: The Inevitable Change?*, ICAS, 1999, p. 53.

CHAPTER 6

Financial reporting – evolution of international standards

6.1 Introduction

The importance of regulating financial reporting to ensure all companies in a country present similar transactions in a consistent fashion has been established in Chapter 5. The pace of internationalisation of trade and investment has accelerated in recent years. This has been accompanied by calls for financial reports to be comparable internationally. This chapter describes the evolution of international standards by examining the following:

- National differences
- Reasons for differences in financial reporting
- Classification of national accounting systems
- Attempts to reduce national differences
- The work of international standard setters
- US GAAP
- Reconciliation and supplementary statements

6.2 National differences

We are all familiar with national differences that have become almost stereotypes. Consider the French, for example, who are described as

> proud, patriotic, sardonic people driven by a clear sense of their own greatness ... social interactions are profoundly affected by social stereotypes ... status depends to a great degree on family origins ... outward signs of social status are the individual's level of education, a tasteful house or flat, and knowledge of literature and fine arts. But the all important structure within which the system operates depends on each individual's family origins.[1]

It is natural that such strongly felt influences as family origin should be reflected in the way business is structured. This can be seen in the extent of family firms in France, with a large proportion of all businesses family owned, run, or dominated through major shareholdings, and in the strongly autocratic style of management.

On the other hand, it is pointed out that

maximising profitability is not always the German's first priority. As in the case of many other Europeans, Germans often feel that the firm has a responsibility to society and the environment.[2]

6.2.1 How do national differences affect financial reporting?

The French business structure indicates that the owners are also frequently the managers. This is different from the UK where there is separation of ownership and management. Consequently, in France, there is far less need for regulations to ensure that financial reports present a true and fair view; the emphasis is not so much on attempting to compensate for potential conflicts of interest between owners and managers as ensuring that the financial reports are accurate.

However, this is only one aspect. There are many other differences in economic and cultural conditions, which have led to an array of different financial reporting practices around the world. An understanding of this improves the awareness of potential misinterpretation when appraising financial statements prepared in other countries. It is useful to appreciate the reasons for these variations in order to improve understanding of the business activities represented by the accounts.

6.3 Reasons for differences in financial reporting

A number of attempts have been made to identify reasons for differences in financial reporting.[3] The issue is far from clear but most writers agree that the following are among the main factors influencing the development of financial reporting:

- the character of the national legal system
- the way in which industry is financed
- the relationship of the tax and reporting systems
- the influence and status of the accounting profession
- the extent to which accounting theory is developed
- accidents of history
- language.

We will consider the effect of each of these.

6.3.1 The character of the national legal system

There are two major legal systems, that based on common law and that based on Roman law. It is important to recognise this because the legal systems influence the way in which behaviour in a country, including accounting and financial reporting, is regulated.

Countries with a legal system based on common law include England and Wales, Ireland, the United States, Australia, Canada and New Zealand. These countries rely on the application of equity to specific cases rather than a set of detailed rules to be applied in all cases. The effect in the UK, as far as financial reporting was concerned, was that there was limited legislation regulating the form and content of financial statements until the government was required to implement the EC Fourth Directive. The Directive was implemented in the UK by the passing of the Companies Act 1981 and this can be seen as a watershed because it was the first time that the layout of company accounts had been prescribed by statute in England and Wales.

English common law heritage was accommodated within the legislation by the provision that the detailed regulations of the Act should not be applied if, in the judgement of the directors, strict adherence to the Act would result in financial statements that did not present a true and fair view.

Countries with a legal system based on Roman law include France, Germany and Japan. These countries rely on the codification of detailed rules, which are often included within their companies legislation. The result is that there is less flexibility in the preparation of financial reports in those countries. They are less inclined to look to fine distinctions to justify different reporting treatments which is inherent in the common law approach.

However, it is not just that common law countries have fewer codified laws than Roman law countries. There is a fundamental difference in the way in which the reporting of commercial transactions is approached. In the common law countries there is an established practice of creative compliance. By this we mean that the spirit of the law is elusive[4] and management is more inclined to act with creative compliance in order to escape effective legal control. By creative compliance we mean that management complies with the form of the regulation but in a way that might be against its spirit, e.g. structuring leasing agreements in the most acceptable way for financial reporting purposes.

6.3.2 The way in which industry is financed

Accountancy is the art of communicating relevant financial information about a business entity to users. One of the considerations to take into account when deciding what is relevant is the way in which the business has been financed, e.g. the information needs of equity investors will be different from those of loan creditors. This is one factor responsible for international financial reporting differences because the predominant provider of capital is different in different countries.[5] Figure 6.1 makes a simple comparison between domestic equity market capitalisation and Gross Domestic Product (GDP).[6] The higher the ratio, the greater the importance of the equity market compared with loan finance.

We see that in the UK, the USA and Sweden companies rely more heavily on individual investors to provide finance than in France or Germany. An active stock

Figure 6.1 Domestic equity market capitalisation/gross domestic product

	Market capitalisation/GDP (%)	
	1994	1998
Germany	22	49
France	33	65
UK	116	170
Sweden	64	125
USA	73	158

exchange has developed to allow shareholders to liquidate their investments. A system of financial reporting has evolved to satisfy a stewardship need where prudence and conservatism predominate and to meet the capital market need for fair information[7] which allows interested parties to deal on an equal footing where the accruals concept and the doctrine of substance over form predominate. It is important to note that equity has gained importance in all the countries in Figure 6.1. This could be an important factor in the development of accounting.

In France and Germany, as well as equity investment having a lower profile, there is also a significant difference in the way in which shares are registered and transferred. In the UK individual shareholders are entered onto the company's Register of Members. In France and Germany many shares are bearer shares which means that they are not registered in the individual investor's name but are deposited with a bank that has the authority to exercise a proxy. It could perhaps appear at first glance that the banks have undue influence, but they state that, in the case of proxy votes, shareholders are at liberty to cast their votes as they see fit and not to follow the recommendations of the bank.[8] In addition to their control over proxy votes, the big three German banks, the Deutsche Bank, the Dresdner Bank and the Commerzbank, also have significant direct equity holdings, e.g. in 1992 the Deutsche Bank had a direct holding of 28% in Daimler Benz.[9]

There was an investigation carried out in the 1970s by the Gessler Commission into the ties between the Big Three and large West German manufacturing companies. The Commission established that the banks' power lay in the combination of the proxy votes, the tradition of the house bank which kept a company linked to one principal lender, the size of the banks' direct equity holdings and their representation on company supervisory boards.[10]

In practice, therefore, the banks are effectively both principal lenders and shareholders in Germany. As principal lenders they receive internal information such as cash flow forecasts which, as a result, is also available to them in their role as nominee shareholders. We are not concerned here with questions such as conflict of interest and criticisms that the banks are able to exert undue influence. Our interest is purely in the financial reporting implications, which are that the banks have sufficient power to obtain all of the information they require without reliance on the annual accounts. Published disclosures are far less relevant than in, say, the UK.

During the 1990s there was a growth in the UK and the USA of institutional investors, such as pension funds, which form an ever increasing proportion of registered shareholders. In theory, the information needs of these institutional investors should be the same as those of individual investors. However, in practice, they might be in a position to obtain information by direct access to management and the directors. One effect of this might be that they will become less interested in seeking disclosures in the financial statements – they will have already picked up the significant information at an informal level.

6.3.3 The relationship of the tax and reporting systems

In the UK separate rules have evolved for computing profit for tax and computing profit for financial reporting purposes in a number of areas. The legislation for tax purposes tends to be more prescriptive, e.g. there is a defined rate for capital allowances on fixed assets, which means that the reduction in value of fixed assets for tax purposes is decided by the government. The financial reporting environment is less prescriptive but this is compensated for by requiring greater disclosure. For example, there is no defined rate for depreciating fixed assets but there is a requirement for companies to state their depreciation accounting policy. Similar systems have evolved in the USA and the Netherlands.

However, certain countries give primacy to taxation rules and will only allow expenditure for tax purposes if it is given the same treatment in the financial accounts. In France and Germany, the tax rules effectively become the accounting rules for the accounts of individual companies, although the tax influence might be less apparent in consolidated financial statements.

This can lead to difficulties of interpretation, particularly when capital allowances, i.e. depreciation for tax purposes, are changed to secure public policy objectives such as encouraging investment in fixed assets by permitting accelerated write-off when assessing taxable profits. In fact, the depreciation charge against profit would be said by a UK accountant not to be fair, even though it could certainly be legal or correct.[11]

Depreciation has been discussed to illustrate the possibility of misinterpretation because of the different status and effect of tax rules on annual accounts. Other items that require careful consideration include stock valuations, bad debt provisions, development expenditure and revaluation of fixed assets. There might also be public policy arrangements that are unique to a single country, e.g. the availability of transfers to reserves to reduce taxable profit as occurs in Sweden.[12]

6.3.4 The influence and status of the accounting profession

The development of a capital market for dealing in shares created a need for reliable, relevant and timely financial information. Legislation was introduced in many countries requiring companies to prepare annual accounts and have them audited. This resulted in the growth of an established and respected accounting profession able to produce relevant reports and attest to their reliability by performing an audit.

In turn, the existence of a strong profession had an impact on the development of accounting regulations. It is the profession that has been responsible for the promulgation of accounting standards and recommendations in a number of countries, such as the UK, the USA, Australia, Canada and the Netherlands.

In countries where there has not been the same need to provide market-sensitive information, e.g. in Eastern Europe in the 1980s, accountants have been seen purely as bookkeepers and have been accorded a low status. This explains the lack of expertise among financial accountants. There was also a lack of demand for financial management skills because production targets were set centrally without the emphasis for maximising the use of scarce resources at the business entity level. The attributes that are valued in a market economy such as the exercise of judgement and the determination of relevant information were not required. This position is changing rapidly and there has been a growth in the training, professionalism and contribution for both financial and management accountants as these economies become market economies.

6.3.5 The extent to which accounting theory is developed

Accounting theory can influence accounting practice. Theory can be developed at both an academic and professional level but for it to take root it must be accepted by the profession. For example, in the UK, theories such as current purchasing power and current cost accounting first surfaced in the academic world and there were many practising accountants who regarded them then, and still regard them now, as academic.

In the Netherlands, professional accountants receive an academic accountancy training as well as the vocational accountancy training which is typical in the UK. Perhaps as a result of that, there is less reluctance on the part of the profession to view academics as isolated from the real world. This might go some way to explaining why it was in the Netherlands that we saw general acceptance by the profession for the idea that for information to be relevant it needed to be based on current value accounting. Largely as a result of pressure from the Netherlands, the Fourth Directive contained provisions which allowed member states to introduce inflation accounting systems.[13]

Attempts have been made to formulate a conceptual framework for financial reporting in countries such as the UK, the USA, Canada and Australia,[14] and the International Standards Committee has also contributed to this field. One of the results has been the closer collaboration between the regulatory bodies, which might assist in reducing differences in underlying principles in the longer term.

6.3.6 Accidents of history

The development of accounting systems is often allied to the political history of a country. Scandals surrounding company failures, notably in the USA in the 1920s and 1930s and in the UK in the 1960s and 1980s, had a marked impact on financial reporting in those countries. In the USA the Securities and Exchange Commission was established to control listed companies, with responsibility to ensure adequate disclosure in annual accounts. Ever increasing control over the form and content of financial statements through improvements in the accounting standard-setting process has evolved from the difficulties in the UK.

International boundaries have also been crossed in the evolution of accounting. In some instances it has been a question of pooling of resources to avoid repeating work already carried out elsewhere, e.g. the Norwegians studied the report of the Dearing Committee in the UK before setting up their new accounting standard-setting system.[15] Other changes in nations' accounting practices have been a result of external pressure, e.g. Spain's membership of the European Community led to radical changes in accounting,[16] while the Germans influenced accounting in the countries they occupied during the Second World War.[17] Such accidents of history have changed the course of accounting and reduced the clarity of distinctions between countries.

6.3.7 Language

Language has often played an important role in the development of different methods of accounting for similar items. Certain nationalities are notorious for speaking only their own language, which has prevented them from benefiting from the wisdom of other nations. There is also the difficulty of translating concepts as well as phrases, where one country has influenced another.

6.4 Classification of national accounting systems

A number of attempts have been made to classify national accounting systems in much the same way that biologists attempt to classify flora and fauna.[18] However, as can be seen from the reasons for different systems described above, national differences are far from straightforward. Any classifications need to be constantly updated as accounting is such a dynamic activity. There are constant changes as a result of events taking place both within and beyond the accounting profession. Such classifications are therefore useful in gaining a greater understanding of particular features of accounting in a country at a particular time, but do need to be treated with a degree of caution.

6.5 Attempts to reduce national differences

Given the increasing numbers of transnational users of accounts, many attempts have been made to reduce the differences between reports prepared in different countries. There are, in essence, two approaches: standardisation and harmonisation.[19] These terms have become technical terms in the study of international accounting. Standardisation advocates the setting out of rules for accounting for similar items in all countries. Harmonisation is less radical in that it allows for some different national approaches but provides a common framework so that major issues will be dealt with in similar ways across national borders. Gradually, as efforts to improve comparability of financial statements have increased, these two approaches have come closer together.

Attempts have been made to standardise or at least harmonise financial reporting to satisfy the needs of a number of different groups. Users of accounts need clear and comparable information to assess a company's past or potential investment performance. Government agencies such as tax and customs authorities also have an interest in greater compatibility of information between countries to trace transactions. International accountancy firms deal with large numbers of multinational clients, whose accounts frequently need to be adjusted to common accounting principles before consolidations can be prepared. A reduction in national accounting differences would reduce the training costs of these firms and increase staff mobility (however, it would ultimately limit the fees they could charge!). Companies seeking capital through cross-border listings may currently need to prepare financial statements under more than one set of regulations to meet the needs of different stock exchanges. This is both costly and time-consuming.

A number of international bodies are involved in the processes of harmonisation or standardisation. These have included organisations which may not immediately be associated with accounting, such as the United Nations and the Organization for Economic Cooperation and Development (OECD). However, the most influential have probably been the International Accounting Standards Committee and the European Union. Their contribution is described below.

6.6 The work of international bodies in harmonising and standardising financial reporting

The major international bodies have accelerated their programmes of work and have sought greater co-operation in recent years. This section sets out something of their histories and structures before relating the latest developments in their strategies and the effect this is likely to have on the annual reports of companies.

6.6.1 The International Accounting Standards Committee

The International Accounting Standards Committee (IASC) was established in 1973 by the professional accounting bodies of Australia, Canada, France, Germany, Japan, Mexico, the Netherlands, the UK, Ireland and the USA. The membership now comprises all professional accounting bodies that are members of the international Federation of Accountants (IFAC). The objectives of the IASC are:

(a) to develop, in the public interest, a single set of high-quality, understandable and enforceable global accounting standards that require high-quality, transparent and comparable information in financial statements and other financial reporting to help participants in the world's capital markets and other users make economic decisions;

(b) to promote the use and rigorous application of those standards; and

(c) to bring about convergence of national accounting standards and International Accounting Standards to high-quality solutions.[20]

The IASC was restructured, following a review between 1998 and 2000, to give an improved balance between geographical representation, technical competence and independence.[21] The nineteen trustees of the IASC represent a range of geographical and professional interests and are responsible for raising the organisation's funds and appointing the members of the Board and the Standing Interpretations Committee (SIC). The International Accounting Standards Board (IASB) has responsibility for all technical matters including the preparation and implementation of International Accounting Standards (IASs). In future, the standards issued by the IASB will be known as International Financial Reporting Standards (IFRSs).[22]

The process of producing a new IFRS is similar to the processes of some national accounting standard setters. Once a need for a new (or revised) standard has been identified, a steering committee is set up to identify the relevant issues and draft the standard. Drafts are produced at varying stages and are exposed to public scrutiny. Subsequent drafts take account of comments obtained during the exposure period. The final standard is approved by the Board and an effective date agreed. International Accounting Standards currently in effect are referred to throughout the rest of this book. The IASC also issued a *Framework for the Preparation and Presentation of Financial Statements.*[23] This will assist in the development of future accounting standards and improve harmonisation by providing a basis for reducing the number of accounting treatments permitted by IASs. Professional accountancy bodies have prepared and published translations of IASs, making them available to a wide audience, and the IASC itself set up a mechanism to issue interpretations of the standards.

IASs and IFRSs (referred to below simply as 'IASs') may be applied in one of the following ways:

● An IAS may be adopted as a national accounting standard. This can be useful where there are limited resources and an 'off the peg' solution is required. This is the practice in countries such as Botswana, Cyprus and Zimbabwe. The disadvantage is that the standard may not meet specific local needs, due to the influence of the larger industrialised nations on the IASC.

● An IAS may be used as a national requirement but adapted for local purposes. This approach is used in Fiji and Kuwait for example.

● National requirements may be derived independently, but adapted to conform with IASs. This is currently the procedure in the UK, although recently the programmes of the IASC and ASB have converged. Indeed IAS 37 and FRS 12 were developed jointly.

It is important to note that if a company wishes to describe its financial statements as complying with IASs, IAS 1 requires the financial statements to comply with all the requirements of each applicable standard and each applicable interpretation of the SIC. This clearly outlaws the practice of 'IAS-lite' reporting, where companies claimed compliance with IASs while neglecting some of their more onerous requirements.

The large number of members of the old IASC meant that it was difficult to achieve a consensus on many of the issues that the Committee has addressed. Consequently, many IASs initially permitted a range of treatments. Whilst this was an improvement on not having a standard at all, it was still far from ideal. In response to this criticism, the IASC began its comparability/improvements project in 1987, which resulted in the revision of ten standards. The IASB adopted all IASs in issue, but soon identified the need for further improvements.

6.6.2 The European Union[24]

The Treaty of Rome was signed in 1957 to establish a European Economic Community. The objectives of the Community were set out in Article 2 of the Treaty:

> The Community shall have as its task, by establishing a common market and progressively approximating the economic policies of member states, to promote throughout the Community a harmonious development of economic activities, a continuous and balanced expansion, an increase in stability, an accelerated raising of the standard of living and closer relations between the States belonging to it.

In order to achieve these objectives, the Treaty set out specific provisions for the free movement of goods, services, people and capital. The single European currency (the euro) in operation in a number of European countries (and some of their trading partners) since January 2000 (with notes and coins in circulation from January 2002) has removed yet another barrier to trade and will link the economies of members more closely.

It was envisaged that the Treaty would be supported by action in other spheres developing common legislation where necessary. The harmonisation of company law across the Community has been part of this process. To date, the most important EC Directives adopted in respect of financial reporting are the Fourth (company accounts), Seventh (consolidated accounts) and Eighth (auditing).

Member states are required to incorporate these Directives into their national legislation within an agreed time-scale. This has succeeded in achieving greater comparability between financial statements prepared in different member states, although a number of cultural differences remain. The Directives have also had an impact on financial reporting in countries seeking membership or involved in trade with existing members of the EU (e.g. Norway has implemented the Directives as a condition of membership of the European Economic Area and Latvia has based its recent accounting legislation on the Danish implementation of the Directives).

Although they have had a major impact on accounting in some countries, e.g. Greece and Spain, the Directives still only provide a framework for financial reporting and provide a range of options. This framework has to be supported by national legislation or accounting standards to provide the detailed regulation that leads to comparability within countries. Consequently, these national practices can then counteract the harmonisation efforts of the Directives. One solution would be to have a European Accounting Standards Board. However, the practicalities of setting up such an organisation and reaching agreement on accounting issues within a reasonable time have meant that such a board has not been established. At the end of 1995, it was decided that the European Union could play a more active role in the IASC with a view to using

IASs to support the Directives. As a first step, the Contact Committee on the Accounting Directives prepared a report entitled 'An examination of the conformity between the international accounting standards and the European accounting Directives' in 1996. This established that there were few major differences between the IASs and the Directives.

6.6.3 IASC and the International Organisation of Securities Commissions (IOSCO)

The IASC and IOSCO have been co-operating on the accounting problems of multinational companies involved in foreign listings since 1987.[25] In July 1995 it was agreed that if the IASC was to produce a set of core standards that were acceptable to the technical committee of IOSCO, any company would be able to use IAS financial statements to obtain listings of its securities on any foreign stock exchange. This would be particularly useful for companies seeking listing on the US stock exchange, which currently requires companies to present financial statements in accordance with US Generally Accepted Accounting Principles (US GAAP) or reconcile domestic accounts to US GAAP. The ramifications of this for preparers and users of financial statements of multinational companies are tremendous: considerable time and effort would be saved. The IASC completed its core standards in December 1998. In May 2000, IOSCO recommended that its members permit the use of IASs by multinational issuers for cross-border offerings and listings, supplemented where necessary to address outstanding substantive issues at a national or regional level. This is clearly a major step towards the acceptance of IASs and the elimination of the necessity for multiple reporting. Nevertheless, there could still be extensive demands on preparers to provide supplementary information. The United States Securities and Exchange Commission is seen as being a potential stumbling block. This is perhaps unsurprising given the remaining differences between IASs and US GAAP[26] and the SEC's requirement for strict application of US GAAP. Nevertheless, the SEC took a constructive approach to the issue in seeking further information on the use and quality of IASs in its *Concept Release on International Accounting Standards* in February 2000.

6.6.4 The EU and IASs

In a communication from the Commission of the European Communities to the Council and the European Parliament (*EU Financial Reporting Strategy: The Way Forward*) in June 2000, it was proposed that all listed companies be required to prepare their consolidated financial statements in accordance with IASs from 2005 onwards. In February 2001 the European Commission published a proposal for a regulation on the application of international accounting standards in the EU which aimed to harmonise financial reporting in the EU on the basis of globally agreed accounting standards by 2005 and to enhance EU companies' access to international capital markets. This proposal became a Regulation in July 2002.[27] Member states are allowed to extend the application of IASs to unlisted companies and to individual accounts. In the UK unlisted and individual companies are to be permitted to use IASs instead of SSAPs and FRSs, if they prefer. This will clearly be helpful for the increasing numbers of companies that have juggled to meet the requirements of international investors without falling foul of national regulations.

The proposals followed changes in legislation in a number of member states to permit certain companies to use international standards. This could be seen as having led to a reduction in comparability as companies take different approaches. For example, in 1999 reports in Finland, Stora Enso (listed in Helsinki and Stockholm) and Nokia (listed in Helsinki, Stockholm, London, Frankfurt and New York) used IASs but UPM Kymmene (listed in Helsinki and New York) used Finnish accounting practice. The proposals also reflect companies' perceptions of market demands. For example, the Danish company Berendsen changed its accounting policies on goodwill and restructuring provisions in 1999. The annual report explains that the changes were made 'in order to come more into line with international accounting standards, thus making comparisons with foreign company accounts easier'.

However, it is important to note that the EU has not simply handed over its powers to the IASC. There is an endorsement mechanism in the EU, which is to ensure that IASs meet the needs of EU listed companies. This may limit the number of options available to EU companies or require additional disclosures. In 2004 there was controversy when the EU only partially endorsed IAS 39.

6.6.5 Current convergence and improvement projects

In 2001 the IASB announced a project to improve twelve IASB standards.[28] The objective of this project was to improve the quality of financial reporting under IASs by converging on best practice around the world and reducing choice in the application of the standards. The project dealt with standards that are not the subject of separate projects and, therefore, changes to individual standards could be considered to be relatively minor. The IASB was responding to suggestions from IOSCO, the EU, national standard setters, accounting firms and the SIC. The date for compliance with IASs by EU listed companies of 2005 gave added impetus to this project. The IASB issued fifteen improved standards in December 2003 as a result of this project.

Other improvements involve clarification of key terms (such as 'present fairly'), removing duplication of regulations between standards, and transferring material between standards to make them easier to follow.

Convergence is a two-way process. At the same time as the IASB was making changes to bring its standards in line with global best practice national standard setters have been working to align their standards with IASs. In the UK, the ASB's FREDs 24 to 30 were part of its 'convergence project'. The ASB was also taking account of any changes to the IASs expected as a result of the IASB's improvements project.

Figure 6.2 highlights the differences that remain between UK accounting standard and IASs.

Figure 6.2 Table of comparison between IASs/IFRSs and UK accounting standards

IAS	Relevant UK standard(s)	Effect of any substantial differences
IFRS 1 First-time adoption of International Financial Reporting Standards	No equivalent standard	
IFRS 2 Share-based payment	FRS 20 Share-based payment	FRS 20 issued in April 2004 (apart from the exemption for entities applying the FRSSE) implements IFRS 2.

(continued)

Figure 6.2 *Continued*

IAS	Relevant UK standard(s)	Effect of any substantial differences
IFRS 3 Business combinations	FRS 6 Acquisitions and mergers	Merger accounting is not permitted under IFRS 3.
IFRS 4 Insurance contracts	No equivalent standard	
IFRS 5 Non-current assets held for sale and discontinued operations	FRS 3 Reporting financial performance	An operation becomes 'discontinued' when it meets the criteria for being 'held for resale' (FRS 3 has more stringent criteria). IFRS 5 prohibits retroactive classification of an operation as discontinuing. FRED 32 will be issued as a UK standard to replace parts of FRS 3 and introduce new requirements for non-current assets held for disposal.
IFRS 6 Exploration for and evaluation of mineral resources	No equivalent standard	
IAS 1 Presentation of financial statements	FRS 18 Accounting policies	Under IAS 1 the statement of total recognised gains and losses can be presented as a separate statement (like the UK STRGL) or as part of the statement of changes in equity.
IAS 2 Inventories	SSAP 9 Stocks and long-term contracts	
IAS 7 Cash Flow Statements	FRS 1 Cash flow statements	Under IAS 7 the statement must report change in cash and cash equivalents (rather than cash, as in the FRS 1).
IAS 8 Accounting policies, changes in accounting estimates and errors	FRS 18 Accounting policies FRS 3 Reporting financial performance	Under IAS 8 all material errors must be adjusted for (FRS 3 only requires restatement for fundamental errors).
IAS 10 Events after the balance sheet date	FRS 21 Accounting for post balance sheet events	FRS 21 issued in May 2004 (apart from the exemption for entities applying the FRSSE) implements IAS 10.
IAS 11 Construction contracts	SSAP 9 Stocks and long-term contracts	

(continued)

Figure 6.2 *Continued*

IAS	Relevant UK standard(s)	Effect of any substantial differences
IAS 12 Income taxes	FRS 16 Current tax FRS 19 Deferred tax	Under IAS 12 deferred tax must be recognised on all liabilities, including gains on revaluation (not required under FRS 19).
IAS 14 Segment reporting	SSAP 25 Segmental reporting	IAS 14 additionally (to SSAP 25) requires separate identification of segments with different risks, returns or expectations.
IAS 16 Property, plant and equipment	FRS 15 Tangible fixed assets	Under IAS 16 fair values must be used where one asset is obtained in exchange for another. The depreciation charge for each year has to reflect any increase in assets' residual value ascertained at the balance sheet date. (Under FRS 15 increases in residual value are generally reflected in profits on disposal in the final year of the assets' lives rather than in reduced depreciation.) Some revaluation losses that would go straight to the STRGL (and hence a change in equity) under FRS 15 have to go through the income statement under IAS 16 and vice versa.
IAS 17 Leases	SSAP 21 Accounting for leases and hire purchase contracts	Under IAS 17 leases of land and buildings are split into one operating lease for the land and another lease (finance or operating, depending on the terms) for the buildings. (Under SSAP 21 long-term property leases are generally treated as operating leases.) IAS 17 requires disclosure of total minimum lease payments (rather than SSAP 21's requirements of commitments within one year).
IAS 18 Revenue	SSAP 9 Stocks and long-term contracts	
IAS 19 Employee benefits	FRS 17 Retirement benefits	Some differences in detail of measurement approach. 'Corridor' approach to recognising actuarial gains and losses in IAS 19 means that recognition may be deferred.

(continued)

Figure 6.2 *Continued*

IAS	Relevant UK standard(s)	Effect of any substantial differences
IAS 20 Accounting for government grants and disclosure of government assistance	SSAP 4 Accounting for government grants	
IAS 21 The effects of changes in foreign exchange rates	FRS 23 The effects of changes in foreign exchange rates	FRS 23 issued in December 2004 implements IAS 21.
IAS 23 Borrowing costs	FRS 15 Tangible fixed assets	
IAS 24 Related party disclosures	FRS 8 Related party disclosures	Related party transactions must be disclosed by type of related party, but names do not have to be given under IAS 24. There is no exemption equivalent to that in FRS 8 for intra-group transactions with 90% subsidiaries whose accounts are publicly available.
IAS 26 Accounting and reporting by retirement benefit plans	SORP Financial reports of pension schemes	
IAS 27 Consolidated and separate financial statements	FRS 2 Accounting for subsidiary undertakings	
IAS 28 Investments in associates	FRS 9 Associates and joint ventures	IAS 28 requires a parent to recognise only the obligations or payments made on behalf of a loss-making associate. This is a stricter definition of when liabilities should be recognised than under FRS 9.
IAS 29 Financial reporting in hyperinflationary economies	FRS 24 Financial reporting in hyperinflationary economies	FRS 24 issued in December 2004 implements IAS 29.
IAS 30 Disclosures in the financial statements of banks and similar financial institutions	FRS 13 Derivatives and other financial instruments: Disclosures	

(continued)

Figure 6.2 *Continued*

IAS	Relevant UK standard(s)	Effect of any substantial differences
IAS 31 Interests in joint ventures	FRS 9 Associates and joint ventures	Proportionate consolidation of joint ventures (prohibited by FRS 9) is the benchmark treatment under IAS 31.
IAS 32 Financial instruments: Disclosure and Presentation	FRS 25 Financial Instruments: Disclosure and Presentation	FRS 25 also has the effect of withdrawing FRS 4 'Capital Instruments', except for material on the measurement of debt and gains and losses on the repurchase of debt. This material is withdrawn for entities applying the measurement requirements in FRS 26, but remains applicable for other entities.
IAS 33 Earnings per share	FRS 22 Earnings per share	FRS 22 issued in December 2004 implements IAS 33.
IAS 34 Interim financial reporting	ASB statement on interim financial reporting	
IAS 36 Impairment of assets	FRS 11 Impairment of fixed assets and goodwill	
IAS 37 Provisions, contingent liabilities and contingent assets	FRS 12 Provisions, contingent liabilities and contingent assets	Definitions in IAS 37 are more strictly associated with definite legal obligations.
IAS 38 Intangible assets	FRS 10 Goodwill and intangible assets SSAP 13 Accounting for research and development	Under IAS 38 goodwill can stay on the balance sheet indefinitely (subject to impairment reviews) whereas FRS 10 has a rebuttable presumption of a maximum life of 20 years. Rules for capitalising research and development expenditure differ – more will be capitalised under IAS 38.
IAS 39 Financial instruments: recognition and measurement	FRS 26 Financial Instruments: Measurement	FRS 26 issued in December 2004 implements the measurement and hedge accounting requirements of IAS 39.

(continued)

Figure 6.2 *Continued*

IAS	Relevant UK standard(s)	Effect of any substantial differences
IAS 40 Investment property	SSAP 19 Accounting for investment properties	Under IAS 40 companies can choose between depreciated cost and fair value (with gains or losses going through the income statement). In contrast, SSAP 19 requires market value with gains and losses going through STRGL. Leased investment properties on leases can be accounted for as investment properties under IAS 40 and the present value of the minimum lease payments is recognised as a separate liability at the start of the lease.
IAS 41 Agriculture	No equivalent standard	
No equivalent standard	Financial reporting standard for smaller entities (FRSSE)	Companies claiming compliance with IFRS must follow all standards in full, regardless of their size.

6.6.6 The future

Financial reporting is clearly about to enter a period of transition. When the US energy giant Enron collapsed in 2001, a number of important issues were raised regarding the conduct of directors and auditors. More importantly in the context of this chapter, the collapse of Enron highlighted a number of deficiencies in financial reporting. The application of US GAAP had led to a lack of transparency regarding matters including revenue recognition, valuation of intangible assets, so-called Special Purpose Entities and off balance sheet finance, and derivatives. This has demonstrated that, in spite of (or perhaps because of) its detailed regulations, US GAAP is not without its faults. The broader debate has been opened as to whether detailed regulations or broader regulations based on principles (as applied by the UK's ASB and the IASB) are a more appropriate way forward. The US Senate Committee investigating the Enron collapse heard evidence from Sir David Tweedie, chairman of the International Accounting Standards Board.

The use of IASs will become more widespread in the European Union and it seems set to become the standard for cross-border listings on a global basis. The new structure of the IASC has been designed to ensure that the IASB will continue to produce high quality standards to provide comparable information to users. However, before true comparability can be achieved, a more effective mechanism is necessary to ensure consistent interpretation and application of IASs. Surveys of companies purporting to follow IASs[29] have demonstrated that many companies disclose exceptions from full compliance. While IAS 1 (revised) bans this practice (i.e. companies are required to follow all IASs if they wish to claim their financial statements comply with IASs), it is difficult to see how it can be enforced without a more rigid enforcement structure. The work of the International Financial Reporting Interpretations Committee will contribute to ensuring consistent interpretations of IASs. Increased interest in IASs has led to an increase in the number of textbooks referring to their use. As auditors and regulatory bodies become more familiar with IASs it is likely that they will be enforced more rigorously. Early in 2004, *Company Reporting* identified the Austrian company Miba as the first company reporting under IAS to receive a qualified audit report as result of its inappropriate recognition of an intangible asset.

Listed companies in the EU and other countries, such as Australia, are currently making the transition to IASs. They need to present their accounts as if they had always used IASs. This means that some items that had not previously been recognised will need to be recognised and other items will be recorded or measured differently. If a company is producing its first IAS financial statements for the year ended 31 December 2005, then it will need to show comparative figures for the year ended 31 December 2004. Consequently, companies will need to restate their opening 1 January 2004 balance sheet in accordance with IASs. The effect on companies' figures will vary according to the nature of their business, but could be substantial. For example, property companies will be hit by IAS 12's requirement to make a provision for deferred taxation on revaluations. In its accounts for the year ended 30 June 2003, Canary Wharf plc disclosed unrecognised deferred tax on property revaluation of £125.8m. If a provision was made for this deferred tax, it would reduce Canary Wharf's net assets by about 8%.

The increase in the use of IASs will be significant for the largest companies, but what will happen to financial reporting in non-listed companies? These companies will probably continue to use national accounting standards, but eventually it seems likely that national requirements will move closer to IASs, thus reducing differences further. This will be necessary to allow an easier transition to listed status. The European Commission communication on financial reporting strategy[30] set out the commission's plan for achieving common internationally agreed accounting standards by 2005 for listed companies in the EU. This may see the position of IASs clarified in the Directives and may lead to further dispensations for the smallest companies.

The move towards IASs will also be significant for national standard setters. In the short to medium term they will still be needed to provide accounting standards for unlisted companies and to provide the expertise to support the IASB. In the 2002 report of the UK's Accounting Standards Board, Sir Bryan Carsberg pointed out that the ASB needed to have an effective voice in the development of international standards. This would involve building on its own ideas to lead the debate and keeping in touch with its UK constituency. The ASB will continue to work with the IASB and the European Financial Reporting Advisory Group. In 2004 and 2005 the ASB invited comments on its future role in a changing standard-setting environment. In the longer term, it is difficult to imagine that it will be possible to justify accounting standard setters operating independently in each country, particularly in smaller countries where there is no direct link between the national standard setters and the IASB.

6.6.7 Economic consequences of accounting differences

While the debate continues about the future regulatory framework, businesses and employees are facing the economic consequences of different accounting practices.

Following the acquisition of British car maker Rover in 1994 by the German company BMW, performance was measured in accordance with the generally more conservative German accounting principles. This information was used for making management decisions. The publication of the £620m loss for 1998 led to a wave of speculation about possible closure of production plants with consequent redundancies. However, it has been pointed out that results under UK accounting rules (which were published later) would not have been quite so dramatic. Figure 6.3 shows a comparison of the company's results under British and German rules.[31]

Figure 6.3 Rover results under UK and German rules

	Rover results using UK rules £m	Rover results using German rules £m
1994	279	unpublished
1995	(51)	(163)
1996	(100)	(109)
1997	19	(91)
1998	(571)	(620)

Nevertheless, the danger of making assumptions about a particular country's measurement rules was highlighted in 1993 when Daimler Benz became the first German company to be listed on the New York Stock Exchange. Figure 6.4 summarises the company's results under German and US rules.[32] In the year of listing (1993) there was a large difference between the two sets of figures, which created the impression that US and German accounting principles were very different and that US rules were more prudent. With hindsight, it is easy to see that 1993 was atypical and most of the differences could be attributed to permitted treatments of provisions which vary between the two countries. However the financial markets did not have the benefit of hindsight and responded to the information available at the time.

Figure 6.4 Daimler Benz results under US and German rules

	Daimler Benz results using German rules DM m	Daimler Benz results using US rules DM m
1990	1,795	884
1991	1,942	1,886
1992	1,451	1,350
1993	615	(1,839)
1994	895	1,052
1995	(5,734)	(5,729)

6.7 US GAAP

Given that it will take some time for the harmonisation and standardisation efforts described above to take effect, it is important to be aware of the structures that determine financial reporting in other countries, to have an awareness of areas of potential difference in the recognition or measurement of financial statement items and areas where practice might change in future. The USA has the largest economy in the world and is also an attractive source of capital for foreign companies. In the light of the apparent competition for international supremacy between US GAAP and IASs, it seems appropriate to spend some time considering the US regulatory environment.

Given the historical links between the UK and the USA, it is unsurprising that the two systems of financial reporting have much in common. However, there are more rules in the USA than in the UK (or perhaps even than anywhere else in the world), and this has resulted in greater standardisation and disclosure of information.

6.7.1 Legislation

There is no direct equivalent of the UK Companies Acts in the USA. The main federal regulation of trade in shares comprises the Securities Act 1933 and the Securities Exchange Act 1934. Neither of these includes any detailed provisions for the form and content of financial statements. The Securities and Exchange Commission (SEC) was born out of this legislation. This body is responsible for requiring the publication of financial information for the benefit of shareholders. It has the power to dictate the form and content of these reports. The largest companies whose shares are listed must register with the SEC and comply with its regulations. The SEC monitors financial reports filed in great detail and makes useful information available to the public via its website (www.sec.gov).

However, it is important to note that the majority of companies fall outside of the SEC's jurisdiction, although shareholders or lenders may require publication of equivalent information and a full audit. Individual states have the power to introduce their own legislation to control businesses and even set taxes. They are also responsible for conferring the right to practise as a public accountant.

6.7.2 Standard-setting body and other sources of GAAP

The Financial Accounting Standards Board (FASB) is responsible for setting accounting standards in the USA. Its independence is ensured by limiting the voluntary contributions to its funding from the various public accounting firms, industry and other interested parties. FASB issues the following documents:

- Statements of Financial Accounting Standards, which deal with specific issues,
- Statements of Concepts, which give general information,
- Interpretations, which clarify existing standards.

A subcommittee of the FASB is the Emerging Issues Task Force, which provided the inspiration for the UK Urgent Issues Task Force. The Accounting Principles Board (APB) also publishes Opinions and the American Institute of Certified Public Accountants (AICPA) also publishes Accounting Practice Bulletins and Opinions. These pronouncements should all be regarded as mandatory. An audit report on the financial statements of a US listed company must express an opinion on whether the accounts 'present fairly in conformity with generally accepted accounting principles'. In trying to determine GAAP, if companies encounter an issue that is not covered by the mandatory pronouncements described above, then they should refer to the FASB Technical Bulletins, AICPA Industry Audit and Accounting Guidelines cleared by FASB and AICPA Statements of Position. Other AICPA interpretations and implementation guidelines published by FASB staff may also be relevant. Finally, companies should refer to practices that are widely recognised and prevalent, either generally or in the industry. Given the large number of sources of authoritative literature, it is perhaps unsurprising that textbooks such as *Wiley GAAP* include an entire chapter on 'researching GAAP problems'.

6.7.3 Foreign companies listed in the USA

Within the EU there has been mutual recognition of member states' accounting principles, so it has been possible for, say, a Belgian company to have its shares listed on the Paris Bourse without needing to make any amendments to its financial statements.

Figure 6.5 Extract from Nokia's Form 20-F

Para 36. Differences between International Accounting Standards and U.S. Generally Accepted Accounting Principles

The Group's consolidated financial statements are prepared in accordance with International Accounting Standards, which differ in certain respects from accounting principles generally accepted in the United States (U.S. GAAP). The principal differences between IAS and U.S. GAAP are presented below together with explanations of certain adjustments that affect consolidated net income and total shareholders' equity as of and for the years ended December 31:

Reconciliation of net income

	2003 EURm	2002 EURm	2001 EURm
Net income reported under IAS	3,592	3,381	2,200
U.S. GAAP adjustments:			
Pension expense	(12)	(5)	(22)
Development costs	322	(66)	(104)
Provision for social security cost on stock options	(21)	(90)	(132)
Stock compensation expense	(9)	(35)	(85)
Cash flow hedges	9	6	(22)
Net investment in foreign companies	—	48	—
Amortization of identifiable intangible assets acquired	(22)	(22)	(7)
Amortization of goodwill	162	206	28
Impairment of goodwill	151	104	—
Deferred tax effect of U.S. GAAP adjustments	(75)	76	47
Net income under U.S. GAAP	4,097	3,603	1,903

The London Stock Exchange has recognised that investors need financial information in a form they can understand, so has permitted foreign companies to use International Accounting Standards for reporting purposes. Foreign companies wishing to list on the US stock exchange need to provide detailed reconciliations and explanations about the differences between the accounting convention used and US GAAP. Companies have to file Form 20-F at the end of the year, which includes the annual financial statements. The consolidated financial statements of Nokia for the year ended 31 December 2003 ran to some 63 pages in its Form 20-F. Fifteen of those pages (i.e. almost a quarter of the financial statements) comprised explanations of the differences between IASs and US GAAP.

The reconciliation between net income reported under IAS and US GAAP for Nokia (shown in Figure 6.5) demonstrates that, in spite of the convergence project, there remain some important differences between US GAAP and IASs. In this example the largest adjustments relate to the capitalisation, amortisation and impairment of fixed assets and the associated tax effects.

6.8 Reconciliations and supplementary statements

As we can see from Nokia above, presenting financial statements in accordance with another accounting convention will result in amendments to figures which require a detailed reconciliation statement.

As a further aid to readers, some companies present financial statements in more than one currency as well as reconciling for accounting convention differences. This is illustrated in Figure 6.6 with an extract from the Annual Report of Eybl International AG (Austria's largest textile company).

Figure 6.6 Examples of multiple reporting in financial statements of Eybl for the year ended 31 December 1998

Accounting convention	ÖHGB	ÖHGB	IAS
Currency	ATS m	Euro m	ATS m
Shareholders' equity	631	46	628
Income attributable to ordinary shareholders	128	9	119
Return on shareholders' equity	20%	20%	19%
Earnings per share	54 ATS	Euro 4	50 ATS

Restating figures in another currency may present information so that it is more familiar, but, of course, there is no effect on financial ratios, as all figures have been adjusted by the same factor. This can be seen from the Eybl accounts presented in Austrian schillings and euros.

Presenting financial statements in accordance with another accounting convention will result in amendments to figures. The differences between Eybl's financial statements prepared in accordance with Austrian regulations and IASs are not substantial. This is perhaps unsurprising given that Austrian regulations have implemented the European Directives and IASs are generally in line with the European Directives. In the 1999 report, Eybl only published financial statements prepared under IASs, taking advantage of dispensations under the Austrian Commercial Code. The main differences between IASs and the Austrian commercial code led to the publication of a cash flow statement and illustration of the development of equity.

Summary

The expansion in the number of multinational enterprises and transnational investments has led to a demand for a greater understanding of financial statements prepared in a range of countries. This has led to pressure for a single set of high quality international accounting standards. IASs are being used increasingly for reporting to capital markets. At the same time, national standards are evolving to come into line with IASs.

REVIEW QUESTIONS

1 How does the regulatory framework for financial reporting in the UK differ from that in the USA? Which is better for particular interest groups and why?

2 'Standardisation is the only way forward for European financial reporting.' Discuss this statement in the light of efforts that have already been made in the harmonisation of company law and the forthcoming requirement for listed companies to follow IASs.

3 Suggest criteria that could be used to classify systems of financial reporting employed in different countries. What difficulties are there in performing an exercise of this nature?

4 Consider the role of scandal in the development of accounting regulation. Compare the reaction to the Enron financial statements in the early part of the twenty-first century with the reaction to the financial statements of AEI and Pergamon Press in the 1960s. (We discussed these UK scandals in Chapter 5.)

5 The current differences between IASs and US GAAP are extensive and the recent pairing of the US Financial Accounting Standards Board and IASB to align IAS and US GAAP will probably result in IAS moving further from current UK GAAP.[33]

   Discuss the implication of this on any choice that non-listed UK companies might make regarding complying with IASs rather than UK GAAP after 2005.

EXERCISES

Question 1

Obtain the financial statements of two companies based in different countries. Review the accounting policies notes. Analyse what the policies tell you about the regulatory environment in which the two companies are operating.

Question 2

Use the EDGAR service (via the SEC website) to identify four European companies listed on the US Stock Exchange. From the Form 20-F identify which items feature in the reconciliation from net income under domestic GAAP (or IASs) to net income under US GAAP. What does your analysis allow you to conclude about regulations or underlying principles in different countries?

Question 3

Consider the interest of the tax authorities in financial reporting regulations. Explain why national tax authorities might be concerned about the transition from domestic accounting standards to IASs in companies' annual reports.

References

1 R.T. Moran, *Cultural Guide to Doing Business in Europe* (2nd edition), Butterworth-Heinemann Ltd, 1992, p. 51.
2 *Ibid.*, p. 60.
3 C. Nobes and R. Parker, *Comparative International Accounting*, (7th edition), Pearson, 2002, pp. 17–33.
4 J. Freedman and M. Power, *Law and Accountancy: Conflict and Cooperation in the 1990s*, Paul Chapman Publishing Ltd, 1992, p. 105.
5 For more detailed discussion see C. Nobes, 'Corporate financing and its effects on European accounting differences', Reading University discussion paper, 1996.
6 Sources: GDP: International Monetary Fund, *International Financial Statistics Yearbook 1999*, IMF, 1999; market capitalisation: International Finance Corporation, *Emerging Stock Markets Factbook 1999*, IFC, 1999.
7 C. Nobes, *Towards 1992*, Butterworths, 1989, p. 15.
8 C. Randlesome, *Business Cultures in Europe* (2nd edition), Heinemann Professional Publishing, 1993, p. 27.
9 J.D. Daniels and L.H. Radebaugh, *International Business*, (8th edition), Addison Wesley, 1998, p. 818.
10 Randlesome, *op. cit.*, p. 25.
11 Nobes, *op. cit.*, p. 8.
12 T. Cooke, *An Empirical Study of Financial Disclosure by Swedish Companies*, Garland, 1989, pp. 112–113.
13 Nobes and Parker, *op. cit.*, pp. 73–75.
14 See S.P. Agrawal, P.H. Jensen, A.L. Meader and K. Sellers, 'An international comparison of conceptual frameworks of accounting', *The International Journal of Accounting*, vol. 24, 1989, pp. 237–249.
15 *Accountancy*, June 1989, p. 10.
16 See, for example, B. Chauveau, 'The Spanish *Plan General de Contabilidad*: Agent of development and innovation?', *European Accounting Review*, vol. 4, no. 1, 1995, pp. 125–138.
17 See, for example, P.E.M. Standish, 'Origins of the *Plan Comptable Général*: a study in cultural intrusion and reaction', *Accounting and Business Research*, vol. 20, no. 80, 1990, pp. 337–351.
18 See Nobes and Parker, *op. cit.*, pp. 52–71.
19 Nobes and Parker, *op. cit.*, pp. 73–75.
20 International Accounting Standards Committee Constitution (2000) as amended on 5 March 2002, www.iasb.org.uk.
21 For further details see *Accountancy*, International Edition, December 1999, p.5.
22 For up-to-date information about the constitution of the IASC, see its web site: www.iasb.org.uk.

23 *Framework for the Preparation and Presentation of Financial Statements*, IASC, 1989, adopted by IASB 2001.

24 The European Economic Community established by the Treaty of Rome in 1957 became known as the European Community in 1985 and the European Union in November 1993 following the Maastricht Treaty.

25 For further details see D. Cairns, 'The future of the IASC and the implications for UK companies' in ICAEW, *Financial reporting today: current and emerging issues*, Accountancy Books, 1998 edition, pp. 115–152.

26 A comprehensive analysis of these differences is provided in C. Bloomer, (ed.), *The IASC-U.S. Comparison Project: A Report on the Similarities and Differences between IASC Standards and U.S. GAAP*, (2nd edition), Financial Accounting Standards Board, 1999.

27 EU, *Regulation of the European Parliament and of the Council on the Application of International Accounting standards*, Brussels, 2002.

28 The following summary is based on IASB (2002) *Improvements to International Accounting Standards*, project summary posted on the IASB web site (www.iasb.org.uk).

29 See, e.g., D. Cairns, *Financial Times International Accounting Standards Survey 1999*, FT Business, 1999.

30 Commission of the European Communities, *EU Financial Reporting Strategy: The Way Forward*, COM(2000) 359 final, 2000.

31 C. Quick and D. Wild, 'Rover trouble was avoidable', *Accountancy Age*, 18 February 1999, p. 7.

32 Source: Daimler Benz, Form 20-F 1995; L.H. Radebaugh, G. Gebhardt and S.J. Gray, 'Foreign stock exchange listings: a case study of Daimler Benz', *Journal of International Financial Management and Accounting*, 6(2), 1995, pp. 158–192.

33 Y. Dinwoodie and P. Holgate, 'Singing from the same songsheet?', *Accountancy*, May 2003, pp. 94–95.

CHAPTER 7

Conceptual framework

7.1 Introduction

In this chapter we will discuss the rationale underlying standards and consider the developments that have occurred in the search for a conceptual framework for financial reporting. We also consider:

- Historical overview of the evolution of financial accounting theory
- IASC *Framework for the Presentation and Preparation of Financial Statements – 1989*
- UK *Statement of Principles for Financial Reporting 1999*
- AICPA *Improving Business Reporting – A Customer Focus: Meeting the Information Needs of Investors and Creditors – 1994*
- ICAS *Making Corporate Reports Valuable – 1988*

7.1.1 Financial reporting under the spotlight

Financial statements have been, and continue to be, subject to an array of accounting standards produced by international bodies such as EU Directives and IASs and by national standard setters such as FASB in the USA and the various standard-setting bodies around the world.

Consistency to protect the auditors

The early standards were set to achieve consistency in the treatment of the major items, e.g. IAS 2 *Inventories*, and were seen as a mechanism to avoid conflicting rules and practices.

Transparency

Later the emphasis evolved to the provision of information useful for making economic decisions. How reliable this is can often, however, only be assessed after some sort of crisis when the internal affairs of the company are subject to investigation.

Financial reporting under the spotlight

Financial reporting does not exist in a vacuum and it is put under the spotlight when events call its fairness into question. This has been seen in recent times with the financial crisis in the global markets.

The implication for standard setting is set out by the International Forum on Accountancy Development (IFAD), a body set up to harness the resources of the accounting profession and international financial institutions. IFAD, whose first meeting was in June 1999, comments:[1]

Lessons from the crisis

. . . the Asian crisis showed that under the forces of financial globalisation it is essential for countries to improve . . . the supervision, regulation and transparency of financial systems . . . Efficiency of markets requires reliable financial information from issuers. With hindsight, it was clear that local accounting standards used to prepare financial statements did not meet international standards. Investors, both domestic and foreign, did not fully understand the weak financial position of the companies in which they were investing.

This assessment has at various times also been made in other countries around the world and has been the initial force driving the standard-setting process.

Rationale for accounting standards

It is interesting to take a historical overview of the evolution of the financial accounting theory underpinning standards and guiding standard setters to see how it has moved through three phases from the empirical inductive to the deductive to a formalised conceptual framework.

7.2 Historical overview of the evolution of financial accounting theory

Financial accounting practices have not evolved in a vacuum. They are dynamic responses to changing macro and micro conditions which may involve political, fiscal, economic and commercial changes, e.g.:

● How to take account of changing prices?
  – Ignore because unmodified historical cost accounting is applied as in Germany.
  – Ignore if inflation is low as is the present situation in many European countries.
  – Have a modified historical cost system where tangible fixed assets are revalued which has been the norm in the UK.
  – Apply a government inflation rate to tangible fixed assets as in Turkey.
  – Have a coherent current cost system as implemented in the 1970s in the Netherlands.
● How to deal with changing commercial practices?
  – Ignore if not a material commercial practice, e.g. leasing in the early 1970s.
  – Apply objective, tightly defined, legalistic-based criteria, e.g. to define finance and operating leases.
  – Apply subjective criteria, e.g. assess the economic substance of a leasing transaction to see if a finance lease because the risks and rewards have substantially been passed to the lessee.
  – Accept that it is not possible to effectively regulate companies to achieve consistent treatment of similar economic transactions and require same reporting treatment for all lease transactions.

It is clear from considering just these two questions that there could be a variety of accounting treatments for similar transactions and, if annual financial reports are to be useful in making economic decisions,[2] there is a need for uniformity and consistency in reporting.

Attempts to achieve consistency have varied over time.

- An **empirical inductive approach** was followed by the accounting profession prior to 1970.

   This resulted in standards or reporting practices that were based on rationalising what happened in practice, i.e. it established best current practice as the norm. Under this approach there was a general disclosure standard, e.g. IAS 1 *Disclosure of Accounting Policies*, and standards for major specific items, e.g. IAS 2 *Inventories*.

- A **deductive approach** followed in the 1970s.

   This resulted in standards based on principles deduced from assumptions, e.g. that price-adjusted financial statements would be more relevant than historical accounting statements. This was not based on existing practice in the real world – in fact, it challenged current reporting practice.

- A **conceptual framework approach** was promoted in the 1980s.

   It was recognised that standards needed to be decision-useful, that they should satisfy cost/benefit criteria and that their implementation could only be achieved by consensus. Consensus was generally only achievable where there was a clearly perceived rationale underpinning a standard and, even so, alternative treatments were required in order to gain support.

- A **conceptual framework approach** in the twenty-first century – the **mandatory model**.

   Under this approach there is less regard for the provision of alternative treatments.

7.2.1 Empirical inductive approach

The empirical inductive approach looked at the practices that existed and attempted to generalise from them.

This tended to be how the technical departments of accounting firms operated. By rationalising what they did, they ensured that the firm avoided accepting different financial reporting practices for similar transactions, e.g. accepting unrealised profit appearing in the income statement of one client and not in another. The technical department's role was to advise partners and staff, i.e. it was a **defensive role** to avoid any potential charge from a user of the accounts that they had been misled.

Initially a technical circular was regarded as a private good and distribution was restricted to the firm's own staff. However, it then became recognised that it could benefit the firm if its practices were accepted as the industry benchmark, so that in the event of litigation it could rely on this fact.

When the technical advice ceased to be a private good, there was a perceived additional benefit to the firm if the nature of the practice could be changed from being a positive statement, i.e. this is how we report profits on uncompleted contracts, to a **normative** statement, i.e. this is how we report *and* this is how all other financial reporters *ought* to report.

Consequently, there has been a growing trend since the 1980s for firms to publish rationalisations for their financial reporting practices. It has been commercially prudent for them to do so. It has also been extremely helpful to academic accountants and their students.

Typical illustrations of the result of such empirical induction are the wide acceptance of the historical cost model and various concepts such as matching and realisation that we discussed in Chapter 2. In terms of standards, we have already mentioned that IAS 1 and IAS 2 evolved under this regime.

This approach has played an important role in the evolution of financial reporting practices and will continue to do so. After all, it is the preparers of the financial statements and their auditors who are first exposed to change, whether economic, political or commercial. They are the ones who have to think their way through each new problem that surfaces. This means that a financial reporting practice already exists by the time the problem comes to the attention of theoreticians.

The major reasons that it has been felt necessary to try other approaches are both pragmatic and theoretical.

Pragmatic reason

The main pragmatic reason is that the past procedure, whereby deduction was dependent upon generalisation from existing practice, has become untenable. The accelerating rate of economic, political and commercial change leaves too little time for effective and uniform practices to evolve.

Theoretical reasons

The theoretical reasons relate to the acceptability of the income determined under the traditional historical cost model. There are three principal reasons:

- **True income**. We have seen that economists had a view that financial reports should report a true income, which differed from the accountants' view.
- **User-defined income – public**. There is a view that there may be a number of relevant incomes depending upon differing user needs which may be regarded as public goods.
- **User-defined income – private**. There is a view that there may be a number of relevant incomes depending upon differing user needs which may be regarded as private rather than public goods.

It was thought that the limitations implicit in the empirical inductive approach could be overcome by the deductive approach.

7.2.2 Deductive approach

The deductive approach is not dependent on existing practice, which is often perceived as having been tainted because it has been determined by finance directors and auditors. However, the problem remains: from whose viewpoint is the deduction to be made?

Possible alternatives to the preparers and auditors of the accounts are economists and users. However, economists are widely perceived as promoting unrealistic models and users as having needs so diverse that they cannot be realistically satisfied in a single set of accounts. Consider the attempts made to define income. Economists have supported the concept of a true income, while users have indicated the need for a range of relevant incomes.

True income

We have already seen in Chapter 3 that there is a significant difference between the accountant's income and the economist's income applying the ideas of Fisher and Hicks.

User needs and multiple incomes

Multiple measures of income, derived from the general price level adjusted accounting model, the replacement cost accounting model and the exit price accounting model, were considered in Chapter 4. Each model provides information that is relevant for different purposes, e.g. replacement cost accounting produces an income figure that indicates how much is available for distribution while still maintaining the operating capacity of the entity.

These income figures were regarded as a public good, i.e. cost-free to the user. Latterly, it has been recognised that there is a cost implication to the production of information, i.e. that it is not a public good; that standards should be capable of being empirically tested; and that consideration should be given to the economic consequences of standards. This has resulted in a concern that standards should deal with economic substance rather than form, e.g. the treatment of leases in IAS 17.[3]

It could be argued that the deductive approach to income, whether an economist's defined income or a theoretician's multiple income, has a basic weakness in that it gives priority to the information needs of only one user group – the investors. In the UK the ASB is quite explicit about this. The *Framework* is less clear about the primary focus, stating that financial statements are prepared to provide information that is useful in making economic decisions. The ASB has been supported by other academics[4] who have stated:

> As we have already noted that the needs of investors, creditors, employees and customers are not fundamentally different, it seems safe to look to the needs of present and potential investors as a guide . . .

There is little independent evidence put forward to support this view.

Where do we stand now?

We have seen that accounting theory was initially founded on generalisations from the accounting practices followed by practitioners. Then came the deductive approach of economists and theoreticians. The latter were not perceived to be realistic and empirical testing, e.g. examination of their economic consequence on share prices, is relied on to give them credibility.

The practitioners have now staked their claim to create accounting theory or a conceptual framework through the IASB. The advantage of this is that the conceptual framework will be based on consensus.

7.3 IASC *Framework for the Presentation and Preparation of Financial Statements*

This exposure draft deals with the following:

● The objective of financial statements.
   The **objective** of financial statements is that they should provide information about the financial position, performance and changes in financial position of an enterprise that is useful to a wide range of potential users in making economic decisions.

● The qualitative characteristics that determine the usefulness of information in financial statements.
   The **qualitative characteristics** that determine the usefulness of information are **relevance** and **reliability**. Comparability is a qualitative characteristic that interacts with both relevance and reliability. Materiality provides a threshold or cut-off point rather than being a primary qualitative characteristic. The balance between cost and benefit is a persuasive constraint rather than a qualitative characteristic.

- The definition, recognition and measurement of elements from which financial statements are constructed.

  The **definition** of an element is given in paragraph 46:

  > Financial statements portray the financial effects of transactions and other events by grouping the effects into broad classes according to their economic characteristics. These broad classes are termed the **elements** of financial statements. The elements directly related to the measurement of financial position in the balance sheet are assets, liabilities and equity. The elements directly related to the measurement of performance in the profit and loss account are income and expense.

  The exposure draft defines each of the elements. For example, an asset is defined in paragraph 53: 'The future economic benefit embodied in an asset is the potential to contribute, directly or indirectly, to the flow of cash and cash equivalents to the enterprise.'

  It defines when an element is to be **recognised**. For example, in paragraph 87 it states: 'An asset is recognised in the balance sheet when it is probable that the future economic benefits will flow to the enterprise and the asset has an attribute that can be measured reliably.'

  Regarding **measurement**, it comments in paragraph 99:

  > The measurement attribute most commonly adopted by enterprises in preparing their financial statements is historical cost. This is usually combined with other measurement attributes, such as realisable value. For example, inventories are usually carried at the lower of cost and net realisable value, and marketable securities may be carried at market value, that is, their realisable value. Furthermore, many enterprises combine historical costs and current costs as a response to the inability of the historical cost model to deal with the effects of changing prices of non-monetary assets.

  The document deals in a similar style with the other elements.

- The concepts of capital, capital maintenance and profit.

  Finally, regarding the concepts of **capital**, **capital maintenance** and **profit**, the IASC comments:

  > At the present time, it is not the intention of the Board of the IASC to prescribe a particular measurement model (i.e. historical cost, current cost, realisable value, present value) ... This intention will, however, be reviewed in the light of world developments.

  An appropriate capital maintenance model is not specified but the Framework mentions historical cost accounting, current cost accounting, net realisable value (as discussed in Chapter 4) and present value models (as discussed in Chapter 3).

  The Framework has initiated the development of conceptual frameworks by other national standard setters for both private sector and public sector financial statements. Since then and up to the present day other jurisdictions have been influenced when drafting their own national conceptual frameworks, e.g. the Swedish National Financial Management Authority in 2002 (www.esv.se) and the South African Accounting Standards Board in 2003 (www.asb.co.za).

  One of the earliest conceptual frameworks developed subsequently was that developed by the ASB in the UK as the *Statement of Principles* – this expanded on the ideas underlying the Framework and the ASB deserves praise for this.

7.4 ASB *Statement of Principles* 1999[5]

The *Statement* fleshes out the ideas contained in the Framework.

As Sir David Tweedie, Chairman of the ASB, commented, 'The Board has developed its *Statement of Principles* in parallel with its development of accounting standards ... It is in effect the Board's compass for when we navigate uncharted waters in the years ahead. This is essential reading for those who want to know where the Board is coming from, and where it is aiming to go.'

The Statement contains eight chapters dealing with key issues. Each of the chapters is commented on below.

7.4.1 Chapter 1: 'The objective of financial statements'

The *Statement of Principles* follows the IASC *Framework* in the identification of user groups.

The statement identifies the investor group as the primary group for whom the financial statements are being prepared. It then states the information needs of each group as follows:

- **Investors**. These need information to:
  - assess the stewardship of management, e.g. in safeguarding the entity's resources and using them properly, efficiently and profitably;
  - take decisions about management, e.g. assessing need for new management;
  - take decisions about their investment or potential investment, e.g. deciding whether to hold, buy or sell shares and assessing the ability to pay dividends.
- **Lenders**. These need information to:
  - determine whether their loans and interest will be paid on time;
  - decide whether to lend and on what terms.
- **Suppliers**. These need information to:
  - decide whether to sell to the entity;
  - determine whether they will be paid on time;
  - determine longer-term stability if the company is a major customer.
- **Employees**. These need information to:
  - assess the stability and profitability of the company;
  - assess the ability to provide remuneration, retirement benefits and employment opportunities.
- **Customers**. These need information to:
  - assess the probability of the continued existence of the company taking account of their own degree of dependence on the company, e.g. for future provision of specialised replacement parts and servicing product warranties.
- **Government and other agencies**. These need information to:
  - be aware of the commercial activities of the company;
  - regulate these activities;
  - raise revenue;
  - produce national statistics.
- **Public**. Members of the public need information to:
  - determine the effect on the local economy of the company's activities, e.g. employment opportunities, use of local suppliers;
  - assess recent developments in the company's prosperity and changes in its activities.

The information needs of which group are to be dominant?

Seven groups are identified, but there is only one set of financial statements. Although they are described as general-purpose statements, a decision has to be made about which group's needs take precedence.

The *Statement of Principles* identifies the **investor** group as the defining class of user, i.e. the primary group for whom the financial statements are being prepared.

It takes the view that financial statements 'are able to focus on the common interest of users'. The common interest is described thus: 'all potential users are interested, to a varying degree, in the financial performance and financial position of the entity as a whole'.

This means that it is a prerequisite that the information must be relevant to the investor group. This suggests that any need of the other groups that is not also a need of the investors will not be met by the financial statements.

The 1995 Exposure Draft stated: 'Awarding primacy to investors does not imply that other users are to be ignored. The information prepared for investors is useful as a frame of reference for other users, against which they can evaluate more specific information that they may obtain in their dealings with the enterprise.'

It is important, therefore, for all of the other users to be aware that this is one of the principles. If they require specific disclosures that might be relevant to them, they will need to take their own steps to obtain them, particularly where there is a conflict of interest. For example, if a closure is being planned by the directors, it may be in the investors' interest for the news to be delayed as long as possible to minimise the cost to the company; employees, suppliers, customers and the public must not expect any assistance from the financial statements – their information needs are not the primary concern.

What information should be provided to satisfy the information needs?

The *Statement* proposes that information is required in four areas: financial performance, financial position, generation and use of cash, and financial adaptability.

Financial performance

Financial performance is defined as the return an entity obtains from the resources it controls. This return is available from the profit and loss account and provides a means to assess past management performance, how effectively resources have been utilised and the capacity to generate cash flows.

Financial position

Financial position is available from an examination of the balance sheet and includes:

- the economic resources controlled by an entity, i.e. assets and liabilities;
- financial structure, i.e. capital gearing indicating how profits will be divided between the different sources of finance and the capacity for raising additional finance in the future;
- liquidity and solvency, i.e. current and liquid ratios;
- capacity to adapt to changes – see below under **Financial adaptability**.

Generation and use of cash

Information is available from the cash flow statement which shows cash flows from operating, investment and financing activities providing a perspective that is largely free from allocation and valuation issues. This information is useful in assessing and reviewing previous assessments of cash flows.

Financial adaptability

This is an entity's ability to alter the amount and timing of its cash flows. It is desirable in order to be able to cope with difficult periods, e.g. when losses are incurred and to take advantage of unexpected investment opportunities. It is dependent on factors such as the ability, at short notice, to:

● raise new capital;

● repay capital or debt;

● obtain cash from disposal of assets without disrupting continuing business, i.e. realise readily marketable securities that might have been built up as a liquid reserve;

● achieve a rapid improvement in net cash flows from operations.

7.4.2 Chapter 2: 'The reporting entity'

This chapter focuses on identifying when an entity should report and which activities to include in the report.

When an entity should report

The principle is that an entity should prepare and publish financial statements if:

● there is a legitimate demand for the information, i.e. it is the case both that it is decision-useful and that benefits exceed the cost of producing the information; and

● it is a cohesive economic unit, i.e. a unit under a central control that can be held accountable for its activities.

Which activities to include

The principle is that those activities should be included that are within the direct control of the entity, e.g. assets and liabilities which are reported in its own balance sheet, or indirect control, e.g. assets and liabilities of a subsidiary of the entity which are reported in the consolidated balance sheet.

Control is defined as (a) the ability to deploy the resources and (b) the ability to benefit (or to suffer) from their deployment. Indirect control by an investor can be difficult to determine. The test is not to apply a theoretical level of influence such as holding $x\%$ of shares but to review the relationship that exists between the investor and investee in practice, such as the investor having the power to veto the investee's financial and operating policies and benefit from its net assets.

7.4.3 Chapter 3: 'The qualitative characteristics of financial information'

The *Statement of Principles* is based on the IASC *Framework* and contains the same four principal qualitative characteristics relating to the content of information and how the information is presented. The two primary characteristics relating to content are the need to be relevant and reliable; the two relating to presentation are the need to be understandable and comparable. The characteristics appear diagrammatically as follows:

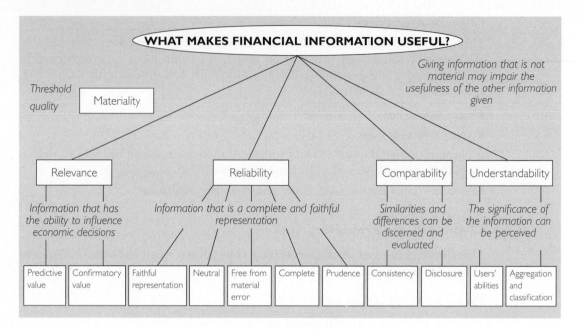

From the diagram we can see that for information content to be **relevant** it must have:

● the ability to influence the economic decisions of users;

● predictive value, i.e. help users to evaluate or assess past, present or future events; or

● confirmatory value, i.e. help users to confirm their past evaluations.

For information to be **reliable** it must be:

● free from material error, i.e. transactions have been accurately recorded and reported;

● a faithful representation, i.e. reflecting the commercial substance of transactions;

● neutral, i.e. not presented in a way to achieve a predetermined result;

● prudent, i.e. not creating hidden reserves or excessive provisions, deliberately understating assets or gains, or deliberately overstating liabilities or losses;

● complete, i.e. the information is complete subject to a materiality test.

To be useful, the financial information also needs to be **comparable** over time and between companies and **understandable**.

It satisfies the criteria for understandability if it is capable of being understood by a user with a reasonable knowledge of business activities and accounting, and a willingness to study the information with reasonable diligence. However, the trade-off between relevance and reliability comes into play with the requirement that complex information that is relevant to economic decision making should not be omitted because some users find it too difficult to understand. There is no absolute answer where there is the possibility of a trade-off and it is recognised by the ASB that the relative importance of the characteristics in different cases is a matter of judgement.

The chapter also introduces the idea of **materiality** as a threshold quality and any item that is not material does not require to be considered further. The statement recognises that no information can be useful if it is not also material by introducing the idea of a threshold quality which it describes as follows: 'An item of information is material to the financial statements if its misstatement or omission might reasonably be expected to influence the economic decisions of users of those financial statements, including their assessment of management's stewardship.'[6]

First, this means that it is justified not to report immaterial items which would impose unnecessary costs on preparers and impede decision makers by obscuring material information with excessive detail.

Secondly, it means that the important consideration is not user expectation (e.g. users might expect turnover to be accurate to within 1%) but the effect on decision making (e.g. there might only be an effect if turnover were to be more that 10% over- or understated in which case, only errors exceeding 10% are material).

It also states that 'Materiality depends on the size of the item or error judged in the particular circumstances of its omission or misstatement'. The need to exercise judgement means that the preparer needs to have a benchmark.

A discussion paper issued in January 1995 by the Financial Reporting & Auditing Group of the ICAEW entitled 'Materiality in Financial Reporting FRAG 1/95' identified that there are few instances where an actual figure is given by statute or by standard setters, e.g. FRS 6,[7] para. 76 refers to a material minority and indicates that this is defined as 10%.

The paper also referred to a rule of thumb used in the USA:

The staff of the US Securities and Exchange Commission have an informal rule of thumb that errors of more than 10% are material, those between 5% and 10% may be material and those under 5% are usually not material. These percentages are applied to gross profit, net income, equity and any specific line in the financial statements that is potentially misstated.

The ASB has moved away from setting percentage benchmarks and there is now a need for more explicit guidance on the application of the materiality threshold.

7.4.4 Chapter 4: 'The elements of financial statements'

This chapter gives guidance on the items that *could* appear in financial statements. These are described as **elements** and have the following essential features:

- **Assets**. These are rights to future economic benefits controlled by an entity as a result of past transactions or events.
- **Liabilities**. These are obligations of an entity to transfer future economic benefits as a result of past transactions or events, i.e. ownership is not essential.
- **Ownership interest**. This is the residual amount found by deducting all liabilities from assets which belong to the owners of the entity.
- **Gains**. These are increases in ownership interest not resulting from contributions by the owners.
- **Losses**. These are decreases in ownership interest not resulting from distributions to the owners.
- **Contributions by the owners**. These are increases in ownership interest resulting from transfers from owners in their capacity as owners.
- **Distributions to owners**. These are decreases in ownership interest resulting from transfers to owners in their capacity as owners.

These definitions have been used as the basis for developing standards, e.g. assessing the substance of a transaction means identifying whether the transaction has given rise to new assets or liabilities, defined as above.

7.4.5 Chapter 5: 'Recognition in financial statements'

The objective of financial statements is to disclose in the balance sheet and the profit and loss account the effect on the assets and liabilities of **transactions**, e.g. purchase of stock on credit and the effect of **events**, e.g. accidental destruction of a vehicle by fire. This implies that transactions are recorded under the double entry principle with an appropriate debit and credit made to the element that has been affected, e.g. the asset element (stock) and the liability element (creditors) are debited and credited to recognise stock bought on credit. Events are also recorded under the double entry principle, e.g. the asset element (vehicle) is derecognised and credited because it is no longer able to provide future economic benefits and the loss element resulting from the fire damage is debited to the profit and loss account. The emphasis is on determining the effect on the assets and liabilities, e.g. the increase in the asset element (stock), the increase in the liability element (creditors) and the reduction in the asset element (vehicle).

This emphasis has a particular significance for application of the matching concept in preparing the profit and loss account. The traditional approach to allocating expenditure across accounting periods has been to identify the costs that should be matched against the revenue in the profit and loss account and carry the balance into the balance sheet, i.e. the allocation is driven by the need to match costs to revenue. The *Statement of Principles* approach is different in that it identifies the amount of the expenditure to be recognised as an asset and the balance is transferred to the profit and loss account, i.e. the question is 'Should this expenditure be recognised as an asset (capitalised) and, if so, should any part of it be derecognised (written off as a loss element)?'

This means that the allocation process now requires an assessment as to whether an asset exists at the balance sheet date by applying the following test:

1 If the future economic benefits are eliminated at a single point in time, it is at that point that the loss is recognised and the expenditure derecognised, i.e. the debit balance is transferred to the profit and loss account.

2 If the future economic benefits are eliminated over several accounting periods – typically because they are being consumed over a period of time – the cost of the asset that comprises the future economic benefits will be recognised as a loss in the performance statement over those accounting periods, i.e. written off as a loss element as their future economic benefit reduces.

The result of this approach should not lead to changes in the accounts as currently prepared but it does emphasise that matching cost and revenue is not the main driver of recognition, i.e. the question is not 'How much expenditure should we match with the revenue reported in the profit and loss account?' but rather 'Are there future economic benefits arising from the expenditure to justify inclusion in the balance sheet?' and, if not, derecognise it, i.e. write it off.

Dealing with uncertainty

There is almost always some uncertainty as to when to recognise an event or transaction, e.g. when is the asset element of raw material stock to be disclosed as the asset element work-in-progress? Is it when a stock requisition is issued, when the storekeeper isolates it in the stock to be issued bay, when it is issued onto the workshop floor, when it begins to be worked on?

The *Statement of Principles* states that the principle to be applied if a transaction has created or added to an existing asset or liability is to recognise it if:

1 sufficient evidence exists that the new asset or liability has been created or that there has been an addition to an existing asset or liability; and

2 the new asset or liability or the addition to the existing asset or liability can be measured at a monetary amount with sufficient reliability.

The use of the word sufficient reflects the uncertainty that surrounds the decision when to recognise and the *Statement* states: 'In the business environment, uncertainty usually exists in a continuum, so the recognition process involves selecting the point on the continuum at which uncertainty becomes acceptable'.[8]

Before that point it may, for example, be appropriate to disclose by way of note to the accounts a contingent liability that is possible (less than 50% chance of crystallising into a liability) but not probable (more than 50% chance of crystallising).

Sufficient reliability

Prudence requires more persuasive evidence of the measurement for the recognition of items that result in an increase in ownership interest than for the recognition of items that do not. However, the exercise of prudence does not allow for the omission of assets or gains where there is sufficient evidence of occurrence and reliability of measurement, or for the inclusion of liabilities or losses where there is not. This would amount to the deliberate understatement of assets or gains, or the deliberate overstatement of liabilities or losses.

Reporting gains and losses

Chapter 5 does not address the disclosure treatment of gains and losses. A change in assets or liabilities might arise from three classes of past event: transactions, contracts for future performance and other events such as a change in market price.

If the change in an asset is offset by a change in liability, there will be no gain or loss. If the change in asset is not offset by a change in liability, there will be a gain or loss. If there is a gain or loss a decision is required as to whether it should be recognised in the profit and loss account or in the statement of total recognised gains and losses.

Recognition in profit and loss account

For a gain to be recognised in the profit and loss account, it must have been earned and realised. **Earned** means that no material transaction, contract or other event must occur before the change in the assets or liabilities will have occurred; **realised** means that the conversion into cash or cash equivalents must either have occurred or be reasonably assured.

Profit, as stated in the profit and loss account, is used as a prime measure of performance. Consequently, prudence requires particularly good evidence for the recognition of gains.

It is important to note that in this chapter the ASB is following a **balance sheet orientated** approach to measuring gains and losses. The conventional profit and loss account approach would identify the **transactions** that had been undertaken and allocate these to financial accounting periods.

7.4.6 Chapter 6: 'Measurement in financial statements'

The majority of listed companies in the UK use the mixed measurement system whereby some assets and liabilities are measured using historical cost and some are measured using a current value basis. The *Statement of Principles* envisages that this will continue to be the practice and states that the aim is to select the basis that:

● provides information about financial performance and financial position that is useful in evaluating the reporting entity's cash-generation abilities and in assessing its financial adaptability;

● carries values which are sufficiently reliable: if the historical cost and current value are equally reliable, the better measure is the one that is the most relevant; current values may frequently be no less reliable than historical cost figures given the level of estimation that is required in historical cost figures, e.g. determining provisions for bad debts, stock provisions, product warranties;

● reflects what the asset and liability represents: e.g. the relevance of short-term investments to an entity will be the specific future cash flows and these are best represented by current values.

ASB view on need for a current value basis of measurement

The *Statement* makes the distinction[9] between return *on* capital – i.e. requiring the calculation of accounting profit – and return *of* capital – i.e. requiring the measurement of capital and testing for capital maintenance. The *Statement* makes the point that the financial capital maintenance concept is not satisfactory when *significant* general or specific price changes have occurred.

ASB gradualist approach

The underlying support of the ASB for a gradualist move towards the use of current values is reflected in 'Although the objective of financial statements and the qualitative characteristics of financial information, in particular relevance and reliability may not change ... as markets develop, measurement bases that were once thought unreliable may become reliable. Similarly, as access to markets develops, so a measurement basis that was once thought insufficiently relevant may become the most relevant measure available'.[10]

Determining current value

Current value systems could be defined as replacement cost (entry value), net realisable value (exit value) or value in use (discounted present value of future cash flows). The approach of the *Statement* is to identify the value to the business by selecting from these three alternatives the measure that is most relevant in the circumstances. This measure is referred to as deprival value and represents the loss that the entity would suffer if it were deprived of the asset.

The value to the business is determined by considering whether the company would replace the asset. If the answer is *yes*, then use replacement cost; if the answer is *no* but the asset is worth keeping, then use value in use; and if *no* and the asset is not worth keeping, then use net realisable value.

This can be shown diagrammatically as follows:

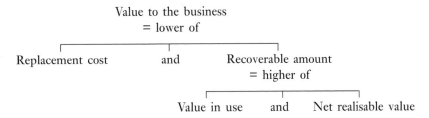

Value to the business
= lower of

Replacement cost   and   Recoverable amount
= higher of

Value in use   and   Net realisable value

How will value to the business be implemented?

The ASB is being pragmatic by following an incremental approach to the question of measurement stating that 'practice should develop by evolving in the direction of greater use of current values consistent with the constraints of reliability and cost'. This seems a sensible position for the ASB to take. Its underlying views were clear when it stated that 'a real terms capital maintenance system improves the relevance of information because it shows current operating margins as well as the extent to which holding gains and losses reflect the effect of general inflation, so that users of real terms financial statements are able to select the particular information they require'.[11]

Policing the mixed measurement system

Many companies have adopted the modified historical cost basis and revalued their fixed assets on a selective basis. However, this piecemeal approach allowed companies to cherry-pick the assets they wish to revalue on a selective basis at times when market values have risen. The ASB have adopted the same approach as IAS 16.[12]

7.4.7 Chapter 7: 'Presentation of financial information'

Chapter 7 states that the objective of the presentation adopted is to communicate clearly and effectively and in as simple and straightforward manner as is possible without loss of relevance or reliability and without significantly increasing the length of the financial statements.

The point about length is well made given the length of current annual reports and accounts. Recent examples include Jenoptik AG extending to 81 pages, Sea Containers Ltd 76 pages and Hugo Boss 115 pages.

The *Statement* analyses the way in which information should be presented in financial statements to meet the objectives set out in Chapter 1. It covers the requirement for items to be aggregated and classified and outlines good presentation practices in the statement of financial performance, balance sheet, cash flow statement and accompanying information, e.g.:

Statement of financial performance

Good presentation involves:

- Recognising only gains and losses.
- Classifying items by function, e.g. production, selling, administrative and nature, e.g. interest payable.
- Showing separately amounts that are affected in different ways by economic or commercial conditions, e.g. continuing, acquired and discontinued operations, segmental geographical information.

- Showing separately:
  - items unusual in amount or incidence
  - expenses that are not operating expenses, e.g. financing costs and taxation
  - expenses that relate primarily to future periods, e.g. research expenditure.

Balance sheet

Good presentation involves:

- Recognising only assets, liabilities and ownership interest.
- Classifying assets so that users can assess the nature, amounts and liquidity of available resources.
- Classifying assets and liabilities so that users can assess the nature, amounts and timing of obligations that require or may require liquid resources for settlement.
- Classifying assets by function, e.g. show fixed assets and current assets separately.

Accompanying information

Typical information includes chairman's statement, directors' report, operating and financial review, highlights and summary indicators.

The *Statement* states that the more complex an entity and its transactions become, the more users need an objective and comprehensive analysis and explanation of the main features underlying the entity's financial performance and financial position.

Good presentation involves discussion of:

- The main factors underlying financial performance, including the principal risks, uncertainties and trends in main business areas and how the entity is responding.
- The strategies adopted for capital structure and treasury policy.
- The activities and expenditure (other than capital expenditure) that are investment in the future.

It is interesting to note the *Statement* view that highlights and summary indicators, such as amounts and ratios that attempt to distil key information, cannot on their own adequately describe or provide a basis for meaningful analysis or prudent decision making. It does, however, state: 'That having been said, well-presented highlights and summary indicators are useful to users who require only very basic information, such as the amount of sales or dividends.' The ASB will be giving further consideration to this view that there is a need for a really brief report.

7.4.8 Chapter 8: 'Accounting for interests in other entities'

Interests in other entities can have a material effect on the company's own financial performance and financial position and need to be fully reflected in the financial statements. As an example, an extract from the 1998 Annual Report and Accounts of Stagecoach plc shows:

	Company balance sheet	*Consolidated balance sheet*
Tangible fixed assets	£0.7m	1,548.4m
Investments	£734.3m	51.4m

In deciding whether to include the assets in the consolidated balance sheet a key factor is the degree of influence exerted over the activities and resources of the investee:

● If the degree of influence allows control of the operating and financial policies, the financial statements are aggregated.

● If the investor has joint control or significant influence, the investor's share of the gains and losses are recognised in the consolidated profit and loss account and reflected in the carrying value of the investment.

However, there is no clear agreement on the treatment of interests in other entities, and further developments can be expected.

7.5 AICPA *Improving Business Reporting – A Customer Focus: Meeting the Information Needs of Investors and Creditors*

This was a study carried out by AICPA in the USA over a three-year period and published in 1994.[13] It resulted in a number of interesting recommendations to improve business reporting. A major recommendation was that standard setters should develop a comprehensive model of business reporting, focusing on factors that create longer-term value and including financial and non-financial measures to cope with rapid changes, e.g. in technology and competition.

The committee identified that users had a high interest in being able to identify:

● **trends,** e.g. from five-year summaries of key statistics, separate reporting of segments and core and non-core assets and liabilities information;

● **substance of transactions,** e.g. accounting for off balance sheet transactions, complex capital instruments and investments in unconsolidated entities;

● **significant risks** arising from uncertainties over the valuation of assets and liabilities.

The committee identified that the users had a lower interest in:

● the variety of income theories;

● the valuation of intangible assets;

● accounting for combinations.

The committee identified user interest in a number of non-financial areas:

● the corporate strategy in general terms;

● the strengths, weaknesses, opportunities and threats (SWOTs) to the company;

● performance measures that management use with an explanation of reasons for changes and trends;

● management plans and degree to which achieved;

● information about the directors and management and their remuneration packages.

A review of the recommendations broadly supports the stance being taken by the IASC, with mandatory standards being introduced for the financial statements and voluntary disclosures for non-financial areas, e.g. management reports. Auditors check that the comments made in the management reports do not give a picture that conflicts with the financial statements. The following is an extract from the audit report of KPMG Austria Gmbh on the 2000 Annual Report of EVN AG (an IAS compliant company):

> We confirm that the Management Report complies with the consolidated statements and that the legal requirements are met to exempt EVN AG from the obligation to compile financial statements in accordance with the Austrian commercial code.

7.6 ICAS *Making Corporate Reports Valuable*

In 1988, following a major research project by its Research Committee, the Institute of Chartered Accountants of Scotland (ICAS) published the *Making Corporate Reports Valuable (MCRV)*[14] report. The general objective of MCRV was to stimulate discussion that would lead to improvements in corporate reporting. The long-term purpose was that reports should be produced that would be better able to assist the user in gauging management performance and assessing an entity's prospects; reports that were more understandable, less daunting in presentation, more readable and with as little technical jargon as possible.

In pursuit of this goal *MCRV* formulated the Research Committee's views on meeting the needs of management and investors. It considered company strategy and planning, the need for clear financial statements covering such areas as entity objectives, present financial wealth, changes in financial wealth, operations, distributable wealth, cash flow and segmental information.

The report criticised historical cost accounting and supported the use of a current value system. It also advocated the publication of projected results so that the user would have available the preceding year's figures, the current year's and the subsequent year's.

To its credit, the Research Committee demonstrated that its proposals could be applied in practice by preparing the financial statements of Melody plc and obtaining feedback from the preparers of the accounts. These were published in 1990 and are perhaps a prototype of what financial statements might look like in the future.

The balance sheet was described as a statement of assets and liabilities and was a value statement. Assets, including stock, were revalued in current terms, thus breaking away from the historical cost philosophy. The net assets at the end of the period were the financial wealth generated by operations plus any increase in the realisable value of financial wealth.

The profit and loss account was described as an operations statement and, by including stock at market value, produced a residual figure called financial wealth generated by operations.

The annual report also contained a statement of cash flow, a value added statement, a chairman's review, a directors' report and a document referred to as 'Management's discussions and analysis of financial conditions and results of operations' for the year under review, supplemented by the financial plans for the following year.

The auditors' report appears as the 'Report of the independent assessors'. It is addressed to the members, creditors and employees of Melody plc and is more informative than the traditional short-form report favoured in the UK.

Another statement that makes its debut spells out 'responsibility for the financial statements'. It informs the user that the ultimate responsibility lies with the directors, and in doing so it also explains the role of the independent assessors and the nature of their report.

MCRV is a useful addition to our experience of financial reporting and its influence will no doubt be felt as the standard setters move towards dealing with the problem of an appropriate measurement base.

It might be useful at this point to list some of the key thoughts in *MCRV*:

Representation of position

● Accounts should aim to portray economic reality.

● Substance over form is emphasised.

● The investors need the same information as the management.

Income

● It is against excessive emphasis on the bottom line with a single earnings figure.

● It emphasises the balance sheet rather than accruals-based income. Income is seen as a reconciliation between consecutive balance sheets expressed in current values.

Capital maintenance

● It takes a proprietary view in seeking to maintain the owners' purchasing power using a consumer price index.

Measurement base

● It supports the use of net realisable values.

Summary

Directors and accountants are constrained by a mass of rules and regulations which govern the measurement, presentation and disclosure of financial information. Regulations are derived from three major sources: the legislature in the form of statutes, the accountancy profession in the form of standards, and the Financial Services Authority in the form of Listing Rules.

There have been a number of reports relating to financial reporting. The preparation and presentation of financial statements continue to evolve. Steps are being taken to provide a conceptual framework and there is growing international agreement on the setting of standards.

User needs have been accepted as paramount; qualitative characteristics of information have been specified; the elements of financial statements have been defined precisely; the presentation of financial information has been prescribed; and comparability between companies is seen as desirable.

However, the intention remains to produce financial statements that present a true and fair view. This is not achieved by detailed rules and regulations, and the exercise of judgement will continue to be needed. This opens the way for creative accounting practices that bring financial reporting and the accounting profession into disrepute. Strenuous efforts will continue to be needed from the auditors, the ASB, the Review Panel and the Financial Reporting Council to contain the use of unacceptable practices. The regulatory bodies show that they have every intention of accepting the challenge.

The question of the measurement base that should be used has yet to be settled. The measurement question still remains a major area of financial reporting that needs to be addressed.

The Framework sees the objective of financial statements as providing information about the financial position, performance and financial adaptability of an enterprise that is useful to a wide range of users in making economic decisions. It recognises that they are limited because they largely show the financial effects of past events and do not necessarily show non-financial information. On the question of measurement the view has been expressed that

> historical cost has the merit of familiarity and (to some extent) objectivity; current values have the advantage of greater relevance to users of the accounts who wish to assess the current state or recent performance of the business, but they may sometimes be unreliable or too expensive to provide. It concludes that practice should develop by evolving in the direction of greater use of current values to the extent that this is consistent with the constraints of reliability, cost and acceptability to the financial community.[15]

There are critics[16] who argue that the concern with recording current asset values rather than historical costs means that

> the essential division between the IASC and its critics is one between those who are more concerned about where they want to be and those who want to be very clear about where they are now. It is a division between those who see the purpose of financial statements as taking economic decisions about the future, and those who see it as a basis for making management accountable and for distributing the rewards among the stakeholders.

Finally, it is interesting to give some thought to extracts from two publications which indicate that there is still a long way to go in the evolution of financial reporting, and that there is little room for complacency.

The first is from *The Future Shape of Financial Reports*:

> As Solomons[17] and *Making Corporate Reports Valuable* discussed in detail, the then system of financial reporting in the UK fails to satisfy the purpose of providing information to shareholders, lenders and others to appraise past performance in order to form expectations about an organisation's future performance in five main respects:
>
> 1 ... measures of performance ... are based on original or historical costs ...
> 2 Much emphasis is placed on a single measure of earnings per share ...
> 3 ... insufficient attention is paid to changes in an enterprise's cash or liquidity position ...
> 4 The present system is essentially backward looking ...
> 5 Emphasis is often placed on the legal form rather than on the economic substance of transactions ... .[18]

We have seen that some of these five limitations are being addressed, but not all, e.g. the provision of projected figures.

The second extract is from *Making Corporate Reports Valuable*:

> The present balance sheet almost defies comprehension. Assets are shown at depreciated historical cost, at amounts representing current valuations and at the results of revaluations of earlier periods (probably also depreciated); that is there is no consistency whatsoever in valuation practice. The sum total of the assets, therefore, is meaningless and combining it with the liabilities to show the entity's financial position does not in practice achieve anything worthwhile.[19]

The IASC has taken steps to deal with the frequency of revaluations but the criticism still holds in that there will continue to be financial statements produced incorporating mixed measurement bases.

The point made by some critics remains unresolved:

> Accountability and the IASC's decision usefulness are not compatible. Forward-looking decisions require forecasts of future cash flows, which in the economic model are what determines the values of assets. These values are too subjective to form the basis of accountability. The definition of assets and the recognition rules restrict assets to economic benefits the enterprise controls as a result of past events and that are measurable with sufficient reliability. But economic decision making requires examination of all sources of future cash flows, not just a restricted sub-set of them.[20]

The need for a conceptual framework is being addressed around the world. In the USA, Australia, Canada, the UK and the IASC, the approach has been the same, i.e. commencing with a consideration of the objectives of financial statements, qualitative characteristics of financial information, definition of the elements, and when these are to be recognised in the financial statements. There is a general agreement on these areas.

REVIEW QUESTIONS

1 (a) Name the user groups and information needs of the user groups identified by the IASC *Framework for the Presentation and Preparation of Financial Statements*.
   (b) Discuss the effect of the *Framework* on current financial reporting practice.

2 Give a brief synopsis of the ICAS *Making Corporate Reports Valuable*.

3 R. MacVe in *A Conceptual Framework for Financial Accounting and Reporting: The Possibilities for an Agreed Structure* suggested that the search for a conceptual framework was a political process. Discuss the effect that this thinking has had and will have on standard setting.

4 (a) In 1999 in the UK, the ASB published the *Statement of Principles*. Explain what you consider to be the purpose and status of the *Statement*.

(b) Chapter 4 of the *Statement* identifies and defines what the ASB believes to be the elements that make up financial statements. Define any four of the elements and explain how, in your opinion, the identification and definition of the elements of financial statements would enhance financial reporting.

(c) Chapter 5 of the *Statement* states that matching is not regarded as the driver of the recognition process. Explain what is meant by this and its probable effect in practice.

5 'The replacement of accrual accounting with cash flow accounting would avoid the need for a conceptual framework.'[21] Discuss.

6 Financial accounting theory has accumulated a vast literature. A cynic might be inclined to say that the vastness of the literature is in sharp contrast to its impact on practice.

(a) Describe the different approaches that have evolved in the development of accounting theory.

(b) Assess its impact on standard setting.

(c) Discuss the contribution of accounting theory to the understanding of accounting practice, and suggest contributions that it might make in the future.

EXERCISES

An extract from the solution is provided in the Appendix at the end of the text for exercises marked with an asterisk (*).

* Question 1

The following information is available in relation to MCRV Ltd (based on the ICAS Report) for the year ending 31 December 20X8:

(a) Statement of assets and liabilities as at 31 December. This statement at the start of the year is assumed to contain valuations at net realisable value throughout:

(i) Fixed assets are estimated by the directors on the basis of an orderly disposal in a second-hand market.

(ii) The NRV of raw materials was assumed by the directors to be the same as their purchase price.

(iii) The NRV of finished goods was estimated as selling price less the estimated costs of disposal in the normal course of business.

(b) A summary of the cash book.

(c) The non-cash transactions during the year are as shown in the journal entries.

Statement of assets and liabilities as at 31 December

	20X7	20X8
	£	£
Fixed assets	200	270
Current assets		
Stock	50	66
Debtors	30	40
Cash	10	76
	290	452
Less:		
Current liabilities		
Creditors	35	30
Long-term loans	60	70
	95	100
	195	352

Cash transactions during the year ended 31 December 20X8

	£	£
Cash received during 20X8:		
Credit customers		190
Long-term loans		30
		220
Cash paid during 20X8:		
Credit suppliers	85	
Fixed assets	30	
Salaries	30	
Loan interest	9	
		154
		66

Journal entries for non-cash transactions for the year ended 31 December 20X8

	Dr	Cr
	£	£
Debtors	200	
Sales		200
Credit sales for 20X8		
Stock	80	
Creditors		80
Credit purchases for 20X8		
Cost of goods sold	70	
Stock		70

*Journal Entries for Non-cash Transactions for the year ended
31 December 20X8*

	Dr £	Cr £
Goods used for sale		
Stock	6	
Cost of goods sold – being uplift in closing stock from cost to net realisable value		6

Required:

(a) Prepare an operations statement for the year ended 31 December 20X8 to show wealth created by operations.

(b) Prepare a statement of changes in wealth, in the following format:

Increase in wealth due to operations

Increase in value of fixed assets

Decrease in value of long-term loans _____

Realisable increase in net assets _____

(c) Explain circumstances in which there can be a decrease in the value of long-term loans.

(d) Explain how the percentage return on capital employed, current ratio and acid test ratio based on the historical cost concept would differ from those calculated using the concept applied in the above question.

(Adapted from extract in Melody plc annual report (ICAS))

Question 2

The following extract is from *Conceptual Framework for Financial Accounting and Reporting: Elements of Financial Statements and Their Measurement*, FASB 3, December 1976.

> The benefits of achieving agreement on a conceptual framework for financial accounting and reporting manifest themselves in several ways. Among other things, a conceptual framework can (1) guide the body responsible for establishing accounting standards, (2) provide a frame of reference for resolving accounting questions in the absence of a specific promulgated standard, (3) determine bounds for judgement in preparing financial statements, (4) increase financial statement users' understanding of and confidence in financial statements, and (5) enhance comparability.

Required:

(a) Define a conceptual framework.

(b) Critically examine why the benefits provided in the above statements are likely to flow from the development of a conceptual framework for accounting.

Question 3

The following extract is from 'Comments of Leonard Spacek', in R.T. Sprouse and M. Moonitz, *A Tentative Set of Broad Accounting Principles for Business Enterprises*, Accounting Research Study No. 3, AICPA, New York, 1962, reproduced in A. Belkaoui, *Accounting Theory*, Harcourt Brace Jovanovich.

> A discussion of assets, liabilities, revenue and costs is premature and meaningless until the basic principles that will result in a fair presentation of the facts in the form of financial accounting and financial reporting are determined. This fairness of accounting and reporting must be for and to people, and these people represent the various segments of our society.

Required:
(a) Explain the term 'fair'.
(b) Discuss the extent to which the IASC conceptual framework satisfies the above definition.

Question 4

The following is an extract from *Accountancy Age*, 25 January 2001.

> A powerful and 'shadowy' group of senior partners from the seven largest firms has
> emerged to move closer to edging control of accounting standards from the world's
> accountancy regulators ... they form the Global Steering Committee ... The GSC has
> worked on plans to improve standards for the last two years after scathing criticism from
> investors that firms produced varying standards of audit in different countries.

Discuss the effect on standard setting if control were to be edged from the world's accountancy
regulators.

References

1 IFAD refer to www.ifad.net.
2 *Framework for the Preparation and Presentation of Financial Statements*, IASC, 1989, Preface.
3 IAS 17 revised, *Leases*, IASC, 1994.
4 D. Solomons, *Guidelines for Financial Reporting Standards*, ICAEW, 1989, p. 32.
5 *Statement of Principles for Financial Reporting*, ASB, 1999.
6 *Ibid.*, para. 3.27.
7 FRS 6 *Acquisition and Mergers*, ASB, 1994.
8 *Statement of Principles for Financial Reporting*, ASB, 1999, para. 5.10.
9 *Ibid.*, para. 6.42.
10 *Ibid.*, para. 6.25.
11 *Statement of Principles for Financial Reporting*, ASB, 1995, para. 5.37.
12 IAS 16 *Property, Plant and Equipment*, IASC, revised 1998, para. 34.
13 *Improving Business Reporting – A Customer Focus: Meeting the Information Needs of Investors and
   Creditors*, AICPA, 1994.
14 *Making Corporate Reports Valuable*, ICAS, 1988.
15 A. Lennard, 'The peg on which standards hang', *Accountancy*, January 1996, p. 80.
16 S. Fearnley and M. Page, 'Why the ASB has lost its bearings', *Accountancy*, April 1996,
   p. 94.
17 D. Solomons, *op. cit.*
18 J. Arnold *et al.*, *The Future Shape of Financial Reports*, ICAEW/ICAS, 1991.
19 *Making Corporate Reports Valuable*, ICAS, 1988, p. 35.
20 S. Fearnley and M. Page, *loc. cit.*
21 R. Skinner, *Accountancy*, January 1990, p. 25.

CHAPTER 8

Published accounts of companies

8.1 Introduction

Each company sends an annual report and accounts to its shareholders. It is the means by which the directors are accountable for their stewardship of the assets and their handling of the company's affairs for the **past year**. It consists of financial data which may have been audited and narrative comment which may be reviewed by the auditors to check that it does not present a picture that differs from the financial data (i.e. that the narrative is not misleading).

The financial data consist of four financial statements. These are the income statement, balance sheet, cash flow statement and statement of changes in equity – supported by appropriate explanatory notes, e.g. showing the make-up of inventories and the movement in non-current assets. In addition, public listed companies are required to provide segmental reports.

The narrative report from the directors satisfies two needs: (a) to explain what has been achieved in the current year and (b) to assist existing and potential investors to make their own predictions of cash flows of future years.

The current year

The directors' report or management report might contain items such as:

● investor data, e.g. market conditions, share issues, share splits, buybacks, company's share price movements, highs/lows and price relative to the market, dividend per share and dividend cover;

● macro data, e.g. the economic climate, currency fluctuations;

● company data such as:
  – key figures/financial highlights, e.g. incoming orders, turnover, EBIT, EBT, net income, employees
  – key ratios, e.g. sales growth, operating margins, return on equity
  – sales performance in key markets
  – explanations of unusual movements in financial data, e.g. why receivables have increased significantly.

Future cash flows

Investors need information to form their view on future cash flows which will be the basis for dividend payouts and capital gains. Directors provide selective information which they see as significant and relevant on items such as:

- capital investment programme;
- changes in production capacity, e.g. new facilities coming on stream, relocation to lower cost areas;
- research and development plans, e.g. new development agreements and alliances;
- prognosis, e.g. directors expect to increase sales by 5% to 7% in the current financial year, with even stronger growth in earnings, provided no unforeseen events occur;
- corporate strategy, e.g. how to deal with any low profitability segments, possible divestments or acquisitions.

In this chapter we consider public listed companies, i.e. companies that have their shares traded on a recognised stock exchange. We use extracts from the Annual Reports and Notes on Accounts of the Nestlé Group and Findel plc as main illustrations. We will consider the following:

- a company's financial calendar;
- the income statement:
  - criteria for the information that is published
  - format of the income statement required by format 1 and format 2
  - classification of costs in the income statement – does it matter under which heading a cost is classified provided it is not omitted?
  - treatment of discontinuing operations;
- the balance sheet:
  - format of the balance sheet
  - accounting rules for asset valuation;
- the statement of changes in equity:
  - rationale and format;
- segment reporting:
  - effect of IAS 14 *Segment Reporting* on presentation;
- accounting policies:
  - disclosure requirements
  - effect of different policies on analysis of the accounts;
- additional information in annual reports:
  - directors'/management reports;
- IFRS 1 *First-time Adoption of International Accounting Standards*.

8.2 A public company's financial calendar

The ownership and management of a public company whose shares are listed on a stock exchange are separate. The owners or shareholders are provided with regular information for stewardship accountability and to allow them to make investment decisions. Each company follows its own financial calendar, often published as a financial calendar or key dates.

Important dates 2004 for the Nestlé Group (as published in the 2003 annual report)

21 April 2004   Announcement of first quarter 2004 sales figures

22 April 2004   137th Ordinary General Meeting, 'Palais de Beaulieu', Lausanne

28 April 2004	Payment of the dividend
18 August 2004	Publication of the half-yearly report January/June 2004
21 October 2004	Announcement of first nine months' 2004 sales figures
	Autumn press conference

Note:

- The above key dates are for a Swiss company, and therefore at each event Swiss legal requirements must be followed. Different countries do have different legal requirements, but the principle of issuing a financial calendar remains across companies in other countries.

- The planned programme of communication with institutional investors and analysts is in recognition of the fact that the market hates surprises and share price is strengthened by regular communication.

8.3 Criteria for information appearing in a published income statement and balance sheet

There are four criteria to consider:

- the format complies with IAS 1 and/or any national statutory requirements;
- the accounting policies comply with appropriate IASs or any national statutory requirements;
- there are appropriate notes;
- the financial statements present a fair view of the profits and of the assets and liabilities.

We comment on each of these in turn.

8.4 The prescribed formats – the income statement

IAS 1 is not prescriptive in how an income statement is presented. The IASB appreciate that different layouts may be needed by different businesses in order for them to present fairly their results. Having said this, there are requirements for items that must be presented on the face of the income statement, and also for the structure of expenses within the income statements.

The minimum information content on the face of the income statement is:

(i) revenue;

(ii) finance costs;

(iii) share of the profit or loss of associates and joint ventures accounted for using the equity method;

(iv) pre-tax gain or loss recognised on the disposal of assets or settlement of liabilities attributable to discontinuing operations;

(v) tax expense;

(vi) profit or loss.

The following must also be disclosed on the face of the income statement as allocations of profit or loss for the period:

(i)   profit or loss attributable to minority interest; and

(ii) profit or loss attributable to equity holders of the parent.

The minimum information does not contain the detail of income and expenses, but this information must be presented in the notes to the accounts at least. Most businesses are likely to put some detail of these on the face of the income statement.

IAS 1 allows a company to choose between two formats for detailing income and expenses. The two choices allow for the analysis of costs in different ways: according to function, e.g. cost of sales, distribution costs and administration expenses, or according to nature, e.g. raw materials, wages and depreciation. The formats[1] are as follows:

Format 1: Vertical with costs analysed according to function.
Format 2: Vertical with costs analysed according to nature.

Many companies use Format 1 (unless there is any national requirement to use Format 2) with the costs analysed according to function. If this format is used the information regarding the nature of expenditure (e.g. raw materials, wages and depreciation) must be disclosed in a note to the accounts.

8.5 What information is required to be disclosed in Format 1 and Format 2?

An illustration of an income statement using the two IAS 1 formats is set out in Figure 8.1. Note that in both formats the same amount is disclosed for profit from operations and the two statements are identical after that point.

8.5.1 Classification of operating expenses and other income by function as in Format 1

In order to arrive at its operating profit, a company needs to classify all of the operating expenses of the business into one of four categories:

● cost of sales

● distribution and selling costs

● administrative expenses

● other operating income.

We comment briefly on each to explain how a company might classify its trading transactions. This will also indicate how the same transaction might be classified differently by different companies and so result in a different gross profit figure. It does not affect inter-period comparisons but it is important to remember when making inter-company comparisons.

Figure 8.1 Illustration of Formats 1 and 2

Format 1 Classification of expense by function	£000	Format 2 Classification of expense by nature	£000
Revenue	1,000	Revenue	1,000
Cost of sales	400		
Gross profit	600		
Other operating income	20	Other operating income	20
Distribution costs	(120)		
Administrative expenses	(70)		
		Changes in inventories of finished goods and work-in-progress	20
		Work performed by enterprise and capitalised	125
		Raw materials and consumables	(140)
		Staff costs	(205)
		Depreciation and amortisation	(110)
		Other operating expenses	(280)
Profit from operations	430		430
Finance cost	(26)		(26)
Income from associates	27		27
Profit before tax	431		431
Income tax expense	130		130
Net profit for the period	301		301

Note:

● Changes in inventories of finished goods and work-in-progress in this example are negative because the closing inventories were less than the opening inventories. The changes will be positive if the closing inventories are greater than the opening inventories.

● If a company classifies expense by function, it is required to also disclose information on the classification of expense by nature, including depreciation and amortisation expenses and staff costs – these are useful in predicting future cash flows and are necessary if preparing a Value Added Statement.

8.6 Cost of sales

Expenditure classified under cost of sales will typically include direct costs, overheads, depreciation and amortisation expense and adjustments. The items that might appear under each heading are:

● **Direct costs:**
direct materials purchased; direct labour; other external charges that comprise production costs from external sources, e.g. equipment rental and subcontracting costs.

- **Overheads:**
  variable production overheads; fixed production overheads.
- **Depreciation and amortisation:**
  depreciation of fixed assets used in production; impairment expense; exceptional amounts written off inventory; research costs and development costs.
- **Adjustments:**
  - **Change between the opening and closing inventory**. If closing inventory is less than opening inventory, the reduction must have been sold and the cost of sales will be increased by the amount that the inventory has fallen. Conversely, if closing inventory is more than opening inventory, the amount by which it has increased will not be included as a cost of the current period's sales.
  - **Capitalisation of own work as a non-current asset**. Any amount of the costs listed above that have been incurred in the construction of non-current assets for retention by the company will not appear as an expense in the income statement: it will be capitalised. Any amount capitalised in this way would be treated for accounting purposes as a non-current asset and depreciated.
  - **Capitalisation of own work as a deferred asset**. Any amount of the costs listed above that needs to be deferred to a future accounting period because the benefits of the expenditure can be reasonably matched with revenue expected in a future period, e.g. development expenditure capitalised under IAS 38, would be treated for accounting purposes as a deferred asset and expensed by matching with the revenue as it arises in the future accounting periods. IAS 38 is considered in detail in Chapter 18.
  - **Treatment of variances from standard**. Where a company uses a standard costing system, the variances can either be transferred in total to the income statement or be allocated to the cost of sales and the inventory. Any variance allocated to the inventory will have an impact on the results of a subsequent period. (This aspect is considered in Chapter 19.)

8.6.1 Why cost of sales figures may not be comparable between companies

The cost of sales figure is derived under the accrual accounting concept. This means that (a) the cash flows have been adjusted by the management in order to arrive at the expense that management considers to be associated with the sales achieved; and (b) additional adjustments may have been made to increase the cost of sales if the net realisable value of the closing inventory is less than cost. Clearly, when management adjust the cash flow figures they are exercising their judgement, and it is impossible to ensure that the management of two companies faced with the same economic activity would arrive at the same adjustment. We will now consider the following reasons for differences in calculating the cost of sales: treatment of direct costs; choice of depreciation policy; management attitudes; and the accounting system capability.

8.6.2 Differences arising from the treatment of direct costs

Different companies may assume different physical flows when calculating the cost of direct materials used in production. This will affect the inventory valuation. One company may assume a first-in-first-out (FIFO) flow, where the cost of sales is charged for raw materials used in production as if the first items purchased were the first items used in production. Another company may use a weighted average basis. This is illustrated in Figure 8.2 for a company that started trading on 1 January 20X1 without any opening inventory and sold 40,000 items on 31 March 20X1 for £4 per item.

Figure 8.2   Effect on cost of sales of using FIFO and weighted average

	Items	£	FIFO £	Weighted average £
Raw materials purchased				
On 1 Jan 20X1 at £1 per item	20,000	20,000		
On 1 Feb 20X1 at £2 per item	20,000	40,000		
On 1 Mar 20X1 at £3 per item	20,000	60,000		
On 1 Mar 20X1 in stock	60,000	120,000	120,000	120,000
On 31 Mar 20X1 in stock	20,000		60,000	40,000
Cost of sales	40,000		60,000	80,000

FIFO inventory is 20,000 items at a cost of £3 per item, assuming that the purchases made on 1 January 20X1 and 1 February 20X1 were sold first. Weighted average inventory is 20,000 items at a cost of £2 per item, being the total cost of £120,000 divided by 60,000, the total number of items at the date of the sale.

Figure 8.3   Effect of physical stock flow assumptions on the percentage gross profit

	Items	FIFO £	Weighted average £	% difference in gross profit
Sales	40,000	160,000	160,000	
Cost of sales	40,000	60,000	80,000	
		100,000	80,000	
Gross profit %		62.5%	50%	25%!

The effect on the gross profit percentage would be as shown in Figure 8.3. This demonstrates that, even from a single difference in accounting treatment, the gross profit for the same transaction could be materially different in both absolute and percentage terms.

How can the investor determine the effect of different assumptions?

Although companies are required to disclose their inventory valuation policy, the level of detail provided varies and we are not able to quantify the effect of different inventory valuation policies. For example, compare the accounting policy of AstraZeneca in Figure 8.4 with that of Findel plc in Figure 8.5. In the latter case, we are not even aware of the definition of cost that the company is actually using.

Figure 8.4   AstraZeneca accounting policy for stock valuation (2003 annual report)

Stocks are stated at the lower of cost and net realisable value and raw materials and other stocks at the lower of cost or replacement price. The first in, first out or an average method of valuation is used. In determining cost, depreciation is included but selling expenses and certain overhead expenses (principally central administration costs) are excluded. Net realisable value is determined as estimated selling price less costs of disposal.

Figure 8.5   Findel plc accounting policy for stocks (2002 annual report)

Stocks are stated at the lower of cost and net realisable value.

Note also that both companies are UK-based. In the UK, 'stock' is a common alternative term for inventory as used in international accounting standards.

While we can carry out academic exercises as in Figure 8.3 and we are aware of the effect of different inventory valuation policies on the level of profits, there is no way in real life that we can be certain of being able to carry out such an exercise.

8.6.3 Differences arising from the choice of depreciation policy

The charge made for depreciation might vary because of different approaches:

● methods, e.g. straight-line or reducing balance;

● assumptions on productive use, e.g. different assessments of the economic life of an asset;

● carrying values, e.g. at cost or at revaluation;

● assumptions of total cost to be expensed, e.g. different assumptions about the residual value of an asset.

8.6.4 Differences arising from management attitudes

Losses might be anticipated and measured at a different rate. For example, when assessing the likelihood of the net realisable value of inventory falling below the cost figure, the management decision will be influenced by the optimism with which it views the future of the economy, the industry and the company. There could also be other influences, e.g. remuneration packages based on net income or preparation of the company for a buy-out by management.

8.6.5 Differences arising from the capability of the accounting system to provide data

Accounting systems within companies differ, e.g. costs that are collected by one company may well not be collected by another company. For example, the costs of some activities may be spread across a number of departments and different expenditure types, e.g. the cost of researching, sourcing and testing new materials for use in a production process. If it is not practicable to collect the information, consistency of presentation of this type of expenditure may not be possible. This could also affect assessment and comparison of segment performance.

8.7 Distribution costs

These are costs incurred after the production of the finished article and up to and including transfer of the goods to the customer. Expenditure classified under this heading will typically include the following:

- warehousing costs associated with the operation of the premises, e.g. rent, rates, insurance, utilities, depreciation, repairs and maintenance; wage costs, e.g. gross wages and pension contributions of warehouse staff;
- promotion costs, e.g. advertising, trade shows;
- selling costs, e.g. salaries, commissions and pension contributions of sales staff; costs associated with the premises, e.g. rent, rates; cash discounts on sales; travelling and entertainment;
- transport costs, e.g. gross wages and pension contributions of transport staff, vehicle costs, e.g. running, maintenance, depreciation.

8.8 Administrative expenses

These are all those operating costs that have not been classified as either cost of sales or distribution costs. Expenditure classified under this heading *will* typically include:

- administration, e.g. salaries, commissions, and pension contributions of administration staff; costs associated with the premises, e.g. rent, rates; amounts written off the receivables that appear in the balance sheet under current assets; professional fees.

8.9 Other operating income

Under this heading a company discloses material income derived from ordinary activities of the business that have not been included in the revenue figure. If the amounts are not material, they would not be separately disclosed but included within the revenue figure. Income classified under this heading will typically include the following:

- income derived from intangible assets, e.g. royalties, commissions;
- income derived from third-party use of property, plant and equipment that is surplus to the current productive needs of the company;
- income received from employees, e.g. canteen, recreation fees.

8.10 What costs and income are brought into account after calculating the trading profit in order to arrive at the profit on ordinary activities before tax?

We have explained the four categories of cost and other income that are taken into account when calculating the trading profit. In order to arrive at the profit on ordinary activities before tax, income from investments and loans is required to be disclosed separately and not included with the other income – unless, of course, the investment or loan income is not material and is included within the other operating income for convenience.

8.11 Does it really matter under which heading a cost is classified in the income statement provided it is not omitted?

This depends on how readers of the accounts use the gross profit and trading profit figures. An examination of annual reports indicates that directors usually make less reference to the gross profit figure and instead draw attention to the operating profit (or trading profit) figure. Operating profit is used to calculate the return on capital employed, as illustrated by the extract from the BOC Group annual report for 2004 where the return on capital for 2004 was 14.9% defined as operating profit, as a percentage of average capital employed.

8.12 Discontinued operations disclosure in the income statement

IFRS 5 *Non-Current Assets Held for Sale and Discontinued Operations* is one of the outcomes of the joint short-term project to reduce differences between IFRSs and US GAAP. It follows the IASB's consideration of FASB Statement No. 144 *Accounting for the Impairment or Disposal of Long-Lived Assets* (SFAS 144) which deals with the classification and presentation of discontinued operations.

The objective is[2] to help users evaluate the financial effects of discontinued operations, e.g. when making projections of future cash flows, earnings-generating capacity and the financial position.

IFRS 5 replaces IAS 35 *Discontinuing Operations* and provides that:

● an operation is classified as discontinued at the date the operation meets the criteria to be classified as held for sale or when the entry has disposed of the operation;

● the results of discontinued operations are to be shown separately on the face of the income statement; and

● an operation cannot be retrospectively classified as discontinued if the criteria for that classification are not met until after the balance sheet date.

8.12.1 Definition of discontinued operations

A discontinued operation[3] is a component of an entity that either has been disposed of, or is classified as held for sale, and

(a) represents a separate major line of business or geographical area of operations as reported in accordance with IAS 14

(b) is part of a single co-ordinated plan to dispose of a separate major line of business or geographical area of operations, or

(c) is a subsidiary acquired exclusively with a view to resale.

Definition of a component

The IFRS defines a component as one which comprises operations and cash flows that can be clearly distinguished, operationally and for financial reporting purposes, from the rest of the entity, e.g. a cash-generating unit or a group of cash-generating units, while being held for use.

Definition of held for sale

It would be attractive for managers to be able to separate out loss-making operations in the Annual Report to present a better picture to shareholders, whilst taking cost reduction measures to bring a division or segment back to profitability. In order to stop enterprises classifying activities as held for resale when it is not appropriate, IFRS 5 defines a disposal group as held for sale if its carrying amount will be recovered principally through a sale transaction rather than through continuing use. It further provides that the disposal group must be available for immediate sale in its present condition and its sale must be **highly probable**.

For the sale to be highly probable requires that:

● the appropriate level of management must be committed to a plan to sell the disposal group;

● an active programme to locate a buyer and complete the plan must have been initiated;

● the disposal group must be actively marketed for sale at a price that is reasonable in relation to its current fair value;

● the sale should be expected to qualify for recognition as a completed sale within one year from the date of classification;

● actions required to complete the plan should indicate that it is unlikely that significant changes to the plan will be made or that the plan will be withdrawn.

There is a pragmatic recognition that there may be events outside the control of the enterprise which prevent completion within one year. In such a case the held for sale classification is retained, provided there is sufficient evidence that the entity remains committed to its plan to sell the disposal group and has taken all reasonable steps to resolve the delay.

8.12.2 Disclosure of activities

Disclosure in the year of disposal

The financial statements should disclose[4] the following:

(a) a single amount on the face of the income statement comprising the total of:
  (i) the post-tax profit or loss of discontinued operations; and
  (ii) the post-tax gain or loss recognised on the measurement to fair value less cost to sell or on the disposal of the assets or disposal group(s) constituting the discontinued operation.
(b) an analysis of the single amount in (a) into:
  (i) the revenue, expenses and pre-tax profit or loss of discontinued operations;
  (ii) the related income tax expense as required by IAS 12;
  (iii) the gain or loss recognised on the measurement to fair value less costs to sell or

on the disposal of the assets or disposal group(s) constituting the discontinued operation; and

(iv) the related income tax expense as required by IAS 12.

(c) the net cash flows attributable to the operating, investing and financing activities of discontinued operations.

The disclosures required by (b) and (c) may be given in the notes to the accounts.

If the criteria for defining as held for sale are met after the balance sheet date but before the authorisation of the financial statements for issue, disclosures are also required in the notes.

Figure 8.6   Extract from the notes of Barlow Ltd

Note 12 Discontinued Operations

During the year certain distinguishable business operations of the group were discontinued. The following information relates thereto:

	1999	1998
Loss on discontinuance [since date of discontinuance and shown as an exceptional item in note 6]		
Gross loss on discontinuance	(105)	(487)
Taxation	9	10
	(96)	(477)
Aggregate summarised balance sheets		
Assets remaining at year end	403	1,189
Liabilities remaining at year end	159	295

The results of discontinued operations arising prior to the effective date of discontinuance and included in the income statement as being from ordinary operations are:

Revenue	1,834
Loss before taxation	(51)
Taxation credit	27
Loss after taxation	(24)
Outside shareholders' interest	7
Attributable loss to ordinary shareholders	(17)

Discontinued operation	Segment	Date of discontinuance	Method of discontinuance
Federated Blakie	Building material	30 June 1998	Sale
Barlow Paper	Paper	31 July 1998	Sale
Eurofilters	Paper	31 July 1998	Sale
Bartons Precision Tube	Steel tube	1 October 1998	Sale
Princetown (Pty) Ltd	Handling	1 October 1998	Sale

Disclosures in subsequent years

Any adjustments made in the current period to amounts previously presented in discontinued operations are required to be classified separately in discontinued operations. Such adjustments may arise as a result of:

(a) the resolution of uncertainties arising subsequent to the disposal, e.g. adjustments to the purchase price;

(b) the resolution of uncertainties existing prior to the disposal, e.g. environmental and product warrenty obligations retained by the seller;

(c) the settlement of employee benefit plan obligations directly related to the disposal transation.

An example of the type of disclosure for discontinued operations can be seen in Figure 8.6.

8.13 Items requiring separate disclosure

When making their future predictions investors need to be able to identify that part of the net income that is likely to be maintained in the future. IAS 1 *Presentation of Financial Statements* provides assistance to users in this by requiring that certain items are separately disclosed. These are items within the ordinary activities of the enterprise which are of such size, nature or incidence that their separate disclosure is required in the financial statements in order for the financial statements to show a fair view.

These items are not extraordinary and must therefore be presented within the profit from ordinary activities. It is usual to disclose the nature and amount of these items in a note to the financial statements, with no separate mention on the face of the income statement; however, if sufficiently material, they can be disclosed on the face.

Examples of the type of items[5] that may give rise to separate disclosures are:

- the write-down of assets to realisable value or recoverable amount,
- the restructuring of activities of the enterprise, and the reversal of provisions for restructuring,
- disposals of items of property, plant and equipment,
- disposals of long-term investments,
- discontinued operations,
- litigation settlements,
- other reversals of provisions.

8.14 The prescribed formats – the balance sheet

We now explain the prescribed formats for balance sheet presentation, the accounting rules that govern the values at which the various assets are included in the balance sheet and the explanatory notes that are required to accompany the balance sheet.

8.14.1 The prescribed format

IAS 1 specifies which items are to be included on the face of the balance sheet but it does not prescribe the order and presentation that is to be followed. It would be acceptable to present the balance sheet as assets less liabilities equalling equity, or total assets equalling total equity and liabilities. The example given in IAS 1 follows the approach of total assets equalling total equity and liabilities.

The information that must be presented on the face is:

(a) Property, plant and equipment;

(b) Investment property;

(c) Intangible assets;

(d) Financial assets (excluding amounts shown under (e), (h) and (i));

(e) Investments accounted for using the equity method;

(f) Biological assets;

(g) Inventories;

(h) Trade and other receivables;

(i) Cash and cash equivalents;

(j) Trade and other payables;

(k) Provisions;

(l) Financial liabilities (excluding amounts shown under (j) and (k));

(m) Liabilities and assets for current tax, as defined in IAS 12 *Income Taxes*;

(n) Deferred tax liabilities and deferred tax assets, as defined in IAS 12;

(o) Minority interests, presented within equity; and

(p) Issued capital and reserves attributable to equity holders of the parent.

Additional line items may need to be presented if required by another IAS.

IAS 1 does not absolutely prescribe that enterprises need to split assets and liabilities into current and non-current. However, it does state that this split would need to be done if the nature of the business indicates that it is appropriate. In almost all cases it would be appropriate to split items into current and non-current. If an enterprise decides that it is more relevant and reliable not to split the assets and liabilities into current and non-current on the face of the balance sheet, they should be presented broadly in order of their liquidity.

If a liquidity presentation is used, the enterprise must still indicate the amount of all items that is payable or recoverable after more than twelve months.[6]

8.14.2 The accounting rules for asset valuation

International standards provide different valuation rules and some choice exists as to which rules to use. Many of the items in the financial statements are held at historical cost, but variations to this principle may be required by different accounting standards. Some of the different bases are:

Property, plant and equipment	Can be presented at either historical cost or market value depending upon accounting policy chosen from IAS 16.[7]

Financial assets	Certain classes of financial asset are required to be recognised at fair value per IAS 39.[8]
Inventory	IAS 2 requires that this is included at the lower of cost and net realisable value.[9]
Provisions	IAS 37 requires the discounting to present value of some provisions.[10]

8.14.3 What are the explanatory notes that accompany a balance sheet?

We will consider four types. These are (a) notes giving greater detail of the make-up of items that appear in the balance sheet, (b) notes providing additional information, (c) notes drawing attention to the existence of related party transactions and (d) notes giving information of interest to other stakeholders.

Notes giving greater detail of the make-up of balance sheet figures

Each of the alpha headings may have additional detail disclosed by way of a note to the accounts. Some items may have a note of their detailed make-up. For example, inventory of £38.6m in the balance sheet may have a note as follows:

	£m
Raw materials	11.2
Work-in-progress	1.5
Finished goods	25.9
	38.6

Property, plant and equipment normally has a schedule as shown in Figure 8.7. From this the net book value is read off the total column for inclusion in the balance sheet.

Notes giving additional information

These are notes intended to assist in predicting future cash flows. They give information on matters such as capital commitments that have been contracted for but not provided in the accounts, and capital commitments that have been authorised but not contracted for; future commitments, e.g. share options that have been granted; and contingent liabilities, e.g. guarantees given by the company in respect of overdraft facilities arranged by subsidiary companies or customers.

Notes drawing attention to existence of related party transactions

Related party relationships may mean that financial statements include transactions that have not been entered into on an arm's-length basis, which would be the normal assumption made by a user. The objective of IAS 24 *Related Party Disclosures* was to ensure that disclosure drew attention to the fact that the reported financial position and results may have been affected by the existence of related parties and material transactions with them. Disclosure is required of the person controlling the reporting entity and of related party transactions such as purchase or sale of goods, property or other assets; rendering or receiving services; agency arrangements; leasing arrangements; transfer of research and development; licence agreements; provision of finance and management contracts.

Figure 8.7   Nestlé Group – property, plant and equipment movements

Property, plant and equipment
In millions of CHF

	Land and buildings	Machinery and equipment	Tools, furniture and other equipment	Vehicles	2003 Total	2002 Total
Gross value						
At 1 January	11,534	22,320	6,177	766	**40,797**	45,093
Currency retranslation and inflation adjustment	(167)	(253)	(47)	(24)	**(491)**	(5,560)
Expenditure	695	1,824	709	109	**3,337**	3,577
Disposals	(184)	(1,137)	(597)	(92)	**(2,010)**	(2,411)
Modification of the scope of consolidation	12	62	54	17	**145**	98
At 31 December	11,890	22,816	6,296	776	**41,778**	40,797
Accumulated depreciation						
At 1 January	(4,520)	(14,462)	(4,333)	(457)	**(23,772)**	(25,195)
Currency retranslation and inflation adjustment	1	15	40	15	**71**	3053
Depreciation	(351)	(1,232)	(726)	(99)	**(2,408)**	(2,542)
Impairment	(87)	(48)	(12)	(1)	**(148)**	(1,316)
Disposals	78	1,023	588	67	**1,756**	2,040
Modification of the scope of consolidation	69	110	(13)	(4)	**162**	188
At 31 December	(4,810)	(14,594)	(4,456)	(479)	**(24,339)**	(23,772)
Net at 31 December	7,080	8,222	1,840	297	**17,439**	17,025

IAS 24 defines such a related party relationship as existing where one party has direct or indirect control of the other party, or the parties are subject to common control, or one party has such influence over the financial and operating policies of the other party that the other party might be inhibited from pursuing its own separate interests, or the parties entering into a transaction are subject to such influence from the same source that one party has subordinated its own separate interests.

Although related parties include companies in the same group and associated companies, these are subject to specific IASs, e.g. IAS 22, IAS 27 and IAS 28. The principal impact will, therefore, be on directors and their close families, pension funds, key management and those controlling 20% or more of the voting rights.

Notes giving information that is of interest to other stakeholders

We could place the disclosure relating to staff into this category. It is common for enterprises to provide a disclosure of the average number of employees in the period or the number of employees at the end of the period. IAS 1 does not require this information but it is likely that most businesses would provide and categorise the information. The categories could follow the primary segments as in IAS 14, or could follow functions in the business such as production, sales, administration, etc. Suggested forms of presentation are shown in Figure 8.8.

Figure 8.8   Staff costs

Operating profit is stated after charging:

Staff costs   £xxx

The average number of employees during the period was as follows:

	Number employed
Production	XXX
Distribution	XXX
Sales	XXX
Research and development	XXX
Administration	XXX

This shows categorisation by function. Also acceptable would be categorisation by business or geographical segment, or no categorisation at all.

This information is useful in the context of reporting to employees. However, there is no standard form of presenting it, and it is not completely adequate for the prediction of cash flows. Staff cost information is not analysed into the expense headings that are used in the income statement so, although the total cost is given, this is not necessarily broken down into cost of sales, distribution costs and administrative expenses.

8.15 Statement of changes in equity

A primary statement called 'statement of changes in equity' should be presented[11] with the same prominence as the other primary statements. The components should be the gains and losses that are recognised in the period in so far as they are attributable to shareholders. This will take the profit for the year and adjust it for unrealised gains and losses, currency translation differences and prior period adjustments (see Figure 8.9).

When IAS 1 had a major revision in 1997 it placed greater emphasis on the components of income rather than the bottom line. The statement was introduced largely to put the reporting of financial performance on the all-inclusive basis favoured by users, who were concerned that gains and losses were sometimes masked or obscured by reserve accounting, which permits items to bypass the income statement. Not all items in Figure 8.9 will of course always appear for every company.

Figure 8.10 shows an alternative presentation that can be adopted. Instead of showing the statements of changes in equity, enterprises may show a statement of recognised

Figure 8.9   Illustration of the statement of changes in equity

Format 1 – Statement of changes in equity for the year ended 31 December 20X2

	Share capital	Other reserves	Trans-lation reserve	Retained earnings	Total	Minority interest	Total equity
			Attributable to equity holders of the parent				
Balance at 31 December 20X1	x	x	(x)	x	x	x	x
Changes in accounting policy				(x)	(x)	(x)	(x)
Restated balance	x	x	(x)	x	x	x	x
Changes in equity for 20X1							
Gains on property revaluation		x			x	x	x
Available for sale investments:							
Valuation gains/(losses) taken to equity		(x)			(x)		(x)
Transferred to profit or loss on sale		(x)			(x)		(x)
Cash flow hedges:							
Gains/(losses) taken to equity		x			x	x	x
Transferred to profit or loss for the period		x			x	x	x
Transferred to initial carrying amount of hedged items		(x)			(x)		(x)
Exchange differences on translating foreign operations			(x)		(x)	(x)	(x)
Tax on items taken directly to or transferred from equity		(x)	x		(x)	(x)	(x)
Net income recognised directly in equity		x	(x)		x	x	x
Profit for the period				x	x	x	x
Total recognised income and expense for the period		x	(x)	x	x	x	x
Dividends				(x)	(x)	(x)	(x)
Issue of share capital	x				x		x
Equity share options issued		x			x		x
Balance at 31 December 20X2 carried forward	x	x	x	x	x	x	x

Figure 8.10   Illustration of statement of recognised income and expense

Format 2 – Statement of recognised income and expense for the year ended 31 December 20X2

	20X2	20X1
Gain/(loss) on revaluation of properties	(x)	x
Available for sale investments:		
Valuation gains/(losses) taken to equity	(x)	(x)
Transferred to profit or loss on sale	x	(x)
Cash flow hedges:		
Gains/(losses) taken to equity	x	x
Transferred to profit or loss for the period	(x)	x
Transferred to the initial carrying amount of hedged items	(x)	(x)
Exchange differences on translation of foreign operations	(x)	(x)
Tax on items taken directly to or transferred from equity	x	(x)
Net income recognised directly in equity	**(x)**	**x**
Profit for the period	x	x
Total recognised income and expense for the period	**x**	**x**
Attributable to:		
Equity holders of the parent	x	x
Minority interest	x	x
	x	x
Effect of changes in accounting policy:		
Equity holders of the parent		(x)
Minority interest		(x)
		(x)

income and expense. The items to be included in both statements are the same and no particular benefits arise from producing one as opposed to the other. If this format is followed the reconciliation of opening and closing balances of share capital, reserves and accumulated profit is given in the notes to the financial statements.

8.15.1   Why have a statement of changes in equity?

The reason for the statement is that a number of gains and losses are either permitted or required by law or accounting standards to be dealt with directly through reserves. This means that financial statements would be incomplete if they stopped at the retained profit for the year figure without giving the shareholders information about other changes in their equity. The statement includes all gains and losses for the period and not just those that have passed through the income statement.

8.16 Reporting comprehensive income

The IASB in association with the ASB (UK Accounting Standards Board) is undertaking a project to examine the way that income and expenses are reported. This project is ongoing and this summary highlights the position it has reached at the time of writing (February 2005).

The IASB felt that a review of income reporting was required to address a number of problems that had arisen with the current income statement

Figure 8.11 Comprehensive income following a matrix approach

	Total	Before remeasurements	Remeasurements
Revenue	1000	1000	—
Write-down of accounts receivable	(10)	—	(10)
Cost of sales	(400)	(340)	(60)
Selling, general, admin	(250)	(200)	(50)
Operating profit	**340**		
Disposal gain/loss	100	—	100
PPE revaluation	150	—	150
Investment property	—	—	—
Goodwill	(100)	—	(100)
Foreign exchange gain/loss on net investment	(50)	—	(50)
Other business profit	**100**		
Income from associates	50	50	—
Equity investments	(60)	—	(60)
Debt investments	20	5	15
Pension assets	(150)	—	(150)
Financial income	**(140)**		
Business profit	**300**		
Interest on liabilities	(80)	(120)	40
Pension financing expenses	(120)	(200)	80
Financing expense	**(200)**		
Tax	**(30)**	—	—
Discontinued operations	**(10)**	(5)	(5)
Cash flow hedges	**50**	—	50
Comprehensive income	**110**		

used by businesses. The main problems include:

● The IFRSs do not currently define all the items that companies include within income statements, and this leads to inconsistent presentation. For example, operating income is commonly referred to even though it is not defined in the accounting standards.

● Different companies use different measures of earnings, e.g. 'core earnings', or 'earnings before exceptional items', and this leads to non-comparability between companies.

● The income statement includes a variety of items that could be more clearly presented. Simply listing income and expenses could imply a similarity of items that is not really justified.

● There is no conceptual justification for having some items reported in the income statement and others reported in equity.

Because of these problems a new comprehensive income statement is proposed that will more clearly present all items of income and expense and therefore better present performance to the user of the accounts.

Figure 8.12   Remeasurements required by IASs/IFRSs

Standard	Title	Required measurements
IAS 2	Inventories	Write-downs
IAS 11	Construction Contracts	Changes in provisions for future losses, in accordance with IAS 37 on provisions
IAS 16	Property, Plant and Equipment	Revaluations Gains and losses on retirements or disposals
IAS 19	Employee benefit	Actuarial gains and losses, settlements and curtailments
IAS 21	The Effects of Changes in Foreign Exchange Rates	Exchange differences on monetary items Exchange differences on net investment in foreign operations
IAS 29	Financial Reporting in Hyperinflationary Economies	Gain or loss on net monetary position
IAS 37	Provisions, Contingent Liabilities and Contingent Assets	Increases in existing provisions Unused amounts reversed in the period Reversal of discounting
IAS 38	Intangible Assets	Revaluations Gains or losses arising from retirement or disposal
IAS 39	Financial Instruments Recognition and Measurement	All income and expenses except those recognised as interest
IAS 40	Investment property	Gains and losses arising from changes in fair value Gains and losses arising from retirement or disposal
IAS 41	Agriculture	Income or expenses reported separately as price changes
IFRS 5	Discontinued Ooperations	Requirements for measurement are as for continuing operations

8.16.1 The proposed format

The new format follows a 'matrix structure', as shown in Figure 8.11, designed to highlight not only income and expense from different business functions (e.g. operating or financing) but also the type of gain or loss, remeasurement or not. This distinction is important as the IASB believe that the remeasurements column allows this statement to recognise all aspects of income and expense clearly.

A summary of the remeasurements required by existing IASs/IFRSs is shown in Figure 8.12.

8.16.2 US comprehensive income reporting

In the USA the Statement of Financial Accounting Standards No. 130 (SFAS 130) 1997, *Reporting Comprehensive Income*, requires the disclosure of both net income and other comprehensive income (OCI). The OCI statement includes four adjustments, being for unrealised gains and losses on marketable securities, foreign currency translation adjustments, minimum required pension liability adjustments and changes in the market values of certain future contracts used as hedges. The following is an extract from the Annual Report 2003 of Vossloh AG showing in the balance sheet:

	12/31/2002 € million	12/31/2003 € million
Group earnings	52.4	55.0
Accumulated other comprehensive income (OCI)	(4.5)	(5.6)

With a supporting note:

Development of accumulated OCI	Currency translation differences	Pension accruals	Fair values of derivative instruments and securities	Total
Balance at Dec 31, 2001	(2.4)	(1.4)	(1.5)	(5.3)
Change	2.3	(0.3)	(1.2)	0.8
Balance at Dec 31 2002	(0.1)	(1.7)	(2.7)	(4.5)
Change	(1.3)	0.1	0.1	(1.1)
Balance at Dec 31 2003	(1.4)	(1.6)	(2.6)	(5.6)

8.16.3 Why have both a net income and net income adjusted for OCI?

Some commentators[12] argue that there is no decision-usefulness in providing the comprehensive net income figure for investors whereas others[13] take the opposite view. Intuitively, one might take a view that investors are interested in the total movement in equity regardless of the cause which would lead to support for the comprehensive income figure. However, given that there is this difference of opinion and research findings, this would seem to be an area open to further empirical research to further test the decision-usefulness of each measure to analysts.

Whilst acknowledging the particular interest of analysts in obtaining an income measure that best predicts future cash flows for investment purposes, there is a growing interest among stakeholders in the income measure that is decision-useful when setting compensation plans for directors with the possibility that net income might be more controllable by the directors and therefore a more appropriate measure.

8.17 Segment reporting

The objective of segment reporting is to assist users of accounts to evaluate the different business segments and geographical regions of a group and how they affect the overall results of that group. IAS 14 sets out how these different segments should be defined and the information which should be disclosed.

IAS 14 gives guidance[14] on the sorts of factors that directors should take into account when defining segments, e.g. the nature of the products or services, or how the group's activities are organised. These factors help to determine whether a segment is distinguishable, but it must also be a significant segment to require disclosure and a significance test[15] will measure if any of the turnover, results or assets account for more than 10% of the group's total.

8.18 The fundamental accounting principles underlying the published income statement and balance sheet

IAS 1 (paras. 23–32) requires compliance with the fundamental accounting principles of accruals, materiality and aggregation, going concern and consistency of presentation.

A concept not specifically stated in IAS 1 is prudence, which is an important principle in the preparation of financial statements. The *Framework* states that reliable information in the financial statements must be prudent[16] and this implies that a degree of caution should be exercised in making judgements or estimates. Prudence does not allow the making of excessive or unnecessary provisions that would deliberately understate net assets and therefore render the financial statements unreliable.

8.19 Disclosure of accounting policies

The accounting policies adopted can make a significant difference to the financial statements, e.g. valuing contracts using the percentage completion method or completed method. It is important for investors to be aware of the policies and to be confident that management will not change them on an *ad hoc* basis to influence the results. IAS 1 (para. 7) therefore requires a company to state the accounting policies adopted by the company in determining the amounts shown in the income statement and balance sheet of the company and to apply them consistently.

8.19.1 What is the difference between accounting principles, accounting bases and accounting policies?

Accounting principles

All companies are required to comply with the broad accounting principles of going concern, consistency, accrual accounting, materiality and aggregation. If they fail to comply, they must disclose, quantify and justify the departure from the principle.

Accounting bases

These are the methods that have been developed for applying the accounting principles. They are intended to restrict the subjectivity by identifying a range of acceptable methods. For example, assets may be valued according to the historical cost convention or the alternative accounting rules. Bases have been established for a number of assets, e.g. goodwill, depreciation, consolidation methods.

Accounting policies

Accounting policies are chosen by a company as being the most appropriate to the company's circumstances and best able to produce a fair view. They typically disclose the accounting policies followed for the basis of accounting, i.e. historical or alternative accounting rules, and asset valuation, e.g. of inventory, stating whether it uses FIFO or other methods; property, plant and equipment, stating whether depreciation is straight-line or other methods; and borrowing costs, stating whether they have been capitalised or not. An example from the accounts of Nestlé group is shown in Figure 8.13.

8.19.2 How do users know the effect of changes in accounting policy?

Accounting policies are required by IAS 1 to be applied consistently from one financial period to another. It is only permissible to change an accounting policy if the directors consider that there are special reasons for a change. When a change occurs IAS 8 requires:

● the comparative figures of the previous financial period to be amended if possible;

● the disclosure of the reason for the change, the effect of the adjustment in the income statement of the period and the effect on all other periods presented with the current period financial statements.

Figure 8.13   Extracts from the financial statements of the Nestlé Group

Property, Plant and Equipment

Property, plant and equipment are shown in the balance sheet at their historical cost. Depreciation is provided on the straight-line method so as to depreciate the initial cost over the estimated useful lives, which are as follows:

Buildings	25–50 years
Machinery and equipment	10–15 years
Tools, furniture, information technology and sundry equipment	3–8 years
Vehicles	5 years

Financing costs incurred during the course of construction are expensed. Land is not depreciated. Premiums capitalised for leasehold land and buildings are amortised over the length of the lease.

Depreciation of property, plant and equipment is allocated to the appropriate heading of expenses by function in the income statement.

Research and development

Research and development costs are charged to the income statement in the year in which they are incurred.

Development costs related to new products are not capitalised because the assured availability of future economic benefits is evident only once the products are in the market place.

This has significantly reduced the opportunity for management to confuse users when making accounting changes with the effect on both the previous year and the current year being disclosed.

8.19.3 IFRS 1 First-Time Adoption of International Financial Reporting Standards

One issue that will involve significant changes in accounting policy and have corresponding disclosure issues is the rules on first-time adoption of IFRS. Many companies are starting to transfer their financial statements from a previous GAAP into IFRS and are therefore having to restate those accounts. IFRS 1 addresses the issues in doing this conversion.

The IASB issued IFRS 1 *First-Time Adoption of International Financial Reporting Standards* on 19 June 2003. The IFRS applies to an entity's first IFRS accounts, and all interim financial statements presented under IAS 34 *Interim Financial Reporting* for part of the period covered by its first IFRS accounts.

Transition to IFRSs involves a number of different activities:

1 selecting accounting policies that comply with IFRSs;
2 preparing an opening balance sheet at the date of transition to IFRSs;
3 making estimates under IFRSs for both the opening IFRS balance sheet and other periods presented;
4 disclosures in the first IFRS accounts.

This overview shows the key activities involved in the project to convert to IFRSs. The most difficult aspect of this conversion is the selection of accounting policies to comply with IFRSs. The international accounting standards give policy choices in some areas, and also further choices must be made by businesses when producing the first IFRS financial statements.

Accounting policies

Accounting policies in line with IFRSs effective at its first IFRS reporting date should be used for opening, comparative and reporting date balance sheets (full retrospective application). There are some exceptions to this that are noted below.

This means that all accounting standards applicable at an entity's first IFRS accounting date (e.g. 31 December 2005) will have to be followed from the opening balance sheet date of the compactive period (e.g. at 1 January 2004).

Exemptions from full retrospective application
Certain exemptions are permitted to avoid excessive costs but are not required. These exemptions are optional except for the derecognition and hedging rules for financial instruments.

They concern:

● Property, plant and equipment
● Business combinations
● Defined benefit pension funds
● Cumulative translation differences
● Financial instruments.

Property, plant and equipment

The IFRS gives examples of where it may be difficult for entities to establish the historic cost of previously revalued assets and permits previous revaluations to be carried forward as deemed cost if this approximates to fair value.

This applies to entities whose previous GAAP allowed assets to be recorded at a 'frozen' revalued amount. If the frozen revaluations are comparable to fair value at the date of the revaluation, then they may be carried forward as deemed cost when adopting IFRSs.

Business combinations

An entity need not apply IFRS 3 *Business Combinations* retrospectively to business combinations recognised under previous GAAP.

However, the entity may apply IFRSs retrospectively if it wishes. If it restates any business combination, it must restate all subsequent business combinations as well. For example, if a first-time adopter decides to restate a business combination that occurred on 30 June 2002, it must restate all business combinations that occurred on or after 30 June 2002.

For business combinations which are not restated, some adjustments will still be required, the main one regarding goodwill. Any goodwill on the balance sheet at the transition date (start of the earliest IFRS comparative period) should, if positive, be frozen and subject to annual impairment reviews, and, if negative, be written back to retained earnings.

Defined benefit pension funds

At the transition date recognise all actuarial gains or losses and only spread any that arise after the transition date.

Cumulative translation differences

Cumulative exchange differences on foreign entities should be presented under IFRS rules as a separate reserve. On transition it is acceptable not to separate historic amounts from retained earnings, and only separate exchange differences arising after the transition date. This would also mean that the exchange differences would not be recycled on the disposal of the foreign entity.

Financial instruments

The transitional rules for financial instruments are very complex; however the main exemptions are as follows:

- IAS 39's derecogition rules are only applied to items that have occurred after 1 January 2004. This means that if a business had entered into some sort of off balance sheet finance scheme before that date they would not need to assess it under IAS 39, and the existing treatment can continue. For anything entered into after that date, however, it will need to assessed according to IAS 39's criteria.

- On transition to IFRS all derivatives must be recognised on the balance sheet. If a derivative is designated as a fair value hedge at transition the corresponding entry is to retained earnings, and the hedged item is also recognised at fair value with an adjustment to retained earnings. If a derivative is designated as a cash flow hedge then the corresponding entry is to a separate reserve in equity.

- For 2005 adopters it will not be necessary to apply IAS 32 and IAS 39 in the comparative financial statements. Instead a company will be able to produce a reconciliation of the position at the end of the comparative year (without IAS 32/39) to the beginning of the first reporting year (following IAS 32/39). This option is only available to 2005 adopters.

Opening IFRS balance sheet at transition date

This should be restated using recognition and measurement criteria in IFRSs. This means that the entity will potentially need to:

- recognise all assets and liabilities required by IFRSs;
- cease to recognise some assets and liabilities that cannot be recognised per IFRSs;
- reclassify items as different types of assets, liabilities and equity under IFRSs;
- apply IFRSs in measuring recognised assets and liabilities.

Any adjustment to the opening net assets should be recognised against retained earnings.

Estimates

Estimates should be consistent with estimates made at the same date under previous GAAP (after any adjustments to reflect difference in accounting policies) unless there is objective evidence that estimates were in error.

This does not prohibit new estimates being made as required by IFRSs, e.g. where no amount was recognised under previous GAAP.

Disclosure

Disclosure requirements of all effective IFRSs at the reporting date must be followed.

Disclosure is required of how transition from previous GAAP to IFRS has affected financial position, financial performance and cash flows. This requires:

- reconciliation of entity's equity under previous GAAP to IFRS for
  - date of transition to IFRSs and
  - end of last period presented in the most recent financial statements under previous GAAP;
- reconciliation of the profit or loss reported under previous GAAP to IFRSs for latest period presented under previous GAAP.

Examples of the reconciliations are provided in the implementation guidance for IFRS 1.

Effect of IFRS on individual companies

The effect is still uncertain and will depend on the industry, e.g. companies with large property portfolios will be able to account for increased property values as profits, and on the nature of their liabilities, e.g. companies with share schemes and employee benefits obligations may be adversely affected. The effects will therefore vary, with some companies like AstraZeneca reporting minor differences on converting from UK GAAP to IFRS and others like Shell who advise that it will take almost $5bn off the company's opening balance sheet as of 1 January 2004. An important consideration for investors will be the potential economic impact and Shell addressed this in stressing that converting would have no impact on strategy, financial framework or cash flow.

Differences between IFRS and national standards

This will vary according to the accounting principles followed by individual countries. The following extract from the 2003 Annual Report of Palfinger AG is an example:

> **Main differences between IFRS and Austrian Accounting Standards**
> **Different principles**
> The goals of IFRS and IAS are exclusively international compared with Austrian accounting provisions. The dominant aim of the IFRS and IAS is to provide investors with the business-oriented information required in decision-making processes, whereas Austrian accounting standards are based on the principle of prudence and are directed at the protection of creditors. Thus, higher significance is placed on comparability of financial statements under the IFRS than under Austrian commercial law.

8.20 Fair view treatment

IAS 1 provisions

IAS 1 requires financial statements to give a fair presentation of the financial position, financial performance and cash flows of an enterprise.[17] In para. 15 it states that:

> In virtually all circumstances, a fair presentation is achieved by compliance with applicable IFRSs. A fair presentation also requires an entity:
>
> (a) to select and apply accounting policies in accordance with IAS 8 *Accounting Policies, Changes in Accounting Estimates and Errors*. IAS 8 sets out a hierarchy of authoritative guidance that management considers in the absence of a Standard or an Interpretation that specifically applies to an item;
>
> (b) to present information, including accounting policies, in a manner that provides relevant, reliable, comparable and understandable information;
>
> (c) to provide additional disclosures when compliance with the specific requirements in IFRSs is insufficient to enable users to understand the impact of particular transactions, other events and conditions on the entity's financial position and financial performance.

The Framework provisions

The *Framework for the Preparation and Presentation of Financial Statements* considers[18] that a fair presentation would mean that the financial statements must show a true and fair view.

Legal opinions

True and fair is a legal concept and can be authoritatively decided only by a court. However, the courts have never attempted to define 'true and fair'. In the UK the Accounting Standards Committee (ASC) obtained a legal opinion which included the following statement:

> It is however important to observe that the application of the concept involves
>
> ● **judgement in questions of degree.** The information contained in the accounts must be accurate and comprehensive to within acceptable limits. What is acceptable and how is this to be achieved?

- **Reasonable businessmen and accountants may differ over the degree of accuracy** or comprehensiveness which in particular cases the accounts should attain.

- Equally, there may sometimes be **room for differences over the method** to adopt in order to give a true and fair view, cases in which there may be more than one true and fair view of the same financial position.

- Again, because true and fair involves questions of degree, we think **that cost effectiveness must play a part** in deciding the amount of information which is sufficient to make accounts true and fair.

- Accounts will not be true and fair unless the information they contain is **sufficient in quantity and quality to satisfy the reasonable expectations** of the readers to whom they are addressed.[19]

A further counsel's opinion was attained by the Accounting Standards Board (ASB) in 1991[20] and published in its foreword to Accounting Standards. It advised that accounting standards are an authoritative source of accounting practice and it is now the norm for financial statements to comply with them. In consequence the court may take accounting standards into consideration when forming an opinion on whether the financial statements give a true and fair view.

Fair override

IAS 1 recognises that there may be occasions when application of an IAS might be misleading and departure from IAS treatment is permitted. This is referred to as the fair override provision. If a company makes use of the override it is required to explain why compliance with IASs would be misleading and also give sufficient information to enable the user to calculate the adjustments required to comply with the standard.

The true and fair concept is familiar to the UK and Netherlands accounting professions. Many countries, however, view the concept of the true and fair view with suspicion since it runs counter to their legal systems. In Germany the fair override provision has not been directly implemented and laws are interpreted according to their function and objectives. It appears that the role of true and fair in the European context is to act as a protection against over-regulation. Since the wider acceptance of IASs has been occurring in recent years, the financial statements of many more companies and countries are fulfilling the principle of a true and fair view.

When do companies use the fair override?
It can occur for a number of reasons:[21]

1 Accounting standards may prescribe one method, which contradicts the Companies Act and thus requires an override, e.g. providing no depreciation on investment properties.

2 Accounting standards may offer a choice between accounting procedures, at least one of which contradicts the Companies Act. If that particular choice is adopted, the override should be invoked, e.g. grants and contributions not shown as deferred income.

An example of this is shown in the extract from the 2004 Annual Report of Severn Trent:

Grants and contributions

Grants and contributions received in respect of non infrastructure assets are treated as deferred income and are recognised in the profit and loss account over the useful economic life of those assets.

In accordance with industry practice, grants and contributions relating to infrastructure assets have been deducted from the cost of fixed assets.

This is not in accordance with Schedule 4 to the Act, which requires assets to be shown at their purchase price or production cost and hence grants and contributions to be presented as deferred income. This departure from the requirements of the Act is, in the opinion of the Directors, necessary to give a true and fair view as, while a provision is made for depreciation of infrastructure assets, these assets do not have determinable finite lives and therefore no basis exists on which to recognise grants and contributions as deferred income. The effect of this departure is that the cost of fixed assets is £362.6 million lower than it would otherwise have been (2003: £327.0 million).

Those grants and contributions relating to the maintenance of the operating capability of the infrastructure network are taken into account in determining the depreciation charged for infrastructure assets.

3 Accounting standards may allow some choice but prefer a particular method which is consistent with the Companies Act, but the alternative may not be consistent, e.g. not amortising goodwill (prior to IAS requirement for impairment review).

4 There may be a Companies Act requirement but no accounting standard. Failure to comply with the Companies Act would require a True and Fair override, e.g. current assets being reported at market value rather than at cost.

5 There may be an accounting standards requirement which is overridden, e.g. not providing depreciation on fixed assets.

8.21 Additional information in the annual report

Legislation such as the Companies Act 1985 in the UK requires that additional information is included in the annual report such as a directors' report. As well as statutory information many companies choose to give additional information with such things as operating and financial reviews, chairperson's statements or business summaries. Around the world the names and formats of the additional information does change, but the actual information included is often of a similar nature.

8.21.1 Information appearing in board or directors' reports

The typical type of information that appears in board or directors' reports might be as follows:

- Information about the business activities which includes:
  - details about principal activities during the year and any significant changes
  - a fair review of the development of the business of the company during the year and of its position at the end of the year,[22] e.g. comment on the development of new markets, comment on any significant rationalisation involving discontinuing segments of the business, etc.
  - likely future developments
  - research and development activity undertaken during the year
  - significant changes in the fixed assets of the company during the year

- any important events affecting the company which have occurred since the end of the financial year;

● Information allowing shareholders to assess asset backing which includes:

- a note of the amount if the market value of land and buildings differs materially from the book values (this gives shareholders a view of the asset backing in determining the value of their shares);

● Information making shareholders aware of material movements in the ownership of the issued share capital which includes:

- share interests that exceed 3% of the nominal capital of the company (3% is UK disclosure guidance); the purchase of own shares; shares of the company in which directors have an interest;

● Information indicating the company's activities in the community which includes:

- political and charitable donations; policy in respect of applications for employment by disabled applicants; actions taken in respect of employee reports and consultation.

The information in the report requires a number of judgements to be made, e.g. a fair review, significant changes and any important events. Because it involves judgement and opinion (which is not easily verified), the director's report is not usually audited but may be reviewed by the auditor to ensure it does not conflict with the financial data.

8.21.2 What does a directors' report look like?

The paragraph headings from Findel plc's 2002 annual report are set out in Figure 8.14 as an illustration of the type of information contained in a published set of accounts. The extract in Figure 8.15 indicates the culture of a company in respect of employee and commercial issues, and illustrates how the report has become almost an index for other sources of financial information. Findel plc is a UK group and therefore the report follows UK requirements.

Figure 8.14   Directors' report headings

Activities
Review of the Year and Future Prospects
Acquisition of Novara plc
Dividends
Share Capital
Supplier Payment Policy
Directors
Employees
Donations
Substantial Shareholdings
Auditors

Figure 8.15   Extracts from Findel plc 2002 Directors' Report

Activities

The principle activities of the group are home shopping and educational supplies sales through mail order and the provision of online and logistics services to third parties.

Review of the Year and Future Prospects

A review of the group's activities and its future prospects is contained in the Chairman's Statement on pages 2 to 3.

Employees

The company recognises its social and statutory duty to employ disabled persons and pursues a policy of providing, wherever possible, the same employment opportunities to disabled persons as to others.

Information to employees regarding the company and factors affecting its performance and that of its subsidiaries is provided through normal management channels and regular consultation.

Donations

During the year the group made charitable donations of £72,000 (£75,000). There were no donations for political purposes.

8.21.3   Chief Executive's Report

The directors' report was supported by a statement from the Chairman. A brief extract from Findel plc's 2002 annual report illustrates the type of information provided.

Home Shopping

Our home shopping division has continued to build successfully. Sales have grown strongly again this year, rising to £136.9m (£113.9m), a 20% increase. Operating profit improved by 45% to £20.9m (£14.4m).

Customer recruitment has outstripped even last year's record performance, with the customer base rising from 964,000 to more than 1.3m customers, a 35% increase.

The formula we have developed of offering seasonally appropriate merchandise competitively priced, coupled with the availability of monthly credit, is proving increasingly successful. Whilst sales of our traditional core Christmas ranges grew by 25%, sales of kitchen, audio visual, household and furniture goods increased by 42% and now account for 31% of all sales.

The importance of financial services to the division becomes more apparent each year. It has had another record year. Whilst bad debt remains firmly under control, income from credit and payment protection plans increased during the year by 73%. With the additional financial products planned, we expect its performance to continue to improve ...

8.22 What information do companies provide to assist comparison between companies reporting under different reporting regimes?

Companies may provide reconciliation statements between their national standards and either US or IASC standards. The following statement shows the type of reconciliations necessary for listing purposes in some countries. These reconciliations highlight and explain the different accounting treatments that can be adopted and the impact on the figures in the financial statements. They are taken from Nokia reconciling IFRS requirements to US GAAP.

The principal differences between IAS and US GAAP are presented below.

Reconciliation of net income

	2003 EURm	2002 EURm	2001 EURm
Net income reported under IAS	3,592	3,381	2,200
US GAAP adjustments:			
Pension expense	(12)	(5)	(22)
Development costs	322	(66)	(104)
Provision for social security on stock options	(21)	(90)	(132)
Stock compensation expense	(9)	(35)	(85)
Cash flow hedges	9	6	(22)
Net investment in foreign entities	—	48	—
Amortisation of identifiable intangible assets acquired	(22)	(22)	(7)
Amortisation of goodwill	162	206	28
Impairment of goodwill	151	104	—
Deferred tax effect of US GAAP adjustment	(75)	76	47
Net income under US GAAP	4,097	3,603	1,903

Reconciliation of shareholders' equity

	2003 EURm	2002 EURm
Total shareholders' equity reported under IAS	15,148	14,281
US GAAP adjustments:		
Pension expense	(49)	(37)
Additional minimum liability	—	(5)
Development costs	(99)	(421)
Marketable securities and unlisted investments	49	77
Provision for social security cost on stock options	14	35
Deferred compensation	(10)	(13)
Share issue premium	186	179
Stock compensation	(176)	(166)
Acquisition purchase price	3	4
Amortisation of identifiable intangible assets acquired	(51)	(29)
Amortisation of goodwill	396	234
Impairment of goodwill	255	104
Translation of goodwill	(293)	(240)
Deferred tax effect of US GAAP adjustments	64	147
Total shareholders' equity under US GAAP	15,437	14,150

8.22.1 Impact of differing accounting practice on interpretation of performance

The differing accounting methods that can be adopted around the world have an effect on the apparent performance of companies and make global inter-company comparison difficult. Reconciliations between different versions of GAAP improve the comparability but real comparability will only be achieved if accounting treatments are unified.

To illustrate the impact that different versions of GAAP can have on the performance, consider the impact on the key ratios of the Incentive Group in 1999 when they restated Danish GAAP to IAS.

The extract from which the financial ratios are calculated is shown below.

Incentive Group – changes in accounting policy to IAS

	Before change in accounting policies	Effect of change in accounting policies	After change in accounting policies
Effect on the consolidated income statement			
1999 (DKKm)			
Net sales	3,451		3,451
Gross margin	1,357	(236)	1,121
Operating profit before amortisation			
of goodwill, etc.	1	13	14
Operating income	17	(61)	(44)
Ordinary income before tax	(68)	(61)	(129)
Net income	**(98)**	**6**	**(92)**
Effect on the consolidated balance sheet			
1999 (DKKm)			
Financial fixed assets	7	1,486	1,493
Property, plant and equipment	676		676
Investments	147		147
Inventories, etc.	624	34	658
Receivables	818	206	1,024
Cash and cash equivalents	220		220
Total asset	**2,492**	**1,726**	**4,218**
Stockholders' equity	(57)	1,659	1,602
Provisions	186	67	253
Long-term and short-term debt*	2,363		2,363
Total liabilities and shareholders'			
equity	**2,492**	**1,726**	**4,218**

	1999	1998
Effect 1998–1999 for the Group DKKm		
Net income before change in		
accounting policies	**(98)**	**152**
– Production overheads	0	0
– Amortisation of goodwill	(74)	(43)

*The short- and long-term debt includes short-term debt of DKK1,227m and long-term debt of DKK1,136m.

– Development costs	13	(2)
– Warranty and pension allowances	0	(5)
– Tax	67	(19)
Net effect of the change in accounting policies	**6**	**(69)**
Net income after change in accounting policies	**(92)**	**83**

	1999	1998
Total assets before change in accounting policies	**2,492**	**2,248**
– Production overheads	34	31
– Goodwill	1,405	686
– Development costs	81	61
– Tax assets	206	92
Net effect of the change in accounting policies	**1,726**	**870**
Total assets after change in accounting policies	**4,218**	**3,118**
Total liabilities before change in accounting policies	**2,492**	**2,248**
Stockholders' equity before change	(57)	930
– Production overheads	34	31
– Goodwill	1,405	686
– Development costs	81	61
– Warranty and pension allowances	(28)	(28)
– Tax	167	(9)
Net effect on stockholders' equity	**1,659**	**741**
Allowances and debt before change	2,549	1,318
– Warranty and pension allowances	28	28
– Tax	39	101
Net effect on allowances and debt	**67**	**129**
Total liabilities after change in accounting policies	**4,218**	**3,118**

Ratio	Danish GAAP	IAS GAAP
Return on capital employed		
Operating income/Total assets less current liabilities	1.3%	(1.5%)
Operating profit margin		
Operating profit/Sales	0.5%	(1.3%)
Current ratio		
Current assets/Current liabilities	1.35	1.55
Gearing		
Long-term debt/Total assets less current liabilities	89.8%	38%
Earnings per share		
Net income/Number of shares	DKK(18.1)	DKK(17)

The alterations in the above ratios have been caused by the following accounting policy changes that were necessary to restate the financial statements from Danish GAAP to IAS:

Goodwill
Under IAS goodwill is capitalised and amortised over its useful life which cannot exceed twenty years. [Note that this treatment changed with the introduction of IFRS 3 Business Combinations.]

Development costs
Development costs have been capitalised and amortised under IAS over a life not exceeding five years.

Inventory measurement
Production overheads are included in the measurement of inventories and allocated on a pro rata basis to cost of goods sold.

Deferred tax
Deferred tax assets related to tax loss carry-forwards are capitalised or set off against deferred tax liabilities provided that the losses are likely to be utilised in the future.

Summary

The published accounts of a listed company are intended to provide a report to enable shareholders to assess current year stewardship and management performance and to predict future cash flows. In order to assess stewardship and management performance, there have been mandatory requirements for standardised presentation, using formats prescribed by International Accounting Standards. There have also been mandatory requirements for the disclosure of accounting policies, which allow shareholders to make comparisons between years. As regards future cash flows, these are normally perceived to be influenced by past profits, the asset base as shown by the balance sheet and any significant changes. In order to assist shareholders to predict future cash flows with an understanding of the risks involved, more information has been required by the IASB. This has taken two forms:

● more quantitative information in the accounts, e.g. segmental analysis, and the impact of changes on the operation, e.g. a breakdown of turnover, costs and profits for both new and discontinued operations; and

● more qualitative information, e.g. the operating and financial review, related party disclosures, effect of changes in accounting policy.

REVIEW QUESTIONS

1 Explain why two companies carrying out identical trading transactions could produce different gross profit figures.

2 An income statement might contain the following profit figures:

Gross profit

Profit from operations

Profit before tax

Net profit from ordinary activities

Net profit for the period.

Explain when you would use each profit figure for analysis purposes, e.g. profit from operations may be used in the percentage return on capital employed.

3 Classify the following items into cost of sales, distribution costs, administrative expenses, other operating income or item to be disclosed after trading profit:

(a) Personnel department costs

(b) Computer department costs

(c) Cost accounting department costs

(d) Financial accounting department costs

(e) Bad debts

(f) Provisions for warranty claims

(g) Interest on funds borrowed to finance an increase in working capital

(h) Interest on funds borrowed to finance an increase in fixed production assets.

4 'Companies should begin to move to greater disclosure of:

● Days training per year for categories of staff.

● Expenditure on training, both in total and differentiated between categories of employees. This could be supplemented with information regarding the spread of expenditure during the year. This is most likely to be best presented in diagrammatic form.

● Career and development policy, both vertically and horizontally. A short statement setting out the relevance of the approach to the future of the company and how management plan to deal with it should be provided and could, over time, be extended to include information on staff turnover rates, average length of service, costs of recruitment, voluntary payments on termination of employment and number of professionally qualified staff'.[23]

(a) Discuss the extent to which this information would assist the investor to:

(i) assess stewardship performance;

(ii) predict future cash flows.

(b) Discuss the extent to which the annual report should contain the information suggested in the CIMA publication and the reasons for its inclusion.

5 What are the fundamental objectives of corporate reports?[24]

6 'A single set of multi-purpose financial statements is unable to satisfy the needs of shareholders for both a stewardship report and a report to assist the prediction of future cash flows.' Discuss.

7 Discuss the relevance of the information in the Statement of Recognised Income and Expense to an investor. Explain the advantages and disadvantages of combining the income statement and this statement into a single report.

8 Describe the content of an OFR statement in UK financial statements and discuss whether it should be made mandatory, more prescriptive and audited.

9 The SEC have objected to the use of the fair override on the grounds that fair is achieved by compliance with standards and that the override could lead to companies concealing poor performance and weakening balance sheets. An opposing view is that the SEC stance leads to companies seeking ways to report that do not infringe standards but are not fair. Discuss whether the override results in less transparency and financial statements which are less informative.

EXERCISES

An extract from the solution is provided in the Appendix at the end of the text for exercises marked with an asterisk (*).

* Question 1

The following trial balance was extracted from the books of Old NV on 31 December 20X1.

	€000	€000
Sales		12,050
Returns outwards		313
Provision for depreciation		
plant		738
vehicles		375
Rent receivable		100
Trade payables		738
Debentures		250
Issued share capital – ordinary €1 shares		3,125
– preference shares (treated as equity)		625
Share premium		250
Retained earnings		875
Inventory	825	
Purchases	6,263	
Returns inwards	350	
Carriage inwards	13	
Carriage outwards	125	
Salesmen's salaries	800	
Administrative wages and salaries	738	
Plant (includes €362,000 acquired in 20X1)	1,562	
Motor vehicles	1,125	
Goodwill	1,062	
Distribution expenses	290	
Administrative expenses	286	
Directors' remuneration	375	
Trade receivables	3,875	
Cash at bank and in hand	1,750	
	19,439	19,439

Note of information not taken into the trial balance data:

(a) Provide for:
   (i) An audit fee of €38,000.
   (ii) Depreciation of plant at 20% straight-line.
   (iii) Depreciation of vehicles at 25% reducing balance.
   (iv) The goodwill suffered an impairment in the year of €177,000.
   (v) Income tax of €562,000.
   (vi) Debenture interest of €25,000.
   (vii) A preference dividend of 8%.
   (viii) An ordinary dividend of €0.1 per share.

(b) Closing inventory was valued at €1,125,000 at the lower of cost and net realisable value.

(c) Administrative expenses were prepaid by €12,000.

Required:
(a) **Prepare an income statement for internal use for the year ended 31 December 20X1.**
(b) **Prepare an income statement for the year ended 31 December 20X1 and a balance sheet as at that date in Format 1 style of presentation.**

* Question 2

HK Ltd has prepared its draft trial balance to 30 June 20X1, which is shown opposite.

The authorised share capital is 4,000,000 9% preference shares of $1 each and 18,000,000 ordinary shares of 50c each.

The following information is available:

1 The depreciation policy of the company is to provide depreciation at the following rates:

   Plant and machinery   20% on cost
   Fixtures and fittings   10% on cost
   Buildings   2% on cost

   In addition, it has been decided to create a reserve of 10% on the cost of plant and machinery to allow for the increased cost of replacement. (Depreciation for 20X1 has not been provided in the draft trial balance.) Charge all depreciation to cost of sales.

2 Acquisitions of property, plant and equipment during the year were:

   Plant $173,000   Fixtures $144,000

3 Government grants of $85,000 have been received in respect of plant purchased during the year and are shown in the trial balance.

4 During the year freehold land which cost $720,000 was sold for $2,036,000. It was valued in last year's balance sheet at $1,500,000. The revaluation surplus had been credited to revaluation reserve.

5 Inventory shown in the trial balance ($11,794,000) consists of:

   Raw materials $1,872,000
   Work-in-progress $6,660,000
   Finished goods $3,262,000

6 Trade receivables and payables are all payable and due within the next financial year. The loan is unsecured and repayable in ten years' time.

Trial balance at 30 June 20X1

	$000	$000
Freehold land	2,880	
Freehold buildings (cost $4,680)	4,126	
Plant and machinery (cost $3,096)	1,858	
Fixtures and fittings (cost $864)	691	
Goodwill	480	
Trade receivables	7,263	
Trade payables		2,591
Inventory	11,794	
Bank balance	11,561	
Income tax on loan interest	151	
Development grant received		85
Profit on sale of freehold land		536
Sales		381,600
Cost of sales	318,979	
Administration expenses	9,000	
Distribution costs	35,100	
Directors' emoluments	562	
Bad debts	157	
Auditors' remuneration	112	
Hire of plant and machinery	2,400	
Loan interest paid net	454	
Dividends paid during the year – preference	162	
– ordinary	426	
9% loan		7,200
Share capital – preference shares (treated as equity)		3,600
– ordinary shares		5,400
Retained earnings		6,364
Revaluation account		780
	408,156	408,156

---

7 During the year a fire took place at one of the company's depots, involving losses of $200,000. These losses have been written off to cost of sales shown in the trial balance. Since the end of the financial year a settlement of $150,000 has been agreed with the company's insurers.

8 It is agreed that $500,000 of the finished goods inventory is obsolete and should be written off. However, since the end of the financial year an offer has been received from another company to buy this inventory for $300,000, subject to certain modifications being made at an estimated cost to HK Ltd of $50,000. This has now been agreed.

9 A contract has been entered into, with a building contractor, to extend the company's premises. The contract price is $5,000,000 and the work is scheduled to start in December 20X1.

10 A final ordinary dividend of 3c per share is declared before the year-end, together with the balance of the preference dividend. Neither dividend was paid at the year-end.

11 The income tax charge in the income statement is to be that based on the net profit for the year, at a rate of 35%.

12 The goodwill has not been impaired.

13 The loan was raised during the year and there is no outstanding interest accrued at the year end.

Required:
(a) Prepare the company's income statement for the year to 30 June 20X1 and a balance sheet as at that date, complying with the relevant accounting standards in so far as the information given permits.
  (All calculations to nearest $000.)
(b) Prepare the property, plant and equipment schedule for the notes to the accounts.
(c) Explain the usefulness of the schedule prepared in (b).

Question 3

Basalt plc is a wholesaler. The following is its trial balance as at 31 December 20X0.

	Dr £000	Cr £000
Ordinary share capital: £1 shares		300
Share premium		20
General reserve		16
Retained earnings as at 1 January 20X0		55
Inventory as at 1 January 20X0	66	
Sales		962
Purchases	500	
Administrative expenses	10	
Distribution expenses	6	
Plant and machinery – cost	220	
Plant and machinery – provision for depreciation		49
Returns outwards		25
Returns inwards	27	
Carriage inwards	9	
Warehouse wages	101	
Salesmen's salaries	64	
Administrative wages and salaries	60	
Hire of motor vehicles	19	
Directors' remuneration	30	
Rent receivable		7
Trade receivables	326	
Cash at bank	62	
Trade payables		66
	1,500	1,500

The following additional information is supplied:
 (i) Depreciate plant and machinery 20% on straight-line basis.
 (ii) Inventory at 31 December 20X0 is £90,000.
 (iii) Accrue auditors' remuneration £2,000.
 (iv) Income tax for the year will be £58,000 payable October 20X1.
 (v) There is a proposed ordinary dividend of £75,000 for the year, declared but not paid before the year-end.

(vi) It is estimated that 7/11 of the plant and machinery is used in connection with distribution, with the remainder for administration. The motor vehicle costs should be assigned to distribution.

Required:

(a) Prepare an income statement and balance sheet in a form that complies with IAS 1. No notes to the accounts are required.

(b) Briefly explain what you would expect to find in the following sections of a UK company annual report:

    (i) Directors' report.   (ii) Chairman's report.   (iii) Auditors' report.

Question 4

Raffles Ltd trades as a wine wholesaler with a large warehouse in Asia. The trainee accountant at Raffles Ltd has produced the following draft accounts for the year ended 31 December 20X6.

Income Statement

	$
Sales	1,628,000
Less: Cost of sales	1,100,000
Gross profit	528,000
Debenture interest paid	9,000
Distribution costs	32,800
Audit fees	7,000
Impairment of goodwill	2,500
Income tax liability on profits	165,000
Interim dividend	18,000
Dividend received from Diat P'or plc	(6,000)
Bank interest	3,000
Over provision of income tax in prior years	(4,250)
Depreciation	
Land and buildings	3,000
Plant and machinery	10,000
Fixtures and fittings	6,750
Administrative expenses	206,300
Net profit	74,900

Draft balance sheet at 31 December 20X6

	$		$
Bank balance	12,700	Inventory	156,350
10% debentures 20X9	180,000	Receivables	179,830
Ordinary share capital		Land and buildings	238,000
50c nominal value	250,000	Plant and machinery	74,000
Trade payables	32,830	Fixtures and fittings	20,250
Income tax			
creditor	165,000	Goodwill	40,000
Retained earnings	172,900	Investments at cost	130,000
Revaluation reserve	25,000		
	838,430		838,430

The following information is relevant:

1 The directors maintain that the investments in Diat P'or plc will be held by the company on a continuing basis and that the current market value of the investments at the balance sheet date was $135,000. However, since the balance sheet date there has been a substantial fall in market prices and these investments are now valued at $90,000.

2 The authorised share capital of Raffles Ltd is 600,000 ordinary shares.

3 The directors propose to pay a final dividend of 7.2c per share, declared but not paid at the balance sheet date.

4 During the year the company paid shareholders the proposed 20X5 final dividend of $30,000. This transaction has already been recorded in the accounts.

5 The company incurred $150,000 in restructuring costs during the year. These have been debited to the administrative expenses account. The trainee accountant subsequently informs you that tax relief of $45,000 will be given on these costs and that this relief has not yet been accounted for in the records.

6 The company employs an average of ten staff, 60% of whom work in the wine purchasing and importing department, 30% in the distribution department and the remainder in the accounts department. Staff costs total $75,000.

7 The company has three directors. The managing director earns $18,000 while the purchasing and distribution directors earn $14,000 each. In addition the directors receive bonuses and pensions of $1,800 each. All staff costs have been debited to the income statement.

8 The directors propose to decrease the bad debt provision by $1,500 as a result of the improved credit control in the company in recent months.

9 Depreciation policy is as follows:

Land and buildings:	No depreciation on land. Buildings are depreciated over 25 years on a straight-line basis. This is to be charged to cost of sales.
Plant and machinery:	10% on cost, charge to cost of sales
Fixtures and fittings:	25% reducing balance, charge to administration.

10 The directors have provided information on a potential lawsuit. A customer is suing them for allegedly tampering with the imported wine by injecting an illegal substance to improve the colour of the wine. The managing director informs you that this lawsuit is just 'sour grapes' by a jealous customer and provides evidence from the company solicitor which indicates that there is only a small possibility that the claim for $8,000 will succeed.

11 Purchased goodwill was acquired in 20X3 for $50,000. The annual impairment test revealed an impairment of $2,500 in the current year.

12 Plant and machinery of $80,000 was purchased during the year to add to the $20,000 plant already owned. Fixtures and fittings acquired 2 years ago with a net book value of $13,500 were disposed of. Accumulated depreciation of fixtures and fittings at 1 January 20X6 was $37,500.

13 Land was revalued by $25,000 by Messrs Moneybags, Chartered Surveyors, on an open market value basis, to $175,000. The revaluation surplus was credited to the revaluation reserve. There is no change in the value of the buildings.

14 Gross profit is stated after charging $15,000 relating to obsolete cases of wine that have 'gone off'. Since that time an offer has been received by the company for its obsolete wine stock of $8,000, provided the company does additional vinification on the wine at a cost of $2,000 to bring it up to the buyer's requirements. A cash discount of 5% is allowed for early settlement and it is anticipated that the buyer will take advantage of this discount.

15 Costs of $10,000 relating to special plant and machinery have been included in cost of sales in error. This was not spotted until after the production of the draft accounts.

Required:
(a) **Prepare an income statement for the year ended 31 December 20X6 and a balance sheet at that date for presentation to the members of Raffles Ltd in accordance with relevant accounting standards.**
(b) **Produce detailed notes to the income statement and balance sheet of Raffles Ltd for the year ended 31 December 20X6.**

Question 5

Phoenix plc trial balance at 30 June 20X7 was as follows:

	£000	£000
Freehold premises	2,400	
Plant and machinery	1,800	540
Furniture and fittings	620	360
Inventory at 30 June 20X7	1,468	
Sales		6,465
Administrative expenses	1,126	
Ordinary shares of £1 each		4,500
Trade investments	365	
Revaluation reserve		600
Development cost	415	
Share premium		500
Personal ledger balances	947	566
Cost of goods sold	4,165	
Distribution costs	669	
Overprovision for tax		26
Dividend received		80
Interim dividend paid	200	
Retained earnings		488
Disposal of warehouse		225
Cash and bank balances	175	

The following information is available:

1   Freehold premises acquired for £1.8 million were revalued in 20X4, recognising a gain of £600,000. These include a warehouse, which cost £120,000, was revalued at £150,000 and was sold in June 20X7 for £225,000. Phoenix does not depreciate freehold premises.

2   Phoenix wishes to report Plant and Machinery at open market value which is estimated to be £1,960,000 on 1 July 20X6.

3   Company policy is to depreciate its assets on the straight-line method at annual rates as follows:

Plant and machinery   10%
Furniture and fittings   5%

4   Until this year the company's policy has been to capitalise development costs, to the extent permitted by relevant accounting standards. The company must now write off the development costs, including £124,000 incurred in the year, as the project no longer meets the capitalisation criteria.

5 During the year the company has issued one million shares of £1 at £1.20 each.

6 Included within administrative expenses are the following:

Staff salary (including £125,000 to directors)	£468,000
Directors' fees	£96,000
Audit fees and expenses	£86,000

7 Income tax for the year is estimated at £122,000.

8 Directors propose a final dividend of 4p per share declared but not paid at the year-end.

Required:

(a) In respect of the year ended 30 June 20X7:
    The income statement.

(b) The balance sheet as at 30 June 20X7.

(c) The statement of movement of property, plant and equipment.

(d) The statement of recognised gains and losses.

References

1 IAS 1, Appendix.
2 IFRS 5 *Non-Current Assets Held for Sale and Discontinued Operations*, para. 30.
3 *Ibid.*, para. 32.
4 *Ibid.*, para. 33.
5 IAS 8 *Net Profit or Loss for the Period, Fundamental Errors and Changes in Accounting Policies*, IASC, revised 1993, para. 16.
6 IAS 1, para. 54.
7 IAS 16 *Property, Plant and Equipment*, IASC, revised 1998, paras. 28–29.
8 IAS 39 *Financial Instruments: Recognition and Measurement*, IASC, 1998, para. 69.
9 IAS 2 *Inventories*, IASC, revised 1993, para. 6.
10 IAS 37 *Provisions, Contingent Liabilities and Contingent Assets*, IASC, 1998, para. 45.
11 IAS 1, para. 86.
12 D. Dhaliwal, K. Subramnayam and R. Trezevant, 'Is comprehensive income superior to net income as a measure of firm performance?', *Journal of Accounting and Economics*, 26:1, 1999, pp. 43–67.
13 D. Hirst and P. Hopkins, 'Comprehensive income reporting and analysts' valuation judgments', *Journal of Accounting Research*, 36 (Supplement), 1998, pp. 47–74.
14 IAS 14 *Segment Reporting*, IASC, revised 1997, para. 9.
15 *Ibid.*, para. 35.
16 *Framework for the Preparation and Presentation of Financial Statements*, IASC, 1989, para. 37.
17 IAS 1 *Presentation of Financial Statements*, IASC, revised 1997, para. 10.
18 *Framework for the Preparation and Presentation of Financial Statements*, IASC, 1989, para. 46.
19 K. Wild and A. Guida, *Touche Ross Financial Reporting Manual* (3rd edition), Butterworth, 1990, p. 433.
20 K. Wild and C. Goodhead, *Touche Ross Financial Reporting Manual* (4th edition), Butterworth, 1994, p. 5.
21 LBS Accounting Subject Area Working Paper No 031 *An Empirical Investigation of the True and Fair Override*, Gilad Livne and Maureen McNichols (http://ssrn.com/abstract_id=38071)
22 Companies Act 1985, section 235.
23 CIMA, Corporate Reporting – *The Management Interface*, CIMA, 1990, p. 27.
24 V. Beatty and M. Jones, 'Company reporting: the US leads the way', *Certified Accountant*, March 1994, p. 50.

CHAPTER 9

Preparation of published accounts

9.1 Introduction

In this chapter we illustrate the preparation of an income statement and balance sheet using format 1 of IAS 1 from trial balance to published accounts. We then take into account the effects of other international accounting standards. We follow a progressive stage approach to the problem.

Stage 1 is the preparation of the internal income statement from the trial balance data. Stage 2 is the preparation of an income statement in format 1. Stage 3 is the preparation of a balance sheet. The aim is that you should be able to prepare a set of accounts that conform to the prescribed formats and that you should also understand how a company arrives at the figures that appear in the published financial statements that it presents to its shareholders.

9.2 Stage 1: preparation of the internal income statement from a trial balance

In this chapter we use format 1, i.e. costs analysed according to function.[1]

The data given in Figure 9.1 are available for Illustrious SpA for the year ended 31 December 20X1. The following information has not yet been taken into account in the amounts shown in the trial balance:

● Inventory at cost at 31 December 20X1 was €22,875,000. Inventory at net realisable value at 31 December 20X1 was €3,000,000. The cost of this inventory was €4,000,000. The reduction to net realisable value was necessitated because the customer who would normally have taken the products assembled from these inventory items had gone into liquidation.

● Depreciation is to be provided as follows:
  2% on freehold buildings using the straight-line method;
  10% on equipment using the reducing balance method;
  25% on motor vehicles using reducing balance.

● €2,300,000 was prepaid for repairs and €5,175,000 has accrued for wages.

Figure 9.1 Trial balance of Illustrious SpA as at 31 December 20X1

	€000	€000
Bank interest	1,150	
Bank overdraft		8,625
Cash in hand	4,600	
Debentures		63,250
Receivables	28,750	
Depreciation – equipment		3,450
– motor vehicles		9,200
Directors' remuneration	1,150	
Dividends	1,725	
Equipment	14,950	
Fees – audit	1,150	
Freehold land	57,500	
Freehold buildings	57,500	
Hire charges	300	
Interest on debentures	6,325	
Issued share capital		17,250
Lighting and power	920	
Miscellaneous expenses	275	
Motor expenses	9,200	
Motor vehicles	20,700	
Post, telephone, courier	1,840	
Retained earnings		57,500
Provision for income tax		5,750
Purchases	258,750	
Insurance	3,450	
Repairs and maintenance	2,760	
Salaries and wages	18,055	
Tax – income	5,750	
Sales		345,000
Inventory at 1 Jan 20X1	43,125	
Trade payables		29,900
	539,925	539,925

An income statement prepared for internal purposes is set out in Figure 9.2. We have arranged the expenses in the income statement in descending monetary value. This is not a prescribed method and companies may organise the items in a number of ways, such as alphabetical sequence or grouping by function, e.g. establishment, administration, selling, distribution and financial expenses.

Figure 9.2   Income statement of Illustrious SpA for the year ended 31 December 20X1

	€000	€000
Sales		345,000
Less:		
Opening inventory	43,125	
Purchases	258,750	
	301,875	
Closing inventory	25,875	
Cost of sales		276,000
Gross profit		69,000
Less: Expenses:		
Salaries and wages	23,230	
Motor expenses	9,200	
Debenture interest	6,325	
Depreciation	5,175	
Insurance	3,450	
Post, telephone, courier	1,840	
Fees – audit	1,150	
Bank interest	1,150	
Directors' remuneration	1,150	
Lighting and power	920	
Repairs and maintenance	460	
Hire charges	300	
Miscellaneous expenses	275	
		54,625
Profit before tax		14,375
Tax		5,750
Profit for the year		8,625
Dividends (treated as a reserve movement externally)		1,725
Amount transferred to reserves		6,900

9.3 Stage 2: preparation of the income statement of Illustrious SpA in Format 1 style

The information contained in the internal income statement in Figure 9.2 needs to be redrafted into the format required by IAS 1. In addition, specific information that would not necessarily appear within the format information needs to be disclosed. First we redraft using Format 1 with its costs analysed according to function, as set out in Figure 9.3.

Figure 9.3   Illustrious SpA income statement redrafted into Format I style

Income statement of Illustrious SpA
for the year ended 31 December 20X1

	€000
Revenue*	345,000.00
Cost of sales	293,422.50
Gross profit	51,577.50
Distribution, selling and marketing costs	25,041.25
Administrative expenses	4,686.25
Operating profit	21,850.00
Finance costs*	7,475.00
Profit on ordinary activities before tax	14,375.00
Tax*	5,750.00
Profit for the year*	8,625.00

*Required information on the face of the income statement

		Total €000	Cost of sales €000	Distribution costs €000	Administration expenses €000
Cost of sales		276,000	276,000		
Salaries and wages	NI	23,230	12,075	10,580	575
Motor expenses		9,200		9,200	
Depreciation	N2	5,175	1,150	3,450	575
Insurance	N3	3,450	1,725	862.5	862.5
Post, telephone, courier	N3	1,840	920	460	460
Fees – audit		1,150			1,150
Directors' salaries	N4	1,150	575		575
Lighting and power	N3	920	460	230	230
Repairs and maintenance	N3	460	230	115	115
Hire charges	N3	300	150	75	75
Miscellaneous expenses	N3	275	137.5	68.75	68.75
		323,150	293,422.5	25,041.25	4,686.25

Finance costs will be disclosed after the trading profit:

	€000
Debenture interest	6,325
Bank interest	1,150
	7,475

Note that dividends would be reported in the Statement of Changes in Equity.

9.3.1 How did we arrive at the figures for cost of sales, distribution costs and administrative expenses?

In order to analyse the costs, we need to consider each item in the detailed income statement. Each item will be allocated to a classification or apportioned if it relates to more than one of the classifications. This requires the company to make a number of assumptions about the basis for allocating and apportioning. The process is illustrated in Figure 9.4.

From the assumptions that have been made, it is clear that the figures appearing under each of the cost classifications may be apportioned differently in different companies.

Figure 9.4   Assumptions made in analysing the costs

N1 An analysis of salaries and wages

	Total €000	Cost of sales €000	Distribution costs €000	Administration expenses €000
Factory assembly staff	11,500	11,500		
Inspectors	575	575		
Warehouse staff	4,600		4,600	
Accounts department	575			575
Drivers	3,680		3,680	
Salespersons' salaries	2,300		2,300	
	23,230	12,075	10,580	575

N2 An analysis of depreciation

Freehold buildings	1,150	575	287.5	287.5
Equipment	1,150	575	287.5	287.5
Motor vehicles	2,875		2,875	
	5,175	1,150	3,450	575

N3 An apportionment of operating expenses

It is assumed that the following expenses can be apportioned on the basis of the space occupied by the activity, as follows:

	€000	€000	€000	€000
Insurance	3,450	1,725	862.5	862.5
Post, telephone, courier	1,840	920	460	460
Lighting and power	920	460	230	230
Repairs and maintenance	460	230	115	115
Hire charges	300	150	75	75
Miscellaneous expenses	275	137.5	68.75	68.75

N4 An allocation of directors' salaries

It is assumed that the directors spend half their time on production and half on administration.

9.3.2 What information would be disclosed by way of note to the income statement?

We have mentioned that sensitive information is required to be disclosed in the notes to the income statement. The usual practice is to have a note referenced to the profit on ordinary activities before tax. For Illustrious SpA the note would read as in Figure 9.5, with additional information regarding the loss on the inventory. This treatment – the inclusion of the expense in its cost type heading with more detail in the notes – complies with IAS 1, which does not allow for the highlighting of exceptional or unusual items. These should be disclosed separately either by way of note or on the face of the income statement only if that degree of prominence is necessary in order to give a fair view.[2]

Figure 9.5   Illustrious SpA disclosure note accompanying the income statement

Profit on ordinary activities before tax is stated after charging:	
	€000
Depreciation and amortisation	5,175
Exceptional loss on inventory	1,000

9.4 Stage 3: preparation of the balance sheet

The balance sheet in Figure 9.6 follows the headings set out in section 8.14.1 above.

Figure 9.6   Illustrious SpA balance sheet and disclosure notes

Disclosure notes to show make up of balance sheet items

Note 1 Property, plant and equipment movements

Property, plant and equipment	Freehold property €000	Equipment €000	Motor vehicles €000	Total €000
Cost				
At 1 January 20X1	115,000	14,950	20,700	150,650
Additions				
Disposals				
At 31 December 20X1	115,000	14,950	20,700	150,650
Accumulated depreciation				
At 1 January 20X1		3,450	9,200	12,650
Charge for year	1,150	1,150	2,875	5,175
At 31 December 20X1	1,150	4,600	12,075	17,825
Net book value				
At 31 December 20X1	113,850	10,350	8,625	132,825
At 31 December 20X0	115,000	11,500	11,500	138,000

Figure 9.6 (cont.)

Balance sheet of Illustrious SpA as at 31 December 20X1	€000	€000
Non-current assets		
Property, Plant and Equipment Note 1		132,825
Current assets		
Inventory	25,875	
Receivables	28,750	
Cash at bank and in hand	4,600	
Prepayments	2,300	
	61,525	
Current liabilities		
Payables	29,900	
Provision for income tax	5,750	
Accrued charges	5,175	
Bank overdraft	8,625	
	49,450	
Net current assets		12,075
Total assets less current liabilities		144,900
Non-current liabilities		
Debentures		63,250
		81,650
Capital and reserves		
Share capital		17,250
Retained earnings		64,400
		81,650

9.5 Preparation of accounts in Format 1 following IAS 8 and IFRS 5

By way of illustration, assume you are the chief accountant of Lewes Road Wines plc, a UK wholesale distributor currently operating from a single warehouse/office complex in London. Until June 20X2 the company had a plant at Dover, where wine that was imported in bulk was bottled prior to its sale to retail outlets. The profitability of this activity had declined and the plant had closed.

One of your unqualified assistants has prepared the following draft for the published income statement for the year to 31 December 20X2, which he has given to you together with his notes and workings as shown in Figure 9.7.

Figure 9.7   Lewes Road Wines plc Income statement (1)

Income statement for the year ended 31 December 20X2

	£000
Revenue (Note 1)	1,288
Cost of sales (Note 2)	744
Gross profit	544
Distribution costs (Note 3)	232
Administration costs (Note 4)	142
	374
Operating profit	170
Other operating income (Note 5)	286
Profit on ordinary activities before interest	456
Interest receivable	4
	460
Finance costs	33
Profit on ordinary activities before taxation	427
Tax on profit on ordinary activities (Note 6)	103
Profit for the year	324

Notes and workings

1   Revenue includes £175,000 in respect of bottling plant revenue.

2   *Cost of sales*

Wine purchased (including duty and carriage in)	536
Labour	72
Bottles, etc	150
Inventory variation (all wine)	(14)
	744

£72,000 (at cost) of wine had to be discarded during the year owing to contamination at source.

Labour costs included £10,000 for wages at the bottling plant and £30,000 in respect of redundancy payments to former employees at the Dover works.

3   *Distribution costs*

Carriage	120
Sales department salaries	51
Bad debts	61
	232

£55,000 represented the bad debt incurred following the collapse of a chain of cut price wine shops.

Figure 9.7 (*cont.*)

4 *Administrative expenses*

Salaries (£10,000 in respect of Dover)	78
Premises costs (£1,000 in respect of Dover)	19
Other overheads (£2,000 in respect of Dover)	21
Cost relating to the closure of the Dover plant	24
	142

5 *Other operating income*

Profit on revaluing Brighton premises	100
Profit on sale of Dover premises	212
Loss on sale of bottling equipment	(26)
	286

6 *Taxation*

Income tax due on 20X2 operating profit	44
Income tax on the capital gain on sale of Dover premises	56
Under provision for taxation in 20X1	3
	103

There was an error on the previous year closing inventory calculation resulting in an understatement of inventory by £100,000.

You need now to redraft the income statement so that it complies with IAS 1 and generally accepted accounting principles. Income tax is 30%. In approaching this task you need to consider the provisions of IFRS 5 relating to the treatment of discontinued operations, IAS 1 regarding unusual items, and IAS 8 regarding errors.

Discontinued operations

Applying the layered treatment of IFRS 5, which requires the results of continuing and discontinued operations to be disclosed separately, it is necessary to identify the revenue, cost of sales and expenses that relate to the discontinuing bottling operation in arriving at the operating profit.

Unusual activities

Paragraph 86 of IAS 1 states that, when items of income and expense are material, their nature and amount shall be disclosed separately – such disclosure is relevant to explain the performance of the enterprise for the period. These items may include losses on termination of operations and profits or losses on the sale of non-current assets. IAS 1 paragraph 81 does requires profits or losses on disposal of assets and liabilities of a discontinued operation to be shown on the face of the income statement.

Revaluation

The revaluation surplus, being unrealised, cannot appear in the income statement. It should, however, appear in the statement of changes in equity or the statement of recognised gains and losses.

Errors

IAS 8 requires errors of prior years to be accounted for by restating the comparative figures and adjusting the opening balance of reserves for the cumulative effect. Note that this means that it is also necessary to take the tax effect into account.

The detailed workings and income statement are given in Figure 9.8.

Figure 9.8 Lewes Road Wines plc income statement (2)

Income statement for the year ended 31 December 20X2	Continuing operations £000	Discontinued operations £000	Total £000
Turnover	1,113	175	1,288
Cost of sales	654	160	814
Gross profit	459	15	474
Administrative costs	(105)	(13)	(118)
Distribution costs	(232)	—	(232)
Operating profit	122	2	124
Profit on property sale		212	212
Loss on disposal of discontinued activity		(80)	(80)
Profit on ordinary activities before interest	122	134	256
Interest receivable	4	—	4
	126	134	260
Finance costs	33	—	33
Profit on ordinary activities before taxation	93	134	227
Taxation	17	56	73
Profit for the year	76	78	154

Statement of movement on reserves

Profit for the year		154
Dividends		(45)
Retained profits b/f:		
As previously reported	274	
Prior year adjustment	100	
Tax thereon	(30)	344
Retained profits carried forward		453

Notes

Unusual items

Cost of sales includes £72,000 in respect of wine that had to be discarded during the year owing to contamination at source.

Sales costs includes £55,000 in respect of a bad debt incurred following the collapse of a chain of cut price wine shops.

Figure 9.8 (cont.)

Workings			
Cost of sales	*Bottling*	*Other*	*Total*
Per draft – labour	40	32	72
bottles, etc.	150		150
stock		(14)	(14)
wine		536	536
Prior year item		100	100
Loss on sale	(30)		(30)
	160	654	814
Administration expenses			
Per draft – salaries	10	68	78
premises	1	18	19
other	2	19	21
closure	24		24
Loss on sale	(24)		(24)
	13	105	118
Loss on closure			
Administration	24		
Redundancy	30		
Bottling equipment	26		
	80		

Statement of recognised income and expense

Profit for the financial year	154	[Figure 9.8 Profit for the year]
Unrealised surplus on revaluation	100	[Figure 9.7 Note 5 premises revalued]
Total recognised gains	254	
Prior year adjustment	70	[Figure 9.8 adjusting profit brought
	324	forward]

9.6 Additional information value of IFRS 5

Changes in the operation

The additional disclosure of the effect of discontinuing operations is intended to assist the user to assess more readily the current performance and to predict future maintainable profits. However, care is required when comparing current performance with that of previous years.

Newly acquired activities

In the international accounting standards there is no requirement for information to be separately disclosed in the income statement about the performance of newly acquired activities. As a result the current year's performance may include the results of activities that were not in the previous periods and therefore any comparison will be invalid. In some accounting regimes, such as that in the UK, information about newly acquired activities is required. As always therefore when interpreting financial information care must be taken when concluding about the results.

9.7 Additional information value of IAS 24

Related party relationships for the purposes of IAS 24[3] could be any of the following:

● enterprises that directly, or indirectly through one or more intermediaries, control, or are controlled by, or are under common control with, the reporting enterprise (this includes holding companies, subsidiaries and fellow subsidiaries);
● associates;
● individuals owning, directly or indirectly, an interest in the voting power of the reporting enterprise that gives them significant influence over the enterprise, and close members of the family of such an individual (close family members of an individual are those that may be expected to influence, or be influenced by, that person in their dealings with the enterprise);
● key management personnel, that is, those persons having authority and responsibility for planning, directing and controlling the activities of the reporting enterprise, including directors and officers of companies and close members of the families of such individuals;
● enterprises in which a substantial interest in the voting power is owned, directly or indirectly, by any person described above or over which such a person is able to exercise significant influence. This includes enterprises owned by the directors or major shareholders of the reporting enterprise and enterprises that have a member of key management in common with the reporting enterprise.

Parties deemed not to be related parties

IAS 24 sets out a number of parties[4] who are not deemed related and for whom no disclosure is therefore required:

● two companies simply because they have a director in common (but it is necessary to consider the possibility, and to assess the likelihood, that the director would be able to affect the policies of both companies in their mutual dealings);
● providers of finance, trade unions, public utilities or government departments in the course of their normal dealings with the enterprise;
● a single customer, supplier, franchisor, distributor or general agent with whom an enterprise transacts a significant volume of business merely by virtue of the resulting economic dependence;
● two ventures simply because they share joint control over a joint venture.

Related party transactions

A related party transaction is a transfer of resources or obligations between related parties, regardless of whether a price is charged. Examples[5] of transactions that may give rise to related party disclosures are:

● purchases or sales of goods; purchases or sales of property and other assets; providing or receiving of services;

● agency arrangements; leasing arrangements; transfer of research and development; licence agreements;

● finance (including loans and equity contributions in cash or in kind); guarantees and collaterals;

● management contracts.

Related party disclosures

Related party relationships where control exists should be disclosed irrespective of whether there have been transactions between the related parties. If there have been transactions between related parties the disclosures required[6] are:

● the amount of the transactions;

● the amount of the outstanding balances and:
   (i) their terms and conditions, including whether they are secured, and the nature of the consideration to be provided in settlement; and
   (ii) details of any guarantees given or received;

● provisions for doubtful debts related to the amount of outstanding balances; and

● the expense recognised during the period in respect of bad or doubtful debts due from related parties;

● key management personnel compensation in total and for each of the following categories:
   (a) short-term employee benefits;
   (b) post-employment benefits;
   (c) other long-term benefits;
   (d) termination benefits; and
   (e) equity compensation benefits.

9.7.1 Illustration of related party disclosures

The following illustration from the 2003 financial statements of Nokia, shows the type of disclosures that should be made under IAS 24.

Related Party Disclosures

Nokia Pension Foundation is a separate legal entity that manages and holds in trust the assets for the Group's Finnish employee benefit plans; these assets include 0.03% of Nokia's shares. In 2002 Nokia Pension Foundation was the counterparty to equity swap agreements with the Group. The equity swaps were entered into to hedge part of the company's liability relating to future social security cost on stock options. During 2003, all outstanding transactions were terminated and no new ones were entered into. During 2002, new transactions were entered into and old ones terminated based on the hedging need. The transactions and terminations were executed on standard commercial terms and conditions. The notional amount of the equity swaps outstanding at December 31, 2002 was EUR 12 million and the fair value EUR 0 million.

At 31 December, 2003 the Group had no contribution payment liability to Nokia Pension Foundation (EUR 14 million in 2002 included in accrued expenses).

At 31 December, 2003 the Group had borrowings amounting to EUR 64 million (EUR 66 million in 2002) from Nokia Unterstützungskasse GmbH, the Group's German pension fund, which is a separate legal entity.

The Group's recorded net rental expense of EUR 2 million in 2003 (EUR 2 million in 2002 and EUR 4 million in 2001) [was] pertaining to a sale-leaseback transaction with the Nokia Pension Foundation involving certain buildings and a lease of the underlying land.

There were no loans granted to top management at December 31, 2003 or 2002. See note 4, Personnel Expenses, for officers' and directors' remunerations.

Summary

A public company that is listed on the Stock Exchange is required to present an annual report and accounts to its shareholders.

The annual report consists of a number of statements. In Chapters 8 and 9 we have considered the following statements: the directors' report; the income statement; the statement of changes in equity and the balance sheet. We have seen the following:

- There is more than one format for presenting the income statement and even companies operating in the same industry sector might choose a different format.
- Even where companies use the same format, they may classify costs into different cost categories.
- The additional information disclosed, e.g. staff costs, cannot necessarily be related to the categories of operations into which the company has classified its costs in its income statement.
- There is no obvious, overriding rationale for the disclosure of information; it has grown in an *ad hoc* fashion with disclosure required:
  - for stewardship accounting, e.g. the disclosure of directors' remuneration;
  - for the shareholders as principal stakeholders, e.g. trading profit;
  - for interested stakeholders, e.g. an analysis of employees and details of staff costs;
  - for the community as an interested stakeholder, e.g. company policy on employment.
- The balance sheet can be prepared under historical cost accounting rules or alternative accounting rules or a mixture of historical and alternative accounting rules.

Perhaps we have reached a stage where the purpose of the annual report needs to be reappraised and given a clearer focus.

REVIEW QUESTIONS

1 The directors of Ufool Ltd are aware that a sizeable number of shareholders, although still a minority, are extremely unhappy with current dividend levels and are agitating for larger distributions.

They have raised several points with the directors, who have turned to you as their trusty financial and accounting adviser for assistance. The points put forward by these shareholders are as follows:

(i) Although the annual accounts disclose that £150,000 profit was available for distribution, it is disclosed elsewhere in these accounts that £520,000 of the loan stock had been repaid. The shareholders assert that this repayment was an attempt to lower the true profit and that, if it were written back, more profit would be available for distribution.

(ii) Despite this year's relatively low profit, there is a very large balance of retained earnings brought forward from preceding years. A significant proportion of these retained earnings from preceding years should be used to pay a larger dividend this year.

(iii) It is unfair to have kept the dividend rate at 10% over the past few years when the average dividend yield on the Stock Exchange has risen from 12% to 18%. The company's dividend rate should follow this average.

(iv) The return on capital employed for the company is 20% and this high rate of profitability accurately reflects the ability of the company to pay far higher dividend levels.

(v) As profit figures can so easily be manipulated by the company's accountants, the £150,000 is more than likely to be a significant underestimate of the real profit, so more profit could be distributed if different accounting bases were used.

Comment on each of the above assertions to enable the board of directors to refute them convincingly.

2 It is said that Format 1 extends the management accounting concept of responsibility accounting to published financial statements. Explain what this means.

3 When preparing accounts under Format 1, how would a bad debt that was materially larger than normal be disclosed?

4 Explain the conditions set out in IFRS 5 for determining whether operations have been discontinued and the problems that might arise in applying them.

5 'Annual accounts have been put into such a straitjacket overemphasis on uniform disclosure that there will be a growing pressure by national bodies to introduce changes unilaterally which will again lead to diversity in the quality of disclosure. This is both healthy and necessary.' Discuss.

6 Explain the relevance to the user of accounts if expenses are classified as 'administrative expenses' rather than as 'cost of sales'.

7 'The regulators are correct in their thinking that voluntary disclosures, e.g. OFR and Interim Reports, are more helpful to shareholders than disclosures made under mandatory, more closely defined formats.' Discuss.

8 IAS 1 *Presentation of Financial Statements* requires the publication of a statement of recognised income and expense or a statement of changes in equity.

Explain the need for the publishing of these statements, identifying the circumstances in which they have to be published, and identify the items you would include in them.

EXERCISES

An extract from the solution is provided in the Appendix at the end of the text for exercises marked with an asterisk (*).

* Question 1

Springtime Ltd is a UK trading company buying and selling as wholesalers fashionable summer clothes. The following balances have been extracted from the books as at 31 March 20X4:

	£000
Auditor's remuneration	30
Income tax based on the accounting profit:	
For the year to 31 March 20X4	3,200
Overprovision for the year to 31 March 20X3	200
Delivery expenses (including £300,000 overseas)	1,200
Dividends: final (proposed – to be paid 1 August 20X4)	200
interim (paid on 1 October 20X3)	100
Non-current assets at cost:	
Delivery vans	200
Office cars	40
Stores equipment	5,000
Dividend income (amount received from listed companies)	1,200
Office expenses	800
Overseas operations: closure costs of entire operations	350
Purchases	24,000
Sales (net of sales tax)	35,000
Inventory at cost:	
At 1 April 20X3	5,000
At 31 March 20X4	6,000
Storeroom costs	1,000
Wages and salaries:	
Delivery staff	700
Directors' emoluments	400
Office staff	100
Storeroom staff	400

Notes:

1 Depreciation is provided at the following annual rates on a straight-line basis: delivery vans 20%; office cars 25%; stores 1%.
2 The following taxation rates may be assumed: corporate income tax 35%; personal income tax 25%.
3 The dividend income arises from investments held in non-current investments.
4 It has been decided to transfer an amount of £150,000 to the deferred taxation account.
5 The overseas operations consisted of exports. In 20X3/X4 these amounted to £5,000,000 (sales) with purchases of £4,000,000. Related costs included £100,000 in storeroom staff and £15,000 for office staff.

6   Directors' emoluments include:

Chairperson	100,000
Managing director	125,000
Finance director	75,000
Sales director	75,000
Export director	25,000 (resigned 31 December 20X3)
	£400,000

Required:

(a) Produce an income statement suitable for publication and complying as far as possible with generally accepted accounting practice.

(b) Comment on how IFRS 5 has improved the quality of information available to users of accounts.

(c) Give two reasons why information contained in the accounting policies notes is of importance to users of accounts.

* Question 2

Olive A/S, incorporated with an authorised capital consisting of one million ordinary shares of €1 each, employs 646 persons, of whom 428 work at the factory and the rest at the head office. The trial balance extracted from its books as at 30 September 20X4 is as follows:

	€000	€000
Land and buildings (cost €600,000)	520	—
Plant and machinery (cost €840,000)	680	—
Proceeds on disposal of plant and machinery	—	180
Fixtures and equipment (cost €120,000)	94	—
Sales	—	3,460
Carriage inwards	162	—
Share premium account	—	150
Advertising	112	—
Inventory on 1 Oct 20X3	211	—
Heating and lighting	80	—
Prepayments	115	—
Salaries	820	—
Trade investments at cost	248	—
Dividend received (net) on 9 Sept 20X4	—	45
Directors' emoluments	180	—
Pension cost	100	—
Audit fees and expense	65	—
Retained earnings b/f	—	601
Sales commission	92	—
Stationery	28	—
Development cost	425	—
Formation expenses	120	—
Receivables and payables	584	296
Interim dividend paid on 4 Mar 20X4	60	—
12% debentures issued on 1 Apr 20X4	—	500
Debenture interest paid on 1 Jul 20X4	15	—
Purchases	925	—
Income tax on year to 30 Sept 20X3	—	128
Other administration expenses	128	—
Bad debts	158	—
Cash and bank balance	38	—
Ordinary shares of €1 fully called	—	600
	5,960	5,960

You are informed as follows:

(a) As at 1 October 20X3 land and buildings were revalued at €900,000. A third of the cost as well as all the valuation is regarded as attributable to the land. Directors have decided to report this asset at valuation.

(b) New fixtures were acquired on 1 January 20X4 for €40,000; a machine acquired on 1 October 20X1 for €240,000 was disposed of on 1 July 20X4 for €180,000, being replaced on the same date by another acquired for €320,000.

(c) Depreciation for the year is to be calculated on the straight-line basis as follows:

Buildings: 2% p.a.
Plant and machinery: 10% p.a.
Fixtures and equipment: 10% p.a.

(d) Inventory in trade, including raw materials and work-in-progress on 30 September 20X4, has been valued at cost at €364,000.

(e) Prepayments are made up as follows:

	€000
Amount paid in advance for a machine	60
Amount paid in advance for purchasing raw materials	40
Prepaid rent	15
	€115

(f) In March 20X3 a customer had filed legal action claiming damages at €240,000. When accounts for the year ended 30 September 20X3 were finalised, a provision of €90,000 was made in respect of this claim. This claim was settled out of court in April 20X4 at €150,000 and the amount of the underprovision adjusted against the profit balance brought forward from previous years.

(g) The following allocations have been agreed upon:

	Factory	Administration
Depreciation of buildings	60%	40%
Salaries other than to directors	55%	45%
Heating and lighting	80%	20%

(h) Pension cost of the company is calculated at 10% of the emoluments and salaries.

(i) Income tax on 20X3 profit has been agreed at €140,000 and that for 20X4 estimated at €185,000. Corporate income tax rate is 35% and the basic rate of personal income tax 25%.

(j) Directors wish to write off the formation expenses as far as possible without reducing the amount of profits available for distribution.

Required:
Prepare for publication:

(a) The income statement of the company for the year ended 30 September 20X4, and

(b) the balance sheet as at that date along with as many notes (other than the one on accounting policy) as can be provided on the basis of the information made available.

Question 3

Cryptic plc extracted its trial balance on 30 June 20X5 as follows:

	£000	£000
Land and buildings at cost	750	—
Plant and machinery at cost	480	—
Accumulated depreciation on plant and machinery at 30 Jun 20X5	—	400
Depreciation on machinery	80	—
Furniture, tools and equipment at cost	380	—
Accumulated depreciation on furniture, etc. at 30 Jun 20X4	—	95
Receivables and payables	475	360
Inventory of raw materials at 30 Jun 20X4	112	—
Work-in-progress at factory cost at 30 Jun 20X4	76	—
Finished goods at cost at 30 Jun 20X4	264	—
Sales including selling taxes	—	2,875
Purchases of raw materials including selling taxes	1,380	—
Share premium account	—	150
Advertising	65	—
Deferred taxation	—	185
Salaries	360	—
Rent	120	—
Retained earnings at 30 Jun 20X4	—	226
Factory power	48	—
Trade investments at cost	240	—
Overprovision for tax for the year ended 30 Jun 20X4	—	21
Electricity	36	—
Stationery	12	—
Dividend received (net)	—	24
Dividend paid on 15 April 20X5	60	—
Other administration expenses	468	—
Disposal of furniture	—	64
Selling tax control account	165	—
Ordinary shares of 50p each	—	1,000
12% Preference shares of £1 each (IAS 32 liability)	—	200
Cash and bank balance	29	—
	5,600	5,600

The following information is relevant:

(i) The company discontinued a major activity during the year and replaced it with another. All non-current assets involved in the discontinued activity were redeployed for the new one. The following expenses incurred in this respect, however, are included in 'Other administration expenses':

	£000
Cancellation of contracts re terminated activity	165
Fundamental reorganisation arising as a result	145

Cryptic has decided to present its results from discontinued operations as a single line on the face of the income statement with analysis in the notes to the accounts as allowed by IFRS 5.

(ii) On 1 January 20X5 the company acquired new land and buildings for £150,000. The remainder of land and buildings, acquired nine years earlier, have NOT been depreciated until this year. The company has decided to depreciate the buildings, on the straight-line method, assuming that one-third of the cost relates to land and that the buildings have an estimated economic life of fifty years. The company policy is to charge a full year of depreciation in the year of purchase and none in the year of sale.

(iii) Plant and machinery was all acquired on 1 July 20X0 and has been depreciated at 10% per annum on the straight-line method. The estimate of useful economic life had to be revised this year when it was realised that if the market share is to be maintained at current levels, the company has to replace all its machinery by 1 July 20X6. The balance in the 'Accumulated provision for depreciation' account on 1 July 20X4 was amended to reflect the revised estimate of useful economic life and the impact of the revision adjusted against the retained earnings brought forward from prior years.

(iv) Furniture acquired for £80,000 on 1 January 20X3 was disposed of for £64,000 on 1 April 20X5. Furniture, tools and equipment are depreciated at 5% p.a. on cost. Depreciation for the current year has not been provided.

(v) Results of the stocktaking at year-end are as follows:

Stock of raw materials at cost including selling tax	£197,800
Work-in-progress at factory cost	£54,000
Finished goods at cost	£364,000

(vi) The company allocates its expenditure as follows:

	Production cost	Factory overhead	Distribution cost	Administrative expenses
Salaries and wages	65%	15%	5%	15%
Rent	—	60%	15%	25%
Electricity	—	10%	20%	70%
Depreciation of building	—	40%	10%	50%

(vii) The directors wish to make an accrual for audit fees of £18,000 and estimate the income tax for the year at £65,000. £11,000 should be transferred from the deferred tax account. The directors have to pay the preference dividend.

(viii) The following analysis has been made:

	New activity	Discontinued activity
Sales excluding selling taxes	£165,000	£215,000
Cost of sales	£98,000	£155,000
Distribution cost	£16,500	£48,500
Administrative expenses	£22,500	£38,500

(ix) Assume that selling taxes applicable to all purchases and sales is 15%, the basic rate of personal income tax is 25% and the corporate income tax rate is 35%.

Required:

(a) Advise the company on the accounting treatment in respect of information stated in (ii) above.

(b) In respect of the information stated in (iii) above, state whether a company is permitted to revise its estimate of the useful economic life of a non-current asset and comment on the appropriateness of the accounting treatment adopted.

(c) Set out a statement of movement of property, plant and equipment in the year to 30 June 20X5.

(d) Set out for publication the income statement for the year ended 30 June 20X5, the balance sheet as at that date and any notes other than that on accounting policy, in accordance with relevant standards.

Question 4

The IASC/IASB has issued accounting standards that concentrate on the issue of reporting financial performance. The main standards that report this are:

IAS 1 *Presentation of Financial Statements*
IAS 14 *Segment Reporting*
IFRS 5 *Non-current Assets held for Sale and Discontinued Operations*

All of these accounting standards require companies to give disclosures or further presentation on the face of the financial statements to help users understand the performance of the enterprise. These further disclosures improve the quality of the information in the financial statements and therefore should improve the decisions taken by users in response to the financial statements.

Required:

(a) Describe how the statement of changes in equity (from IAS 1), segmental disclosures and discontinuing operations disclosures will help investors and lenders make decisions based on the financial statements.

(b) Bedok Ltd has three divisions: a paper manufacturing division, a printing division and a clothing manufacturing division. On 1 April 20X9 the directors of Bedok Ltd decided to sell the clothing division as it was not in line with the core activities of the company. This decision was announced to the employees and the public on 1 June 20X9. The net assets of the clothing division as at 31 December 20X9 were £16 million (£20 million assets less £4 million liabilities).

On 10 May 20Y0 the board signed an agreement with Woodlands Ltd to sell the clothing division for £20 million. The net assets of the clothing division at this date were £18 million (£23 million assets and £5 million liabilities). Bedok Ltd incurred redundancy costs of £1 million which had been expected from the date the decision to sell the division was made. The redundancy costs are not reflected in the income statement information given below. The sale was completed on 1 July 20Y0 and the clothing division did not trade between 10 May 20Y0 and 1 July 20Y0.

The results of the clothing manufacturing division for 20X9 and 20Y0 are as follows:

	20X9	20Y0 (to 1 July)
	£000	£000
Turnover	65,000	40,000
Expenses	(50,000)	(32,000)
Operating profit	15,000	8,000
Tax charge	(5,000)	(3,000)

Prepare extracts from the financial statements (including notes) of Bedok Ltd for 31 December 20X9 and 20Y0 in accordance with IFRS 5, including all relevant information on the face of the income statement.

Question 5

The following is the draft trading and income statement of Parnell Ltd for the year ending 31 December 2003:

	$m	$m
Revenue		563
Cost of sales		310
		253
Distribution costs	45	
Administrative expenses	78	
		123
Profit on ordinary activities before tax		130
Tax on profit on ordinary activities		45
Profit on ordinary activities after taxation – all retained		85
Profit brought forward at 1 January 2003		101
Profit carried forward at 31 December 2003		186

You are given the following additional information, which is reflected in the above income statement only to the extent stated:

1. Distribution costs include a bad debt of $15 million which arose on the insolvency of a major customer. There is no prospect of recovering any of this debt. Bad debts have never been material in the past.

2. The company has traditionally consisted of a manufacturing division and a distribution division. On 31 December 2003, the entire distribution division was sold for $50 million; its book value at the time of sale was $40 million. The surplus on disposal was credited to administrative expenses. (Ignore any related income tax.)

3. During 2003, the distribution division made sales of $100 million and had a cost of sales of $30 million. There will be no reduction in stated distribution costs or administration expenses as a result of this disposal.

4. The company owns offices which it purchased on 1 January 2001 for $500 million, comprising $200 million for land and $300 million for buildings. No depreciation was charged in 2001 or 2002, but the company now considers that such a charge should be introduced. The buildings were expected to have a life of fifty years at the date of purchase, and the company uses the straight-line basis for calculating depreciation, assuming a zero residual value. No taxation consequences result from this change.

5. During 2003, part of the manufacturing division was restructured at a cost of $20 million to take advantage of modern production techniques. The restructuring was not fundamental and will **not** have a material effect on the nature and focus of the company's operations. This cost is included under administration expenses in the income statement.

Required:

(a) State how each of the items 1–5 above must be accounted for in order to comply with the requirements of international accounting standards.

(b) Redraft the income statement of Parnell Ltd for 2003, taking into account the additional information so as to comply, as far as possible, with relevant standard accounting practice. Show clearly any adjustments you make. Notes to the accounts are not required. Where an IAS recommends information to be on the face of the income statement it could be recorded on the face of the statement. *(The Chartered Institute of Bankers)*

Question 6 Related party scenarios

(a) In 20X3 Arthur is a large loan creditor of X Ltd and receives interest at 20% p.a. on this loan. He also has a 24% shareholding in X Ltd. Until 20X1 he was a director of the company and left after a disagreement. The remaining 76% of the shares are held by the remaining directors. Is Arthur a related party to X Ltd?

(b) Brenda joined Y Ltd, an insurance broking company, on 1 January 20X0 on a low salary but high commission basis. She brought clients with her that generated 30% of the company's 20X0 turnover. Is Brenda a related party to Y Ltd?

(c) Carrie is a director and major shareholder of Z Ltd. Her husband, Donald, is employed in the company on administrative duties for which he is paid a salary of £25,000 p.a. Her daughter, Emma, is a business consultant running her own business. In 20X0 Emma carried out various consultancy exercises for the company for which she was paid £85,000. Are Donald or Emma related parties to Z Ltd?

(d) Fred is a director of V Ltd. V Ltd is a major customer of W Ltd. In 20X0 Fred also became a director of W Ltd. Are related party disclosures required in either V Ltd or W Ltd?

Required:
Discuss whether parties are related in the above situations.

Question 7

Maxpool plc, a listed company, owned 60% of the shares in Ching Ltd. Bay plc, a listed company, owned the remaining 40% of the £1 ordinary shares in Ching Ltd. The holdings of shares were acquired on 1 January 20X0.

On 30 November 20X0 Ching Ltd sold a factory outlet site to Bay plc at a price determined by an independent surveyor.

On 1 March 20X1 Maxpool plc purchased a further 30% of the £1 ordinary shares of Ching Ltd from Bay plc and purchased 25% of the ordinary shares of Bay plc.

On 30 June 20X1 Ching Ltd sold the whole of its fleet of vehicles to Bay plc at a price determined by a vehicle auctioneer.

Required:
Explain the implications of the above transactions for the determination of related party relationships and disclosure of such transactions in the financial statements of (a) Maxpool Group plc, (b) Ching Ltd and (c) Bay plc for the years ending 31 December 20X0 and 31 December 20X1.
(ACCA)

References

1 IAS 1 *Presentation of Financial Statements*, IASC, revised 1997, para. 77.
2 IAS 1 *Presentation of Financial Statements*, IASB, 2003.
3 IAS 24 *Related Party Disclosures*, IASB, revised 2003, para. 9.
4 *Ibid.*, para. 11.
5 *Ibid.*, para. 20.
6 *Ibid.*, para. 17.

PART 3

Balance sheet – equity, liability and asset measurement and disclosure

CHAPTER 10

Share capital, capital maintenance and distributable profits

10.1 Introduction

Companies may be financed by equity investors, loan creditors and trade creditors. Governments have recognised that for an efficient capital market to exist, the rights of each of these stakeholders need to be protected. This means that equity investors require a clear statement of their powers to appoint and remunerate directors and of their entitlement to share in residual income and net assets; loan creditors and trade creditors require assurance that the directors will not distribute funds to the equity investors before settling outstanding debts in full.

Statutory rules have, therefore, evolved which attempt a balancing act by protecting the creditors on the one hand, e.g. by restricting dividend distributions to realised profits whilst, on the other hand, not unduly restricting the ability of companies to organise their financial affairs, e.g. by reviewing a company's right to purchase and hold Treasury shares. Such rules may not be totally consistent between countries but there do appear to be some common themes running through much of the legislation – these are:

- Share capital can be broadly of two types, equity or preference.
- Equity shares are entitled to the residual income after paying expenses, loan interest and tax.
- Equity itself is a residual figure in that the standard setters have taken the approach of defining assets and liabilities and leaving equity capital as the residual difference.
- Equity may consist of ordinary shares or equity elements of **participating** preference shares and compound instruments which include debt and equity i.e. where there are conversion rights when there must be a split into their debt and equity elements, with each element being accounted for separately.
- Preference shares are not entitled (unless participating) to share in the residual income but may be entitled to a fixed or floating rate of interest on their investment.
- The distributable reserves of enterprises are those that have arisen due to realised gains and losses (retained profits), as opposed to unrealised gains (such as revaluation reserves).
- There must be protection for creditors to prevent an enterprise distributing assets to shareholders to the extent that the creditors are not paid in full. An enterprise must retain net assets at least equal to its share capital and non-distributable reserves (a capital maintenance concept).
- The capital maintenance concept also applies with regard to reducing share capital, with most countries requiring a replacement of share capital with a non-distributable reserve (capital redemption reserve) if it is redeemed.

Because all countries have company legislation and these themes are common, the authors felt that, as the UK has relatively well-developed company legislation, it would be helpful to consider such legislation as illustrating a typical range of statutory provisions. We therefore now consider the constituents of total shareholders' funds (also known as total owners' equity) and the nature of distributable and non-distributable reserves. We then analyse the role of the capital maintenance concept in the protection of creditors, before discussing the effectiveness of the protection offered by the Companies Act 1985 in respect of both private and public companies and international influences for change.

10.2 Total owners' equity: an overview

Total owners' equity consists of the issued share capital stated at nominal (or par) value, non-distributable and distributable reserves. Here we comment briefly on the main constituents of total shareholders' funds. We go on to deal with them in greater detail in subsequent sections.

10.2.1 Right to issue shares

Companies incorporated under the Companies Act 1985 are able to raise capital by the issue of shares and debentures. There are two main categories of company: private limited companies and public limited companies. Public limited companies are designated by the letters **plc** and have the right to issue shares and debentures to the public. Private limited companies are often family companies; they are not allowed to seek share capital by invitations to the public. The shareholders of both categories have the benefit of limited personal indemnity, i.e. their liability to creditors is limited to the amount they agreed to pay the company for the shares they bought.

10.2.2 Types of share

Broadly, there are two types of share: ordinary and preference.

Ordinary shares

Ordinary shares, often referred to as equity shares, carry the main risk and their bearers are entitled to the residual profit after paying any fixed interest or fixed dividend to investors who have invested on the basis of a fixed return. Distributions from the residual profit are made in the form of dividends, which are normally expressed as pence per share.

Preference shares

Preference shares usually have a fixed rate of dividend, which is expressed as a percentage of the nominal value of the share. The dividend is paid before any distribution to the ordinary shareholders. The specific rights attaching to a preference share can vary widely.

10.2.3 Non-distributable reserves

There are two types of **statutory** non-distributable reserve: share premium and capital redemption reserve. These are considered in greater detail below. In addition to the statutory non-distributable reserves, a company might have restrictions on distribution within its memorandum and articles, stipulating that capital profits are non-distributable as dividends.

10.2.4 Distributable reserves

Distributable reserves are normally represented by the balance on the profit and loss account that appears in the balance sheet and belong to the ordinary shareholders. However, as we shall see, there may be circumstances where credits that have been made to the profit and loss account are not actually distributable, usually because they do not satisfy the **realisation** concept.

Although the balance sheet profit and loss account figure contains the cumulative residual distributable profits, it is the earnings per share (EPS), based on the post-tax earnings for the year as disclosed in the profit and loss account, that influences market valuation of the shares, applying the price/earnings ratio.

When deciding whether to issue or buy back shares, the directors will therefore probably consider the impact on the EPS figure. If the EPS increases, the share price can normally be expected also to increase.

10.3 Total shareholders' funds: more detailed explanation

10.3.1 Ordinary shares – risks and rewards

Ordinary shares (often referred to as equity shares) confer the right to

(a) share proportionately in the rewards, i.e.:
   ● the residual profit remaining after paying any loan interest or fixed dividends to investors who have invested on the basis of a fixed return
   ● any dividends distributed from these residual profits
   ● any net assets remaining after settling all creditors' claims in the event of the company ceasing to trade;

(b) share proportionately in the risks, i.e.:
   ● lose a proportionate share of invested share capital if the company ceases to trade and there are insufficient funds to pay all the creditors and the shareholders in full.

10.3.2 Ordinary shares – powers

The owners of ordinary shares generally have one vote per share which can be exercised on a routine basis, for example at the Annual General Meeting to vote on the appointment of directors, and on an *ad hoc* basis, e.g. at an Extraordinary General Meeting to vote on a proposed capital reduction scheme.

However, there are some companies that have issued non-voting ordinary shares which may confer the right to a proportional share of the residual profits but not to vote. The practice varies around the world.

In Europe, for example, it may be regarded as poor corporate governance, and companies have been taking steps to enfranchise non-voting shares. The following is an extract from a letter from John Laing plc to shareholders setting out its enfranchisement proposals:

LAING SETS OUT ENFRANCHISEMENT PROPOSALS 23 March 2000

John Laing plc today issues enfranchisement proposals to change the Group voting structure.

The key points are as follows:

- Convert the Ordinary A (non-voting) Shares into Ordinary Shares
- All redesignated shares to have full voting rights ranking *pari passu* in all respects with the existing Ordinary Shares
- Compensatory Scrip Issue for holders of existing Ordinary Shares of one New Ordinary Share for every 20 Ordinary Shares held [*authors' note: this is in recognition of the fact that the proportion of votes of the existing ordinary shareholders has been reduced – an alternative approach would be to ask the non-voting shareholders to pay a premium in exchange for being given voting rights*]
- EGM to be held on 18th May 2000

Reasons for Enfranchisement

- To increase the range of potential investors in the Company which the Directors believe should enhance the marketability and liquidity of the Company's shares
- To enable all classes of equity shareholders, who share the same risks and rewards, to share the same voting rights
- To ensure the Company has maximum flexibility to manage its capital structure in order to reduce its cost of capital and to enhance shareholder value.

In other countries, however, there may be sound commercial reasons why non-voting shares are issued. In Japan, for example, the Japanese Commercial Code was amended in 2002 to allow companies to issue shares with special rights, e.g. power to veto certain company decisions, and to increase the proportion of non-voting shares in issue. The intention was to promote successful restructuring of ailing companies and stimulate demand for Japanese equity investments.

10.3.3 Methods and reasons for issuing shares

Methods of issuing shares

Some of the common methods of issuing shares are: *offer for subscription*, where the shares are offered directly to the public; *placings*, where the shares are arranged (placed) to be bought by financial institutions; and *rights issues*, whereby the new shares are offered to the existing shareholders at a price below the market price of those shares. The rights issue might be priced significantly below the current market price but this may not mean that the shareholder is benefiting from cheap shares as the price of existing shares will be reduced, e.g. the British Telecommunications plc £5.9 billion rights issue announced in 2001 made UK corporate history in that no British company had attempted to raise so much cash from its shareholders. The offer was three BT shares for every ten held and, to encourage take-up, the new shares were offered at a deeply discounted rate of £3 which was at a 47% discount to the share price on the day prior to the launch.

Reasons for issuing shares

- **For future investment,** e.g. Watford Leisure plc (Watford Football Club) offered and placed 540,000,000 ordinary shares and expected to raise cash proceeds of about £4.7 million. The company is to be floated on the AIM.
- **As consideration on an acquisition,** e.g. Microsoft Corp. acquired Great Plains Software Incorporated, a leading supplier of mid-market business applications. The acquisition was structured as a stock purchase and was valued at approximately

$1.1 billion. Each share of Great Plains common stock was exchanged for 1.1 shares of Microsoft common stock.

- **To shareholders to avoid paying out cash from the company's funds,** e.g. the BIDVest Group Ltd which decided in 2001 that in lieu of an interim dividend, a cash payment of 40 cents per share should be paid out of share premium, and a capitalisation issue of shares awarded in the ratio of 0.8631 new shares per 100 shares held, being equivalent to 41 cents per share. The total value awarded to shareholders in lieu of a dividend was 81 cents per share.

- **To directors and employees to avoid paying out cash in the form of salary from company's funds,** e.g. in the Psion 2000 Annual Report the note on directors' remuneration stated:

Name	As at 1/1/00	Exercised	As at 31.12.00	Option price	Market price
M.M. Wyatt	150,000	150,000	–	£0.73	£12.09

10.3.4 Types of preference shares

The following illustrate some of the ways in which specific rights can vary.

Cumulative preference shares
Dividends not paid in respect of any one year because of a lack of profits are accumulated for payment in some future year when distributable profits are sufficient.

Non-cumulative preference shares
Dividends not paid in any one year because of a lack of distributable profits are permanently forgone.

Participating preference shares
These shares carry the right to participate in a distribution of additional profits over and above the fixed rate of dividend after the ordinary shareholders have received an agreed percentage. The participation rights are based on a precise formula.

Redeemable preference shares
These shares may be redeemed by the company at an agreed future date and at an agreed price.

Convertible preference shares
These shares may be converted into ordinary shares at a future date on agreed terms. The conversion is usually at the preference shareholder's discretion.

There can be a mix of rights, e.g. Dixon plc in its 1994 accounts included 5% dividend convertible cumulative redeemable preference shares with a note that stated 'Subject to certain conditions, preference shares are convertible at the shareholders' option into fully paid Ordinary shares of the Company on 31 October in any years 1994–2002 on the basis of 26.667 Ordinary shares for every 100 Preference shares. The Company will be entitled after 1 January 2003, and will be obliged on 31 December 2007, to redeem at 100p per share any outstanding.'

10.4 Accounting entries on issue of shares

10.4.1 Shares issued at nominal value

If shares are issued at nominal value, the company simply debits the cash account with the amount received and credits the ordinary share capital or preference share capital, as appropriate, with the **nominal value** of the shares.

10.4.2 Shares issued at a premium

The market price of the shares of a company, which is based on the prospects of that company, is invariably different from the par (nominal) value of those shares.

On receipt of consideration for the shares, the company again debits the cash account with the amount received and credits the ordinary share capital or preference share capital, as appropriate, with the **nominal value** of the shares.

Assuming that the market price exceeds the nominal value, a premium element will be credited to a share premium account. The share premium is classified as a **non-distributable reserve** to indicate that it is not repayable to the shareholders who have subscribed for their shares: it remains a part of the company's permanent capital.

The accounting treatment for recording the issue of shares is straightforward. For example, the journal entries to record the issue of 1,000 £1 ordinary shares at a market price of £2.50 per share payable in the following instalments:

on application	on 1 January 20X1	25p
on issue	on 31 January 20X1	£1.75 including the premium
on first call	on 31 January 20X2	25p
on final call	on 31 January 20X4	25p

would be as follows:

1 Jan 20X1	Dr £	Cr £
Cash account	250	
Application account		250

31 Jan 20X1	Dr £	Cr £
Cash account	1,750	
Issue account		1,750

31 Jan 20X1	Dr £	Cr £
Application account	250	
Issue account	1,750	
Share capital account		500
Share premium		1,500

The first and final call would be debited to cash account and credited to share capital account on receipt of the date of the calls.

The other **non-distributable reserve** is the **capital redemption reserve**, which may be created when a company redeems some of its shares without replacing them with new ones. There are detailed accounting rules regarding this, which will be considered in the next chapter.

10.5 Creditor protection: capital maintenance concept

We have seen in earlier chapters that the Companies Act 1985 contains detailed provisions to protect shareholders, e.g. legislation relating to the presentation and disclosure of information in financial statements. To protect creditors, the Act has rules relating to the use of the total shareholders' funds which determine how much is distributable.

As a general rule, the issued share capital is not repayable to the shareholders and the reserves are classified into two categories: distributable and non-distributable. The directors have discretion as to the amount of the distributable profits that they recommend for distribution as a dividend to shareholders. However, they have no discretion as to the treatment of the non-distributable funds. There is a statutory requirement for the company to retain within the company net assets equal to the non-distributable reserves. This requirement is to safeguard the interests of creditors and is known as **capital maintenance**.

10.6 Creditor protection: why capital maintenance rules are necessary

It is helpful at this point to review the position of unincorporated businesses in relation to capital maintenance.

10.6.1 Unincorporated business

An unincorporated business such as a sole trader or partnership is not required to maintain any specified amount of capital within the business to safeguard the interests of its creditors. The owners are free to decide whether to introduce or withdraw capital. However, they remain personally liable for the liabilities incurred by the business, and the creditors can have recourse to the personal assets of the owners if the business assets are inadequate to meet their claims in full.

When granting credit to an unincorporated business the creditors may well be influenced by the personal wealth and apparent standing of the owners and not merely by the assets of the business as disclosed in its financial statements. This is why in an unincorporated business there is no external reason for the capital and the profits to be kept separate.

In partnerships, there are frequently internal agreements that require each partner to maintain his or her capital at an agreed level. Such agreements are strictly a matter of contract between the owners and do not prejudice the rights of the business creditors.

Sometimes owners attempt to influence creditors unfairly, by maintaining a lifestyle in excess of what they can afford, or try to frustrate the legal rights of creditors by putting their private assets beyond their reach, e.g. by transferring their property to relatives or trusts. These subterfuges become apparent only when the creditors seek to enforce their claim against the private assets. Banks are able to protect themselves by seeking adequate security, e.g. a charge on the owners' property.

10.6.2 Incorporated limited liability company

Because of limited liability, the rights of creditors against the private assets of the owners, i.e. the shareholders of the company, are restricted to any amount unpaid on their shares. Once the shareholders have paid the company for their shares, they are not personally liable for the company's debts. Creditors are restricted to making claims against the assets of the company.

Hence the legislature considered it necessary to ensure that the shareholders did not make such distributions to themselves so that the assets needed to meet creditors' claims were put beyond creditors' reach. This was achieved by setting out statutory rules.

10.7 Creditor protection: how to quantify the amounts available to meet creditors' claims

Creditors are exposed to two types of risk: the business risk that a company will operate unsuccessfully and will be unable to pay them; and the risk that a company will operate successfully, but will pay its shareholders rather than its creditors.

The legislature has never intended trade creditors to be protected against ordinary business risks, e.g. the risk of the debtor company incurring either trading losses or losses that might arise from a fall in the value of the assets following changes in market conditions.

The Companies Act 1985 requires the amount available to meet creditors' claims to be calculated by reference to the company's annual financial statements. There are two possible approaches:

● The **direct** approach which requires the **asset** side of the balance sheet to contain assets with a realisable value sufficient to cover all outstanding liabilities.

● The **indirect** approach which requires the **liability** side of the balance sheet to classify reserves into distributable and non-distributable reserves (i.e. respectively, available and not available to the shareholders by way of dividend distributions).[1]

The Act follows the indirect approach by specifying capital maintenance in terms of the total shareholders' funds. It thus avoids the thorny problem of asset valuation, which would have led straight back to the arguments considered in Chapter 4 concerning the use of historic cost, realisable values and replacement costs.

However, this has not stopped certain creditors taking steps to protect themselves by following the direct approach, e.g. it is bank practice to obtain a mortgage debenture over the assets of the company. The effect of this is to disadvantage the trade creditors. The statutory restrictions preventing shareholders from reducing capital accounts on the liability side are weakened when management grants certain parties priority rights against some or all of the company's assets.

We will now consider total shareholders' funds and capital maintenance in more detail, starting with share capital. Two aspects of share capital are relevant to creditor protection: minimum capital requirements and reduction of capital. Reduction of capital is dealt with in the next chapter.

10.8 Issued share capital: minimum share capital

The creditors of public companies are protected by the requirements that there should be a minimum share capital and that capital should be reduced only under controlled conditions.

The minimum share capital requirement for a public company is currently set at £50,000, although this can be increased by the Secretary of State for Trade and Industry.[2] A company is not permitted to commence trading unless it has issued this amount.

However, given the size of many public companies, it is questionable whether this figure is adequate.

The minimum share capital requirement refers to the nominal value of the share capital. In the UK, the law requires each class of share to have a stated nominal value. This value is used for identification and also for capital maintenance. The law ensures that a company receives an amount that is at least equal to the nominal value of the shares issued, less a controlled level of commission, by prohibiting the issue of shares at a discount and by limiting any underwriting commissions on an issue. This is intended to avoid a material discount being granted in the guise of commission. However, the requirement is concerned more with safeguarding the relative rights of existing shareholders than with protecting creditors.

There is effectively no minimum capital requirement for private companies. We can see many instances of such companies having an issued and paid-up capital of only a few £1 shares, which cannot conceivably be regarded as adequate creditor protection. The lack of adequate protection for the creditors of private companies is considered again later in the chapter.

10.9 Distributable profits: general considerations

We have considered capital maintenance and non-distributable reserves. However, it is not sufficient to attempt to maintain the permanent capital accounts of companies unless there are clear rules on the amount that they can distribute to their shareholders as profit. Without such rules, they may make distributions to their shareholders out of capital. The question of what can legitimately be distributed as profit is an integral part of the concept of capital maintenance in company accounts.

10.9.1 The position before 1980

Before the Companies Act 1980 – now part of the 1985 Act – the position of distributable profits rested largely on case law from the early 1900s. The judgments in those cases were sometimes contradictory and confusing, and often did not coincide with an accountant's view of what constituted distributable profits. This was due to the fact that until 1980 statutes stated only that dividends must not be paid out of capital, and Table A also mentioned that 'dividends must only be paid out of profits'. However, these requirements begged questions as to the nature of profit and capital, rather than providing any clear guidance.

Two questions of general importance should be addressed:

● Should distributable profits include only realised profits, or should they also include unrealised gains?

● Should distributions also include realised capital profits, e.g. arising from the sale of fixed assets?

Realised profits and unrealised gains

Historically, the accounting profession has considered that only realised profits should be distributed. This is because realisation implies the availability of liquid assets, i.e. cash, for distribution. Unrealised profits are not represented by any cash receipt and depend on the subjective views of valuers. This is a good practical view and is reflected in the preparation of profit and loss accounts today.

Legally, in the past, any accumulated realised losses of previous years could have been ignored in deciding the amount of distributable profits of the year in which a distribution was to be made.

Realised revenue profits and realised capital profits

Differentiation between these two is the result of accountants' classification of assets into fixed and current. The accountant's view is that normal trading activities create current assets of a revenue nature, whereas fixed assets are of a capital nature. Therefore, any proceeds from the sale of fixed assets are of a capital nature.

If only realised profits were to be distributed, it was not clear whether this meant only revenue profits, or whether capital profits should also be included. In some companies the latter were taken to a capital reserve, while in others they were taken to the profit and loss account. The now defunct SSAP 6 recommended that the profit and loss account should include all realised profits, which in turn influenced distribution policies. The legal situation was that realised capital profits could be distributed, provided there remained a surplus of assets over liabilities.

10.9.2 Present position

The issue of what constituted distributable profits was clarified by the Companies Act 1980. It is surprising that it took successive governments such a long time to clarify the situation. However, if the EC had not issued its Second Directive, it would probably have taken much longer. In the following sections we will describe the present rules for private and public companies.

10.10 Distributable profits: general rule for private companies

The definition of distributable profits under the Companies Act 1985 is:

Accumulated, realised profits, so far as not previously utilised by distribution or capitalisation, less its accumulated, realised losses, as far as not previously written off in a reduction or reorganisation of capital.

This means the following:

- Unrealised profits cannot be distributed.

- There is no difference between realised revenue and realised capital profits.

- All accumulated net realised profits (i.e. realised profits less realised losses) on the balance sheet date must be considered.

As an example, an analysis of the shareholders' funds section of a company's balance sheet as at the end of its latest financial year is set out in Figure 10.1.

The distributable profit of this private company on the balance sheet date is simply its accumulated net realised profit, i.e. £1,600,000. No account need be taken of any accumulated net unrealised gains or losses. This means that there could be a reduction in the permanent capital of the company of £100,000 if the maximum amount is distributed. Its net assets after such a distribution are shown in Figure 10.2.

Figure 10.1 Shareholders' funds

	£000	£000
Share capital		2,000
Share premium		600
Capital redemption reserve		200
Permanent capital at beginning of year		2,800
Unrealised: gains	100	
: losses	(200)	
		(100)
Permanent capital at end of year		2,700
Realised: current year's profits	500	
: current year's losses	(100)	
	400	
: previous year's b/f	1,200	
		1,600
Net assets of company		4,300

Figure 10.2 Net assets after distribution of profits

	£000	£000
Share capital		2,000
Share premium		600
Capital redemption reserve		200
Permanent capital at beginning of year		2,800
Unrealised: gains	100	
: losses	(200)	
		(100)
Permanent capital at end of year – net assets		2,700

10.11 Distributable profits: general rule for public companies

According to the Companies Act, the undistributable reserves of a public company are its share capital, share premium, capital redemption reserve and also 'the excess of accumulated unrealised profits over accumulated unrealised losses at the time of the intended distribution and … any reserves not allowed to be distributed under the Act or by the company's own Memorandum or Articles of Association'.

This means that, when dealing with a public company, the distributable profits have to be reduced by any net unrealised loss. In our example above, the distributable profits would be £1,500,000 if the company were a public company. We arrive at this by applying the wording of the Act that its net assets will not be less than:

	£000
Share capital	2,000
Share premium	600
Capital redemption reserve	200
Excess of unrealised profits over unrealised losses	No excess
	2,800

The net accumulated unrealised loss figure of £100,000 in the above example would be unusual in practice, since any net deficiency on the revaluation of an asset would normally be taken to the profit and loss account and may be deemed to have implications for distribution policy.

10.11.1 Investment companies

The Act allows for the special nature of some businesses in the calculation of distributable profits. There are additional rules for investment companies in calculating their distributable profits. For a company to be classified as an investment company, it must invest its funds mainly in securities with the aim of spreading investment risk and giving its members the benefit of the results of managing its funds.

Such a company has the option of applying one of two rules in calculating its distributable profits. These are either:

● the rules that apply to public companies in general, but excluding any realised capital profits, e.g. from the disposal of investments; or

● the company's accumulated realised revenue less its accumulated realised and unrealised revenue losses, provided that its assets are at least one and a half times its liabilities both before and after such a distribution.

The reasoning behind these special rules seems to be to allow investment companies to pass the dividends they receive to their shareholders, irrespective of any changes in the values of their investments, which are subject to market fluctuations. However, the asset cover ratio of liabilities can easily be manipulated by the company simply paying creditors, whereby the ratio is improved, or borrowing, whereby it is reduced.

EXAMPLE ● Figure 10.3 provides an analysis of the shareholders' funds and liabilities of an investment company.

Distributable profits of the company are:

● Under the general rule:

	£000
Realised revenue profits	700
Less: Excess of unrealised losses over unrealised profits (£900,000 + £100,000 – £0)	(1,000)
Nil distributable	(300)

Figure 10.3 Shareholders' funds and liabilities of an investment company

	£000
Share capital	2,000
Capital profits (losses):	
Realised	400
Unrealised	(900)
Revenue profits (losses):	
Realised	700
Unrealised	(100)
Shareholders' funds, i.e. net assets	2,100
Liabilities	1,000
Total assets	3,100

or, applying the net asset maintenance rule:

	£000
Share capital	2,000
Excess of unrealised profits over unrealised losses	No excess
Other undistributable profits:	
Realised capital profit	400
	2,400

Under this option the company cannot distribute any profits unless net assets can be maintained at £2,400,000, whereas its net assets at the balance sheet date are £2,100,000.

● Under the second (investment company) rule:

	£000
Realised revenue profits	700
Less: Realised or unrealised revenue losses	(100)
Distributable profit	600

Subject to asset cover ratio of liabilities:

Before distribution $\dfrac{3,100,000}{1,000,000} = 3.1$ times

After distribution $\dfrac{3,100,000 - 600,000}{1,000,000} = 2.5$ times

In both cases the asset cover ratio of liabilities is more than 1.5 times and therefore the company can distribute £600,000 profit to its shareholders.

10.12 Distributable profits: how to arrive at the amount using relevant accounts

The Companies Act stipulates that distributable profits of a company must be based on **relevant accounts**. These would normally be the audited annual accounts, which have been prepared according to the requirements of the Act to give a true and fair view of the company's financial affairs. In the case of a qualified audit report, the auditor is required to prepare a written statement stating whether such a qualification is material in determining a company's distributable profit. Interim dividends are allowed to be paid provided they can be justified on the basis of the latest annual accounts, otherwise interim accounts will have to be prepared that would justify such a distribution.

10.13 Distributable profits: realisation principle applies

Realisation is central to the determination of profits which can be legally distributed to shareholders in either cash or non-cash form. The Companies Act provides that 'only profits realised at the balance sheet date shall be included in the profit and loss account'.

10.13.1 Retained profit figure may not consist only of realised profits

It is not always the case that the retained profit on a balance sheet consists only of realised profits and is therefore wholly distributable. The overriding requirement that accounts should give a true and fair view can lead to a mismatch between profits that are reported in order to present a true and fair view and profits that are distributable within the legal definition of the Companies Act.

An example is the calculation of the depreciation charge on revalued assets. The true and fair requirement as set out in FRS 15 is that the depreciation charge should be calculated on the carrying value of the asset in the balance sheet. If it were revalued from £100 to £200, the depreciation would be based on the £200. However, the legal requirement is that it should be based on the cost figure of £100.

In general, however, the retained balance may be regarded as realised and distributable.

10.13.2 The Companies Act and the concept of realised profit

On the key question of whether a profit is realised or not, the Act (Schedule 4, para. 91) simply says that realised profits or realised losses are

> such profits or losses of the company as fall to be treated as realised in accordance with principles generally accepted, at the time when the accounts are prepared, with respect to the determination for accounting purposes of realised profits or losses.

Hence the Act does not lay down detailed rules on what is and what is not a realised profit; indeed, it does not even refer specifically to 'accounting principles'. Nevertheless, it would seem reasonable for decisions on realisation to be based on **generally accepted accounting principles** at the time, subject to the court's decision in cases of dispute.

Generally, revenue is deemed to have been realised on receipt of cash or if the receipt of cash is reasonably certain. But the basis of realisation is viewed differently now, whereby realisation is associated with the occurrence of the critical (risky) event in the operating cycle of a business. The latest FRS 18, which supersedes SSAP 2, follows the recent recommendations of the ASB, whereby a gain is accepted to have been realised if it is reasonably certain that it will occur and that it can be measured with sufficient reliability.

There seems to be a case for clarifying the basis and nature of costs and expenses, too, which can be deducted from realised revenue in calculating realised profit. One example covered by the Companies Act is the depreciation charge in the profit statement. According to FRS 15, the depreciation charge in the profit and loss account should be based on the carrying value of a fixed asset. However, the Companies Act only requires a deduction of depreciation based on the historic cost of a fixed asset, in calculating the distributable profit of a company. The Act regards any excess depreciation, over the historical cost based figure, as part of the realised profit.

Besides the question of depreciation, the Companies Act includes only a few specific provisions on the treatment of other events. We consider two such provisions: development costs and fixed asset revaluations.

Development costs

The Act provides that (product) development costs can be treated as a **realised** loss unless directors can justify treating it differently by special circumstances. An ICAEW Technical Release (TECH 7/03)[3] states that, if the accounts have been prepared according to the requirements of the Companies Act and professional accounting and reporting standards, any consequent profit or loss is to be taken as realised unless a standard specifically states that an item is unrealised.

This seems to imply that, if the development costs have been accounted for in accordance with the requirements of SSAP 13, the amount taken to the profit and loss account is the realised part of the total cost.

Fixed asset revaluations

The Act provides that any diminution in the value of a fixed asset arising as a result of revaluations of **all** fixed assets (whether including goodwill or not) is an **unrealised** loss. This seems to imply that the revaluation of an **individual** asset would amount to a **realised** loss. In practice, the Act allows such a loss to be regarded as unrealised, provided directors can satisfy themselves (without an actual revaluation of all assets) that the aggregate value of assets is not less than their book value.

10.14 What are the implications of IAS compliance on distributions?

There is a requirement for **consolidated** accounts of listed companies to comply with IASs and IFRSs by 2005. These standards will affect both the disclosure and measurement of items appearing in the profit and loss account and balance sheet.

10.14.1 Disclosure changes

Preference shares

Under the UK accounting framework, preference shares have been classified as equity rather than liabilities. Now that preference shares are to be treated as liabilities, the change will affect the gearing ratios calculated in the balance sheet and the times interest cover ratio in the income statement. This might have commercial and legal implications, e.g. if there are loan covenant conditions or performance-related criteria expressed in terms of either of these ratios. The profit available for ordinary shareholders will be unaffected.

Proposed dividends

The statutory requirement to accrue proposed dividends and disclose them in the income statement and current liabilities has been changed and companies now disclose the aggregate amount of proposed dividends as a note to the accounts. This is an improvement as dividends are payable out of distributable profits and not merely the profit for the year.

10.14.2 Measurement changes

The impact of these will be affected by the decision a company makes about the standards applied to the **individual** company financial statements. They have the choice of applying international standards or remaining with national standards. If they choose the international route then there are measurement changes that will affect the profit available for distribution to equity shareholders. Even if companies decide to apply national standards there will be subsequent impact as national standards are brought into line with the international standards.

It is now clear that the effect of international standards on areas such as accounting for deferred tax, pensions and share options will be for profits after tax to become more volatile.

10.14.3 International influences for change

There is a view (www.biicl.org) that the current law of capital maintenance restricts the returns that companies can pay their investors and damages company financing under new accounting standards.

Consequently, there is a view that the UK should base distribution decisions on the basis of solvency rather than simply the retained profits. In this it would be following the approach taken in some other countries, e.g. New Zealand.

Summary

Creditors of companies are not expected to be protected against ordinary business risks as these are taken care of by financial markets, e.g. through the rates of interest charged on different capital instruments of different companies. However, the creditors are entitled to depend on the non-erosion of the permanent capital where the shareholders may pay themselves out of capital.

A major part of this protection is the regulation of distributions (e.g. dividends) to shareholders. Until the early 1980s the situation regarding this was confusing and unclear, but this has changed a great deal as a result of the Companies Act 1985.

Nevertheless, the question of distributable profits carries the problem of the application of the generally accepted accounting principles in deciding what constitutes 'realised profit'. These accounting principles are subject to change over time.

As we mentioned at the beginning of the chapter, rules relating to capital maintenance and distribution are always evolving. Governments and standard setters are constantly attempting to balance the need for flexibility in managing a company's finances at a time when rules for measuring capital and income are changing with the need to protect the rights of creditors.

We are living in an interesting time of change – just as in other countries, we see time-honoured UK features changing, e.g. authorised capital and nominal value shares being seen as a redundant concept, the redemption of ordinary shares being permitted to be held for resale rather than cancelled, distributions being based on the ability to pay rather than the amount of retained earnings.

REVIEW QUESTIONS

1　What is the relevance of dividend cover if dividends are paid out of distributable profits?

2　How do industries differ in the levels of distributable profits?

3　What is the significance of high distributable profits to an existing/potential investor/loan creditor/creditor?

4　Why is the distributable profits figure not apparent from the accounts?

5　Give four examples of reasons why the retained profit figure might not equal distributable profits.

6　Is there any relationship between non-distributable reserves and total assets?

7　(a) How can distributable profits become non-distributable?

　　(b) In what circumstances can non-distributable reserves become distributable?

　　(c) Explain how the restrictions on dividends by a public company differ from those made by a private company.

8　In a report 'Reforming Capital' [www.biicl.org] there was a view that there are problems when there is a rigid link between distributions and a company's statutory accounts, particularly now that modern accounting standards are increasingly focused on the needs of the capital market. Discuss this view and consider alternative approaches to creditor protection.

9　The Companies Act requires capitalised development costs to be deducted from realised profits unless circumstances justify the policy of capitalisation. Discuss (a) why you think the Act contains this provision and (b) what you consider would provide adequate justification for deferring the charge to the current year's profit and loss account.

10　(a) The regional electricity companies and the National Grid argued strongly against the ASB proposal to require full provisioning for deferred tax on its revision of SSAP 15. Explain why these companies would have been so strongly opposed.

　　(b) Full provisioning for deferred tax would result in increased tax charges on earnings and large deferred tax liabilities, neither of which are likely to materialise. Explain (i) why they are unlikely to materialise, and (ii) how to reduce the impact while still following the principle of full provisioning.

(c) It has been stated that 'by reducing distributable reserves the proposals directly affect not only annual dividends but also the apparent gearing position and balance sheet strength of companies. These proposals would do serious damage to the strength of an important sector of the economy.'[4] Discuss whether the effect on distributable profit is an acceptable reason for not providing in full for deferred tax.

EXERCISES

An extract from the solution is provided in the Appendix at the end of the text for exercises marked with an asterisk (*).

* Question 1

(a) Define the term 'distribution', and state what items the Companies Act 1985 excludes from its definition of a distribution.

(b) Explain the need for the introduction of statutory rules concerning the distribution of a company's profits.

(c) State the Companies Act 1985 requirements regarding distributions by both public and private limited companies.

(d) State what other principal non-legal limitations the directors of a company would take into account when deciding on a distribution policy.

(e) You have draft balance sheets of two companies as follows:

	Company A £000	Company B £000
Fixed assets		
Property at valuation	90	90
Investment at cost	10	10
Net current assets (liabilities)	60	(20)
	160	80

	Company A £000	Company B £000
Share capital	10	10
Share premium	20	20
Revaluation reserve	40	50
Profit and loss account	90	—
	160	80

You also ascertain the following:

1 Additional depreciation charged to the profit and loss account to date as a result of revaluations is £5,000 for company A and £10,000 for company B.

2 The fixed asset investments of both company A and company B have subsequent to the year-end proved to be worthless.

3 A court case has commenced against company B for £20,000. The directors have not come to a conclusion on the accounting treatment of this case, but they believe the loss after tax would be £13,000.

4 Company B had sold a plot of land at its revalued amount. However, the net gain of £15,000 over the original cost was still shown in the revaluation reserve and not in the profit and loss account.

Required:
State with clear reasoning the distributable profits that could be paid as dividends by companies A and B respectively:
(i) treating them as private companies;
(ii) treating them as public limited companies.

Question 2

V.R. Confident Ltd
Profit and loss account for the year ended 30 November 20X2

	£000
Net profit for the year, before taxation	604
Corporation tax, at 33%	290
	314

Balance sheet as on 30 November 20X2

		£000
Ordinary share capital		800
6% preference share capital		300
Share premium		200
Capital redemption reserve		400
Asset revaluation reserve		250
General reserve		160
Profit and loss account:		
Balance brought forward	(288)	
Current year	314	26
		2,136

Notes

(a) One-half of the asset revaluation reserve represents an increase in the value of a freehold property which was sold during the year to 30 November 20X2 (at the revalued amount). This sale was not recorded in the accounts. A tax liability of £35,000 is expected in connection with the disposal.

(b) The £300,000 depreciation charge to the profit and loss account was based on revalued figures. This charge would have been £240,000 if it had been based on the original cost of fixed assets.

(c) Some of the stock-in-trade, which appeared on the draft balance sheet at cost, was later sold for £90,000 below this figure.

(d) The draft balance sheet includes £500,000 research and development expenditure under fixed assets.

(e) Since the preparation of the draft accounts, one of the debtors of the company has gone into liquidation and is not expected to pay more than 50p in the £1 to its creditors. This debtor owed £120,000 to V.R. Confident Ltd on 30 November 20X2.

Required:

(a) Explain briefly the provisions of the Companies Act 1985 relating to profits that a company can distribute as dividends.

(b) Calculate the maximum amount of dividends that the directors of V.R. Confident Ltd may propose to pay to ordinary shareholders within the legal requirements and in conformity with the relevant Statements of Standard Accounting Practice. Also state whether your answer would be different if V.R. Confident Ltd were a public limited company (plc).

* Question 3

The following are details of three separate companies' summarised balance sheets at 31 March 20X7.

	Alpha plc £000	Beta plc £000	Gamma Ltd £000
Fixed assets	5,000	760	1,000
Current assets	1,800	360	600
Current liabilities	(1,400)	(320)	(400)
	5,400	800	1,200
Share capital	400	600	4,000
Reserves: revaluation	2,200	(400)	—
Realised capital profit	1,600	—	—
Brought forward realised revenue profit (loss)	800	1,000	(3,200)
Current year realised revenue profit (loss)	400	(400)	400
	5,400	800	1,200

Alpha's property, previously included in the financial statements at original cost of £1,800,000, was revalued on 1 April 20X6 at £4 million. The revalued amount is included in the figures above, subject to the full amount being written off equally over the next 50 years from 1 April 20X6. Prior to this date, no depreciation had been provided on property. At 31 March 20X7, no transfer had been made between revaluation reserve and realised revenue profit.

Required:

(a) Compare briefly the bases for calculating the maximum distribution under the provisions of the Companies Act 1985 in respect of public and private companies.

(b) Calculate the maximum distribution that Alpha, Beta and Gamma could each make under the Companies Act 1985.

References

1 Companies Act 1985.
2 *Ibid.*, Section 118.
3 Tech 7/03 *Guidance on the Determination of Realised Profits and Losses in the Context of Distributions under the Companies Act 1985*, ICAEW 2003.
4 *Revenue Recognition*, discussion paper by ASB, 2001.

CHAPTER 11

Reduction of share capital

11.1 Introduction

In this chapter, we consider restrictions on the reduction of share capital and the accounting treatment of the share premium and the capital redemption reserve. We outline the legal requirements under the Companies Act 1985 for the redemption of shares by public and private companies, and for fundamental changes in a company's capital structure.

11.2 Capital: restrictions on reduction of capital

Once the shares have been issued and paid up, the share capital account is credited with the nominal value of such shares and this value forms part of the capital to be maintained. The intention is that this amount should not be reduced. However, there might be commercially sound reasons for a company to reduce its capital. The Companies Act therefore has provision for share capital to be reduced, subject to the consent of the court, in three ways:

1 Writing off part of capital which has already been lost and is not represented by assets

This situation normally occurs when a company has accumulated trading losses which prevent it from making dividend payments under the rules relating to distributable profits. The general approach is to credit the profit and loss account in order to eliminate any debit balance, and to debit share capital and non-distributable reserves. This has the effect of eliminating current losses, thus making future profits distributable. The debit balance on profit and loss account is transferred to a capital reduction account, and this account is credited with amounts transferred from the share capital and reserves.

The consent of the creditors may be required by order of the court. The rules governing a reduction of capital are that no reduction can be made unless it is authorised by the Articles of Association of the company, is approved by a special resolution of the shareholders and secures the consent of the court. The rights of the creditors are thus protected directly or indirectly through the court.

2 Repayment of part of paid-up capital to shareholders or cancellation of unpaid share capital

This can occur when a company wishes to reduce its unwanted liquid resources. The accounting entries for the repayment are to credit cash and debit share capital. The consent of the creditors is required.

3 Redemption of shares

This is discussed in section 11.5 below.

11.3 Non-distributable reserves: share premium

Prior to the Companies Act 1948, if a company issued shares at a premium, the premium could be distributed to the shareholders. However, it came to be recognised that the premium represented a capital receipt and should be treated in the same way as the nominal value of the shares. Consequently, the Companies Act now requires any premium to be taken to a separate share premium account as a non-distributable reserve. For example, if a company issued 100 £1 shares (nominal value) at a premium of £2.50 per share, the capital receipt of £350 would be recorded as follows:

	£	£
Cash	350	
Share capital		100
Share premium		250

Although both the proceeds from the nominal value of the shares and the premium element are regarded as capital receipts, the company has more flexibility in using its share premium account. For example, it can be used to:

1 issue fully paid bonus shares;

2 write off preliminary expenses (i.e. company formation costs);

3 write off any share or debenture issue expenses or any discounts on the issue of debentures;

4 write off any premiums (payable) on redemption or purchase of own shares, provided the shares being redeemed or purchased were themselves issued at a premium and that adequate funds exist in the share premium account.

Let us consider each of these uses in terms of their impact on creditor protection. The capitalisation of the reserve indicated by (1) maintains the creditors' protection, since the share premium is reclassified as share capital, i.e.:

	£	£
Share premium	250	
Share capital		250

However, uses (2)–(4) reduce their protection, even though no direct payment has been made to any of the shareholders. To illustrate this, let us assume that the company's balance sheet includes the following items:

	£
Share capital	100
Share premium	250
Permanent capital	350

Further, assume that the company issues one 10% debenture (nominal value £100) for £90 cash and decides, applying (3) above, to write off the discount against the share premium account. The entries in the company's books would be:

	£	£
Cash	90	
Debentures discount	10	
10% debentures		100
Share premium	10	
Debenture discount		10

The balance sheet items following these transactions would be:

	£
Share capital	100
Share premium	<u>240</u>
Permanent capital	340
10% debentures	<u>100</u>
	<u><u>440</u></u>

Because the rules permit the discount to be classified as a capital item, the permanent capital available for the protection of capital has been depleted to the extent of the discount. The same would apply to uses (2) and (4). This did not matter unduly when the amount of discount on debentures was immaterial, but we have seen many examples in recent years of financial instruments being issued at material discounts, e.g. deep discounting.

11.4 Non-distributable reserves: capital redemption reserve

Until the beginning of the twentieth century, companies were not allowed to buy back their own shares after they had been issued. Shareholders could convert their investment into cash only by selling their shares to a third party either privately or via the Stock Exchange. This meant that the share capital base of the company could not be depleted by a return of capital, so the level of protection afforded to the creditors was unchanged by share transfers between existing and new shareholders.

However, commercial considerations caused a relaxation in the rules to accommodate shareholders who wanted to be reasonably certain of recovering the capital amount that they originally invested. To attract their investment, companies were permitted to issue **redeemable preference shares**.

When redeemable preference shares were redeemed, the company was required either to replace them with other shares or to make a transfer from distributable reserves to non-distributable reserves in order to maintain the permanent capital. The non-distributable reserve was called a capital redemption reserve and there were restrictions on how it could be used.

The accounting entries were to credit cash and debit the redeemable preference share account on redemption, and to credit a capital redemption reserve and debit the profit and loss account with an equal amount.

This right to redeem preference shares was later extended by the Companies Act 1981 to permit companies to purchase their own ordinary shares.

11.4.1 Purchase of own shares

The Companies Act now permits a company to effect **market** or **off-market** purchases of its own ordinary shares. Market purchases are those shares purchased from a recognised

Stock Exchange and off-market purchases are all other shares. Market purchases must be authorised by the articles of association and an **ordinary resolution** of the shareholders setting out terms such as the price to be paid and the timing of the purchase.

Off-market purchases offer a greater opportunity for abuse by the directors and there are accordingly more stringent legal requirements, such as the need for a **specific purchase contract** which requires a **special resolution** of the shareholders.

In this chapter we will not distinguish between redemption and purchase of own shares, since the same accounting considerations apply to both.

11.4.2 Buyback of own shares – intention to cancel

There are a number of reasons for companies buying back shares. These provide a benefit when taken as:

● a strategic measure, e.g. recognising that there is a lack of viable investment projects, i.e. expected returns being less than the company's weighted average cost of capital and so returning excess cash to shareholders to allow them to search out better growth investments;

● a defensive measure, e.g. an attempt to frustrate a hostile takeover or to reduce the power of dissident shareholders;

● a reactive measure, e.g. taking advantage of the fact that the share price is at a discount to its underlying intrinsic value or stabilising a falling share price;

● a proactive measure, e.g. creating shareholder value by reducing the number of shares in issue which increases the earnings per share or making a distribution more tax-efficient than the payment of a cash dividend.

The following is an extract from the St Ives plc 2004 Annual Report:

> Resolution 11 ... will be proposed to renew the authority to purchase ... ordinary shares. The directors will continue only to exercise such power if it is expected that it would result in an increase in the earnings per share attributable to the ordinary share capital ... and would be in the best interest of the shareholders generally.

There is also a potential risk if the company has to borrow funds in order to make the buyback leaving itself liable to service the debt. Where it uses free cash rather than loans it is attractive to analysts and shareholders. For example, in the BP share buyback scheme (one of the UK's largest), the chief executive, Lord Browne, said that any free cash generated from BP's assets when the oil price was above $20 a barrel would be returned to investors over the following three years.

11.4.3 Companies Act requirements

The Companies Act states that for shares that are redeemed and cancelled:

● No redemption can take place unless the shares are fully paid up. This is to protect creditors who regard any uncalled capital as part of the capital base of the company.

● No redemption can take place which would result in there being no shareholders. This would in effect be a winding-up or liquidation of the company and other rules would then apply.

Different rules apply to the redemption of shares by public companies and by private companies. We will consider each in turn.

11.5 Capital: redemption of shares by a public company

Although a public company is now permitted to redeem shares so that an individual shareholder can liquidate a shareholding, it is required to maintain the same overall level of permanent capital for the protection of the creditors. This can be achieved in two different ways.

Firstly, redemption can be made **out of the distributable profits** of a company. In this case the Act requires the transfer of an amount equal to the nominal value of the redeemed shares from distributable profits to a capital redemption reserve.

A capital redemption reserve may only be used for issuing fully paid bonus shares to the shareholders. In other words, it is like share capital in its permanence. Such a transfer from distributable profits is described as a capitalisation, which means that profits have been capitalised and the permanent capital has been maintained.

Furthermore, if the shares are redeemed at a premium, i.e. at a price above their nominal value, any such premium cannot be carried forward in the accounts, but must be written off against distributable profits.

For example, a company buys 50 of its own £1 shares at a premium of £2 each, i.e. it makes a capital repayment of £150. The accounting entries are shown in Figure 11.1.

Figure 11.1 Balance sheet before and after redemption

Balance sheet before redemption		Purchase	W/off premium	Transfer to CRR	Balance sheet after redemption
	£	£	£	£	£
Share capital	100	(50)			50
Capital redemption reserve (CRR)				50	50
Share premium	240				240
Permanent capital	340				340
P&L account	160		(100)	(50)	10
	500				350
Cash	200	(150)			50
Other assets	300				300
Premium on redemption		100	(100)		—
	500				350

Secondly, shares may be redeemed **out of the proceeds of a new share issue**. In practice, a redemption may be made partly out of profits and partly out of the proceeds of a new issue. The accounting requirements are as follows:

1 An amount equal to the excess of the nominal value of redeemed shares over the total proceeds of any new issue is to be transferred from distributable profits to capital redemption reserve, i.e. they become classified as an undistributable reserve.

2 Any premium on redemption may be written off against distributable profits. However, if the company wishes to reduce the impact on its distributable profits, it may set off the premium on redemption against the share premium account, i.e. an undistributable reserve. However, this is subject to certain constraints. The amount of set-off is restricted to the lowest of:

(a) any share premium originally received on the issue of the shares that are now being redeemed; or

(b) the amount standing to the credit of the share premium account, including any premium received on the newly issued shares; or

(c) the total proceeds of the new issue.

EXAMPLE ● Ozer plc had issued class B shares at a premium of £1 each, i.e. at £2 per share, in 20X1. In 20X4 the company issued 20 class A shares of £1 each at a premium of £1 each, receiving a total capital receipt of £40. It then redeemed 50 class B shares of £1 each at a premium of £3 for a total capital repayment of £200, i.e. there was a premium on redemption of £150.

Management would normally propose writing off the premium on redemption of £150 against the share premium account to avoid reducing the distributable profits. However, the outcomes of the above criteria are as follows:

● Share premium originally received on the issue of the class B shares which are now being redeemed: £50.

● Amount standing to the credit of the share premium account, including any premium received on the newly issued shares: £240 + £20 = £260.

● Total proceeds of the new issue: £40.

We can see that the maximum that can be written off the share premium is £40. The remaining £110 has to be written off the distributable profits.

It then remains to determine the amount required to be transferrred to the capital redemption reserve account. This is calculated as follows:

	£
Nominal value of shares redeemed	50
Less: Total proceeds of the new issue	(40)
Required transfer from distributable profits	10

The balance sheet items before and after the issue of the class A shares and the redemption of the class B shares are shown in Figure 11.2.

We can see from the revised balance sheet that, in spite of the legal requirements, the permanent capital of the company has not been maintained. It has actually been reduced by £40 from £340 to £300. This means that part of the redemption has been made out of capital. It could be maintained by the transfer to capital redemption reserve of £30, which is the difference in the nominal value of shares redeemed (£50) and issued (£20), and by the premium chargeable to share premium account not being more than the premium received from the new issue, i.e. £20. Nevertheless, as the law stands, on redemption the capital of a public company may be reduced or increased rather than being maintained. It is the reduction in capital that is important to the creditors.

Figure 11.2 Balance sheet before and after issue and redemption of shares

Balance sheet before redemption	£	New issue £	Purchase £	W/off premium £	Transfer to CRR £	Balance sheet after redemption £
Share capital:						
Class A	50	20				70
Class B	50		(50)			—
Capital redemption reserve					10	10
Share premium	240	20		(40)		220
Permanent capital	340					300
P&L account	160	—	—	(110)	(10)	40
	500					340
Cash	200	40	(200)			40
Other assets	300					300
Premium on redemption			150	(150)		—
	500					340

11.6 Capital: redemption of shares by a private company

The Companies Act explicitly accepts that private companies may reduce their permanent capital in order to keep control within the same family or group of people.

This can arise when a shareholder dies or decides to leave the company and the other shareholders are not in a position to buy the shares. In such cases, if the company buys the shares, the control remains with the remaining shareholders. However, the legislature recognised that a counterbalance was required to provide additional protection for the creditors. Consequently, the rights of the creditors are protected by requiring the directors to make a declaration of solvency.

The company must declare that it will still be able to pay its creditors after the redemption and that it will continue to be able to do so for a year after the date of the redemption. The declaration is also required to be agreed and reported upon by the company's auditors. Furthermore, the company must publicise the intended redemption in order to inform the creditors who may object to such a redemption through the courts.

It is perhaps ironic that private companies are required to make a declaration of solvency in relation to an intentional reduction of capital, whereas public companies are not required to do so, although a reduction might also have occurred in their case. The creditors of a private company may actually be in a stronger position than those of a public company.

The accounting requirements for private companies are that any reduction in their permanent capital should not exceed the **permissible capital payment** as defined by the Act. This payment is the excess of the total amount paid on redemption of shares over the distributable profits of a company and the proceeds of any new share issue specifically made for the purposes of redemption. The accounting entries needed to confine the reduction in permanent capital to the permissible capital payment are as follows:

- If the nominal value of shares redeemed exceeds the permissible capital payment, an amount equal to the excess must be transferred from distributable profits to the capital redemption reserve account.

- If the nominal value of shares redeemed is less than the permissible capital payment, an amount equal to this plus the proceeds of any new share issue may be used to reduce any undistributable reserves. Undistributable reserves for this purpose include any unrealised gain, share premium, capital redemption reserve and share capital.

The general effect is that, in limiting the reduction in permanent capital to the permissible amount, a private company first utilises its distributable profit before reducing any undistributable reserves. The following two examples show the nature of adjustments needed for this purpose.

EXAMPLE ● A private company redeems 50 of its shares of £1 each at a premium of £3 per share, i.e. for £200. It does not issue any new shares. Its balance sheet is shown in Figure 11.3.

Figure 11.3 Balance sheet before and after redemption at a premium

Balance sheet before redemption		Redemption of shares	Write-off redemption premium	Transfer to CRR	Balance sheet after redemption
	£	£	£	£	£
Share capital	100	(50)			50
Capital redemption reserve				10	10
Share premium	240				240
Permanent capital	340				300
P&L account	160	——	(150)	(10)	—
	500				300
Cash	260	(200)			60
Other assets	240				240
Premium on redemption	—	150	(150)	——	—
	500				300

Calculation of permissible capital payment:	£
Amount payable on redemption	200
Less: Distributable profits	(160)
Permissible capital payment	40
Transfer to capital redemption reserve:	
Nominal value of shares redeemed	50
Less: Permissible capital payment	(40)
Capital redemption reserve	10

In this case the nominal value of shares redeemed is more than the permissible capital payment. A transfer is made from distributable profits to the capital redemption reserve to limit the reduction to the permissible capital amount of £40.

EXAMPLE ● A private company redeems 50 of its class B shares of £1 each at a premium of £5 per share, i.e. for £300. It also issues 20 class A shares of £1 each at a premium of £2 per share, i.e. for £60, to help finance the redemption. Its balance sheet is shown in Figure 11.4.

Figure 11.4 Balance sheet before and after issue and redemption of shares at a premium

	Balance sheet before redemption £	Issue of A shares £	Redemption of B shares £	Transfer from P&L a/c £	Transfer from permanent capital £	Balance sheet after redemption £
Share capital:						
Class A	50	20				70
Class B	50		(50)			—
Share premium	240	40			(90)	190
Permanent capital	340					260
Income statement	(160)			(160)		—
	500					260
Cash	260	60	(300)			20
Other assets	240					240
Premium on redemption	—		250	(160)	(90)	—
	500					260

Calculation of permissible capital payment:		
Amount payable on redemption		300
Less: Distributable profits	160	
Less: New issue proceeds	60	
		(220)
Permissible capital payment		80

Required transfer in the accounts:	
Nominal value of shares redeemed	50
Less: Permissible capital payment	(80)
Allowed reduction in permanent capital:	(30)
Also: New issue proceeds because it has increased the permanent capital	(60)
Total allowed reduction in permanent capital	(90)

In this case the nominal value of redeemed shares is less than the permissible capital payment and therefore the permanent capital (i.e. undistributable reserves) can be reduced by the difference. However, as the newly issued shares have already increased the permanent capital, the total reduction in undistributable reserves includes the new issue too. The result is a reduction of £80 in the original permanent capital, which is the permissible capital payment in this case.

11.7 Distributable profits: effect of accumulated trading losses

A company's distributable profits made in the current year are affected by its accumulated profit or loss position. We have seen that existing losses must be made good before a distribution can be made. However, a company might have experienced significant losses which require a fundamental change to its capital structure.

11.7.1 Elimination that affects only the ordinary shareholders

The Companies Act 1985, section 135, allows a company to reduce its capital where it has incurred losses and the share capital is no longer represented by available assets. This provides the statutory authority for a company that has suffered losses, but now believes that it has overcome the problems and will be profitable, to adjust its capital to reflect the current level of asset backing.

One of the results of doing this is that future profits become available for distribution rather than being required to be set off against the accumulated losses. It is a material change for the shareholders, who will be able to receive a dividend from future profits without losses being required to be made good first. Consequently, authority for the reduction must be contained in the Articles of Association, there must be a special resolution with a majority of at least 75% of the members voting in favour of the proposal, and court approval must be obtained.

11.7.2 Accounting treatment for a capital reduction to eliminate accumulated trading losses

The accounting treatment is straightforward. A capital reduction account is opened. It is debited with the accumulated losses and credited with the amount written off the share capital.

For example, assume that the capital and reserves of Hopeful Ltd were as follows at 31 December 20X1:

	£
200,000 ordinary shares of £1 each	200,000
Income statement	(180,000)

The directors estimate that the company will return to profitability in 20X2, achieving profits of £4,000 per annum thereafter. Without a capital reduction, the profits from 20X2 must be used to reduce the accumulated losses. This means that the company would be unable to pay a dividend for forty-five years if it continued at that level of profitability and ignoring tax. Perhaps even more importantly, it would not be attractive for shareholders to put additional capital into the company because they would not be able to obtain any dividend for some years.

The directors therefore obtained a special resolution and court approval to reduce the £1 ordinary shares to ordinary shares of 10p each. The accounting entries would be:

	Dr £	Cr £
Capital reduction account	180,000	
Income statement:		180,000
Transfer of debit balance		
Share capital	180,000	
Capital reduction account:		180,000
Reduction of share capital		

11.7.3 Accounting treatment for a capital reduction to eliminate accumulated trading losses and loss of value on fixed assets

Companies often take the opportunity to revalue all of their assets at the same time as they eliminate the accumulated trading losses. Any loss on revaluation is then treated in the same way as the accumulated losses and transferred to the capital reduction account.

For example, assume that the capital and reserves and assets of Hopeful Ltd were as follows at 31 December 20X1:

	£	£
200,000 ordinary shares of £1 each		200,000
Profit and loss account		(180,000)
		20,000
Non-current assets		
Plant and machinery		15,000
Current assets		
Cash	17,000	
Current liabilities		
Trade payables	12,000	
Net current assets		5,000
		20,000

The plant and machinery is revalued at £5,000 and it is resolved to reduce the share capital to ordinary shares of 5p each. The accounting entries would be:

	Dr £	Cr £
Capital reduction account	190,000	
Income statement		180,000
Plant and machinery:		10,000
Transfer of accumulated losses and loss on revaluation		
Share capital	190,000	
Capital reduction account:		190,000
Reduction of share capital to 200,000 shares of 5p each		

The balance sheet after the capital reduction shows that the share capital fairly reflects the underlying asset values:

	£	£
200,000 ordinary shares of 5p each		10,000
		10,000
Non-current assets		
Plant and machinery		5,000
Current assets		
Cash	17,000	
Current liabilities		
Trade payables	12,000	5,000
		10,000

The *pro forma* balance sheet shown in Figure 11.5 is from the Pilkington's Tiles Group plc's 2002 Annual Report. It shows the position when the company proposed the creation of distributable reserves after a substantial deficit in the reserves had been caused by the writing down of an investment – this was to be achieved by transferring to the profit and loss account the sums currently standing to the credit of the capital redemption reserve and share premium account.

Figure 11.5 Pilkington's Tiles Group *pro forma* balance sheet assuming the completion of the restructuring plan

	31 March 2002 £000	Adjustment £000	Adjusted balance £000
Capital and reserves			
Share capital	9,247		9,247
Share premium account	25,429	(25,429)	—
Capital redemption reserve	645	(645)	—
Merger reserve	(1,001)	1,001	—
Revaluation reserve	1,581	—	1,581
Profit and loss account	(21,738)	25,073	3,335
Equity shareholders' funds	14,163	—	14,163

The proposal was the subject of a special resolution to be confirmed by the High Court – the court would consider the proposal taking creditor protection into account. The Company recognised this with the following statement:

> to the satisfaction of the High Court that no creditor of the Company who has consented to the cancellations will be prejudiced by them. At present, it is anticipated that the creditor protection will take the form of an undertaking ... not to treat as distributable any sum realised ... which represents the realisation of hidden value in the balance sheet ... .

11.7.4 Elimination that affects the ordinary shareholders and other stakeholders

In the Hopeful Ltd example earlier, the ordinary shareholders alone bore the losses. The Companies Act, sections 425–427, provides a procedure for a reconstruction that involves a compromise between shareholders and creditors, with an amendment of the rights of the latter.

Such a reconstruction requires the support of 75% of each class of creditor whose rights are being compromised, 75% of each class of shareholder and the permission of the court. Once it has been approved by the court, it is binding on all parties. The court seeks to ensure that there is reasonable evidence of commercial viability and that anticipated profits are sufficient to service the proposed new capital structure.

Assuming in the Hopeful Ltd example that the creditors agree to bear £5,000 of the losses, the accounting entries would be as follows:

	£	£
Share capital	185,000	
Creditors	5,000	
Capital reduction account:		190,000
Reduction of share capital to 200,000 shares of 7.5p each		

Reconstruction schemes can be complex, but the underlying evaluation by each party will be the same. Each will assess the scheme to see how it affects their individual position.

Trade creditors

In their decision to accept £5,000 less than the book value of their debt, the trade creditors of Hopeful Ltd would be influenced by their prospects of receiving payment if Hopeful were to cease trading immediately, the effect on their results without Hopeful as a continuing customer, and the likelihood that they would continue to receive orders from Hopeful following reconstruction.

Loan creditors

Loan creditors would take into account the expected value of any security they possess and a comparison of the opportunities for investing any loan capital returned in the event of liquidation with the value of their capital and interest entitlement in the reconstructed company.

Preference shareholders

Preference shareholders would likewise compare prospects for capital and income following a liquidation of the company with prospects for income and capital from the company as a going concern following a reconstruction.

Relative effects of the scheme

In practice, the formulation of a scheme will involve more than just the accountant except in the case of very small companies. A merchant bank, major shareholders and major debenture holders will undoubtedly be concerned. Each vested interest will be asked for its opinion on specific proposals: unfavourable reactions will necessitate a rethink by the accountant. The process will continue until a consensus begins to emerge.

Each stakeholder's position needs to be considered separately. For example, any attempt to reduce the nominal value of all classes of shares and debentures on a proportionate basis would be unfair and unacceptable. This is because a reduction in the nominal values of preference shares or debentures has a different effect from a reduction in the nominal value of ordinary shares. In the former cases, the dividends and interest receivable will be reduced; in the latter case, the reduction in nominal value of the ordinary shares will have no effect on dividends as holders of ordinary shares are entitled to the residue of profit, whatever the nominal value of their shares.

Total support may well be unachievable. The objective is to maintain the company as a going concern. In attempting to achieve this, each party will continually be comparing its advantages under the scheme with its prospects in a liquidation.

Illustration of a capital reconstruction

XYZ plc has been making trading losses, which have resulted in a substantial debit balance on the profit and loss account. The balance sheet of XYZ plc as at 31 December 20X3 was as follows:

		£000
Ordinary share capital (£1 shares)		1,000
Less: Accumulated losses	Note 1	(800)
		200
10% debentures (£1)		600
Net assets at book value	Note 2	800

Notes:
1 The company is changing its product and markets and expects to make £150,000 profit before interest and tax every year from 1 January 20X4.
2 (a) The estimated break-up or liquidation value of the assets at 31 December 20X3 was £650,000.
  (b) The going concern value of assets at 31 December 20X3 was £700,000.

The directors are faced with a decision to liquidate or reconstruct. Having satisfied themselves that the company is returning to profitability, they propose the following reconstruction scheme:

● Write off losses and reduce asset values to £700,000.

● Cancel all existing ordinary shares and debentures.

● Issue 1,200,000 new ordinary shares of 25p each and 400,000 12.5% debentures of £1 each as follows:
  – the existing shareholders are to be issued with 800,000 ordinary 25p shares;
  – the existing debenture holders are to be issued with 400,000 ordinary 25p shares and the new debentures.

The stakeholders, i.e. the ordinary shareholders and debenture holders, have first to decide whether the company has a reasonable chance of achieving the estimated profit for 20X4. The company might carry out a sensitivity analysis to show the effect on dividends and interest over a range of profit levels.

Next, stakeholders must consider whether allowing the company to continue provides a better return than that available from the liquidation of the company. Assuming that it does, they assess the effect of allowing the company to continue without any reconstruction of capital and with a reconstruction of capital.

The accountant writes up the reconstruction accounts and produces a balance sheet after the reconstruction has been effected.

The accountant will produce the following information:

Effect of liquidating	£	Debenture holders £	Ordinary shareholders £
Assets realised	650,000		
Less: Prior claim	(600,000)	600,000	
Less: Ordinary shareholders	(50,000)		50,000
	—	600,000	50,000

This shows that the ordinary shareholders would lose almost all of their capital, whereas the debenture holders would be in a much stronger position. This is important because it might influence the amount of inducement that the debenture holders require to accept any variation of their rights.

Company continues without reconstruction

	£	Debenture holders £	Ordinary shareholders £
Expected annual income:			
Expected operating profit	150,000		
Debenture interest	(60,000)	60,000	
Less: Ordinary dividend	(90,000)		90,000
Annual income	—	60,000	90,000

However, as far as the ordinary shareholders are concerned, no dividend will be allowed to be paid until the debit balance of £800,000 has been eliminated, i.e. there will be no dividend for more than nine years (for simplicity the illustration ignores tax effects).

Company continues with a reconstruction

	£	Debenture holders £	Ordinary shareholders £
Expected annual income:			
Expected operating profit	150,000		
Less: Debenture interest	(50,000)	50,000	
(12.5% on £400,000)			
Dividend on shares	(33,000)	33,000	
Less: Ordinary dividend	(67,000)		67,000
Annual income	—	83,000	67,000

How will debenture holders react to the scheme?

At first glance, debenture holders appear to be doing reasonably well: the £83,000 provides a return of almost 14% on the amount that they would have received in a liquidation (83,000/600,000 × 100), which exceeds the 10% currently available, and it is £23,000 more than the £60,000 currently received. However, their exposure to risk has increased because £33,000 is dependent upon the level of profits. They will consider their position in relation to the ordinary shareholders.

For the ordinary shareholders the return should be calculated on the amount that they would have received on liquidation, i.e. 134% (67,000/50,000 × 100). In addition to receiving a return of 134%, they would hold two-thirds of the share capital, which would give them control of the company.

A final consideration for the debenture holders would be their position if the company were to fail after a reconstruction. In such a case, the old debenture holders would be materially disadvantaged as their prior claim will have been reduced from £600,000 to £400,000.

Accounting for the reconstruction

The reconstruction account will record the changes in the book values as follows:

Reconstruction account

	£000		£000
Income statement	800	Ordinary share capital	1,000
Assets (losses written off)	100	10% debentures (old	
		debentures cancelled)	600
Ordinary share capital (25p			
shares)	300		
12.5% debentures (new issue			
of debentures)	400		
	1,600		1,600

The post-reconstruction balance sheet will be as follows:

	£
Ordinary share capital (25p)	300,000
12.5% debentures of £1	400,000
	700,000

11.8 Proposals for changes to company law

The Company Law Review Steering Group (the Review Group) was appointed by the government to look into the question of any changes that may be needed to company law 'for a competitive economy'. In October 1999, it published a number of consultation documents. One of these is on the formation of companies and the maintenance of their capital. The Review Group makes some important proposals for changes regarding the documents that companies should produce (on their formation), and also regarding the question of their capital maintenance (for the protection of their creditors).

11.8.1 Company formation

Here it is proposed to replace the Memorandum of Association and Articles of Association with two different documents and to make it easier for companies to alter some of the contents of these. At present, the Memorandum acts as a declaration by a company to the outside world of its name, place, share capital, limitation of members' liability and its objects; whereas the Articles are the internal rules of a company, e.g. meetings, etc. It is proposed to replace these with (a) the Registration Form, which will have roughly the same information as on the Memorandum, but it will be easier for companies to change some of its contents; and (b) the Company Constitution, which will, generally, resemble the Articles.

Two major changes proposed in relation to the contents of these new documents are that (a) the objects clauses (i.e. the nature of trade of a company), and (b) authorised share capital of companies should be abolished. Historically, objects clauses of companies have created many problems and the legal requirement as to the contents of the objects clause was simplified in recent legislation. The present proposal of abolishing it completely will mean that companies will be able to undertake any lawful trade. The only problem here seems to be the Second Directive of the European Commission ('the Directive') which requires every public company to have an objects clause. So, unless the Directive can be changed, the proposal will only apply to private companies. The second proposal is to abolish the requirement for companies to have an authorised share capital. This will make it easier for companies to increase or reduce their intended capital.

Another proposal is to allow a company to be formed by one person. At present only private companies are allowed to have one member. This is to be extended to cover all types of companies, public as well as private ones.

11.8.2 Capital maintenance

A major proposal here is to allow companies to issue shares of no par value (NPV shares), i.e. shares without nominal values. This will affect the way a share issue is recorded and the permanent capital of a company is maintained.

Shares with no par value

At present any kind of shares issued by UK companies are required to have a nominal value. It seems difficult to defend this requirement today. There seem to be two main arguments for it, namely that (a) the total (nominal) value of share capital of a company can be known and therefore can be maintained, and (b) dividends paid by a company can be based on the (nominal) value of its shares. But the starting point of these arguments seems to be wrong. Nominal values of shares have no real financial meaning, as they are usually the result of an arbitrary value put on them in the past. What is more, in accounting, the net proceeds of a share issue are artificially divided between share capital and share premium accounts as a result of a legal requirement. This is so even though this receipt is the result of one single financial transaction (a capital receipt on sale of a stake in the company). This would not have mattered if share capital and share premium accounts were treated in the same way by the Companies Act, but they are not. So the amount (i.e. nominal value) in the share capital account cannot be an appropriate base in measuring the capital to be maintained by a company. Secondly, basing any dividends on such unrealistic figures can only be misleading. Dividends can easily be based on 'per share'.

In 1952, a committee appointed by the government recommended the introduction of shares of no par value, but the then government failed to legislate for it. The current report by the Review Group also states that creditors of a company attach more importance to other indicators (e.g. asset values and cash flows) than share capital. But today it is not possible for the UK government to allow all companies to issue NPV shares as the Directive requires public companies to have nominal values for their shares. So the proposal to allow such shares will only apply to private companies. This will lead to different rules of writing-up and maintaining the share capital accounts of private and public companies. The Review Group expresses its wish for the Directive to be changed so that all companies can be allowed to issue NPV shares. Until then it is proposed that the new Statute should retain the obligation to have shares with a par or nominal value.

Minimum capital and share issue

At present, there is no requirement for private companies to have a minimum amount of share capital and no change is proposed in this.

Public companies are at present required to have a minimum share capital of £50,000. Whether this amount is adequate for a public company has been questionable from its inception. The Review Group does not make any proposal for this but seeks further consultation.

Accounting for the issue of shares by public companies will not change, as they have to have nominal values for their shares. Nominal values will continue to be credited to share capital account and any excess of net receipt over this value to share premium account.

At present, no company is allowed to give discounts or commissions on the issue of shares (except for underwriting or placing an issue) as this will amount to a reduction of share capital. It is proposed to maintain this requirement for public and private companies.

Share premium

Public companies will continue to have a share premium account which, at present, can be used for the following purposes:

(a) issue bonus shares;

(b) write off formation expenses;

(c) write off expenses, commissions and discounts on issue of shares or debentures;

(d) provide for premium on redemption of debentures.

It is proposed to:

(a) allow this as it does not reduce capital;

(b) disallow this as it reduces capital;

(c) allow only for the shares of the same class;

(d) disallow as debentures are of different class.

Reduction of share capital

There are two major proposals here, namely to reduce the power of courts in these cases and to require a solvency declaration by all companies before a reduction can be affected.

At present a company can reduce its share capital for three purposes, namely to:

● eliminate or reduce the part which has not been called up;

● pay back that part which is in excess of it needs;

● write off lost capital (i.e. accumulated losses).

Currently, in all these cases, the court's consent is required to protect the interests of creditors.

It is proposed to retain the purposes for which share capital can be reduced, but to eliminate the need for court approval for private companies completely and, in the case of public companies, to allow their creditors the right to challenge the intended reduction through the courts. It is also proposed that the directors of all companies, whether private or public, would issue a formal solvency statement stating that the company will be able to pay its debts during a year after the reduction or on winding up in that year. If the company has auditors, their opinion on the solvency statement would also be needed.

Redemption of shares

At present, a public company is allowed to buy back its own shares or redeem them out of the proceeds of a new share issue or out of its distributable profits. To the extent that this is not possible, there must be a transfer from distributable profits to an account called capital redemption reserve which becomes part of the permanent capital of the company and which can only be used to issue bonus shares. It is proposed to maintain this requirement for public companies.

Private companies are at present allowed to reduce their capital to the extent of their 'permissible capital payment'. It is proposed to drop the notion of permissible capital payment and to allow these companies to reduce their capital, provided any redemption is first met from a new share issue or distributable profits and that a solvency statement – as mentioned in section 11.6 above – is issued by the directors. There will be no need for a capital redemption reserve account for them.

At the moment, all shares redeemed by any type of company are required to be cancelled on redemption. There are other current proposals by the Department of Trade to allow companies to retain (i.e. not to cancel) these shares but to hold them as part of their treasury activities to the extent that they do not exceed 10% of the issued capital. The Review Group proposes that this should also be introduced into the new legislation (see section 11.9 below).

When shares are redeemed at a premium, this premium is required to be written off against the distributable profits. But companies are also given the option to utilise their share premium account to the extent of the lower of (a) premium received on the issue of shares now being redeemed, and (b) balance existing on the share premium account. It is argued by the Review Group that this enables a company to avoid a situation whereby a redemption may cause its capital to increase, and therefore this option should be maintained for public companies. On the other hand, it can be demonstrated that this provision may cause a company's permanent capital to decrease. It is surprising that this possibility has been missed out by the Review Group after so many years.

This demonstrates how easy and straightforward the situation would have been if companies could also have NPV shares; any excess of the payment for a redemption over the net proceeds of a new issue would have caused an equivalent transfer from distributable profits to the subscribed capital (or to a redemption account) thereby maintaining the permanent capital exactly as it was.

11.8.3 Distributable profits

It is intended to maintain the substance of provisions relating to distributable profits.

The Review Group concedes that there are problems relating to the definition of 'realised profits' and to the valuation of assets and liabilities for this purpose. It also states that there is a need to look at accounting standards in this context. As these are complex accounting matters, it will be interesting to see how they can be adequately covered by legislation.

11.8.4 Comments on the proposed changes

The proposed abolition of authorised capital and the elimination of the need to obtain court approval for a reduction in issued capital will make it less onerous and less expensive for all companies to increase or reduce their issued capital.

For creditors of private companies, the only protection will be a forecast (solvency declaration by directors) that the company will be able to pay its debts in the short term. Small family-run companies could always, effectively, reduce their capital through their remuneration. Creditors of these companies had to depend on the character and personal guarantees of their owners. The proposed changes should not materially alter the position of the creditors of these companies. But the position of creditors of large private companies will be less secure than that of creditors of public companies.

For creditors of public companies there will not be a material change, as these companies will still be required to maintain their permanent capital through transfers from distributable to undistributable reserves, on any capital reduction. But the problem of the flexibility of the use of share premium will remain, which may still lead to an erosion of capital.

11.8.5 Final Report

In June 2001, The Company Law Review Steering Group produced its Final Report which recommended changes to the Companies Act according to its earlier proposals (as summarised above), except for one important omission as regards the issue of NPV shares. The Review Group was not prepared to recommend the issue of such shares because of the difficulties and anomalies that may arise as a result of private companies being able to issue them while public companies may not. Nevertheless, the Final Report stated that the abolition of par values for shares of all companies should be the long-term objective of the law.

The government published its response to the Review Group's major recommendations and set out its core proposals for reform in a White Paper 'Modernising Company Law' (Cm 5553) published on 16 July 2002. The consultation period for the receipt of views on the proposals concluded on 29 November 2002. The Act is now awaited.

11.9 Buyback of own shares – treasury shares

11.9.1 National regimes where buyback is already permitted

In Europe and the USA it has been permissible to buy back shares, known as treasury shares, and hold them for reissue: There are two common accounting treatments – the cost method and the par value method.

The most common method is the cost method which provides that:

On purchase:

● The treasury shares are debited at gross cost to a Treasury Stock account – this is deducted as a one-line entry from equity, e.g. a balance sheet might appear as follows:

Owners' Equity Section of Balance Sheet	£
Common stock, £1 par, 100,000 shares authorised, 30,000 shares issued	30,000
Paid in capital in excess of par	60,000
Retained earnings	165,000
Treasury Stock (15,000 shares at cost)	(75,000)
Total owners' equity	180,000

In some countries, e.g. Switzerland, the treasury shares have been reported in the balance sheet as a financial asset. When a company moves to IAS this is not permitted and the shares are required to be disclosed as negative equity.

On resale:

● If on resale the sales price is higher than the cost price, the Treasury Stock account is credited at cost price and the excess is credited to Paid-in Capital (Treasury Stock).

● If on resale the sales price is lower than the cost price, the Treasury Stock account is credited with the proceeds and the balance is debited to Paid-in Capital (Treasury Stock). If the debit is greater than the credit balance on Paid-in Capital (Treasury Stock), the difference is deducted from retained earnings.

11.9.2 The UK regime

Under the Companies Act 1985 companies were required to cancel any of their own shares that they purchased. This changed with effect from December 2003 when the Companies (Acquisition of Own Shares) (Treasury Shares) Regulations 2003 – SI 2003/1116 and SI 2003/3031 – came into effect. These regulations permit companies with listed shares that purchase their own shares out of distributable profits to hold them 'in treasury' for sale at a later date or for transfer to an employees' share scheme.

There are certain restrictions whilst shares are held in treasury, namely:

● Their aggregate nominal value must not exceed 10% of the nominal value of issued share capital (if exceeding 10% then the excess must be disposed of or cancelled).

● Rights attaching to the class of share – e.g. receiving dividends, and the right to vote – cannot be exercised by the company.

There are stipulations as to the accounting treatment on disposal:

● If the proceeds are equal to or less than the purchase price, the proceeds are treated as realised profit (this recognises that they had been purchased out of distributable profits).

● If the proceeds exceed the purchase price, an amount equal to the purchase price is treated as a realised profit and the excess is transferred to a share premium account.

11.9.3 What are the benefits to the company holding treasury shares?

A company has greater flexibility to respond to investors' attitude to gearing, e.g. reissuing the shares if the gearing is perceived to be too high. It also has the capacity to satisfy loan conversions and employee share options without the need to issue new shares which would dilute the existing shareholdings.

11.10 Developments in other countries – the Singapore experience

It is interesting to note that until 1998 companies in Singapore were not permitted to purchase their own shares and had to rely on obtaining a court order to reduce capital. It was realised, however, that regimes such as those in the UK allowed a quicker and less expensive way to return capital to shareholders. UK experience meant that public companies were able to return capital if there were insufficient investment opportunities and private companies were able to repurchase shares to resolve disputes between family members or minority and majority shareholders.

The same criteria discussed in Chapters 10 and 11 apply:

● the company should have authority under its Articles of Association;
● the repayment should be from distributable profits that are realised;
● the creditors should be protected by requiring the company to be solvent before and after the repayment (assets and liabilities to be restated to current values for this exercise);
● on-market acquisitions require an ordinary resolution;
● selective off-market acquisitions require a special resolution because of the risk that directors may manipulate the transaction.

The amount paid by the company will be set against the carrying amount of the contributed capital, i.e. the nominal value plus share premium attaching to the shares acquired and the retained earnings. In order to maintain capital, there will be a transfer from retained earnings to a capital redemption reserve. For example, a payment of $100,000 to acquire shares with a nominal value of $20,000 would be recorded as:

	Dr	Cr
Share capital	$20,000	
Retained earnings	$80,000	
Cash		$100,000

Being purchase of 20,000 $1 shares for $100,000 and their cancellation

	Dr	Cr
Retained earnings	$20,000	
Capital redemption reserve		$20,000

Being the creation of capital redemption reserve to maintain capital.

Summary

The regulation of any reduction in share capital is part of the question of capital maintenance and creditor protection. The Companies Act 1985 provides, in detail, the conditions under which capital can be reduced and shares can be bought back by companies. It lays down detailed rules to maintain the permanent capital of a company by the creation of a capital redemption reserve and utilisation of a share premium account. But, contrary to the aim of the Act, the final result may not necessarily lead to the maintenance of permanent capital.

Also, the chapter covers the question of capital reconstructions and the need to consider the effect of any proposed reconstruction on the rights of different parties.

Finally, a view of the possible future shape of all these matters is given in a summary of the recommendations of the Company Law Review Steering Group.

REVIEW QUESTIONS

1 How can distributable profits become non-distributable?

2 In what circumstances can non-distributable profits become distributable?

3 Why do companies reorganise when they have accumulated realised losses?

4 What does the court consider in those circumstances?

5 The directors of Edac plc are considering purchasing some or all of the company's preference shares (nominal value £1 per share) on the open market during the year ending 30 June 20X1. Edac plc's share premium account balance at purchase date will be £320,000.

Three completely independent scenarios are under consideration.

Scenario A

- 80,000 of the shares are to be bought back at a premium of 40p per share. There will be no accompanying new share issue.
- Legally distributable profits at buyback date are estimated to be £376,000.
- The preference shares had originally been issued at par.

Scenario B

- 120,000 of the shares are to be bought back at a premium of 25p per share. There will be no accompanying new share issue.
- Legally distributable profits at buyback date are estimated to be £205,900.
- The preference shares had originally been issued at 115p per share.

Scenario C

- As Scenario B, except that partial financing is to be provided by an issue of 90,000 ordinary shares of £1 per share at 110p per share.

(a) For each scenario A, B and C, calculate and identify the amounts which Edac plc would appropriate from distributable profits in connection with the buyback. Assume that the share premium account would be utilised to the full extent permitted under the Companies Act 1985.

(b) Assume now that Edac plc is a private limited company (Edac Ltd) and that it has distributable profits which are estimated at £15,000 (not £205,900). Recalculate the figures for scenario C as follows:

(i) Show the permissible capital payment.

(ii) Compare the nominal value of bought-back shares with the aggregate of the new share proceeds and the permissible capital payment. Show the surplus or deficit which arises from this.

(c) Say how Edac Ltd would be most likely to deal with the balance in (b)(ii).

Your answers should show your calculations and contain a brief written explanation.

6 The Woolwich repurchased 1.79 million shares at a cost of around £221m.

Discuss possible reasons for the buyback of shares.

EXERCISES

An outline solution is provided in the Appendix at the end of the text for exercises marked with an asterisk (*).

Question 1

(a) Company law defines 'share premium' and attempts to protect it from reduction.

(i) Define 'share premium'.

(ii) State the circumstances in which company law requires a company to place an amount in the share premium account.

(iii) State why and how company law seeks to protect any balance placed in the share premium account.

(b) State whether each of the following are realised or unrealised profits (or losses) for the purpose of calculating distributable profits:

(i) depreciation charged on a revalued fixed asset

(ii) development expenditure in the profit and loss account which was previously capitalised in the balance sheet

(iii) the share of profits from an associated company to an investing company which does not prepare consolidated financial statements

(iv) the profit on the disposal of a fixed asset which had been revalued in a previous year

(v) a provision for libel damages in a forthcoming court case

(vi) surpluses arising on revaluation of assets before sale

(vii) a charge to the profit and loss account of a provision for bad debts.

Question 2

You are the auditor of Smith Family Ltd, which is a family-owned private company. One of the members, Otto Smith Senior, who is also a director, wishes to retire from business and would like to dispose of his holding of 200,000 ordinary £1 shares. These had originally been purchased at a premium of 20p per share. Independent valuations of the company suggested that a reasonable price for his holding would be £300,000.

The remaining family members are happy with this proposal and are considering financing the purchase as follows:

either (i) from internal resources;

or (ii) partly from internal resources and partly by the issue of 50,000 ordinary £1 shares at a premium of £1 per share to Otto Smith Junior.

The summarised balance sheet of Smith Family Ltd at 31 July 20X7 (before the proposed buyback) shows:

Net assets

Cash	400,000
Other sundry assets	850,000
	1,250,000

Financed by:

Ordinary £1 shares	1,000,000
Share premium	100,000
Profit and loss account	150,000
	1,250,000

The directors have approached you for advice.

Required:
Draft a report to the directors of Smith Family Ltd which:
(a) outlines the power of a private limited company to purchase its own shares;
(b) explains the procedure which must be followed;
(c) describes the special rules allowing the purchase of the shares;
(d) includes for both financing options the necessary journal entries, the balance sheets after the purchase of the shares, and an explanation of the changes to the balance sheet.
(Chartered Institute of Public Finance and Accounting)

* Question 3

The draft balance sheet of Telin plc at 30 September 20X5 was as follows:

	£000		£000
Ordinary shares of £1 each, fully paid	12,000	Product development costs	1,400
12% preference shares of £1 each, fully paid	8,000	Sundry assets	32,170
Share premium	4,000	Cash and bank	5,450
Retained (distributable) profits	4,600		
Creditors	10,420		
	39,020		39,020

Preference shares of the company were originally issued at a premium of 2p per share. The directors of the company decided to redeem these shares at the end of October 20X5 at a premium of 5p per share. They also decided to write off the balances on development costs and discount on debentures (see below).

All write-offs and other transactions are to be entered into the accounts according to the provisions of Companies Acts and in a manner financially advantageous to the company and to its shareholders.

The following transactions took place during October 20X5:

(a) On 4 October the company issued for cash 2,400,000 10% debentures of £1 each at a discount of 2½%.

(b) On 6 October the balances on development costs and discount of debentures were written off.

(c) On 12 October the company issued for cash 6,000,000 ordinary shares at a premium of 10p per share. This was a specific issue to help redeem preference shares.

(d) On 29 October the company redeemed the 12% preference shares at a premium of 5p per share and included in the payments to shareholders one month's dividend for October.

(e) On 30 October the company made a bonus issue, to all ordinary shareholders, of one fully paid ordinary share for every twenty shares held.

(f) During October the company made a net profit of £275,000 from its normal trading operations. This was reflected in the cash balance at the end of the month.

Required:
(i)   Write up the ledger accounts of Telin plc to record the transactions for October 20X5.
(ii) Prepare the company's balance sheet as at 31 October 20X5.
(iii) Briefly explain accounting entries which arise as a result of redemption of preference shares.

Question 4

The following is the balance sheet of Alpha Ltd as on 30 June 20X8:

	£000	£000	£000
	Cost	Accumulated depreciation	
Non-current assets			
Freehold property	46	5	41
Plant	85	6	79
	131	11	120
Investments			
Shares in subsidiary company		90	
Loans		40	130
Current assets			
Inventory		132	
Trade receivables		106	
		238	
Current liabilities			
Trade creditors		282	
Bank overdraft		58	
		340	
Net current liabilities			(102)
Total assets *less* liabilities			148

Capital and reserves

250,000 8½% cumulative redeemable preference shares of £1 each fully paid	250
100,000 ordinary shares of £1 each 75p paid	75
	325
Retained earnings	(177)
	148

The following information is relevant:

1 There are contingent liabilities in respect of (i) a guarantee given to bankers to cover a loan of £30,000 made to the subsidiary and (ii) uncalled capital of 10p per share on the holding of 100,000 shares of £1 each in the subsidiary.

2 The arrears of preference dividend amount to £106,250.

3 The following capital reconstruction scheme, to take effect as from 1 July 20X8, has been duly approved and authorised:

   (i) the unpaid capital on the ordinary shares to be called up;

   (ii) the ordinary shares thereupon to be reduced to shares of 25p each fully paid up by cancelling 75p per share and then each fully paid share of 25p to be subdivided into five shares of 5p each fully paid;

   (iii) the holders to surrender three of such 5p shares out of every five held for reissue as set out below;

   (iv) the 8½% cumulative preference shares together with all arrears of dividend to be surrendered and cancelled on the basis that the holder of every 50 preference shares will pay to Alpha a sum of £30 in cash, and will be issued with

      (a) one £40 convertible 7¾% note of £40 each, and

      (b) 60 fully paid ordinary shares of 5p each (being a redistribution of shares surrendered by the ordinary shareholders and referred to in (iii) above);

   (v) the unpaid capital on the shares in the subsidiary to be called up and paid by the parent company whose guarantee to the bank should be cancelled;

   (vi) the freehold property to be revalued at £55,000;

   (vii) the adverse balance on retained earnings to be written off, £55,000 to be written off the shares in the subsidiary and the sums made available by the scheme to be used to write down the plant.

Required:

(a) Prepare a capital reduction and reorganisation account.

(b) Prepare the balance sheet of the company as it would appear immediately after completion of the scheme.

* Question 5

A summary of the balance sheet of Doxin plc, as at 31 December 20X0, is given below:

	£000		£000
800,000 ordinary shares of £1 each	800,000	Assets other than bank (at book values)	1,500,000
300,000 6% preference shares of £1 each	300,000	Bank	200,000
General reserves	200,000		
Creditors	400,000		
	1,700,000		1,700,000

During 20X1, the company:

(i) Issued 200,000 ordinary shares of £1 each at a premium of 10p per share (a specific issue to redeem preference shares).

(ii) Redeemed all preference shares at a premium of 5%. These were originally issued at 25% premium.

(iii) Issued 4,000 7% debentures of £100 each at £90.

(iv) Used share premium, if any, to issue fully paid bonus shares to members.

(v) Made a net loss of £500,000 by end of year which affected the bank account.

Required:

(a) Show the effect of each of the above items in the form of a moving balance sheet (i.e. additions/deductions from original figures) and draft the balance sheet of 31 December 20X1.

(b) Consider to what extent the interests of the creditors of the company are being protected.

Question 6

Discuss the advantages to a company of:

(a) purchasing and cancelling its own shares;

(b) purchasing and holding its own shares in treasury.

Bibliography

Companies Act 1985.

Company Law Review Steering Group, *Company Formation and Capital Maintenance*, October 1999; *The Final Report*, June 2001.

CHAPTER 12

Off balance sheet finance

12.1 Introduction

Accountants have traditionally followed an objective, transaction-based book-keeping system for recording financial data and a conservative, accrual-based system for classifying into income and capital and reporting to users and financial analysts.

However, since the 1950s there has been a growth in the use of off balance sheet finance and complex capital instruments. The financial analyst can no longer rely on the residual balances that appear in the traditional balance sheet when assessing risks and returns.

The traditional balance sheet is undergoing conceptual change. To understand this change we need to consider the evolving treatment in the primary financial statements of the various forms of loan capital and the changing needs of financial analysts. In this chapter we consider:

- Primary financial statements: their interrelationship
- Reasons that companies borrow
- Capital gearing and its implications
- Off balance sheet finance
- Substance over form examples
- Why companies take steps to strengthen their balance sheet
- IAS 10 *Events after the Balance Sheet Date*
- IAS 37 *Provisions, Contingent Liabilities and Contingent Assets.*

12.2 Primary financial statements: their interrelationship

12.2.1 Income statement

At a mechanistic level, the historical income statement is an integral feature of the book-keeping system, in that receipts and payments of a revenue nature are transferred to this account.

At a conceptual level, it is an integral part of the financial reporting system, in that the matching and accruals concepts are applied to the receipts and payments transaction balances in order to arrive at the reported profit or loss for the period.

12.2.2 Balance sheet

At a mechanistic level, the historical cost balance sheet simply contains all those monetary balances remaining within the ledger after revenue and expenses have been transferred to the income statement. It is a form of second trial balance representing the balances of residual data at the end of the financial year as liabilities or assets.

Liabilities are expenses incurred and expected as a consequence of activities not yet finalised by cash transactions with creditors and other third parties; assets constitute expenditure whose economic benefits have not been fully utilised.

These **residual** values are a direct result of the accruals, or matching, concept.

12.3 Primary financial statements: changes in their interrelationship

12.3.1 Importance of the income statement

Although the income statement and the balance sheet were presented in tandem, the income statement used to be considered more important than the balance sheet. It was seen as having a dynamic quality, in that it reported the change in wealth that had occurred during the year with details of costs, taxation, earnings and dividends.

In contrast, the balance sheet's static quality revealed only the left-over balances arising from the double entry book-keeping system.

12.3.2 Emerging importance of the balance sheet

This picture was irrevocably altered by the emergence of capital-hungry joint stock companies. Equity capital, which was the traditional source of finance, was unable to satisfy total demand and loan capital became important. Later, other financial institutions such as insurance companies, merchant banks and pension funds entered the field. The balance sheet came to be viewed in a new light.

Equity or ordinary shareholders were the risk carriers of the limited company. Risk-averse investors seeking greater security of investment income at the expense of capital growth were able to invest in preference shares.

Risk-averse investors seeking greater security of both investment income and investment capital became loan creditors; however, they demanded greater security, and evidence of such security, before parting with money.

While all investors looked to the income statement as a means of assessing the borrower's ability to service the interest and dividend payments, the loan creditors, as a further precaution, looked to the balance sheet to determine the safety of the principal sum secured on the net assets available in the event of foreclosure or liquidation.

12.4 Reasons that companies borrow

Companies borrow money for many reasons:

- **Temporary cash flow problems.** Cash may be needed as a consequence of temporary cash flow problems, and early repayment might be foreseen.
- **Lower cost.** Prevailing interest rates may be attractively low.
- **Fiscal advantages.** Loan interest may attract tax relief for the borrower; such relief is not available for dividend payments.

- **Income gearing.** A fixed rate of loan interest may be less than the anticipated return obtainable by the company in employing the loan funds. The excess will benefit shareholders via earnings per share and increased dividends and, perhaps, capital growth.
- **Timing.** When there is a lack of buoyancy in the capital market, a company might satisfy a medium-term capital requirement by borrowing with a view to redeeming the debt and making a share issue when market conditions are favourable.
- **Dilution of voting power.** Shareholders and management might be reluctant to issue shares if this would dilute the control of the existing shareholders. They might also consider that an increase in the number of shares would increase the risk of a takeover bid.
- **Earnings per share considerations.** The anticipated return on any proposed new share capital, although desirable in absolute terms, might be insufficient to prevent a fall in EPS. A resultant fall in the market value per share might be unacceptable.

In practice, capital gearing decisions will be influenced by a mixture of motives.

12.5 Capital gearing and its implications

Capital gearing is an attempt to measure the risk to the equity shareholders arising from a company's capital structure. It is the arithmetic relationship between borrowed capital and total capital employed. There is no single definition or standard description, but companies operating with a low proportion of borrowed capital as compared with equity capital are described as **low geared**.

The usual arithmetical model compares long-term debt with equity funds. However, it is customary to include within long-term debt any form of long-term capital demanding fixed servicing costs. Hence, preference shares are included because they receive a priority payment of fixed dividend before any distribution to the ordinary shareholders, thus increasing the risk that the latter will receive little or nothing. Under IAS 32 preference shares are often presented as liabilities on the balance sheet.

The measurement usually takes the form of a ratio, which we illustrate using two definitions of gearing. The first definition excludes bank overdraft, the second includes it.

Overdraft excluded

Company Y: $\dfrac{\text{Debentures + Preference shares}}{\text{Debentures + Preference shares + Equity}}$

	Year 2 £m	Year 1 £m
	$\dfrac{10 + 20}{10 + 20 + 50}$	$\dfrac{5 + 20}{5 + 20 + 30}$
	37.5%	**45.5%**
Company Z:	$\dfrac{2 + 6}{2 + 6 + 80}$	$\dfrac{0 + 10}{10 + 72}$
	9.1%	**12.2%**
Industry average:	**25%**	**27%**

Company Y is shown in year 2 to be more highly geared than the industry's average. However, a reduction has occurred in the gearing from 45.5% to 37.5% because the increase in borrowing of £5m has been more than offset by a growth in equity of £20m.

Company Z is shown in year 2 to be lower geared than the industry's average. It too has experienced a reduction in gearing due to a change in its capital structure. The change arises from the redemption of £4m preference shares, the issue of £2m debentures and an increase of £8m in equity shares. Notice the gearing of each company as a proportion of the industry average:

	Year 2	Year 1
Company Y	150%	168.5%
Company Z	36.4%	45.2%

In general, 'long-term debt' means borrowed funds (and preference shares) assumed to be repayable after one year. However, where companies make a habit of maintaining a bank overdraft, it can be argued that such funding is in effect long or medium term and should be treated as such when assessing risk.

Overdraft included

$$\frac{\text{Debentures} + \text{Preference shares} + \text{Overdraft}}{\text{Debentures} + \text{Preference shares} + \text{Overdraft} + \text{Equity}}$$

	£m (Year 2)	£m (Year 1)
Company Y:	$\dfrac{10 + 20 + 5}{10 + 20 + 5 + 50}$	$\dfrac{5 + 20 + 7}{5 + 20 + 7 + 30}$
	41.2%	**51.6%**
Company Z:	$\dfrac{2 + 6 + 3}{2 + 6 + 3 + 80}$	$\dfrac{0 + 10 + 4}{10 + 4 + 72}$
	12.1%	**16.3%**
Industry average:	**31%**	**36%**

The measure of risk is increased for both entities:

	Year 2	Year 1
Company Y	132.9%	143.3%
Company Z	39.0%	45.3%

In comparison with the industry's average, the gearing of Y is higher for both years and the gearing of Z is lower.

12.5.1 Implication of gearing

The risk to the ordinary shareholders in the above example is higher with company Y than with company Z. The fixed dividend of preference shareholders and the fixed interest of loan creditors remains constant irrespective of the level of profits. This leads to fluctuations in the amount of profits attributable to equity. In times of high profits, the return will be generous; in periods of low profits, the return may be low or nonexistent. This volatility is a measure of the risk inherent in an equity shareholding arising from the level of loan finance; it influences dividend yield and the market price of the equity shares.

12.5.2 Interest cover

Interest cover is calculated from the income statement. It indicates the extent to which profits before interest and tax cover the interest charges shown in the income statement. It can be adapted to take account of fixed dividends on preference shares, even if they are not presented as an expense in the income statement. An illustration for companies Y and Z shows:

$$\frac{\text{Profit before interest and tax}}{\text{Interest}}$$

Company Y	Company Z	Industry average	Company Y	Company Z	Industry average
$\frac{27}{4}$	$\frac{18}{3}$		$\frac{21}{5}$	$\frac{14}{4}$	
6.75 times	6 times	4 times	4.2 times	3.5 times	4.5 times

The interest cover ratios suggest that, while Y is more highly geared than Z, it has a marginally greater safety factor (6.75 times compared with 6; 4.2 times compared with 3.5). It has a considerably greater cover than the industry average. However, if profits suffered a severe decline, the relative interest cover ratios could change drastically.

An analysis of the capital structure indicates an entity's ability to discharge its obligations in respect of interest and principal on long-term borrowings. This information is of value to all types of providers of funds, e.g. bankers, debenture holders, preference and ordinary shareholders.

It is primarily the balance sheet that provides the capital structure information; it thus performs a key role in financial decision making. But is its information adequate?

12.6 Off balance sheet finance

Off balance sheet finance is the descriptive phrase for all financing arrangements where strict recognition of the legal aspects of the individual contract results in the exclusion of liabilities and associated assets from the balance sheet.

The impact of such transactions is to understate resources (assets) and obligations (liabilities) to the detriment of the true and fair view.[1] The analyst cannot assess the value of capital employed or the real gearing ratio, and attempts to determine risk are nullified.

This can happen as an innocent side-effect of the transaction-based book-keeping system. For example, when a company undertakes the long-term hire of a machine by payment of annual rentals, the rental is recorded in the income statement, but the machine, because it is not owned by the hirer, will not be shown in the hirer's balance sheet.

If the facility to hire did not exist, the asset could still be used and a similar cash outflow pattern incurred by purchasing it with the aid of a loan. A hiring agreement, if perceived in terms of its **accounting substance** rather than its **legal form**, has the same effect as entering into a loan agreement to acquire the machine.

The exclusion of a liability and its associated asset undermines the use of the balance sheet as a vehicle for assessing risk by means of the gearing ratio.

The true and fair view can also be compromised by deliberate design. The problem of off balance sheet finance became exacerbated by attempts to camouflage the substance of transactions by relying on a strictly legal distinction. For example, loan capital arrangements were concealed from shareholders and other creditors by a legal subterfuge to which management and lenders were party, and with which the auditors colluded.

12.7 Substance over form

IAS 17 *Leases*[2] was the first formal imposition of the principle of accounting for substance over legal form, aiming to ensure that the legal characteristics of a financial agreement did not obscure its commercial impact. In particular, it was intended to prevent the inherent gearing implications of the traditional balance sheet being circumvented and, consequently, the true and fair view being jeopardised.

The standard's aim has generally been achieved, but total elimination of leasing as a vehicle for generating off balance sheet finance has proved difficult. For instance, some companies have manipulated the criteria in the standard which distinguish a finance lease from an operating lease.

The explosive growth of additional and complex forms of financial arrangements during the 1980s focused attention on the need to increase the disclosure and awareness of such arrangements and led to substance over form being included as one of the qualities of reliable information in the *Framework for the Preparation and Presentation of Financial Statements*.

12.7.1 Accounting for substance over form

The IASB has not issued a standard on accounting for substance over form and therefore guidance must be sought from the *Framework for the Preparation and Presentation of Financial Statements*. To account for substance we need to consider the definitions of assets and liabilities as these will dictate the substance of a transaction. If a transaction or item meets the definition of an asset or liability it should be recognised on the balance sheet regardless of the legal nature of the transaction or item.

The definitions of assets and liabilities[3] are as follows:

● An **asset** is a resource controlled by an enterprise as a result of past events and from which future economic benefits are expected to flow to the enterprise.

● A **liability** is a present obligation of the enterprise arising from past events, the settlement of which is expected to result in an outflow from the enterprise of resources embodying economic benefits.

The definitions emphasise **economic benefits controlled** (assets) and **economic benefits transferable** (liabilities). Thus the issues of legal ownership of, or title to, assets and possession of legal responsibilities for liabilities are necessarily evaded in the quest for an identification of substance inherent within the individual transaction.

12.7.2 Applying the definitions

This involves the consideration of key factors in analysing the commercial implications of an individual transaction. The key factors are:

1 **Substance** must first be identified by determining whether the transaction has given rise to new assets or liabilities for the reporting entity and whether it has changed the entity's existing assets and liabilities.

2 **Rights** or other access to benefits (i.e. possession of an asset) must be evidenced by the entity's exposure to risks inherent in the benefits, taking into account the likelihood of those risks having a commercial effect in practice.

3 **Obligations** to transfer benefits (i.e. acceptance of a liability) must be evidenced by the existence of some circumstance by which the entity is unable to avoid, legally or commercially, an outflow of benefits.

4 **Options, guarantees or conditional provisions** incorporated in a transaction should have their commercial effect assessed within the context of all the aspects and implications of the transaction in order to determine what assets and liabilities exist.

12.7.3 Recognition in the balance sheet

Having applied the definition to determine the existence of an asset or liability, it is then necessary to decide whether to include the asset or liability in the balance sheet. This decision necessitates:

● sufficient evidence that a transfer of economic benefits is probable; and

● that monetary evaluation of the item is measurable with sufficient reliability.[4]

12.7.4 Substance over form examples

The following examples illustrate the appropriate treatment for transactions concerning consignment stocks, sale and repurchase agreements, and debt factoring.

Consignment stocks

Consignment stocks are a regular feature of some trades, whereby transfers from one party to another are arranged so that legal title is retained by the consignor, but the economic risks and benefits move to the consignee. Determining the absolute commercial impact of the transaction requires consideration of the rights of each party to have the stock returned to the consignor. The agreement may contain an absolute right of return of the inventory to the consignor, but in practice penalty provisions may effectively neutralise the right so that inventory is never returned.

EXAMPLE ● Producer P plc supplies leisure caravans to caravan dealer C Ltd on the following terms:

1 Each party has the option to have the caravans returned to the producer.
2 C Ltd pays a rental charge of 1% per month of the cost price of the caravan as consideration for exhibiting the caravan in its display compound.
3 Eventual sale of a caravan necessitates C Ltd remitting to P plc the lower of:
   (a) the ex-factory price of the caravan when first delivered to C Ltd, or
   (b) the current ex-factory price of the caravan, less all rentals paid to date.
4 If the caravans remain unsold for six months, C Ltd must pay for each unsold caravan on the terms specified above.

To some extent the risks and rewards of ownership are shared between both parties. However, in practice we must decide in favour of one party because it is not acceptable to show the caravans partly on each balance sheet.

The factors in favour of treating the consigned goods as inventory of P plc are:

● P plc's right to demand the return of the vans.
● C Ltd's ability to return the vans to P plc.
● P plc is deriving a rental income per caravan for six months or until the time of sale, whichever occurs first.

The factors in favour of treating the goods as the inventory of C Ltd are:

● C Ltd's obligation to pay for unsold vans at the end of six months.
● The payment of a monthly rental charge. This may be considered as interest on the amount outstanding.
● C Ltd's payment need not exceed the ex-works price existing at the time of supply.

However, if C Ltd has an **unrestricted** right to return the caravans before the six months have elapsed it can, in theory, avoid the promise to pay for the caravans. Indeed, providing the ex-works cost has not increased beyond the rental (i.e. 1% per month), the company can recover the sum of the rental.

On balance the factors seem to favour treating the transaction as a sale to C Ltd, so its balance sheet would carry the caravans as stock and P plc would carry them as a liability.

Consider also the option of return held by C Ltd. This may not be unrestricted. Disputes may develop if the exhibited caravans suffer wear and tear considered excessive by P plc; or other restrictions may be considered inherent in the various clauses. Thus substance over form is not always easy to identify or isolate. In practice, a decision may be delayed to observe how the terms actually operated, on the basis that what actually transpired constitutes the substance.

Sale and repurchase agreements

Sale and repurchase agreements appear in a variety of guises. The essential ingredient is that the original holder or purported vendor of the asset does not relinquish physical control: it retains access to the economic benefits and carries exposure to the commercial risks. In short, the characteristics of a normal sale are absent. Substance would deem that such a transaction be treated as non-sale, the asset in question remaining in the balance sheet of the purported vendor.

EXAMPLE ● A company specialising in building domestic houses sells a proportion of its landholding to a merchant bank for £750,000 on 25 March 20X5, agreeing to repurchase the land for £940,800 on 24 March 20X7. The land remains under the control and supervision of the vendor.

Substance deems this contract to be a financing arrangement. The risks and rewards of ownership have not been transferred to the bank. Money has been borrowed on the security of the land. The bank is to receive a fixed sum of £190,800 at the end of a two-year term. This equates to 12% per annum compound interest. The balance sheet should retain the land as an asset, the cash inflow of £750,000 being displayed as a loan, redeemed two years later by its repayment at £750,000 plus accrued interest of £190,800.

In deciding whether it is a sale or a finance agreement, consider which party enjoys the benefits and suffers the risk between sale and repurchase. In the simplest version of this kind of contract, this will usually be indicated by the prices at which the two transactions are arranged. If the prices are market prices current at the date of each transaction, risks and rewards of ownership rest with the buyer for the period between the two transactions. But if the later price displays any arithmetic linking with the former, this suggests a relationship of principal and interest between the two dates. Thus benefits and risk reside with the original entity-seller, who is in effect a borrower; the original entity-buyer is in effect a lender.

Debt factoring

Factoring is a means of accelerating the cash inflow by selling debtors to a third party. Sales ledger administration and protection from bad debts may be involved. Is the transaction really a sale in substance, or merely a borrowing arrangement with collateral in the form of accounts receivable? Once again, identification of substance will necessitate consideration of the overall terms of the factoring contract as the factor may be supplying a variety of services. We may safely dispense with the benefits of ownership and concentrate on the risks: there is no likelihood of any improvement in benefit in relation to debtors, apart perhaps from a reduction in finance costs as a side-effect of earlier cash inflow.

The main risk of ownership of debtors is the bad debt risk and the risk of slow payment. If these risks have been transferred to a third party the substance of the factoring arrangement is the genuine sale of accounts receivable, but if these risks are retained by the enterprise the factoring arrangement is in substance a loan arrangement. To decide on the transference of risks the details of the agreement with the third party must be established.

If the agreement transfers the debts **without recourse** then the third party accepts the risks and will have no recourse to the enterprise in the event of non-payment by the debtor. The receipt of cash by the enterprise from the third party in this situation would be recorded to reduce the balance of debtors in the balance sheet.

If the agreement transfers the debts **with recourse** then the third party has not accepted the risks and in the event of default by the debtor the third party will seek redress from the enterprise. The substance of this arrangement is a financing transaction and therefore any cash received by the enterprise from the third party will be recorded as a liability until the debtor pays. Only at that point does the risk and the obligation to repay the third party disappear.

The above examples of substance over form concentrate on a key issue – whether assets and liabilities should be recognised on the balance sheet. The substance approach taken in all the examples follows the principle that if a transaction or transactions creates something that meets the definition of an asset or liability it should be recognised on the balance sheet. If a transaction, on the other hand, passes the risks and rewards of an asset to another party it should be derecognised from the balance sheet regardless of the legal nature of the transaction. This issue is considered again in Chapter 13 since IAS 39 *Financial Instruments: Recognition and Measurement* addresses recognition and derecognition of financial assets and liabilities.

12.8 Impact of converting to IFRS

Owing to the importance of the balance sheet, the impact of converging to IFRS on the balance sheet must be considered. Changes to the balance sheet can change the perceptions of risk by different investors and can therefore potentially affect the ability of companies to raise capital and provide adequate returns to investors. The general changes to assets and liabilities, together with an example, are shown below.

As regards liabilities, this may require

(a) the recognition of new liabilities onto the balance sheet, e.g. provisions for environmental and decommissioning costs; and

(b) the derecognition of existing liabilities, e.g. general provisions for bad debts and provisions for future restructuring costs.

As regards assets, this may require

(a) the recognition of new assets, e.g. derivative financial assets; and

(b) the derecognition of existing assets, e.g. start-up costs and research.

For some companies the main impact might, however, arise from the reclassification of existing assets and liabilities. This is illustrated with the following extract from the Annual Report of Arinso International which converted to IFRS in 2003 and restated its 2002 balance sheet.

Arinso International extract

December 31, 2002 (IFRS opening balance 2003) (in EUR)	Note	2002 Belgian GAAP	IFRS corrections	IFRS reclass.	2002 IFRS
Assets					
Non-current Assets					
Start-up expenses	1	45,017	(45,017)		
Property, plant and equipment		2,298,195			2,298,195
Goodwill	3	10,986,740	(347,062)		10,639,678
Intangible assets		5,536			5,536
Long term receivables		665,354		228,755	894,109
Deferred tax assets	8		1,583,035		1,583,035
Current Assets					
Amounts receivable after one year		228,755		(228,755)	
Work in process	4	37,621	26,200	(63,821)	
Tax assets				992,805	992,805
Trade and other receivables	7	34,787,200	5,187	332,781	35,125,168
Investments		19,578,727		(19,578,727)	
Cash and cash equivalents		29,771,618		19,578,727	49,350,345
Deferred charges and accrued income		1,261,765		(1,261,765)	
Total assets		99,666,528	1,222,343	0	100,888,871

December 31, 2002 *(IFRS opening balance 2003) (in EUR)*	*Note*	*2002 Belgian GAAP*	*IFRS corrections*	*IFRS reclass.*	*2002 IFRS*
Liabilities					
Equity					
Capital		60,245,423			60,245,423
Reserves		1,023,738			1,023,738
Retained earnings	1, 2,3,4, 5,6,7,8	9,484,114	1,567,936		11,052,050
Translation differences		433,035			433,035
Third parties		2,500			2,500
Non-current liabilities					
Interest bearing liabilities		13,619			13,619
Provisions	5	831,673	(223,947)	(607,726)	
Deferred tax liabilities	8	266,511	98,594		365,105
Current liabilities					
Tax liabilities	8		18,300	2,567,731	2,586,031
Trade and other liabilities	2,6	9,675,272	(183,940)	13,565,034	23,056,366
Advances		248,284		(248,284)	
Social and tax liabilities	2	16,873,639	(54,600)	(16,819,039)	
Provisions				2,111,004	2,111,004
Other debts		30,193		(30,193)	
Accrued charges and deferred income		538,527		(538,527)	
Total liabilities		99,666,528	1,222,343	0	100,888,871

Arinso is a Belgian company and the reclassifications required will vary in different regulatory regimes.

Investors may be interested in the effect on retained earnings and distributable profits e.g. increased by 1,567,936; loan creditors may be interested in the effect on non-current liabilities, gearing and possible breaking of debt covenants; and creditors may be interested in the effect on the liquidity expressed as current and quick ratios.

There might be difficulties in differentiating real changes in performance from the impact of the new IFRS requirements. It will be important for companies to highlight the economic impact of any changes on their business strategy, treasury management, financing, profitability and dividends, e.g Barclays have indicated that there will be little impact on profit after tax and earnings per share but that there will be an impact on the balance sheet as off balance sheet items are brought on to the balance sheet.

12.9 Balance sheet as valuation document

Another evolutionary feature of the modern balance sheet is its increasing tendency to be perceived as a valuation document. The traditional balance sheet was seen as a form of second trial balance, i.e. a statement listing economic benefits still to come, unused expenditures of earlier accounting periods, prepayments, obligations not yet discharged, unsettled accounts and accruals.

The main motives for the change in perception are to report the financial strengths of an entity and to allow an assessment of risk by extracting appropriate ratios, such as gearing and net asset cover. We have already discussed the gearing ratio and will now discuss net asset cover.

12.9.1 Net asset cover

Net asset cover compares the current market price of a company's equity share with the value of underlying net assets attributable to that share as revealed by the entity's most recent published balance sheet.

EXAMPLE ● Each of NAC plc's £0.25 fully paid ordinary shares has a current middle market price of 80p on 31 January 20X7. Its summarised balance sheet as at 31 December 20X6 is shown in Figure 12.1.

Figure 12.1   Balance sheet to determine net asset cover

	£	£
Non-current assets		1,100
Current assets	300	
Less: Current liabilities	(100)	
Net current assets		200
Total assets *less* current liabilities		1,300
10% debentures		200
		1,100
Capital and reserves:		
Ordinary shares of 25p fully paid		600
6% preference shares of £1 fully paid		200
Reserves		300
		1,100

Two methods – the micro and macro – may be used to compute the net asset cover, but the formula is:

$$\frac{\text{Net assets per equity share}}{\text{Current market price per equity share}}$$

NAC plc's net assets attributable to the equity shares are £900. The computations of net asset cover are, then:

(i) Micro method: $\dfrac{£900/2400}{£0.80} = 47:1 \quad \text{or} \quad 47\%$

(ii) Macro method: $\dfrac{£900}{£0.80 \times 2400} = 47:1 \quad \text{or} \quad 47\%$

What does the ratio reveal?

In NAC's case, the ratio reveals that the current market price per share of 80p is represented by assets of 35.5p, i.e. the price is covered by 47% in the form of net assets. Thus, it may be argued, if the company is forced into liquidation, the equity holders will receive some 47% of the current market price. It pretends to reveal the extent of the **safety net** underpinning the current share price by assuming the following:

● The net asset carrying value in the balance sheet is a current market price value and all assets in the balance sheet will be saleable, even in a piecemeal situation.
● The aggregate values will be received after allowing for liquidation expenses.
● The share price is inclined to be static.

In order to differentiate the quality or realisability of individual assets, assets such as goodwill, copyright and patents were often deducted in arriving at the net assets applicable to each ordinary share. In other words, the safety net was seen to consist only of tangible assets; but not all city analysts applied such rules.

Is the ratio any use?

Yes, as long as we appreciate that the inherent assumptions may be questionable and that it is a very rough measurement of risk in a capital market where share prices are volatile and where balance sheet data may not be representative of market values. Fundamentally, it is a basis for comparison between like companies in the same industry. It is subjective and considerable care must be applied in the assessment using this ratio.

In spite of its shortcomings, management perceives that the balance sheet is used as a risk measure. Management attention is therefore often given to strengthening the balance sheet. For example, assets may be revalued to improve the apparent asset cover.

12.10 Why companies take steps to strengthen their balance sheets

One of several reasons is management's belief that the gearing ratio is important, and that it can be improved by increasing equity reserves as a consequence of revaluing existing assets in the balance sheet. The revaluation can have an effect on the gearing ratio and earnings per share (EPS).

12.10.1 Gearing ratio improved

In addition to revaluing the book values of assets appearing in the balance sheet, companies may introduce assets into the balance sheet. For example, brand accounting is a system of asset creation designed to bolster the net worth of the entity, and was adopted by a number of major companies during the late 1980s. It caused major concern throughout the accountancy profession because it violated the transaction basis of traditional accountancy reporting; valuation was extremely subjective and it was thought that a brand was too ephemeral to be recorded as an asset.

12.10.2 EPS improved

Earnings per share may be improved by the method chosen to eliminate assets. For example, a company may wish to create reserves, perhaps for use in a capitalisation issue, but more often for the purpose of writing off rather than amortising goodwill. If amortisation can be avoided, profits will be higher than otherwise and EPS may avoid a decline; hence the share price might be maintained.

12.10.3 Commercial pressures to revalue

Pressure on management to strengthen the balance sheet is often associated with a perceived commercial benefit from doing so. Strengthening might be undertaken to frustrate a potential takeover, either real or anticipated. A company experiencing or expecting a hostile bid may revalue its assets to improve the interpretation of its balance sheet and so influence its equity share price. The management may feel that the current price is too low and consequently attractive to a would-be predator. Thus revaluation becomes part of an attempt to make shareholders believe that the current share price does not reflect the true worth of the entity, and hence that the bidder's offer price is not adequate.

Strengthening might also be undertaken to support a potential takeover bid. A predator might try to improve its own balance sheet to encourage shareholders of the target company to accept its offer. Such an offer invariably embraces an exchange of shares between target company shareholders and the bidder.

We saw in earlier chapters that there have been proposals to reflect current values in the balance sheet by implementing a coherent price-level model to adjust the historical carrying amounts. To date, these proposals have not been adopted and historic values, with some modification, still appear in the balance sheet.

12.11 Definitions cannot remove uncertainty: IAS 10 and IAS 37

We have seen that the IASB has issued standards and the *Framework for the Preparation and Presentation of Financial Statements* to help determine the nature of a transaction, by defining assets and liabilities and requiring the substance of commercial transactions to be reflected in the accounts. However, there are times when the nature of the transaction is clear, but the events have not crystallised to the extent that the effect on the accounts is certain. There has to be an estimate and this requires the directors to exercise judgement.

The IASB had already issued standards in two areas: IAS 10 *Events after the Balance Sheet Date* and IAS 37 *Provisions, Contingent Liabilities and Contingent Assets*.

12.11.1 IAS 10 Events after the Balance Sheet Date

IAS 10 requires financial statements to reflect the conditions that existed at the balance sheet date. There is a period of perhaps two months after the year-end before the accounts are signed by the directors and auditors, and information that becomes available during that period should be appraised to determine whether the accounts need to be adjusted.

Adjusting events

If information becomes available during this period that gives further evidence of the conditions that existed **at the balance sheet date**, it is described as an **adjusting event** and, if it is **material**, will require changes in the amounts to be included in the financial statements. Examples are the subsequent determination of the purchase price or proceeds of sale of fixed assets sold before the year-end, and a valuation of property that provides evidence of impairment in value.

Non-adjusting events

Non-adjusting events are post balance sheet events which concern conditions that did not exist at the balance sheet date, but which are **so material** that non-disclosure would affect the ability of the users of financial statements to reach a proper understanding of the financial position. These events are required to be disclosed by way of note. The following is an extract from the 2003 Annual Report of Manchester United:

> ### Post balance sheet events
>
> Subsequent to the balance sheet date, the playing registrations of two footballers have been acquired for a total consideration including associated costs of £18,063,000 of which £7,393,000 is due for payment after more than one year.
>
> The playing registration of one footballer has been disposed of for a total consideration, net of associated costs, of £11,941,000. The associated book value of the playing registration at 31 July 2003 was £16,469,000. As the transaction was in progress at the balance sheet date, a provision for the loss on disposal of £4,528,000 has been included in these financial statements. The revised carrying value of the registration of £11,941,000 has been transferred from intangible fixed asset (see note 11) and reclassified as an intangible asset held for sale.

12.11.2 IAS 37 Provisions, Contingent Liabilities and Contingent Assets[5]

The IASC approved IAS 37 in July 1998. IAS 37 superseded IAS 10 in respect of contingencies, but also gave further guidance on the accounting treatment for provisions. The key objective of IAS 37 is to ensure that appropriate recognition criteria and measurement bases are applied and that sufficient information is disclosed in the notes to enable users to understand their nature, timing and amount.

The IAS sets out a useful **decision tree**, shown in Figure 12.2, for determining whether an event requires the creation of a provision, the disclosure of a contingent liability or no action.

We will now consider provisions, contingent liabilities and contingent assets.

12.11.3 Provisions

The IAS is mainly concerned with provisions. It defines a provision as 'a liability of uncertain timing or amount'.

In particular it targets 'big bath' provisions that companies have been able to make. These are the type of provisions that it has been tempting for directors to make in order to smooth profits without any reasonable certainty that the provision would actually be required in subsequent periods. Sir David Tweedie, the chairman of the IASB, has said:

> A main focus of [IAS 37] is 'big-bath' provisions. Those who use them sometimes pray in aid of the concept of prudence. All too often however the provision is wildly excessive and conveniently finds its way back to the [income statement] in a later period. The misleading practice needs to be stopped and [IAS 37] proposes that in future provisions should only be allowed when the company has an unavoidable obligation – an **intention** which may or may not be fulfilled will **not be enough**. Users of accounts can't be expected to be mind readers.

Figure 12.2   Decision tree

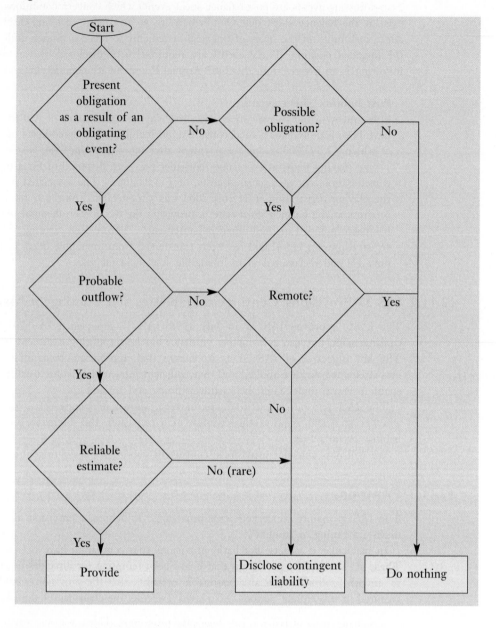

12.11.4 What are the general principles that IAS 37 applies to the recognition of a provision?

The general principles are that a provision should be recognised when:[6]

(a) an entity has a **present obligation** (legal or constructive) **as a result of past events**;

(b) it is **probable** that a transfer of **economic benefits will be required to settle the obligation**;

(c) **a reliable estimate** can be made of the amount of the obligation.

Provisions by their nature relate to the future. This means that there is a need for estimation and IAS 37 comments[7] that **the use of estimates is an essential part of the preparation of financial statements and does not undermine their reliability**.

The IAS addresses the uncertainties arising in respect of present obligation, past event, probable transfer of economic benefits and reliable estimates when deciding whether to recognise a provision.

Present obligation

The test to be applied is whether it is more likely than not, i.e. more than 50% chance of occurring. For example, if involved in a disputed lawsuit, the company is required to take account of all available evidence including that of experts and of post balance sheet events to decide if there is a greater than 50% chance that the lawsuit will be decided against the company.

Where it is more likely that no present obligation exists at the balance sheet date, the company discloses a contingent liability, unless the possibility of a transfer of economic resources is remote.

Past event[8]

A past event that leads to a present obligation is called an **obligating event**. This is a new term with which to become familiar. This means that the company has no realistic alternative to settling the obligation. The IAS defines no alternative as being only where the settlement of the obligation can be enforced by law or, in the case of a constructive obligation, where the event creates valid expectations in other parties that the company will discharge the obligation.

The IAS stresses that it is only those obligations arising from past events existing independently of a company's future actions that are recognised as provisions, e.g. clean-up costs for unlawful environmental damage that has occurred require a provision; environmental damage that is not unlawful but is likely to become so and involve clean-up costs will not be provided for until legislation is virtually certain to be enacted as drafted.

Probable transfer of economic benefits[9]

The IAS defines probable as meaning that the event is more likely than not to occur. Where it is not probable the company discloses a contingent liability unless the possibility is remote.

12.11.5 What are the general principles that IAS 37 applies to the measurement of a provision?

IAS 37 states[10] that the amount recognised as a provision should be the *best estimate* of the expenditure required to settle the present obligation at the balance sheet date.

Best estimate is defined as the amount that a company would rationally pay to settle the obligation or to transfer it to a third party. The estimates of outcome and financial effect are determined by the judgement of management supplemented by experience of similar transactions and reports from independent experts. Management deal with the uncertainties as to the amount to be provided in a number of ways:

● A class obligation exists
  – where the provision involves a large population of items such as a warranty provision, statistical analysis of expected values should be used to determine the amount of the provision.

- A single obligation exists
  - where a single obligation is being measured, the individual most likely outcome may be the best estimate;
  - however, there may be other outcomes that are significantly higher or lower indicating that expected values should be determined.

Management must avoid creation of excessive provisions based on a prudent view:

- Uncertainty does not justify the creation of excessive provisions[11]
  - if the projected costs of a particular adverse outcome are estimated on a prudent basis, that outcome should not then be deliberately treated as more probable than is realistically the case.

The IAS states[12] that 'where the effect of the time value of money is material, the amount of a provision should be the present value of the expenditures expected to be required to settle the obligation'.

Present value is arrived at[13] by discounting the future obligation at 'a pre-tax rate (or rates) that reflect(s) current market assessments of the time value of money and the risks specific to the liability. The discount rate(s) should not reflect risks for which future cash flow estimates have been adjusted.'

12.11.6 Application of criteria illustrated

Scenario 1

An offshore oil exploration company is required by its licence to remove the rig and restore the seabed. Management have estimated that 85% of the eventual cost will be incurred in removing the rig and 15% through the extraction of oil. The company's practice on similar projects has been to account for the decommissioning costs using the 'unit of production' method whereby the amount required for decommissioning was built up year by year, in line with production levels, to reach the amount of the expected costs by the time production ceased.

Decision process

1 Is there a present obligation as a result of a past event?
The construction of the rig has created a legal obligation under the licence to remove the rig and restore the seabed.

2 Is there a probable transfer of economic benefits?
This is probable.

3 Can the amount of the outflow be reasonably estimated?
A best estimate can be made by management based on past experience and expert advice.

4 Conclusion
A provision should be created of 85% of the eventual future costs of removal and restoration.
This provision should be discounted if the effect of the time value of money is material.
A provision for the 15% relating to restoration should be created when oil production commences.
The unit of production method is not acceptable in that the decommissioning costs relate to damage already done.

Scenario 2

A company has a private jet costing £24m. Air regulations required it to be overhauled every four years. An overhaul costs £1.6m. The company policy has been to create a provision for depreciation of £2m on a straight-line basis over twelve years and an annual provision of £400,000 to meet the cost of the required overhaul every four years.

Decision process

1 Is there a present obligation as a result of a past obligating event?
There is no present obligation. The company could avoid the cost of the overhaul by, for example, selling the aircraft.

2 Conclusion
No provision for cost of overhaul can be recognised. Instead of a provision being recognised, the depreciation of the aircraft takes account of the future incidence of maintenance costs, i.e. an amount equivalent to the expected maintenance costs is depreciated over four years.

12.11.7 Disclosures

Specific disclosures,[14] for each material class of provision, should be given as to the amount recognised at the year-end and about any movements in the year, e.g.:

- **Increases in provisions** – any new provisions; any increases to existing provisions; and, where provisions are carried at present value, any change in value arising from the passage of time or from any movement in the discount rate.
- **Reductions in provisions** – any amounts utilised during the period; management are required to review provisions at each balance sheet date and
  – adjust to reflect the current best estimates; and
  – if it is no longer probable that a transfer of economic benefits will be required to settle the obligation, the provision should be reversed.

Disclosures need not be given in cases where to do so would be seriously prejudicial to the company's interests. For example, an extract from the Technotrans 2002 Annual Report states:

> A competitor filed patent proceedings in 2000, ... the court found in favour of the plaintiff ... paves the way for a claim for compensation which may have to be determined in further legal proceedings ... the particulars pursuant to IAS 37.85 are not disclosed, in accordance with IAS 37.92, in order not to undermine the company's situation substantially in the ongoing legal dispute.

- **A provision for future operating losses** should not be recognised (unless under a contractual obligation) **because there is no obligation at the date of the balance sheet**. However, where a contract becomes onerous (see next point) and cannot be avoided, then a provision should be made.
  This can be contrasted to cases where a company supplies a product as a loss leader to gain a foothold in the market. In the latter case, the company may cease production at any time. Accordingly, no provision should be recognised as no obligation exists.
- A provision should be recognised if there is an onerous contract. An onerous contract is one entered into with another party under which the unavoidable costs of fulfilling the contract exceed the revenues to be received and where the entity would have to

pay compensation to the other party if the contract was not fulfilled as, e.g. in the following extract from the Kuoni Travel Holding AG 2001 Annual Report when it created a provision of over CHF80m:

> The provision for onerous contracts covers the loss anticipated in connection with excess flight capacity at Scandinavian charter airline Novair for the period up to the commencement of the 2005 summer season and resulting from the leasing agreement for an Airbus A-330. Until this time, the aircraft will be leased, for certain periods only to other airlines at the current low rates prevailing in the market. The leasing agreement will expire in autumn 2007.

- **A provision for restructuring** should only be recognised when there is a commitment supported by:
  (a) a detailed formal plan for the restructuring identifying at least:
      (i)   the business or part of the business concerned;
      (ii) the principal locations affected;
      (iii) details of the approximate number of employees who will receive compensation payments;
      (iv) the expenditure that will be undertaken; and
      (v)   when the plan will be implemented; and
  (b) has raised a valid expectation in those affected that it will carry out the restructuring by implementing its restructuring plans or announcing its main features to those affected by it.

- **A provision for restructuring should not be created merely on the intention to restructure**. For example, a management or board decision to restructure taken before the balance sheet date does not give rise to a constructive obligation at the balance sheet date unless the company has, before the balance sheet date:
  – started to implement the restructuring plan, e.g. dismantling plant or selling assets;
  – announced the main features of the plan with sufficient detail to raise the valid expectation of those affected that the restructuring will actually take place.

- **A provision for restructuring** should only include the direct expenditures arising from the restructuring which are necessarily entailed and not associated with the ongoing activities of the company. For example, the following costs which relate to the future conduct of the business are not included:
  – retraining costs; relocation costs; marketing costs; investment in new systems and distribution networks.

- **A provision for environmental liabilities** should be recognised at the time and to the extent that the entity becomes obliged, legally or constructively, to rectify environmental damage or to perform restorative work on the environment. This means that a provision should be set up only for the entity's costs to meet its *legal* obligations. It could be argued that any provision for any additional expenditure on environmental issues is a public relations decision and should be written off.

- **A provision for decommissioning costs** should be recognised to the extent that decommissioning costs relate to damage already done or goods and services already received.

The last point may require a change of accounting policy in the way in which companies provide for restoration costs. Gold Mines of Sardinia Ltd, an Australian company listed on the Alternative Issues Market in the UK, stated in its accounting policies in the 1997 accounts:

Restoration costs
Restoration costs that are expected to be incurred are provided for as a part of the exploration, evaluation, development, construction or production phases that give rise to the need for restoration. Accordingly, these costs are recognised gradually over the life of the facility as these phases occur. The costs include obligations relating to reclamation, waste site closure, plant closure, platform removal and other costs associated with the restoration of the site. These estimates of the restoration obligations are based on anticipated technology and **legal** requirements and future costs, which have been **discounted to their present value**.

It would appear that the company is applying the units of production method in respect of restoration costs.

12.11.8 The use of provisions

Only expenditures that relate to the original provision are to be set against it because to set expenditures against a provision that was originally recognised for another purpose would conceal the impact of two different events.

12.11.9 Contingent liabilities

IAS 37 deals with provisions and contingent liabilities within the same IAS because the IASB regarded all provisions as contingent as they are uncertain in timing and amount. For the purposes of the accounts, it distinguishes between provisions and contingent liabilities in that:

● Provisions are a present obligation requiring a probable transfer of economic benefits that can be reliably estimated – a provision can therefore be recognised as a liability.

● Contingent liabilities fail to satisfy these criteria, e.g. lack of a reliable estimate of the amount; not probable that there will be a transfer of economic benefits; yet to be confirmed that there is actually an obligation – a contingent liability cannot therefore be recognised in the accounts but may be disclosed by way of note to the accounts or not disclosed if an outflow of economic benefits is remote.

Where the occurrence of a contingent liability becomes sufficiently probable, it falls within the criteria for recognition as a provision as detailed above and should be accounted for accordingly and recognised as a liability in the accounts.

Where the likelihood of a contingent liability is possible, but not probable and not remote, disclosure should be made, for each class of contingent liability, where practicable, of:

(a) an estimate of its financial effect, taking into account the inherent risks and uncertainties and, where material, the time value of money;

(b) an indication of the uncertainties relating to the amount or timing of any outflow; and

(c) the possibility of any reimbursement.

For example, an extract from the 2003 Annual Report of Manchester United plc informs as follows:

Contingent liabilities

Transfer fees payable
Under the terms of certain contracts with other football clubs in respect of player

transfers, certain additional amounts would be payable by the Group if conditions as to future team selection are met. The maximum that could be payable is £12,005,000 (2002 £12,548,000).

Guarantee on behalf of associate
Manchester United PLC has undertaken to guarantee the property lease of its associate, Timecreate Limited. The lease term is 35 years with annual rentals of £400,000.

12.11.10 Contingent assets

A contingent asset is a possible asset that arises from past events whose existence will be confirmed only by the occurrence of one or more uncertain future events not wholly within the entity's control.

Recognition as an asset is only allowed if the asset is *virtually certain*, i.e. and therefore by definition no longer contingent.

Disclosure by way of note is required if an inflow of economic benefits is *probable*. The disclosure would include a brief description of the nature of the contingent asset at the balance sheet date and, where practicable, an estimate of their financial effect taking into account the inherent risks and uncertainties and, where material, the time value of money.

No disclosure is required where the chance of occurrence is anything less than probable. For the purposes of IAS 37, probable is defined as more likely than not, i.e. more than a 50% chance.

Summary

Traditional book-keeping resulted in the production of a balance sheet that was simply a list of unused and unpaid balances on account at the close of the financial year. It was intrinsically a document confirming the veracity of the double entry system, but it revealed the capital structure of the reporting entity. Hence it became a document for measuring the risk encountered by the providers of capital.

Unfortunately the transaction-based nature of book-keeping created a balance sheet incapable of keeping pace with a developing financial market of highly sophisticated transactions. By operating within the legal niceties, management was able to keep future benefits and obligations off the balance sheet. It was also possible for capital instruments of one kind to masquerade as those of another – sometimes by accident, but often by design. This dilution in the effectiveness of the balance sheet had to be remedied.

The IASB has addressed the problem from first principles by requiring consideration to be given to the definitions of assets and liabilities; to the accounting substance of a transaction over its legal form; to the elimination of off balance sheet finance; and to the standardisation of accounting treatment in respect of items such as leases and capital instruments.

As a consequence, the former balance sheet paradigm has been changed beyond recognition. It is rapidly becoming the primary reporting vehicle. In so doing it is tending to be seen as a valuation document and as a definitive statement of assets used and liabilities incurred by the reporting entity.

This will create an ongoing pressure on the regulators and companies to produce a relevant valuation document. The process of change is unlikely to be painless and considerable controversy will doubtless arise about whether a transaction falls within the IASB definition of an asset or liability; whether it should be recognised; and how it should be disclosed. This will remain an important developing area of regulation and the IASB is to be congratulated on its approach, which requires accountants to exercise their professional judgement.

REVIEW QUESTIONS

1 Some members of the board of directors of a company deliberating over a possible source of new capital believe that irredeemable debentures carrying a fixed annual coupon rate would suffice. They also believe that the going concern concept of the balance sheet would obviate the need to include the debt thereon: the entity is a going concern and there is no intention to repay the debt; therefore disclosure is unwarranted. Discuss.

2 A company is obliged to reveal, in note form, a quantitative assessment of the dilution of future earnings per share on the assumption that convertible stock in issue will experience total conversion into ordinary shares at the earliest possible date. Why should this philosophy not apply to the balance sheet and thus enable such stock to be classified entirely as equity? Discuss.

3 In 20X6 Alpha AS made the decision to close a loss-making department in 20X7. The company proposed to make a provision for the future costs of termination in the 20X6 income statement. Its argument was that a liability existed in 20X6 which should be recognised in 20X6. The auditor objected to recognising a liability, but agreed to recognition if it could be shown that the management decision was irrevocable. Discuss whether a liability exists and should be recognised in the 20X6 balance sheet.

4 As a sales incentive, a computer manufacturer, Burgot SA, offers to buy back its computers after three years at 25% of the original selling price, so providing the customer with a guaranteed residual value which would be exercised if he or she were unable to achieve a higher price in the second-hand market.

Discuss the substance of this transaction and conclude on how the transaction should be presented in the financial statements of the customer.

5 A boat manufacturer, Swann SpA, supplies its dealers on a consignment basis, which allows either Swann SpA or a dealer to require a boat to be returned. Each dealer has to arrange insurance for the boats held on consignment.

When a boat is sold to a customer, the dealer pays Swann SpA the lower of:

● the delivery price of the boat as at the date it was first supplied, or
● the current delivery price less the insurance premiums paid to date of sale.

If a boat is unsold after three months, the dealer has to pay on the same terms.

Discuss, with reasons, whether boats held by the dealers on consignment should appear as inventory in the balance sheet of Swann SpA or the dealer.

7 Discuss the problems of interpreting financial reports when there are events after the balance sheet date, and the extent to which you consider IAS 10 should be amended. Illustrate your decisions with practical examples as appropriate.

8 D Ltd has a balance on its debtors' account of £100,000. Previous experience would anticipate bad debts to a maximum of 3%. The company adopts a policy of factoring its debts. Explain how the transaction would be dealt with in the books of D Ltd under each of the following independent sets of circumstances:

(i) The factoring agreement involves a sole payment of £95,000 to complete the transaction. No further payments are to be made or received by either party to the agreement.

(ii) The debtors are transferred to the factoring entity on receipt of £93,000. The agreement provides for further payments, which will vary on the basis of timing and receipts from debtors. Interest is chargeable by the factor on a daily basis, based on the outstanding amount at the close of the day's transactions. The factor also has recourse to D Ltd for the first £10,000 of any loss.

9 Mining, nuclear and oil companies have normally provided an amount each year over the life of an enterprise to provide for decommissioning costs. Explain why the IASB considered this to be an inappropriate treatment and how these companies would be affected by IAS 37 *Provisions, Contingent Liabilities and Contingent Assets.*

EXERCISES

An extract from the solution is provided in the Appendix at the end of the text for exercises marked with an asterisk (*).

Question 1

(a) Post balance sheet events are those events, both favourable and unfavourable, which occur between the balance sheet date and the date on which the financial statements are approved by the board of directors.

Required:

Set out the treatment of events after the balance sheet date as laid down by IAS 10. Explain why this treatment is required by that IAS in order to ensure that financial statements show a true and fair view and give appropriate information to the shareholders and other legitimate users.

(b) You are the financial accountant of Tooting Engineering plc (a substantial private company). You are responsible for preparing the company's financial statements and are at present finalising those for the year ended 31 December 20X6 for presentation to the board. The following items are material:

(i) You have recently discovered that during September and October 20X6, while you were away sick, the cashier took advantage of the weakened internal controls to defraud the company of £8,000.

(ii) At a board meeting on 3 February 20X7 the directors agreed to purchase the business of Mr N. M. Patel (a small engineering business) for £45,000.

(iii) On 18 January 20X7 the company made a 1 for 4 rights issue to existing ordinary shareholders. This involved the issue of 20,000 £1 ordinary shares for a consideration of £25,000.

(iv) A customer, General Products Ltd, owed Tooting Engineering plc £16,000 on 31 December 20X6. This company had always been considered a good credit risk until on 15 February 20X7 it went into voluntary liquidation. Of the £16,000 debt, £12,000 is still outstanding and General Products Ltd is expected to pay approximately 25p in the pound on this £12,000.

Required:

Explain how you will treat items (i)–(iv) above in the financial statements and give a brief explanation of why you are adopting your proposed treatment.

Question 2

As the financial controller of SEAS Ltd, you are responsible for preparing the company's financial statements and are at present finalising these for the year ended 31 March 20X8 for presentation to the board of directors. The following items are material:

(i) Costs of £250,000 arose from the closure of the company's factory in Garratt, which manufactured coffins. Owing to a declining market, the company has withdrawn from this type of business prior to the year-end.

(ii) You discover that during February 20X8, whilst you were away skiing, the cashier took advantage of the weakness in internal control to defraud the company of £30,000.

(iii) During the year ended 31 March 20X8, stocks of obsolete electrical components had to be written down by £250,000 owing to foreign competitors producing them more cheaply.

(iv) At a board meeting held on 30 April 20X8, the directors signed an agreement to purchase the business of Mr Hacker (a small computer manufacturer) for the sum of £100,000.

(v) £300,000 of development expenditure, which had been capitalised in previous years, was written off during the year ended 31 March 20X8. This became necessary due to foreign competitors' price cutting, which cast doubt on the recovery of costs from future revenue.

(vi) Dynatron Ltd, a customer, owed the company £50,000 on 31 March 20X8. However, on 15 May 20X8 it went into creditors' voluntary liquidation. Of the £50,000, £40,000 is still outstanding and the liquidator of Dynatron is expected to pay approximately 25p in the pound to unsecured creditors.

(vii) On 30 April 20X8, the company made a 1 for 4 rights issue to the ordinary shareholders, which involved the issue of 50,000 £1 ordinary shares for a sum of £62,500.

Required

Explain how you will treat the above financial statements, and give a brief explanation of why you are adopting your proposed treatment.

Question 3

(a) Provisions are particular kinds of liabilities. It therefore follows that provisions should be recognised when the definition of a liability has been met. The key requirement of a liability is a present obligation and thus this requirement is critical also in the context of the recognition of a provision. However, although accounting for provisions is an important topic for standard setters, it is only recently that guidance has been issued on provisioning in financial statements. IAS 37 *Provisions, Contingent Liabilities and Contingent Assets* deals with this area.

Required:
(i) Explain why there was a need for more detailed guidance on accounting for provisions.
(ii) Explain the circumstances under which a provision should be recognised in the financial statements according to IAS 37 *Provisions, Contingent Liabilities and Contingent Assets*.

(b) World Wide Nuclear Fuels, a public limited company, disclosed the following information in its financial statements for the year ending 30 November 20X9:

The company purchased an oil company during the year. As part of the sale agreement, oil has to be supplied to the company's former holding company at an uneconomic rate for a period of five years. As a result a provision for future operating losses has been set up of $135m, which relates solely to the uneconomic supply of oil. Additionally the oil company is exposed to environmental liabilities arising out of its past obligations, principally in respect of soil and ground water restoration costs, although currently there is no legal obligation to carry out the work. Liabilities for environmental costs are provided for when the group determines a formal plan of action on the closure of an inactive site. It has been decided to provide for $120m in respect of the environmental liability on the acquisition of the oil company. World Wide Nuclear Fuels has a reputation for ensuring the preservation of the environment in its business activities.

Required:
Discuss whether the provision has been accounted for correctly under IAS 37 *Provisions, Contingent Liabilities and Contingent Assets*.

Question 4

The directors of Apple Pie plc at the September 20X5 board meeting were expressing concern about falling sales and the lack of cash to meet a dividend for the current year ending 31 December at the same rate as the previous year. They suggested to the Finance Director that:

● equipment with a book value of £40m as at the beginning of the year and an estimated useful economic life of three years should be sold for £62.5m;

● the £62.5m and £40m should be included in the sales and cost of sales for the period resulting in an improvement of £12.5m in profit which would cover the proposed dividend;

● the equipment should then be leased back at 1 October 20X5. The commercial rate of interest for a similar lease agreement had been 10%.

Required:
Draft the Finance Director's response to their suggestion and indicate the effect on the income statement and balance sheet as at 31 December 20X5 if the lease agreement is entered into on 1 October 20X5.

References

1   K.V. Peasnell and R.A. Yaansah, *Off-Balance Sheet Financing*, ACCA, 1988.
2   IAS 17 *Leases*, IASC, revised 1997.
3   *Framework for the Preparation and Presentation of Financial Statements*, IASC, 1989, para. 49.
4   *Ibid.*, para. 86.
5   IAS 37 *Provisions, Contingent Liabilities and Contingent Assets*, IASC, 1998.
6   *Ibid.*, para. 2.
7   *Ibid.*, para. 25.
8   *Ibid.*, para. 17.
9   *Ibid.*, para. 23.
10 *Ibid.*, para. 36.
11 *Ibid.*, para. 43.
12 *Ibid.*, para. 45.
13 *Ibid.*, para. 47.
14 *Ibid.*, para. 84.

CHAPTER 13

Financial instruments

13.1 Introduction

The area of financial instruments has proved to be one of the most controversial and difficult ones that the IASB has had to provide guidance on. The impact on the balance sheet and the income statement is great and the implications for company systems have also been significant. The controversy caused by IAS 39 *Financial Instruments: Recognition and Measurement* in particular is highlighted by the difficulties the European Union had in endorsing the standard. In late 2004 the EU agreed to endorse a 'carved out' version of IAS 39 as the full standard was not considered acceptable to member states and under EU law.

The IASB has gone much further than some accounting standards boards such as the ASB in the UK. The ASB has only issued guidance on disclosure of financial instruments whereas the IASB has also considered recognition and measurement. The IASB has drawn significantly from US GAAP, but even then its requirements go further.

This chapter looks at the main requirements for accounting for financial instruments governed by IAS 32 *Financial Instruments: Disclosure and Presentation*, and IAS 39 *Financial Instruments: Recognition and Measurement*. The two standards should be viewed together as they are effectively two parts of the same issue. The reason that two standards were issued as opposed to one is the result of pragmatism – the IASB could get agreement on disclosure and presentation before recognition and measurement. It felt it was better to introduce some guidance even though the whole issue had not been sorted out.

13.2 IAS 32 *Financial Instruments: Disclosure and Presentation*[1]

The dynamic nature of the international financial markets has resulted in a great variety of financial instruments from traditional equity and debt instruments to derivative instruments such as futures or swaps. These instruments are a mixture of on balance sheet and off balance sheet instruments, and they can significantly contribute to the risks that an enterprise faces. IAS 32 was introduced to highlight to users of financial statements the range of financial instruments used by an enterprise and how they affect the financial position, performance and cash flows of the enterprise.

IAS 32 only considers the areas of presentation and disclosure of financial instruments; recognition and measurement are considered in a subsequent standard, IAS 39.

13.2.1 Scope of the standard

IAS 32 should be applied by all enterprises and should consider all financial instruments with the exceptions of:

(a) share-based payments as defined in IFRS 2;

(b) interests in subsidiaries as defined in IAS 27;

(c) interests in associates as defined in IAS 28;

(d) interests in joint ventures as defined in IAS 31;

(e) post-retirement employee benefit plans;

(f) employers' obligations under employee share option and share purchase plans;

(g) rights and obligations arising under insurance contracts;

(h) contracts for contingent consideration in a business combination (this exemption applies only to the acquirer);

(i) contracts that require a payment based on climatic, geological or other physical variables.

13.2.2 Definition of terms[2]

The following definitions are used in IAS 32 and also in IAS 39, which is to be considered later.

A **financial instrument** is any contract that gives rise to both a financial asset of one enterprise and a financial liability or equity instrument of another enterprise.

A **financial asset** is any asset that is:

(a) cash;

(b) a contractual right to receive cash or another financial asset from another enterprise;

(c) a contractual right to exchange financial instruments with another enterprise under conditions that are potentially favourable; or

(d) an equity instrument of another enterprise.

A **financial liability** is any liability that is a contractual obligation:

(a) to deliver cash or another financial asset to another enterprise; or

(b) to exchange financial instruments with another enterprise under conditions that are potentially unfavourable.

An **equity instrument** is any contract that evidences a residual interest in the assets of an enterprise after deducting all of its liabilities.

Following the introduction of IAS 39 extra clarification was introduced into IAS 32 in the application of the definitions. First, a commodity-based contract (such as a commodity future) is a financial instrument if either party can settle in cash or some other financial instrument. Commodity contracts would not be financial instruments if they were expected to be settled by delivery, and this was always intended.

The second clarification is for the situation where an enterprise has a financial liability that can be settled either with financial assets or the enterprise's own equity shares. If the number of equity shares to be issued varies with changes in their value so that the enterprise always has an obligation to give shares equal to the fair value of the obligation, they are treated as a financial instrument.

13.2.3 Presentation of instruments in the financial statements

Two main issues are addressed in the standard regarding the presentation of financial instruments. These issues are whether instruments should be classified as liabilities or equity instruments, and how compound instruments should be presented.

Liabilities v equity

IAS 32 follows a substance approach[3] to the classification of instruments as liabilities or equity. If an instrument has terms such that there is an obligation on the enterprise to transfer financial assets to redeem the obligation then it is a liability instrument regardless of its legal nature. Preference shares are the main instrument where in substance they could be liabilities but legally are equity. The conditions on the preference share that would indicate it is to be treated as a liability instrument are as follows:

- the share provides for mandatory redemption by the issuer at a fixed or determinable amount at a future fixed or determinable date;
- the share gives the holder the option to redeem upon the occurrence of a future event that is highly likely to occur (e.g. after the passing of a future date).

If a preference share is treated as a liability instrument it is presented as such in the balance sheet and also any dividends paid or payable on that share are calculated in the same way as interest and presented as a finance cost in the income statement. The presentation on the income statement could be as a separate item from other interest costs but this is not mandatory. Any gains or losses on the redemption of financial instruments classified as liabilities are also presented in the income statement.

Impact on companies

The presentation of preference shares as liabilities does not alter the cash flows or risks that the instruments give, but there is a danger that the perception of a company may change. This presentational change has the impact of reducing net assets and increasing gearing. This could be very important, for example, if a company had debt covenants on other borrowings that required the maintenance of certain ratios such as gearing or interest cover. Moving preference shares to debt and dividends to interest costs could mean the covenants are breached and other loans become repayable.

In addition, the higher gearing and reduced net assets could mean the company is perceived as more risky, and therefore a higher credit risk. This in turn might lead to a reduction in the company's credit rating, making obtaining future credit more difficult and expensive.

These very practical issues need to be managed by companies converting to IFRS from a local accounting regime that treats preference shares as equity or non-equity funds. Good communication with users is key to smoothing the transition.

Compound instruments[4]

Compound instruments are financial instruments that have the characteristics of both debt and equity. A convertible loan, which gives the holder the option to convert into equity shares at some future date, is the most common example of a compound instrument. The view of the IASB is that the proceeds received by an enterprise for these instruments are made up of two parts, a debt part and an equity option, and following substance IAS 32 requires that the two parts are presented separately, a 'split accounting' approach.

The split is made by measuring the debt part and making the equity the residual of the proceeds. This approach is in line with the definitions of liabilities and equity, where equity is treated as a residual. The debt is calculated by discounting the cash flows on the debt at a market rate of interest for similar debt without the conversion option.

Illustration for compound instruments

Rohan plc issues 1,000 £100 5% convertible debentures at par on 1 January 2000. The debentures can either be converted into 50 ordinary shares per £100 of debentures, or redeemed at par at any date from 1 January 2005. Interest is paid annually in arrears on 31 December. The interest rate on similar debentures without the conversion option is 6%.

To split the proceeds the debt value must be calculated by discounting the future cash flows on the debt instrument.

The value of debt is therefore:

Present value of redemption payment	£74,726
Present value of interest (5 years)	£21,062
Value of debt	£95,788
The value of the equity proceeds: (£100,000 – £95,788)	£4,212

(presented as an option in shareholders' funds)

Perpetual debt

Following a substance approach, perpetual or irredeemable debt could be argued to be an equity instrument as opposed to a debt instrument. IAS 32, however, takes the view that it is a debt instrument because the interest must be paid (as compared to dividends which are only paid if profits are available for distribution), and the present value of all the future obligations to pay interest will equal the proceeds of the debt if discounted at a market rate. The proceeds are therefore a liability obligation.

13.2.4 Calculation of finance costs on liability instruments

The finance costs will be debited in the income statement. The finance cost of debt is the total payments to be incurred over the life-span of that debt less the initial carrying value. Such costs should be allocated to the income statement over the life-time of the debt at a constant rate of interest based on the outstanding carrying value per period. If a debt is settled before maturity, any profit or loss should be reflected immediately in the income statement – unless the substance of the settlement transaction fails to generate any change in liabilities and assets.

Illustration of the allocation of finance costs and the determination of carrying value

On 1 January 20X6 a company issued a debt instrument of £1,000,000 spanning a four-year term. It received from the lender £890,000, being the face value of the debt less a discount of £110,000. Interest was payable yearly in arrears at 8% per annum on the principal sum of £1,000,000. The principal sum was to be repaid on 31 December 20X9.

To determine the yearly finance costs and year-end carrying value it is necessary to compute:

- the aggregate finance cost;
- the implicit rate of interest carried by the instrument;
- the finance charge per annum; and
- the carrying value at successive year-ends.

Aggregate finance cost

This is the difference between the total future payments of interest plus principal, less the net proceeds received less costs of the issue, i.e. £430,000 in column (i) of Figure 13.1.

Implicit rate of interest carried by the instrument

This can be computed by using the net present value (NPV) formula:

$$\sum_{t=1}^{t=n} \frac{At}{(1+r)^t} - I = 0$$

where A is forecast net cash flow in year A, t time (in years), n the life-span of the debt in years, r the company's annual rate of discount and I the initial net proceeds. Note that the application of this formula can be quite time-consuming. A reasonable method of assessment is by interpolation of the interest rate.

The aggregate formula given above may be disaggregated for calculation purposes:

$$\sum_{t=1}^{t=n} \frac{A1}{(1+r)^1} + \frac{A2}{(1+r)^2} + \frac{A3}{(1+r)^3} + \frac{A4}{(1+r)^4} - I = 0$$

Using the data concerning the debt and assuming (allowing for discount and costs) an implicit constant rate of, say, 11%:

$$\Sigma = \frac{80,000}{(1.11)^1} + \frac{80,000}{(1.11)^2} + \frac{80,000}{(1.11)^3} + \frac{1,080,000}{(1.11)^4} - 890,000 = 0$$

$$= 72,072 + 64,930 + 58,495 + 711,429 - 890,000 = +16,926$$

The chosen implicit rate of 11% is too low. We now choose a higher rate, say 12%:

$$\Sigma = \frac{80,000}{(1.12)^1} + \frac{80,000}{(1.12)^2} + \frac{80,000}{(1.12)^3} + \frac{1,080,000}{(1.12)^4} - 890,000 = 0$$

$$= 71,429 + 63,776 + 56,942 + 686,360 - 890,000 = -11,493$$

This rate is too high, resulting in a negative net present value. Interpolation will enable us to arrive at an implicit rate:

$$11\% + \left[\frac{16,926}{16,926+11,493} \times (12\% - 11\%) \right]$$

$$= 11\% + 0.59\% = 11.59\%$$

Figure 13.1 shows the entries for each year 20X6–20X9.

Figure 13.1   Allocation of finance costs and determination of carrying value

	(i)		(ii)		(iii)
			Finance charge to		Carrying value in balance
	Cash flows		Income statement		sheet
	£000		£000		£000
At 1 Jan 20X6	(890)	(1,000 – 50 – 60)	—		890
At 31 Dec 20X6	80	(8% × 1,000)	103.2	(11.59% × 890)	913.2
At 31 Dec 20X7	80	(8% × 1,000)	105.8	(11.59% × 913.2)	939.2
At 31 Dec 20X8	80	(8% × 1,000)	108.8	(11.59% × 939)	967.8
At 31 Dec 20X9	1,080	(1,000 + (8% × 1,000))	112.2	(11.59% × 967.8)	—
Net cash flow	430		= Cost	430	

This is a trial and error method of determining the implicit interest rate. In this example the choice of rates, 11% and 12%, constituted a change of only 1%. It would be possible to choose, say, 11% and then 14%, generating a 3% gap within which to interpolate. This wider margin would result in a less accurate implicit rate and an aggregate interest charge at variance with the desired £430,000 of column (ii). The aim is to choose interest rates as close as possible to either side of the monetary zero, so that the exact implicit rate may be computed.

The object is to determine an NPV of zero monetary units, i.e. to identify the discount rate that will enable the aggregate future discounted net flows to equate to the initial net proceeds from the debt instrument. In the above illustration, a discount (interest) rate of 11.59% enables £430,000 to be charged to the income statement after allowing for payment of all interest, costs and repayment of the face value of the instrument.

13.2.5 Offsetting financial instruments[5]

Financial assets and liabilities can only be offset and presented net if the following conditions are met:

(a) the enterprise has a legally enforceable right to set off the recognised amounts; and

(b) the enterprise intends either to settle on a net basis, or to realise the asset and settle the liability simultaneously.

IAS 32 emphasises the importance of the intention to settle on a net basis as well as the legal right to do so. Offsetting should only occur when the cash flows and therefore the risks associated with the financial asset and liability are offset and therefore to present them net in the balance sheet shows a true and fair view.

Situations where offsetting would not normally be appropriate are:

● several different financial instruments are used to emulate the features of a single financial instrument;

● financial assets and financial liabilities arise from financial instruments having the same primary risk exposure but involve different counterparties;

● financial or other assets are pledged as collateral for non-recourse financial liabilities;

● financial assets are set aside in trust by a debtor for the purpose of discharging an obligation without those assets having been accepted by the creditor in settlement of the obligation;

● obligations incurred as a result of events giving rise to losses are expected to be recovered from a third party by virtue of a claim made under an insurance policy.

13.2.6 Disclosure requirements

Disclosure is a major part of IAS 32 and the requirements for disclosure cover both non-derivative and derivative instruments. The disclosures are very extensive but aim to ensure that users understand the risks faced by an enterprise because of its use of financial instruments and the reductions in risk that can also be achieved. A summary of the main disclosures[6] relating to price, currency, liquidity and cash flow risks and risk management policies follows:

Market risk

This risk is made up of three types: currency risk, interest rate risk and price risk.

Currency risk	The risk that the value of a financial instrument will fluctuate due to changes in foreign exchange rates.
Interest rate risk	The risk that the value of a financial instrument will fluctuate due to changes in interest rates.
Price risk	The risk that the value of a financial instrument will fluctuate in value as a result of changes in market prices whether those changes are caused by factors specific to the individual security or its issuer or factors affecting all securities traded in the market.

Credit risk

Credit risk is the risk that one party to a financial instrument will fail to discharge an obligation and cause another party to incur a financial loss.

Liquidity risk

This is also referred to as funding risk, and is the risk that an enterprise will encounter difficulty in raising funds to meet commitments associated with the financial instruments. Liquidity risk may result from an inability to sell a financial asset quickly at close to its fair value.

Cash flow risk

Cash flow risk is the risk that future cash flows associated with a monetary financial instrument will fluctuate in amount. In the case of a floating rate debt instrument, for example, such fluctuations result in a change in the effective interest rate of the financial instrument, usually without a corresponding change in its fair value.

The standard does not prescribe the format of the disclosures but does give some detailed standards and guidance on what has to be disclosed.

Risk management policies

This disclosure would include the financial risk management objectives and policies, including its policy for hedging each major type of forecasted transaction for which hedge accounting is used.

13.2.7 The detailed disclosure standards

Terms, conditions and accounting policies

Standard
For each class of financial asset, financial liability and equity instrument, both recognised and unrecognised, an enterprise should disclose:

(a) information about the extent and nature of the financial instruments, including significant terms and conditions that may affect the amount, timing and certainty of future cash flows; and

(b) the accounting policies and methods adopted, including the criteria for recognition and the basis of measurement applied.

Guidance
The contractual terms of the instrument are important factors in deciding the certainties of future cash flows. The financial instruments should either be treated separately if individually material or as a group if the group of instruments is material.

If the instruments held or issued create a potentially significant exposure to the risks outlined above the following should be disclosed:

(a) the principal amount on which future payments are based;

(b) the date of maturity of the instrument;

(c) the early settlement options on the instrument held by either party;

(d) options held by either party to convert the instrument into another financial instrument, asset or liability;

(e) the amount and timing of future cash receipts/payments of the principal amount;

(f) stated rate of interest or dividend;

(g) collateral held or pledged;

(h) the currency in which cash flows are denominated (if a foreign currency);

(i) in the case of an instrument that provides for an exchange – all the above information for the instrument to be acquired in the exchange; and

(j) any condition or covenant that, if breached, would significantly alter any of the other terms (e.g. a maximum debt–equity ratio in a bond that, if breached, would cause the bond to become immediately repayable).

As well as the above disclosures a company must explain in its accounting policies the basis of measurement of financial instruments and the basis for dealing with income and expenses associated with the instrument.

Interest rate risk

Standard

For each class of financial asset and financial liability, both recognised and unrecognised, an enterprise should disclose information about its exposure to interest rate risk, including:

(a) contractual repricing or maturity dates, whichever dates are earlier; and

(b) effective interest rates, when applicable.

Guidance

The disclosures of interest rate risk are designed to give the users of the financial statements information about the interest rate price risks and cash flow risks. An interest rate price risk would occur if the instrument has a fixed interest rate (as interest rate changes would alter the value of the instrument), and a cash flow risk would occur if the instrument was a variable rate instrument.

If an instrument does not have an effective interest rate (as, e.g. with derivative instruments) they do not require disclosure.

The guidance indicates the type of presentation that may be applicable (although it does say that it will depend on the particular situation):

(a) the carrying amounts of financial instruments exposed to interest rate price risk in tabular form:
  – within one year of the balance sheet date;
  – between two and five years, giving separate disclosure for each year;
  – five years and more from the balance sheet date;

(b) in the case of an enterprise significantly affected by the level of interest rate price risk (such as a bank) lower time periods may be appropriate (e.g. one month, two to twelve months, over twelve months);

(c) an enterprise could indicate its exposure to interest rate cash flow risk by presenting a table of the aggregate carrying amount of the various instruments that have a floating rate, and the time to repricing or maturity;

(d) the information could be presented by individual instrument or by groups. If instruments are exposed to different credit risks they should be disclosed as separate groups.

An enterprise may feel that it would provide valuable information to the users if it gave disclosure of the sensitivity of instruments to interest rate changes. This disclosure may be given; however, the enterprise must clearly disclose the basis of the calculations and any assumptions that have been made.

Credit risk

Standard

For each class of financial asset, both recognised and unrecognised, an enterprise should disclose information about its exposure to credit risk, including:

(a) the amount that best represents its maximum credit risk exposure at the balance sheet date, without taking account of the fair value of any collateral, in the event that parties fail to perform their obligations under financial instruments; and

(b) significant concentrations of credit risk.

Guidance

The credit risk disclosures are designed to give the users of the accounts an understanding of the maximum risk that the company bears in relation to non-payment of financial assets and liabilities. The credit risk is before any collateral held because it is designed to be the maximum potential loss.

In most cases if the instrument is recognised on the balance sheet, the maximum credit risk will be the balance on the balance sheet. If this is the case no additional disclosure is required to meet the standard. If, however, credit risk arises that is different to the balance on the balance sheet extra disclosure may be required. The type of instrument where the credit risk is different to the balance on the balance sheet could be:

(a) where a company has a legal right of offset but this has not been reflected because the company has no intention to settle on a net basis;

(b) where an unrecognised financial asset may be offset against an unrecognised financial liability;

(c) where a company gives a guarantee to another party that exposes the guarantor to credit risk.

The other considerations for the disclosure are the concentrations of credit risk. The guidance on the concentrations of credit risk says that concentrations would arise either via a single debtor or a group of debtors. The characteristics that give rise to the concentration of credit risk could be the nature of the industry or the geographical location of the debtors. IAS 14 *Segment Reporting* would give indications of the type of areas that could give rise to credit risk.

Fair value

Standard

For each class of financial assets and financial liabilities, an entity shall disclose the fair value of that class of assets and liabilities in a way that permits it to be compared with the corresponding carrying amount in the balance sheet.

Guidance

The fair value information is valuable because many management decisions are based on the fair values of financial instruments, and the fair value can represent the discounted value of future cash flows on the enterprise.

The fair value will often be found from an active market for the financial instrument and therefore the bid price will be the best estimate of the fair value. If an active market does not exist it may be necessary for the company to use a reasonable estimate (such as discounted cash flow, option pricing models, or comparison to a similar traded instrument).

The fair value of the instrument is calculated by assuming that the company is a going concern and considering the company's intentions for the instrument. The transaction costs should be deducted from the value of the instrument to get the fair value.

Risk management policies and hedging activites

An entity must describe its financial risk management objectives and policies, including its policy for hedging each main type of forecast transaction for which hedge accounting is used.

An entity must disclose the following separately for designated fair value hedges, cash flow hedges and hedges of a net investment in a foreign operation (as defined in IAS 39):

(a) a description of the hedge;

(b) a description of the financial instruments designated as hedging instruments and their fair values at the balance sheet date;

(c) the nature of the risks being hedged; and

(d) for cash flow hedges, the periods in which they are expected to occur and when they are expected to enter into the determination of profit or loss.

For cash flow hedges the movements in the amounts recognised in equity must also be disclosed.

An illustration of the disclosures for a simple situation is given in Figure 13.2.

13.3 IAS 39 *Financial Instruments: Recognition and Measurement*

IAS 39 is the first comprehensive standard on the recognition and measurement of financial instruments and completes the guidance that was started with the introduction of IAS 32.

13.3.1 Scope of the standard

IAS 39 should be applied by all enterprises to all financial instruments except those excluded from the scope of IAS 32 (see above) and the following additional instruments:

● rights and obligations under leases to which IAS 17 applies (except for embedded derivatives);

Figure 13.2 Extract from the 2002 financial statements of Incentive A/S

Note 22 Derivatives

Interest rate exposure

The Group's interest-bearing debt includes floating-interest bank debt of DKK 919m (2001: 1,270m). Contracts to hedge future interest payments have not been entered. The fixed-rate debt totals DKK 387m (2001: DKK 144m). The fixed-interest mortgage debt totals DKK 68m (2001: DKK 73m). The average effective rate of interest relating to the interest-bearing debt was 6.0% in 2002.

Credit exposure

Due to the allocation of trade receivables, there are no significant concentrations of credit exposure.

Currency exposure

Foreign exchange contracts have been entered into hedging expected future cash flows in foreign currencies. The contracts expire in 2003.

As a result of the contracts entered into the net results would be affected by DKK 1m (2001: DKK 0m) in the event of an increase of the DKK by 1% relative to GBP, USD and NOK (GBP and CHF).

The allocation of contracts entered into for hedging purposes are GBP 2.2m, USD 5m and NOK 40m. Unrealised losses on hedging contracts total DKK 1m (2001: DKK 0m), which are recognised in the income statement.

There are no contracts hedging investments in subsidiaries.

● equity instruments of the reporting enterprise including options, warrants and other financial instruments that are classified as shareholders' equity;

● financial guarantee contracts and contingent assets;

● loan commitments that cannot be settled net in cash or other financial instruments.

13.3.2 Additional definitions

As well as the definitions given in IAS 32, other definitions are required in order to discuss the treatments in IAS 39 as follows:

A **derivative** is a financial instrument:

(a) whose value changes in response to the change in a specified interest rate, security price, commodity price, foreign exchange rate, index of prices or rates, a credit rating or credit index or similar variable (sometimes called the 'underlying');

(b) that requires no initial net investment or an initial net investment that is smaller than would be required for other types of contract that would be expected to have a similar response to changes in market factors; and

(c) that is settled at a future date.

Definitions of four categories of financial instruments

Financial asset or liability at fair value through profit or loss
'A financial asset or financial liability that meets either of the following conditions:

(a) It is classified as held for trading. A financial asset or financial liability is classified as held for trading if it is:

   (i) acquired or incurred principally for the purpose of selling or repurchasing it in the near term;

   (ii) part of a portfolio of identified financial instruments that are managed together and for which there is evidence of a recent pattern of short-term profit-taking, or

   (iii) a derivative (except for a derivative that is a designated and effective hedging instrument).

(b) Upon initial recognition it is designated by the entity as at fair value through profit or loss. Any financial asset or financial liability within the scope of the standard may be designated when initially recognised as a financial asset or financial liability at fair value through profit or loss except for investments in equity instruments that do not have a quoted market price in an active market, and whose fair value cannot be reliably measured.'

It is not allowed to transfer instruments into and out of this category while the instrument is held.

It appears likely that the IASB will restrict the assets and liabilities included in (b) above in the near future.

Held-to-maturity investments

'Non-derivative financial assets with fixed or determinable payments and fixed maturity that an enterprise has the positive intent and ability to hold to maturity, other than:

(a) those that the entity upon initial recognition designates as at fair value through profit or loss;

(b) those that the entity designates as available for sale; and

(c) those that meet the definition of loans and receivables.'

Held-to-maturity investments must be investments that have a fixed term to maturity and therefore cannot include ordinary shares in other enterprises. Ordinary share investments are available-for-sale assets. Investments such as corporate or government bonds and redeemable preference shares may be held to maturity.

For items to be classified as held-to-maturity a company must justify that it will hold them to maturity. The tests a company must pass to justify this classification are summarised in Figure 13.3.

Loans and receivables

'Non-derivative financial assets with fixed or determinable payments that are not quoted in an active market, other than:

(a) those that the entity intends to sell immediately or in the near term, which shall be classified as held for trading, and those that the entity upon initial recognition designates as at fair value through profit or loss;

(b) those that the entity upon initial recognition designates as available for sale; or

(c) those for which the holder may not recover substantially all of its initial investment, other than because of credit deterioration, which shall be classified as available for sale.

Figure 13.3 Tests for classification as held-to-maturity investment

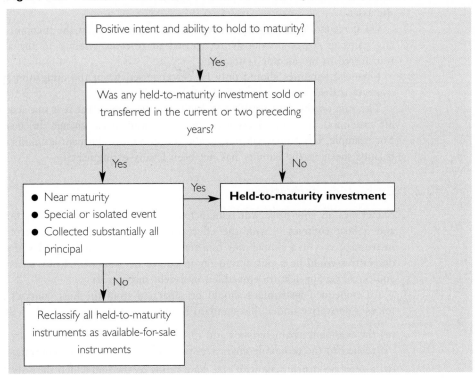

An interest in a pool of assets that are not loans or receivables (e.g. an interest in a mutual fund or a similar fund) is not a loan or receivable.'

Available-for-sale financial assets
'Non-derivative financial assets that are designated as available for sale or are not classified as (a) loans and receivables, (b) held-to-maturity investments or (c) financial assets at fair value through profit or loss.'

The main financial asset that would be classified as available-for-sale would be equity investments in other companies that are not subsidiary, associate or joint venture investments.

13.3.3 Recognition of financial instruments

Initial recognition
A financial asset or liability should be recognised on the balance sheet when it becomes party to the contractual provisions of the instrument. This means that derivative instruments must be recognised on the balance sheet if a contractual right or obligation exists.

Derecognition
Financial assets should only be derecognised from the balance sheet when the enterprise transfers the risks and rewards that comprise the asset. This could be because the benefits are realised, the rights expire or the enterprise surrenders the benefits.
If it is not clear whether the risks and reward have been transferred the entity

considers whether control has passed. If control has passed the entity should derecognise the asset.

On derecognition any gain or loss should be recorded in the income statement. Also any gains or losses previously recognised in reserves relating to the asset should be transferred to the income statement.

Financial liabilities should only be derecognised when the obligation specified in the contract is discharged or cancelled, or expires.

The rule on the derecognition of liabilities does mean that it is not acceptable to write off creditors. In some industries this will lead to a change in business practice. For example, UK banks will not be allowed to remove dormant accounts ever from their balance sheets as the liability has not been legally extinguished.

13.3.4 Embedded derivatives

Sometimes an enterprise will issue a hybrid instrument that includes both a derivative and a host contract – with the effect that some of the cash flows of the combined instrument vary in a similar way to a stand-alone derivative. Examples of such embedded derivatives could be a put option on an equity instrument held by an enterprise, or an equity conversion feature embedded in a debt instrument.

An embedded instrument should be separated from the host contract and accounted for as a derivative under this standard if all of the following conditions are met:

(a) the economic characteristics and risks of the embedded derivative are not closely related to the economic characteristics and risks of the host contract;

(b) a separate instrument with the same terms as the embedded derivative would meet the definition of a derivative; and

(c) the hybrid instrument is not measured at fair value with changes in fair value reported in net profit or loss.

If an enterprise is required to separate the embedded derivative from its host contract but is unable to separately measure the embedded derivative, the entire hybrid instrument should be treated as a financial instrument held for trading and as a result changes in fair value should be reported through the income statement.

13.3.5 Measurement of financial instruments

Initial measurement

Financial assets and liabilities (other than those at fair value through profit or loss) should be initially measured at fair value plus transaction costs. In almost all cases this would be at cost. For instruments at fair value through profit and loss, transaction costs are not included.

Subsequent measurement

Figure 13.4 summarises the way that financial assets and liabilities are to be subsequently measured after initial recognition.

Gains or losses on subsequent measurement

When financial instruments are remeasured to fair value the rules for the treatment of the subsequent gain or loss are as shown in Figure 13.5. Gains or losses arising on financial instruments that have not been remeasured to fair value will arise either when

Figure 13.4   Subsequent measurement

Category	Measurement
Financial assets at fair value through profit or loss*	Fair value without any deduction for transaction costs on sale or disposal.
Held-to-maturity investments	Amortised cost using the effective interest method
Loans and receivables	Amortised cost using the effective interest method
Available-for-sale financial assets*	Fair value without any deduction for transaction costs on sale or disposal
Financial liabilities at fair value through profit or loss	Fair value
Other financial liabilities	Amortised cost using the effective interest method

*If these categories include unquoted equity instruments (or derivative liabilities that are settled in unquoted equity instruments) where fair value cannot be measured reliably then they are measured at cost.

Figure 13.5   Gains or losses on subsequent measurements

Instrument	Gain or loss
Instruments at fair value through profit or loss	Profit or loss
Available-for-sale	Equity (except for impairments and foreign exchange gains and losses) until derecognition, at which time the cumulative gain/loss in equity is recognised in profit or loss. Dividend income is recognised in profit or loss when the right to receive payment is established.

the assets are impaired or the instruments are derecognised. These gains and losses are recognised in the income statement for the period.

13.3.6 Hedging

If a financial instrument has been taken out to act as a hedge, and this position is clearly identified and expected to be effective, hedge accounting rules should be followed.

There are three types of hedging instrument:

Fair value hedge

A hedge of the exposure to changes in fair value of a recognised asset or liability or an unrecognised firm commitment that will affect reported net income. Any gain or loss arising on remeasuring the hedging instrument and the hedged item should be recognised in the income statement in the period.

Cash flow hedge

A hedge of the exposure to variability in cash flows that is attributable to a particular risk associated with the recognised asset or liability and that will affect reported net income. A hedge of foreign exchange risk on a firm commitment may be a cash flow or a fair value hedge. The gain or loss on the hedging instrument should be recognised directly in reserves. If the instrument being hedged results in the recognition of a non-financial asset or liability, the gain or loss on the hedging instrument can be recognised as part of the cost of the hedged item. Any gains or losses recognised in reserves should be included in the income statement in the period that the hedged instrument affects the income statement.

Net investment hedge

A hedge of an investment in a foreign entity. The gain or loss on the hedging instrument should be recognised directly in reserves to match against the gain or loss on the hedged investment.

Conditions for hedge accounting

In order to be able to apply the hedge accounting techniques detailed above an entity must meet a number of conditions. These conditions are designed to ensure that only genuine hedging instruments can be hedge accounted, and that the hedged positions are clearly identified and documented.

The conditions are:

- at the inception of the hedge there is formal documentation of the hedge relationship and the enterprise's risk management objective and strategy for undertaking the hedge;
- the hedge is expected to be highly effective at inception and on an ongoing basis in achieving offsetting changes in fair values or cash flows;
- the effectiveness of the hedge can be reliably measured, that is the fair value of the hedged item and the hedging instrument can be measured reliably;
- for cash flow hedges, a forecasted transaction that is the subject of the hedge must be highly probable; and
- the hedge was assessed on an ongoing basis and determined actually to have been effective throughout the accounting period (effective between 80% and 125%).

Summary

This chapter has given some insight into the difficulties and complexities of accounting for financial instruments. The approach of the IASB is to adhere to the principles contained in the *Framework* but to also issue guidance that is robust enough to prevent manipulation and abuse. Whether the IASB has achieved this is open to debate. Some might view the detailed requirements of the standards, particularly IAS 39, to be so onerous that companies will not be able to show their real intentions in the financial statements. This would be particularly true, for instance, with the detailed criteria on hedging. In the USA these criteria have led to many businesses not hedge accounting even though they are hedging commercially to manage their risks. The hedge accounting criteria do not fit with the way they run or manage their risk profiles.

The standards are still developing and problems have already been identified. There is much concern, for instance, that a company will be able to designate any financial asset or liability at fair value through profit or loss. If companies are able to do this it will lead to a great variation in practice and a lack of comparability between businesses. It appears already that the IASB will have to change this rule.

As can be seen there is much to criticise these standards about, but it should be borne in mind that the IASB has grasped this issue better than other standard setters. Financial instruments may be complex and subject to debate but guidance is required in this area, and the IASB has given guidance where many others have not.

REVIEW QUESTIONS

1   Discuss the implications for businesses of a substance approach being used for the presentation of liabilities and equity. Indicate how the terms of an instrument could present problems in classification, e.g. a preference share that has accelerating dividends redeemable at the option of the company.

2   Explain why financial instruments, particularly derivatives, can alter the risk profile of a business. Use a forward currency contract as an example. Discuss whether disclosure alone is sufficient to address these risks.

3   'Disclosure of the fair values of financial instruments (as required by FRS 13 in the UK) is better than measuring them at fair values in the financial statements (as is often required by IAS 39) because measurement at fair value would introduce unwanted volatility to the reported earnings.' Discuss.

4   A reduction in the credit rating of a business would reduce the fair value of its debt instruments. Explain why this is the case.

5   Following from Question 4, if the debt instrument was included in the balance sheet at fair value through profit or loss this would mean that a profit would be recognised in the income statement. This appears counter-intuitive. Discuss.

6   Many groups have treasury policies that use hedging of net positions. They would look at their group-wide exposure in, e.g. foreign currency and then take forward contracts to cover the position. Discuss the difficulties that would arise in hedge accounting if this practice is followed.

7   Interest rate swaps can be designated as hedges. A swap of floating for fixed rate is a cash flow hedge, but a swap of fixed for floating is a fair value hedge. Why?

EXERCISES

An extract from the solution is provided in the Appendix at the end of the text for exercises marked with an asterisk (*).

* Question 1

On 1 April year 1, a deep discount bond was issued by DDB AG. It had a face value of £2.5 million covering a five-year term. The lenders were granted a discount of 5%. The coupon rate was 10% on the principal sum of £2.5 million, payable annually in arrears. The principal sum was repayable in cash on 31 March year 5. Issuing costs amounted to £150,000.

Required:

Compute the finance charge per annum and the carrying value of the loan to be reported in each year's income statement and balance sheet respectively.

* Question 2

On 1 October year 1, RPS plc issued one million £1 5% redeemable preference shares. The shares were issued at a discount of £50,000 and are due to be redeemed on 30 September Year 5. Dividends are paid on 30 September each year.

Required:

Show the accounting treatment of the preference shares throughout the life-span of the instrument calculating the finance cost to be charged to the income statement in each period.

Question 3

October 20X1, Little Raven plc issued 50,000 debentures, with a par value of £100 each, to investors at £80 each. The debentures are redeemable at par on 30 September 20X6 and have a coupon rate of 6%, which was significantly below the market rate of interest for such debentures issued at par. In accounting for these debentures to date, Little Raven plc has simply accounted for the cash flows involved, namely:

● On issue: Debenture 'liability' included in the balance sheet at £4,000,000.

● Income statements: Interest charged in years ended 30 September 20X2, 20X3 and 20X4 (published accounts) and 30 September 20X5 (draft accounts) – £300,000 each year (being 6% on £5,000,000).

The new finance director, who sees the likelihood that further similar debenture issues will be made, considers that the accounting policy adopted to date is not appropriate. He has asked you to suggest a more appropriate treatment.

Little Raven plc intends to acquire subsidiaries in 20X6.

Income statements for the years ended 30 September 20X4 and 20X5 are as follows:

	Y/e 30 Sept 20X5 (Draft) £000	Y/e 30 Sept 20X4 (Actual) £000
Turnover	6,700	6,300
Cost of sales	(3,025)	(2,900)
Gross profit	3,675	3,400
Overheads	(600)	(550)
Interest payable – debenture	(300)	(300)
– others	(75)	(50)
Profit for the financial year	2,700	2,500
Retained profits brought forward	4,300	1,800
Retained profit carried forward	7,000	4,300

Extracts from the balance sheet are:

	At 30 Sept 20X5 (Draft) £000	At 30 Sept 20X4 (Actual) £000
Share capital	2,250	2,250
Share premium	550	550
Profit and loss account	7,000	4,300
	9,800	7,100
6% debentures	4,000	4,000
	13,800	11,100

Required:

(a) Outline the considerations involved in deciding how to account for the issue, the interest cost and the carrying value in respect of debenture issues such as that made by Little Raven plc. Consider the alternative treatments in respect of the income statement and refer briefly to the appropriate balance sheet disclosures for the debentures. Conclude in terms of the requirements of IAS 32 (on accounting for financial instruments) in this regard.

(b) Detail an alternative set of entries in the books of Little Raven plc for the issue of the debentures and subsequently; under this alternative the discount on the issue should be dealt with under the requirements of IAS 32. The constant rate of interest for the allocation of interest cost is given to you as 11.476%. Draw up a revised income statement for the year ended 30 September 20X5 – together with comparatives – taking account of the alternative accounting treatment.

References

1 IAS 32 *Financial Instruments: Disclosure and Presentation*, IASC, revised 1998.
2 *Ibid.*, para. 5.
3 *Ibid.*, para. 18.
4 *Ibid.*, para. 23.
5 *Ibid.*, para. 33.
6 *Ibid.*, para. 43.

CHAPTER **14**

Employee benefits

14.1 Introduction

In this chapter we consider the application of IAS 19 *Employee Benefits*.[1] IAS 19 is concerned with the determination of the cost of retirement benefits in the financial statements of **employers** having retirement benefit plans (sometimes referred to as 'pension schemes', 'superannuation schemes' or 'retirement benefit schemes'). We also consider the disclosure requirements of IAS 26 *Accounting and Reporting by Retirement Benefit Plans*.[2]

14.1.1 Employee interest in pensions has widened

The percentage of pensioners and public pension expenditure are increasing.

	% of population over 60		Public pensions as % of GDP
	2000	2040	2040
	%	% (projected)	% (projected)
Germany	24	33	18
Italy	24	37	21
Japan	23	34	15
UK	21	30	5
US	17	29	7

This has led to gloomy projections that countries could even be bankrupted by the increasing demand for state pensions. In an attempt to avert what governments see as a national disaster, there have been increasing efforts to encourage private funding of pensions.

As people become more and more aware of the possible failure of governments to provide adequate basic state pensions, they recognise the advisability of making their own provision for their old age. This has raised their expectation that their employers should offer a pension scheme and other post-retirement benefits. These have increased, particularly in Ireland, the UK and the USA, and what used to be a 'fringe benefit' for only certain categories of staff has been broadened across the workforce. This has been encouraged by various governments with favourable tax treatment of both employers' and employees' contributions to pension schemes.

14.2 Financial reporting implications

The provision of pensions for employees as part of an overall remuneration package has led to the related costs being a material part of the accounts. The very nature of such arrangements means that the commitment is a long-term one that may well involve estimates. The way the related costs are allocated between accounting periods and are reported in the financial statements needs careful consideration to ensure that a fair view of the position is shown.

In recent years there has been a shift of view on the way that pension costs should be accounted for. The older view was that pension costs (as recommended by IAS 19 prior to its revision in 1998) should be matched against the period of the employee's service so as to create an even charge for pensions in the income statement, although the balance sheet amount could have been misleading. The more recent approach is to make the balance sheet more sensible, but perhaps accept greater variation in the pension cost in the income statement. The new view is the one endorsed by IAS 19 (revised) and is the one now in use by companies preparing accounts to international accounting standards.

Before examining the detail of how IAS 19 (revised) requires pensions and other long-term benefits to be accounted for, we need to consider the types of pension scheme that are commonly used.

14.3 Types of scheme

Ex gratia arrangements

These are not schemes at all but are circumstances where an employer agrees to grant a pension to be paid for out of the resources of the firm. Consequently these are arrangements where pensions have not been funded but decisions are made on an *ad hoc* or case-by-case basis, sometimes arising out of custom or practice. No contractual obligation to grant or pay a pension exists, although a constructive obligation may exist which would need to be provided for in accordance with IAS 37 *Provisions, Contingent Liabilities and Contingent Assets*.

Defined contribution schemes

These are schemes in which the employer undertakes to make certain contributions each year, usually a stated percentage of salary. These contributions are usually supplemented by contributions from the employee. The money is then invested and, on retirement, the employee gains the pension benefits that can be purchased from the resulting funds.

Such schemes have uncertain future benefits but fixed, predetermined costs. Schemes of this sort were very common among smaller employers but fell out of fashion for a time. In recent years, due to the fixed cost to the company and the resulting low risk to the employer for providing a pension, these schemes have become increasingly popular. They are also popular with employees who regularly change employers, since the funds accrued within the schemes are relatively easy to transfer.

The contributions may be paid into a wide variety of plans, e.g. government plans to ensure state pensions are supplemented (these may be optional or compulsory), or schemes operated by insurance companies.

The following is an extract from the 2003 Annual Report of Nokia:

Pensions

The Group's contributions to defined contribution plans and to multi-employer and insured plans are charged to the profit and loss account in the period to which the contributions relate.

Defined benefit schemes

Under these schemes the employees will, on retirement, receive a pension based on the length of service and salary, usually final salary or an average of the last few (usually three) years' salary.

These schemes form the majority of company pension schemes. They are, however, becoming less popular when new schemes are formed because the cost to employers is uncertain and there are greater regulation requirements being introduced.

Whilst the benefits to the employee are not certain, they are more predictable than under a defined contribution scheme. The cost to the employer, however, is uncertain as the employer will need to vary the contributions to the scheme to ensure it is adequately funded to meet the pension liabilities when employees eventually retire.

The following is an extract from the accounting policies in the 2003 Annual Report of the Nestlé Group:

Employee benefits
Post-employment benefits
The liabilities of the Group arising from defined benefit obligations, and the related current service cost, are determined using the projected unit credit method. Valuations are carried out annually for the largest plans and on a regular basis for other plans. Actuarial advice is provided both by external consultants and by actuaries employed by the Group. The actuarial assumptions used to calculate the benefit obligations vary according to the economic conditions of the country in which the plan is located.

Such plans are either externally funded, with the assets of the schemes held separately from those of the Group in independently administered funds, or unfunded with the related liabilities carried in the balance sheet.

For the funded defined benefit plans, the deficit or excess of the fair value of plan assets over the present value of the defined benefit obligation is recognised as a liability or an asset in the balance sheet, taking into account any unrecognised actuarial gains or losses and past service cost. However, an excess of assets is recognised only to the extent that it represents a future economic benefit which is actually available to the Group, e.g. in the form of refunds from the plan or reductions in future contributions to the plan. When such excess is not available or does not represent a future economic benefit, it is not recognised but is disclosed in the notes.

Actuarial gains and losses arise mainly from changes in actuarial assumptions and differences between actuarial assumptions and what has actually occurred. They are recognised in the income statement, over the expected average remaining working lives of the employees only to the extent that their net cumulative amount exceeds 10% of the greater of the present value of the obligation or the fair value of plan assets at the end of the previous year. Unrecognised actuarial gains and losses are reflected in the balance sheet.

For defined benefit plans the actuarial cost charged to the income statement consists of current service cost, interest cost, expected return on plan assets and past service cost as well as actuarial gains or losses to the extent that they are recognised.

The past service cost for the enhancement of pension benefits is accounted for when such benefits vest or become a constructive obligation.

The accounting policy is quite complex to apply and we will illustrate the detailed calculations involved below.

Equity compensation plans

IAS 19 does not specify recognition or measurement requirements for equity compensation plans such as shares or share options issued to employees at less than fair value. The valuation of share options has proved an extremely contentious topic and we consider the issues that have arisen in Chapter 30. IFRS 2 *Share-Based Payment* covers these plans.[3]

The following is an extract from the accounting policies in the 2003 Annual Report of the Nestlé Group:

> **Equity compensation plans**
> *Members of the Group's Management*
> Members of the Group's Management are entitled to participate each year in a share option plan without payment. The benefits consist of the right to buy Nestlé S.A. shares at a predetermined price.
>
> As from 1st January 1999, this plan has a rolling seven-year duration and the rights are vested after three years (previously five years and two years respectively).
>
> In order to hedge the related exposure, the Group buys – or transfers from existing treasury portfolios – the number of shares necessary to satisfy all potential outstanding obligations under the plan when the benefit is awarded and holds them until maturity of the plan or the exercise of the rights. No additional shares are issued as a result of the equity compensation plan. When the options are exercised equity is increased by the amount of the proceeds received.
>
> The Group is not exposed to any additional cost and there is no dilution to the rights of the shareholders.

Share-based payments are discussed further in Chapter 31.

14.4 Defined contribution pension schemes

Defined contribution schemes (otherwise known as money purchase schemes) have not presented any major accounting problems. The cost of providing the pension, usually a percentage of salary, is recorded as a remuneration expense in the income statement in the period in which it is due. Balance sheet assets or liabilities may exist for the pension contributions if the company has not paid the amount due for the period. If a contribution was payable more than twelve months after the balance sheet date for services rendered in the current period, the liability should be recorded at its discounted amount (using a discount rate based on the market rate for high-quality corporate bonds).

Disclosure is required of the pension contribution charged to the income statement for the period.

Illustration of Andrew plc defined contribution pension scheme costs

Andrew plc has payroll costs of £2.7 million for the year ended 30 June 2005. Andrew plc pays pension contributions of 5% of salary, but for convenience paid £10,000 per month standard contribution with any shortfall to be made up in the July 2005 contribution.

Income statement charge

The pension cost is £2,700,000 × 5%   £135,000

Balance sheet

The amount paid over the period is £120,000 and therefore an accrual of £15,000 will be made in the balance sheet at 30 June 2005.

14.5 Defined benefit pension schemes

14.5.1 Position before 1998

To consider the accounting requirements for defined benefit pension schemes it is useful to look at the differences between the original IAS 19 and IAS 19 as revised in 1998. By looking at the original IAS 19 it is possible to see why a revision was necessary and what the revision to the standard was trying to achieve.

Income statement

Under the original standard both the costs and the fund value were computed on an actuarial basis. The valuation was needed to give an estimate of the costs of providing the benefits over the remaining service lives of the relevant employees. This was normally done in such a way as to produce a pension cost that was a level percentage of both the current and future pensionable payroll. Both the accounting standard and the actuarial professional bodies gave guidance on the assumptions and methods to be employed in the valuation and required that those guidelines were followed.

Treatment of variations from regular costs

If a valuation gave rise to a variation in the regular costs, it would normally be allocated over the remaining service lives of the employees. If, however, a variation arose out of a surplus or deficit arising from a significant reduction in pensionable employees, it was recognised when it arose unless such treatment was not prudent and involved the anticipating of income.

Balance sheet

This was a much simpler approach and was based purely on the accruals principle for defined benefit pension schemes. The difference between cumulative pension costs charged in the income statement and the money paid either as pensions or contributions to a scheme or fund was shown as either a prepayment or an accrual. In effect the balance sheet value was a balancing figure representing the difference between the amounts charged against the income statement and the amounts paid into the fund.

Illustration of Hart plc defined benefit pension scheme

Hart plc operates a defined benefit pension scheme on behalf of its employees. At an actuarial valuation in early 2005 the following details were calculated:

Regular service costs (per annum)	£10,000
Estimated remaining average service lives of staff	10 years
Surplus on scheme at 31 December 2004	£30,000

Hart plc has been advised to eliminate the surplus on the scheme by taking a three-year contribution holiday, and then returning to regular service cost contributions.

The financial statements over the remaining service lives of the employees would show the following amounts:

Year	Contribution	Income statement charge	Balance sheet liability
	£	£	£
2004	Nil	7,000	7,000
2005	Nil	7,000	14,000
2006	Nil	7,000	21,000
2007	10,000	7,000	18,000
2008	10,000	7,000	15,000
2009	10,000	7,000	12,000
2010	10,000	7,000	9,000
2011	10,000	7,000	6,000
2012	10,000	7,000	3,000
2013	10,000	7,000	—
	70,000		

The income statement charge is the total contributions paid over the period (£70,000) divided by the average remaining service lives of ten years. The effect of this is to spread the surplus over the remaining service lives in the income statement.

14.5.2 Problems of the old standard

The old IAS 19 gave a number of problems in its approach which needed to be addressed by the revised standard.

A misleading balance sheet position

Making the balance sheet accrual or prepayment a balancing figure based on the comparison of the amount paid and charged to date could be very misleading. In the above illustration it can be seen that the balance sheet shows a liability even though there is a surplus on the fund. A user of the financial statements who was unaware of the method used to account for the pension scheme could be misled into believing that contributions were owed to the pension fund.

Current emphasis is on getting the balance sheet to report assets and liabilities more accurately

There is an issue regarding the consistency of the presentation of the pension asset or liability with that of other assets and liabilities. Accounting is moving towards ensuring that the balance sheet shows a sensible position with the income statement recording the change in the balance sheet position. Accounting for pension schemes under the old IAS 19 does not do this.

The old IAS 19 was also inconsistent with the way that US GAAP would require pensions to be accounted for, although in its defence it was consistent with the approach adopted by UK GAAP.

Valuation basis

The old IAS 19 required the use of an actuarial valuation basis for both assets and liabilities of the fund in deciding what level of contribution was required and whether any surplus or deficit had arisen. In addition the liabilities of the fund (i.e. the obligation to pay future pensions) were discounted at the expected rate of return on the assets. These approaches to valuation are difficult to justify and could give rise to unrealistic pension provision being made.

14.6 IAS 19 (revised) *Employee Benefits*

After a relatively long discussion and exposure period IAS 19 (revised) was issued in 1998 and it redefined how all employee benefits were to be accounted for.

IAS 19 has chosen to follow a 'balance sheet' approach to accounting for the pension scheme contributions by the employer and, therefore, it defines how the balance sheet asset or liability should be built up. The income statement charge is effectively the movement in the balance sheet asset or liability. The pension fund must be valued sufficiently regularly so that the balance sheet asset or liability is kept up to date. The valuation would normally be done by a qualified actuary and is based on actuarial assumptions.

14.7 The liability for pension and other post-retirement costs

The liability for pension costs is made up from the following amounts:

(a) the present value of the defined benefit obligation at the balance sheet date;

(b) plus any actuarial gains (less actuarial losses) not yet recognised;

(c) minus any past service cost not yet recognised;

(d) minus the fair value at the balance sheet date of plan assets (if any) out of which the obligations are to be settled directly.

If this calculation comes out with a negative amount the company should recognise a pension asset in the balance sheet. There is a limit on the amount of the asset, if the asset calculated above is greater than the total of:

(i) any unrecognised actuarial losses and past service cost; plus

(ii) the present value of any future refunds from the scheme or reductions in future contributions.

Within IAS 19 there are rules regarding the maximum pension asset that can be created.

Each of the elements making up the balance sheet position (a) to (d) above can now be considered.

14.7.1 Obligations of the fund

The pension fund obligation must be calculated using the 'projected unit credit method'. This method of allocating pension costs builds up the pension liability each year for an extra year of service and a reversal of discounting. Discounting of the liability is done using the market yields on high-quality corporate bonds with similar currency and duration.

The Grado illustration below shows how the obligation to pay pension accumulates over the working life of an employee.

Grado illustration

A lump sum benefit is payable on termination of service and equal to 1% of final salary for each year of service. The salary in year 1 is £10,000 and is assumed to increase at 7% (compound) each year. The discount rate used is 10%. The following table shows how an obligation (in £) builds up for an employee who is expected to leave at the end of year 5. For simplicity, this example ignores the additional adjustment needed to reflect the probability that the employee may leave service at an earlier or later date.

Year	1	2	3	4	5
Benefit attributed to prior years	0	131	262	393	524
Benefit attributed to current year (1% of final salary)*	131	131	131	131	131
Benefit attributed to current and prior years	131	262	393	524	655
Opening obligation (present value of benefit attributed to prior years)	—	89	196	324	476
Interest at 10%	—	9	20	33	48
Current service cost (present value of benefit attributed to current year)	89	98	108	119	131
Closing obligation (present value of benefit attributed to current and prior years)**	89	196	324	476	655

* Final salary is £10,000 × (1.07)^4 = £13,100.
** Discounting the benefit attributable to current and prior years at 10%.

14.7.2 Actuarial gains and losses

Actuarial gains or losses result from changes either in the present value of the defined benefit obligation or changes in the market value of the plan assets. They arise from experience adjustments – that is, differences between actuarial assumptions and actual experience. Typical reasons for the gains or losses would be:

● unexpectedly low or high rates of employee turnover;
● the effect of changes in the discount rate;

● differences between the **actual** return on plan assets and the **expected** return on plan assets.

Accounting treatment

Since a revision of IAS 19 in 2004 there has been a choice of accounting treatment for actuarial gains and losses. One approach follows a '10% corridor' approach and requires recognition of gains and losses in the income statement whereas an alternative makes no use of the corridor and requires gains and losses to be recognised in equity.

10% corridor approach

● If actual gains and losses are greater than the larger of 10% of the present value of the defined benefit obligation or 10% of the market value of the plan assets, the excess gains and losses should be charged or credited to the income statement over the average remaining service lives of current employees. Any shorter period of recognition of gains or losses is acceptable.

● If beneath the 10% thresholds they can be part of the defined benefit liability for the year; however, the standard also allows them to be recognised in the income statement.

Any actuarial gains and losses that are recognised in the income statement are recognised in the periods following the one in which they arise. For example, if an actuarial loss arose in the year ended 31 December 2004 that exceeded the 10% corridor and therefore required recognition in the income statement, that recognition would begin in the 2005 year. This means that to calculate the income statement charge or credit for the current year the cumulative unrecognised gains or losses at the end of the previous year are compared to the corridor at the end of the previous year (or the beginning of the current year).

The comprehensive illustration in section 14.9 below illustrates this treatment.

Equity recognition approach

It is acceptable to recognise actuarial gains and losses immediately in equity, usually as part of retained earnings.

This approach has the benefit over the corridor approach in that it does not require any acturial gains and losses to be recognised in the income statement; however, its drawback comes in volatility on the balance sheet. Under this approach all actuarial gains and losses are recognised and therefore no unrecognised ones are available for offset against the balance sheet asset or liability. As the actuarial valuations are based on fair values the volatility could be significant.

This new treatment in IAS 19 is not mandatory until accounting periods commencing in 2006; however, earlier adoption would be allowed.

14.7.3 Past service costs

Past service costs are costs that arise for a pension scheme as a result of improving the scheme or when a business introduces a plan. They are the extra liability in respect of previous years' service by employees. Do note, however, that past service costs can only arise if actuarial assumptions did not take into account the reason why they occurred. Typically they would include:

● estimates of benefit improvements as a result of actuarial gains (if the company proposes to give the gains to the employees);

● the effect of plan amendments that increase or reduce benefits for past service.

Accounting treatment

The past service cost should be recognised on a straight-line basis over the period to which the benefits become vested. If already vested the cost should be recognised immediately in the income statement. A benefit becomes vested when an employee satisfies preconditions. For example, if a company offered a scheme whereby an employee would only be entitled to a pension if they worked for at least five years, the benefits would be vested as soon as they started their sixth year of employment. The company will still have to make provision for pensions for the first five years of employment (and past service costs could arise in this period), as these will be pensionable service years provided the employee works for more than five years.

14.7.4 Fair value of plan assets

This is usually the market value of the assets of the plan (or the estimated value if no immediate market value exists). The plan assets exclude unpaid contributions due from the reporting enterprise to the fund.

14.8 The income statement

The income statement charge for a period should be made up of the following parts:

(a) current service cost;

(b) interest cost;

(c) the expected return on any plan assets;

(d) actuarial gains and losses to the extent that they are recognised;

(e) past service cost to the extent that it is recognised;

(f) the effect of any curtailments or settlements.

These items are all the things that cause the balance sheet liability for pensions to alter and the income statement is consequently based on the movement in the liability. Because of the potential inclusion of actuarial gains and losses and past service costs the income statement is liable to fluctuate much more than the charge made under the original IAS 19.

14.9 Comprehensive illustration

The following comprehensive illustration is based on an example in IAS 19 (revised)[4] and demonstrates how a pension liability and income statement charge is calculated. The example does not include the effect of curtailments or settlements. This illustration demonstrates the 10% corridor approach for actuarial gains and losses.

Illustration

The following information is given about a funded defined benefit plan. To keep the computations simple, all transactions are assumed to occur at the year-end. The present value of the obligation and the market value of the plan assets were both 1,000 at 1 January 20X1. The average remaining service lives of the current employees is ten years.

	20X1	20X2	20X3
Discount rate at start of year	10%	9%	8%
Expected rate of return on plan assets at start of year	12%	11%	10%
Current service cost	160	140	150
Benefits paid	150	180	190
Contributions paid	90	100	110
Present value of obligations at 31 December	1,100	1,380	1,455
Market value of plan assets at 31 December	1,190	1,372	1,188

In 20X2 the plan was amended to provide additional benefits with effect from 1 January 20X2. The present value as at 1 January 20X2 of additional benefits for employee service before 1 January 20X2 was 50, all for vested benefits.

Required
Show how the pension scheme would be shown in the accounts for 20X1, 20X2 and 20X3.

Solution to the comprehensive illustration

Step 1 Change in the obligation
The changes in the present value of the obligation must be calculated and used to determine what, if any, actuarial gains and losses have arisen. This calculation can be done by comparing the expected obligations at the end of each period with the actual obligations as follows:

Change in the obligation:

	20X1	*20X2*	*20X3*
Present value of obligation, 1 January	1,000	1,100	1,380
Interest cost	100	99	110
Current service cost	160	140	150
Past service cost – vested benefits	—	50	—
Benefits paid	(150)	(180)	(190)
Actuarial (gain) loss on obligation (balancing figure)	*(10)*	*171*	*5*
Present value of obligation, 31 December	1,100	1,380	1,455

Step 2 Change in the assets
The changes in the fair value of the assets of the fund must be calculated and used to determine what, if any, actuarial gains and losses have arisen. This calculation can be done by comparing the asset values at the end of each period with the actual asset values.

Change in the assets:

	20X1	*20X2*	*20X3*
Fair value of plan assets, 1 January	1,000	1,190	1,372
Expected return on plan assets	120	131	137
Contributions	90	100	110
Benefits paid	(150)	(180)	(190)

Actuarial gain (loss) on plan assets			
(balancing figure)	130	131	(241)
Fair value of plan assets, 31 December	1,190	1,372	1,188

Step 3 10% corridor calculation

The limits of the '10% corridor' need to be calculated in order to establish whether actuarial gains or losses exceed the corridor limit and therefore need recognising in the income statement. Actuarial gains and losses are recognised in the income statement if they exceed the 10% corridor, and they are recognised by being amortised over the remaining service lives of employees.

The limits of the 10% corridor (at 1 January) are set at the greater of:

(a) 10% of the present value of the obligation before deducting plan assets (100, 110 and 138); and

(b) 10% of the fair value of plan assets (100, 119 and 137).

	20X1	*20X2*	*20X3*
Limit of '10% corridor' at 1 January	100	119	138
Cumulative unrecognised gains (losses) –			
1 January	—	140	99
Gains (losses) on the obligation	10	(171)	(5)
Gains (losses) on the assets	130	131	(241)
Cumulative gains (losses) before amortisation	140	70	(147)
Amortisation of excess over ten years			
(see working)	—	(2)	—
Cumulative unrecognised gains (losses) –			
31 December	140	99	(147)

Working: $\dfrac{(140 - 119)}{10 \text{ yrs}} = 2$ – amortisation charge in 20X2.

Step 4 Calculate the income statement entry

	20X1	*20X2*	*20X3*
Current service cost	160	140	150
Interest cost	100	99	110
Expected return on plan assets	(120)	(131)	(137)
Recognised actuarial (gains) losses		(2)	
Recognised past service cost		50	
Income statement charge	140	156	126

Step 5 Calculate the balance sheet entry

	20X1	*20X2*	*20X3*
Present value of obligation, 31 December	1,100	1,380	1,455
Fair value of assets, 31 December	(1,190)	(1,372)	(1,188)
Unrecognised actuarial gains (losses) –			
from Step 3	140	99	(147)
Liability in balance sheet	50	107	120

14.10 Plan curtailments and settlements

A curtailment of a pension scheme occurs when a company is committed to make a material reduction in the number of employees of a scheme or when the employees will receive no benefit for a substantial part of their future service. A settlement occurs when an enterprise enters into a transaction that eliminates any further liability from arising under the fund.

The accounting for a settlement or curtailment is that a gain or loss is recognised when the settlement or curtailment occurs. The gain or loss on a curtailment or settlement should comprise:

(a) any resulting change in the present value of the defined benefit obligation;

(b) any resulting change in the fair value of the plan assets;

(c) any related actuarial gain/loss and past service cost that had not previously been recognised.

Before determining the effect of the curtailment the enterprise must remeasure the obligations and the liability to get it to the up-to-date value.

14.11 Multi-employer plans

The definition of a multi-employer plan per IAS 19[5] is that it is a defined contribution or defined benefit plan that:

(a) pools the assets contributed by various enterprises that are not under common control; and

(b) uses those assets to provide benefits to employees of more than one enterprise, on the basis that contribution and benefit levels are determined without regard to the identity of the enterprise that employs the employees concerned.

An enterprise should account for a multi-employer defined benefit plan as follows:

● account for its share of the defined benefit obligation, plan assets and costs associated with the plan in the same way as for any defined benefit plan; or

● if insufficient information is available to use defined benefit accounting it should:
  – account for the plan as if it were a defined contribution plan; and
  – give extra disclosures.

In 2004 the IASB revised IAS 19 and changed the position for group pension plans in the financial statements of the individual companies in the group. Prior to the revision a group pension scheme could not be treated as a multi-employer plan and therefore any group schemes would have had to be split across all the individual contributing companies. The amendment to IAS 19, however, made it acceptable to treat group schemes as multi-employer schemes. This means that the defined benefit accounting is only necessary in the consolidated accounts and not in the individual company accounts of all companies in the group. If a group wishes, a split can still be made but it is not compulsory.

This amendment to IAS 19 is not mandatory until accounting periods commencing in 2006; however, earlier adoption would be allowed.

14.12 Disclosures

The major disclosure requirements[6] of the standard are:

● the enterprise's accounting policy for recognising actuarial gains and losses;

● a general description of the type of plan;

● a reconciliation of the assets and liabilities including the present value of the obligations, the market value of the assets, the actuarial gains/losses and the past service cost;

● a reconciliation of the movement during the period in the net liability;

● the total expense in the income statement broken down into different parts;

● the actual return on plan assets;

● the principal actuarial assumptions used as at the balance sheet date.

14.13 Other long-service benefits

So far in this chapter we have considered the accounting for pension costs for both defined contribution and defined benefit pension schemes. As well as pensions, IAS 19 (revised) considers other forms of long-service benefit paid to employees.[7] These other forms of long-service benefit include:

(a) long-term compensated absences such as long-service or sabbatical leave;

(b) jubilee or other long-service benefits;

(c) long-term disability benefits;

(d) profit-sharing and bonuses payable twelve months or more after the end of the period in which the employees render the related service;

(e) deferred compensation paid twelve months or more after the end of the period in which it is earned.

The measurement of these other long-service benefits is not usually as complex or uncertain as it is for post-retirement benefits and therefore a more simplified method of accounting is used for them. For other long-service benefits any actuarial gains and losses and past service costs (if they arise) are recognised immediately in the income statement and no '10% corridor' is applied.

This means that the balance sheet liability for other long-service benefits is just the present value of the future benefit obligation less the fair value of any assets that the benefit will be settled from directly.

The income statement charge for these benefits is therefore the total of:

(a) current service cost;

(b) interest cost;

(c) expected return on plan assets (if any);

(d) actuarial gains and losses;

(e) past service cost;

(f) the effect of curtailments or settlements.

14.14 Short-term benefits

In addition to pension and other long-term benefits considered earlier, IAS 19 gives accounting rules for short-term employee benefits.

Short-term employee benefits include items such as:

1 wages, salaries and social security contributions;
2 short-term compensated absences (such as paid annual leave and paid sick leave) where the absences are expected to occur within twelve months after the end of the period in which the employees render the related employee service;
3 profit-sharing and bonuses payable within twelve months after the end of the period in which the employees render the related service; and
4 non-monetary benefits (such as medical care, housing or cars) for current employees.

All short-term employee benefits should be recognised at an undiscounted amount:

● as a liability (after deducting any payments already made), and
● as an expense (unless another international standard allows capitalisation as an asset).

If the payments already made exceed the undiscounted amount of the benefits an asset should be recognised only if it will lead to a future reduction in payments or a cash refund.

Compensated absences

The expected cost of short-term compensated absences should be recognised:

(a) in the case of accumulating absences, when the employees render service that increases their entitlement to future compensated absences; and
(b) in the case of non-accumulating compensated absences, when the absences occur.

Accumulating absences occur when the employees can carry forward unused absence from one period to the next. They are recognised when the employee renders services regardless of whether the benefit is vesting (the employee would get a cash alternative if they left employment) or non-vesting. The measurement of the obligation reflects the likelihood of employees leaving in a non-vesting scheme.

It is common practice for leave entitlement to be an accumulating absence (perhaps restricted to a certain number of days) but for sick pay entitlement to be non-accumulating.

Profit-sharing and bonus plans

The expected cost of a profit-sharing or bonus plan should only be recognised when:

(a) the enterprise has a present legal or constructive obligation to make such payments as a result of past events; and
(b) a reliable estimate of the obligation can be made.

14.15 Termination benefits[8]

These benefits are treated separately from other employee benefits in IAS 19 (revised) because the event that gives rise to the obligation to pay is the termination of employment as opposed to the service of the employee.

The accounting treatment for termination benefits is consistent with the requirements of IAS 37 and the rules concern when the obligation should be provided for and the measurement of the obligation.

Recognition

Termination benefits can only be recognised as a liability when the enterprise is demonstrably committed to either:

(a) terminate the employment of an employee or group of employees before the normal retirement date; or

(b) provide termination benefits as a result of an offer made in order to encourage voluntary redundancy.

The enterprise would only be considered to be demonstrably committed to a termination when a detailed plan for the termination is made and there is no realistic possibility of withdrawal from that plan. The plan should include as a minimum:

● the location, function and approximate number of employees whose services are to be terminated;

● the termination benefits for each job classification or function;

● the time at which the plan will be implemented.

Measurement

If the termination benefits are to be paid more than twelve months after the balance sheet date, they should be discounted, at a discount rate using the market yield on good quality corporate bonds. Prudence should also be exercised in the case of an offer made to encourage voluntary redundancy, as provision should only be based on the number of employees expected to accept the offer.

14.16 IAS 26 *Accounting and Reporting by Retirement Benefit Plans*

This standard provides complementary guidance in addition to IAS 19 regarding the way that the pension fund should account and report on the contributions it receives and the obligations it has to pay pensions. The standard mainly contains the presentation and disclosure requirements of the schemes as opposed to the accounting methods that they should adopt.

14.16.1 Defined contribution plans

The report prepared by a defined contribution plan should contain a statement of net assets available for benefits and a description of the funding policy.

With a defined contribution plan it is not normally necessary to involve an actuary, since the pension paid at the end is purely dependent on the amount of fund built up for the employee. The obligation of the employer is usually discharged by the employer paying the agreed contributions into the plan. The main purpose of the report of the plan is to provide information on the performance of the investments, and this is normally achieved by including the following statements:

(a) a description of the significant activities for the period and the effect of any changes relating to the plan, its membership and its terms and conditions;

(b) statements reporting on the transactions and investment performance for the period and the financial position of the plan at the end of the period; and

(c) a description of the investment policies.

14.16.2 Defined benefit plans

Under a defined benefit plan (as opposed to a defined contribution plan) there is a need to provide more information, as the plan must be sufficiently funded to provide the agreed pension benefits at the retirement of the employees. The objective of reporting by the defined benefit plan is to periodically present information about the accumulation of resources and plan benefits over time that will highlight an excess or shortfall in assets.

The report that is required should contain[9] either:

(a) a statement that shows:
   (i) the net assets available for benefits;
   (ii) the actuarial present value of promised retirement benefits, distinguishing between vested benefits and non-vested benefits; and
   (iii) the resulting excess or deficit; or

(b) a statement of net assets available for benefits including either:
   (i) a note disclosing the actuarial present value of promised retirement benefits, distinguishing between vested benefits and non-vested benefits; or
   (ii) a reference to this information in an accompanying report.

The most recent actuarial valuation report should be used as a basis for the above disclosures and the date of the valuation should be disclosed. IAS 26 does not specify how often actuarial valuations should be done but suggests that most countries require a triennial valuation.

When the fund is preparing the report and using the actuarial present value of the future obligations, the present value could be based on either projected salary levels or current salary levels. Whichever has been used should be disclosed. The effect of any significant changes in actuarial assumptions should also be disclosed.

Report format

IAS 26 proposes three different report formats that will fulfil the content requirements detailed above. These formats are:

(a) A report that includes a statement that shows the net assets available for benefits, the actuarial present value of promised retirement benefits, and the resulting excess or deficit. The report of the plan also contains statements of changes in net assets available for benefits and changes in the actuarial present value of promised retirement benefits. The report may include a separate actuary's report supporting the actuarial present value of promised retirement benefits.

(b) A report that includes a statement of net assets available for benefits and a statement of changes in net assets available for benefits. The actuarial present value of the promised retirement benefits is disclosed in a note to the statements. The report may also include a report from an actuary supporting the actuarial value of the promised retirement benefits.

(c) A report that includes a statement of net assets available for benefits and a statement of changes in net assets available for benefits with the actuarial present value of promised retirement benefits contained in a separate actuarial report.

In each format a trustees' report in the nature of a management or directors' report and an investment report may also accompany the statements.

14.16.3 All plans – disclosure requirements[10]

For all plans, whether defined contribution or defined benefit, some common valuation and disclosure requirements exist.

Valuation

The investments held by retirement benefit plans should be carried at fair value. In most cases the investments will be marketable securities and the fair value is the market value. If it is impossible to determine the fair value of an investment, disclosure should be made of the reason why fair value is not used.

Market values are used for the investments because this is felt to be the most appropriate value at the report date and the best indication of the performance of the investments over the period.

Disclosure

In addition to the specific reports detailed above for defined contribution and defined benefit plans, the report should also contain:

(a) a statement of net assets available for benefits disclosing:
- assets at the end of the period suitably classified
- the basis of valuation of assets
- details of any single investment exceeding either 5% of the net assets available for benefits or 5% of any class or type of security
- details of any investment in the employer
- liabilities other than the actuarial present value of promised retirement benefits;

(b) a statement of changes in net assets for benefits showing the following:
- employer contributions
- employee contributions
- investment income such as interest or dividends
- other income
- benefits paid or payable
- administrative expenses
- other expenses

- taxes on income
- profits or losses on disposal of investment and changes in value of investments
- transfers from and to other plans;

(c) a summary of significant accounting policies;

(d) a description of the plan and the effect of any changes in the plan during the period.

Summary

Accounting for post-retirement employee benefits has always been a difficult problem with different views as to the appropriate method. The different types of scheme and the associated risks add to the difficulties in terms of accounting. The accounting treatment for these benefits has recently changed with the current view that the balance sheet position takes priority over the income statement charge. However, one consequence of giving the balance sheet priority is that this change to the income statement can be much more volatile and this is considered by some to be undesirable.

Within the international community agreement does not exist on how these benefits should be accounted for. An interesting recent development is the proposed option to use the Statement of Movements in Equity to record variations from the normal pension costs, i.e. for actuarial gains and losses, rather than taking them to the income statement. The latest revisions do give significant choice to the companies in how they account for their pension schemes, which could be a criticism of the standard. Pension accounting is a very difficult area to gain global agreement on, and therefore IAS 19 (revised) could be construed as an early step towards more global convergence.

REVIEW QUESTIONS

1. Outline the differences between a defined benefit and a defined contribution pension scheme.

2. If a defined contribution pension scheme provided a pension that was 6% of salary each year, the company had a payroll cost of €5 million, and the company paid €200,000 in the year, what would be the income statement charge and the balance sheet liability at the year-end?

3. 'The approach taken in IAS 19 before its 1998 revision was to match an even pension cost against the period the employees provided service. This follows the accruals principle and is therefore fundamentally correct.' Discuss.

4. Under the revised IAS 19 (post 1998) what amount of actuarial gains and losses should be recognised in the income statement?

5. Past service costs are recognised under IAS 19 (revised) immediately if the benefit is 'vested'. In what circumstances would the benefits not be vested?

6. What is the required accounting treatment for a curtailment of a defined benefit pension scheme?

7. What distinguishes a termination benefit from the other benefits considered in IAS 19 (revised)?

8 The following are extracts from the financial statements of Heidelberger Druckmaschinen AG showing the accounting policy and detailed notes regarding the provision of pensions according to IAS 19. As can be seen the disclosures are quite complex but they attempt to give a sensible balance sheet and income statements position.

Accounting policy disclosure

Provisions for pensions and similar obligations comprise both the provision obligations of the Group under defined benefit plans and defined contribution plans. Pension obligations are determined according to the projected unit credit method (IAS 19) for defined benefit plans. Actuarial expert opinions are obtained annually in this connection. Calculations are based on an assumed trend of 3.5 per cent (previous year: 2.5%) for the growth in pensions, and a discount rate of 6.0 per cent (previous year: 6.0%). The probability of death is determined according to Heubec's current mortality tables as well as comparable foreign mortality tables.

In the case of defined contribution plans (for example, direct insurance policies), compulsory contributions are offset directly as an expense. No provisions for pension obligations are formed, as in these cases our Company does not have any liability over and above its liability to make premium payments.

Provisions for pensions and similar obligations (Note 15 in the financial statements)

We maintain benefit programs for the majority of employees for the period following their retirement — either a direct program or one financed by payments of premiums to private institutions. The level of benefits payments depends on the conditions in particular countries. The amounts are generally based on the term of employment and the salary of the employees. The liabilities include both those arising from current pensions as well as vested pension rights for pensions payable in the future. The pension payments expected following the beginning of benefit payment are accrued over the entire service time of the employee.

The provisions for pensions and similar obligations are broken down as follows:

	31 Mar 98	31 Mar 99
Net present value of the pension claims	408,208	445,054
Adjustment amount based on (not offset) actuarial profits/losses	−12,843	−18,225
Provisions for pensions and similar obligations	395,365	426,829

The amount of €18,225 thousand (previous year: €12,843 thousand), which is not yet adjusted arises largely from profits/losses in connection with deviations of the actual income trends from the assumptions that were the basis of the calculation. As soon as it exceeds 10 per cent of total liabilities, this amount is carried as an expense over the average remaining period of service of the staff (IAS 19).

The expense for the pension plan is broken down as follows:

	31 Mar 98	31 Mar 99
Expense for pension claims added during the financial year*	16,902	17,084
Interest expense for claims already acquired	21,583	22,855
Net additions to pension provision	38,485	39,939
Expenses for other pension plans*	14,848	19,407
	53,333	59,346

*The expense for the pension plan included under personnel expenses totals €36,491 thousand (previous year: €31,750 thousand).

We include interest expenses for already acquired pension claims under interest and similar expenses.

Required:
(a) Explain the projected unit credit method for determining pension obligations for defined benefit plans.
(b) Why does the company need to use a discount rate?
(c) Explain the reference to the 10% corridor.

EXERCISES

An extract from the solution is provided in the Appendix at the end of the text for exercises marked with an asterisk (*).

Question 1

Kathryn

Kathryn plc, a listed company, provides a defined benefit pension for its staff, the details of which are given below.

Pension scheme

As at the 30 April 2004, actuaries valued the company's pension scheme and estimated that the scheme had assets of £10.5m and obligations of £10.2m (using the valuation methods prescribed in IAS 19).

The actuaries made assumptions in their valuation that the assets would grow by 11% over the coming year to 30 April 2005, and that the obligations were discounted using an appropriate corporate bond rate of 10%. The actuaries estimated the current service cost at £600,000. The actuaries informed the company that pensions to retired directors would be £800,000 during the year, and the company should contribute £700,000 to the scheme.

At 30 April 2005 the actuaries again valued the pension fund and estimated the assets to be worth £10.7m, and the obligations of the fund to be £10.9m.

Assume that contributions and benefits are paid on the last day of each year.

Required:
(a) Explain the reasons why IAS 19 was revised in 1998, moving from an actuarial income driven approach to a market-based balance sheet driven approach. Support your answer by referring to the *Framework Document* principles.
(b) Show the extracts from the income statement, statement of movement in equity and balance sheet of Kathryn plc in respect of the information above for the year ended 30 April 2005. You do not need to show notes to the accounts.

   [The accounting policy adopted by Kathryn plc is to recognise actuarial gains and losses immediately in equity as allowed by IAS in its 2004 amendment.]

Question 2

Donna Inc

Donna Inc operates a defined benefit pension scheme for staff. The pension scheme has been operating for a number of years but not following IAS 19. The finance director is unsure of which accounting policy to adopt under IAS 19 because he has heard very conflicting stories. He went to one presentation in 2003 that referred to a '10% corridor' approach to actuarial gains and losses, but went to another presentation in 2004 that said actuarial gains and losses could be recognised in equity.

The pension scheme had market value of assets of £3.2m and a present value of obligations of £3.5m on 1 January 2002. There were no actuarial gains and losses brought forward into 2002..

The details relevant to the pension are as follows (in 000s) are:

	2002	2003	2004
Discount rate at start of year	6%	5%	4%
Expected rate of return on plan assets at start of year	10%	9%	8%
Current service cost	150	160	170
Benefits paid	140	150	130
Contributions paid	120	120	130
Present value of obligations at 31 December	3,600	3,500	3,200
Market value of plan assets at 31 December	3,400	3,600	3,600

In all years the average remaining service lives of the employees was 10 years. Under the 10% corridor approach any gains or losses above the corridor would be recognised over the average remaining service lives of the employees.

Required:
Advise the finance director of the differences in the approach to actuarial gains and losses following the '10% corridor' and the recognition in equity. Illustrate your answer by showing the impact on the pension for 2002 to 2004 under both bases.

References

1   IAS 19 *Employee Benefits*, IASB, amended 2002.
2   IAS 26 *Accounting and Reporting by Retirement Benefit Plans*, IASC, reformatted 1994.
3   IFRS 2 *Share-Based Payment*, IASB, 2004.
4   IAS 19, Appendix 1.
5   *Ibid.*, para. 7.
6   *Ibid.*, para. 120.
7   *Ibid.*, para. 126.
8   *Ibid.*, para. 132.
9   IAS 26, para. 28.
10 *Ibid.*, para. 32.

CHAPTER **15**

Taxation in company accounts

15.1 Introduction

Limited companies, and indeed all corporate bodies, are treated for tax purposes as being legally separate from their proprietors. Thus, a limited company is itself liable to pay tax on its profits. This tax is known as **corporation tax**. The shareholders are only accountable for tax on the income they receive by way of any dividends distributed by the company. If the shareholder is an individual, then **income tax** may become due on their dividend income received.

This is in contrast to the position in a partnership, where each partner is individually liable for the tax on that share of the pre-tax profit that has been allocated. A partner is taxed on the profit and not simply on drawings. Note that it is different from the treatment of an employee who is charged tax on the amount of salary that is paid.

In this chapter we consider the different types of company taxation and their accounting treatment. The International Accounting Standard that applies specifically to taxation is IAS 12 *Income Taxes*. The standard was last modified radically in 1996, further modified in part by IAS 10 in 1999 and revised by the IASB in 2000. Those UK unquoted companies that choose not to follow international standards will follow FRS 16 *Current Tax* and FRS 19 *Deferred Tax*.

15.2 Corporation tax

Corporation tax is calculated under rules set by Parliament each year in the Finance Act. The Finance Act may alter the existing rules; it also sets the rate of tax payable. Because of this annual review of the rules, circumstances may change year by year, which makes comparability difficult and forecasting uncertain.

The reason for the need to adjust accounting profits for tax purposes is that although the tax payable is based on the accounting profits as disclosed in the profit and loss account, the tax rules may differ from the accounting rules which apply prudence to income recognition. For example, the tax rules may not accept that all the expenses which are recognised by the accountant under the IASB's *Framework for the Preparation and Presentation of Financial Statements* and the IAS 1 *Presentation of Financial Statements* accrual concept are deductible when arriving at the taxable profit. An example of this might be a bonus, payable to an employee (based on profits), which is payable in arrear but which is deducted from accounting profit as an accrual under IAS 1. This expense is only allowed in calculating taxable profit on a cash basis when it is paid in order to ensure that one taxpayer does not reduce his potential tax liability before another becomes liable to tax on the income received.

The accounting profit may therefore be lower or higher than the taxable profit. For example, the Companies Acts require that the formation expenses of a company, which are the costs of establishing it on incorporation, must be written off in its first accounting period; the rules of corporation tax, however, state that these are a capital expense and cannot be deducted from the profit for tax purposes. This means that more tax will be assessed as payable than one would assume from an inspection of the published profit and loss account.

Similarly, although most businesses would consider that entertaining customers and other business associates was a normal commercial trading expense, it is not allowed as a deduction for tax purposes.

A more complicated situation arises in the case of depreciation. Because the directors have the choice of method of depreciation to use, the legislators have decided to require all companies to use the same method when calculating taxable profits. If one thinks about this, then it would seem to be the equitable practice. Each company is allowed to deduct a uniform percentage from its profits in respect of the depreciation that has arisen from the wear and tear and diminution in value of fixed assets.

The substituted depreciation that the tax rules allow is known as a **capital allowance**. The capital allowance is calculated in the same way as depreciation; the only difference is that the rates are those set out in the Finance Acts. At the time of writing, most commercial fixed assets (excluding land and buildings) qualify for a capital allowance of 25% calculated on the reducing balance method. There are restricted allowances, called industrial buildings allowances, for certain categories of buildings used in manufacturing. Just as the depreciation that is charged by the company under accrual accounting is substituted by a capital allowance, profits or losses arising on the sale of fixed assets are not used for tax purposes.

15.3 Corporation tax systems – the theoretical background

It might be useful to explain that there are three possible systems of company taxation (classical, imputation and partial imputation).[1] These systems differ solely in their tax treatment of the relationship between the limited company and those shareholders who have invested in it.

15.3.1 The classical system

In the classical system, a company pays tax on its profits, and then the shareholders suffer a second and separate tax liability when their share of the profits is distributed to them. In effect, the dividend income of the shareholder is regarded as a second and separate source of income from that of the profits of the company. The payment of a dividend creates an additional tax liability which falls directly on the shareholders. It could be argued that this double taxation is inequitable when compared to the taxation system on unincorporated bodies where the rate of taxation suffered overall remains the same whether or not profits are withdrawn from the business. It is suggested that this classical system discourages the distribution of profits to shareholders since the second tranche of taxation (the tax on dividend income of the shareholders) only becomes payable on payment of the dividend, although some argue that the effect of the burden of double taxation on the economy is less serious than it might seem.[2] Austria, Belgium, Denmark, the Netherlands and Sweden have classical systems.

15.3.2 The imputation system

In an imputation system, the dividend is regarded merely as a flow of the profits on each sale to the individual shareholders, as there is considered to be merely one source of income which could either be retained in the company or distributed to the shareholders. It is certainly correct that the payment of a dividend results from the flow of monies into the company from trading profits, and that the choice between retaining profits to fund future growth and the payment of a dividend to investing shareholders is merely a strategic choice unrelated to a view as to the nature of taxable profits. In an imputation system the total of the tax paid by the company and by the shareholder is unaffected by the payment of dividends and the tax paid by the company is treated as if it were also a payment of the individual shareholders' liabilities on dividends received. It is this principle of the flow of net profits from particular sales to individual shareholders that has justified the repayment of tax to shareholders with low incomes or to non-taxable shareholders of tax paid by the limited company, even though that tax credit has represented a reduction in the overall tax revenue of the state because the tax credit repaid also represented a payment of the company's own corporation tax liability. If the dividend had not been distributed to such a low-income or non-taxable shareholder who was entitled to repayment, the tax revenue collected would have been higher overall. France and Germany have such an imputation system. The UK modified its imputation system in 1999, so that a low-income or non-taxable shareholder (such as a charity) could no longer recover any tax credit.

15.3.3 The partial imputation system

In a partial imputation system only part of the underlying corporation tax paid is treated as a tax credit.

15.3.4 Common basis

All three systems are based on the taxation of profits earned as shown under the same basic principles used in the preparation of financial statements.

15.4 Corporation tax systems – avoidance and evasion

Governments have to follow the same basic principles of management as individuals. To spend money, there has to be a source of funds. The sources of funds are borrowing and income. With governments, the source of income is taxation. As with individuals, there is a practical limit as to how much they can borrow; to spend for the benefit of the populace, taxation has to be collected. In a democracy, the tax system is set up to ensure that the more prosperous tend to pay a greater proportion of their income in order to fund the needs of the poorer; this is called a progressive system. As Franklin Roosevelt, the American politician, stated, 'taxes, after all, are the dues that we pay for the privileges of membership in an organised society'.[3] Corporation tax on company profits represents 22% of the taxation collected by the Inland Revenue in the UK.

It appears to be a general rule that taxpayers do not enjoy paying taxation (despite the fact that they may well understand the theory underpinning the collection of taxation). This fact of human nature applies just as much to company directors handling company resources as it does to individuals. Every extra pound paid in taxation by a company reduces the resources available for retention for funding future growth.

15.4.1 Tax evasion

Politicians often complain about tax evasion. Evasion is the illegal (and immoral) manipulation of business affairs to escape taxation. An example could be the directors of a family-owned company taking cash sales for their own expenditure. Another example might be the payment of a low salary (below the threshold of income tax) to a family member not working in the company, thus reducing profits in an attempt to reduce corporation tax. It is easy to understand the illegality and immorality of such practices. When politicians complain of tax evasion, they tend not to distinguish between evasion and avoidance.

15.4.2 Tax avoidance

Tax avoidance could initially be defined as a manipulation of one's affairs, within the law, so as to reduce liability; indeed, as it is legal, it can be argued that it is not immoral. There is a well established tradition within the UK that 'every man is entitled if he can to order his affairs so that the tax attaching under the appropriate Acts is less than it otherwise would be'.[4]

Indeed the government deliberately sets up special provisions to reduce taxes in order to encourage certain behaviours. The more that employers and employees save for employee retirement, the less social security benefits will be paid out in the future. Thus both companies and individuals obtain full relief against taxation for pension contributions. Another example might be increased tax depreciation (capital allowances) on capital investment, in order to increase industrial investment and improve productivity within the UK economy.

The use of such provisions, as intended by the legislators, is not criticised by anyone, and might better be termed 'tax planning'. The problem area lies between the proper use of such tax planning, and illegal activities. This 'grey area' could best be called 'tax avoidance'.

The Institute for Fiscal Studies has stated:

> We think it is impossible to define the expression 'tax avoidance' in any truly satisfactory manner. People routinely alter their behaviour to reduce or defer their taxation liabilities. In doing so, commentators regard some actions as legitimate tax planning and others as tax avoidance. We have regarded tax avoidance (in contra-indication to legitimate ... tax planning) as action taken to reduce or defer tax liabilities in a way Parliament plainly did not intend ... .[5]

The law tends to define tax avoidance as an artificial element in the manipulation of one's affairs, within the law, so as to reduce liability.[6]

15.4.3 The problem of distinguishing between avoidance and evasion

The problem lies in distinguishing clearly between legal avoidance and illegal evasion. It can be difficult for accountants to walk the careful line between helping clients (in tax avoidance) and colluding with them against the Inland Revenue.[7]

When clients seek advice, accountants have to be careful to ensure that they have integrity in all professional and business relationships. Integrity implies not merely honesty but fair dealing and truthfulness. 'In all dealings relating to the tax authorities, a member must act honestly and do nothing that might mislead the authorities.'[8]

As an example to illustrate the problems that could arise, a client company has carried out a transaction to avoid taxation, but failed to minute the details as discussed at a directors' meeting. If the accountant were to correct this act of omission in arrear, this would be a move from tax avoidance towards tax evasion. Another example of such a move from tax avoidance to tax evasion might be where an accountant in informing the Inland Revenue of a tax-avoiding transaction fails to detail aspects of the transaction which might show it in a disadvantageous light.

15.5 Corporation tax – the system from 6 April 1999

A company pays corporation tax on its income. When that company pays a dividend to its shareholders it is distributing some of its taxed income among the proprietors. In an imputation system the tax paid by the company is 'imputed' to the shareholders who therefore receive a dividend which has already been taxed.

This means that, from the paying company's point of view, the concept of gross dividends does not exist. From the paying company's point of view, the amount of dividend paid shown in the profit and loss account will equal the cash that the company will have paid.

However, from the shareholder's point of view, the cash received from the company is treated as a net payment after deduction of tax. The shareholders will have received, with the cash dividend, a note of a tax credit, which is regarded as equal to basic rate income tax on the total of the dividend plus the tax credit. For example:

	£
Dividend being the cash paid by the company and disclosed in the company's profit and loss account	400.00
Imputed tax credit of 1/9 of dividend paid (being the rate from 6 April 1999)	44.44
Gross dividend	444.44

The imputed tax credit calculation (as shown above) has been based on a basic tax rate of 10% for dividends paid, being the basic rate of income tax on dividend income from 6 April 1999. This means that an individual shareholder who only pays basic rate income tax has no further liability in that the assumption is that the basic tax has been paid by the company. A non-taxpayer cannot obtain a repayment of tax.

Although a company pays corporation tax on its income, when that company pays a dividend to its shareholders it is still considered to be distributing some of its taxed income among the proprietors. In this system the tax payable by the company is 'imputed' to the shareholders who therefore receive a dividend which has already been taxed. This means that, from the paying company's point of view, the concept of 'gross' dividends does not exist. From the paying company's point of view, the amount of dividends paid shown in the profit and loss account will equal the cash that the company will have paid to the shareholders.

The essential point is that the dividend paying company makes absolutely no deduction from the dividend **nor is any payment made by the company to the Inland Revenue**. The addition of $1/9$ of the dividend paid as an imputed tax credit is purely nominal. A tax credit of $1/9$ of the dividend will be deemed to be attached to that dividend (in effect an income tax rate of 10%). That credit is notional in that no payment of the 10% will be made to the Inland Revenue.[9] The payment of taxation is not associated with dividends.

Large companies (those with taxable profits of over £1,500,000) pay their corporation tax liability in quarterly instalments starting within the year of account, rather than paying their corporation tax liability nine months thereafter. The payment of taxation is not associated with the payment of dividends. Smaller companies pay their corporation tax nine months after the year-end.

It has been argued that the imputation system has encouraged the payment of dividends, and consequently discourages firms from reinvesting earnings. Since 1985, both investment and the ratio of dividend payments to GDP have soared in Britain relative to the USA, but it is not obvious that such trends are largely attributable to tax policy.[10] It has been suggested that the corporation tax system (from 5 April 1999) would tend to discourage companies from paying 'excessive' dividends because the major pressure for dividends has come in the past from pension fund investors who previously could reclaim the tax paid, and that the decrease in cash flow to the company caused by payment of quarterly corporation tax payments might tend to assist company directors in resisting dividend increases to compensate for this loss.

15.5.1 Advance corporation tax – the system until 5 April 1999

A company pays corporation tax on its income. Statute previously required that when a company paid a dividend it was required to make a payment to the Inland Revenue equal to the total tax credit associated with that dividend. This payment was called 'advance corporation tax' (ACT) because it was a payment on account of the corporation's tax liability that would be paid on the profits of the accounting period. When the company eventually made its payment of the corporation tax liability, it was allowed to reduce the amount paid by the amount already paid as ACT. The net amount of corporation tax that was paid after offsetting the ACT was known as **mainstream corporation tax**. The total amount of corporation tax was no greater than that assessed on the taxable profits of the company; there was merely a change in the timing of the amount of tax paid by paying it in two parts – the ACT element and the mainstream corporation tax element.

What would have been the position if the company had declared a dividend but had not paid it out to the shareholders by the date of the balance sheet? In such a case the ACT could only have been offset against the corporation tax in the accounting period during which the tax was actually paid. The offset of ACT against corporation tax was effectively restricted to the ACT rate multiplied by the company's profits chargeable to corporation tax. A further refinement was that for offset purposes the ACT rate was multiplied by the UK profit – this does not include profits generated overseas. Should a distribution have exceeded the chargeable profits for that period, then the ACT could not be recovered immediately. Under tax law, such unrelieved ACT could be carried back against corporation tax payments in the preceding six years or forward against future liabilities indefinitely.

Unrecovered ACT would have appeared in the balance sheet as an asset. At this point the accountant must have considered the prudence concept. In order for it to have remained as such on the balance sheet it must have been (a) reasonably certain and (b) foreseeable that it would be recoverable at a future date. If the ACT could be reasonably seen as recoverable then it should have been shown on the balance sheet as a deferred asset. If, for any reason, it seemed improbable that there would be sufficient future tax liabilities to 'cover' the ACT, then it had to be written off as irrecoverable. This payment of ACT stopped on 5 April 1999 with a change in the imputation system. Companies which had paid tax for which they had not yet had relief against mainstream corporation tax at 5 April 1999 are permitted to carry it forward against future corporation tax liabilities – this carry-forward is called **shadow ACT**.

15.6 IFRS and taxation

European Union law requires listed companies to draw up their consolidated accounts according to IFRS for accounting periods beginning after 1 January 2005 (with adjusted comparative figures for the previous year). United Kingdom law has been amended to allow the Inland Revenue to accept accounts drawn up in accordance with GAAP ('generally accepted accounting practice'), which is defined as IFRS or UK GAAP (UK Generally Accepted Accounting Practice).[11]

Although the Accounting Standards Board (ASB) intends to bring its standards into accordance with IFRS (but not necessarily identical with them), it will take several years to do this. Consequently two different standards will be acceptable for some years. The move towards IFRS is leading to a detailed study of accounting theory and principles, so that the accounting treatment may eventually become the benchmark standard for taxation purposes, although this will take several years to reach fruition (if it proves to be attainable).

The Inland Revenue and the professional bodies have anticipated the potential impact of the move to IFRS. For some years at least, the legislation will have to provide for different treatment of specific items under UK GAAP and IFRS.

The Finance Act 2004 included legislation which ensured that companies that adopted IFRS to draw up their accounts would receive broadly equivalent tax treatment to companies that continue to use UK GAAP.[12] The intention of these provisions is to defer the major tax effects of most transitional adjustments until the tax impact becomes clearer.

The Pre-Budget Report of 2 December 2004 proposed further tax changes to ensure this policy of deferring tax effects of these accounting changes, for which the Chancellor of the Exchequer further confirmed his support in his Budget of 16 March 2005.

The clearest intimation of the intention to defer major tax effects is shown by the proposals for special purpose securitisation companies. These are certain companies where borrowing is located in a separate company in order to protect from insolvency. Under the proposed provisions, these companies would continue to use the previous accounting practice for taxation purposes for a further year, thus avoiding a significant tax charge on items that would not have been treated as income under UK GAAP. Another example is that there will be difficulties under IAS 39 where hedging profits are taken into account before they are realised, and tax law will ignore these volatile items.

A deliberate decision had already been made during the discussion of the Finance Act 2003 not to follow the changes in the treatment of share-based payments to employees that would not only follow from IFRS 2 but also from FRS 20 (under UK GAAP).[13]

IAS 8 includes adjustments for fundamental errors in the statement of changes in equity, but the legislation specifically excludes the tax effects of these.

It remains to be seen whether the taxation effects of any significant changes in profit resulting from the change from UK GAAP to IFRS will be deferred until UK GAAP becomes truly aligned with IFRS.

IFRS will not remain static. The IASB Project on the 'Financial Reporting of all Profit-Oriented Entities' (for under consideration is the development of a standard 'performance statement') will lead to further significant changes from UK GAAP. Such a move from the present Profit and Loss Account would lead to the need for a decision whether it could be used for tax purposes and what further adjustments would be needed for tax assessment purposes.

At least for the time being, any significant effects of the change to IFRS will be deferred for tax purposes.

15.7 IAS 12 – accounting for current taxation

The essence of IAS 12 is that it requires an enterprise to account for the tax consequences of transactions and other events in the same way that it accounts for the transactions and other events themselves. Thus, for transactions and other events recognised in the income statement, any related tax effects are also recognised in the income statement.

The details of how IAS 12 requires an enterprise to account for the tax consequences of transactions and other events follow below.

Income statement disclosure

The standard (para. 77) states that the tax expense related to profit or loss from ordinary activities should be presented on the face of the income statement. It also provides that the major components of the tax expense should be disclosed separately. These separate components of the tax expense may include (para. 80):

(a) current tax expense for the period of account,

(b) any adjustments recognised in the current period of account for prior periods (such as where the charge in a past year was underprovided),

(c) the amount of any benefit arising from a previously unrecognised tax loss, tax credit or temporary difference of a prior period that is used to reduce the current tax expense, and

(d) the amount of tax expense (income) relating to those changes in accounting policies and fundamental errors which are included in the determination of net profit or loss for the period in accordance with the allowed alternative treatment in IAS 8 *Net Profit or Loss for the Period, Fundamental Errors and Changes in Accounting Policies.*

Balance sheet disclosure

The standard states that current tax for current and prior periods should, to the extent unpaid, be recognised as a liability. If the amount already paid in respect of current and prior periods exceeds the amount due for those periods, the excess should be recognised as an asset.

The treatment of tax losses

As regards losses for tax purposes, the standard states that the benefit relating to a tax loss that can be carried back to recover current tax of a previous period should be recognised as an asset. Tax assets and tax liabilities should be presented separately from other assets and liabilities in the balance sheet. An enterprise should offset (para. 71) current tax assets and current tax liabilities if, and only if, the enterprise:

(a) has a legally enforceable right to set off the recognised amounts; and

(b) intends either to settle on a net basis, or to realise the asset and settle the liability simultaneously.

The standard provides (para. 81) that the following should also be disclosed separately:

(a) tax expense (income) relating to extraordinary items recognised during the period,

(b) an explanation of the relationship between tax expense (income) and accounting profit in either or both of the following forms:
   (i) a numerical reconciliation between tax expense (income) and the product of accounting profit multiplied by the applicable tax rate(s), disclosing also the basis on which the applicable tax rate(s) is (are) computed; or
   (ii) a numerical reconciliation between the average effective tax rate and the applicable tax rate, disclosing also the basis on which the applicable tax rate is computed,

(c) an explanation of changes in the applicable tax rate(s) compared to the previous accounting period.

The relationship between tax expense and accounting profit

The standard sets out the following example in Appendix B of an explanation of the relationship between tax expense (income) and accounting profit:

Current Tax Expense

	X5	X6
Accounting profit	8,775	8,740
Add		
Depreciation for accounting purposes	4,800	8,250
Charitable donations	500	350
Fine for environmental pollution	700	—
Product development costs	250	250
Health care benefits	2,000	1,000
	17,025	18,590
Deduct		
Depreciation for tax purposes	(8,100)	(11,850)
Taxable profit	8,925	6,740
Current tax expense at 40%	3,570	
Current tax expense at 35%		2,359

IAS 12 and FRS 16

IAS 12 is similar to FRS 16 *Current Tax*, which UK non-quoted companies that choose not to follow international standards can choose to adopt.

There are very few rules for calculating current tax in UK GAAP, although in practice the calculation will be largely similar to that under IAS 12. FRS 16 does not go into the detail of calculating current tax, but it does, however, clarify the treatment of withholding taxes and the effect they have on the income statement.

15.8 Deferred tax

15.8.1 IAS 12 – background to deferred taxation

The profit on which tax is paid may differ from that shown in the published profit and loss account. This is caused by two separate factors.

Permanent differences

One factor that we looked at above is that certain items of expenditure may not be legitimate deductions from profit for tax purposes under the tax legislation. These differences are referred to as **permanent** differences because they will not be allowed at a different time and will be permanently disallowed, even in future accounting periods.

Timing differences

Another factor is that there are some other expenses that are legitimate deductions in arriving at the taxable profit which are allowed as a deduction for tax purposes at a later date. These might be simply **timing** differences in that tax relief and charges to the profit and loss account occur in different accounting periods. The accounting profit is prepared on an accruals basis but the taxable profit might require certain of the items to be dealt with on a cash basis. Examples of this might include bonuses payable to senior management, properly included in the financial statements under the accruals concept but not eligible for tax relief until actually paid some considerable time later, thus giving tax relief in a later period.

Temporary differences

The original IAS 12 allowed an enterprise to account for deferred tax using the income statement liability method which focused on timing differences. IAS 12 (revised) requires the balance sheet liability method, which focuses on temporary differences, to be used. Timing differences are differences between taxable profit and accounting profit that originate in one period and reverse in one or more subsequent periods. Temporary differences are differences between the tax base of an asset or liability and its carrying amount in the balance sheet. The tax base of an asset or liability is the amount attributed to that asset or liability for tax purposes. All timing differences are temporary differences.

The most significant temporary difference is depreciation. The depreciation charge made in the financial statements must be added back in the tax calculations and replaced by the official tax allowance for such an expense. The substituted expense calculated in accordance with the tax rules is rarely the same amount as the depreciation charge computed in accordance with IAS 16 *Property, Plant and Equipment*.

Capital investment incentive effect

It is common for legislation to provide for higher rates of tax depreciation than are used for accounting purposes, for it is believed that the consequent deferral of taxation liabilities serves as an incentive to capital investment (this incentive is not forbidden by European Union law or the OECD rules). The classic effect of this is for tax to be payable on a lower figure than the accounting profit in the earlier years of an asset's life because the tax allowances usually exceed depreciation in the earlier years of an asset's life. In later accounting periods, the tax allowances will be lower than the depreciation charges and the taxable profit will then be higher than the accounting profit that appears in the published profit and loss account.

Deferred tax provisions

The process whereby the company pays tax on a profit that is lower than the reported profit in the early years and on a profit that is higher than reported profit in later years is known as **reversal**. Given the knowledge that, ultimately, these timing differences will reverse, the accruals concept requires that consideration be given to making provision for the future liability in those early years in which the tax payable is calculated on a lower figure. The provision that is made is known as a **deferred tax provision**.

Alternative methods for calculating deferred tax provisions

As you might expect, there has been a history of disagreement within the accounting profession over the method to use to calculate the provision. There have been, historically, two methods of calculating the provision for this future liability – the **deferral** method and the **liability** method.

The deferral method

The deferral method, which used to be favoured in the USA, involves the calculation each year of the tax effects of the timing differences that have arisen in that year. The tax effect is then debited or credited to the profit and loss account as part of the tax charge; the double entry is effected by making an entry to the deferred tax account. This deferral method of calculating the tax effect ignores the effect of changing tax rates on the timing differences that arose in earlier periods. This means that the total provision may consist of differences calculated at the rate of tax in force in the year when the entry was made to the provision.

The liability method

The liability method requires the calculation of the total amount of potential liability each year at current rates of tax, increasing or reducing the provision accordingly. This means that the company keeps a record of the timing differences and then recalculates at the end of each new accounting period using the rate of corporation tax in force as at the date of the current balance sheet.

To illustrate the two methods we will take the example of a single asset, costing £10,000, depreciated at 10% using the straight-line method, but subject to a tax allowance of 25% on the reducing balance method. The workings are shown in Figure 15.1. This shows, that, if there were no other adjustments, for the first four years the profits subject to tax would be lower than those shown in the accounts, but afterwards the situation would reverse.

Charge to income statement under the deferral method

The deferral method would charge to the profit and loss account each year the variation multiplied by the current tax rate, e.g. 1996 at 25% on £1,500 giving £375.00, and 1999 at 24% on £55 giving £13.20. This is in accordance with the accruals concept which matches the tax expense against the income that gave rise to it. Under this method the deferred tax provision will be credited with £375 in 1997 and this amount will not be altered in 1999 when the tax rate changes to 24%. In the example, the calculation for the five years would be as in Figure 15.2.

Figure 15.1   Deferred tax provision using deferral method

		ACCOUNTS (depreciation) £	TAX (allowances) £	DIFFERENCE (temporary) £	TAX (rate)
01.0.1.1996	Cost of asset	10,000	10,000		
31.12.1996	Depreciation/tax				
	Allowance	1,000	2,500	1,500	25%
		9,000	7,500	1,500	
31.12.1997	Depreciation/tax				
	Allowance	1,000	1,875	875	25%
		8,000	5,625	2,375	
31.12.1998	Depreciation/tax	1,000	1,406	406	25%
	Allowance	7,000	4,219	2,781	
31.12.1999	Depreciation/tax	1,000	1,055	55	24%
	Allowance	6,000	3,164	2,836	
31.12.2000	Depreciation/tax	1,000	791	(209)	24%
	Allowance	5,000	2,373	2,627	

Figure 15.2   Summary of deferred tax provision using the deferral method

Year ended	Timing difference £	Basic rate %	Deferred tax charge in year £	Deferred tax provision (deferral method) £
31.12.1996	1,500	25%	375.00	375.00
31.12.1997	875	25%	218.75	593.75
31.12.1998	406	25%	101.50	695.25
31.12.1999	55	24%	13.20	708.45
31.12.2000	(209)	24%	(50.16)	658.29

Charge to income statement under the liability method

The liability method would make a charge so that the total balance on deferred tax equalled the cumulative variation multiplied by the current tax rate. The intention is that the balance sheet liability should be stated at a figure which represents the tax effect as at the end of each new accounting period. This means that there would be an adjustment made in 1999 to recalculate the tax effect of the timing difference that was provided for in earlier years. For example, the provision for 1997 would be recalculated at 24%, giving a figure of £360 instead of the £375 that was calculated and charged in 1997. The decrease in the expected liability will be reflected in the amount charged against the profit and loss account in 1997. The £15 will in effect be credited to the 1997 profit statement.

Figure 15.3 Deferral tax provision using the liability method

Year ended	Temporary difference £	Basic rate	Deferred tax charge in year £	Deferred tax provision (deferral method) £	Rate in 2000	Deferred tax provision (liability method) £
31.12.1997	1,500	25%	375.00	375.00	24%	360.00
31.12.1998	875	25%	218.75	593.75	24%	210.00
31.12.1999	406	25%	101.50	695.25	24%	97.44
31.12.2000	55	24%	13.20	708.45	24%	13.20
				708.45		680.64

The effect on the charge to the 2000 profit statement (Figures 15.2 and 15.3) is that there will be a charge of £13.20 using the deferral method and a **credit** of £14.61 using the liability method. The £14.61 is the reduction in the amount provided from £695.25 at the end of 1999 to the £680.64 that is required at the end of 2000.

World trend towards the liability method

There has been a move in national standards away from the deferral method towards the liability method, which is a change of emphasis from the income statement to the balance sheet because the deferred tax liability is shown at current rates of tax in the liability method. This is in accordance with the IASB's conceptual framework which requires that all items in the balance sheet, other than shareholders' equity, must be either assets or liabilities as defined in the framework. Deferred tax as it is calculated under the traditional deferral method is not in fact a calculation of a liability, but is better characterised as deferred income or expenditure. This is illustrated by the fact that the sum calculated under the deferral method is not recalculated to take account of changes in the rate of tax charged, whereas it is recalculated under the liability method.

The world trend towards using the liability method also results in a change from accounting only for timing differences to accounting for temporary differences.

Temporary versus timing: conceptual difference

These temporary differences are defined in the IASB standard as 'differences between the carrying amount of an asset or liability in the balance sheet and its tax base'.[14] The conceptual difference between these two views is that under the liability method provision is made for only the future reversal of these timing differences whereas the temporary difference approach provides for the tax that would be payable if the company were to be liquidated at balance sheet values (i.e. if the company were to sell all assets at balance sheet values).

The US standard SFAS 109 argues the theoretical basis for these temporary differences to be accounted for on the following grounds:

A government levies taxes on net taxable income. Temporary differences will become taxable amounts in future years, thereby increasing taxable income and taxes payable, upon recovery or settlement of the recognised and reported amounts of an enterprise's assets or liabilities ... A contention that those temporary differences will never result in taxable amounts ... would contradict the accounting assumption inherent in the statement of financial position that the reported amounts of assets and liabilities will be recovered and settled, respectively; thereby making that statement internally inconsistent.[15]

A consequence of accepting this conceptual argument in IAS 12 is that provision must also be made for the potential taxation effects of asset revaluations.

15.8.2 IAS 12 – deferred taxation

The standard requires that the financial statements are prepared using the liability method described above (which is sometimes known as the balance sheet liability method).

An example of how deferred taxation operates follows.

EXAMPLE ● An asset which cost £150 has a carrying amount of £100. Cumulative depreciation for tax purposes is £90 and the tax rate is 25% as shown in Figure 15.4.

Figure 15.4   Cumulative depreciation

	In accounts	For tax
Cost	150	150
Depreciation	50	90
Carrying amount	100	60

The tax base of the asset is £60 (cost of £150 less cumulative tax depreciation of £90). To recover the carrying amount of £100, the enterprise must earn taxable income of £100, but will only be able to deduct tax depreciation of £60. Consequently, the enterprise will pay taxes of £10 (£40 at 25%) when it recovers the carrying amount of the asset. The difference between the carrying amount of £100 and the tax base of £60 is a taxable temporary difference of £40. Therefore, the enterprise recognises a deferred tax liability of £10 (£40 at 25%) representing the income taxes that it will pay when it recovers the carrying amount of the asset as shown in Figure 15.5.

Figure 15.5   Deferred tax liability

Income to recover	
Carrying amount	£100
Carrying amount for tax	£60
Temporary difference	£40
Tax rate	25%
Deferred tax	£10

The accounting treatment over the life of an asset

The following example, taken from IAS 12,[16] illustrates the accounting treatment over the life of an asset.

EXAMPLE ● An enterprise buys equipment for £10,000 and depreciates it on a straight-line basis over its expected useful life of five years. For tax purposes, the equipment is depreciated at 25% per annum on a straight-line basis. Tax losses may be carried back against taxable profit of the previous five years. In year 0, the enterprise's taxable profit was £5,000. The tax rate is 40%. The enterprise will recover the carrying amount of the equipment by using it to manufacture goods for resale. Therefore, the enterprise's current tax computation is as follows:

Year	1	2	3	4	5
Taxable income (£)	2,000	2,000	2,000	2,000	2,000
Depreciation for tax purposes	2,500	2,500	2,500	2,500	0
Tax profit (loss)	(500)	(500)	(500)	(500)	2,000
Current tax expense (income) at 40%	(200)	(200)	(200)	(200)	800

The enterprise recognises a current tax asset at the end of years 1 to 4 because it recovers the benefit of the tax loss against the taxable profit of year 0.

The temporary differences associated with the equipment and the resulting deferred tax asset and liability and deferred tax expense and income are as follows:

Year	1	2	3	4	5
Carrying amount (£)	8,000	6,000	4,000	2000	0
Tax base	7,500	5,000	2,500	0	0
Taxable temporary difference	500	1,000	1,500	2,000	0
Opening deferred tax liability	0	200	400	600	800
Deferred tax expense (income)	200	200	200	200	(800)
Closing deferred tax liability	200	400	600	800	0

The enterprise recognises the deferred tax liability in years 1 to 4 because the reversal of the taxable temporary difference will create taxable income in subsequent years. The enterprise's income statement is as follows:

Year	1	2	3	4	5
Income (£)	2,000	2,000	2,000	2,000	2,000
Depreciation	2,000	2,000	2,000	2,000	2,000
Profit before tax	0	0	0	0	0
Current tax expense (income)	(200)	(200)	(200)	(200)	800
Deferred tax expense (income)	200	200	200	200	(800)
Total tax expense (income)	0	0	0	0	0
Net profit for the period	0	0	0	0	0

Further examples of items that could give rise to temporary differences are:

● Retirement benefit costs may be deducted in determining accounting profit as service is provided by the employee, but deducted in determining taxable profit either when contributions are paid to a fund by the enterprise or when retirement benefits are paid by the enterprise. A temporary difference exists between the carrying amount of the liability (in the financial statements) and its tax base (the carrying amount of the liability for tax purposes); the tax base of the liability is usually nil.

● Research costs are recognised as an expense in determining accounting profit in the period in which they are incurred but may not be permitted as a deduction in determining taxable profit (tax loss) until a later period. The difference between the tax base (the carrying amount of the liability for tax purposes) of the research costs, being the amount the taxation authorities will permit as a deduction in future periods, and the carrying amount of nil is a deductible temporary difference that results in a deferred tax asset.

Treatment of asset revaluations

The original IAS 12 permitted, but did not require, an enterprise to recognise a deferred tax liability in respect of asset revaluations. If such assets were sold at the revalued sum then a profit would arise that could be subject to tax. IAS 12 as currently written requires an enterprise to recognise a deferred tax liability in respect of asset revaluations.

Such a deferred tax liability on a revalued asset might not arise for many years, for there might be no intention to sell the asset. Many would argue that IAS 12 should allow for such timing differences by discounting the deferred liability (for a sum due many years in advance is certainly recognised in the business community as a lesser liability than the sum due immediately, for the sum could be invested and produce income until the liability would become due; this is termed the time value of money). The standard does not allow such discounting.[17] Indeed, it could be argued that in reality most businesses tend to have a policy of continuous asset replacement, with the effect that any deferred liability will be further deferred by these future acquisitions, so that the deferred tax liability would only become payable on a future cessation of trade. Not only does the standard preclude discounting, it also does not permit any account being made for future acquisitions by making a partial provision for the deferred tax.

Accounting treatment of deferred tax following a business combination

In a business combination that is an acquisition, the cost of the acquisition is allocated to the identifiable assets and liabilities acquired by reference to their fair values at the date of the exchange transaction. Temporary differences arise when the tax bases of the identifiable assets and liabilities acquired are not affected by the business combination or are affected differently. For example, when the carrying amount of an asset is increased to fair value but the tax base of the asset remains at cost to the previous owner, a taxable temporary difference arises which results in a deferred tax liability. Paragraph B16(i) of IFRS 3 *Business Combinations* prohibits discounting of deferred tax assets acquired and deferred tax liabilities assumed in a business combination as does IAS 12 (revised). IAS 12 states that deferred tax should not be provided on goodwill if amortisation of it is not allowable for tax purposes (as is the case in many states). Deferred tax arising on a business combination that is an acquisition is an exception to the rule that changes in deferred tax should be recognised in the income statement (rather than as an adjustment by way of a note to the financial statements).

Another exception to this rule relates to items charged (or credited) directly to equity. Examples of such items are:

● a change in the carrying amount arising from the revaluation of property, plant and equipment (IAS 16 *Property, Plant and Equipment*);

- an adjustment to the opening balance of retained earnings resulting from either a change in accounting policy that is applied retrospectively or the correction of an error (IAS 8 *Accounting Policies, Changes in Accounting Estimates and Errors*);

- exchange differences arising on the translation of the financial statements of a foreign entity (IAS 21 *The Effects of Changes in Foreign Exchange Rates*);

- amounts arising on initial recognition of the equity component of a compound financial instrument.

Deferred tax asset

A deferred tax asset should be recognised for the carry-forward of unused tax losses and unused tax credits to the extent that it is probable that future taxable profit will be available against which the unused tax losses and unused tax credits can be utilised.

At each balance sheet date, an enterprise should reassess unrecognised deferred tax assets. The enterprise recognises a previously unrecognised deferred tax asset to the extent that it has become probable that future taxable profit will allow the deferred tax asset to be recovered. For example, an improvement in trading conditions may make it more probable that the enterprise will be able to generate sufficient taxable profit in the future for the deferred tax asset.

15.9 FRS 19 (the UK standard on deferred taxation)

Those UK unquoted companies that choose not to follow international standards will follow FRS 19 *Deferred Tax*.

Accounting for deferred tax in the UK pre-dates the issue of accounting standards.

Prior to the issue of standards, companies applied an accounting practice known as 'tax equalisation accounting', whereby they recognised that accounting periods should each be allocated an amount of income tax expense that bears a 'normal relationship to the income shown in the income statement', and to let reported income taxes follow reported income has been the objective of accounting for income taxes ever since.[18] There is also an economic consequence that flows from the practice of tax equalisation in that the trend of reported after-tax income is smoothed, and there is less likelihood of pressure for a cash dividend distribution based on the crediting of the tax benefit of capital investment expenditure to the early years of the fixed assets.

There followed a period of very high rates of capital allowances and, with a naive belief that this situation would continue and allow permanent deferral, companies complained that to provide full provision was unrealistic and so in 1977 the concept of **partial provision** was introduced in which deferred tax was only provided in respect of timing differences that were likely to be reversed. The argument was that if the company continued with the replacement of fixed assets, and if the capital allowances were reasonably certain to exceed the depreciation in the foreseeable future, it was unrealistic to make charges against the profit and create provisions that would not crystallise. This would merely lead to the appearance of an ever-increasing provision on the balance sheet.

The *Foreword to Accounting Standards* published in June 1993 by the Accounting Standards Board (ASB) states that 'FRSs are formulated with due regard to international developments ... the Board supports the IASC in its aim to harmonise' and that 'where the requirements of an accounting standard and an IAS differ, the accounting standard should be followed'.

Professor Andrew Lennard, then Assistant Technical Director of the ASB, confirmed during a lecture on 17 March 1999 that this was a matter where there was a divergence of view between the ASB and international regulators, where the ASB was unhappy to account in full for deferred tax where there was no discounting for long delays until the anticipated payment; indeed he expressed his exasperation with the topic in stating that 'he wished deferred tax accounting would go away'.[19] Applying the full provision method is more consistent with both international practice and the ASB's draft *Statement of Principles* (as modified in March 1999). However, a criticism of the full provision method in the past was that it could, if the company had a continuous capital expenditure programme, lead to a build-up of large liabilities that may fall due only far into the future, if at all.

The significant differences between FRS 19 and IAS 12 are:

1 Under FRS 19 there is a general requirement that a deferred tax charge **should not be recognised on revaluation gains** on non-monetary assets which are revalued to fair values on the acquisition of a business. IAS 12 requires tax on revaluations.

2 Under FRS 19 **discounting of deferred taxation liabilities is made optional**. The ASB had stated its belief that, in principle, deferred tax should be discounted, but has taken the view that discounting should be optional so as to give a choice to the preparer of the accounts. However, although discounting appears to be an attractive method for allowing for the delay in payment of the liability, it has been pointed out that in some cases where capital expenditure is uneven, then an unexpected effect of discounting both the initial and final cash flow effects could be to turn an eventual liability into an initial asset.[20] IAS 12 does not allow such discounting.[21]

The ASB is aware that the break with international standards is undesirable. Indeed it has been suggested that the ASB developed and implemented FRS 19 with a view that it would 'encourage the International Accounting Standards Committee to think again' about IAS 12.[22]

15.10 A critique of deferred taxation

It could be argued that deferred tax is not a legal liability until it accrues. The consequence of this argument would be that deferred tax should not appear in the financial statements, and financial statements should:

● present the tax expense for the year equal to the amount of income taxes that has been levied based on the income tax return for the year;

● accrue as a receivable any income refunds that are due from taxing authorities or as a payable any unpaid current or past income taxes;

● disclose in the notes to the financial statements differences between the income tax bases of assets and liabilities and the amounts at which they appear in the balance sheet.

The argument is that the process of accounting for deferred tax is confusing what **did** happen to a company, i.e. the agreed tax payable for the year, and what **did not** happen to the company, which is the tax that would have been payable if the adjustments required by the tax law for timing differences had not occurred. It is felt that the investor should be provided with details of the tax charge levied on the profits for the year and an explanation of factors that might lead to a different rate of tax charge appearing in future financial statements. The argument against adjusting the tax charge for deferred tax and the creation of a deferred tax provision holds that shareholders are accustomed to giving consideration to many other imponderables concerning the amount, timing and uncertainty of future cash receipts and payments, and the treatment of tax should be considered in the same way. This view has received support from others,[23] who have held that tax attaches to taxable income and not to the reported accounting income and that there is no legal requirement for the tax to bear any relationship to the reported accounting income. Indeed it has been argued that 'deferred tax means income smoothing'.[24]

Before discussing the arguments it is appropriate to consider the economic reality of deferred taxation.

Those industries which are capital-intensive tend to have benefited from tax deferral by way of accelerated tax depreciation on plant investment, and it could be suggested that their accounts do not truly reflect the economic reality without provision for deferred taxation. Studies in the UK certainly support this view.

In the UK it has not been the practice to make full provision for deferred taxation. 'Full provision' refers to the fact that **the potential liability to deferred taxation has not been reduced** to allow for the view of management that the entire liability will not be paid in the future as a result of timing differences because the taxation benefits of future capital investments will result in a further deferral of taxation liability. In the UK, the deferred taxation liability has been reduced to allow for the effects of these anticipated future investments.

Terry Smith points out in Table 17.2 of his *Accounting for Growth*[25] that according to the companies' own figures their estimated EPS would fall as follows if full provision for deferred tax were made:

British Airways	36.4%
Severn Trent	25.3%
British Gas	20.5% (based on CCA earnings of 15.1p per share adjusted to exclude restructuring costs)
TI Group	13.8%

In his Table 17.3 he lists companies which expected an EPS fall of over 10% and with more than 10% of shareholders' funds in unprovided deferred tax:

	Estimated impact on historic gearing of full provision	
	From	*To*
	%	%
British Airways	148	214
BP	67	78
British Gas	56	68

He points out in his Table 17.4 that five of the companies he lists without any exposure to an increase in deferred tax charge are some of the UK's most successful and conservatively financed large companies.

	Tax rate (%)
General Electric	32
Marks & Spencer	32
Reuters	32
GUS	33
Wolesey	33

In the light of such economic facts, it is possible to understand why business managers might oppose deferred tax accounting, for it would lower their company stock valuation, whereas investment advisors might support deferred tax accounting as enabling them to form a better view of future prospects. It is suggested that the arguments for and against deferred taxation accounting must be based solely on the theory underpinning accounting, and unaffected by commercial considerations.

It is also suggested that the above arguments against the use of deferred tax accounting are unconvincing if one considers the IASB's underlying assumption about accrual accounting, as stated in the *Framework*:

> In order to meet their objectives, financial statements are prepared on the accrual basis of accounting ... Financial statements prepared on the accrual basis inform users not only of past transactions involving the payment and receipt of cash but also of obligations to pay cash in the future and of resources that represent cash to be received in the future.[26]

This underlying assumption confirms that deferred tax accounting makes the fullest possible use of accrual accounting.

Pursuing this argument further the *Framework* states:

> The future economic benefit embodied in an asset is the potential to contribute, directly or indirectly, to the flow of cash and cash equivalents to the enterprise. The potential may be a productive one that is part of the operating activities of the enterprise.[27]

If a balance sheet includes current market valuations based on this view of an asset, it is difficult to argue logically that the implicit taxation arising on this future economic benefit should not be provided for at the same time. The previous argument for excluding the deferred tax liability cannot therefore be considered persuasive on this basis.

On the other hand, it is stated in the *Framework* that 'An essential characteristic of a liability is that the enterprise has a present obligation.'[28] One could argue solely from these words that deferred tax is not a liability, but this conflicts with the argument based on the definition of an asset; consequently when considered in context this does not provide a sustainable argument against a deferred tax provision. The fact is that accounting practice has moved definitively towards making such a provision for deferred taxation.

The legal argument that deferred tax is not a legal liability until it accrues runs counter to the criterion of substance over form which gives weight to the economic aspects of the event rather than the strict legal aspects. The *Framework* states:

Substance Over Form
If information is to represent faithfully the transactions and other events that it purports to represent, it is necessary that they are accounted for and presented in

accordance with their substance and economic reality and not merely their legal form. The substance of transactions or other events is not always consistent with that which is apparent from their legal or contrived form.[29]

It is an interesting fact that substance over form has achieved a growing importance since the 1980s and the legal arguments are receiving less recognition. Investments are made on economic criteria, investors make their choices on the basis of anticipated cash flows, and such flows would be subject to the effects of deferred taxation.

15.11 Examples of companies following IAS 12

Figure 15.6 is from the Roche Group 2000 Annual Report; Figure 15.7 is from the Bayer Group 2002 Annual Report. It should be noted that these published examples do not always comply in full with all aspects of IAS 12 (revised).

Figure 15.6   Extract from Roche Group 2000 Annual Report

Note 11 – Income taxes

Income Tax Expenses

The amounts charged in the income statements are as follows:

	2000	1999
Current income taxes	2,913	1,103
Deferred income taxes	(641)	799
Total charge for income taxes	2,272	1,902

The Group's parent company, Roche Holding Limited, and several of the Group's operating companies are domiciled in Switzerland. The maximum effective rate of all income taxes on companies domiciled in Basel, Switzerland, is 8% for holding companies and 25% for operating companies (1998: 8% and 25%).

Since the Group operates across the world, it is subject to income taxes in many different tax jurisdictions. The Group calculates its average expected tax rate as a weighted average of the tax rates in the tax jurisdictions in which the Group operates.

The Group's effective tax rate differs from the Group's expected tax rate as follows:

	2000	1999
Group's average expected tax rate	20%	20%
Tax effect of		
Income not taxable	–3%	–2%
Expenses not deductible for tax purposes	3%	3%
Benefit of prior year tax losses not previously recognised	—	—
Other differences	–3%	–3%
Gain from sales of Genentech shares	8%	2%
Gain from sales of LabCorp shares	2%	—
Impairment of long-term assets	–3%	—
Vitamin case	—	6%
Genentech legal settlements	—	–1%
Group's effective tax rate	24%	25%

Figure 15.6 *(cont.)*

Income tax assets and liabilities

Amounts recognised in the balance sheet for income taxes are as follows:

	2000	1999
Current income tax		
Current income tax assets	435	408
Current income tax liabilities	(882)	(728)
Net current income tax asset (liability) in the balance sheet	(447)	(320)
Deferred income taxes		
Deferred income tax assets	460	1,170
Deferred income tax liabilities	(2,535)	(3,895)
Net deferred income tax asset (liability) in the balance sheet	(2,075)	(2,725)

Amounts recognised in the balance sheet for deferred taxes are reported as long-term assets and non-current liabilities, of which approximately 50% and 15% respectively are current.

Deferred income tax assets are recognised for tax loss carry-forwards only to the extent that realisation of the related tax benefit is probable. The Group has no significant unrecognised tax losses. Deferred income tax liabilities have not been established for the withholding tax and other taxes that would be payable on the unremitted earnings of certain foreign subsidiaries, as such amounts are currently regarded as permanently reinvested. These unremitted earnings totalled 24.8 billion Swiss francs at 31 December 2000 (1999: 19.2 billion Swiss francs).

The deferred income tax assets and liabilities and the deferred income tax charges (credits) are attributable to the following items:

2000	Fixed assets	Restructuring provisions	Temporary differences	Total
Net deferred income tax asset (liability) at the beginning of the year	(3,128)	302	101	(2,725)
Changes to accounting policies	49	—	—	49
Debt instrument issue	—	—	(128)	(128)
To income statement	312	(144)	473	641
Changes in group organisation	(54)	(8)	(55)	(117)
Currency translation effects	(521)	(4)	730	205
	(3,342)	146	1,121	(2,075)

Figure 15.7   Extract from Bayer Group 2002 Annual Report

	2002 €000	2001 €000
Income before tax	956	1,115
Tax charge on income	107	(154)
Income after taxes	1,063	961
Current assets		
Provisions for taxes	650	524

	2002 €000	2001 €000
Income before tax		
Germany	1,392	971
Other countries	(436)	144
	956	1,115
Tax paid or accrued		
Germany	(129)	(122)
Other countries	(169)	(502)
	(298)	(624)
Deferred taxes		
From temporary differences	(185)	(272)
From losses carried	(220)	(198)
	405	470
Tax charge	107	(154)

15.12 Value added tax (VAT)

VAT is one other tax that affects most companies and for which there is an accounting standard (SSAP 5 *Accounting for Value Added Tax*), which was established on its introduction. This standard was issued in 1974 when the introduction of value added tax was imminent and there was considerable worry within the business community on its accounting treatment. We can now look back, having lived with VAT for well over two decades, and wonder, perhaps, why an SSAP was needed. VAT is essentially a tax on consumers collected by traders and is accounted for in a similar way to PAYE income tax, which is a tax on employees collected by employers.

IAS 18 (para. 8) makes clear that the same principles are followed:

> Revenue includes only the gross inflows of economic benefits received and receivable by the enterprise on its own account. Amounts collected on behalf of third parties such as sales taxes, goods and services taxes and value added taxes are not economic benefits which flow to the enterprise and do not result in increases in equity. Therefore, they are excluded from revenue.[30]

15.12.1 The effects of the standard

The effects of the standard vary depending on the status of the accounting entity under the VAT legislation. The term 'trader' appears in the legislation and is the terminology for a business entity. The 'traders' or companies, as we would normally refer to them, are classified under the following headings:

(a) Registered trader

For a registered trader, accounts should only include figures net of VAT. This means that the VAT on the sales will be deducted from the invoice amount. The VAT will be payable to the government and the net amount of the sales invoice will appear in the profit and loss account in arriving at the sales turnover figure. The VAT on purchases will be deducted from the purchase invoice. The VAT will then be reclaimed from the government and the net amount of the purchases invoice will appear in the profit and loss account in arriving at the purchases figure.

The only exception to the use of amounts net of VAT is when the input tax is not recoverable, e.g. on entertaining and on 'private' motor cars.

(b) Non-registered or exempt trader

For a company that is classified as non-registered or exempt, the VAT that it has to pay on its purchases and expenses is not reclaimable from the government. Because the company cannot recover the VAT, it means that the expense that appears in the profit and loss account must be inclusive of VAT. It is treated as part of each item of expenditure and the costs treated accordingly. It will be included, where relevant, with each item of expense (including capital expenditure) rather than being shown as a separate item.

(c) Partially exempt trader

An entity which is partially exempt can only recover a proportion of input VAT, and the proportion of non-recoverable VAT should be treated as part of the costs on the same lines as with an exempt trader. The VAT rules are complex but, for the purpose of understanding the figures that appear in published accounts of public companies, treatment as a registered trader would normally apply.

Summary

The major impact on reported post-tax profits will be the adoption of IAS 12 which will remove the possibility for the discounting of deferred tax on the adoption of the full provisioning method.

There may be significant increase in the deferred tax charge, with the earnings per share correspondingly reduced.

REVIEW QUESTIONS

1 Why does the charge to taxation in a company's accounts not equal the profit multiplied by the current rate of corporation tax?

2 Explain clearly how advance corporation tax arose and its effect on the profit and loss account and the year-end balance sheet figures. (Use a simple example to illustrate.)

3 Explain how the corporation tax system changed as from April 1999.

4 Deferred tax accounting may be seen as an income-smoothing device which distorts the true and fair view. Explain the impact of deferred tax on reported income and justify its continued use.

5 Explain how dividends received and paid are shown in the accounts.

6 Distinguish between (a) the deferral and (b) the liability methods of company deferred tax.

7 Explain the criteria that a deferred tax provision needs to satisfy under IAS 12 in order to be accepted as a liability in the balance sheet.

8 Explain the effect of SSAP 5 *Accounting for Value Added Tax*.

EXERCISES

An extract from the solution is provided in the Appendix at the end of the text for exercises marked with an asterisk (*).

Question 1

In your capacity as chief assistant to the financial controller, your managing director has asked you to explain to him the differences between tax planning, tax avoidance and tax evasion.

He has also asked you to explain to him your feelings as a professional accountant about these topics.

Write some notes to assist you in answering these questions.

Question 2

A fixed asset (a machine) was purchased by Adjourn plc on 1 July 20X1 at a cost of £25,000.

The company prepares its annual accounts to 31 March in each year. The policy of the company is to depreciate such assets at the rate of 15% straight line (with depreciation being charged pro rata on a time apportionment basis in the year of purchase). The company was granted capital allowances at 25% per annum on the reducing balance method (such capital allowances are apportioned *pro rata* on a time apportionment basis in the year of purchase).

The rate of corporation tax has been as follows:

Year ended	31 Mar 20X2	20%
	31 Mar 20X3	30%
	31 Mar 20X4	20%
	31 Mar 20X5	19%
	31 Mar 20X6	19%

Required:
(a) Calculate the deferred tax provision using both the deferred method and the liability method.
(b) Explain why the liability method is considered by commentators to place the emphasis on the balance sheet, whereas the deferred method is considered to place the emphasis on the profit and loss account.

Question 3

The move from the preparation of accounts under UK GAAP to the users of IFRS by United Kingdom quoted companies for years beginning 1 January 2005 will have an effect on the level of profits reported. How will those profits arising from the change in accounting standards be treated for taxation purposes?

Question 4

Discuss the arguments for and against discounting the deferred tax charge.

References

 1 OECD, *Theoretical and Empirical Aspects of Corporate Taxation*, Paris, 1974; van den Temple, *Corporation Tax and Individual Income Tax in the EEC*, EEC Commission, Brussels, 1974.
 2 G.H. Partington and R.H. Chenhall, *Dividends, Distortion and Double Taxation*, Abacus, 1983.
 3 Franklin D. Roosevelt, 1936 speech at Worcester, Massachusetts (Roosevelt Museum).
 4 L.J. Tomlin in *Duke of Westminster v CIR*, HL 1935, 19 TC 490.
 5 *Tax Avoidance: A Report by the Tax Law Review Committee*, The Institute For Fiscal Studies, 1997, para. 7.
 6 *WT Ramsay Ltd v CIR*, HL 1981, 54 TC 101; [1981] STC 174; [1981] 2 WLR 449; [1981] 1 All ER 865.
 7 Robert Maas, *Beware Tax Avoidance Drifting into Evasion*, Taxline, Tax Planning 2003–2004, Institute of Chartered Accountants in England and Wales.
 8 *Professional Conduct in Relation to Taxation*, Ethical Statement 1.308, Institute of Chartered Accountants in England and Wales, para. 2.13 (this is similar to the statements issued by the other accounting bodies).
 9 R. Altshul, 'Act now', *Accountancy Age*, 5 February 1998, p. 19.
10 William Gale, 'What can America learn from the British tax system?', *Fiscal Studies*, vol. 18, no. 4, November 1997.
11 S. 836A *Income and Corporation Taxes Act 1988* (as modified by Finance Act 2004).
12 Sections 50 to 54, under the heading of Accounting Practice, and Schedule 10 (Amendment of enactments that operate by reference to accounting practice), Finance Act 2004.
13 Schedule 23 to Finance Act 2003.
14 IAS 12 *Income Taxes*, IASB, revised 2000, para. 5.
15 SFAS 109 *Accounting for Income Taxes*, FASB, 1992.
16 IAS 12 *Income Taxes*, IASB, revised 2000, Example 1 to Appendix B.
17 IAS 12 *Income Taxes*, IASB, revised 2000, para. 54.
18 P. Rosenfield and W.C. Dent, 'Deferred income taxes' in R. Bloom and P.T. Elgers (eds), *Accounting Theory and Practice*, Harcourt Brace Jovanovich, 1987, p. 545.
19 Andrew C. Lennard during a guest lecture at Sunderland Business School.
20 Mike Metcalf, 'Alchemical accounting', *Accountancy*, November 1999, p. 100.
21 IAS 12 *Income Taxes*, IASB, revised 2000, para. 54.
22 Joan Brown, 'A step closer to harmony', *Accountancy*, January 2001, p. 90.
23 R.J. Chambers, *Tax Allocation and Financial Reporting*, Abacus, 1968.
24 Prof. D.R. Middleton, letter to the editor, *The Financial Times*, 29 Sept. 1994.
25 Terry Smith, *Accounting for Growth: Stripping the Camouflage from Company Accounts* (2nd edition), Random House, 1996.
26 *Framework for the Preparation and Presentation of Financial Statements*, IASB, 2001, para. 22.
27 *Ibid.*, para. 53.
28 *Ibid.*, para. 60.
29 *Ibid.*, para. 35.
30 IAS 18 *Revenue*, IASB 2001, para. 8.

CHAPTER 16

Property, plant and equipment (PPE)

16.1 Introduction

In this chapter we consider property, plant and equipment (PPE). It is helpful to consider the importance of PPE relative to intangible assets, inventory and receivables. This will, of course, vary with the nature of the industry as shown if we consider the pharmaceutical and brewing industries.

The relative importance of the different categories of asset within the two industries based on average industry profile has been compiled from IPA UK Industrial Performance Analysis 1996/97 (ICC Business Publications Ltd 1996 – ISSN 0262 3684) based on 83 pharmaceutical manufacturers and developers and 55 brewers and appears in Figure 16.1.

Figure 16.1   Ratio of assets to total assets for 1994/95 for 83 pharmaceutical manufacturers and developers and 55 brewers

1994/95 averages (£000)
Pharmaceutical manufacturers and developers (83 companies)

	Tangible non-current assets	Intangible non-current assets	Inventory	Trade receivables	Total assets
Average (£000)	82,375	31,246	23,471	35,452	243,667
% of total assets	33.8%	12.8%	9.6%	14.5%	

1994/95 averages (£000)
Brewers (55 companies)

	Tangible non-current assets	Intangible non-current assets	Inventory	Trade receivables	Total assets
Average (£000)	202,284	123	8,410	11,525	258,256
% of total assets	78.3%	0%	3.3%	4.5%	

For PPE the accounting treatment is based on the accruals or matching concepts, under which expenditure is capitalised until it is charged as depreciation against revenue in the periods in which benefit is gained from its use. Thus, if án item is purchased that has an economic life of two years, so that it will be used over two accounting periods to help earn profit for the enterprise, then the cost of that asset should be apportioned in some way between the two accounting periods.

However, this does not take into account the problems surrounding PPE accounting and depreciation, which have so far given rise to five relevant international accounting standards. We will consider these problems in this chapter covering:

IAS 16 and IAS 23:

● What is PPE (IAS 16)?

● How is the cost of PPE determined (IAS 16 and IAS 23)?

● How is depreciation of PPE computed (IAS 16)?

● What are the regulations regarding carrying PPE at revalued amounts (IAS 16)?

Other relevant international accounting standards and pronouncements:

● How should grants receivable towards the purchase of PPE be dealt with (IAS 20)?

● Are there ever circumstances in which PPE should not be depreciated (IAS 40)?

● What is impairment and how does this affect the carrying value of PPE (IAS 36)?

● What are the key changes proposed by the IASB concerning the disposal of non-current assets (IFRS 5)?

16.2 What is PPE?

IAS 16 *Property, Plant and Equipment*[1] defines PPE as tangible assets that are:

(a) held by an enterprise for use in the production or supply of goods and services, for rental to others, or for administrative purposes, and

(b) expected to be used during more than one period.

It is clear from the definition that PPE will be included in the non-current assets section of the balance sheet.

16.2.1 Problems that may arise

Problems may arise in relation to the interpretation of the definition and in relation to the application of the materiality concept.

The definitions give rise to some areas of practical difficulty. For example, an asset that has previously been held for use in the production or supply of goods or services but is now being disposed of should, under the provisions of IFRS 5, be classified as a current asset on the balance sheet as an asset 'held for sale'.

Differing accounting treatments arise if there are different assessments of materiality. This may result in the same expenditure being reported as an asset in the balance sheet of one company and as an expense in the income statement of another company. In the accounts of a self-employed carpenter, a kit of hand tools that, with careful maintenance, will last many years will, quite rightly, be shown as PPE. Similar assets used by the maintenance department in a large factory will, in all probability, be treated as 'loose tools' and written off as acquired.

Many enterprises have *de minimis* policies, whereby only items exceeding a certain value are treated as PPE; items below the cut-off amount will be expensed through the income statement.

16.3 How is the cost of PPE determined?

16.3.1 Components of cost[2]

According to IAS 16, the cost of an item of PPE comprises its purchase price, including import duties and non-refundable purchase taxes, plus any directly attributable costs of bringing the asset to working condition for its intended use. Examples of such directly attributable costs include:

(a) the costs of site preparation;

(b) initial delivery and handling costs;

(c) installation costs;

(d) professional fees such as for architects and engineers;

(e) the estimated cost of dismantling and removing the asset and restoring the site, to the extent that it is recognised as a provision under IAS 37 *Provisions, Contingent Liabilities and Contingent Assets*.

Administration and other general overhead costs are not a component of the cost of PPE unless they can be directly attributed to the acquisition of the asset or bringing it to its working condition. Similarly, start up and similar pre-production costs do not form part of the cost of an asset unless they are necessary to bring the asset to its working condition.

16.3.2 Self-constructed assets[3]

The cost of a self-constructed asset is determined using the same principles as for an acquired asset. If the asset is made available for sale by the enterprise in the normal course of business then the cost of the asset is usually the same as the cost of producing the asset for sale. This cost would usually be determined under the principles set out in IAS 2 *Inventories*.

The normal profit that an enterprise would make if selling the self-constructed asset would not be recognised in 'cost' if the asset were retained within the enterprise. Following similar principles, where one group company constructs an asset that is used as PPE by another group company, any profit on sale is eliminated in determining the initial carrying value of the asset in the consolidated accounts (this will also clearly affect the calculation of depreciation).

If an item of PPE is exchanged in whole or in part for a dissimilar item of PPE then the cost of such an item is the fair value of the asset received. This is equivalent to the fair value of the asset given up, adjusted for any cash or cash equivalents transferred or received.

16.3.3 Capitalisation of borrowing costs

Where an asset takes a substantial period of time to get ready for its intended use or sale then the enterprise may incur significant borrowing costs in the preparation period. Under the accruals basis of accounting there is an argument that such costs should be included as a directly attributable cost of construction. IAS 23 *Borrowing Costs* was issued to deal with this issue.

The benchmark treatment[4] laid out in IAS 23 is that borrowing costs should be recognised as an expense in the period in which they are incurred, as in this extract from the SudZucker AG 2003 Annual Report: 'Production cost of internally constructed equipment includes the cost of production materials, production wages and an appropriate share of overheads; third party borrowing costs relating to the production are not included.' This is probably because there are a number of potential problems associated with the capitalisation of borrowing costs:

- It can be difficult to identify specific borrowings with specific projects, especially where funds are raised centrally.
- It could be said to be inappropriate that the cost of an asset whose construction is financed by borrowings is different from the cost of another (possibly very similar) asset whose construction is financed by equity.
- There is the possibility that capitalisation of borrowing costs could be used to manipulate the trend of reported profits.

The allowed alternative treatment[5] laid down in IAS 23 is that borrowing costs that are directly attributable to the acquisition, construction or production of a 'qualifying asset' are included in the cost of that asset. A 'qualifying asset' is one that necessarily takes a substantial period of time to get ready for its intended use or sale.

Borrowing costs that would have been avoided if the expenditure on the qualifying asset had not been undertaken are eligible for capitalisation under IAS 23. Where the funds are borrowed specifically for the purpose of obtaining a qualifying asset then the borrowing costs that are eligible for capitalisation are those incurred on the borrowing during the period less any investment income on the temporary investment of those borrowings. Where the funds are borrowed generally and used for the purpose of obtaining a qualifying asset then the enterprise should use a capitalisation rate to determine the borrowing costs that may be capitalised. This rate should be the weighted average of the borrowing costs applicable to the enterprise, other than borrowings made specifically for the purpose of obtaining a qualifying asset. Capitalisation should commence when:

- expenditures for the asset are being incurred;
- borrowing costs are being incurred;
- activities that are necessary to prepare the asset for its intended use or sale are in progress.

When substantially all the activities necessary to prepare the qualifying asset for its intended use or sale are complete then capitalisation should cease.

Many commentators would argue that standardisation in this area is not yet complete given the choice of treatments afforded by IAS 23 and the slightly subjective manner of computing a capitalisation rate in many circumstances. However, many enterprises that prepare financial statements in accordance with international accounting standards take advantage of the alternative treatment that is allowed by IAS 23. The following is an extract from the 2002 financial statements of Coil SA, a company incorporated in Belgium that prepares financial statements in euros in accordance with international accounting standards:

> Borrowing costs are recognised as an expense in the period in which they are incurred. Borrowing costs that relate to the construction or installation of fixed assets are capitalised into the cost of the related fixed asset until the asset is substantially complete.

16.3.4 Subsequent expenditure

Subsequent expenditure relating to an item of PPE that has already been recognised should normally be recognised as an expense in the period in which it is incurred. The exception to this general rule is where it is probable that future economic benefits in excess of the originally assessed standard of performance of the existing asset will, as a result of the expenditure, flow to the enterprise. In these circumstances, the expenditure should be added to the carrying value of the existing asset. Examples of expenditure that might fall to be treated in this way include:

● modification of an item of plant to extend its useful life, including an increase in its capacity;

● upgrading machine parts to achieve a substantial improvement in the quality of output;

● adoption of new production processes enabling a substantial reduction in previously assessed operating costs.

Conversely, expenditure that restores, rather than increases, the originally assessed standard of performance of an asset is written off as an expense in the period incurred.

Some assets have components that require replacement at regular intervals. Two examples of such components would be the lining of a furnace and the roof of a building. IAS 16 states[6] that, provided such components have readily ascertainable costs, they should be accounted for as separate assets because they have useful lives different from the items of PPE to which they relate. This means that when such components are replaced they are accounted for as an asset disposal and acquisition of a new asset.

16.4 What is depreciation?

IAS 16 defines depreciation[7] as the systematic allocation of the depreciable amount of an asset over its life. The depreciable amount is the cost of an asset or other amount substituted for cost in the financial statements, less its residual value.

Note that this definition places an emphasis on the consumption in a particular accounting period rather than an average over the asset's life. We will consider two aspects of the definition: the measure of wearing out; and the useful economic life.

16.4.1 Allocation of depreciable amount

Depreciation is a measure of wearing out that is calculated annually and charged as an expense against profits. Under the 'matching concept', the depreciable amount of the asset is allocated over its productive life.

It is important to make clear what depreciation is **not**:

● It is not 'saving up for a new one'; it is not setting funds aside for the replacement of the existing asset at the end of its life; it is the matching of cost to revenue. The effect is to reduce the profit available for distribution, but this is not accompanied by the setting aside of cash of an equal amount to ensure that liquid funds are available at the end of the asset's life.

● It is not 'a way of showing the real value of assets on the balance sheet' by reducing the cost figure to a realisable value.

We emphasise what depreciation is not because both of these ideas are commonly held by non-accountant users of accounts; it is as well to realise these possible misconceptions when interpreting accounts for non-accountants.

Depreciation is currently conceived as a charge for funds **already expended**, and thus it cannot be considered as the setting aside of funds to meet future expenditure. If we consider it in terms of capital maintenance, then we can see that it results in the maintenance of the initial invested monetary capital of the company. It is concerned with the allocation of that expenditure over a period of time, without having regard for the **value** of the asset at any intermediate period of its life.

Where an asset has been revalued the depreciation is, however, based on the revalued amount. This ensures that capital maintenance continues in monetary terms.

16.4.2 Useful life

IAS 16 defines this as:

(a) the period of time over which an asset is expected to be used by an entity; or

(b) the number of production or similar units expected to be obtained from the asset by an entity.[8]

The IAS 16 definition is based on the premise that almost all assets have a finite useful economic life. This may be true in principle, but it is incredibly difficult in real life to arrive at an average economic life that can be applied to even a single class of assets, e.g. plant. This is evidenced by the accounting policy in the ICI 2003 Annual Report which states:

> *Depreciation* – The Group's policy is to write-off the book value of each tangible non-current asset to its residual value evenly over its estimated remaining life. Reviews are made annually of the estimated remaining lives of individual productive assets, taking account of commercial and technological obsolescence as well as normal wear and tear. Under this policy it becomes impractical to calculate average asset lives exactly; however, the total lives approximate to 31 years for buildings and 13 years for plant and equipment. Depreciation of assets qualifying for grants is calculated on their full cost.

In addition to the practical difficulty of estimating economic lives, there are also exceptions where nil depreciation is charged. Two common exceptions found in the accounts of UK companies relate to freehold land and certain types of property.

16.4.3 Freehold land

Freehold land (but not the buildings thereon) is considered to have an infinite life unless it is held simply for the extraction of minerals, etc. Thus land held for the purpose of, say, mining coal or quarrying gravel will be dealt with for accounting purposes as a coal or gravel deposit. Consequently, although the land may have an infinite life, the deposits will have an economic life only as long as they can be profitably extracted. If the cost of extraction exceeds the potential profit from extraction and sale, the economic life of the quarry has ended. When assessing depreciation for a commercial company, we are concerned only with these private costs and benefits, and not with public costs and benefits which might lead to the quarry being kept open.

The following extract from the Goldfields 2003 Annual Report illustrates accounting policies for land and mining assets.

Land
Land is shown at cost and is not depreciated.

Amortisation and depreciation of mining assets
Amortisation is determined to give a fair and systematic charge in the income statement taking into account the nature of a particular ore body and the method of mining that ore body. To achieve this the following calculation methods are used:

● mining assets, including mine development and infrastructure costs and evaluation costs, are amortised over the lives of the mines using the units of production method, based on estimated proved and probable ore reserves above infrastructure.

● where the group believes it will be reporting significant additional proved and probable ore reserves in the near to medium term, mining assets are amortised over the lives of the mines using the units of production method based on multiples of estimated proved and probable reserves.

● at certain of the group's operations, the calculation of amortisation takes into account future costs which will be incurred to develop all the proved and probable ore reserves.

Proved and probable ore reserves reflect estimated quantities of economically recoverable reserves, which can be recovered in future from known mineral deposits.

Other mining plant and equipment is depreciated on a straight-line basis over their estimated useful lives.

Mineral and surface rights
Mineral and surface rights are recorded at cost of acquisition. When there is little likelihood of a mineral right being exploited, or the value of mineral rights have diminished below cost, a write-down is effected against income in the period that such determination is made.

Few jurisdictions have comprehensive accounting standards for extractive activities. IFRS 6 – *Exploration for and Evaluation of Mineral Resources* – is an interim measure pending a more comprehensive view by the ASB in future. IFRS 6 allows an entity to develop an accounting policy for exploration and evaluation assets without considering the consistency of the policy with the IASB framework. This may mean that for an interim period accounting policies might permit the recognition of both current and non-current assets that do not meet the criteria laid down in the IASB Framework. This is considered by some commentators to be unduly permissive. Indeed, about the only firm requirement IFRS 6 can be said to contain is the requirement to test exploration and evaluation assets for impairment whenever a change in facts and circumstances suggests that impairment exists.

16.4.4 Certain types of property

In some jurisdictions certain types of property, e.g. hotels, are not subject to annual depreciation charges. The rationale for this treatment is that in certain cases regular refurbishment expenditure on such properties is necessary because of their key function within the business. This regular refurbishment expenditure, it is alleged, makes the useful economic lives of such properties infinite, thus removing the need for depreciation.

An example is provided by this extract from the Accounting Policies in the 2003 Annual Report of Punch Taverns plc.

> **Depreciation – Leased estate**
> It is the Group's policy to maintain the properties comprising the licensed estate in such a condition that the residual values of the properties, based on prices prevailing at the time of acquisition or subsequent revaluation, are at least equal to their book values. The primary responsibility for the maintenance of such properties, ensuring that they remain in sound operational condition, is normally that of the lessee as required by their lease contracts with the Group. Having regard to this, it is the opinion of the Directors that depreciation of any such property as required by the Companies Act 1985 and generally accepted accounting practice would not be material ... An annual impairment review is carried out on all properties in accordance with FRS 11 and FRS 15.

IAS 16 does not appear to support non-depreciation of PPE other than freehold land in any circumstances. Paragraph 58 of IAS 16 states:

> Land and buildings are separable assets and are accounted for separately, even when they are acquired together. With some exceptions, such as quarries and sites used for landfill, land has an unlimited useful life and is therefore not depreciated. Buildings have a limited useful life and are therefore depreciable assets. An increase in the value of the land on which the building stands does not affect the determination of the depreciable amount of the building.

It is difficult to see how any company not depreciating the buildings element of its properties could be said to be complying with IAS 16.

16.5 What are the constituents in the depreciation formula?

In order to calculate depreciation it is necessary to determine three factors:

- cost (or revalued amount if the company is following a revaluation policy);
- economic life;
- residual value.

A simple example is the calculation of the depreciation charge for a company that has acquired an asset on 1 January 20X1 for £1,000 with an estimated economic life of four years and an estimated residual value of £200. Applying a straight-line depreciation policy, the charge would be £200 per year using the formula

$$\frac{\text{Cost} - \text{Estimated residual value}}{\text{Estimated economic life}} = \frac{£1,000 - £200}{4} = £200 \text{ per annum}$$

We can see that the charge of £200 is influenced in all cases by the definition of cost; the estimate of the residual value; the estimate of the economic life; and the management decision on depreciation policy.

In addition, if the asset were to be revalued at the end of the second year to £900, then the depreciation for 20X3 and 20X4 would be recalculated using the revised valuation figure. Assuming that the residual value remained unchanged, the depreciation for 20X3 would be:

$$\frac{\text{Revalued asset} - \text{Estimated residual value}}{\text{Estimated economic life}} = \frac{£900 - £200}{2} = £350 \text{ per annum}$$

16.6 How is the useful life of an asset determined?

The IAS 16 definition of useful life is given in section 16.4.2 above. This is not necessarily the total life expectancy of the asset. Most assets become less economically and technologically efficient as they grow older. For this reason, assets may well cease to have an economic life long before their working life is over. It is the responsibility of the preparers of accounts to estimate the economic life of all assets.

It is conventional for enterprises to consider the economic lives of assets by class or category, e.g. buildings, plant, office equipment, or motor vehicles. However, this is not necessarily appropriate, since the level of activity demanded by different users may differ. For example, compare two motor cars owned by a business: one is used by the national sales manager, covering 100,000 miles per annum visiting clients; the other is used by the accountant to drive from home to work and occasionally the bank, covering perhaps one-tenth of the mileage.

In practice, the useful economic life would be determined by reference to factors such as repair costs, the cost and availability of replacements, and the comparative cash flows of existing and alternative assets. The problem of optimal replacement lives is a normal financial management problem; its significance in financial reporting is that the assumptions used within the financial management decision may provide evidence of the expected economic life.

16.6.1 Other factors affecting the useful life figure

We can see that there are technical factors affecting the estimated economic life figure. In addition, other factors have prompted companies to set estimated lives that have no relationship to the active productive life of the asset. One such factor is the wish of management to take into account the effect of inflation. This led some companies to reduce the estimated economic life, so that a higher charge was made against profits during the early period of the asset's life to compensate for the inflationary effect on the cost of replacement. The total charge will be the same, but the timing is advanced. This does not result in the retention of funds necessary to replace; but it does reflect the fact that there is at present no coherent policy for dealing with inflation in the published accounts – consequently, companies resort to *ad hoc* measures that frustrate efforts to make accounts uniform and comparable. *Ad hoc* measures such as these have prompted changes in the standards.

16.7 Residual value

IAS 16 defines residual value as the net amount which an enterprise expects to obtain for an asset at the end of its useful life after deducting the expected costs of disposal. Where PPE is carried at cost the residual value is initially estimated at the date of acquisition. In subsequent periods the estimate of residual value is revised, the revision being based on conditions prevailing at each balance sheet date. Such revisions have an effect on future depreciation charges.

Besides inflation, residual values can be affected by changes in technology and market conditions. For example, during the period 1980–90 the cost of small business computers fell dramatically in both real and monetary terms, with a considerable impact on the residual (or second-hand) value of existing equipment.

16.8 Calculation of depreciation

Having determined the key factors in the computation, we are left with the problem of how to allocate that cost between accounting periods. For example, with an asset having an economic life of five years:

	£
Asset cost	11,000
Estimated residual value	
(no significant change anticipated over useful economic life)	1,000
Depreciable amount	10,000

How should the depreciable amount be charged to the income statement over the five years? IAS 16 tells us that it should be allocated on a systematic basis and the depreciation method used should reflect as fairly as possible the pattern in which the asset's economic benefits are consumed. The two most popular methods are **straight-line**, in which the depreciation is charged evenly over the useful life, and **diminishing balance**, where depreciation is calculated annually on the net written-down amount. In the case above, the calculations would be as in Figure 16.2.

Figure 16.2   Effect of different depreciation methods

	Straight-line (£2,000) £	Diminishing balance (38%) £	Difference £
Cost	11,000	11,000	
Depreciation for year 1	2,000	4,180	2,180
Net book value (NBV)	9,000	6,820	
Depreciation for year 2	2,000	2,592	592
NBV	7,000	4,228	
Depreciation for year 3	2,000	1,606	(394)
NBV	5,000	2,622	
Depreciation for year 4	2,000	996	(1,004)
NBV	3,000	1,626	
Depreciation for year 5	2,000	618	(1,382)
Residual value	1,000	1,008	

The diminishing balance formula was $1 - \sqrt[n]{(\text{Residual value}/\text{Cost})}$

Note that, although the diminishing balance is generally expressed in terms of a percentage, this percentage is arrived at by inserting the economic life into the formula as n; the 38% reflects the expected economic life of five years. As we change the life, so we change the percentage that is applied. The normal rate applied to vehicles is 25% diminishing balance; if we apply that to the cost and residual value in our example, we can see that we would be assuming an economic life of eight years. It is a useful test when using reducing balance percentages to refer back to the underlying assumptions.

We can see that the end result is the same. Thus, £10,000 has been charged against income, but with a dramatically different pattern of income statement charges. The charge for straight-line depreciation in the first year is less than half that for reducing balance.

16.8.1 Arguments in favour of the straight-line method

The method is simple to calculate. However, in these days of calculators and computers this seems a particularly facile argument, particularly when one considers the materiality of the figures.

16.8.2 Arguments in favour of the diminishing balance method

First, the charge reflects the efficiency and maintenance costs of the asset. When new, an asset is operating at its maximum efficiency, which falls as it nears the end of its life. This may be countered by the comment that in year 1 there may be 'teething troubles' with new equipment, which, while probably covered by a supplier's guarantee, will hamper efficiency.

Secondly, the pattern of diminishing balance depreciation gives a net book amount that approximates to second-hand values. For example, with motor cars the initial fall in value is very high.

16.8.3 Other methods of depreciating

Besides straight-line and diminishing balance, there are a number of other methods of depreciating, such as the sum of the units method, the machine-hour method and the annuity method. We will consider these briefly.

Sum of the units method

A compromise between straight-line and reducing balance that is popular in the USA is the sum of the units method. The calculation based on the information in Figure 16.2 is now shown in Figure 16.3. This has the advantage that, unlike diminishing balance, it is simple to obtain the exact residual amount (zero if appropriate), while giving the pattern of high initial charge shown by the diminishing balance approach.

Machine-hour method

The machine-hour system is based on an estimate of the asset's service potential. The economic life is measured not in accounting periods but in working hours, and the depreciation is allocated in the proportion of the actual hours worked to the potential total hours available. This method is commonly employed in aviation, where aircraft are depreciated on the basis of flying hours.

Figure 16.3   Sum of the units method

		£
Cost		11,000
Depreciation for year 1	£10,000 × 5/15	3,333
Net book value (NBV)		7,667
Depreciation for year 2	£10,000 × 4/15	2,667
NBV		5,000
Depreciation for year 3	£10,000 × 3/15	2,000
NBV		3,000
Depreciation for year 4	£10,000 × 2/15	1,333
NBV		1,667
Depreciation for year 5	£10,000 × 1/15	667
Residual value		1,000

Annuity method

With the annuity method, the asset, or rather the amount of capital representing the asset, is regarded as being capable of earning a fixed rate of interest. The sacrifice incurred in using the asset within the business is therefore two-fold: the loss arising from the exhaustion of the service potential of the asset; and the interest forgone by using the funds invested in the business to purchase the fixed asset. With the help of annuity tables, a calculation shows what equal amounts of depreciation, written off over the estimated life of the asset, will reduce the book value to nil, after debiting interest to the asset account on the diminishing amount of funds that are assumed to be invested in the business at that time, as represented by the value of the asset.

Figure 16.4 contains an illustration based on the treatment of a five-year lease which cost the company a premium of £10,000 on 1 January year 1. It shows how the total depreciation charge is computed. Each year the charge for depreciation in the income statement is the equivalent annual amount that is required to repay the investment over the five-year period at a rate of interest of 10% less the notional interest available on the remainder of the invested funds.

Figure 16.4   Annuity method

Year	Opening written-down value £	Notional interest (10%) £	Annual payment £	Net movement £	Closing written-down value £
1	10,000	1,000	(2,638)	(1,638)	8,362
2	8,362	836	(2,638)	(1,802)	6,560
3	6,560	656	(2,638)	(1,982)	4,578
4	4,578	458	(2,638)	(2,180)	2,398
5	2,398	240	(2,638)	(2,398)	Nil

An extract from the annuity tables to obtain the annual equivalent factor for year 5 and assuming a rate of interest of 10% would show:

Year	Annuity $A_{\overline{n}|}^{-1}$
1	1.1000
2	0.5762
3	0.4021
4	0.3155
5	0.2638

Therefore at a rate of interest of 10% five annual payments to repay an investor of £10,000 would each be £2,638.

A variation of this system involves the investment of a sum equal to the net charge in fixed interest securities or an endowment policy, so as to build up a fund that will generate cash to replace the asset at the end of its life.

This last system has significant weaknesses. It is based on the misconception that depreciation is 'saving up for a new one', whereas in reality depreciation is charging against profits funds already expended. It is also dangerous in a time of inflation, since it may lead management not to maintain the capital of the enterprise adequately, in which case they may not be able to replace the assets at their new (inflated) prices.

The annuity method, with its increasing net charge to income, does tend to take inflationary factors into account, but it must be noted that the *total* net profit and loss charge only adds up to the cost of the asset.

16.8.4 Which method should be used?

The answer to this seemingly simple question is 'it depends'. On the matter of depreciation IAS 16 is designed primarily to force a fair charge for the use of assets into the income statement each year, so that the earnings reflect a true and fair view.

Straight-line is most suitable for assets such as leases which have a definite fixed life. It is also considered most appropriate for assets with a short working life, although with motor cars the diminishing balance method is sometimes employed to match second-hand values. Extraction industries (mining, oil wells, quarries, etc.) sometimes employ a variation on the machine-hour system, where depreciation is based on the amount extracted as a proportion of the estimated reserves.

Despite the theoretical attractiveness of other methods the straight-line method is, by a long way, the one in most common use by enterprises that prepare financial statements in accordance with IFRSs. Reasons for this are essentially pragmatic:

● It is the most straightforward to compute.

● In the light of the three additional subjective factors [cost (or revalued amount); residual value; useful life] that need to be estimated, any imperfections in the charge for depreciation caused by the choice of the straight-line method are not likely to be significant. .

The following accounting policy note comes from the financial statements of BorsodChem Rt., a Hungarian enterprise preparing financial statements in accordance with international accounting standards:

Freehold land is not depreciated. Depreciation is provided using the straight-line methods at rates calculated to write off the cost of the asset over its expected economic useful life. The rates used are as follows:

Buildings	2%
Machinery and other equipment	5–15%
Vehicles	15–20%
Computer equipment	33%

16.8.5 Impairment of fixed assets

IAS 36 *Impairment of Assets*[9] deals with the problems of the measurement, recognition and presentation of material reductions in value of non-current assets both tangible and intangible.

Non-current assets will be required to be reviewed for impairment only if there is some indication that impairment has occurred, e.g. slump in property market or expected future losses.

The IASB's aim is to ensure that relevant assets are recorded **at no more than recoverable amount**. This is defined as being the higher of net selling price and value in use. Value in use is defined as the **present value** of future cash flows obtainable from the asset's continued use using a **discount rate** that is equivalent to the rate of return that the market would expect on an equally risky investment.

We will consider impairment of assets in more detail in section 16.10. However, this issue is also relevant to the computation of the depreciation charge. Paragraph 17 of IAS 36 states:

> If there is an indication that an asset may be impaired this may indicate that the remaining useful life, the depreciation method, or the residual value for the asset need to be reviewed and adjusted under the IAS applicable to the asset, even if no impairment loss is recognised for the asset.

In the case of PPE the relevant IAS is IAS 16 and this indicates that an impairment review may well affect future depreciation charges in the income statement, even if no impairment loss is recognised.

16.9 Measurement subsequent to initial recognition

16.9.1 Choice of models

An entity needs to choose either the cost or the revaluation model as its accounting policy for an entire class of PPE. The cost model (definitely the most common) results in an asset being carried at cost less accumulated depreciation and any accumulated impairment losses.

16.9.2 The revaluation model

Under the revaluation model the asset is carried at revalued amount, being its fair value at the date of the revaluation less any subsequent accumulated depreciation and subsequent accumulated impairment losses. The fair value of an asset is defined in IAS 16 as 'the amount for which an asset could be exchanged between knowledgeable and willing parties in an arm's length transaction'. Thus fair value is basically market value. If a market value is not available, perhaps in the case of partly used specialised plant and equipment that is rarely bought and sold other than as new, then IAS 16 requires that revaluation be based on depreciated replacement cost.

EXAMPLE ● An enterprise purchased an item of plant for £12,000 on 1 January 20X1. The plant was depreciated on a straight-line basis over its useful economic life, which was estimated at six years. On 1 January 20X3 the enterprise decided to revalue its plant. No fair value was available for the item of plant that had been purchased for £12,000 on 1 January 20X1 but the replacement cost of the plant at 1 January 20X3 was £21,000.

The carrying value of the plant immediately before the revaluation would have been:

● Cost £12,000

● Accumulated deprecation £4,000 [(£12,000/6) × 2]

● Written-down value £8,000.

Under the principles of IAS 16 the revalued amount would be £14,000 [£21,000 × 4/6]. This amount would be reflected in the financial statements either by:

● showing a revised gross figure of £14,000 and reversing out all the accumulated deprecation charged to date so as to give a carrying value of £14,000; or

● restating both the gross figure and the accumulated depreciation by the proportionate change in replacement cost. This would give a gross figure of £21,000, with accumulated depreciation restated at £7,000 to once again give a net carrying value of £14,000.

16.9.3 Detailed requirements regarding revaluations

The frequency of revaluations depends upon the movements in the fair values of those items of PPE being revalued. In jurisdictions where the rate of price changes is very significant revaluations may be necessary on an annual basis. In other jurisdictions revaluations every three or five years may well be sufficient.

Where an item of PPE is revalued then the entire class of PPE to which that asset belongs should be revalued.[10] A class of PPE is a grouping of assets of a similar nature and use in an enterprise's operations. Examples would include:

● land,

● land and buildings,

● machinery.

This is an important provision because without it enterprises would be able to select which assets they revalued on the basis of best advantage to the balance sheet. Revaluations will usually increase the carrying values of assets and equity and leave borrowings unchanged. Therefore gearing (or leverage) ratios will be reduced. It is important that, if the revaluation route is chosen, assets are revalued on a rational basis.

The following is a further extract from the financial statements of Coil SA, a company incorporated in Belgium that prepares financial statements in euros in accordance with international accounting standards: 'Items of PPE are stated at historical cost modified by revaluation and are depreciated using the straight-line method over their estimated useful lives.'

16.9.4 Accounting for revaluations

When the carrying amount of an asset is increased as a result of a revaluation, the increase should be credited directly to equity under the heading of revaluation surplus. The only exception is where the gain reverses a revaluation decrease previously recognised as an expense **relating to the same asset**.

This means that, in the example we considered under 16.9.2, the revaluation would lead to a credit of £6,000 (£14,000 – £8,000) to equity.

If however the carrying amount of an asset is decreased as a result of a revaluation then the decrease should be recognised as an expense. The only exception is where that asset had previously been revalued. In those circumstances the loss on revaluation is charged against the revaluation surplus to the extent that the revaluation surplus contains an amount **relating to the same asset**.

EXAMPLE ● An enterprise buys freehold land for £100,000 in year 1. The land is revalued to £150,000 in year 3 and £90,000 in year 5. The land is not depreciated.

In year 3 a surplus of £50,000 [£150,000 – £100,000] is credited to equity under the heading 'revaluation surplus'. In year 5 a deficit of £60,000 [£90,000 – £150,000] arises on the second revaluation. £50,000 of this deficit is deducted from the revaluation surplus and £10,000 is charged as an expense. It is worth noting that £10,000 is the amount by which the year 5 carrying amount is lower than the original cost of the land.

Where an asset that has been revalued is sold then the revaluation surplus becomes realised.[11] It may be transferred to retained earnings when this happens but this transfer is not made through the income statement.

Turning again to our example in 16.9.2 let us assume that the plant was sold on 1 January 20X5 for £5,000. The carrying amount of the asset in the financial statements immediately before the sale would be £7,000 [£14,000 – 2 × £3,500]. This means that a loss on sale of £2,000 would be taken to the income statement. The revaluation surplus of £6,000 would be transferred to realised reserves.

IAS 16 allows for the possibility that the revaluation surplus is transferred to realised reserves as the asset is depreciated. To turn once again to our example we see that the revaluation on 1 January 20X3 increased the annual depreciation charge from £2,000 [£12,000/6] to £3,500 [£21,000/6]. Following revaluation an amount equivalent to the 'excess depreciation' may be transferred from the revaluation surplus to realised reserves as the asset is depreciated. This would lead in our example to a transfer of £1,500 each year. Clearly if this occurs then the revaluation surplus that is transferred to realised reserves on sale is £3,000 [£6,000 – (2 × £1,500)].

16.10 IAS 36 *Impairment of Assets*

16.10.1 IAS 36 approach

IAS 36 sets out the principles and methodology for accounting for impairments of non-current assets and goodwill. Where possible, individual non-current assets should be tested for impairment. However, where cash flows do not arise from the use of a single non-current asset, impairment is measured for the smallest group of assets which generates income that is largely independent of the company's other income streams. This smallest group is referred to as a cash generating unit (CGU).

Impairment of an asset, or CGU (if assets are grouped), occurs when:

● the carrying amount of an asset or CGU is greater than its recoverable amount; where
  ● carrying amount is the depreciated historical cost (or depreciated revalued amount);
  ● recoverable amount is the higher of net selling price and value in use; where
    – net selling price is the amount at which an asset could be disposed of, less any direct selling costs, and
    – value in use is the present value of the future cash flows obtainable as a result of an asset's continued use, including those resulting from its ultimate disposal.

When impairment occurs a **revised carrying amount** is calculated for the balance sheet as follows:

Note that it is only necessary to calculate value in use if the carrying amount is greater than net selling price.

The revised carrying amount is then depreciated over the remaining useful economic life.

16.10.2 Dividing activities into CGUs

In order to carry out an impairment review it is necessary to decide how to divide activities into CGUs. There is no single answer to this – it is extremely judgemental, e.g. if the company has multi-retail sites, the cost of preparing detailed cash flow forecasts for each site could favour grouping.

The risk of grouping is that poorly performing operations might be concealed within a CGU and it would be necessary to consider whether there were any commercial reasons for breaking a CGU into smaller constituents, e.g. if a location was experiencing its own unique difficulties such as local competition or inability to obtain planning permission to expand to a more profitable size.

16.10.3 Indications of impairment

A review for impairment is required when there is an indication that an impairment has actually occurred. The following are indicators of impairment:

● External indicators
  – a fall in the market value of the asset
  – material adverse changes in regulatory environment
  – material adverse changes in markets
  – material long-term increases in market rates of return used for discounting.
● Internal indicators
  – material changes in operations
  – major reorganisation
  – loss of key personnel
  – loss or net cash outflow from operating activities if this is expected to continue or is a continuation of a loss-making situation.

If there is such an indication, it is necessary to determine the depreciated historical cost if a single fixed asset, or the net assets employed if a CGU, and compare this with the net realisable value and value in use.

ICI stated in its 2003 Annual Report:

> No depreciation has been provided on land. Impairment reviews are performed where there is an indication of potential impairment. If the carrying value of an asset exceeds its discounted estimated future cash flows the impairment is charged to the profit and loss account.

16.10.4 Value in use calculation

Value in use is arrived at by estimating and discounting the income stream. In some cases a detailed calculation of value in use will not be necessary if a simple estimate is sufficient to demonstrate that either value in use is higher than carrying value, in which case there is no impairment, or value in use is lower than selling price, in which case impairment is measured by reference to selling price.

The **income streams**:

- are likely to follow the way in which management monitors and makes decisions about continuing or closing the different lines of business;
- may often be identified by reference to major products or services;
- should be based on reasonable and supportable assumptions;
- should be consistent with the most up-to-date budgets and plans that have been formally approved by management:
  - if for a period beyond that covered by formal budgets and plans should, unless there are exceptional circumstances, assume a steady or declining growth rate;[12]
- should be projected cash flows unadjusted for risk, discounted at a rate of return expected from a similarly risky investment or should be projected risk-adjusted pre-tax cash flows discounted at a risk-free rate.

The **discount rate** should be:

- calculated on a pre-tax basis;
- an estimate of the rate that the market would expect on an equally risky investment excluding the effects of any risk for which the cash flows have been adjusted:[13]
  - increased to reflect the way the market would assess the specific risks associated with the projected cash flows
  - reduced to a risk-free rate if the cash flows have been adjusted for risk.

The following illustration is from the Roche Holdings Ltd 2003 Annual Report:

> When the recoverable amount of an asset, being the higher of its net selling price and its value in use, is less than the carrying amount, then the carrying amount is reduced to its recoverable value. This reduction is reported in the income statement as an impairment loss. Value in use is calculated using estimated cash flows, generally over a five-year period, with extrapolating projections for subsequent years. These are discounted using an appropriate long-term pre-tax interest rate. When an impairment arises the useful life of the asset in question is reviewed and, if necessary, the future depreciation/amortisation charge is accelerated.

16.10.5 Treatment of impairment losses

If the depreciated historical cost (or net assets employed) exceeds the higher of net realisable value and value in use, then an impairment loss has occurred. The accounting treatment of such a loss is as follows:

Asset not previously revalued

An impairment loss should be recognised in the income statement in the year in which the impairment arises.

Asset previously revalued

An impairment loss on a revalued asset is effectively treated as a revaluation deficit. As we have already seen, this means that the decrease should be recognised as an expense. The only exception is where that asset had previously been revalued. In those circumstances the loss on revaluation is charged against the revaluation surplus to the extent that the revaluation surplus contains an amount **relating to the same asset**.

Allocation of impairment losses

Where an impairment loss arises the loss should ideally be set against the specific asset to which it relates. Where the loss cannot be identified as relating to a specific asset, it should be apportioned within the CGU to reduce the most subjective values first, as follows:

● first, to reduce any goodwill within the CGU;

● then to the unit's other assets, allocated on a pro rata basis;

● however, no individual asset should be reduced below the higher of:
  – its net selling price (if determinable)
  – its value in use (if determinable)
  – zero.

Restoration of past impairment losses

Past impairment losses in respect of a tangible fixed asset may be restored where the recoverable amount increases due to an improvement in economic conditions or a change in use of the asset. Such a restoration should be reflected in the income statement to the extent of the original impairment previously charged to the income statement, adjusting for depreciation which would have been charged otherwise in the intervening period.

16.10.6 Illustration of data required for an impairment review

Pronto SA has a product line producing wooden models of athletes for export. The carrying amount of the net assets employed on the line as at 31 December 20X3 was £114,500. The scrap value of the net assets at 31 December 20X6 is estimated to be £5,000.

There is an indication that the export market will be adversely affected in 20X6 by competition from plastic toy manufacturers. This means that the net assets employed to produce this product might have been impaired.

The finance director estimated the net realisable value of the net assets at 31 December 20X3 to be £70,000. The value in use is now calculated to check if it is higher or lower than £70,000. If it is higher it will be compared with the carrying amount to see if impairment has occurred; if it is lower the net realisable value will be compared with the carrying amount.

Pronto SA has prepared budgets for the years ended 31 December 20X4, 20X5 and 20X6. The assumptions underlying the budgets are as follows:

Unit costs and revenue:

	£
Selling price	10.00
Buying in cost	(4.00)
Production cost: material, labour, overhead	(0.75)
Head office overheads apportioned	(0.25)
Cash inflow per model	5.00

Estimated sales volumes:

	20X3	20X4	20X5	20X6
Estimated at 31 December 20X2	6,000	8,000	11,000	14,000
Revised estimate at 31 December 20X3	—	8,000	11,000	4,000

Determining the discount rate to be used:

	20X4	20X5	20X6
The rate obtainable elsewhere at the same level of risk is	10%	10%	10%

The discount factors to be applied to each year are then calculated using cost of capital discount rates as follows:

20X4	$1/1.1$	= 0.909
20X5	$1/(1.1)^2$	= 0.826
20X6	$1/(1.1)^3$	= 0.751

16.10.7 Illustrating calculation of value in use

Before calculating value in use, it is necessary to ensure that the assumptions underlying the budgets are reasonable, e.g. is the selling price likely to be affected by competition in 20X6 in addition to loss of market? Is the selling price in 20X5 likely to be affected? Is the estimate of scrap value reasonably accurate? How sensitive is value in use to the scrap value? Is it valid to assume that the cash flows will occur at year-ends? How accurate is the cost of capital? Will components making up the income stream, e.g. sales, materials, labour be subject to different rates of inflation?

Assuming that no adjustment is required to the budgeted figures provided above, the estimated income streams are discounted using the normal DCF approach as follows:

	20X4	20X5	20X6
Sales (models)	8,000	11,000	4,000
Income per model	£5	£5	£5
Income stream (£)	40,000	55,000	20,000
Estimated scrap proceeds			5,000
Cash flows to be discounted	40,000	55,000	25,000
Discounted (using cost of capital factors)	0.909	0.826	0.751
Present value	36,360	45,430	18,775

Value in use = £100,565

16.10.8 Illustration determining the *revised* carrying amount

If the carrying amount at the balance sheet date exceeds net realisable value and value in use, it is revised to an amount which is the higher of net realisable value and value in use. For Pronto SA:

	£
Carrying amount as at 31 December 20X3	114,500
Net realisable value	70,000
Value in use	100,565
Revised carrying amount	**100,565**

16.11 IFRS 5 *Non-Current Assets Held for Sale and Discontinued Operations*

IFRS 5 sets out requirements for the classification, measurement and presentation of non-current assets held for sale. The requirements which replaced IAS 35 *Discontinuing Operations* were discussed in Chapter 8. The IFRS is the result of the joint short-term project to resolve differences between IFRSs and US GAAP.

Classification as 'held for sale'

The IFRS (para. 6) classifies a non-current asset as 'held for sale' if its carrying amount will be recovered principally through a sale transaction rather than through continuing use. The criteria for classification as 'held for sale' are:

- the asset must be available for immediate sale in its present condition, and
- its sale must be *highly probable*.

The criteria for a sale to be highly probable are:

- the appropriate level of management must be committed to a plan to sell the asset;
- an active programme to locate a buyer and complete the plan must have been initiated;
- the asset must be actively marketed for sale at a price that is reasonable in relation to its current fair value;
- the sale should be expected to qualify for recognition as a completed sale within one year from the date of classification unless the delay is caused by events or circumstances beyond the entity's control and there is sufficient evidence that the entity remains committed to its plan to sell the asset; and
- actions required to complete the plan should indicate that it is unlikely that significant changes to the plan will be made or that the plan will be withdrawn.

Measurement and presentation of assets held for sale

The IFRS requires that assets 'held for sale' should:

- be measured at the lower of carrying amount and *fair value* less costs to sell;
- not continue to be depreciated; and
- be presented separately on the face of the balance sheet.

The following additional disclosures are required in the notes in the period in which a non-current asset has been either classified as held for sale or sold:

- a description of the non-current asset;
- a description of the facts and circumstances of the sale;
- the expected manner and timing of that disposal;
- the gain or loss if not separately presented on the face of the income statement; and
- the caption in the income statement that includes that gain or loss.

16.12 Disclosure requirements

For each class of PPE the financial statements need to disclose:

- the measurement bases used for determining the gross carrying amount;
- the depreciation methods used;
- the useful lives or the depreciation rates used;
- the gross carrying amount and the accumulated depreciation (aggregated with accumulated impairment losses) at the beginning and end of the period;
- a reconciliation of the carrying amount at the beginning and end of the period.

The style employed by British Sky Broadcasting Group Plc in its 2003 accounts is almost universally employed for this:

Tangible fixed assets (or PPE)
The movements in the year were as follows:

	Freehold land and buildings £m	*Short leasehold improvements* £m	*Equipment, fixtures and fittings* £m	*Assets in course of construction*	*Total* £m
Group					
Cost					
Beginning of year	37.9	83.3	554.4	29.9	705.5
Additions	0.4	3.2	73.0	24.8	101.4
Disposals	—	—	(10.9)	—	(10.9)
Transfers	—	—	25.8	(25.8)	—
End of year	**38.3**	**86.5**	**642.3**	**28.9**	**796.0**

	Freehold land and buildings £m	*Short leasehold improvements* £m	*Equipment, fixtures and fittings* £m	*Assets in course of construction*	*Total* £m
Depreciation					
Beginning of year	6.0	43.3	313.2	—	362.5
Charge	2.3	4.0	91.6	—	97.9
Disposals	—	—	(10.6)	—	(10.6)
End of year	**8.3**	**47.3**	**394.2**	**—**	**449.8**
Net book value					
Beginning of year	31.9	40.0	241.2	29.9	343.0
End of year	**30.0**	**39.2**	**248.1**	**28.9**	**346.2**

Additionally the financial statements should disclose:

- the existence and amounts of restrictions on title, and PPE pledged as security for liabilities;
- the accounting policy for the estimated costs of restoring the site of items of PPE;
- the amount of expenditures on account of PPE in the course of construction;
- the amount of commitments for the acquisition of PPE.

16.13 Government grants towards the cost of PPE

The accounting treatment of government grants is covered by IAS 20. The basis of the standard is the accruals concept, which requires the matching of cost and revenue so as to recognise both in the income statements of the periods to which they relate. This should, of course, be tempered with the prudence concept, which requires that revenue is not anticipated. Therefore, in the light of the complex conditions usually attached to grants, credit should not be taken until receipt is assured.

Similarly, there may be a right to recover the grant wholly or partially in the event of a breach of conditions, and on that basis these conditions should be regularly reviewed and, if necessary, provision made.

Should the tax treatment of a grant differ from the accounting treatment, then the effect of this would be accounted for in accordance with IAS 12 *Income Taxes*.

IAS 20

Government grants should be recognised in the income statement so as to match the expenditure towards which they are intended to contribute. If this is retrospective, they should be recognised in the period in which they became receivable.

Grants in respect of PPE should be recognised over the useful economic lives of those assets, thus matching the depreciation or amortisation.

IAS 20 outlines two acceptable methods of presenting grants relating to assets in the balance sheet:

(a) The first method sets up the grant as deferred income, which is recognised as income on a systematic and rational basis over the useful life of the asset.

> EXAMPLE ● An enterprise purchased a machine for £60,000 and received a grant of £20,000 towards its purchase. The machine is depreciated over four years.
>
> The 'deferred income method' would result in an initial carrying amount for the machine of £60,000 and a deferred income credit of £20,000. In the first year of use of the plant the depreciation charge would be £15,000. £5,000 of the deferred income would be recognised as a credit in the income statement, making the net charge to income £10,000. At the end of the first year the carrying amount of the plant would be £45,000 and the deferred income included in the balance sheet would be £15,000.

(b) The second method deducts the grant in arriving at the carrying amount of the relevant asset. If we were to apply this method to the above example then the initial carrying amount of the asset would be £40,000. The depreciation charged in the first year would be £10,000. This is the same as the net charge to income under the 'deferred credit' method. The closing carrying amount of the plant would be £30,000. This is of course the carrying amount under the 'deferred income method' (£45,000) less the closing deferred income under the 'deferred income method' (£15,000).

The following are an accounting policy and balance sheet note from the 2002 Annual Report of Coil SA:

Government grants are not recognised until there is reasonable assurance that the grants will be received and that the Company will comply with the applicable conditions. Grants are recognised in the Profit & Loss Account on a systematic basis by matching them with the related costs.

Note 16. GOVERNMENT GRANT RELATED TO ASSETS

€'000	2002	2001
Balance at 1st January	152	175
Grants received during the year	—	—
Amortised to income statement	(22)	(23)
Balance at 31st December	130	152

16.14 Investment properties

While IAS 16 requires all PPEs to be subjected to a systematic depreciation charge, this may be considered inappropriate for properties held as assets but not employed in the normal activities of the enterprise, rather being held as investments. For such properties a more relevant treatment is to take account of the current market value of the property. The accounting treatment is set out in IAS 40 *Investment Property*.

Such properties may be held either as a main activity (e.g. by a property investment company) or by a company whose main activity is not the holding of such properties. In each case the accounting treatment is similar.

Definition of an investment property[14]

For the purposes of the statement, an investment property is property held (by the owner or by the lessee under a finance lease) to earn rentals or capital appreciation or both.

Investment property does **not** include:

(a) property held for use in the production or supply of goods or services or for administrative purposes (dealt with in IAS 16);

(b) property held for sale in the ordinary course of business (dealt with in IAS 2);

(c) property being constructed or developed for future use as investment property – IAS 16 applies to such property until the construction or development is complete, at which time the property becomes investment property and IAS 40 applies. However, IAS 40 does apply to existing investment property that is being redeveloped for continued future use as investment property;

(d) an interest held by a lessee under an operating lease, even if the interest was a long-term interest acquired in exchange for a large up-front payment (dealt with in IAS 17);

(e) forests and similar regenerative natural resources (dealt with in IAS 41 *Agriculture*); and

(f) mineral rights, the exploration for and development of minerals, oil, natural gas and similar non-regenerative natural resources (dealt with in project on Extractive Industries).

Accounting models

Under IAS 40, an enterprise must choose either:

- a fair value model: investment property should be measured at fair value and changes in fair value should be recognised in the income statement; or

- a cost model (the same as the benchmark treatment in IAS 16 *Property, Plant and Equipment*): investment property should be measured at depreciated cost (less any accumulated impairment losses). An enterprise that chooses the cost model should disclose the fair value of its investment property.

An enterprise should apply the model chosen to all its investment property. A change from one model to the other model should be made only if the change will result in a more appropriate presentation. The standard states that this is highly unlikely to be the case for a change from the fair value model to the cost model.

In exceptional cases, there is clear evidence when an enterprise that has chosen the fair value model first acquires an investment property (or when an existing property first becomes investment property following the completion of construction or development, or after a change in use) that the enterprise will not be able to determine the fair value of the investment property reliably on a continuing basis. In such cases, the enterprise measures that investment property using the benchmark treatment in IAS 16 until the disposal of the investment property. The residual value of the investment property should be assumed to be zero. The enterprise measures all its other investment property at fair value.

16.15 Effect of accounting policy for PPE on the interpretation of the financial statements

A number of difficulties exist when attempting to carry out inter-firm comparisons using the external information that is available to a shareholder.

16.15.1 Effect of inflation on the carrying value of the asset

The most serious difficulty is the effect of inflation, which makes the charges based on historical cost inadequate. Companies have followed various practices to take account of inflation. None of these is as effective as an acceptable surrogate for index adjustment using specific asset indices on a systematic annual basis: this is the only way to ensure uniformity and comparability of the cost/valuation figure upon which the depreciation charge is based.

The method that is currently allowable under IAS 16 is to revalue the assets. This is a partial answer, but it results in lack of comparability of ratios such as gearing, or leverage.

16.15.2 Effect of revaluation on ratios

The rules of double entry require that when an asset is revalued the 'profit' (or, exceptionally, 'loss') must be credited somewhere. As it is not a 'realised' profit, it would not be appropriate to credit the income statement, so a 'revaluation reserve' must be created. As the asset is depreciated, this reserve may be realised to income; similarly, when an asset is ultimately disposed of, any residue relevant to that asset may be taken into income.

One significant by-product of revaluing assets is the effect on gearing. The revaluation reserve, while not distributable, forms part of the shareholders' funds and thus improves the debt/equity ratio. Care must therefore be taken in looking at the revaluation policies and reserves when comparing the gearing or leverage of companies.

The problem is compounded because the carrying value may be amended at random periods and on a selective category of asset.

16.15.3 Choice of depreciation method

There are a number of acceptable depreciation methods that may give rise to very different patterns of debits against the profits of individual years.

16.15.4 Inherent imprecision in estimating economic life

One of the greatest difficulties with depreciation is that it is inherently imprecise. The amount of depreciation depends on the estimate of the economic life of assets, which is affected not only by the durability and workload of the asset, but also by external factors beyond the control of management. Such factors may be technological, commercial or economic. Here are some examples:

- the production by a competitor of a new product rendering yours obsolete, e.g. watches with battery-powered movements replacing those with mechanical movements;
- the production by a competitor of a product at a price lower than your production costs, e.g. imported goods from countries where costs are lower;
- changes in the economic climate which reduce demand for your product.

This means that the interpreter of accounts must pay particular attention to depreciation policies, looking closely at the market where the enterprise's business operates. However, this understanding is not helped by the lack of requirement to disclose specific rates of depreciation and the basis of computation of residual values. Without such information the potential effects of differences between policies adopted by competing enterprises cannot be accurately assessed.

16.15.5 Mixed values in the balance sheet

The effect of depreciation on the balance sheet is also some cause for concern. The net book amount shown for non-current assets is the result of deducting accumulated depreciation from cost (or valuation); it is not intended to be (although many non-accountants assume it is) an estimate of the value of the underlying assets. The valuation of a business based on the balance sheet is extremely difficult.

16.15.6 Different policies may be applied within the same sector

Inter-company comparisons are even more difficult. Two enterprises following the historical cost convention may own identical assets, which, as they were purchased at different times, may well appear as dramatically different figures in the accounts. This is particularly true of interests in land and buildings.

16.15.7 Effect on the return on capital employed

There is an effect not only on the net asset value, but also on the return on capital employed. To make a fair assessment of return on capital it is necessary to know the current replacement cost of the underlying assets, but, under present conventions, up-to-date valuations are required only for investment properties.

16.15.8 Effect on EPS

IAS 16 is concerned to ensure that the earnings of an enterprise reflect a fair charge for the use of the assets by the enterprise. This should ensure an accurate calculation of earnings per share. But there is a weakness here. If assets have increased in value without revaluations, then depreciation will be based on the historical cost.

Summary

Before IAS 16 there were significant problems in relation to the accounting treatment of PPE such as the determination of a cost figure and the adjustment for inflation; companies providing nil depreciation on certain types of asset; revaluations being made selectively and not kept current.

With IAS 16 the IASC has made the accounts more consistent and comparable. This standard has resolved some of these problems, principally requiring companies to provide for depreciation and if they have a policy of revaluation to keep such valuations reasonably current and applied to all assets within a class, i.e. removing the ability to cherry-pick which assets to revalue.

However, certain difficulties remain for the user of the accounts in that there are different management policies on the method of depreciation, which can have a major impact on the profit for the year; subjective assessments of economic life that may be reviewed each year with an impact on profits; and inconsistencies such as the presence of modified historical costs and historical costs in the same balance sheet. In addition, with pure historical cost accounting, where non-current asset carrying values are based on original cost, no pretence is made that non-current asset net book amounts have any relevance to current values. The investor is expected to know that the depreciation charge is arithmetical in character and will not wholly provide the finance for tomorrow's assets or ensure maintenance of the business's operational base. To give recognition to these factors requires the investor to grapple with the effects of lost purchasing power through inflation; the effect of changes in supply and demand on replacement prices; technological change and its implication for the company's competitiveness; and external factors such as exchange rates. To calculate the effect of these variables necessitates not only considerable mental agility, but also far more information than is contained in a set of accounts. This is an area that needs to be revisited by the standard setters.

REVIEW QUESTIONS

I   Define PPE and explain how materiality affects the concept of PPE.

2   Define depreciation. Explain what assets need not be depreciated and list the main methods of calculating depreciation.

3   What is meant by the phrases 'useful life' and 'residual value'?

4   Define 'cost' in connection with PPE.

5   What effect does revaluing assets have on gearing (or leverage)?

6   How should grants received towards expenditure on PPE be treated?

7   Define an investment property and explain its treatment in financial statements.

8   'Depreciation should mean that a company has sufficient resources to replace assets at the end of their economic lives.' Discuss.

EXERCISES

An extract from the solution is provided in the Appendix at the end of the text for exercises marked with an asterisk (*).

Question I

(a) Discuss why IAS 40 *Investment Property* was produced.

(b) Universal Entrepreneurs plc has the following items on its PPE list:
   (i)   £1,000,000 – the right to extract sandstone from a particular quarry. Geologists predict that extraction at the present rate may be continued for ten years.
   (ii) £5,000,000 – a freehold property, let to a subsidiary on a full repairing lease negotiated on arm's-length terms for fifteen years. The building is a new one, erected on a greenfield site at a cost of £4,000,000.
   (iii) A fleet of motor cars used by company employees. These have been purchased under a contract which provides a guaranteed part exchange value of 60% of cost after two years' use.
   (iv) A company helicopter with an estimated life of 150,000 flying hours.
   (v)   A nineteen-year lease on a property let out at arm's-length rent to another company.

Required:
Advise the company on the depreciation policy it ought to adopt for each of the above assets.

(c) The company is considering revaluing its interests in land and buildings, which comprise freehold and leasehold properties, all used by the company or its subsidiaries.

Required:
Discuss the consequences of this on the depreciation policy of the company and any special instructions that need to be given to the valuer.

Question 2

Mercury

You have been given the task, by one of the partners of the firm of accountants for which you work, of assisting in the preparation of a trend statement for a client.

Mercury has been in existence for four years. Figures for the three preceding years are known but those for the fourth year need to be calculated. Unfortunately, the supporting workings for the preceding years' figures cannot be found and the client's own ledger accounts and workings are not available.

One item in particular, plant, is causing difficulty and the following figures have been given to you:

12 months ended 31 March	20X6	20X7	20X8	20X9
	£	£	£	£
(A) Plant at cost	80,000	80,000	90,000	?
(B) Accumulated depreciation	(16,000)	(28,800)	(28,080)	?
(C) Net (written down) value	64,000	51,200	61,920	?

The only other information available is that disposals have taken place at the beginning of the financial years concerned:

	Date of		Original	Sales
	Disposal	Original acquisition	cost	proceeds
	12 months ended 31 March		£	£
First disposal	20X8	20X6	15,000	8,000
Second disposal	20X8	20X6	30,000	21,000

Plant sold was replaced on the same day by new plant. The cost of the plant which replaced the first disposal is not known but the replacement for the second disposal is known to have cost £50,000.

Required:
(a) Identify the method of providing for depreciation on plant employed by the client, stating how you have arrived at your conclusion.
(b) Show how the figures shown at line (B) for each of the years ended 31 March 20X6, 20X7 and 20X8 were calculated. Extend your workings to cover the year ended 31 March 20X9.
(c) Produce the figures that should be included in the blank spaces on the trend statement at lines (A), (B) and (C) for the year ended 31 March 20X9.
(d) Calculate the profit or loss arising on each of the two disposals.

* Question 3

In the year to 31 December 20X9, Amy bought a new machine and made the following payments in relation to it:

	£	£
Cost as per supplier's list	12,000	
Less: Agreed discount	1,000	11,000
Delivery charge		100
Erection charge		200
Maintenance charge		300
Additional component to increase capacity		400
Replacement parts		250

Required:
(a) State and justify the cost figure which should be used as the basis for depreciation.
(b) What does depreciation do, and why is it necessary?
(c) Briefly explain, without numerical illustration, how the straight-line and diminishing balance methods of depreciation work. What different assumptions does each method make?
(d) Explain the term 'objectivity' as used by accountants. To what extent is depreciation objective?
(e) It is common practice in published accounts in Germany to use the diminishing balance method for PPE in the early years of an asset's life, and then to change to the straight-line method as soon as this would give a higher annual charge. What do you think of this practice? Refer to relevant accounting conventions in your answer.

(ACCA)

* Question 4

The finance director of the Small Machine Parts Ltd company is considering the acquisition of a lease of a small workshop in a warehouse complex that is being redeveloped by City Redevelopers Ltd at a steady rate over a number of years. City Redevelopers are granting such leases for five years on payment of a premium of £20,000.

The accountant has obtained estimates of the likely maintenance costs and disposal value of the lease during its five-year life. He has produced the following table and suggested to the finance director that the annual average cost should be used in the financial accounts to represent the depreciation charge in the profit and loss account.

Table prepared to calculate the annual average cost

Years of life	1	2	3	4	5
	£	£	£	£	£
Purchase price	20,000	20,000	20,000	20,000	20,000
Maintenance/repairs					
Year 2		1,000	1,000	1,000	1,000
3			1,500	1,500	1,500
4				1,850	1,850
5					2,000
	20,000	21,000	22,500	24,350	26,350
Resale value	11,500	10,000	8,010	5,350	350
Net cost	8,500	11,000	14,490	19,000	26,000
Annual average cost	8,500	5,500	4,830	4,750	5,200

The finance director, however, was considering whether to calculate the depreciation chargeable using the annuity method with interest at 15%.

Required:
(a) Calculate the entries that would appear in the profit and loss account of Small Machine Parts Ltd for each of the five years of the life of the lease for the amortisation charge, the interest element in the depreciation charge and the income from secondary assets using the ANNUITY METHOD. Calculate the net profit for each of the five years assuming that the operating cash flow is estimated to be £25,000 per year.

(b) Discuss briefly which of the two methods you would recommend.
The present value at 15% of £1 per annum for five years is £3.35214.
The present value at 15% of £1 received at the end of year 5 is £0.49717.
Ignore taxation.

(ACCA)

Question 5

Simple SA has just purchased a roasting/salting machine to produce roasted walnuts. The finance director asks for your advice on how the company should calculate the depreciation on this machine. Details are as follows:

Cost of machine	SF800,000
Residual value	SF104,000
Estimated life	4 years
Annual profits	SF2,000,000
Annual turnover from machine	SF850,000

Required:
(a) Calculate the annual depreciation charge using the straight-line method and the reducing balance method. Assume that an annual rate of 40% is applicable for the reducing balance method.
(b) Comment upon the validity of each method, taking into account the type of business and the effect each method has on annual profits. Are there any other methods which would be more applicable?

Question 6

(a) IAS 16 Property, Plant and Equipment requires that where there has been a permanent diminution in the value of property, plant and equipment, the carrying amount should be written down to the recoverable amount. The phrase 'recoverable amount' is defined in IAS 16 as 'the amount which the enterprise expects to recover from the future use of an asset, including its residual value on disposal'. The issues of how one identifies an impaired asset, the measurement of an asset when impairment has occurred and the recognition of impairment losses were not adequately dealt with by the standard. As a result the International Accounting Standards Committee issued IAS 36 *Impairment of Assets* in order to address the above issues.

Required:
(i) Describe the circumstances which indicate that an impairment loss relating to an asset may have occurred.
(ii) Explain how IAS 36 deals with the recognition and measurement of the impairment of assets.

(b) AB, a public limited company, has decided to comply with IAS 36 Impairment of Assets. The following information is relevant to the impairment review:
(i) Certain items of machinery appeared to have suffered a permanent diminution in value. The inventory produced by the machines was being sold below its cost and this occurrence had affected the value of the productive machinery. The carrying value at historical cost of these machines is $290,000 and their net selling price is estimated at $120,000. The anticipated net cash inflows from the machines is now $100,000 per annum for the next three years. A market discount rate of 10% per annum is to be used in any present value computations.

(ii) AB acquired a car taxi business on 1 January 20X1 for $230,000. The values of the assets of the business at that date based on net selling prices were as follows:

	$000
Vehicles (12 vehicles)	120
Intangible assets (taxi licence)	30
Trade receivables	10
Cash	50
Trade payables	(20)
	190

On 1 February 20X1, the taxi company had three of its vehicles stolen. The net selling value of these vehicles was $30,000 and because of non-disclosure of certain risks to the insurance company, the vehicles were uninsured. As a result of this event, AB wishes to recognise an impairment loss of $45,000 (inclusive of the loss of the stolen vehicles) due to the decline in the value in use of the cash generating unit, that is the taxi business. On 1 March 20X1 a rival taxi company commenced business in the same area. It is anticipated that the business revenue of AB will be reduced by 25% leading to a decline in the present value in use of the business, which is calculated at $150,000. The net selling value of the taxi licence has fallen to $25,000 as a result of the rival taxi operator. The net selling values of the other assets have remained the same as at 1 January 20X1 throughout the period.

Required:
Describe how AB should treat the above impairments of assets in its financial statements.

(In part (b) (ii) you should show the treatment of the impairment loss at 1 February 20X1 and 1 March 20X1.)

(ACCA)

References

1 IAS 16 *Property, Plant and Equipment*, IASB, revised 2004, para 6.
2 *Ibid.*, para 16.
3 *Ibid.*, para 22.
4 IAS 23 *Borrowing Costs*, IASB, revised 2004, para 7.
5 *Ibid.*, para 11.
6 IAS 16 *Property, Plant and Equipment*, IASB, revised 2004, para 18.
7 *Ibid.*, para 6.
8 *Ibid.*, para 6.
9 IAS 36 *Impairment of Assets*, IASB, 2004.
10 IAS 16 *Property, Plant and Equipment*, IASB, revised 2004, para 29.
11 *Ibid.*, para 41.
12 IAS 36 *Impairment of Assets*, IASB, 2004, para 33.
13 *Ibid.*, paras 55–56.
14 IAS 40 *Investment Property*, IASB, 2004.

CHAPTER **17**

Leasing

17.1 Introduction

This chapter introduces the accounting principles and policies that apply to lease agreements primarily from the viewpoint of the lessee. We are interested in developing a wider understanding of leasing and leasing-related issues, so that you can understand how they should be represented in the financial statements and why a company might favour a particular type of lease agreement.

In this chapter we consider the following:

- Leasing – an introduction
- IAS 17 – the controversy
- IAS 17 – classification of a lease
- IAS 17 – accounting for leases by lessees
- Leasing – a form of off balance sheet financing

We must understand not only what a lease is and the mechanical adjustments required to account for any given leasing agreement in the financial statements, but also the economic consequences of the accounting treatment that is applied and the impact of these economic consequences on company behaviour.

17.2 Background to leasing

In this section we consider the nature of the lease; historical developments in leasing; reasons for its popularity; and why it was necessary to introduce IAS 17.

17.2.1 What is a lease?

IAS 17 *Leases* provides the following definition:

> A *lease* is an agreement whereby the lessor conveys to the lessee in return for a payment or series of payments the right to use an asset for an agreed period of time.

In practice, there might well be more than two parties involved in a lease. For example, on leasing a car the parties involved are the motor dealer, the finance company and the company using the car.

Some leases will give the lessee the option to purchase the asset at the end of the lease term, or may require the lessee to purchase the asset at the end of the lease term. In some countries an agreement where legal title will pass to the lessee is known as a hire purchase contract.

17.2.2 Historical developments in leasing

The growth in the leasing industry until the advent of IAS 17, and indeed after its introduction, was staggering.[1] Statistics produced by the Finance and Leasing Association, whose members account for 80% of all leasing in the UK, show[2] that the cost of assets acquired for leasing each year rose from £288m in 1973 to £2,894m in 1983 to £10,200m in 1991. In fact, it was estimated that in 1985 the value of leased equipment represented over 20% of capital expenditure in the UK.[3]

17.2.3 Why did leasing become popular?

In the UK, there were two major reasons: the tax advantage to the lessor; and the commercial advantage to the lessee.

Tax advantage

The government is responsible for the initial stimulus to the leasing industry. In 1972, first year allowances (FYAs) on equipment were increased to 100%. These allowances could be offset against taxable profits, which reduced a company's tax bill.

Companies, especially in the manufacturing sector, which had sustained tax losses in preceding years could not utilise the tax benefits of FYAs. This resulted in lessors claiming the FYAs and then leasing out equipment to these other companies at a reduced rental, thus enabling both lessors and lessees to benefit from a leasing agreement.

The leasing industry flourished even more in times of high interest rates. In these periods, lessors can achieve even greater cash flow benefits by deferring tax payments. Consequently, lessors are even more committed to leasing.

Many of these tax advantages were removed by the Finance Act 1984. This implemented a gradual reduction in the corporation tax rate and a gradual removal of FYAs. Some other countries had similar or alternative tax advantages.

Commercial advantage

Despite the Finance Act 1984, there are still a number of advantages associated with leases. These are attributable in part to the ability to spread cash payments over the lease period instead of making a one-off lump sum payment. They include the following:

- **Cash flow management**. If cash is used to purchase non-current assets, it is not available for the normal operating activities of a company.

- **Conservation of capital**. Lines of credit may be kept open and may be used for purposes where finance might not be available easily (e.g. financing working capital).

- **Continuity**. The lease agreement is itself a line of credit that cannot easily be withdrawn or terminated due to external factors, in contrast to an overdraft that can be called in by the lender.

- **Flexibility of the asset base**. The asset base can be more easily expanded and contracted. In addition, the lease payments can be structured to match the income pattern of the lessee.

- **Off balance sheet financing**. Leasing provides the lessee with the possibility of off balance sheet financing,[4] whereby a company has the use of an economic resource that does not appear in the balance sheet, with the corresponding omission of the liability.

17.2.4 Why was IAS 17 necessary?

As with many of the standards, action was required because there was no uniformity in the treatment and disclosure of leasing transactions. The need became urgent following the massive growth in the leasing industry and the growth in off balance sheet financing. In the former case, leasing had become a material economic resource; in the latter case, the accounting treatment of the lease transaction was seen to distort the financial reports of a company so that they did not represent a true and fair view of its commercial activities.

However, for the first time attention was paid to the economic consequences of introducing a standard, the ASC in the UK expressing a concern that the standard might have undesirable economic consequences.[5] (The UK standard, SSAP 21, was similar in principle to IAS 17.) The inclusion of the lease obligation might affect the lessee company's gearing adversely and, indeed, cause it to exceed its legal borrowing powers under the Memorandum and Articles or under a loan agreement. The Memorandum and Articles might, for example, have a stipulation that the total borrowings should not exceed the total shareholders' funds. In the event, the commercial reasons for leasing and the capacity of the leasing industry to structure lease agreements to circumvent the standard have prevented a reduction in lease activity. Evidence of lessors varying the term of the lease agreements is supported by Cranfield[6] and by Abdel-Khalik et al.[7]

Macdonald[8] made the point that most transactions will be undertaken with a commercial purpose; some may be undertaken, or undertaken in a particular form, so as to change materially the accounting message communicated by the accounts; even those commercially motivated may be accounted for in one way rather than another so as to improve the accounting message. Macdonald also observed that, while it might be thought that the overriding requirement of the fair view could cope with such pressures, this was prevented by the lack of auditor independence, the inadequacy of qualified reports as opposed to revised accounts, and the absence of a codified conceptual framework with which to constrain auditor judgement.

A standard was necessary to ensure uniform reporting and to prevent the accounting message being manipulated.

17.3 IAS 17 (and its national equivalents) – the controversy

This section considers the development of IAS 17, its main thrust and why it was so controversial. It also discusses how the accounting and legal professions differ in their approach to the reporting of lease transactions.

17.3.1 Development of IAS 17

IAS 17 and its national equivalents proved to be extremely controversial accounting standards. The extent of the controversy is shown by the time that many took to become standards.

IAS 17 was originally issued in September 1982 (the latest revision was in 2004 effective 1 January 2005) and was effective for periods beginning on or after 1 January 1984. This followed the development of a standard in the USA, Financial Accounting Standard 13 (SFAS 13), which was issued in 1977.

In the UK the standard SSAP 21 was not issued until 1984, and this was only issued after a three-year exposure period. Prior to the exposure draft being issued there had been a five-year discussion period about the approach taken by the standard.

17.3.2 What is the main thrust of IAS 17?

First, IAS 17 distinguishes between two types of lease – finance and operating – and recommends different accounting treatment for each. In brief, the definitions were as follows:

● **Finance lease**: a lease that transfers substantially all the risks and rewards of ownership of an asset. Title may or may not eventually be transferred.

● **Operating lease**: a lease other than a finance lease.

The accounting treatment and definition of each lease will be explored in greater depth in 17.4 and 17.5 below.

Second, the standard requires finance leases to be capitalised in the lessee's accounts. This means that the leased item should be recorded as an asset in the balance sheet, and the obligation for future payments should be recorded as a liability in the balance sheet. It is not permissible for the leased asset and lease obligation to be left out of the balance sheet. In the case of operating leases, the lessee is required only to expense the annual payments as a rental through the income statement.

17.3.3 Why was the IAS 17 approach so controversial?

The proposal to classify leases into finance and operating leases, and to capitalise those which are classified as finance leases, appears to be a feasible solution to the accounting problems that surround leasing agreements. So, why did the standard setters encounter so much controversy in their attempt to stop the practice of charging all lease payments to the income statement?

The whole debate centres on one accounting policy: **substance over form**. Although this is not cited as an accounting concept in the IASC *Framework*, para. 35 states:

> If information is to represent faithfully the transactions and other events that it purports to represent, it is necessary that they are accounted for and presented in accordance with their substance and economic reality and not merely their legal form.

The real sticking point was that IAS 17 invoked a substance over form approach to accounting treatment that was completely different to the traditional approach, which has strict regard to legal ownership. The IASC argued that in reality there were two separate transactions taking place. In one transaction, the company was borrowing funds to be repaid over a period. In the other, it was making a payment to the supplier for the use of an asset.

The correct accounting treatment for the borrowing transaction, based on its substance, was to include in the lessee's balance sheet a liability representing the obligation to meet the lease payments, and the correct accounting treatment for the asset acquisition transaction, based on its substance, was to include an asset representing the asset supplied under the lease.

IAS 17, para. 10, states categorically that 'whether a lease is a finance lease or an operating lease depends on the substance of the transaction rather than the form of the contract'.

17.3.4 How do the accounting and legal professions differ in their approach to the reporting of lease transactions?

The accounting profession sees itself as a service industry that prepares financial reports in a dynamic environment, in which the user is looking for reports that reflect commercial reality. Consequently, the profession needs to be sensitive and responsive to changes in commercial practice.

There was still some opposition within the accounting profession to the inclusion of a finance lease in the balance sheet as an 'asset'. The opposition rested on the fact that the item that was the subject of the lease agreement did not satisfy the existing criterion for classification as an asset because it was not 'owned' by the lessee. To accommodate this, the definition of an asset has been modified from 'ownership' to 'control' and 'the ability to contribute to the cash flows of the enterprise'.

The legal profession, on the other hand, concentrates on the strict legal interpretation of a transaction. The whole concept of substance over form is contrary to its normal practice.

It is interesting to reflect that, whereas an equity investor might prefer the economic resources to be included in the balance sheet under the substance over form principle, this is not necessarily true for a loan creditor. The equity shareholder is interested in resources available for creating earnings; the lender is interested in the assets available as security.

Another way to view the asset is to think of it as an asset consisting of the ownership of the right to use the facility as opposed to the ownership of the physical item itself. In a way this is similar to owning accounts receivable or a patent or intellectual property. You don't have a physical object but rather a valuable intangible right.

17.4 IAS 17 – classification of a lease

As discussed earlier in the chapter, IAS 17 provides definitions for classifying leases as finance or operating leases, then prescribes the accounting and disclosure requirements applicable to the lessor and the lessee for each type of lease.

The crucial decision in accounting for leases is whether a transaction represents a finance or an operating lease. We have already defined each type of lease, but we must now consider the risks and rewards of ownership.

IAS 17 provides in paragraph 10 a list of the factors that need to be considered in the decision whether risks and rewards of ownership have passed to the lessee. These factors are considered individually and in combination when making the decision, and if met would normally indicate a finance lease:

(a) the lease transfers ownership of the asset to the lessee by the end of the lease term;

(b) the lessee has the option to purchase the asset at a price that is expected to be sufficiently lower than the fair value at the date the option becomes exercisable for it to be reasonably certain, at the inception of the lease, that the option will be exercised;

(c) the lease term is for the major part of the economic life of the asset even if title is not transferred;

(d) at the inception of the lease the present value of the minimum lease payments amounts to at least substantially all of the fair value of the leased asset; and

(e) the leased assets are of such a specialised nature that only the lessee can use them without major modifications.

Lease classification is made at the inception of the lease and changes of estimates (e.g. of the economic life or residual value of the asset), or changes in circumstances (e.g. default by the lessee) do not alter the classification.

Leases of land

If land is leased and legal title is not expected to pass at the end of the lease the lease will be an operating lease. The reason is that the lease can never be for the substantial part of the economic life of the asset (criterion (c) above). This means that if a land and buildings lease is entered into it should be classified as two leases, a land lease which is an operating lease and a buildings lease which could be an operating or a finance lease. The lease payments should be allocated between the land and buildings elements in proportion to the relative fair values of the land element and the buildings element of the lease at its inception.

This split is not required by lessees if the land and buildings are an investment property accounted for under IAS 40, and where the fair value model has been adopted.

IAS 17 (revised 1997) included a helpful flow chart, prepared by the IAS secretariat, which represents examples of some possible positions that would normally be classified as finance leases (Figure 17.1).

Figure 17.1 IAS 17 aid to categorising operating and finance leases

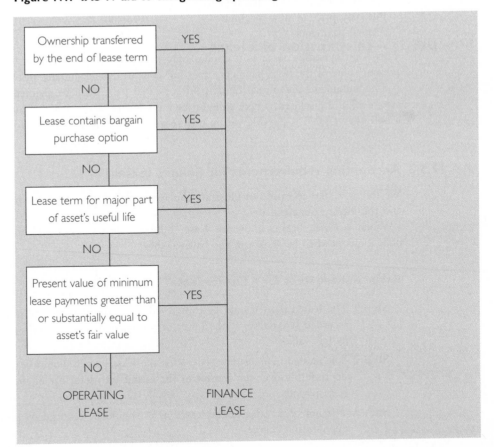

17.5 IAS 17 – accounting for leases by lessees

17.5.1 Accounting requirements for operating leases

The treatment of operating leases conforms to the legal interpretation and corresponds to the lease accounting practice that existed before IAS 17. No asset or obligation is shown in the balance sheet; the operating lease rentals payable are charged to the income statement on a straight-line basis.

17.5.2 Disclosure requirements for operating leases

IAS 17 requires that the total of operating lease rentals charged as an expense in the income statement should be disclosed, and these rentals should be broken down for minimum lease payments, contingent costs, and sublease payments. Disclosure is required of the payments that a lessee is committed to make during the next year, in the second to fifth years inclusive, and over five years.

EXAMPLE ● OPERATING LEASE Clifford plc is a manufacturing company. It negotiates a lease to begin on 1 January 20X1 with the following terms:

Term of lease	4 years
Estimated useful life of machine	9 years
Age of machine on inception of lease	4 years
Purchase price of new machine	£75,000
Annual payments	£8,000

This is an operating lease as it applies only to a part of the asset's useful life, and the present value of the lease payments does not constitute substantially all of the fair value.

The amount of the annual rental paid – £8,000 p.a. – will be charged to the income statement and disclosed. There will also be a disclosure of the ongoing commitment with a note that £8,000 is payable within one year and £24,000 within two to five years.

17.5.3 Accounting requirements for finance leases

We follow a step approach to illustrate the accounting entries in both the balance sheet and the income statement.

When a lessee begins a finance lease, both the leased asset and the related lease obligations need to be shown in the balance sheet.

Balance sheet steps for a finance lease

Step 1 The leased asset should be capitalised in property, plant and equipment (and recorded separately) at the lower of the present value of lease payments and its fair value.

Step 2 The annual depreciation charge for the leased asset should be calculated by depreciating over the shorter of the estimated useful life of the asset or the lease period.

Step 3 The net book value of the leased asset should be reduced by the annual depreciation charge.

Step 4 The finance lease obligation is a liability which should be recorded. At the inception of a lease agreement, the value of the leased asset and the leased liability will be the same.

Step 5 (a) The finance charge for the finance lease should be calculated as the difference between the total of the minimum lease payments and the fair value of the asset (or the present value of these lease payments if lower), i.e. it represents the charge made by the lessor for the credit that is being extended to the lessee.

(b) The finance charge should be allocated to the accounting periods over the term of the lease. Three methods for allocating finance charges are used in practice:

- **Actuarial method.** This applies a constant periodic rate of charge to the balance of the leasing obligation. The rate of return applicable can be calculated by applying present value tables to annual lease payments.
- **Sum of digits method.** This method ('Rule of 78') is much easier to apply than the actuarial method. The finance charge is apportioned to accounting periods on a reducing scale.
- **Straight-line method.** This spreads the finance charge equally over the period of the lease (it is only acceptable for immaterial leases).

Step 6 The finance lease obligation should be reduced by the difference between the lease payment and the finance charge. This means that first the lease payment is used to repay the finance charge, and then the balance of the lease payment is used to reduce the book value of the obligation.

Income statement steps for a finance lease

Step 1 The annual depreciation charge should be recorded.

Step 2 The finance charge allocated to the current period should be recorded.

EXAMPLE ● FINANCE LEASE Clifford plc negotiates another lease to commence on 1 January 20X1 with the following terms:

Term of lease	3 years
Purchase price of new machine	£16,500
Annual payments (payable in advance)	£6,000
Clifford plc's borrowing rate	10%

Finance charges are allocated using the sum of digits method.

Categorise the transaction
First we need to decide whether the lease is an operating or a finance lease. We do this by applying the present value criterion.

- Calculate the fair value:
  Fair value of asset = £16,500

- Calculate the present value of minimum lease payments:

$$£6,000 + \frac{£6,000}{1.1} + \frac{£6,000}{(1.1)^2} = £16,413$$

- Compare the fair value and the present value. It is a finance lease because PV of the lease payments is substantially all of the fair value of the asset.

Balance sheet steps for a finance lease

Step 1 Capitalise lease at fair value (present value is immaterially different):
Asset value = £16,500

Step 2 Calculate depreciation (using straight-line method):
£16,500/3 = £5,500

Step 3 Reduce the asset:

Balance sheet (extract) as at		31 Dec 20X1	31 Dec 20X2	31 Dec 20X3
ASSET	Opening value	16,500	11,000	5,500
(Right to	Depreciation	5,500	5,500	5,500
use asset)	Closing value	11,000	5,500	—

Or if we keep the asset at cost as in published accounts:

ASSET	Cost	16,500	16,500	16,500
(Right to	Depreciation	5,000	11,000	16,500
use asset)	Net book value	11,000	5,500	—

Step 4 Obligation on inception of finance lease:
Liability = £16,500

Step 5 Finance charge:

Total payments	3 × £6,000	= £18,000
Asset value		= £16,500
		£1,500

Finance charge
Allocated using sum of digits:

Year 1 = 2/(1 + 2) × £1,500 = (£1,000)
Year 2 = 1/(1 + 2) × £1,500 = (£500)

Note that the allocation is only over two periods because the instalments are being made in advance. If the instalments were being made in arrears, the liability would continue over three years and the allocation would be over three years.

Step 6 Reduce the obligation:

Balance sheet (extract) as at		31 Dec 20X1	31 Dec 20X2	31 Dec 20X3
Liability	Opening value	16,500	11,500	6,000
(Obligation	Lease payment	6,000	6,000	6,000
under finance		10,500	5,500	—
lease)	Finance charge	1,000	500	—
	Closing value	11,500	6,000	—

Note that the closing balance on the asset represents unexpired service potential and the closing balance on the liability represents the capital amount outstanding at the balance sheet date.

Income statement steps for a finance lease

> **Step 1** A depreciation charge is made on the basis of use. The charge would be calculated in accordance with existing company policy relating to the depreciation of that type of asset.
>
> **Step 2** A finance charge is levied on the basis of the amount of financing outstanding.

Both then appear in the income statement as expenses of the period:

	Income statement (extract) for year ending		
	31 Dec 20X1	*31 Dec 20X2*	*31 Dec 20X3*
Depreciation	5,500	5,500	5,500
Finance charge	1,000	500	—
Total	6,500	6,000	5,500

In the Clifford example, we used the sum of the digits method to allocate the finance charge over the period of the repayment. In the following example, we will illustrate the actuarial method of allocating the finance charge.

EXAMPLE ● FINANCE LEASE Witts plc negotiates a four-year lease for an item of plant with a cost price of £35,000. The annual lease payments are £10,000 payable in advance. The cost of borrowing for Witts plc is 15%.

First we need to determine whether this is a finance lease. Then we need to calculate the implicit interest rate and allocate the total finance charge over the period of the repayments using the actuarial method.

● Categorise the transaction to determine whether it is a finance lease.

> Fair value of asset $\qquad = £35,000$
> PV of future lease payments:
> $£10,000 + (10,000 \times a_{\overline{3}|15})$
> $£10,000 + (10,000 \times 2.283) \qquad = £32,830$

The PV of the minimum lease payments is substantially the fair value of the asset. The lease is therefore categorised as a finance lease.

● Calculate the 'interest rate implicit in the lease'.

> Fair value = Lease payments discounted at the implicit interest rate
> $£35,000 \quad = £10,000 + (10,000 \times a_{\overline{3}|i})$
> $a_{\overline{3}|i} \quad = £25,000/10,000 = 2.5$
> $i \qquad = 9.7\%$

● Allocate the finance charge using the actuarial method.

Figure 17.2 shows that the finance charge is levied on the obligation during the period at 9.7%, which is the implicit rate calculated above.

Figure 17.2 Finance charge allocation using actuarial method

Period	Obligation (start) £	Rentals paid £	Obligation (during) £	Finance 9.7% £	Obligation (end) £
Year 1	35,000	10,000	25,000	2,425	27,425
Year 2	27,425	10,000	17,425	1,690	19,115
Year 3	19,115	10,000	9,115	885	10,000
Year 4	10,000	10,000	—	—	—

17.5.4 Disclosure requirements for finance leases

IAS 17 requires that assets subject to finance leases should be identified separately and the net carrying amount disclosed. This can be achieved either by separate entries in the property, plant and equipment schedule or by integrating owned and leased assets in this schedule and disclosing the breakdown in the notes to the accounts.

The obligations relating to finance leases can also be treated in two different ways. The leasing obligation should either be shown separately from other liabilities in the balance sheet or integrated into 'current liabilities' and 'non-current liabilities' and disclosed separately in the notes to the accounts.

The notes to the accounts should also analyse the leasing obligations in terms of the timing of the payments. The analysis of the amounts payable should be broken down into those obligations falling due within one year, two to five years, and more than five years.

Note that Figure 17.2 also provides the information required for the balance sheet. For example, at the end of year 1 the table shows, in the final column, a total obligation of £27,425. This can be further subdivided into its non-current and current components by using the next item in the final column, which represents the amount outstanding at the end of year 2. This amount of £19,115 represents the non-current element, and the difference of £8,310 represents the current liability element at the end of year 1.

This method of calculating the current liability from the table produces a different current figure each year. For example, the current liability at the end of year 2 is £9,115, being £19,115 – £10,000. This has been discussed in *External Financial Reporting*, where the point was made that the current liability should be the present value of the payment that is to be made at the end of the next period, i.e. £10,000 discounted at 9.7%, which gives a present value for the current liability of £9,115 for inclusion in the balance sheet each year until the liability is discharged.[9] We use the conventional approach in working illustrations and exercises, but you should bear this point in mind.

EXAMPLE ● DISCLOSURE REQUIREMENTS IN THE LESSEE'S ACCOUNTS It is interesting to refer to the disclosures found in published accounts as illustrated by the Nestlé Group accounts.

Extract from the Nestlé Group – Annual Report and Accounts 2003

Accounting policies

Leased assets
Assets acquired under long-term finance leases are capitalised and depreciated in accordance with the Group's policy on property, plant and equipment. The associated obligations are included in financial liabilities.

Rentals payable under operating leases are charged to the income statement as incurred.

Other notes

Lease commitments
The following charges arise from these commitments:

Operating leases

In millions of CHF	2003	2002
	Minimum lease payments future value	
Within one year	458	450
In the second year	378	382
In the third to fifth year inclusive	705	753
After the fifth year	893	1,395
	2,434	2,980

Finance leases

In millions of CHF	2003		2002	
	Minimum future payments			
	Present value	Future value	Present value	Future value
Within one year	48	64	52	64
In the second year	42	53	43	52
In the third to fifth year inclusive	76	106	63	86
After the fifth year	106	137	138	191
	272	360	296	393

The difference between the future value of the minimum lease payments and their present value represented the discount on the lease obligations.

17.6 Accounting for the lease of land and buildings

Land and buildings are dealt with separately. Each has to be reviewed to determine whether to classify as an operating or finance lease. This is illustrated in the Warehouse Company example.

Let us assume that

● The Warehouse Company Ltd, whose borrowing rate was 10% per annum, entered into a 10-year lease under which it made payments of $106,886 annually in advance.

● The present value of the land was $500,000 and of the buildings was $500,000.

● The value of the land at the end of 10 years was $670,000 and the value of the buildings was $50,000.

Classifying the land segment of the lease

We first need to classify the land lease. As there is no contract to pass title at the end of the contract and the land is expected to increase in value, it is clear that the land segment of the contract does not involve the lessor transferring the risk and benefits to the lessee. This means that the lessee has to account for the lease of the land as an operating lease.

Classifying the building segment of the lease

The building segment of the lease is different. The residual value has fallen to $50,000 which has a present value of $19,275 (50,000 × 0.3855). This means that 96% of the benefit has been transferred (500,000 – 19,275) and the building segment is, therefore, a finance lease.

How to apportion the lease payment in the income statement

The payment should be split at the commencement of the lease according to the fair value of the components covered by the lease. In the case of the land, the present value of the land is $500,000 of which $258,285 (670,000 × 0.3855) represents the present value of the land at the end of the contract so the balance of $241,715 represents the present value of the operating lease. Similarly the amount covered by the finance lease is $480,725. Splitting the lease payment of $106,886 in those proportions (241,715:480,725) gives $35,763 for the land component and $71,123 for the finance lease representing the buildings leased.

How to report in the balance sheet

For the finance lease covering the building the lessee will have to show a $480,725 asset initially which will be depreciated over the ten years of the lease according to the normal policy of depreciating buildings which are going to last 10 years. At the same time a liability representing an obligation to the legal owner of the buildings (the lessor) for the same amount will be created. As lease payments are made the interest component will be treated as an expense and the balance will be used to reduce the liability.

In this example the risk and rewards relating to the building segment were clearly transferred to the lessee. If the residual value had been say, $350,000 rather than $50,000 then the present value at the end of the lease would have been $134,925 which represents 27% of the value. This does not indicate that substantially all the benefits of ownership have been transferred and hence it would be classified as an operating lease. The lessee would not, therefore, capitalise the lease but would charge each period with the same leasing expense.

17.7 Leasing – a form of off balance sheet financing

Prior to IAS 17, one of the major attractions of leasing agreements for the lessee was the off balance sheet nature of the transaction. However, the introduction of IAS 17 required the capitalisation of finance leases and removed part of the benefit of off balance sheet financing.

The capitalisation of finance leases effectively means that all such transactions will affect the lessee's gearing, return on assets and return on investment. Consequently, IAS 17 substantially alters some of the key accounting ratios which are used to analyse a set of financial statements.

Operating leases, on the other hand, are not required to be capitalised. This means that operating leases still act as a form of off balance sheet financing.[10] Hence they are extremely attractive to many lessees. Indeed, leasing agreements are increasingly being structured specifically to be classified as operating leases, even though they appear to be more financial in nature.[11]

An important conclusion is that some of the key ratios used in financial analysis become distorted and unreliable in instances where operating leases form a major part of a company's financing.[12]

To illustrate the effect of leasing on the financial structure of a company, we present a buy versus leasing example.

EXAMPLE ● RATIO ANALYSIS OF BUY VERSUS LEASE DECISION Kallend Tiepins plc requires one extra machine for the production of tiepins. The MD of Kallend Tiepins plc is aware that the gearing ratio and the return on capital employed ratio will change depending on whether the company buys or leases (on an operating lease) this machinery. The relevant information is as follows.

The machinery costs £100,000, but it will improve the operating profit by 10% p.a. The current position, the position if the machinery is bought and the position if the machinery is leased are as follows:

	Current £	Buy £	Lease £
Operating profit	40,000	44,000	44,000
Equity capital	200,000	200,000	200,000
Long-term debt	100,000	200,000	100,000
Total capital employed	300,000	400,000	300,000
Gearing ratio	0.5:1	1:1	0.5:1
ROCE	13.33%	11%	14.66%

It is clear that the impact of a leasing decision on the financial ratios of a company can be substantial.[13] Although this is a very simple illustration, it does show that the buy versus lease decision has far-reaching consequences in the financial analysis of a company.

17.8 Accounting for leases – a new approach

As discussed earlier in this chapter, IAS 17 makes a distinction between finance leases and operating leases. However, an international group has questioned this distinction. Standard setters from the UK, Australia, Canada, New Zealand, the USA and the IASC (an extension of the G4+1 group) issued a Special Report[14] which concluded that non-cancellable operating leases should be treated in the same way as finance leases. The similar treatment is based on the premise that the rights and obligations created under a lease contract meet the definitions of an asset and liability of a conceptual framework such as the IASC *Framework*. The G4+1 group issued a discussion paper in 1999.

W. McGregor[15] explained that:

A lease contract conveys a right to a lessee to use the leased property; in the language of the conceptual frameworks, the lessee controls the future economic benefits embodied in the leased property for the period of the lease term. Similarly, the lease contract establishes an obligation on the lessee to sacrifice future economic benefits to an external party in payment for the use of the leased property.

This approach addresses one of the main problems with the current accounting treatment, namely, the potential for framing a finance lease as an operating lease and not having to capitalise the lease contract on the lessee's balance sheet.

The G4+1 group issued a further position paper in 1999. The main thrust of the paper is that operating leases which are not currently included in the balance sheet would give rise to assets and liabilities reported at the fair value of the rights and obligations conveyed in the lease, e.g. where a lease is only for a small part of an asset's economic life, only that part would be reflected in the lessee's balance sheet. The ASB (UK Accounting Standards Board) has said that a persuasive factor in adopting the main principles of the paper is the common and growing practice of analysts recasting financial statements by capitalising operating leases.

In principle it is an attractive idea that all leased assets and liabilities should be treated in the same way to avoid the manipulation we have seen with lease agreements drawn up so that finance leases in substance are classified as operating leases. However, there is a problem that needs to be resolved which is how to measure the asset and liability that is reported in the balance sheet. When treated as an operating lease there was no asset or liability recorded on the face of the balance sheet. Under new proposals the decision has to be made as to whether to include the leased item as an asset at full value in which case the liability would be the present value of the minimum payments plus the obligation to return the asset at the end of the rental period, or at another value such as simply the present value of the minimum payments.

Should the requirement to capitalise operating leases become a binding requirement the impact is hard to predict. However, one factor is certain: any new standard will be examined closely by the affected parties who will look for ways to reduce the impact of the standard. The most likely scenario is that firms will seek to reduce the length of contracts if the binding period determines the magnitude of the liability. Also, it is possible that the finance industry will invent new types of financial arrangements to escape the leasing standard. In the past, the finance industry has been very creative and there is no reason to think it will be any less entrepreneurial in the future.

17.9 Accounting for leases by lessors

There are essentially two different types of situations.

The first is where a manufacturer enters into a lease to enable a potential purchaser to 'buy' their product. In this situation it is necessary to separate the sale transaction from the leasing transaction. All costs relating to making the sale must be included in calculating the profit or loss on the sale and must not be included in the lease accounting. The second scenario is where an asset is purchased by the finance company at the request of a client and is then leased to the client. The lease is then classified as a financial lease or as an operating lease.

17.9.1 Finance lease

The lessor will recognise a finance lease in their assets. The amount initially shown will be the cost of the asset plus any direct costs necessarily incurred in setting up the lease. Suppose the XYZ plc finance company purchases a machine for $157,000 at the request of Flexible Manufacturing plc who then leases it for $58,000 per annum for three years, payments being made at the commencement of each year. XYZ plc incurs costs of $1,661 to establish the lease.

XYZ plc, the lessor, will record an asset of $158,661 being the amount which is to be recovered from Flexible Manufacturing plc. In addition they are entitled to interest on the transaction. To ascertain the rate of interest we ascertain by trial and error the rate of interest which equates the present value of the lease payments ($58,000 in years 0, 1 and 2) to the amount to be recovered, in this case $158,661. The interest rate is 10%.

So at the start of the first year XYZ plc will receive $58,000. Of that $10,066 will be recorded as interest and $47,934 as recovery of the initial investment. (Initial investment 158,661 less immediate recovery of 58,000 leaving a balance of 100,661 outstanding for a year at 10% or 10,066 interest. This means of the 58,000 paid, 10,066 represents interest and the remaining 47,934 is a repayment of capital.) At balance date the lease asset would show as $110,727 (158,661 − 47,934). Interest recognised in the next year would be $5,273.

There are also disclosure requirements relating to the timing of cash flows, unearned finance income, allowances for uncollectible amounts, unguaranteed residuals expected under the contracts, and contingent rents.

17.9.2 Operating leases

The asset will be capitalised at its cost plus the direct cost of arranging the lease. The asset will then be depreciated like any other fixed asset.

The revenue will be matched against periods according to the pattern of benefits received, which in most cases will be on a straight-line basis.

Summary

The initial upturn in leasing activity in the 1970s was attributable to the economy and tax requirements rather than the popularity of lease transactions *per se*. High interest rates, a high inflation rate, 100% first year tax allowances and a sequence of annual losses in the manufacturing industry made leasing transactions extremely attractive to both the lessors and the lessees.

Once the leasing industry was firmly established, the amount of leasing activity continued to increase, even when many of the original benefits were no longer applicable. The Finance Act 1984 removed the major tax advantages of leases, but by then many other benefits of leasing as a form of finance had been discovered.

Off balance sheet financing was considered a particular advantage of lease financing. IAS 17 recognised this and attempted to introduce stricter accounting policies and requirements. However, although IAS 17 introduced the concept of 'substance over form', the hazy distinction between finance and operating leases still allows companies to structure lease agreements to achieve either type of lease. This is important because, while stricter accounting requirements apply to finance leases, operating leases can still be used as a form of off balance sheet accounting.

We do not know the real extent to which IAS 17 is either observed or ignored. However, it is true to say that creative accountants and finance companies are able to circumvent IAS 17 by using 'structured' leases. Future development may change this position considerably.

REVIEW QUESTIONS

1 Can the legal position on leases be ignored now that substance over form is used for financial reporting? Discuss.

2 (a) Consider the importance of the categorisation of lease transactions into operating lease or finance lease decisions when carrying out financial ratio analysis. What ratios might be affected?

(b) Discuss the effects of renegotiating/reclassifying all operating leases into finance leases. For which industries might this classification have a significant impact on the financial ratios?

3 Explain the major provisions of IAS 17 *Leases*.

4 The favourite off balance sheet financing trick used to be leasing. Use any illustrative numerical examples you may wish to:

(a) Define the term 'off balance sheet financing' and state why it is popular with companies.

(b) Illustrate what is meant by the above quotation in the context of leases and discuss the accounting treatments and disclosures required by IAS 17 which have limited the usefulness of leasing as an off balance sheet financing technique.

(c) Suggest two other off balance sheet financing techniques and discuss the effect that each technique has on balance sheet assets and liabilities, and on the profit and loss account.

5 The BOC Group 2004 Accounting Policies state:

Where finance leases have been entered into, the capital element of the obligations to the lessor are shown as part of borrowings and the rights in the corresponding assets are treated in the same way as owned fixed assets [UK name for non-current assets].

(a) Explain the terms 'obligations to the lessor' and 'rights in corresponding assets'.

(b) Explain how these amounts would be quantified in the balance sheet.

(c) Describe the entries that would appear in the income statement.

6 The Body Shop International PLC 2004 Annual Report included the following accounting policy:

Leased assets

Assets held under finance leases are capitalised at amounts approximating to the present value of the minimum lease payments payable over the term of the lease. The corresponding leasing commitments are shown as amounts payable to the lessor. Depreciation on assets held under finance leases is charged to the profit and loss account.

Leasing payments are analysed between capital and interest components so that the interest element is charged to the profit and loss account over the period of the lease and approximates to a constant proportion of the balances of capital payments outstanding.

All other leases are treated as operating leases with annual rentals charged to the profit and loss account on a straight-line basis over the term of the lease.

(a) Explain the meaning of 'minimum lease payments' and 'approximates to a constant proportion of the balances of capital repayments outstanding.'

(b) Explain why it is necessary to use present values and approximate to a constant proportion.

7 Peter Mullen says in an article sent in to the ASB, the following:

the ASB advocates that all leasing type deals should essentially be accounted for in relation to the extent of asset and liability transfer that they involve ...

On the first point, the ASB seems to have a point – 90% [for recognition of a finance lease] is unquestionably an arbitrary figure. But 'arbitrariness' is not in itself wrong: indeed often it is necessary. The speeding limit on a motorway is set at 70 mph, a driver driving at 71 mph is therefore breaking the law, where one driving at a 'substantially similar' speed is not. One could easily think of many similar examples where the demands of pragmatism means that a 'bright line' being drawn somewhere is preferable to no line at all. There is only a convincing case for dispensing with arbitrariness in these situations if the replacement does not give rise to something which is equally arbitrary, and this is where the ASB starts to run into problems.

... If assets and liabilities mean what the ASB wants them to mean they have to do so in all circumstances. The range of contracts that give rise to similar liabilities and assets, however is vast.

At a very simple level, Leaseguard has retainer agreements with its clients which are typically between two and four years' duration. Under any sensible extension of ASB's logic these should be capitalised rather than treated as revenue items. Imagine a world, however, where just about every contract for the provision of future services or assets that an organization enters into is scrutinized for its asset and liability content.

Discuss whether this is a valid argument for not treating all leases in the same manner.

EXERCISES

An extract from the solution is provided in the Appendix at the end of the text for exercises marked with an asterisk (*).

* Question 1

On 1 January 20X8, Grabbit plc entered into an agreement to lease a widgeting machine for general use in the business. The agreement, which may not be terminated by either party to it, runs for six years and provides for Grabbit to make an annual rental payment of £92,500 on 31 December each year. The cost of the machine to the lessor was £350,000, and it has no residual value. The machine has a useful economic life of eight years and Grabbit depreciates its property, plant and equipment using the straight-line method.

Required:
(a) Show how Grabbit plc will account for the above transaction in its balance sheet at 31 December 20X8, and in its income statement for the year then ended, if it capitalises the leased asset in accordance with the principles laid down in IAS 17.
(b) Explain why the standard setters considered accounting for leases to be an area in need of standardisation and discuss the rationale behind the approach adopted in the standard.
(c) The lessor has suggested that the lease could be drawn up with a minimum payment period of one year and an option to renew. Discuss why this might be attractive to the lessee.

* Question 2

(a) When accounting for finance leases, accountants prefer to overlook legal form in favour of commercial substance.

Required:
Discuss the above statement in the light of the requirements of IAS 17 *Leases*.
(b) State briefly how you would distinguish between a finance lease and an operating lease.
(c) Smarty plc finalises its accounts annually on 31 March. It depreciates its machinery at 20% per annum on cost and adopts the 'Rule of 78' for allocating finance charges among different accounting periods. On 1 August 20X7 it acquired machinery on a finance lease on the following agreement:

(i) a lease rent of £500 per month is payable for 36 months commencing from the date of acquisition;

(ii) cost of repairs and insurance are to be met by the lessee;

(iii) on completion of the primary period the lease may be extended for a further period of three years, at the lessee's option, for a peppercorn rent.

The cash price of the machine is £15,000.

Required:

(1) Set out how all ledger accounts reflecting these transactions will appear in each of the four accounting periods 20X7/8, 20X8/9, 20X9/Y0 and 20Y0/Y1.

(2) Show the income statement entries for the year ended 31 March 20X8 and balance sheet extracts as at that date.

Question 3

The Mission Company Ltd, whose year-end is 31 December, has acquired two items of machinery on leases, the conditions of which are as follows:

Item Y: Ten annual instalments of £20,000 each, the first payable on 1 January 20X0. The machine was completely installed and first operated on 1 January 20X0 and its purchase price on that date was £160,000. The machine has an estimated useful life of ten years, at the end of which it will be of no value.

Item Z: Ten annual instalments of £30,000 each, the first payable on 1 January 20X2. The machine was completely installed and first operated on 1 January 20X2 and its purchase price on that date was £234,000. The machine has an estimated useful life of twelve years, at the end of which it will be of no value.

The Mission Company Ltd accounts for finance charges on finance leases by allocating them over the period of the lease on the sum of the digits method.

Depreciation is charged on a straight-line basis. Ignore taxation.

Required:

(a) Calculate and state the charges to the income statement for 20X6 and 20X7 if the leases were treated as operating leases.

(b) Calculate and state the charges to the income statement for 20X6 and 20X7 if the leases were treated as finance lease and capitalised using the sum of the digits method for the finance charges.

(c) Show how items Y and Z should be incorporated in the balance sheet, and notes thereto, at 31 December 20X7, if capitalised.

Question 4

X Ltd entered into a lease agreement on the following terms:

Cost of leased asset	£100,000
Lease term	5 years
Rentals six-monthly in advance	£12,000
Anticipated residual on disposal of the assets at end of lease term	£10,000
Lessee's interest in residual value	97%
Economic life	8 years
Inception date	1 January 20X4

Lessee's financial year-end	31 December
Implicit rate of interest is applied half-yearly	4.3535%

Required:
Show the income statement entries for the years ended 31 December 20X4 and 20X7 and balance sheet extracts at those dates.

Question 5

At 1 January 20X5 Bridge Finance plc agreed to Finance the lease of machinery costing $37,200 to Rapid Growth plc at a lease cost of $10,000 per annum payable at the end of the year, namely 31 December. The period of the lease is five years. Bridge finance plc incurred direct costs of $708 dollars in setting up the contract.

Required:
Show for Bridge finance plc the amount that would be charged to the income statement for the year ending 31 December 20X7 and the amount of the leased asset that would appear in the balance sheet at that date.

References

1 C. Drury and S. Braund, 'A survey of UK leasing practice', *Management Accounting*, April 1989, pp. 40–43.
2 N. Cope, 'Big ticket to ride out the recession', *Accountancy*, December 1992, pp. 55–57.
3 R. Perera, 'To buy or not to buy – how to decide', *Certified Accountant*, December 1986.
4 G. Allum *et al.*, 'Fleet focus: to lease or not to lease', *Australian Accountant*, September 1989, pp. 31–58; R.L. Benke and C.P. Baril, 'The lease vs. purchase decision', *Management Accounting*, March 1990, pp. 42–46.
5 B. Underdown and P. Taylor, *Accounting Theory and Policy Making*, Heinemann, 1985, p. 273.
6 Cranfield School of Management, *Financial Leasing Report*, Bedford, 1979.
7 Abdel-Khalik *et al.*, 'The economic effects on lessees of FASB Statement No. 13', *Accounting for Leases*, FASB, 1981.
8 G. Macdonald, in J. Freedman and M. Power (eds), *Law and Accountancy*, Paul Chapman Publishing, 1992, p. 76.
9 R. Main, in *External Financial Reporting*, ed. B. Carsberg and S. Dev, Prentice Hall, 1984.
10 R.H. Gamble, 'Off-balance-sheet diet: greens on the side', *Corporate Cashflow*, August 1990, pp. 28–32.
11 R.L. Benke and C.P. Baril, 'The lease vs. purchase decision', *Management Accounting*, March 1990, pp. 42–46; N. Woodhams and P. Fletcher, 'Operating leases to take bigger market share with changing standards', *Rydge's (Australia)*, September 1985, pp. 100–110.
12 C.H. Volk, 'The risks of operating leases', *Journal of Commercial Bank Lending*, May 1988, pp. 47–52.
13 Chee-Seong Tah, 'Lease or buy?', *Accountancy*, December 1992, pp. 58–59.
14 G4+1, *Accounting for Leases – A New Approach*, July 1996.
15 W. McGregor, 'Lease accounting: righting the wrongs', *Accountancy*, September 1996, p. 96.

CHAPTER 18

R&D; goodwill and intangible assets; brands

18.1 Introduction

In this chapter we consider the accounting treatments of the following:

- Research and development
- Goodwill and intangible assets
- Brands

18.2 Accounting treatment for research and development

Under IAS 38 *Intangible Assets*, the accounting treatment for R&D differs depending on whether the expenditure relates to research expenditure or development expenditure. Broadly speaking, research expenditure must always be charged to the profit and loss account and development expenditure should be capitalised provided a strict set of criteria are met. In this section we will consider why there is pressure to write off research and development expenditure, the accounting requirements for R&D, and how development costs are defined.

18.2.1 Why is there a pressure to write off R&D expenditure?

Many readers will think of research and development (R&D) as an investment rather than as a cost. They may well perceive it as a strategic investment that is essential if we are to be competitive in world markets. This applies particularly to an advanced technical industry such as chemicals, where a sustained high level of R&D investment is required.

The '2004 R&D Scoreboard'[1] prepared for the DTI by Company Reporting analysed the results for figures published in annual reports up to 31 May 2004. It was reported that the UK had the next to lowest ratio of R&D to sales of any large industrialised country. According to the figures, average R&D-to-sales figures for individual countries were:

	2004
Switzerland	6.5%
USA	4.9%
Germany	4.3%
Japan	4.2%
France	3.1%
UK	2.3%

In the table of 'Top 12 International Companies by R&D Expenditure', only one UK company features. An extract, which includes a comparison with each of the top US, German and Japanese companies, is shown below:

Position	Company	Country	R&D expenditure (£bn)
1	Ford	USA	4.2
3	Daimler/Chrysler	Germany	3.9
8	Toyota	Japan	3.5
11	GlaxoSmithKline	UK	2.8

One publication mentioned that the recognition of R&D as an asset had appeared in a report from the House of Lords Select Committee on Science and Technology, stating that 'R&D has to be regarded as an investment which leads to growth, not a cost'.[2] Unfortunately, two constraints militate against companies incurring high levels of expenditure. First, there is a commercial constraint: it is felt that a company which pursues a commitment to R&D is vulnerable to takeover bids. It is perhaps an irony that the threat comes from companies that have not had such a commitment. There is presumably an attraction for the company with the lower R&D commitment to mount a takeover with the prospect of a short-term increase in its earnings per share merely by reducing R&D by, say, 25%. That would show an immediate increase in disclosed trading profit.

So why do companies write off all of their research and development costs to the profit and loss account in the year in which the cost arises? As far as the company is concerned, one may hypothesise that directors have been pleased to take the expense in a year when they know its impact rather than carry it forward. They are aware of profit levels in the year in which the R&D arises and could find it embarrassing to take the loss in a subsequent year when profits were lower or the company even reported a trading loss.

This brings us to our second constraint: the difficulty of being reasonably certain that the intended economic benefits of R&D activities will flow to the enterprise. Because of this uncertainty, the accounting profession has traditionally considered it more prudent to write off the investment in research as a cost rather than report it as an asset in the balance sheet.

In the UK ED 14, the initial exposure draft issued in 1975, was influenced by the prudence concept, and required companies to write off all R&D expenditure in the year in which it arose. This was changed in the following year by the proposal in ED 17 that companies should be required to capitalise development costs.

The UK standard that eventually appeared was different again. A compromise was arrived at in SSAP 13, which permitted, rather than required, a company to capitalise development costs, provided stringent conditions were met. Companies were permitted the choice of treatment provided there was disclosure in the notes to the accounts. The Companies Act also permitted capitalisation, but only in special circumstances. IAS 38 *Intangible Assets*,[3] takes the ED 17 approach and requires companies to capitalise development costs provided they meet the conditions for capitalisation.

Directors wanted the capacity to choose the accounting treatment on a variety of grounds. Some felt that it would give their competitors an advantage if the build-up of a large development cost flagged the fact that a new product was about to be launched. Others rated a strong balance sheet higher than commercial secrecy and wanted to be able to include the asset on the balance sheet. Neither of these reasons has any basis in accounting principles, but the accounting profession was subject to the constraints of consensus standard-setting.

In its *Statement of Intent: Comparability of Financial Statements*, the IASC moved away from these constraints.[4] It proposed that the choice should be removed and that, if development costs meet the conditions for capitalisation, they must be capitalised and depreciated. This is the approach that has since been adopted by IAS 9[5] and IAS 38[6] which superseded IAS 9 in 1998.

There has been some research on both analysts'[7] and accountants'[8] reactions to R&D expenditure. Nixon[9] found that 'Two important dimensions of the corporate reporting accountants' perspective emerge: first, disclosure is seen as more important than the accounting treatment of R&D expenditure and, second, the financial statements are not viewed as the primary channel of communication for information on R&D'.

18.3 Research and Development

IAS 38 has given a definition of development costs and also sets out the conditions that need to be met in order to capitalise.

18.3.1 Background to Accounting for Research and Development

The part of IAS 38 Intangible Assets, which relates to Research and Development, is essentially the same as the UK Standard SSAP 13 Accounting for Research and Development, which was originally issued in 1977.

The original UK Standard

The original Standard, SSAP 13, was reactive. It arose out of the 'scandal' of the collapse of Rolls-Royce in 1971, and most of the criteria for capitalising development expenditure come from a consideration of the collapse of Rolls-Royce.

The main business of Rolls-Royce is the manufacture of aero engines (and not the more famous cars). Since the 1950s most of these have been 'jet' engines. In the late 1960s three 'jumbo' jets were being developed, the Boeing 747, the Douglas DC10 and the Lockheed L1011. In 1968 Rolls-Royce got the contract to supply the RB211 engine for the L1011. At this stage, it was a 'paper' engine (only preliminary drawings) and not a working model. The engine was to have twice the power of any previous Rolls-Royce engine and incorporate many new developments, including carbon fibre fan blades. It was a 'fixed (selling) price' contract with penalty clauses for late delivery and the engine failing to meet its stated performance. Prior to 1971 Rolls-Royce had capitalised (some) development expenditure – at that time there was no relevant accounting standard. In February 1971, Rolls-Royce 'ran out of money' and went into the hands of a Receiver (similar to today's Administration). The reasons were that:

(a) the development engines were very poor, with insufficient power, very unreliable and too heavy. There was serious doubt that an engine could be produced with sufficient power and reliability;

(b) the engines would be produced at a loss, because of the high inflation that started in the late 1960s and the costs of manufacturing and developing the engines being much higher than originally estimated;

(c) late delivery and poor performance made the company liable to substantial penalty charges.

At that stage it appeared that the financial future of Rolls-Royce was hopeless – it could not afford to complete development of the engine and it was estimated that there would be future losses on the sale of the engines.

You may ask 'how is Rolls-Royce still here today?' The answer was that Rolls-Royce were able to re-negotiate the original contract and raise the selling price of the engine (to make a small profit) and extend the development period by six months to overcome the problems. The UK Government took over the company and provided the funds to complete development of the engine (later this company was floated on the UK Stock Exchange). Stanley Hooker was brought in from Rolls-Royce at Bristol and he effectively sorted out the technical problems (Bristol made the engines for Concorde). Today, Rolls-Royce is one of the three major manufacturers of aero engines and they have about 1/3 of the market for engines for 'jumbo jets'. Their current range of 'Trent' engines are developments of the original RB211 engine of the late 1960s.

The current International Standard

The current Standard for Research and Development, IAS 38 para. 51–67, is very similar to the original SSAP 13, and the criteria for capitalising development expenditure are closely related to the collapse of Rolls-Royce in 1971.

The IAS 38 approach is to divide expenditure into the 'Research phase' and the 'Development phase'.

18.3.2 Research defined

IAS 38 states[10] 'expenditure on research shall be recognised as an expense when it is incurred'. This means that it cannot be included as an intangible asset in the balance sheet. The Standard gives examples of research activities[11] as:

(a) activities aimed at obtaining new knowledge;

(b) the search for, evaluation and final selection of, applications of research findings or other knowledge;

(c) the search for alternatives for materials, devices, products, processes, systems and services;

(d) the formulation, design, evaluation and final selection of possible alternatives for new or improved materials, devices, products, processes, systems or services.

Normally, research expenditure is not related directly to any of the company's products or processes. For instance, development of a high temperature material, which can be used in any aero engine, would be 'research', but development of a honeycomb for a particular engine would be 'development'. Whilst it is in the research phase, the IAS position[12] is that an entity cannot demonstrate that an intangible asset exists that will generate probable future economic benefits. It is this inability that justifies the IAS requirement for research expenditure not to be capitalised but to be charged as an expense when it is incurred.

18.3.3 Development defined

Expenditure is recognised[13] as development if the entity can identify an intangible asset and demonstrate that the asset will generate probable future economic benefits. The Standard gives examples of development activities:[14]

(a) the design, construction and testing of pre-production and pre-use prototypes and models;

(b) the design of tools, jigs, moulds and dies involving new technology;

(c) the design, construction and operation of a pilot plant that is not of a scale economically feasible for commercial production;

(d) the design, construction and testing of a chosen alternative for new or improved materials, devices, products, processes, systems or services.

18.3.4 Activities that are neither research or development

The UK accounting standard SSAP 13 says[15] that there are activities that are related to research and to development but which are not classified as either for the purposes of the standard. These include:

- engineering follow-through in an early phase of commercial production;
- quality control during commercial production, including routine testing of products;
- troubleshooting in connection with breakdowns during commercial production;
- routine efforts to refine, enrich or otherwise improve on the qualities of an existing product;
- adaptation of an existing capability to a particular requirement or customer's need as part of a continuing commercial activity; seasonal or other periodic design changes to existing products;
- routine design of tools, jigs, moulds and dies, and activities, including design and construction engineering, related to the construction, relocation, rearrangement or start-up of facilities or equipment other than facilities whose sole use is for a particular R&D development project.

IAS 38 does not provide this guidance, but it is apparent that such guidance would be useful in deciding whether expenditure can be capitalised.

18.3.5 Capitalising development costs

The important paragraph of IAS 38 (para. 57) says an intangible asset for development expenditure shall be recognised if and only if an entity can demonstrate **all** of the following (comments about Rolls-Royce are included in brackets after the statement):

(a) the technical feasibility of completing the intangible asset so that it will be available for use or sale (*with RR in 1971 this was questionable/unlikely*);

(b) the intention to complete the intangible asset and use or sell it (*this would not happen if RR collapsed*);

(c) its ability to use or sell the intangible asset (*RR would not use the asset if it collapsed*);

(d) how the intangible asset will generate probable future economic benefits (*as RR would have made a loss on sale of the engines, there were no 'future economic benefits'*);

(e) the availability of adequate technical, financial and other resources to complete the development and to use or sell the intangible asset (*it was questionable/unlikely that RR had the technical resources to complete the development, and it didn't have the 'financial resources'*);

(f) its ability to measure reliably the expenditure attributable to the intangible asset during its development (*RR was unable to estimate reliably the future cost of developing the engine*).

It is important to note that if the answers to all the conditions (a) to (f) above are 'Yes' then the entity must capitalise the development expenditure. With the UK Standard, if the answers to all the questions are 'Yes', then the entity may capitalise the development expenditure.

This is a significant difference between the International and UK Standards. However, in practice, the difference between the International and UK Standards may be less than imagined. If a company does not want to capitalise its development expenditure, it could argue that there is sufficient uncertainty about future development costs, being able to develop the product and/or making profits from future sales, and thus answer 'No' to one of the questions above. Then development expenditure would not be capitalised.

What IAS 38 is saying is that if future profits from the sale of the product exceed the development cost, all the development cost should be included as an intangible asset in the balance sheet. For example, assuming that development costs are $80 million:

(a) if future profits are $100m, then $80 million should be included in the balance sheet as development expenditure at the start of sales;

(b) if future profits are $50m, then $50 million should be included in the balance sheet as development expenditure at the start of sales (applying IAS 36 Impairment of Assets);

(c) if there are no future profits, then no asset should be included in the balance sheet at the start of sales.

What costs can be included?

The costs that can be included in development expenditure are similar to those used in determining the cost of inventory (IAS 2 *Inventories*).

How is the amortisation charge calculated?

The intangible asset of development costs is usually amortised over the sales of the product (i.e. the charge in 20X5 would be: 20X5 sales/total estimated sales × capitalised development expenditure).

18.3.6 Disclosure of Research and Development

Research and Development is important to many manufacturing companies, such as pharmaceutical companies who develop drugs, car and defence manufacturers. Disclosure is required of the aggregate amount of research and development expenditure recognised as an expense during the period.[16] Normally, this total expenditure will be:

(a) research expenditure,

(b) development expenditure amortised,

(c) development expenditure not capitalised, and

(d) impairment of capitalised development expenditure.

Under IAS 38 more companies may capitalise R&D expenditure, although many will avoid capitalisation by saying they cannot be certain to make future profits from the sale of the product. Although Research and Development is a popular topic for intellectual study and examination questions, most companies do not capitalise development expenditure.

18.3.7 Expensing development costs

As an illustration, the following is the R&D policy extract from the 2004 Bayer Annual Report:

> **Research and development expenses**
> According to IAS 38 (Intangible Assets), research costs cannot be capitalized; development costs can only be capitalized if specific conditions are fulfilled. Development costs must be capitalized if it is sufficiently certain that the future economic benefits to the company will cover not only the usual production, selling and administrative costs but also the development costs themselves. There are also several other criteria relating to the development project and the product or process being developed, all of which have to be met to justify asset recognition. As in previous years, these conditions are not satisfied.

18.3.8 The capitalisation of Research & Development expenditure

When a company incurs R&D expenditure, it makes payments for wages, materials and other expenses (Cr cash book). The question is 'where does the debit entry go'? If the entity decides to treat these payments as an expense, then the entry is Dr Income Statement. However, if it decides to capitalise the expenditure, the entry is Dr R&D asset in the balance sheet. The early Accounting Standards decreed that only development expenditure could be capitalised, and only if it was expected to make a profit. IAS 38 says this profitable development expenditure **must** be capitalised, whereas earlier standards often gave the option of either capitalising the expenditure or charging it as an expense.

Is capitalisation acceptable?

The question is whether it is 'right' to capitalise this expenditure. The IASB's *Framework for the Preparation and Presentation of Financial Statements* says 'an asset is recognised in the balance sheet when it is probable that the future economic benefits will flow to the entity and the asset has a cost or value that can be measured reliably'. Let us consider these conditions further.

Cost incurred to date

Certainly the capitalised cost of R&D can be 'measured reliably' as it comprises the wages, materials and other costs which have been incurred in the development activity and are available from the accounting system. The problem, however, with R&D is whether 'it is probable that future economic benefits will flow to the entity'.

In the early stages of a development project, usually there are uncertainties over:

(a) whether the project can be completed successfully, and

(b) the costs of developing the product.

Experience tends to indicate that people who develop products are notoriously optimistic. In practice, they encounter many more problems than they imagined and the cost is much greater than estimates. This means that the development project will probably be approaching completion before future development costs can be estimated reliably.

Profit measurement – estimating future sales

Once development has been completed, it is necessary to check whether sales of the product will be profitable. Sales value is the product of the selling price and quantity sold and there are uncertainties about both of these figures. For some high technology products the selling price might initially be high, but subsequently it will decline. For instance, high speed microprocessors will command a high price when they are released, but they will decline quite quickly as competitors develop faster microprocessors. Also, there is a relationship between quantity sold and the selling price – lowering the selling price will increase sales. This discussion highlights the problems of estimating future sales value.

Profit measurement – estimating future costs

Production costs might initially be high because of 'learning', but they are likely to reduce when production quantities increase – but by how much? These factors show how uncertain it is that a product will be profitable, and the potential inaccuracies in estimating this figure.

So, it may be very difficult to satisfy the Framework's statement of an asset as being 'recognised in the balance sheet when it is probable that the future economic benefits will flow to the entity'. If this statement cannot be satisfied, then the development expenditure cannot be included as an asset in the balance sheet.

18.4 Introduction to goodwill and intangible assets

The discussion of goodwill and intangibles proceeds as follows:

● the current position is considered briefly;
● historical developments are considered;
● intangibles and goodwill are introduced along with an illustration of their accounting treatment;
● the economic consequences of accounting for goodwill are discussed;
● the amortisation of goodwill is discussed;
● the main requirements of IFRS 3 *Business Combinations* and IAS 38 *Intangible Assets* are set out and evaluated.

18.5 Application of IAS 38 *Intangible Assets*

A person new to this subject would believe that IAS 38 would apply to all Intangible Assets, as its title implies. However, this is not the case. Para. 3 says it does not apply to:

(a) intangible assets held for sale in the ordinary course of business (IAS 2 *Inventories* and IAS 11 *Construction Contracts*)

(b) deferred tax assets (IAS 12 *Income Taxes*)

(c) leases under IAS 17 *Leases*

(d) assets arising from employee benefits (IAS 19 *Employee Benefits*)

(e) financial assets as defined by IAS 39 *Financial Instruments: Recognition and Measurement*

(f) goodwill acquired in a business combination (IFRS 3 *Business Combinations*)

(g) deferred acquisition costs and intangible assets arising from insurance contracts (IFRS 4 *Insurance Contracts*)

(h) non-current intangible assets classified as held for sale (IFRS 5 *Non-current Assets Held for Sale and Discontinued Operations*).

Some aspects of item (f) above will be considered in this chapter, as it is similar to the goodwill considered in IAS 38 (although the treatment is different).

The principal subject of IAS 38 (and IFRS 3) is goodwill. Other intangible assets covered by IAS 38 will be considered later in this chapter.

18.5.1 Definition of goodwill

IFRS 3 defines goodwill[17] as:

> The excess of the cost of the business combination over the acquirer's interest in the net fair value of the identifiable assets, liabilities and contingent liabilities.

Except for the addition of 'contingent liabilities', this definition has remained unchanged since the first accounting standards on goodwill were issued. It is probable that the addition of 'contingent liabilities' has little effect in practice, as the figure used in the calculation of goodwill would be the estimated liability for future uncertain events (and not the maximum possible liability). The words 'fair value' are important, as it is not the book value of the assets and liabilities, but the fair value at the date of acquisition (addition of the words 'at the date of acquisition' would be beneficial).

Under IAS 38, the value of goodwill will always be positive, as the entity would always pay for the goodwill (i.e. Dr goodwill – asset, Cr Cash book). However, under IFRS 3, the value of goodwill can be negative, when the fair value of the assets and liabilities acquired is greater than the consideration. There are special rules for dealing with negative goodwill – it is a subject which has caused a lot of problems to standard setters.

18.5.2 Internally generated goodwill

IAS 38 states clearly that 'Internally Generated Goodwill (or 'self generated goodwill') shall not be recognised as an asset'.

In about 1990, a number of companies, including Ranks Hovis McDougall, capitalised their self-generated brands. However, IAS 38 prohibits[18] this by saying 'Internally generated brands, mastheads, publishing titles, customer lists and items similar in substance shall not be recognised as intangible assets'.

If companies were allowed to include these items as an asset in the balance sheet, it would:

(a) 'boost' assets and produce a more favourable balance sheet (e.g. by reducing gearing),

(b) if the credit entry was directly to the profit and loss account reserve (retained earnings) or a capital reserve in the balance sheet, there would be no effect on reported profit, but

(c) if the credit entry was to the income statement, this would 'boost' the profit for the year. This would allow the manipulation of reported profit.

How does development expenditure differ from the cost of developing brands?

The distinction is important because one is required to be capitalised and the other pro-hibited. It is not obvious that the two are so very different but perhaps it could be argued that it is more probable that future economic benefits will flow from development expen-diture than from advertising expenditure which would be the type of expenditure capi-talised to create a brand.

18.5.3 Purchased goodwill

An inconsistency is created by not allowing capitalisation of internally generated good-will, but allowing capitalisation of purchased goodwill. A company could create purchased goodwill by selling a brand name (to a third party) and buying it back. However, companies probably do not do this, as the sale of the brand to the third party would probably result in a corporation tax charge (capital gains tax or gain from trading).

The value of goodwill can be looked at in two ways:

(a) it is the cost of creating and developing the company's business, including the skills and expertise of the workforce, the production processes and acquiring customers (i.e. the 'cost' approach), or

(b) the 'value' of the business in excess of its separable assets (i.e. working capital and tangible non-current assets). This 'value' can also be based on the future super-profits of the business.

18.5.4 Accounting for goodwill

Now that we have a definition of goodwill, we need to consider how it is to be written down in the balance sheet over its life. One might have thought that a requirement to amortise over its estimated useful life in the same way as we treat a tangible fixed asset would have been sufficient. This has been far from the case. Over the past 40 years, there have been a number of approaches to accounting for purchased goodwill, including:

(a) keeping the goodwill in the balance sheet unchanged (i.e. no amortisation and probably no impairment);

(b) writing off the cost of the goodwill directly to reserves in the year of acquisition (and not through the income statement);

(c) writing off the cost of goodwill to the income statement in the year of acquisition

(d) amortising the goodwill over its expected life;

(e) not amortising goodwill, but checking it annually for impairment.

The present position is that IAS 38 uses option (d), but the recently introduced IFRS 3 *Business Combinations* uses option (e).

Before accounting standards were issued on the subject, most companies included goodwill in the balance sheet at its original cost (option (a) above). Normally, they did not amortise the goodwill or write it off until it became apparent that the goodwill was worthless when they would write it off.

The initial UK standard treatment

The first UK accounting standard SSAP 22 Accounting for Goodwill was issued in 1984. This allowed entities two alternative treatments:

1 write off the goodwill directly to reserves in the year of acquisition (option (b)), or
2 amortise the goodwill to the income statement over its expected life (option (d))

Almost all UK companies used treatment 1 above, as it had no effect on reported profit (option 2 reduced reported profit because of the amortisation charge). The problem with using option 1 was that it reduced shareholders' funds, which could become negative. In fact, some advertising agencies reached the situation of having negative shareholders' funds (i.e. the balance sheet showed the company had negative net worth). As option 1 reduces shareholders' funds, it increases the capital gearing of the company (i.e. loans/shareholders' funds) and it could lead to a breach of loan covenants and banks and other investors being unwilling to provide loans to the entity.

It was possible to write off the goodwill in the year of acquisition to the income statement (option (c)). However, very few companies would have taken this option as it would result in a very substantial reduction in profit.

The initial IAS 22 treatment

Unlike the UK's SSAP 22, IAS 22 *Business Combinations* (revised 1998) did not allow goodwill to be written off against reserves in the year of acquisition, so all companies were then required to amortise goodwill to the income statement over its useful life (option (d)), thus reducing profits.

The IAS 38 treatment – where useful lives are finite

IAS 38 requires intangible assets with a finite useful life to be amortised (i.e. option (d) above). The residual value (at the end of the asset's life) is taken as zero, unless it can be shown that it can be sold at the end of its useful life.

The IAS 38 treatment – where useful lives are indefinite

Where an intangible asset has an indefinite useful life, it is not amortised. The word 'indefinite' does not mean 'infinite' (para. 91). The Standard suggests that an intangible asset would have an indefinite life if maintenance expenditure would maintain the asset and its standard of performance. Allowing an intangible asset to have an indefinite life is a loophole of the Standard, which could lead to some abuse (as having an intangible asset with an indefinite life allows an entity to avoid the amortisation charge). The Standard should more strongly discourage companies from arguing that intangible assets have an indefinite life.

If an intangible asset has an indefinite life, then IAS requires the entity to check the asset annually for impairment (or more frequently if there is an indication of impairment). If the recoverable value of the intangible asset is less than its carrying value, then the asset's value must be reduced to the recoverable value by an impairment charge (note that impairment also applies to intangible assets, which are being amortised). Essentially, this treatment is option (e) above.

The IFRS3 treatment

IFRS 3 *Business Combinations* treats goodwill as if it has an indefinite life. So, it tests goodwill annually for impairment. An impairment charge is made if the carrying value is greater than the recoverable value of the goodwill. IFRS 3 prohibits the amortisation of goodwill.

The effect of this is that IFRS 3 is one of the International Accounting Standards that can have a substantial positive effect on reported profit. For example, under IAS, the reported profit of Vodafone has increased by £6.8 billion, because the previous charge for amortisation of goodwill is eliminated under IAS.

18.5.5 Transition to IFRS 3 *Business Combinations*

Prior to IFRS 3, IAS 22 required goodwill to be capitalised and amortised in the profit and loss account over its useful life. IFRS 3 has been introduced for accounting periods starting on or after 31 March 2004. A company which is using IFRS 3 for the first time in its financial statements for the year ended 31 March 2005 will discontinue amortising goodwill at 31 March 2004. The balance of goodwill at 31 March 2004 will be used at 31 March 2005, subject to an annual impairment test. Goodwill amortised prior to 31 March 2004 is not written back.

18.5.6 Negative goodwill

IAS 22 (paras 61–62) said that:

(a) if negative goodwill relates to expectations of losses and expenses which are identified in the acquirer's plan for the acquisition and can be measured reliably, the negative goodwill should be included as income in the periods when the future losses and expenses are recognised;

(b) any remaining negative goodwill (after (a) above) should be credited to the income statement over the period in which the non-monetary assets are depreciated or sold;

(c) any remaining negative goodwill (after (a) and (b) above) should be credited to the income statement immediately.

This treatment is different from the UK FRS 10 which includes only item (b) above and amortises any remaining negative goodwill over the periods expected to benefit.

Where negative goodwill arises from a business combination, IFRS3 says the acquirer should:

(a) reassess the identification and measurement of the acquiree's identifiable assets, liabilities and contingent liabilities and the measurement of the cost of the combination; and

(b) recognise immediately in the income statement any excess remaining after that reassessment.

The reassessment in (a) will normally result in a reduction in the net value of the assets, liabilities and contingent liabilities and a consequent reduction in negative goodwill. The immediate crediting of the remaining negative goodwill to the income statement seems difficult to justify when, as in many situations, the reason why the consideration is less than the value of the net identifiable assets is that there are expected to be future losses or redundancy payments. Whilst the redundancy payments could be included in the 'contingent liabilities' at the date of acquisition, standard setters are very reluctant to allow a provision to be made for future losses (this has been prohibited in recent accounting standards). This means that the only option is to say the negative goodwill should be credited to the income statement at the date of acquisition. This results in the group profit being inflated when a subsidiary with negative goodwill is acquired.

In some ways, it would be better to credit the negative goodwill to the income statement over the years the losses are expected. However, the 'provision for future losses' (i.e. the negative goodwill) does not fit in very well with the Framework's definition of a liability as being recognised 'when it is probable that an outflow of resources embodying economic benefits will result from the settlement of a present obligation and the amount at which the settlement will take place can be measured reliably'. It is questionable whether future losses are a 'present obligation' and whether they can be 'measured reliably', so it is very unlikely that future losses can be included as a liability in the balance sheet.

18.6 Is there a correct treatment for amortising goodwill?

We will consider the alternative treatments for amortising or writing off purchased goodwill:

(a) keeping the goodwill in the balance sheet unchanged (i.e. no amortisation and probably no impairment);

(b) writing off the cost of the goodwill directly to reserves in the year of acquisition (and not through the income statement);

(c) writing off the cost of goodwill to the income statement in the year of acquisition;

(d) amortising the goodwill over its expected useful life;

(e) not amortising goodwill, but checking it annually for impairment.

(a) Keeping the goodwill in the balance sheet unchanged

It is (probably) wrong to keep goodwill in the balance sheet unchanged, as its value will decline with time. Its value may be maintained by further expenditure e.g. advertising, but this expenditure is essentially 'internally generated goodwill' which is not allowed to be capitalised. Sales of most manufactured products decline during their life and their selling price falls. Eventually, the products are replaced by a technically superior product. An example is computer microprocessors, which initially command a high price, and high sales. The selling price and sales quantities decline as faster microprocessors are produced. Much of the goodwill of businesses is represented by the products they sell. Hence it is wrong to not amortise the goodwill.

(b) Writing off the cost of the goodwill directly to reserves in the year of acquisition

Writing off goodwill direct to reserves in the year of acquisition is wrong, as the loss in value of the goodwill does not occur at acquisition. It occurs over a longer period. The goodwill is losing value over its life, and this loss in value should be charged to the income statement. Making the charge direct to reserves stops this charge from appearing in the income statement.

(c) Writing off the cost of goodwill to the income statement in the year of acquisition

Writing off goodwill to the income statement in the year of acquisition is wrong. It does have the advantage over (b) of showing the charge in the income statement. However, the loss in value of the goodwill does not occur at acquisition. It occurs over a longer period, and this amortisation charge should be made over the life of the goodwill.

(d) Amortising the goodwill over its expected useful life

Amortising goodwill over its life is the best way of making the charge in the income statement. There are problems over (i) what is the life of the goodwill and (ii) the method for amortising.

(i) *What is the life of the goodwill?*

Companies will wish to minimise the amortisation charge by increasing the life of the goodwill, so auditors should be vigilant and prevent excessively long lives being used. For many businesses, a life of about 5 years might be appropriate, although this would be long for microprocessors but short for some well-known brands (such as the Mars Bar, which was introduced in the 1930s). However, one should be careful not to assume that the Mars Bar brand has a future life of 70 years because it has already been in existence for 70 years. Also, new microprocessors may have a longer life, now that the technology is becoming more mature. This requires careful consideration by the accountant and auditor.

(ii) *The method for amortising*

Straight-line amortisation is the simplest method. However, as the benefits are likely to be greater in earlier years than later ones, amortisation could use 'actual sales'/'expected total sales' or the reducing balance method.

It could be argued that amortising goodwill is equivalent to depreciating tangible fixed assets as prescribed by IAS 16 *Property, Plant and Equipment* and that option (d) appears to be the best way of treating goodwill in the balance sheet and income statement.

There are difficulties but these should not prevent us from using this method. After all, accountants have to make many judgements when valuing items in the balance sheet, such as assessing the life of tangible fixed assets, the value of stock and bad debt provisions.

(e) An annual impairment check

IFRS 3 *Business Combinations* has introduced a new treatment for purchased goodwill when it arises from a business combination (i.e. the purchase of a company which becomes a subsidiary). This treatment is to include the value of purchased goodwill at its original figure, and only make a charge to the income statement when it becomes impaired. This is called a 'balance sheet approach' to accounting, as the charge is only made when the value (in the balance sheet) diminishes below its original cost.

The IFRS 3 treatment is consistent with the 'Framework',[19] which says 'Expenses are recognised in the income statement when a decrease in future economic benefits related to a decrease in an asset or an increase of a liability has arisen that can be measured reliably'.

However, there has been much criticism of the 'balance sheet approach' of the 'Framework'. An 'income statement' approach to 'expense' (e.g. depreciation) would probably suggest the expense is charged over the life of the asset or the profits the item produces.

For example, if a company purchased specialised plant which had a resale value of 5% of its cost, then it could be argued that the depreciation charge should be 95% of its cost immediately after it comes into use. This is not sensible, as the purpose of buying the plant is to produce a product, so the depreciation charge should be over the life of the product.

Alternatively, if the 'future economic benefit' approach was used to value the plant, there would be no depreciation until the future economic benefit was less than its original cost. So, initial sales would incur no depreciation charge, but later sales would have an increased charge.

A further problem is estimating 'future economic benefit' (FEB) accurately. The FEB depends on future sales and the profitability of the sales. It is probable that estimates of future sales and profitability will be optimistic, thus increasing estimated FEB and avoiding an impairment charge. Eventually, the company's management will realise their sales predictions are too optimistic and there will be a substantial impairment charge against the goodwill, but this will not be when the profits were made. Most car manufacturers have very optimistic sales predictions when a new model is introduced. When sales do not reach expected levels, they reduce the selling price, which further reduces the profit.

This example shows the weakness of using 'impairment' and the 'balance sheet approach' of charging goodwill to the income statement – the charge occurs at the 'wrong time'. The charge should be made earlier when sales, selling prices and profits are high, not when the product becomes 'out of date' and sales and profits are falling.

Although the IFRS 3 treatment of 'impairment' appears to be correct according to the 'Framework', it could be argued that the impairment approach is not correct, as the charge occurs at the wrong time (i.e. when there is a loss in value, rather than when profits are being made), it is very difficult to estimate the 'future economic benefit' of the goodwill and those estimates are likely to be over-optimistic.

In addition, it means that the treatment of goodwill for IFRS 3 transactions is different from its treatment in IAS 38. This shows the inconsistency of the Standards – they should use a single treatment, either IAS 38 amortisation or IFRS 3 impairment.

Why does the IFRS 3 treatment of goodwill differ from IAS 38?

The answer is probably related to the convergence of International Accounting Standards to US accounting standards, and pressures from listed companies.

In issuing recent International Standards, the IASB has not only aimed to produce 'worldwide' Standards but also Standards which are acceptable to US Standard setters. The IASB wanted their Standards to be acceptable for listing on the New York Stock Exchange (NYSE), so there was strong pressure on the IASB to make their Standards similar to US Standards. The equivalent US Standard to IFRS 3 uses impairment of goodwill as the charge against profits (rather than amortisation). Thus, IFRS 3 uses the same method and it prohibits amortisation.

A further pressure for impairment rather than amortisation comes from listed companies. Essentially, listed companies want to maximise their reported profit, and amortisation reduces profit. For most of the time, companies can argue that the 'future economic benefit' of the goodwill is greater than its original cost (or carrying value if it has been previously impaired), and thus avoid a charge to the income statement. Also, companies could argue that the 'impairment charge' is an unexpected event and charge it as an exceptional item. In the UK, most companies publicise their 'profit before exceptional items' which will avoid charging the 'exceptional impairment charge'. As mentioned above, it is reported that the UK telecoms company Vodafone will increase its reported profit by £6.8 billion (i.e. £6,800 million) when it changes to International Standards and avoids amortisation of its goodwill.

Note that under IAS 38 an intangible asset with an 'indefinite' useful life is not amortised but subject to an annual impairment check (and written down to its impaired value if this is less than its carrying value). This treatment is similar to the treatment of purchased goodwill under IFRS 3 *Business Combinations*. IFRS 3 justifies its treatment of purchased goodwill (in a business combination) by saying it (always) has an indefinite useful life – this seems more of a justification for the accounting treatment than reflecting the substance.

18.6.1 Effect of different methods on financial statements

The financial statements of CW Group for the year ended 31 December 20X2 are shown in Figure 18.1. The last three columns show the consolidated balance sheet and profit and loss account using:

Figure 18.1 Effect of IFRS 3

	CW plc £000	Fair value WW Ltd £000	IFRS 3 £000	Write off immediately £000	Amortise over life £000
Consolidated CW Group					
Balance sheet at 31 December 20X2					
Non-current assets					
Goodwill			100		95
Plant and machinery	1,100	180	1,280	1,280	1,280
Investment in WW Ltd	300				
Net current assets	800	120	920	920	920
	2,200	300	2,300	2,200	2,295
Non-current liabilities	430	30	460	460	460
	1,770	270	1,840	1,740	1,835
Capital and reserves					
Share capital	900	150	900	900	900
Share premium account	300		300	300	300
Retained earnings	570	80	640	540	635
Revaluation reserve		40			
	1,770	270	1,840	1,740	1,835
Income statement for year ended 31 December 20X2					
Profit before goodwill amortisation	350	100	450	450	450
Goodwill amortisation					5
Profit before tax	350	100	450	450	445
Taxation	100	30	130	130	130
Profit after tax	250	70	320	320	315
Dividends	80			80	80
Retained profit	170	70	240	240	235
Reserves b/fwd	400	10	400	300	400
Reserves c/fwd	570	80	640	540	635
Ratios:					
Profit before tax/shareholders' funds			24.46%	25.86%	24.25%
Gearing – loans/shareholders' funds			25.00%	26.44%	25.07%

Note: Dividends column shows 80 under IFRS 3, Write off, Amortise columns.

- IFRS 3 where it is assumed that the goodwill remains worth at least £100,000, and no impairment provision is required;
- writing off goodwill at acquisition to accumulated profits;
- IAS 22 where goodwill is amortised over twenty years (i.e. at £5,000 a year).

In this example, the effect is relatively small. However,

- Under IFRS 3, shareholders' funds and profits are maximised. The profit margin (i.e. profit before tax/shareholders' funds) is slightly lower than for immediate write-off, as immediate write-off gives lower shareholders' funds. The gearing is lowest under this method.
- Immediate write-off gives the highest profit margin, but the highest gearing, as the write-off reduces shareholders' funds.
- IAS 22 (amortisation) gives the lowest profit margin, because of the amortisation charge for goodwill. The gearing is slightly higher than for IFRS 3 because shareholders' funds have been reduced by the amortisation charge.

18.6.2 Economic consequences of each method

We have seen that amortisation has an effect on future EPS, while immediate write-off has an effect on the balance sheet structure. If there is no impairment of goodwill, IFRS 3 produces the same profit (and EPS) as immediate write-off, and slightly higher shareholders' funds than amortisation. Writing off goodwill against reserves acts to distort some of the primary ratios, since it reduces the shareholders' reserves and therefore the capital employed as well. This has important effects on inter-firm comparison. As an example, let us compare WPP's UK accounts with its US-adjusted accounts. If we concentrate purely on the goodwill adjustments, what is the effect on the return on capital employed (ROCE) ratio as per the above? In brief, the profit in the USA is decreased by the annual amortisation charge and the capital employed is increased by the capitalised value of goodwill (which had been written off in the UK). This will reduce the US ROCE. For comparability, the accounts need to be adjusted so that they use exactly the same goodwill policy.

Gearing ratios are also affected by writing off goodwill against reserves. These ratios include:

$$\text{Gearing ratio} = \frac{\text{Total liability} - \text{Current liability}}{\text{Capital employed}}$$

The gearing ratio measures the proportion of capital employed which has been raised by fixed-interest debt. A highly geared company has a high proportion of borrowings, while a company with low gearing relies more on shareholders' funds and equity. The gearing ratio is interpreted in different ways by different users: shareholders might seek higher ratios because this will increase the EPS; creditors might prefer lower ratios as this means that there are fewer secured claims against the company's assets.

We have discussed the choices available for dealing with goodwill and have demonstrated the effect of each on the accounts.

18.7 Other types of intangible asset under IAS 38

IAS 38 gives the following examples of classes of intangible assets:[20]

- brand names;
- mastheads and publishing titles;
- computer software;
- licences and franchises;
- copyrights, patents and other industrial property rights, services and operating rights;
- recipes, formulae, models, designs and prototypes; and
- intangible assets under development.

IAS 38 says that intangible assets should be divided into these categories (or other suitable categories) and disclosed separately. Different lives may be attributed to each of these types of intangible assets. Apart from this, the treatment of these items is essentially the same as for purchased and non-purchased goodwill in IAS 38.

18.8 Disclosure of intangible assets under IAS 38

IAS 38 requires the disclosure of the following for each type of intangible asset:[21]

(a) Whether useful lives are indefinite or finite. For finite useful lives, the useful lives or amortisation rates used.

(b) The amortisation methods used for intangible assets with finite useful lives.

(c) The gross carrying amount and accumulated amortisation at the beginning and end of the period.

(d) Where amortisation of intangible assets is included in the income statement.

(e) A reconciliation of the carrying value at the beginning and end of the period, showing:

- additions, showing separately those from internal development, acquired separately and those acquired through business combinations;
- assets classified as held for sale or included in a disposal group classified as held for sale;
- increases or decreases resulting from revaluations and from impairment losses recognised or reversed directly in equity (IAS 36 Impairment of Assets);
- impairment losses recognised in the income statement in the period;
- impairment losses reversed in the income statement in the period;
- the amortisation charge;
- exchange differences;
- other changes in the carrying value in the period.

Where an intangible asset is assessed as having an indefinite useful life, the carrying value of the asset must be stated[22] and the reasons for supporting the assessment of an indefinite life.

   As stated in the section on R&D, the financial statements must disclose the charge for research and development in the period.[23]

18.8.1 Intangible assets: extracts of accounting policies from accounts of UK companies

In recent years, companies have applied a range of different accounting policies to the treatment of intangible assets in their financial statements. This variety of accounting treatment is illustrated by the following extracts from the accounts of Bass plc, Reckitt & Colman plc, The EMI Group, Racal Electronics plc and Charterhouse Communications plc. Although companies disclose their accounting treatment in their statement of accounting policies, this does not give us information on the motives influencing this choice; nor does it allow us to assess the value, or indeed the continued existence, of an asset.

For example, Bass plc did not include intangible assets in either its 1997, 1998 or 1999 balance sheets, as stated in its accounting policies. Its 1997 accounting policies stated:

Fixed assets and depreciation

Intangible assets – No value is attributed to trademarks, concessions, patents and similar rights and assets, including hotel franchises and management contracts.

As readers of the accounts, we were unable to assess readily whether this policy was one of convenience, which would result in the understatement of assets and the creation of secret reserves, or whether it indicated that these assets did, indeed, have no value; or whether the company is applying the prudence concept and it is difficult to attach values to the intangible assets with any reasonable certainty. In practice, it may be very difficult to establish a link between the cost incurred and the value created for intangibles – the economic benefits associated with an asset depend on how successfully the appropriate market can be developed. Moreover, a reliable measurement of the cost of intangibles is often impossible because of the problems involved in establishing a separate cost figure. This is often the case when there is not an active market in a particular intangible to indicate a market value.

Following the issue of FRS 10 the 1998 and 1999 Bass plc annual report accounting policy reads as follows:

Intangible assets

On acquisition of a business, no value is attributed to intangible assets which cannot be separately identified or reliably measured. No value is attributed to internally generated intangible assets.

This policy applied from 1998 but there is no indication as to the position before FRS 10 relating to the intangible assets described in the Bass 1997 accounting policy.

Reckitt & Colman offers a different treatment from Bass. It includes trademarks in the balance sheet at their purchase cost and does not provide any annual systematic amortisation because in the company's view their useful economic life is unlimited. The intangible asset is written down only if there is evidence of an impairment in value. The Reckitt & Colman 1998 Annual Report accounting policies read as follows:

Intangible assets and goodwill

Trademarks are not amortised, as it is considered that their useful economic lives are not limited. Their carrying value is reviewed annually by the directors to determine whether there has been any impairment in value and any such reductions in value are taken to the profit and loss account.

Cost	Trademarks
	£m
At beginning of financial year	1,143.0
Additions during year	64.6
Disposals during the year	(6.2)
Exchange adjustments	(5.4)
At 2 January 1999	1,196.0

Following the issue of FRS 10, the 1998 Reckitt & Colman Annual Report accounting policy was unchanged except that the wording 'permanent diminution' was changed to 'impairment'.

The EMI Group's policy partly followed the Bass treatment and partly followed the Reckitt & Colman treatment. For example, in its 1997 accounts the company had written off some copyrights and capitalised other copyrights (at their purchase cost), which it amortises only if the royalties indicate that the book value is not supported by the level of royalties.

The EMI Group's Annual Report 1997

Accounting policies

Music Publishing Copyrights purchased prior to 1 April 1989 were written off against shareholders' funds on acquisition. Copyrights acquired as a result of the acquisition of a business, on or after 1 April 1989, are treated as intangible assets in the Group balance sheet. The capitalised amount of such copyrights, being their purchase cost, is subject to amortisation only to the extent that the royalty income generated by the total music publishing portfolio is insufficient to support its book value. All costs attributable to copyrights obtained in the normal course of trade, and not as a result of the acquisition of a business, are written off as incurred.

In its 1999 Annual Report, EMI changed its accounting policy due to the FRS 10 rigorous impairment review requirement. Its accounting policy read as follows:

Music copyrights

Music publishing copyrights purchased prior to 1 April 1989 were written off against shareholders' funds on acquisition. Copyrights acquired as a result of acquisitions on or after 1 April 1989 have previously been capitalised as intangible assets in the Group balance sheet, but amortised only to the extent that royalty income generated by the total music publishing copyrights portfolio was insufficient to support its book value.

On adoption of FRS 10, our accounting policy for copyrights had to change because we could not perform the detailed annual impairment review required by FRS 10 to support an indefinite useful economic life. Consequently, copyrights are now amortised by equal annual amounts over up to 20 years, other than in exceptional circumstances when sufficient ongoing impairment tests can be performed to support a useful economic life of over 20 years. Where a useful economic life of up to 20 years has been adopted, copyrights are reviewed for impairment at the end of the first full financial year following acquisition and in other periods if events or changes in circumstances indicate that the carrying value may not be recoverable.

The comparatives for the year ended 31 March 1998 and opening balances have been restated, via prior period adjustment, to reflect the accumulated amortisation at 31 March 1997 and the charge for the year ended 31 March 1998 arising from this change in accounting policy.

Racal follows a policy of amortising the historical cost of intangible assets which it holds in the form of 'know-how' over the useful economic life of the know-how. This is illustrated in its annual accounts.

Racal Electronics plc Annual Reports and Accounts 1999

Accounting policies

Know-how – Payments made to acquire manufacturing licences for specific products are amortised against profits over a period of 3 to 5 years being the period of utilisation of such manufacturing knowledge.

Charterhouse Communications includes newly acquired publishing rights in its financial statements. Note that the intangible assets dwarf the tangible assets.

Charterhouse Communications plc Annual Reports and Accounts 1998

Accounting policies

Intangible Fixed Assets – Publishing rights and titles are stated at cost in these financial statements. On an annual basis, the directors consider the fair value of these assets on the basis of cash flow projections. Amortisation is not provided as there has been no permanent diminution in their value.

Balance Sheet at 31 May 1998

Fixed assets	£000
Intangible assets	6,501
Tangible assets	92
Investments	—
	6,593

18.8.2 Intangible assets: extracts of accounting policies from accounts of Continental companies

In the financial statements of Articon Information Systems AG (a German company) for the year ended 31 December 1998, the accounting policies on intangible assets state:

Acquired intangible assets are capitalised at cost and depreciated using the straight-line method over a scheduled period of three to four years. Minor intangibles are fully expensed immediately.

The financial statements disclose intangible assets as:

	1998	1997
Fixed assets	DM	DM
I. Intangible assets		
1. Industrial property rights	1	502
2. Computer programs	121,436	8,949
3. Goodwill	274,066	0
4. 'Black box'	19,800	0
5. Self-developed intangible assets	115,310	0
6. Advance payments	1,920	0
	532,533	9,451

In the financial statements of Essilor International (a French company) for the year ended 31 December 1999, the accounting policies on intangible assets state:

Intangible assets correspond primarily to purchased goodwill, trade marks, concessions, patents and licences. Purchased goodwill and trade marks correspond to part of the excess of the cost of acquisition of investments over the Group's equity in the underlying net assets that is classified as an intangible asset. They are not amortised. The value of purchased goodwill and trade marks is reviewed annually based on projections made at the time of acquisition, and provision is made in the case of any impairment in value. Other intangible assets are stated at cost and are amortised by the straight-line method over 3 to 5 years.

Intangible assets in the balance sheet are disclosed

Assets	1999	1998
Intangible assets	657,028	473,643
Goodwill	2,179,864	1,854,258

There is the following disclosure of movement in purchased goodwill and other intangibles during the year:

Other net intangible assets	Purchased goodwill	Other intangibles	Amortisation
At 1 January	374,110	222,122	(122,589)
Changes in scope and other		77,604	(38,457)
acquisitions	9,119	109,840	
Disposals		(7,872)	3,489
Translation adjustment	59,686	13,455	(5,686)
Amortisation and provisions			(37,793)
	442,915	415,149	(201,036)

On 'purchased goodwill and trade marks', Essilor did not comply with the then current provisions of IAS 22 and IAS 38, as both these International Standards required amortisation of intangible assets. For example, IAS 22 para. 44 stated that:

Goodwill should be amortised on a systematic basis over its useful life. The amortisation period should reflect the best estimate of the period during which future economic benefits are expected to flow to the enterprise. **There is a rebuttable presumption that the useful life of goodwill will not exceed twenty years from initial recognition.**

Furthermore, para. 51 states that **'the useful life of goodwill is always finite'.**

Under the new IFRS 3, goodwill acquired in a business combination is not amortised but subject to an annual impairment test. Thus, Essilor's accounting treatment for goodwill is in accordance with IFRS 3 (2004).

Essilor did already comply with the international standards on other intangible assets.

18.9 Brand accounting

Brand accounting refers to the practice of representing a specific type of intangible asset – brand names – as a fixed asset in the balance sheet and typically not amortising it but subjecting it to regular review.

Prior to IAS 38, brand accounting emerged for two main reasons.

- For acquisitive companies it could be attributed to the accounting treatment required for measuring and reporting goodwill. The London Business School carried out research into the 'brands phenomenon' and found that 'a major aim of brand valuation has been to repair or pre-empt equity depletion caused by UK goodwill accounting rules'.[24]

- Non-acquisitive companies do not incur costs for acquiring goodwill, so their reserves are not eroded by writing off purchased goodwill. However, these companies may have incurred promotional costs in creating home-grown brands and it would strengthen the balance sheet if they were permitted to include a valuation of these brands.[25]

Justifications for brand accounting

We now consider some other justifications that have been put forward for the inclusion of brands as a separate asset in the balance sheet.

Effect on shareholders' funds

Immediate goodwill write-off results in a fall in net tangible assets as disclosed by the balance sheet, even though the market capitalisation of a company increases. One way to maintain the asset base and avoid such a depletion of companies' reserves is to divide the purchased goodwill into two parts: the amount attributable to brands and the remaining amount attributable to pure goodwill.[26] For instance, WPP have capitalised two corporate brand names (J. Walter Thompson; Hill and Knowlton) which were originally valued in 1988 at £350m (and remain at that amount in the balance sheet). Without this capitalisation, the share owners' funds of £187.7m in the 1998 accounts would be reduced by £350m to a negative figure of (£162.3m).

Effect on borrowing powers

The borrowing powers of public companies may be expressed in terms of multiples of net assets. In Articles of Association there may be strict rules regarding the multiple that a company must not exceed. In addition, borrowing agreements and Stock Exchange listing agreements are generally dependent on net assets.

Effect on ratios

Immediate goodwill write-off distorts the gearing ratios, but the inclusion of brands as intangible assets minimised this distortion by providing a more realistic value for shareholders' funds. Guinness plc provided information on its gearing ratio in its five-year financial summary:

			31 December		
Gearing ratio	*1992*	*1993*	*1994*	*1995*	*1996*
Including cost of acquired brands	56%	49%	35%	28%	34%
Excluding cost of acquired brands	140%	111%	63%	49%	58%

Effect on management decisions

It is claimed that including brands on the balance sheet leads to more informed and improved management decision making. The quality of internal decisions is related to the quality of information available to management.[27] As brands represent one of the most important assets of a company, management should be aware of the success or failure of each individual brand. Knowledge about the performance of brands ensures that management reacts accordingly to maintain or improve competitive advantage.

There is also evidence[28] that companies with valuable brand names are not including these in their balance sheets and are not, therefore, taking account of the assets for insurance purposes.

18.10 Intellectual property

According to the World Intellectual Property Organization (WIPO), intellectual property refers to creations of the mind: inventions, literary and artistic works and symbols, names, images and designs used in commerce. Intellectual property is divided into two categories, namely:

- **industrial property** which includes inventions (patents), trademarks, industrial designs and geographic indications of source; and

- **copyright** which includes literary and artistic works such as novels, poems, plays, films, musical works, artistic works such as drawings, paintings, photographs and sculptures, and architectural designs. Rights related to copyright include those of performing artistes in their performances, producers of phonograms in their recordings, and those of broadcasters in their radio and television programmes.

WIPO[29] is an international organisation dedicated to promoting the use and protection of works of the human spirit. These works – intellectual property – are expanding the bounds of science and technology and enriching the world of arts. Through its work, WIPO plays an important part in enhancing the quality and enjoyment of life as well as creating real wealth for nations. With headquarters in Geneva, Switzerland, WIPO is one of the 16 specialised agencies of the United Nations system of organisations. It administers 21 international treaties dealing with different aspects of intellectual property protection. The organisation counts 175 nations as member states. Its importance is recognised in the following comment by Peter Drucker:

> Knowledge has become the 'key resource' of the world economy. The traditional factors of production – land, labour, capital – are becoming restraints rather than driving forces.

and in the UK, a 1998 White Paper placed 'know-how' at the heart of competitiveness.[30]

> Our competitiveness depends on making the most of our distinctive and valuable assets which competitors find hard to imitate. In a modern economy those distinctive assets are increasingly knowledge, skills and creativity rather than traditional factors.

In looking at the relative importance of asset values in businesses, in the 1980s 70% was attributed to tangible assets and 30% to intangible assets. In the mid 1990s, the situation reversed and 30% was tangible assets and 70% intangible assets. More recently 95% has been attributed to intangible assets and 5% to physical and financial assets.

The rise of the new economy

This has been principally driven by information and knowledge. It has been identified by the Organization for Economic Co-operation and Development (OECD) as explaining the increased prominence of intellectual capital as a business and research topic.[31]

Through a brief examination of the period since the industrial revolution, the following chain of events is observable:[32]

(a) Capital and labour were brought together and the factors of production became localised and accessible.

(b) Firms pushed to increase volumes of production to meet the demands of growing markets.

(c) Firms began to build intangibles like brand equity and reputation (goodwill) in order to create a competitive advantage in markets where new entrants limited the profit-making potential of a strategy of mass production.

(d) Firms invested heavily in information technology to increase the quality of products and improve the speed with which those products could be brought to market.

(e) Firms realised the value of information and worked at managing information and transforming it into the intellectual capital needed to drive the organisation.

At each state of this corporate evolution fixed assets became less important, in relative terms, compared with intangible assets in determining a company's success. Accounting and financial reporting practices, however, have remained largely unchanged.

Guthrie, while arguing[33] that accountants must find a way to incorporate accurate measures and values of intellectual capital in formal company reports or they will become irrelevant, suggests that the importance of intellectual capital is specifically emphasised in

● the revolution in information technology and the information society;
● the rising importance of knowledge and the knowledge-based economy;
● the changing patterns of interpersonal activities and the network society;
● the emergence of innovation and creativity as the principal determinant of competitiveness.

In a world of dot.com companies, virtual corporations and a flourishing service industry, book values correlate poorly with market capitalisation.

The OECD definition

The OECD describes intellectual capital[34] as

the economic value of two categories of intangible assets of a company:
(a) organizational ('structural') capital and
(b) human capital.

Structural capital refers to things like proprietary software systems, distribution networks and supply chains. Human capital includes human resources within the organisation (i.e. staff resources) and resources external to the organisation (namely, customers and suppliers). The term intellectual capital has often been treated as being synonymous with intangible assets. The definition by the OECD makes a distinction by identifying intellectual capital as a subset of rather than the same as the intangible assets base of a business.

Traditionally, accounting reports have been prepared on the basis of historical cost. This does not provide for the identification and measurement of intangibles in organisations – especially knowledge-based organisations. The limitations of the existing financial reporting systems have resulted in a move towards finding new ways to measure and report on a company's intellectual capital.

The legal view

As Gallafent, Eastaway and Dauppe suggest,[35] the principal characteristic of all forms of intellectual property is the so-called 'incorporeal' nature of that property. It is an abstraction, intangible and as such more difficult to protect than other less nebulous forms of property. To be eligible for legal protection, the author's or inventor's work must have been rendered into some tangible form. The term 'intellectual property' denotes the rights over a tangible object of the person whose mental efforts created it. The high-speed development in communications initially left the practical application of copyright law in disarray as in the recent example of the *Napster* case (http--www.riaa.com-news-filings-pdf-napster-PlaintiffsSJM.pdf.url). The new technology of genetic engineering and the genome project leaves this area wide open.

The bankers' view

From about 1945 until 1975, bankers traditionally thought of intangibles as worthless and deducted them from net worth to arrive at tangible net worth. Liquidation analysis assumes that a loan will be repaid solely from the proceeds of sale of assets at forced sale prices. It stressed the value of the collateral as the main reason for lending.

By the early 1980s credit analysts from American banks in London began to input some value to some intangible assets, at first on a case-by-case judgement. The major change in the attitude to intangibles arose from the wave of acquisitions and particularly leverage acquisitions. Donaldson suggests the following principles:[36]

● An asset which generates cash in ways that can be understood and forecast has value to its owner.

● Where the asset and cash flow can be sold, a market price higher than the valuation of actual cash flow suggests that the owner is failing to extract the maximum value from the asset. The cash flow valuation may underestimate the real value.

● The cost to replace an asset provides a useful check on other methods of value.

● Given that valuation techniques are likely to remain underdeveloped for some time it will often be possible to give a range rather than pinpoint value.

● Value is the critical element, not cost. Where money is spent creating an asset it is well spent only if the asset has value, i.e. it is the value of the asset rather than the cost reflected in the balance sheet.

● Once established an asset should be depreciated in ways to reflect the facts of each case.

● A tendency to lose value in liquidation is one factor to consider in assessing overall value. The ability to generate cash which helps to avoid liquidation remains important at all times.

18.10.1 Financial reporting models

Principal among the new reporting models are:

● the Intangible Asset Monitor (Sveiby; Celemi)[37]
● the Balanced Scorecard (Kaplan and Norton)[38]
● the Skandia Value scheme (Edvinsson and Malone)[39]
● the Intellectual Capital Accounts (DATI).[40]

At the OECD symposium referred to above (see note 34) the focus of reported issues was on four issues:

(a) assessing what motivates firms to want to measure their intellectual capital;

(b) examining who within an organisation is best positioned to measure and manage intellectual capital;

(c) determining the potential effects that the reporting of intellectual capital is expected to have; and

(d) improved methods of measuring intellectual capital.

The findings of almost twenty national research studies cover some common ground as follows:

- Organisations are motivated to
  - measure their intellectual capital to assist with competitive benchmarking exercises
  - create a consciousness within the organisation that intellectual capital and human resources in particular do matter
  - provide structured information to the capital and labour markets that may enhance perceptions of the company.
- There was agreement that everyone in an organisation needs to be committed to the task of measuring and managing intellectual capital if a company is to do so successfully.
- The effects of reporting intellectual capital included improved employee morale, lower staff turnover, increased investment in developing intellectual capital, a higher value being attributed to a company's intellectual capital by senior corporate officers than previously and an improved understanding of what specific factors are crucial to continued growth and development.

Techniques commonly used by public and private sector organisations to measure their intellectual capital included Kaplan and Norton's Balanced Scorecard and Karl-Erik Sveiby's Intangible Asset Monitor. Two innovative approaches are those followed by Celemi and Skandia which are described below.

The Celemi experience

Celemi is a Swedish-based company specialising in facilitating a learning process within other organisations. It was one of the first to open its eyes to the wisdom of measuring the value of its intellectual capital. Celemi published in 1995 what has been described as the world's first audit of intangible assets as part of the company annual report. Celemi uses the Sveiby framework to classify its intangibles into three groups: individual competence, external structure and internal structure. Celemi's reports provide answers to three questions asked by stakeholders: first, the overall size of the balance sheet (what type of assets does Celemi have) and second, are intangibles increasing or decreasing and are they being utilised efficiently?

As regards individual competence, Celemi views its employees and their competencies (its knowledge base) as its most important strength in business. Celemi uses non-financial metrics to assess the value represented by its employees. The idea is to report the same metrics each year to facilitate benchmarking over time. This reveals whether the human capital is improving or declining.

The Skandia experience

Skandia started work on developing a system for reporting the value of its knowledge capital in 1991. While early reports by Skandia adopted the same format as Celemi, it has more recently developed a management and reporting model called the Skandia Navigator. This creates a balance between the past (financial focus), the present (customer focus, process focus and human focus) and future (renewal and development focus).

The measurement of the past, financial focus, includes performance ratios, balance sheet and profit and loss account. The customer focus is assessed in terms of market penetration. The human focus deals with levels of employee training, leadership training and teaming. The process focus looks at operational methods used and the levels of information technology support. The renewal and development focus measures the extent to which resources are being directed towards the work of teams and methods of the future. A unique aspect of the Navigator is the measure of the extent to which human capital is converted to structural capital, i.e. retained to provide corporate value.

18.10.2 Knowledge management

Another term that is currently being bandied about is knowledge management (KM). It has been described as developing business practices and processes that ensure that a business creates, accesses and embeds the knowledge that it needs. Binney[41] sees different elements of the knowledge management spectrum, namely:

● transactional knowledge management

● analytical knowledge management

● asset knowledge management

● process knowledge management

● innovation/creation-based knowledge management

● developmental knowledge management.

In transactional KM the use of knowledge is embedded in the system. Knowledge is presented to the user of a system in the course of completing a transaction or a unit of work such as entering an order or handling an enquiry from a customer.

In analytical KM large amounts of data or information are used to derive trends and patterns, making apparent that which is hidden due to the vastness of source material – turning data into information which if acted upon can become knowledge.

In asset KM the focus is on processes associated with the management of knowledge assets. The treatment of knowledge is either the management of explicit knowledge assets which have been codified in some way or the management of intellectual property and the processes surrounding its identification, exploitation and protection.

Process KM as its name implies is concerned with the codification and improvement of process. This is usually related to other disciplines such as TQM or BPR. The knowledge assets produced are known as engineered assets as they involve third parties.

Innovation/creation-based KM focuses on providing an environment in which knowledge workers, often from different disciplines, can come together in collaboration to create new knowledge resulting in new products or company capabilities.

Developmental KM focuses on either the transfer of explicit knowledge via training or education, or the conscious development of tacit knowledge through developmental interventions such as experiential assignments aimed at increasing companies' human capital.

As far as financial reporting is concerned the key requirement is that the intellectual property should be capable of meeting the criteria established in the *Statement of Principles* for classification as an asset if it is to be reported in the balance sheet.

Summary

As business has become more complex and industrial processes more sophisticated, the amount paid to develop or acquire an intangible asset has become significant in comparison to the fixed asset base of some companies. Under IAS 38 internally generated intangible assets may be capitalised if they have a readily ascertainable market value. Under IAS 38 purchased goodwill and intangibles should be capitalised in the balance sheet. Once they have been capitalised, IAS 38 requires that these assets either be amortised or subject to a regular impairment review, depending on their useful economic life. Under IFRS 3, goodwill acquired in a business combination is not amortised, but tested for impairment annually.

REVIEW QUESTIONS

1 In connection with IAS 38 *Intangible Assets*:

   (a) Define 'applied research' and 'development'.

   (b) Why is it considered necessary to distinguish between applied research and development expenditure, and how does this distinction affect the accounting treatment?

   (c) State whether the following are included within the IAS 38 definition of research and development, and give your reasons:

       (i) market research

       (ii) testing of preproduction prototypes

       (iii) operational research

       (iv) testing in search of process alternatives.

2 Describe the problems encountered when accounting for:

   (a) tangible fixed assets;

   (b) leasing (in lessees' accounts);

   (c) research and development;

   and outline the recommended accounting treatment given in the relevant International Accounting Standards (IASs). How effective are the IASs in limiting the use of different accounting treatments of the above areas?

3 Discuss the suggestion that the requirement for companies to write off research investment rather than showing it as an asset exposes companies to short-term pressure from acquisitive companies that are damaging to the country's interest.

4 Here is an extract from the Reckitt Benckiser 2000 Annual Report:

	2000	1999
	£m	£m
Fixed assets		
Intangible assets		
Brands	1,584	1,489
Goodwill	54	48
Tangible assets	535	514
	2,173	2,051
Total shareholders' funds	1,116	1,056

The accounting policy states:

> Acquired brands are only recognised on the balance sheet as intangible assets where title is clear, brand earnings are separately identifiable, the brand could be sold separately from the rest of the business and where the brand achieves earnings in excess of those achieved by unbranded products. The value of an acquired brand is determined by allocating the purchase consideration of an acquired business between the underlying fair values of the tangible assets, goodwill and brands acquired.
>
> Brands are not amortised, as it is considered that their useful economic lives are not limited. Their carrying values are reviewed annually by the directors to determine whether there has been any permanent impairment in value and any such reductions in their values are taken to the profit and loss account.

A note to the accounts states:

> A brand is only recognised where it is supported by a registered trademark, is established in the market place and holds significant market share.

Given the materiality of the brands (these include products such as Dettol, Air Wick, Calgonit-2-in-1, Lysol, Dettox, Finish, Vanish, Harpic) in relation to the total shareholders' funds, discuss the information that you consider appropriate to be disclosed in the annual report in order to assess the level and nature of risk to an investor.

5 The Nestlé 2000 Annual Report included goodwill of 3,395 CHF million arising on the acquisition of various companies such as PowerBar Inc., the US leader in the emerging energy bar category, and 188 CHF million on payment for intellectual property rights, operating rights and data processing software.

Discuss reasons for not including in the balance sheet brand valuations for such brands as Nestlé, Nescafé, Nestea, Maggi, Buitoni and Friskies which contribute about 70% of the group's total sales.

6 Discuss the advantages and disadvantages of the proposal that there should be a separate category of asset in the balance sheet clearly identified as 'research investment – outcome uncertain'.

7 The Chloride 2003 Annual Report included the following accounting policy for goodwill:

> Goodwill is subject to review at the end of the year of acquisition and at any other time when the directors believe that impairment may have occurred. Any impairment would be charged to the profit and loss account in the period in which the loss occurs.

(a) Explain the indications that a review for impairment is required.
(b) Once there are indications of impairment, how is impairment measured?

8 How is 'value in use' calculated for an impairment review? What are the areas of subjectivity?

9 Critically evaluate the basis of the following assertion: 'I am sceptical that it [the impairment test] will work reliably in practice, given the complexity and subjectivity that lie within the calculation.'[42]

10 IFRS 3 has introduced a new concept into accounting for purchased goodwill – annual impairment testing, rather than amortisation. Consider the effect of a change from amortisation of goodwill (in IAS 22) to impairment testing and no amortisation in IFRS 3, and in particular:

- the effect on the financial statements;
- the effect on financial performance ratios;
- the effect on the annual impairment or amortisation charge and its timing;

- which method gives the fairest charge over time for the value of the goodwill when a business is acquired;
- whether impairment testing with no amortisation complies with the IASC's *Framework for the Preparation and Presentation of Financial Statements;*
- why there has been a change from amortisation to impairment testing – is this pandering to pressure from the US FASB and/or listed companies?

EXERCISES

An extract from the solution is provided in the Appendix at the end of the text for exercises marked with an asterisk (*).

Question 1

Environmental Engineering plc is engaged in the development of an environmentally friendly personal transport vehicle. This will run on an electric motor powered by solar cells, supplemented by passenger effort in the form of pedal assistance.

At the end of the current accounting period, the following costs have been attributed to the project:

(a) A grant of £500,000 to the Polytechnic of the South Coast Faculty of Solar Engineering to encourage their research.

(b) Costs of £1,200,000 expended on the development of the necessary solar cells prior to the decision to incorporate them in a vehicle.

(c) Costs of £5,000,000 expended on designing the vehicle and its motors, and the planned promotional and advertising campaign for its launch on the market in twelve months' time.

Required:
 (i) Explain, with reasons, which of the above items could be considered for treatment as deferred revenue expenditure, quoting any relevant International Accounting Standard.
 (ii) Set out the criteria under which any items can be so treated.
 (iii) Advise on the accounting treatment that will be afforded to any such items after the product has been launched.

Question 2

As chief accountant at Italin NV, you have been given the following information by the director of research:

Project Luca

	€000
Costs to date (pure research 25%, applied research 75%)	200
Costs to develop product (to be incurred in the year to 30 September 20X1)	300
Expected future sales per annum for 20X2–20X7	1,000

Fixed assets purchased in 20X1 for the project:

Cost	2,500
Estimated useful life	7 years
Residual value	400

(These assets will be disposed of at their residual value at the end of their estimated useful lives.)

The board of directors considers that this project is similar to the other projects that the company undertakes, and is confident of a successful outcome. The company has enough finances to complete the development and enough capacity to produce the new product.

Required:
Prepare a report for the board outlining the principles involved in accounting for research and development and showing what accounting entries will be made in the company's accounts for each of the years ending 30 September 20X1–20X7 inclusive.
Indicate what factors need to be taken into account when assessing each research and development project for accounting purposes, and what disclosure is needed for research and development in the company's published accounts.

* Question 3

Oxlag plc, a manufacturer of pharmaceutical products, has the following research and development projects on hand at 31 January 20X2:

(A) A general survey into the long-term effects of its sleeping pill Chalcedon upon human resistance to infections. At the year-end the research is still at a basic stage and no worthwhile results with any particular applications have been obtained.

(B) A development for Meebach NV in which the company will produce market research data relating to Meebach's range of drugs.

(C) An enhancement of an existing drug, Euboia, which will enable additional uses to be made of the drug and which will consequently boost sales. This project was completed successfully on 30 April 20X2, with the expectation that all future sales of the enhanced drug would greatly exceed the costs of the new development.

(D) A scientific enquiry with the aim of identifying new strains of antibiotics for future use. Several possible substances have been identified, but research is not sufficiently advanced to permit patents and copyrights to be obtained at the present time.

The following costs have been brought forward at 1 February 20X1:

Project	A	B	C	D
			£000	
Specialised laboratory				
Cost	—	—	500	—
Depreciation	—	—	25	—
Specialised equipment				
Cost	—	—	75	50
Depreciation	—	—	15	10
Capitalised development costs	—	—	200	—
Market research costs	—	250	—	—

The following costs were incurred during the year:

Project	A	B	C	D
			£000	
Research costs	25	—	265	78
Market research costs	—	75	—	—
Specialised equipment cost	50	—	—	50

Depreciation on specialised laboratories and special equipment is provided by the straight-line method and the assets have an estimated useful life of twenty-five and five years respectively. A full year's depreciation is provided on assets purchased during the year.

Required:

(i) Write up the research and development, fixed asset and market research accounts to reflect the above transactions in the year ended 31 January 20X2.

(ii) Calculate the amount to be charged as research costs in the profit and loss account of Oxlag plc for the year ended 31 January 20X2.

(iii) State on what basis the company should amortise any capitalised development costs and what disclosures the company should make in respect of amounts written off in the year to 31 January 20X3.

(iv) Calculate the amounts to be disclosed in the balance sheet in respect of fixed assets, deferred development costs and work-in-progress.

(v) State what disclosures you would make in the accounts for the year ended 31 January 20X2 in respect of the new improved drug developed under project C, assuming sales begin on 1 May 20X2, and show strong growth to the date of signing the accounts, 14 July 20X2, with the expectation that the new drug will provide 25% of the company's pre-tax profits in the year to 31 January 20X3.

Question 4

International Accounting Standards IFRS 3 and IAS 38 address the accounting for goodwill and intangible assets.

Required:

(a) Describe the requirements of IFRS 3 regarding the initial recognition and measurement of goodwill and intangible assets.

(b) Explain the proposed approach set out by IFRS 3 for the treatment of positive goodwill in subsequent years.

(c) Territory plc acquired 80% of the ordinary share capital of Yukon Ltd on 31 May 20X6. The balance sheet of Yukon Ltd at 31 May 20X6 was:

Yukon Ltd – Balance sheet at 31 May 20X6

	£000
Non-current assets	
Intangible assets	6,020
Tangible assets	38,300
	44,320
Current assets	
Inventory	21,600
Receivables	23,200
Cash	8,800
	53,600
Current liabilities	24,000
Net current assets	29,600
Total assets less current liabilities	73,920
Non-current liabilities	12,100
Provision for liabilities and charges	3,586
Accruals and deferred income	
	58,234

Capital reserves	
Called-up share capital	10,000
(ordinary shares of £1)	
Share premium account	5,570
Retained earnings	42,664
	58,234

Additional information relating to the above balance sheet

(i)   The intangible assets of Yukon Ltd were brand names currently utilised by the company. The directors felt that they were worth £7 million but there was no readily ascertainable market value at the balance sheet date, nor any information to verify the directors' estimated value.

(ii)   The provisional market value of the land and buildings was £20 million at 31 May 20X6. This valuation had again been determined by the directors. A valuers' report received on 30 November 20X6 stated the market value of land and buildings to be £23 million as at 31 May 20X6. The depreciated replacement cost of the remainder of the tangible fixed assets was £18 million at 31 May 20X6.

(iii)   The replacement cost of inventories was estimated at £25 million and its net realisable value was deemed to be £20 million. Trade receivables and trade payables due within one year are stated at the amounts expected to be received and paid.

(iv)   The non-current liability was a long-term loan with a bank. The initial loan on 1 June 20X5 was £11 million at a fixed interest rate of 10% per annum. The total amount of the interest is to be paid at the end of the loan period on 31 May 20X9. The current bank lending rate is 7% per annum.

(v)   The provision for liabilities and charges relates to costs of reorganisation of Yukon Ltd. This provision had been set up by the directors of Yukon Ltd prior to the offer by Territory plc and the reorganisation would have taken place even if Territory plc had not purchased the shares of Yukon Ltd. Additionally Territory plc wishes to set up a provision for future losses of £10 million which it feels will be incurred by rationalising the group.

(vi)   The offer made to all of the shareholders of Yukon Ltd was 2.5 £1 ordinary shares of Territory plc at the market price of £2.25 per share plus £1 cash, per Yukon Ltd ordinary share.

(vii)   The directors of Yukon Ltd informed Territory plc that as at 31 May 20X7, the brand names were worthless as the products to which they related had recently been withdrawn from sale because they were deemed to be a health hazard.

(viii) In view of the adverse events since acquisition, the directors of Territory plc have impairment-tested the goodwill relating to Yukon SA, and they estimate its current value is £1 million.

Required:
Calculate the charge for impairment of goodwill in the Group Profit and Loss Account of Territory plc for the accounting period ending on 31 May 20X7.

Question 5

The brands debate

Under IAS 22, the depletion of equity reserves caused by the accounting treatment for purchased goodwill resulted in some companies capitalising brands on their balance sheets. This practice was started by Rank Hovis McDougall (RHM) – a company which has since been taken over. Martin Moorhouse, the group chief accountant at RHM, claimed that putting brands on the balance sheet forced a company to look to their value as well as to profits. It served as a reminder to management of the value of the assets for which they were responsible and that at the end of the day those companies which were prepared to recognise brands on the balance sheet could be better and stronger for it.[43]

There were many opponents to the capitalisation of brands. A London Business School research study found that brand accounting involves too many risks and uncertainties and too much subjective judgement. In short, the conclusion was that 'the present flexible position, far from being neutral, is potentially corrosive to the whole basis of financial reporting and that to allow brands – whether acquired or home-grown – to continue to be included in the balance sheet would be highly unwise'.[44]

Required:

Consider the arguments for and against brand accounting. In particular, consider the issues of brand valuation; the separability of brands; purchased vs home-grown brands; and the maintenance/substitution argument.

References

1 'The 2004 R&D Scoreboard', *DTI*, October 2004.
2 B. Nixon and A. Lonie, 'Accounting for R&D: the need for change', *Accountancy*, February 1990, p. 91; B. Nixon, 'R&D disclosure: SSAP 13 and after', *Accountancy*, February 1991, pp. 72–73.
3 IAS 38 *Intangible Assets*, IASC, revised March 2004.
4 *Statement of Intent: Comparability of Financial Statements*, IASC, 1990.
5 IAS 9 (revised), *Research and Development Costs*, IASC, December 1993.
6 IAS 38 *Intangible Assets*, IASC, revised March 2004.
7 A. Goodacre and J. McGrath, 'An experimental study of analysts' reactions to corporate R&D expenditure', *British Accounting Review*, 1997, 29, pp. 155–179.
8 B. Nixon, 'The accounting treatment of research and development expenditure: views of UK company accountants', *European Accounting Review*, 1997, vol. 6, no. 2, pp. 265–277.
9 *Ibid.*
10 IAS 38 *Intangible Assets*, IASC, revised March 2004, para. 54.
11 *Ibid.*, para. 56.
12 *Ibid.*, para. 55.
13 *Ibid.*, para. 58.
14 *Ibid.*, para. 59.
15 SSAP 13 *Accounting for Research and Development*, ASB, revised 1989, para. 7.
16 IRS 38 *Intangible Assets*, IASC, revised March 2004, para. 126.
17 IFRS 3 *Business Combinations*, IASB, 2004, para. 51.
18 IAS 38 *Intangible Assets*, IASC, revised March 2004, para. 63.
19 *The Framework for the Preparation and Presentation of Financial Statements*, IASB, April 2001, para 94.
20 *Ibid.*, para. 119.
21 *Ibid.*, para. 118.
22 *Ibid.*, para. 122.
23 *Ibid.*, para. 126.
24 P. Barwise, C. Higson, A. Likierman and P. Marsh, *Accounting for Brands*, ICAEW, June 1989; M. Cooper and A. Carey, 'Brand valuation in the balance', *Accountancy*, June 1989.
25 A. Pizzey, 'Healing the rift', *Certified Accountant*, October 1990.
26 'Finance directors say yes to brand valuation', *Accountancy*, January 1990, p. 12.
27 M. Moorhouse, 'Brands debate: wake up to the real world', *Accountancy*, July 1990, p. 30.
28 M. Gerry, 'Companies ignore value of brands', *Accountancy Age*, March 2000, p. 4.
29 www.wipo.org.

30 Great Britain, White Paper, *Our Competitive Future: Building the Knowledge Driven Economy*, London, HMSO, 1998.

31 OECD, *Final Report: Measuring and Reporting Intellectual Capital: Experience, Issues and Prospects*, Paris: OECD, 2000.

32 J. Guthrie and R. Petty, 'Knowledge management: the information revolution has created the need for a codified system of gathering and controlling knowledge', *Company Secretary*, January 1999, vol. 9, no.1, pp. 38–41; R. Tissen *et al.*, *Value-Based Knowledge Management*, Longman Nederland BV, 1998, pp. 25–44.

33 J. Guthrie, 'Measuring up to change', *Financial Management*, December 2000, CIMA, London, p. 11.

34 OECD, 'Guidelines and instructions for OECD Symposium', International Symposium Measuring and Reporting Intellectual Capital: Experiences, Issues and Prospects, June 1999, Amsterdam, OECD, Paris.

35 R.J. Gallafent, N.A. Eastaway and V.A. Dauppe, *Intellectual Property Law and Taxation*, Longman, London, 1992.

36 T.H. Donaldson, *The Treatment of Intangibles: A Banker's View*, St Martin's Press, New York, 1992.

37 K.E. Sveiby, *The New Annual Report in Swedish*, Stockholm, 1988: see www.sveiby.com.au for English translation; Celemi, 1999, Growing a knowledge company, www.celemi.com (site includes Celemi Intangible Assets Monitor).

38 R.S. Kaplan and D.P. Norton, 'The Balanced Scorecard – measures that drives performance', *Harvard Business Review*, 1992, vol. 70, no. 1, pp. 71–79; R.S. Kaplan and D.P. Norton, 'Using the Balanced Scorecard as a strategic management system', *Harvard Business Review*, 1996, vol. 70, no. 1.

39 L. Edvinsson and M. Malone, *Intellectual Capital: Realising Your Company's True Value by Finding Its Hidden Power*, New York, HarperCollins, 1997; L. Edvinsson, 'Developing Intellectual Capital at Skandia', *Long Range Planning*, 1997, vol. 30, no. 3, pp. 266–373.

40 Danish Agency for Trade and Industry (DATI), English version, 'Intellectual Capital Accounts: new tool for companies', DTI Council, Copenhagen, 1998; Danish Agency for Trade and Industry, *Developing Intellectual Capital Accounts: Experiences from 19 Companies*, Copenhagen: Ministry of Business and Industry, 1999.

41 Derek Binney, 'The knowledge management spectrum – a technique for optimising knowledge management strategies', *Journal of Knowledge Management*, vol. 5, no. 1, 2001, pp. 33–42.

42 R. Paterson, 'Will FRS 10 hit the target?', *Accountancy*, February 1998, pp. 74–75.

43 M. Moorhouse, 'Brands debate: wake up to the real world', *Accountancy*, July 1990, p. 30.

44 P. Barwise, C. Higson, A. Likierman and P. Marsh, *Accounting for Brands*, ICAEW, June 1989.

CHAPTER **19**

Inventories

19.1 Introduction

This chapter explains the accounting principles involved in the valuation of inventory, and how this impacts not only on balance sheet valuation, but also on the computation of annual profit.

We attempt to combine mechanics with a theoretical understanding of the accounting principles and illustrate this with practical examples showing how the interpretation of financial statements can be affected by differing treatments. In this chapter we consider:

- Inventory defined and the controversy
- The requirements of IAS 2
- Inventory valuation
- Inventory control
- Creative accounting
- Audit of year-end physical count
- Published financial statements.

19.2 Inventory defined

IAS 2 *Inventories* defines inventories as assets:

(a) held for sale in the ordinary course of business;
(b) in the process of production for such sale;
(c) in the form of materials or supplies to be consumed in the production process or in the rendering of services.[1]

The valuation of inventory involves:

(a) the establishment of physical existence and ownership;
(b) the determination of unit costs;
(c) the calculation of provisions to reduce cost to net realisable value, if necessary.[2]

The resulting evaluation is then disclosed in the financial statements.

These definitions appear to be very precise. We shall see, however, that although IAS 2 was introduced to bring some uniformity into financial statements, there are many areas where professional judgement must be exercised. Sometimes this may distort the financial statements to such an extent that we must question whether they do represent a 'true and fair' view.

19.3 The controversy

The valuation of inventory has been a controversial issue in accounting for many years. The inventory value is a crucial element not only in the computation of profit, but also in the valuation of assets for balance sheet purposes.

Figure 19.1 presents information relating to Coats Viyella plc. It shows that the inventory is material in relation to total assets and pre-tax profits. In relation to the profits we can see that an error of 4% in the 2001 interim report inventory value would potentially cause the profits for the group to change from a pre-tax profit to a pre-tax loss. As inventory is usually a multiple rather than a fraction of profit, inventory errors may have a disproportionate effect on the accounts. Valuation of inventory is therefore crucial in determining earnings per share, net asset backing for shares and the current ratio. Consequently, the basis of valuation should be consistent, so as to avoid manipulation of profits between accounting periods, and comply with generally accepted accounting principles, so that profits are comparable between different companies.

Figure 19.1 Coats Viyella plc

	2000	2001 (Half year)
Pre-tax profits (losses) (£m)	(29.9)	9.9
Inventory(£m)	304.2	320.2
Total assets (£m)	1,321.8	1,310.4

Unfortunately, there are many examples of manipulation of inventory values in order to create a more favourable impression. By increasing the value of inventory at the year-end, profit and current assets are automatically increased (and vice versa). Of course, closing inventory of one year becomes opening inventory of the next, so profit is thereby reduced. But such manipulation provides opportunities for profit-smoothing and may be advantageous in certain circumstances, e.g. if the company is under threat of takeover.

Figure 19.2 illustrates the point. Simply by increasing the value of inventory in year 1 by £10,000, profit (and current assets) is increased by a similar amount. Even if the two values are identical in year 2, such manipulation allows profit to be 'smoothed' and £10,000 profit switched from year 2 to year 1.

According to normal accrual accounting principles, profit is determined by matching costs with related revenues. If it is unlikely that the revenue will in fact be received, prudence dictates that the irrecoverable amount should be written off immediately against current revenue.

It follows that inventory should be valued at cost less any irrecoverable amount. But what is cost? Entities have used a variety of methods of determining costs, and these are explored later in the chapter. There have been a number of disputes relating to the valuation of inventory which affected profits (e.g. the AEI/GEC merger of 1967).[3] Naturally, such circumstances tend to come to light with a change of management, but it was considered important that a definitive statement of accounting practice be issued in an attempt to standardise treatment.

Figure 19.2   Inventory values manipulated to smooth income

	Year 1			Year 1 With inventory inflated
Sales		100,000		100,000
Opening inventory	—		—	
Purchases	65,000		65,000	
Less: Closing inventory	5,000		15,000	
COST OF SALES		60,000		50,000
PROFIT		40,000		50,000
	Year 2			Year 2 With inventory inflated
Sales		150,000		150,000
Opening inventory	5,000		15,000	
Purchases	100,000		100,000	
	105,000		115,000	
Less: Closing inventory	15,000		15,000	
COST OF SALES		90,000		100,000
PROFIT		60,000		50,000

19.4 IAS 2 *Inventories*

No area of accounting has produced wider differences in practice than the computation of the amount at which inventory is stated in financial accounts. An accounting standard on the subject needs to define the practices, to narrow the differences and variations in those practices and to ensure adequate disclosure in the accounts.

IAS 2 requires that the amount at which inventory is stated in periodic financial statements should be the total of the lower of cost and net realisable value of the separate items of inventory or of groups of similar items. The standard also emphasises the need to match costs against revenue, and it aims, like other standards, to achieve greater uniformity in the measurement of income as well as improving the disclosure of inventory valuation methods. To an extent IAS 2 relies on management to choose the most appropriate method of inventory valuation for the production processes used and the company's environment. Various methods of valuation are available, including FIFO, LIFO and weighted average or any similar method (see below). In selecting the most suitable method, management must exercise judgement to ensure that the methods chosen provide the fairest practical approximation to cost. IAS 2 does not normally allow the use of LIFO because it often results in inventory being stated in the balance sheet at amounts that bear little relation to recent cost levels.

At the end of the day, even though there is an International Accounting Standard in existence, the valuation of inventory can provide areas of subjectivity and choice to management. We will return to this theme many times in the following sections of this chapter.

19.5 Inventory valuation

The valuation rule outlined in IAS 2 is difficult to apply because of uncertainties about what is meant by cost (with some methods approved by IAS 2 and others not) and what is meant by net realisable value.

19.5.1 Methods acceptable under IAS 2

The acceptable methods of inventory valuation include FIFO, AVCO and standard cost.

First-in-first-out (FIFO)

Inventory is valued at the most recent 'cost', since the cost of oldest inventory is charged out first, whether or not this accords with the actual physical flow. FIFO is illustrated in Figure 19.3.

Figure 19.3 First-in-first-out method (FIFO)

Date	Receipts Quantity	Rate	£	Issues Quantity	Rate	£	Balance Quantity	Rate	£
January	10	15	150				10		150
February				8	15	120	2		30
March	10	17	170				12		200
April	20	20	400				32		600
May				2	15	30			
				10	17	170			
				12	20	240			
				Cost of goods sold		560			
				Inventory			8	20	160

Average cost (AVCO)

Inventory is valued at a 'weighted average cost', i.e. the unit cost is weighted by the number of items carried at each 'cost', as shown in Figure 19.4. This is popular in manufacturing and in organisations holding a large volume of inventory at fluctuating 'costs'. The practical problem of actually recording and calculating the weighted average cost has been overcome by the use of sophisticated computer software.

Standard cost

In many cases this is the only way to value manufactured goods in a high-volume/high-turnover environment. However, the standard is acceptable only if it approximates to actual cost. This means that variances need to be reviewed to see if they affect the standard cost and for inventory evaluation.

IAS 2 recognises that an acceptable method of arriving at cost is the use of selling price, less an estimated profit margin. This method is only acceptable if it can be demonstrated that the method gives a reasonable approximation of the actual cost. It is the method employed by major retailers, e.g. Tesco 2003 Annual Report states in its accounting policies:

Inventory comprises goods held for resale and development properties and are valued at the lower of cost and net realisable value. Inventory in stores is calculated at retail price and reduced by appropriate margins to the lower of cost and net realisable value.

Figure 19.4 Average cost method (AVCO)

Date	Receipts Quantity	Rate	£	Issues Quantity	Rate	£	Balance Quantity	Rate	£
January	10	15	150				10		150
February				8	15	120	2		30
March	10	17	170				12		200
April	20	20	400				32		600
May				24	18.75	450			600
				Cost of goods sold		570			
				Inventory			8	18.75	150

And Somerfield plc's 2003 accounting policy states:

Inventory is valued at the lower of cost or net realisable value. Cost represents invoiced cost or selling price less the relevant profit margin to reduce it to estimated cost, including an appropriate element of overheads. Inventory at warehouses is valued at weighted average cost and inventory at stores on a first-in-first-out basis.

IAS 2 does not recommend any specific method. This is a decision for each organisation based upon sound professional advice and the organisation's unique operating conditions.

19.5.2 Methods rejected by IAS 2

Methods rejected by IAS 2 include LIFO and (by implication) replacement cost.

Last-in-first-out (LIFO)

The cost of the inventory most recently received is charged out first at the most recent 'cost'. The practical upshot is that the inventory value is based upon an 'old cost', which may bear little relationship to the current 'cost'. LIFO is illustrated in Figure 19.5.

US companies commonly use the LIFO method, as illustrated in the following extract from the Eastman Kodak Company Annual Report 2003:

Inventories are stated at lower of cost and market. The cost of most inventories in the USA is determined by the 'last-in, first-out' (LIFO) method. The cost of all of the Company's remaining inventory in and outside the USA is determined by the 'first-in, first-out' (FIFO) or average cost method, which approximates current cost. The Company provides inventory reserves for excess, obsolete or slow-moving inventory based on changes in customer demand, technology developments or other economic factors.

Figure 19.5 Last-in-first-out method (LIFO)

Date	Receipts Quantity	Receipts Rate	Receipts £	Issues Quantity	Issues Rate	Issues £	Balance Quantity	Balance Rate	Balance £
January	10	15	150				10		150
February				8	15	120	2		30
March	10	17	170				12		200
April	20	20	400				32		600
May				20	20	400			
				4	17	68			
				Cost of goods sold		588			
				Inventory			8		132

May closing balance = $[(2 \times 15) + (6 \times 17)]$

Where LIFO is used the effect of using FIFO is quantified as in the Wal-Mart Stores Inc. Annual Report:

	2001 $m	2000 $m
Inventories at replacement cost	21,644	20,171
Less LIFO reserve	202	378
Inventories at LIFO cost	21,442	19,793

The company's summary of significant accounting policies states that the company uses the retail LIFO method. The LIFO reserve shows the cumulative, pre-tax effect on income between the results obtained using LIFO and the results obtained using a more current cost inventory valuation method (e.g. FIFO) – this gives an indication of how much higher profits would be if FIFO were used.

Replacement cost

The inventory is valued at the current cost of the individual item (i.e. the cost to the organisation of replacing the item) rather than the actual cost at the time of manufacture or purchase. This is an attractive idea since the 'value' of inventory could be seen as the cost at which a similar item could be currently acquired. The problem again is in arriving at a 'reliable' profit figure for the purposes of performance evaluation. Wild fluctuation of profit could occur simply because of such factors as the time of the year, the vagaries of the world weather system or the manipulation of market forces. Let us take three examples, involving coffee, oil and silver.

Coffee. Wholesale prices collapsed over three years (1999-2002) from nearly $2.40 per pound to just under 50 cents. This was the lowest level in thirty years and, allowing for the effects of inflation, coffee became uneconomic to sell and farmers resorted to burning their crop for fuel. The implication for financial reporting was that the objective was to increase the inventory unit cost by 100% by forcing the price back above $1 per pound. What value should be attached to the coffee inventory? 50 cents or the replacement cost of $1 which would create a profit equal to the existing inventory value?

Oil. When the Gulf Crisis of 1990 began, the cost of oil moved from around $13 per barrel to a high of around $29 per barrel in a short time. If oil companies had used replacement cost, this would have created huge fictitious profits. This might have resulted in higher tax payments and shareholders demanding dividends from a profit that existed only on paper. When the Gulf Crisis settled down to a quiet period (before the 1991 military action), the market price of oil dropped almost as dramatically as it had risen. This might have led to fictitious losses for companies in the following financial year with an ensuing loss of business confidence.

This scenario was not unique to the Gulf Crisis and we see the same situation arising with fluctuations in the price of Arab Light which moved from $8.74 per barrel on 31 December 1998 to $24.55 per barrel on 31 December 1999 and down to $17.10 on 31 December 2001 (www.eia.doe.gov).

Silver. In the early 1980s a Texan millionaire named Bunker Hunt attempted to make a 'killing' on the silver market by buying silver to force up the price and then selling at the high price to make a substantial profit. This led to remarkable scenes in the UK, with long lines of people outside jewellers wanting to sell items at much higher prices than their 'real' cost. Companies using silver as a raw material (e.g. jewellers, mirror manufacturers, and electronics companies, which use silver as a conductive element) would have been badly affected had they used replacement cost in a similar way to the preceding two cases. The 'price' of silver in effect doubled in a short time, but the Federal Authorities in the USA stepped in and the plan was defeated.

The use of replacement cost is not specifically prohibited by IAS 2 but is out of line with the basic principle underpinning the standard, which is to value inventory at the actual costs incurred in its purchase or production. The IASC *Framework for the Preparation and Presentation of Financial Statements* describes historical cost and current cost as two distinct measurement bases and where a historical cost measurement base is used for assets and liabilities the use of replacement cost is inconsistent.

Although LIFO does not have IAS 2 approval it is still used in practice. For example, LIFO is commonly used by UK companies with US subsidiaries, since LIFO is the main method of inventory valuation in the USA.

19.5.3 Procedure to ascertain cost

Having decided upon the accounting policy of the company, there remains the problem of ascertaining the cost. In a retail environment, the 'cost' is the price the organisation had to pay to acquire the goods, and it is readily established by reference to the purchase invoice from the supplier. However, in a manufacturing organisation the concept of cost is not as simple. Should we use prime cost, or production cost, or total cost? IAS 2 attempts to help by defining cost as 'all costs of purchase, costs of conversion and other costs incurred in bringing the inventories to their present location and condition'.

In a manufacturing organisation each expenditure is taken to include three constituents: direct materials, direct labour and appropriate overhead.

Direct materials

These include not only the costs of raw materials and component parts, but also the costs of insurance, handling (special packaging) and any import duties. An additional problem is waste and scrap. For instance, if a process inputs 100 tonnes at £45 per tonne, yet outputs only 90 tonnes, the output's inventory value **must** be £4,500 (£45 × 100) and not £4,050 (90 × £45). (This assumes the 10 tonnes loss is a normal, regular part of the process.) An adjustment may be made for the residual value of the scrap/waste material, if any. The treatment of component parts will be the same, provided they form part of the finished product.

Direct labour

This is the cost of the actual production in the form of gross pay and those incidental costs of employing the direct workers (employer's national insurance contributions, additional pension contributions, etc.). The labour costs will be spread over the goods' production.

Appropriate overhead

It is here that the major difficulties arise in calculating the true cost of the product for inventory valuation purposes. Normal practice is to classify overheads into five types and decide whether to include them in inventory. The five types are as follows:

● Direct overheads – subcontract work, royalties.
● Indirect overheads – the cost of running the factory and supporting the direct workers, and the depreciation of capital items used in production.
● Administration overheads – the office costs and salaries of senior management.
● Selling and distribution overheads – advertising, delivery costs, packaging, salaries of sales personnel, and depreciation of capital items used in the sales function.
● Finance overheads – the cost of borrowing and servicing debt.

We will look at each of these in turn, to demonstrate the difficulties that the accountant experiences.

Direct overheads. These should normally be included as part of 'cost'. But imagine a situation where some subcontract work has been carried out on *some* of a company's products because of a capacity problem (i.e. the factory could normally do the work, but due to a short-term problem some of the work has been subcontracted at a higher price/cost). In theory, those items subject to the subcontract work should have a higher inventory value than 'normal' items. However, in practice, the difficulty of identifying such 'subcontracted' items is so great that many companies do not include such non-routine subcontract work in the inventory value as a direct overhead. For example, if a factory produces 1,000,000 drills per month and 1,000 of them have to be sent out because of a machine breakdown, since all the drills are identical it would be very costly and time-consuming to treat the 1,000 drills differently from the other 999,000. Hence the subcontract work would *not* form part of the overhead for inventory valuation purposes (in such an organisation, the standard cost approach would be used when valuing inventory). On the other hand, in a customised car firm producing 20 vehicles per month, special subcontract work would form part of the inventory value because it is readily identifiable to individual units of inventory.

To summarise, any regular, routine direct overhead will be included in the inventory valuation, but a non-routine cost could present difficulties, especially in a high-volume/high-turnover organisation.

Indirect overheads. These always form part of the inventory valuation, as such expenses are incurred in support of production. They include factory rent and rates, factory power and depreciation of plant and machinery; in fact, any indirect factory-related cost, including the warehouse costs of storing completed goods, will be included in the value of inventory.

Administration overheads. This overhead is in respect of the whole business, so only that portion easily identifiable to production should form part of the inventory valuation. For instance, the costs of the personnel or wages department could be apportioned to production on a head-count basis and that element would be included in the inventory valuation. Any production-specific administration costs (welfare costs, canteen costs, etc.) would also be included in the inventory valuation. If the expense cannot be identified as forming part of the production function, it will not form part of the inventory valuation.

Selling and distribution overheads. These costs will not normally be included in the inventory valuation as they are incurred after production has taken place. However, if the goods are on a 'sale or return' basis and are on the premises of the customer but remain the supplier's property, the delivery and packing costs will be included in the inventory value of goods held on a customer's premises.

An additional difficulty concerns the modern inventory technique of 'just-in-time' (JIT). Here, the customer does not keep large inventories, but simply 'calls off' inventory from the supplier and is invoiced for the items delivered. There is an argument for the inventory still in the hands of the supplier to bear more of this overhead within its valuation, since the only selling and distribution overhead to be charged/incurred is delivery. The goods have in fact been sold, but ownership has not yet changed hands. As JIT becomes more popular, this problem may give accountants and auditors much scope for debate.

Finance overheads. Normally these overheads would never be included within the inventory valuation because they are not normally identifiable with production. In a job-costing context, however, it might be possible to use some of this overhead in inventory valuation. Let us take the case of an engineering firm being requested to produce a turbine engine, which requires parts/components to be imported. It is logical for the financial charges for these imports (e.g. exchange fees or fees for letters of credit) to be included in the inventory valuation.

Thus it can be seen that the identification of the overheads to be included in inventory valuation is far from straightforward. In many cases it depends upon the judgement of the accountant and the unique operating conditions of the organisation.

In addition to the problem of deciding **whether** the five types of overhead should be included, there is the problem of deciding **how much** of the total overhead to include in the inventory valuation at the year-end. IAS 2 stipulates the use of 'normal activity' when making this decision on overheads. The vast majority of overheads are 'fixed', i.e. do not vary with activity, and it is customary to share these out over a normal or expected output. If this expected output is not reached, it is not acceptable to allow the actual production to bear the full overhead for inventory purposes. A numerical example will illustrate this:

Overhead for the year	£200,000	
Planned activity	10,000	units
Closing inventory	3,000	units
Direct costs	£2	per unit
Actual activity	6,000	units

Inventory value based on actual activity

Direct costs	$3,000 \times £2$	£6,000
Overhead	$\dfrac{3,000 \times £200,000}{6,000}$	£100,000
Closing inventory value		£106,000

Inventory value based on planned or normal activity

Direct cost	$3,000 \times £2$	£6,000
Overhead	$\dfrac{3,000 \times £200,000}{10,000}$	£60,000
Closing inventory value		£66,000

Comparing the value of inventory based upon actual activity with the value based upon planned or normal activity, we have a £40,000 difference. This could be regarded as increasing the current year's profit by carrying forward expenditure of £40,000 to set against the following year's profit.

The problem occurs because of the organisation's failure to meet expected output level (6,000 actual versus 10,000 planned). By adopting the **actual activity basis**, the organisation makes a profit out of failure. This cannot be an acceptable position when evaluating performance. Therefore, IAS 2 stipulates **the planned or normal activity model** for inventory valuation. The failure to meet planned output could be due to a variety of sources (e.g. strikes, poor weather, industrial conditions); the cause, however, is classed as abnormal or non-routine, and all such costs should be excluded from the valuation of inventory.

19.5.4 What is meant by net realisable value?

We have attempted to identify the problems of arriving at the true meaning of cost for the purpose of inventory valuation. Net realisable value is an alternative method of inventory valuation if 'cost' does not reflect the true value of the inventory. Prudence dictates that net realisable value will be used if it is lower than the 'cost' of the inventory (however that may be calculated). These occasions will vary among organisations, but can be summarised as follows:

● There is a permanent fall in the market price of inventory. Short-term fluctuations should not cause net realisable value to be implemented.

● The organisation is attempting to dispose of high inventory levels or excessively priced inventory to improve its liquidity position (quick ratio/acid test ratio) or reduce its inventory holding costs. Such high inventory volumes or values are primarily a result of poor management decision making.

● The inventory is physically deteriorating or is of an age where the market is reluctant to accept it. This is a common feature of the food industry, especially with the use of 'sell by' dates in the retail environment.

● Inventory suffers obsolescence through some unplanned development. (Good management should never be surprised by obsolescence.) This development could be technical in nature, or due to the development of different marketing concepts within the organisation or a change in market needs.

● The management could decide to sell the goods at 'below cost' for sound marketing reasons. The concept of a 'loss leader' is well known in supermarkets, but organisations also sell below cost when trying to penetrate a new market or as a defence mechanism when attacked.

Such decisions are important and the change to net realisable value should not be undertaken without considerable forethought and planning. Obsolescence should be a decision based upon sound market intelligence and not a managerial 'whim'. The auditors of companies always examine such decisions to ensure they were made for sound business reasons. The opportunities for fraud in such 'price-cutting' operations validate this level of external control.

Realisable value is, of course, the price the organisation receives for its inventory from the market. However, getting this inventory to market may involve additional expense and effort in repackaging, advertising, delivery and even repairing of damaged inventory. This additional cost must be deducted from the realisable value to arrive at the net realisable value.

A numerical example will demonstrate this concept:

Item	Cost (£)	Net realisable value (£)	Inventory value (£)
1 No. 876	7,000	9,000	7,000
2 No. 997	12,000	12,500	12,000
3 No. 1822	8,000	4,000	4,000
4 No. 2076	14,000	8,000	8,000
5 No. 4732	27,000	33,000	27,000
	(a) 68,000	(b) 66,500	(c) 58,000

The inventory value chosen for the accounts is (c) £58,000, although each item is assessed individually.

19.6 Work-in-progress

Inventory classified as work-in-progress (WIP) is mainly found in manufacturing organisations and is simply the production that has not been completed by the end of the accounting period.

The valuation of WIP must follow the same IAS 2 rules and be the lower of cost or net realisable value. We again face the difficulty of deciding what to include in cost. The three basic classes of cost – direct materials, direct labour and appropriate overhead – will still form the basis of ascertaining cost.

19.6.1 Direct materials

It is necessary to decide what proportion of the total materials have been used in WIP. The proportion will vary with different types of organisation, as the following two examples illustrate:

- If the item is complex or materially significant (e.g. a custom-made car or a piece of specialised machinery), the WIP calculation will be based on actual recorded materials and components used to date.

- If, however, we are dealing with mass production, it may not be possible to identify each individual item within WIP. In such cases, the accountant will make a judgement and define the WIP as being $x\%$ complete in regard to raw materials and components. For example, a drill manufacturer with 1 million tools per week in WIP may decide that in respect of raw materials they are 100% complete; WIP then gets the full materials cost of 1 million tools.

In both cases **consistency** is vital so that, however WIP is valued, the same method will always be used.

19.6.2 Direct labour

Again, it is necessary to decide how much direct labour the items in WIP have actually used. As with direct materials, there are two broad approaches:

- Where the item of WIP is complex or materially significant, the actual time 'booked' or recorded will form part of the WIP valuation.

- In a mass production situation, such precision may not be possible and an accounting judgement may have to be made as to the average percentage completion in respect of direct labour. In the example of the drill manufacturer, it could be that, on average, WIP is 80% complete in respect of direct labour.

19.6.3 Appropriate overhead

The same two approaches as for direct labour can be adopted:

- With a complex or materially significant item, it should be possible to allocate the overhead actually incurred. This could be an actual charge (e.g. subcontract work) or an application of the appropriate overhead recovery rate (ORR). For example, if we use a direct labour hour recovery rate and we have an ORR of £10 per direct labour hour and the recorded labour time on the WIP item is twelve hours, then the overhead charge for WIP purposes is £120.

- With mass production items, the accountant must either use an overhead recovery rate approach or simply decide that, in respect of overheads, WIP is $y\%$ complete.

The above approaches must always be sanctioned by the firm's auditors to ensure that a true and fair view is achieved. The approach must also be consistent provided the basic product does not vary.

EXAMPLE 1 ● A company produces drills. The costs of a completed drill are:

	£
Direct materials	2.00
Direct labour	6.00
Appropriate overhead	10.00
Total cost	18.00 (for finished goods inventory value purposes)

The company accountant takes the view that for WIP purposes the following applies:

Direct material   100% complete
Direct labour   80% complete
Appropriate overhead   30% complete

Therefore, for one WIP drill:

Direct material   £2.00 × 100% = £2.00
Direct labour   £6.00 × 80% = £4.80
Appropriate overhead £10.00 × 30% = £3.00
WIP value   £9.80

If the company has 100,000 drills in WIP, the value is:

100,000 × £9.80 = £980,000

This is a very simplistic view, but the principle can be adapted to cover more complex issues. For instance, there could be 200 different types of drill, but the same calculation can be done on each. Of course, sophisticated software makes the accountant's job mechanically easier.

This technique is particularly useful in processing industries, such as petroleum, brewing, dairy products or paint manufacture, where it might be impossible to identify WIP items precisely. The role of the auditor in validating such practices is paramount.

EXAMPLE 2 ● A custom-car company making sports cars has the following costs in respect of No. 821/C, an unfinished car, at the end of the month:

Materials charged to job 821/C   £2,100
Labour 120 hours @ £4   £480
Overhead £22/DLH × 120 hours   £2,640
WIP value of 821/C   £5,220

This is an accurate WIP value provided *all* the costs have been accurately recorded and charged. The amount of accounting work involved is not great as the information is required by a normal job cost system. An added advantage is that the figure can be formally audited and proven. Work-in-progress valuation has its difficulties, but they are not insurmountable, given the skill of an accountant and a good working knowledge of the production process.

19.7 Inventory control

The way in which inventory is physically controlled should not be overlooked. Discrepancies are generally of two types: disappearance through theft and improper accounting.[4] Management will, of course, be responsible for adequate systems of internal control, but losses may still occur through theft or lack of proper controls and recording. Inadequate systems of accounting may also cause discrepancies between the physical and book inventories, with consequent correcting adjustments at the year-end.

Many companies are developing in-house computer systems or using bought-in packages to account for their inventories. Such systems are generally adequate for normal recording purposes, but they are still vulnerable to year-end discrepancies arising from errors in establishing the physical inventory on hand at the year-end, and problems connected with the paperwork and the physical movement of inventories.

A major cause of discrepancy between physical and book inventory is the 'cut-off' date. In matching sales with cost of sales, it may be difficult to identify exactly into which period of account certain inventory movements should be placed, especially when the annual inventory count lasts many days or occurs at a date other than the last day of the financial year. It is customary to make an adjustment to the inventory figure, as shown in Figure 19.6. This depends on an accurate record of movements between the inventory count date and the financial year-end.

Figure 19.6   Adjusted inventory figure

	£
Inventory on 7 January 20X1	XXX
Less: Purchases	(XXX)
Add: Sales	XXX
Inventory at 31 December 20X0	XXX

Auditors have a special responsibility in relation to inventory control. They should look carefully at the inventory counting procedures and satisfy themselves that the accounting arrangements are satisfactory. For example, in September 1987 Harris Queensway announced an inventory reduction of some £15m in projected profit caused by write-downs in its furniture division. It blamed this on the inadequacy of control systems to 'identify ranges that were selling and ensure their replacement'. Interestingly, at the preceding AGM, no hint of the overvaluation was given and the auditors insisted that 'the company had no problem from the accounting point of view'.[5]

In many cases the auditor will be present at the inventory count. Even with this apparent safeguard, however, it is widely accepted that sometimes an accurate physical inventory take is almost impossible. The value of inventory should nevertheless be based on the best information available; and the resulting disclosed figure should be acceptable and provide a true and fair view on a going concern basis.

In practice, errors may continue unidentified for a number of years,[6] particularly if there is a paper-based system in operation. This was evident when T.J. Hughes reduced its profit for the year ended January 2001 by £2.5–3m from a forecast £8m.

19.8 Creative accounting

No area of accounting provides more opportunities for subjectivity and creative accounting than the valuation of inventory. This is illustrated by the report *Fraudulent Financial Reporting: 1987–1997 – An Analysis of U.S. Public Companies* prepared by the Committee of Sponsoring Organizations of the Treadway Commission.[7] This report, which was based on the detailed analysis of approximately 200 cases of fraudulent financial reporting, identified that the fraud often involved the overstatement of revenues and assets with inventory fraud featuring frequently – assets were overstated by understating allowances for receivables, overstating the value of inventory and other tangible assets, and recording assets that did not exist.

This section summarises some of the major methods employed.

19.8.1 Year-end manipulations

There are a number of stratagems companies have followed to reduce the cost of goods sold by inflating the inventory figure. These include:

Manipulating cut-off procedures

Goods are taken into inventory but the purchase invoices are not recorded.

The authors of *Fraudulent Financial Reporting: 1987–1997 – An Analysis of U.S. Public Companies* found that over half the frauds involved overstating revenues by recording revenues prematurely or fictitiously and that such overstatement tended to occur right at the end of the year – hence the need for adequate cut-off procedures. This was illustrated by Ahold's experience in the USA where subsidiary companies took credit for bulk discounts allowed by suppliers before inventory was actually received.

Fictitious transfers

Year-end inventory is inflated by recording fictitious transfers of non-existent inventory, e.g. it was alleged by the SEC that certain officers of the Miniscribe Corporation had increased the company's inventory by recording fictitious transfers of nonexistent inventory from a Colorado location to overseas locations where physical inventory counting would be more difficult for the auditors to verify or the goods are described as being 'in transit'.[8]

Including obsolete inventory at cost

This practice was alleged to have been followed in the case of the Miniscribe Corporation, e.g. by the repackaging of scrap and obsolete inventory and treating it as an asset instead of expensing it.

Inaccurate inventory records

Where inventory records are poorly maintained it has been possible for senior management to fail to record material shrinkage due to loss and theft as in the matter of Rite Aid Corporation.[9]

Journal adjustments

In addition to suppressing purchase invoices, making fictitious transfers, failing to write off obsolete inventory or recognise inventory losses, the senior management may simply reduce the cost of goods sold by adjusting journal entries, e.g. when preparing quarterly reports by crediting cost of goods and debiting accounts payable.

19.8.2 Net realisable value (NRV)

Although the determination of net realisable value is dealt with extensively in the appendix to IAS 2, the extent to which provisions can be made to reduce cost to NRV is highly subjective and open to manipulation. A provision is an effective smoothing device and allows overcautious write-downs to be made in profitable years and consequent write-backs in unprofitable ones.

19.8.3 Overheads

The treatment of overheads has been dealt with extensively above and is probably the area that gives the greatest scope for manipulation. Including overhead in the inventory valuation has the effect of deferring the overhead's impact and so boosting profits. IAS 2 allows expenses incidental to the acquisition or production cost of an asset to be included in its cost. We have seen that this includes not only directly attributable production overheads, but also those which are indirectly attributable to production and interest on borrowed capital. IAS 2 provides guidelines on the classification of overheads to achieve an appropriate allocation, but in practice it is difficult to make these distinctions and auditors will find it difficult to challenge management on such matters.

The statement suggests that the allocation of overheads included in the valuation needs to be based on the company's normal level of activity. The cost of unused capacity should be written off in the current year. The auditor will insist that allocation should be based on normal activity levels, but if the company underproduces, the overhead per unit increases and can therefore lead to higher year-end values. The creative accountant will be looking for ways to manipulate these year-end values, so that in bad times costs are carried forward to more profitable accounting periods.

19.8.4 Other methods of creative accounting

A simple manipulation is to show more or less inventory than actually exists. If the commodity is messy and indistinguishable, the auditor may not have either the expertise or the will to verify measurements taken by the client's own employees. This lack of auditor measuring knowledge and involvement allowed one of the biggest frauds ever to take place, which became known as 'the great salad oil swindle'.[10]

Another obvious ploy is to include, in the inventory valuation, obsolete or 'dead' inventory. Of course, such inventory should be written off. However, management may be 'optimistic' that it can be sold, particularly in times of economic recession. In high-tech industries, unrealistic values may be placed on inventory that in times of rapid development becomes obsolete quickly.

This can be highly significant, as in the case of Cal Micro.[11] On 6 February 1995, Cal Micro restated its financial results for fiscal year 1994. The bulk of the adjustments to Cal Micro's financial statements – all highly material – occurred in the areas of accounts inventory, accounts receivable and property and, from an originally reported net income of approximately $5.1 million for the year ended 30 June 1994, the restated allowance for additional inventory obsolescence decreased net income by approximately $9.3 million.

This is a problem that investors need to be constantly aware of, particularly when a company experiences a downturn in demand but a pressure to maintain the semblance of growth. An example is provided by Lexmark[12] which was alleged to have made highly positive statements regarding strong sales and growth for its printers although there was intense competition in the industry – the company reporting quarter after quarter of strong financial growth whereas the actual position appeared to be very different with unmarketable inventory in excess of $25 million to be written down in the fourth quarter of fiscal year 2001. The share price of a company that conceals this type of information is maintained and allows insiders to offload their shareholding on an unsuspecting investing public.

19.9 Audit of the year-end physical inventory count

The problems of accounting for inventory are highlighted at the company's year-end. This is when the closing inventory figure to be shown in both the income statement and balance sheet is calculated. In practice, the company will assess the final inventory figure by physically counting all inventory held by the company for trade. The year-end inventory count is therefore an important accounting procedure, one in which the auditors are especially interested.

The auditor generally attends the inventory count to verify both the physical quantities and the procedure of collating those quantities. At the inventory count, values are rarely assigned to inventory items, so the problems facing the auditor relate to the identification of inventory items; their ownership; and their physical condition.

19.9.1 Identification of inventory items

The auditor will visit many companies in the course of a year and will spend a considerable time looking at accounting records. However, it is important for the auditor also to become familiar with each company's products by visiting the shop floor or production facilities during the audit. This makes identification of individual inventory items easier at the year-end. Distinguishing between two similar items can be crucial where there are large differences in value. For example, steel-coated brass rods look identical to steel rods, but their value to the company will be very different. It is important that they are not confused at inventory count because, once recorded on the inventory sheets, values are assigned, production carries on, and the error cannot be traced.

19.9.2 Ownership of inventory items

The year-end cut-off point is important to the final inventory figure, but the business activities continue regardless of the year-end, and some account has to be taken of this. Hence the auditor must be aware that the recording of accounting transactions may not coincide with the physical flow of inventory. Inventory may be in one of two locations: included as part of inventory; or in the loading bay area awaiting dispatch or receipt. Its treatment will depend on several factors (see Figure 19.7). The auditor must be aware of all these possibilities and must be able to trace a sample of each inventory entry through to the accounting records, so that:

● if purchase is recorded, but not sale, the item must be in inventory;
● if sale is recorded, purchase must also be recorded and the item should not be in inventory.

Figure 19.7 Treatment of inventory items

Sales	In inventory	Loading bay
If invoiced to customer	Delete from inventory	Inventory not counted
If credited (i.e. returned)	Include	Include
If not invoiced/credited	Include unless accounting entry falls into this year	Include
Purchases		
If invoiced to company	Include in inventory	Include in inventory
If credited (i.e. to be returned)	Delete from inventory	Delete from inventory
If invoiced/credited	Include unless accounting entry falls into next year	Include

19.9.3 Physical condition of inventory items

Inventory in premium condition has a higher value than damaged inventory. The auditor must ensure that the condition of inventory is recorded at inventory count, so that the correct value is assigned to it. Items that are damaged or have been in inventory for a long period will be written down to their net realisable value (which may be nil) as long as adequate details are given by the inventory counter. Once again, this is a problem of identification, so the auditor must be able to distinguish between, for instance, rolls of first quality and faulty fabric. Similarly, items that have been in inventory for several inventory counts may have little value, and further enquiries about their status should be made at the time of inventory count.

19.10 Published accounts

Disclosure requirements in IAS 2 have already been indicated. The standard requires the accounting policies that have been applied to be stated and applied consistently from year to year. Inventory should be sub-classified in the balance sheet or in the notes to the financial statements so as to indicate the amounts held in each of the main categories in the standard balance sheet formats. But will the ultimate user of those financial statements be confident that the information disclosed is reliable, relevant and useful? We have already indicated many areas of subjectivity and creative accounting, but are such possibilities material?

In 1982 Westwick and Shaw examined the accounts of 125 companies with respect to inventory valuation and its likely impact on reported profit.[13] The results showed that the effect on profit before tax of a 1% error in closing inventory valuation ranged from a low of 0.18% to a high of 25.9% (in one case) with a median of 2.26%. The industries most vulnerable to such errors were household goods, textiles, mechanical engineering, contracting and construction.

Clearly, the existence of such variations has repercussions for such measures as ROCE, EPS and the current ratio. The research also showed that, in a sample of audit managers, 85% were of the opinion that the difference between a pessimistic and an optimistic valuation of the same inventory could be more than 6%.

IAS 2 has since been strengthened and these results may not be so indicative of the present situation. However, using the same principle, let us take a random selection of eight companies' recent annual accounts, apply a 5% increase in the closing inventory valuation and calculate the effect on EPS (taxation is simply taken at 35% on the change in inventory).

Figure 19.8 shows that, in absolute terms, the difference in pre-tax profits could be as much as £57.7m and the percentage change ranges from 2.7% to 24%. Of particular note is the change in EPS, which tends to be the major market indicator of performance. In the case of the electrical retailer (company 1), a 5% error in inventory valuation could affect EPS by as much as 27%. The inventory of such a company could well be vulnerable to such factors as changes in fashion, technology and economic recession.

Figure 19.8   Impact of a 5% change in closing inventory

Company:	1	2	3	4	5	6	7	8
	£m	£m	£m	£m	£m	£m	£m	£m
Actual inventory	390.0	428.0	1,154.0	509.0	509.0	280.0	360.0	232.0
Actual pre-tax profit	80.1	105.6	479.0	252.5	358.4	186.3	518.2	436.2
Change in pre-tax profit	19.5	21.4	57.7	25.2	25.5	14.0	18.0	11.6
			Impact of a 5% change in closing inventory (%)					
(i) Pre-tax profit	24.0	20.0	12.0	10.0	7.0	7.5	3.5	2.7
(ii) Post-tax profit	22.0	27.0	12.0	8.8	6.8	6.3	3.4	2.5
(iii) Current assets	2.6	2.3	2.8	3.1	2.8	1.8	2.9	1.4
(iv) Current assets less								
current liabilities	4.9	4.6	14.1	14.0	48.8	8.2	2.2	3.8
(v) Earnings per share	27.0	25.0	12.0	9.3	8.4	6.9	3.4	3.4

Key to companies:
1 Electrical retailer
2 Textile, etc., manufacturer
3 Brewing, public houses, etc.
4 Retailer – diversified
5 Pharmaceutical and retail chemist
6 Industrial paints and fibres
7 Food retailer
8 Food retailer

Summary

Examples of differences in inventory valuation are not uncommon.[14] For example, in 1984, Fidelity, the electronic equipment manufacturer, was purchased for £13.4m.[15] This price was largely based on the 1983/84 profit figure of £400,000. Subsequently, it was maintained that this 'profit' should actually be a loss of £1.3m – a difference of £1.7m. Much of this difference was attributable to inventory discrepancies. The claim was contested, but it does illustrate that a disparity can occur when important figures are left to 'professional judgement'.

Another case involved the selling of British Wheelset by British Steel, just before privatisation in 1988, at a price of £16.9m.[16] It was claimed that the accounts 'were not drawn up on a consistent basis in accordance with generally accepted accounting practice'. If certain inventory provisions had been made, these would have resulted in a £5m (30%) difference in the purchase price.

Other areas that cause difficulties to the user of published information are the capitalisation of interest and the reporting of write-downs on acquisition. Post-acquisition profits can be influenced by excessive write-downs of inventory on acquisition, which has the effect of increasing goodwill. The written-down inventory can eventually be sold at higher prices, thus improving post-acquisition profits.

Although legal requirements and IAS 2 have improved the reporting requirements, many areas of subjective judgement can have substantial effects on the reporting of financial information.

REVIEW QUESTIONS

1 Discuss why some form of theoretical pricing model is required for inventory valuation purposes.

2 Discuss the acceptability of the following methods of inventory valuation: LIFO; replacement cost.

3 Discuss the application of individual judgement in inventory valuation, e.g. changing the basis of overhead absorption.

4 Explain the criteria to be applied when selecting the method to be used for allocating costs.

5 Discuss the effect on work-in-progress and finished goods valuation if the net realisable value of the raw material is lower than cost at the balance sheet date.

6 Discuss why the accurate valuation of inventory is so crucial if the financial statements are to show a true and fair view.

7 The following is an extract from the Interbrew 2003 Annual Report:

Inventories are valued at the lower of cost and net realisable value. Cost is determined by the weighted average method. The cost of finished products and work-in-progress comprises raw materials, other production materials, direct labour, other direct cost and an allocation of fixed and variable overhead based on normal operating capacity. Net realisable value is the estimated selling price in the ordinary course of business, less estimated costs of completion and selling costs.

Discuss the possible effects on profits if the company did not use normal operating activity. Explain an alternative definition for net realisable value and discuss the criterion to be applied when making a policy choice.

8 The following is an extract from the Sudzucker AG 2003 Annual Report:

Inventories are stated at acquisition or production cost using average cost or first-in, first-out. As set out in IAS 2 the production cost of work in progress and finished goods includes ... a proportion of administrative expenses.

Explain (a) why the company is using both the average cost and first-in-first-out methods and (b) the expenses that might be included under the administrative expenses heading.

EXERCISES

An extract from the solution is provided in the Appendix at the end of the text for exercises marked with an asterisk (*).

Question 1

Sunhats Ltd manufactures patent hats. It carries inventory of these and sells to wholesalers and retailers via a number of salespeople. The following expenses are charged in the profit and loss account:

Wages of:	Storemen and factory foremen
Salaries of:	Production manager, personnel officer, buyer, salespeople, sales manager, accountant, company secretary
Other:	Directors' fees, rent and rates, electric power, repairs, depreciation, carriage outwards, advertising, bad debts, interest on bank overdraft, development expenditure for new type of hat.

Required:
Which of these expenses can reasonably be included in the valuation of inventory?

* Question 2

Purchases of a certain product during July were:

July	1	100 units @ £10.00
	12	100 units @ £9.80
	15	50 units @ £9.60
	20	100 units @ £9.40

Units sold during the month were:

July	10	80 units
	14	100 units
	30	90 units

Required:
Assuming no opening inventories:
  (i) Determine the cost of goods sold for July under three different valuation methods.
 (ii) Discuss the advantages and/or disadvantages of each of these methods.
(iii) A physical inventory count revealed a shortage of five units. Show how you would bring this into account.

* Question 3

Alpha Ltd makes one standard article. You have been given the following information:

1 The inventory sheets at the year-end show the following items:

Raw materials:
100 tons of steel:
Cost £140 per ton
Present price £130 per ton

Finished goods:
100 finished units:
Cost of materials £50 per unit
Labour cost £150 per unit
Selling price £500 per unit

40 semi-finished units
Cost of materials £50 per unit
Labour cost to date £100 per unit
Selling price £500 per unit (completed)

10 damaged finished units:
Cost to rectify the damage £200 per unit
Selling price £500 per unit (when rectified)

2 Manufacturing overheads are 100% of labour cost.
Selling and distribution expenses are £60 per unit (mainly salespeople's commission and freight charges).

Required:
From the information in notes 1 and 2, state the amounts to be included in the balance sheet of Alpha Ltd in respect of inventory. State also the principles you have applied.

Question 4

Beta Ltd commenced business on 1 January and is making up its first year's accounts. The company uses standard costs. The company own a variety of raw materials and components for use in its manufacturing business. The accounting records show the following:

	Standard cost of purchases	Adverse (favourable) variances Price variance	Usage variance
	£	£	£
July	10,000	800	(400)
August	12,000	1,100	100
September	9,000	700	(300)
October	8,000	900	200
November	12,000	1,000	300
December	10,000	800	(200)
Cumulative figures for whole year	110,000	8,700	(600)

Raw materials control account balance at year-end is £30,000 (at standard cost).

Required:
The company's draft balance sheet includes 'Inventories, at the lower of cost and net realisable value £80,000'. This includes raw materials £30,000: do you consider this to be acceptable? If so, why? If not, state what you consider to be an acceptable figure.

(*Note:* for the purpose of this exercise, you may assume that the raw materials will realise more than cost.)

Balance sheet – equity, liability and asset measurement and disclosure

Question 5

The income statement of Bottom, a manufacturing company, for the year ending 31 January 20X2 is as follows:

	Bottom
	$000
Revenue	75,000
Cost of sales	(38,000)
Gross profit	37,000
Other operating expenses	(9,000)
Profit from operations	28,000
Investment income	
Finance cost	(4,000)
Profit before tax	24,000
Income tax expense	(7,000)
Net profit for the period	17,000

Note – accounting policies

Bottom has used the LIFO method of inventory valuation but the directors wish to assess the implications of using the FIFO method. Relevant details of the inventories of Bottom are as follows:

Date	Inventory valuation under:	
	FIFO	LIFO
	$000	$000
1 February 20X1	9,500	9,000
31 January 20X2	10,200	9,300

Requirement:

Re-draft the income statement of Bottom using the FIFO method of inventory valuation and explain how the change would need to be recognised in the published financial statements, if implemented.

References

1 IAS 2 *Inventories*, IASB, revised 2004.
2 'A guide to accounting standards – valuation of inventory and work-in-progress', *Accountants Digest*, Summer 1984.
3 M. Jones, 'Cooking the accounts', *Certified Accountant*, July 1988, p. 39.
4 T.S. Dudick, 'How to avoid the common pitfalls in accounting for inventory', *The Practical Accountant*, January/February 1975, p. 65.
5 *Certified Accountant*, October 1987, p. 7.
6 M. Perry, 'Valuation problems force FD to quit', *Accountancy Age*, 15 March 2001, p. 2.
7 The report appears on http://www.coso.org/index.htm.
8 See http:www.sec.gov/litigation/admin/34-41729.htm.
9 See http:www.sec.gov/litigation/admin/34-46099.htm.
10 E. Woolf, 'Auditing the stocks – part II', *Accountancy*, May 1976, pp. 108-110.
11 See www.sec.gov/litigation/admin/34-41720.htm.
12 See http://securities.stanford.edu/1022/LXK01-01/.
13 C. Westwick and D. Shaw, 'Subjectivity and reported profit', *Accountancy*, June 1982, pp. 129–131.
14 E. Woolf, 'Auditing the stocks – part I', *Accountancy*, April 1976, p. 106; 'Auditing the stocks – part II', *Accountancy*, May 1976, pp. 108–110.
15 K. Bhattacharya, 'More or less true, quite fair', *Accountancy*, December 1988, p. 126.
16 R. Northedge, 'Steel attacked over Wheelset valuation', *Daily Telegraph*, 2 January 1991, p. 19.

CHAPTER **20**

Construction contracts

20.1 Introduction

IAS 11 *Construction Contracts* defines a construction contract as

A contract specifically negotiated for the construction of an asset or a combination of assets that are closely inter-related or inter-dependent in terms of their design, technology and function or their ultimate purpose or use.

Some construction contracts are **fixed-price contracts**, where the contractor agrees to a fixed contract price, which in some cases is subject to cost escalation clauses. Other contracts are **cost-plus contracts**, where the contractor is reimbursed for allowable costs, plus a percentage of these costs or a fixed fee.

Construction contracts are normally assessed and accounted for individually. However, in certain circumstances construction contracts may be combined or segmented. Combination or segmentation is appropriate when:

● A group of contracts is negotiated as a single package and the contracts are performed together or in a continuous sequence (combination).

● Separate proposals have been submitted for each asset and the costs and revenues of each asset can be identified (segmentation).

A key accounting issue is when the revenues and costs (and therefore net income) under a construction contract should be recognised. There are two possible approaches:

● Only recognise net income when the contract is complete – the *completed contracts method*.

● Recognise a proportion of net income over the period of the contract – the *percentage of completion method*.

IAS 11 favours the latter approach, provided the overall contract result can be predicted with reasonable certainty.

20.2 Identification of contract revenue

Contract revenue should comprise:

(a) The initial amount of revenue agreed in the contract; and

(b) Variations in contract work, claims and incentive payments, to the extent that

    (i) it is probable that they will result in revenue;

    (ii) they are capable of being reliably measured.

Variations to the initially agreed contract price occur due to events such as:

- cost escalation clauses;
- claims for additional revenue by the contractor due to customer-caused delays or errors in specification or design;
- Incentive payments where specified performance standards are met or exceeded.

However they occur, the basic criteria of probable receipt and measurability need to be satisfied before variations can be included as revenue.

20.3 Identification of contract costs

IAS 11 classifies costs that can be identified with contracts under three headings:

Costs that directly relate to the specific contract, such as:

- site labour;
- costs of materials;
- depreciation of plant and equipment used on the contract;
- costs of moving plant and materials to and from the contract site;
- costs of hiring plant and equipment;
- costs of design and technical assistance that are directly related to the contract;
- the estimated costs of rectification and guarantee work;
- claims from third parties.

Costs that are attributable to contract activity in general and can be allocated to specific contracts, such as:

- insurance;
- costs of design and technical assistance that are not directly related to a specific contract;
- construction overheads.

Costs of this nature need to be allocated on a systematic and rational basis, based on the normal level of construction activity.

Such other costs as are specifically chargeable to the customer under the terms of the contract. Examples of these would be general administration and development costs for which reimbursement is specified in the terms of the contract.

Contract costs normally include relevant costs from the date the contract is secured to the date the contract is finally completed. If they can be separately identified and reliably measured then costs that are incurred in securing the contract can also be included as part of contract costs. However, where such costs were previously recognised as an expense in the period in which they were incurred then they are not included in contract costs when the contract is obtained in the subsequent period.

20.4 Recognition of contract revenue and expenses

IAS 11 states that the revenue and costs associated with a construction contract should be recognised in the income statement as soon as the outcome of the contract can be estimated reliably. This is likely to be possible when:

- the total contract revenue can be measured reliably and it is probable that the related economic benefits will flow to the enterprise;
- the total contract costs (both those incurred to date and those expected to be incurred in the future) can be measured reliably;
- the stage of completion of the contract can be accurately identified.

As stated in section 20.1 above the method of accounting for construction contracts that is laid down in IAS 11 is the percentage of completion method, which, as we have seen, involves, *inter alia*, identifying the stage of completion of the contract. IAS 11 does not identify a single method that may be used to identify the stage of completion. For many contracts this may involve an external expert (e.g. an architect) confirming that the contract has reached a particular stage of completion. However, alternative methods that might be appropriate include:

- the proportion that contract costs incurred for work performed to date bear to total contract costs;
- completion of a physical proportion of the contract work.

The appropriate method for recognising net income on a construction contract is to recognise the relevant proportion of total contract income as revenue and the relevant proportion of total contract costs as expenses. Clearly under this process the proportion of net income that is attributable to the work performed to date will be credited in the income statement.

If, exceptionally, the contract is expected to show a loss then the total expected loss is recognised immediately on the grounds of prudence. Where the contract is at too early a stage for an accurate prediction of the overall result then IAS 11 forbids enterprises from recognising any profit. In such circumstances, provided there is no reason to expect that the contract will make an overall loss, then the revenue that is recognised should be restricted to the costs incurred during the year that relate to the contract, which should in turn be recognised as an expense. Clearly in such circumstances the net income recognised is nil.

The balance sheet presentation for construction contracts should show as an asset – *Gross amounts due from customers* – the following net amount:

- total costs incurred to date;
- plus attributable profits (or less foreseeable losses);
- less any progress billings to the customer.

Where for any contract the above amount is negative, it should be shown as a liability – *Gross amounts due to customers.*

Advances – amounts received by the contractor before the related work is performed – should be shown as a liability – effectively a payment on account by the customer.

The financial statements of Eni, an Italian company that prepares financial statements in accordance with US GAAP, show an accounting policy note for inventories that is fairly close to the requirements of IAS 11:

> Contract work-in-progress, representing 14% and 12% of inventories at December 31 1998 and 1999 respectively, is recorded using the percentage-of-completion method. Payments received in advance of construction are subtracted from inventories and any excess of such advances over the value of work performed is recorded as a liability. Contract work-in-progress not invoiced, whose payment is agreed in a foreign currency, is recorded at current exchange rates at year-end. Future losses that exceed the revenues earned are accrued for when the company becomes aware such losses will occur.

This policy is IAS 11 compliant in all respects other than the treatment of advances. IAS 11 requires that these be shown as liabilities until the related work is performed.

EXAMPLE ● STEP APPROACH

ABC has two construction contracts outstanding at the end of its financial year, 30 June 20X1. Details are as follows:

	Contract A £000	Contract B £000
Total contract price	25,000	20,000
Costs incurred to date	14,000	15,000
Anticipated future costs	6,000	9,000
Progress billings	12,000	10,000
Advance payments	4,000	nil
% complete 30.6.X1	60%	50%
% complete 30.6.X0	30%	Not possible to determine

In the year to 30 June 20X0 ABC recognised revenue of £7,000,000 and costs of £5,500,000 on contract A. Contract B was at an early stage of completion at 30 June 20X0 but there was no indication **at that date** that it was likely to make a loss. Costs incurred on contract B to 30 June 20X0 totalled £2,000,000.

Step 1 Overall anticipated result

The first step is to predict the overall contract result for both contracts using the information available at the balance sheet date:

	Contract A £000	Contract B £000
Total contract price	25,000	20,000
Total expected contract costs:		
Costs to date	(14,000)	(15,000)
Expected future costs	(6,000)	(9,000)
Overall anticipated result	5,000	(4,000)

Step 2 Income statement: revenue entry

The next step is to compute the revenue that will be included in the income statement for each contract for the year ended 30 June 20X1:

	Contract A £000	Contract B £000
Cumulative revenue (60%/50% of total)	15,000	10,000
Less: recognised in previous years:	(7,000)	(2,000)
So revenue for the year	8,000	8,000

Notice that the revenue that is recognised in the year to 30 June 20X0 for contract B is equal to the costs incurred in that year. This is because, in previous years, the contract was at too early a stage to recognise any profit. Therefore, under IAS 11, the revenue and expense that is recognised is equal to the costs actually incurred on that contract.

Step 3 Income statement: expense entry

We now move on to compute the expense that will be recognised for each contract:

	Contract A £000	Contract B £000
60%/50% of total anticipated costs	12,000	12,000
Allowance for future losses	nil	2,000
Less: recognised in previous years:	(5,500)	(2,000)
So expense for the year	6,500	12,000

As far as contract B is concerned, recognising 50% of the total contract price and revenue and 50% of the total expected contract costs as expense results in a net expense of £2,000,000 [£10,000,000 – £12,000,000]. The contract is expected to make an overall loss of £4,000,000. Since the contract is expected to be loss-making then the whole of the expected loss must be recognised. This means making an additional charge to expense of £2,000,000 [£4,000,000 – £2,000,000].

Before we move on to the balance sheet presentation of the contracts let us summarise the income statement position, both for the current year and cumulatively:

	Contract A		Contract B	
	This year £000	Cumulative £000	This year £000	Cumulative £000
Revenue	8,000	15,000	8,000	10,000
Expense	(6,500)	(12,000)	(12,000)	(14,000)
Net income (expense)	1,500	3,000	(4,000)	(4,000)

Step 4 Balance sheet entries

As far as the balance sheet is concerned, the figures presented will be based on the cumulative amounts. The gross amounts due from customers will be as follows:

	Contract A £000	Contract B £000
Costs incurred to date	14,000	15,000
Add: recognised profits less recognised losses	3,000	(4,000)
Less: progress billings	(12,000)	(10,000)
Gross amounts due from customers	5,000	1,000

The advance received regarding contract A is shown separately as a payment on account. It is not offset against the amount due from customers until the relevant work is performed.

20.5 Public–private partnerships (PPPs)

PPPs have become a common government policy for public bodies to enter into contracts with private companies which have included contracts for the building and management of transport infrastructure, prisons, schools and hospitals. There are inherent risks in any project and the intention is that the government, through a PPP arrangement, should transfer some or all of such risks to private contractors. For this to work equitably there needs to be an incentive for the private contractors to be able to make a reasonable profit provided they are efficient whilst ensuring that the providers, users of the service, tax payers and employees also receive a fair share of the benefits of the PPP.

Improved public services

It has been recognised that where such contracts satisfy a value for money test it makes economic sense to transfer some or all of the risks to a private contractor. In this way it has been possible to deliver significantly improved public services with:

- increases in the quality and quantity of investment, e.g. by the private contractor raising equity and loan capital in the market rather than relying simply on government funding;
- tighter control of contracts during the construction stage to avoid cost and time overruns, e.g. completing construction contracts within budget and within agreed time – this is evidenced in a report from the National Audit Office[1] which indicates that the majority are completed on time and within budget; and
- more efficient management of the facilities after construction, e.g. maintaining the buildings, security, catering and cleaning of an approved standard for a specified number of years.

PPP defined

There is no clear definition of a PPP. It can take a number of forms, e.g. in the form of the improved use of existing public assets under the Wider Markets Initiative (WMI) or contracts for the construction of new infrastructure projects and services provided under a Private Finance Initiative (PFI).

The Wider Markets Initiative (WMI)[2]

The WMI encourages public sector bodies to become more entrepreneurial and to undertake commercial services based on the physical assets and knowledge assets (e.g. patents, databases) they own in order to make the most effective use of public assets. WMI does not relate to the use of surplus assets – the intention would be to dispose of these. However, becoming more entrepreneurial leads to the need for collaboration with private enterprise with appropriate expertise.

Private Finance Initiative (PFI)

The PFI has been described[3] as a form of public private partnership (PPP) that 'differs from privatisation in that the public sector retains a substantial role in PFI projects, either as the main purchaser of services or as an essential enabler of the project ... differs from contracting out in that the private sector provides the capital asset as well as the services ... differs from other PPPs in that the private sector contractor also arranges finance for the project'.

In its 2004 Government Review the HM Treasury stated[4] that 'The Private Finance Initiative is a small but important part of the Government's strategy for delivering high quality public services. In assessing where PFI is appropriate, the Government's approach is based on its commitment to efficiency, equity and accountability and on the Prime Minister's principles of public sector reform. PFI is only used where it can meet these requirements and deliver clear value for money without sacrificing the terms and conditions of staff. Where these conditions are met, PFI delivers a number of important benefits. By requiring the private sector to put its own capital at risk and to deliver clear levels of service to the public over the long term, PFI helps to deliver high quality public services and ensure that public assets are delivered on time and to budget'. The following is an extract showing the capital value of PFI contracts and a breakdown by major departments.

Breakdown by department

Department	Number of signed projects	Capital value (£m)
Transport	45	21,432.1
Education and Skills	121	2,922.8
Health	136	4,901.2
Work & Pensions	11	1,341.0
Home Office	37	1,095.8
Defence	52	4,254.8
Scotland	84	2,249.3
Other departments	191	4,502.4
Total	**677**	**42,699.4**

The PFI has meant that more capital projects have been undertaken for a given level of public expenditure and public service capital projects have been brought on stream earlier. However, it has to be recognised that this increased level of activity must be paid for by higher public expenditure in the future, as the stream of payments to the private sector grows – PFI projects have committed the government (and future governments) to a stream of revenue payments to private sector contractors between 2000/01 and 2025/26 of more than £100 billion.

Briefly, then, PFI allows the public sector to enter into a contract (known as a concession) with the private sector to provide quality services on a long-term basis, typically 25–30 years, so as to take advantage of private sector management skills working under contracts where private finance is at risk.

20.5.1 How does PFI operate?

In principle, private sector companies accept the responsibility for the design; raise the finance; undertake the construction, maintenance and possibly operation of assets for the delivery of public services. In return for this the public sector pays for the project by making annual payments that cover all the costs plus a return on the investment through performance payments.

In practice the construction company and other parties such as the maintenance companies become shareholders in a project company set up specifically to tender for a concession. The project company:

● enters into the contract (the 'concession') with the public sector; then
● enters into two principal subcontracts with
  – a construction company to build the project assets, and
  – a facilities management company to maintain the asset – this is normally for a period of 5 or so years after which time it is re-negotiated.

  NOTE: the project company will pass down to the constructor and maintenance subcontractors any penalties or income deductions that arise as a result of their mismanagement.

● raises a mixture of
  – equity and subordinated debt from the principal private promoters i.e. the construction company and the maintenance company; and
  – long-term debt.

NOTE: The long-term debt may be up to 90% of the finance required on the basis that it is cheaper to use debt rather than equity. The loan would typically be obtained from banks and would be without recourse to the shareholders of the project company. As there is no recourse to the shareholders, lenders need to be satisfied that there is a reliable income stream coming to the project company from the public sector, i.e. the lender needs to be confident that the project company can satisfy the contractual terms agreed with the public sector.

The subordinated debt made available to the project company by the promoters will be subordinated to the claims of the long-term lenders in that they will only be repaid after the long-term lenders.

● receives regular payments, usually over a 25–30-year period, from the public sector once the construction has been completed to cover the interest, construction, operating and maintenance costs.

NOTE: Such payments may be conditional on a specified level of performance and the private sector partners need to have carried out detailed investigation of past practice for accommodation type projects and or detailed economic forecasting for throughput projects.

If, for example, it is an accommodation type project (e.g. prisons, hospitals and schools) then payment is subject to the buildings being available in an appropriate clean and decorated condition – if not, income deductions can result.

If it is a throughput project (e.g. roads, water) with payment made on basis of throughput such as number of vehicles and litres of water, then payment would be at a fixed rate per unit of throughput and the accuracy of the forecast usage has a significant impact on future income.

● makes interest and dividend payments to the principal promoters.

● returns the infrastructure assets in agreed condition to the public sector at the end of the 25–30 year contractual period.

This can be shown graphically as follows:

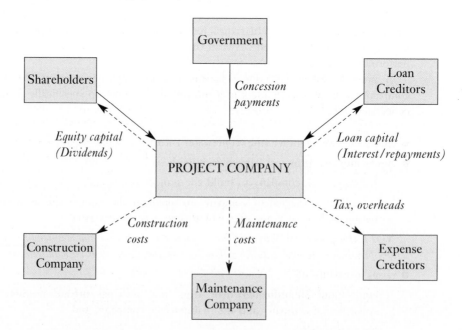

20.5.2 Profit and cash flow profile for the shareholders

Over a typical 30-year contract the profit and cash flow profiles would follow different growth patterns.

Profit profile

No profits earned during construction. On completion the depreciation and loan interest charges can result in losses in the early years. As the loans are reduced the interest charge falls and profits then grow steadily to the end of the concession.

Cash flow

As far as the shareholders are concerned, cash flow is negative in the early years with the introduction of equity finance and subordinated loans. Cash begins to flow in when receipts commence from the public sector and interest payments commence to be made on the subordinated loans, say from year 5, and dividend payments start to be made to the equity shareholders, say from year 15.

20.5.3 How is a concession dealt with in the annual accounts of a construction company?

Income statement entries

The accounting treatment will depend on the nature of the construction company's shareholding in the project company. If it has control, then it would consolidate. Frequently, however, it has significant influence without control and therefore accounts for its investment in concessions by taking to the income statement its share of the turnover, operating profit, interest and taxation of each concession, in line with IAS 28 Investments in Associates.

20.5.4 How is a concession dealt with in the annual accounts of a concession company?

Accounting for concessions in the UK is governed by Financial Reporting Standard 5, Reporting the Substance of Transactions, Application Note F, which is primarily concerned with how to account for the costs of constructing new assets.

Assets constructed by the concession may be either considered as a fixed asset of the concession, or as a long-term financial asset ('contract receivable'), depending on the specific allocation of risks between the concession company and the public sector authority. In practice the main risk is normally the demand risk associated with the usage of the asset, e.g. number of vehicles using a road where the risk remains with the concession company.

Treated as a non-current asset

Where the concession company takes the greater share of the risks associated with the asset, the cost of constructing the asset is considered to be a fixed asset of the concession. The cost of construction is capitalised and depreciation is charged to the income statement over the life of the concession. Income is recognised as turnover in the income statement as it is earned.

Treated as a financial instrument

Where the public sector takes the greater share of the risks associated with the asset, the concession company accounts for the cost of constructing the asset as a long-term contract receivable, being a receivable from the public sector. Finance income on this contract debtor is recorded using a notional rate of return which is specific to the underlying asset, and included as part of non-operating financial income in the income statement.

Under the contract receivable treatment, the revenue received from the public sector is split. The element relating to the provision of services that are considered a separate transaction from the provision of the asset is recognised as turnover in the income statement. The element relating to the contract debtor is split between finance income and repayment of the outstanding principal.

The following is an extract from the Balfour Beatty 2003 Annual Report to illustrate a usage based concession:

Roads

Balfour Beatty's road concessions typically comprise a mixture of new build roads and taking responsibility for the long-term maintenance of roads that the concession has not constructed ('assumed roads').

The income on roads concessions is directly related to the volume of traffic. The new roads are therefore considered to be fixed assets of the concession and are depreciated over the life of the concession, once construction is complete.

The revenue is split into two streams: that relating to the constructed road and that relating to the assumed road. Revenue on the constructed road is recognised as turnover as it is received. Revenue on the assumed road is recognised as turnover as the underlying maintenance obligations are performed. Where revenue is received in advance of performing these obligations, its recognition as turnover is deferred until they are performed.

The total profit earned from a concession will be the same whether it is treated as a fixed asset or a finance asset. There will, however, be a difference in the timing of the profit recognition. When treated as a fixed asset, profits increase over time largely due to the reducing financing costs of the transaction as the outstanding loans are repaid; when treated as a finance asset, the finance income is calculated on the full value of the contract debtor and this finance income falls in line with the principal repayments over the life of the project.

REVIEW QUESTIONS

1 Discuss the point in a contract's life when it becomes appropriate to recognise profit and the feasibility of specifying a common point, e.g. when contract is 25% complete.

2 'Profit on a contract is not realised until completion of the contract.' Discuss.

3 'Profit on a contract that is not completed is an unrealised holding gain.' Discuss.

4 'There should be one specified method for calculating attributable profit.' Discuss.

5 The Treasury state that 'Talk of PFI liabilities with a present value of £110bn is wrong. Adding up

PFI unitary payments and pretending they present a threat to the public finances is like adding up electricity, gas, cleaning and food bills for the next 30 years.' Discuss.

EXERCISES

An extract from the solution is provided in the Appendix at the end of the text for exercises marked with an asterisk (*).

Question 1

MACTAR have a series of contracts to resurface sections of motorways. The scale of the contract means several years' work and each motorway section is regarded as a separate contract.

Required:
From the following information, calculate for each contract the amount of profit (or loss) you would show for the year and show how these contracts would appear in the balance sheet with all appropriate notes.

M1	£m
Contract	3.0
Costs to date	2.1
Estimated cost to complete	0.3
Certified value of work completed to date	1.8
Progress billings applied for to date	1.75
Payment received to date	1.5

M6	£m
Contract sum	2.0
Costs to date	0.3
Estimated cost to complete	1.1
Certified value of work completed to date	0.1
Progress billings applied for to date	0.1
Payments received to date	—

M62	£m
Contract sum	2.5
Costs to date	2.3
Estimated costs to complete	0.8
Certified value of work completed to date	1.3
Progress billings applied for to date	1.0
Payments received to date	0.75

The M62 contract has had **major** difficulties due to difficult terrain, and the contract only allows for a 10% increase in contract sum for such events.

Question 2

At 31 October 20X0, Lytax Ltd was engaged in various contracts including five long-term contracts, details of which are given below:

	1 £000	2 £000	3 £000	4 £000	5 £000
Contract price	1,100	950	1,400	1,300	1,200
At 31 October					
Cumulative costs incurred	664	535	810	640	1,070
Estimated further costs to					
completion	106	75	680	800	165
Estimated cost of post-completion					
guarantee rectification work	30	10	45	20	5
Cumulative costs incurred					
transferred to cost of sales	580	470	646	525	900
Progress billings:					
Cumulative receipts	615	680	615	385	722
Invoiced					
– awaiting receipt	60	40	25	200	34
– retained by customer	75	80	60	65	84

It is not expected that any customers will default on their payments.

Up to 31 October 20X9, the following amounts have been included in the turnover and cost of sales figures:

	1 £000	2 £000	3 £000	4 £000	5 £000
Cumulative revenue	560	340	517	400	610
Cumulative costs incurred					
transferred to cost of sales	460	245	517	400	610
Foreseeable loss transferred to					
cost of sales	—	—	—	70	—

It is the accounting policy of Lytax Ltd to arrive at contract revenue by adjusting contract cost of sales (including foreseeable losses) by the amount of contract profit or loss to be regarded as recognised, separately for each contract.

Required:
Show how these items will appear in the balance sheet of Lytax Ltd with all appropriate notes. Show all workings in tabular form.

* Question 3

During its financial year ended 30 June 20X7 Beavers, an engineering company, has worked on several contracts. Information relating to one of them is given below:

Contract X201

Date commenced	1 July 20X6
Original estimate of completion date	30 September 20X7
Contract price	£240,000
Proportion of work certified as satisfactorily completed (and invoiced) up to 30 June 20X7	£180,000
Progress payments from Dam Ltd	£150,000

Costs up to 30 June 20X7

Wages	£91,000
Materials sent to site	£36,000
Other contract costs	£18,000
Proportion of Head Office costs	£6,000
Plant and equipment transferred to the site (at book value on 1 July 20X6)	£9,000

The plant and equipment is expected to have a book value of about £1,000 when the contract is completed.

Inventory of materials at site 30 June 20X7	£3,000
Expected additional costs to complete the contract:	
Wages	£10,000
Materials (including stock at 30 June 20X7)	£12,000
Other (including Head Office costs)	£8,000

At 30 June 20X7 it is estimated that work to a cost value of £19,000 has been completed, but not included in the certifications.

If the contract is completed one month earlier than originally scheduled, an extra £10,000 will be paid to the contractors. At the end of June 20X7 there seemed to be a 'good chance' that this would happen.

Required:
(a) Show the account for the contract in the books of Beavers up to 30 June 20X7 (including any transfer to the income statement which you think is appropriate).
(b) Show the balance sheet entries.
(c) Calculate the profit (or loss) to be recognised in the 20X6–X7 accounts.

Question 4

Newbild SA commenced work on the construction of a block of flats on 1 July 20X0.

During the period ended 31 March 20X1 contract expenditure was as follows:

	€
Materials issued from stores	13,407
Materials delivered direct to site	73,078
Wages	39,498
Administration expenses	3,742
Site expenses	4,693

On 31 March 20X1 there were outstanding amounts for wages €396 and site expenses €122, and the stock of materials on site amounted to €5,467.

The following information is also relevant:

1 On 1 July 20X0 plant was purchased for exclusive use on site at a cost of €15,320. It was estimated that it would be used for two years after which it would have a residual value of €5,000.

2 By 31 March 20X1 Newbild SA had received €114,580, being the amount of work certified by the architects up to 31 March 20X1 less a 15% retention.

3 The total contract price is €780,000. The company estimates that additional costs to complete the project will be €490,000. From costing records it is estimated that the costs of rectification and guarantee work will be 2.5% of the contract price.

Required:

(a) Prepare the contract account for the period, together with a statement showing your calculation of the net income to be taken to the company's income statement on 31 March 20X1. Assume for the purpose of the question that the contract is sufficiently advanced to allow for the taking of profit.

(b) Give the values which you think should be included in the figures of revenue and cost of sales, in the income statement, and those to be included in net amounts due to or from the customer in the balance sheet in respect of this contract.

Question 5

Good Progress SpA entered into a contract on 1.1.20X0 at a contract price of €1,000,000 and an estimated total profit of €250,000. The contract was due for completion on 31.12.20X4.

The following information was available.

As at 31.12.20X0:

The contract was 25% complete and an architect's certificate was issued for €250,000.

As at 31.12.20X1

The contract was 40% complete and an architect's certificate was issued for €400,000.

Required:

Prepare the income statement entries for the years ended 31 December 20X0 and 20X1 and the balance sheet entries as at those dates.

Question 6

(a) A concession company, WaterAway, has completed the construction of a wastewater plant. The public sector (the grantor) makes payments related to the volume of wastewater processed.

Discuss how this will be dealt with in the income statement and balance sheet of the concession company.

(b) A concession company, LearnAhead, has built a school and receives income from the public sector (the grantor) based on the availability of the school for teaching.

Discuss how this will be dealt with in the income statement and balance sheet of the concession company.

References

1 National Audit Office, PFI: Construction Performance Feb. 2003
http://www.nao.org.uk/publications/nao_reports/02-03/0203371.pdf
2 *Selling government services into wider markets, Policy and Guidance Notes*, Enterprise and Growth Unit, HM Treasury July 1998
http://www.hm-treasury.gov.uk/mediastore/otherfiles/sgswm.pdf
3 Research Paper 01/0117 *Private Finance Initiative*, G. Allen, Economic Policy and Statistics Section, House of Commons, December 2001.
4 http://www.hm-treasury.gov.uk/documents/public_private_partnerships/ppp_index.cfm?ptr=29

PART **4**

Consolidated accounts

CHAPTER 21

Accounting for groups at date of acquisition

21.1 Introduction

This chapter will consider:

● The definition of a group
● Consolidated accounts and some reasons for their preparation
● The definition of control
● The purchase method
● The treatment of goodwill
● The comparison between an acquisition by cash and an exchange of shares
● Minority interests
● The treatment of differences between fair value and book value
● The determination of fair values.

21.2 The definition of a group

Under IAS 27 *Consolidated and Separate Financial Statements*, a group exists where one enterprise (the parent) **controls**, either directly or **indirectly**, another enterprise (the subsidiary). A group consists of a parent and its subsidiaries.[1] This book will deal only with situations where both the parent and subsidiary enterprises are companies.

21.3 Consolidated accounts and some reasons for their preparation

In most cases a parent company is required by IAS 27 to prepare consolidated financial statements. These show the accounts of a group as though that group were one enterprise. The net assets of the companies in a group will therefore be combined and any inter-company profits and balances eliminated.

Why are groups required to prepare consolidated accounts?

(i) To prevent the preparation of misleading accounts by such means as inflating the sales through selling to another member of a group.

(ii) To provide a more meaningful EPS figure. Consolidated accounts show the full earnings on a parent company's investment while parent's individual accounts only show the dividend received from the subsidiaries.

(iii) To provide a better measurement of the performance of a parent company's directors. In consolidated accounts the total earnings of a group can be compared with its total assets in arriving at a group's return on capital employed (ROCE).

ROCE is regarded as important strategic information. For example, the Danish group FLS Industries A/S stated in its 1999 Financial Results Statement:

> **Return on capital employed (ROCE)**
> The FLS Group has decided to introduce value-based management with the overall objective of strengthening the framework for monitoring and controlling the Group's long-term capability for generating earnings. For this purpose a version of EVA™ – Economic Value Added – is used. This entails relating the financial result to the capital it requires and the risk it entails ...
>
> Although the return on capital employed is not satisfactory, over the past five years the FLS Group has achieved an increasing return on its capital employed. In 1995, ROCE amounted to 6.6 per cent, compared with 10.2 per cent in 1998 and 21.1 per cent in 1999. Adjusted for non-recurring items, ROCE for 1999 amounts to 5.9 per cent.
>
> In 2000 the Group will intensify the focus on optimising capital employed.

When may a parent company not be required to prepare consolidated accounts?

It may not be necessary for a parent company to prepare consolidated accounts if the parent is itself a wholly-owned subsidiary and the ultimate parent produces consolidated financial statements available for public use that comply with International Financial Reporting Standards (IFRSs).[2] This situation arises when the ultimate parent exercises control over a company through a subsidiary company's investment as illustrated by the extract from the 1999 Accounts of Eybl International:

> **Consolidated companies**
> The group of consolidated companies was determined in accordance with IAS 27.11. The consolidated financial statements of Eybl International Aktiengesellschaft as the parent company thus comprises the financial statements of nine subsidiaries on which Eybl International Aktiengesellschaft exercises unified control or in which Eybl International Aktiengesellschaft **or one of its subsidiaries** has majority voting rights.

Note that in the UK FRS 2 the same rule applies except where the parent is established outside the EU.

If the parent company is a partially-owned subsidiary of another entity, then, if its other owners have been informed and do not object, the parent company need not present consolidated financial statements.

When may a parent company exclude a subsidiary from a consolidation?

IAS 27 provides[3] that a subsidiary **should be excluded** from consolidation when control is intended to be temporary because the subsidiary is acquired and held exclusively with a view to its disposal within twelve months from acquisition and management is actively seeking a buyer. Investments in such subsidiaries must be classified as held for trading and accounted for in accordance with IAS 39 *Financial Instruments: Recognition and*

Measurement. This is because the investment is a current asset and the directors' performance in this matter can best be judged from the profit or loss on the investment.

IAS 27 now states[4] that an entity is not permitted to exclude from consolidation an entity it continues to control simply because that entity is operating under severe long-term restrictions that significantly impair its ability to transfer funds to the parent. Control must be lost for exclusion to occur.

Exclusion is permissible on grounds of non-materiality[5] as the International Accounting Standards are not intended to apply to immaterial items. For example, the French Group, Essilor, with sales of €2,138m and tangible assets of €850m, included in its 2002 Annual Report the following statement on the scope of the consolidation:

> The consolidated financial statements include the financial statements of all entities that satisfy one of the following two criteria:
>
> ● annual sales of over €3m,
>
> ● or tangible assets in excess of €9m.

Exclusion on the grounds that a subsidiary's activities are dissimilar from those of the others within a group cannot be justified.[6] This is because information is required under IAS 14 *Segment Reporting* on the different activities of subsidiaries, and users of accounts can, therefore, make appropriate adjustments for their own purposes if required.

Accounting treatment of subsidiaries excluded under IAS 27

The following disclosures are required:[7]

(a) the fact that a subsidiary is not consolidated; and

(b) summarised financial information of subsidiaries, either individually or in groups, that are not consolidated, including the amounts of total assets, total liabilities, revenues and profit or loss.

21.4 The definition of control

Under IFRS 3 *Business Combinations*, control is defined[8] as 'the power to govern the financial and operating policies of an entity or business so as to obtain benefits from its activities'. Control is **assumed** when one party to the combination owns more than half of the voting rights of the other either directly or through a subsidiary. This is illustrated with the following extract from the 2003 accounts of Wartsila NSD Corporation:

> **Principles of consolidation**
> The consolidated financial statements include the accounts of the parent company, Wartsila NSD Corporation, and the accounts of its directly or indirectly owned subsidiaries (over 50% of the voting rights) ...

What if the voting rights acquired are less than half?

Even in this situation, it may still be possible[9] to identify an acquirer when one of the combining enterprises, as a result of the business combination, acquires:

(a) power over more than one-half of the voting rights of the other enterprise by virtue of an agreement with other investors;

(b) power to govern the financial and operating policies of the other enterprise under a statute or an agreement;

(c) power to appoint or remove the majority of the members of the board of directors or equivalent governing body of the other enterprise; or

(d) power to cast the majority of votes at a meeting of the board of directors or equivalent governing body of the other enterprise.

An extract from the 2003 accounts of BorsodChem Rt (registered under Hungarian law), whose consolidated financial statements have been prepared in accordance with IFRSs, states:

> **Basis of consolidation**
> BorsodChem Group companies are those companies in which the Company has a controlling financial interest through direct or indirect ownership of a majority voting interest or effective managerial and contractual control.

21.5 Alternative methods of preparing consolidated accounts

Before IFRS 3 there were two main methods of preparing consolidated statements, the purchase method and the pooling of interests method. The former method was the more common and was used in all cases where one company was seen as acquiring another. The pooling method was used only where the shareholders of the two companies were seen as coming together to 'achieve a continuing mutual share in the risks and benefits attaching to the combined entity such that neither party can be identified as the acquirer'.[10] IFRS 3 now allows only the purchase method. This should ensure greater comparability of financial statements and remove the incentive to structure combinations in such a way as to produce the desired accounting result.

The purchase method

The **fair value** of the parent company's investment in a subsidiary is set against its share of the **fair value** of the identifiable net assets in the subsidiary at the date of acquisition. If the investment is greater than the share of net assets then the difference is regarded as the purchase of goodwill – see the Rose Group example below.

EXAMPLE ● THE ROSE GROUP CONSOLIDATED USING THE PURCHASE METHOD

On 1 January 20X0 Rose plc acquired 100% of the 10,000 £1 common shares in Tulip plc for £1.50 per share in cash and gained control. The fair value of the net assets of Tulip plc at that date was the same as the book value. The individual balance sheets immediately after the acquisition and the group accounts at that date were as follows:

	Rose plc £	Tulip plc £	Group £	
ASSETS				
Non-current assets	20,000	11,000	31,000	Note 2
Goodwill	—	—	1,000	Note 1
Investment in Tulip	15,000	—	—	
Net current assets	8,000	3,000	11,000	Note 2
Net assets	43,000	14,000	43,000	
Common share capital	16,000	10,000	16,000	Note 3
Retained earnings	27,000	4,000	27,000	Note 3
	43,000	14,000	43,000	

Note 1. Calculate the goodwill for inclusion in the group accounts:

		£	£
The parent company's investment			15,000
Less: The parent's share of the subsidiary's			
share capital	(100% × 10,000)	10,000	
The parent's share of accumulated profits	(100% × 4,000)	4,000	14,000
The difference is goodwill for inclusion in the consolidated balance sheet			1,000*

*(This is equivalent to the 100% share of net assets, i.e. Fixed assets 11,000 + Net current assets 3,000)

Note 2. Add together the assets and liabilities of the two companies for the group accounts:

		£
Fixed assets other than goodwill	(20,000 + 11,000)	31,000
Goodwill	(as calculated in Note 1)	1,000
Net current assets	(8,000 + 3,000)	11,000
		43,000

Note 3. Calculate the consolidated share capital and reserves for the group accounts:

		£
Common share capital	(The parent company only)	16,000
Retained earnings	(The parent company only)	27,000
		43,000

Note that:

- In Note 1 the investment in the subsidiary (£15,000) has been set off against the parent company's share of the subsidiary's share capital and reserves (£14,000) and these cancelled inter-company balances do not, therefore, appear in the consolidated accounts.
- In Note 2 the total of the net assets in the group account is the same as the net assets in the individual balance sheet but the Tulip plc investment in Rose plc's accounts has been replaced by the net assets of Tulip plc of £14,000 **plus** the previously unrecorded £1,000 goodwill.
- In Note 3 the consolidated balance sheet only includes the share capital and retained earnings of the parent company, because the subsidiary's share capital and retained earnings have been used in the calculation of goodwill.

An extract from the 2003 accounts of Schoeller-Bleckmann Oilfield equipment AG states:

Consolidation method
All companies in the company's accounts have adopted December 31 as the balance sheet date. Upon capital consolidation the investments in the subsidiaries were offset against the equity of the respective entities in applying the purchase method of consolidation accounting in line with International Financial Reporting Standards.

21.6 The treatment of positive goodwill

Positive purchased goodwill, where the investment exceeds the total of the net assets acquired, should be recognised as an asset with no amortisation. Goodwill must be subject to impairment tests in accordance with IAS 36 *Impairment of Assets*. These tests will be annual, or more frequently if circumstances indicate that the goodwill might be impaired.[11] Once recognised, an impairment loss for goodwill may not be reversed in a subsequent period,[12] which helps in preventing the manipulation of period profits.

21.7 The treatment of negative goodwill

The acquiring company does not always pay more than the fair value of the identifiable net assets. If it pays less then negative goodwill is said to arise.

Negative goodwill, where the fair value of the net assets exceeds the amount of the investment, can arise[13] because

(a) there have been errors measuring the fair value of either the cost of the combination or the acquiree's identifiable assets, liabilities or contingent liabilities;

(b) future costs such as losses have been taken into account;

(c) there has been a bargain purchase.

Under IFRS 3, negative goodwill arising under (b) or (c) should be recognised immediately in the income statement.

Note that in the case of negative goodwill, the UK standard FRS 10 requires that it should be recognised in the profit and loss account in the periods expected to benefit from it.

21.8 The comparison between an acquisition by cash and an exchange of shares

Shares in another company can be purchased with cash or through an exchange of shares. In the former case, the cash will be reduced and exchanged for another asset called 'Investment in the subsidiary company'. If there is an exchange of shares there will be an increase in the share capital of the acquiring company rather than a decrease in cash. There is no effect in either case on the accounts of the acquired company. The purchase price may contain a mixture of cash and shares and possibly other assets as well.

21.9 Minority interests

A parent company does not need to purchase all the shares of another company to gain control. The holders of the remaining shares are collectively referred to as the **minority interest**. They are part owners of the subsidiary. In such a case, therefore, the parent does not **own** all the net assets of the acquired company but does **control** them.

One of the purposes of preparing group accounts is to show the effectiveness of that control and of the directors of the parent company who are responsible for it. Therefore all of the net assets of the subsidiary will be included in the group balance sheet and the minority interest will be shown as partly financing those net assets. In the group income statement the full profit of the subsidiary is included and the minority interest in it then deducted. The income statement will be dealt with in more detail in Chapter 23. The effect on the balance sheet is illustrated in the Bird Group example below.

EXAMPLE ● THE BIRD GROUP

On 1 January 20X0 Bird plc acquired 80% of the 10,000 £1 Common shares in Flower plc for £1.50 per share in cash and gained control. The fair value of the net assets of Flower at that date was the same as the book value. The individual balance sheets immediately after the acquisition and the group accounts at that date were as follows:

	Bird £	Flower £	Group £	
ASSETS				
Non-current assets	20,000	11,000	31,000	Note 3
Goodwill	—	—	800	Note 1
Investment in Flower	12,000	—	—	
Net current assets	11,000	3,000	14,000	Note 3
Net assets	43,000	14,000	45,800	
Common share capital	16,000	10,000	16,000	Note 4
Retained earnings	27,000	4,000	27,000	Note 4
	43,000	14,000	43,000	
Minority interest		—	2,800	Note 2
	43,000	14,000	45,800	

Note 1. Calculate goodwill

	£	£
The parent company's investment in Flower		12,000
Less: The parent's share of the subsidiary's share capital (80% × 10,000)	8,000	
The parent's share of the retained earnings (80% × 4,000)	3,200	
(Equivalent to the share of net assets, i.e. 80% × (10,000 + 4,000))		11,200
The difference is goodwill		800

Note 2. Calculate the minority interest

The minority interest in the share capital of Flower	(20% × 10,000)	=	2,000
The minority interest in the retained earnings of Flower	(20% × 4,000)	=	800
Represents the minority interest in the net assets of Flower			2,800

In published group accounts the minority interest will be shown as a separate item in the equity of the group as follows:

Common share capital	16,000
Retained earnings	27,000
Bird shareholders' share of equity	43,000
Minority interest	2,800
Total equity	45,800

Minority interest is, therefore, now shown as part of the ownership of the group rather than as a liability.

Note 3. Add together the assets and liabilities of the two companies for the group accounts

	£
Fixed assets other than goodwill (20,000 + 11,000)	31,000
Goodwill (as calculated in Note 1)	800
Net current assets (11,000 + 3,000)	14,000
	45,800

Note 4. Calculate the consolidated share capital and reserves for the group accounts

		£
Common share capital	*(parent company only)*	16,000
Retained earnings	*(parent company only)*	27,000
		43,000

Note that **no goodwill** is credited to the minority interest and correspondingly only the goodwill relating to the 80% holding of the parent appears in the balance sheet. The argument for this treatment is that the amount paid for goodwill is to enable the parent to gain control, rather than to acquire a separately identifiable asset. As it is a payment for control it is not, therefore, applicable to the minority interest.

21.10 The treatment of differences between a subsidiary's fair value and book value

In our examples so far we have assumed that the book value of the net assets in the subsidiary are equal to their fair value. In practice, book value in the parent company and in the subsidiary rarely equals fair value and it is necessary to revalue the group's share of the assets and liabilities of the subsidiary prior to consolidation. Note that, when consolidating, the parent company's assets and liabilities remain unchanged at book value – it is only the subsidiary's that are adjusted for the purpose of the consolidated accounts. If, for example, the fixed assets of Flower in the example above had a fair value of £11,600, the fixed assets would be increased by £600 and a revaluation reserve created of £600.

	Bird £	Flower £	Group £	
ASSETS				
Non-current assets	20,000	11,000	31,600	
Goodwill	—	—	320	Note 1
Investment in Flower	12,000	—	—	
Net current assets	11,000	3,000	14,000	
Net assets	43,000	14,000	45,920	
Common share capital	16,000	10,000	16,000	
Retained earnings	27,000	4,000	27,000	
	43,000	14,000	43,000	
Minority interest	—	—	2,920	Note 2
	43,000	14,000	45,920	

Note 1. Goodwill

			£
The parent company's investment in Flower			12,000
Less: The parent's share of the subsidiary's share capital	(80% × 10,000)	8,000	
The parent's share of retained earnings	(80% × 4,000)	3,200	
The parent's share of the revaluation	(80% × 600)	480	
(Equivalent to the share of net assets) 80% × (10,000 + 4,000 + 600)			11,680
The difference is goodwill			**320**

Note 2. Minority interest

			£
The minority interest in the share capital of Flower	(20% × 10,000)	=	2,000
The minority interest in the retained earnings of Flower	(20% × 4,000)	=	800
The minority interest in the revaluation of the subsidiary's assets	(20% × 600)		120
			2,920

Note 3. Non-current assets (20,000 + 11,000 + 600)   = **£31,600**

It must be stressed that the revaluation of the subsidiary's assets is only necessary for the consolidated accounts. No entries need be made in the individual accounts of the subsidiary or its books of account. The preparation of consolidated accounts is a separate exercise that in no way affects the records of the individual companies.

21.11 How to calculate fair values

IFRS 3 *Business Combinations* gives a definition of fair value as 'The amount for which an asset could be exchanged or a liability settled between knowledgeable, willing parties in an arm's-length transaction.'[14] The detailed guidance for determining fair value is also set out in IFRS 3. The main provisions are as follows:

As from the date of acquisition, an acquirer should:

(a) incorporate into the income statement the results of operations of the acquiree; and

(b) recognise in the balance sheet the identifiable assets and liabilities of the acquiree and any goodwill or negative goodwill arising on the acquisition.

The identifiable assets and liabilities acquired that are recognised should be those of the acquiree that existed at the date of acquisition. Liabilities should not be recognised at the date of acquisition if they result from the acquirer's intentions or actions. Therefore liabilities for terminating or reducing the activities of the acquiree should only be recognised where the acquiree has, at the acquisition date, an existing liability for restructuring recognised in accordance with IAS 37 *Provisions, Contingent Liabilities and Contingent Assets*.

Liabilities should also not be recognised for future losses[15] or other costs expected to be incurred as a result of the acquisition, whether they relate to the acquirer or acquiree.

The IFRS sets out the rules for specific assets and liabilities in Appendix B.

● Tangible fixed assets: Fair value should be based on market value or, where there is no evidence of market value, at depreciated replacement cost or at a value based on future income.

- Identifiable intangible assets: Fair value should be based on market value or, if there is no active market, the best estimate on an arm's-length basis.
- Marketable securities: At their current market values.
- Non-marketable securities: At estimated values based on performance.
- Inventories and work-in-progress:
  - Finished goods at selling prices less the cost of disposal and a reasonable profit allowance, based on the profit on similar goods.
  - Work-in-progress at the selling price of finished goods less the costs to complete, the costs of sale and a reasonable profit allowance.
  - Raw materials at current replacement cost.
- Monetary assets and liabilities other than taxation: The fair value is the amount to be received or disbursed, discounted to present value. There is no need to discount if the difference between the discounted amount and the actual amount is immaterial.
- Tax assets and liabilities: The fair value is the amount of the tax benefit or liability after taking into account the tax effect of restating the other identifiable assets and liabilities to their fair value. The tax benefit or liability is not discounted.

The reason why the net assets of the subsidiary must be revalued at the date of acquisition is to ensure that all profits, both realised and unrealised, are reflected in the value of the net assets at the date of acquisition and to prevent distortion of EPS in periods following the acquisition.

Summary

When one company acquires a controlling interest in another and the combination is treated as an acquisition, the investment in the subsidiary is recorded in the acquirer's consolidated balance sheet at the fair value of the investment map plus any cost directly attributable to the combination.

On consolidation, if the acquirer has acquired less than 100% of the common shares, any differences between the fair values of the assets or liabilities and their face value are recognised in full and the parent and minorities credited or debited with their respective percentage interests.

Also, on consolidation, any differences between the fair values of the net assets and the consideration paid to acquire them is treated as positive or negative goodwill and dealt with in accordance with IFRS 3 *Business Combinations*.

REVIEW QUESTIONS

1 Explain how negative goodwill may arise and its accounting treatment.

2 Explain how the fair value is calculated for:
- tangible fixed assets
- inventories
- monetary assets.

3 Explain why only the net assets of the subsidiary and not those of the parent are adjusted to fair value at the date of acquisition for the purpose of consolidated accounts.

4 Eybl International states in its notes to the consolidated financial statements:

Methods of Consolidation
Capital consolidation is carried out according to the book-value method, by offsetting the book values of the investments against the group's share in the stockholders' equity of the subsidiary at the time of its acquisition.

Required: Explain how any difference between the book value of the investments and the group's share in the stockholder equity of the subsidiary would be dealt with.

5 Coil SA/NV is a company incorporated under the laws of Belgium. Its accounts are IAS compliant. It states in its 1999 accounts (in accordance with IAS 27, para. 13):

Principles of consolidation
The consolidated Financial statements include all subsidiaries which are controlled by the Parent Company, unless such control is assumed to be temporary or due to long-term restrictions significantly impairing a subsidiary's ability to transfer funds to the Parent Company.

Required: Discuss whether these are acceptable reasons for excluding a subsidiary from the consolidated financial statements under IFRS 3.

6 BorsodChem Rt is a company incorporated under Hungarian law. Its accounts are IAS compliant. It states in its 1999 accounts:

Basis of consolidation
The accompanying consolidated financial statements include the accounts of all of the companies comprising the BorsodChem Group except certain subsidiaries which are immaterial individually and in aggregate.

Required: Discuss what BorsodChem would take into account when deciding that a subsidiary was immaterial.

7 In each of the following cases you are required to give your opinion, with reasons, on whether or not there is a parent/subsidiary under IFRS 3. Suggest any other information, if any, that might be helpful in making a decision.

(a) Tin acquired 15% of the equity voting shares and 90% of the non-voting preferred shares of Copper. Copper has no other category of shares. The directors of Tin are also the directors of Copper, there is a common head office with shared administration departments and the functions of Copper are mainly the provision of marketing and transport facilities for Tin. Another company, Iron, holds 55% of the equity voting shares of Copper but has never used its voting power to interfere with the decisions of the directors.

(b) Hat plc owns 60% of the voting equity shares in Glove plc and 25% of the voting equity shares in Shoe plc. Glove owns 30% of the voting equity shares in Shoe plc and has the right to appoint a majority of the directors.

(c) Morton plc has 30% of the voting equity shares of Berry plc and also has a verbal agreement with other shareholders, who own 40% of the shares, that those shareholders will vote according to the wishes of Morton.

(d) Bean plc acquired 30% of the shares of Pea plc several years ago with the intention of acquiring influence over the operating and financial policies of that company. Pea sells 80% of its output to Bean. While Bean has a veto over the operating and financial decisions of Pea's board of directors it has only used this veto on one occasion, four years ago, to prevent that company from supplying one of Bean's competitors.

8 The following is an extract from the Accounting Policy in the 1999 Annual Report of Schmalbach-Lubeca AG:

> Capital consolidation of the subsidiaries included in the financial statements is carried out on the basis of the date of acquisition according to the book value method (in line with Art. 301, Para. 1, Item 1 of the HGB).

Required: Explain what differences there would be in the consolidation procedures if IFRS 3 *Business Combinations* were applied.

EXERCISES

An extract from the solution is provided in the Appendix at the end of the text for exercises marked with an asterisk (*).

Questions 1–5

Required: Prepare the balance sheets of Parent Ltd and the consolidated balance sheet as at 1 January 20X7 after each transaction, using for each question the balance sheets of Parent Ltd and Daughter Ltd as at 1 January 20X7 which were as follows:

	Parent Ltd	Daughter Ltd
	£	£
Ordinary shares of £1 each	40,500	9,000
Retained earnings	4,500	1,800
	45,000	10,800
Cash	20,000	2,000
Other net assets	25,000	8,800
	45,000	10,800

* Question 1

(a) Assume that on 1 January 20X7 Parent Ltd acquired all the ordinary shares in Daughter Ltd for £10,800 cash. The fair value of the net assets in Daughter Ltd was their book value.

(b) The purchase consideration was satisfied by the issue of 5,400 new ordinary shares in Parent Ltd. The fair value of a £1 ordinary share in Parent Ltd was £2. The fair value of the net assets in Daughter Ltd was their book value.

* Question 2

(a) On 1 January 20X7 Parent Ltd acquired all the ordinary shares in Daughter Ltd for £16,200 cash. The fair value of the net assets in Daughter Ltd was their book value.

(b) The purchase consideration was satisfied by the issue of 5,400 new ordinary shares in Parent Ltd. The fair value of a £1 ordinary share in Parent Ltd was £3. The fair value of the net assets in Daughter Ltd was their book value.

Question 3

(a) On 1 January 20X7 Parent Ltd acquired all the ordinary shares in Daughter Ltd for £16,200 cash. The fair value of the net assets in Daughter Ltd was £12,000.

(b) The purchase consideration was satisfied by the issue of 5,400 new ordinary shares in Parent Ltd. The fair value of a £1 ordinary share in Parent Ltd was £3. The fair value of the net assets in Daughter Ltd was £12,000.

Question 4

On 1 January 20X7 Parent Ltd acquired all the ordinary shares in Daughter Ltd for £6,000 cash. The fair value of the net assets in Daughter Ltd was their book value.

Question 5

On 1 January 20X7 Parent Ltd acquired 75% of the ordinary shares in Daughter Ltd. for £9,000 cash. The fair value of the net assets in Daughter Ltd was their book value.

Question 6

The following accounts are the consolidated balance sheet and parent company balance sheet for Alpha Ltd as at 30 June 20X2.

	£	Consolidated balance sheet £	£	Parent company balance sheet £
Ordinary shares		140,000		140,000
Capital reserve		92,400		92,400
Retained earnings		79,884		35,280
Minority interest		12,329		—
		324,613		267,680
Non-current assets				
Property		127,400		84,000
Plant and equipment		62,720		50,400
Goodwill		85,680		
Investment in subsidiary (50,400 shares)				151,200
Current assets				
Inventory	121,604		71,120	
Trade receivables	70,429		51,800	
Cash at bank	24,360		—	
	216,393		122,920	
Current liabilities				
Trade payables	140,420		80,920	
Income tax	27,160		20,720	
Bank overdraft	—		39,200	
	167,580		140,840	
Working capital		48,813		(17,920)
		324,613		267,680

Notes:
- (i) There was only one subsidiary called Beta Ltd.
- (ii) There were no capital reserves in the subsidiary.
- (iii) Alpha produced inventory for sale to the subsidiary at a cost of £3,360 in May 20X2. The inventory was invoiced to the subsidiary at £4,200 and was still on hand at the subsidiary's warehouse on 30 June 20X2. The invoice had not been settled at 30 June 20X2.
- (iv) The retained earnings of the subsidiary had a credit balance of £16,800 at the date of acquisition.
- (v) There was a right of set-off between overdrafts and bank balances.

Required:
- (a) Prepare the balance sheet as at 30 June 20X2 of the subsidiary company from the information given above.
- (b) Discuss briefly the main reasons for the publication of consolidated accounts.

* Question 7

Rouge plc acquired 100% of the common shares of Noir plc on 1 January 20X0 and gained control. At that date the balance sheets of the two companies were as follows:

	Rouge £ million	Noir £ million
ASSETS		
Non-current assets		
Property, plant and equipment	100	60
Investment in Noir	132	
Current assets	80	70
Total assets	312	130
EQUITY AND LIABILITIES		
Common £1 shares	200	60
Retained earnings	52	40
	252	100
Current liabilities	60	30
Total equity and liabilities	312	130

Note: The fair values are the same as the book values.

Required: Prepare a consolidated balance sheet for Rouge plc as at 1 January 20X0.

* Question 8

Ham plc acquired 100% of the common shares of Burg plc on 1 January 20X0 and gained control. At that date the balance sheets of the two companies were as follows:

	Ham £000	Burg £000
ASSETS		
Non-current assets		
Property, plant and equipment	250	100
Investment in Burg	90	
Current assets	100	70
Total assets	440	170

EQUITY AND LIABILITIES

Capital and reserves		
Common £1 shares	200	100
Retained earnings	160	10
	360	110
Current liabilities	80	60
Total equity and liabilities	440	170

Notes:

1. The fair value is the same as the book value.
2. £15,000 of the negative goodwill arises because the net assets have been acquired at below their fair value and the remainder covers expected losses of £3,000 in the year ended 31/12/20X0 and £2,000 in the following year.

Required: **(a) Prepare a consolidated balance sheet for Ham plc as at 1 January 20X0.**

(b) Explain how the negative goodwill will be treated.

Question 9

Set out below is the summarised balance sheet of Berlin plc at 1 January 20X0.

	£000
ASSETS	
Non-current assets	
Property, plant and equipment	250
Current assets	150
Total assets	400
EQUITY AND LIABILITIES	
Capital and reserves	
Common £5 shares	200
Retained earnings	80
	280
Current liabilities	120
Total equity and liabilities	400

On 1/1/20X0 Berlin acquired 100% of the shares of Hanover for £100,000 and gained control.

Required: Prepare the balance sheet of Berlin immediately after the acquisition if:

(a) Berlin acquired the shares for cash

(b) Berlin issued 10,000 common shares of £5 (market value £10).

Question 10

Bleu plc acquired 80% of the common shares of Verte plc on 1 January 20X0 and gained control. At that date the balance sheets of the two companies were as follows:

	Bleu £m	Verte £m
ASSETS		
Non-current assets		
Property, plant and equipment	150	120
Investment in Verte	210	
Current assets	108	105
Total assets	468	225

	Bleu £m	Verte £m
EQUITY AND LIABILITIES		
Capital and reserves		
Common £10 shares	300	120
Retained earnings	78	60
	378	180
Current liabilities	90	45
Total equity and liabilities	468	225

Note: The fair values are the same as the book values

Required: Prepare a consolidated balance sheet for Bleu plc as at 1 January 20X0.

Question 11

Base plc acquired 60% of the common shares of Ball plc on 1 January 20X0 and gained control. At that date the balance sheets of the two companies were as follows:

	Base £000	Ball £000
ASSETS		
Non-current assets		
Property, plant and equipment	250	100
Investment in Ball	90	
Current assets	100	70
Total assets	440	170
EQUITY AND LIABILITIES		
Capital and reserves		
Common £5 shares	200	80
Share premium		20
Retained earnings	160	10
	360	110
Current liabilities	80	60
Total equity and liabilities	440	170

Note:

The fair value of the property, plant and equipment in Ball at 1/1/20X0 was £120,000.

Required: Prepare a consolidated balance sheet for Base as at 1 January 20X0.

References

1   IAS 27 *Consolidated and Separate Financial Statements*, IASB, 2003, para. 4.
2   *Ibid.*, para. 10.
3   *Ibid.*, para. 16.
4   *Ibid.*, IN9.
5   IAS 1 *Presentation of Financial Statements*, IASB, 2003, para. 31.
6   IAS 27 *Consolidated and Separate Financial Statements*, IASB, 2003, para. 20.
7   *Ibid.*, para. 40.
8   IFRS 3 *Business Combinations*, 2004.
9   *Ibid.*, para. 19.
10 IAS 22 *Business Combinations*, IASC, revised 1998, para. 8 – now replaced by IFRS 3.
11 IFRS 3 *Business Combinations*, 2004, paras 54 and 55.
12 IAS 36 *Impairment of Assets*, IASB, revised 2004, para. 124.
13 IFRS 3 *Business Combinations*, 2004, para. 57.
14 *Ibid.*, Appendix A.
15 *Ibid.*, para. 41.

CHAPTER **22**

Preparation of consolidated balance sheets after the date of acquisition

22.1 Introduction

In the previous chapter we considered the application of IFRS 3 *Business Combinations* when preparing a consolidated balance sheet at the date of acquisition. We also considered the provisions of IAS 27 *Consolidated and Separate Financial Statements*[1] in relation to the scope of consolidated financial statements. In this chapter we consider the application of IAS 27 when preparing a consolidated balance sheet at the end of the first financial year – the principles, however, are also applicable to all subsequent financial periods.

This chapter will consider:

- Pre- and post-acquisition profits/losses
- Inter-company balances
- Unrealised profit on inter-company sales
- Provision for unrealised profit affecting a minority
- Uniform accounting policies.

22.2 Pre- and post-acquisition profits/losses

Pre-acquisition profits

Any profits or losses made **before** the date of acquisition are referred to as **pre-acquisition profits/losses**. These are represented by net assets that exist in the subsidiary as at the date of acquisition and, as we have seen in Chapter 21, the fair values of these net assets will be dealt with in the goodwill calculation.

Post-acquisition profits

Any profits or losses made **after** the date of acquisition are referred to as **post-acquisition profits**. Because these will have arisen whilst the subsidiary was under the control of the parent company, they will, if realised, be included in the group consolidated income statement and so will appear in the retained earnings figure in the balance sheet. The following example for the Bend Group illustrates the approach to dealing with the pre- and post-acquisition profits.

EXAMPLE ● THE BEND GROUP illustrating the treatment of pre- and post-acquisition profits

1 January 20X1

Bend plc acquired 80% of the 10,000 £1 common shares in Stretch plc for £1.50 per share in cash and so gained control.

- Investment in the subsidiary cost £12,000.

- The retained earnings of Stretch plc were £4,000.

Note that the retained earnings are required for the goodwill calculation.

- The fair value of the non-current assets in Stretch plc was £600 above book value. The fair value of the subsidiary's assets are required for the consolidated balance sheet. In the subsidiary's own accounts the assets may be left at book values or restated at their fair values. If revalued, they will then become subject to the requirements of IAS 16 *Property, Plant and Equipment*[2] which states that revaluations should be made with sufficient regularity that the balance sheet figure is not materially different from the fair value at that date. This is one reason why the fair value adjustment is usually treated simply as a consolidation adjustment each year.

At 31 December 20X1

The closing balance sheets of Bend plc and Stretch plc together with the group accounts were as follows:

	Bend £	Stretch £	Group £	
ASSETS				
Non-current assets	26,000	12,000	38,600	Note 3
Goodwill	—	—	320	Note 1
Investment in Stretch	12,000	—	—	
Net current assets	13,000	4,000	17,000	Note 3
Net assets	51,000	16,000	55,920	
EQUITY				
Common share capital	16,000	10,000	16,000	Note 4
Retained earnings	35,000	6,000	36,600	Note 4
	51,000	16,000	52,600	
Minority interest	—	—	3,320	Note 2
	51,000	16,000	55,920	

Note 1. Goodwill calculated as at 1 January 20X1

	£	£
The cost of the parent company's investment in Stretch		12,000

Less:

(a) Share capital

the parent's share of the subsidiary's share capital:

80% × share capital of Stretch (80% × 10,000) = 8,000

(b) Pre-acquisition profit

the parent's share of the subsidiary's retained earnings

80% × retained earnings at 1 January 20X1 (80% × 4,000) = 3,200

(c) Fair value adjustment
the parent's share of any change in the book values
80% × revaluation of fixed assets at 1 January 20X1 (80% × 600) = 480

	11,680
Goodwill	320

Note 2. Minority interest in the net assets of subsidiary calculated as at 31 December 20X1

			£
(a) Subsidiary share capital			
Minority interest in the share capital of Stretch	(20% × 10,000)	=	2,000
(b) Total retained earnings as at 31 December 20X1			
Minority interest in the retained earnings of Stretch	(20% × 6,000)	=	1,200
(c) Fair value adjustment of subsidiary's fixed assets			
Minority interest in any revaluation reserve	(20% × 600)	=	120
Balance sheet figure for minority interest in the net assets of Stretch as at 31.12.20X1			**3,320**

Note 3. Add together the assets and liabilities of the parent and subsidiary for the group accounts

	Parent		Subsidiary	Group
	£		£	£
Non-current other than goodwill	26,000	+	(12,000 + Revaluation 600)	38,600
Goodwill		as calculated in Note 1		320
Net current assets	13,000	+	4,000	17,000
Total				**55,920**

Note 4. Calculate the consolidated share capital and reserves for the group accounts

	£	£	£
Common share capital (parent company only)			16,000
Reserves:			
Retained earnings (parent company)		35,000	
Parent's share of the **post-acquisition retained profit** of the subsidiary			
80% of (accumulated profit at 31.12.20X1 less accumulated profit at 1.1.20X1)		1,600	
			36,600
Total shareholders' interest			**52,600**

Notes:
1. The £4,000 pre-acquisition retained profit of the subsidiary is needed to calculate the goodwill.
2. The minority interest shareholders are entitled to their percentage share of the closing net assets. The pre-acquisition and post-acquisition division is irrelevant to the minority – they are entitled to their percentage share of the **total** retained earnings at the date the consolidated balance sheet is prepared.

22.3 Inter-company balances

We have seen above that we set off the parent's investment in a subsidiary against the parent's share of the subsidiary's share capital and reserves (retained earnings plus/minus revaluation changes) as at the date of acquisition.

However, there are likely to be other balances in the balance sheets of both the parent and the subsidiary company arising from inter-company (also referred to as intra-group) transactions. These will require adjustment in order that the group accounts do not double count assets and/or liabilities. These are normally referred to as consolidation adjustments and would be authorised as consolidation journal entries by a responsible officer such as the Finance Director. The following are examples of intra-group or inter-company transactions which we will now consider:

- Preferred shares held by a parent in its subsidiary
- Bonds held by a parent in its subsidiary
- Inter-company balances arising from inter-company sales or other transactions such as inter-company loans
- Inter-company dividends payable/receivable.

These are discussed below in relation to preparation of the consolidated balance sheet and are included in the comprehensive example, the Prose Group, below. Their significance as far as the group income is concerned will be explained when we refer to the preparation of the annual income statement in the next chapter.

22.3.1 Preferred shares

A parent company, in addition to the common shares by which it gained control, may have acquired preferred shares in the subsidiary. If so, any amount paid by the parent company will be included within the investment in subsidiary figure that appears in the parent company's balance sheet. Just as the common shares represent part of the net assets acquired, so the parent's share of the preferred shares in the subsidiary's balance sheet will represent part of the net assets acquired and will be included in the calculation of goodwill.

Any preferred shares not held by the parent are part of the minority interest – this applies even though the parent might itself hold less than 50% of the preferred shares – it is not necessary for the parent to hold a majority of the preferred shares.

22.3.2 Bonds

As with the preferred shares, any bonds in the subsidiary's balance sheet that have been acquired by the parent will represent part of the net assets acquired and will be included in the calculation of goodwill.

However, the amount of bonds not held by the parent will not be part of the minority interest as they do not bestow any rights of ownership on shareholders. They are, effectively, a form of long-term loan, and will be shown as such in the consolidated balance sheet.

22.3.3 Inter-company balances arising from sales or other transactions

IAS 27 requires inter-company balances to be eliminated in full.[3]

Eliminating inter-company balances

If entries in the parent's records and the subsidiary's records are up to date, the same figure will appear as a balance in the current assets of one company and in the current liabilities of the other. For example, if the parent company has supplied goods invoiced at £1,500 to its subsidiary, there will be a debtor for £1,500 in the parent balance sheet and a creditor for £1,500 in the subsidiary's balance sheet. These need to be cancelled, i.e. eliminated, before preparing the consolidated accounts. In accounting terminology, this would be described as offsetting.

Reconciling inter-company balances

In practice, temporary differences may arise for such items as stock or cash in transit that are recorded in one company's books but of which the other company is not yet aware, e.g. goods or cash in transit. In such a case the records will require reconciling and updating before proceeding. In a multinational company, this can be an extremely time-consuming exercise.

The following is an extract from the Sanitec 2002 financial statements:

All significant inter-company balances and transactions have been eliminated in consolidation.

22.3.4 Inter-company dividends payable/receivable

If the subsidiary company has declared a year-end dividend, this will appear in the current liabilities of the subsidiary company and in the current assets of the parent company and must be cancelled before preparing the consolidated balance sheet. If the subsidiary is wholly owned by the parent the whole amount will be cancelled. If, however, there is a minority interest in the subsidiary, the non-cancelled amount of the dividend payable in the subsidiary's balance sheet will be the amount payable to the minority and will be reported as part of the minority interest in the consolidated balance sheet. Where a dividend has not been declared by the year-end date there is no liability under IAS 37 *Provisions, Contingent Liabilities and Contingent Assets* and there should, therefore, be no provision reported under International Accounting Standards.

22.4 Unrealised profit on inter-company sales

Where sales have been made between two companies within the group, there may be an element of profit that has not been realised by the group if the goods have not then been sold on to a third party before the year-end. We will illustrate with the Many Group which consists of a parent, Many plc, and a subsidiary, Few plc.

Intra-group sales realised by sale to a third party (not a group member)

Assume, for example, that Many plc buys £1,000 worth of goods for resale and sells them to Few plc for £1,500, making a profit of £500. At the date of the balance sheet, if Few plc still has these goods in stock, the group has not yet made any profit on these goods and the £500 is therefore said to be 'unrealised'. It must be removed from the group balance sheet by:

● reducing the retained earnings of Many by £500;
● reducing the inventories of Few by £500.

The £500 is called a provision for unrealised profit.

If these goods are eventually sold by Few to customers outside the group for £1,800, the profit made by the group will be £800, the difference between the original cost of the goods to Many, £1,000, and the eventual sales price of £1,800. It follows from this that it is only necessary to provide for an unrealised profit from intra-group sales to the extent that the goods are still in the inventories of the group at the balance sheet date.

The following extract from the 1999 accounts of Schering AG is an example of consolidation policy:

Inter-company profits and losses, sales, income and expenses, receivables and liabilities between companies included in the consolidation have been eliminated.

The comprehensive example below for the Prose Group incorporates the main points dealt with so far on the preparation of a consolidated balance sheet.

EXAMPLE ● THE PROSE GROUP

On 1 January 20X1 Prose plc acquired 80% of the common shares in Verse plc for £21,100, 20% of the preferred shares for £2,000 and 10% of the bonds for £900, and gained control. The retained earnings as at 1 January 20X1 were £4,000. The fair value of the land in Verse was £1,000 above book value. During the year Prose sold some of its inventory to Verse for £3,000, which represented cost plus a mark-up of 25%. Half of these goods are still in the inventory of Verse at 31/12/20X1. Prepare a consolidated balance sheet as at 31 December 20X1. Note that depreciation is not charged on land.

Note: Just as in the Bend plc example above, it is helpful to structure the information before preparing your consolidation, as follows:

1 January 20X1 – the date of acquisition

- Prose acquired 80% of the common shares and 80% of the additional paid-up capital for £21,100 for cash and so gained control.
- Prose acquired 20% of the preferred shares in Verse for £2,000.
- Prose acquired 10% of the bonds in Verse for £900.
- The total cost of the investment is therefore £24,000.
- The retained earnings in Verse were £4,000, i.e. this is the pre-acquisition profit of which 80% will be included in the goodwill calculation.
- The fair value of the fixed assets in Verse was £1,000 above book value, i.e. the non-current assets of the subsidiary will be increased in the consolidated balance sheet.

During 20X1

- Prose sold some of its inventory to Verse for £3,000, which represented cost plus a mark-up of 25%.

At 31 December 20X1

- Half of the goods sold by Prose were still in the inventory of Verse, i.e. there is unrealised profit, and both the consolidated gross profit and inventories in the consolidated balance sheet will need to be reduced by the amount unrealised.

- The closing balance sheets of Prose and Verse at 31 December 20X1 together with the group accounts were as follows:

	Prose £	Verse £	Group £	
ASSETS				
Non-current assets				
(including land)	25,920	43,400	70,320	Note 4
Goodwill	—	—	8,900	Note 1
Investment in Verse	24,000	—	—	Note 1

Current assets				
Inventories	9,600	4,000	13,300	Note 2(c)
				Note 4
Verse current account	8,000			Note 2(a)
Bond interest receivable	35			Note 2(b)
Other current assets	1,965	3,350	5,315	Note 4
Net assets	69,520	50,750	97,835	

EQUITY and LIABILITIES

Common share capital	22,000	10,000	22,000	Note 5
Additional paid-in capital	2,000	1,000	2,000	Note 5
Preferred shares	4,000	8,000	4,000	Note 5
Retained earnings	30,000	8,500	33,300	Note 5
	58,000	27,500	61,300	
Minority interest	—	—	10,500	Note 3
Non-current liabilities				
Bonds	5,000	7,000	11,300	Note 6
Current liabilities				
Prose current account		8,000		
Bond interest payable		350	315	Note 2 (b)
Other current liabilities	6,520	7,900	14,420	Note 4
	69,520	50,750	97,835	

Note 1. Calculation of goodwill (note that this calculation will be the same as when calculated at the date of acquisition)

	£	£
The cost of the parent company's investment for common shares, additional paid in capital, preferred shares and bonds		24,000

Less:
(a) parent's share of the **subsidiary's share capital**:
  80% × common shares of Verse (80% × 10,000) = 8,000
(b) parent's share of the **subsidiary's additional paid in capital**:
  80% × additional paid in capital of Verse (80% × 1,000) = 800
(c) parent's share of the **subsidiary's retained earnings**:
  80% × retained earnings balance at
  1 January 20X1 (80% × 4,000) = 3,200
(d) parent's share of any change in **subsidiary's book values**:
  80% × revaluation of land at **1 January 20X1** (80% × 1,000) = 800
(e) parent's share of preferred shares:
  20% × **preferred shares** of Verse (20% × 8,000) = 1,600
(f) parent's share of **bonds**:
  10% × bonds of Verse (10% × 7,000) = 700

  15,100

Goodwill in balance sheet — 8,900

Note 2. Inter-company adjustments
(a) The **current accounts** of £8,000 between the two companies are cancelled. Note that the accounts are equal which indicates that there are no items such as goods in transit or cash in transit which would have required a reconciliation.
(b) The **bond interest receivable** by Prose is cancelled with £35 (10% of £350) of the bond interest payable by Verse leaving £315 (90% of £350) payable to outsiders. This

is not part of the minority interest as bond holders have no ownership rights in the company.

(c) **Provision for unrealised profit** on the stock of Verse

The mark-up on the inter-company sales was $£3,000 \times \dfrac{25}{125}$ = £600

Half the goods are still in inventories at the balance sheet date so provide
$\frac{1}{2} \times £600$ for the unrealised profit = **£300**

Note 3. Calculation of minority interest as at 31/12/20X1
Note that

● the minority interest is calculated as at the year-end while goodwill is calculated at the date of acquisition.

		£
(a) Subsidiary share capital		
Minority interest in the **common shares** of Verse	(20% × 10,000) =	2,000
Minority interest in the **additional paid-in capital** of Verse	(20% × 1,000) =	200
(b) Total **accumulated profit** as at 31 December 20X1		
Minority interest in the accumulated profit of Verse	(20% × 8,500)	1,700
(c) Fair value adjustment of subsidiary's fixed assets		
Minority interest in the **revaluation** of land	(20% × 1,000) =	200
(d) Subsidiary preferred shares		
Minority interest in the **preferred shares** of Verse	(80% × 8,000) =	6,400
Balance sheet figure		**10,500**

Note 4. Add together the following assets and liabilities of the parent and subsidiary for the group accounts.

	Parent	Subsidiary	£
Fixed assets other than goodwill	25,920 +	(43,400 + revaluation 1,000)	= 70,320
Inventories	9,600 +	(4,000 – provision for unrealised profit 300)	= 13,300
Other current assets	1,965 +	3,350	= 5,315
Other current liabilities	6,520 +	7,900	= 14,420

Note 5. Calculate the consolidated share capital and reserves for the group accounts.

Share capital:			
Common share capital	(parent company's only)		22,000
Additional paid-in capital of Prose only	(that of Verse is all pre-acquisition)		2,000
Preferred shares	(parent company's only)		4,000
Retained earnings	(parent company's)	= 30,000	
Less: Provision for unrealised profit		(300)	
			29,700
Parent's share of the **post-acquisition profit** of the subsidiary			
80% × 8,500		6,800	
Less: 80% of pre-acquisition profits	(80% × 4,000)	(3,200)	
			3,600
Retained earnings in the consolidated balance sheet			**33,300**

Note 6. Bonds

	Parent		Subsidiary		
Bonds	5,000	+	(7,000 – inter-company 700)	=	**11,300**

22.5 Provision for unrealised profit affecting a minority

Where a subsidiary with a minority interest sells goods to a parent company at a mark-up, the minority interest must be charged with their share of any provision for unrealised profit. For example, if Verse had sold goods to Prose for £3,000, including a mark-up of 25%, the minority interest would have been charged with 20% of the provision for unrealised profit (20% × £300) = £60. The group would have been charged with the remaining £240.

22.6 Uniform accounting policies and reporting dates

Consolidated financial statements should be prepared using uniform accounting policies. If it is not practicable then disclosure must be made of that together with details of the items involved.[4]

The financial statements of the parent and subsidiaries used in the consolidated accounts are usually drawn up to the same date but IAS 27 allows up to three months' difference providing that appropriate adjustments are made for significant transactions outside the common period.[5]

The following is an extract from the 2003 Annual Report of a South African company, Eskom, which is IAS compliant:

All significant intercompany transactions and resulting profits and losses between the group companies have been eliminated. Where necessary, accounting policies for subsidiaries have been changed to ensure consistency with the policies adopted by the group.

22.7 How is the investment in subsidiaries reported in the parent's own balance sheet?

IAS 27 gives the parent a choice as to how to report the investment.[6] It can either report the investment at cost, or report it in accordance with the provisions of IAS 39 *Financial Instruments: Recognition and Measurement*. Cost in this context means the fair value of the consideration at the date of acquisition.

Summary

When consolidated accounts are prepared after the subsidiary has traded whilst under the control of the parent, the goodwill calculation remains as at the date of the acquisition but all inter-company transactions have to be eliminated.

REVIEW QUESTIONS

1   The 2002 accounts of BorsodChem Rt state:

Basis of consolidation

All material inter-company accounts and transactions have been eliminated on consolidation.

(a) Discuss three examples of inter-company (also referred to as intra-group) accounts.

(b) Explain what is meant by 'have been eliminated'.

(c) Explain what effect there could be on the reported group profit if inter-company transactions were not eliminated.

2   Explain why the minority interest is calculated as at the year-end whilst goodwill is calculated at the date of acquisition.

3   Explain why pre-acquisition profits of a subsidiary are treated differently from post-acquisition profits.

4   Explain the effect of a provision for unrealised profit on a minority interest:

(a) where the sale was made by the parent to the subsidiary; and

(b) where the sale was made by the subsidiary to the parent.

EXERCISES

An extract from the solution is provided in the Appendix at the end of the text for exercises marked with an asterisk (*).

* Question 1

Sweden acquired 100% of the common shares of Oslo on 1 March 20X1 and gained control. At that date the balances on the reserves of Oslo were as follows:

The Revaluation reserve   – Kr10 million
Retained earnings   – Kr70 million

The balance sheets of the two companies at 31/12/20X1 were as follows:

	Sweden Krm	Oslo Krm
ASSETS		
Non-current assets		
Property, plant and equipment	264	120
Investment in Oslo	200	
Current assets	160	140
Total assets	624	260
EQUITY AND LIABILITIES		
Common Kr10 shares	400	110
Retained earnings	104	80
Revaluation reserve	20	10
	524	200
Current liabilities	100	60
Total equity and liabilities	624	260

Notes:
1. The fair values were the same as the book values on 1/3/20X1.
2. There have been no movements on share capital since 1/3/20X1.
3. 20% of the goodwill is to be written off as an impairment loss.

Required:
Prepare a consolidated balance sheet for Sweden as at 31 December 20X1.

Question 2

Summer plc acquired 60% of the common shares of Winter Ltd on 30 September 20X1 and gained control. At the date of acquisition, the balances on the reserves were as follows:

Additional paid-in capital   − £20,000
Retained earnings   − £35,000

At 31 December 20X1 the balance sheets of the two companies were as follows:

	Summer £000	Winter £000
ASSETS		
Non-current assets		
Property, plant and equipment	200	200
Investment in Winter	141	
Current assets	100	140
Total assets	441	340
EQUITY AND LIABILITIES		
Common £5 shares	175	160
Additional paid-in capital	25	20
Retained earnings	161	40
	361	220
Current liabilities	80	120
Total equity and liabilities	441	340

Notes:
1. The fair value is the same as the book value.
2. There have been no movements on share capital since 30/9/20X1.
3. 8.33% of the goodwill is to be written off as an impairment loss.

Required:
Prepare a consolidated balance sheet for Summer plc as at 31 December 20X1.

Question 3

On 30 September 20X0 Gold plc acquired 75% of the common shares, 30% of the preferred shares and 20% of the bonds in Silver plc and gained control. The balance of retained earnings on 30 September 20X0 was £16,000. The fair value of the land owned by Silver was £3,000 above book value. No adjustment has so far been made for this revaluation.

The balance sheets of Gold and Silver at 31 December 20X1 together with the group accounts were as follows:

	Gold £	Silver £
ASSETS		
Non-current assets (including land)	82,300	108,550
Investment in Silver	46,000	—
Current assets:		
Inventory	23,200	10,000
Silver current account	20,000	
Bond interest receivable	175	
Other current assets	5,000	7,500
Total assets	176,675	126,050
EQUITY AND LIABILITIES		
Common share capital	55,000	24,000
Additional paid-in capital	5,000	3,600
Preferred shares	10,000	20,000
Retained earnings	75,000	21,200
	145,000	68,800
Non-current liabilities – bonds	12,500	17,500
Current liabilities		
Gold current account		20,000
Bond interest payable	625	875
Other current liabilities	18,550	18,875
Total equity and liabilities	176,675	126,050

Notes:

1. 20% of the goodwill is to be written off as an impairment loss.
2. During the year Gold sold some of its inventory to Silver for £3,000, which represented cost plus a mark-up of 25%. Half of these goods are still in the inventory of Silver at 31/12/20X1.
3. There is no depreciation of land.
4. There has been no movement on share capital or additional paid-in capital since the acquisition.

Required:
Prepare a consolidated balance sheet as at 31 December 20X1.

References

1 IAS 27 *Consolidated and Separate Financial Statements*, IASB, revised 2003.
2 IAS 16 *Property, Plant and Equipment*, IASB, revised 2003, para. 31.
3 IAS 27, revised 2003, para. 24.
4 *Ibid.*, para. 28.
5 *Ibid.*, paras 26 and 27.
6 *Ibid.*, para. 37.

CHAPTER **23**

Preparation of consolidated income statements

23.1 Introduction

In the previous chapter we explained the consolidation adjustments required at the end of the first financial period in which the parent had been able to exercise control over the subsidiary. The adjustments were of two kinds, namely, those that affected the profit such as unrealised profit on inter-company inventories and pre-acquisition profits, and those that affected the balance sheet such as current accounts and preferred shares held by the parent.

This chapter will consider:

● The treatment arising from the above items in the consolidated income statement

● Dividends or interest paid out of pre-acquisition profits

● How to adjust when a subsidiary is acquired part of the way through the year.

23.2 Preparation of a consolidated income statement – the Ante Group

The following information is available:

At the date of acquisition on 1 January 20X1
Ante plc acquired 75% of the common shares and 20% of the preferred shares in Post plc.
    (Shows that Ante had control)
At that date the retained earnings of Post were £30,000.
    (These are pre-acquisition profits and should not be included in the Group profit for the year)
Ante had paid £10,000 more than the fair value of the net assets acquired.
    (This represents positive goodwill)

During the year ended 31 December 20X2
Ante had sold Post goods at their cost price of £9,000 plus a mark up of one-third. These were the only inter-company sales.
    (Indicates that the group sales and cost of sales require adjusting)

At the end of the financial year on 31 December 20X2
Half of these goods were still in the inventory at the end of the year.
    (There is unrealised profit to be removed from the Group gross profit)

20% is to be written-off goodwill as an impairment loss.

Set out below are the individual income statements of Ante and Post together with the consolidated income statement for the year ended 31 December 20X2 with explanatory notes.

Income statements for the year ended 31 December 20X2

	Ante £	Post £	Consolidated £	
Sales	200,000	120,000	308,000	Notes 1/3
Cost of sales	60,000	60,000	109,500	Notes 1/2/3
Gross profit	140,000	60,000	198,500	
Expenses	59,082	40,000	99,082	Note 4
Impairment of goodwill	—		2,000	Note 5
Profit from operations	80,918	20,000	97,418	
Dividends received – common shares	3,750	—	—	Note 6
Dividends received – preferred shares	600	—	—	Note 6
Profit before tax	85,268	20,000	97,418	
Income tax expense	14,004	6,000	20,004	Note 7
Profit for the period	71,264	14,000	77,414	
Minority interest			5,150	Note 8
Net profit for the period			72,264	
Dividends paid – common shares	40,000	5,000	40,000	Note 9
Dividends paid – preferred shares	—	3,000	—	Note 9
	31,264	6,000	32,264	
Retained earnings brought forward from previous years	69,336	54,000	87,336	Note 10
Retained earnings carried forward	100,600	60,000	119,600	

Profit realised from operations – £97,418

Adjustments are required to establish the profit **realised** from operations. This entails eliminating the effects of inter-company sales and inventory transferred within the group with a profit loading but not sold at the balance sheet date and charging any goodwill impairment – see Notes 1–5.

Notes:

1. **Eliminate inter-company sales on consolidation.**
   Cancel the inter-company sales of £12,000 (9,000 + $^1/_3$) by
   (i) reducing the sales of Ante from £200,000 to £188,000; and
   (ii) reducing the cost of sales of Post by the same amount from £60,000 to £48,000.

2. **Eliminate unrealised profit on inter-company goods that were still in closing inventory.**
   (i) Ante had sold the goods to Post at a mark up £3,000
   (ii) Half of the goods remain in the stock of Post at the year-end
   (iii) From the group's view there is an unrealised profit of half of the mark-up, i.e. £1,500. Therefore:
   - deduct £1,500 from the gross profit of Ante by adding this amount to the cost of sales
   - add this amount to a provision for unrealised profit
   - reduce the inventories in the consolidated balance sheet by the amount of the provision (as explained in the previous chapter).

3. **Aggregate the adjusted sales and cost of sales figures for items in Notes 1 and 2.**
   (i) Add the adjusted sales figures
   ((200,000 − 12,000 inter-company sales) + 120,000)   =   £308,000
   (ii) Add the adjusted cost of sales figures;
   60,000 + (60,000 − 12,000) + 1,500 provision   =   £109,500

4. **Aggregate expenses**
   No adjustment is required to the parent or subsidiary total figures.

5. **Deduct the impairment loss.**
   The goodwill was given as £10,000, and it has been estimated that there has been a £2,000 impairment loss.

Profit after tax – £97,418

Adjustments are required[1] to establish the profit after tax earned by the group as a whole. This entails eliminating dividends and interest that have been paid to the parent by the subsidiaries. If this were not done, there would be a double counting as these would appear in the profit from operations of the subsidiary, which has been included in the consolidated profit from operations, and again as dividends and interests received by the group.

6. **Accounting for inter-company dividends**
   (i) **The common dividend £3,750** received by Ante is 75% of the £5,000 dividend paid by Post.
   (ii) Cancel the inter-company dividend received by Ante with £3,750 dividend paid by Post, leaving the £1,250 dividend paid by Post to the minority.
   (iii) **The preferred dividend** of £600 received by Ante is 20% of the £3,000 paid by Post.
   (iv) Cancel the £600 preferred dividend received by Ante with £600 of the preferred dividend paid by Post.
   (v) the balance of £2,400 remaining was paid to the minority.

7. **Aggregate the taxation figures.**
   No adjustment is required to the parent or subsidiary total figures.

Net profit from ordinary activities

Adjustment is required[2] to establish how much of the profit after tax is attributable to equity holders of the parent. This entails deducting the minority interest in the subsidiary company as a percentage of the subsidiary's after-tax figure, as adjusted for any preference dividend (see note 8).

8. **Calculate the share of post-taxation profits belonging to the minority interest.**

	£
Preferred shares – dividend on these shares:	
Minority shareholders hold 80% of preferred shares (80% × 3,000)	= 2,400
Common shares – % of profit after tax of the subsidiary *less* preferred share dividend	
Minority shareholders hold 25% of the common shares 25% × (14,000 − 3,000)	= 2,750
Total minority interest in the profit after tax of the subsidiary	5,150

9. Dividends paid to parent company common shareholders

The dividend paid in the consolidated accounts will always be the parent company's dividends. This is because the dividends payable to the minority are payable out of the minority's share of the profit after taxation, which has been deducted in arriving at the group's share of the profit after taxation. To deduct the £1,250 common and £2,400 preference dividends payable to the minority would be double counting.

10. Retained earnings

The retained earnings at the beginning of the year are added to the net profit for the period. They are calculated as follows:

	£
Ante retained earnings brought forward	69,336
The group's share of Post's post-acquisition retained earnings	
75% × (54,000 − 30,000)	18,000
	87,336

23.2.1 Statement of changes in equity – extract[3]

The statement would include the following:

Retained earnings	£	
Balance at 1 January 20X2	87,336	Note 10
Net profit for the year	72,264	
Dividends	(40,000)	Note 9
Balance at 31 December 20X2	119,600	

23.3 Dividends or interest paid by the subsidiary out of pre-acquisition profits

In the Ante Group example above, we illustrated the accounting treatment where a dividend was paid by a subsidiary out of post-acquisition profits. This showed that, when dividends and interest are received by a parent company from a company it has acquired, they will normally be credited as income in the parent company's income statement.

However, this treatment will not be appropriate where the dividend or interest has been paid out of profits earned by the subsidiary before acquisition. The reason is that the dividend or interest is paid out of the net assets acquired at the date of acquisition and these were paid for in the price paid for the investment. The dividend or interest received by the parent, therefore, is not income but a return of part of the purchase price, which must be reported as such in the parent's balance sheet. This is illustrated in the Bow plc example below:

Illustration of a dividend paid out of pre-acquisition profits

Bow plc acquired 75% of the shares in Tie plc on 1 January 20X1 for £80,000 when the balance of the retained earnings of Tie was £40,000. There was no goodwill. On 10 January 20X1 Bow received a dividend of £3,000 from Tie out of the profits for the year ended 31/12/20X0. There were no inter-company transactions, other than the dividend. The summarised income statements for the year ended 31/12/20X1 were as follows:

	Bow £	Tie £	Consolidated £
Gross profit	130,000	70,000	200,000
Expenses	50,000	40,000	90,000
Profit from operations	80,000	30,000	110,000
Dividends received from Tie (see note)	3,000	—	—
Profit before tax	83,000	30,000	110,000
Income tax expense	24,000	6,000	30,000
Profit for the period	59,000	24,000	80,000
Minority interest (25% × 24,000)			6,000
Profit after taxation belonging to the group	—	—	74,000
Dividends paid	40,000	4,000	40,000
Retained profit for the year	19,000	20,000	34,000

Note:

The £3,000 dividend received from Tie is not income and must not therefore appear in Bow income statement. The correct treatment is to deduct it from the investment in Tie, which will then become £77,000 (80,000 – 3,000). The consolidation would then proceed as usual.

23.4 A subsidiary acquired part of the way through the year

It would be attractive for a company whose results had not been as good as expected to acquire a profitable subsidiary at the end of the year and take its annual profit into the group accounts. However, this type of window dressing is not permitted and the group can only bring in a subsidiary's profits from the date of the acquisition. The Tight plc example below illustrates the approach.

23.4.1 Illustration of a subsidiary acquired part of the way through the year – Tight plc

The following information is available:

At date of acquisition – 30 September 20X1
Tight acquired 75% of the common shares and 20% of the 5% bonds in Loose.
The purchase consideration (amount paid) was £10,000 more than book value.
The book value and fair value were the same amount.
The retained earnings of the Tight Group was £69,336.

During the year
All income and expenses are deemed to accrue evenly through the year and the dividend receivable may be apportioned to pre- and post-acquisition on a time basis.
On 30 June 20X1 Tight sold Loose goods for £4,000 plus a mark-up of one-third.

At end of financial year
The Tight Group prepares its accounts as at 31 December each year.
Half of the intra-group goods were still in stock at the end of the year.

Set out below are the individual income statements of Tight and Loose together with the consolidated income statement for the year ended 31 December 20X1.

Income statements for the year ended 31 December 20X1

	Tight £	Loose £	Consolidated £	
Revenue	200,000	120,000	230,000	Notes 1/2
Cost of sales	60,000	60,000	75,000	Note 2
Gross profit	140,000	60,000	155,000	
Expenses	59,082	30,000	66,582	Note 3
Interest paid on 5% bonds		10,000	2,000	Note 4
Interest received on Loose bonds	2,000		—	
	82,918	20,000	86,418	
Dividends received	3,600	NIL	NIL	Note 5
Profit before tax	86,518	20,000	86,418	
Income tax expense	14,004	6,000	15,504	Note 6
Profit for the period after tax	72,514	14,000	70,914	
Minority interest (25% × (14,000 × $^3/_{12}$))			875	Note 7
Profit after taxation belonging to the group	—	—	70,039	
Dividends paid	40,000	4,800	40,000	Notes 8/9
	32,514	9,200	30,039	
Retained earnings				
Brought forward from previous years	69,336	51,000	69,336	Note 10
	101,850	60,200	99,375	

Notes:

1. **Inter-company sales**
   These can be ignored as they took place before the date of acquisition.

2. **Time-apportion and aggregate the sales and cost of sales figures.**
   Group sales include a full year for the parent company and
   three months for the subsidiary (1 October to 31 December),
   i.e. £200,000 + (120,000 × $^3/_{12}$)   =   **£230,000**
   Group cost of sales include a full year for the parent company
   and three months for the subsidiary (1 October – 31 December),
   i.e. £60,000 + (60,000 × $^3/_{12}$)   =   **£75,000**

3. **Aggregate the expense.**
   This includes the whole of the parent and the time-apportioned
   subsidiary's expenses, i.e. £59,082 + (30,000 × $^3/_{12}$)   =   **£66,582**

4. **Accounting for inter-company interest**
   The interest received by Tight is apportioned on a time basis: $^9/_{12}$ × £2,000 = £1,500
   is treated as being pre-acquisition and deducted from the cost of the investment in
   Loose.
   The remainder (£500) is cancelled with £500 of the post-acquisition element of the
   interest payable by Loose. The interest payable figure in the consolidated financial
   statements will be the post-acquisition interest less the inter-company elimination,
   which represents the amount payable to the holders of 80% of the bonds.
   Total interest paid 10,000 – pre-acquisition 7,500 – inter-company 500 = **£2,000**

Profit before tax
Inter-company expense items need to be eliminated. These include items such as
management charges, consulting fees and interest payments. In this example we illustrate the

treatment of interest. Interest is an expense which is normally deemed to accrue evenly over the year and to be apportioned on a time basis.

5. **Accounting for inter-company dividends**

Amount received by Tight	=	£3,600
The dividend received by Tight is apportioned on a time basis, and the pre-acquisition element is credited to the cost of investment in Tight's balance sheet, i.e. $9/12 \times £3,600$	=	(£2,700)
The post-acquisition element is cancelled with part of the dividend paid in Loose income statement prior to consolidation.	=	(£900)
Amount credited to consolidated income statement		NIL

6. **Aggregate the tax figures.**
   This includes the whole of the parent's tax and the time-apportioned part of the subsidiary's tax, i.e. $£14,004 + (6,000 \times 3/12)$ $\qquad = £15,504$
   The group taxation is that of Tight plus $3/12$ of Loose.

7. **Calculate the share of post-acquisition consolidated profits belonging to the minority interest.**
   As only the post-acquisition proportion of the subsidiary's profit after tax has been included in the consolidated income statement, the amount deducted as the minority interest in the profit after tax is also time-apportioned, i.e.
   $25\% \times (14,000 \times 3/12)$ $\qquad\qquad = £875$

8. **Dividend paid – Tight**
   As we have seen, the dividend shown as paid in the consolidated accounts will always be the parent company's dividends. $\qquad = £40,000$

9. **Dividend paid – Loose**
   The £4,800 dividends shown as paid in Loose's income statement has been dealt with as follows:

	£
See Note 5 above:	
Paid out of pre-acquisition profits, not included in the consolidated income statement	2,700
Cancelled with the post-acquisition dividend received by Tight	900

		£
Included in the minority interest:		
Paid to the minority interest out of the post-acquisition profits, (already included in the minority interest of £875 – see Note 7) £1,200 × 3/12	=	300
Paid to the minority out of the pre-acquisition profits £1,200 × 9/12	=	900
		4,800

10. **Retained earnings**
    As Loose was acquired during the year to 31/12/20X1, none of its profits brought forward (£51,000) can be included in the consolidated accounts for the year.
    Consolidated retained earnings at 31.12.20X1 comprises:

		£
The group's share of the subsidiary's post acquisition profit retained in the current year $(9,200 \times 3/12) \times 75\%$	=	1,725
The parent's retained earnings at 1.1.20X1	=	69,336
The parent's retained profit in the current year $(32,514 - \text{pre-acquisition interest } [2,000 \times 9/12]$ $- \text{pre-acquisition dividend } [3,600 \times 9/12])$	=	28,314
	=	99,375

23.4.2 Statement of changes in equity – extract

	Retained earnings
	£
Balance at 1.1.20X1	69,336
Profit for the period	70,039
Dividends paid	(40,000)
Balance at 31.12.20X1	99,375

23.5 Published format income statement

The income statement follows the classification of expenses by function as illustrated in IAS 1:[4]

		£
Revenue		230,000
Cost of sales		75,000
Gross profit		155,000
Distribution costs	xxxxxx	
Administrative expense	xxxxxx	
		66,582
		88,418
Finance cost		2,000
		86,418
Income tax expense		15,504
Profit for the period		70,914
Attribute to:		
Equity holders of the parent		70,039
Minority interest		875

Summary

The retained earnings of the subsidiary brought forward is divided into pre-acquisition profits and post-acquisition profits – the group share of the former are used in the goodwill calculation, and the share of the latter are brought into the consolidated shareholders' equity.

Revenue and cost of sales are adjusted in order to eliminate intra-group sales and unrealised profits.

Finance expenses and income are adjusted to eliminate intra-group payments of interest and dividends.

The minority interest in the profit after tax of the subsidiary is deducted to arrive at the profit for the year attributable to the equity holders of the parent.

The amounts paid as dividends to the parent company's shareholders are shown as deductions in the consolidated statement of changes in equity.

If a subsidiary is acquired during a financial year, the items in its income statement require apportioning. In the illustration in the text we assumed that trading was evenly spread throughout the year – in practice you would need to consider any seasonal patterns that would make this assumption unrealistic, remembering that the important consideration is that the group accounts should only be credited with profits arising whilst the subsidiary was under the parent's control.

REVIEW QUESTIONS

1 Explain why the dividends deducted from the net profit of the group in the income statement are only those of the parent company.

2 Explain how unrealised profits arise from transactions between companies in a group and why it is important to remove them.

3 Explain why it is necessary to apportion a subsidiary's profit or loss if acquired part-way through a financial year.

4 Explain why dividends paid by a subsidiary to a parent company are eliminated on consolidation.

5 Give five examples of inter-company income and expense transactions that will need to be eliminated on consolidation and explain why each is necessary.

6 A shareholder was concerned that following an acquisition the profit from operations of the parent and subsidiary were less than the aggregate of the individual profit from operations figures. She was concerned that the acquisition, which the directors had supported as improving earnings per share, appeared to have reduced the combined profits. She wanted to know where the profits had gone.

Give an explanation to the shareholder.

EXERCISES

An extract from the solution is provided in the Appendix at the end of the text for exercises marked with an asterisk (*).

* Question 1

Bill plc acquired 80% of the common shares and 10% of the preferred shares in Ben plc on 31 December three years ago when Ben's accumulated retained profits were £45,000. During the year Bill sold Ben goods for £8,000 plus a mark-up of 50%. Half of these goods were still in stock at the end of the year. There was goodwill impairment loss of £3,000.

The income statements of the two companies for the year ended 31 December 20X1 were as follows:

	Bill	Ben
	£	£
Revenue	300,000	180,000
Cost of sales	90,000	90,000
Gross profit	210,000	90,000
Expenses	88,623	60,000
	121,377	30,000
Dividends received – common shares	6,000	—
Dividends received – preferred shares	450	—
Profit before tax	127,827	30,000
Income tax expense	21,006	9,000
Profit for the period	106,821	21,000
Dividends paid – common shares	60,000	7,500
Dividends paid – preferred shares	—	4,500
	46,821	9,000
Retained earnings brought forward from previous years	104,004	81,000
	150,825	90,000

Required: Prepare a consolidated income statement for the year ended 31 December 20X1.

* Question 2

Morn Ltd acquired 90% of the shares in Eve Ltd on 1 January 20X1 for £90,000 when Eve Ltd's accumulated profits were £50,000. On 10 January 20X1 Morn Ltd received a dividend of £10,800 from Eve Ltd out of the profits for the year ended 31/12/20X0. The summarised income statements for the year ended 31/12/20X1 were as follows:

	Morn	Eve
	£	£
Gross profit	360,000	180,000
Expenses	120,000	110,000
	240,000	70,000
Dividends received from Eve Ltd	10,800	—
Profit before tax	250,800	70,000
Income tax expense	69,000	18,000
Profit for the period	181,800	52,000
Dividends paid	120,000	12,000
Retained earnings for the year	61,800	40,000

There were no inter-company transactions, other than the dividend. There was no goodwill.

Required: Prepare a consolidated income statement for the year ended 31 December 20X1.

Question 3

River plc acquired 90% of the common shares and 10% of the 5% bonds in Pool Ltd on 31 March 20X1. All income and expenses are deemed to accrue evenly through the year. On 31 January 20X1 River sold Pool goods for £6,000 plus a mark up of one-third. 75% of these goods were still in stock at the end of the year. There was a goodwill impairment loss of £4,000. Set out below are the individual income statements of River and Pool:

Income statements for the year ended 31 December 20X1

	River £	Pool £
Net turnover	100,000	60,000
Cost of sales	30,000	30,000
Gross profit	70,000	30,000
Expenses	20,541	15,000
Interest payable on 5% bonds		5,000
Interest receivable on Pool Ltd bonds	500	
	49,959	10,000
Dividends received	2,160	NIL
Profit before tax	52,119	10,000
Income tax expense	7,002	3,000
Profit for the period	45,117	7,000
Dividends paid	20,000	2,400
	25,117	4,600
Retained earnings brought forward from previous years	34,668	25,500
	59,785	30,100

Required: Prepare a consolidated income statement for the year ended 31 December 20X1.

Question 4

The balance sheets of Mars plc and Jupiter plc at 31 December 20X2 are as follows:

	Mars £	Jupiter £
ASSETS		
Non-current assets at cost	550,000	225,000
Depreciation	220,000	67,500
	330,000	157,500
Investment in Jupiter	187,500	
Current assets		
Inventories	225,000	67,500
Trade receivables	180,000	90,000
Current account – Jupiter	22,500	
Bank	36,000	18,000
	463,500	175,500
Total assets	**981,000**	**333,000**

EQUITY AND LIABILITIES

Capital and reserves

£1 common shares	196,000	90,000
General reserve	245,000	31,500
Retained earnings	225,000	135,000
	666,000	256,500

Current liabilities

Trade payables	283,500	40,500
Taxation	31,500	13,500
Current account – Mars		22,500
	315,000	76,500
Total equity and liabilities	**981,000**	**333,000**

Income statements for the year ended 31 December 20X2

	£	£
Sales	1,440,000	270,000
Cost of sales	1,045,000	135,000
Gross profit	395,000	135,000
Expenses	123,500	90,000
Dividends received	9,000	NIL
Profit before tax	280,500	45,000
Income tax expense	31,500	13,500
	249,000	31,500
Dividends paid	180,000	11,250
	69,000	20,250
Retained earnings brought forward		
from previous years	156,000	114,750
	225,000	135,000

Mars acquired 80% of the shares in Jupiter on 1 January 20X0 when Jupiter's retained earnings were £80,000 and the balance on Jupiter's general reserve was £18,000. During the year Mars sold Jupiter goods for £18,000 which represented cost plus 50%. Half of these goods were still in stock at the end of the year.

Required:
Prepare a consolidated income statement for the year ended 31/12/20X2 and a balance sheet as at that date.

Question 5

The balance sheets of Red Ltd and Pink Ltd at 31 December 20X2 are as follows:

	Red $	Pink $
ASSETS		
Non-current assets	200,000	100,000
Depreciation	80,000	30,000
	120,000	70,000
Investment in Pink Ltd	110,000	
Current assets		
Inventories	100,000	30,000
Trade receivables	80,000	40,000
Current account – Pink Ltd	10,000	
Bank	16,000	8,000
	206,000	78,000
Total assets	**436,000**	**148,000**
EQUITY AND LIABILITIES		
Capital and reserves		
$1 common shares	176,000	40,000
General reserve	20,000	14,000
Retained earnings	100,000	60,000
	296,000	114,000
Current liabilities		
Trade payables	125,996	18,000
Taxation payable	14,004	6,000
Current account – Red Ltd		10,000
	140,000	34,000
Total equity and liabilities	**436,000**	**148,000**

Income statements for the year ended 31 December 20X2

	$	$
Sales	200,000	120,000
Cost of sales	60,000	60,000
Gross profit	140,000	60,000
Expenses	59,082	40,000
Dividends received	3,750	NIL
Profit before tax	84,668	20,000
Income tax expense	14,004	6,000
	70,664	14,000
Dividends paid	40,000	5,000
	30,664	9,000
Retained earnings brought forward from previous years	69,336	51,000
	100,000	60,000

Red Ltd acquired 75% of the shares in Pink Ltd on 1 January 20X0 when Pink Ltd's retained earnings were $30,000 and the balance on Pink's general reserve was $8,000.

During the year Pink sold Red goods for $9,000 plus a mark-up of one-third. Half of these goods were still in inventory at the end of the year. Goodwill suffered an impairment loss of 20%.

Required: Prepare a consolidated income statement for the year ended 31/12/20X2 and a balance sheet as at that date.

Question 6

The income statements of Try and Hard for the year ended 31 December 20X5 are as follows:

	Try plc £	Hard plc £
Profit before tax	80,000	56,000
Tax	42,000	28,600
	38,000	27,400
Dividend	20,000	
	18,000	27,400

Try plc acquired 75% of the equity shares of Hard plc on 1 January 20X3.

Required: Prepare a consolidated income statement for the year ended 31 December 20X5.

Questions 7–10

The following income statements and balance sheets of Mother plc and Daughter plc as at 31 December 20X6 are to be used for questions 7 to 10:

	Mother plc £000	Daughter plc £000
Profit before tax	300	100
(includes dividends received from Daughter plc)		
Tax	(120)	(30)
Profit after tax	180	70
Transfer to general reserves	(30)	(20)
Dividends	(50)	(20)
Retained	100	30
Balance brought forward at 1 Jan 20X6	50	10
	150	40
Balance sheets		
Non current assets	300	150
Investment in Daughter plc	200	
Net current assets	280	110
	780	260
Share capital	500	200
General reserve	130	20
Retained earnings	150	40
	780	260

Question 7

Required:

(a) Prepare a consolidated income statement and consolidated balance sheet as at 31 December 20X6 on the assumption that Mother plc acquired all of the shares in Daughter plc on its incorporation on 1 January 20X2.

(b) Explain accounting treatment.

Question 8

Required:

(a) Prepare a consolidated income statement and consolidated balance sheet as at 31 December 20X6 on the assumption that Mother plc acquired 80% of the shares in Daughter plc on its incorporation on 1 January 20X2.

(b) Explain accounting treatment.

Question 9

Required:

(a) Prepare a consolidated income statement and consolidated balance sheet as at 31 December 20X6 on the assumption that Mother plc acquired all of the shares in Daughter plc on 1 January 20X4, at which date the Daughter plc accounts showed credit balances on the general reserve of £15,000 and on retained earnings of £5,000, and corresponding net assets of £220,000.

(b) Explain accounting treatment.

Question 10

Required:

(a) Prepare a consolidated income statement and consolidated balance sheet as at 31 December 20X6 on the assumption that Mother plc acquired 80% of the shares in Daughter plc on 1 January 20X4, at which date the Daughter plc accounts showed credit balances on the general reserve of £15,000 and on retained earnings of £5,000, and corresponding net assets of £220,000.

(b) Explain accounting treatment.

Question 11

On 1 January 20X5 Tinker Ltd bought 6,300 of the shares of Tailor Ltd. The total issued share capital of Tailor was then, and remains, 7,000 fully paid shares of £1 nominal value. Tinker's summarised accounts for 20X5 are as follows:

Tinker Ltd and its subsidiary Tailor Ltd

	Parent company's accounts £		Consolidated group accounts £	
Income statement:				
Trading profit		8,400		10,200
Dividend from subsidiary		900		—
		9,300		10,200
Dividend on share capital		4,000		4,000
		5,300		6,200
Brought forward		22,700		22,700
Carried forward		28,000		28,900
Balance sheet:				
Plant and equipment (cost)		184,900		207,900
Depreciation		32,000		44,000
		152,900		163,900
Investment in subsidiary (cost)		9,100		—
Inventory (cost) – Note 1	63,000		70,000	
Receivables	23,000		25,000	
Southern Bank	16,000		16,000	
	102,000		111,000	
Eastern Bank	—	6,000		
Payables	56,000	58,000		
		46,000	64,000	47,000
		208,000		210,900
Common share capital				
(£1 shares fully paid)		180,000		180,000
Reserves – Note 2		28,000		29,700
Minority interest		—		1,200
		208,000		210,900

Notes:

1 It is known that at 31 December 20X5 Tinker had goods in inventory invoiced to it by Tailor during 20X5 for £1,200, the cost of which to Tailor was £900. An appropriate adjustment has been made for this (so far as it affects the parent company) in the group accounts.

2 The group reserves at 31 December 20X5 were as follows:

	£
Profit retained	28,900
Capital reserve on consolidation attributable to interest of parent company	800
	29,700

Required:
Prepare summarised accounts for Tailor Ltd for 20X5 in the same form.

Question 12

H Ltd has one subsidiary, S Ltd. The company has held a controlling interest for several years. The latest financial statements for the two companies and the consolidated financial statements for the H Group are as shown below:

	H Ltd	S Ltd	H Group
Income statements for the year ended 30 September 20X4			
	£000	£000	£000
Turnover	4,000	2,200	5,700
Cost of sales	(1,100)	(960)	(1,605)
	2,900	1,240	4,095
Administration	(420)	(130)	(550)
Distribution	(170)	(95)	(265)
Dividends received	180	—	—
Profit before tax	2,490	1,015	3,280
Income tax	(620)	(335)	(955)
Profit after tax	1,870	680	2,325
Minority interest	—	—	(170)
	1,870	680	2,155
Dividends	(250)	(240)	(250)
	1,620	440	1,905
Balance brought forward	2,700	1,020	2,335
Balance carried forward	4,320	1,460	4,240

Balance sheets at 30 September 20X4

	H Ltd		S Ltd		H Group	
	£000	£000	£000	£000	£000	£000
Non-current assets:						
Tangible	7,053		2,196		9,249	
Investment in S Ltd	1,700	8,753	—	2,196	—	9,249
Current assets:						
Inventory	410		420		785	
Receivables	535		220		595	
Bank	27	972	19	659	46	1,426
Current liabilities:						
Payables	(300)		(260)		(355)	
Dividend to minority	—		—		(45)	
Taxation	(605)	(905)	(375)	(635)	(980)	(1,380)
		8,820		2,220		9,295

	H Ltd	S Ltd	H Group
	£000	£000	£000
Share capital	4,500	760	4,500
Retained earnings	4,320	1,460	4,240
	8,820	2,220	8,740
Minority interest	—	—	555
	8,820	2,220	9,295

Goodwill of £410,000 was written off at the date of acquisition following an impairment review.

Required:

(a) Calculate the percentage of S Ltd which is owned by H Ltd.

(b) Calculate the value of sales made between the two companies during the year.

(c) Calculate the amount of unrealised profit which had been included in the inventory figure as a result of inter-company trading and which had to be cancelled on consolidation.

(d) Calculate the value of inter-company receivables and payables cancelled on consolidation.

(e) Calculate the balance on S Ltd's retained earnings when H Ltd acquired its stake in the company.

(CIMA)

References

1   IAS 27 *Consolidated and Separate Financial Statements*, IASB, revised 2003, para. 25.
2   *Ibid.*, paras 22(b) and 33.
3   IAS 1 *Presentation of Financial Statements*, IASB, revised 2003, Implementation Guidance.
4   *Ibid.*

CHAPTER **24**

Accounting for associated companies

24.1 Introduction

This chapter will consider:

- The definitions of associate and of significant influence
- The treatment of associated companies in consolidated accounts
- The treatment of provisions for unrealised profits
- The acquisition of an associate part-way through the year
- The effect of the treatment on the earnings per share
- Criticism of the equity method.

24.2 Definitions of associates and of significant influence

An associate is an entity over which the investor has significant influence and which is neither a subsidiary nor a joint venture of the investor.[1]

Significant influence is the power to participate in the financial and operating policy decisions of the investee but is not control over these policies.[2]

This chapter will only consider **associated companies. Note that an associated company, as such, cannot be a member of a group, i.e. it is not consolidated on a line by line basis**.

Significant influence will be assumed in situations where one company has 20% or more of the voting power in another company, unless it can be shown that there is no such influence. Unless it can be shown to the contrary, a holding of less than 20% will be assumed insufficient for associate status. The circumstances of each case must be considered.[3]

IAS 28 suggests that one or more of the following might be evidence of an associate:

(a) representation on the board of directors or equivalent governing body of the investee;

(b) participation in policy-making processes;

(c) material transactions between the investor and the investee;

(d) interchange of managerial personnel; or

(e) provision of essential technical information.[4]

24.3 The treatment of associated companies in consolidated accounts

Associated companies will be shown in the consolidated accounts under the equity method, unless the investment is acquired exclusively for disposal within twelve months from acquisition and management is actively seeking a buyer,[5] in which case it will be shown at cost. The equity method is a method of accounting whereby:

- The investment is reported in the consolidated balance sheet in the non-current asset section.[6] It is reported initially at cost adjusted, at the end of each financial year, for the post-acquisition change in the investor's share of the net assets of the investee.[7]
- In the consolidated income statement, income from associates is reported after profit from operations together with finance costs and finance expenses.[8] The income reflects the investor's share of the pre-tax results of operations of the investee.[9]

24.4 The Brill Group – the equity method illustrated

Brill plc had acquired 80% of Bream plc's common shares in 20X0.

At date of acquisition of shares in associate on 1 January 20X0:

- Brill acquired 20% of the common shares in Cod for £20,000,
    i.e. Brill was assumed to have significant influence
- The retained earnings of Cod were £22,500 and the general reserve was £6,000.
    These are pre-acquisition items. The group share will be deducted from the cost of the investment to calculate the goodwill figure.

Set out below are the consolidated accounts of Brill and its subsidiary Bream and the individual accounts of the associated company, Cod, together with the consolidated group accounts.

24.4.1 Consolidated balance sheet

Balance sheets of the Brill Group (parent plus subsidiaries already consolidated) and Cod (an associate company) as at 31 December 20X2:

	Brill and Subsids £	*Cod* £	*Group* £	
Non-current assets				
Tangible fixed assets	172,500	59,250	172,500	
Goodwill on consolidation	13,400		13,400	
Investment in Cod	20,000		23,600	Note 1
Current assets				
Inventories	132,440	27,000	132,440	
Trade receivables	151,050	27,000	151,050	
Current account – Cod	2,250		2,250	Note 2
Bank	36,200	4,500	36,200	
	527,840	117,750	531,440	

	Brill and Subsids £	Cod £	Group £
Current liabilities			
Trade payables	110,250	25,500	110,250
Taxation	27,750	6,000	27,750
Current account – Brill		2,250	
	138,000	33,750	138,000
Total net assets	389,840	84,000	393,440
EQUITY			
£1 common shares	187,500	37,500	187,500
General reserve	24,900	9,000	25,500 Note 3
Retained earnings	145,940	37,500	148,940 Note 4
	358,340	84,000	361,940
Minority interest	31,500	—	31,500 Note 5
	389,840	84,000	393,440

Notes:

1. **Investment in associate**

Initial cost of the 20% holding		20,000
Share of post-acquisition reserves of Cod		
20% (37,500 – 22,500) (retained earnings) =	3,000	
20% (9,000 – 6,000) (general reserves)	600	3,600
		23,600

Note that (a) the assets and liabilities are not joined line by line
with those of the companies in the group and (b) the £23,600 comprises 20% of
net assets of £84,000 plus goodwill of £6,800. The goodwill can be calculated as
follows:

Investment at cost		20,000
20% × 37,500 (shares)	7,500	
20% × 6,000 (General Reserve)	1,200	
20% × 22,500 (Retained earnings)	4,500	13,200
		6,800

Note that because goodwill in an associate is not separately recognised,
it is the entire carrying amount that is tested for impairment under IAS 36.[10]

2. The Cod current account is received from outside the group and must therefore
continue to be shown as receivable by the group. **It is not cancelled.**

3. **General reserve consists of:**

	£
Parent's general reserve	24,900
General reserve of Cod:	
The group share of the post-acquisition retained profits	
i.e. 20% (9,000 – 6,000) =	600
Consolidated general reserve	**25,500**

4. **Accumulated profits consists of:**

Parent's retained earnings	145,940
Retained earnings of Cod:	
The group share of the post-acquisition retained profits,	
i.e. 20% (37,500 – 22,500) =	3,000
Consolidated retained earnings	**148,940**

5. Minority interest

Note that there is no minority interest in Cod. Only the group share of Cod's net assets has been brought into the total net assets above (see note 1).

24.4.2 Consolidated income statement

Income statements for the year ended 31 December 20X2

	Brill and Subsids £	Cod £	Group £	
Sales	329,000	75,000	329,000	
Cost of sales	114,060	30,000	114,060	
Gross profit	214,940	45,000	214,940	
Expenses	107,700	22,500	107,700	
Profit from operations	107,240	22,500	107,240	
Dividends received	1,200	—	NIL	Note 1
Share of associate's profit	—	—	4,500	Note 2
Profit before tax	108,440	22,500	111,740	
Income tax expense	27,750	6,000	28,950	Note 3
Profit for the period	80,690	16,500	82,790	
Minority interest	3,450		3,450	Note 4
	77,240		79,340	
Dividends paid	30,000	6,000	30,000	Note 5
	47,240	10,500	49,340	
Income statement balance brought forward from previous years	98,700	27,000	99,600	Note 6
	145,940	37,500	148,940	

Notes:

Profit before tax

1. **Dividend received from Cod** is not shown because the share of Cod's profits (before dividend) has been included in the group account (see note 2). To include the dividend as well would be double counting.

2. **Share of Cod's profit before tax** = 20% × £22,500 = **4,500**

Taxation

3. **Taxation** consists of:

Group tax	27,750
Share of Cod's taxation, i.e. 20% × 6,000	1,200
Total group tax	**28,950**

Profit for the period

4. **Minority interest** – note that there is no minority interest in Cod.

5. Note that there is no Cod dividend included because the £1,200 paid to Brill has been set against the dividend of £1,200 received by Brill and the group's share of Cod's profit has been included in the group's accounts.

6. The balance brought forward is made up as follows:

	£
Group	98,700
Cod 20% of the post-acquisition retained profit 20% (27,000 – 22,500)	900
	99,600

Note that in the annual report the dividends would be shown in the group statement of equity as follows:

Accumulated profits

Net profit for year	79,340
Dividends paid	30,000
	49,340
Income statement balance brought forward from previous years	99,600
	148,940

24.5 The treatment of provisions for unrealised profits

It is never appropriate in the case of associated companies to remove 100% of any unrealised profit on inter-company transactions because only the group's share of the associate's profit and net assets are shown in the group accounts. This is illustrated in the Zenith example:

EXAMPLE ● Zenith Group made sales to an associate, Nadir plc, at a mark-up of £10,000. All the goods are in the inventory of Nadir at the year-end. Zenith's holding in Nadir was 20%. The Zenith Group will provide for 20% of £10,000 (i.e. £2,000) against the group share of the associate's profit in the income statement and against the group share of the associate's net assets in the balance sheet.

24.6 The acquisition of an associate part-way through the year

In order to match the cost (the investment) with the benefit (share of the associate's net assets), the associate's profit will only be taken into account from the date of acquiring the holding in the associate. The associate's profit at the date of acquisition represents part of the net assets that are being acquired at that date. The Puff example below is an illustration of the accounting treatment.

In this chapter the adjustment for unrealised profit is made against the group's share of the associate's profit and net assets irrespective of whether the associate is receiving goods from the group (i.e. downstream transactions) or providing goods to the group (i.e. upstream transactions).[11]

24.6.1 The Puff Group

At date of acquisition on 31 March 20X0 of shares in associate:

● Puff plc acquired 30% of the shares in Blow plc.

● At that date the accumulated retained profit of Blow was £61,500 (after providing for £1,500 accrued dividend).

During the year:

● On 1/10/20X0 Blow sold Puff goods for £15,000 which was cost plus 25%.

● All income and expenditure for the year in Blow's income statement accrued evenly throughout the year.

At end of financial year on 31 December 20X0:

● 75% of the goods sold to Puff by Blow were still in stock.

● £450 of the dividend received by Puff from Blow has correctly been credited by Puff to the 'Investment in Blow'. This amount represents the dividend receivable out of pre-acquisition profits of Blow.

Set out below are the consolidated income statement of Puff and its subsidiaries and the individual income statement of an associated company, Blow, together with the consolidated group income statement.

	Puff and Subsids £	Blow £	Group accounts £	
Revenue	225,000	112,500	225,000	Note 1
Cost of sales	75,000	56,250	75,000	Note 2
Gross profit	150,000	56,250	150,000	
Expenses	89,850	30,000	89,850	
	60,150	26,250	60,150	
Dividends received	1,350	NIL	NIL	Note 3
Share of associate's profit	—	—	5,400	Note 4
Profit before taxation	61,500	26,250	65,550	
Income tax period	15,000	6,750	16,519	Note 5
Profit for the period	46,500	19,500	49,031	
Dividends paid	30,000	6,000	30,000	
	16,500	13,500	19,031	
Income statement balance brought forward from previous years	67,500	58,125	67,500	Note 6
	84,000	71,625	86,531	

Notes:

1. The revenue, cost of sales and all other income and expenses of the associated company are not added on a line by line basis with the those of the parent company and its subsidiaries. The group's share of the profit before taxation of the associate is shown as one figure (see note 4) and added to the remainder of the group's profit before taxation.

2. The group accounts 'cost of sales' figure does not include the provision for unrealised profit, as this has been deducted from the share of the associate's profit.

3. The dividend received of £1,350 represented 30% of the associate's dividend for the nine months that Blow has been an associate, i.e. $(30\% \times 6,000) \times {}^9/_{12}$ months.

4. Share of profits before tax of the associate

	£
Profit before tax	26,250
Less: unrealised profit $({}^{25}/_{125} \times 15,000) \times 75\%$	2,250
	24,000
Apportion for 9 months	18,000
Group share 30% of 18,000	**5,400**

5. The group's share of the associate's taxation
is $30\% \times 6,750 \times {}^9/_{12}$ =

	1,519
Parent and subsidiary tax	15,000
	16,519

6. There is no share of the associated company's accumulated profits brought forward because the shares in the associate were purchased during the year.

24.7 Joint ventures

IAS 31 *Interests in Joint Ventures* defines a joint venture as one in which there is a contractual arrangement whereby two or more parties undertake an economic activity that is subject to joint control so that no single venturer is in a position to control the activity unilaterally.[12]

There are a number of ways[13] in which a contractual arrangement may be evidenced, e.g. by a formal contract between the venturers or minutes of discussions between the venturers setting out in writing matters such as:

(a) scope – identifying the activity and its duration

(b) management – the appointment of managers/directors

(c) finance – capital contributions and sharing of profits and losses

(d) stewardship – reporting obligations.

The standard identifies three broad types, namely, **jointly controlled operations, jointly controlled assets** and **jointly controlled entities**.

24.7.1 Jointly controlled operations

The collaborative approach to the manufacture of an aircraft is a good example of this type of joint venture where the wings, body and engine are built by different companies. Each company bears its own costs and takes an agreed contractual share of the revenue from the sale of the aircraft. Each company is responsible for raising its own capital, using its own production capacity and working capital and incurring its own expenses.

Financial reports

The following are reported in the financial statements of each venturer:

(a) the assets that it controls and the liabilities that it incurs; and

(b) the expenses that it incurs and its share of the income that it earns from the sale of goods or services by the joint venture.

24.7.2 Jointly controlled assets

The common use of an oil pipeline by companies which control and finance it and pay according to the amount of throughput is an example[14] from IAS 31.

Financial reports

The following are reported in the financial statements of each venturer:

(a) its share of the jointly controlled assets, classified according to the nature of the assets;

(b) any liabilities that it has incurred;

(c) its share of any liabilities incurred jointly with the other venturers in relation to the joint venture;

(d) any income from the sale or use of its share of the output of the joint venture, together with its share of any expenses incurred by the joint venture; and

(e) any expenses that it has incurred in respect of its interest in the joint venture.

24.7.3 Jointly controlled entities

These joint ventures are operated through a corporation or partnership which controls the assets of the joint venture, incurs liabilities and expenses and earns income and enters into contracts in its own name.

Financial reports

A jointly controlled entity maintains its own accounting records[15] and prepares and presents financial statements in the same way as other entities in conformity with International Financial Reporting Standards.

24.7.4 Proportionate consolidation[16]

Proportionate consolidation is a method of accounting whereby a venturer's share of each of the assets, liabilities, income and expenses of a jointly controlled entity is combined line by line with similar items in the venturer's financial statements or reported as separate line items in the venturer's financial statements.

24.7.5 Equity accounting method

In the UK joint ventures are generally required to be accounted for using the equity method. IAS 31 takes a different approach in that it permits equity accounting but actively argues against it,[17] saying:

> Some venturers report their interests in jointly controlled entities using the equity method, as described in IAS 28. The use of the equity method is supported by those who argue that it is inappropriate to combine controlled items with jointly controlled items and by those who believe that venturers have significant influence, rather than joint control, in a jointly controlled entity. This Standard does not recommend the use of the equity method because proportional consolidation better reflects the substance and economic reality of a venturer's interest in a jointly controlled entity, that is control over the venturer's share of the future economic benefits. Nevertheless, this Standard permits the use of the equity method, as an allowed alternative treatment, when reporting interests in jointly controlled entities.

It is interesting to note that the IASB prefers the proportionate consolidation method on the grounds of economic reality, which is the reason that national standard setters support the equity method.

Summary

Associates are accounted for using the equity method whereby there is a single-line entry in the balance sheet for the Investment in Associate which is carried initially at cost and the balance adjusted annually for the investor's share of the associate's current year's profit or loss.

Joint ventures take a number of forms and, in each case, users need to be able to identify the assets and liabilities committed to the venture and the results in so far as they relate to the venturer. For joint venture entities IAS 31 permits alternative treatments with investors able to adopt the equity accounting method or proportionate consolidation. The IASB has expressed its preference for the proportionate consolidation method.

REVIEW QUESTIONS

1   The following is an extract from the notes to the 1999 consolidated financial statements of the Chugoku Electric Power Company, Incorporated.

Equity method
Investments in four (three in 1998) affiliated companies (20% to 50% owned) are accounted for by the equity method and, accordingly, are stated at cost adjusted for equity in undistributed earnings and losses from the date of acquisition.

(a) What is another name for most companies which are 20% to 50% owned?
(b) What is meant by the word 'equity' in the above statement?
(c) What are the entries in the income statement under the equity method of accounting?
(d) What are the differences between the equity method and consolidation?

2   Why are associated companies accounted for under the equity method rather than consolidated?

3   How does the treatment of inter-company unrealised profit differ between subsidiaries and associated companies?

4   IAS 28, para. 17, states:

The recognition of income on the basis of distributions received may not be an adequate measure of the income earned by an investor on an investment in an associate.

Explain why this may be so.

5   Where an associate has made losses, IAS 28, para. 30, states:

After the investor's interest is reduced to zero, additional losses are provided for, and a liability is recognised, only to the extent that the investor has incurred legal or constructive obligations or made payments on behalf of the associate. If the associate subsequently reports profits, the investor resumes recognising its share of those profits only after its share of the profits equals the share of losses not recognised.

Explain why profits are recognised only after its share of the profits equals the share of losses not recognised.

EXERCISES

An extract from the solution is provided in the Appendix at the end of the text for exercises marked with an asterisk (*).

* Question I

The following are the financial statements of the parent company Swish plc, a subsidiary company Broom and an associate company Handle.

Balance sheets as at 31 December 20X3

	Swish £	Broom £	Handle £
ASSETS			
Non-current assets			
Fixed assets at cost	320,000	180,000	100,000
Depreciation	200,000	70,000	21,000
	120,000	110,000	79,000
Investment in Broom	140,000		
Investment in Handle	40,000		
Current assets			
Inventories	120,000	60,000	36,000
Trade receivables	130,000	70,000	36,000
Current account – Broom	15,000		
Current account – Handle	3,000		
Bank	24,000	7,000	6,000
Total current assets	292,000	137,000	78,000
Total assets	592,000	247,000	157,000
EQUITY AND LIABILITIES			
£1 common shares	250,000	60,000	50,000
General reserve	30,000	20,000	12,000
Retained earnings	150,000	120,000	50,000
	430,000	200,000	112,000
Current liabilities			
Trade payables	132,000	25,000	34,000
Taxation payable	30,000	7,000	8,000
Current account – Swish		15,000	3,000
Total equity and liabilities	592,000	247,000	157,000

Income statement for the year ended 31 December 20X3

	£	£	£
Sales	300,000	160,000	100,000
Cost of sales	90,000	80,000	40,000
Gross profit	210,000	80,000	60,000
Expenses	95,000	50,000	40,000
Dividends received	11,000	NIL	10,000
Profit before tax	126,000	30,000	30,000
Income tax expense	30,000	7,000	8,000
Profit for the period	96,000	23,000	22,000
Dividends paid	40,000	10,000	8,000
	56,000	13,000	14,000
Retained earnings brought forward from previous years	94,000	107,000	36,000
	150,000	120,000	50,000

Swish acquired 90% of the common shares in Broom on 1 January 20X1 when the balance on the income statement of Broom was £60,000 and the balance on the general reserve of Broom was £16,000. Swish also acquired 25% of the common shares in Handle on 1 January 20X2 when the balance on Handle's accumulated retained profits was £30,000 and the general reserve £8,000.

During the year Swish sold Broom goods for £16,000, which included a mark-up of one-third. 80% of these goods were still in stock at the end of the year.

Required:
(a) Prepare a consolidated income statement, including the associated company Handle's results, for the year ended 31 December 20X3.
(b) Prepare a consolidated balance sheet as at 31 December 20X3.

* Question 2

Set out below are the consolidated accounts of Stop Ltd and its subsidiaries as well as the individual accounts of an associated company, Start Ltd.

Balance sheets of the Stop Ltd Group and Start Ltd at 31 December 20X1

	Stop Ltd and Subsids £	Start Ltd £
ASSETS		
Non-current assets		
Fixed assets at cost	375,000	150,000
Depreciation	125,000	25,000
	250,000	125,000
Investment in Start Ltd	62,500	
Current assets		
Inventories	160,000	62,500
Trade receivables	165,000	75,000
Current account – Start Ltd	15,000	
Bank	12,500	15,625
Total current assets	352,500	153,125
Total assets	665,000	278,125
EQUITY AND LIABILITIES		
£1 common shares	281,000	62,500
General reserve	31,500	22,500
Retained earnings	140,000	119,375
	452,500	204,375
Current liabilities		
Trade payables	187,500	47,500
Taxation	25,000	11,250
Current account – Stop Ltd		15,000
Total equity and liabilities	665,000	278,125

Profit and loss accounts for the year ended 31 December 20X1

	£	£
Sales	375,000	187,500
Cost of sales	125,000	93,750
Gross profit	250,000	93,750
Expenses	150,000	50,000
Dividends received from Start and others	2,500	NIL
Profit before tax	102,500	43,750
Income tax expense	25,000	11,250
Profit for the period	77,500	32,500
Dividends paid	50,000	10,000
	27,500	22,500
Retained earnings brought forward		
from previous years	112,500	96,875
	140,000	119,375

Notes:

1. Stop Ltd acquired 30% of the shares in Start Ltd on 31/3/20X1 when the balance of retained earnings of Start Ltd was £102,500, after accruing £2,500 dividend and the balance on the general reserve of Start Ltd was £20,000.
2. On 1/1/20X1 Stop Ltd sold Start Ltd goods for £58,500 which represented cost plus 30%. Half of these goods were still in inventory at the end of the year.
3. All income and expenditure for the year in Start Ltd's income statement accrued evenly throughout the year.
4. £750 of the dividend received by Stop Ltd from Start Ltd has correctly been credited by Stop Ltd to the 'Investment in Start Ltd'. This amount represents the dividend paid out of pre-acquisition profits of Start Ltd.

Required:
(a) Show the consolidated income statement of Stop Ltd for the year ending 31/12/20X1 including the associated company, Start Ltd, on the equity method of accounting basis.
(b) Show the consolidated balance sheet of Stop Ltd as at 31/12/20X1 including the associated company, Start Ltd, on the equity method of accounting basis.

Question 3

Set out below are the financial statements of Ant Co., its subsidiary Bug Co. and an associated company Nit Co. for the accounting year-end 31 December 20X9.

Balance sheets as at 31 December 20X9

	Ant $	Bug $	Nit $
ASSETS			
Non-current assets			
Property, plant and equipment	240,000	135,000	75,000
Depreciation	150,000	52,500	15,750
	90,000	82,500	59,250
Investment in Bug	90,000		
Investment in Nit	30,000		

	Ant $	Bug $	Nit $
Current assets			
Inventories	105,000	45,000	27,000
Trade receivables	98,250	52,500	27,000
Current account – Bug	11,250		
Current account – Nit	2,250		
Bank	17,250	5,250	4,500
Total current assets	234,000	102,750	58,500
Total assets	444,000	185,250	117,750
EQUITY AND LIABILITIES			
$1 common shares	187,500	45,000	37,500
General reserve	22,500	15,000	9,000
Retained earnings	112,500	90,000	37,500
	322,500	150,000	84,000
Current liabilities			
Trade payables	99,000	18,750	25,500
Taxation payable	22,500	5,250	6,000
Current account – Ant		11,250	2,250
Total equity and liabilities	444,000	185,250	117,750

Income statement for the year ended 31 December 20X9

	$	$	$
Sales	225,000	120,000	75,000
Cost of sales	67,500	60,000	30,000
Gross profit	157,500	60,000	45,000
Expenses	70,500	37,500	30,000
Dividends received	7,500	NIL	7,500
Profit before tax	94,500	22,500	22,500
Taxation	22,500	5,250	6,000
	72,000	17,250	16,500
Dividends paid	30,000	7,500	6,000
	42,000	9,750	10,500
Retained earnings brought forward from previous years	70,500	80,250	27,000
	112,500	90,000	37,500

Ant Co. acquired 80% of the shares in Bug Co. on 1 January 20X7 when the balance on the retained earnings of Bug Co. was $45,000 and the balance on the general reserve of Bug Co. was $12,000. Ant Co. also acquired 25% of the common shares in Nit Co. on 1 January 20X8 when the balance on Nit's retained earnings was $22,500 and the general reserve $6,000.

During the year Ant Co. sold Bug Co. goods for $12,000, which included a mark-up of one-third. 90% of these goods were still in inventory at the end of the year.

Required:
(a) Prepare a consolidated income statement for the year ending 31/12/20X9, including the associated company Nit's results.
(b) Prepare a consolidated balance sheet at 31/12/20X9, including the associated company.

Question 4

Set out below are the consolidated accounts of Twist plc and its subsidiaries and the individual accounts of an associated company, Turn plc.

Balance sheets of the Twist Group and Turn at 31 December 20X3

	Twist and Subsids £000	Turn £000
ASSETS		
Property, plant and equipment at cost	450	180
Depreciation	150	30
	300	150
Investment in Turn	75	
Current assets		
Inventories	180	75
Trade receivables	207	90
Current account – Turn	18	
Bank	18	18
Total current assets	423	183
Total assets	798	333
EQUITY AND LIABILITIES		
£1 common shares	200	70
General reserve	37	32
Retained earnings	168	142
	405	244
Minority interest	138	
Current liabilities		
Trade payables	225	57
Taxation	30	14
Current account – Twist		18
	798	333

Income statements for the year ended 31 December 20X3

	£000	£000
Sales	450	246
Cost of sales	150	112
Gross profit	300	134
Expenses	171	60
Dividends received	3	NIL
Profit before tax	132	74
Taxation	30	14
	102	60
Minority interest	10	
	92	60
Dividends paid	60	40
	32	20
Retained earnings brought forward from previous years	136	122
	168	142

Notes:

1. Twist acquired 30% of the shares in Turn on 30/9/20X3 when the balance on the retained earnings of Turn was £137,000 after providing for £30,000 dividend and the balance on the general reserve of Turn was £32,000.
2. On 1/1/20X3 Turn sold Twist goods for £30,000, at cost plus 25%. At the end of the year, 75% of these goods were still in inventory.
3. All income and expenditure for the year in Turn's income statement accrued evenly throughout the year.
4. £9,000 of the dividend receivable by Twist from Turn has correctly been credited by Twist to the 'Investment in Turn.' This amount represents the dividend receivable out of pre-acquisition profits of Turn.

Required:

(a) Show the consolidated Income Statement of Twist for the year ending 31/12/20X3 INCLUDING the associated company, Turn, on the equity method of accounting basis.
(b) Show the consolidated balance sheet of Twist as at 31/12/20X3 INCLUDING the associated company, Turn, on the equity method of accounting basis.

References

1 IAS 28 *Investments in Associates*, IASB, revised 2003, para. 2.
2 *Ibid.*, para. 2.
3 *Ibid.*, para. 6.
4 *Ibid.*, para. 7.
5 *Ibid.*, para. 13.
6 *Ibid.*, para. 38.
7 *Ibid.*, para. 2.
8 IAS 1 *Presentation of Financial Statements*, IASB, revised 2003, Implementation Guidance.
9 IAS 28, para. 2.
10 IFRS 3 – *Business Combinations 2004*, appendix C.
11 *Ibid.*, para. 22.
12 IAS 31 *Interests in Joint Ventures*, IASB, revised 2003, para. 3.
13 *Ibid.*, para. 10.
14 *Ibid.*, para. 20.
15 *Ibid.*, para. 28.
16 *Ibid.*, para. 3.
17 *Ibid.*, paras 38–41.

CHAPTER **25**

Accounting for the effects of changes in foreign exchange rates under IAS 21

25.1 Introduction

This chapter will consider:

- The difference between conversion and translation and the definition of a foreign currency transaction
- The functional currency
- The presentation currency
- Monetary and non-monetary items
- The rules on the recording of foreign currency transactions
- The treatment of exchange differences on foreign currency transactions
- The treatment of foreign exchange transactions in the individual accounts of companies
- The translation of the accounts of foreign operations.

25.2 The difference between conversion and translation and the definition of a foreign currency transaction

Conversion is the exchange of one currency for another while **translation** is the expression of another currency in the terms of the currency of the reporting operation. Only in the case of conversion is there a **foreign currency transaction**, which IAS 21 *The Effects of Changes in Foreign Exchange Rates* defines as follows:[1]

A foreign transaction is a transaction, which is denominated in or requires settlement in a foreign currency, including transactions arising when an entity:

(a) buys or sells goods or services whose price is denominated in a foreign currency;
(b) borrows or lends funds when the amounts payable or receivable are denominated in a foreign currency;
(c) otherwise acquires or disposes of assets, or incurs or settles liabilities, denominated in a foreign currency.

25.3 The functional currency

The **functional currency** is the currency of the primary economic environment in which the entity operates.

IAS 21 sets out the factors which a reporting entity (a company preparing financial statements) will consider in determining its functional currency.[2] These are:

(a) the currency:
   (i) that mainly influences sales prices for goods and services and
   (ii) of the country whose competitive forces and regulations mainly determine the sales prices of its goods and services;
(b) the currency that mainly influences labour, material, and other costs of providing goods and services.

The following factors may also provide evidence of an entity's functional currency:[3]

(a) the currency in which funds from financing activities are generated;
(b) the currency in which the receipts from operating activities are usually retained.

A company must also decide whether or not any of its foreign operations, such as a branch or subsidiary, has the same functional currency. In doing so the following factors will be considered:[4]

(a) Whether the activities of the foreign operation are carried out as an extension of the reporting entity, rather than being carried out with a significant degree of autonomy. An example of the former is when the foreign operation only sells goods imported from the reporting entity and remits the proceeds to it. An example of the latter is when the operation accumulates cash and other monetary items, incurs expenses, generates income and arranges borrowings, all substantially in its local currency.
(b) Whether transactions with the reporting entity are a high or low proportion of the foreign operation's activities.
(c) Whether cash flows from the activities of the foreign operation directly affect the cash flows of the reporting entity and are readily available for remittance to it.
(d) Whether cash flows from the activities of the foreign operation are sufficient to service existing and normally expected debt obligations without funds being made available by the reporting entity.

25.4 The presentation currency[5]

The **presentation currency** is the currency a reporting entity uses for its financial statements. The reporting entity is entitled to present its financial statement in any currency, so that in some cases the presentation currency may differ from the functional currency.

25.5 Monetary and non-monetary items

Monetary items are balances owed by or to an entity that will be settled in cash. Examples will be creditors for goods supplied, loans, cash dividends payable, cash and debtors for goods supplied. Non-monetary assets will include fixed assets, stock and amounts prepaid for goods.

25.6 The rules on the recording of foreign currency transactions

Initial recognition[6]

All transactions are entered in the books at the spot currency exchange rate between the foreign currency and the functional currency on the transaction date. An average rate may be used for a period where it is appropriate. It will be inappropriate where exchange rates fluctuate significantly.

At subsequent dates

Amounts paid or received in settlement of foreign currency monetary items during an accounting period are translated at the date of settlement.

At the balance sheet date monetary balances are translated at closing rate.

Non-monetary items at historical cost remain at their original rate. Non-monetary items at fair value are translated at the rate on the date the fair value was determined.[7]

25.7 The treatment of exchange differences on foreign currency transactions

Exchange differences arising on the settlement of monetary items or on translating monetary items at rates different from those at which they were translated on initial recognition during the period, or in previous financial statements, must be recognised in the income statement during the period in which they arise,[8] except in the case of the group accounts where the exchange difference arises on a monetary item (e.g. a long-term loan) that in substance forms part of a company's net investment in a foreign entity. In this case the exchange difference will be recognised in a separate component of equity and only recognised in the income statement on disposal of the net investment.

Note that the profits or losses on foreign currency transactions affect the cash flow and are therefore realised.

The following extract is from the Nemetschek AC 1999 group accounts:

In the individual annual accounts of Nemetschek AC and its subsidiaries, business transactions in a foreign currency are valued at the exchange rate at the time of their original posting. Any exchange losses from the valuation of receivables and payables are taken into account up to the balance sheet cutoff date. Profits and losses from fluctuations in the exchange rate are taken into account as affecting net income.

25.8 Foreign exchange transactions in the individual accounts of companies illustrated – Boil plc

Boil plc is a UK company that buys and sells catering equipment. The following information is available for foreign currency transactions entered into by Boil plc during the year ended 31 December 20X0:

1/11 Buys goods for $30,000 on credit from Nevada Inc
15/11 Sells goods for $40,000 on credit to Union Inc
15/11 Pays Nevada Inc $20,000 for on account for the goods purchased
10/12 Receives $25,000 on account from Union Inc in payment for the goods sold
10/12 Buys machinery for $80,000 from Florida Inc on credit
10/12 Borrowed $60,000 from an American bank. This is held in a dollar bank account.
22/12 Pays Florida Inc $80,000 for the machinery

The exchange rates at the relevant dates were

1/11 £1 = $2.00
15/11 £1 = $2.20
10/12 £1 = $2.40
22/12 £1 = $2.50
31/12 £1 = $2.60

Required: Calculate the profit or loss on foreign currency to be reported in the financial statements of Boil plc at 31/12/20X0.

(Assume that Boil plc buys foreign currency to pay for goods and non-current assets on the day of settlement and immediately converts into sterling any currency received from sales.)

Solution
We need to calculate any exchange differences on monetary accounts, non-monetary accounts, and income statement sales and purchases as follows:

Monetary accounts
Profits or losses on foreign transactions will arise on monetary accounts from the difference between the exchange rate on the date of the initial transaction and the rate on the date of its settlement or the balance sheet date, whichever is earlier. Profits or losses on exchange differences will arise on the following monetary accounts:

Nevada Inc   – Trade payables
Union Inc   – Trade receivable
Florida Inc   – Creditor for machinery
American bank   – Creditor for a loan

The profit or loss on foreign exchange in these cases will be as follows:

Name of account	Nevada Inc payable	Union Inc receivable	Florida Inc creditor	American bank loan creditor
Foreign currency at exchange rate on date of initial transaction	$30,000/2.00 = £15,000	$40,000/2.20 = £18,182	$80,000/2.40 = £33,333	$60,000/2.40 = £25,000
Foreign currency at exchange rate on date of settlement	$20,000/2.20 = £9,091	$25,000/2.40 = £10,417	$80,000/2.50 = £32,000	

Foreign currency at exchange rate on date of balance sheet	$10,000/2.60 = £3,846	$15,000/2.60 = £5,769		$60,000/2.60 = £23,077
Profit/(loss) on foreign exchange (£)	£2,063	(£1,996)	£1,333	£1,923

Other balances

All other balances, i.e. purchases and sales in the income statement and machinery (non-monetary) will be translated on the day of the initial transaction and no profit or loss on foreign exchange will arise. These balances will therefore appear in the financial statements as follows:

Purchases $30,000/2.00 = £15,000
Sales $40,000/2.20 = £18,182
Machinery $80,000/2.40 = £33,333

The profit or loss on exchange differences is realised as they have either already affected the cash flows of Boil plc or will do so in the foreseeable future. This profit or loss must therefore be taken to the income statement.

25.9 The translation of the accounts of foreign operations where the functional currency is the same as that of the parent

In the Boil illustration above (25.8) we considered the effects of converting foreign currency in the individual company accounts. In this section we consider the situation of a subsidiary, Berlin Gmbh, which has its accounts in euros but has the pound sterling as its **functional** currency. Note also that **the presentation currency** of the reporting company, Granby Ltd, is also the pound sterling. In this situation Berlin is considered to be an extension of the parent and the translation method used is therefore exactly the same as applied to the individual company.

25.10 Granby Ltd illustration

On 30 June 20X0 Granby Ltd acquired 60% of the common shares of a German subsidiary Berlin Gmbh. At that date the balance on the accumulated profits of Berlin was €20,000,000 and the balance on additional paid-in capital €2,000,000. The summarised income statements and balance sheet of Granby Ltd and Berlin Gmbh at 30 June 20X3 were as follows:

Income statements for the year ended 30 June 20X3

	Granby Ltd £000	Berlin Gmbh €000
Sales	430,000	140,000
Opening inventories	70,000	21,200
Purchases	250,000	80,000
Closing inventories	25,000	17,200
Cost of sales	295,000	84,000
Gross profit	135,000	56,000

	Granby Ltd £000	Berlin Gmbh €000
Dividend received	2,400	NIL
Depreciation	40,000	12,000
Other expenses	10,600	4,000
Interest paid	7,000	2,000
Total expenses	57,600	18,000
Profit before taxation	79,800	38,000
Taxation	20,000	12,000
Profit after taxation	59,800	26,000
Dividend paid 30.6.20X3	25,000	8,000
Retained profit for the year	34,800	18,000

Balance sheets as at 30 June 20X3

	£000	€000
Non-current assets	140,000	90,000
Investment in Berlin Gmbh	4,500	
Current assets:		
Inventories	25,000	17,200
Trade receivables	60,500	20,000
Berlin Gmbh	4,000	
Cash	11,000	800
	100,500	38,000
Current liabilities:		
Trade payables	60,000	18,000
Granby Ltd		8,000
Taxation	20,000	12,000
	80,000	38,000
Bonds	50,000	16,000
Total assets *less* liabilities	115,000	74,000
Share capital	45,000	4,000
Additional paid-in capital	7,000	2,000
Revaluation reserve	10,000	12,000
Retained earnings	53,000	56,000
	115,000	74,000

The following information is also available:

1. Non-current assets
   - Non-current assets were acquired on 1/7/20X1 when the exchange rate was €6 to the £.
   - The revaluation reserve in Berlin Gmbh arose from the revaluation of non-current assets on 1/7/20X2.

2. Inventories
   - Opening inventories were acquired when the exchange rate was £1 = €3
   - Closing inventories were acquired when the rate was £1 = €2.5

3. Exchange rates were as follows:

At 30 June 20X0   £1 = €5
Average for the year ending 30 June 20X3, an approximation of
the rate on the date of trading transactions and expenses   £1 = €4
At 30 June/1 July 20X2   £1 = €3.5
At 30 June 20X3   £1 = €2

4. It is assumed that the functional currency of Berlin is the pound sterling.

5. An amount of €1,380,000 was written of goodwill as an impairment charge in the current year, and €2,760,000 in previous years.

Required:

(a) Translate the accounts of the German company into sterling for the consolidated accounts and calculate the profit/loss on exchange differences for the consolidated accounts at 30 June 20X3.

(b) Show how the profit/loss on exchange differences arose.

(c) Prepare consolidated accounts.

The process of consolidation is as follows:

1. Translate the financial statements into the currency of the reporting concern.

2. Consolidate as previously but watch the treatment of any profit/loss on exchange differences.

25.10.1 Stage 1 – Translate the financial statements of Berlin Gmbh into sterling

(a) The income statement

	Berlin Gmbh income €000	Exchange rate	Translated statement £000
Sales	140,000		
Purchases	(80,000)		
Other expenses	(4,000)		
Interest	(2,000)		
Taxation	(12,000)		
	42,000	4.0	10,500 Note 1
Opening inventories	(21,200)	3.0	(7,067) Note 2
Closing inventories	17,200	2.5	6,880
Depreciation	(12,000)	3.5	(3,429) Note 3
Dividend	(8,000)	2.0	(4,000) Note 4
Net profit carried forward	**18,000**		**2,884**

Notes:
1. Sales, purchases and expenses have been translated at an average which is an approximation of the rate when they were originally recorded. This requirement of the IAS has been rather more loosely interpreted in the case of interest and taxation, which have been translated at the rates or approximate rates when they originally accrued. Under the wording of the IAS it might be more strictly correct if the taxation and interest were translated at the date they were first recorded in the books.

2. Translated at the actual date of acquiring the inventories.
3. The rate is that applicable to the date of revaluation rather than that at the date of acquiring the fixed assets.
4. Translated at the actual rate.

(b) The balance sheet

Non-current assets				
Property, plant and equipment	90,000	3.5	25,714	Note 3
Current assets				
Inventories	17,200	2.5	6,880	Note 5
Receivables	20,000	2.0	10,000	Note 6
Cash	800	2.0	400	
Current liabilities				
Payables	(18,000)	2.0	(9,000)	
Granby Ltd	(8,000)	2.0	(4,000)	
Taxation	(12,000)	2.0	(6,000)	
Non-current assets – bonds	(16,000)	2.0	(8,000)	
Total assets less liabilities	**74,000**		**15,994**	
Equity				
Share capital	4,000	5.0	800	Note 7
Additional paid-in capital	2,000	5.0	400	Note 8
Accumulated				
Profit (56,000 – 18,000)	38,000	Balancing figure	1,667	Note 9
	44,000		2,867	Note 10
Revaluation reserve	12,000	3.5	3,429	Note 11
Profit for the year	18,000	see above	2,884	Note 12
Profit on exchange differences			6,814	Note 13
Total equity	**74,000**		**15,994**	

Notes:

5. As inventories are non-monetary assets they are translated at actual.

6. The receivables and all the following net assets in the balance sheet are monetary items and therefore retranslated at the closing rate.

7. Share capital issued should be translated at the date of acquiring the subsidiary or at the date of issue if later. At this stage of the process we are attempting to find the figure of profit or loss on exchange differences up to the beginning of the current year so that we can isolate the profit or loss on exchange in the current year. One way to do this is to split the share capital and reserves into the amount arising this year and the balance at the end of the previous year. In this question the balance at the end of the previous year can be calculated as €44,000 (see Note 10). The rest (profit for the year €18,000 and revaluation reserve €12,000) arose in the present year. If we can then translate the 44,000 into pounds sterling at the end of the previous year, we can eventually find this year's profit or loss on exchange. In practice we could obtain the sterling equivalent of the €44,000 from the workings for the previous year's consolidated accounts.

8. The additional paid-in capital (share premium) is translated at the same rate as the shares to which it relates.

9. The accumulated profit at the end of the previous year can be taken as the balancing figure after translating the €44,000. The accumulated profit will have

been translated at many different rates over the years. In practice the translated figure would be available from the previous years' consolidated accounts.

10. The €44,000 represents a mixture of monetary and non-monetary assets. The amount can be translated by applying the exchange rates used in the balance sheet in the previous year. This is calculated as follows:

Non-current assets			
Fixed assets	90,000		
Depreciation	12,000		
Revaluation	(12,000)		
	90,000	6.0	15,000
Opening inventory	21,200	3.0	7,067
	111,200		22,067
Balance = monetary			
liabilities at 30/6/20X2	(67,200)	3.5	(19,200)
Net assets at 30/6/20X2	**44,000**		2,867

11. The revaluation reserve is translated at the rate when the revaluation took place.

12. The income statement was translated to give the profit figure in sterling

13. The loss on exchange differences is the balancing figure but can be found directly as in 25.10.2 below.

25.10.2 An analysis of the exchange difference for the year

The monetary net liabilities at the beginning of the year of €67,200 (see Note 10 above) have been retranslated into sterling at 30 June 20X3 and a loss of £14,400 has been made since translation last year.

		£
Opening net monetary liabilities €67,200	@ opening rate 3.5 =	19,200
Opening net monetary liabilities €67,200	@ closing rate 2.0 =	33,600
	Loss (i)	(14,400)

Any profit made during the year initially goes into monetary net assets. The translation of these at the year-end rate will give a profit in this case of the difference between the actual or average rate (as an approximation of the actual rate) used for translating the profit and loss items and the year-end rate used for translating monetary items in the balance sheet.

			£
Translated at average rate	42,000 @ 4.0	=	10,500
At closing rate	42,000 @ 2.0	=	21,000
	Gain (ii)		10,500

(iii) The non-current assets were acquired when the rate of exchange was 6.0 euros to the pound and this was the rate applied to them at 30 June 20X2. On 1 July 20X3 the non-current assets were revalued when the rate was 3.5 euros to the pound and this was therefore the rate applied to the non-current assets at 30 June 2003. There has therefore been a profit on translation as follows:

		£
€90,000 at 6.0	=	15,000
€90,000 at 3.5	=	25,714
		10,714

The total of (i) + (ii) + (iii) is a gain of £6,814 (10,500 + 10,714 – 14,400), of which 60% (£4,088) belongs to the group. The full gain will be recognised in the income statement and the minority intersts will be allocated 40%.

25.10.3 Stage 2 – Prepare consolidated accounts – Granby

Solution to Granby

			£000
ASSETS			
Non-current assets			
Goodwill	**(W1)**		552
Other	(140,000 + 25,714)		165,714
			166,266
Current assets	**(W2)**		
Inventories	(25,000 + 6,880)	31,880	
Trade receivables	(60,500 + 10,000)	70,500	
Bank	(11,000 + 400)	11,400	
			113,780
Total assets			**280,046**
EQUITY AND LIABILITIES			
Common share capital			45,000
Additional paid-in capital			7,000
Revaluation reserve	(10,000 + 2,057 **(W3)**)		12,057
Retained earnings	(53,000 + 4,419 **(W4)**)		
Less impairment of goodwill	828 (4140 ÷ 5) **(W1)**		56,591
			120,648
Minority interest			6,398
Non-current liabilities	**(W2)**		
Bonds	(50,000 + 8,000)		58,000
Current liabilities	**(W5)**		
Trade payables	(60,000 + 9,000)	69,000	
Taxation	(20,000 + 6,000)	26,000	95,000
Total equity and liabilities			**280,046**

W1 Goodwill

	€000	€000
Investment in Berlin (4,500 × 5)*		22,500
Common share in Berlin (60% × 4000)	2,400	
Retained earnings (60% × 20,000)	12,000	
Additional paid-in capital (60% × 2,000)	1,200	
		15,600
Goodwill		6,900
Impairment loss in current year was 1,380		
Impairment loss in previous year was 2,760		4,140
Balance sheet figure		2,760

The investment has been translated into euros at the day of acquisition. The goodwill in sterling at the exchange rate on that date is £552,000 (2,760,000 ÷ 5). *Note that goodwill is regarded as the asset of the subsidiary. This will become relevant when the presentation currency is other than the functional currency (see 25.11).

W2 Cancel inter-company balances:
Current accounts of 4,000

W3 Berlin Gmbh Revaluation reserve

	£000
Balance at 30/6/20X3 as per balance sheet	3,429
Minority interest 40% × 3,429	1,372
Consolidated balance sheet	2,057

W4 Retained earnings of Berlin Gmbh   £000

Balance at 30/6/20X3 as per the balance sheet (1,667 + 2,884 + 6,814 profit on exchange)		11,365
Pre-acquisition profit	2,400	
Minority interest 40% × 11,365	4,546	6,946
		4,419

W5 The minority interest   £000

Common shares 40% × 800	320
Retained earnings 40% × 11,365	4,546
Additional paid-in capital 40% × 400	160
Revaluation reserve 40% × 3,429	1,372
	6,398

25.10.4 Prepare the Granby consolidated income statement

The consolidated income statement for the year ended 31/6/20X3 includes the subsidiary figures using the exchange rates as shown in 25.10.1 above.

		£000
Sales	(430,000 + [140,000/4])	465,000
Cost of sales	(295,000 + [7,067+80,000/4 − 6,880])	315,187
Gross profit		149,813
Depreciation	(40,000 + 3,429)	43,429
Expenses	(10,600 + 4,000/4)	11,600
Profit on foreign exchange		(6,814)
Impairment loss	(1,380 ÷ 5)	276
Interest	(7,000 + 2,000/4)	7,500
Profit before tax		93,822
Taxation	(20,000 + 12,000/4)	23,000
Profit after tax		70,822
Minority interest	(40% × (2,884 + Div 4,000 − 6,814)	5,479
Net profit for the period		65,343
Dividend paid		25,000

25.10.5 Group statement of changes in equity for the year ended 30 June 20X3

This statement will appear as follows:

Retained earnings brought forward (W6)	16,248
Net profit for the period	65,343
Dividend payable	(25,000)
Accumulated profit carried forward	56,591

W6 Group accumulated profits brought forward at 1/7/20X2

Granby	(53,000 − this year 34,800)	18,200
Berlin	(60% × (1,667 − pre-acquisition 4,000 (see W1)))	(1,400)
		16,800
Less: impairment loss		552
Accumulated profits brought forward		16,248

25.11 The use of a presentation currency other than the functional currency

Whenever the presentation currency is different from the functional currency, it is necessary to translate the financial statements into the presentation currency. In this situation there is no realisation of the exchange gain/loss in the cash flows and therefore any gain/loss will go to reserves. This is demonstrated in the alternative solution to Granby Ltd below, which in this case assumes that the euro is the functional currency of Berlin Gmbh and the presentation currency is the same as the functional currency of the reporting entity, i.e the pound sterling.

The translation rules used in this situation are set out in para. 39 of IAS 21 as follows:

(a) assets and liabilities ... shall be translated at the closing rate at the date of the balance sheet;

(b) income and expenses ... shall be translated at exchange rates at the dates of the transactions [or average rate if this is a reasonable approximation] and

(c) all resulting exchange differences shall be recognised as a separate component of equity.

25.12 Granby Ltd illustration continued

Stage 1. Translate the financial statements of Berlin Gmbh into sterling

(a) Income statement
This will be calculated in the same way as was done in 25.10.1 above.

	€000	Translated	£000
Retained profit for year	18,000	Actual rate at date of transaction	2,884

(b) Balance sheet

	Berlin Gmbh	Exchange rate	Translated financial statements
ASSETS			
Net assets at 30/6/20X3	74,000	Closing rate 2	37,000
Share capital	4,000	5.0	800
Additional paid-in capital	2,000	5.0	400
Accumulated Profit (56,000 − 18,000)	38,000	Balancing figure	11,371
	44,000	Opening rate 3.5	12,571
Revaluation reserve	12,000	Opening rate 3.5	3,429
Profit for the year	18,000	see Stage 1(a) above	2,884
Profit on exchange differences		See workings below	18,116
	74,000		37,000

The profit on exchange differences in the group accounts will be £18,116 of which 40% is attributable to the minority. The differences arise because the subsidiary figures are restated at the closing rate in the consolidated balance sheet. The calculation of each difference is as follows:

(i) On the retranslation of the net non-monetary assets at 30/06/20X3

				£
Opening net assets	€44,000	@ opening rate 3.5	=	12,571
Opening net assets	€44,000	@ closing rate 2.0	=	22,000
			Gain	9,429

(ii) The difference arising because of the different rates for translation applied to the monetary assets in the income statement (see 25.10.1(a)) and the balance sheet year-end rate

		£
Translated at average rate	€42,000 @ 4.0 =	10,500
At closing rate	€42,000 @ 2.0 =	21,000
Gain		10,500

(iii) The difference arising because of the different rates for translation applied to the depreciation in the income statement (see 25.10.1(a)) and the balance sheet year-end rate

Translated at date of revaluation of fixed assets	€12,000 @ 3.5 =	3,429
Translated at the year-end	€12,000 @ 2.0 =	6,000
Loss		2,571

(iv) The difference arising because of the different rates for translation applied to the opening inventory in the income statement (see 25.10.1(a)) and the balance sheet year-end rate

Translation at the date of acquisition of opening inventory	€21,200 @ 3	=	7,067
Translated at the year-end	€21,200 @ 2	=	10,600
Loss			3,533

(v) The difference arising because of the different rates for translation applied to the closing inventory in the income statement (see 25.10.1(a)) and the balance sheet year-end rate

Translation at the date of acquisition of closing inventory	€17,200 @ 2.5 =		6,880
Translated at the year-end	€17,200 @ 2	=	8,600
Gain			1,720

(vi) The difference arising because of the different rates for translation applied to the revaluation in the balance sheet and the balance sheet year-end rate

Translation at the date of revaluation.	€12,000 @ 3.5 =	3,429
Translated at the year-end	€12,000 @ 2.0 =	6,000
Gain		2,571

The total of (i) – (vi) is a gain of £18,116 of which 60% (£10,870) belongs to the group. The group share will go to a reserve and the minority share to the minority interest.

Stage 2. Prepare consolidated accounts.

The consolidated accounts are prepared in the same way as for foreign operations where the functional currency is the same as that of the parent as in 25.10.3 and 25.10.4 above, except that the translated amounts from the subsidiary company will be different, because of the different exchange rates applied, and the profit or loss on foreign currency will go to equity. Only when the investment in the foreign operation is sold will the profit or loss on foreign exchange be realised and become part of the calculation of profit or loss on sale of the investment. Note that the goodwill on acquisition is treated as the asset of the subsidiary and will therefore be translated at the closing rate. This will in turn affect the profit or loss on foreign currency.

25.13 Implications of IAS 21

IAS 21 was revised in December 2003, and it was at this revision that the concept of the functional and presentation currencies was introduced. Whilst the implications for the standard are not significant for all businesses, they can have an effect. For example, a company may, in the past, have viewed foreign operations as separate to their existing parent business, but under IAS 21 as revised, if the foreign operations have a functional currency the same as the parent business, this is no longer permitted.

Also, the revision to IAS 21 changed the translation rules for income statements of businesses with a different functional and presentation currency, and gave new rules for the restatement of goodwill and fair value adjustments. These changes affected profits, net asset values and exchange differences that companies declared.

The following extract from Shell highlights some potential impacts:

The Group has a range of inter-company funding arrangements in place in order to optimise the sourcing of financing for the Group and optimise the funding of its subsidiaries. IAS 21 is more prescriptive on the treatment of gains and losses taken to reserves [equity], for example, gains/losses where the currency of the loan is neither in the functional currency of the borrower nor of the lender are to be recognised in the income statement. IAS 21 is thus expected to increase volatility in the Income Statement. However, the Group is currently investigating whether to change its treasury policies to reduce this volatility.

Summary

The conversion and translation of foreign currency for presentation in the financial statements has always been a difficult area of accounting with different views on approach. The approach taken in IAS 21 attempts to translate transactions and operations in a way that reflects the economic circumstances of the transaction. This gives no significant problems for individual foreign transactions but has led to two methods being adopted for foreign operations.

A foreign operation which has the same functional currency as its parent is treated as in integral part of the parent operations and therefore is translated in the same way as individual company transactions. A foreign operation with a functional currency different to the parent's (or a company with different functional and presentation currencies) follows different rules.

REVIEW QUESTIONS

1   Discuss the desirability or otherwise of isolating profits or losses caused by exchange differences from other profit or losses in financial statements.

2   How can different relationships between a parent operation and its controlled foreign operation affect the treatment of exchange profits or losses in the consolidated financial statements? Why should the treatment be different?

3   How does the treatment of changes in foreign exchange rates relate to the prudence and accruals concepts?

EXERCISES

An extract from the solution is provided in the Appendix at the end of the text for exercises marked with an asterisk (*).

* Question 1

Fry Ltd has the following foreign currency transactions in the year to 31/12/20X0

15/11	Buys goods for $40,000 on credit from Texas Inc
15/11	Sells goods for $60,000 on credit to Alamos Inc
20/11	Pays Texas Inc $40,000 for the goods purchased
20/11	Receives $30,000 on account from Alamos Inc in payment for the goods sold
20/11	Buys machinery for $100,000 from Chicago Inc on credit
20/11	Borrows $90,000 from an American bank
21/12	Pays Chicago Inc $80,000 for the machinery

The exchange rates at the relevant dates were

15/11	£1 = $2.60
20/11	£1 = $2.40
21/12	£1 = $2.30
31/12	£1 = $2.10

Required:
Calculate the profit or loss to be reported in the financial statements of Fry Ltd at 31/12/20X0.

Question 2

On 1 January 20X0 Walpole Ltd acquired 90% of the ordinary shares of a French subsidiary Paris SA. At that date the balance on the retained earnings of Paris SA was €10,000. No shares have been issued by Paris since acquisition. The summarised income statements and balance sheet of Walpole Ltd and Paris SA at 31 December 20X2 were as follows:

Income statements for the year ended 31 December 20X2

	Walpole Ltd £000	Paris SA €000
Sales	317,200	200,000
Opening inventories	50,000	22,000
Purchases	180,000	90,000
Closing inventories	60,000	12,000
Cost of sales	170,000	100,000
Gross profit	147,200	100,000
Dividend received from Paris SA	1,800	NIL
Depreciation	30,000	30,000
Other expenses	15,000	7,000
Interest paid	6,000	3,000
Total expenses	51,000	40,000
Profit before taxation	98,000	60,000
Taxation	21,000	15,000
Profit after taxation	77,000	45,000
Dividend paid	20,000	10,000
Retained profit for the year	57,000	35,000

Balance sheet as at 31 December 20X2

	£000	€000
Non-current assets	94,950	150,000
Investment in Paris SA	41,050	
Current assets:		
Inventories	60,000	12,000
Trade receivables	59,600	40,000
Paris SA	2,400	
Cash	11,000	11,000
Total current assets	133,000	63,000
Current liabilities:		
Trade payables	45,000	18,000
Walpole Ltd		12,000
Taxation	21,000	15,000
Total current liabilities	66,000	45,000
Debentures	40,000	10,000
Total assets less liabilities	163,000	158,000
Share capital	80,000	60,000
Share premium	6,000	20,000
Revaluation reserve	10,000	12,000
Retained earnings	67,000	66,000
	163,000	158,000

The following information is also available:

(i)   The revaluation reserve in Paris SA arose from the revaluation of fixed assets on 1/1/20X2.

(ii) All the non-current assets of Paris were acquired on 1/1/20X0.

(iii) The opening inventory was acquired when the exchange rate was £1 = €2.5 and the closing stock when the rate was £1 = €4.5.

(iv) Exchange rates were as follows:

At 1 January 20X0	£1 = €2
Average for the year ending 31 December 20X2	£1 = €3
At 31 December 20X1/1 January 20X2	£1 = €3.5
At 31 December 20X2	£1 = €5

Required:

(a) Assuming that the functional currency of Paris SA is the £ sterling, translate the accounts of the French company into sterling for the consolidated accounts and calculate the profit/loss on changes in the exchange rate for the consolidated accounts at 31 December 20X2.

(b) Prepare the consolidated accounts for the Walpole group at 31 December 20X2.

Question 3

The information is the same as in Question 2 above **but** assume that the functional currency of Paris SA is the euro.

Required:

(a) Translate the accounts of the French company into sterling for the consolidated accounts and calculate the profit/loss on changes in the exchange rate for the consolidated accounts at 31 December 20X2.

(b) Prepare the consolidated accounts for the Walpole group at 31 December 20X2.

References

1   IAS 21 *The Effects of Changes in Foreign Exchange Rates*, IASB, revised 2003, para. 20.
2   *Ibid.*, para. 20.
3   *Ibid.*, para. 10.
4   *Ibid.*, para. 11.
5   *Ibid.*, para. 38.
6   *Ibid.*, para. 21.
7   *Ibid.*, para. 23.
8   *Ibid.*, para. 28.

PART **5**

Interpretation

CHAPTER 26

Earnings per share

26.1 Introduction

In this chapter we consider

- Why the earnings per share figure is important
- How it is used by shareholders
- IAS 33 calculation of basic earnings per share (BEPS)
- BEPS when there has been a bonus issue, share split, new issue and buyback of shares
- BEPS when there has been a rights issue
- Calculation of diluted EPS
- IAS 33 procedure where there are several potential dilutions, e.g. conversion rights and options
- EPS when conversion rights are exercised
- Institute of Investment Management and Research (IIMR) definition of an alternative EPS
- the IASB Improvement Project.

26.2 Why is the earnings per share figure important?

One of the most widely publicised ratios for a public company is the price/earnings or PE ratio. The PE ratio is significant because, by combining it with a forecast of company earnings, analysts can decide whether the shares are currently over- or undervalued.[1]

The ratio is published daily in the financial press and is widely employed by those making investment decisions. The following is a typical extract from the *Risk Measurement Service*:[2]

Breweries, Pubs and Restaurants

Company	Price 31/3/98	PE ratio
Company A	453	12.6
Company B	340	39.3
Company C	1,125	19.6

The PE ratio is calculated by dividing the market price of a share by the earnings that the company generated for that share. Alternatively, the PE figure may be seen as a multiple of the earnings per share, where the multiple represents the number of years' earnings required to recoup the price paid for the share. For example, it would take a shareholder in Company B just under forty years to recoup her outlay if all earnings were to be distributed, whereas it would take a shareholder in Company A just over twelve years to recoup his outlay, and one in Company C just under twenty years.

26.2.1 What factors affect the PE ratio?

The PE ratio for a company will reflect investors' confidence and hopes about the international scene, the national economy and the industry sector, as well as about the current year's performance of the company as disclosed in its financial report. It is difficult to interpret a PE ratio in isolation without a certain amount of information about the company, its competitors and the industry within which it operates.

For example, a **high PE ratio** might reflect investor confidence in the existing management team: people are willing to pay a high multiple for expected earnings because of the underlying strength of the company. Conversely, it might also reflect lack of investor confidence in the existing management, but an anticipation of a takeover bid which will result in transfer of the company assets to another company with better prospects of achieving growth in earnings than has the existing team.

A **low PE ratio** might indicate a lack of confidence in the current management or a feeling that even a new management might find problems that are not easily surmounted. For example, there might be extremely high gearing, with little prospect of organic growth in earnings or new capital inputs from rights issues to reduce it.

These reasons for a difference in the PE ratios of companies, even though they are in the same industry, are market-based and not simply a function of earnings. However, the current earnings per share figure and the individual shareholder's expectation of future growth relative to that of other companies also have an impact on the share price.

26.3 How is the EPS figure calculated?

Because of the importance attached to the PE ratio, it is essential that there is a consistent approach to the calculation of the EPS figure. IAS 33 *Earnings per Share*[3] was issued in 1998 for this purpose.

The EPS figure is of major interest to shareholders not only because of its use in the PE ratio calculation, but also because it is used in the earnings yield percentage calculation. It is a more acceptable basis for comparing performance than figures such as dividend yield percentage because it is not affected by the distribution policy of the directors. The formula is:

$$\text{EPS} = \frac{\text{Earnings}}{\text{Weighted number of ordinary shares}}$$

The standard defines two EPS figures for disclosure, namely,

● **basic** EPS based on ordinary shares currently in issue; and
● **diluted** EPS based on ordinary shares currently in issue *plus* potential ordinary shares.

26.3.1 Basic EPS

Basic EPS is defined in IAS 33 as follows:[4]

- Basic earnings per share is calculated by dividing the net profit or loss for the period attributable to ordinary shareholders by the weighted average number of ordinary shares outstanding during the period.

For the purpose of the BEPS definition:

- **Net profit** is the consolidated profit for the period after deduction of preference dividends (assuming preference shares are equity instruments).[5]
- The **weighted average number of ordinary shares** should be adjusted for events, other than the conversion of potential ordinary shares, that have changed the number of ordinary shares outstanding, without a corresponding change in resources.[6]
- An **ordinary share** is an equity instrument that is subordinate to all other classes of equity instruments.[7]

26.3.2 Diluted EPS

Diluted EPS is defined as follows:

- For the purpose of calculating diluted earnings per share, the net profit attributable to ordinary shareholders and the weighted average number of shares outstanding should be *adjusted for the effects of all dilutive potential ordinary shares.*[8]

This means that *both* the earnings *and* the number of shares used *may* need to be adjusted from the amounts that appear in the profit and loss account and balance sheet.

- **Dilutive** means that earnings in the future may be spread over a larger number of ordinary shares.
- **Potential ordinary shares** are financial instruments that may entitle the holders to ordinary shares.

26.4 The use to shareholders of the EPS

Shareholders use the reported EPS to estimate future growth which will affect the future share price. It is an important measure of growth over time. There are however limitations in its use as a performance measure and for inter-company comparison.

26.4.1 How does a shareholder estimate future growth in the EPS?

The current EPS figure allows a shareholder to assess the wealth-creating abilities of a company. It recognises that the effect of earnings is to add to the individual wealth of shareholders in two ways: first, by the payment of a dividend which transfers cash from the company's control to the shareholder; and, secondly, by retaining earnings in the company for reinvestment, so that there may be increased earnings in the future.

The important thing when attempting to arrive at an estimate is to review the profit and loss account of the current period and identify the earnings that can reasonably be expected to continue. In accounting terminology, you should identify the **maintainable post-tax earnings** that arise in the **ordinary course of business**.

Companies are required to make this easy for the shareholder by disclosing separately, by way of note, any exceptional items and by analysing the profit and loss on trading between discontinuing and continuing activities.

Shareholders can use this information to estimate for themselves the maintainable post-tax earnings, assuming that there is no change in the company's trading activities.

Clearly, in a dynamic business environment it is extremely unlikely that there will be no change in the current business activities. The shareholder needs to refer to any information on capital commitments which appear as a note to the accounts and also to the chairman's statement and any coverage in the financial press. This additional information is used to adjust the existing maintainable earnings figure.

26.4.2 Limitations of EPS as a performance measure

EPS is thought to have a significant impact on the market share price. However, there are limitations to its use as a performance measure.

The limitations affecting the use of EPS as an inter-period performance measure include the following:

- It is based on historical earnings. Management might have made decisions in the past to encourage current earnings growth at the expense of future growth, e.g. by reducing the amount spent on capital investment and research and development. Growth in the EPS cannot be relied on as a predictor of the rate of growth in the future.

- EPS does not take inflation into account. Real growth might be materially different from the apparent growth.

The limitations affecting inter-company comparisons include the following:

- The earnings are affected by management's choice of accounting policies, e.g. the choice of the depreciation method.

- EPS is affected by the capital structure, e.g. changes in number of shares by making bonus issues.

However, the **rate of growth** of EPS is important and this may be compared between different companies and over time within the same company.

26.5 Illustration of the basic EPS calculation

Assume that Watts plc had post-tax profits for 20X1 of £1,250,000 and an issued share capital of £1,500,000 comprising 1,000,000 ordinary shares of 50p each and 1,000,000 £1 10% preference shares. The basic EPS (BEPS) for 20X1 is calculated at £1.15 as follows:

	£000
Profit on ordinary activities after tax	1,250
Less preference dividend	(100)
Profit for the period attributable to ordinary shareholders	1,150

$$\text{BEPS} = £1,150,000 / 1,000,000 \text{ shares} = £1.15$$

Note that it is the *number* of issued shares that is used in the calculation and *not the nominal value* of the shares. The market value of a share is not required for the BEPS calculation.

26.6 Adjusting the number of shares used in the basic EPS calculation

The earnings per share is frequently used by shareholders and directors to demonstrate the growth in a company's performance over time. Care is required to ensure that the number of shares is stated consistently to avoid distortions arising from changes in the capital structure that have changed the number of shares outstanding without a corresponding change in resources during the whole or part of a year. Such changes occur with (a) bonus issues and share splits; (b) new issues and buybacks at full market price during the year; and (c) the bonus element of a rights issue.

We will consider the appropriate treatment for each of these capital structure changes in order to ensure that EPS is comparable between accounting periods.

26.6.1 Bonus issues

A bonus issue, or capitalisation issue as it is also called, arises when a company capitalises reserves to give existing shareholders more shares. In effect, a simple transfer is made from reserves to issued share capital. In real terms, neither the shareholder nor the company is giving or receiving any immediate financial benefit. The process indicates that the reserves will not be available for distribution, but will remain invested in the physical assets of the company. There are, however, more shares.

Treatment in current year

In the Watts plc example, assume that the company increased its shares in issue in 20X1 by the issue of another 1 million shares and achieved identical earnings in 20X1 as in 20X0. The EPS reported for 20X1 would be immediately halved from £1.15 to £0.575. Clearly, this does not provide a useful comparison of performance between the two years.

Restatement of previous year's BEPS

The solution is to restate the EPS for 20X0 that appears in the 20X1 accounts, using the number of shares in issue at 31.12.20X1, i.e. £1,150,000/2,000,000 shares = BEPS of £0.575.

26.6.2 Share splits

When the market value of a share becomes high some companies decide to increase the number of shares held by each shareholder by changing the nominal value of each share. The effect is to reduce the market price per share but for each shareholder to hold the same total value. A share split would be treated in the same way as a bonus issue.

For example, if Watts plc split the 1,000,000 shares of 50p each into 2,000,000 shares of 25p each, the 20X1 BEPS would be calculated using 2,000,000 shares. It would seem that the BEPS had halved in 20X1. This is misleading and the 20X0 BEPS is therefore restated using 2,000,000 shares. The total market capitalisation of Watts plc would remain unchanged. For example, if, prior to the split, each share had a market value of £4 and the company had a total market capitalisation of £4,000,000, after the split each share would have a market price of £2 and the company market capitalisation would remain unchanged at £4,000,000.

26.6.3 New issue at full market value

Selling more shares to raise additional capital should generate additional earnings. In this situation we have a real change in the company's capital and there is no need to adjust any comparative figures. However, a problem arises in the year in which the issue took place. Unless the issue occurred on the first day of the financial year, the new funds would have been *available to generate profits* for only a part of the year. It would therefore be misleading to calculate the EPS figure by dividing the earnings generated during the year by the number of shares in issue at the end of the year. The method adopted to counter this is to use a time-weighted average for the number of shares.

For example, let us assume in the Watts example that the following information is available:

	No. of shares
Shares (nominal value 50p) in issue at 1 January 20X1	1,000,000
Shares issued for cash at market price on 30 September 20X1	500,000

The time-weighted number of shares for EPS calculation at 31 December 20X1 will be:

	No. of shares
Shares in issue for 9 months to date of issue	
$(1,000,000) \times (9/12 \text{ months})$	750,000
Shares in issue for 3 months from date of issue	
$(1,500,000) \times (3/12 \text{ months})$	375,000
Time-weighted shares for use in BEPS calculation	1,125,000

BEPS for 20X1 will be £1,150,000/1,125,000 shares = **£1.02**

26.6.4 Buybacks at market value

Companies are prompted to buy back their own shares when there is a fall in the stock market. The main arguments that companies advance for purchasing their own shares are:

● To reduce the cost of capital when equity costs more than debt.

● The shares are undervalued.

● To return surplus cash to shareholders.

● To increase the apparent rate of growth in BEPS.

The following is an extract from the 2000 Annual Report of EVN AG in respect of both a buyback and a share split, both of which will impact on the EPS figure:

Share buyback programme prolonged
At the 71st Annual General Meeting on January 14, 2000, the EVN Executive Board was given authorisation to purchase company shares up to a maximum of 10% of share capital over 18 months. This authorisation also extends to the resale of the shares via the stock markets. The main aim was the stabilisation of the shareholder structure and the stock market share price. On this basis, the Executive Board decided to repurchase shares initially to the value of 3% of share capital in the period up to September 30, 2000.

Share split
In line with a resolution passed by the 71st Annual General Meeting, EVN AG share capital was reallocated through a 1:3 share split. Shareholders have received three shares for every one in their possession. Share capital, which remains unchanged at Eur 82,878,000 is now divided into 34,200,000 ordinary shares. The measure was aimed at easing the price of the EVN share, thereby stimulating trading and share price development

The impact on the weighted number of shares is explained by the EVN in Note 52 as follows:

Earnings per share
Due to the 1:3 ratio share split, the number of ordinary shares outstanding totalled 34,200,000. Following the deduction of own shares, the weighted number of shares outstanding is 33,974,310 ...

In the UK, examples are found amongst the FTSE 100 companies: e.g. in 1998 NatWest Bank purchased 175,000; Rio Tinto 2.965m; BTR 700,020 ordinary shares.[9]

The shares bought back by the company are included in the basic EPS calculation time apportioned from the beginning of the year to the date of buyback.

For example, let us assume in the Watts example that the following information is available:

	No. of shares
Shares (50p nominal value) in issue at 1 January 20X1	1,000,000
Shares bought back on 31 May 20X1	240,000
Profit attributable to ordinary shares	£1,150,000

The time-weighted number of shares for EPS calculation at 31 December 20X1 will be:

1.1.20X1 Shares in issue for 5 months to date of buyback
$$1,000,000 \times 5/12 \quad 416,667$$

31.5.20X1 Number of shares bought back by company (240,000)

31.12.20X1 Opening capital less shares bought back $760,000 \times 7/12$ 443,333

Time-weighted shares for use in BEPS calculation 860,000

BEPS for 20X1 will be £1,150,000/860,000 shares = **£1.34**

Note that the effect of this buyback has been to increase the BEPS for 20X1 from £1.15 as calculated in 26.5 above. This is a mechanism for management to lift the BEPS and achieve EPS growth.

26.7 Rights issues

A rights issue involves giving existing shareholders 'the right' to buy a set number of additional shares at a price below the fair value which is normally the current market price. A rights issue has two characteristics being both an issue for cash and, because the price is below fair value, a bonus issue. Consequently the rules for *both* a cash issue *and* a bonus issue need to be applied in calculating the weighted average number of shares for the basic EPS calculation.

This is an area where students frequently find difficulty with Step 1 and we will illustrate the rationale without accounting terminology.

The following four steps are required:

Step 1: Calculate the average price of shares before and after a rights issue to identify the amount of the bonus the company has granted.

Step 2: The weighted average number of shares is calculated for current year.

Step 3: The BEPS for current year is calculated.

Step 4: The previous year BEPS is adjusted for the bonus element of the rights issue.

Step 1: Calculate the average price of shares before and after a rights issue to identify the amount of the bonus the company has granted

Assume that Mr Radmand purchased two 50p shares at a market price of £4 each in Watts plc on 1 January 20X1 and that on 2 January 20X1 the company offered a 1:2 rights issue (i.e. one new share for every two shares held) at £3.25 per share.

If Mr Radmand had bought at the market price, the position would simply have been:

		£
2 shares at market price of £4 each on 1 January 20X1	=	8.00
1 share at market price of £4.00 per share on 2 January	=	4.00
Total cost of 3 shares as at 2 January		12.00
Average cost per share unchanged at		4.00

However, this did not happen. Mr Radmand only paid £3.25 for the new share. This meant that the total cost of 3 shares to him was:

		£
2 shares at market price of £4 each on 1 January 20X1	=	8.00
1 share at discounted price of £3.25 on 2 January 20X1	=	3.25
Total cost of 3 shares	=	11.25
Average cost per share (£11.25/3 shares)	=	3.75

The rights issue has had the effect of reducing the cost per share of each of the three shares held by Mr Radmand on 2 January 20X1 by (£4.00 − £3.75) **£0.25 per share**.

The accounting terms applied are:

● Average cost per share after the rights issue (£3.75) is *the theoretical ex-rights value*.
● Amount by which the average cost of each share is reduced (£0.25) is *the bonus element*.

In accounting terminology Step 1 is described as follows:

> Step 1: The bonus element is ascertained by calculating the theoretical ex-rights value, i.e. the £0.25 is ascertained by calculating the £3.75 and deducting it from £4 pre-rights market price

Step 1: Theoretical ex-rights calculation

In accounting terminology, this means that existing shareholders get an element of bonus per share (£0.25) at the same time as the company receives additional capital (£3.25 per new share). The bonus element may be quantified by the calculation of a **theoretical ex-rights price** (£3.75), which is compared with the last market price (£4.00) prior to the issue; the difference is a bonus. The theoretical ex-rights price is calculated as follows:

		£
2 shares at fair value of £4 each prior to rights issue	=	8.00
1 share at discounted rights issue price of £3.25 each	=	3.25
3 shares at fair value after issue (i.e. ex-rights)	=	11.25
The theoretical ex-rights price is £11.25/3 shares	=	3.75
The bonus element is fair value £4 less £3.75	=	0.25

Note that for the calculation of the number of shares and time-weighted number of shares for a bonus issue, share split and issue at full market price per share the market price per share is not relevant. The position for a rights issue is different and the market price becomes a relevant factor in calculating the number of bonus shares.

Step 2: The weighted average number of shares is calculated for current year

Assume that Watts plc made a rights issue of one share for every two shares held on 1 January 20X1.

There would be no need to calculate a weighted average number of shares. The total used in the BEPS calculation would be as follows:

	No. of shares
Shares to date of rights issue:	
1,000,000 shares held for a full year	= 1,000,000
Shares from date of issue:	
500,000 shares held for full year	= 500,000
Total shares for BEPS calculation	1,500,000

However, if a rights issue is made part way through the year, a time-apportionment is required. For example, if we assume that a rights issue is made on 30 September 20X1, the time-weighted number of shares is calculated as follows:

	No. of shares
Shares to date of rights issue:	
1,000,000 shares held for a full year	= 1,000,000
Shares from date of issue:	
500,000 shares held for 3 months (500,000 × 3/12) =	125,000
Weighted average number of shares	1,125,000

Note, however, that the 1,125,000 has not taken account of the fact that the new shares had been issued at less than market price and that the company had effectively granted the existing shareholders a bonus. We saw above that when there has been a bonus issue the number of shares used in the BEPS is increased. We need, therefore, to calculate the number of bonus shares that would have been issued to achieve the reduction in market price from £4.00 to £3.75 per share. This is calculated as follows:

Total market capitalisation was 1,000,000 shares		
@ £4.00 per share	=	£4,000,000
Number of shares that would reduce the		
market price to £3.75	=	£4,000,000/£3.75
	=	1,066,667 shares
Number of shares prior to issue	=	1,000,000
Bonus shares deemed to be issued to existing shareholders	=	66,667
Bonus share for period of 9 months to date of issue		
(66,667/12 × 9)	=	**50,000**

The bonus shares for the 9 months are added to the existing shares and the time apportioned new shares as follows:

		No. of shares
Shares to date of rights issue:		
1,000,000 shares held for a full year	=	1,000,000
Shares from date of issue:		
500,000 shares held for 3 months (500,000 × 3/12)	=	125,000
Weighted average number of shares		1,125,000
Bonus share:		
66,667 shares held for 9 months (66,667/12 × 9)	=	50,000
		1,175,000

The same figure of 1,175,000 can be derived from the following approach using the relationship between the market price of £4.00 and the theoretical ex-rights price of £3.75 to calculate the number of bonus shares as in Figure 26.1.

Figure 26.1 Formula approach to calculating weighted average number of shares

					No. of shares
Shares to date of rights issue:					
No. of shares × Increase by bonus fraction		× Time adjustment			
1,000,000		× 9/12	=	750,000	
Bonus:	$((1{,}000{,}000 \times 4/3.75) - 1{,}000{,}000)$ × 9/12	=	50,000		
Shares from date of issue:					
1,500,000 ×	× 3/12	=	375,000		
Weighted average number of shares				1,175,000	

Step 3: Calculate BEPS for current year

BEPS for 20X1 is then calculated as £1,150,000 / 1,175,000 shares = **£0.979**

Step 4: Adjusting the previous year's BEPS for the bonus element of a rights issue

The 20X0 BEPS of £1.15 needs to be restated, i.e. reduced to ensure comparability with 20X1.

In Step 2 above we calculated that the company had made a bonus issue of 66,667 shares to existing shareholders. In re-calculating the BEPS for 20X0 the shares should be increased by 66,667 to 1,066,667. The restated BEPS for 20X0 is as follows:

Earnings   /   restated number of shares
£1,150,000   /   1,066,667   =   £1.078125

Assuming that the earnings for 20X0 and 20X1 were £1,150,000 in each year the 20X0 BEPS figures will be reported as follows:

As reported in the 20X0 accounts as at 31.12.20X0 =
£1,150,000/1,000,000   =   **£1.15**
As restated in the 20X1 accounts as at 31.12.20X1 =
£1,150,000/1,066,667   =   **£1.08**

The same result is obtained using the bonus element approach by reducing the 20X0 BEPS as follows by multiplying it by:

$$\frac{\text{Theoretical ex-rights fair value per share}}{\text{Fair value per share immediately before the exercise of rights}} = \frac{£3.75}{£4.00}$$

As restated in the 20X1 accounts as at 31.12.20X1 = £1.15 × (3.75/4.00)   =   **£1.08**

26.7.1 Would BEPS for current and previous year be the same if the company had made a separate full market price issue and a separate bonus issue?

This section is included to demonstrate that the BEPS is the same, i.e. £1.08 if we approach the calculation on the assumption that there was a full price issue followed by a bonus issue. This will demonstrate that the BEPS is the same as that calculated using theoretical ex-rights. There are five steps, as follows:

Step 1: Calculate the number of full value and bonus shares in the company's share capital

	No. of shares
Shares in issue *before* bonus	1,000,000
Rights issue at full market price	
(500,000 shares × £3.25 issue price/full market price of £4)	406,250
	1,406,250
Total number of bonus shares	93,750
Total shares	1,500,000

Step 2: Allocate the total bonus shares to the 1,000,000 original shares

(Note that the previous year will be restated using the proportion of original shares: original shares + bonus shares allocated to these original 1,000,000 shares)

Shares in issue before bonus		1,000,000
Bonus issue applicable to pre-rights:		
93,750 bonus shares × (1,000,000/1,406,250) =		
66,667 shares × 9/12 months	= 50,000	
Bonus issue applicable to post-rights		
93,750 bonus shares × (1,000,000/1,406,250) =		
66,667 shares × 3/12 months	= 16,667	
Total bonus shares allocated to existing 1,000,000 shares		66,667
Total original holding plus bonus shares allocated to that holding		1,066,667

Step 3: Time-weight the rights issue and allocate bonus shares to rights shares

Rights issue at full market price	
500,000 shares × (£3.25 issue price/full market price of £4)	
= 406,250 × 3/12 months	101,563
Bonus issue applicable to rights issue:	
93,750 bonus shares × (406,250/1,406,250) = 27,083 shares × 3/12 months	6,770
Weighted average ordinary shares (includes shares from Steps 2 and 3)	1,175,000

Step 4: BEPS calculation for 20X1

Calculate the BEPS using the post-tax profit and weighted average ordinary shares, as follows:

$$\text{20X1 BEPS} = \frac{£1,150,000}{1,175,000} = £0.979$$

Step 5: BEPS restated for 20X0

There were 93,750 bonus shares issued in 20X1. The 20X0 BEPS needs to be reduced, therefore, by the same proportion as applied to the 1,000,000 ordinary shares in 20X1, i.e. 1,000,000:1,066,667

20X0 BEPS × bonus adjustment = restated 20X0 BEPS
i.e. 20X0 = £1.15 × (1,000,000/1,066,667) = £1.08

This approach illustrates the rationale for the time-weighted average and the restatement of the previous year's BEPS. The adjustment using the theoretical ex-rights approach produces the same result and is simpler to apply but the rationale is not obvious.

26.8 Adjusting the earnings and number of shares used in the diluted EPS calculation

We will consider briefly what dilution means and the circumstances which require the weighted average number of shares and the net profit attributable to ordinary shareholders used to calculate BEPS to be adjusted.

26.8.1 What is dilution?

In a modern corporate structure, a number of classes of person such as the holders of convertible bonds, the holders of convertible preference shares, members of share option schemes and share warrant holders may be entitled as at the date of the balance sheet to become equity shareholders at a future date.

If these people exercise their entitlements at a future date, the EPS would be reduced. In accounting terminology, the EPS will have been diluted. The effect on future share price could be significant. Assuming that the share price is a multiple of the EPS figure, any reduction in the figure could have serious implications for the existing shareholders; they need to be aware of the potential effect on the EPS figure of any changes in the way the capital of the company is or will be constituted. This is shown by calculating and disclosing both the basic and 'fully diluted EPS' figures.

IAS 33 therefore requires a diluted EPS figure to be reported using as the denominator potential ordinary shares that are dilutive, i.e. would decrease net profit per share or increase net loss from continuing operations.[10]

26.8.2 Circumstances in which the number of shares used for BEPS is increased

The holders of convertible bonds, the holders of convertible preference shares, members of share option schemes and the holders of share warrants will each be entitled to receive ordinary shares from the company at some future date. Such additional shares, referred to as potential ordinary shares, *may* need to be added to the basic weighted average number *if they are dilutive*. It is important to note that if a company has potential ordinary shares they are not automatically included in the fully diluted EPS calculation. There is a test to apply to see if such shares actually are dilutive – this is discussed further in 26.9 below.

26.8.3 Circumstances in which the earnings used for BEPS are increased

The earnings are increased to take account of the post-tax effects of amounts recognised in the period relating to dilutive potential ordinary shares that will no longer be incurred on their conversion to ordinary shares, e.g. the loan interest payable on convertible loans will no longer be a charge after conversion and earnings will be increased by the post-tax amount of such interest.

26.8.4 Procedure where there are share warrants and options

Where options, warrants or other arrangements exist which involve the issue of shares below their fair value (i.e. at a price lower than the average for the period) then the impact is calculated by notionally splitting the potential issue into shares issued at fair value and shares issued at no value for no consideration.[11] Since shares issued at fair value are not dilutive that number is ignored but the number of shares at no value is employed to calculate the dilution. The calculation is illustrated for Watts plc:

Assume that Watts plc had at 31 December 20X1:

● an issued capital of 1,000,000 ordinary shares of 50p each nominal value;

● post-tax earnings for the year of £1,150,000;

● an average market price per share of £4; and

● share options in existence 500,000 shares issuable in 20X2 at £3.25 per share.

The computation of basic and diluted EPS is as follows:

	Per share	Earnings	Shares
Net profit for 20X1		£1,150,000	
Weighted average shares during 20X1			1,000,000
Basic EPS (£1,150,000/1,000,000)	*1.15*		
Number of shares under option			500,000
Number that would have been issued			
At fair value (500,000 × £3.25)/£4			(406,250)
Diluted EPS	*1.05*	*£1,150,000*	*1,093,750*

26.8.5 Procedure where there are convertible bonds or convertible preference shares

The post-tax profit should be adjusted[12] for:

● any dividends on dilutive potential ordinary shares that have been deducted in arriving at the net profit attributable to ordinary shareholders;

● interest recognised in the period for the dilutive potential ordinary shares; and

● any other changes in income or expense that would result from the conversion of the dilutive potential ordinary shares, e.g. the reduction of interest expense related to convertible bonds results in a higher post-tax profit but this could lead to a consequential increase in expense if there were a non-discretionary employee profit-sharing plan.

26.8.6 Convertible preference shares calculation illustrated for Watts plc

Assume that Watts plc had at 31 December 20X1:

● an issued capital of 1,000,000 ordinary shares of 50p each nominal value;

● post-tax earnings for the year of £1,150,000;

● convertible 8% preference shares of £1 each totalling £1,000,000, convertible at one ordinary share for every five convertible preference shares.

The computation of basic and diluted EPS for convertible bonds is as follows:

	Per share	Earnings	Shares
Post-tax net profit for 20X1 (after interest)		£1,150,000	
Weighted average shares during 20X1			1,000,000
Basic EPS (£1,150,000/1,000,000)	£1.15		
Number of shares resulting from conversion			200,000
Add back the preference dividend paid in 20X1		80,000	
Adjusted earnings and number of shares		1,230,000	1,200,000
Diluted EPS (£1,230,000/1,200,000)	£1.025		

26.8.7 Convertible bonds calculation illustrated for Watts plc

Assume that Watts plc had at 31 December 20X1:

● an issued capital of 1,000,000 ordinary shares of 50p each nominal value;
● post-tax earnings after interest for the year of £1,150,000;
● convertible 10% loan of £1,000,000;
● an average market price per share of £4;

and the convertible loan is convertible into 250,000 ordinary shares of 50p each.
The computation of basic and diluted EPS for convertible bonds is as follows:

	Per share	Earnings	Shares
Post-tax net profit for 20X1 (after interest)		£1,150,000	
Weighted average shares during 20X1			1,000,000
Basic EPS (£1,150,000/1,000,000)	£1.15		
Number of shares resulting from conversion			250,000
Interest expense on convertible loan		100,000	
Tax liability relating to interest expense – Assuming the firm's marginal tax rate is 40%		(40,000)	
Adjusted earnings and number of shares		1,210,000	1,250,000
Diluted EPS (£1,210,000/1,250,000)	£0.97		

26.9 Procedure where there are several potential dilutions

Where there are several potential dilutions the calculation must be done in progressive stages starting with the most dilutive and ending with the least.[13] Any potential 'antidilutive' (i.e. potential issues that would increase earnings per share) are ignored.
Assume that Watts plc had at 31 December 20X1:

● an issued capital of 1,000,000 Ordinary shares of 50p each nominal value;
● post-tax earnings after interest for the year of £1,150,000;
● an average market price per share of £4; and
● share options in existence 500,000 shares
  – exercisable in year 20X2 at £3.25 per share;
● convertible 10% loan of £1,000,000
  – convertible in year 20X2 into 250,000 ordinary shares of 50p each;

● convertible 8% preference shares of £1 each totalling £1,000,000
  – convertible in year 20X4 at 1 ordinary share for every **40** preference shares.

There are two steps in arriving at the diluted EPS, namely:

Step 1: Determine the increase in earnings attributable to ordinary shareholders on conversion of potential ordinary shares;

Step 2: Determine the potential ordinary shares to include in the diluted earnings per share.

Step 1: Determine the increase in earnings attributable to ordinary shareholders on conversion of potential ordinary shares

	Increase in earnings	Increase in number of ordinary shares	Earnings per incremental share
Options Increase in earnings Incremental shares issued for no consideration 500,000 × (£4 − 3.25)/£4	nil	93,750	nil
Convertible preference shares Increase in net profit 8% of £1,000,000	80,000		
Incremental shares 1,000,000/40		25,000	3.20
10% convertible bond Increase in net profit £1,000,000 × 0.10 × (60%) (assumes a marginal tax rate of 40%)	60,000		
Incremental shares 1,000,000/4		250,000	0.24

Step 2: Determine the potential ordinary shares to include in the computation of diluted earnings per share

	Net profit attributable to continuing operations	Ordinary shares	Per share
As reported for BEPS	1,150,000	1,000,000	1.15
Options	—	93,750	
	1,150,000	1,093,750	1.05 dilutive
10% convertible bonds	60,000	250,000	
	1,210,000	1,343,750	0.90 dilutive
Convertible preference shares	80,000	25,000	
	1,290,000	1,368,750	0.94 antidilutive

Since the diluted earnings per share is increased when taking the convertible preference shares into account (from 90p to 94p), the convertible preference shares are antidilutive and are ignored in the calculation of diluted earnings per share. The lowest figure is selected and the diluted EPS will, therefore, be disclosed as 90p. The following illustration is from the 1998 Accounts of the Sony Corporation.

Reconciliation of the differences between basic and diluted net income per share (EPS) for the year ended 31 March 1998:

	Yen (million) income	Shares (000s) weighted average	Yen	Dollars
			\multicolumn{2}{c}{EPS}	
Basic EPS				
Net income available to common stockholders	222,068	398,181	557.7	4.23
Effect of dilutive securities				
Warrants		51		
Convertible bonds	2,271	65,890		
Diluted EPS				
Net income for computation	224,339	464,122	¥483.4	$3.66

This shows that warrants currently carry no interest expense cost and will increase the shares when issued; that convertible bonds currently incur an interest expense of 2,271m yen that will no longer be paid on conversion and that both are dilutive.

26.10 Exercise of conversion rights during financial year

Shares actually issued will be in accordance with the terms of conversion and will be included in the BEPS calculation on a time-apportioned basis from the date of conversion to the end of the financial year.

26.10.1 Calculation of BEPS assuming that convertible loan has been converted and options exercised during the financial year

This is illustrated for the calculation for the year 20X2 accounts of Watts plc as follows. Assume that Watts plc had at 31 December 20X2:

● an issued capital of 1,000,000 ordinary shares of 50p each as at 1 January 20X2;

● convertible 10% loan of £1,000,000 **converted** on 1 April 20X2 into 250,000 ordinary shares of 50p each;

● share options for 500,000 ordinary shares of 50p each **exercised** on 1 August 20X2.

The weighted average number of shares for BEPS is calculated as follows:

1.1.20X2	Ordinary shares in issue	1,000,000	× 3/12	250,000
1.4.20X2	Issued on conversion of the 10% loan	250,000		
		1,250,000	× 4/12	416,667
1.8.20X2	Issued on exercise of options	500,000		
		1,750,000	× 5/12	729,167
31.12.20X2 Weighted average number of shares				**1,395,834**

26.11 Disclosure requirements of IAS 33

The standard[14] requires the following disclosures:

For the current year:

- Companies should disclose the basic and diluted EPS figures for profit or loss from continuing operations and for profit or loss with equal prominence, whether positive or negative, on the face of the income statement for each class of ordinary share that has a different right to share in the profit for the period.
- The amounts used as the numerators in calculating basic and diluted earnings per share, and a reconciliation of those amounts to the net profit or loss for the period.
- The weighted average number of shares used as the denominator in calculating the basic and diluted earnings per share and a reconciliation of these denominators to each other.

For the previous year (if there has been a bonus issue, rights issue or share split):

- BEPS and diluted EPS should be adjusted retrospectively.

26.11.1 Alternative EPS figures

In the UK the Institute of Investment Management and Research (IIMR) published Statement of Investment Practice No. 1, entitled *The Definition of Headline Earnings*,[15] in which it identified two purposes for producing an EPS figure:

- as a measure of the company's **maintainable earnings** capacity, suitable in particular for forecasts and for inter-year comparisons, and for use on a per share basis in the calculation of the price/earnings ratio;
- as a factual headline figure for historical earnings, which can be a benchmark figure for the **trading outcome for the year**.

The Institute recognised that the maintainable earnings figure required exceptional or non-continuing items to be eliminated, which meant that, in view of the judgement involved in adjusting the historical figures, the calculation of maintainable earnings figures could not be put on a standardised basis. It took the view that there was a need for an earnings figure, calculated on a standard basis, which could be used as an unambiguous reference point among users. The Institute accordingly defined a **headline earnings** figure for that purpose.

26.11.2 Definition of IIMR headline figure

The Institute criteria for the headline figure are that it should be:

1 **A measure of the trading performance**, which means that it will:
    (a) *exclude* capital items such as profits/losses arising on the sale or revaluation of fixed assets; profits/losses arising on the sale or termination of a discontinued operation and amortisation charges for goodwill, because these are likely to have a different volatility from trading outcomes;
    (b) *exclude* provisions created for capital items such as profits/losses arising on the sale of fixed assets or on the sale or termination of a discontinued operation; and
    (c) *include* abnormal items with a clear note and profits/losses arising on operations discontinued during the year.

2 **Robust**, in that the result could be arrived at by anyone using the financial report produced in accordance with IAS 1 and IFRS 5.

3 **Factual**, in that it will not have been adjusted on the basis of subjective opinions as to whether a cost is likely to continue in the future.

The strength of the Institute's approach is that, by defining a headline figure, it is producing a core definition. Additional earnings, earnings per share and price/earnings ratio figures can be produced by individual analysts, refining the headline figure in the light of their own evaluation of the quality of earnings.

26.11.3 IAS 33 Disclosure requirements

If an enterprise discloses an additional EPS figure using a reported component of net profit other than net profit for the period attributable to ordinary shareholders, IAS 33 requires that:

● It must still use the weighted average number of shares determined in accordance with IAS 33.

● If the net profit figure used is not a line item in the income statement, then a reconciliation should be provided between the figure and a line item which is reported in the income statement.

● The additional EPS figures cannot be disclosed on the face of the income statement.

The extract in Figure 26.2 from the De La Rue 2003 Annual Report is an example of an IIMR-based reconciliation (FRS 14 is the UK equivalent of IAS 33).

Figure 26.2   Reconciliation of earnings per share

	2003 Pence per share	2002 Pence per share
As calculated from FRS 14	(4.3)	40.7
Profit on the disposal of discontinued operations	—	(0.7)
Profit on sale of investments	—	(12.0)
Loss on impairment of investment	0.7	
Loss/(profit) on disposal of fixed assets held for resale	0.2	(0.1)
Amortisation of goodwill	10.4	1.5
Headline earnings per share as defined by IIMR	**7.0**	**29.4**
Reorganisation costs	11.9	5.0
Headline earnings per share before items shown above	**18.9**	**34.4**

26.11.4 Will companies include an alternative EPS figure?

In 1994 Coopers & Lybrand surveyed 100 top UK companies.[16] The survey found that 54 companies reported additional EPS figures, which varied from 62% lower to 278% higher than the reported figure. The basis of the most frequently used additional EPS figures was as follows:

Basis of additional EPS	*No. of companies*
IIMR headline EPS	16
Adjusted for exceptional items reported below operating profit	16
Adjusted for all exceptional items above and below operating profit	13

A number of other bases were used. Commenting on the choice of basis, the authors stated:

> This may result in stability for an individual company, but they certainly do not give rise to comparability across companies. To our surprise, only 16 of the 54 companies used the IIMR headline figures as their EPS. The remainder evidently preferred to tell their own story despite the analysts' announcement of the basis on which they will perform their analysis.

The survey, therefore, also tested the hypothesis that companies would produce an alternative EPS figure where the alternative exceeded the standard figure. The outcome suggested that companies show additional EPS figures primarily to stabilise their earnings figures and not merely to enhance their reported performance.

An interesting recent research study (Young-soo Choi, M. Walker and S. Young, 'Bridging the earnings GAAP', *Accountancy*, February 2005, pp. 77–78) supports the finding that the additional EPS figures provide a better indication of future operating earnings one-year-ahead.

26.12 The Improvement Project

IAS 33 was one of the IASs revised by the IASB as part of its Improvement Project. The objective of the revised standard was to continue to prescribe the principles for the determination and presentation of earnings per share so as to improve comparisons between different entities and different reporting periods. The Board's main objective when revising was to provide additional guidance on selected complex issues such as the effects of contingently issuable shares and purchased put and call options. However, the Board did not reconsider the fundamental approach to the determination and presentation of earnings per share contained in the original IAS 33.

Summary

The increased globalisation of stock market transactions places an increasing level of importance on international comparisons. The EPS figure is regarded as a key figure with a widely held belief that management performance could be assessed by the comparative growth rate in this figure. This has meant that the earnings available for distribution, which was the base for calculating EPS, became significant. Management action has been directed towards increasing this figure: sometimes by healthy organic growth; sometimes by buying-in earnings by acquisition; sometimes by cosmetic manipulation, e.g. structuring transactions so that all or part of the cost bypassed the income statement; and at other times by the selective exercise of judgement, e.g. underestimating provisions. Regulation by the IASB has been necessary.

IAS 33 permits the inclusion of an EPS figure calculated in a different way, provided that there is a reconciliation of the two figures. Analysts have expressed the view that EPS should be calculated to show the future maintainable earnings and in the UK have arrived at a formula designed to exclude the effects of unusual events and of activities discontinued during the period.

REVIEW QUESTIONS

1 Explain: (i) basic earnings per share; (ii) diluted earnings per share; (iii) potential ordinary shares; and (iv) limitation of EPS as a performance measure.

2 Why are issues at full market value treated differently from rights issues?

3 In the 1999 Annual Report and Accounts of Associated British Ports Holdings plc, the directors report earnings per share – basic, and earnings per share – underlying, as follows:

	Underlying	Goodwill amortisation	Exceptional items	Total 1999	1998
	£m	£m	£m	£m	£m
Profit on ordinary activities after tax attributable to shareholders	86.3	(3.8)	(76.9)	5.6	84.1
Dividends	(39.4)	—	—	(39.4)	(37.2)
Retained profit/(loss)	46.9	(3.8)	(76.9)	(33.8)	46.9
Earnings per share – basic	24.6	(1.1)	(21.9)	**1.6p**	22.4p
Earnings per share – underlying				**24.6p**	22.4p

Note 11 Reconciliation of profit used for calculating the basic and underlying earnings per share:

	1999 £m	1998 £m
Profit for year attributable to shareholders for calculating basic earnings per share	**5.6**	84.1
Amortisation of goodwill	3.8	2.0
Impairment of goodwill	60.6	—
Impairment of fixed assets	19.6	—
Profit on sale of fixed assets	(3.3)	(1.2)
Withdrawal from a discontinued business	—	(1.2)
Attributable tax	—	0.3
Profit for year attributable to shareholders for calculating the underlying earnings per share	**86.3**	84.0

The directors state that the underlying basis is a more appropriate basis for comparing performance between periods.

Discuss the relevance of the basic figure of 1.6p reported for 1999.

4 When disclosing EPS, how should a company deal with the issue of a separate class of equity shares which do not rank for any dividend in the current accounting period, but will do so in the future?

5 The following note appeared in the 2002 Annual Report of Mercer International Inc.

	2002	2001	2000
Net income (loss) available to shareholders of beneficial interest	€(6,322)	€(2,823)	€32,013
BEPS weighted average number of shares outstanding – basic	16,774,515	16,874,899	16,778,962
Effect of dilutive securities:			
Options	—	—	365,528
Weighted average number of shares outstanding – diluted	16,774,515	16,874,899	17,144,490

For 2002 and 2001 options and warrants were not included in the computation of diluted earnings per share because they were antidilutive. Warrants were not dilutive in 2000.

Explain

(a) why the BEPS shares were weighted and

(b) what is meant by antidilutive.

6 Would the following items justify the calculation of a separate EPS figure under IAS 33?

(a) A charge of £1,500m that appeared in the accounts, described as additional provisions relating to exposure to countries experiencing payment difficulties.

(b) Costs of £14m that appeared in the accounts, described as redundancy and other non-recurring costs.

(c) Costs of £62.1m that appeared in the accounts, described as cost of rationalisation and withdrawal from business activities.

(d) The following items that appeared in the accounts:

(i) Profit on sale of property	£80m
(ii) Reorganisation costs	£35m
(iii) Disposal and discontinuance of hotels	£659m

7 Income smoothing describes the management practice of maintaining a steady profit figure.

(a) Explain why managers might wish to smooth the earnings figure. Give three examples of how they might achieve this.

(b) It has been suggested that debt creditors are most at risk from income smoothing by the managers. Discuss why this should be so.

8 In connection with IAS 33 *Earnings per Share*:

(a) Define the profit used to calculate basic and diluted EPS.

(b) Explain the relationship between EPS and the price/earnings (P/E) ratio. Why may the P/E ratio be considered important as a stock market indicator?

9 The following is an extract from the FirstGroup 2004 Annual Report:

Profit for adjusted basic EPS calculation	£112.0	£27.3	£111.8
Depreciation	£103.0	£25.1	£99.2
Profit for adjusted cash EPS calculation	£215.0	£52.4	£211.0

Discuss the relevance of an adjusted cash EPS.

EXERCISES

An outline solution is provided in the Appendix at the end of the text for exercises marked with an asterisk (*).

* Question 1

Alpha plc had an issued share capital of 2,000,000 ordinary shares at 1 January 20X1. The nominal value was 25p and the market value £1 per share. On 31 March 20X1 the company made a rights issue of 1 for 4 at a price of 80p per share. The post-tax earnings were £4.5m and £5m for 20X0 and 20X1 respectively.

Required: (i) Calculate the basic earnings per share for 20X1.
(ii) Restate the basic earnings per share for 20X0.

* Question 2

Beta Ltd had the following changes during 20X1:

1 January	1,000,000 shares of 50c each
31 March	500,000 shares of 50c each issued at full market price of $5 per share
30 April	Bonus issue made of 1 for 2
31 August	1,000,000 shares of 50c each issued at full market price of $5.50 per share
31 October	Rights issue of 1 for 3. Rights price was $2.40 and market value was $5.60 per share.

Required:

Calculate the time-weighted average number of shares for the basic earnings per share denominator. Note that adjustments will be required for time, the bonus issue and the bonus element of the rights issue.

* Question 3

The computation and publication of earnings per share (EPS) figures by listed companies are governed by IAS 33 *Earnings per Share*.

Nottingham Industries plc
Income statement for the year ended 31 March 20X6
(extract from draft unaudited accounts)

		£000
Profit on ordinary activities before taxation	(Note 2)	1,000
Tax on profit on ordinary activities	(Note 3)	(420)
Profit on ordinary activities after taxation		580

Notes:

1 Called-up share capital of Nottingham Industries plc:

In issue at 1 April 20X5:

16,000,000 ordinary shares of 25p each
1,000,000 10% cumulative preference shares of £1 each

1 July 20X5: Bonus issue of ordinary shares, 1 for 5.
1 October 20X5: Market purchase of 500,000 of own ordinary shares at a price of £1.00 per share.

2 In the draft accounts for the year ended 31 March 20X6, 'profit on ordinary activities before taxation' is arrived at after charging or crediting the following items:
(i) accelerated depreciation on fixed assets, £80,000;
(ii) book gain on disposal of a major operation, £120,000.

3 Profit after tax included a write-back of deferred taxation (accounted for by the liability method) in consequence of a reduction in the rate of corporation tax from 45% in the financial year 20X4 to 40% in the financial year 20X5.

4 The following were charged:
(i) Provision for bad debts arising on the failure of a major customer, £150,000. Other bad debts have been written off or provided for in the ordinary way.
(ii) Provision for loss through expropriation of the business of an overseas subsidiary by a foreign government, £400,000.

5   In the published accounts for the year ended 31 March 20X5, basic EPS was shown as 2.2p; fully diluted EPS was the same figure.

6   Dividends paid totalled £479,000.

Required:

(a) On the basis of the facts given, compute the basic EPS figures for 20X6 and restate the basic EPS figure for 20X5, stating your reasons for your treatment of items that may affect the amount of EPS in the current year.

(b) Compute the diluted earnings per share for 20X6 assuming that on 1 January 20X6 executives of Nottingham plc were granted options to take up a total of 200,000 unissued ordinary shares at a price of £1.00 per share: no options had been exercised at 31 March 20X6. The average fair value of the shares during the year was £1.10.

(c) Give your opinion as to the usefulness (to the user of financial statements) of the EPS figures that you have computed.

* Question 4

The following information relates to Simrin plc for the year ended 31 December 20X0:

	£
Turnover	700,000
Operating costs	476,000
Trading profit	224,000
Net interest payable	2,000
	222,000
Exceptional charges	77,000
	145,000
Tax on ordinary activities	66,000
Profit after tax	79,000

Simrin plc had 100,000 ordinary shares of £1 each in issue throughout the year. Simrin plc has in issue warrants entitling the holders to subscribe for a total of 50,000 shares in the company. The warrants may be exercised after 31 December 20X5 at a price of £1.28 per share. The average fair value of shares was £1.10. The company had paid an ordinary dividend of £15,000 and a preference dividend of £9,000.

Required:

(a) Calculate the basic EPS for Simrin plc for the year ended 31 December 20X0, in accordance with best accounting practice.

(b) Calculate the diluted EPS figure, to be disclosed in the statutory accounts of Simrin plc in respect of the year ended 31 December 20X0.

(c) Briefly comment on the need to disclose a diluted EPS figure and on the relevance of this figure to the shareholders.

(d) In the past, the single most important indicator of financial performance has been earnings per share. In what way has the profession attempted to destroy any reliance on a single figure to measure and predict a company's earnings, and how successful has this attempt been?

* Question 5

Gamma plc had an issued share capital at 1 April 20X0 of:

● £200,000 made up of 20p shares.
● 50,000 £1 convertible preference shares receiving a dividend of £2.50 per share
    – these shares were convertible in 20X6 on the basis of 1 ordinary share for 1 preference share.

There was also loan capital of:

● £250,000 10% convertible loans
    – the loan was convertible in 20X9 on the basis of 500 shares for each £1,000 of loan;
    – the tax rate was 40%.

Earnings for the year ended 31 March 20X1 were £5,000,000 after tax.

Required:
(a) Calculate the diluted EPS for 20X1.
(b) Calculate the diluted EPS assuming that the convertible preference shares were receiving a dividend of £6 per share instead of £2.50.

Question 6

Delta NV has share capital of €1m in shares of €0.25 each. At 31 May 20X9 shares had a market value of €1.1 each. On 1 June 20X9 the company makes a rights issue of 1 share for every 4 held at €0.6 per share. Its profits were €500,000 in 20X9 and €440,000 in 20X8. The year-end is 30 November.

Required:
Calculate
(a) the theoretical ex-rights price
(b) the bonus issue factor
(c) the basic earnings per share for 20X8
(d) the basic earnings per share for 20X9.

Question 7

The following information is available for X Ltd for the year ended 31 May 20X1:

Net profit after tax and minority interest	£18,160,000
Ordinary shares of £1 (fully paid)	£40,000,000
Average fair value for year of ordinary shares	£1.50

1   Share options have been granted to directors giving them the right to subscribe for ordinary share between 20X1 and 20X3 at £1.20 per share. The options outstanding at 31 May 20X1 were 2,000,000 in number.

2   The company has £20 million of 6% convertible loan stock in issue. The terms of conversion of the loan stock per £200 nominal value of loan stock at the date of issue were:

Conversion date	No. of shares
31 May 20X0	24
31 May 20X1	23
31 May 20X2	22

No loan stock has as yet been converted. The loan stock had been issued at a discount of 1%.

3 There are 1,600,000 convertible preference shares in issue. The cumulative dividend is 10p per share and each preference share can convert into two ordinary shares. The preference shares can be converted in 20X2.

4 Assume a corporation tax rate of 33% when calculating the effect on income of converting the convertible loan stock.

Required:
(a) Calculate the diluted EPS according to IAS 33.
(b) Discuss why there is a need to disclose diluted earnings per share.

References

1 J. Day, 'The use of annual reports by UK investment analysts', *Accounting Business Research*, Autumn 1986, pp. 295–307.
2 London Business School, *Risk Measurement Service*, April–June 1998, ISBN 0361-3344.
3 IAS 33 *Earnings per Share*, IASB, 2003.
4 *Ibid.*, para. 10.
5 *Ibid.*, para. 12.
6 *Ibid.*, para. 26.
7 *Ibid.*, para. 5.
8 *Ibid.*, para. 31.
9 *Accountancy*, November 1998, p. 73.
10 IAS 33, para. 31.
11 *Ibid.*, para. 45.
12 *Ibid.*, para. 33.
13 *Ibid.*, para. 44.
14 *Ibid.*, paras 66 and 70.
15 Statement of Investment Practice No. 1, *The Definition of Headline Earnings*, IIMR, 1993.
16 Coopers and Lybrand, *EPS and Exceptional Items*, 1994.

CHAPTER **27**

Cash flow statements

27.1 Introduction

In this chapter we consider why funds flow statements came to be replaced by cash flow statements in recent years. We analyse the application of IAS 7 and the extent to which it gives users of financial statements more information about the solvency and liquidity of companies, and enables them to make comparisons between firms.

27.2 Development of cash flow statements

In 1977 IAS 7 *Statement of Changes in Financial Position* was issued, requiring companies to publish a funds flow statement with the annual accounts.[1] The funds flow statement explained the changes between the opening and closing balance sheet by classifying the changes in fixed assets and long-term capital under two headings:

- **source of funds**, comprising funds from operating and other sources such as sale of fixed assets and issue of shares and loans; and

- **application of funds**, comprising tax paid, dividends paid, fixed asset acquisitions and long-term capital repayments. The difference represented the net change in working capital.

In 1987 SFAS 95 *Statement of Cash Flows* was published in the USA.[2] It concluded that a cash flow statement should replace the funds flow statement, concentrating on **changes in cash** rather than **changes in working capital**. The cash flow statement should represent all of a company's cash receipts and cash payments during a period. There was also widespread support for the belief that **cash flow statements were more decision-useful** and that they should replace the funds flow statement.

In 1992 the IASC issued IAS 7 (revised), which appeared to be based on SFAS 95.[3] It proposed that cash flow statements should replace funds flow statements in financial reporting. Guidelines were given about reporting cash flows, appropriate formats and minimum disclosure.

A report by the ICAEW Research Board and the ICAS Research Advisory Committee, entitled *The Future Shape of Financial Reports*, recommended a number of reporting reforms.[4] One of the main areas for improvement was reporting a company's cash position. Professor Arnold wrote:

> little attention is paid to the reporting entity's cash or liquidity position. Cash is the lifeblood of every business entity. The report ... advocates that companies should provide a cash flow statement ... preferably using the direct method.[5]

An important issue is the relationship of cash flows to the existing financial statements. As the following quotation illustrates, statements of cash flows are not a substitute for the income statement:

> The emphasis on cash flows, and the emergence of the statement of cash flows as an important financial report, does not mean that operating cash flows are a substitute for, or are more important than, net income. In order to analyse financial statements correctly we need to consider **both** operating cash flows and net income.[6]

The overwhelming reason for replacing a funds flow statement with a cash flow statement was that the latter provides more relevant and useful information to users of financial statements. When used in conjunction with the accrual-adjusted data included in the income statement and the balance sheet, cash flow information helps to assess liquidity, viability and financial flexibility. This view is held by Henderson and Maness, who stress the need to integrate different types of analysis to achieve an overall assessment of an organisation's financial health: 'cash flow analysis should be used in conjunction with traditional ratio analysis to get a clear picture of the financial position of a firm'.[7]

The financial viability and survival prospects of any organisation rest on the ability to generate net positive cash flows. Cash flows help to reduce an organisation's dependency on external funding, service existing debts and obligations, finance investments, and reward the investors with an acceptable dividend policy. The end-result is that, independent of reported profits, if an organisation is unable to generate sufficient cash, it will eventually fail.

Cash flow statements can also be used to evaluate any economic decisions related to the financial performance of an organisation. Decisions made on the basis of expected cash flows can be monitored and reviewed whenever additional cash flow information becomes available.

Finally, the quality of information contained in cash flow statements should be better than that contained in funds flow statements because it is more consistent and neutral. Cash flows can be reliably traced to when a transaction occurred, while funds flows are distorted by the accounting judgements inherent in accrual-adjusted data.[8]

The following extract from Heath and Rosenfield's article on solvency is a useful conclusion to our analysis of the benefits of cash flow statements:

> Solvency is a money or cash phenomenon. A solvent company is one with adequate cash to pay its debts; an insolvent company is one with inadequate cash ... Any information that provides insight into the amounts, timings and certainty of a company's future cash receipts and payments is useful in evaluating solvency. Statements of past cash receipts and payments are useful for the same basic reason that income statements are useful in evaluating profitability: both provide a basis for predicting future performance.[9]

27.3 Applying IAS 7 (revised) *Cash Flow Statements*

27.3.1 IAS 7 issued

IAS 7 was revised and renamed in 1992 by the IASC to require companies to issue a cash flow statement. Its objective was to require companies to provide standardised reports on their cash generation and cash absorption for a period. Its principal feature was the analysis of cash flows under **three** standard headings of 'operating activities', 'investing activities' and 'financing activities'. Accounting commentators said that information on cash is an essential part of a company's financial statements.

27.3.2 Method of presenting cash flows from operating activities

IAS 7 permitted either the direct or indirect method of presentation to be used.

● The **direct** method reports cash inflows and outflows directly, starting with the major categories of gross cash receipts and payments. This means that cash flows such as receipts from customers and payments to suppliers are stated separately within the operating activities.

● The **indirect** method starts with the profit before tax and then adjusts this figure for non-cash items such as depreciation and changes in working capital.

The two methods provide different types of information to the users. The indirect method applies changes in working capital to net income.

The principal advantage of the indirect method is that it highlights the differences between operating profit and net cash flow from operating activities. Many users of financial statements believe that such a reconciliation is essential to give an indication of the quality of the reporting entity's earnings. Some investors and creditors assess future cash flows by estimating future income and then allowing for accruals adjustments; thus information about past accruals adjustments may be useful to help estimate future adjustments.

The direct method demonstrates more of the qualities of a true cash flow statement because it provides more information about the sources and uses of cash. This information is not available elsewhere and helps in the estimation of future cash flows.

The principal advantage of the direct method is that it shows operating cash receipts and payments. Knowledge of the specific sources of cash receipts and the purposes for which cash payments were made in past periods may be useful in assessing future cash flows.

When is the direct method beneficial?

One such time is when the user is attempting to predict bankruptcy or future liquidation of the company. A research study looking at the cash flow differences between failed and non-failed companies[10] established that seven cash flow variables and suggested ratios captured statistically significant differences between failed and non-failed firms as much as five years prior to failure. The study further showed that the research findings supported the use of a direct cash flow statement and the authors commented:

> An indirect cash flow statement will not provide a number of the cash flow variables for which we found significant differences between bankrupt and non-bankrupt companies. Thus, using an indirect cash flow statement could lead to ignoring important information about creditworthiness.

The major deficiency therefore with the IASC approach is that few, if any, companies would elect to use the direct method if it was more likely than the indirect method to indicate that the company was at risk of failing!

Cash equivalents

IAS 7 recognised that companies' cash management practices vary in the range of short- to medium-term deposits and instruments in their cash and near-cash portfolio. The standard standardised the treatment of near-cash items by applying the following definition when determining whether items should be aggregated with cash in the cash flow statement:

> Cash equivalents are short-term, highly liquid investments which are readily convertible into known amounts of cash and which are subject to an insignificant risk of changes in value.

Near-cash items falling outside this definition were reported under the heading of 'investing activities'.

There has been criticism over the definition of cash equivalents. IAS 7 does give some guidance that a cash equivalent should normally be within three months of maturity at the date of acquisition, but this guidance can create problems. For example, it is not always commercially appropriate to deal with deposits over three months as investing activities as opposed to cash equivalents. The effect of the definition of cash equivalents is to split the activities of corporate treasury departments between investing cash flows and increases or decreases in cash. If cash is put on deposit for more than three months it is treated as a cash outflow under investing, whereas if deposited for less than three months it is not shown as actually being a cash flow. This makes analysis of the movements in cash and cash equivalents potentially misleading.

27.4 IAS 7 (revised) format of cash flow statements

The IAS 7 format is set out below and its application to Tyro Bruce illustrated.

27.4.1 The IAS 7 format is as follows:

Cash flows from operating activities	
Net profit before tax	x
Adjustments for:	
Depreciation	x
Investment income	(x)
Interest expense	<u>x</u>
Operating profit before working capital changes	x
Increase in trade and other receivables	(x)
Decrease in inventories	x
Decrease in trade payables	<u>(x)</u>
Cash generated from operations	x
Interest paid*	(x)
Income taxes paid	<u>(x)</u>
Cash flow before extraordinary item	x
Proceeds from earthquake disaster settlement	x
Net cash from operating activities	x
Cash flows from investing activities	
Acquisition of subsidiary net of cash acquired (note a)	(x)
Purchase of property, plant and equipment	(x)
Proceeds from sale of equipment	x
Interest received*	x

Dividends received*		x	
Net cash used in investing activities			(x)
Cash flows from financing activities			
Proceeds from issuance of share capital		x	
Proceeds from long-term borrowings		x	
Payment of finance lease liabilities		(x)	
Dividends paid*		(x)	
Net cash used in financing activities			(x)
Net increase in cash and cash equivalents			x
Cash and cash equivalents at the beginning of the period			x
Cash and cash equivalents at the end of the period			x

* The position in the cash flow statement for these items is not precisely defined in IAS 7, and choice exists in the presentation. Interest paid, and interest and dividends received, could either be classified as operating cash flows or as financing (for interest paid) and investing cash flows (for the receipts). Dividends paid could either be presented as financing cash flows or as operating cash flows. However, it is a requirement that whichever presentation is adopted by an enterprise should be consistently applied from year to year.

27.4.2 Tyro Bruce accounts

The income statement for the year ended 31 March 20X2 and balance sheets as at 31 March 20X1 and 20X2 (including the fixed asset schedule) for Tyro Bruce with explanatory notes to explain how each item is classified in the cash flow statement are as follows:

Income statement of Tyro Bruce for the year ended 31 March 20X2

	£000	*How treated in cash flow statement*	
Sales	6,000		
Cost of sales	4,000		
Gross profit	2,000		
Net operating expenses	(986)		
Operating profit before interest and tax	1,014		
Profit on sale of land	80		
Loss on sale of plant	(54)		
(1) Profit before interest and tax	**1,040**	**(1) Operating activities section starts here**	**(+1,040)**
(2) Interest payable	(40)	**(2)** Operating activities	(–40)
Profit before tax	1,000		
(3) Tax	(400)	**(3)** Operating activities	(–400)
Profit after tax	600		

Balance sheets for 20X1 and 20X2

How treated in cash flow statement

	20X2 £000	20X1 £000	Change £000		
Intangible non-current assets					
(4) R&D written off	360	840	480	(4) Operating activities – non-cash expense	(+480)
(5) Tangible assets	4,596	4,136	460	(5) The figure of 460 is not used. Refer to the PPE schedule for **Additions**	
(6) Inventory	2,400	1,600	800	(6) Operating activities	(–800)
(7) Receivables	1,800	1,360	440	(7) Operating activities	(–440)
(8) Government securities	30	—	30	(8) Investing activities (assumed not cash equivalents)	(+30)
(9) Cash	30	20	10	(9) Cash and cash equivalents increase	(10)
(10) Payables	1,360	1,080	280	(10) Operating activities	(+280)
(11) Taxation	340	380	40	(11) Operating activities	(–40)
(12) Dividends	—	140	140	(12) Financing activities	(–140)
(13) Overdraft	1,116	1,356	240	(13) Cash and cash equivalents increase	(240)
	6,400	5,000			
(14) Ordinary shares	2,000	1,600	400	(14) Financing activities	(+400)
(15) 7% preference shares	2,000	2,000		(15)	no change
(16) Share premium account	400	100	300	(16) Financing activities	(+300)
(17) Revaluation reserve	400	200		(17)	non-cash movement
(18) Retained profits at 31.3.20X1	700	700		(18)	no change
(19) Retained profit for year	600	—		(19) Already included in operating activities	
(20) 10% debentures 20X0–04	300	400	100	(20) Financing activities	(–100)
	6,400	5,000			

The non-cash items required for the reconciliation are calculated as follows:

- Depreciation is given in schedule of fixed assets
- R&D amortised obtained from change in balance sheets: £840,000 – £360,000 = £480,000
- Profit on sale of land is an exceptional item in the income statement: £80,000
- Loss on sale of plant is an exceptional item in the income statement: £54,000

The Property, plant and equipment schedule for Tyro Bruce as at 31 March 20X2 is as follows:

	Land £000	Buildings £000	Plant £000	Vehicles £000	Total £000	*How treated in cash flow statement*
At cost 31.3.20X1	3,200	800	840	200	5,040	
(1) Additions	800	200	120		1,120	(1) Investing activities (–1,120)
(2) Revaluations	200				200	(2) Non-cash movement
	4,200	1,000	960	200	6,360	
(3) Disposals	600	—	240	—	840	(3) Used to calculate proceeds
At cost/valuation 31.3.20X2	3,600	1,000	720	200	5,520	for investing activities
Depreciation						
At 31.3.20X1		384	400	120	904	
(4) Income statement charge		20	144	40	204	(4) Operating activities (+204)
		404	544	160	1,108	
(5) Disposals		—	184	—	184	(5) Used to calculate proceeds
At 31.3.20X2	3,600	404	360	160	924	for investing activities
Net book value 20X1	3,200	416	440	80	4,136	
Net book value 20X2	3,600	596	360	40	4,596	

The sales proceeds from the sale of land and plant are calculated for the investing activities section as follows:

- Cost £600,000 in Property, plant and equipment schedule + Profit on disposal £80,000 = £680,000 proceeds
- Cost £240,000 – £184,000 depreciation – Loss on disposal £54,000 = £2,000 proceeds

One criticism of IAS 7 was that it did not standardise on the use of the direct method. The 'operating activities' of the cash flow statement are presented differently under the direct method. Actual cash flows from customers and to suppliers are disclosed as follows:

	£000
Cash received from customers (Working 1)	5,560
Cash payments to suppliers (Working 2)	(4,822)
Interest paid	(40)
Taxation paid	(440)
Net cash inflow from operations	258

Working 1: Sales £6,000,000 – Receivables increase £440,000

Working 2: Cost of sales £4,000,000 – Trade payables increase £280,000 + Inventory increase £800,000 – Depreciation £204,000 – R&D £480,000 – Loss on sale of plant £54,000 + Profit on sale of land £80,000 + Selling and distribution expenses £600,000 + Administration costs £360,000

27.4.3 Tyro Bruce cash flow statement

The cash flow statement can now be prepared for Tyro Bruce for the year ended 31.3.20X2 (using indirect method).

	£000	£000
Cash flows from operating activities		
Net profit before tax	1,000	
Adjustments for:		
Depreciation	204	
R&D amortisation charge	480	
Loss on sale of plant	54	
Profit on sale of land	(80)	
Interest expense	40	
Operating profit before working capital changes	1,698	
Increase in trade and other receivables	(440)	
Increase in inventories	(800)	
Increase in trade payables	280	
Cash generated from operations	738	
Interest paid (*from income statement*)	(40)	
Income taxes paid [380 + 400 – 340]	(440)	
Net cash from operating activities		258
Cash flows from investing activities		
Purchase of property, plant and equipment	(1,120)	
Proceeds from sale of equipment and land	682	
Purchase of government securities	(30)	
Net cash used in investing activities		(468)
Cash flows from financing activities		
Proceeds from issuance of share capital	700	

Repayment of debentures	(100)	
Dividends paid (*from income statement*)	(140)	
Net cash from financing activities		460
Net increase in cash and cash equivalents		250
Cash and cash equivalents at the beginning of the period		(1,336)
Cash and cash equivalents at the end of the period		(1,086)

27.4.4 Additional notes required by IAS 7

As well as the presentation on the face of the cash flow statement IAS 7 requires notes to the cash flow statement to help the user understand the information. The notes that are required are as follows:

Major non-cash transactions

If the entity has entered into major non-cash transactions that are therefore not represented on the face of the cash flow statement sufficient further information to understand the transactions should be provided in a note to the financial statements. Examples of major non-cash transactions might be:

● the acquisition of assets by way of finance leases;

● the conversion of debt to equity.

Components of cash and cash equivalents

An enterprise must disclose the components of cash and cash equivalents and reconcile these into the totals in the balance sheet. An example of a suitable disclosure in the case of Tyro Bruce is:

	20X2	20X1
Cash	30	20
Overdraft	(1,116)	(1,356)
Cash and cash equivalents	(1,086)	(1,336)

Disclosure must also be given on restrictions on the use by the group of any cash and cash equivalents held by the enterprise. These restrictions might apply if, for example, cash was held in foreign countries and could not be remitted back to the parent company.

Segmental information

IAS 7 encourages enterprises to disclose information about operating, investing and financing cash flows for each business and geographical segment. This disclosure is optional, but if it is given enterprises need not disclose depreciation and other non-cash expenses information as required by IAS 14.

27.5 Consolidated cash flow statements

A consolidated cash flow statement differs from that for a single company in two respects: there are additional items; and adjustments may be required to the actual amounts.

27.5.1 Additional items

Additional items appear in the operating, investing and financing sections of the cash flow statement as follows:

1 **Operating activities**
- Adjust for non-cash income:
  - Share of profit of associate

2 **Investing activities**
- Dividends received
  - Dividends received from associates
- Purchase of a subsidiary, interest in an associated/joint venture undertaking or of a business
- Receipt from the disposal of a subsidiary, interest in an associated/joint venture undertaking or of a business.

3 **Financing activities**
- Dividends paid to minority interests
  (this is calculated as minority interests in the opening consolidated balance sheet plus minority interests in the income statement less minority interests in the closing balance sheet).

27.5.2 Adjustments to amounts

Adjustments are required if the closing balance sheet items have been increased or reduced as a result of **non-cash movements**. Such movements occur (a) if there has been a purchase of a subsidiary to reflect the fact that the asset and liabilities from the new subsidiary have not necessarily resulted from cash flows; and (b) if there are exchange differences arising on consolidating foreign subsidiaries.

(a) Subsidiary acquired during year

For example, if Tyro Bruce had acquired a subsidiary on 31 March 20X2 on the following terms:

Net assets acquired	£000	In consolidated cash flow the effect will be:
Working capital:		
Inventory	10	Reduce inventory increase
Trade payables	(12)	Reduce trade payables increase
Capital expenditure:		
Vehicles	20	Reduce capital expenditure
Cash/bank:		
Cash	5	Reduce amount paid to acquire subsidiary in investing section
Net assets acquired	23	
Consideration from Tyro Bruce:		
Shares	10	Reduce share cash inflow
Premium	10	Reduce share cash inflow
Cash	3	Payment to acquire subsidiary in investing section
	23	

The Tyro Bruce consolidated cash flow statement can then be prepared.

Cash flow statement for Tyro Bruce using indirect method

Cash flows from operating activities		£000	£000
Net profit before tax		1,000	
Adjustments for:			
Depreciation		204	
R&D amortisation charge		480	
Loss on sale of plant		54	
Profit on sale of land		(80)	
Interest expense		40	
Operating profit before working capital changes		1,698	
Increase in trade and other receivables		(440)	
Increase in inventories	(800)		
Less: inventory brought in on acquisition	10	(790)	
Increase in trade payables	280		
Less: trade payables brought in on acquisition	12	268	
Cash generated from operations		736	
Interest paid (*from income statement*)		(40)	
Income taxes paid (*380 + 400 – 340*)		(440)	
Net cash from operating activities			256
Cash flows from investing activities			
Purchase of property, plant and equipment	(1,120)		
Less: vehicles brought in on acquisition	20	(1,100)	
Proceeds from sale of equipment and land		682	
Purchase of government securities		(30)	
Payment to acquire subsidiary		(3)	
Cash acquired with subsidiary		5	
Net cash used in investing activities			(446)
Cash flows from financing activities			
Proceeds from issuance of share capital	700		
Less: shares issued on acquisition not for cash	(20)	680	
Repayment of debentures		(100)	
Dividends paid (*from income statement*)		(140)	
Net cash from financing activities			440
Net increase in cash and cash equivalents			250
Cash and cash equivalents at the beginning of the period			(1,336)
Cash and cash equivalents at the end of the period			(1,086)

If there had been a disposal of a subsidiary, the same adjustments would have been required except that they would have been in the opposite direction, e.g. capital expenditure on vehicles would have been increased from £1,120,000 to £1,140,000.

(b) Exchange differences arising on consolidation

If the subsidiary's accounts have been translated using the closing rate and the exchange differences taken to reserves, then the assets and liabilities in the consolidated balance sheet will contain **non-cash movements**. Let us assume that the non-cash differences that arose from exchange rate translation were the same amounts as those that arose on an acquisition of a subsidiary, namely:

	£000	Cash flow treatment
Working capital:		
Inventory	10	Reduce stock increase
Trade payables	(12)	Reduce trade payables increase
Capital expenditure:		
Vehicles	20	Reduce capital expenditure
Cash/bank:		
Cash	5	Shown separately after financing section before the movement in cash and cash equivalents
Exchange gain	23	

Operating cash flows

Cash flow from operations would be the same as for the subsidiary acquired during the year, i.e. £736,000 (£738,000 − Trade payables increase of £12,000 + Inventory decrease of £10,000).

Investing cash flows

Capital expenditure would be the same as for subsidiary acquired during the year: £418,000 (£438,000 − fixed asset decrease of £20,000).

A new line, Effect of foreign rate changes, £5,000, is shown before the movement in cash and cash equivalents.

Note: The exchange gain of £23,000 would have been credited to reserves in Tyro Bruce.

27.6 Analysing a cash flow statement

Arranging cash flows into specific classes provides users with relevant and decision-useful information by highlighting operating cash flows before working capital changes, cash generated from operations after working capital changes, cash flows from investing activities and cash flows from financing activities. The classification assists users in making informed predictions about future cash flows. It would be difficult to make these conjectures using traditional accrual-based techniques.[11]

We will briefly comment on the implication of each classification.

27.6.1 Operating profit before working capital changes

Users look to see if this is positive or negative. If it is positive, the next step would be to determine the trend − investors naturally hoping to invest in a company with a rising trend. If there is a downward trend or it is negative, this is a cause for concern and investors should make further enquiries to identify any proposed steps to improve the position. The operating and financial review and chairman's statement may indicate whether the company is carrying out a cost reduction programme or disposing of loss-making activities. If it is not possible to improve the trend or reverse the negative cash flow, then there could be future liquidity difficulties. Such difficulties could have an impact on future discretionary costs, e.g. the curtailment of research, marketing and advertising expenditure, on investment decisions, e.g. postponing capital expenditure, and on financing decisions, e.g. raising additional equity or loan capital.

27.6.2 Cash generated from operations after working capital changes

The cash available to meet interest charges and taxation will be affected by the impact of working capital changes. In the Tyro Bruce example we can see that, although there has been a significant increase in working capital of £960,000, this has only taken 56% of the £1,698,000.

We can see the cash implication, but would need to make further enquiries to establish the reasons for the change and the likelihood of similar cash outflow movements recurring in future years. If, for example, the increased investment in inventory resulted from an increase in turnover, then a similar increase could recur if the forecast turnover continued to increase. If, on the other hand, the increase was due to poor inventory control, then it is less likely that the increase will recur: in fact, quite the opposite as management addresses the problem.

The same comments could be made in relation to the trade receivables and trade payables. The cash flow statement indicates the cash extent of the change: additional ratios are required to allow us to evaluate the change.

The cash generated is available to pay interest and taxation, both of which are unavoidable. It is also an indication of the safety margin, i.e. how long a business could continue to pay unavoidable costs.

Interest cover

Interest cover is normally defined as the number of times the profit before interest and tax covers the interest charge: in the Tyro Bruce example, £1,040,000/£40,000 = 26 times.

The position as disclosed in the cash flow statement is weaker. It is the number of times the net cash flow from operating activities covers the payment, i.e. £738,000/£40,000 = 18.45 times.

This does not allow us to assess the financing policy of the company, e.g. whether the capital was raised the optimum way. Nor does it allow us to assess whether the company would have done better to provide finance by improved control over its assets, e.g. working capital reduction.[12]

27.6.3 Evaluating the investing activities cash flows

These arise from the acquisition and disposal of non-current assets and investments.

It is useful to consider how much of the expenditure is to replace existing non-current assets and how much is to increase capacity. One way is to relate the cash expenditure to the depreciation charge; this indicates that the cash expenditure is 549% greater than the depreciation charge calculated as follows: [(£1,120,000/£204,000) × 100]. This seems to indicate a possible increase in productive capacity. However, the cash flow statement does not itemise the expenditure and referring to the non-current asset schedule reveals that only £120,000 of the total of £1,120,000 was spent on plant with the major outlay being on land and buildings where we see a 25% increase.

How much relates to replacing existing non-current assets?

There has been a criticism that it is not possible to assess how much of the investing activities cash outflow related to simply maintaining operations by replacing non-current assets that were worn out rather than to increasing existing capacity with a potential for an increase in turnover and profits. The solution proposed was that investment that merely maintained should be shown as an operating cash flow and that the investing cash flow should be restricted to increasing capacity. The IASC doubted the reliability of such a distinction but there is a view that such an analysis provides additional information, provided the breakdown between the two types of expenditure can be reliably ascertained.

27.6.4 Evaluating the financing cash flows

A comparison of the net cash outflow of £210,000 before financing with the cash inflow from financing of £468,000 indicates the extent to which the cash flow after investing has been utilised or financed, e.g. financing has contributed over 100% and there has been no reduction in cash.

27.7 Critique of cash flow accounting

In this section we look at cash flow accounting from the viewpoint of users. We discuss the conflicting objectives of flexibility and uniformity, and comment on the two methods available under IAS 7.

27.7.1 Users

One of the main measures for evaluating the effectiveness of cash flow statements is the extent to which user needs are satisfied. Initial questions surrounding the replacement of funds flow statements with cash flow statements involved consideration of the following:

- For which user groups was the original IAS 7 designed?
- Which user groups actually used funds flow statements and found the resultant information useful?
- Which user groups were considered during the formulation of IAS 7 (revised)?
- For which user groups was IAS (revised) designed?

During this chapter we have identified the strengths and weaknesses of funds flow statements and cash flow statements. Funds flow statements did provide some useful information and were perceived as useful by users. Different user groups were able to extract information from the statement:

- **Shareholders** could assess the stability of the company's dividend distribution policy by determining what proportion of net profit was accounted for by tax and dividends.
- **Creditors** could assess the company's ability to meet long-term obligations and maintain working capital investment.
- **Lenders** could assess the company's reliance on either borrowings or share capital for financing investment and expansion projects.

Unfortunately, even though the funds flow statement satisfied some user needs, many areas could not be evaluated using it. Solomons[13] explains this aspect of user needs:

> If ... the main concerns of primary groups of users of general purpose financial reports are with the profitability and the viability of the enterprises in which they have an interest, that points to the need for financial statements that at least disclose:

(a) the enterprise's capacity to generate income for its owners, employees, and lenders who are entitled to interest on their loans;

(b) its present and probable future solvency.

Solomons states that the link between profitability and viability is expressed by an enterprise's cash flows. The disclosure of this information is one of the arguments in favour of producing a cash flow statement.

27.7.2 Flexibility versus uniformity

One premise for the replacement of funds flow statements with cash flow statements is that funds flow statements allowed too much scope for flexibility in the presentation of funds flow information. This led to an increase in the variety of formats and a decrease in comparability between companies.

There appears to be an assumption that management, left to its own devices, will choose an accounting format for purely self-satisfying motives that will mislead the user. But perhaps the format of funds flow statements was properly left to the discretion of management. This discretion allowed management to decide which user groups the statement was aimed at, so that management could then select the most appropriate format to disclose and highlight relevant information about recent activities. This might be more helpful than having the figures arrayed in a standard uniform fashion.

IAS 7 (revised) applies stricter requirements to the format and presentation of cash flow statements. It still, however, allows companies to choose between the direct and the indirect methods, and the presentation of interest and dividend cash flows. It can be argued, therefore, that it has failed to rectify the problem of a lack of comparability between statements.

An important point is that, in its search for improved comparability, IAS 7 (revised) reduced the scope for innovation. It might be argued that standard setters should not be reducing innovation, but that there should be concerted effort to increase innovation and improve the information available to user groups. The acceptability of innovation is a fundamental issue in a climate that is becoming increasingly prescriptive.

27.7.3 Cash flows or funds flows

Our final consideration is the option of direct or indirect methods allowed in IAS 7 (revised). The direct method appears to be a genuine format for a cash flow statement, whereas the indirect method is a cross between a cash flow statement and a funds flow statement. Is it appropriate to continue to offer this hybrid format in IAS 7 (revised) as a replacement for a funds flow statement?

Summary

The funds flow statements produced until 1992 were criticised for not highlighting potential financial problems and for allowing too much choice to companies in how items were disclosed. IAS 7 (revised) defines more tightly the format and treatment of individual items within the cash flow statement. This leads to uniformity and greater comparability between companies. However, there is still some criticism of the current IAS 7:

- There are options within IAS 7 for presentation, since either the direct or the indirect method can be used; and there are choices about the presentation of dividends and interest.
- The cash flow statement does not distinguish between discretionary and non-discretionary cash flows, which would be valuable information to users.
- There is no separate disclosure of cash flows for expansion from cash flows to maintain current capital levels. This distinction would be useful when assessing the position and performance of companies, and is not always easy to identify in the current presentation.
- The definition of cash and cash equivalents can cause problems in that companies may interpret which investments are cash equivalents differently, leading to a lack of comparability. Cash flow statements could be improved by removing cash equivalents and concentrating solely on the movement in cash, which is the current UK practice.

REVIEW QUESTIONS

1 The management of any enterprise may put considerable emphasis on the cash flow effects of its decisions and actions, monitoring these with the internal reporting system. Cash flow information is also relevant to those with external interests in the enterprise. Discuss the importance of cash flow information for both internal and external decisions. What internal and external user needs does cash flow reporting satisfy? Is the current cash flow information adequate for these purposes?

2 Many people preferred the direct method for cash flow preparation, but IAS 7 did not require it. Discuss possible reasons for allowing choice and the effectiveness of the IASC's encouragement to companies to use the direct method.

3 Explain the information that a user can obtain from a cash flow statement that cannot be obtained from the current or comparative balance sheets.

4 'The traditional income statement in published accounts should be replaced (or at least supplemented) by a cash flow statement.'
   (a) Explain what you understand by such a cash flow statement.
   (b) Explain the basis on which the above view can be justified, and state any drawbacks of disclosing cash flow information.

5 Explain why the fixed assets acquired on the acquisition of a subsidiary during the year have the same effect on the consolidated cash flow statement as an exchange gain of equal amount resulting from the translation at closing rate.

EXERCISES

An extract from the solution is provided in the Appendix at the end of the text for exercises marked with an asterisk (*).

* Question I

The draft balance sheets of Example Ltd as at 31 March 20X0 and 31 March 20X1 are as follows:

(£000)	Cost	20X1 Depn	NBV	Cost	20X0 Depn	NBV
Non-current assets	2,760	462	2,298	2,520	452	2,068
Current assets						
Inventory		1,200			800	
Trade receivables		900			640	
Government securities		20			—	
Cash		10			80	
		2,130			1,520	
Current liabilities						
Trade receivables		500			540	
Taxation		170			190	
Dividends		—			—	
Overdraft		478			8	
		1,148			738	
Net current assets			982			782
			3,280			2,850
Ordinary share capital			1,400			1,300
Share premium account			400			200
Retained profits at 31 Mar 20X0			1,150			1,150
Profit for year			180			—
10% debentures repayable 20X0–X4			150			200
			3,280			2,850

The income statement of Example Ltd for the year ended 31 March 20X1 is as follows:

	£000	£000
Sales		3,000
Cost of sales		2,000
Gross profit		1,000
Selling and distribution expenses	300	
Administrative expenses	180	−480
		520
Interest payable		−20
Profit before tax		500
Tax		−200
Profit after tax		300

Notes:
1 Non-current assets having a cost of £320,000 on which £92,000 of depreciation had been provided were sold during the year at a profit of £13,000.
2 The company had paid a dividend of £120,000.
3 The non-current asset schedule included the following:

Cost	£000	Depreciation	£000	Net book value	£000
At cost 31 Mar 20X0	2,520	At 31 Mar 20X0	452	At 31 Mar 20X0	2,068
Additions	560	I.S. charge	102		
	3,080		554		
Disposals	320	Disposal	92		
At 31 Mar 20X1	2,760		462	At 31 Mar 20X1	2,298

Required:

A cash flow statement using the format of IAS 7.

* Question 2

Shown below are the summarised final accounts of Martel plc for the last two financial years:

Balance sheet as at 31 December

	20X1		20X0	
	£000	£000	£000	£000
Non-current assets				
Tangible				
Land and buildings	1,464		1,098	
Plant and machinery	520		194	
Motor vehicles	140		62	
		2,124		1,354
Current assets				
Inventory	504		330	
Trade receivables	264		132	
Government securities	40		—	
Bank	—		22	
	808		484	
Current liabilities				
Trade payables	266		220	
Taxation	120		50	
Proposed dividend	72		40	
Bank overdraft	184		—	
	642		310	
Net current assets		166		174
Total assets less current liabilities		2,290		1,528
Non-current liabilities				
9% debentures		(432)		(350)
		1,858		1,178
Capital and reserves				
Ordinary shares of 50p each fully paid		900		800
Share premium account	120		70	
Revaluation reserve	360		—	
General reserve	100		50	
Retained earnings	378		258	
		958		378
		1,858		1,178

	Summarised income statement for the year ending 31 December	
	20X1	20X0
	£000	£000
Operating profit	479	215
Interest paid	52	30
Profit before taxation	427	185
Tax	149	65
Profit after taxation	278	120

Additional information:

1 The movement in non-current assets during the year ended 31 December 20X1 was as follows:

	Land and buildings £000	Plant, etc. £000	Motor vehicles £000
Cost at 1 January 20X1	3,309	470	231
Revaluation	360	—	—
Additions	81	470	163
Disposals	—	(60)	—
Cost at 31 December 20X1	3,750	880	394
Depreciation at 1 January 20X1	2,211	276	169
Disposals	—	(48)	—
Added for year	75	132	85
Depreciation at 31 December 20X1	2,286	360	254

The plant and machinery disposed of during the year was sold for £20,000.

2 During 20X1, a rights issue was made of one new ordinary share for every eight held at a price of £1.50.

3 A dividend of £36,000 (20X0 £30,000) was paid in 20X1. A dividend of £72,000 (20X0 £40,000) was proposed for 20X1. A transfer of £50,000 was made to the general reserve.

Required:
(a) Prepare a cash flow statement for the year ended 31 December 20X1, in accordance with IAS 7.
(b) Prepare a report on the liquidity position of Martel plc for a shareholder who is concerned about the lack of liquid resources in the company.

Question 3

The balance sheets of Flow Ltd for the years ended 31 December 20X5 and 20X6 were as follows:

	€	20X5 €	€	20X6 €
Non-current assets				
Tangible assets				
PPE at cost	1,743,750		1,983,750	
Accumulated depreciation	551,250	1,192,500	619,125	1,364,625
Current assets				
Inventory		101,250		85,500
Trade receivables		252,000		274,500
		1,545,750		1,724,625
Capital and reserves				
Common shares of €1 each		900,000		1,350,000
Share premium				30,000
Retained earnings		387,000		176,625
Current liabilities				
Trade payables		183,750		159,750
Bank overdraft		75,000		8,250
		1,545,750		1,724,625

Note that during the year ended 31 December 20X6:

1 Equipment that had cost €25,500 and with a net book value of €9,375 was sold for €6,225.

2 The company paid a dividend of €45,000.

3 A bonus issue was made at the beginning of the year of 1 bonus share for every three shares.

4 A new issue of 150,000 shares was made on 1 July 20X6 at a price of €1.20 for each €1 share.

5 A dividend of €60,000 was declared but no entries had been made in the books of the company.

Required:
Prepare a cash flow statement for the year ended 31 December 20X6 that complies with IAS 7.

Question 4

The following financial statements relate to Blue Ting plc for the year ended 31 May 20X5.

Income statement for the year ended 31 May 20X5

	£m	£m
Turnover		335
Cost of sales		(177)
Gross profit		158
Distribution costs	(31)	
Administrative expenses	(27)	(58)
Operating profit		100
Interest payable	(7)	
Interest receivable	3	(4)
Profit before tax		96
Taxation		(22)
Profit for the financial year		74

Balance sheets at 31 May

	20X5 £m	20X5 £m	20X4 £m	20X4 £m
Tangible non-current assets		272		196
Intangible fixed assets				
(development expenditure)		3		4
		275		200
Current assets				
Inventory	140		155	
Trade receivables	130		110	
Cash and liquid resources	102		23	
	372		288	
Current liabilities	(249)		(172)	
Net current assets		123		116
Total assets less current liabilities		398		316
Non-current liabilities		(80)		(90)
		318		226
Capital and reserves				
Ordinary share capital		120		100
Share premium account		45		35
Capital redemption reserve		12		—
Retained earnings		141		91
		318		226

The following information relates to the financial statements of Blue Ting plc

(1) Ordinary share capital		£m
£1 shares fully paid at 1.6.X4	100
Issued during year	10
Purchase of own shares	(12)
Shares converted	22
	120

(2) Reserves

	Share premium account £m	Capital redemption reserve £m	Retained earnings £m
At 1.6.X4	35		91
Premium on issue (net of issue costs of £1m)	3		
Premium on conversion of debentures	7		
Transfer to CRR		12	(12)
Profit for period	—	—	62
	45	12	141

(3) Non-current liabilities

	20X5 £m	20X4 £m
Obligations under finance leases	49	30
6% debentures 20X5–20Y1	31	60
	80	90

£29m of 6% debentures 20X5–20Y1 were converted into £22m of ordinary shares during the year and interest paid in the year amounted to £2m.

(4) Current liabilities

	20X5 £m	20X4 £m
Bank overdraft	8	20
Obligations under finance leases	5	3
Trade payables	220	131
Taxation	16	10
Dividends	–	8
	249	172

(5) Tangible non-current assets

	£m
Carrying value at 1.6.X4	196
Additions – finance leases	28
– purchases at cost	104
Disposals at carrying value	(19)
Depreciation for the year	(37)
Carrying value at 31.5.X5	272

The non-current assets disposed of realised £21m.

(6) Cash and liquid resources

	20X5 £m	20X4 £m
Treasury stock 8.5% 20X9	60	—
Treasury stock 12.75% 20X9 (June)	20	20
Loan notes repayable on demand	15	—
Cash at bank and in hand	7	3
	102	23

(Note that all of the interest due on the treasury stock for the year ending 31.5.X5 has been received and there was no interest due on 31.5.X4.)

(7) Interest payable

	20X5 £m
Bank overdraft	2
Finance charges payable under finance leases	3
Debentures not wholly repayable within five years	2
	7

(8) Obligations under finance leases

	20X5 £m	20X4 £m
Amounts payable within one year	6	4
Within two to five years	55	33
	61	37
Less finance charges allocated to future periods	(7)	(4)
	54	33

Interest paid on finance leases in the year to 31 May 20X5 amounted to £3m.

(9) A dividend of £12m was paid in the year ended 31 May 20X5.

Required:
(a) Prepare a cash flow statement for Blue Ting plc for the year ended 31 May 20X5 in compliance with IAS 7 *Cash Flow Statements*.
(b) Discuss the principal advantages and disadvantages of publishing forecast cash flow statements for the next accounting period.

(ACCA, adapted)

References

1 IAS 7 *Statement of Changes in Financial Position*, IASC, 1977.
2 SFAS 95 *Statement of Cash Flows*, FASB, November 1987.
3 IAS 7 *Cash Flow Statements*, ASC, July 1990.
4 J. Arnold *et al.*, *The Future Shape of Financial Reports*, ICAEW and ICAS, 1991.
5 J. Arnold, 'The future shape of financial reports', *Accountancy*, May 1991, p. 26.
6 G.H. Sorter, M.J. Ingberman and H.M. Maximon, *Financial Accounting: An Events and Cash Flow Approach*, McGraw-Hill, 1990.

7   J.W. Henderson and T.S. Maness, *The Financial Analyst's Deskbook*, Van Nostrand Reinhold, 1989, p. 12.

8   J. Crichton, 'Cash flow statements – what are the choices?' *Accountancy*, October 1990, p. 30.

9   L.J. Heath and P. Rosenfield, 'Solvency: the forgotten half of financial reporting', in R. Bloom and P.T. Elgers (eds), *Accounting Theory and Practice*, Harcourt Brace Jovanovich, 1987, p. 586.

10 J.M. Gahlon and R.L. Vigeland, 'Early warning signs of bankruptcy using cash flow analysis', *Journal of Commercial Lending*, December 1988, pp. 4–15.

11 J.W. Henderson and T.S. Maness, *op. cit.*, p. 72.

12 G. Holmes and A. Sugden, *Interpreting Company Reports and Accounts* (5th edition), Woodhead Faulkner, 1995, p. 134.

13 D. Solomons, *Guidelines for Financial Reporting Standards*, ICAEW, 1989.

CHAPTER 28

Review of financial ratio analysis

28.1 Introduction

In this chapter we consider the following:

- Accounting ratios and ratio analysis
- Six key ratios
- Pyramid of ratios
- Other important ratios
- Application of pyramid of ratios
- Segmental analysis
- Interfirm comparisons and industry averages
- World Wide Web pages
- Non-financial ratios
- Interpretation problems when using consolidated financial statements.

This chapter reviews the use of financial ratio analysis for the interpretation of a company's financial statements. The techniques that we discuss are fundamental to user appraisal of financial statements and should be used in conjunction with any alternative interpretative techniques available.

The key to understanding and interpreting financial statements is an extremely inquisitive and enquiring frame of mind. When examining a set of accounts, we should try to understand exactly what the figures mean.

Some issues will be evident from a cursory look at the accounts. For example, an initial glance might reveal a company that has made losses in the past two years; that has a declining sales turnover, a large overdraft and a greatly increased accounts payable figure. This would clearly raise questions about, for example, the increase in accounts payable. The initial look is a prelude to a more systematic review and is helpful in quickly putting the accounts into context.

Following the overview, financial ratios become important. One of the main strengths of financial ratios is that they help to direct the user's focus of attention. They identify and highlight areas of good and bad performance, and areas of significant change. In each instance, the user should attempt to explain exactly why the accounts reveal this behaviour.

Before we embark on a full investigation of financial ratios, a word of warning. Ian Griffiths has written a book on creative accounting which questions the reliability of financial statements: 'Every company in the country is fiddling its profits. Every set of published accounts is based on books which have been gently cooked or completely roasted ... it is the biggest con trick since the Trojan Horse.'[1]

We should take heed of these reservations when we undertake any analytical interpretations. They should make us even more open-minded and investigative when confronted by a set of financial statements. To quote Griffiths again,

> Whether the differences in accounting treatment and presentation are real or imagined, it is clear that there is scope for tremendous variation in reported figures ... perhaps the best safeguard is to look upon the annual accounts with a more cynical and jaundiced eye. The myth that the financial statements are an irrefutable and accurate reflection of the company's trading performance for the year must be exploded once and for all. The accounts are little more than an indication of the broad trend.[2]

28.2 Accounting ratios and ratio analysis

Accounting ratios identify irregularities, anomalies and surprises that require further investigation to ascertain the current and future financial standing of a company. This sounds very useful, but what are ratios and how can we use them?

28.2.1 What are ratios?

Ratios describe the relationship between different items in the financial statements. Obviously, we could calculate hundreds of ratios from a set of financial statements; the expertise lies in knowing which ratios provide useful information. The relative usefulness of each ratio depends on what aspects of a company's business affairs are being investigated. Some of the most important and frequently used ratios are outlined in section 28.3.

28.2.2 How can we use ratios?

An important lesson about ratios is that, if they are applied incorrectly, they may be completely useless or, perhaps even worse, misleading. However, if they are used correctly, they are a powerful tool for understanding and interpreting company accounts. Some basic rules for financial ratio analysis are as follows.

Compare like with like

The relative performance of a company can be gauged in a number of different terms by comparing that company's financial ratios with:

- financial ratios for a preceding period;
- budgeted financial ratios for the current period;
- financial ratios for other profit centres within the company;
- financial ratios for other companies within the same industrial sector.

In each case, comparison is possible only if an identical basis of compilation is employed. There must be conformity and uniformity in the preparation of accounts to ensure a comparison of like with like. In addition, if one is comparing companies in different countries, one needs to be aware of any differences in international accounting policies (see Chapter 6).

Clear definition of the financial ratio

A full understanding of the precise implications of a given ratio is possible only if it is accompanied by a clear definition of its constituent parts. The user must be able to judge the accuracy and reliability of the underlying business operations before the reliability of the ratio can be assessed. In addition, the definitions of ratios may vary from source to source as concepts and terminology are not universally defined.[3]

Awareness of underlying trends

As a ratio compares two values, changes in either of these underlying values over time may be obscured in the final ratio figure. Let us take the example of Radmand plc:

	Net profit £	*Capital employed* £	*Return on capital employed*
20X1	100,000	1,000,000	10%
20X2	150,000	1,500,000	10%
20X3	225,000	2,250,000	10%

Although the return on capital employed (ROCE) remains a constant 10% over the years 20X1–20X3, no assumptions can be made about the underlying figures. As we can see, the net profit increased by 50% in both 20X2 and 20X3, and this trend is not ascertainable in the ROCE ratio. The user should be aware that a ratio is not saying anything about the trends of its individual components – only about the combined effect of both components.

28.3 Six key ratios

In our analysis we identify six key ratios and a number of subsidiary ratios. The key ratios are presented as a pyramid in Figure 28.1. The pyramid illustrates how the constituent parts of each ratio relate to a set of financial statements.

The six key ratios are divided into three categories, as follows:

Primary investment level ratios

1 Primary investment ratio **(operating return on equity)**

$$\frac{\text{Net profit before interest and tax}}{\text{Shareholders' funds}}$$

2 Primary financing ratio **(financial leverage multiplier)**

$$\frac{\text{Capital employed}}{\text{Shareholders' funds}}$$

Primary operative level ratios

3 Primary operating ratio **(return on capital employed)**

$$\frac{\text{Net profit before interest and tax}}{\text{Capital employed}}$$

Figure 28.1 Pyramid of key ratios

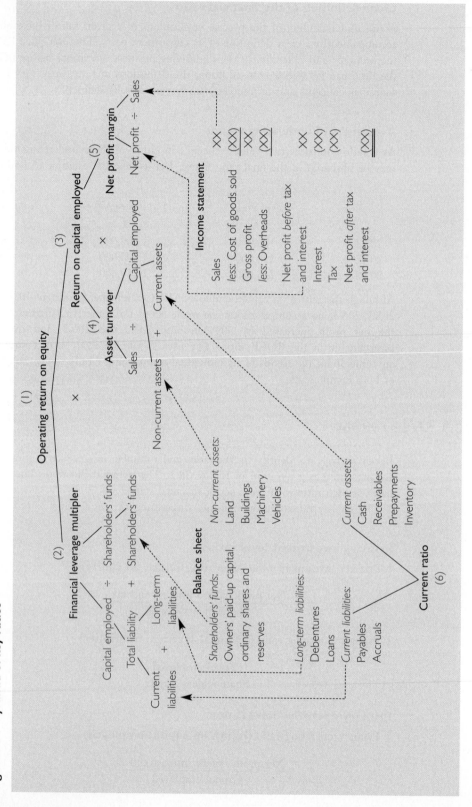

4 Primary utilisation ratio (**asset turnover**)

$$\frac{\text{Sales}}{\text{Capital employed}}$$

5 Primary efficiency ratio (**net profit margin**)

$$\frac{\text{Net profit before interest and tax}}{\text{Sales}}$$

Primary liquidity level ratios

6 Primary liquidity ratio (**current ratio**)

$$\frac{\text{Current assets}}{\text{Current liabilities}}$$

28.4 Description of the six key ratios

28.4.1 Primary investment level ratios

1 Primary investment ratio (operating return on equity)

The operating return on equity represents the net profit of a company as a percentage of the shareholders' funds (i.e. the total investment by the owners). This ratio is at the apex of the ratio pyramid, and it is the product of the financial leverage multiplier and the ROCE. Note that our 'operating return on equity' is defined differently from more traditional 'returns on equity' (profit before tax/shareholders' funds and profit after tax/shareholders' funds).

2 Primary financing ratio (financial leverage multiplier)

The financial leverage multiplier expresses how many times bigger the capital employed is than the shareholders' funds. This multiplier implies that assets funded by sources other than the owners will increase the profit or loss of the company relative to shareholders' funds.

28.4.2 Primary operative level ratios

3 Primary operating ratio (return on capital employed)

The ROCE is a fundamental measure of the profitability of a company. It is a popular indicator of management efficiency because it contrasts the net profit generated by the company with the total value of fixed and current assets, which are presumed to be under management control. Therefore, the ROCE demonstrates how well the management has utilised total assets.

ROCE is the product of the remaining two primary operative level ratios:

ROCE = Asset turnover × Net profit margin

Many different factors impact on the ROCE figure, including asset valuation policies, depreciation policies, revaluation policies, pricing policies, the treatment of goodwill and the treatment of expenses. In particular, the accounting treatment of goodwill (prior to FRS 10) resulted in the vast majority of companies writing off goodwill against their reserves. For some acquisitive companies, the goodwill write-off was so substantial that their shareholders' funds became negative. For instance, in the GGT Group's 1997 annual report their shareholders' funds were −£98,688,000. This makes interpretation and comparisons more difficult.

ROCE is also used by companies as part of their strategic planning, e.g. the 1998 Annual Report of VIAG AG states:

> VIAG made excellent progress in 1998 towards reaching its stated profitability goal. Return on capital employed increased significantly from 6.5% in 1997 to 7.0% in 1998. …The goal is to increase the Group's return on capital employed to at least 10% by the year 2003. The target figures we have adopted are based on our own experience and on the results of our leading competitors.

Care needs to be taken with ROCE as there is no single definition. For example, VIAG explain how their ROCE might be affected by their definition:

> Capital employed is defined on the basis of very restrictive criteria, as evidenced by the fact that Bayernwerk's accruals for decommissioning are included in the capital employed totalling DM59.5 billion. We are legally obliged to establish these accruals for decommissioning expenses, which account for 20% of capital employed. Consequently, VIAG's return on equity and capital costs tend to be lower than those of other industrial corporations.

4 Primary utilisation ratio (asset turnover)

The asset turnover is a measure of how much sales are generated by the capital asset base of a company. Although this ratio can act as a good guide to company performance, it can also be misleading. Its magnitude should therefore be evaluated in terms of its constituent parts.

If asset turnover increases, either the total value of sales is increasing, or the capital asset base is decreasing, or both. If it is because sales are increasing, this might signify improved performance. However, if it is because the capital asset base is reduced, this needs further investigation. For example, it could be caused by failure to maintain fixed assets, or by a massive drop in stock levels.

5 Primary efficiency ratio (net profit margin)

Net profit margin is another widely used ratio in the assessment of company performance and in comparisons with other companies.

Profit margin depends on the type of industry a company is operating within (e.g. high-volume/low-margin), the company pricing policies, the sales volumes and cost structure. A higher margin generally suggests good performance, but the profit margin should not be taken at face value. When analysing profit margin we should ask questions such as why the profit margin is higher than average; or why it is lower than it was last year; or whether the company management is setting the profit margin strategically.

28.4.3 Primary liquidity level ratios

6 Primary liquidity ratio (current ratio)

The current ratio is a short-term measure of a company's liquidity position. This ratio (which should be appraised in conjunction with the acid test ratio) compares current assets with current liabilities. In cases where the value is greater than unity, the current asset value exceeds the value of current liabilities. It is often claimed that the current ratio should be greater than 2, but the recommended current ratio depends (as always) on the industry sector and each individual company's experience. This can be assessed by referring to the times series summaries, as shown in this extract from the 2004 Annual Report of Barloworld, a South African conglomerate:

	2004	2003	2002	2001	2000	1999
Current ratio	1.5	1.4	1.3	1.3	1.6	1.7

This indicates that the company's current ratio for 2003 is within its own normal range.

The sector norms become relevant if a prospective acquirer is considering a takeover and subsequently revising the existing financial structure.

What if the current ratio increases beyond the normal range?

This may arise for a number of reasons, some beneficial, others unwelcome.

Beneficial reasons

- A build-up of inventory in order to support a recent advertising campaign or increasing popular demand as for, say, a PlayStation. Management action will be to establish from a cash budget that the company will not experience liquidity problems from holding such stock, e.g. a short-term loan, extended credit or bank overdraft may be appropriate.
- A permanent expansion of the business which will require continuing higher levels of inventory. Management action will be to arrange additional finance, e.g. equity or long-term borrowings to finance the increased working capital.

Unwelcome reasons

- Operating losses may have eroded the working capital base. Management action will vary according to the underlying problem, e.g. implementing a cost reduction programme, disposing of underperforming segments, arranging a sale of assets or inviting a takeover.
- Inefficient control over working capital, e.g. poor inventory or accounts receivable control.
- Adverse litigation, e.g. liability to employees for asbestosis.
- Adverse trading conditions, e.g. inventory becoming obsolete or introduction of new models by competitors.

Moreover, the current ratio should be analysed in terms of its constituent parts to test the quality of the value. We should ask: what part of current assets is cash, accounts receivable or inventory; what is the likelihood of debtors defaulting; what is the condition of the inventory; and what are the timings of all the current liabilities?

28.5 Description of subsidiary ratios

28.5.1 Gearing ratios

$$\text{Gearing ratio} = \frac{\text{Total liability} - \text{Current liability}}{\text{Capital employed}}$$

The gearing ratio represents the proportion of capital employed which is accounted for by long-term fixed-interest debt. The gearing structure of a company refers to the amount of borrowings compared with the amount of shareholders' funds. A company with high gearing is predominantly financed by debt, whereas a company with low gearing relies on equity finance. Different user groups prefer different gearing structures. Creditors and shareholders will be influenced by gearing as it affects factors such as annual interest payments and earnings per share.

This particular definition of gearing concentrates on long-term debt financing. An alternative measure might be total liabilities/capital employed, which includes short-term financing as well as long-term financing. This might be more pertinent because some companies rely on high levels of overdraft. As a further refinement one might disaggregate current liabilities into interest-bearing finance (overdrafts; short-term loans) and more indirect finance (trade creditors; tax payable).

$$\text{Shareholders' ratio} = \frac{\text{Shareholders' funds}}{\text{Capital employed}}$$

This represents the proportion of capital employed that is financed by shareholders' funds.

$$\text{Interest cover} = \frac{\text{Net profit before interest and tax}}{\text{Interest}}$$

Most companies are committed to paying a certain amount of interest charges. This ratio describes how many times greater the profit is than the interest charges. It gives creditors an indication of how secure these payments are. An alternative measure is to compare the actual cash flow (rather than profit) to interest payments to give an indication of the availability of cash to cover interest charges.

The earnings before interest and tax (EBIT) might move in the same way as the earnings before interest, tax, depreciation and amortisation (EBITDA). However, if they differ significantly, as in periods of unusual growth, it may be more useful to calculate the cash flow interest cover. Even so, attention should also be given to free cash flow, as suggested in the following extract from the 2003 Annual Report of Sauer-Danfoss Inc.:

> EBITDA – represents Net Income, plus Provision for Income Taxes and Net Interest expense, plus Depreciation and Amortization. EBITDA may not be comparable to similarly titled measures reported by other companies. While EBITDA should not be construed as a substitute for Operating Income or a better indicator of liquidity than Cash Flow from Operating Activities, which is determined in accordance with accounting principles generally accepted in the United States, it is included herein to provide additional information with respect to the ability of Sauer-Danfoss to meet its future debt service, Capital Expenditures and Working Capital requirements.

28.5.2 Liquidity ratios

$$\text{Acid test ratio} = \frac{\text{Current assets} - \text{Inventory}}{\text{Current liabilities}}$$

The acid test or quick ratio indicates the company's ability to repay immediate commitments using cash or near-cash. It excludes the value of inventory in order to show the immediate solvency of the company.

The following is an extract from the 2004 Annual Report of Barloworld:

	2004	2003	2002	2001	2000	1999
Quick ratio	1.0	0.8	0.7	0.8	0.9	1.1

This indicates that the company's quick (or acid test) ratio is within its own normal range.

28.5.3 Asset utilisation ratios

The asset turnover ratio can be subdivided into more specific component parts, so that each element of fixed and current assets can be analysed separately. The asset turnover ratio measures the amount of sales generated by the capital employed as a whole, whereas individual asset utilisation ratios compare total sales with the selected asset under management control. The breakdown of the asset turnover ratio is illustrated in Figure 28.2.

Figure 28.2 Asset turnover ratio

The non–current asset, tangible, property and plant utilisation ratios are measures of efficiency. They all indicate the sales volume produced by the available fixed assets. Although an improvement in these ratios will also improve the ROCE, it must be remembered that the depreciation policies and historical cost valuation of fixed assets will cause a distortion.

Three utilisation (or turnover) ratios that are particularly informative for understanding and interpreting financial statements are inventory turnover, accounts receivable turnover and accounts payable turnover. Inventory turnover can be calculated as:

$$\text{Inventory turnover} = \frac{\text{Sales}}{\text{Inventory}} \text{ or } \frac{\text{Cost of sales}}{\text{Average inventory}} \text{ or more usually } \frac{\text{Cost of sales}}{\text{Closing inventory}}$$

Inventory control involves careful planning and management. A company must avoid tying up too much capital in inventory, yet the stock levels must always be sufficient to meet customer demand and maintain continuous production. Any changes in this ratio must be investigated to determine exactly why inventory turnover is fluctuating – it could be due to changing sales volumes; different inventory valuation policies, or obsolete inventory. The average inventoryholding period (in days) can be calculated as:

$$\frac{\text{Closing inventory}}{\text{Cost of sales}} \times 365$$

The company's management report may be helpful in assessing changes in inventory levels. The following is an extract from the 1999 Annual Report of Schering AG:

Good balance-sheet ratios maintained
The balance-sheet ratios demonstrate the healthy financial state of the Schering Group. Inventories and receivable rose to 41% of the balance-sheet total. Among other things, this was due to a build-up of stocks to keep the market supplied during implementation of our European Production Concept and to cater for any problems that might have arisen in connection with Y2K.

The receivables ratio (usually trade receivables) is usually expressed in terms of the accounts receivable collection period (in days):

$$\frac{\text{Accounts receivable}}{\text{Sales}} \times 365$$

This ratio can be used to evaluate credit control and how quickly the company receives cash. Changes in the accounts receivable collection period might be misleading, so the root cause must be ascertained. A falling debt collection period might mean that the company is successfully reducing bad debts and eliminating poor risks; or the liquidity position might be so poor that the company is extending discounts and incentives to customers who pay early (or on time). An increasing accounts receivable collection period might mean that the company has poor credit control and is besieged with bad debts; or that it has a strategy for attracting new customers.

The payables turnover ratio (usually trade payables) is calculated as:

$$\text{Payables turnover} = \frac{\text{Sales}}{\text{Accounts payable}} \text{ or more usually } \frac{\text{Cost of sales}}{\text{Accounts payable}}$$

It is usually expressed in terms of the accounts payable payment period (in days):

$$\frac{\text{Accounts payable}}{\text{Sales}} \times 365 \text{ or more usually } \frac{\text{Accounts payable}}{\text{Cost of sales}} \times 365$$

This ratio indicates the credit facilities extended to a company by its suppliers. Any changes in the payment period might be due to suppliers altering credit terms (either more or less generous), the company trying to gain maximum credit facilities, or the company utilising early payment incentives.

28.5.4 Investment ratios

Investment ratios such as earnings per share (EPS), price/earnings ratio (PE ratio) and dividend cover are of great interest to investors.

Earnings per share

EPS indicates the amount of profit after tax, interest and dividends to preference shares has been earned for each ordinary share. Its importance is recognised by some management who use the EPS as part of their strategic planning; e.g. the 2002 Annual Report of Gamma Holding NV states:

> Gamma Holding aims to maximise shareholder value, taking into account the interests of the employees and other stakeholders in the company. In doing so, Gamma Holding strives to offer its shareholders an attractive return based on continuous growth of earnings per share of an average 10% over a number of years whilst maintaining healthy balance sheet ratios and generating positive cash flows. Furthermore, the company aims to achieve an average return on capital employed (including goodwill) of 15%.

This has been added to in the 2003 Annual Report which also states:

> With a view to a healthy balance sheet the company aims for a solvency percentage of at least 30% and gearing of less than 100%. It is the company's policy that net debt should not exceed 2.5 times EBITDA.

PE ratio

The ratio is calculated using the current share price and current earnings. It is a measure of market confidence in the shares of a company. However, the market price also takes into account anticipated changes in the earnings arising from their assessment of macro events such as political factors, e.g. imposition of trade embargoes and sanctions; economic factors, e.g. the downturn in manufacturing activity; and market conditions as in the following extract from the Sepracor 2003 Annual Report:

> The price of our common stock historically has been volatile, which could cause you to lose part of your investment. The market price of our stock, like that of the common stock of many other pharmaceutical and biotechnology companies, may be highly volatile. In addition, the stock market has experienced extreme price and volume fluctuations. This volatility has significantly affected the market price .... For reasons unrelated to or disproportionate to the operating performance of the specific companies. Prices ... may be influenced by many factors, including variations in our financial results and investors' perceptions of us, changes in recommendations by securities analysts as well as their perceptions of general economic, industry and market conditions.

It is also, of course, influenced by company-related events, e.g. the possibility of organic or acquired growth and the implication of financial indicators on future cash flow estimates. These financial indicators may be identified from the balance sheet, income statement and trade sources, as follows:

- Balance sheet:
  - change in debt/equity ratio in relation to prior periods;
  - new borrowings to finance expansion;
  - debt restructuring following inability to meet current repayment terms;
  - adequacy of working capital;
  - change in current ratio in relation to prior periods, i.e. higher indicating a build-up of slow-moving inventory and lower possible inventory-outs;
  - contingent liabilities that could be damaging if they crystallise;
  - non-current assets being increased or not being replaced;
  - low acid test (quick) ratio in relation to prior periods indicating liquidity difficulties.

Although it might be thought that a high quick ratio is attractive to investors, some companies have decided that their share price does not reflect this strength and have decided to return cash to shareholders as in the following extract from the Syskoplan 2003 Annual Report relating to a higher dividend pay-out:

> The Executive Board and the Supervisory Board reappraised the liquidity situation and capital structure of Syskoplan AG. In the past, stock markets and investors tended to set little store by the Group's excellent availability of liquid funds, as evident from the share price and market capitalization.

- Income statement:
  - change in sales trend;
  - limited product range, products moving out of patent protection period;
  - expanding product range;
  - changes in technology beneficial or otherwise to company;
  - high or low capital expenditure/depreciation ratio indicating that productive capacity is not being maintained;
  - loss of key suppliers/customers, e.g. loss of longstanding Marks & Spencer contracts;
  - change in ratio of R&D to sales.

- Trade sources:
  - suppliers applying more/less stringent credit terms;
  - loss/gain of key staff.

Earnings yield expresses earnings as a percentage of the share price.

Dividend cover

Dividend cover is ascertained by comparing EPS to dividend per share. It indicates the cushion that exists to meet dividends in the future if earnings were to deteriorate. The cover is expressed as number of times or, in some annual reports, as a payout ratio. Dividend yield expresses dividend as a percentage of the share price.

28.5.5 Profitability ratios

Profitability ratios allow a more specific analysis of profit margin, e.g. expressing individual expenses as a proportion of sales or cost of sales. These ratios will identify any irregularities or changes in specific expenses from year to year.

A list of the subsidiary ratios is included in Figure 28.3.

Figure 28.3 Subsidiary ratios

Gearing ratios

$$\text{Gearing ratio} = \frac{\text{Total liability} - \text{Current liability}}{\text{Capital employed}}$$

$$\text{Shareholders' ratio} = \frac{\text{Shareholders' funds}}{\text{Capital employed}}$$

$$\text{Interest cover} = \frac{\text{Net profit before interest and tax}}{\text{Interest}}$$

Liquidity ratios

$$(6)\ \text{Current ratio} = \frac{\text{Current assets}}{\text{Current liabilities}}$$

$$\text{Acid test ratio} = \frac{\text{Current assets} - \text{Inventory}}{\text{Current liabilities}}$$

Investment ratios

Earnings per share =

$$\frac{\text{Net profit after tax} - \text{Preference dividends}}{\text{Number of ordinary shares}}$$

$$\text{Price/earnings ratio} = \frac{\text{Share price}}{\text{Earnings per share}}$$

Dividend cover (ordinary shares) =

$$\frac{\text{Net profit after tax} - \text{Preference dividends}}{\text{Dividends on ordinary shares}}$$

$$\text{Dividend yield} = \frac{\text{Dividend on ordinary shares}}{\text{Market value of ordinary shares}}$$

Asset utilisation ratios (turnover ratios)

$$\frac{\text{Sales}}{\text{Non-current assets}}$$

$$\frac{\text{Sales}}{\text{Current assets}}$$

$$\frac{\text{Sales}}{\text{Working capital}}$$

$$\frac{\text{Cost of sales}}{\text{Inventory}}$$

$$\frac{\text{Sales}}{\text{Accounts receivable}}$$

$$\frac{\text{Cost of sales}^a}{\text{Trade payables}}$$

^{a}Ideally cost of materials used should be used.

Profitability ratios

$$\frac{\text{Gross profit}}{\text{Sales}}$$

$$\frac{\text{Cost of sales}}{\text{Sales}}$$

$$\frac{\text{Total overheads}}{\text{Sales}}$$

$$\frac{\text{Cost of materials}}{\text{Cost of sales}}$$

$$\frac{\text{Cost of labour}}{\text{Cost of sales}}$$

28.6 Application of pyramid of ratios to JD Wetherspoon plc

To illustrate financial ratio analysis and trend analysis we are using the accounts of JD Wetherspoon plc. The company's principal activities are the development and management of public houses.[4] JD Wetherspoon's profit and loss account and balance sheet for 2002 and 2003 are reproduced in Figure 28.4.

Figure 28.4 JD Wetherspoon consolidated profit and loss account for year ended 31 July 2003

	2003 £000	2002 £000
Turnover from continuing operations	730,913	601,295
Cost of sales	(621,894)	(503,699)
Gross profit	109,019	97,596
Administrative expenses	(34,036)	(27,511)
Operating profit	74,983	70,085
Net interest payable	(18,844)	(16,517)
Profit on ordinary activities before tax	56,139	53,568
Tax on profit on ordinary activities	(19,744)	(18,152)
Profit on ordinary activities after tax	36,395	35,416
Dividends	(7,434)	(6,902)
Retained profit for the year	28,961	28,514

JD Wetherspoon
Group balance sheet at 31 July 2003

	2003 £000	2002 £000
Fixed assets		
Tangible assets	773,823	745,041
	773,823	745,041
Current assets		
Stocks	9,601	8,594
Debtors due after more than one year	8,448	7,682
Debtors due after less than one year	9,017	8,237
Investments	301	203
Cash	15,160	13,609
	42,527	38,325
Creditors due within one year	(135,361)	(122,919)
Net current liabilities	(92,834)	(84,594)
Total assets less current liabilities	680,989	660,447
Creditors due after one year	(299,942)	(292,915)
Provisions for liabilities and charges	(62,419)	(57,399)
	318,628	310,133
Capital and reserves		
Called-up share capital	4,149	4,292
Share premium account	126,739	124,819
Capital redemption reserve	165	
Revaluation reserve	22,439	23,386
Profit and loss account	165,136	157,636
Equity shareholders' funds	318,628	310,133

Calculation of the six key ratios

1 Operating return on equity

2003 $\dfrac{74,983}{318,628}$ = 23.5% 2002 $\dfrac{70,085}{310,133}$ = 22.6%

2 Financial leverage multiplier

2003 $\dfrac{816,250}{318,628}$ = 2.56 times 2002 $\dfrac{783,366}{310,133}$ = 2.53 times

3 Return on capital employed

2003 $\dfrac{74,983}{816,350}$ = 9.19% 2002 $\dfrac{70,085}{783,366}$ = 8.95%

4 Asset turnover

2003 $\dfrac{730,913}{816,350}$ = 0.9 times 2002 $\dfrac{601,295}{783,366}$ = 0.77 times

5 Net profit margin

2003 $\dfrac{74,983}{730,913}$ = 10.26% 2002 $\dfrac{70,085}{601,295}$ = 11.66%

6 Current ratio

2003 $\dfrac{42,527}{135,361}$ = 0.31:1 2002 $\dfrac{38,325}{122,919}$ = 0.31:1

Five of these key ratios are shown in the pyramid structure of Figure 28.5 (allowing for rounding).

Figure 28.5 Pyramid of ratios

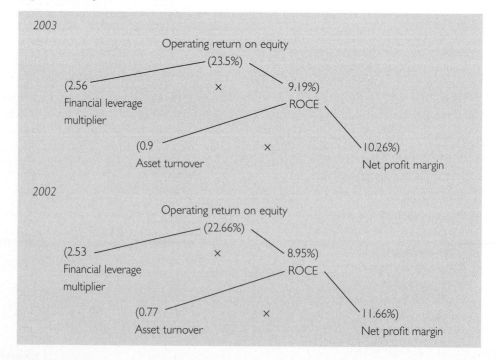

28.6.1 Interpretation of JD Wetherspoon plc's accounts

Using the pyramid structure to analyse JD Wetherspoon in 2003 and 2002 we can identify a number of areas of the business in which further investigations should be carried out. To begin with, the operating return on equity has improved from 22.6% to 23.5%. Disaggregating this ratio we can see that the improvement is due to both an increase in the financial leverage multiplier (2.53 to 2.56) and an increase in the ROCE (8.95% to 9.19%).

The increase in the financial leverage multiplier means that there has been an increased proportion of total liabilities within the capital employed figure. Looking at the balance sheet, it is evident that long-term loans have risen by nearly £7 million (from £292,915,000 to £299,942,000).

The increase in the ROCE is driven by an improved asset turnover (from 0.77 to 0.9), despite a drop in the net margin (11.66% to 10.26%). The improved asset turnover means that each £ of capital employed (or total assets) produces a higher level of sales. If the decline in net margin is investigated further it is evident that the main cause has been a decline in the gross margin (gross profit/sales) from 16.2% to 14.9%. The declining gross margin might be due to a decline in sales prices or higher cost of sales (which, according to the Wetherspoon annual report, is the main reason).

Some other considerations become apparent when evaluating the accounts in general. First of all, consider the profit and loss account:

- The company distributed only 20.42% of the after-tax profits in the form of dividends. The explanation for this, in the Finance Director's report, is that the company is preserving cash for future expansion whilst still maintaining its policy of increasing the dividend rate year on year.

- The above accounts are before exceptional items and the accounts showed an exceptional loss of £2,251,000 arising principally from the sale of 18 pubs.

Second, consider the balance sheet:

- The cash balance has risen by over £1.5m. The cash balance at the end of the year was over £15m which taken together with £103.1m of unutilised bank facilities (as disclosed in the Financial Review) has left the company in a strong position to continue expansion or continue to buy back shares. This is supported by a strong net cash inflow from operations as shown in the cash flow statement (not reproduced here).

- The current liabilities are much higher than the current assets, generating a net current liability. This is illustrated by the current ratio (0.31 in 2003 and 0.31 in 2002). One would need to compare this with the industry average (note that the current ratio for brewers is quite low) and determine whether this drop in current ratio is a deliberate policy or needs attention. The notes to the accounts (not reproduced here) show that trade creditors (accounts payable) have fallen from £54.4m to £53m.

28.7 Segmental analysis

In this section we review the reasons for and importance of segmental accounting in the analysis of financial statements.

Reasons for segmental accounting
Segmental information is provided on a consistent basis that allows it to be comparable over time so as to assist the users to:

- appreciate more thoroughly the results and financial position by permitting a better understanding of past performance and thus a better assessment of future prospects;
- be aware of the impact that changes in significant components of a business may have on the business as a whole.

Importance of segmental accounting

Segmental information makes the user aware of the balance between the different operations and thus able to assess:

- the quality of the company's reported earnings;
- the specific risks to which the company is subject;
- the areas where long-term growth may be expected.

Constraints on comparison between companies

Segmental analysis is intrinsically subjective. This means that there are likely to be major differences in the way segments are determined, and because costs, for instance, may be allocated differently by companies in the same industry it is difficult to make inter-company comparisons at the segment level and the user still has to take a great deal of responsibility for the interpretation of that information.[5]

Management reservations

Standard setters have not been totally prescriptive in recognising that management's attitude to segmental reporting is coloured by their fear that they will suffer some competitive disadvantage, e.g. host countries or competitors becoming aware of profit margins. They may also fear that they may not have reciprocal access to sensitive information if their own reporting jurisdiction, e.g. in the UK, requires a higher level of disclosure than that required of their international competitors, e.g. in Switzerland.

However, empirical evidence[6] indicates that such disadvantage arising from disclosure is limited and restricted to geographic segmental disclosure, particularly for smaller companies where such a segment might relate to a single contract.

We also consider the rules applicable to segmental accounting, provide an extract from a set of accounts to illustrate what information might be disclosed, and evaluate the information provided in Bass plc accounts (see 28.7.2).

28.7.1 Segmental reporting

Although the Companies Act 1967 introduced some requirements for the disclosure of segmental information, an accounting standard on the topic was not issued until June 1990.[7] The objective of segmental reporting is to assist users of accounts in evaluating the different business segments and geographical regions of a group and how they affect its overall results.[8] SSAP 25 *Segmental Reporting* sets out how these different segments should be defined and the information that should be disclosed.

SSAP 25 *Segmental Reporting*

SSAP 25 gives guidance on the factors that directors should take into account when defining segments, e.g. the nature of the products or services, and how the group's activities are organised. These factors help to determine whether a segment is distinguishable. However, it must also be a significant segment to require disclosure: a significance test will measure if any of the turnover, results (profit or loss) or net assets accounts for more than 10% of the group's total. SSAP 25 also states that turnover, results (profit or loss before tax, minority interests and extraordinary items) and net assets (not defined in the standard) should be disclosed for both business and geographic segments.

IAS 14 (revised) *Segment Reporting*[9]

IAS 14 is intended to allow an assessment of the overall risks and returns that may arise from the diversity of products/services and markets. Products/services are grouped into business segments and markets are grouped into geographical segments.

The intention is to group related items and IAS 14 suggests factors which might indicate that items are related. For example, in relation to business segments the factors to be considered are:

- the nature of the products/services,
- the nature of the production processes,
- the class of customer for the products/services,
- the distribution methods used.

For geographical segments, the factors to be considered are:

- similarity of political conditions,
- similarity of economic conditions,
- exchange control regulations,
- currency risks.

There is a difficulty with the geographic segmentation in that the risks may relate either to the location of the assets producing the products or to the markets in which sales are made – both might incur risks, and management has to decide which is the most significant.

The management approach

The information reported is derived from the internal financial reporting system on the grounds that the managers should be concentrating on the identification, reporting and controlling of such risks. The approach is therefore referred to as the management approach.

Deciding whether the business or geographical segment is the most significant

Having determined the business and geographical segments, management have to decide which of the two is the most significant – this is then referred to as the primary segment, and the other is referred to as the secondary segment.

Deciding whether a segment is reportable

IAS 14, para. 35, provides that following the identification of the primary segment and the business and geographical analysis, management need to determine whether a segment is reportable. The IAS provides that a business segment or geographical segment should be identified as a reportable segment if a majority of its revenue is earned from sales to external customers and:

(a) its revenue from sales to external customers and from transactions with other segments is 10% or more of the total revenue, external and internal, of all segments; or

(b) its segment result, whether profit or loss, is 10% or more of the combined result of all segments in profit or the combined result of all segments in loss, whichever is the greater in absolute amount; or

(c) its assets are 10% or more of the total assets of all segments.

The segmental information to be disclosed

Companies are required to report segment revenue, expense, results, assets and liabilities. However, there can be problems, e.g. how to treat assets that are jointly used by two or more segments. The important point is to ensure that there is appropriate matching, e.g. if an asset is allocated to a segment, then any related costs such as amortisation or depreciation should also be allocated to that segment. This is often referred to as symmetry and, just as related costs are included, so also is related income, e.g. if the segment results include interest income then the assets should include the asset producing that interest.

Despite the existence of SSAP 25 and IAS 14, there are many concerns about the extent of segmental disclosure and its limitations must be recognised.[10] A great deal of discretion is imparted to the directors concerning the **definition of each segment**. However, 'the factors which provide guidance in determining an industry segment are often the factors which lead a company's management to organise its enterprise into divisions, branches or subsidiaries'.[11] There is discretion concerning the **allocation of common costs** to segments on a reasonable basis. There is flexibility in the **definition of some of the items** to be disclosed (particularly net assets). Finally, in the UK there is a get-out clause. Where the directors consider the disclosure of information to be seriously prejudicial to the interests of their group, they do not have to disclose it (as long as the accounts report this non-disclosure). For example, the 2004 Annual Report of St Ives provides a segmental analysis of turnover but then states:

> The directors consider that an analysis of profit on a segmental basis would be seriously prejudicial to the interest of the Group and, as permitted by SSAP 25 *Segmental Reporting*, no further disclosure is given.

The revised version of IAS 14 requires a much greater disclosure of information than both the original IAS 14 and SSAP 25. In particular, separate disclosure of both segment assets and segment liabilities are required (as opposed to net assets for SSAP 25) and the basis of inter-segment pricing. In the UK, ED 45[12] proposed that the basis of inter-segment pricing (transfer pricing[13]) should be disclosed, but this particular proposal was not implemented in SSAP 25.

28.7.2 Segmental accounting – extract from a set of accounts

Where a segment can be distinguished, it is significant and the 'seriously prejudicial' clause is not invoked, one would expect to see disclosure of turnover, results and net assets for both business segments and geographical segments. However, a business may have only one business segment or operate in only one geographical region. Also, not all groups disclose net asset information, e.g. Leicester City plc state in the 1999 accounts: 'In the opinion of the Directors, it is not possible to analyse the assets between the businesses due to the shared nature of many of the assets'.

The following extract shows a summarised segmental report from the Bass plc 1999 accounts of their business segments and geographical segments (turnover by origin):

	External turnover £m	Operating profit £m	Non-operating exceptionals £m	Profit on ordinary activities before int £m
Bass Hotels & Resorts	1,162	321	(107)	214
Bass Leisure Retail	1,428	298	—	298
Bass Brewers	1,576	160	(7)	153
Britvic Drinks	507	44	—	44
Other activities	13	1	2	3
	4,686	824	(112)	712
United Kingdom	3,564	556	3	559
Rest of Europe, Middle East and Africa	496	71	(6)	65
United States	482	170	(110)	60
Rest of Americas	86	17	1	18
Asia Pacific	58	10	—	10
	4,686	824	(112)	712

Assets	£m
UK	5,328
Rest of Europe, Middle East and Africa	1,076
United States	1,144
Rest of Americas	85
Asia Pacific	107
	7,740

The segmental information provides a rough idea about how a group is performing in its main business segments and geographical regions. Bearing in mind the initial discussions on segmental accounting, a number of general observations can be made. Bass has significant interests in hotels, leisure retailing and branded drinks. Although most of Bass business is UK-based, there are high levels of sales in the USA and in the rest of Europe, the Middle East and Africa.

To get a feel for the profitability of the different business segments and markets, it is possible to calculate profit margins (based on operating profit/external sales as disclosed in the above note). For instance the profit margin for the hotel segment is 27.6% compared to 10.2% for Bass Brewers. In addition, the profit margin for the UK is 15.6% compared to 35.3% for the USA. This illustrates just how important it is to understand what different business segments are part of a group and which different markets the company is operating in. Furthermore, is the group changing its direction from one year to the next? The profit margin on the hotel segment might indicate that the company would make acquisitions to strengthen this area. The 1998 accounts showed that this happened with the acquisition of Inter-Continental Hotels for £1,765 million. Is the group a conglomerate operating in numerous different business segments? What are the group's core competencies? Have there been any acquisitions during the year? Have there been any divestments? In relation to Bass, the 1998 operating and financial review stated that there had been a switch in its focus from one of maximising group benefits through operating tied beer outlets to one of being a leisure retailer.

The 1999 Review stated that the group made significant progress during 1999, capitalising on the strategic activity undertaken in 1998 which saw the acquisition of the Inter-Continental Hotel (ICH) business, the disposal of the leased pub operation and the leisure businesses, and the return of over £800m of capital to shareholders.

With regard to the Bass Hotels & Resorts segment of the business, the operating and financial review states: 'As an indicator of future expansion, at 30 September 1999, BHR had approved franchise applications for 571 hotels (1998, 575) with approximately 58,000 rooms, though the hotels had yet to enter the system'.

The refocusing was completed in December 2000 when Bass, the UK's third largest brewer, sold off its brewing division to Belgium's Interbrew – this has resulted in more than 50% of UK brewing being owned by non-UK owners (refer to www.bass.com).

Implication of segment reporting for share valuation

There may be different risks attaching to the cash flows from the individual segments. This should be taken into account when assessing the overall value of the company, e.g. an extract from the Lex Column of the *Financial Times*, 17 November 2000, reads:

> **Bayer**
> As other old-style chemical giants have broken themselves up to focus on pharmaceuticals, the inventor of aspirin has stuck to its unloved conglomerate formula. So when results on its healthcare business – on which it is increasing its focus – undershoot expectations, the market punishes its shares.
>
> In fact the slippage in healthcare margins came mainly from one-offs ... The pharmaceuticals business is in reasonable shape ... The 20% operating profit margin for healthcare by 2002 is not unrealistic ... So Bayer should be valued more highly. Put healthcare on an earnings multiple of, say, 20% below the sector average, and it would be worth close to the group's €49.20 share price on its own. Adding on chemicals and polymers on an average sector multiple suggests a value closer to €75 ... Achieving its margin targets should provoke a rerating. Otherwise, counterparts such as Novartis or even Roche – with hostile takeovers no longer taboo in Germany – might sniff a bargain.

28.7.3 Identifying segment trends and management strategy

Segmental reports are helpful in assessing current and future performance of companies which operate across a number of business or geographical segments. These may report year on year overall improvements in total operating revenues and operating profits whereas the underlying performance of individual segments may be deteriorating. In such cases, the directors' explanation of the reasons and their proposals for dealing with the situation are important. For example, the following are extracts from the 1999 Annual Report of Royal Ten Cate NV:

In millions of euros	1999	1998	1997
Revenues	655.9	627.7	629.7
Operating result	40.9	34.5	36.9
Return on capital employed	13.5%	11.5%	11.3%

The segmental information is:

	High grade textiles sector			Plastics sector			Rubber sector		
	1999	1998	1997	1999	1998	1997	1999	1998	1997
Revenues	329.1	303.1	278.0	237.7	221.0	222.4	97.4	107.0	117.2
Operating result	24.5	17.6	13.5	10.1	14.6	7.7	9.1	3.6	5.8
Return on capital employed (%)	15.0	12.2	10.3	9.5	16.8	20.6	17.6	7.0	11.3

With regard to the rubber sector, management action was taken in 1998 to reverse the deterioration:

> The result improved sharply, thanks to fundamental cost reductions, the introduction of the production of cell structure and increased volume. As a result of the above-mentioned cost reductions, efficiency improvements and changes to product design, substantial sales price reductions were implemented. This restored the confidence of major customers and generated higher volumes. However, the volume growth was unable to offset the effects of the price reductions and sales fell in net terms by 9%.

Management also indicated medium-term and longer-term thinking:

> In the medium term part of the production will be transferred from Europe and the United States to eastern Europe and central America respectively ... In the longer term it will be necessary to examine the strategic position of Ten Cate Enbi in the sector, partly in the light of the increasing importance of assembly plants.

With regard to the plastics sector, management action was implemented in the latter half of 1999:

> 1999 was an extremely difficult year, partly because customers experienced a decline in sales. A negative result was recorded in net terms. This led to a reorganisation, which was implemented in the second half of the year. Management changes were made and led to the loss of over 70 jobs in three countries. The French operation was converted from a supplier of technical injection-moulded products to a producer specialising in caps. In America a small production unit was started in the Chicago area ... thereby adding a further geographical area.

28.7.4 Identifying organic growth

Investors may be interested to establish the reasons for any change, e.g. the extent to which it relates to organic growth, new acquisitions or currency movements. This often requires a close reading of the Notes to the accounts. For example, the 2003 Annual Report of Interbrew indicated that the profit from operations on their Asia Pacific activities had increased by 16.9%. The explanatory note reads as follows:

> Net turnover decreased by €(26)m, including a currency impact of €(69)m, due to the strengthening of the euro versus the Korean Won. Of the remaining increase of €43m, €31m is related to the KK acquisition and the remaining increase of €12m is attributable to organic growth, representing 2.3%, mainly fuelled by the price increase which compensated for the volume loss.

28.8 Inter-firm comparisons and industry averages

Financial ratios are a convenient way of assessing the current financial health and performance of a company relative to similar companies in the same industrial sector. This enables a company to be judged directly against its competitors, rather than merely against its own previous performance. Provided that each company uses exactly the same bases in calculation ratios, inter-firm comparisons provide a more controlled and objective means of evaluation. Every company is subject to identical economic and market conditions in the given review period, allowing a much truer comparison than a single company's fluctuating results over several years.

Inter-firm comparisons are ideal for identifying the strengths and weaknesses of a company relative to its industrial sector. These comparisons can be analysed by both internal users (management can take the necessary actions to maintain strengths and rectify weaknesses) and external users (lenders, creditors, investors, etc.). There are numerous sources of inter-firm information, but the organisations providing it can be divided into those which gather their data from external published accounts and those which collect the data directly from the surveyed companies on a strictly confidential basis.

28.8.1 Data collected from external published accounts

Organisations that prepare inter-firm comparisons from external published accounts face all the limitations associated with company accounts. These limitations include the following:

- The comparative ratios that can be included in an inter-firm comparison are limited to the information content of a set of published accounts. The inadequacies of compulsory disclosure restrict the amount of useful information and make it impossible to prepare every desirable ratio.
- There is insufficient standardisation in the preparation of published accounts. This is particularly relevant to ratio analysis because comparisons are meaningful only if the ratios are calculated from financial data that have been prepared on the same basis.
- The timeliness of any inter-firm comparison is dependent on the timeliness of published accounts. As published accounts are not usually available immediately after a financial year-end, there will be a time lag in the publication of inter-firm comparison information.

Although these drawbacks affect the reliability and completeness of survey results, such agencies have several advantages:

- The scope of an inter-firm comparison is extremely wide as it can include an analysis of any firm that produces published accounts.
- The quality of ratio analysis is improved because survey organisations attempt to standardise the bases of every ratio in the survey. This increases the uniformity and comparability of the ratio information.
- The survey information is easy to access and available at a relatively low cost.

What organisations provide inter-firm comparisons prepared from external published accounts?

Useful sources for inter-firm ratio comparisons include *Company REFS*,[14] *Handbook of Market Leaders*,[15] Dun & Bradstreet's *Key Business Ratios: The Guide to British Business*

Performance,[16] *The Company Guide*[17] and the online and CD-ROM computer services, including Datastream, OneSource,[18] Fame and Extel Financial Workstation. In addition, the World Wide Web provides an excellent source for corporate information.

28.8.2 Data collected direct from member companies of the private inter-firm comparison scheme

These inter-firm comparisons are prepared on a confidential basis and the analysed information is usually available only to the participating companies.

The advantages of private schemes are that inter-firm comparisons consist of a comprehensive analysis of every firm in the scheme, and a higher degree of reliability can be attached to their findings than if external published accounts alone were used.

The drawbacks of private schemes are as follows:

● There are onerous requirements concerning the quality of information that companies contribute to private schemes. All information must comply with strict uniformity requirements.

● The cost of these schemes is relatively high.

The advantages of private schemes are that inter-firm comparisons consist of a comprehensive analysis of every firm in the scheme, and a higher degree of reliability can be attached to their findings than if external published accounts alone were used.

What organisations provide private schemes?

Numerous organisations co-ordinate private inter-firm comparison schemes for the majority of different trade groups and industrial sectors. One of the best known is the Centre for Interfirm Comparison, which was founded by the British Institute of Management.

28.9 Inter-firm comparisons

The necessity for comparing like with like has been stressed throughout this chapter. For true comparisons, we must ensure not only that the bases of ratios are identical, but that a company is compared with companies in the same industrial sector and with similar principal activities. If it is compared with a company in a different industrial sector, the results might be interesting, but they might not be suitable for any decision-useful analysis. Of course, when using any published inter-company comparison data, it is essential to understand how the ratios are calculated. Each publication defines key terms, how ratios are computed and the methodologies used.

As stressed before, ratio definitions are not 'set in stone'. Different publications and inter-company comparison schemes will use different definitions of seemingly identical ratios. For instance, when using FAME's profit margin, we would need to ascertain what measure of profit is used (e.g. is other income and/or interest received included?).

There are a number of subscription databases available on CD-rom or online which provide annual reports and ratios with excellent search facilities e.g. FAME, Amadeus and OneSource.

FAME (Financial Analysis Made Easy) (www.bvdep.com)

FAME displays annual consolidated accounts, and performs company comparisons (Peer Analysis), as well as market sector reports (Statistical Analysis). The detailed information includes Company profile including subsidiaries and directors, Accounting and financial information including company turnover, Ratios and trends, Complete lists of holding companies and shareholder details, and the latest company news.

Search can be on a single criterion or over 100 criteria with results displayed or printed in various formats, e.g. text, charts or graphs, and exported to other applications, e.g. wordprocessors, databases, Excel spreadsheets. The index supplies information on live and dissolved companies, which is particularly helpful for tracing old, new and very small companies. It also includes share prices from mid-2000 for quoted companies.

Amadeus (www.bvdep.com)

Amadeus is a comprehensive, pan-European database containing financial information on public and private companies in 34 European countries. It provides standardised company accounts for up to 10 years for European companies with 25 standard ratios. As with FAME, it is modular, with data for the top 250,000 companies, the top 1.5 million or all companies.

OneSource (www.onesource.com)

OneSource is a user-friendly database that can be accessed on line. It integrates business content from over 2,500 leading sources worldwide to provide world-class company and industry profiles, executive biographies, financial data, analyst reports, and business press coverage. OneSource gathers in-depth data on more than 100 major industries, including detailed SIC code-level information. Users can search to find companies that match their criteria – search by size, location or line of business or via a large selection of variables and get detailed financial information and analysts' reports. In addition to financial data it records key executive contacts and board members by name, location, line of business, job function or biographical details, news and articles.

The following extract from OneSource illustrates Key Indicators and a Peer Listing of 10 closest companies by sales (it is also possible to extend the number of companies listed and list by assets):

J D Wetherspoon plc
Financial Health Report – GBP (000)

	2004	2003	2002	1 Year Growth Rate	3 Year Growth Rate
Key Indicators					
Sales	787,126.0	730,913.0	601,295.0	7.7%	17.6%
Net Income	29,274.0	34,044.0	35,416.0	−14.0%	−0.7%
Earnings Per Share	0.15	0.16	0.17	−7.89%	1.05%
Total Assets	828,078.0	820,838.0	783,366.0	0.9%	8.0%
Total Liabilities	539,124.0	502,511.0	473,233.0	7.3%	12.0%
Long-Term Debt	322,219.0	299,221.0	291,618.0	7.7%	8.6%
Margins	**2004**	**2003**	**2002**		
Gross Margin	14.6%	14.9%	16.2%	17.0%	17.7%
Operating Margin	9.9%	10.3%	11.7%	12.1%	12.5%
Pretax Margin	3.7%	4.7%	5.9%	6.2%	NA
Profit Margin	3.7%	4.7%	5.9%	6.2%	6.5%

Ratios

Long-Term Debt to Equity	1.1%	0.9%	0.9%	0.9%	0.9%
Return on Equity	9.6%	10.8%	12.1%	11.5%	NA
Asset Turnover	1.0%	0.9%	0.8%	0.8%	0.7%
Inventory Turnover	59.1	64.3	62.6	65.9	71.4
Receivable Turnover	NA	NA	NA	NA	NA
Total Debt/Equity	1.2%	1.0%	1.0%	0.9%	0.9%
Current Ratio	0.3	0.3	0.3	0.4	0.9

J D Wetherspoon plc – Peer Listing Report

Peer Listing – 10 closest companies by sales anywhere in the United Kingdom in the same primary SIC

	Town	County	Sales (GBP 000)	Pre-Tax Profit (GBP 000)	Net Worth (GBP 000)	Number of Employees	Total Assets (GBP 000)
J D Wetherspoon plc	Watford	Hertfordshire	787,126.0	46,316.0	288,954.0	9,708	828,078.0
Punch Taverns plc	Burton On Trent	Staffordshire	637,600.0	133,300.0	799,600.1	700	3,997,100.1
Spirit Group Ltd.	London	London	498,540.0	(8,912.0)	90,587.0	16,447	1,343,069.0
Unique Pubs Ltd.	Solihull	West Midlands	458,547.0	121,057.0	805,995.0	266	2,768,359.0
De Vere Group Plc	Warrington	Cheshire	321,778.0	41,629.0	597,781.0	7,014	944,131.0
Punch Taverns (Pm) Ltd.	Burton On Trent	Staffordshire	278,429.0	15,898.0	(65,585.0)	557	1,158,947.0
Punch Taverns (Ptl) Ltd.	Burton On Trent	Staffordshire	211,423.0	38,170.0	313,070.0	355	1,223,760.0
Punch Taverns (Vpr) Ltd.	Burton On Trent	Staffordshire	183,085.0	9,812.0	146,652.0	NA	1,108,277.0
Spirit Group Retail Ltd.	Burton On Trent	Staffordshire	139,373.0	52,534.0	1,027,054.0	10,181	1,396,747.0
Punch Taverns (Pml) Ltd.	Warrington	Cheshire	135,506.0	2,151.0	(29,295.0)	267	1,186,015.0
Sfi Group Ltd.	Woking	Surrey	128,738.0	(26,392.0)	(11,081.0)	31,080	86,386.0

Note: The above information is derived from a OneSource Information Services, Ltd. ('OneSource') product, and is the copyrighted property of OneSource and/or its information providers. OneSource and its information providers disclaim the accuracy, adequacy, completeness, and timeliness of the information, and shall not be held liable for any loss, damage, or injury that results from any use of the information.

28.10 World Wide Web (WWW) pages for company information

The WWW offers enormous opportunities to access company information and selected accounting information. A number of sources include:

Financial report data

Corporate reports	www.corporatereports.co.uk
Companies annual reports on line	www.carolworld.com
Hemmington Scott	www.hemscott.net
COMPANY REFS (demo)	www.companyrefs.com
BIZ/ED	http://bized.ac.uk
Accounting web	www.accountingweb.co.uk

Professional accounting bodies

ACCA – Association of Chartered Certified Accountants	www.accaglobal.com
CIMA – Chartered Institute of Management Accountants	http://cimaglobal.com
CIPFA – Chartered Institute of Public Finance and Accountancy	www.cipfa.org.uk
Institute of Chartered Accounts in Ireland	www.icai.ie
ICAS – Institute of Chartered Accountants of Scotland	www.icas.org.uk
ICSA – Institute of Chartered Secretaries and Administrators	www.icsa.org.uk
The Fédération des Experts Comptables Européens	www.fee.be
Hong Kong Institute of Certified Public Accountants	www.hkicpa.org.hk
Institute of Chartered Accountants of India	http://icai.org
Institute of Chartered Accountants of New Zealand	www.icanz.co.nz
Instituite of Certified Public Accountants of Singapore	www.accountants.org.sg
The South African Institute of Chartered Accountants	www.saica.co.za
American Institute of Certified Public Accountants	www.aicpa.org

Other bodies

IASB – International Accounting Standards Board	www.iasb.org
IOSCO – International Organisation of Securities Commissions	www.iosco.org
UK Accounting Standards Board	www.asb.org.uk
UK Financial Reporting Council	www.frc.org.uk
Australian Accounting Standards Board	http://aasb.com.au
Malaysian Accounting Standards Board	www.masb.org.my
IFAD – International Forum for Accountancy Development	www.ifad.net
ISTAR – International Standard Setting Report	www.istar-global.net
EFRAG – European Financial Reporting Advisory Group	www.efrag.org
FASB – Financial Accounting Standards Board	www.fasb.org

Other accounting sites

American Accounting Association	www.aaahq.org
British Accounting Association	www.shef.ac.uk/~baa
European Accounting Association	www.eaa-online.org
Deloitte & Touche	www.deloitte.com
Ernst & Young	www.ey.com
KPMG	www.kpmg.com
PriceWaterhouseCoopers	www.pwcglobal.com
DTI	http://dti.gov.uk
SEC	www.sec.gov

28.11 Non-financial ratios

As well as some of the more traditional financial statistics, each industry will have important operational statistics which provide some clues to the direction a company is moving and its performance in its area of expertise. For instance, BT provides information which charts the changes in technology (from the BT Annual Report and Accounts 2001):

BT Cellnet	1997	1998	1999	2000	2001
Digital GSM ('000)	1,125	2,303	4,163	7,249	11,162
Analogue ('000)	1,573	774	359	155	–
% growth over previous year	12.9	14.0	47.0	63.7	50.8

Optical fibre					
Kilometres in the network ('000)	1997	1998	1999	2000	2001
Fibre	3,302	3,591	4,058	4,555	5,100

28.12 Interpretation problems when using ratios and consolidated financial statements

Limitations of ratio analysis

Ratios are useful flags but there are limitations that the reader needs to bear in mind – these include limitations:

● relating to the underlying financial statements:

  – the reliability of the financial statements themselves made suspect by, say, fraudulent misrepresentation as in Enron or window-dressing, e.g. despatching goods at the end of the period knowing them to be defective so that they appear in current year's sales and accepting that they will be returned later in the next period.

  – the possibility that the accounts are subject to fundamental uncertainty which could affect the going concern concept – there might be full disclosure in the notes but ratios might not be accurate predictors of earnings and solvency.

- arising because ratios make use of the balance sheet figures:
  - the end of year figures are static and might not be a fair reflection of normal relationships such as when a business is seasonal, e.g. an arable farm might have no inventory until the harvest and a toy manufacturer might have little inventory after supplying wholesalers in the lead up to Christmas. Any ratios based on the inventory figure such as inventory turnover could be misleading if calculated, at say, a 31 December year-end.
- invalidating inter-company comparisons, such as:
  - use of different measurement bases, e.g.
    - non-current assets reported at historical cost or revaluation
    - revaluations carried out at different dates
  - use of off-balance sheet finance, e.g.
    - structuring the terms of a lease to ensure that it is treated as an operating lease and not a finance lease
    - special-purpose enterprises to keep debts off the balance sheet
  - use of different commercial practices, e.g.
    - factoring accounts receivable so that cash is increased – a perfectly normal transaction but one that could cause the comparative ratio of days' credit allowed to be significantly reduced
  - applying different accounting policies, e.g.
    - adopting different depreciation methods such as straight-line and reducing balance
    - adopting different inventory valuation methods such as FIFO and weighted average
  - assuming different degrees of optimism/pessimism when making judgement-based adjustments to non-current and current assets, e.g.
    - on the impairment review of intangible and tangible fixed assets
    - on writing down inventory and accounts receivable
  - having different definitions for ratios, e.g.
    - the numerator for ROCE may be operating profit, profit before interest and tax, profit before interest, profit after tax etc.
    - the denominator for ROCE may be total assets, total assets less intangibles, net assets etc.
  - the use of norms can be misleading, e.g.
    - a current ratio of 2:1 may be totally inappropriate for a company like Tesco which does not have long inventory turnover periods – as its sales are for cash it would also not produce trade receivable collection period ratios.
  - making appropriate choice of comparator companies for benchmarking – this is a simple idea but more difficult in practice, e.g.
    - how to find companies with a similar trade

- how to set criteria for selection – should it be
  - the industry average ratios – but these may be based on many companies operating under very different economies of scale; or companies with
  - similar amount of capital employed, or
  - similar amount of sales, or
  - some other criteria e.g. the most profitable.

The choice of benchmark is important in that it may affect the conclusions that are made.

Problems when using consolidated accounts

Certain limitations need to be recognised when analysing a consolidated balance sheet, making inter-company comparisons and forming a judgement on distributable profits based on the consolidated profit and loss account. These are as follows:

● The consolidated balance sheet aggregates the assets and liabilities of the parent company and its subsidiaries. The current and liquidity ratios that are extracted to indicate to creditors the security of their credit and the likelihood of the debt being settled will be valid only if all creditors have equal rights to claim against the aggregated assets. This may be the case if there are cross-guarantees from each company, but it is more likely that the creditors will need to seek payment from the individual group company to which it allowed the credit. One needs to be aware that the consolidated accounts are prepared for the shareholders of the parent company and that they may be irrelevant to the needs of creditors. This is not a criticism of consolidation, merely a recognition of the purpose for which the accounts are relevant.

● Inter-company comparisons may be invalidated if groups follow different accounting policies in relation to the choice of consolidation process. For example, one group might organise a combination to fall within the criteria for treatment as a merger, without goodwill and using book values for the aggregation; another group might organise the combination to be treated as an acquisition, with goodwill arising on consolidation and fair values used for the aggregation.

● The consolidated profit and loss account does not give a true picture of the profits immediately available for distribution by the holding company to its shareholders. It shows the group profit that could become available for distribution if the holding company were to exercise its influence and control, and require all its subsidiary companies and associated companies to declare a dividend of 100% of their profits for the year. Legally, it is possible for the company to exercise its voting power to achieve the passing up to it of the subsidiary companies' profits – although commercially this is highly unlikely. The position of the associated companies is less clear: the holding company only has influence and does not have the voting power to guarantee that the profit disclosed in the consolidated profit and loss account is translated into dividends for the holding company shareholders.

Summary

Financial ratio analysis is integral to the assessment and improvement of company performance. Financial ratios help to direct attention to the areas of the business that need additional analysis. In particular, they provide some measure of the profitability and cash position of a company.

Financial ratios can be compared against preceding period's ratios, budgeted ratios for the current period, ratios of other companies in the same industry and the industry sector averages. This comparison is meaningful and decision-useful only when like is compared with like. Users of financial ratios must ensure that the composition of ratios is clearly defined and agreed.

Unfortunately, many of the problems that arise are not simply problems of different definitions for ratios, but far more fundamental. They result from the lack of uniformity and comparability of published financial statements.

Ratios are useful only if they are used properly. They are a starting point for further investigations and should be used in conjunction with other sources of information and other analytical techniques. Financial reports are only one of many sources of information available about an enterprise; others include international, national and industrial statistics and projections, trade association reports, market and consumer surveys, and reports prepared by professional analysts.

In Chapter 29 we consider some additional techniques that complement the pyramid approach to ratio analysis.

REVIEW QUESTIONS

1   Explain how the reader of an annual report prepared for a group might become aware if any subsidiary or associated company was experiencing:

  (a) solvency problems;

  (b) profitability problems.[19]

2   Using the segmental analysis from the Bass plc 1999 accounts in section 28.7.2, discuss the following:

  (a) Explain the value of the segmental analysis to an existing shareholder, a potential shareholder and a creditor of the company.

  (b) Which is the most profitable business segment?

  (c) What further segmental information would it be useful for a shareholder to receive in the operating and financial review?

  (d) How subjective are the figures for turnover and profit?

  (e) How useful do you consider the separate disclosure of business and geographic segment information?

3   'The problems of using ratio analysis on a set of published accounts exceed the benefits to be gained.' Discuss.

4 (a) Explain the uses and limitations of ratio analysis when used to interpret the published financial accounts of a company.

   (b) State and express two ratios that can be used to analyse each of the following:
   (i) profitability;
   (ii) liquidity;
   (iii) management control.

   (c) Explain briefly points which are important when using ratios to interpret accounts under each of the headings in (b) above.

5 (a) Describe the current requirements for the disclosure of segmental information in the annual report.

   (b) Discuss the advantages and disadvantages to the users and preparers of annual reports of disclosing segmental data classified by (i) industry groupings, (ii) legal entities within the group structure.

   (c) Discuss the importance of the disclosure of exceptional items to the users of the annual report in addition to the operating profit.

6 'Unregulated segmental reporting is commercially dangerous to companies making disclosures.'[20] Discuss.

EXERCISES

An outline solution is provided in the Appendix at the end of the text for exercises marked with an asterisk (*).

Question I

Saddam Ltd is considering the possibility of diversifying its operations and has identified three firms in the same industrial sector as potential takeover targets. The following information in respect of the companies has been extracted from their most recent financial statements.

	Ali Ltd	Baba Ltd	Camel Ltd
ROCE before tax %	22.1	23.7	25.0
Net profit %	12.0	12.5	3.75
Asset turnover ratio	1.45	1.16	3.73
Gross profit %	20.0	25.0	10.0
Sales/fixed assets	4.8	2.2	11.6
Sales/current assets	2.1	5.2	5.5
Current ratio	3.75	1.4	1.5
Acid test ratio	2.25	0.4	0.9
Average number of weeks' debtors outstanding	5.6	6.0	4.8
Average number of weeks' stock held	12.0	19.2	4.0
Ordinary dividend %	10.0	15.0	30.0
Dividend cover	4.3	5.0	1.0

Required:

(a) Prepare a report for the directors of Saddam Ltd, assessing the performance of the three companies from the information provided and identifying areas which you consider require further investigation before a final decision is made.

(b) Discuss briefly why a firm's balance sheet is unlikely to show the true market value of the business.

* Question 2

The major shareholder/director of Esrever Ltd has obtained average data for the industry as a whole. He wishes to see what the forecast results and position of Esrever Ltd would be if in the ensuing year its performance were to coincide with the industry averages.

At 1 July 20X0, actual figures for Esrever Ltd included:

	£
Land and buildings (at written-down value)	132,000
Fixtures, fittings and equipment (at written-down value)	96,750
Stock	22,040
12% loan (repayable in 20X5)	50,000
Ordinary share capital (50p shares)	100,000

For the year ended 30 June 20X1 the following forecast information is available:

1 Depreciation of fixed assets (on reducing balance)

Land and buildings	2%
Fixtures, fittings and equipment	20%

2 Net current assets will be financed by a bank overdraft to the extent necessary.

3 At 30 June 20X0 total assets minus current liabilities will be £231,808.

4 Profit after tax for the year will be 23.32% of gross profit and 11.16% of total assets minus all external liabilities, both long-term and short-term.

5 Corporation tax will be an effective rate of 20% of profit before tax.

6 Cost of sales will be 68% of turnover (excluding VAT).

7 Closing stock will represent 61.9 days' average cost of sales (excluding VAT).

8 Any difference between total expenses and the aggregate of expenses ascertained from this given information will represent credit purchases and other credit expenses, in each case excluding VAT input tax.

9 A dividend of 2.5p per share will be proposed.

10 The collection period for the VAT-exclusive amount of trade debtors will be an average of 42.6 days of the annual turnover. All the company's supplies are subject to VAT output tax at 15%.

11 The payment period for the VAT-exclusive amount of trade creditors (purchases and other credit expenses) will be an average of 29.7 days. All these items are subject to (reclaimable) VAT input tax at 15%. This VAT rate has been increased to 17.5% and may be subject to future changes, but for the purpose of this question the theory and workings remain the same irrespective of the rate.

12 Creditors, other than trade creditors, will comprise corporation tax due, proposed dividends and VAT payable equal to one-quarter of the net amount due for the year.

13 Calculations are based on a year of 365 days.

Required:
Construct a forecast profit and loss account for Esrever Ltd for the year ended 30 June 20X1 and a forecast balance sheet at that date in as much detail as possible. (All calculations should be made to the nearest £1.)

* Question 3

Amalgamated Engineering plc makes specialised machinery for several industries. In recent years, the company has faced severe competition from overseas businesses, and its sales volume has hardly changed. The company has recently applied for an increase in its bank overdraft limit from £750,000 to £1,500,000. The bank manager has asked you, as the bank's credit analyst, to look at the company's application.

You have the following information:

(i) Balance sheets as at 31 December 20X5 and 20X6:

	20X5		20X6	
	£000	£000	£000	£000
Tangible fixed assets				
Freehold land and buildings, at cost		1,800		1,800
Plant and equipment, at net value		3,150		3,300
		4,950		5,100
Current assets				
Inventory	1,125		1,500	
Trade receivables	825		1,125	
Short-term investments	300		—	
	2,250		2,625	
Current liabilities				
Bank overdraft	225		675	
Trade payables	300		375	
Taxation payable	375		300	
Dividends payable	225		225	
	1,125		1,575	
Net current assets		1,125		1,050
		6,075		6,150
Long-term liability				
8% debentures, 20X9		1,500		1,500
		4,575		4,650
Capital and reserves				
Ordinary shares of £1 each		2,250		2,250
Share premium account		750		750
Retained earnings		1,575		1,650
		4,575		4,650

(ii) Profit and loss accounts for the years ended 31 December 20X5 and 20X6:

	20X5		20X6	
	£000	£000	£000	£000
Turnover		6,300		6,600
Cost of sales: materials	1,500		1,575	
: labour	2,160		2,280	
: production				
: overheads	750		825	
		4,410		4,680
		1,890		1,920
Administrative expenses		1,020		1,125
Operating profit		870		795
Investment income		15		—
		885		795
Interest payable: debentures	120		120	
: bank overdraft	15		75	
		135		195
Profit before taxation		750		600
Taxation		375		300
Profit attributable to shareholders		375		300
Dividends		225		225
Retained earnings for year		150		75

You are also provided with the following information:

(iii) The general price level rose on average by 10% between 20X5 and 20X6. Average wages also rose by 10% during this period.

(iv) The debenture stock is secured by a fixed charge over the freehold land and buildings, which have recently been valued at £3,000,000. The bank overdraft is unsecured.

(v) Additions to plant and equipment in 20X6 amounted to £450,000: depreciation provided in that year was £300,000.

Required:
(a) Prepare a cash flow statement for the year ended 31 December 20X6.
(b) Calculate appropriate ratios to use as a basis for a report to the bank manager.
(c) Draft the outline of a report for the bank manager, highlighting key areas you feel should be the subject of further investigation. Mention any additional information you need, and where appropriate refer to the limitations of conventional historical cost accounts.
(d) On receiving the draft report the bank manager advised that he also required the following three cash-based ratios:
  (i) Debt service coverage ratio defined as EBITDA/annual debt repayments and interest.
  (ii) Cash flow from operations to current liabilities.
  (iii) Cash recovery rate defined as ((cash flow from operations + proceeds from sale of fixed assets)/average gross assets)×100

The director has asked you to explain why the bank manager has requested this additional information given that he has already been supplied with profit-based ratios.

Question 4

Sally Gorden seeks your assistance to decide whether she should invest in Ruby plc or Sapphire plc. Both companies are quoted on the London Stock Exchange. Their shares were listed on 20 June 20X4 as Ruby 475p and Sapphire 480p.

The performance of these two companies during the year ended 30 June 20X4 is summarised as follows:

	Ruby plc £000	Sapphire plc £000
Operating profit	588	445
Interest and similar charges	(144)	(60)
	444	385
Taxation	(164)	(145)
Profit after taxation	280	240
Interim dividend paid	(30)	(40)
Preference dividend proposed	(90)	—
Ordinary dividend proposed	(60)	(120)
Retained profit for the year	100	80

The companies have been financed on 30 June 20X4 as follows:

	Ruby plc £000	Sapphire plc £000
Ordinary shares of 50p each	1,000	1,500
15% preference shares of £1 each	600	—
Share premium account	60	—
Profit and loss account balance	250	450
17% debentures	800	—
12% debentures	—	500
	2,710	2,450

On 1 October 20X3 Ruby plc issued 500,000 ordinary shares of 50p each at a premium of 20%. On 1 April 20X4 Sapphire plc made a 1 for 2 bonus issue. Apart from these, there has been no change in the issued capital of either company during the year.

Required:
(a) Calculate the earnings per share (EPS) of each company.
(b) Determine the price/earnings ratio (PE) of each company.
(c) Based on the PE ratio alone, which company's shares would you recommend to Sally?
(d) On the basis of appropriate accounting ratios (which should be calculated), identify three other matters Sally should take account of before she makes her choice.
(e) Describe the advantages and disadvantages of gearing.

Question 5

Briefly state:
(i) the case for segmental reporting;
(ii) the case against segmental reporting.

Question 6

Filios Products plc brews beers, owns and manages pubs and hotels, manufactures and supplies alcoholic and soft drinks, and is a supplier and operator of amusement machines and other leisure facilities.

The accounts for 1997 contain the following information:

Balance Sheet of Filios Products

	£m
Fixed assets at book value	1,663
Current assets	
Stocks and debtors	381
Bank balance	128
	509
Less: *Creditors falling due within one year*	193
Net current assets	316
Total assets less current liabilities	1,979
Less: 10% debentures	140
	1,839
Capital and reserves	
Share capital	800
Retained profit	1,039
	1,839

Profit and Loss Account of Filios Products

	£m	£m
Turnover		1,028
Less: Cost of sales	684	
Administration expenses	110	
Distribution costs	101	
Interest charged	14	909
Net profit		119

The following breakdown is provided of the company's results into three divisions and head office:

	Beer and pub operations	Hotel business	Other drinks & leisure	Head office
	£m	£m	£m	£m
Turnover	508	152	368	—
Cost of sales	316	81	287	—
Administration expenses	43	14	38	15

Distribution costs	64	12	25	—
Interest charged	10	—	—	4
Fixed assets at book value	890	332	364	77
Stocks and debtors	230	84	67	—
Bank balance	73	15	28	12
Creditors	66	40	56	31
10% debentures	100	—	—	40

The following information is obtained for competitor companies: Dean, which brews beer and manages pubs; and Clarke, which is in the hotel business:

	Dean £m	Clarke £m
Turnover	600	150
Operating profit	80	60
Net assets	1,300	300

Required:
(a) Outline the nature of segmental reports and explain the reason for presenting such information in the published accounts.
(b) Prepare a segmental statement for Filios Products plc for 1997 complying, so far as the information permits, with the provisions of SSAP 25 *Segmental Reporting*, so as to show for each segment and the business as a whole:
  − turnover;
  − profit;
  − net assets.
(c) (i) Examine the relative performance of the operating divisions of Filios Products; and
   (ii) Compare the performance of the operating divisions of Filios Products, where appropriate, with that of the competitor companies.

   The examination and comparison should be based on the following accounting ratios:
   − operating profit percentage;
   − net asset turnover;
   − return on net assets.
   (The Chartered Institute of Bankers)

Question 7

The Housing Department of Chaldon District Council has invited tenders for re-roofing 80 houses on an estate. Chaldon Direct Services (CDS) is one of the Council's direct services organisations and it has submitted a tender for this contract, as have several contractors from the private sector.

The Council has been able to narrow the choice of contractor to the four tenderers who have submitted the lowest bids, as follows:

	£
Nutfield & Sons	398,600
Chaldon Direct Services	401,850
Tandridge Tilers Ltd	402,300
Redhill Roofing Contractors plc	406,500

The tender evaluation process requires that the three private tenderers be appraised on the basis of financial soundness and quality of work. These tenderers were required to provide their latest final accounts (year ended 31 March 20X4) for this appraisal; details are as follows:

	Nutfield & Sons	Tandridge Tilers Ltd	Redhill Roofing Contractors plc
Profit and loss account for year ended 31 March 20X4	£	£	£
Turnover	611,600	1,741,200	3,080,400
Direct costs	(410,000)	(1,190,600)	(1,734,800)
Other operating costs	(165,000)	(211,800)	(811,200)
Interest	—	(85,000)	(96,000)
Net profit before taxation	36,600	253,800	438,400
Balance sheet as at 31 March 20X4	£	£	£
Fixed assets (net book value)	55,400	1,542,400	2,906,800
Stocks and work-in-progress	26,700	149,000	449,200
Debtors	69,300	130,800	240,600
Bank	(11,000)	10,400	(6,200)
Creditors	(92,600)	(140,600)	(279,600)
Proposed dividend	—	(91,800)	(70,000)
Loan	—	(800,000)	(1,200,000)
	47,800	800,200	2,040,800
Capital	47,800	—	—
Ordinary shares @ £1 each	—	250,000	1,000,000
Reserves	—	550,200	1,040,800
	47,800	800,200	2,040,800

Nutfield & Sons employ a workforce of six operatives and have been used by the Council for four small maintenance contracts worth between £60,000 and £75,000 which they have completed to an appropriate standard. Tandridge Tilers Ltd have been employed by the Council on a contract for the replacement of flat roofs on a block of flats, but there have been numerous complaints about the standard of the work. Redhill Roofing Contractors plc is a company which has not been employed by the Council in the past and, as much of its work has been carried out elsewhere, its quality of work is not known.

CDS has been suffering from the effects of increasing competition in recent years and achieved a return on capital employed of only 3.5% in the previous financial year. CDS's manager has successfully renegotiated more beneficial service level agreements with the Council's central support departments with effect from 1 April 20X4. CDS has also reviewed its fixed asset base which has resulted in the disposal of a depot which was surplus to requirements and in the rationalisation of vehicles and plant. The consequence of this is that CDS's average capital employed for 20X4/X5 is likely to be some 15% lower than in 20X3/X4.

A further analysis of the tender bids is provided below:

	Nutfield & Sons £	Chaldon Direct Services £	Tandridge Tilers Ltd £	Redhill Roofing Contractors plc £
Labour	234,000	251,400	303,600	230,400
Materials	140,000	100,000	80,000	140,000
Overheads (including profit)	24,600	50,450	18,700	36,100

The Council's Client Services Committee can reject tenders on financial and/or quality grounds. However, each tender has to be appraised on these criteria and reasons for acceptance or rejection must be justified in the appraisal process.

Required:
In your capacity as accountant responsible for reporting to the Client Services Committee, draft a report to the Committee evaluating the tender bids and recommending to whom the contract should be awarded.

(CIPFA)

Question 8

Chelsea plc has embarked on a programme of growth through acquisitions and has identified Kensington Ltd and Wimbledon Ltd as companies in the same industrial sector, as potential targets. Using recent financial statements of both Kensington and Wimbledon and further information obtained from a trade association, Chelsea plc has managed to build up the following comparability table:

	Kensington	Wimbledon	Industrial average
Profitability ratios			
ROCE before tax %	22	28	20
Return on equity %	18	22	15
Net profit margin %	11	5	7
Gross profit ratio %	25	12	20
Activity ratios			
Total assets turnover = times	1.5	4.0	2.5
Fixed asset turnover = times	2.3	12.0	5.1
Debtor collection period in weeks	8.0	5.1	6.5
Stockholding period in weeks	21.0	4.0	13.0
Liquidity ratios			
Current ratio	1.8	1.7	2.8
Acid test	0.5	0.9	1.3
Debt–equity ratio %	80.0	20.0	65.0

Required:
(a) Prepare a performance report for the two companies for consideration by the directors of Chelsea plc indicating which of the two companies you consider to be a better acquisition.
(b) Indicate what further information is needed before a final decision can be made.

Question 9

(a) The following ratios have been extracted from an analysis of the accounts of three companies – North, South and East:

	North	South	East
Profit/Sales × 100	5%	4%	3%
Asset turnover	5 times	3 times	4 times
Financial leverage	2	4	5

Required:
Comment on the respective performance of each of the three companies.

(b) 'The consolidation of financial statements hides rather than provides information.' Discuss.

Question 10

The following profit and loss account and balance sheet extracts from the accounts of J D Wetherspoon have been downloaded from the FAME (Financial Analysis Made Easy) database:

PROFIT & LOSS ACCOUNTS	31/07/2004	31/07/2003	31/07/2002	31/07/2001
Turnover	787,126	730,913	601,295	483,968
Total Expenses	−709,498	−655,930	−531,210	−425,588
Operating Profit	77,628	74,983	70,085	58,380
Other Income	592	810	749	1,247
Exceptional Items	−7,758			
Profit (Loss) before Interest	70,462	75,793	70,834	59,627
Interest Paid	−24,146	−19,654	−17,266	−15,310
Profit (Loss) before Tax	46,316	56,139	53,568	44,317
Taxation	−17,042	−19,744	−18,152	−14,457
Profit (Loss) after Tax	29,274	36,395	35,416	29,860

BALANCE SHEETS				
Fixed Assets				
Tangible Assets	783,574	773,823	745,041	625,903
Current Assets				
Stock & W.I.P.	12,009	9,601	8,594	7,503
Bank & Deposits	9,660	15,160	13,609	9,791
Other Current Assets	22,835	17,766	16,122	13,991
Current Assets	44,504	42,527	38,325	31,285
Current Liabilities				
Trade Creditors	−52,661	−53,066	−54,352	−50,418
Short Term Loans & Overdrafts	−25,000	−24,799	−24,831	
Total Other Current Liabilities	−72,707	−57,496	−43,736	−31,547
Current Liabilities	−150,368	−135,361	−122,919	−81,965
Total Assets	828,078	816,350	783,366	657,188
Total Assets less Cur. Liab.	677,710	680,989	660,447	575,223
Long Term Liabilities				
Long Term Debt	−322,219	−299,221	−291,618	−251,368
Total Other Long Term Liab.	−66,537	−63,140	−58,696	−50,016
Long Term Liabilities	−388,756	−362,361	−350,314	−301,384
Total Assets less Liabilities	288,954	318,628	310,133	273,839
Shareholders Funds				
Issued Capital	3,783	4,149	4,292	4,224
Total Reserves	285,171	314,479	305,841	269,615
Shareholders Funds	288,954	318,628	310,133	273,839

Required:
Prepare a table in following FAME Profile Report format:

PROFILE	31/07/2004	31/07/2003	31/07/2002	31/07/2001
12 months	12 months	12 months	12 months	12 months
Turnover				
Profit (Loss) before Taxation				
Net Tangible Assets (Liab.)				
Shareholders Funds				
Profit Margin (%)				
Return on Shareholders Funds (%)				
Return on Capital Employed (%)				
Liquidity Ratio				
Gearing Ratio (%)				
Number of Employees				

Note that the ratios are to be calculated as in the FAME Report where they are defined as follows:

Return = Profit before tax; Capital Employed = Total assets less liabilities;
Gearing ratio =(Long-term liabilities + Short-term loans)/Shareholders funds

References

1 I. Griffiths, *Creative Accounting*, Sidgwick & Jackson, 1986.
2 *Ibid.*
3 M. Stead, *How to Use Company Accounts for Successful Investment Decisions*, FT Pitman Publishing, 1995, pp. 134–136.
4 N. Cope, 'Bitter battles in the beer business', *Accountancy*, May 1993, p. 32.
5 D. Chopping, R. Carroll and R. Skerratt, *Applying GAAP*, ICAEW, 1999/2000, p. 100.
6 Neil Garrod, *Competitive Disadvantage and Segmental Disclosure*, Working Paper 2000/5, University of Glasgow.
7 SSAP 25 *Segmental Reporting*, ASC, June 1990.
8 S. Hussain, 'What do segmental definitions tell us?', *Accountancy*, June 1996, p. 103.
9 IAS 14 (revised) *Segment reporting*, IASL, 1997.
10 C. Emmanuel and N. Garrod, 'Segmental reporting in the UK – how does SSAP 25 stand up to international comparison?', *European Accounting Review*, vol. 3, no. 3, 1994, pp. 547–562.
11 M. Davies, R. Patterson and A. Wilson, *UK GAAP*, Ernst & Young (5th edition), 1997, p. 1079.
12 ED 45 *Segmental Reporting*, ASC, November 1988.
13 C.R. Emmanuel and M. Mehafdi, *Transfer Pricing*, The Chartered Institute of Management Accountants and Academic Press, London, 1994.
14 *Company REFS – Really Essential Financial Statistics*: Tables Volume devised by Jim Slater, Hemmington Scott.
15 *Handbook of Market Leaders*, Extel Financial Ltd.
16 *Key Business Ratios: The Guide to British Business Performance*, Dun & Bradstreet Ltd.
17 *The Company Guide*, HS Financial Publishing.
18 See http://www.onesource.com/.
19 P. Anderson, 'Are you ready for ratio analysis?', *Accountancy*, September 1996, p. 92.
20 G.J. Kelly, 'Unregulated segment reporting: Australian evidence', *British Accounting Review*, 26(3), 1994, p. 217.

CHAPTER 29

Trend analysis and multivariate analysis

29.1 Introduction

In the preceding chapter we introduced ratio analysis as a means for interpreting financial statements. In this chapter we present further techniques that can be used in conjunction with ratio analysis. The main similarity between these techniques is their purpose: each technique acts as a focus for more detailed investigation. By various means, they can be applied to a set of financial statements to identify areas of interest and concern. If the initial investigation throws up unexpected and unexplained results, the root cause should then be ascertained by more rigorous investigation.

In this chapter we consider the following:

- Horizontal analysis between two periods
- Trend analysis over a series of periods
- Historical summaries
- Vertical analysis – common size statements
- Multivariate analysis – Z-scores
- H-scores
- A-scores
- Balanced scorecards
- Valuing shares of an unquoted company – quantitative process
- Valuing shares of an unquoted company – qualitative process
- Shareholder value analysis
- Financial reporting and risk.

We will illustrate the techniques using the accounts of JD Wetherspoon plc, which were used in the preceding chapter to demonstrate ratio analysis.

29.2 Horizontal analysis between two periods

The mechanics of horizontal analysis between two periods are very simple. The percentage change (positive or negative) for each item in the financial statements between two periods needs to be calculated. Usually, the percentage changes are calculated for all balance sheet items and profit and loss items over two successive years.

Although the calculations are straightforward, the skill rests with their interpretation. What do the percentages mean? Which changes are significant and warrant detailed analysis? Which changes require an explanation so that we can determine whether or not we need to implement rectifying measures?

29.2.1 Percentage changes in profit and loss account items

The percentage changes between JD Wetherspoon plc's 2002 and 2003 consolidated profit and loss accounts are calculated below.

	% change	2003 £000	2002 £000
Turnover from continuing operations	21.6%	730,913	601,295
Cost of sales	23.5%	(621,894)	(503,699)
Gross profit	11.7%	109,019	97,596
Administrative expenses	23.7%	(34,036)	(27,511)
Operating profit	7.0%	74,983	70,085
Loss on disposal of tangible fixed assets		(3,688)	—
Net interest payable	14.1%	(18,844)	(16,517)
Profit on ordinary activities before tax	2.1%	52,451	53,568
Tax on profit on ordinary activities	1.4%	(18,407)	(18,152)
Profit on ordinary activities after tax	(3.9%)	34,044	35,416
Dividends	7.7%	(7,434)	(6,902)
Retained profit for the year	6.7%	26,610	28,514

The company has been following an active policy of opening pubs, with 45 new pubs opened in 2003, bringing the total to 638. This has been a large element in the turnover increase. To quote the chairman's statement:

> The new pubs are in a variety of locations throughout Britain and Northern Ireland and have opened at initial sales levels which are encouraging for the future. Like-for-like sales increased by 4% although like-for-like profits declined by 1%, principally as a result of higher costs for labour, repairs and insurance.

Although higher labour and other pub costs exceeded the rate of increase in the turnover, operating profit increased by 7%. Dividends appear to have increased at a little over this rate and retained earnings have been depleted.

29.2.2 Percentage changes in profit and loss account items affected by exceptional items and balance sheet movements

Our interpretation can be affected by (a) balance sheet movements and (b) exceptional items.

Balance sheet movements

For example, the apparent increase of 7.7% in the dividend payout is misleading as we are more interested in the rate of increase in the dividend per share which can be affected by the number of shares in issue – the balance sheet note tells us that the company has purchased shares during the year and the chairman's statement includes the following:

The board proposes, subject to shareholders' consent, to pay a final dividend of 2.33p per share on 28 November 2003 to those shareholders on the register on 31 October 2003, bringing the total dividend for the year to 3.54p per share, a 10% increase on the previous year. At this level, dividends will be covered 4.8 times by earnings (before exceptional items), compared to 5.2 times in 2002. The company has decided to cease offering a scrip alternative to dividends, now and for the foreseeable future.

Note that by ceasing to offer scrip dividends the company is avoiding a future reduction in its earnings per share arising from any resultant increase in the number of shares in issue.

Exceptional items

The company sold 18 pubs during the year and there is a total after-tax loss of £2,351,000. The profit and loss account before exceptional items is as follows:

	% change	2003 £000	2002 £000
Operating profit	7.0%	74,993	70,085
Net interest payable	14.1%	(18,844)	(16,517)
Profit on ordinary activities before tax	4.8%	56,139	53,568
Tax on profit on ordinary activities	8.8%	(19,744)	(18,152)
Profit on ordinary activities after tax	2.8%	36,395	35,416
Dividends	7.7%	(7,434)	(6,902)
Retained profit for the year	1.6%	28,961	28,514

This shows a positive profit after tax and an increase in the retained earnings. Enquiry would be made as to the possible effect of the disposal of pubs which gave rise to the exceptional loss although this might be immaterial given that it involved the disposal of only 18 pubs out of a total of 638.

29.3 Trend analysis over a series of periods

Trend analysis is used to analyse company accounts over a series of years. It is usually applied to five-year or ten-year summaries supplied in company accounts. The main advantage of this technique is that it gives a very quick rough guide to specific trends in individual items in the financial statements. The main disadvantage is that the figures may ignore the effects of inflation and not represent company performance in real terms. An easy way to take some account of inflation is to use the retail price index (RPI) as a proxy for inflation and adjust calculated trends for the trend in RPI.

The two forms of trend analysis considered here are percentage changes and index numbers.

Percentage changes are calculated to highlight whether the rate is increasing or decreasing. For instance, Jacklin Cripes plc records the following profits in the five-year record:

	20X1 £000	20X2 £000	20X3 £000	20X4 £000	20X5 £000
Net profit	150	195	249	309	375
% change		+30.0%	+27.7%	+24.1%	+21.4%

The percentage changes show that the net profit for Jacklin Cripes plc has increased every year between 20X1 and 20X5. However, the rate of increase in net profit has decreased. The increase is 30% in 20X2, but only 21.4% in 20X5.

Index numbers give a good indication of how the results over a series of years compare with each other, and the general direction of the trend. To calculate index numbers, year 1 in the series is set to 100 and the other years are scaled down to correspond to the index number. To demonstrate this, consider Jacklin Cripes plc:

	20X1 £000	20X2 £000	20X3 £000	20X4 £000	20X5 £000
Net profit	150	195	249	309	375
Index number	100	130	166	206	250

where index (20X2) = 195/150 × 100 = 130
where index (20X3) = 249/150 × 100 = 166
where index (20X4) = 309/150 × 100 = 206
where index (20X5) = 375/150 × 100 = 250

The index numbers show that net profit increases every year over this period.

Now consider the trends in the five-year record for JD Wetherspoon plc shown in Figure 29.1. Both the percentage changes and the index numbers show that JD Wetherspoon's turnover and operating profit have increased significantly each year from 1999 to 2003. However, the rate of increase in both turnover and operating profit is falling and the pressure on margins is causing the rate of increase in the operating profits to lag behind that of the turnover.

Figure 29.1 JD Wetherspoon's five-year record

	1999 £000	2000 £000	2001 £000	2002 £000	2003 £000
Turnover	269,699	369,628	483,968	601,295	730,913
Operating profit	36,226	46,278	58,380	70,085	74,983
(a) *Percentage changes*	*1999*	*2000*	*2001*	*2002*	*2003*
Turnover		+37.1%	+30.9%	+24.2%	+21.6%
Operating profit		+27.7%	+26.2%	+20.0%	+7.0%
(b) *Index number*	*1999*	*2000*	*2001*	*2002*	*2003*
Turnover	100	137	179	223	271
Operating profit	100	128	161	193	207

This has implications for the future expansion of the company and on this point the Chairman's statement makes interesting reading:

Current Trading and Outlook
Profits both in the current year and going forward, are likely to be impacted by regulatory and employee cost increases.

Whereas we continue to see opportunities for profitable expansion, the uncertainty created by increased red tape and taxation means that it is prudent to reduce the rate of that expansion, so that the level of capital investment for the foreseeable future remains approximately in line with our free cash flow.

29.4 Historical summaries

The Companies Act 1985 does not require a company to include a historical summary in its annual report. However, following a comment by the chairman of the Stock Exchange, the practice has arisen for companies to include a five-year historical summary.

There is no accounting standard relating to such summaries, but there may well be circumstances where the reported figures need to be adjusted to make the series comparable: e.g. a change in accounting policy such as the adoption of IFRSs; a change in the composition of the group; bonus issues, rights issues and share splits. In the ASC handbook *Accounting for the Effects of Changing Prices*, it was recommended that companies which publish historical summaries should restate certain figures such as turnover, earnings and dividends in units of current purchasing power.[1]

The following extract from the 2000 Annual Report of a South African company, Barloworld, considers inflation in relation to earnings and dividends per share:

Inflation-adjusted information

	2000	1999
South African consumer price index (base 1994 = 100)	145.6	138.2
Deflation factor	*68.7*	*72.4*
Earnings per share (cents)	380.4	285.8
EPS deflated	*261.3*	*206.8*
Dividends per share (cents)	180.0	141.0
Dividend deflated	*123.7*	*102.0*
Total assets	16,550	14,951
Total assets deflated	*11,369*	*10,820*

Historical summaries should assist shareholders to answer such questions as: Is growth being achieved in excess of the rate of inflation? Is the growth in all segments of the business? What is the dividend cover over the past five years? Is the change in turnover and profitability constant or fluctuating?

Given the usefulness of the historical summaries, this is an area that requires a standard approach of the kind provided for segmental reporting. Without such a standard, the information may be unavailable or partially presented, e.g. it may disclose profit and loss data, but no balance sheet data to assess the rate of change in assets and rates of return.

29.5 Vertical analysis – common size statements

Vertical analysis concentrates solely on one year's financial statements, rather than comparing a number of years. Common size statements express all items in each financial statement as a percentage of a selected figure. For instance, all items in the profit and loss account can be expressed in terms of turnover; and all items in the balance sheet can be expressed in terms of capital employed or total shareholders' funds.

The advantages of vertical analysis are as follows:

● Common size statements allow comparisons between companies of different sizes. However, like ratio analysis, particular care should be taken to ensure the comparison of like companies with like.

● The balance sheet will identify changes in financial structure relative to the total capital employed or total shareholders' funds. The profit and loss account will identify changes in expenses relative to turnover.

● As all figures are expressed as annual percentages, this will redress many of the distortions of inflation. However, different financial statement items might be affected by different specific rates of inflation.

The disadvantages are as follows:

● Accounting policies might distort changes in financial structure and expenditure.

● Common size statements eliminate the concept of different-sized companies so that comparison is possible. However, the actual size of a company determines the specific risks to which the company is subject.

To illustrate common size statements, the 2003 balance sheet and profit and loss accounts for JD Wetherspoon plc are analysed below. The balance sheet expresses all items in terms of shareholders' funds, while the profit and loss account expresses all items in terms of turnover.

JD Wetherspoon
Consolidated profit and loss account for the year ended 31 July 2003

	2003 £000	Calculations	%
Turnover from continuing operations	730,913	730,913/730,913	100
Cost of sales	(621,894)	(621,894)/730,913	(85.1)
Gross profit	109,019	109,019/730,913	14.9
Administrative expenses	(34,036)	(34,036)/730,913	(4.7)
Operating profit	74,983	74,983/730,913	10.2
Loss on disposal of tangible assets	(3,688)	(3,688)/730,913	(0.5)
Net interest payable	(18,844)	(18,844)/730,913	(2.6)
Profit on ordinary activities before tax	52,451	52,451/730,913	7.1
Tax on profit on ordinary activities	(18,407)	(18,407)/730,913	(2.5)
Profit on ordinary activities after tax	34,044	34,044/730,913	4.6
Dividends	(7,434)	(7,434)/730,913	(1.0)
Retained profit for the year	26,610	26,610/730,913	3.6

Balance sheet at 31 July 2003

	2003 £000	Calculations	%
Fixed assets			
Tangible assets	773,823	773,823/318,628	242.9
	773,823	773,823/318,628	242.9
Current assets			
Stocks	9,601	9,601/318,628	3.0
Debtors due after more than one year	8,448	8,448/318,628	2.7
Debtors due within one year	9,017	9,017/318,628	2.8
Investments	301		
Cash	15,160	15,160/318,628	4.8
	42,527	42,527/318,628	13.3
Creditors due within one year	(135,361)	(135,361)/318,628	(42.5)
Net current liabilities	(92,834)	(92,834)/318,628	(29.1)
Total assets less current liabilities	680,989	680,989/318,628	213.7
Creditors due after one year	(299,942)	(299,942)/318,628	(94.1)
Provisions for liabilities and changes	(62,419)	(62,419)/318,628	(19.6)
	318,628	318,628/318,628	100.0
Capital and reserves			
Called-up share capital	4,149	4,149/318,828	1.3
Share premium account	126,739	126,739/318,628	39.8
Capital redemption reserve	165	165/318,628	0.1
Revaluation reserve	22,439	22,439/318,628	7.0
Profit and loss account	165,136	165,136/318,628	51.8
Equity shareholders' funds	318,628	318,628/318,628	100.0

Another strength of common size statements is to identify their trends over time. In effect, this applies horizontal and vertical analysis, analysing the changes in financial structure and cost structure over time. To examine the technique we compare the 2002 and 2003 common size statements for JD Wetherspoon's profit and loss account.

	2003 %	2002 %
Turnover from continuing operations	100.0	100.0
Cost of sales	(85.1)	(83.8)
Gross profit	14.9	16.2
Administrative expenses	(4.7)	(4.6)
Operating profit	10.2	11.7
Loss on disposal of tangible assets	(0.5)	–
Net interest payable	(2.6)	(2.8)
Profit on ordinary activities before tax	7.1	8.9
Tax on profit on ordinary activities	(2.5)	(3.0)
Profit on ordinary activities after tax	4.6	5.9
Dividends	(1.0)	(1.1)
Retained profit for the year	3.6	4.7

What are the main questions which arise from these two common size statements? Some of the issues were identified also in the previous chapter using other analytical methods. All the ratios are expressed as a proportion of sales:

- The gross profit and operating profit in 2003 have decreased with increases in both the cost of sales and administrative expenses.

- Further information would be required as to the cash management policies of the company in both the short and long term. This is addressed within the Financial Review:

    The company monitors its cash resources through short-, medium- and long-term cash forecasting ... The company monitors its overall level of financial gearing weekly, with short and medium-term forecasts showing underlying levels of gearing which remain within our targets.

29.6 Multivariate analysis – Z-scores

In the preceding chapter we extolled the virtues of ratio analysis for the interpretation of financial statements. However, ratio analysis is an excellent indicator only when applied properly. Unfortunately, a number of limitations impede its proper application. How do we know which ratios to select for the analysis of company accounts? Which ratios can be combined to produce an informative end-result? How should individual ratios be ranked to give the user an overall picture of company performance? How reliable are all the ratios – can users place more reliance on some ratios than others?

Z-score analysis can be employed to overcome some of the limitations of traditional ratio analysis. It evaluates corporate stability and, more importantly, predicts potential instances of corporate failure. All the forecasts and predictions are based on publicly available financial statements.[2] The aim is to identify potential failures so that 'the appropriate action to reverse the process [of failure] can be taken before it is too late'.[3]

29.6.1 What are Z-scores?

Inman describes what Z-scores are designed for:

    Z-scores attempt to replace various independent and often unreliable and misleading historical ratios and subjective rule-of-thumb tests with scientifically analysed ratios which can reliably predict future events by identifying bench marks above which 'all's well' and below which there is imminent danger.[4]

Z-scores provide a single-value score to describe the combination of a number of key characteristics of a company. Some of the most important predictive ratios are weighted according to perceived importance and then summed to give the single Z-score. This is then evaluated against the identified benchmark.

The two best known Z-scores are Altman's Z-score and Taffler's Z-score.

Altman's Z-score

The original Z-score equation was devised by Professor Altman in 1968 and developed further in 1977.[5] The original equation is:

$$Z = 0.012X_1 + 0.014X_2 + 0.033X_3 + 0.006X_4 + 0.999X_5$$

where

X_1 = Working capital/Total assets

(Liquid assets are being measured in relation to the business's size and this may be seen as a better predictor than the current and acid test ratios which measure the interrelationships within working capital.)

X_2 = Retained earnings/Total assets

(In early years the proportion of retained earnings used to finance the total asset base may be quite low and length of time in existence has been seen as a factor in insolvency.)

X_3 = Earnings before interest and tax/Total assets

(Adequate operating profit is fundamental to the survival of a business.)

X_4 = Market capitalisation/Book value of debt

(This is an attempt to include market expectations which may be an early warning as to possible future problems.)

X_5 = Sales/Total assets

(This is a measure that might have been more appropriate when Altman was researching companies within the manufacturing sector. It is a relationship that varies widely between manufacturing sectors and even more so within knowledge-based companies.)

Altman identified two benchmarks. Companies scoring over 3.0 are unlikely to fail and should be considered safe, while companies scoring under 1.8 are very likely to fail. The value of 3.0 has since been revised down to 2.7.[6] Z-scores between 2.7 and 1.8 fall into the grey area. The 1968 work is claimed to be able to distinguish between successes and failures up to two or three years before the event. The 1977 work claims an improved prediction period of up to five years before the event.

Taffler's Z-score

The exact definition of Taffler's Z-score[7] is unpublished, but the following components form the equation:

$$Z = c_0 + c_1 X_1 + c_2 X_2 + c_3 X_3 + c_4 X_4$$

where

X_1 = Profit before tax/Current assets (53%)
X_2 = Current assets/Current liabilities (13%)
X_3 = Current liabilities/Total assets (18%)
X_4 = No credit interval = Length of time which the company can continue to finance its operations using its own assets with no revenue inflow (16%)

c_0 to c_4 are the coefficients, and the percentages in brackets represent the ratios' contributions to the power of the model.

The benchmark used to detect success or failure is 0.2.[8] Companies scoring above 0.2 are unlikely to fail, while companies scoring less than 0.2 demonstrate the same symptoms as companies that have failed in the past.

PAS-score: performance analysis score

Taffler adapted the Z-score technique to develop the PAS-score. The PAS-score evaluates company performance relative to other companies in the industry and incorporates changes in the economy.

The PAS-score ranks all company Z-scores in percentile terms, measuring relative performance on a scale of 0 to 100. A PAS-score of X means that $100 - X\%$ of the companies have scored higher Z-scores. So, a PAS-score of 80 means that only 20% of the companies in the comparison have achieved higher Z-scores.

The PAS-score details the relative performance trend of a company over time. Any downward trends should be investigated immediately and the management should take appropriate action. For other danger signals see Holmes and Dunham.[9]

29.7 H-scores

An H-score is produced by Company Watch to determine overall financial health. The H-score is an enhancement of the Z-score technique in giving more emphasis to the strength of the balance sheet. The Company Watch system calculates a score ranging from 0 to 100 with below 25 being in the danger zone. It takes into account profit management, asset management and funding management using seven factors – these are profit from the profit and loss account, three factors from the asset side of the balance sheet, namely, current asset cover, stock and debtor management and liquidity; and three factors from the liability side of the balance sheet, namely, equity base, debt dependence and current funding.

The factors are taken from published financial statements which makes the approach taken by the ASB to bring off balance sheet transactions on to the balance sheet particularly important.

A strength of the H-score is that it can be applied to all sectors (other than the financial sector) and there is clear evidence that it can predict possible failures, e.g. the model indicated that Hollas plc was at risk in 1994 and it eventually failed in 1998.

The ability to chart each factor against the sector average and to twenty-five level criteria over a five-year period means that it is valuable for a range of user needs from trade creditors considering extending or continuing to allow credit to potential lenders and equity investors and in reviewing audit risk. The model also has the ability to process 'what-ifs'. This is referred to in an article by Maggie Urry, who gives as an example the fact that the impact on the H-score can be measured for a potential rights issue which is used to repay debt. She states:

> That is a feature which Paul Woodley, a director of Postern, the group that provides company doctors for distressed companies, also finds useful. If a company is in trouble, the H score can be used to show exactly what needs to be done to sort it out.[10]

It appears to be a robust, useful and exciting new tool for all user groups. Further information appears on the company's website at www.companywatch.net which includes additional examples.

29.8 A-scores

A-scores concentrate on non-financial signs of failure.[11] This method sets out to quantify different judgemental factors. The whole basis of the analysis is that financial difficulties are the direct result of management defects and errors which have existed in the company for many years.

A-scores assume that many company failures can be explained by similar factors. Company failure can be broken down into a three-stage sequence of events:

1 **Defects**. Specific defects exist in company top management. Typically, these defects centre on management structure; decision making and ability; accounting systems; and failure to respond to change.

2 **Mistakes**. Management will make mistakes that can be attributed to the company defects. The three mistakes that lead to company failure are very high leverage; overtrading; and the failure of the company's main project.

3 **Symptoms**. Finally, symptoms of failure will start to arise. These are directly attributable to preceding management mistakes. Typical symptoms are financial signs (e.g. poor ratios, poor Z-scores); creative accounting (management might attempt to 'disguise' signs of failure in the accounts); non-financial signs (e.g. investment decisions delayed; market share drops); and terminal signs (when the financial collapse of the company is imminent).

To calculate a company A-score, different scores are allocated to each defect, mistake and symptom according to their importance. Then this score is compared with the benchmark values. If companies achieve an overall score of over 25, or a defect score of over 10, or a mistakes score of over 15, then the company is demonstrating typical signs leading up to failure. Generally, companies not at risk will score below 18, and companies which are at risk will score well over 25.

The scoring system attaches a weight to individual items within defects, mistakes and symptoms. By way of illustration we set out the weights applied within defects which are as follows:

Defects in management:

	Weight
The chief executive is an autocrat	8
The chief executive is also the chairman	4
There is a passive board	2
The board is unbalanced, e.g. too many accountants	2
There is poor management depth	1

Defects in accountancy:

There are not budgets for budgetary control	3
There are no current cash flow plans	3
There is no costing system or product costs	3
There is a poor response to change, e.g. out-of-date plant, old-fashioned products, poor marketing	15

Consider our A-score assessment of DNB Computer Systems plc:

Defects:		
	Weak finance director	2
	Poor management depth	1
	No budgeting control	3
	No current updated cash flows	3
	No costing system	3

12

Mistakes:	Main project failure	<u>15</u>	
			15
Symptoms:	Financial signs – adverse Z-scores	4	
	Creative accounting – unduly low debtor provisions	4	
	High staff turnover	<u>3</u>	
			<u>11</u>
Total A-score:			<u><u>38</u></u>

According to our benchmarks, DNB Computer Systems plc is at risk of failure because the mistakes score is 15 and the overall A-score is 38. Therefore, there is some cause for concern, e.g. Why did the main project fail? To which of the symptoms was it due?

Whilst it is difficult to see the rationale for either the weightings or the additive nature of the A-score and whilst the process can be criticised for being subjective, the identification of a defect or mistake can in itself give direction to further enquiry.

29.9 Accounting policies

Auditors are required to assess whether a company has any going concern problems which would indicate that it might not be able to continue trading for a further financial year. This typically requires an assessment of solvency and future cash flows. The following is an extract from the Notes to the 2003 Financial Statements of Consolidated Communications Corporation plc:

Note 2 Going concern
The financial statements have been prepared on the going concern basis which assumes that the Company and its subsidiaries will continue in operational existence for the foreseeable future. The validity of this assumption depends on the following:

i)   Raising additional equity and/or additional funding through the sale of land for €1,000,000 net of expenses,
ii) The enlarged group maintaining existing turnover and simultaneously reducing overheads in Russia by successfully merging the Satcom Tel and NDNT operations
iii) Increasing turnover in Hungary from recent contracts.

The financial statements do not include any adjustments that would result if additional funding were not forthcoming or the anticipated cost savings and increased turnover were not achieved.

The auditors drew attention to the Note in their report as follows:

Fundamental uncertainty – Going Concern
In forming our opinion, we have considered the adequacy of the disclosures .... In view of the significance of these issue, we consider that these disclosures should be brought to your attention. Our opinion is not qualified in that respect.

29.10 Balanced scorecards

Move away from a single performance measure
The EPS figure has been generally seen as providing an acceptable measure of performance. Its attraction was that it seemed to encapsulate performance in a single

figure. However, this came to be regarded as too simplistic and the ASB has attempted to encourage investors to see the annual report as an information set through the FRS 3 *Reporting Financial Performance* disclosure requirements and the *Operating and Financial Review* (OFR) document. Similarly, business is moving away from relying simply on traditional financial measures, such as the return on capital and earnings per share. These can encourage companies to achieve short-term financial results, while damaging employee morale and customer service to the extent of causing long-term damage to the organisation's profitability.[12]

Move towards different perspectives

Four perspectives are seen to affect the long-term economic value of a company.

1 **Financial perspective**. This includes consideration of factors such as the return on capital employed, cash flows, project profitability and the setting of realistic targets. For example, was the company aiming to maximise its return on capital employed or maintain a steady rate of improvement?

2 **Customer perspective**. This requires the company to set specific goals, besides price, that are important to the customer, e.g. quality, performance and service. For example, was the customer interested in the lowest price or in obtaining a regular, guaranteed supply at a reasonable price?

3 **Internal business perspective**. This includes consideration of factors such as tender success rate. For example, was the presentation and preparation effective?

4 **Innovation and learning perspective**. This includes the generation of new business from innovation, and staff attitudes and morale.

The balanced scorecard approach requires a company to focus both on hard financial targets and on important soft or non-financial factors that affect long-term profitability, and to understand the links between the different perspectives. For example, reducing staff numbers might produce an immediate improvement in the short-term financial performance as measured by ROCE and EPS, but could so adversely affect customer satisfaction and staff morale that it has a long-term adverse effect.

According to Kaplan and Norton,[13] the balanced scorecard allows managers to look at the business from four important perspectives. It provides answers to four basic questions:

● How do customers see us? (customer perspective)

● What must we excel at? (internal perspective)

● Can we continue to improve and create value? (innovation and learning perspective)

● How do we look to shareholders? (financial perspective).

There is nothing particularly new in the perspectives. Customers and staff are invariably referred to by the chairman in the annual report as important contributors to the company's success. The difference that the balanced scorecard approach makes is to raise awareness that the perspectives are interdependent and that management performance can be appraised on more than just the bottom line. Of course, the bottom line needs to be healthy for a company to be successful, but it does not exist in isolation; other important factors affect long-term health.

29.11 Valuing shares of an unquoted company – quantitative process

The valuation of shares brings together a number of different financial accounting procedures that we have covered in previous chapters. The assumptions may be highly subjective, but there is a standard approach. This involves the following:

● Estimate the maintainable income flow based on earnings defined in accordance with the IIMR guidelines, as described in Chapter 26. Normally the profits of the past five years are used, adjusted for any known or expected future changes.

● Estimate an appropriate dividend yield, as described in Chapter 28, if valuing a minority holding; or an appropriate earnings yield if valuing a majority holding.

● Make a decision on any adjustment to the required yields. For example, the shares in the unquoted company might not be as marketable as those in the comparative quoted companies and the required yield would therefore be increased to reflect this lack of marketability; or the balance sheet might not be as strong with lower current/acid test ratios or higher gearing, which would also lead to an increase in the required yield.

● Calculate the economic capital value, as described in Chapter 3, by applying the required yield to the income flow.

● Compare the resulting value with the net realisable value (NRV), as described in Chapter 4, when deciding what action to take based on the economic value.

EXAMPLE ● The Doughnut Ltd is an unlisted company engaged in the baking of doughnuts. The balance sheet of the Doughnut Ltd as at 31 December 20X4 showed:

	£000	£000
Freehold land		100
Fixed assets at cost	240	
Accumulated depreciation	40	
		200
Current assets	80	
Current liabilities	(60)	
		20
		320
Share capital in £1 shares		300
Profit and loss account		20
		320
Estimated net realisable values:		
Freehold land		310
Fixed assets		160
Current assets		70

It achieved the following profit after tax (adjusted to reflect maintainable earnings) for the past five years ended 31 December:

	20X0	20X1	20X2	20X3	20X4
Maintainable earnings (£000)	36	40	44	38	42
Dividend payout history: Dividends	10%	10%	12%	12%	12%

Current yields for comparative quoted companies as at 31 December 20X4:

	Earnings yield %	Dividend yield %
Ace Bakers plc	14	8
Busi-Bake plc	10	8
Hard-to-beat plc	13	8

You are required to value a holding of 250,000 shares for a shareholder, Mr Quick, who makes a practice of buying shares for sale within three years.

Now, the 250,000 shares represent an 83% holding. This is a majority holding and the steps to value it are as follows:

1 Calculate average maintainable earnings (in £000):

$$\frac{36{,}000 + 40{,}000 + 44{,}000 + 38{,}000 + 42{,}000}{5} = £40{,}000$$

2 Estimate an appropriate earnings yield:

$$\frac{14\% + 10\% + 13\%}{3} = 12.3\%$$

3 Adjust the rate for lack of marketability by, say, 3% and for the lower current ratio by, say, 2%. Both these adjustments are subjective and would be a matter of negotiation between the parties.

		%
Require yield	=	12.3
Lack of marketability weighting	=	3
Balance sheet weakness	=	2
Required earnings yield		17.3

The adjustments depend on the actual circumstances. For instance, if Mr Quick were intending to hold the shares as a long-term investment, there might be no need to increase the required return for lack of marketability.

4 Calculate share value:

$$(£40{,}000 \times 100/17.3)/300{,}000 = 77\text{p}$$

5 Compare with the net realisable values on the basis that the company were to be liquidated:

		£
Net realisable values = 70,000 + 160,000 + 310,000	=	540,000
Less: Current liabilities		60,000
		480,000
Net asset value per share = £480,000/300,000	=	£1.60

The comparison indicates that, on the information we have been given, Mr Quick should acquire the shares and dispose of the assets and liquidate the company to make an immediate capital gain of 83p per share.

Let us extend our illustration by assuming that it is intended to replace the fixed assets at a cost of £20,000 per year out of retained earnings, if Mr Quick acquires the shares. Advise Mr Small, who has £10,000 to invest, how many shares he would be able to acquire in the Doughnut Ltd.

There are two significant changes: the cash available for distribution as dividends will be reduced by £20,000 per year, which is used to replace fixed assets; and Mr Small is acquiring only a minority holding, which means that the appropriate valuation method is the **dividend yield** rather than the **earnings yield**.

The share value will be calculated as follows:

1 Estimate income flow:

	£
Maintainable earnings	40,000
Less: Fixed asset investment	20,000
Cash available for distribution	20,000

Note that we are here calculating not distributable profits, but the available cash flow.

2 Required dividend yield:

	%
Average dividend yield	8
Lack of negotiability, say	2
Financial risk, say	1.5
	11.5

3 Share value:

$$\frac{£20,000}{300,000} \times \frac{100}{11.5} = 58p$$

At this price it would be possible for Mr Small to acquire (£10,000/58p) = 17,241 shares.

29.12 Valuing shares of an unquoted company – qualitative process

In the section above we illustrated how to value shares using the capitalisation of earnings and capitalisation of dividends methods. However, share valuation is an extremely subjective exercise: for example, when Rhône-Poulenc Rorer made a bid for Fisons in 1995 the share price moved from 193p per share to 265p, with the analysts expecting the final bid price to be between 270p and 300p. The values we have calculated for the Doughnut Ltd shares could therefore be subject to material revision in the light of other relevant factors.

A company's future cash flows may be affected by a number of factors. These may occur as a result of action within the company (e.g. management change, revenue investment) or as a result of external events (e.g. change in the rate of inflation, change in competitive pressures).

● **Management change** often heralds a significant change in a company's share price. For example, the new chief executive of Fisons made significant changes to Fisons in 1994/5 by reducing the business to its valuable core, which then saw the share price move from 103p to 193p.

● **Revenue investment** refers to discretionary revenue expenditure, such as charges to the profit and loss account for research and development, training, advertising and major maintenance and refurbishment. The ASB in its exposure draft for FRS 3 *Reporting Financial Performance* had proposed that this information should be disclosed in the profit and loss account. The proposal did not find support at the exposure stage and it is suggested that such information should instead be disclosed in the operating and financial review.

● **Changes in the rate of inflation** can affect the required yield. If, for example, it is expected that inflation will fall, this might mean that past percentage yields will be higher than the percentage yield that is likely to be available in the future.

● **Change in competitive pressures** can affect future sales. For example, increased foreign competition could mean that past maintainable earnings are not achievable in the future and the historic average level might need to be reduced.

These are a few of the internal and external factors that can affect the valuation of a share. The factors that are relevant to a particular company may be industry-wide (e.g. change in rate of inflation), sector-wide (e.g. change in competitive pressure) or company-specific (e.g. loss of key managers or employees). They may not be immediately apparent from an appraisal of financial statements alone: e.g. the application and success of the balanced scorecard approach might not be immediately apparent without discussions with all the stakeholders. The valuer will need to carry out detailed enquiries in order both to identify which factors are relevant and to evaluate their impact on the share price.

If the company supports the acquisition of the shares, the valuer will be able to gain access to relevant internal information. For example, details of research and development expenditure may be available analysed by type of technology involved, by product line, by project and by location, and distinguishing internal from externally acquired R&D.

If the acquisition is being considered without the company's knowledge or support, the valuer will rely more heavily on information gained from public sources: e.g. statutory disclosures such as the annual accounts, voluntary disclosures such as the OFR, and industry information such as trade journals. Information on areas such as R&D may be provided in the OFR, but probably in an aggregated form, constrained by management concerns about use by potential competitors.[14]

There is an increasing wealth of financial and narrative disclosures to assist investors in making their investment decisions. There are external data such as the various multivariate Z-scores and H-scores and professional credit agency ratings; there is greater internal disclosure of financial data such as TSR and EVA data indicating how well companies have managed value in comparison with a peer group and of narrative information such as the OFR, statements of business risk and the Value Platform approach to explaining the key drivers to increased shareholder value; and there will increasingly be easier access to companies' financial data through the web.

29.13 Shareholder value analysis (SVA)

Rappaport[15] identified a number of reasons why there has been a growing interest in shareholder value analysis:

● a belief that takeovers are based on undervalued assets;
● a belief that accounting measures (e.g. EPS) are unrelated to share value;
● wider reporting of returns to shareholders;

- wider adoption and endorsement;
- the linkage of executive rewards to shareholders' returns.

Copeland *et al.*[16] argued that 'managers at both business-unit and corporate levels need to broaden their conceptions of strategy; they need to manage value'. Mills explained that 'the pursuit of such an approach involves moving the focus of attention away from simply looking at short-term profits to a longer-term view of value creation'.[17]

Essentially, SVA discounts forecasted cash flows, factors in a terminal value for the period beyond the forecast period, and adjusts for the value of debt. Rappaport proposed a seven value-driver approach (which was adopted by Mills *et al.*[18]) based on:

- sales growth,
- operating margin,
- fixed capital investment,
- working capital investment,
- cash taxes,
- planning period,
- cost of capital.

There are several other variations for determining wealth. Two of these measures[19] are:

Market Value Added (MVA) – the difference between total market value and invested capital (i.e. the difference between what investors can take out of a business and what they put in).

Economic Value Added (EVA) – this is the wealth a company creates each year as measured by net income from operations less the cost of capital needed to generate that income. Essentially, MVA is the valuation of all future annual EVAs.

The strength of the MVA/EVA framework is that it 'improves a company's focus on the maximisation of shareholder value ... [and] discourages new investments that are likely to earn inadequate rates of return while encouraging periodic culling of existing assets'.[20]

29.14 Measuring and reporting values in the annual report

29.14.1 Shareholder value (SV)

It has been a longstanding practice for analysts to arrive at shareholder value of a share by calculating the internal rate of return (IRR%) on an investment from the dividend stream and realisable value of the investment at date of disposal, i.e. taking account of dividends received and capital gains. However, it is not a generic measure in that the calculation is specific to each shareholder. The reason for this is that the dividends received will depend on the length of period the shares are held and the capital gain achieved will depend on the share price at the date of disposal – and, as we know, the share price can move significantly even over a week.

For example, consider the SV for each of the following three shareholders, Miss Rapid, Mr Medium and Miss Undecided, who each invested £10,000 on 1 January 20X1 in Spacemobile Ltd which pays a dividend of £500 on these shares on 31 December each year. Miss Rapid sold her shares on 31 December 20X2. Mr Medium sold his on 31 December 20X4, whereas Miss Undecided could not decide what to do with her shares. The SV for each shareholder is as follows:

Shareholder	Date acquired	Investment at cost	Dividends amount (total)	Date of disposal	Sale proceeds	IRR%
Miss Rapid	1.1.20X1	10,000	1,000	31.12.20X2	11,000	10%*
Mr Medium	1.1.20X1	10,000	2,000	31.12.20X4	15,000	15%
Miss Undecided	1.1.20X1	10,000	2,000	undecided		

*$((500 \times .9091) + (11,500 \times .8265)) - 10,000 = 0$

We can see that Miss Rapid achieved a shareholder value of 10% on her shares and Mr Medium, by holding until 31.12.20X4, achieved an increased capital gain raising the SV to 15%. We do not have the information as to how Miss Rapid invested from 1.1.20X3 and so we cannot evaluate her decision – it depends on the subsequent investment and the economic value added by that new company.

29.14.2 Total shareholder return

Miss Undecided has a notional SV at 31.12.20X4 of 15% as calculated for Mr Medium. However, this has not been realised and, if the share price changed the following day, the SV would be different. The notional 15% calculated for Miss Undecided is referred to as the total shareholder return (TSR) – it takes into account market expectation on the assumption that share prices reflect all available information but it is dependent on the assumption made about the length of the period the shares are held.

TSR has been used for performance monitoring, as a criterion for performance-based remuneration and, recently, to satisfy statutory requirements.

Performance monitoring

It has been used by companies to monitor their performance by comparing their own TSR with that of comparator companies. It is also used to set strategic targets. For example, Unilever set itself a TSR target in the top third of a reference group of 21 international consumer goods companies. Unilever calculates the TSR over a three-year rolling period which it considers 'sensitive enough to reflect changes but long enough to smooth out short-term volatility'. In its 2004 Annual Report it quantified its target as follows:

> For the period 2005–2010 our priority continues to be sustained top-third TSR performance and we intend to deliver shareholder value by the generation of over €30 billion ungeared free cash flow and growth in economic profit, the latter translating into an increased return on invested capital from 12.5% to at least 17% by 2010.

Remuneration performance criterion

It is also used by companies as part of its remuneration package. For example, Mitchell & Butler plc in their Annual Report for 2003 (http://www.mbplc.com/investors) state:

Performance restricted share plan

This plan aims to encourage continuing improvement in the Group's performance over the longer term. Its participants are Directors and those senior executives who are best placed to influence such performance.

Generally a three-year performance cycle will commence each year and at the end of the cycle two aspects of the Company's performance will be measured:

● total shareholder return against a comparator group of eleven competitor companies; and

● the Company's cash return on capital employed against its weighted average cost of capital.

The choice of comparator companies rests with the directors. The following is an extract from the Boots plc Annual Report for 2003:

> The long term bonus scheme can provide executive directors with a maximum potential bonus award worth up to 125% of basic salary, and provides a direct link between the pay of executive directors and the creation of value for shareholders by rewarding directors for the company's performance in terms of total shareholder return (TSR) over a three or four-year performance period relative to a peer group of ten other leading companies which the Committee consider to be appropriate comparators by virtue of their size and markets in which they operate. TSR was chosen as the appropriate performance measure for the Long Term Incentive Plan as it aligns the interests of the executive with the actual return received by shareholders.
>
> The peer group is reviewed before each performance cycle to maintain its relevance.

Statutory requirement

The Directors' Report Regulations 2002 now require a line graph to be prepared showing such a comparison. Marks & Spencer Group's 2003 Annual Report contained the following:

Summary remuneration report

The full report on directors' remuneration complies with the Directors' Report Regulations 2002

Performance graph

This graph illustrates the performance of the Company against the FTSE 100 over the past five years. The FTSE 100 has been chosen as it is a recognised broad

Total shareholder return

The above graph looks at the value, at the end of the 2002/03 financial year, of £100 invested in Marks & Spencer shares at the end of the 1997/98 financial year compared with the value of £100 invested in the FTSE 100 Index over the same period. The other points plotted are the values at intermediate financial year-ends.

equity market index of which the Company has been a member throughout the period. Performance, as required by the legislation, is measured by Total Shareholder Return (share price growth plus dividends paid).

29.14.3 Economic value added

Need to generate above average returns

Companies are increasingly becoming aware that investors need to be confident that the company can deliver above average rates of return, i.e. achieve growth, and that communication is the key. This is why companies are using the annual report to provide shareholders and potential shareholders with a measure of the company's performance that will give them confidence to maintain or make an investment in the company. The directors of the Belgian company, Coil SA, make this explicit in the company's 2000 Annual Report:

> A larger company, particularly a public company, competes for financial resources in the market. In order to induce investors to invest in the Company, management must show that it has the expectation to earn more than companies with the equivalent risk profile taking into account the size of the company, the risk of the industry, the capital structure of the company measured as a premium to the 'risk-free' rate, equivalent to the highest quality debt obligations issued by sovereign issuers.
>
> If the Company cannot convince investors of its ability to deliver above average rates of return, more investors will sell shares than will buy shares and the share price will fall. Financial communication is key to the process of convincing investors.
>
> If the Company's rate of return is in excess of that of the market average, the Company creates additional value for the shareholder. If it is less than the market average, the investor earns less than he could have done by investing in another company with the same risk profile. This loss is a destruction of value for the investor.

Formula for calculating economic value added

The formula applied is explained by Geveke nv Amsterdam in their 1999 Annual Report:

> EVA measures economic value achieved over a specific period. It is equal to net operating profit after tax (NOPAT), corrected for the cost of capital employed (the sum of interest bearing liabilities and shareholders' equity). The cost of capital employed is the required yield R times capital employed (CE).
>
> In the form of a formula: $NOPAT - (R \times CE) = EVA$
>
> A positive EVA indicates that over a specific period economic value has been created. Net operating profit after tax is then greater than the cost of finance (i.e. the company's weighted average cost of capital). Research has shown that a substantial part of the long-term movement in share price is explained by the development of EVA. The concept of EVA can be a very good method of performance measurement and monitoring of decisions.

We will illustrate the formula for Alpha nv, which has the following data (in euros):

	31 March 20X1	31 March 20X2	31 March 20X3
NOPAT	10m	11m	13m
Weighted average cost of capital (WACC)	12%	11.5%	11%
Capital employed	70m	77m	96m

The EVA is:

		% change
31 March 20X1	EVA = 10m – (12% of 70m) = 1.6m	–
31 March 20X2	EVA = 11m – (11.5% of 77m) = 2.145m	34%
31 March 20X3	EVA = 12.5m – (11% of 96m) = 1.94m	(10%)

The formula allows weight to be given to the capital employed to generate operating profit. The percentage change is an important management tool in that the annual increase is seen as the created value rather than the absolute level, i.e. the 34% is the key figure rather than the 2.145m. Further enquiry is necessary to assess how well Alpha nv will employ the increase in capital employed in future periods.

It is useful to calculate rate of change over time. However, as for all inter-company comparisons of ratios, it is necessary to identify how the WACC and capital employed have been defined. This may vary from company to company.

WACC calculation

This figure depends on the capital structure and risk in each country in which a company has a significant business interest. For example, the following is an extract from the 2003 Annual Report of the Orkla Group:

Capital structure and cost of capital
The Group's average cost of capital is calculated as a weighted average of the costs of borrowed capital and equity. The calculations are based on an equity-to-total-assets ratio of 60%. The cost of equity is calculated with the help of the Capital Asset Pricing Model. The cost of borrowed capital is based on a long-term, weighted interest rate for relevant countries in which Orkla operates ...
The table shows how Orkla's average cost of capital is calculated:

Description	Rates	Relative %	Weighted cost
Weighted average beta	1.0		
× Market risk premium	4.0%		
= Risk premium for equity	4.0%		
+ Risk free long-term interest rate	4.9%		
= Cost of equity	8.9%	60%	5.3%
Imputed borrowing rate before tax	5.9%		
Imputed tax charge	28%		
= Imputed borrowing rate after tax	4.2%	40%	1.7%
WACC after tax			7.0%

Capital employed definition

The norm is to exclude non-interest-bearing liabilities including current liabilities when determining net total assets. However, there are variations in the treatment of intangible assets, e.g. goodwill may be excluded from the net assets or included at book value or included, as by Koninkleijke Wessanen, at market value rather than the historically paid goodwill.

Achieving increases in EVA

EVA can be improved in three ways: by increasing NOPAT, reducing WACC and/or improving the utilisation of capital employed.

- Increasing NOPAT: this is achieved by optimising strategic choices by comparing the cash flows arising from different strategic opportunities, e.g. appraising geographic and product segmental information, cost reduction programmes, appraising acquisitions and divestments.

- Reducing WACC: this is achieved by reviewing the manner in which a company is financed, e.g. determining a favourable gearing ratio and reducing the perceived risk factor by a favourable spread of products and markets.

- Improving the utilisation of capital employed: this is achieved by consideration of activity ratios, e.g. fixed asset turnover, working capital ratio.

29.15 Shareholder information needs

Historical financial data is not sufficient

Shareholders rely on information provided by companies when they make their investment decisions. Traditionally this information has been historical. This is no longer acceptable and there is a growing demand for managers to share their assessment of future business prospects so that investors can make informed investment decisions.

The financial information is perceived as not being reliable

Investors rely on annual reports and the various mid-year reports and are entitled to assume that these give a true and fair view of a company's financial position. Following various accounting scandals such as Enron there is a lack of confidence among investors that the information provided is true and fair. There is a need for greater transparency, e.g. preventing off balance sheet transactions that have a material impact on a company's viability and continuing existence.

The audit profession is perceived as being too closely allied with management

Many of the schemes which have kept liabilities off the balance sheet have been actively promoted by the auditors. This has meant that the auditors are not seen as protecting the interests of the shareholders but as more concerned with increasing their non-audit income. This is discussed further in Chapter 31.

Investors do not have the means to easily analyse the financial data

Traditionally attention has focused on financial data which have been paper-based. Investors have had to be dependent on analysts or access to the various commercial databases, e.g. Datastream, for data in electronic format for further analysis. The Internet is about to change this by focusing on how to report rather than what to report. It has the capacity to give investors the means to readily analyse the financial data by providing it in a uniform format which can be easily transported into other systems, e.g. Excel. It achieves this through the Extensible Business Reporting Language (XBRL) which has been developed to allow information to be described uniformly and tagged.

A demonstration website has been developed by Microsoft, Nasdaq and PricewaterhouseCoopers (www.nasdaq.com/xbrl).

The above concerns have been widely recognised and a number of different bodies have been developing ideas. These include professional bodies such as the ICAEW, government bodies such as the DTI and professional firms such as PwC. These ideas are discussed further below.

29.15.1 *Financial reporting of risk*

The ICAEW has proposed that listed companies should be at the forefront of improved risk reporting in financial statements. In a 1998 discussion paper, *Financial Reporting of Risk*,[21] it attempted to encourage the inclusion of better-quality information on business risks so that users of accounts had a better understanding of the risks underlying a business's activity. With specific reference to ratio analysis, the discussion paper argued that 'the preparation of a statement of business risk should help preparers and users to focus on the ratios that are most relevant to the particular business risks that are most relevant to individual companies' (para. 6.16).

The summary of the main thrust of the discussion paper is as follows:

Why increase risk reporting in annual reports?

Enhanced information about what companies do to assess and manage key business risks of all types will:

- provide practical forward-looking information;
- reduce the cost of capital;
- encourage better risk management;
- help ensure the equal treatment of all investors; and
- improve accountability for stewardship, investor protection and the usefulness of financial reporting.

What should a statement of business risk include?

- Identification: a company should identify and prioritise its key risks.
- Risk management: a company should describe the actions it has taken to manage each of the identified risks.
- Measurement: the company should identify how each risk is measured.

What should preparers consider when preparing the statement of business risk?

Preparers need to ensure that the information satisfies a range of qualitative characteristics (e.g. relevant, reliable); is forward-looking; is suitable for users; is clear with respect to time-scales; and is not too commercially sensitive.

29.15.2 *Inside Out: Reporting on Shareholder Value*

In 1999 the ICAEW produced a report, *No Surprises: The Case for Better Risk Reporting*, which recognised the need for management to disclose their strategies and how they managed risk – the intention was not to encourage profit smoothing but rather a better management of risk and a better understanding by investors of volatility.

In the same year it produced a discussion paper, *Financial Performance: Alternative Views of the Bottom Line*, which, whilst appreciating that the financial performance of a business was best represented by the change in the net present value of its expected future cash flows, recognised that such changes were uncertain. This led to the recognition that there was a need for more narrative disclosures and performance indicators.

In the same year the ICAEW produced a discussion paper, *Inside Out: Reporting on Shareholder Value*, which focused on improved transparency with a more open disclosure by management of their strategies, and more forward looking disclosures, particularly identifying the information which they considered important in making their decisions and the indicators that would be most useful in assessing their effective implementation.

29.15.3 Value platform

There is an increasing recognition that investors need to know the drivers which create and maintain corporate wealth in the form of net present value of future cash flows. PwC have carried out research which indicates that there is broad agreement on the constituents of a company's value platform. The constituents are six intangible assets, or key drivers, namely: innovation, brand, customers, supply chain efficiency, human capital and reputation. Traditional financial reporting has not generally included any of these in the balance sheet although there is now ongoing research to determine how this could be achieved. Companies therefore have the problem of how to measure these intangible assets reliably and how to communicate this information to investors – any company that fails to do this may find that its shares become less attractive to investors and that its share prices fall (www.pwcglobal.com).

29.15.4 *Business Reporting: the inevitable change?*

This was a discussion paper produced by ICAS (the Institute of Chartered Accountants in Scotland) in 1999 with proposals for financial and non-financial business information to be more timely, more forward looking and more accessible to non-expert users to assist them to understand the drivers of corporate performance.

29.15.5 Information for Better Markets

Prospective Financial Information: Guidance for UK Directors

In September 2003 as part of its campaign for Information for Better Markets, the ICAEW produced a discussion paper, *Prospective Financial Information: Guidance for UK Directors*, which provided guidance based on a framework of principles derived from the International Accounting Standards Board's *Framework for the Preparation and Presentation of Financial Statement*. For example, there is a requirement that the prospective information should be understandable, relevant, reliable and comparable (para. 2.1). It further proposed that directors should identify why the information was being prepared and how it was intended to be used, taking account of the qualitative characteristics of understandability, relevance, reliability and comparability (para. 3.1).

New Reporting Models for Business

In December 2003 the ICAEW produced a report, *New Reporting Models for Business*, which analysed existing models such as the balanced scorecard (Kaplan and Norton), the

Inevitable Change (ICAS), GRI (Global Reporting Initiative) and ValueReporting™ (PricewaterhouseCoopers). None of these models had been completely successful in satisfying the information needs of all stakeholders and further research is required to validate any of the differing views held on the ability of business reporting in key areas such as:

- the ability of a report to satisfy the decision-making needs of multiple stakeholders;
- the adequacy of existing reports given the current level of supporting narrative and forward looking information and the current treatment of intangible assets;
- the level of transparency given the current perceived constraints of cost, commercial confidentiality and potential litigation.

29.16 Professional risk assessors

Credit agencies such as Standard & Poor and Moody's Investor Services assist investors, lenders and trade creditors by providing a credit rating service. Companies are given a rating that can range from AAA for companies with a strong capacity to meet their financial commitments down to D for companies that have been unable to make contractual payments or have filed for bankruptcy with more than ten ratings in between, e.g. BBB for companies that have adequate capacity but which are vulnerable to internal or external economic changes.

29.16.1 How are ratings set?

The credit agencies take a broad range of internal company and external factors into account.

Internal company factors may include:

- an appraisal of the financial reports to determine:
  - trading performance, e.g. specific financial targets such as return on equity and return on assets; earnings volatility; past and projected performance; how well a company has coped with business cycles and severe competition
  - cash flow adequacy, e.g. EBITDA interest cover; EBIT interest cover; free operating cash flow
  - capital structure, e.g. gearing ratio; debt structure; implications of off balance sheet financing
  - a consideration of the notes to the accounts to determine possible adverse implications, e.g. contingent liabilities, heavy capital investment commitments which may impact on future profitability, liquidity and funding requirements;
- meetings and discussions with management;
- monitoring expectation, e.g. against quarterly reports, company press releases, profit warnings;
- monitoring changes in company strategy, e.g. changes to funding structure with company buyback of shares, new divestment or acquisition plans and implications for any debt covenants.

However, experience with companies such as Enron makes it clear that off balance sheet transactions can make appraisal difficult even for professional agencies if companies continue to avoid transparency in their reporting.

External factors may include:

- growth prospects, e.g. trends in industry sector; technology possible changes; peer comparison;
- capital requirements, e.g. whether company is fixed capital or working capital intensive; future tangible fixed asset requirements; R&D spending requirements;
- competitors, e.g. the major domestic and foreign competitors; product differentiation; what barriers there are to entry;
- keeping a watching brief on macroeconomic factors, e.g. environmental statutory levies, tax changes, political changes such as restrictions on the supply of oil, foreign currency risks;
- monitoring changes in company strategy, e.g. implication of a company embarking on a heavy overseas acquisition programme which changes the risk profile, e.g. difficulty in management control and in achieving synergies, increased foreign exchange exposure.

29.16.2 What impact does a rating have on a company?

The rating is a risk measure and influences decisions as to whether to grant credit and also as to the terms of such credit, e.g. if a company's rating is downgraded then lenders may refuse credit or impose a higher interest rate or set additional debt covenants.

The ratings are taken seriously by even the largest multinational because they are perceived by investors as possibly adversely affecting access to capital markets. Sony, for example, addressed this concern when it commented in its 2004 Annual Report:

On June 25, 2003 Moody's downgraded Sony's long-term debt rating from Aa3 to A1 (outlook: negative). R&I downgraded Sony's long-term debt rating from AA+ to AA on June 16, 2003. These actions reflected the concerns of the two agencies that Sony may take longer than initially expected to regain its previous level of profit and cash flow under the severe competition, particularly in the electronics business ... Despite the downgrading ... Sony believes that its access to the global capital markets will remain sufficient for its financing needs going forward ... .

29.16.3 What are debt covenants?

Lenders may require borrowers to do certain things by affirmative covenants or refrain from doing certain things by negative covenants.

Affirmative covenants may, e.g. include requiring the borrower to:

- provide quarterly and annual financial statements;
- remain within certain ratios whilst ensuring that each agreed ratio is not so restrictive that it impairs normal operations:
  - maintain a current ratio of not less than an agreed ratio – say 1.6 to 1
  - maintain a ratio of total liabilities to tangible net worth at an agreed rate – say no greater than 2.5 to 1
  - maintain tangible net worth in excess of an agreed amount – say £1m;
- maintain adequate insurance.

Negative covenants may, for example, include requiring the borrower **not** to:

- grant any other charges over the company's assets;

- repay loans from related parties without prior approval;
- change the group structure by acquisitions, mergers or divestment without prior agreement.

29.16.4 What happens if a company is in breach of its debt covenants?

Borrowers will normally have prepared forecasts to assure themselves and the lenders that compliance is reasonably feasible – such forecasts will also normally include the worst case scenario, e.g. taking account of seasonal fluctuations that may trigger temporary violations with higher borrowing required to cover higher levels of stock and debtors.

If any violation has occurred, the lender has a range of options, such as:

- amending the covenant, e.g. accepting a lower current ratio, or
- granting a waiver period when the terms of the covenant are not applied, or
- granting a waiver but requiring the loans to be restructured, or
- requiring the terms to be met within a stipulated period of grace, or, as a last resort,
- declaring that the borrower is in default and demanding repayment of the loan.

29.16.5 Audit implications when there is a breach of a debt covenant

Auditors are required to bring a healthy scepticism to their work. This applies particularly at times such as when there is a potential debt covenant breach. There may then well be a temptation to manipulate to avoid reporting a breach. This will depend on the specific covenant, e.g. if the current ratio is below the agreed figure, management might be more optimistic in setting inventory obsolescence and accounts receivable provisions and have a lower expectation of the likelihood of contingent liabilities crystallising.

29.16.6 Impact on share price

If there is a risk of bank covenants being breached there can be a significant adverse effect on the share price, e.g. the Jarvis share price tumbled 24%, wiping £64 million off the engineering services group's stock market value as a result of fears that bank covenants would be breached.[22]

29.17 Aggressive earnings management

In 2001, before the collapse of Enron, there was a consensus amongst respondents to the UK Auditing Practices Board Consultation Paper *Aggressive Earnings Management* that aggressive earnings management was a significant threat and actions should be taken to diminish it. It was considered that aggressive earnings management could occur when there was a need to meet or exceed market expectations and when directors' and managements' remuneration were linked to earnings – also, but to a lesser extent, to understate profits to reduce tax liabilities or to increase profits to ensure compliance with loan covenants.

In 2004, as a part of the *Information for Better Markets* initiative, the Audit and Assurance Faculty commissioned a survey[23] to check whether views had changed since 2001. This showed that the vulnerability of corporate reporting to manipulation is perceived as being always with us but at a lower level following the greater awareness and scrutiny by non-executive directors and audit committees.

The *analysts* interviewed in the survey believed the potential for aggressive earnings management varied from sector to sector, e.g. in the older, more established sectors followed by the same analysts for a number of years, they believed that company management would find it hard to disguise anything aggressive even if they wanted to – however, this was not true of newer sectors (IT, for example) where the business models may be imperfectly understood.

Whilst analysts and journalists tend to have low confidence in the reported earnings where there are pressures to manipulate, there is a research report[24] which paints a rather more optimistic picture. This report aimed to assess the level of confidence investors had in different sources of company information, including audited financial information, when making investment decisions. As far as audited financial information was concerned, the levels of confidence in UK audited financial information amongst UK and US investors remained very high, with 87% of UK respondents having either a 'great deal' or a 'fair amount' of confidence in UK audited financial information.

The audit profession continues to respond to the need to contain aggressive earnings management. This is not easy because it requires a detailed understanding not only of the business but also of the process management follow when making their estimates. The proposed IAS 540 Revised, *Auditing Accounting Estimates and Related Disclosures*, requires auditors to exercise greater rigour and scepticism and to be particularly aware of the cumulative effect of estimates which in themselves fall within a normal range but which, taken together, are misleading.

29.18 Impact of differences between IASs and national standards on trend analysis

Companies have been producing reconciliations between IASs and US GAAP to satisfy US SEC requirements as illustrated with extracts from Nokia and Eybl in Chapter 6 and Incentive in Chapter 8.

There has been a recognition that national standards may reflect fundamental differences, as shown in the following extract from the Beta Systems Software AG 2002 Annual Report:

Fundamental differences

There are fundamentally different lines of thinking behind German GAAP and US GAAP. Whereas accounting according to the German GAAP focuses on the principles of conservatism and creditor protection, the providing of information relevant to the decision-making process for shareholders is the prior aim of US GAAP.

Therefore both the comparability of annual financial statements over a number of years as well as those of different companies, and the calculation of profits on an accrual basis according to US GAAP is given a higher importance than that according to German GAAP.

Whereas the SEC require detailed reconciliations, companies may, on the introduction of IASs, include a general statement of significant differences in their annual report, as in the following extract from the Sudzucker 2002/03 Annual Report:

Principles of preparation

The consolidated financial statements for 2003/04 of Sudzucker AG have been prepared in accordance with those standards issued by the IASB ...

The significant differences between German accounting principles for consolidated financial statements and IAS are as follows:

- No recognition of internal expense provisions (e.g. maintenance provisions) as set out in IAS 37.
- Requirement to recognise unrealised foreign currency gains as set out in IAS 12.
- Requirement to recognise deferred income taxes using the liability method as set out in IAS 12.
- Requirement to recognise certain financial instruments at fair values as set out in IAS 39.
- No annual amortisation of goodwill, but a requirement to test for impairment at least annually as set out in IFRS 3.
- Different depreciation methods, as prescribed in IAS 16.

Although comparative figures may be restated for the previous year, users need to be aware of the nature of the changes, the increased focus on a decision-useful approach and that such differences may impact on expected ratios, e.g. excluding provisions will result in a higher reported profit for the year and EPS figure.

Summary

This chapter has introduced a number of additional analytical techniques to complement ratio analysis. These techniques include horizontal analysis, vertical analysis, Z-scores, H-scores, A-scores and balanced scorecards. In addition, this chapter has described how to value unquoted shares and introduced the concept of shareholder value analysis. Finally, there have been a number of discussion papers on the financial reporting of risk. Business risk reporting is an area which will become increasingly important and prominent.

The prime purpose of each analytical method in the first half of the chapter is to identify potential financial problem areas. Once these have been identified, thorough investigations should be carried out to determine the cause of each irregularity. Management should then take the necessary actions to correct these irregularities and deficiencies.

All users of financial statements (both internal and external users) should be prepared to utilise any or all of the interpretative techniques suggested in this chapter and the preceding one. These techniques help to evaluate the financial health and performance of a company. Users should approach these financial indicators with real curiosity – any unexplained or unanswered questions arising from this analysis should form the basis of a more detailed examination of the company accounts.

REVIEW QUESTIONS

I As well as the balance sheet, profit and loss account and cash flow statement, a company's annual report and accounts contain other useful information.

Discuss the interpretative importance of the report of the directors, the chairman's statement, group structure information, employee statistics, geographical and activity breakdowns, and other supplementary information.

How useful and reliable is this additional information in the assessment of financial performance and the interpretation of financial statements?

2 Discuss Z-score analysis with particular reference to Altman's Z-score and Taffler's Z-score. In particular:

(i) What are the benefits of Z-score analysis?

(ii) What criticisms can be levelled at Z-score analysis?

3 Robertson identifies four main elements which cause changes in the financial health of a company: trading stability; declining profits; declining working capital; increase in borrowings.[25]

Robertson's Z-score is represented by:

$$Z = 3.0X_1 + 3.0X_2 + 0.6X_3 + 0.3X_4 + 0.3X_5$$

where

X_1 = (Sales − Total assets)/Sales
X_2 = Profit before tax/Total assets
X_3 = (Current assets − Total debt)/Current liabilities
X_4 = (Equity − Total borrowing)/Total debt
X_5 = (Liquid assets − Bank overdraft)/Creditors

Interpretation of the Z-score concentrates on rate of change from one period to the next. If the score falls by 40% or more in any one year, immediate investigations must be made to identify and rectify the cause of the decrease in Z-score. If the score falls by 40% or more for two years running, the company is unlikely to survive.

Compare and contrast Robertson's Z-score with:

(i) Altman's Z-score;

(ii) Taffler's Z-score and PAS-score.

4 (a) Explain how ROI, ROCE and EVA are calculated.

(b) Compare ROI, ROCE and EVA as a means of improving company performance.

5 Explain what you would look for when examining a company's common-sized balance sheet.

6 Discuss the difficulties when attempting to identify comparator companies for benchmarking as, for example, when selecting a TSR peer group.

7 The details given below are a summary of the balance sheets of six public companies engaged in different industries:

	A %	B %	C %	D %	E %	F %
Land and buildings	10	2	26	24	57	5
Other fixed assets	17	1	34		13	73
Stocks and work-in-progress	44		22	55	16	1
Trade debtors	6	77	15	4	1	13
Other debtors	11			8	2	5
Cash and investments	12	20	3	9	11	3
	100	100	100	100	100	100

	A	B	C	D	E	F
Capital and reserves	37	5	62	58	55	50
Creditors: over one year	12	5	4	13	6	25
Creditors: under one year						
Trade	32	85	34	14	24	6
Other	16	5		14	15	11
Bank overdraft	3			1		8
Total capital employed	100	100	100	100	100	100

The activities of each company are as follows:

1 Operator of a chain of retail supermarkets.

2 Sea ferry operator.

3 Property investor and house builder. Apart from supplying managers, including site management, for the house building side of its operations, this company completely subcontracts all building work.

4 A vertically integrated company in the food industry which owns farms, flour mills, bakeries and retail outlets.

5 Commercial bank with a network of branches.

6 Contractor in the civil engineering industry.

Note: No company employs off balance sheet financing such as leasing.

(a) State which of the above activities relate to which set of balance sheet details, giving a brief summary of your reasoning in each case.

(b) What do you consider to be the major limitations of ratio analysis as a means of interpreting accounting information?

8 It has been suggested that 'growth in profits which occurred in the 1960s was the result of accounting sleight of hand rather than genuine economic growth'. Consider how 'accounting sleight of hand' can be used to report increased profits and discuss what measures can be taken to mitigate against the possibility of this happening.

9 Discuss the main features/perspectives of the 'balanced scorecard'.

10 The Unilever 2002 annual review stated:

Total Shareholder Return (TSR) is a concept used to compare the performance of different companies' stocks and shares over time. It combines share price appreciation and dividends paid to show the total return to the shareholder. The absolute size of the TSR will vary with stock markets, but the relative position is a reflection of the market perception of overall performance relative to a reference group. The Company calculates the TSR over a three-year rolling period…. Unilever has set itself a TSR target in the top third of a reference group of 21 … companies.

Discuss (a) why a three-year rolling period has been chosen, and (b) the criteria you consider appropriate for selecting the reference group of companies.

EXERCISES

An extract from the solution is provided in the Appendix at the end of the text for exercises marked with an asterisk (*).

Question 1

The following five-year summary relates to Wandafood Products plc and is based on financial statements prepared under the historical cost convention:

Financial ratios			20X9	20X8	20X7	20X6	20X5
Profitability							
Margin	$\dfrac{\text{Trading profit}}{\text{Sales}}$	%	7.8	7.5	7.0	7.2	7.3
Return on assets	$\dfrac{\text{Trading profit}}{\text{Net operating assets}}$	%	16.3	17.6	16.2	18.2	18.3
Interest and dividend cover							
Interest cover	$\dfrac{\text{Trading profit}}{\text{Net finance charges}}$	times	2.9	4.8	5.1	6.5	3.6
Dividend cover	$\dfrac{\text{Earnings per ordinary share}}{\text{Dividend per ordinary share}}$	times	2.7	2.6	2.1	2.5	3.1
Debt–equity ratios							
	$\dfrac{\text{Net borrowings}}{\text{Shareholders' funds}}$	%	65.9	61.3	48.3	10.8	36.5
	$\dfrac{\text{Net borrowings}}{\text{Shareholders' funds plus minority interests}}$	%	59.3	55.5	44.0	10.1	33.9

			20X9	20X8	20X7	20X6	20X5
Liquidity ratios							
Quick ratio	$\dfrac{\text{Current assets less stock}}{\text{Current liabilities}}$	%	74.3	73.3	78.8	113.8	93.4
Current ratio	$\dfrac{\text{Current assets}}{\text{Current liabilities}}$	%	133.6	130.3	142.2	178.9	174.7
Asset ratios							
Operating asset turnover	$\dfrac{\text{Sales}}{\text{Net operating assets}}$	times	2.1	2.4	2.3	2.5	2.5
Working capital turnover	$\dfrac{\text{Sales}}{\text{Working capital}}$	times	8.6	8.0	7.0	7.4	6.2

Per share

Earnings per share	– pre-tax basis .... p	23.62	21.25	17.96	17.72	15.06
	– net basis .... p	15.65	13.60	10.98	11.32	12.18
Dividends per share	.... p	5.90	5.40	4.90	4.60	4.10
Net assets per share	.... p	102.1	89.22	85.95	85.79	78.11

Net operating assets include tangible fixed assets, stock, debtors and creditors. They exclude borrowings, taxation and dividends.

Required:

Prepare a report on the company, clearly interpreting and evaluating the information given.

(ACCA)

Question 2

The following are the accounts of Bouncy plc, a company that manufactures playground equipment, for the year ended 30 November 20X6

Profit and loss accounts for years ended 30 November

	20X6	20X5
	£000	£000
Profit before interest and tax	2,200	1,570
Interest expense	170	150
Profit before tax	2,030	1,420
Taxation	730	520
Profit after tax	1,300	900
Dividends paid	250	250
Retained profit	1,050	650

Balance sheets as at 30 November 20X6

	20X6	20X5
	£000	£000
Fixed assets (written-down value)	6,350	5,600
Current assets		
Stock	2,100	2,070
Debtors	1,710	1,540
	10,160	9,210
Creditors: amounts due within one year		
Trade creditors	1,040	1,130
Taxation	550	450
Bank overdraft	370	480
Total assets less current liabilities	8,200	7,150
Creditors: amounts due after more than one year		
10% debentures 20X7/20X8	1,500	1,500
	6,700	5,650

Capital and reserves

Share capital: ordinary shares of 50p fully paid up	3,000	3,000
Share premium	750	750
Profit and loss account	2,950	1,900
	6,700	5,650

The directors are considering two schemes to raise £6,000,000 in order to repay the debentures and finance expansion estimated to increase profit before interest and tax by £900,000. It is proposed to make a dividend of 6p per share whether funds are raised by equity or loan. The two schemes are:

(1) an issue of 13% debentures redeemable in 30 years;
(2) a rights issue at £1.50 per share. The current market price is £1.80 per share (20X5: £1.50; 20X4: £1.20).

Required:

(a) Calculate the return on equity and any three investment ratios of interest to a potential investor.
(b) Calculate three ratios of interest to a potential long-term lender.
(c) Report briefly on the performance and state of the business from the viewpoint of a potential shareholder and lender using the ratios calculated above and explain any weaknesses in these ratios.
(d) Advise management which scheme they should adopt on the basis of your analysis above and explain what other information may need to be considered when making the decision.

* Question 3

Liz Collier runs a small delicatessen. Her profits in recent years have remained steady at around £21,000 per annum. This type of business generally earns a uniform rate of net profit on sales of 20%.

Recently, Liz has found that this level of profitability is insufficient to enable her to maintain her desired lifestyle. She is considering three options to improve her profitability.

Option 1 Liz will borrow £10,000 from her bank at an interest rate of 10% per annum, payable at the end of each financial year. The whole capital sum will be repaid to the bank at the end of the second year. The money will be used to hire the services of a marketing agency for two years. It is anticipated that turnover will increase by 40% as a result of the additional advertising.

Option 2 Liz will form a partnership with Joan Mercer, who also runs a local delicatessen. Joan's net profits have remained at £12,000 per annum since she started in business five years ago. The sales of each shop in the combined business are expected to increase by 20% in the first year and then remain steady. The costs of the amalgamation will amount to £6,870, which will be written off in the first year. The partnership agreement will allow each partner a partnership salary of 2% of the revised turnover of their own shop. Remaining profits will be shared in the ratio of Liz 3/5, Joan 2/5.

Option 3 Liz will reduce her present sales by 80% and take up a franchise to sell Nickson's Munchy Sausage. The franchise will cost £80,000. This amount will be borrowed from her bank. The annual interest rate will be 10% flat rate based on the amount borrowed. Sales of Munchy Sausage yield a net profit to sales percentage of 30%. Sales are expected to be £50,000 in the first year, but should increase annually at a rate of 15% for the following three years then remain constant.

Required:
(a) Prepare a financial statement for Liz comparing the results of each option for each of the next two years.
(b) Advise Liz which option may be the best to choose.
(c) Discuss any other factors that Liz should consider under each of the options.

Question 4

The directors of Chekani plc, a large listed company, are engaged in a policy of expansion. Accordingly, they have approached the directors of Meela Ltd, an unlisted company of substantial size, in connection with a proposed purchase of Meela Ltd.

The directors of Meela Ltd have indicated that the shareholders of Meela Ltd would prefer the form of consideration for the purchase of their shares to be in cash and you are informed that this is acceptable to the prospective purchasing company, Chekani plc.

The directors of Meela Ltd have now been asked to state the price at which the shareholders of Meela Ltd would be prepared to sell their shares to Chekani plc. As a member of a firm of independent accountants, you have been engaged as a consultant to advise the directors of Meela Ltd in this regard.

In order that you may be able to do so, the following details, extracted from the most recent financial statements of Meela, have been made available to you.

Meela Ltd accounts for year ended 30 June 20X4

Balance sheet extracts as at 30 June 20X4:

	£000
Purchased goodwill unamortised	15,000
Freehold property	30,000
Plant and machinery	60,000
Investments	15,000
Net current assets	12,000
10% debentures 20X9	(30,000)
Ordinary shares of £1 each (cumulative)	(40,000)
7% preference shares of £1 each (cumulative)	(12,000)
Share premium account	(20,000)
Profit and loss account	(30,000)

Meela Ltd disclosed a contingent liability of £3.0m in the notes to the balance sheet.

(Amounts in brackets indicate credit balances.)

Profit and loss account extracts for the year ended 30 June 20X4:

	£000
Profit before interest payments and taxation and exceptional items	21,000
Exceptional items	1,500
Interest	(3,000)
Taxation	(6,000)
Dividends paid – Preference	(840)
– Ordinary	(3,000)
Retained profit for the year	9,660

(Amounts in brackets indicate a charge or appropriation to profits.)

The following information is also supplied:

(i) Profit before interest and tax for the year ended 30 June 20X3 was £24.2m and for the year ended 30 June 20X2 it was £30.3m.

(ii) Assume corporation tax at 30%.

(iii) Exceptional items in 20X4 relate to the profit on disposal of an investment in a related company. The related company contributed to profit before interest as follows:

To 30 June 20X4	£0
To 30 June 20X3	£200,000
To 30 June 20X2	£300,000

(iv) The preference share capital can be sold independently, and a buyer has already been found. The agreed purchase price is 90p per share.

(v) Chekani plc has agreed to purchase the debentures of Meela Ltd at a price of £110 for each £100 debenture.

(vi) The current rental value of the freehold property is £4.5m per annum and a buyer is available on the basis of achieving an 8% return on their investment.

(vii) The investments of Meela Ltd have a current market value of £22.5m.

(viii) Meela Ltd is engaged in operations substantially different from those of Chekani plc. The most recent financial data relating to two listed companies that are engaged in operations similar to those of Meela Ltd are:

	NV per share	Market price per share	P/E	Net dividend per share	Cover	Yield
Ranpar plc	£1	£3.06	11.3	12 pence	2.6	4.9
Menner plc	50p	£1.22	8.2	4 pence	3.8	4.1

Required:

Write a report, of approximately 2,000 words, to the directors of Meela Ltd, covering the following:

(a) Advise them of the alternative methods used for valuing unquoted shares and explain some of the issues involved in the choice of method.

(b) Explain the alternative valuations that could be placed on the ordinary shares of Meela Ltd.

(c) Recommend an appropriate strategy for the Board of Meela Ltd to adopt in their negotiations with Chekani plc.

Include, as appendices to your report, supporting schedules showing how the valuations were calculated.

Question 5

R. Johnson inherited 810,000 £1 ordinary shares in Johnson Products Ltd on the death of his uncle in 20X5. His uncle had been the founder of the company and managing director until his death. The remainder of the issued shares were held in small lots by employees and friends, with no one holding more than 4%.

R. Johnson is planning to emigrate and is considering disposing of his shareholding. He has had approaches from three parties, who are:

1 A competitor – Sonar Products Ltd. Sonar Products Ltd considers that Johnson Products Ltd would complement their own business and they are interested in acquiring all of the 810,000 shares. Sonar Products Ltd currently achieve a post-tax return of 12.5% on capital employed.

2 Senior employees. Twenty employees are interested in making a management buyout with each acquiring 40,500 shares from R. Johnson. They have obtained financial backing, in principle, from the company's bankers.

3 A financial conglomerate – Divest plc. Divest plc is a company that has extensive experience of acquiring control of a company and breaking it up to show a profit on the transaction. It is their policy to seek a pre-tax return of 20% from such an exercise.

The company has prepared draft accounts for the year ended 30 April 20X9. The following information is available.

(a) Past earnings and distributions:

Year ended 30 April	Profit/(Loss) after tax	Gross dividends declared
£	%	
20X5	79,400	6
20X6	(27,600)	—
20X7	56,500	4
20X8	88,300	5
20X9	97,200	6

(b) Balance sheet of Johnson Products Ltd as at 30 April 20X9:

	£000	£000
Fixed assets		
Land at cost		376
Premises at cost	724	
Aggregate depreciation	216	
		508
Equipment at cost	649	
Aggregate depreciation	353	
		296
Current assets		
Stock	141	
Debtors	278	
Cash at bank	70	
	489	
Creditors due within one year	(335)	
Net current assets		154
Non-current liabilities		(158)
		1,176
Represented by:		
£1 ordinary shares		1,080
Profit and loss account		96
		1,176

(c) Information on the nearest comparable listed companies in the same industry:

Company	Profit after tax for 20X9 £000	Retention %	Gross dividend yield %
Eastron plc	280	25	15
Westron plc	168	16	10.5
Northron plc	243	20	13.4

Profit after tax in each of the companies has been growing by approximately 8% per annum for the past five years.

(d) The following is an estimate of the net realisable values of Johnson Products Ltd's assets as at 30 April 20X9:

	£000
Land	480
Premises	630
Equipment	150
Debtors	168
Stock	98

Required:

(a) As accountant for R. Johnson, advise him of the amount that could be offered for his shareholding with a reasonable chance of being acceptable to the seller, based on the information given in the question, by each of the following:
  (i) Sonar Products Ltd;
  (ii) the twenty employees;
  (iii) Divest plc.

(b) As accountant for Sonar Products Ltd, estimate the maximum amount that could be offered by Sonar Products Ltd for the shares held by R. Johnson.

(c) As accountant for Sonar Products Ltd, state the principal matters you would consider in determining the future maintainable earnings of Johnson Products Ltd and explain their relevance.

(ACCA)

Question 6

Discuss the following issues with regard to financial reporting for risk:
(a) How can a company identify and prioritise its key risks?
(b) What actions can a company take to manage the risks identified in (a)?
(c) How can a company measure risk?

References

1 *Accounting for the Effects of Changing Prices: A Handbook*, ASC, 1986.

2 C. Pratten, *Company Failure*, Financial Reporting and Auditing Group, ICAEW, 1991, pp. 43–45.

3 R.J. Taffler, 'Forecasting company failure in the UK using discriminant analysis and financial ratio data', *Journal of the Royal Statistical Society*, Series A, vol. 145, part 3, 1982, pp. 342–358.

4 M.L. Inman, 'Altman's Z-formula prediction', *Management Accounting*, November 1982, pp. 37–39.

5 E.I. Altman, 'Financial ratios, discriminant analysis and the prediction of corporate bankruptcy', *Journal of Finance*, vol. 23(4), 1968, pp. 589–609.

6 M.L. Inman, 'Z-scores and the going concern review', *ACCA Students' Newsletter*, August 1991, pp. 8–13.

7 R.J. Taffler, *op. cit.;* R.J. Taffler, 'Z-scores: an approach to the recession', *Accountancy*, July 1991, pp. 95–97.

8 M.L. Inman, *op. cit*, 1991.

9 G. Holmes and R. Dunham, *Beyond the Balance Sheet*, Woodhead Faulkner, 1994.

10 M. Urry, 'Early warning signals', *Financial Times*, 5 October 1999.

11 J. Argenti, 'Predicting corporate failure', *Accountants Digest*, no. 138, Summer 1983, pp. 18–21.

12 R. Newing, 'Benefits of a balanced scorecard', *Accountancy*, November 1994, pp. 52–53.

13 R.S. Kaplan and D.P. Norton, 'The balanced scorecard – measures that drive performance', *Harvard Business Review*, January–February 1992, pp. 71–79.

14 W.A. Nixon and C.J. McNair, 'A measure of R&D', *Accountancy*, October 1994, p. 138.

15 A. Rappaport, *Creating Shareholder Value: The New Standard for Business Performance*, The Free Press, 1986.

16 T. Copeland, T. Koller and J. Murrin, *Valuation: Measuring and Managing the Value of Companies*, John Wiley and Sons, New York, 1990.

17 R.W. Mills, 'Shareholder value analysis', *Management Accounting*, February 1998, pp. 39–40; see also R.W. Mills *et al.*, *The Use of Shareholder Value Analysis in Acquisition and Divestment Decisions by Large UK Companies*, CIMA, 1997.

18 R.W. Mills, J. Robertson and T. Ward, 'Strategic value analysis: trying to run before you can walk', *Management Accounting*, November 1992, pp. 48–49.

19 'America's best wealth creators', *Forbes*, 28 November 1994, pp. 77–91.

20 J. Stern, 'Management: its mission and its measure', *Director*, October 1994, pp. 42–44.

21 ICAEW, *Financial Reporting of Risk*, Discussion Paper, 1998.

22 *The Times*, 28 January 2004.

23 J. Collier, *Aggressive Earnings Management: Is it still a significant threat?*, ICAEW October 2004.

24 Alpa A Virdi, *Investors' Confidence in Audited Financial Information Research Report*, ICAEW December 2004.

25 J. Robertson, 'Company failure – measuring changes in financial health through ratio analysis', *Management Accounting*, November 1983.

CHAPTER **30**

An introduction to financial reporting on the Internet

30.1 Introduction

We saw in the previous chapter that various online subscription databases such as Datastream, FAME and OneSource are available, where selected financial reports have been reformatted by each of the databases into a standardised format. This allows subscribers to select peer groups and search across a variety of variables. Students having access to such databases at their own institution may carry out a range of assignments and projects such as selecting companies suitable for takeover based on stated criteria such as ROCE, % Sales and Earnings growth.

At an individual company level we find that most companies have a website to communicate all types of information to interested parties, including financial information. Stakeholders or other interested parties can then download this information for their own particular use. Most of the financial information is in the format of PDF files created by a software program called Adobe(r) Acrobat(r). This program is used for the conversion of all their documents, which make up the financial information contained within the Annual General Reports, into one document, a PDF file, for publication on the Internet. This PDF file can be formatted to include encryption and digital signatures to ensure that the document cannot be changed. In order for the user to be able to read the PDF files a special software program called Adobe Reader(r) needs to be downloaded from the Adobe website www.adobe.com

Other formats used to display company information are often in Hyper Text Mark-up Language (HTML). HTML mainly defines the appearance of the information on the computer screen such as placement, colour, font etc. But even though it is helpful to be able to download the file and read or print the financial information on screen or on paper, when calculations need to be performed the information has to be re-typed. When we need to consider and evaluate multiple years of a company's financial results or when we wish to evaluate a whole category of companies then this re-typing becomes a time-consuming task. Any of the re-typed information can contain errors, which makes the information produced less reliable.

Other interested parties or stakeholders such as investment analysts, merchant bankers, banks, regulatory bodies and government taxation departments also need to re-type all the information or request information in specific electronic formats so that the re-typing is kept to a minimum. This, very costly, process has led to the development of a special business reporting language called eXtensible Business Reporting Language or XBRL.

Accountants will become increasingly involved with its development and this chapter provides a brief oversight of a development that is going to make a major impact on the availability of financial data for comparative analysis. The IASB is making an impact on the uniformity of accounting policies and XBRL will make an impact on the uniformity in the presentation of the data on the Internet.

This chapter will consider:

- What is XBRL?
- What it is not
- How can it be used
- What is needed to use XBRL
- Progress of XBRL development
- Companies currently using XBRL.

30.2 What is XBRL?

XBRL is based upon the eXtensible Mark-up Language or XML. XML is an extension of the Hyper Text Mark-up Language (HTML) which controls the format and display of web pages. HTML is extensively used in website creation for the purposes of display.

XML goes one step further; it allows for 'tags' to be created which convey identification and meaning of the data within the tags. Thus instead of looking at format and presentation, the XML code looks for the text displayed within the code. This XML language is developed by The World Wide Web Consortium (W3C). (www.w3.org/Consortium/)

The following text using HTML would have tags that describe the format and placement of the text.

Assets $50,000
Liabilities $25,000

```
<p><b>Assets   $50,000</b></p>
<p><b>Liabilities   $25,000</b></p>
```

where <p> instructs the item to be printed on the screen (and also where on the screen or in what format) and <b> instructs the item to be displayed in bold print. The </p> and the </b> denote the end of the commands.

The user can design the tags used in XML. For example:

Assets $50,000 in this example of XML would be written as
<Assets>$50,000</Assets> and similarly for **Liabilities $25,000** the XML code would be <Liabilities>$50,000</Liabilities>

The computer program reading the XML code would thus know that the value found within the tags relates to Assets.

The bold in the print and the way in which the financial report is set out would be formatted through the use of a 'stylesheet' where the display is pre-designed. Stylesheets can be used again and again or a variety of different stylesheets can be used for different purposes. For example, the information presented in a full annual report would be based on the same stylesheet year after year whilst that for a half-yearly concise report to the shareholders might well be different each year.

XBRL has taken XML one step further and designed 'tags' based upon the common financial language used. For example, the term ASSETS or LIABILITIES is a common term used in financial reports even though the calculations or valuations and the definitions used in different accounting standards may be dependent on those accounting standards applicable to the company.

Tags can thus be developed for a particular set of Accounting Standards, e.g. International Accounting Standards, or specific to a country such as the US GAAP.

The XBRL definitions or tags are contained within a number of files. Other technical specifications are also required and these are found in a set of files referred to as 'Schema', 'Label Linkbase', 'Presentation Linkbase' and 'Calculation Linkbase'. Within these files are references, or variables, to other files and specifications as defined by XML protocols. The files are necessary to allow the computer to be able to combine all the language contained within the taxonomy with these files and then together to enable the operation and application of XBRL. Schemas for calculation and definitions of fields etc. are often used in computer programming. Schemas with these abstract meanings are kept separate as it is easier, and more efficient, for the main program to call upon schema files than to incorporate all variables in the main program. The table below provides a simplified listing of the elements.

The elements of the XBRL Specification

XBRL Specification and schema	Describes the architecture and structure of the XML references used in XBRL. A special XL schema has been constructed for XBRL to overcome connectivity problems in using the w3c xlink technology.
Taxonomies	Contains the meaning and presentation of the financial data elements; acts like a dictionary
Instance documents	The physical document in which the financial data is presented, e.g. the Balance Sheet or Profit and Loss
Stylesheet	Different types of templates for the presentation of the financial data

Source: Based on Ernst & Young, 2004 pp. 21–22

Displayed below is an example of the XBRL element for the classification of Current Assets in the UK GAAP taxonomy:

```
<element id="uk-gaap-ci_CurrentAssets" name="CurrentAssets"
type="xbrli:monetaryItemType" substitutionGroup="xbrli:item" nillable="true"
xbrli:periodType="instant" xbrli:balance="debit" />
```

(source – www.xbrl.org/uk/fr/gaap/ci/2004-05-15 accessed 28/03/05)

In the above example the 'element id' as defined in the UK GAAP 'Current Assets' is named here. It is of a 'type' belonging to the Monetary Items with the normal balance being a 'debit'. The identifier for period type is referred to as 'instant' and is obtained from the Period date found in the beginning of the financial statement.

The naming conventions follow closely those used in database design.

For a more extensive example access the following link www.xbrl.org/Example1/

The XBRL specifications and schemas and taxonomies go through a process of validations and approval by XBRL International. The taxonomies are specifically developed according to a specific accounting standard. For example, the US GAAP taxonomy is different from the Australian taxonomy or the UK GAAP taxonomy.

With the requirement to follow the International Financial Reporting Standards in most western countries, the IFRS taxonomy can be used and adapted to reflect the differences of the individual country. Australian listed companies must use the Australian Accounting Standards which have been harmonised with IFRS from June 2005.

Financial reporting taxonomies currently approved or acknowledged by XBRL International

Country Jurisdiction	Taxonomy	Spec	Level	Status
Canada	GAAP Primary Financial Statements	2.1	Ack	Draft
Germany	AP Commercial and Industrial	2.0	Ack	Final
IASB	IFRS General Purpose, 2004 rules	2.1	Ack	Draft
	IFRS General Purpose, 2003 rules	2.1	Ack	Draft
Korea	GAAP Primary Financial Statements	2.0	Ack	Draft
New Zealand	GAAP Commercial and Industrial	2.1	Ack	Draft
United Kingdom	GAAP Commercial and Industrial	2.1	Ack	Draft
United States	GAAP – Commercial and Industrial	2.1	App	Final
	Management Report	2.1	App	Final
	Accountants Report	2.1	App	Final
	MD&A	2.1	App	Final

(*Source:* www.xbrl.org/FRTaxonomies/ accessed 30/3/05)

The advantage of using the XBRL, according to XBRL International, is that:

Computers can treat XBRL data "intelligently": they can recognise the information in a XBRL document, select it, analyse it, store it, exchange it with other computers and present it automatically in a variety of ways for users. XBRL greatly increases the speed of handling of financial data, reduces the chance of error and permits automatic checking of information.
(www.xbrl.org/WhatIsXBRL/ accessed on 30/03/05)

For a good basic overview tutorial on XBRL, visit
www.us.kpmg.com/microsite/xbrl/train/86/start.htm

30.3 What XBRL is not

XBRL is not an accounting standard, it is a language specifically constructed for the exchange of accounting information. As with other financial statements, the reader needs to be aware of accounting standards applicable to the statements under review. XBRL does not in any way attempt to specify accounting rules.

30.4 How can it be used?

The information flow from an organisation to stakeholders and regulatory institutions and banks is considerable. Each of the external parties has their own individual needs for particular information and not one report would suit all of these parties.

The flow of information would look something as follows:

Today: A Convoluted Information Supply Chain

Source: www.xbrl.org.au/training/NSWWorkshop.pdf – accessed on 30/03/05

The above figure demonstrates how information is collated from Operational Data Stores and coded to the General Ledger (GL) using the Chart of Accounts (C of A). Once the data has been captured in the GL, reports can be produced. These reports may be special purpose reports such as those required by the statutory organisations or banks. The reports can be published in different formats. Each of the regulatory organisations has their own requirements. The Australian Securities and Investment Commission (ASIC) has quite different demands for disclosure from, say, the Australian Taxation Office (ATO). Reports can be in different formats such as printed statements for internal use or for the Auditors. Investors may receive information in print such as the full Annual report, or the organisation may publish summary or full reports on their home webpage in PDF or HTML format.

If we were to use XBRL then, with the use of the different Instance Documents and Stylesheets, the information preparation would be much simpler, as the figure below indicates.

With XRBL: Multiple Outputs from a Single Specification

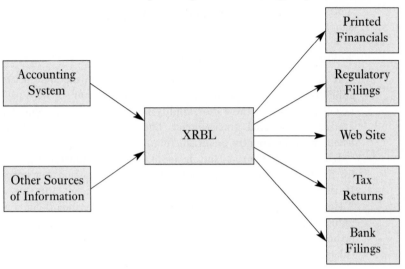

Source: www.xbrl.org.au/training/NSWWorkshop.pdf – accessed on 30/03/05

XBRL also makes it possible for the stakeholders to receive information that can be understood by computer software and allow them to analyse the data obtained.

XRBL: Information flow TO stakeholders

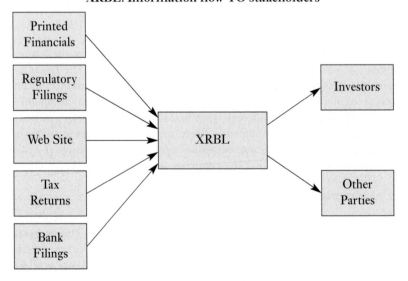

Source: www.xbrl.org.au/training/NSWWorkshop.pdf – accessed on 30/03/05

30.5 What is needed to use XBRL?

There are four processes, supported by the appropriate software, to be completed to adopt XBRL.

1 The taxonomy needs to be designed

The design could be based upon the IFRS or upon the appropriate accounting standard applicable for a given country. There are a number of software packages available, called taxonomy builders; these can simplify the process greatly. The taxonomies are all freely available from XBRL International. The status (final, draft etc.) of the taxonomy is also listed, as is the country or jurisdiction.

It is also possible to adapt, or adopt, a particular taxonomy. Designing the taxonomy for the first time with no reference to a previous version is a very time-consuming task. It is easier to take an existing taxonomy and adapt this for a particular purpose. Adaptation may occur when there is no specific standard for a particular commercial industry. So if, say, mining was not catered for, then a mining company can take the taxonomy applicable to the specific country and adapt this to their particular needs. Adaptation is also required for an organisation where structural changes or consolidation changes have taken place.

2 Mapping

The term 'mapping' relates to equating the terminology used in the financial statements to 'names' used in the taxonomy. For example, if the taxonomy refers to 'Inventory' as being products held for sale, but the organisation refers to this as 'Stock In Trade' in the financial reports, then this needs to be 'mapped' to the taxonomy. All the names used in the financial statements, or any other reports, need thus be compared and mapped to the taxonomy. This 'mapping' is done the first time the taxonomy is used. Structural changes relating to the business structure due to mergers etc. or a change relating to an additional Asset classification would require an adjustment to the 'mapping'.

3 Creating an Instance document

The Instance document is the document that captures all the data values that are to be contained within the end-product, the financial statements. The Instance document contains the facts that conform to the XBRL taxonomy. The Instance document serves as a coded input for the next stage of the process, the stylesheet. It should be remembered when looking at all the different types of coding that this coding is designed to be read by computers rather than humans. There are more tools now available to help with this process. Software for large organisations, especially those that cover Enterprise Resource Planning (ERP) systems, has the capability to produce an Instance document.

4 Use of the Instance document

The Instance document produced in Process 3 discussed above needs to be used in conjunction with a stylesheet to produce the required report(s). This process can be done by use of automated software processes whereby the instance document is linked automatically to the stylesheet also set up in the same software. It is also possible to produce the Instance document and use special purpose software for linking to the stylesheets.

The Instance document can be read by humans but it requires at minimum a good understanding of the formats and naming conventions used. This would also apply to the whole of the process: taxonomy adoption/adaptation, mapping and Instance documents.

In most cases a database repository (database dictionary) of all the 'instances' of the financial statement naming conventions is used to accomplish the mapping process and produce the Instance document. For some of the software available see the listing at the end of this chapter.

See Figure 30.1 for a summary of the four processes.

Figure 30.1

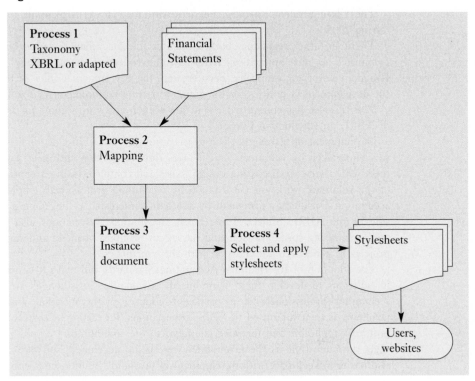

30.6 Progress of **XBRL** development

Since the formation of XBRL as an independent organisation in 1999 in the USA, when it had only a dozen or so members, membership and development of taxonomies have progressed. In December 2000 membership had grown to around 70 organisations and the first taxonomy was released for public comment in the USA in April 2000 with subsequent public release in August 2000 (USA). In December 2000 membership exceeded 70 organisations. In February 2001 the first IASB draft taxonomy was released and UK XBRL was launched. In June 2001 XBRL was harmonised with new W3C recommendations and work on XBRL for the General Ledger was announced.

Also in 2001 countries such as Australia and Japan launched their jurisdictions and started working on taxonomies and other adoption work. Work did not only commence on the countries' own XBRL taxonomies but projects were also initiated by regulators and industry.

For example, the Australian Prudential Regulatory Authority (APRA), the government body that controls and regulates banking and superannuation funds in Australia, announced the adoption of XBRL for their data collections. APRA needs to collect regular data from more than 10,000 institutions. The final result of the project allows for specially set up Microsoft Excel spreadsheets, provided by APRA, to run over the spreadsheets used by the institutions; the APRA files then go through a series of conversions to finally upload the data to the APRA files in XBRL format. The advantage of this process is that the information providers to APRA are not required to develop their own taxonomies. If the institutions had their own taxonomies it would have been left to APRA to 'map' this data to their own requirements, a task far too daunting with more than 10,000 institutions delivering data to APRA.

The UK equivalent Financial Services Authority (FSA) is planning to collect returns during 2005.

There are other regulatory bodies, such as the Australian Taxation Office, which are committed to development of XBRL in the collection of tax filings. In the United Kingdom a working group has been created, the government's office of the E-envoy, for the development of policies for the digital reporting requirement for regulatory purposes.

The EU also has committed about one million euros in a grant for the development of XBRL jurisdictions in Europe.

Development of taxonomies is a time-consuming task. Most of the early development was undertaken by volunteers and it takes time to develop and meet with other volunteers with a view to discussing design issues and complete tasks. A considerable amount of the volunteer work was contributed by accounting professionals employed by the big accounting consultancy firms and by academics interested in developing the educational side of the XBRL project. Professional Accounting Associations also contributed by making meeting space available and having an 'in-house' contact and supporting XBRL projects in general communication with their members.

The adoption of International Accounting Standards will make it easier for individual jurisdictions to develop their 'harmonised' taxonomies. Jurisdictions are established by accounting professionals in a particular country or organisation and the resulting taxonomy is then submitted to XBRL International for testing of correct usage of all the protocols applicable and for open comment to the community.

At the same time as the taxonomies were being developed, software companies were also trying to keep pace with development of taxonomy builders and with software delivering all the needed mapping and production of Instance documents. Software development is always subject to extensive testing and there is no difference in the case of XBRL. Validation requires a lot of testing for data integrity and for the software routines. There are now, however, a few commercial products available.

Additional development in the general ledger area will have the result that organisational data is classified at the source as to which particular 'identity label' the transaction belongs to. This means that classification decisions with respect to XBRL names will have to be made at the Chart of Accounts level. This is very large task as the financial statements are usually concerned with aggregated data. For example, the total for administration expenses in the Profit and Loss Statement is usually made up by the aggregation of quite a number of different account classifications in the General Ledger. In order to develop the XBRL code for the General Ledger, decisions as to what constitutes the aggregate accounts need to be based upon the relevant accounting standard. For example, the Chart of Account structure for the disclosure of segmentation by product class or geographical areas is distinctly different. The XBRL code also needs to reflect this. There is also the probability of an organisation changing its focus owing to strategic decisions. The information systems must then also be adapted to reflect the change. This can be very costly.

The XBRL for the General Ledger may also bring great cost savings as data collection at source is automated and the extraction and processing of data into information can be achieved in a much shorter time. A company such as General Electric has more than 150 general ledgers which are not compatible in use. XBRL has the potential to streamline consolidation processes considerably.

30.7 Companies currently using **XBRL**

There are quite a number of organisations currently using XBRL for reporting purposes. For example, EDGAR® Online®, Inc. (NASDAQ: EDGR – News), a financial information company specialising in making complex regulatory reporting by public companies actionable and easy-to-use, now offers US public company financial statements in XBRL. However, not all are commercial organisations – some of the Professional Accounting Organisations have also applied XBRL to their annual reports.

The XBRL International website www.xbrl.org has an extensive listing of companies and authorities currently using XBRL; the reader is encouraged to investigate any of these further. A number of the links provided will lead to good discussions of the projects and demonstrate how XBRL is applied. Some of the links will also bring the reader to websites in languages other than English and may be of particular interest to readers of this text living in these countries.

Individual countries' jurisdictions can also be reached from the XBRL international website.

Summary

XBRL is still a developing area relating to organisational reporting. In the coming years this will continue and extend beyond the current focus on the published financial statements. The General Ledger area is developing and this will benefit the organisational information supply chain. Accounting software suppliers are also adopting XBRL in their developments and this will increase accessibility to XBRL. Accounting software companies aimed at the smaller organisations, such as MYOB™, are also using XBRL in their new developments. Future software development may also make it easier for accountants to use XBRL, especially when the country's taxonomies are in 'final' approved stage. Developing a company's taxonomy may be an inbuilt function, like the many report writers.

Accountants and students wishing to keep up to date with these developments are gaining a competitive advantage by creating and developing a 'niche' skill which can only add value to an organisation employing these professionals.

REVIEW QUESTIONS

1 Discuss how an investor might benefit from Annual Reports being made available in XBRL.

2 Explain how a body such as a tax authority might benefit from XBRL.

3 Explain what you understand by taxonomy and mapping.

4 Explain the uses of stylesheets.

5 List the steps in the approval process for a taxonomy to be considered to have 'final' status. (Hint: look at www.xbrl.org.)

EXERCISES

Question 1

In this chapter you were given an example of what Current Assets may look like in XBRL coding. Current Assets refers to a heading in the Financial Statements and is thus used as a TOTAL account (sometimes also referred to as a 'roll up to' account).

Required:
Construct your own XBRL coding to an item belonging to the current assets such as Inventory. (Hint: – look at the taxonomy applicable in your jurisdiction on the www.xbrl.org website.)

Question 2

How does a country establish a 'jurisdiction'? Is your country listed as such? If not, do you know of any activity in the XBRL area in your country?

The following questions (3–8) provide an opportunity for further student enquiry using the Internet.

Question 3

Find out more about any of the following topics and write a one-page summary on:

● the XBRL General Ledger work

● use of XBRL by stock exchanges

● the commitment by the IFRS to the XBRL project

● accounting software companies involved providing XBRL capabilities

● public utilities who are using XBRL

● government involvement in XBRL.

Question 4

Visit the website www.us.kpmg.com/microsite

What other types of training courses in XBRL are listed? Attempt one of them and write a short summary of what you have learned.

Question 5

Find a company listed on the www.xbrl.org website as having accounts prepared with XBRL and write a brief summary about the company. See if you can also find information on the **company's own** website about the use of XBRL.

Question 6

Visit www.microsoft.com and write a summary of Microsoft's involvement in XBRL.

Question 7 – for the adventurous!

Follow the link from www.microsoft.com/office/solutions/xbrl/default.mspx information page on 'Solutions for Financial Reporting'; here you can follow the link www.microsoft.com/office/solutions/xbrl/nextsteps.mspx and download the Office Tool for XBRL *Prototype*. There is also further information and a help-file for the demo.

Did you have to re-key any data using the analysis? If you were a shareholder, would this tool help you?

Question 8

Visit the websites for XBRL authoring tools such as those from Semansys, UBMatrix or j3Technology and others and compare or try their free products.

Write up your experience.

Supplementary reading:

Ernst & Young, *Web Enabled Business Reporting. De invloed van XBRL op het verslaggevingsprocess*, Kluwer, 2004.

Mike Rondel, *XBRL – Do I need to know more?*, *Chartered Accountants Journal of New Zealand*, Volume 83, No 5, June 2004, pp. 37–40.

Mark Huckelsby and Josef Macdonald, *The three tenets of XBRL – adoption, adoption, adoption!*, *Chartered Accountants Journal of New Zealand* , March 2004, pp. 46–47.

Neil Hannon, *XBRL Grows Fast in Europe*, *Strategic Finance*, October 2004, pp. 55–56.

The following websites were accessed.
www.adobe.com
www.w3.org/Consortium/
www.xbrl.org/uk/fr/gaap/ci/2004-05-15
www.xbrl.org/Example1/
www.xbrl.org/FRTaxonomies/
www.xbrl.org/WhatIsXBRL/
www.us.kpmg.com/microsite/xbrl/train/86/start.htm
www.xbrl.org/Example1/
www.xbrl.org
www.oracle.com/applications/financials/OracleGeneralLedgerDS-1.pdf
www.xbrl.org/WhatIsXBRL/
www.xbrl.org.au/training/NSWWorkshop.pdf
www.microsoft.com/office/solutions/xbrl/default.mspx
www.ubmatrix.com/home/
www.semansys.com
www.j3technology.com/

PART **6**

Accountability

CHAPTER 31

Corporate governance

31.1 Introduction

In this chapter we consider:

Corporate governance – directors

- The need for corporate governance guidelines
- Corporate governance in different countries
- Corporate governance requirements
- UK Voluntary Code
- Directors' remuneration
- Influence of institutional investors.

Corporate governance – auditors

- Auditor's report to shareholders
- Competence of the auditor – educational requirements
- Independence of the auditor
- Assessing quality of management performance.

31.2 The need for corporate governance guidelines

Where shares are widely held, and management of the company is delegated to directors who are not major shareholders of the company, there is a need for corporate governance guidelines.

The 'theory' of listed companies is that the shareholders own the company. However, there are too many shareholders to run the company, and they may not have the expertise or desire to run the company. So, the task of running the company is delegated to the directors. The 'duty' of the directors is to run the company in a way that maximises the long-term return to the shareholders (i.e. maximises the company's profit and cash flow).

Corporate governance guidelines are developed so that it can be seen whether the directors are maximising returns to shareholders, that business risk is set at a reasonable level, that a director or the board of directors do not become dominant to the detriment of the shareholders, and that the remuneration of the directors is reasonable.

Disclosure of this information is made in the company's annual financial statements. To ensure the reliability of this information, it must be checked by an independent auditor. The national accounting bodies and the International Federation of Accountants provide ethical rules and auditing standards which aim to ensure that auditors are competent to perform their work and have the appropriate independence from the audit client.

31.3 Corporate governance in different countries

There are four interesting correlations when considering the development of corporate governance requirements in different countries. These are:

(a) the ratio of the value of listed companies to the country's gross domestic product (GDP). The higher this ratio, the more developed are the corporate governance requirements;

(b) how widely the shares of listed companies are held. If a large number of financial institutions and individuals hold shares in listed companies, there is a greater need for corporate governance requirements;

(c) cultural considerations. The USA and the UK and its former colonies tend to have much more developed corporate governance requirements than other countries;

(d) the different levels of management in the organisation structures of companies.

We will consider each of these correlations below.

31.3.1 The ratio of the value of listed companies to the country's GDP (gross domestic product)

As we can see from Figure 31.1 the value of listed companies as a percentage of GDP varies between countries but has tended to increase within countries over time. The higher the ratio the more pressure there will be from equity investors for good corporate governance and transparency. The UK percentage of over 130% in 1993 was one of the reasons why there was an early interest in good corporate governance in the UK. Since 1996 there has been a growth in equity investment in other countries which has led to a similar pressure for greater transparency, good corporate governance and improved investor education.

Figure 31.1 Value of listed companies as percentage of GDP

	1993 %	1996[1] %
France	38	38
Germany	25	28
Italy	15	21
Netherlands	62	95
Norway	28	36
Spain	26	33
UK	132	142

31.3.2 How widely the shares in listed companies are held

The second factor influencing corporate governance requirements is how widely the shares in listed companies are held. In the USA and the UK, a large number of financial institutions and individuals hold shares in listed companies, so there is a greater need for corporate governance requirements. In Japan and most European countries (except the UK) shares in listed companies tend to be held by a small number of banks, financial institutions and individuals. Where there are few shareholders in a company, they can question the directors directly, so there is less need for corporate governance requirements.

A further related factor is that US and UK companies tend to have a low gearing, so most of the finance is provided by shareholders. However, in other countries the gearing of companies is much higher, which indicates that most finance for companies comes from banks. If the majority of the finance is provided by shareholders, then there is a greater need for corporate governance requirements than if finance is in the form of loans where the lenders are able to stipulate conditions and loan covenants, e.g. the maximum level of gearing and action available to them if interest payments or capital repayments are missed.

31.3.3 Cultural

The third factor is cultural. It is apparent that the most detailed corporate governance requirements come from the USA, the UK and former UK colonies (Australia, Canada, Singapore, Malaysia, Hong Kong and South Africa).

31.3.4 Organisational structures

In the UK system there is just one level of management represented by a board of directors who may delegate to members of the board such functions as remuneration committee and audit committee membership. Corporate governance is achieved by the financial regulatory authorities requiring compliance with a voluntary code of conduct from the directors of listed companies.

Other countries have a two-tier system of management with a management (or executive) board responsible for the operational management of the company, and a supervisory board which acts on an *ad hoc* basis, e.g. approving an important business transaction, and at the year-end when it receives the audit report, and the management report on the activities and dividend proposed by the management board and approves the financial statements and dividend distribution. This two-tier structure might be seen as providing a greater degree of control than the single-tier system and so there is less need for an imposed code of conduct.

31.3.5 Future developments

Corporate governance requirements are less developed in the European Union countries (except the UK) and Japan. What about the future? Developments in the European Union, Japan, China, Russia and other Eastern Bloc (former communist) countries are leading to a model of much wider ownership of shares (i.e. like the USA and the UK).

In the European Union, restrictions on who may hold shares in major companies are inconsistent with the Union's desire for 'free movement of goods and capital', so there will be a trend for a greater proportion of companies' shares being listed on a stock exchange.

In Japan, major losses by some large companies have led to 'negative equity' and those companies being purchased in part or whole by companies in the USA and other countries. In China, Russia and the former communist countries in Eastern Europe, the economies are being changed from state-controlled businesses to privately owned companies. The 'model' of these companies is similar to those in the USA and UK. So, the trend is towards the US and UK model of companies' shares being listed on their national stock exchange. This trend to wider share ownership will doubtless encourage the development of corporate governance criteria similar to those in the USA and the UK.

31.4 Corporate governance requirements

Figure 31.2 summarises the main corporate governance requirements for listed companies in OECD recommendations,[2] the Commonwealth,[3] the USA, and the UK.

Figure 31.2 Corporate governance guidelines in different countries

Country	Australia	Canada	Hong Kong	India	Malaysia
1 Disclosure of Compliance	Yes	Yes	Yes	Yes	Yes
2 Board responsible to	Share-holders	Share-holders	n/c	n/c	Share-holders
3 Separation of Chairman & CEO	Yes	Yes	n/c	n/c	Yes
4 Non-executive directors	Majority	Majority	n/c	Majority	At least a third
5 Audit committee	Yes all NED	Yes all NED	Yes majority NED	Yes all NED	Yes majority NED
6 Governance committee	n/c	Yes	n/c	n/c	n/c
7 Nomination committee	Yes majority NED	Yes all NED	n/c	n/c	Yes all NED
8 Remuneration Committee	Yes majority NED	Yes	n/c	n/c	Yes majority NED
9 Director re-election	n/c	n/c	n/c	n/c	3 years
10 One share, one vote	Yes	n/c	n/c	n/c	n/c
11 Shareholder approval of remuneration	n/c	n/c	n/c	n/c	No

Country	OECD	Singapore	UK	USA
1 Disclosure of Compliance	Yes	Yes	Yes	n/c
2 Board responsible to	n/c	Shareholders	Shareholders	Shareholders
3 Separation of Chairman & CEO	Encouraged	n/c	Yes	No firm recommendation
4 Non-executive directors	Majority	n/c	Yes	Majority

Figure 31.2 (*cont.*)

Country	OECD	Singapore	UK	USA
5 Audit committee	Yes majority NED	Yes majority NED	Yes majority NED	Yes only NED
6 Governance committee	n/c	n/c	n/c	Yes only NED
7 Nomination committee	Yes only NED	n/c	Yes majority NED	Yes only NED
8 Remuneration Committee	Yes only NED	n/c	Yes only NED	Yes only NED
9 Director re-election	n/c	3 years (CEO 5 years)	3 years	n/c
10 One share, one vote	n/c	n/c	n/c	n/c
11 Shareholder approval of remuneration	n/c	n/c	Only long-term incentive schemes	n/c

Abbreviations:
NED Non-executive directors (or independent directors) not involved in the day-to-day running of the company;
n/c not covered; OECD Organization for Economic Co-operation and Development.
Note also that OECD requirements might be implemented differently in different countries.
Corporate governance requirements for other countries are either undeveloped or far less developed.

31.4.1 Status of corporate governance requirements

The above list of points are **recommendations** and not requirements. Thus, they are not as strong as statutory requirements or even accounting standards. However, stock exchanges will expect listed companies to comply with the recommendations, and failure to comply with some of them may have an adverse effect on the company's share price.

Generally, the recommendations have been drawn up by committees comprising directors and representatives of listed companies, their auditors, and financial institutions which invest in the shares. There is little, if any, representation of 'ordinary' shareholders on these committees. So, the recommendations may be biased. Many companies and their directors would prefer not to have to comply with corporate governance requirements, compliance limits their independence, and there are additional costs involved in setting up and monitoring corporate governance systems within the company. However, pressures from governments, the general public, shareholders and financial institutions will mean that directors have to accept some corporate governance requirements. The agreed corporate governance requirements will be a compromise between the pressures of the directors of the listed companies (who would have few, if any, requirements) and those of the government, shareholders and financial institutions (who would prefer to have detailed corporate governance requirements).

31.4.2 Setting directors' remuneration

Consideration of requirements to disclose directors' remuneration illustrates these pressures and the final compromise which is reached. In the UK there has been considerable concern at

(a) the high salaries paid to listed company directors;
(b) the high annual increase in these salaries, often at least twice the annual increase of other employees;
(c) the salaries continuing to remain high, even when the company is performing badly.

Although the general public may believe that directors' salaries are set by the shareholders, this does not happen, as it is not a requirement of the Companies Acts. With no statutory control over directors' setting their salaries, there has been a rapid increase in their salaries. So, one would expect corporate governance requirements to require some controls over the levels of directors' salaries, probably by their salaries being approved by the shareholders at the annual general meeting. However, the corporate governance requirements of the countries in the Figure 30.2 above show that there is no requirement for approval of directors' salaries by the shareholders. Recently, in the UK, listed companies are now required to propose a resolution at the Annual General Meeting for shareholders to approve the Directors' Remuneration Report. In this way, UK shareholders have some control over the remuneration of the directors. In a few companies, there has been the threat that shareholders may vote against this report when the directors' remuneration appears to be over-generous. Occasionally, either the generous remuneration package has been withdrawn or a majority of shareholders have voted against the resolution.

31.4.3 Role of remuneration committees

The other requirement suggested in a number of countries is that the company should have a remuneration committee, comprising wholly or mainly non-executive directors, who consider the performance and remuneration of the executive directors. The corporate governance requirements do not suggest that shareholders or other more independent people should be members of the remuneration committee. As directors will want to maximise their earnings, it appears that remuneration committees will have little effect in limiting the increase in salaries of executive directors. Nevertheless, they should hopefully help to link directors' remuneration more closely to the financial performance of the company.

In the UK, it has been reported[4] that the 'sole instance where a majority of companies fail to comply with the code [on corporate governance] is in having a board Remuneration Committee composed entirely of non-executive directors'. The article goes on to say, 'Indeed, they [i.e. investors] may think that having colleagues and chums deciding executive pay may have a great deal to do with pay rises that regularly outdo rises for non-board managers or employees, and with over-generous packages that reward success, mediocrity and failure with equal munificence.' It then says, 'But the remorseless upward pay ratchet should be less highly geared in their hands' (i.e. when the remuneration is decided by the non-executive directors).

31.5 UK Voluntary Code – The Cadbury Report[5]

The Cadbury Committee was set up by the Financial Reporting Council, the London Stock Exchange and the accountancy profession in 1991 under the chairmanship of Sir Adrian Cadbury. The London Stock Exchange adopted as part of its Listing Rules a statement in the annual report as to whether the company had complied with the Code or not.

The Cadbury Report produced a *voluntary* Code of Best Practice. The points it made were as follows:

The board

1.1 The board should meet regularly, retain full and effective control over the company and monitor the executive management.

1.2 There should be a clearly accepted division of responsibilities at the head of a company, which will ensure a balance of power and authority, such that no one individual has unfettered powers of decision. Where the chairman is also the chief executive, it is essential that there should be a strong and independent element on the board, with a recognised senior member.

1.3 The board should include non-executive directors of sufficient calibre and number for their views to carry significant weight in the board's decisions.

1.4 The board should have a formal schedule of matters specifically reserved to it for decision to ensure that the direction and control of the company is firmly in its hands.

1.5 There should be an agreed procedure for directors in the furtherance of their duties to take independent professional advice if necessary, at the company's expense.

1.6 All directors should have access to the advice and services of the company secretary, who is responsible to the board for ensuring that board procedures are followed and that applicable rules and regulations are complied with. Any question of the removal of the company secretary should be a matter for the board as a whole.

Non-executive directors

2.1 Non-executive directors should bring an independent judgement to bear on issues of strategy, performance and resources, including key appointments and standards of conduct.

2.2 The majority should be independent of management and free from any business or other relationship that could materially interfere with the exercise of their independent judgement, apart from their fees and shareholdings. Their fees should reflect the time which they commit to the company.

2.3 Non-executive directors should be appointed for specified terms and reappointment should not be automatic.

2.4 Non-executive directors should be selected through a formal process and both the process and their appointment should be a matter for the board as a whole.

Executive directors

3.1 Directors' service contracts should not exceed three years without shareholders' approval.

3.2 There should be full and clear disclosure of directors' total emoluments and those of the chairman and the highest-paid UK director, including pension contributions and stock options. Separate figures should be given for salary and for performance-related elements, and the basis on which performance is measured should be explained.

3.3 Executive directors' pay should be subject to the recommendations of a remuneration committee made up wholly or mainly of non-executive directors.

Reporting and controls

4.1 It is the board's duty to present a balanced and understandable assessment of the company.

4.2 The board should ensure that an objective and professional relationship is maintained with the auditors.

4.3 The board should establish an audit committee of at least three non-executive directors with written terms of reference which deal clearly with its authority and duties.

4.4 The directors should explain their responsibility for preparing the accounts next to a statement by the auditors about their reporting responsibilities.

4.5 The directors should report on the effectiveness of the company's system of internal control.

31.6 The Greenbury Report[6]

In July 1995 the Greenbury Committee issued a four-part code on directors' remuneration and covering good practice in relation to the following:

● **The remuneration committee**. The board should set up remuneration committees of non-executive directors to determine the company's policy on executive remuneration and specific remuneration packages for each of the executive directors, including pension rights and compensation payments.

● **Disclosure**. The remuneration committee should report to the shareholders each year the company's policy on executive directors' remuneration, including levels, comparative groups of companies, individual components (e.g. basic salary, benefits in kind, annual bonuses and long-term incentive schemes including share options), performance criteria and measurement, pension provision, contracts of service and compensation commitments on early termination.

● **Remuneration policy**. Remuneration committees must provide the packages needed to attract, retain and motivate directors of the quality required, but avoiding paying more than is necessary.

● **Service contracts**. Remuneration committees should consider what compensation commitments their directors' contracts of service would entail in the event of early termination, particularly for unsatisfactory performance, with a strong case for setting contract periods at one year or less.

Two of the most controversial recommendations – issuing options at discounts and pension entitlements – were initially resisted by a number of companies maintaining that they were unable to value these benefits. However, the existence of the code was yet another step exerting pressure on companies to give more information to the shareholders. The Greenbury Report was followed by the Hampel Report.

31.7 The Hampel Report[7]

In January 1998 the Hampel Report was produced. It was defined by the chairman as a 'fine tuning exercise' of the Cadbury and Greenbury Reports. The main provisions are:

- Chairman and chief executive should be separate roles. This was stronger than the Cadbury recommendation that where the chairman is also the chief executive, it is essential that there should be a strong and independent element on the board, with a recognised senior member.
- Directors should be on contracts lasting one year or less. This was more restrictive than the Cadbury recommendation that directors' service contracts should not exceed three years without shareholders' approval.
- Remuneration committees should be made up of independent non-executive directors. This was more restrictive than the Cadbury recommendation that executive directors' pay should be subject to the recommendations of a remuneration committee made up wholly or mainly of non-executive directors.
- Non-executive directors may be paid in company shares although this is not recommended. This view is more restrictive than the existing Cadbury recommendation that accepts non-executive directors holding shares but is against them holding share options that means they are tied to the company performance. The Hampel view appeared more logical. It was difficult to see why independence was not compromised by holding shares whilst it was by holding share options – if anything the pressure on the non-executive director was even greater if he or she actually had an existing shareholding to protect rather than a speculative gain.
- A senior non-executive director should be nominated to deal with shareholders' concerns. Hampel has expressed the view that, if directors pay themselves too much or do not invest enough in the company, it was the power wielded by the shareholders rather than books of corporate governance rules that really counted. However, it is difficult to see how a busy non-executive director, often with extensive commitments elsewhere, will be in a position to respond to other than limited requests for information or action.
- Directors should be trained.

The Hampel Report was followed by the *Combined Code* (see 31.10).

31.8 The Higgs Report[8]

The Higgs Report on the role and effectiveness of non-executive directors' (NEDs) was published in January 2003. The main recommendations are summarised below:

Board operation
- The company's annual report should state the number of meetings of the board and its main committees, and the attendance of each director. There should be a description of how the board operates.
- At least half the members of the board, excluding the chairman, should be independent NEDs.
- The performance of the Board, its committees and its members should be evaluated at least once a year.

- A nomination committee of the board should conduct the process of board appointments and make recommendations. It should consist of a majority of independent NEDs.

Comment on possible success of the proposal that at least 50% of the directors of listed companies should be NEDs:

- It is beneficial when executive directors and NEDs work together, valuing each other's experience and contribution. The NEDs can provide an independent check on the executives' plans and decisions, and their experience will be different from that of the executive, which should lead to better decision making.

- However, there can be 'splits' between the executives and NEDs. The executives may propose a future plan, but (some or all of) the NEDs may disagree. This can lead to distrust between the executives and NEDs, which will adversely affect the running of the company. Because of these problems, the executives may 'hide' certain decisions and information from the NEDs. The executives are likely to feel that the NEDs are 'interfering' – they will see the NEDs as less valuable than themselves, as the NEDs will be paid substantially less than the executives, and the NEDs will spend only a small part of their time on the company's affairs while the executives will be working full-time.

- Boards try to keep 'splits' (i.e. disagreements) between directors secret until the matter is resolved. If this information becomes public, it can have a very adverse effect on the company's share price, and it could precipitate the collapse of the company. For instance, the Board may be considering dismissing the Chief Executive (e.g. if the company is performing poorly), but it will not make an announcement until it has been agreed by a majority of the members of the Board. There may be a further delay while termination payments of the Chief Executive are being agreed.

- There may be situations when the NEDs' approach to running the business is too cautious. The executives may make a proposal which the NEDs reject. However, it may be that the executives understand the market better than the NEDs, and that the executives' proposal would have been very profitable. The decision by the NEDs will have led to a reduction in future profitability and expansion of the business.

- Even with a board of at least 50% NEDs, it is questionable whether they will have the courage and power to override the proposals of the executives. For instance, would the NEDs of Marconi have prevented the executives from buying companies for cash and increasing the company's borrowings by many billions of pounds? However, some years ago the NEDs were effective when British Airways (BA) produced unjustified publicity against Virgin. Virgin took legal action against BA, and the NEDs replaced the directors involved in this unjustified publicity.

Comment on proposal for nominations:

- Making appointments to the Board has often been seen as the chairman's prerogative and the proposal may well be opposed by chairmen.

Chairman

- The role of the chairman and chief executive should be separated, with their responsibilities set out in writing and approved by the board.

- A chief executive should not become chairman of the same company.

Comment:
There are still companies that consider it is more efficient for the roles to be combined, and it is not unusual for the chief executive to 'retire' and become chairman.

NEDs – appointment
- Before appointment, NEDs should satisfy themselves that they have the knowledge, skills, experience and time to make a positive contribution to the board.
- The board should set out to shareholders why they propose a new NED and how they meet the requirements.
- There should be an induction programme for new NEDs, which is the responsibility of the chairman and company secretary.
- NEDs should be expected to serve two three-year terms.

NEDs – independence
- NEDs should meet at least once a year without the chairman or executive directors present.
- NEDs may hold shares in the company but should not be awarded share options.
- NEDs should inform the chairman of their reasons for resignation.

NEDs – effectiveness
- A full-time executive director should not have more than one non-executive directorship and should not become chairman of a major company.
- The remuneration committee should comprise at least three members, all of whom should be NEDs. It should have delegated responsibility for setting the remuneration of all the executive directors and the chairman.

Comment:
It is still quite common for full-time executive directors to have more than one non-executive directorship. For instance, in BP plc's financial statements for the year ended 31 December 2003, it reports that the Chief Executive is a non-executive director of Intel Corporation and Goldman Sachs Group Inc. (non-executive director of two companies). A non-executive director of BP plc is (executive) Chairman of Schroders plc and non-executive Chairman of Johnson Matthey plc (i.e. non-executive director of two companies and Chairman of two companies).

Senior NED
- There should be a senior independent NED, who should be available to shareholders for concerns that have not been resolved by the chairman or chief executive.
- The senior NED should attend meetings of management with a range of major shareholders.

Comment:
There have been objections to the proposal for a senior NED on the grounds that the power of the chairman would be reduced and the unitary board principle comprised.

31.9 The Smith Report

The Smith Committee on 'Audit Committees – Combined Code Guidance' was set up by the Financial Reporting Council (FRC), and was designed as a 'junior companion' to Higgs' wider brief on non-executive directors. The committee was chaired by Sir Robert Smith, Chairman of the Weir Group. The Smith Report was published by the FRC on 20 January 2003.

The recommendations on audit committees include:

- At least three members, all independent NEDs.
- At least one member should have significant, recent and relevant financial experience.
- The audit committee should:
  - monitor the integrity of the financial statements
  - review the company's internal financial control system and monitor the effectiveness of internal audit
  - recommend the appointment of the external auditor, and approve the remuneration and terms of engagement
  - monitor the external auditor's independence, objectivity and effectiveness
  - develop and implement a policy on the external auditor supplying non-audit services.
- The directors' report should describe the role of the audit committee and the action it has taken. The chairman of the audit committee should be present at the AGM.

31.9.1 What impact will the Higgs and Smith Reports have on UK corporate governance?

Greater transparency

Future annual reports should reflect the emphasis for greater transparency. An example of this is the requirement for disclosure by the Board of the NEDs considered to be independent and, where circumstances might imply otherwise, the reasons why they are so considered, e.g. where the NED represents a major shareholder.

Audit committee's responsibilities more explicit

The Committee will have a more proactive role and broader overview rather than the previous rather reactive role of keeping the scope and results of the audit under review, e.g. a requirement to monitor the integrity of the financial statements and review significant financial reporting issues and judgements. There is a possibility that misunderstandings may arise:

- for the NEDs who have a conflict of roles with the Committee acting as Board members with the executive management to achieve strategic objectives and as Committee members, overseeing the executive management to protect shareholders' long-term interests;

- for the other Board members who may believe that they have been relieved of responsibility for the work carried out by the Audit Committee.

What will the impact be in practice?

There are two aspects that may affect the impact:

- the degree to which the NEDs achieve constructive informal relationships beyond the formal meetings;
- the extent to which Boards exercise discretion with disclosure.[9]

31.10 The *Combined Code*

The *Combined Code*[10] is described in the Preamble to the Code as 'a consolidation of the work of the three committees, not a new departure'.

It made clear that companies should be ready to explain their governance policies, including any circumstances justifying departure from best practice, and that those concerned with the evaluation of governance should do so with common sense and with due regard to companies' individual circumstances.

The Code proposes principles and code provisions under five headings:

(a) directors

(b) directors' remuneration

(c) relations with shareholders

(d) accountability and audit

(e) institutional shareholders.

We considered directors in Chapter 5. We will now consider headings (b), (c) and (e).

31.11 Directors' remuneration

The proposals are as in previous reports, i.e.:

- companies should establish a formal and transparent procedure for developing policy;
- companies should pay enough to attract suitable directors;
- companies should pay no more than enough;
- part of the remuneration should be linked to individual and corporate performance;
- policy and remuneration of each director should be disclosed in the annual report.

31.11.1 Where do accountants feature in setting directors' remuneration?

The equity of the remuneration is not normally seen as an accounting matter, but accountants should ensure transparent disclosure of the performance criteria and of the payments.

31.11.2 Performance criteria

Directors are expected to produce increases in the share price and dividends. Traditional measures have been largely based on growth in earnings per share (EPS), which has encouraged companies to seek to increase short-term earnings at the expense of long-term earnings, e.g. by cutting back capital programmes. Even worse, concentrating on growth in earnings per share can result in a reduction in shareholder value, e.g. by companies borrowing and investing in projects that produce a return in excess of the interest charge, but less than the return expected by equity investors.

31.11.3 What alternatives are there?

It is interesting to identify the suggested criteria because they could have an impact on the financial information that has to be disclosed in the annual accounts. Suggested criteria include the following:

- **Relative share price increase**, i.e. using market comparisons. Grand Met has revised its scheme so that, before executives gain any benefit from their share options, Grand Met's share price must outperform the FT All-Share Index over a three-year period, i.e. the scheme focuses management on value creation.[11] If this policy is adopted, it would be helpful for the annual accounts to contain details of share price and index movements. Comparative share price schemes should also, in the opinion of the Association of British Insurers, be conditional on a secondary performance criterion, validating sustained and significant improvement in underlying financial performance over the same period.

- **Indicators related to business drivers**, i.e. using internal data. Schemes would need to identify business drivers appropriate to each company, such as customer satisfaction or process times, growth in sales, gross profit, profit before interest and tax, cash flow and return on shareholders' funds.

- **Indicators based on factors such as size and complexity**. Schemes would need to take account of factors such as market capitalisation, turnover, number of employees, breadth of product and markets, risk, regulatory and competitive environment, and rates of change experienced by the organisation. This information could again be disclosed in the business review section of the annual report.

The indications are that there will be a growth in the number of firms offering schemes. However, regulators will need to keep a close eye on the position to avoid schemes creeping in that avoid the existing disclosure requirements. For example, there has been a growth in long-term incentive plans, under which free shares are offered in the future if the executive remains with the company and achieves a certain performance level. This is a perfectly healthy development that retains staff, but such schemes fall outside the definition of a share option plan and allow companies to avoid disclosure.

One of the problems is the innovative nature of the remuneration packages that companies might adopt and the fact that there is no uniquely correct scheme. The Association of British Insurers, in its publication *Share Option and Profit Sharing Incentive Schemes* (February 1995), commented on this very point:

> There is growing acceptance that the benefit arising from the exercise of options should be linked to the underlying financial performance of the company.
>
> Initially, attention focused on performance criteria showing real growth in normalised earnings; however, a number of other criteria have subsequently emerged. The circumstances of each individual company will vary and there is a reluctance, therefore, on the part of institutional investors to indicate a general preference for any particular measurement. On the other hand, a considerable number of companies have stated that they welcome indications of the sort of formulae that are considered to be acceptable ... It is felt that remuneration committees should have discretion to select the formula which is felt to be most appropriate to the circumstances of the company in question. Nevertheless ... it is important that whatever criterion is chosen ... the formula should be supported by, or give clear evidence of, sustained improvement in the underlying financial performance of the group in question.

31.11.4 Requiring adequate disclosure

There is a need for greater disclosure because, in addition to their salaries, directors have been rewarded with bonuses and share options which were not disclosed in the annual accounts in a form that was readily understandable.

In the UK, this prompted the ASB to issue, in 1994, a UITF Abstract *Disclosure of Directors' Share Options*, recommending disclosure of information about option prices and market prices. In the USA, the SEC had already addressed the issue by requiring a precise description of salary, bonuses and share options for the five most highly paid executives, identified by name; and requiring the options to be valued and the information to be presented in a standardised format.

31.11.5 Why should disclosure be required?

In the USA, the disclosure approach has indicated that the very fact of disclosure exerted a moderating influence on the levels of executive reward.[12] It might be argued that financial reporting should not concern itself with the level of an individual executive's remuneration. However, there is a statutory duty to report on directors' remuneration and, under the *Statement of Principles*, a requirement that the information should be reliable. This is an excellent example of where the *Statement of Principles* can assist the financial reporting process. Details about the remuneration package need to be relevant and reliable.

31.11.6 Relevance implication

For information to be relevant, it needs to be predictive. Given that the major purpose of the motivational aspects of the package is to guide the directors towards maximising a defined attribute, e.g. EPS, it is vital to be aware of this when assessing the future performance of the company. If the scheme succeeds, the defined attributes will be the ones that the directors concentrate on. The financial statements should make the shareholder aware of the aim and in subsequent periods provide confirmation as to the level of achievement.

31.11.7 Reliability implication

The *Statement of Principles* states that for information to be reliable it needs to be a valid description and measure, to be complete and to convey the substance of the transaction in an understandable fashion with due regard for the user's abilities. This has not yet been achieved with directors' remuneration and the ASB approach of substance over form could well be followed.

31.11.8 Evaluation of current practice

Following the Greenbury Committee in 1995, remuneration committees now make their own reports to shareholders. The accounts have clearer messages concerning basic salary, constituents of the bonus calculation (although no information that allows the shareholder to assess targets or achievement of targets), long-term incentive plans, share options and pension contributions.

This would seem to indicate that all is well. However, this is certainly not the view presented in an article in *Management Today*.[13] This makes positive reference to the effect of Cadbury, Greenbury and Hampel in forcing companies to adopt long-term incentive plans linked to future performance over a three- to five-year period which, on the surface, appears to be a far more effective way of aligning the interests of executives with those of their investors and their workers; it also recognises that some companies are introducing more stringent performance criteria, e.g. the Whitbread requirement that, unless over a three-year period it improves its minimum total shareholder ranking from 75th to 60th out of the FTSE 100, executives participating in the scheme will not be entitled to any shares. There is a note of caution, however, in that 40% of FTSE 100 companies are still paying above average rewards for poorly performing executives, and more challenging objectives should be found that support shareholder value creation.

The search to tailor remuneration packages will continue and may see a move away from measures such as share price movements which are often a reflection of market movements rather than executive performance. An interesting suggestion was made by Robert Heller in *Management Today* in July 1997,[14] that, if the true top task is to provide successful medium- and long-term strategic direction, and to ensure its implementation, then this should loom largest in determining rewards, and never mind the short-term price of shares. This could be implemented by the use of techniques such as the balanced scorecard with its combination of financial and non-financial measures.

The Code itself sets out provisions to act as warnings to the remuneration committee, e.g. 'comparisons with other companies should be used with caution, in view of the risk that they can result in an upward ratchet of remuneration levels with no corresponding improvement in performance' and 'avoid paying more than is necessary' and 'options should not be exercisable in under three years' and 'total rewards potentially available should not be excessive' and 'incentive schemes should be subject to challenging performance criteria'.

However, in the *Combined Code* there is recognition that the achievement of a fair remuneration policy has not been completed and it states in its preamble: 'We ... make it clear in our report that it is still too soon to assess definitively the results of the Cadbury and, more especially, the Greenbury codes.'

31.11.9 How well do executives' rewards correlate with performance?

A comparison[15] of the top FTSE 100 performers with those at the bottom showed that the presence or otherwise of long-term incentive plans (LTIPs) made very little difference to an executive's performance. The comparison showed the following information for the chief executive officers (CEOs):

Footsie leaders

Company	Salary(£)	Bonus(£)	LTIP(£)	Total(£)
Misys	285,717	329,287	193,228	808,232
Legal & General	440,000	400,000	361,215	1,201,215
Vodafone	587,000	0	3,246,985	3,833,985
Lloyds TSB	475,000	199,000	940,797	1,614,797

Footsie laggards

Company	Salary(£)	Bonus(£)	LTIP(£)	Total(£)
Hanson	310,000	155,000	544,223	1,009,223
Rio Tinto	669,000	144,000	1,179,548	1,992,548
EMI Group	543,300	105,500	361,600	1,010,400
Allied Domecq	460,000	165,000	732,065	1,357,065
Reuters	522,000	255,000	815,938	1,592,938

In June 2003 the Department of Trade and Industry issued a consultation document *'Rewards for Failure' Director's Remuneration – Contracts for Performance and Severance*. Such an approach has become necessary because there has been no effective restraining influence with directors in the largest listed companies reaping ever-increasing rewards which are unrelated to the economic performance of their companies. The hoped-for ability of remuneration committees to restrain excesses has been unrealised – this is unsurprising given that members are frequently themselves executive directors of other companies with little interest in maintaining a strong link with either the company performance or the levels of increases being achieved by staff. There is too great an emphasis on raising remuneration to an average peer group level that fuels continuous catching-up increases.

It is interesting to note the following extract from the ACCA response to the consultation document:

> Shareholders, institutional and individual, need to be well informed on a timely basis about pay and exit packages. In addition, directors should be required to demonstrate to shareholders that their pay is reasonable in relation to their own performance, company performance and employee pay. ACCA would like a standard measure used to track the relationship of board pay to average employee pay and return on capital employed, this would help to ensure that boards remain sensitive to the issue of compensation. Apart from this, we would not seek to prescribe how directors demonstrate that pay is reasonable, but transparency is essential. Transparency is best achieved by providing information based on appropriate benchmarking and supplying trends over time. We recognise, however, that it can be difficult to identify the best criteria for assessing performance and determining remuneration.

31.12 Directors' remuneration – illustration from the Annual Report of Diageo plc[16]

One would imagine that the remuneration which is paid to directors is a simple subject. A director's salary should comprise a basic salary and a bonus based on the profits of the company. However, looking at the financial statements of listed companies, it can be seen that directors' remuneration includes:

(a) basic salary;

(b) benefits in kind;

(c) bonus;

(d) pension entitlements;

(e) share options.

Each of these elements of remuneration is considered below. An example of disclosure of directors' remuneration is taken from the financial statements of Diageo plc, a UK listed company. These disclosures are long and very detailed. However, careful consideration of them reveals a number of unclear matters and unanswered questions.

31.12.1 Remuneration committee

As shown in Figure 31.2, it is suggested that listed companies should have a remuneration committee. Diageo has a remuneration committee; its financial statements say: 'The Remuneration Committee is responsible for making recommendations to the board on remuneration policy as applied to Diageo's executive directors. It consists wholly of independent non-executive directors.' (The names of the directors are given, including the Chairman.)

Remuneration committees are common in US and UK listed companies, but it is far from clear that remuneration is based on the financial performance of the companies. In the UK, the evidence suggests that the larger the company, the larger is the remuneration of the directors, and there is little correlation between remuneration and profitability of the company.

The weakness of the remuneration committee is that it comprises non-executive directors of the company, rather than individuals independent of the company. The initial appointment of the non-executive directors will have been by the executive directors and existing non-executive directors of the company. Also, it is not uncommon for a non-executive director of company A to be an executive director of company B, and a non-executive director of company B an executive director of company A – an incestuous circle in which executive directors of A approve the remuneration of the executive directors of B and vice versa. However, the existence of a remuneration committee should discourage excessive remuneration being paid to executive directors, particularly where the financial performance of the company is poor. Note that Diageo's Remuneration Committee includes the Chairman – Higgs' proposals (2003) prohibit this.

31.12.2 Basic salary

The Diageo financial statements say 'Basic salaries are determined according to the competitive market for senior executives, taking into account their experience, contribution and performance.' As expected, this is more a qualitative statement than a quantitative one. One could not determine the basic salary of any director from this statement.

31.12.3 Benefits in kind

The notes to the financial statements of Diageo plc say that benefits include 'Company cars, private use of chauffeur, fuel, product allowance, financial counselling, spouse travel, medical insurance and life insurance premiums'. Once again, these vary significantly from 6% to 77% of the basic salary. Some explanation is given of the larger sums, such as £279,000 in payment for relocation of a director to the UK.

An example of excessive 'benefits in kind' by a director was Greg Hutchings, chief executive of Tomkins plc. The 'benefits' paid by the company included providing two flats in London, a Rolls-Royce, four jet aircraft, a helicopter, paying his wife and housekeeper, and paying for his son's flight on Concorde. An earlier non-executive Chairman of Tomkins had resigned over being unable to quantify and control Mr Hutchings' 'benefits'. A new non-executive chairman, David Newlands, investigated the extent of his benefits in kind. This led to Mr Hutchings' resignation from the board of Tomkins plc in October 2000.

It can be very difficult to determine the extent of a director's benefits in kind, particularly when the director is in a dominant position and unwilling to disclose these benefits. The financial director, chief accountant and company secretary may be aware of the chief executive's benefits in kind, but a dominant chief executive may prevent them from disclosing the benefits to the non-executive directors and the auditors. However, the Tomkins plc example shows how strong non-executive directors (including the chairman) can act as a control on the actions of executive directors.

31.12.4 Director's bonus

Diageo's financial statements say:

> Bonus payments are based on improvement in the economic profit (EP) of Diageo and its businesses for the year in question. The targets for EP and for the level of bonus are determined by the remuneration committee at the commencement of each year. EP is calculated as net trading profit after tax, less a capital charge which takes into account returns expected by lenders and shareholders. However, for the financial years commencing 1 July 2002, the primary performance measure for the annual performance bonus will be trading profit before exceptional items. This reflects Diageo's objectives of driving organic growth.

Note that:

(i) Trading profit is **before** charging or crediting losses or profits on sale of fixed assets and sale of businesses and interest payments. The profit before taxation is **after** charging/crediting these items. So, for instance, the bonus could be increased by reducing the depreciation charge, so increasing the trading profit. Any losses on sale of fixed assets would be after the trading profit, so they would have no effect on the bonus.

(ii) EP is defined as the **improvement** in economic profit. Would any improvement in EP lead to a bonus? How is 'improvement' calculated? Is it the 'improvement' over last year, or from a basic target or from a long-term trend?

(iii) There is no explanation of how the **capital charge** is determined.

(iv) There is no statement about how much of the 'improvement' in EP is paid to the directors.

(v) There is no explanation why the bonus as a percentage of the basic salary varies so much. The monetary amount of the bonus of directors varies in the ratio 3:1.

From 1 July 2002 the calculation of the bonus is even less detailed and less clear, and it could be much more generous. There is no mention of deducting a 'capital charge', so is a bonus paid as long as there is a profit before exceptional items? There should be a 'normal profit' below which no bonus should be paid (the intention of the previous capital charge). Using the 'profit before exceptional items' is more generous than using the 'profit after exceptional items', as almost all 'exceptional items' are deductions from profit. The 'real' profit of a business is the profit *after* exceptional items, as such exceptional items as closure, redundancy and reorganisation costs are 'real' costs to a business.

It can be seen that the note on the bonus raises more questions than it answers!

Considering bonuses generally, most bonuses are based on the current year's profit, rather than the trend in profits. The bonus cannot be based on future profits, as they are unknown. Basing the bonus on the current year's profit could lead directors to maximise this year's profit by:

(a) the way in which they exercise their judgement in relation to asset vales in the balance sheet, e.g.:

- valuing stock and debtors at the highest possible value by having low provisions for stock obsolescence and bad debts;
- reducing the depreciation on fixed assets;
- capitalising development costs;

(b) making decisions that affect the timing of cash flows, e.g.:

- delaying capital expenditure;
- delaying routine commitments such as the maintenance programme;
- delaying decisions on staff benefits;
- holding back on developing new products.

Developing new products is expensive, and will adversely affect the current year's profit. Some of the costs of developing new products will have to be charged against the current year's profits, as not all these costs can be included in capitalised development expenditure. Also, few companies capitalise development expenditure, and it may not be possible to capitalise development expenditure (particularly in the early stages) as it may not be possible to guarantee there will be sufficient profits from the new product to cover the development costs. So, basing directors' bonuses on the current year's profits could encourage directors to delay (or cancel) development of new products.

If no new products are developed, the company will probably fail in the long term. Thus, providing a bonus based on the current year's profit tends to encourage 'short-termism', which is not in the best interests of the shareholders. The allocation of share options to directors will tend to encourage directors to consider longer-term profitability, which is in the interests of the shareholders. 'Share options' are considered below.

A further problem with paying directors on the basis of the company's profits is that no one would want to be a director in a loss-making company. In many ways, it can be much more difficult to be a director of a company which is in trouble and making losses (in terms of skills required, hours worked and stress) than of a successful and profitable company. Normally, a company makes losses because there have been changes in market conditions and the company has not been able to keep up with the changes. Implementing changes in the company is very difficult and time-consuming. The directors have to decide the new direction of the company. This is very risky, and taking the wrong direction may result in failure of the company. This requires very skilled directors, working very long hours and making difficult decisions. Some decisions, such as making employees redundant, will increase losses (or reduce profits). So, a directors' bonus scheme based on the profitability of the company would be inappropriate. In this situation a remuneration committee would be very valuable. The members of the remuneration committee will be able to see the contributions of each director towards 'turning around' the company. So, they will be good at deciding the appropriate remuneration of each of the directors. The shareholders would be less effective at this task, as they would not have the necessary detailed understanding of the contribution of each director.

From the above discussion, it can be seen that the remuneration committee can be an effective way of determining the remuneration of the individual directors.

31.12.5 Pension entitlements

The disclosure of this item in Diageo's financial statements states the director's annual pension at retirement, and the increase in the pension over inflation since last year. However, this disclosure does not give the pension cost to the company this year, which is the amount the company would have to pay into a pension scheme this year to provide a fund sufficient to pay the director's pension on retirement.

How this pension cost can be calculated is shown by the following example. In the 2001 accounts, a director's pension on retirement was £468,000, and in the 2002 accounts this pension had increased to £509,000. The computation of this cost is performed by actuaries. The following additional information is used in the calculation:

  (i) the director would retire in 2005;

 (ii) the director's planned pension in 2001 was £468,000 and in 2002 it is £509,000;

(iii) a return on investments of 6% is assumed;

(iv) no inflation or increase is assumed in the director's pension after retirement;

 (v) it is assumed the director receives a pension for 15 years, starting in 2005.

The pension fund required in 2005 to pay a pension of £468,000 for 15 years
    = £468,000 × (1 + annuity for 14 years)
    = £468,000 × (1 + 9.2950)   = £4,818,000

The pension fund required in 2001 to pay a pension of £468,000 for 15 years
    = £4,818,000 × discount factor for 4 years
    = £4,818,000 × 0.792094   = £3,816,000

By 2002 this pension fund will have grown to
    = £3,816,000 × 1.06   = £4,045,000

Considering the year 2002 pension of £509,000:
The pension fund required in 2005 to pay a pension of £509,000 for 15 years
    = £509,000 × (1 + annuity for 14 years)
    = £509,000 × (1 + 9.2950)   = £5,240,000

The pension fund required in 2002 to pay a pension of £468,000 for 15 years
    = £5,240,000 × discount factor for 3 years
    = £5,240,000 × 0.839619   = £4,400,000

So, the company's contribution to the pension fund in 2002
    = pension fund required in 2002 – pension fund accrued by 2002
    = £4,400,000 – £4,045,000   = £355,000

These figures illustrate how the calculation would be performed. In practice, the following factors would be included:

  (i) the real increase in the pension fund investments from 2001 to 2002;

 (ii) the assumed increase in the director's salary each year to retirement;

(iii) the increase in the director's pension in retirement (frequently, pensions are increased by the retail price index).

31.12.6 Share options

As indicated earlier, share options are believed to be an effective way of paying directors and of avoiding 'short-termism', as the value of a share should be a reflection of the long-term profitability of the company. Until recently, there has been no charge to the income statement for share options, so the shareholders are not aware of the value of the options granted to the directors. However, share options can be very valuable to directors. Excluding the cost of share options from the financial statements understates the directors' remuneration.

An illustration of how share options work

A company granted a share option on 1 January 20X3 (the **grant date**) to its chief executive officer (CEO) for 100,000 shares at the current market price of 350p. The option required the director to meet profit targets for the three years to 31 December 20X5 (the **vesting date**). If these profit targets are met, the director will be able to purchase the shares at the **exercise date** of 30 June 20X4 at the option price of 350p a share.

Normally, the option is granted at the market price of the shares at the grant date (i.e. 350p a share). If the value of the shares is less than 350p on 30 June 20X6, the director will not purchase the shares (as they would make a loss), so the director's gain on the option will be zero. If the value of the shares is 410p on 30 June 20X6, the director will buy the shares for £350,000 and immediately sell them in the market for £410,000, making a gain of £60,000.

Interestingly, most directors of listed companies in the UK buy and sell the shares at the **exercise date** (30 June 20X6 in this case). Only a small minority of directors buy the shares at the option price and continue to hold them.

The 'theory' of share options is that the share price on 30 June 20X6 will be based on the company's long-term profitability, so if the company is doing well, the share price will be higher and the director's profit on buying the shares (and subsequently selling them) will be higher. So the director's gain on selling the shares will reflect the director's success in increasing the profits and hence the share price of the company. To a certain extent, this 'theory' is correct in that the share price tends to increase if the company's profitability increases. However, share price movements also depend on other factors, such as the general price movement of other shares and investors' views about the future profitability and growth in the particular type of trade the company is in. For instance, in late 1999 and early 2000 there was an enormous increase in the value of telecom and dot.com shares, yet many of these companies had never made a profit. Thus, the increase in the share price did not depend on the profitability of the companies, and it could be argued that the prices of these shares increased because this was a fashionable sector of the market in which to invest.

At the same time as the increase in value of telecom and dot.com shares there was a substantial fall in the value of other shares, including well-known retailers. In some of these cases the share prices were falling, despite the fact that the companies' profits were increasing. So, it can be seen that the increase in the share price of a company may be more related to market conditions than to the long-term profitability of the company. Thus, awarding options on shares may not be a very effective way of paying directors, as the change in the share price may have little to do with the profitability of the company and the directors' contribution to increasing its profits.

31.12.7 Accounting for share options

As has been discussed earlier, share options have become an important way of paying directors, motivating them to ensure the long-term profitability of the company. There has been disclosure of these options in the financial statements of companies for a number of years, but no cost of the share options has been included in the income statement. However, as explained below, there is a cost to the company of awarding these options. The problems are:

(i) when should the cost of the options be charged in the financial statements?

(ii) how much should be charged in the financial statements?

Taking the example above, we will provide some definitions. First, the dates:

● The **grant date** (i.e. 1 January 20X3) is the date when the employee and employer enter into an agreement that will entitle the employee to receive an option on a future date, provided certain conditions are met.

- The **vesting period** (1 January 20X3 to 31 December 20X5) is the date or dates on which the employee performs the services necessary to become unconditionally entitled to the option.
- The **vesting date** (31 December 20X5) is the date when the employee, having satisfied all the conditions, becomes unconditionally entitled to the option.
- The **exercise date** (30 June 20X6) is when the option is exercised.

Using the figures in our example, we will show how these affect the charge to the income statement for three methods:

(a) a UK Accounting Standards Board proposal, that the vesting date should be used to measure and date the charge for the option made in the financial statements;

(b) the US Financial Accounting Standards Board in FAS 123 *Accounting for Stock-Based Compensation*, which uses the grant date as when the charge should be made to the income statement (the ASB issued IFRS 2 *Share-Based Payment*, which is similar to FAS 123, in 2004);

(c) a proposal based on IAS 37 *Provisions, Contingent Liabilities and Contingent Assets*.[17]

Grant date

At this date, it may appear the value of the option is zero, as the option is granted at the current market price of the shares. This argument has been used to justify not charging directors' share options in the income statement. However, the value of the option is not zero, as the director will make either a nil profit or a gain on exercising the share option on 30 June 20X6. So, the value of the option is the market price of an option to purchase the company's shares at 350p on 30 June 20X6 – we will take the value of this option at 1 January 20X3 as 30p a share. But the director may not be eligible to take the option as the profitability target may not be met. The probability of the CEO meeting the target is 60%.

Using the figure in our example, we will show how these affect the charge to the income statement for three methods:

(a) Using IFRS 2 *Share-Based Payment*, the Standard issued by the IASB in 2004. This Standard uses the grant date as when the charge should be made to the income statement. IFRS 2 is similar to the US Standard FAS 123 *Accounting for Stock-Based Compensation* and the UK Standard FRS 20 *Share-based Payment*.

(b) Using an earlier UK Accounting Standards Board proposal, which used the vesting date to measure and date the charge for the option in the financial statements.

(c) A proposal based on IAS 37 *Provisions, Contingent Liabilities and Contingent Assets*.

US and IAS treatment
At the grant date, the value of the option is

$$100,000 \times 0.30 \times 60\% = £18,000$$

As the vesting period is three years, a charge of £6,000 a year would be made in the financial statements, reaching a total balance sheet provision at 31 December 20X5 of £18,000. This is the amount charged using the US FAS 123 and IFRS 2 methods.

UK treatment
There would be no charge at this stage under the UK ASB proposals, as the charge does not arise until the vesting date.

IAS 37 treatment

Under IAS 37, the value of the option would be calculated at each year-end, and the charge to the income statement would be the difference between this year's provision and last year's. At 31 December 20X3 the value of the option is 35p a share, and the probability of the option being granted is 70%. At this date, a third of the service will have been performed, so the contingent liability and charge to the income statement for the year is:

100,000 × 0.35 × 70% × ⅓ = £8,167

At 31 December 20X4 the option value is 45p a share, the probability is 85% and two-thirds of the service has been performed, so the contingent liability is

100,000 × 0.45 × 85% × ⅔ = £25,500

The charge to the income statement is £17,333 (i.e. £25,500 − 8,167).

At 31 December 20X5 the option value is 55p a share, the probability is 100% and all of the service has been performed, so the contingent liability is

100,000 × 0.55 × 100% × 1 = £55,000

The charge to the income statement is £29,500 (i.e. £55,000 − 25,500).

At the vesting date of 30 June 20X6 the price of the shares is £4.10 (giving an option value of 60p), the probability is 100% and all of the service has been performed, so the contingent liability is

100,000 × 0.60 × 100% × 1 = £60,000

The charge to the income statement is £5,000 (i.e. £60,000 − 55,000).

Vesting date

At the vesting date (31 December 20X5), we will assume the value of an option to purchase shares at £3.50 on 30 June 20X6 is 55p a share. Assuming the director has achieved the target, the value of this option at 31 December 20X5 will be

100,000 × 0.55 = £55,000

- US – Under FAS 123 and IFRS 2 the total charge is £18,000 in the three years to 31 December 20X5.

- UK – Under the UK ASB method, the charge of £55,000 will be made to the income statement on 31 December 20X3.

- IAS 37 – Under IAS 37, the charge for the three years to 31 December 20X5 is £55,000.

Exercise date

At the exercise date, the value of the company's shares is £4.10. By buying the shares from the company and immediately selling them, the director's profit will be:

100,000 × (£4.10 − 3.50) = £60,000.

This is the total cost of the options under IAS 37.

Under US FAS 123 the total cost is £18,000. The UK ASB would include a cost of £55,000 on 31 December 20X5 and no prior or subsequent charge to the income statement.

Summarising the discussion, the annual charge and the total charge for the CEO's options using the three methods is shown in Figure 31.3.

With the IAS 37 method, there is an annual charge each year, but it increases because the probability of the CEO exercising the options increases, and (in this example) the option price at each year-end is increasing. The ultimate cost to the company is the difference in the amount it would receive on 30 June 20X6 from selling the shares in the market and the amount it receives by selling the shares to the director at £3.50 each (i.e. 60p a share). This method treats the provision at each year-end as the amount the company would have to pay in the market to discharge itself of the provision. This is consistent with a financial management view of the problem.

Figure 31.3 Comparison of income statement charge for different accounting methods

Year ended	IAS 37 method	US FAS 123	UK ASB
31 Dec 20X3	8,167	6,000	0
31 Dec 20X4	17,333	6,000	0
31 Dec 20X5	29,500	6,000	55,000
31 Dec 20X6	5,000	0	0
Total charge	**60,000**	**18,000**	**55,000**

So, the IAS 37 method complies with IAS 37 *Provisions, Contingent Liabilities and Contingent Assets* and with financial management principles. However, the US FAS 123, IFRS 2 and UK ASB proposals are not consistent with IAS 37. All three produce a lower charge to the income statement for the director's options. Why is this happening?

It appears that the IAS 37 method is not acceptable to the US or UK accounting standards committees. As has been indicated earlier, accounting standards are often an acceptable compromise between the views of the representatives of the listed companies and those of the financial institutions represented on the accounting standards committees. The US proposal has met with hostility from the listed companies, as it makes them charge the cost of the options in the financial statements, and in many cases the costs are very high. The directors of the listed companies would prefer there to be no charge for the cost of the options, as had previously been the case. The hostility of the listed companies to the FAS 123 and IFRS 2 proposals have probably set a line beyond which they would not go, so the FAS 123 proposals are set at valuing the option at the grant date. In our example, this gives a charge of £18,000.

The UK ASB's proposal of using the vesting date gives a charge which is much closer to the actual cost to the company. However, its weakness is that this charge is made at a relatively late date, and it would be preferable if this charge was made over the period when the CEO earned the right to the options.

In 2004 the IASB introduced a new standard, IFRS 2 *Share-Based Payment*. The provisions of this standard are similar those of to US FAS 123, in that the fair value of the equity instrument granted is measured at the grant date. Any tax incurred by the company in awarding or issuing the options is charged in the financial statements (e.g. the tax the company has to pay as a result of awarding the options to the employee). Many of the provisions of IFRS 2 appear to be inconsistent with IAS 37 and the IASC's *Framework*. For instance, charging the cost at the 'grant date' is not the actual cost to the company – the actual cost is the value of the option at the exercise date. Also, if the option is not exercised, it is unreasonable to charge any cost for the option (IFRS 2 still charges the cost at the grant date). The aim of IFRS 2 appears to be to make it as similar to US FAS 123, which results in a set of rules, rather than a principles-based standard.

In conclusion, it can be seen that the US FAS 123, IFRS 2 and the UK ASB's proposals give a lower charge to the income statement for the share options than the IAS 37 method, which is, however, the correct method to use as it is consistent with IAS 37 on *Provisions, Contingent Liabilities and Contingent Assets* and with financial management principles.

31.12.8 IFRS 2 Share-Based Payment – a brief discussion of its principles

IFRS 2 *Share-Based Payment* is a complex standard with a multitude of rules. These are too detailed to be covered in this chapter, but consideration of some of the rules could result in an interesting (academic) discussion of the topic and the standard.

First, it could be argued that the correct approach to share-based payment is to use the principles of IAS 37 (*Provisions, Contingent Liabilities and Contingent Assets*) which are consistent with the IASB's Framework, and Economic and Financial Management principles. However, it is apparent that IFRS 2 has been issued as a compromise, which is acceptable to company directors and is consistent with the US Standard FAS 123.

The subject of IFRS 2 is much wider than the discussion in 31.12.7 (above) suggests. It covers:

(a) payment in shares to employees (as well as directors);

(b) payments to employees and directors in cash which are based on the increase in share price;

(c) payments to others (e.g. suppliers) either in shares or in cash which are based on the increase in share price.

The treatment of payment of employees in shares ((a) above) is the same as for directors.

Where employees or directors are paid in cash, based on the increase in the share price ((b) above), the cost is taken as the final amount paid (i.e. the IAS 37 method) with a progressive increase as the 'bonus' is earned.

In (c), where shares are issued, the value is taken as the fair value of the goods or services received.

Where the eventual payment is in cash, the accounting entry is:

Dr   expense
Cr   liability

This is consistent with the IASB Framework. However, where the eventual payment is in shares, the accounting entry is:

Dr   expense
Cr   equity

The credit entry is 'very surprising' and inconsistent with the IASB Framework. The company 'owes' the shares or share options to the employee, so surely the credit entry should be a liability. According to the Framework, the entry is consistent with the definition of a liability, as: 'recognised in the balance sheet when it is probable that an outflow of resources embodying economic benefits will result from the settlement of a present obligation and the amount at which the settlement will take place can be measured reliably'.

The 'outflow of resources' is issuing the shares at a discount (rather than the current market price) and the 'obligation' is to the employee.

When one asks 'where will I make the credit entry to equity', IFRS 2 gives no guidance. If the credit entry is to the profit and loss account, then there is no net charge, so the credit entry is probably to a directors' share options reserve (effectively from the profit and loss account). However, the directors' share options reserve is not an amount which belongs to the company (i.e. capital) – it belongs to the directors and thus is a liability.

IFRS 2 becomes even more complex (and inconsistent with the Framework) in situations where some or all of the share options are not exercised. The cost of the share option is charged to the income statement when granted. However, the share option may not be granted if the employee leaves, or does not satisfy the vesting conditions, or the share price at the exercise date is below the option price. If the option is not granted, IFRS 2 does not allow the earlier charge to be reversed and credited to the income statement. This is inconsistent with normal accounting. If, for instance, an electricity accrual is overstated in one year, then this is corrected by an understatement of the electricity charge in the following year. Why shouldn't this be allowed to happen with directors' share options?

From this discussion, it can be seen that, in many ways, IFRS 2 is inconsistent with the 'Framework', particularly in valuing the option at the grant date and crediting the cost to equity. This has produced a standard which is very complex, so that it can 'get round' the inconsistencies it has created in its basic principles. For example, if the settlement is in cash, the cost is taken at the exercise date, whereas if it is in shares the cost is taken at the grant date. It could be argued that the correct treatment would be to take the exercise date in both cases.

If IFRS 2 had taken the exercise date as final cost of the option, it would have been consistent with the 'Framework' and IAS 37. Also, the credit entry should be to a liability (and not to equity).

By using these principles, which are consistent with the 'Framework' and IAS 37, the IASB would have produced a standard which would have been much shorter and simpler than the current IFRS 2.

However, the principal aims of the IASB in producing IFRS 2 seem to have been to produce a standard which is consistent with the US FAS 123 and acceptable to directors of listed companies.

31.13 Directors' remuneration – conclusion

From the above discussion on directors' remuneration, it can be seen that current disclosure of the costs to the company of employing directors is incomplete, and the disclosed cost is understated. In particular:

(a) the current year's cost of providing directors' pensions is not disclosed. Only directors' annual pensions on retirement are disclosed;

(b) the cost of providing directors' share options is either understated (under US FAS 123, IFRS 2 or UK ASB proposals) or taken as zero. A method which is consistent with IAS 37 *Provisions, Contingent Liabilities and Contingent Assets* should be used to determine the annual cost of these options to the company.

In the example of Diageo plc shown in this chapter, the disclosure of directors' remuneration and benefits is probably close to the best available for listed companies. For most other listed companies in the UK and other countries, the disclosure of directors' remuneration is probably less detailed and less helpful than for Diageo. This shows how much further listed companies need to go to provide a complete disclosure of directors' remuneration in the annual financial statements.

31.14 Relations with shareholders

There is simply a proposal that companies enter into dialogue with institutional shareholders and for chairmen of the remuneration, audit and nomination committees to be available to answer questions at the AGM.

31.15 Institutional investors

There are three principles, namely that institutional shareholders:

- have a responsibility to make considered use of their votes,
- should be ready to enter into dialogue with companies, and
- should give due weight to all factors drawn to their attention when evaluating companies' governance arrangements.

For greater detail, we need to refer to the governance documents produced by the various institutional investor organisations, e.g. the Association of British Insurers and National Association of Pension Funds.

31.15.1 Association of British Insurers (ABI)

The ABI has published a *Statement of Voting Policy and Corporate Governance Good*,[18] which sets out that ABI members' overall objective is, and must be, to achieve on behalf of those for whom they act a competitive return on the funds invested and that the exercise of their voting policy will be in support of the proper management of companies and directed towards the enhancement of long-term shareholder value and the wider economic benefits which this should engender.

The *Statement* includes the following points:

- ABI members fully support the principles of the Cadbury, Greenbury and Hampel committees.

- The exercise of voting rights is inseparable from the investment management function and the objective of maximisation of long-term shareholder value.

- It is considered important to support boards by a positive use of their voting rights unless they have good reason for doing otherwise so that it would be a matter of concern for the board if that support was not forthcoming.

- If considering voting against a proposal it is important to make representations to the board in time for consultation and satisfactory resolution.

- Voting decisions by ABI members will reflect the Association's guidance notes, e.g. on share incentive schemes and policy statements; e.g. roles of chairman and chief executive should not normally be combined.

- Structured dialogue is encouraged to better understand management's objectives, the problems confronting management and the quality of management whilst at the same time making clear the expectations and requirements of shareholders.

- Institutional investors will not wish to receive price sensitive information and, if they do, there would be a requirement that they suspend their ability to deal in the shares.

- They are concerned to ensure the appointment of a core of non-executives of sufficient number and of appropriate calibre, experience and independence to identify where there may be undue concentrations of decision-making power not formally constrained by appropriate checks and balances.

- On directors' remuneration, institutional investors support the key recommendations of the Greenbury Committee.

31.16 The Myners Report

Developing a Winning Partnership is a report of a joint City/industry working group established under the chairmanship of Paul Myners. The report considered how companies and institutional investors are working together.

The report recognises that there has been a perceived antagonism between companies and institutional investors. Institutional investors have been accused of short-termism which has discouraged investment. Companies need supportive long-term shareholders to encourage them to invest for the future. There is an urgent need for a long-term working relationship to be developed.

What is meant by short-termism?

Short-termism of investors has been blamed for the UK's lack of investment. It is evidenced by the churning of shares, driven in part by the buy and sell recommendations of stockbrokers' analysts, the ready acceptance of hostile takeovers, and unreasonable demands for early earnings growth and increasing dividends. However, the National Association of Pension Funds has estimated that the average holding period for a share in a pension fund portfolio is over eight years.

There is also, of course, the short-termism of management evidenced by excessive management remuneration and share option schemes which are not in the best interest of the shareholders.

The Combined Code refers to 'dialogue'. This implies a two-way commitment from both the institutional investors and the company managers.

Institutional investors

Institutional investors want company managers to articulate more clearly their long-term corporate objectives and financial policies, of which dividend policy is an important part, and to emphasise in the discussion their vision for the company and the corporate values. They want managers to be consistent in their communication with investors and the press, and to be open about bad news as well as good.

Company managers

Whilst many companies are spending more time and effort in investor relations the report comments:

They recognise the benefit of more constructive dialogue with their shareholders, which leads to better understanding. What company managers want now is greater value from the time and effort they are putting in to investor relations. They want more openness from investors, candour about objectives and expectations, and a professional approach to the relationship. They justifiably expect better shareholder preparation for meetings, better sector and industry knowledge and better use of time in meetings.

Constraints on dialogue

The report identified that as regards the companies:

● Many company managers are not confident that their messages will be listened to and fear that information given to investors beyond the minimum required will be used against them.

● Many companies are reluctant to give details of investment plans fearing that:
  – explicit forecasting is a hostage to fortune;
  – investors will use the plans against them;
  – plans were too commercially sensitive.

The report identified that as regards the investors:

● Most fund managers are ambivalent about the responsibilities of ownership where these have been delegated by beneficial owners.

● There is a difficulty in determining the boundaries of legitimate involvement.

How will constraints on dialogue be removed?

The report comments that there was frequently a lack of confidence between company managers and investors but that open and informed dialogue can overcome this lack of trust. It is important also to see the company manager/institutional investor relationship in the context of the growing pressure for more transparency as seen with the corporate governance developments discussed above and the social and environmental reporting and business ethics discussed in the following two chapters.

31.17 Corporate governance – summary

On directors' remuneration, it is apparent that corporate governance in the UK is not working. On the 'beneficial' side:

● Directors' service contracts have been limited to a year, thus limiting the termination payments when directors are dismissed.

● Higgs' proposals that an individual should be chairman of only one listed company and executive directors should be non-executive directors of only one listed company are welcome proposals (i.e. executive directors should devote most of their time to their company, rather than being distracted by being non-executive directors of other companies).

● Although it is not covered in the Companies Act, listed companies now include a resolution for shareholders to approve the directors' remuneration report. However, a vote 'for' or 'against' does not allow shareholders to criticise or obtain further details of directors' remuneration.

However, there are many 'adverse' signs:

- Directors' remuneration is increasing at a much greater rate than employees' wages, and often it appears not to be related to the performance of the company. Directors' remuneration is increasing at a much faster rate than the increase in companies' profits (e.g. in Rolls-Royce plc, the 2001 profits increased by 15.7% over 2000, but the Chairman's remuneration increased by 42% and the Chief Executive's by 38.2%).

Directors are still deciding their own remuneration (even though the decision is by non-executives for the executive directors). When companies make many millions of pounds profit, it seems hardly surprising that directors decide to take an increasingly large proportion of this profit, as there is little or no control over their actions.

- The full remuneration of directors is not being disclosed in accounts (the disclosed remuneration is significantly less than the 'actual' remuneration). In particular, it has not been possible to quantify the value of share options. Pension entitlements (i.e. the pension the director will receive on retirement) are disclosed, but the cost to the company of providing a fund for these pensions is not disclosed.

- Large payments are made to directors who are dismissed, even if this is for incompetence or following disastrous strategies. This was the case with, for instance, the Chairman and Chief Executive of Marconi who may be seen as having effectively overseen the destruction of the company through the strategy of buying for cash internet/telecoms companies at the top of the market. The result was enormous borrowings for which interest could not be paid, as the companies made little or no profits. On dismissal, these directors were paid substantial termination payments (over £1 million in total). These seem inappropriate when related to the millions of pounds lost by the company and its shareholders.

To sum up, the proposals on corporate governance are 'a step in the right direction', but there is a long way to go before a satisfactory conclusion is reached.

30.18 Auditors

The purpose of an audit is summarised by the audit report on the financial statements of the company being audited. The international body which gives guidance to auditors is the International Federation of Accountants (IFAC). This body has published International Standards on Auditing (ISAs) and on ethical and educational matters relating to auditors. National bodies of accountants have published their own auditing standards and ethical and educational rules. These national standards are generally very similar to the equivalent IFAC pronouncements. For instance, in the UK, the Statements of Auditing Standard (SASs) were published soon after the IFAC's Standards on Auditing, and it is apparent that they are based on the IFAC's ISAs with only minor differences. The ethical and educational requirements of the UK's Association of Chartered Certified Accountants (ACCA) and the Institute of Chartered Accountants in England and Wales (ICAEW) are very similar, but slightly more restrictive than the IFAC's requirements.

Returning to the Audit Report, ISA 700 *The Auditor's Report on Financial Statements*[19] proposes (para. 28) the following unqualified audit report:

Report to the Shareholders of ABC
We have audited the accompanying balance sheet of ABC company as of December 31 20X1, and the related statements of income, and cash flows for the year then

ended. These financial statements are the responsibility of the Company's management. Our responsibility is to express an opinion on these financial statements based on our audit.

We conducted our audit in accordance with International Standards on Auditing. These Standards require that we plan and perform the audit to obtain reasonable assurance about whether the financial statements are free of material misstatement. An audit includes examining, on a test basis, evidence supporting the amounts and disclosures in the financial statements. An audit also includes assessing the accounting principles used and significant estimates made by management, as well as evaluating the overall financial statement presentation. We believe that our audit provides a reasonable basis for our opinion.

In our opinion, the financial statements give a true and fair view of the financial position of the Company as of December 31 20X1, and of the results of its operations and its cash flows for the year then ended in accordance with the Companies Act (date).

Auditor's name .... Date .... Address ....

The principal statement in the audit report is in the last paragraph when it says 'the financial statements give a true and fair view'. This means that the auditor is saying the financial statements do not contain any significant errors. For the word 'significant', auditors use the word 'material'. The auditor is not saying the financial statements are exactly correct. There may be small errors in the financial statements, but these errors will not create a 'material' error in the financial statements.

Many items in the balance sheet cannot be determined exactly. These include depreciation rates on fixed assets, stock value and bad debts which cannot be determined exactly at the time of the audit. It may be many years after the date of the audit when fixed assets are sold, all stock is sold and all debts from customers are repaid. So, depreciation, bad debts and estimating the net realisable value of stock have to be best estimates at the time of the audit, so their value in the financial statements must be a best estimate.

Materiality is a complex subject, but the principal measure is profit before tax, and errors in the financial statements which are 5% or less of profit before tax are not material, and errors which are greater than 10% of profit before tax are material. Between 5% and 10% of profit before tax, the error may be material – the auditor has to apply judgement to determine whether the error is material. If there are material errors or uncertainties in the financial statements, he/she will give a 'qualified audit report', in which the auditor will explain why the financial statements 'do not show a true and fair view'. The subject of qualified audit reports is covered in detail in ISA 700 *The Auditor's Report on Financial Statements*.

31.18.1 Principal qualities of an auditor

The ethical[20] and educational[21] requirements of the IFAC are very detailed, but they can be summarised under three headings:

(a) Competence of the auditor
(b) Independence of the auditor
(c) Other ethical/professional matters.

31.18.2 Competence of the auditor

This can be summarised as:

(a) the basic educational requirements to become a member of a professional body and auditor;

(b) the continued education required of auditors to keep them up to date; and

(c) the practical experience of the auditor.

Basic educational requirements

The IFAC (*Guidelines on Education*, para. 19) says:

> The core of knowledge to which all accountants should be exposed should cover:
>
> Core subjects:
> | | | |
> | --- | --- | --- |
> | Financial Accounting | Management Accounting | Information Technology |
> | Auditing | Taxation | Business Finance |
>
> Supportive Subjects:
> | | | |
> | --- | --- | --- |
> | Economics | Law | Mathematics and Statistics |
> | Behavioural Science | Management | |

The IFAC places considerable emphasis on information technology, and includes a separate section on 'Information technology in the accounting curriculum'. Accounting systems are information systems, and most information systems are computerised, hence the importance of information technology in the work of the accountant. Thus, the accountant is interested both in ensuring that the information system is reliable, and in ensuring that the information produced by the system is relevant and easily understood.

Continued professional education

The newly qualified accountant should have the required technical knowledge when he/she has passed the professional examinations. However, accountants may be in practice for up to forty years after they have qualified. Their knowledge will have become out of date only a few years after they qualified, because of changes in legislation (particularly tax law and practice) and in accounting and auditing standards. There is therefore a need for accountancy bodies to show that their members are keeping their knowledge up to date.

This is achieved by means of continued professional education (CPE). Section 2 of the IFAC's *Guidelines on Education* covers this topic in detail. The IFAC says that the minimum CPE should be 30 hours a year (or 90 hours in a three-year period) of structured learning activity, supplemented by regular unstructured learning. Essentially, 'structured learning' comprises attending lectures or conferences, or taking correspondence courses. Being a lecturer or leader in a conference also comprises 'structured learning'. Unstructured learning will usually comprise reading technical, professional, financial or business literature. Many accountancy bodies provide or approve courses with 'approved CPE hours'. If the accountancy body requires CPE to be mandatory, they will have to provide and monitor a system for members to record their CPE activities and hours.

It is apparent that accountancy bodies must have a system of compulsory CPE to ensure that their members keep up to date with changes in legislation and with accounting and auditing standards. Also, there will be a need for members to increase the depth of their knowledge in the specialised areas they work in, over and above the basic knowledge they learnt when taking the exams of their professional body.

Practical experience

The IFAC says (*Guidelines on Education*, para. 54) that this should be at least three years' duration. Also, they suggest professional bodies should have a system for approving employers who are suitable for providing the appropriate experience to students (para. 56). These 'approved employers' should be checked periodically by the professional body. The employer is responsible for designing and implementing a programme which meets the practical experience requirements of the student and the needs of the employer. The employer is responsible for recording the actual experience provided for each student.

31.18.3 Independence of the auditor

Part B of the IFAC's *Code of Ethics for Professional Accountants* considers matters applicable to professional accountants in public practice. The principal points made in this section include:

1 **Independence**. Professional accountants in public practice when undertaking a reporting assignment should be and appear to be free of any interest which might be regarded, whatever its actual effect, as being incompatible with integrity, objectivity and independence.

2 The following paragraphs indicate some of those situations which, because of the actual or apparent lack of independence, would give a reasonable observer grounds for doubting the independence of a professional accountant in public practice.

3 **Financial involvement with or in the affairs of clients**. Financial involvement with a client affects independence and may lead a reasonable observer to conclude that it has been impaired. Such involvement can arise in a number of ways, such as:

(a) by direct financial interest in a client;

(b) by indirect material financial interest in a client, e.g. by being a trustee of any trust or executor or administrator of any estate if such a trust or estate has a financial interest in a client company;

(c) by loans to or from the client or any officer, director or principal shareholder of a client company;

(d) by holding a financial interest in a joint venture with a client or employee of a client;

(e) by having a financial interest in a non-client that has an investor or investee relationship with the client.

4 **Appointments in companies**. When professional accountants in public practice are or were, within the period under current review or immediately preceding an assignment:

(a) a member of the board, an officer or employee of a company; or

(b) a partner of, in the employment of, a member of the board or an officer or employee of a company;

they would be regarded as having an interest which could detract from independence when reporting on that company.

5 **Provision of other services to audit clients**. When a professional accountant in public practice, in addition to carrying out an audit or other reporting function, provides other services to a client, care should be taken not to perform management functions or make management decisions, responsibility for which remains with the board of directors and management.

6 **Personal and family relationships**. Personal and family relationships can affect independence. There is a particular need to ensure that an independent approach to any assignment is not endangered as a consequence of any personal or family relationship.

7 **Fees**. When the receipt of recurrent fees from a client or group of connected clients represents a large proportion of the total gross fees of a professional accountant in public practice or of the practice as a whole, the dependence on that client or group of clients should inevitably come under scrutiny and could raise doubts as to independence.

8 **Contingency fees**. Professional services should not be offered or rendered to a client under an arrangement whereby no fee will be charged unless a specified finding or result is obtained or when the fee is otherwise contingent upon the findings or results of such services.

9 **Goods and services**. Acceptance of goods and services from a client may be a threat to independence. Acceptance of undue hospitality poses a similar threat.

10 **Ownership of the capital**. Ideally, the capital of a practice should be owned entirely by professional accountants in public practice. However, ownership of capital by others may be permitted provided that the majority of both the ownership of the capital and the voting rights lies only with the professional accountants in public practice.

11 **Former partners**. A partner in a practice may leave the practice by resignation, termination, retirement, or sale of the practice. Such a partner may accept an appointment with a client in practice, of which he/she is a former partner when an audit or other reporting function is being performed by that practice of which he or she is a former partner.

12. **Actual or threatened litigation**. Litigation involving the professional accountant in public practice and a client may cause concern that the normal relationship with the client is affected to the extent that the professional accountant's independence and objectivity may be impaired.

13 **Long association of senior personnel with audit clients**. The use of the same senior personnel on an audit engagement over a prolonged period of time may pose a threat to independence. The professional accountant in public practice should take steps to ensure that objectivity and independence are maintained on the engagement.

31.18.4 Current position on auditor providing consultancy services

Pre Enron

In 2000, the chairman of the US Securities and Exchange Commission (SEC), Arthur Levitt, proposed that other services provided by audit firms to their audit clients should be severely restricted, probably solely to audit and tax work.[22] The provision of any other service to audit clients would be prohibited.

Whilst the profession was opposed to the blanket approach appearing to be taken by the SEC there was also support for a selective approach to restricting particular types of work, e.g. that external auditors should not provide internal audit services for client companies.[23]

Post Enron

Enron filed for bankruptcy in early December 2001 by which time the share price had fallen from a 2000 figure of about $83 a share to less than $1 a share. The bankruptcy was unexpected by those investors who might have based their investment decisions on the historical financial statements on the mistaken assumption that these were accurate.

Equity shareholders are rewarded for taking risks and understand that no company in which they invest is immune to the risk of failure. However, in the case of Enron there appear to have been three major problems.

The first problem was that the US financial reporting standards were not as robust in dealing with off balance sheet transactions such as special purpose entities (SPEs) as FRS 5 *Reporting the Substance of Transactions* which has been effective in the UK since 1995.

What is an SPE?

An SPE might be set up for a variety of purposes ranging from those that are commercially acceptable (e.g. to finance fixed assets) to those that are unacceptable (e.g. to conceal from investors who rely on the company's financial statements presenting an accurate or true and fair view of material items such as the existence of liabilities or losses or the payment of fees to directors of the sponsor company). In the case of Enron it is reported that there was concealment of all three such material items.

How does an SPE operate?

Typically there are four parties involved, namely,

- the sponsor (a company such as Enron that wishes to acquire a fixed asset but wants to keep the asset and liability off the balance sheet);
- the SPE (this is the entity that will borrow the funds to acquire the fixed asset);
- the lender (a bank or institution prepared to advance funds to the SPE to acquire the fixed asset); and
- the independent investor (who puts in at least 3% of the cost of the fixed asset and who technically controls the SPE).

As far as the sponsor is concerned, both the asset and the liability are off the balance sheet and the sponsor enters into a lease arrangement with the SPE to make lease payments to cover the loan repayments. If required by the lender, the sponsor might also arrange for a guarantee to be provided using its own share price strength or through another party. As we recognised in the UK prior to the introduction of FRS 5, by keeping debt off the balance sheet a company's creditworthiness is improved.

The second problem was that investors were unable to rely on advice from analysts. It is reported that analysts failed to follow sound financial analysis principles, being under pressure to hype the shares, e.g. to keep the share price up particularly where their employers, such as investment banks, were making significant advisory fees.[24]

The third problem was that investors were not alerted by the auditors to the fact that such liabilities, losses and the payment of fees existed. It could be that the auditors were convinced that the financial statements complied with the requirements of US GAAP and that the SPEs did not therefore need to be consolidated. If that were the case, it could be argued that the auditor was acting professionally in reporting that the financial statements complied with US GAAP.

31.18.5 Future developments on auditors providing consultancy services

SEC testimony concerning legislative solutions to problems raised by events relating to Enron Corporation

It is interesting to review the testimony made by Harvey L. Pitt, Chairman of the US Securities and Exchange Commission before the Subcommittee on Capital Markets, Insurance and government Sponsored Enterprises, United States House of Representatives.[25]

Within the testimony the Chairman makes the following points:

● Accounting standard setting should reflect business realities – observing that for too many years the FASB has failed to set standards for accounting for special purpose entities. In the wake of Enron, it must act and act quickly to give guidance.

● A system that ensures that those entrusted with the important public responsibility of performing audits of public companies are single-minded in their devotion to the public interest, and are not subject to conflicts that might confuse or divert them from their efforts – observing that those who perform audits must be truly independent and in particular must not be subject to the conflict of increasing their own compensation at the risk of jeopardising the public's protection.

US Senate investigation

We need to recognise that the auditors could well be actively involved in designing schemes such as SPEs and representation was made by Lynn Turner on 24 January 2002 to the Committee of Governmental Affairs of the United States Senate[26] that auditors should be prohibited from designing and structuring transactions, such as SPEs, that result in less, rather than more, transparency for those they are reporting to.

The fact that the auditors become actively involved in designing such schemes could well be seen as evidence that they are moving into consultancy which gives rise to a conflict of interest. This move deprives investors, creditors, employees and pension scheme members of an independent audit.

UK accountancy press

There is a view[27] that audit failures are made in the boardrooms of accountancy firms where, in pursuit of money, low-balling is rife and audits are used as stalls to sell other wares. The same writer takes a similar view to the SEC, namely, that auditors should act exclusively as auditors.

EU recommendations

In May 2002 the European Commission issued Recommendations.[28] There is an overriding recommendation that a statutory auditor should not carry out an audit if there are any financial, business, employment or other relationships that a reasonable and informed third party would conclude could compromise the auditor's independence and detailed recommendations such as the requirement for the audit fee to be sufficient to cover the necessary audit work, i.e. effectively prohibiting low-balling. The Recommendations do not, however, prohibit auditors accepting consultancy work.

UK government initiatives

Following the collapse of Enron the Secretary of State for Trade and Industry, Patricia Hewitt, announced in early 2002 the creation of a Co-ordinating Group on Audit and Accounting Issues with a remit to ensure that the effectiveness of the UK systems of financial reporting and audit regulation is carefully reviewed. Issues that have been raised include:

- the adequacy of existing ethical standards of the professional audit bodies in ensuring the independence of auditors particularly as to whether they provide sufficient protection where auditors also provide non-audit services to clients;
- the possible requirement for the mandatory rotation of auditors or re-tendering for company audits;
- the need for more detailed disclosure in company accounts of the fees paid to the auditors for audit and non-audit services.[29]

The above references are a sample of the steps now being taken following the collapse of Enron. It will be interesting to see the extent to which confidence in financial reporting and auditing is restored during the next few years.

Summary

Corporate governance requirements are being developed in many countries. Most of the proposals have come from the USA and from the UK and its former colonies where shares are widely held. In this situation there needs to be some controls and monitoring of the directors. Developments in other countries are leading to wider ownership of shares of companies, and this will lead to the extension of corporate governance requirements in those countries.

The disclosure of the remuneration of directors was studied. We have shown the many ways directors are remunerated, and highlighted current weaknesses in disclosing pension costs and the cost of issuing share options. Different methods of accounting for share options were examined and criticised.

The other side of corporate governance concerns controls over auditors. The educational and practical experience requirements were considered as were the independence requirements of the IFAC and the provision of consultancy services to audit clients.

REVIEW QUESTIONS

1 The Association of British Insurers held the view that options should be exercised only if the company's earnings per share growth exceeded that of the retail price index. The National Association of Pension Funds preferred the criterion to be a company's outperformance of the FTA All-Share Index.

   (a) Discuss the reasons for the differences in approach.

   (b) Discuss the implication of each approach to the financial reporting regulators and the auditors.

2 'Management will become accountable only when shareholders receive information on corporate strategy, future-based plans and budgets, and actual results with explanations of variances.' Discuss.

3 (i) Discuss the extent to which directors should be accountable to: (a) shareholders; (b) employees; (c) suppliers; (d) customers; (e) the government; (f) the public.

   (ii) Research[30] suggests that companies whose managers own a significant proportion of the voting share capital tend to violate the Cadbury recommendations on board composition far more frequently than other companies. Discuss the advantages and disadvantages of enforcing greater compliance.

4 The following is a proposal from a major research report, *The Future of Corporate Governance: Insights from the UK*, prepared for the Institute of Chartered Accountants of Scotland.[31]

> In order to improve the effectiveness of non-executive directors and strengthen their independence, guidelines should be introduced on the maximum number of non-executive directorships that may be held by an individual and regulation should be introduced to control 'cross-holdings' of executive and non-executive directorships.

Discuss the guidance you consider appropriate on the maximum number and the advantages and disadvantages of controlling cross-holdings.

5 There has been much criticism of the effectiveness of non-executive directors following failures such as Enron. Some consider that their interests are too close to those of the executive directors and they have neither the time nor professional support to allow them to be effective monitors of the executive directors. Draft a job specification and personal criteria that you think would allay these criticisms.

6 The Chartered Institute of Management Accountants (CIMA) has warned that linking directors' pay to EPS or return on assets is open to abuse, since these are not the objective measures they might appear.

(a) Can shareholders rely on the ASB to prevent abuse? Discuss.

(b) Identify five ways in which the directors might manipulate the EPS and return on assets without breaching existing standards.

7 It has been suggested that 'changes in market capitalisation from period to period should be the subject of comment [and] it would be sensible for investors to be guided on the nature of the market capitalisation figure and to be given an indication of share price trends'.[32] Discuss the advantages and disadvantages of such disclosure in relation to corporate governance.

8 (a) The Companies Act 1985 (Disclosure of Remuneration for Non-audit Work) Regulations SI No 1991/2181 requires companies to disclose all payments made to their auditors. Discuss the additional information that would be required in order to make the disclosure of the non-audit fees meaningful.

(b) The *Combined Code* provides that the audit committee should keep the nature and extent of non-audit services provided by the auditor under review, seeking to balance the maintenance of objectivity and value for money. Discuss criteria that could be applied in seeking to establish this balance.

9 In the modern commercial world, auditors provide numerous other services to complement their audit work. These services include the following:

(a) Accountancy and book-keeping assistance, e.g. in the maintenance of ledgers and in the preparation of monthly and annual accounts.

(b) Secretarial help, e.g. ensuring that the company has complied with the Companies Act in the maintenance of shareholder registers and in the completion of annual returns to Companies House.

(c) Consultancy services, e.g. advice on the design of information systems and organisational structures, advice on the choice of computer equipment and software packages, and advice on the recruitment of new executives.

(d) Investigation work, e.g. appraisals of companies that might be taken over.

(e) Receivership work, e.g. when the firm assumes the role of receiver or liquidator on behalf of an audit client.

(f) Taxation work, e.g. tax planning advice and preparation of tax returns to the Inland Revenue for both the company and the company's senior management.

Discuss:

(i) Whether any of these activities is unacceptable as a separate activity because it might weaken an auditor's independence.

(ii) The advantages and disadvantages to the shareholders of the audit firm providing this range of service.

10 The audit fee disclosed for Cable & Wireless plc was £1.7 million in its 1997 accounts.

(a) Discuss how many man-days of audit time you think would be reasonable to audit an industrial company where:

(i) the sales were £7,002 million;

(ii) the fixed assets were £6,442 million;

(iii) the current assets were £3,225 million; and

(iv) there were 37,448 staff in Hong Kong, the UK, Continental Europe, North America, the Caribbean and the rest of the world.

(b) Discuss the suggestion that audit fees are inadequate.

EXERCISES

Question 1

The financial statements of AB, a listed company, disclose the following information on the Chairman's pension entitlements:

(a) for the year ended 31 December 20X0 the pension fund is sufficient to pay the director a pension of £200,000 a year from his retirement date of 1 January 20X4;

(b) for the year ended 31 December 20X1 the pension fund is sufficient to pay the director a pension of £250,000 a year from his retirement date of 1 January 20X4.

It is expected that the pension fund will pay the director's pension for twelve years, and the expected return on investments is 8% per annum.

Required:
Calculate the cost of the director's pension entitlements for the year ended 31 December 20X1.

Note: The value of an annuity for eleven years at 8% is 7.139.
The present value of £1 at 8% for two years is 0.85734; for three years, 0.79383.

Question 2

On 31 December 20X0, the Chief Executive of BC, a listed company, was awarded the option to purchase 1,000,000 shares in the company at £4.50 a share on 30 June 20X4. This option was subject to her achieving specified performance targets for the three years ending on 31 December 20X3. The following information has been provided:

Date	Option price	Probability of achieving option
31.12.X0	5p	60%
31.12.X1	10p	70%
31.12.X2	15p	85%
31.12.X3	30p	100%
30.06.X4	35p	100%

Required:
(a) Calculate the charge for the share option to be included in the financial statements for the years ended 31 December 20X0, 20X1, 20X2, 20X3 and 20X4 using the IAS 37 method;
(b) Calculate the total cost of the share option using:
    (i) the IAS 37 method;
    (ii) the US FAS 123 and the IFRS 2 methods;
    (iii) the UK recommendation.
(c) Discuss the different answers you have calculated in part (b).

Question 3

The financial statements of Rolls-Royce plc (aero engine manufacturer) for the year ended 31 December 1999 disclose the following matters in relation to the directors:

(a) Remuneration committee

The remuneration committee, which operates within agreed terms of reference, has responsibility for making recommendations to the board on the Group's general policy towards executive remuneration. The committee also determines, on the board's behalf, the specific remuneration packages of the executive directors and a number of senior executives.

The membership of the committee consists exclusively of independent non-executive directors (*the financial statements disclose the names of these directors*). The committee meets regularly and has access to professional advice from inside and outside the Company.

The Chairman of the Company (*a part-time executive director*) and the Chief Executive (*an executive director*) generally attend meetings but are not present during any discussion of their own emoluments.

(b) Base salary

The committee believes that in order to attract and retain executive directors of the right calibre and to provide them with adequate incentives to deliver the Group's objectives, the Group should pursue a policy of offering median-level base salaries for its executive directors, and through the performance-related schemes, the opportunity of upper quartile earnings for upper quartile performance.

(c) Annual performance award scheme

The scheme enables a maximum performance award of up to 60% of salary to be paid to executive directors for exceptional performance against pre-determined targets based upon return on capital employed with a tapered and reducing scale of maximum percentages for senior employees. The targets are set by the committee based upon the Group's annual operating plans. Such payments do not form part of pensionable earnings. One-third of total awards made are paid in Rolls-Royce shares which are held in trust for two years, with release normally being conditional on the individual remaining in the Group's employment until the end of the period. The required shares are purchased on the open market. This arrangement provides a strong link between performance and remuneration and provides a culture of share ownership amongst the Group's senior management.

(d) Long-term incentive plan

The LTIP involves the grant of awards of shares in the Company, which can be realised in the form of shares and cash if demanding performance targets are met. The maximum value of the awards is 60% of salary for executive directors, with a tapered and reducing scale of maximum percentages for senior executives. The required shares for the LTIP are purchased on the open market.

The percentage of the award, and therefore the value which can be realised, depends upon the Company's total shareholder return (TSR) over a three-year performance measurement period, compared to that achieved over the same period by a group of 19 comparator companies comprising other leading engineering and industrial companies. No award is realised unless the average growth in the Group's EPS over the three-year period is at least 2% per annum greater than the average increase in the UK retail price index over the same period.

Under the rules of the LTIP, the percentage of shares comprised in the award which can be realised is determined by the Company's TSR ranking against the comparator group. 100% of the award is secured for a first, second or third ranking with a uniform sliding scale of percentages then being applied to each ranking down to, and including, ninth place which earns 40% of the share award. No award is made if the Company's TSR ranking is tenth or below. If an award is realised, the participant receives one-half of its value at the release date in the form of shares and the other half in cash. He or she is required to retain at least half of the shares for a maximum of two years.

The performance period for the 1997 LTIP grant ended on 31 December, 1999 and no award was realised.

(e) Service contracts

In the light of the Combined Code (*which recommends rolling contracts of no more than one year*), the committee has reviewed its previous policy of offering UK executive directors two-year rolling contracts. It has concluded that new appointees to the board will be offered notice periods of one year. The committee recognises that in the case of appointments to the board from outside the Company, it may be necessary to offer a longer initial notice period, which would be subsequently reduced to twelve months after that initial period. Five executive directors (*which the report names*) all have two-year rolling contracts, which provide for 24 months' notice in the event of termination of employment by the company. These contracts were entered into before the change in policy described above.

(f) Compensation and mitigation

The committee has a defined policy on compensation and mitigation to be applied in the event of a director's contract being permanently terminated. In these circumstances, steps are taken to ensure that poor performance is not rewarded. When calculating termination payments, the committee takes into account a range of factors such as age, years of service and the director's obligation to mitigate his own loss.

A director (*named in the accounts*) retired early from the Company on 31 December 1999 and received a termination payment of £530,000 and a payment of £20,298 in lieu of benefits. The committee considered this compensation in the light of its policy on mitigation and in line with that policy concluded that it would not be appropriate to apply mitigation.

The accounts disclose the retiring director's base salary for the year ended 31 December 1999 was £240,000.

For the retiring director, there was no disclosure of:

(i) his age at 31 December 1999,

(ii) his executive position in the company, and

(iii) the reasons why he took early retirement.

The financial statements did disclose the executive position and age of the other directors at 31 December 1999.

There were no exceptional points included in the financial statements about directors' pensions. Items included in *italics* in the text above are comments or additional information provided by the author.

Required:
Comment on the notes to the financial statements included above.

Question 4

A rational auditor would stop audit work when the total cost is a minimum. However, it is apparent that auditors are 'risk-averse' and they perform more work than is necessary to minimise their total costs. Explain why auditors perform more work than is necessary.

Question 5

(a) Describe the value to the audit client of the audit firm providing consultancy services.

(b) Why is it undesirable for audit firms to provide consultancy services to audit clients?

(c) Why do audit firms want to continue to provide consultancy services to audit clients?

Question 6

How is the relationship between the audit firm and the audit client different for:

(a) the provision of statutory audit when the auditor reports to the shareholders;

(b) the provision of consultancy services by audit firms?

Question 7

Why is there a prohibition of auditors owning shares in client companies? Is this prohibition reasonable? Discuss.

References

1 http://www.oecd.org
2 'Corporate governance in Europe', Report of Centre for European Policy Studies Working Party, June 1995.
3 'Principles for corporate governance in the Commonwealth', Commonwealth Association for Corporate Governance Guidelines, November 1999.
4 *The Times*, 10 October, 2000, p. 29.
5 *Report of the Committee on the Financial Aspects of Corporate Governance (Cadbury Committee Report)*, Gee Publishing, December 1992.
6 *Directors' Remuneration: Report of a Study Group Chaired by Sir Richard Greenbury (Greenbury Committee Report)*, Gee Publishing, July 1995.
7 *Committee on Corporate Governance: Final Report (Hampel Committee Report)*, Gee Publishing, January 1998.
8 D. Higgs, *Review of the Role and Effectiveness of Non-Executive Directors*, DTI, January 2003.
9 S. Turley and M. Zaman, 'Higgs and Smith: what difference will they really make?', *Accounting & Business*, April 2003, pp. 40–42.
10 *Committee on Corporate Governance: The Combined Code* (revised), Gee Publishing, July 2003.
11 *Accountancy*, September 1995.

12 *The Times*, 30 March 1995.

13 M. Pagano, 'Package plus performance', *Management Today*, January 1998, pp. 70–72.

14 R. Heller, 'Heads they win, tails they win', *Management Today*, July 1997, p. 22.

15 'What is the incentive?', *Management Today*, July 1999, p. 46.

16 '2000 Annual Report and Accounts', Diageo plc, September 2000, pp. 10–16.

17 IAS 37 *Provisions, Contingent Liabilities and Contingent Assets*, IASC, July 1998.

18 ABI, *Statement of Voting Policy and Corporate Governance Good*, 1998.

19 ISA 700 *The Auditor's Report on Financial Statements*, IFAC, 1996, pp. 223–224.

20 *Code of Ethics for Professional Accountants*, IFAC, 1996, pp. 451–504.

21 *Guidelines on Education*, IFAC, 1996, pp. 505–637.

22 'PwC and E&Y in favour of rules to restrict services', *Accountancy*, October 2000, p. 7.

23 I.H. Davison, 'Non-audit fees and auditor independence', *Accountancy*, November 2000, p. 1.

24 B. Singleton-Green, 'Enron – how the fraud worked', *Accountancy*, May 2002, pp. 20–21.

25 See http://www.sec.gov/news/testimony/020402tshlp.htm

26 See http://govt-aff.senate.gov/012402turner.htm

27 A. Mitchell, 'Reform or nemesis', *Accountancy*, May 2002, p. 10.

28 European Commission, *Statutory Auditors' Independence in the EU: A Set of Fundamental Principles*; see http://www.europa.eu.int/comm/internal_market/en/company/audit/official/6D42-01/6942-01_en.pdf

29 See http://www.dti.gov.uk/cld/post_enron.html

30 K. Peasnell, P. Pope and S. Young, *Accountancy*, July 1998, p. 115.

31 I. Fraser and W. Henry, *The Future of Corporate Governance: Insights from the UK*, ICAS 2003.

32 ICAS, *Making Corporate Reports Valuable*, p. 103.

CHAPTER 32

Environmental and social reporting

32.1 Introduction

In this chapter we consider the following:

- Accountants' role in a capitalist society
- Sustainability
- Environmental reporting
- European Commisson recommendations
- Stand-alone environmental reports and award schemes
- International charters, guidelines and self-regulation schemes
- Economic consequences of environmental reporting
- Environmental auditing
- Social accounting
- Corporate social responsibility
- Need for comparative data
- International initiatives towards triple bottom line reporting.

32.2 Accountants' role in a capitalist industrial society

In a capitalist, industrial society, production requires the raising and efficient use of capital largely through joint stock companies. These operate within a legal framework which grants them limited liability subject to certain obligations. The obligations include **capital maintenance provisions** to protect creditors, e.g. restriction on distributable profits, and **disclosure provisions** to protect shareholders, e.g. the publication of annual reports.

The state issues statutes to ensure there is effective control of the capital market; the degree of intervention depends on the party in power. Accountants issue standards to ensure there is reliable information to the owners to support an orderly capital market. Both the state and the accountancy profession have directed their major efforts towards servicing the needs of capital. This has influenced the nature of the legislation, e.g. removing obligations that are perceived to make a company uncompetitive, and the nature of the accounting standards, e.g. concentrating on earnings and monetary values.

However, production and distribution involve complex social relationships between private ownership of property and wage labour[1] and other stakeholders. This raises the question of the role of accountants. Should their primary concern be to serve the interests of the shareholders, or the interests of management, or to focus on equity issues and social welfare?[2]

Prior to the formation of the ASB, the profession identified with management and, willingly or unwillingly, it appeared to allow information to be reported to suit management. If management were unhappy with a standard, as with SSAP 11 and SSAP 16, they were able to frustrate its implementation. Often, reported results bore little resemblance to the commercial substance of the underlying transactions.

The ASB has concentrated on making reports congruent with commercial reality; it sees financial information as being an economic commodity in its own right. It has developed a conceptual framework for financial reporting to underpin its reporting standards; assets, liabilities, income and expense have been defined with criteria for their recognition which include the ability to state them in monetary terms.

The ASB has not produced mandatory requirements for narrative or qualitative disclosures – the operating and financial review (OFR) is voluntary. However, the proposal for the publication of an OFR was an important shift: it was recognition that there was a need for narrative disclosure, even where this was not capable of audit verification.

Why is the qualitative information voluntary?

It is voluntary in recognition of the fact that market and political pressures exist; that each company balances the perceived costs, e.g. competitive disadvantage, and the perceived benefits of voluntary disclosure, e.g. improved investor appeal, in determining the extent of its voluntary disclosures.[3]

Companies have traditionally been ranked according to various criteria, e.g. their ability to maximise their shareholders' wealth or return on capital employed or EPS growth rates. However, there is a philosophical view that holds that a company

> possesses a role in society because society finds it useful that it should do so ... [It] cannot expect to find itself fully acceptable to society if it single-mindedly pursues its major objective without regard for the range of consequences of its actions.[4]

This means that a company is permitted to seek its private objectives subject to legal, social and ethical boundaries. This takes accounting beyond the traditional framework of reporting monetary transactions that are of interest primarily to the shareholders. It takes it into a realm where there is, at present, no obvious paymaster.

32.3 Sustainability

There has been a growing concern since the early 1990s that insufficient attention has been given to the impact of current commercial activities on future generations. This has led to the need for sustainable development which meets the needs of the present without compromising the ability of future generations to meet their own needs.

Why have companies become sensitive to the environmental concerns of stakeholders other than their shareholders? This has been a reaction to pressure from a variety of stakeholders ranging from the government to local communities and from environmental groups to individual consumers and individual investors.

32.3.1 Environmental information in the annual accounts

Much of the environmental information falls outside the expertise of the accountant, so why was it included in the annual report? The annual report had already become the accepted vehicle for providing shareholders with information on matters of social interest such as charitable donations and this extended to present qualitative information such as a statement of company policy.

However, in addition to recognising the concerns of other stakeholders companies also began to realise that there could be adverse financial implications for their companies on capacity to raise funds.

Potential individual investors

The government in *This Common Inheritance*[5] indicated that shareholders could seek information about environmental practices from companies that they invest in and make their views known.

Potential corporate investors

Acquisitive companies needed to be aware of contingent liabilities,[6] which can be enormous. In the USA the potential cost of clearing up past industrially hazardous sites has been estimated at $675 billion. Even in relation to individual companies the scale of the contingency can be large, as in the Love Canal case. In this case a housing project was built at Love Canal in Upper New York State on a site that until the 1950s had been used by the Hooker Chemicals Corporation for dumping a chemical waste containing dioxin. Occidental, which had acquired Hooker Chemicals, was judged liable for the costs of clean-up of more than $260 million.[7] Existing shareholders and the share price would also be affected by these increased costs.

There is recognition that there is a wider interest than short-term profits.

32.4 Background to companies' reporting practices

During the past decade some companies have independently instituted comprehensive environmental management systems but most have not. There was been a tendency initially for companies to target the area that they considered to be the most sensitive and to treat it rather as a PR exercise or damage limitation. There was a concern that resources devoted to achieving environmental benefits would merely increase costs and companies made a point of referring to cost benefits to justify their outlay as in the following extract from the Scottish Power 1994 Annual Report:

> The company is committed to meeting or bettering increasingly stringent
> environmental controls for electricity generation and is developing new technologies
> and plant which can achieve significant benefits at realistic cost. At Longannet Power
> Station, more than £24 million is being invested in low Nox burners, which produce
> fewer nitrous oxides, and in renewing equipment to reduce dust from flue gases...
> This process is expected to be environmentally superior and lower in costs than
> alternative technologies.

This was quite understandable as it had been estimated that the enforcement of stringent environmental controls to reduce pollution could have substantial cost implications estimated at £15 billion for Britain in 1991.[8]

Companies were reactive and concentrated on satisfying statutory obligations or explaining their treatment of what they perceived to be the major environmental concern affecting their company. For example, in the case of Pearson, a major publishing company, a major concern was the use for printing of renewable resources and their 1993 Annual Report they included the following:

One aspect of our company's environmental responsibilities is to keep their purchasing policies under review. Pearson's most significant purchase is paper. Our publishing companies between them buy some 180,000 tonnes of paper a year... Pearson makes certain that it buys paper only from responsibly managed forests and avoids paper bleached with chlorinated organic compounds where possible...

Although this was an *ad hoc* approach to environmental reporting it did not mean that significant benefits were not achieved. The following extract from the 2001 Annual Report of the Body Shop indicates the level of benefit:

At the Body Shop, we have made a significant commitment to reducing our CO_2 impact by switching electricity supply at both our Littlehampton sites and all UK company-owned shops to a renewable source. This initiative, together with our 15% investment in Bryn Titli wind farm, means that we offset an estimated 48% of electricity, gas and road freight used for all our UK operations including company-owned shops in the last financial year.

In some jurisdictions there have been mandatory requirements. In the USA, e.g. the Securities and Exchange Commission requires companies to disclose:

(a) the material effects of complying or failing to comply with environmental requirements on the capital expenditures, earnings and competitive position of the registrant and its subsidiaries;

(b) pending environmental legal proceedings or proceedings known to be contemplated, which meet any of three qualifying conditions: (1) materiality, (2) 10% of current assets, or (3) monetary sanctions; and

(c) environmental contingencies that may reasonably have material impact on net sales, revenue, or income from continuing operations.

A typical disclosure of amounts appears in the following extract from the Schering AG Group 2000 Annual Report:

Outlay on safety and environmental protection in 2000

		€m
1.	Safety, clean-up, miscellaneous	16
2.	Environmental protection departments	6
3.	Recycling, processing and disposal	40
	Operating expenses	62
4.	Environmental protection investment	4

32.5 European Commission recommendations for disclosures in annual accounts

In May 2001 the European Commission issued a *Recommendation on the Recognition, Measurement and Disclosure of Environmental Issues in the Annual Accounts and Annual Reports of Companies.*[9]

The Commission view was that there were two problems. The first was that there was a lack of explicit rules, which meant that any one or all of the different stakeholder groups, e.g. investors, regulatory authorities, financial analysts and the public in general, could feel that the disclosures were insufficient or unreliable; the second was that there was a low level of voluntary disclosure, even in sectors where there was significant impact on the environment.

32.5.1 Lack of explicit rules

The lack of harmonised guidelines has meant that investors have been unable to compare companies or to adequately assess environmental risks affecting the financial position of the company. Whilst recognising that there are existing financial reporting standards on the disclosure of provisions and contingent liabilities and that companies in environmentally sensitive sectors are producing stand-alone environmental reports, the Commission was of the opinion that there is a justified need to facilitate further harmonisation on what to disclose in the annual accounts.

As mentioned above, the cost of collecting and reporting is frequently perceived to be a deterrent and the *Recommendation* intends to avoid unjustified burdensome obligations. It also proposes that Recommendations should be within existing European Directives, e.g. the Fourth and Seventh Directives.

32.5.2 Stakeholder groups' information needs

All groups require relevant disclosures that are consistent and comparable – particularly disclosure in the notes to the accounts relating to environmental expenditures either charged to the profit and loss account or capitalised including fines and penalties for non-compliance and compensation payments.

32.5.3 Key points relating to recognition, measurement and disclosure

The approach to recognition and measurement is a restatement of current financial reporting requirements with some additional illustrations and explanations. The disclosures are fuller than currently met within annual accounts.

Recognition and measurement

For the recognition of environmental liabilities the criteria are the same as for FRS 12 *Provisions, Contingent Liabilities and Contingent Assets* (Section 8.9.3), e.g. requirement for probable outflow of resources, reliable estimate of costs and recognition of liability at the date operations commence if relating to site restoration.

For the capitalisation of environmental expenditure the criteria to recognise as an asset apply, e.g. it produces future economic benefits. There are also detailed proposals relating to environmental expenditure which improves the future benefits from another asset and to asset impairment.

Disclosures

Disclosure is recommended if the issues are material to either the financial performance or financial position. Detailed proposals in relation to environmental protection are for the disclosure of:

- the policies that have been adopted and reference to any certification such as EMAS (see 31.7.2 below);
- the improvements made in key areas with physical data if possible, e.g. on emissions;
- progress implementing mandatory requirements;
- environmental performance measures, e.g. trends for percentage of recycled packaging;
- reference to any separate environmental report produced.

There are, in addition, detailed cross-references to the requirements of the Fourth and

Seventh Directives, e.g. description of valuation methods applied and additional disclosures, e.g. if there are long-term dismantling costs, the accounting policy and, if the company gradually builds up a provision, the amount of the full provision required.

32.6 Evolution of stand-alone environmental reports

There is a steady growth in the rate at which environmental reports are being produced. As one would perhaps expect, they are more prevalent in sectors where there is high risk such as forestry, pulp and paper, chemicals, oil and gas and pharmaceuticals.

This has been response to consumer pressure and also in response to the PR value of obtaining an award from one of the award schemes.

32.6.1 The effect of award schemes

Companies were encouraged to develop their environmental reporting by entering for various award schemes in which companies are invited to submit their report for scrutiny by a panel of judges.

Several such schemes have been established in Europe and North America, such as the competitions organised in Europe and the UK each year for the European Environmental Reporting Awards and the ACCA UK Environmental Reporting Awards. These last two schemes are discussed briefly below.

The European Environmental Reporting Awards

At the Europe-wide level, there are the European Environmental Reporting Awards (EERA), which commenced in 1997, in which entries are selected from the winners of national schemes organised by EU member states.

In 2000, the four winners in the EERA scheme, picked from a field of 24 entries, were as follows:

- Overall winner: Shell International (UK),
- Best first-time reporter: Acquedotto Pugliese (Italy),
- Best SME reporter: Obermurtaler Brauereigenossenschaft (Austria),
- Best sustainability report: Novo Nordisk (Denmark).

It is interesting to refer to the judges' comments on the strengths of each of the winners. For example, in respect of the best SME reporter some of the strengths listed included:

- its comprehensive reporting on corporate performance including five-year trend data for various indicators and quantified targets;
- an analysis of the environmental impact arising from the product development activity;
- detailed description of supplier audits;
- disclosure of internal audit procedures and results; and
- evidence of environmental interest including obtaining EMAS registration (the first site to do this in Austria).

ACCA UK Environmental Reporting Awards

In 2000 the ACCA commemorated ten years of progress in environmental reporting. After these ten years the ACCA established in 2002 a new structure for the UK awards to reflect the ever-increasing public awareness of the environmental, social and economic impacts of business. The ACCA Award scheme was restructured in 2001 under the title 'The ACCA Awards for Sustainability Reporting'. There are three different award categories: the ACCA UK Environmental Reporting Awards, the ACCA Social Reporting Awards and a new category, the ACCA Sustainability Reporting Awards.

These schemes have given environmental reporting a high profile and contributed greatly to the present quality of reports.

32.7 International charters and guidelines

There have been a number of international and national summits, charters and recommendations issued. In some jurisdictions such as Denmark, the Netherlands, Norway and Sweden, there is now legislation requiring environmental statements from environmentally sensitive industries either in their financial statements or in a stand-alone report; in other countries, voluntary disclosures are proposed. Below are brief descriptions of just some of the voluntary disclosures proposed by the United Nations, Europe and the USA, and of some self-regulation schemes in which companies can elect to participate.

32.7.1 United Nations

At the United Nations we can see that the United Nations Environmental Programme (UNEP)[10] has made major impacts, e.g. it was the driving force behind the 1987 Montreal Protocol on Substances that Deplete the Ozone Layer whereby industrialised countries ceased production and consumption of a significant proportion of all ozone-depleting substances in 1996. It is estimated that 1.5 million cases of melanoma skin cancer due to the sun's UV-B radiation will be averted by the year 2060 as a result of the Protocol. It has had similar success as the leading force for the sound global management of hazardous chemicals and the protection of the world's biological diversity by forging the Convention on Biological Diversity. It is innovative in its approach, e.g. entering into a partnership agreement with the International Olympic Committee (IOC) in 1995 as a result of which the environment now figures as the third pillar of Olympism, along with sport and culture, in the IOC's Charter. UNEP has initiated the development of environmental guidelines for sports federations and countries bidding for the Olympic Games.

32.7.2 Europe

In Europe the Eco-Management and Audit Scheme (EMAS)[11] was adopted by the European Council on 29 June 1993, allowing voluntary participation in an environmental management scheme. Its aim is to promote continuous environmental performance improvements of activities by committing organisations to evaluating and improving their own environmental performance.

The main elements of the current EMAS regulations include:

● making environmental statements more transparent;

● the involvement of employees in the implementation of EMAS; and

● a more thorough consideration of indirect effects including capital investments, administrative and planning decisions and procurement procedures.

Companies that participate in the scheme are required to adopt an environmental policy containing the following key commitments:

- compliance with all relevant environmental legislation;
- prevention of pollution; and
- achieving continuous improvements in environmental performance.

The procedure is for an initial environmental review to be undertaken and an environmental programme and environmental management system established for the organisation.

Verification is seen as an important element and environmental audits, covering all activities at the organisation concerned, must be conducted within an audit cycle of no longer than three years. On completion of the initial environmental review and subsequent audits or audit cycles a public environmental statement is produced.

An organisation's environmental statement will include the following key elements:

- a clear description of the organisation, and its activities, products and services;
- the organisation's environmental policy and a brief description of the environmental management system;
- a description of all the significant direct and indirect environmental aspects of the organisation and an explanation of the nature of the impacts as related to these aspects;
- a description of the environmental objectives and targets in relation to the significant environmental aspects and impacts;
- a summary of the organisation's year-by-year environmental performance data which may include pollution emissions, waste generation, consumption of raw materials, energy use, water management and noise;
- other factors regarding environmental performance including performance against legal provisions; and
- the name and accreditation number of the environmental verifier, the date of validation and deadline for submission of the next statement.

The following extract from the Schering 2000 Annual Report indicates the persuasive influence of schemes such as EMAS:

We aim at achieving the ISO 14001 certification or the Eco Management and Audit Scheme (EMAS) validation for all production sites. We have begun to integrate the existing management systems for quality, safety and environmental protection, and to organise throughout the Group. This Integrated Management System (IMS) is based on International Standard ISO 9000 (for quality) as well as ISO 14001 and EMAS (for environmental protection).

32.7.3 The USA

In the USA the Environmental Accounting Project began in 1992 to encourage companies to adopt environmental accounting techniques which would make environmental costs more apparent to managers and, therefore, make them more controllable. It was thought that this could result in three positive outcomes namely, the significant reduction of environmental costs, the gaining of competitive advantage and the improvement of environmental performance with the initial concern being to reduce pollution.

32.7.4 Self-regulation schemes

There are a number of examples of self-regulatory codes of conduct from institutions, e.g. The International Chamber of Commerce (ICC),[12] The International Organization for Standardization (ISO), and bodies representing particular industries, e.g. the European Chemical Industry Council (CEFIC).[13] We will describe briefly the ICC Charter and ISO standards.

The International Chamber of Commerce (ICC)

The ICC launched The Business Charter for Sustainable Development in 1991 to help business around the world improve its environmental performance relating to health, safety and product stewardship. The Charter set out sixteen Principles which include:

- *Policy statements* – such as giving environmental management high corporate priority; aiming to integrate environmental policies and practices as an essential element of management; continuing to improve corporate policies performance; advising customers, distributors and the public in the safe use, transportation, storage and disposal of products provided; promoting the adoption of these principles by contractors acting on behalf of the enterprise; developing products that have no undue environmental impact and are efficient in their consumption of energy and natural resources, and that can be recycled, reused, or disposed of safely; fostering openness and dialogue with employees and the public, anticipating and responding to their concerns about the potential hazards and impacts of operations, products, wastes or services; and measuring environmental performance.

- *Financially quantifiable practices* – such as employee education; assessment of environmental impacts before starting a new activity or decommissioning; conduct or support of research on the environmental impacts of raw materials, products, processes, emissions and wastes associated with the enterprise and on the means of minimising such adverse impacts; modification of the manufacture, marketing or use of products or services to prevent serious or irreversible environmental degradation.

The following extract from the Nestlé 2000 Environment Progress Report is a good example of a company that has applied the ICC approach and is proactive in seeking improvements:

Message from CEO

I am pleased about the clear progress in a number of key areas, including a significant decline in the amounts of water and energy used to bring each kilo of Nestlé product into your home, and a similar reduction in factors which potentially affect global warming. However, we are never completely satisfied with our current performance, and are committed to further environmental improvements.

We try to remain sensitive to the environmental concerns of our consumers and the public as a whole. ... we have pledged our allegiance to *The Business Charter for Sustainable Development* of the International Chamber of Commerce, and we are committed to being a leader in environmental performance.

The Report then proceeded to deal in detail with three key areas on which the company focus, namely,

- An integrated approach throughout the supply chain, quantifying:
  - The average annual investment reporting, for example, that 'From 1997 to 1999, Nestlé invested an average of CHF 100 million per year for the protection of the environment. This included readily-identifiable environmental investments, and amounted to more than 3% of total capital expenditure'.
  - Environmental performance indicators for greenhouse gases, air acidification potential, ozone-depleting substances and energy consumption. As an example of the level of detail, it reported for energy: 'Energy consumption is the sum of all energy

purchased or obtained – less any energy which, in rare cases, is sold. This includes electricity, steam, fuels such as oil and natural gas, and by-products such as spent coffee grounds. Through different approaches, global energy consumption per tonne of product was reduced and, thus, energy use efficiency was improved by 20%. Even with the significant increase in manufacturing production, the total energy use company-wide has remained stable'.

- Water as a key priority, quantifying:
  - environmental performance indicators for water consumption, water waste management and by-products/water generation.
- Systematic management of environmental performance, committing itself to:
  - compatability with international standards, e.g. ISO 14001 and EMAS of the European Union;
  - focus on performance and improvements in all aspects of sutainability.

The International Organization for Standardization (ISO)

ISO is a non-governmental organisation established in 1947, and comprises a worldwide federation of national standards with the aim of establishing international standards to reduce barriers to international trade. Its standards, including environmental standards, are voluntary and companies may elect to join in order to obtain ISO certification.

One group of standards, the ISO 14000 series, is intended to encourage organisations to systematically assess the environmental impacts of their activities through a common approach to environmental management systems. Within the group, the ISO 14001 standard states the requirements for establishing an EMS and companies must satisfy its requirements in order to qualify for ISO certification.

What benefits arise from implementation of ISO 14001?

Those who support the ISO approach consider that there are a number of positive advantages, such as:

- **Top-level management become involved** – they are required to define an overall policy and, in addition, they recognise significant financial considerations from certification, e.g. customers might in the future prefer to deal with ISO compliant companies, insurance premiums might be lower and there is the potential to reduce costs by greater production efficiency.

- **Environmental management** – ISO 14001 establishes a framework for a systematic approach to environmental management which can identify inefficiencies that were not apparent beforehand resulting in operational cost savings and reduced environmental liabilities. We have seen above, for example, that Nestlé reduced its energy consumption by 20%.

- **A framework for continual improvements is established** – there is a requirement for continual improvement of the management system.

What criticisms are there of a compliance approach?

Compliance approaches which set out criteria such as a commitment to minimise environmental impact can allow companies to set low objectives for improvement and report these as achievements with little confidence that there has been significant environmental benefit.

32.8 Economic consequences of environmental reporting

There can be internal and external favourable economic consequences for companies in the form of internal cost reductions and of the influence on the share price activities which affect a company's reputation.

32.8.1 Cost reductions

It has been reported that the discipline of measuring these risks can yield valuable management information with DuPont, for example, reporting that since it began measuring and reporting on the environmental impact of its activities, its annual environmental costs dropped from a high of US$1 billion in 1993 to $560 million in 1999.

32.8.2 Investment

Investors are gradually beginning to require information on a company's policy and programmes for environmental compliance and performance in order to assess the risk to earnings and balance sheet. One would expect that the more transparent these are the less volatile the share prices will be which could be beneficial for both the investor and the company. This will be a fruitful field for research as environmental reporting evolves with more consistent, comparable, relevant and reliable numbers and narrative disclosures.

This has also given rise to Socially Responsible Investing (SRI) which considers both the investor's financial needs and the investee company's impact on society to an extent that in 1999 over US$2,000 billion in assets were invested in 'ethical' investment funds. In the UK there is pressure from bodies such as the Association of British Insurers for institutional investors to take SRI principles into account.

However, research carried out by Trucost and commissioned by the Environment Agency (www.environment-agency.gov.uk/business) into quantitative disclosures found that direct links between management of environmental risks and shareholder value are almost non-existent, with only 11% of FTSE 350 making a link between the environment and some aspect of their financial performance and only 5% explicitly linking it to shareholder value.

32.9 Summary on environmental reporting

Environmental reporting is in a state of evolution ranging from *ad hoc* comments in the annual report to a more systematic approach in the annual report to stand-alone environmental reports.

Environmental investment is no longer seen as an additional cost but as an essential part of being a good corporate citizen and environmental reports are seen as necessary in communicating with stakeholders to address their environmental concerns.

Companies are realising that it is their corporate responsibility to achieve sustainable development whereby they meet the needs of the present without compromising the ability of future generations to meet their own needs. Economic growth is important for shareholders and other stakeholders alike in that it provides the conditions in which protection of the environment can best be achieved, and environmental protection, in balance with other human goals, is necessary to achieve growth that is sustainable.

However, there is still a long way to go and the EU's Sixth Action Programme 'Environment 2010: Our Future, Our Choice'[14] recognises that effective steps have not been taken by all member states to implement EC environmental directives and there is weak ownership of environmental objectives by stakeholders. The programme focuses on four major areas for action – climate change, health and the environment, nature and biodiversity, and natural resource management – and emphasises how important it is that all stakeholders should be involved to achieve more environmentally friendly forms of production and consumption as well as integration into all aspects of our life such as as transport, energy and agriculture.

As with the other environmental reporting initiatives discussed above and the corporate governance approach we have seen with the Hampel Report and the OFR, the programme concentrates on setting general objectives rather than quantified targets apart from the targets relating to climate change where there is the EU's 8% emission reduction target for 2008–12 under the Kyoto Protocol. This is a sensible way to progress with an opportunity for best practice to evolve.

However, significant improvements are still required, with research indicating that although the majority of FTSE All Share companies discuss their interaction with the environment in their Annual Report and Accounts, the vast majority lack depth, rigour or quantification.

32.10 Environmental auditing: international initiatives

The need for environmental auditors has grown side by side with the growth of environmental reporting. This is prompted by the need for investors to be confident that the information is reliable and relevant. There have been various initiatives around the world and we will briefly refer to examples from Canada, the USA and Europe.

Canada

The Canadian Environmental Auditing Association (CEAA) was founded in 1991 to encourage the development of environmental auditing and the improvement of environmental management through environmental auditor certification and the application of environmental auditing ethics, principles and standards. It is a multidisciplinary organisation whose international membership base now includes environmental managers, ISO 14001 registration auditors, EMS consultants, corporate environmental auditors, engineers, chemists, government employees, accountants and lawyers. The CEAA is now accredited by the Standards Council of Canada as a certifying body for EMS Auditors.[15]

USA

The Registrar Accreditation Board (RAB)[16] was established in 1989 by the American Society for Quality to provide accreditation services for ISO 9000 Quality Management Systems (QMS) registrars.

In 1991, the American National Standards Institute (ANSI) and RAB joined forces to establish the American National Accreditation Program for Registrars of Quality Systems.

In 1996, with the release of new ISO 14000 Environmental Management Systems (EMS) standards, the ANSI-RAB National Accreditation Program (NAP) was formed covering the accreditation of QMS and EMS registrars as well as accreditation of course providers offering QMS and EMS auditor training courses. Certification programmes for both EMS and QMS auditors are now operated solely by RAB.

RAB exists to serve the conformity assessment needs of business and industry, registrars, course providers and individual auditors.

Europe

Since 1999 the European Federation of Accountants (FEE) Sustainability Working Party (formerly Environmental) has been active in the project Providing Assurance on

Environmental Reports[17] and is actively participating with other organisations and collaborating on projects such as GRI Sustainability Guidelines which are discussed further in 32.16 below.

32.11 The activities involved in an environmental audit

There are many activities commonly seen in practice. These can be grouped into those assessing the *current position* and those evaluating decisions affecting the *future*.

32.11.1 Assessing the current position

The assessment embraces physical, systems and staff appraisal.

- Physical appraisal is carried out by means of:
- – **site inspections**;
- – **scientific testing** to sample and test substances including air samples;
- – **off-site testing and inspections** to examine the organisation's impact on its immediate surroundings; after all, the company's responsibility does not stop at the boundary fence.
- Systems appraisal is carried out by means of:
- – **systems inspections** to review the stated systems of management and control in respect of environmental issues;
- – **operational reviews** to review actual practices when compared to the stated systems;
- – **compliance audits for certification schemes.**
- Staff appraisal is carried out by means of:
  - – **awareness tests for staff** to test, by questionnaire, the basic knowledge of all levels of staff of the systems and practices currently used by the organisation. This will highlight any areas of weakness.

32.11.2 Assessing the future

The assessment embraces planning and design processes and preparedness for emergencies.

- Planning and design appraisal is carried out by means of:
  - – **review of planning procedures** to ensure that environmental factors are considered in the planning processes adopted by the organisation;
  - – **design reviews** to examine the basic design processes of the organisation (if applicable) to ensure that environmental issues are addressed at the design stage so the organisation can avoid problems rather than have to solve them when they happen.
- Preparedness for emergencies is appraised by means of:
  - – **review of emergency procedures** to assess the organisation's preparedness for specific, predictable emergencies;
  - – **review of crisis plans** to review the organisation's general approach to crisis management with the audit covering such topics as the formation of **crisis management teams** and resource availability.

32.11.3 The environmental audit report

We can see from the above that an environmental audit may be wide-ranging in its scope and time-consuming, particularly when auditing a major organisation. A typical report could include:

- Current practice
- a comprehensive review and comment on current operational practices.
- List of action required
  - areas of **immediate concern** which the organisation needs to address as a matter of urgency;
  - areas for improvement over a set period of time.
- Qualitative assessment
  - a **statement of risk** as seen by the audit team based on an overview of the whole situation with a qualitative assessment of the level of environmental risk being faced by the organisation.
- An action plan
  - a **schedule of improvement** may also be produced which gives a timetable and series of stages for the organisation to follow in improving its environmental performance.
- Encouraging good practice
  - a positive statement of 'good practice' may be included. This has a dual value in that it is a motivational tool for management and an educational tool to foster staff awareness of what constitutes 'good practice'.

32.11.4 What is the status of an environmental audit report?

Legal position

There is no legal obligation to carry out an environmental audit or to inform outside parties of any critical findings when such an audit is carried out. The reports are usually regarded as 'confidential' even when carried out by external auditors who provide the service as an 'optional extra' which is offered to the organisation for an additional fee.

Public interest

There is a strong case for requiring both environmental audits and the publication of the resultant reports. Requiring reports to be put into the public domain would encourage transparency in the process and avoid accusations of secrecy. However, this 'public interest' argument has been heard before in accounting and has met with some resistance in the guise of commercial sensitivity.

Mandatory position

The lack of legal obligation could be regarded as a crucial weakness of the environmental audit process as there could be a major danger to the environment which remains 'secret' until after the crisis when it is then too late. The responsible organisation will of course inform all appropriate parties of any revealed risk but it would be foolhardy to assume that all organisations are responsible. The ASB has become involved with potential liability for the company in its consideration of provisions. Whilst this is only viewing it from the viewpoint of the shareholder, it may well be the only pragmatic way forward at present.

32.11.5 Experience in the USA

The increasing importance of environmental accounting can be seen in the USA in the work of the United States Environmental Protection Agency (EPA) and its Environmental Accounting Project (EAP) which has been operating since 1992.

In this large project the EPA attempts to identify the currently 'hidden' societal costs faced by organisations. These costs are those which an organisation incurs in its interaction with the environment and which in theory are totally avoidable. By identifying these costs, the organisation is motivated to address them and by implication make every attempt to reduce them, thus improving the environment.

The EPA has a very impressive website, which can be found at the following address: http://www.epa.gov/epahome/aboutepa/htm. Here the basic ideas and concepts governing the EPA's study of environmental accounting are set out.

The work of the EPA has also been of a more practical nature in helping organisations address environmental issues from an environmental viewpoint. A brief review of three such cases may help explain the proactive approach to environmental accounting, which goes beyond traditional reporting.

A. The Chrysler Corporation (a major vehicle manufacturer) was faced with a problem with the use of mercury switches in its electrical systems on vehicles. Mercury is dangerous to use and is very dangerous as a waste product when the vehicle is scrapped. The company had always resisted the use of non-mercury switches on pure cost terms.

However, during the EPA project, by looking at the environmental cost it was seen that non-mercury switches actually made a saving of $0.11 per unit. The company on an annual basis would make an $18,000 annual saving on one plant alone by this component change.

B. Amoco Corporation (a major oil company) needed to identify the cost of complying with environmental protection regulations and used one of its refineries in Yorktown, Virginia, as an experimental site. From an analysis of the financial accounts it was found that environmental costs represented 21.9% of the non-crude cost of the product (crude oil being the major cost).

This figure was six times the level previously assumed to be the environmental cost of production. The realisation of the scale of the cost led to changes in managerial policies and practices.

C. Majestic Metals Inc. of Denver, Colorado, had a problem with pollution caused by its paint-spraying machinery and practices. Through an environmental accounting exercise, the company decided to use high-volume, low-pressure (HVLP) sprayers and this reduced the cost of environmental damage (as shown by fines and rectification costs) by $40,000 per year. From a capital investment appraisal viewpoint the project gave a positive NPV over eight years of $140,000, an internal rate of return (IRR) of 906% and a discounted payback of 0.12 years – an impressive range of results in any terms.

The EPA's website has many more cases showing the impact of an environmental accounting approach.

32.12 Concept of social accounting

This is a difficult place to start because there are so many definitions of social accounting[18] – the main points are that it includes non-financial as well as financial information and addresses the needs of stakeholders other than the shareholders. Stakeholders can be broken down into three categories:

● **internal stakeholders** – managers and workers;
● **external stakeholders** – shareholders, creditors, banks and debtors;
● **related stakeholders** – society as represented by national and local government and the increasing role of pressure groups such as Amnesty International and Greenpeace.

32.12.1 Reporting at corporate level

Prior to 1975, social accounting was viewed as being in the domain of the **economist** and concerned with national income and related issues. In 1975, *The Corporate Report* gave a different definition:

> the reporting of those costs and benefits, which may or may not be quantifiable in money terms, arising from economic activities and subsequently borne or received by the community at large or particular groups not holding a direct relationship with the reporting entity.[19]

This is probably the best working definition of the topic and it establishes the first element of the social accounting concept, namely **reporting at a corporate level** and interpreting corporate in its widest sense as including all organisations of economic significance regardless of the type of organisation or the nature of ownership.

32.12.2 Accountability

The effect of the redefinition by *The Corporate Report* was to introduce the second element of our social accounting concept: accountability. The national income view was only of interest to economists and could not be related to individual company performance – *The Corporate Report* changed that. Social accounting moved into the accountants' domain and it should be the aim of accountants to learn how accountability might be achieved and to define a model against which to judge their own efforts and the efforts of others.[20]

32.12.3 Comprehensive coverage

The annual report is concerned mainly with monetary amounts or clarifying monetary issues. Despite the ASB identifying employees and the public within the user groups,[21] no standards have been issued that deal specifically with reporting to employees or the public.

Instead, the ASB prefers to assume that financial statements that meet the needs of investors will meet most of the needs of other users.[22] For all practical purposes, it disassociates itself from the needs of non-investor users by assuming that there will be more specific information that they may obtain in their dealings with the enterprise.[23]

The information needs of different categories, e.g. employees and the public, need not be identical. The provision of information of particular interest to the public has been referred to as **public interest accounting**,[24] but there is a danger that, whilst valid as an approach, it could act as a constraint on matters that might be of legitimate interest to the employee user group. For example, safety issues at a particular location might be of little interest to the public at large but of immense concern to an employee exposed to work-related radiation or asbestos. The term 'social accounting' as defined by *The Corporate Report* is seen as embracing all interests, even those of a small group.

Equally, the information needs within a category, say employees, can differ according to the level of the employees. One study identified that different levels of employee ranked the information provided about the employer differently, e.g. lower-level employees rated safety information highest, whereas higher-level employees rated organisation information highest.[25] There were also differences in opinion about the need for additional information, with the majority of lower-level but minority of higher-level employees agreeing that the social report should also contain information on corporate environmental effects.[26]

The need for social accounting to cope with both inter-group and intra-group differences was also identified in a Swedish study.[27]

32.12.4 Independent review

The degree of credibility accorded a particular piece of information is influenced by factors such as whether it is historical or deals with the future; whether appropriate techniques exist for obtaining it; whether its source causes particular concern about deliberate or unintentional bias towards a company view; whether past experience has been that the information was reasonably complete and balanced; and, finally, the extent of independent verification.[28]

Given that social accounting is complex and technically underdeveloped, that it deals with subjective areas or future events, and that it is reported on a selective basis within a report prepared by the management, it is understandable that its credibility will be called into question. Questions will be raised as to why particular items were included or omitted – after all, it is not that unusual for companies to want to hide unfavourable developments.

32.13 Background to social accounting

A brief consideration of the history of social accounting in the UK could be helpful in putting the subject into context. *The Corporate Report* (1975) was the starting point for the whole issue. This was at a time when there was the general dissatisfaction with the quality of financial reporting which had resulted in the creation of a standard-setting regulatory body (the Accounting Standards Steering Committee) and additional statutory provisions, e.g. Companies Act provisions relating to directors.

The Corporate Report was a discussion paper issued by the ASSC which represented the first UK conceptual framework. Its approach was to identify users and their information needs. It identified seven groups of user, which included employees and the public, and their information needs. However, although it identified that there were common areas of interest among the seven groups, such as assessing liquidity and evaluating management performance, it concluded that a single set of general-purpose accounts would not satisfy each group – a different conclusion from that stated by the ASB in 1991, as discussed above.[29] The conclusions reached in *The Corporate Report* were influenced by the findings of a survey of the chairmen of the 300 largest UK listed companies. They indicated a trend towards acceptance of multiple responsibilities towards groups affected by corporate decision-making and their interest as stakeholders.[30]

It was proposed in *The Corporate Report* that there should be additional reports to satisfy the needs of the other stakeholders. These included a statement of corporate objectives, a statement of future prospects, an employment report and a value added statement.

Statement of corporate objectives

Would this be the place for social accounting to start? Would this be the place for vested interests to be represented so that agreed objectives take account of the views of all stakeholders and not merely the management and, indirectly, the shareholders? At present, social accounting appears as a series of add-ons, e.g. a little on charity donations, a little on disabled recruitment policy. Corporate objectives or the mission statement are often seen as something to be handed down; could they assume a different role?

The employment report

The need for an employment report was founded on the belief that there is a trust relationship between employers and employees and an economic relationship between employment prospects and the welfare of the community. The intention was that such a report should contain statistical information relating to such matters as numbers, reasons for change, training time and costs, age and sex distribution, and health and safety.

Statement of future prospects

There has always been resistance to publishing information focusing on the future. The arguments raised against it have included competitive disadvantage and the possibility of misinterpretation because the data relate to the future and are therefore uncertain.

The writers of *The Corporate Report* nevertheless considered it appropriate to publish information on future employment and capital investment levels that could have a direct impact on employees and the local community.

Value added reports

A value added report was intended to give a different focus from the profit and loss account with its emphasis on the bottom line earnings figure. It was intended to demonstrate the interdependence of profits and payments to employees, shareholders, the government and the company via inward investment. It reflected the mood picked up from the survey of chairmen that distributable profit could no longer be regarded as the sole or prime indicator of company performance.[31]

The value added statement became a well-known reporting mechanism to measure how effectively an organisation utilised its resources and added value to its raw materials to turn them into saleable goods. Figure 32.1 is an example of a value added statement.

Several advantages have been claimed for these reports, including improving employee attitudes by reflecting a broader view of companies' objectives and responsibilities.[32]

There have also been criticisms, e.g. they are merely a restatement of information that appears in the annual report; they only report data capable of being reported in monetary terms; and the individual elements of societal benefit are limited to the traditional ones of shareholders, employees and the government, with others such as society and the consumers ignored.

There was also criticism that there was no standard so that expenditures could be aggregated or calculated to disclose a misleading picture, e.g. the inclusion of PAYE tax and welfare payments made to the government in the employee classification so that wages were shown gross whereas distributions to shareholders were shown net of tax. The effect of both was to overstate the apparent employee share and understate the government and shareholders' share.[33]

In the years immediately following the publication of *The Corporate Report*, companies published value added statements on a voluntary basis but their importance has declined. There was a move away from industrial democracy and the standard-setting regulators did not make the publication of value added statements mandatory.

32.13.1 Why *The Corporate Report* was not implemented

The Corporate Report's proposals for additional reports have not been implemented. There are a number of views as to why this was so. There is a view that the business community, despite the results of the chairmen survey, were concerned about the possibility of their reporting responsibility being extended through the report's concept of public accountability and welcomed the release of the Sandilands Report on inflation accounting which overshadowed *The Corporate Report*. There is a view that *The Corporate Report* fell short of making a significant contribution 'by virtue of its failure to select the

Figure 32.1 Barloworld Limited value added statement for year ended 30 September 2004

R million	2004	%	2003	%
Revenue	36,673		34,603	
Paid to suppliers for materials and services	26,184		25,486	
Value added	10,489		9,117	
Income from investments*	287		274	
Total wealth created	10,776		9,391	
Wealth distribution				
Salaries, wages and other benefits (note 1)	5,993	56	5,450	58
Providers of capital	1,298	12	1,512	16
Finance cost	468		531	
Dividends paid to Barloworld Ltd shareholders	626		736	
Dividends paid to outside shareholders in subsidaries	204		245	
Government (note 2)	1,059	10	809	9
Reinvested in group to maintain and develop operations	2,426	22	1,620	17
Depreciation	1,535		1,226	
Retained profit	814		415	
Deferred taxation	77		(21)	
	10,776	100	9,391	100
Value added ratios				
Number of employees (30 September)	25,233		22,749	
Turnover per employee (Rand)#	1,528,615		1,506,410	
Wealth created per employee (Rand)#	449,168		406,086	

Notes:
1. Salaries, wages and other benefits

	2004	2003
Salaries, wages, overtime payments, commissions, bonuses and allowances	4,483	4,385
Employer contributions⁺	1,150	1,065
	5,593	5,450

2. Central and local government

	2004	2003
Current taxation	828	637
Regional Services Council levels	39	33
Rates and taxes paid to local authorities	62	54
Customs duties, import surcharges and excise taxes	122	76
Skills development levy	13	11
South African withholding taxation		2
Cash grants and cash subsidies granted by the government	(5)	(4)
Gross contribution to central and local government	1,059	809

* Includes internet received, dividend income and share of associate companies and joint ventures retained profit.
# Based on average number of employees
⁺ In respect of pension funds, retirement annuities, provident funds, medical aid and insurance.

accounting models appropriate to the informational needs of the individual user groups which it had identified'.[34]

However, the most likely reason for it not being fully implemented was the change of government. The Labour government produced a Green Paper in 1976, *Aims and Scope of Company Reports*, which endorsed much of *The Corporate Report* concept. The reaction from the business community and the Stock Exchange was hostile to any move away from the traditional stewardship concept with its obligations only to shareholders. The CBI view was that other users could ask for information, but that was no reason for companies to be required to provide it.[35] In the event, there was a change of government and the Green Paper sank without trace.

The new government supported the view of Milton Friedman, who wrote in 1962 that 'few trends could so ... undermine the very foundations of our free society as the acceptance by corporate officials of a social responsibility other than to make as much money ... as possible'.

Many responsible members of the business community pressed for change,[36] but the mid 1980s saw a decline in the commercial support for social accounting, as profit, dividends and growth superseded all other social goals in business. The movement continued but advocates were regarded at best as well-meaning radicals and at worst as dangerous politicised activists devoted to the destruction of the capitalist system.

By the early 1990s, interest was appearing in the commercial sector but from a free market rather than regulatory viewpoint. The thought was that socially responsible policies need not mean lower profits – in fact, quite the opposite. Given this change in perception, companies began to embrace social accounting concepts – suddenly accountants were able to make a contribution, e.g. evaluating the profit implication of crêche facilities for working mothers being provided by the employer rather than the state. There was also a growth within society in general of a socially responsible point of view which even extended to share investment decisions with the marketing of ethically sound investments.

32.14 Corporate social responsibility

Companies are increasingly recognising the importance of adopting a social, ethical and environmentally responsible approach to business activity and entering into dialogue with all groups of stakeholders. We have discussed the environmentally responsible approach above – the socially responsible approach includes a wide range of activities including the companies' dealings in the marketplace, the workplace, and the community, and in the field of human rights.

Reporting is slowly evolving from simply reporting the amount of charitable donations in the annual report to including additional activities which the company considers to be of key interest. The reporting might be brief but it gives an attractive picture of a company's social responsibility. For example, the 2001 Kingfisher Annual Report has a brief two-page section for social responsibility in which it gives information on:

- environmental issues, e.g. a commitment to sustainable forestry, winning the Business in the Environment award for energy saving; and

- social issues, e.g. from training young unemployed people to recycling electrical goods; making charitable donations that supported the Woolworth Kids First, You Can Do It and Green Grants schemes; and winning a Business in the Community award for Innovation relating to its work forming partnerships with local disability organisations.

We can see from this that community involvement can take many forms, e.g. charitable donations, gifts in kind, employee volunteering initiatives, staff secondments, and sustainable and mutually beneficial partnerships with community and voluntary organisations active in a variety of fields including education, training, regeneration, employment and homelessness.

The approach to CSR is becoming increasingly formalised with the setting up of committees reporting to the Board and more comprehensive CSR Reports.

Committees reporting to the Board

The 2004 Kingfisher Annual Report describes the role of the Social Responsibility Committee whose purpose is to review progress in fulfilling the Social Responsibility Plan, including monitoring the resources required to support the Plan and ensuring that actions taken maximise the opportunity to meet the expectations of key Group stakeholders and emerging corporate governance standards (e.g. investor surveys, Turnbull, Business in the Community Survey). The seniority of the Committee members is an indication that it has significant influence in advising the Board and ensuring the Plan is delivered.

CSR Reports

The following is an extract from the CSR Report accompanying the Marks & Spencer 2004 Annual Report:

> **What Corporate Social Responsibility means to us**
> Marks & Spencer has a strong tradition of CSR ... Our founders believed that building good relationships with employees, suppliers and wider society was the best guarantee of long-term success ... Managing CSR well will allow us to identify potential risks to the Company and respond to areas of performance where we fall behind ... it also means we can identify opportunities to differentiate ourselves from our competitors. CSR can help us to draw shoppers to our stores, attract and retain the best staff, make us a partner of choice with suppliers and create value for our shareholders.

Their approach is built around three principles, namely **Products, People and Places**, and a framework developed by their Board-level CSR Committee during 2002 with a detailed statement for each Principle. For example, the **Principle for Places** reads as follows:

> **Help make our communities good places in which to live and work**
> We recognise our obligations to the communities in which we trade. We were founding members of Business in the Community ... Our relationship with communities is interdependent. Successful retailing requires economically healthy and sustainable communities ... we provide employment and products and services and often become an important part of the fabric of the high street. We place much emphasis on our stores, their location, design, construction and activities. A 'Store of the Future' project has helped to improve the environmental standards we use to locate, build and refurbish them. Day-to-day operations are managed within an overall compliance system that includes emergency planning, energy and water usage, heath and safety, waste disposal, recycling, recovery of shopping trolleys and donations of unsold food to charities ... We are also active in a wider sense ... A recent development is our growing
> co-operation with suppliers and business partners in community programmes.

32.15 Need for comparative data

There is evidence[37] that environmental performance could be given a higher priority when analysts assess a company if there were comparable data by sector on a company's level of corporate responsibility.

We will consider two approaches that have taken place to satisfy this need for comparable data: benchmarking and comprehensive guidelines.

32.15.1 Benchmarking

There are a number of benchmarking schemes and we will consider two by way of illustration – these are the London Benchmarking Group, established in 1994, and the Impact on Society, established in December 2001.

The London Benchmarking Group[38]

The Group started in 1994 and consists of companies which join in order to measure and report their involvement in the community, which is a key part of any corporate social responsibility programme, and which have a tool to assist them effectively to assess and target their community programmes. Organisations such as Deloitte & Touche, British Airways and Lloyds TSB are members.

The scheme is concerned with corporate community involvement. It identifies three categories into which different forms of community involvement can be classified, namely, charity donations, social or community investment and commercial initiatives, and includes only contributions made over and above those that result from the basic business operations.

It uses an input/output model, putting a monetary value on the 'input' costs which include contributions made in cash, in time or in kind, together with full cost of staff involved; and collecting 'output' data on the community benefit, e.g. number who benefited, leveraged resources and benefit accruing to the business.

Impact on Society[39]

This is a website created in 2001 which provides free access to corporate social responsibility information from leading companies. It is the first time a common set of indicators against which companies can be measured has been provided, offering insight into areas such as the environment, the workplace, the community in which the company operates, the marketplace and human rights. The information ranges from relatively easy-to-measure numeric data, such as water usage, through to more complex, often perception-based information, e.g. from employee surveys. The information is then summarised into clear company profiles and can be compared and contrasted according to a range of parameters, such as specific indicators or industry sectors.

The site provides **qualitative** information for each company with key indicators as shown in Figure 32.2. It also provides quantitative information as a percentage, absolute cash value or physical volume.

An illustration of the scheme applied to Marks & Spencer for human rights and the environment is as follows:

Human rights
Particularly applicable to countries with operations or suppliers in developing countries.

The issues measured under human rights largely apply to companies who operate in, or buy from suppliers in, developing countries. What does or does not constitute a human right is always under some debate. However, the Universal Declaration of Human Rights is a main reference point. Before they can report that they definitely fall outside the scope of this section, companies need to answer a 'gatekeeper' question. Unless they can answer that they are definitely not exposed to human rights issues, they need to do more research and report against this indicator area.

The human rights indicators are being developed further: in consultation with non-governmental organisations and businesses engaged in human rights issues. While some companies have chosen to report, others await more fully developed indicators in this area.

Figure 32.2 Impact on Society key indicators

Indicator area	Indicators reported against
Marketplace	Advertising complaints upheld; upheld cases of anti-competitive behaviour; customer satisfaction levels; average time to pay bills to suppliers; customer retention; customer complaints about products and services; provision for customers with special needs.
Environment	Overall energy consumption; water usage; quantity of waste produced by weight; upheld cases of prosecution for environmental offences; CO_2/greenhouse gas emissions; percentage of waste recycled; environmental impact; benefits or costs of company's core products and services; environmental impact over the supply chain.
Workplace	Workforce profile by race, gender, disability and age; number of legal non-compliances with health and safety and equal opportunities legislation; upheld cases of corrupt or unprofessional behaviour; staff turnover; value of staff training; perception measures of the company by its employees; absenteeism rates; pay and conditions compared to local equivalent average; work profile compared to local community profile.
Community	Cash value of support as % of pre-tax profits; estimated combined value of staff company time; gifts in kind and management time; leverage of other resources; perception measure of company as a good neighbour.
Human rights	Existence of confidential grievance procedures for staff; proportion of suppliers or partners screened for human rights compliance; proportion of suppliers or partners meeting company's own standards on human rights; perception by staff and local community of company's performance on human rights; wage rates.

Environment
Use of recycled material
% of material used from recycled sources
Non-weight bearing food product cardboard packaging

	Recycled cardboard
2000	60%
1999	50%
1998	25%

Many types of packaging use recycled materials as a matter of course, e.g. glass bottles, tin cans and transport boxes. Where we believe that the use of recycled materials is the best environmental option and that we are able to achieve improvements we set targets. We have been working to increase our use of recycled cardboard (made from at least 50% post-consumer waste) for all our non-weight bearing food product packaging.

32.16 International initiatives towards triple bottom line reporting

There are no mandatory standards for sustainability reporting but there are Sustainability Reporting Guidelines which were issued in 2000 by the Global Reporting Initiative Steering Committee on which a number of international organisations are represented including ACCA, the Institute of Social and Ethical Accountability, the New Economics Foundation and SustainAbility Ltd from the UK.

32.16.1 The Global Reporting Initiative (GRI)

The GRI has a mission to develop global sustainability reporting guidelines for voluntary use by organisations reporting on the three linked elements of sustainability, namely, the economic, environmental and social dimensions of their activities, products and services.

Economic dimension

This includes financial and non-financial information on R&D expenditure, investment in the workforce, current staff expenditure and outputs in terms of labour productivity.

Environmental dimension

This includes any adverse impact on air, water, land, biodiversity and human health by an organisation's production processes, products and services.

Social dimension

This includes information on health and safety and recognition of rights, e.g. human rights for both employees and outsourced employees.

32.16.2 How will the guidelines assist organisations?

The aim is to assist organisations to report information that complements existing reporting standards and is consistent, comparable and easy to understand so that:

● Parties contemplating a relationship such as assessing investment risk, obtaining goods or services or entering into any other commercial partnership arrangement will have available to them a clear picture of the human and ecological impact of the business so that they can make an informed decision.
● Management have the means to develop information systems to provide the basis for monitoring performance, making inter-company comparisons and reporting to stakeholders.

32.16.3 What information should appear in an ideal GRI report?

There are six parts to the ideal GRI report:

1. CEO statement – describing key elements of the report.
2. A profile – providing an overview of the organisation and the scope of the report (it could for example be dealing only with environmental information) which sets the context for the next four parts.
3. Executive summary and key indicators – to assist stakeholders to assess trends and make inter-company comparisons.
4. Vision and strategy – a statement of the vision for the future and how that integrates economic, environmental and social performance.
5. Policies, organisation and systems – an overview of the governance and management systems to implement this vision with a discussion of how stakeholders have been engaged. This reflects the GRI view that the report should not be made in isolation but there should have been appropriate inputs from stakeholders.
6. Performance review.

32.16.4 How are GRI reports to be verified?

CSR Reports are now able to be verified by independent, competent and impartial external assurance providers. The assurance providers now have a standard – the AA1000 Assurance Standard (www.accountability.org.uk) to provide a framework for their work. This Standard was launched in 2003 to address the need for a single approach to deal effectively with the qualitative as well as quantitative data that makes up sustainability performance plus the systems that underpin the data and performance. It is designed to complement the GRI Reporting Guidelines and other standardised or company-specific approaches to disclosure. It requires reports against three Assurance Principles which are Materiality, Completeness and Responsiveness, as well as statements as to how conclusions were reached and on the independence of the assurance providers.

As an example, in the 2004 Annual Report of O$_2$ Ernst & Young, who were the assurance providers, stated that they were forming a conclusion on matters such as (a) Materiality – whether O$_2$ had provided a balanced representation of material issues concerning O$_2$'s corporate responsibility performance, (b) Completeness – whether O$_2$ had complete information on which to base a judgment of what was material for inclusion in the Report, and (c) Responsiveness – whether O$_2$ had responded to stakeholder concerns. They also explained what they did to form their conclusions:

What we did to form our conclusions
There are currently no statutory requirements in the UK in relation to the independent review of corporate responsibility reports. The AA1000 Assurance Standard sets out principles for social and environmental report assurance. We have been asked by O$_2$ to set out our conclusions by reference to the assurance principles described in the AA1000 Assurance Standard.

32.16.5 Will there be any impact on matters that are currently disclosed?

There may be an overlap with existing disclosures in the OFR and there is also a pressure for additional information to permit a greater understanding of future risks, e.g. the GRI acknowledges that in financial reporting terms a going concern is one that is considered to be financially viable for at least the next financial year but seeks additional information such as:

● The extent to which significant internal and external operational, financial, compliance, and other risks are identified and assessed on an ongoing basis. Significant risks may, for example, include those related to market, credit, liquidity, technological, legal, health, safety, environmental and reputation issues.

● The likely impact of prospective legislation, e.g. product, environmental, fiscal or employee-related.

32.16.6 The nature of the accountant's involvement

There will be inputs from accountants in each of the three elements with a greater degree of quantification at present for the economic and environmental dimensions. For example:
The economic dimension may require economic indicators such as:

● profit: segmental gross margin, net profit, EBIT, return on average capital employed;
● intangible assets: ratio of market valuation to book value;

- investments: human capital, R&D, debt/equity ratio;
- wages and benefits: totals by country;
- labour productivity: levels and changes by job category;
- community development: jobs by type and country showing absolute figures and net change;
- suppliers: value of goods and services outsourced, performance in meeting credit terms.

The environmental dimension may require environmental indicators such as:

- products and services: major issues, e.g. disposal of waste, packaging practices, percentage of product reclaimed after use;
- suppliers: supplier issues identified through stakeholder consultation, e.g. forest stewardship;
- travel: objectives and targets, e.g. product distribution, fleet operation, quantitative estimates of miles travelled by transport type.

Social dimensions may require social indicators such as:

- quality of management: employee retention rates, ratio of jobs offered to jobs accepted, ranking as an employer in surveys;
- health and safety: reportable cases, lost days, absentee rate, investment per worker in injury prevention;
- wages and benefits: ratio of lowest wage to local cost of living, health and pension benefits provided;
- training and education: ratio of training budget to annual operating cost, programmes to encourage worker participation in decision making;
- freedom of association: grievance procedures in place, number and types of legal action concerning anti-union practices.

Summary

As environmental and social reporting evolves there are proposals being made to harmonise the content and disclosure and to set up benchmark schemes which will allow stakeholders to compare corporate social reports and evaluate an individual company's performance. The management systems that are being developed within companies should result in data that are consistent and reliable and capable of external verification. The benchmarking systems should assist in both identifying best practice and establishing the performance indicators that are relevant.

Corporate social reporting has been relatively ignored by commercial organisations until the mid 1990s but, with the recognition that a company's reputation can have favourable and unfavourable economic consequences, it is now receiving serious attention from companies.

REVIEW QUESTIONS

1 Discuss the relevance of corporate social reports to an existing and potential investor.

2 Obtain a copy of the environmental report of a company that has taken part in the ACCA Awards for Sustainability Reporting and critically discuss from an investor's and public interest viewpoint.

3 'Charters and guidelines help make reports reliable but inhibit innovation and reduce their relevance.' Discuss.

4 Discuss the implications of the Global Reporting Initiative for the accountancy profession.

5 Discuss *The Corporate Report*'s relevance to modern business; identify changes that would improve current reporting practice and the conditions necessary for such changes to become mandatory.

6 (a) Explain the term 'stakeholders' in a corporate context.

   (b) 'Social accounting recognises all *Corporate Report* users as stakeholders.' Discuss.

7 Discuss the value added concept, giving examples, and ways to improve the statement.

8 Outline the arguments for and against a greater role for the audit function in corporate social reporting.

9 (a) 'Human assets are incapable of being valued.' Discuss.

   (b) Football clubs have followed various policies in the way in which they include players within their accounts. For example, some clubs capitalise players, as shown by a 1992 Touche Ross survey:[40]

Club	Value £m	Basis	Which players
Tottenham Hotspur	9.8	Cost	Those purchased
Sheffield United	8.7	Manager's valuation	Whole squad
Portsmouth	7.0	Directors' valuation	Whole squad
Derby County	6.5	Cost	Those purchased

Other clubs disclose squad value in notes to the accounts or in the directors' report:

Manchester United	24.0	Independent valuation
Charlton Athletic	4.1	Directors' valuation
Millwall	11.0	Manager's valuation

Discuss arguments for and against capitalising players as assets. Explain the effect on the profit and loss account if players are not capitalised.

10 (a) Examine the recent financial press to identify examples of a failure to meet information needs in respect of an area of public interest.

   (b) Obtain a set of accounts from a public listed company and assess the success in meeting the needs of the traditional users. Repeat the process for non-traditional users and discuss how you could improve the situation (i) marginally, (ii) significantly.

11 Discuss the impact of the following groups on the accounting profession:
   (a) Environmental groups;
   (b) Customers;
   (c) Workforce;
   (d) Ethical investors.

12 Nissan, the Japanese car company, decided that 'any environmentalism should pay for itself and for every penny you spend you must save a penny. You can spend as many pennies as you like as long as other environmental actions save an equal number.'[41] Discuss the significance of this for each of the stakeholders.

13 (a) 'Accounting should contribute to the protection of the environment.' Discuss whether this is a proper role for accounting and outline ways in which it could.
   (b) Outline, with reasons, your ideas for an environmental report for a company of your choice.
   (c) Discuss the arguments against the adoption of environmental accounting.

14 (a) Obtain the annual reports of companies that claim to be environmentally aware and assess whether these reports and accounts reflect the claim. The various oil, chemical and pharmaceutical companies are useful for this.
   (b) Look at your own organisation/institution, outline the possible environmental issues and discuss how these could or should be disclosed in the annual report.

EXERCISES

An extract from the solution is provided in the Appendix at the end of the text for exercises marked with an asterisk (*).

* Question 1

The following information relates to the Plus Factors Group plc for the years to 30 September 20X8 and 20X9:

	Notes	20X9 £000	20X8 £000
Associated company share of profit		10.9	10.7
Auditors' remuneration		12.2	11.9
Creditors for materials			
At beginning of year		1,109.1	987.2
At end of year		1,244.2	1,109.1
Debtors			
At beginning of year		1,422.0	1,305.0
At end of year		1,601.0	1,422.0
11% debentures	1	500.0	600.0
Depreciation		113.7	98.4
Employee benefits paid		109.9	68.4
Hire of plant, machinery and vehicles	2	66.5	367.3
Materials paid for in year		3,622.9	2,971.4
Minority interest in profit of the year		167.2	144.1
Other overheads incurred		1,012.4	738.3
Pensions and pension contributions paid		319.8	222.2
Profit before taxation		1,437.4	1,156.4
Provision for corporation tax		464.7	527.9
Salaries and wages		1,763.8	1,863.0
Sales	3	9,905.6	8,694.1
Shares at nominal value			
Ordinary at 25p each fully paid	4	2,500.0	2,000.0
7% preference at £1 each fully paid	4	500.0	200.0
Stocks of materials			
Beginning of year		804.1	689.7
End of year		837.8	804.1

Ordinary dividends were declared as follows:

Interim 1.12 pence per share (20X8, 1.67p)
Final 3.57 pence per share (20X8, 2.61p)
Average number of employees was 196 (20X8, 201)

Notes:

1 £300,000 of debentures were redeemed at par on 31 March 20X9 and £200,000 new debentures at the same rate of interest were issued at £98 for each £100 nominal value on the same date. The new debentures are due to be redeemed in five years' time.

2 This is the amount for inclusion in the profit and loss account in accordance with SSAP 21.

3 All the groups' sales are subject to value added tax at 15% and the figures given include such tax. All other figures are exclusive of value added tax. This VAT rate has been increased to 17.5% and may be subject to future changes, but for the purposes of this question the theory and workings remain the same irrespective of the rate.

4 All shares have been in issue throughout the year.

The statement of value added is available for 20X8 and the 20X9 statement needs to be completed.

	Workings	£000	
Turnover	1	7,560.1	
Less: Bought-in materials and services	2	4,096.4	
Value added by group		3,463.7	
Share of profits of associated company		10.7	
		3,474.4	
Applied in the following ways			
To pay employees	3	2,153.6	62.0%
To pay providers of capital	4	566.5	16.3%
To pay government		527.9	15.2%
To provide for maintenance and expansion of assets	5	226.4	6.50%
		3,474.4	100.0%

Workings

1 *Turnover*

	£000
Sales inclusive of VAT	8,694.1
VAT at 15%	1,134.0
	7,560.1

2 *Bought-in materials and services*
   Cost of materials

	£000
Creditors at end of year	1,109.1
Add: Payments in year	2,971.4
	4,080.5
Less: Creditors at beginning of year	987.2
Materials purchased in year	3,093.3
Add: Opening stock	689.7
Less: Closing stock	(804.1)
Materials used	2,978.9
Add: Cost of bought-in services	
Auditors' remuneration	11.9
Hire of plant, machinery and vehicles	367.3
Other overheads	738.3
	4,096.4

3 *To pay employees*

	£000
Benefits paid	68.4
Pensions and pension contributions	222.2
Salaries and wages	1,863.0
	2,153.6

4 *To pay providers of capital*
  Debenture interest
  11% of £600,000   66.0
  Dividends
  Preference 20X8 7% of £200,000   14.0
  Ordinary 20X8 8 million shares at 4.28p   342.4
  Minority interest   144.1
                                                              ─────
                                                              566.5
                                                              ═════

5 *To provide for maintenance and expansion of assets*
  Profit before tax   1,156.4
  Less: tax   (527.9)
       : minority interest   (144.1)
       : dividends   (356.4)
                                                             ───────
  Retained profits   128.0
  Depreciation   98.4
                                                             ───────
                                                              226.4
                                                             ═══════

Required:

(a) **Prepare a statement of value added for the year to 30 September 20X9. Include a percentage breakdown of the distribution of value added.**

(b) **Produce ratios related to employees' interests based on the statement in (a) and explain how they might be of use.**

(c) **Explain briefly what the difficulties are of measuring and reporting financial information in the form of a statement of value added.**

Question 2

David Mark is a sole trader who owns and operates supermarkets in each of three villages near Ousby. He has drafted his own accounts for the year ended 31 May 20X4 for each of the branches. They are as follows:

	Arton		Blendale		Clifearn	
	£	£	£	£	£	£
Sales		910,800		673,200		382,800
Cost of sales		633,100		504,900		287,100
Gross profit		277,700		168,300		95,700
Less: Expenses:						
David Mark's salary	10,560		10,560		10,560	
Other salaries and wages	143,220		97,020		78,540	
Rent			19,800			
Rates	8,920		5,780		2,865	
Advertising	2,640		2,640		2,640	
Delivery van expenses	5,280		5,280		5,280	
General expenses	11,220		3,300		1,188	
Telephone	2,640		1,980		1,584	
Wrapping materials	7,920		3,960		2,640	
Depreciation:						
Fixtures	8,220		4,260		2,940	
Vehicle	3,000	203,620	3,000	157,580	3,000	111,237
Net profit/(loss)		74,080		10,720		(15,537)

The figures for the year ended 31 May 20X4 follow the pattern of recent years. Because of this, David Mark is proposing to close the Clifearn supermarket immediately.

David Mark employs twelve full-time and twenty part-time staff. His recruitment policy is based on employing one extra part-time assistant for every £30,000 increase in branch sales. His staff deployment at the moment is as follows:

	Arton	Blendale	Clifearn
Full-time staff (including managers)	6	4	2
Part-time staff	8	6	6

Peter Gaskin, the manager of the Clifearn supermarket, asks David to give him another year to make the supermarket profitable. Peter has calculated that he must cover £125,500 expenses out of his gross profit in the year ended 31 May 20X5 in order to move into profitability. His calculations include extra staff costs and all other extra costs.

Additional information:

1 General advertising for the business as a whole is controlled by David Mark. This costs £3,960 per annum. Each manager spends a further £1,320 advertising his own supermarket locally.
2 The delivery vehicle is used for deliveries from the Arton supermarket only.
3 David Mark has a central telephone switchboard which costs £1,584 rental per annum. Each supermarket is charged for all calls actually made. For the year ended 31 May 20X4 these amounted to:

Arton	£2,112
Blendale	£1,452
Clifearn	£1,056

Required:
(a) A report addressed to David Mark advising him whether to close Clifearn supermarket. Your report should include a detailed financial statement based on the results for the year ended 31 May 20X4 relating to the Clifearn branch.
(b) Calculate the increased turnover and extra staff needed if Peter's suggestion is implemented.
(c) Comment on the social implications for the residents of Clifearn if (i) David Mark closes the supermarket, (ii) Peter Gaskin's recommendation is undertaken.

* **Question 3**

(a) You are required to prepare a value added statement to be included in the corporate report of Hythe plc for the year ended 31 December 20X6, including the comparatives for 20X5, using the information given below:

	20X6	20X5
	£000	£000
Fixed assets (net book value)	3,725	3,594
Debtors	870	769
Creditors	530	448
14% debentures	1,200	1,080
6% preference shares	400	400
Ordinary shares (£1 each)	3,200	3,200
Sales	5,124	4,604
Materials consumed	2,934	2,482
Wages	607	598
Depreciation	155	144
Fuel consumed	290	242
Hire of plant and machinery	41	38
Salaries	203	198
Auditors' remuneration	10	8
Corporation tax provision	402	393
Ordinary share dividend	9p	8p
Number of employees	40	42

(b) Although value added statements were recommended by *The Corporate Report*, as yet there is no accounting standard related to them. Explain what a value added statement is and provide reasons as to why you think it has not yet become mandatory to produce such a statement as a component of current financial statements either through a Financial Reporting Standard or company law.

Question 4

Gettry Doffit plc is an international company with worldwide turnover of £26 million. The activities of the company include the breaking down and disposal of noxious chemicals at a specialised plant in the remote Scottish countryside. During the preparation of the financial statements for the year ended 31 March 20X5, it was discovered that:

1 Quantities of chemicals for disposals on site at the year-end included:

    (A) Axylotl peroxide   40,000 gallons
    (B) Pterodactyl chlorate   35 tons

Chemical A is disposed of for a South Korean company, which was invoiced for 170 million won on 30 January 20X5, for payment in 120 days. It is estimated that the costs of disposal will not exceed £75,000. £60,000 of costs have been incurred at the year-end.

Chemical B is disposed of for a British company on a standard contract for 'cost of disposal plus 35%', one month after processing. At the year-end the chemical has been broken down into harmless by-products at a cost of £77,000. The by-products, which belong to Gettry Doffit plc, are worth £2,500.

2 To cover against exchange risks, the company entered into two forward contracts on 30 January 20X5:

    No. 03067   Sell 170 million won at 1,950 won = £1: 31 May 20X5
    No. 03068   Buy $70,000 at $1.60   = £1: 31 May 20X5

Actual sterling exchange rates were:

	won	$
30 January 20X5	1,900	1.70
31 March 20X5	2,000	1.38
30 April 20X5 (today)	2,100	1.80

The company often purchases a standard chemical used in processing from a North American company, and the dollars will be applied towards this purpose.

3 The company entered into a contract to import a specialised chemical used in the breaking down of magnesium perambulate from a Nigerian company which demanded the raising of an irrevocable letter of credit for £65,000 to cover 130 tons of the chemical. By 31 March 20X5 bills of lading for 60 tons had been received and paid for under the letter of credit. It now appears that the total needed for the requirements of Gettry Doffit plc for the foreseeable future is only 90 tons.

4 On 16 October 20X4 Gettry Doffit plc entered into a joint venture as partners with Dumpet Andrunn plc to process perfidious recalcitrant (PR) at the Gettry Doffit plc site using Dumpet Andrunn plc's technology. Unfortunately, a spillage at the site on 15 April 20X5 has led to claims being filed against the two companies for £12 million. A public inquiry has been set up, to assess the cause of the accident and to determine liability, which the finance director of Gettry Doffit plc fears will be, at the very least, £3 million.

Required:

Discuss how these matters should be reflected in the financial statements of Gettry Doffit plc as on and for the year ended 31 March 20X5.

Question 5

Examine the EPA's website (http://www.epa.gov/epahome/aboutepa.htm) and prepare one of the cases as a presentation to the group showing clearly how environmental accounting was used and the results of the exercise.

References

1 C. Lehman, *Accounting's Changing Roles in Social Conflict*, Markus Weiner Publishing, 1992, p. 64.
2 *Ibid.*, p. 17.
3 S.J. Gray and C.B. Roberts, *Voluntary Information Disclosure and the British Multinationals: Corporate Perceptions of Costs and Benefits, International Pressures for Accounting Change*, Prentice Hall, 1989, p. 117.
4 AICPA, *The Measurement of Corporate Social Performance*, 1977, p. 4.
5 *This Common Inheritance*, Government White Paper, 1990.
6 KPMG Peat Marwick McLintock, *Environmental Considerations in Acquiring*, Corporate Finance Briefing, 17 May 1991.
7 M. Jones, 'The cost of cleaning up', *Certified Accountant*, May 1995, p. 47.
8 M. Campanale, 'Cost or opportunity', *Certified Accountant*, November 1991, p. 32.
9 See http://www.europa.eu.int/comm/internal_market/accounting/officialdocs_en.htm
10 See www.unep.org
11 See http://europa.eu.int/comm/environment/emas/
12 See www.iccwbo.org
13 See http://www.cefic.be/
14 See http://europa.eu.int/comm/environment/newprg/
15 See http://www.ceaa-acve.ca/aboutus.htm

16 See http://www.rabnet.com/

17 See http://www.fee.be/issues/other.htm#Sustainability

18 M.R. Matthews and M.H.B. Perera, *Accounting Theory and Development*, Chapman and Hall, 1991, p. 350.

19 Accounting Standards Steering Committee, *The Corporate Report*, 1975.

20 R. Gray, D. Owen and K. Maunders, *Corporate Social Reporting*, Prentice Hall, 1987, p. 75.

21 ASB, *Statement of Principles: The Objective of Financial Statements*, 1991, para. 9.

22 *Ibid.*, para. 10.

23 *Ibid.*, para. 11.

24 F. Okcabol and A. Tinker, 'The market for positive theory: deconstructing the theory for excuses', *Advances in Public Interest Accounting*, vol. 3, 1990.

25 H. Sebreuder, 'Employees and the corporate social report: the Dutch case', in S.J. Gray (ed.), *International Accounting and Transnational Decisions*, Butterworth, 1983, p. 287.

26 *Ibid.*, p. 289.

27 *Ibid.*, p. 287.

28 AICPA, *op. cit.*, p. 243.

29 *Statement of Principles, op cit.*

30 R. Gray, D. Owen and K. Maunders, *op. cit.*, p. 44.

31 *Ibid.*

32 S.J. Gray and K.T. Maunders, *Value Added Reporting: Uses and Measurement*, ACCA, 1980; B. Underwood and P.J. Taylor, *Accounting Theory and Policy Making*, Heinemann, 1985, p. 298.

33 *Ibid.*, p. 174.

34 M. Davies, R. Patterson and A. Wilson, *UK GAAP* (4th edition), Ernst & Young, 1994, p. 71.

35 R. Gray, D. Owen and K. Maunders, *op. cit.*, p. 48.

36 R.W. Perks and R.H. Gray, 'Corporate social reporting – an analysis of objectives', *British Accounting Review*, 1978, Vol. 10(2), pp. 43–59.

37 Business in the Environment, *Investing in the Future*, May 2001.

38 See http://www.lbg-online.net/

39 See www.iosreporting.org

40 R. Bruce, *The Independent*, 25 October 1993, p. 29.

41 M. Brown, 'Greening the bottom line', *Management Today*, July 1995, p. 73.

Bibliography

The following references have been helpful for students carrying out assignments in the developing areas of environmental and social reporting:

Accounting Advisory Forum, *Environmental Issues in Financial Reporting*, Accounting Advisory Forum (Brussels), 1995.

C.A. Adams, W.-Y. Hill and C.B. Roberts, 'Corporate social reporting practices in Western Europe: legitimating corporate behaviour?', *British Accounting Review*, vol. 30(1), 1998, pp. 1–22.

C.C. Adams, A. Coutts and G. Harte, 'Corporate equal opportunities (non-) disclosure', *British Accounting Review*, vol. 27(2), 1995, pp. 87–108.

K. Bagshaw, *Reporting on environmental issues*, London: Accountancy Books [for the] ICAEW, 1999, 28p. (Accountants Digest; no. 415).

P. Bartram, 'Go green, not into the red', *Accountancy Age*, 31 October 2002, p. 15.

J. Bebbington, 'Sustainable development: a review of the international development business and accounting literature', *Accounting Forum*, vol. 25(2), 2001, pp. 128–157.

J. Bebbington and I. Thomson, 'Commentary on: Some thoughts on social and environmental accounting education', *Accounting Education: An international journal*, vol. 10(4), 2001, pp. 353-355.

F.K. Birkin, 'Environmental Management Accounting', *Management Accounting*, 1996, pp. 34–37.

F. Birkin and D. Woodward, 'Management accounting for sustainable development', *Management Accounting*, June 1997, pp. 24–26.

F. Birkin, P. Edwards and D. Woodward, 'Some Evidence on Executives' Views of Corporate Social Responsibility', *British Accounting Review*, vol 33, 2001, pp 357-397.

J.H. Blokdijk and F. Drieenhuizen, 'The environment and the audit profession – a Dutch research study', *The European Accounting Review*, December 1992, pp. 437–443.

R.L. Burritt and G. Lehman, 'The Body Shop wind farm – an analysis of accountability and ethics', *British Accounting Review*, vol. 27(3), 1995, pp. 167–186.

J. Collier, *The Corporate Environment*, Prentice Hall, 1995.

'Corporate social responsibility – the ABI guidelines', *Practical Governance*, no. 23, April 2002, pp. 5–6.

D. Crowther, *Social and Environmental Accounting*, Harlow: Financial Times Prentice Hall, 2000.

D. Dodds, J.A. Lesser and R.O. Zerbe, *Environmental Economics and Policy*, Addison Wesley, 1997.

C. Evans, 'Sustainability: the bottom line', *Accountancy*, vol. 131, no. 1313, January 2003, p. 16.

R. Gray, J. Bebbington, D. Walters and M. Houldin (eds), *Accounting for the Environment*, Paul Chapman Publishing, 1993.

R. Gray, D. Owen and C. Adams, *Accounting and Accountability: Changes and Challenges in Corporate Social and Environmental Reporting*, Prentice Hall, 1996.

R. Gray, J. Bebbington and M. Houldin, *Accounting for the Environment*, 2nd edn, London: Sage Publications, 2001.

R. Howes, *Environmental Cost Accounting: An introduction and practical guide*, London: CIMA, 2002.

M.J. Jones, 'Accounting for biodiversity', *British Accounting Review*, vol. 28(4), 1996, pp. 281–304.

L. Lewis, C. Humphrey and D. Owen, 'Accounting and the social: a pedagogic perspective', *British Accounting Review*, vol. 24(3), 1992, pp. 219–234.

M. Lynn, 'A note on corporate social disclosure in Hong Kong', *British Accounting Review*, vol. 24, no. 2, 1992, pp. 105–110.

M. Matthews and M.H.B. Perera, *Accounting Theory and Development* (3rd edition), Thompson Business Press, 1996.

T. Mouck, 'Financial reporting, democracy and environmentalism: a critique of the commodification of information', *Critical Perspectives on Accounting*, vol. 6(6), 1995, pp. 535–553.

M.K. Neimark, *The Hidden Dimensions of Annual Reports: Sixty Years of Social Conflict at General Motors*, Paul Chapman Publishing, 1993.

D. Owen (ed.), *Green Reporting: Accountancy and the Challenge of the Nineties*, Thompson Business Press, 1992.

L.S. Paine, *Value Shift – why companies must merge social and financial imperatives to achieve superior performance*, New York: McGraw-Hill, 2002.

A. Papmehl, 'Beyond the GAAP', *CMA Management*, vol. 76, no. 5, July/August 2002, pp. 20–25.

PricewaterhouseCoopers, *The Politics of Responsible Business – a survey of political and business opinion on corporate social responsibility*, London: PricewaterhouseCoopers in association with the Industry and Parliament Trust, 2001.

J. Rayner and W. Raven., eds, *Corporate Social Responsibility Monitor*, London: Gee, 2002, 1 vol., looseleaf, updated.

A. Riahi-Belkaoui, *Corporate Social Awareness and Financial Outcomes*, Westport, CT: Quorum, 1999.

R. Roslender and J.R. Dyson, 'Accounting for the worth of employees: a new look at an old problem', *British Accounting Review*, vol. 24(4), 1992, pp. 311–330.

D. Rubenstein, *Environmental Accounting for the Sustainable Corporation*, Quorum Books, 1994.

S. Schaltegger, K. Muller and H. Hindrichsen, *Corporate Environmental Reporting*, Wiley, 1996.

C.A. Tilt, 'Environmental policies of major companies: Australian evidence', *British Accounting Review*, vol. 29(4), 1997, pp. 367–394.

T. Tinker and T. Puxy, *Policing Accounting Knowledge: The Market for Excuses Affair*, Paul Chapman Publishing, 1995.

J.S. Toms, *Environmental Management, Environmental Accounting and Financial Performance*, London: Chartered Institute of Management Accountants, 2000.

G. Tower, 'A public accountability model of the accounting profession', *British Accounting Review*, 1992, vol. 25(1), pp. 61–86.

CHAPTER 33

Ethics for accountants

33.1 Introduction

In this chapter we consider the following:

- The nature of business ethics
- Ethical codes for businesses
- The background to business ethics
- The role of ethics in modern business
- The role of professional accounting ethics
- The role of the accountant as a guardian of business ethics
- Growth of voluntary standards.

The issue of ethics is at the very centre of all societies. Every society, such as a nation, must operate according to some ethical guidelines, however idiosyncratic or singular they may seem to outsiders – without such guidelines the society would lapse into anarchy and eventual collapse. This also applies to sub-societies, e.g. a family, a group of friends or even a business organisation, and in this chapter we introduce the student of accounting to the basics of ethics as they could be applied to business.

What do we mean by 'ethics'?

In any study a good starting point is the production of a working definition of the issue under consideration. The *Oxford English Dictionary* has one of the more accessible definitions of ethics. It states four possible views of ethics:

> Ethics can be defined as (i) the science of morals; (ii) moral principles; (iii) a philosophy **or (iv) a code.**

In this chapter we will adopt the fourth definition of ethics as **an ethical code**, i.e. we will concentrate on the bureaucratic view of how to operate ethics in practice. The other three views are more properly the domain of philosophers as they are really concerned with what ethics should be.

33.2 The nature of business ethics

Business ethics refers to the relationship of a business to three significant 'environments' or 'levels'. Each business seeks for a harmonisation (or even a compromise) between the three levels of ethics which are traditionally viewed as follows:

1 The macro level

The macro ethical guidelines applied to a business in the national and international context are usually the result of political, cultural, legal and religious pressures.

2 The organisational level

The organisational ethical guidelines are the ethics specific to an organisation. In many texts they are referred to as 'corporate social responsibility'. The guidelines may be of long duration, e.g. the ethics of the original founders of the organisation (such as the Co-operative Wholesale Movement or the John Lewis Partnership) or short duration, e.g. the ethical beliefs of the current senior managers of the business and of the current trading partners in the industrial sector within which the organisation operates.

3 The individual level

Individual ethical guidelines or personal ethics refers to the ethics of each individual in the organisation. These are naturally the result of a much more varied set of influences or pressures. As an individual each of us 'enjoys' a series of ethical pressures or influences including the following:

- parents – the first and, according to many authors, the most crucial influence on our ethical guidelines;
- family – the *extended* family which is common in Eastern societies (aunts, uncles, grandparents and so on) can have a significant impact on personal ethics; the *nuclear* family which is more common in Western societies (just parent(s) and siblings) can be equally as important but more narrowly focused;
- social group – the ethics of our 'class' (either actual or aspirational) can be a major influence;
- peer group – the ethics of our 'equals' (again either actual or aspirational) can be another major influence;
- religion – ethics based in religion are more important in some cultures, e.g. Islamic societies have some detailed ethics demanded of believers as well as major guidelines for business ethics. However, even in supposedly secular cultures, individuals are influenced by religious ethics;
- culture – this is also a very effective formulator of an individual's ethics;
- professional – when an individual becomes part of a professional body then he/she is subject to the ethics of the professional body.

How do professional ethics differ from those arising from parents and peers?

The essential difference is that the ethics handbook which governs the behaviour of all staff in an organisation are more likely to be formally codified. A code of behaviour may be written as a formal Statement of Professional Ethics or subsumed within the staff. The fact that the Code is formally specified means that it is capable of being policed with information systems in place to assist monitoring and enforcement.

Harmonisation

We have seen above that 'business' has a complex 'web' of relationships with various parties each operating with their own ethics guidelines. The task of the business is therefore to ensure effective operations whilst meeting the various ethical demands of all interested parties.

33.3 Ethical codes for businesses

There are two approaches to defining an ethical code, namely, the positivist and normative approaches.

The rationale for the positivist approach

This places emphasis on the preparation of a formal, written ethical code for the guidance of all employees within an organisation. Such an approach is to be expected as, in all control models, it is considered to be essential to have a fixed, rigid standard against which to measure performance. Any ambiguities of performance measurement can lead to disputes and confusion. This is especially true with ethics as the term has a variety of meanings and constructs within the mind of each individual. It is, therefore, hardly surprising that a business tries to produce a 'hard copy' of ethics for the use of all interested parties.

There are many examples of ethical codes in practice and for further study reference can be made to the codes of the following organisations:

- Trusthouse Forte plc – with its 'Company Philosophy' document;
- British Gas plc – with its 'Code of Conduct';
- Royal Dutch Shell Group of Companies – with its 'Statement of General Business Principles';
- BICC plc – with its 'Statement of Company Principles';
- the Body Shop – which publishes a considerable amount of information showing its belief in classic business ethics.

The limitations of the positivist approach

Key arguments against the positivist approach of written codes can be summarised as follows:

- **Status of the source**: the source, or who writes the code of ethics, can be a crucial question with the risk that ethical codes could be imposed on a business against the 'natural' beliefs of its employees. This is always a key danger in multinational companies where the management in the parent country may impose ethical beliefs on subsidiaries in other counties which are contrary to the cultural or religious beliefs of the host country.
- **Flexibility**: it is a well-known axiom that rules once in place do tend to have an existence well beyond their appointed time and this could cause serious ethical problems. It is important that there are procedures in place determining how written codes may be changed to meet changing beliefs and customs.
- **Comprehensiveness**: it is questionable whether one written code can cover all the possible issues raised under ethics. It is a weakness of all codified rules that they tend to apply only to known or, at least, anticipated situations. As discussed under flexibility, procedures are required to cope with totally new and unexpected situations – ethical issues often fall into this category and new situations and potential conflicts are always arising which limits the effectiveness of a written code.

The rationale for the normative approach

The alternative approach is to adopt a more 'normative' ethical stance where a philosophy is developed for the business following a theoretical, religious or pragmatic approach as follows:

The theoretical approach

A business may take any one of the many theoretical stances on ethics. It is not the purpose of the chapter to go into detail but typically the business could adopt any philosophy including:

- **Utilitarianism**, as propounded by Jeremy Bentham (1748–1832) or John Stuart Mill (1806–1873), where individual happiness is balanced against the needs of society.

- **Deontological philosophy**, as propounded by Immanuel Kant (1724–1804), revised by David Hare (b. 1919), which is a philosophy based upon perceived absolutes of 'right', 'wrong' and 'duty'.

- **Marxism and post-Marxism**, based on the ideas of Karl Marx (1818–1883) and the post-marxists such as Herbert Marcuse (1898–1979), Roland Barthes (1915–1980) and Michel Foucault (1926–1984). Their views are of importance in multi-national situations and look at the imposition of ethics based upon economic power.

- **Postmodernism**, put forward by those such as A.J. Ayer (1910–1989), Jean-François Lyotard (1924–1998) and Jacques Derrida (b. 1930), has a particular resonance for business by offering an almost 'free market' approach to ethics.

- **Social philosophy**, with the work of John Rawls (b. 1921) and Alasdair MacIntyre (b. 1929), who adopt a more community-centred approach.

There are many theorists whose views can be explored for a deeper understanding of the approach.

The religious approach

This approach is applied when business ethics are formulated on some basic religious foundation, e.g. Judeo-Christian or Islamic or Hindu or Buddhist or Jainist.

The pragmatic approach

This is the approach where a business simply addresses each ethical problem as it arises and solves such problems by committee – the establishment of ethical committees is commonplace in many large organisations.

There are, however, difficulties with the approach which can be summarised as:

- Inefficiency: this is a very time-consuming process and some issues are urgent and need a swift solution.

- Inconsistency: the approach can, over time, lead to inconsistencies and apparent changes of approach which can be embarrassing and confusing.

- Theoretical underpinning: there is the question of who is qualified to sit on such committees, which can be a major question for a business. In some hospitals in the USA philosophers are employed by hospitals to help medical staff address key ethical issues on a case-by-case basis. These philosophers, however, will operate from one of the theoretical standpoints highlighted above.

Thus the 'normative' approach, whilst being sound in concept, does raise enormous practical difficulties for business. This explains the reliance on written codes, which despite their drawbacks are at least accessible and in many ways 'reliable'.

33.4 The background to business ethics

A brief survey of the recent history of business ethics may prove useful at this point in our study.

The separatist view

In classical economic theory the business has only one purpose, as typified by the following précis of the ideas of Milton Friedman:

> Managers should single-mindedly pursue only one goal: the maximisation of profit for the benefit of shareholders. The invisible hand of the market then guarantees their actions contribute to social welfare in the best possible way.

This view of ethics is often referred to as the 'separatist view' and assumes that the business will conform to some ethical standard because of the combined influence of the law (via governmental pressure) and the (almost magical) powers of 'market forces'. Thus it assumes that businesses will behave ethically because it makes sound business sense to do so!

The integration view

The alternative view, proposed by Jeurissen in his Sankt Gallen lecture, is known as the 'integration view'. This view recognises the impact of law and market forces but also gives the organisation a duty or responsibility to respond and reflect the views of the moral community within which it operates. In other words the business may well have a wider social responsibility with objectives broader than simply profit maximisation.

Thus society allows the business the freedom to operate on 'market lines' provided that the 'public' can rely upon the integrity of the management to operate for the wider benefit of society in the long term. It is the conditional nature of the freedom that makes business ethics important.

Promotion of business ethics

At an institute level, the Chair of the Institute of Business Ethics, Neville Cooper put the issue with remarkable clarity in 1987 when he said:

> Our conviction is that, essentially, industry and commerce are highly ethical undertakings. The ethical demands on us ... are to run them supremely efficiently, responsibly and with clear moral standards.[1]

At a corporate level, the chairman of a major UK food company in referring to his company's code of ethics said:

> ... business ethics are not negotiable – a well founded reputation for scrupulous dealing is itself a priceless company asset and the most important single factor in our success is faithful adherence to our beliefs.

Management commitment to business ethics

This view of business ethics has its spiritual home in the development of codes of behaviour formulated in the USA since the 1960s and imported into Britain in the 1980s. Research carried out by the Institute of Business Ethics in 1987 in respect of the 300 largest UK companies did support this view, where the replies received did show ethics being taken seriously by senior management. Many ethical statements were shown to be published in the annual accounts and report documents produced by these companies. This research supported other surveys, especially that carried out by the journal *International Management* in 1982.

Well-known failures to follow acceptable ethical practices

The importance of business ethics is also, sadly, reinforced by a series of high-profile scandals caused by an obvious lack of business ethics. There are many examples including BCCI and the activities of the late Robert Maxwell with the Mirror Group of companies.

The issue of public confidence in business integrity is at the key of the continued acceptance of the freedom to operate within a market economy. It was as a result of such scandals that the Institute of Business Ethics was formed in 1987 to

> ... clarify ethical issues in business, to propose positive solutions to problems and to establish common ground with people of goodwill of all faiths.

This, voluntary, organisation has been attempting to spread the issue of ethics and ethical behaviour across all business enterprises both nationally and internationally.

UK commitment to self-regulation

The self-regulation approach is a feature of the business culture of the UK. The work of the Cadbury Committee (1991, updated in 1992) helped the issue of corporate governance and managerial behaviour and the Greenbury Report (1995), which looked in detail at the issue of directors' remuneration packages, included an ethical view of such, again reflecting the usual UK approach. The Hampel Report (1998) reinforced the voluntary, self-regulatory nature of such views of business ethics.

Thus the issue of business ethics is seen to be a key feature of business success but ethics are (in the view of business) best 'enforced' on a voluntary basis.

33.5 The role of ethics in modern business

When considering the issues raised under business ethics a useful starting point is to examine the areas covered by the Ethical Codes published by the various organisations which indicate the key areas of concern.

1 Conflicts of interest

These are always issues of concern as management must be concerned with the benefit of the organisation and they must not put personal gain ahead of the gain for the organisation. Where there is a possibility of conflict, the usual practice is for the manager (including directors) to declare an interest to their fellow managers who can then assess the actions of the manager in such a light. Ideally the manager should withdraw from taking decisions where he/she may gain personally, but this may not always be practical. The awarding of contracts, employment of relatives and share dealings are all areas of concern here.

Public perceptions

The manager needs to not only be behaving ethically but also to be **seen** to be behaving ethically. Recent issues in Parliament have highlighted the dangers of conflicts of interest and how even innocent conflicts can be seen to have a more sinister, ulterior motive. The whole issue of **insider dealing** has recently caused problems in respect of share options for directors and their actions in taking up the options at advantageous times.

2 Gifts

The practice of giving and receiving gifts in business has always been a very fine ethical question. Ideally gifts should not be seen as an inducement to promote business in a manner which is less than open and honest. However, gifts are often intended as a sign of goodwill and respect and have no other motive than this. The issue becomes even more cloudy when we consider corporate hospitality, e.g. are tickets for the Football World Cup given to potential customers a legitimate gift? An apparently innocent social event could be seen to have sinister overtones in the 'cold light of day'.

There is a normal, human need to show respect and the giving and receiving of gifts is a key part of this. Japan for example is an illustration of cultural ethical differences where gifts are commonplace in business. In most businesses the key factor is scale. Small, low-value gifts (diaries, low cost pens, etc.) are not perceived as a threat to ethical behaviour but high-value gifts are not acceptable.

This is the policy set out in the PSA Peugeot Citroen 2003 Code of Ethics:

> Employees act with integrity and honesty in their dealings with customers and suppliers, refraining from directly or indirectly soliciting gifts and refusing to accept gifts of any significant value.

The issue also applies to the payment of 'bribes' to encourage business, totally unacceptable in the eyes of most managers but common practice in many countries and industries (e.g. the defence industry). Thus, ethically no bribes (however named) should be paid or received.

There is a growing concern over the use of gifts of cash, goods or services in relation to governmental officials. Such officials, by the very nature of their work, must be above reproach in respect of ethical behaviour. Unfortunately these officials are often very poorly paid and thus the temptation is great.

Commercial organisations must have very precise codes for dealing with governmental officials. These codes must cover the relationship with the official before, during and after the main business has been carried out. This is to prevent the temptation of payment paid later, even after the official has left government service, since the suspicion will always remain of unfair treatment.

3 Confidentiality

The business has secrets which could have commercial value if revealed, so the manager is required to maintain confidentiality. A common policy is that set out in the PSA Peugeot Citroen 2003 Code of Ethics:

> Employees of PSA Peugeot Citroen member companies must not divulge confidential business information to outsiders or to other Group employees who are not authorised to have such information. Employees refrain directly or indirectly using privileged information obtained in their jobs for personal gain.

This does, however, itself raise a keen ethical point: what should the manager do if the organisation is carrying out an illegal or immoral act? In most codes of practice, published by organisations and professional bodies, secrecy must be maintained but there is, surely, a wider social element of the individual's duty to society? It is here that **whistle-blowing** starts to be a possible course of action. This involves the employee in informing an outside agency of the organisation's unacceptable behaviour. Most organisations would regard this as 'gross misconduct' and would dismiss the employee even though the employee was acting with the highest of motives.

Governments have seen the danger to individuals of this and have taken steps to prevent the victimisation of employees who whistle-blow. The UK and US governments are taking a lead in this approach. In the USA many organisations have **whistle-blowing hotlines** where employees can tell about unethical behaviour in confidence; in the UK there are professional organisations who provide this service to their members. An interesting approach to whistle-blowing can be seen in the work of the charity Public Concern at Work. They outline the process and protection offered to whistle-blowers on their website: http://www.pcaw.demon.co.uk.

4 Products and processes

It is becoming a recognised fact of business that society expects certain standards in respect of processes of production and products, and businesses could face severe censure if these standards are broken.

Processes
The environment is a major topic of concern so businesses have to be 'green' in their products and processes; this is very apparent in the oil industry.

Products
The product can also be an issue; for instance tobacco products cause major issues of concern for much of society. An additional example was the sale of 'alco-pops', the alcoholic drink in an apparent 'soft drink' form.

Selling practices
Selling practices can also cause concern as instanced by the concern voiced over the sale of baby milk substitute products in the Third World. Changes in marketing practices were demanded and were forthcoming because of ethical concerns.

5 Employment practices

The treatment of employees is also a major ethical concern for business; businesses need to be seen to be fair to their workers. This means looking, for example, at the status of women, ethnic minorities, older employees and disabled people within the workplace.

It also covers the employment of children, a very sensitive issue as evidenced by the recent court case of a major high street retailer taking legal action against a TV programme for suggesting they **knowingly** bought products from manufacturers overseas who employed child labour. Thus the ethics of an organisation in this area is a matter of interest to society.

Most business organisations of any size will take action to address these very real areas of societal concern within their formal, written, ethical code. It is here that the main ethical effort in business is concentrated.

33.5.1 International Accreditation Programme

An international accreditation programme is available to companies through Social Accountability International (SAI).

Social Accountability International

SAI is a US-based, non-profit organisation (http://www.cepaa.org) dedicated to the development, implementation and oversight of voluntary verifiable social accountability standards to improve workplace conditions. It convenes key stakeholders to develop consensus-based voluntary standards and accredits qualified organisations to verify compliance.

In 1996, SAI convened an international multi-stakeholder Advisory Board which developed Social Accountability 8000 (SA 8000), a voluntary standard for workplaces based on ILO (International Labour Organization) and other human rights conventions with independent verification.

SA 8000 is a way for retailers, brand companies, suppliers and other organisations to maintain just and decent working conditions throughout the supply chain. It is based on international workplace norms in the ILO conventions and the UN's Universal Declaration of Human Rights and the Convention on Rights of the Child. It includes, e.g. a standard for compensation which reads as follows:

> **Compensation:** Wages paid for a standard work week must meet the legal and industry standards and be sufficient to meet the basic need of workers and their families; no disciplinary deductions.

There are also standards relating to child labour, forced labour; health and safety; freedom of association and right to collective bargaining; discrimination; discipline; working hours and management systems. For further information refer to www.sa-intl.org.

33.6 The role of professional accounting ethics

Within the UK the various professional accounting bodies do provide their members with very detailed ethical guidelines. Accountants both in practice and in businesses are required to follow these guidelines in their normal patterns of work and can be punished individually for breaches of these professional codes of ethics. There are, however, two distinct approaches to ethics, one for the accountant in practice and another for those within business.

Accountants in practice

The accountant in practice has a considerable body of ethical support to work from, particularly if he/she is a member of one of the various Chartered Accountancy bodies.

These bodies (for England and Wales, Scotland and Ireland) publish guidelines covering key areas of accounting work and behaviour such as

- their relationship with the client;
- the type of work they can do for the client;
- the way to safeguard independence;
- the standards of behaviour expected of accountants;
- the manner of dealing with conflicts of interest;
- the way in which they will behave in given situations such as takeovers, insolvencies and so on;
- the nature and type of advice they can give clients.

In 2002 following the recommendations of the Co-ordinating Group on Audit and Accounting Issues, the Accountancy Foundation, which had been set up in 1999 as a self-regulatory body, was replaced by extending the powers of the Financial Reporting Council. The new structure is as follows:

Financial Reporting Council

Accounting Standards Board (ASB)	Auditing Practices Board (APB)	Financial Reporting Review Panel (FRRP)	Investigation and Discipline Board	Professional Oversight Board

The ASB will continue to be responsible for accounting standards; the APB will be responsible for standards for audit integrity, independence and objectivity previously set by the professional bodies; the FRRP will become more proactive in investigating possible departures from standards; the Investigation and Discipline Board provides an independent hearing for those disciplinary cases where there is a public interest; the Professional Oversight Board will oversee ethical standards.

The intention has been to put in place a regime (supplemented by the Higgs and Smith Reports) that will maintain public confidence that there is sound corporate governance, that the financial reports are true and fair and the audit process is effective to avoid the prospect of the large-scale accounting frauds that have occurred in the USA.

Accountants in business

The accountant working within business has a different set of problems due to the dual position as an employee and a professional accountant. There is a potential clash of issues where the interests of the business could be at odds with professional standards.

The various professional bodies approach things in different ways. For example, the ICAEW established the Industrial Members Advisory Committee on Ethics (IMACE) in the late 1970s to give specific advice to members with ethical problems in business. This is supported by a strong local support network as well as a national helpline for the guidance of accountants. At the moment IMACE is dealing with 200 to 300 problems per year but this is more a reflection of the numbers of chartered accountants in business than a reflection on the lack of ethical problems. A survey[2] carried out by the Board of Chartered Accountants in Business indicated that 11% of members had put their jobs on the line over ethical issues.

The type of problem raised is a good indication of the ethical issues raised for accountants in business. They include:

- requests by employers to manipulate tax returns;
- requests to produce figures to mislead shareholders;
- requests to conceal information;
- requests to manipulate overhead absorption rates to extort more income from customers (an occurrence in the defence industries);
- requests to authorise and conceal bribes to buyers and agents, a common request in some exporting businesses;
- requests to produce misleading projected figures to obtain additional finance;
- requests to conceal improper expense claims put in by senior managers;
- requests to over- or undervalue assets;
- requests to misreport figures in respect of government grants;
- requests for information which could lead to charges of 'insider dealing';
- requests to redefine bad debts as 'good' or vice versa.

These issues are also reflected by the other professional bodies, the Chartered Association of Certified Accountants (ACCA), the Chartered Institute of Management Accountants (CIMA) and the Chartered Institute of Public Finance and Accountancy (CIPFA). The last of these organisations has added problems in that there is an overt political dimension to many decisions taken as its members are working in local government and the concept of 'value for money' is becoming a key feature of their work. Cases in respect of local councils in Westminster and Doncaster have demonstrated the ethical difficulties encountered by CIPFA members in carrying out their duties within their very singular environment.

The accountant in business has this problem of dual ethical structures; they are professionals but they are also employees and on a surprising number of occasions there is a conflict between the two roles on ethical issues. The solution of this conflict causes many problems for the accountant who is left with only three possible solutions, namely:

1 Take some action either by informing a superior (letting them take some action) or by whistle-blowing to an outside agency such as the professional body, the police, the media or whatever. This may well cause the accountant some personal problems and is difficult if the superior is the 'guilty party'.

2 Resign on principle and leave the organisation with personal and professional ethics intact but with a possibly damaged career.

3 Ignore the action and hope someone else notices the unethical behaviour and takes the appropriate action.

All accountants may have to face these choices at some time during their career and it is a test of character which choice is made. The choice itself may well be a function of the individual's own ethical background influenced by the factors mentioned earlier.

National and international regulation

It is likely that there will be an increase in formal regulation as the search for greater transparency and ethical business behaviour continues.

National regulation

Money laundering – overview

There are various estimates of the scale of money laundering ranging up to over 2% of global gross domestic product. Certain businesses are identified as being more prone to money laundering, e.g. import/export companies and cash businesses such as antiques and art dealers, auction houses, casinos and garages. However, the avenues are becoming more and more sophisticated with methods varying between countries, e.g. in the UK there is the increasing use of smaller non-bank institutions whereas in Spain it includes cross-border carrying of cash, money-changing at bureaux de change and investment in real estate.

Money laundering – implications for accountants

In 1997 the APB in the UK issued Practice Note 12 *Money Laundering* which required auditors to take the possibility of money laundering into account when carrying out their audit and to report to the appropriate authority if they become aware of suspected laundering.

In 1999 there was also guidance from the professional accounting bodies, e.g. *Money Laundering: Guidance Notes for Chartered Accountants* issued by the Institute of Chartered Accountants which deal with the statute law, regulations and professional requirements in relation to the avoidance, recognition and reporting of money laundering.

Since that date, there has been an intensification of efforts to control it in the EU and the UK prompted by terrorist implications and the determination to target criminal activities. For example:

- In 2001 the EU Parliament approved a New Money Laundering Directive (effective from June 2003) which stipulated that accountants are included in existing legislation requiring suspicious activities to be reported.
- In 2002 the UK Parliament passed the Proceeds of Crime Act under which the Assets Recovery Agency (http://www.assetsrecovery.gov.uk/) began operations in February 2003 with opportunities for accountants to be employed as financial investigators to follow often complex financial arrangements in order to link the proceeds of crime to extant assets.

Whistle-blowing – defined

Some disclosures which may be embarrassing to senior management may also be a statutory obligation, e.g. in the UK an accountant or internal auditor has the same legal duty to report to external authorities suspicions of terrorism or money laundering as any other employee. This means that there is an implicit authorisation by management. By whistle-blowing, we mean the unauthorised disclosure, in good faith, of serious information relating to questionable practices, where disclosure is perceived to be in the public interest. Such information can be extremely varied: e.g. a financial accountant may be reporting the managing director of a subsidiary company for materially padding his expenses, or an internal auditor may be disclosing audit findings.

Whistle-blowing – proportionate response

Because every whistle-blowing situation is different there is no right answer and any response needs to be proportionate. What is proportionate will of course reflect the potential whistle-blower's own value system, e.g. deciding what he ought to do if there was a dangerous product defect which management considered too expensive to rectify and were concealing or a theft of funds or over-optimistic projections.

Whistle-blowing – protection

In the UK the Public Interest Disclosure Act came into force in 1999 protecting whistle-blowers who raised genuine concerns about malpractice from dismissal and victimisation in order to promote the public interest. The scope of malpractice is wide-ranging, including, e.g. the covering up of a suspected crime, a civil offence such as negligence, a miscarriage of justice, and health and safety or environmental risks.

Whistle-blowing – policies

Companies should have in place a policy which gives clear guidance to employees on the appropriate internal procedures to follow if there is a suspected malpractice. Employees, including accountants and internal auditors, are expected to follow these procedures as well as acting professionally and in accordance with their own professional code.

However, although the whistle-blowing policies might have been followed and the accountants protected by the provisions of the Public Interest Disclosure Act, it could result in a breakdown of trust making their position untenable; this means that a whistle-blower might be well advised to have an alternative position in mind.

Breach of confidentiality

Auditors are protected from the risk of liability for breach of confidence provided that:

(a) disclosure is made in the public interest;

(b) disclosure is made to a proper authority;

(c) there is no malice motivating the disclosure.

International regulation

The OECD drew up a new anti-bribery convention making it a criminal offence for business executives to bribe foreign officials. The implication for accountants is that companies will have to ensure that financial statements do not omit or falsify cases involving bribery and prohibit the establishment of off-the-books accounts for the purpose of bribing foreign public officials or of hiding the bribery. The convention has been ratified by major trading nations including the UK, USA, Japan and Germany. The pressure for the OECD convention came initially from the USA where there was already anti-bribery legislation and then from multinational companies which were finding that some government officials were demanding not 1% but up to 30% of contract prices to award contracts; this not only made it far more difficult to conceal but was seen to be hitting the bottom line too hard. The convention had commercial support and has been ratified by major trading nations including the UK, USA, Japan and Germany. In the UK, the Anti-Terrorism, Crime and Security Act 2001 has extended the common law relating to bribery of UK officials to include the bribery of foreign officials.

Events with the European Commission have highlighted the potential for ethical issues and the inevitability of whistle-blowing as being a logical step in the absence of an effective internal process for dealing with ethical issues. In this case, the whole Commission resigned due to the ethical malpractice of a few, brought to light by the public revelation of a whistle-blower in the accounting function.

33.7 The role of the accountant as guardian of business ethics

There is therefore an established need for business ethics, but the question arises: who can police the organisation for ethical breaches? This is a crucial question as any set of rules is only as effective as its enforcement mechanism allows it to be.

There needs to be some sort of 'ethical guardian' who can police the code of ethics within an organisation to bring out any unethical practices and ensure that corrective action is taken as appropriate.

There are 'ethics committees' in some organisations which act as a court to judge ethical breaches, but in themselves they are only part of the guardian function.

It is therefore a possible function of an accountant's role to be the guardian of ethics within a business because the following attributes are possessed by the accountant:

● skill – the accountant is trained in the establishment and management of control systems and ethics is simply another layer of control;

● stewardship – the accountant already acts as the steward of the shareholders' interests and the function is similar when discussing ethics;

● rule orientation – the accountant is a trained follower of rules and is accomplished at ensuring others obey stated rules and regulations;

● judgement – ethics requires the application of fine judgement, an attribute common in many accountants;

● professionalism – the accountant is one of the main professionals working within businesses and the attributes of a professional are essential to make judgements on ethical breaches.

The role of the accountant in practice

This could well prove to be a new area of responsibility for accountants in both practice and business and it is not without precedent. The work, for example, of the Audit Commission in the public sector is perhaps an indication of the future role of accountants in practice. The Commission does make judgements on the traditional accounting areas but it is also looking at other more subjective measures of performance within public sector organisations and perhaps this is a growth area, especially as the demand by society for more accountability in business becomes more powerful and politically impossible to ignore.

The role of the accountant in business

The accountant within business could also be seeing a growth in the ethical policing role as internal auditors take on the role of assessing the performance of managers as to their adherence to the ethical code of the organisation. This is already partially happening as conflicts of interest are often highlighted by internal audits and comments raised on managerial practices. This is after all a traditional role for accountants, ensuring that the various codes of practice of the organisation are followed. The level of adherence to an ethical code is but another assessment for the accountant to undertake.

Implications for training

If, as is likely, the accountant has a role in the future as 'ethical guardian', additional training will be necessary. This should be done at a very early stage, as in the USA, where accountants wishing to be Certified Public Accountants (CPAs) are required to pass formal exams on ethical practices and procedures before they are allowed the privilege of working in practice. Failure in these exams prevents the prospective accountant from practising in the business environment.

33.8 Growth of voluntary standards

Social, environmental and ethical reporting is at an early stage but it is receiving increasing attention from industry and commerce with the growing recognition that long-term shareholder value cannot be achieved without acknowledging responsibility to wider stakeholder groups.[3] There has already been stakeholder pressure for management to balance the interests of investors, employees, suppliers, customers and the public. Finally, industry, commerce and stakeholders are moving towards a common goal which is to provide innovative reports. However, this requires a commitment from the directors, who are the ones who control the information, and an acceptance of the fact that it is not appropriate to produce only favourable comments. This has now been recognised by some of our major companies, e.g. BT's 1999 Social Report.

The Institute of Social and Ethical Accountability was founded in 1996 as an international membership organisation, based in the UK. In November 1999 the institute launched a world first international processing standard, AA 1000, enabling organisations to build quality into their existing and developing social and ethical management systems. The standard defines how companies should report on issues such as pollution and labour issues. Its objective is to encourage a collaborative approach, with inputs from stakeholders including interest and pressure groups. Two major concerns that have been voiced are:

● Companies should not see consultation with a wide range of stakeholders as an excuse to avoid their responsibility for dealing with adverse social and environmental effects.

● Credibility will only be achieved if there is an independent audit and there could be a risk of ineffectual auditing.

AA 1000 addresses the latter point by setting out criteria for the social and ethical auditor, namely:

● integrity,

● objectivity and independence,

● professional competence,

● professional behaviour exercising rigour, judgement and clear communication,

● confidentiality,

● due care to stakeholders.[4]

AA 1000 will provide a consistent measure of performance and a uniform basis for reporting but the institute recognises that this is a dynamic field and plans to keep the standard under constant review. In this it resembles the ASB policy of revisiting FRSs when there has been experience and feedback from stakeholders and management.

33.8.1 *IFAC Code of Ethics for Professional Accountants* — revised November 2001

The International Federation of Accountants (IFAC) believes that the accountancy profession worldwide endeavours to achieve a number of common objectives and to observe certain fundamental principles. It recognises that due to national differences of culture, language, legal and social systems, the task of preparing, implementing and enforcing detailed ethical requirements is primarily that of the member bodies in each country. IFAC sees its role as establishing an international code of ethics for professional accountants as a foundation for national codes covering ethical requirements applying to all professional accountants, professional accountants in public practice and employed professional accountants.

We have already discussed the code as it relates to auditors in Chapter 31 and now consider the broader aspects relating to the profession in general.

Characteristics of a profession include:

● mastery of a particular intellectual skill, acquired by training and education;

● adherence by its members to a common code of values and conduct;

● maintaining an objective outlook;

● acceptance of a responsibility to the public consisting of clients, credit grantors, governments, employers, employees, investors, the business and financial community, and others who rely on the objectivity and integrity of professional accountants to maintain the orderly functioning of commerce.

Conflicts of interest

A code setting out ethical requirements is required because accountants may find that conflicts arise between their duties of loyalty to an employer, to the profession and to society as well as their own self-interest. It should be implicit in any such code that a professional accountant's responsibility to satisfy the needs of an individual client or employer is not paramount and satisfying public interest is also important, e.g.:

- financial institutions and investors rely on the integrity of independently audited financial statements when making loan and investment decisions;
- financial executives contribute to the efficient and effective use of the organisation's resources;
- internal auditors provide assurance about a sound internal control system which enhances the reliability of the external financial information of the employer;
- tax experts help to establish confidence and efficiency in, and the fair application of, the tax system.

Fundamental principles

Professional accountants should carry out their work with

- *integrity* – being straightforward and honest;
- *objectivity* – acting fairly and not allowing prejudice or bias, conflict of interest or influence of others to override objectivity;
- *professional competence* – applying up-to-date technical and professional standards;
- *confidentiality* – respecting the confidentiality of information acquired during the course of performing professional services.

33.8.2 National response in the UK

In 2003 the final report from the government's Co-ordinating Group on Auditing and Accounting Issues required auditors to comply with the Auditing Practice Board's Ethical Standards on auditor independence, rather than those of the professional accountancy bodies. The APB issued its Consultation Paper *Draft Ethical Standards for Auditors* in November 2003.

The responses from the professional accounting bodies addressed a number of concerns, illustrated in the following comments from the ACCA, ICAS and ICAEW.

ACCA response

In February 2004 the ACCA commented on the draft,[5] making the points that the ACCA:

- sought to ensure that its members complied as a minimum with the IFAC Code of Ethics;
- was concerned that the proposed Ethical Standards did not address all relevant matters included in that Code and that unless the APB Standards were at least as stringent as the IFAC Code of Ethics, auditor members would have to consider two documents on independence;
- believed that the Auditing Practices Board (APB) should recognise that the wider public interest was best served by it seeking international influence rather than issuing national rules which fragmented the market and potentially confused the users of financial statements; and

- believed that the APB should be a strong voice for harmonisation, aligning its agenda not only with that of the International Auditing and Assurance Standards Board, but also with relevant aspects of the work of the IFAC Ethics Committee.

ICAS response

The Institute of Chartered Accountants in Scotland also commented[6] in March 2004 making the following points:

- the APB had not struck the appropriate balance between requirements applicable to all audits and additional provisions applicable only to the audits of public interest entities and, as a result, there would be a detrimental effect on the ability of audit firms to provide the necessary package of advisory and business support services needed by smaller companies;
- ethical standards should be set with a bottom-up approach (i.e. determine what is required for smaller entities and then add additional requirements) rather than the top-down approach that appeared to being adopted; and
- it was a matter of regret that the APB Ethics Group did not have among its members representatives from either small audit firms or small businesses.

ICAEW response

The ICAEW commented[7] that:

- there was concern that the draft standards had in many cases not carried the principles-based approach into the detailed drafting;
- the approach to fee dependency and the wide scope of a number of non-audit service prohibitions would impact on many small businesses and the smaller audit firms that generally provide professional services to them; and
- the risk did not justify the potentially draconian impact of these provisions, though in some instances it may be that the APB had not intended the requirements to be as prohibitive as the drafting made them seem.

Summary

In this chapter we have attempted to explain how business ethics has adopted the definition of ethics as **an ethical code** in order to have a mechanism that (a) makes the ethical expectations of the business clear to staff and other stakeholders and (b) allows performance to be monitored. Although ethics are often perceived as a qualitative or philosophical matter, there is a public expectation and demand for quantitative measures – after all, we live in the age of performance criteria and league tables!

Accountability requires that a report should be made to relevant parties if the monitoring provides evidence that there has been a breach of the code. The relevant party would depend on the nature of the breach, e.g. petty dishonesty by junior staff might be reported to the immediate line manager, fraud by senior managers reported to the audit committee and material misrepresentation of the profit reported to the shareholders.

The accountant is heavily involved with ethical issues as a member of society, as a member of a professional body with a formal code of ethics and as a member and/or employee of a business. The prevalence of the self-regulation ethos in the UK also supports directors delegating to the accountant responsibility for ethical policing.

Accountants' expertise in designing systems and measuring compliance leaves them in a strong position to undertake the monitoring of the ethical code and, as with all control systems, there will be a continuing need to balance costs and benefits. It would, for example, be uneconomic to require all staff to take a truth test to support every expense claim that was lodged!

It is interesting to note that the Auditing Practices Board is actively considering an approach to the government to provide auditors with greater powers in relation to fraud. Given that companies might be reluctant to increase the fees paid to auditors, there might well be a case for state funding for monitoring that is a form of ethical policing. One attraction of this might be that there would be pressure from the government to formulate an ethical code. It is a strength of the self-regulatory ethos that best practice trickles down but it can trickle mighty slowly!

REVIEW QUESTIONS

1 Outline **three** areas where ethics and ethical behaviour are of importance to business.

2 Discuss the role of the accounting profession in the issue of ethics.

3 How might a company develop a code of ethics for its own use?

4 Outline the advantages and disadvantages of a written code of ethics.

5 (a) Obtain an ethical statement from:
   (i) a commercial organisation;
   (ii) a charitable organisation.
   (b) Review each statement for content and style.
   (c) Compare each of the two statements and highlight any areas of difference which, in your view, reflect the different nature of the two organisations.

6 In each of the following scenarios outline the ethical problem and suggest ways in which the organisation may solve the problem and prevent its reoccurrence.
   (a) A director's wife uses his company car for shopping.
   (b) Groceries bought for personal use are included on a director's company credit card.
   (c) The director is sent overseas on business with a business air ticket but he converts it to two economy class tickets and takes his wife with him.
   (d) A director negotiates a contract for management consultancy services but it is later revealed that her husband is a director of the management consultancy company.
   (e) The director of a company hires her son for some holiday work within the company but does not mention the fact to her fellow directors.
   (f) You are the accountant to a small engineering company and you have been approached by the Chairman to authorise the payment of a fee to an overseas government employee in the hope that a large contract will be awarded.
   (g) Your company has had some production problems which have resulted in some electrical goods being faulty (possibly dangerous) but all production is being dispatched to customers regardless of condition.

(h) Your company is about to sign a contract with a repressive regime in South America for equipment which **could** have a military use. Your own government has given you no advice on this matter.

(i) Your company is in financial difficulties and a large contract has just been gained in partnership with an overseas supplier who employs children as young as seven years old on their production line. The children are the only wage earners for their families and there is no welfare available in the country where they live.

(j) You are the accountant in a large manufacturing company and you have been approached by the manufacturing director to prepare a capital investment proposal for a new production line. After your calculations the project meets **none** of the criteria necessary to allow the project to proceed but the director instructs you to change the financial forecast figures to ensure the proposal is approved.

(k) Review the last week's newspapers and select **three** examples of failures of business ethics and justify your choice of examples.

(l) At the year-end, goods are dispatched although not tested in order to improve the current year's sales figures. The management fully expect returns to be made but not within the period prior to the auditor signing the accounts.

7 Select one philosophical viewpoint of ethics and prepare a single A4 piece of paper with a set of notes summarising the viewpoint.

8 With your researches produced for Question 7 discuss how this viewpoint may be applied to a **named** business of your choice to help develop appropriate ethics for this business.

9 'The management of a listed company has a fiduciary duty to act in the best interest of the shareholders and it would be unethical for them to act in the interest of other shareholders if this did not maximise the existing earnings per share.' Discuss.

10 The Financial Director of a listed company makes many decisions which are informed by statute, e.g. the Companies Act and the Public Interest Disclosure Act, and by mandatory pronouncements by, e.g. the ASB, the APB and his professional accounting body. What guidance is available when there is a need for an ethical decision which does not contravene statutory or mandatory demands – how can there be confidence that the decision is right?

11 An approach has been made to the Board to support a takeover bid where the offer price exceeds the current market capitalisation.

(a) Discuss situations where you consider it (i) ethical to recommend the offer to shareholders and (ii) unethical; and

(b) Discuss whether an aggrieved shareholder should be able to obtain relief from the Court if the decision was unethical.

12 The Finance Director has been carrying out some sensitivity analysis and produced figures that show that the return on capital employed could be improved if the company were to downsize, make existing staff redundant and replace them with lower-paid temporary staff. The current return on capital employed and PE ratio exceed the industry average but the change of policy would take the company into the top quartile with a favourable impact on the directors' performance targets and bonuses. This is a common commercial practice. Discuss whether there is an ethical problem in (a) the company pursuing such a policy; (b) the Finance Director submitting such a proposal; and (c) the Finance Director failing to submit such a proposal.

13 Discuss the following:

(a) Why an accountant should be involved with designing or monitoring ethical codes.

(b) What additional training this would require.

(b) How an accountant could become an effective 'guardian of business ethics'.

14 Confidentiality means that an accountant in business has a loyalty to the business which employs him/her which is greater than any commitment to a professional code of ethics. Discuss.

15 Lord Borrie QC has said[8] of the Public Interest Disclosure Bill that came into force in July 1999 that the new law would encourage people to recognise and identify with the wider public interest, not just their own private position and it will reassure them that if they act reasonably to protect the legitimate interest of others, the law will not stand idly by should they be vilified or victimised. Confidentiality should only be breached, however, if there is a statutory obligation to do so. Discuss.

References

1 Simon Webley, *Company Philosophies and Codes of Business Ethics*, Institute of Business Ethics (1988).
2 'Dispute resolution', *Accountancy*, May 1998, p. 99.
3 Andrew Bolger, *Financial Times*, 2 July 1998, p. 10.
4 John Plender, *Financial Times*, 15 July 1999.
5 See http://www.accaglobal.com/technical/responses/recent/
6 See http://www.icas.org.uk/CMS/articleView.asp?article=1516
7 See http://www.icaew.co.uk/members/index.cfm/
8 W. Raven, 'Social auditing', *Internal Auditor*, February 2000, p. 8.

Bibliography

Tom Burke and Julie Hill, *Ethics, Environment and the Company*, Institute of Business Ethics, 1990.
T. Cannon, *Corporate Responsibilty: A Textbook on Business Ethics, Governance, Environment: Roles and Responsiblities*, Pitman, 1994.
Neville Cooper, *What's All This About Business Ethics?* Institute of Business Ethics, 1989.
J. Donaldson, *Key Issues in Business Ethics?*, Academic Press, 1989.
Trevor Gambling and Rifaat Ahmed Abdel Karim, *Business and Accounting Ethics in Islam*, Mansell, 1991.
R.M. Green, *The Ethical Manager: A New Method for Business Ethics*, Macmillan, 1994.
B. Harvey (ed.), *Business Ethics: A European Approach*, Prentice Hall, 1994.
V. Henderson, *What's Ethical in Business?*, McGraw Hill, 1992.
Institute of Applied Professional Ethics – http://www.cats.ohiou.edu/ethics.
Institute of Business Ethics, *Take-overs – What Ethical Considerations Should Apply?* Institute of Business Ethics, 1990.
Institute of Chartered Accountants in England and Wales, *Guide to Professional Ethics*, ICAEW Members' Handbook, vol. 1, 1996.
International Business Ethics Institute – http://www.business-ethics.org.
H. van Luijk, *Business Ethics: The Field and Its Importance*, Prentice Hall, 1994.
Jack Maurice, *Accounting Ethics*, Pitman Publishing, 1996.
Marcia P. Miceli and Janet P. Near, *Blowing the Whistle: The Organizational and Legal Implications for Companies and Employees*, Lexington Books, 1992.
Peter Pratley, *The Essence of Business Ethics*, Prentice Hall, 1995.
William Shaw and Vincent Barry, *Moral Issues in Business* (7th edition), Wadsworth, 1998.
M. Velasquez, *Business Ethics: Concepts and Cases*, Prentice Hall, 1992.
Simon Webley, *Business Ethics and Company Codes*, Institute of Business Ethics, 1992.
Simon Webley, *Codes of Business Ethics*, Institute of Business Ethics, 1993.
Simon Webley, *Applying Codes of Business Ethics*, Institute of Business Ethics, 1995.
Simon Webley, *Codes of Ethics and International Business*, Institute of Business Ethics, 1997.

Outline solutions to selected exercises

Chapter 1

Question 1

(i) (£000)

	Jan	Feb	Mar	Apr	May	Jun
Cash balance c/f	17.55	(17.85)	(70.05)	(51.75)	(55.95)	(47.25)

(ii) Operating cash flow at 30 June 20X1   (143.55)

Question 2

(b) (£000)

	Jan	Feb	Mar	Apr	May	Jun
Cash balance c/f	(28.80)	(26.40)	(18.10)	(12.10)	(7.70)	(0.80)

(c) Operating cash flow at 30 June 20X8   29.20

Chapter 2

Question 1

(a) (€000)

	Jan	Feb	Mar	Apr	May	Jun
Cash balance c/f	17.25	(17.25)	(69.75)	(74.25)	(63.75)	(4.65)

(b) Net profit   47.90
Net capital employed   263.90

Question 2

(b) ($000)

	Jan	Feb	Mar	Apr	May	Jun
Cash balance c/f	85.90	67.50	87.15	104.95	119.55	142.30

(c) Net profit   34.87
Net capital employed   184.87

Chapter 3

Question 2

Economic income: $Y_1 = £153$, $Y_2 = £168$, $Y_3 = £185$

Question 3

(a) (i) Accounting income = £36,700; (ii) Realisable income = £26,200; (iii) Economic income *ex ante* = £27,894; (iv) Economic income *ex post* = £35,000

Chapter 4

Question 1 Income statements and balance sheets show:

(i) Historical profit = £3,800; Total assets £13,800

(ii) *CPP*: Monetary gains = £11,200; Monetary losses = £(6,000); Net income = £10,720; Total assets £23,520

(iii) *Replacement cost*: Realised holding gains = £3,200 (Fixed assets £1,200 + Inventory £2,000); Unrealised holding gains = £6,900 (Fixed assets £4,800 + Inventory £2,100); Net income = £10,700; Total assets £20,700

(iv) *Continuous contemporary accounting*: Operating income = £5,000; Price variation adjustments = (£1,900); Capital maintenance (£2,800); Net income = £300; Total assets £13,100

Question 3

(a) MWCA = £6,190

Question 4 (£000)

(a) (i) Cost of goods sold = 39,162; (ii) Inventory = 11,735; (iii) Depreciation charge = 10,083 or 10,614; (iv) Equipment = 49,822

Question 6

	£
GPP net profit before loss on monetary items =	263,859
Loss on monetary items =	(142,003)
GPP net profit	121,856
RCA profit =	236,083
NRV operating gain =	241,800
Holding gain =	18,188
	259,988

Chapter 7

Question 1

(a) Turnover = £200; Charge for goods sold = £64; Wealth created by operations = £97

(b) Realisable increase in net assets = £157

Chapter 8

Question 1 (€000)

(a) Gross profit = 5,724; Profit before tax = 2,795; Profit for year = 2,233

(b) Trading profit = 2,820; Profit on ordinary activities before tax = 2,795

Question 2 ($000)

(a) Profit before tax = 14,243; Profit for year = 8,895

Chapter 9

Question 1 (£000)
(a) Gross profit = 12,000; Operating profit – continuing operations = 6,710, discontinued operations = 210; Profit for the year = 4,970

Question 2 (€000)
(a) Gross profit = 1,902.9; Profit for the year = 447
(b) Net capital employed = 2,058; Net current assets = 405

Chapter 10

Question 1
(i) Distributable profit for private company A = £95,000
(ii) Distributable profit for public company A = £95,000

Question 3
(b) Alpha plc maximum distribution = £2,844,000; Beta plc = £200,000; Gamma plc = (£2,800,000)

Chapter 11

Question 3
(ii) Sundry assets = £32,170,000; Cash = £6,185,000; Share capital = £18,900,000; CRR = £500,000; Share premium = £4,380,000; Retained profits = £1,755,000; Debentures = £2,400,000; Creditors = £10,420,000

Question 5
(a) *Balance sheet as at 31 Dec 20X1*: Ordinary shares = £1,005,000; CRR = £80,000; Reserves = (£380,000); Debentures = £400,000; Creditors = £400,000

Chapter 13

Question 1
Finance charge for year 1 = £284,375; Carrying value in balance sheet = £2,309,375

Question 2
Finance charge for year 1 = £58,900; Balance sheet = £958,900

Chapter 14

Question 2

Present value of obligation

	20X2	20X3	20X4
	£000	£000	£000
PV of obligation at end of year	3,600	3,500	3,200

Fair value of plan assets

FV of plan assets at year-end	3,400	3,600	3,600

Income statement
Operating cost

Current service cost	(150)	(160)	(170)

Financing cost

Interest cost	(210)	(180)	(140)
Expected return on plan assets	(320)	(306)	(288)
Expense recognised in year	40	34	22

Chapter 15

Question 2

(a) (i) Deferred tax provision – *deferral method*
31/3/20X0 = £375.00; 31/3/20X1 = £773.44; 31/3/20X2 = £785.16;
31/3/20X3 = £615.38; 31/3/20X4 = £310.12

Chapter 16

Question 3

(a) £11,700

Question 4

The solution for Years 1 and 2:

(a) Year 1 Depreciation = £5,914.43; Income from secondary assets = £0; Interest = £3,000;
Net profit = £22,085.57

Year 2 Income from secondary assets = £437.16; Interest = £2,562.84

Chapter 17

Question 1

(a) Fixed asset = £306,250; Liability = £310,000; Interest = £52,500; Depreciation = £43,750

Question 2

(2) Depreciation 20X8 = £2,000; Finance charges 20X8 = £1,200; Liability 31 Mar 20X8 =
£12,200

Chapter 18

Question 3

(i) *Balance c/f*: R&D costs account = £500,000; Laboratory account cost = £500,000; Depreciation = £45,000; Equipment cost = £225,000; Depreciation = £70,000

Chapter 19

Question 2

(i) *Cost of goods sold*: FIFO = £2,648, LIFO = £2,626, Weighted average = £2,638

Question 3

Raw materials = £14,000; Finished units = £35,000; Semi-finished units = £10,000

Chapter 20

Question 3

(b) Stock = £3,000; Long-term contracts = £44,900; Amount recoverable on long-term contract £30,000

Question 5

Profit 20X0 €62,500; 20X1 €37,500

Chapter 21

Question 7

Non-current assets £192,000; Current assets £150,000; Current liabilities £90,000

Question 8

(a) Non-current assets £330,000; Current assets £170,000; Current liabilities £140,000

Chapter 22

Question 1

(Krm) Non-current assets 392; Current assets 300; Current liabilities 160

Chapter 23

Question 1

Profit before tax £146,377; Minority interest £7,350; Retained profit for year £49,021

Question 2

Profit before tax £310,000; Minority interest £5,200; Retained profit for year £97,800

Chapter 24

Question 1

(a) Profit before tax £149,300; Minority interest £2,300; Retained profit for year £68,000
(b) Non-current assets £247,600; Investment in associate £46,000; Current assets £410,800;
Current liabilities £194,000; Minority interest £20,000

Question 2

(a) Profit before tax £110,094; Retained profit for year £32,563
(b) Non-current assets £257,000; Investment in associate £61,313; Current assets £352,500;
Current liabilities £212,500

Chapter 25

Question 1

Profit on exchange: Alamos £3,709; Bank £5,357
Loss on exchange: Texas £1,282; Chicago £2,640; American Bank £5,357

Chapter 26

Question 1

(i) BEPS for 20X1 = £2.29
(ii) BEPS for 20X0 = £2.16 (restated)

Question 2

2,885,416 shares

Question 3

(a) Basic EPS for 20X6 = 2.53p; Basic EPS for 20X5 = 1.83p; (b) Fully diluted EPS = 2.53p

Question 4

(a) Basic EPS = 70p (b) Diluted EPS = 66.15p

Question 5

(a) Diluted EPS = £4.37
(b) Diluted EPS = £4.46

Chapter 27

Question 1

Net cash flow from operations = (£331,000); Net cash used in investing activities (£339,000);
Net cash from financing activities £130,000.

Question 2

(a) Net cash flow from operations = £372,000; Net cash used in investing activities (£734,000);
Net cash from financing activities £156,000.

Chapter 28

Question 2

Turnover = £271,897; Cost of goods sold = £184,890; Profit before tax = £25,362; Retained profit = £15,290; Fixed assets = £206,760; Net current assets = £25,048; Net capital employed = £181,808

Question 3

(a) Net cash flow from operating = £495,000; Servicing finance = £195,000; Taxation = £375,000; Capital expenditure = (£150,000); Dividend paid = £225,000

Chapter 29

Question 3

(a) Option 1: Profit Year 1 = £28,400; Profit Year 2 = £28,400; Option 2: Profit Year 1 = £19,782; Profit Year 2 = £23,904; Option 3: Profit Year 1 = £23,800; Profit Year 2 = £26,050

Chapter 30

Question 2

(a) 20X0 10,000; 20X1 36,667; 20X2 80,833; 20X3 172,500; 20X4 50,000

(b) (i)   £350,000

   (ii) £30,000

   (iii) £300,000

Chapter 32

Question 1

(a)

	20X9 £000
Employees	2,193.5
Providers of capital	735.7
Government	464.7
Asset maintenance	415.2

Question 3

(a)

	20X5 £000
Employees	796
Providers of capital	431
Government	393
Asset maintenance	214

Index